The

Holy Qur'an
In Today's English

Presented by Yahiya Emerick

Bismillahir Rahmanir Raheem

In the Name of Allah,
The Compassionate, the Merciful

"The Meaning of the Holy Qur'an in Today's English: Extended Study Edition" is also available and has hundreds more footnotes and a wider menu of valuable resources than this more concise edition you hold in your hands now.

An Elementary version of this translation for ages 8-14 is available entitled: "The Meaning of the Holy Qur'an for School Children."

A version of this translation for Teenagers is available entitled: "The Holy Qur'an: As If You Were There."

The streamlined version of this translation without footnotes and only with "reasons for revelation" is called, "A Journey through the Holy Qur'an."

Visit www.amirahpublishing.com for more information
or visit your favorite major online bookseller.

ISBN: 1451506910
EAN-13:   9781451506914

3

Table of Contents

The Holy Qur'an Chapter List

The Two Bright Lights

The Law-Giving Chapters

The Chapters of Struggle

The Teaching Chapters

The Spiritual Journey of the Prophets

Learning to Worship God

Stories of the Past

What is the End Result?

Proving the Faith

The Family of the Seven Ha Meems

Prophetic Leadership

Nature is the Proof of God

Practical Matters

The Beautiful Poems

The Rhythmic Chapters

The Two Chapters of Protection

Preface

The Holy Qur'an is a book of guidance and spiritual progress. This book outlines the values and beliefs that can make you the best person you can be. It teaches a way of thinking that is positive, progressive and solution-oriented.

Any person who adopts the world-view of this book becomes a person who believes in justice for all, equality for all and personal responsibility.

The Qur'an teaches its message in a very unique way. It is not a book like the Bible that starts with the beginning of time and tells the stories of hundreds of people and dozens of nations and their ups and downs before closing with predictions about the future. It isn't a book of hundreds of laws or varying types of essays or poems, again like you would find in the Bible.

The Qur'an is more of a book of persuasion – it is a book that speaks to you like a friend. Stories of famous people are given only as a way to prove a point. Laws are few and are connected with trying to make you a better person. Poetic phrases become beautiful ways to remember sound advice and good teachings. You can open the book at any page, start reading and learn something useful.

In short, the Qur'an is a personal letter from God to you, asking you to become something more than you thought you could be: someone whom God loves and someone who loves God's world so much that he or she will do everything in their power to take good care of it and place their ultimate hopes in an even better one.

This translation of the meaning of the Qur'an is not the same as the original Arabic Qur'an. You can use this book to get at the meanings and message of the Qur'an, but it is the original Arabic text where the message truly resides. May your search bear fruit and may the message of the Qur'an guide your way for all the rest of your days.

Ameen, let it be so.

Yahiya Emerick
June, 2000

A Brief Look at the Life of Muhammad

The name *Mecca* has become synonymous in the English language with any place that attracts enormous throngs of devotees. This is a fair and accurate use of the word, for its roots can be traced to a real city, in a real place, which at last count was visited by over two million pilgrims in just one week!

However, Mecca is not a new kind of Disneyland or vacation resort. It is an old city – an ancient one – that has been continuously inhabited for over two and a half thousand years. It is an oasis in the Arabian Desert. It is also the birthplace of Muhammad, who was arguably the most influential human being who ever lived. Our story, then, will begin with the Mecca of Muhammad's day, since it has remained the most important city in the world until even now both in terms of religion and cultural exchange.

Situated at the nexus of a series of important merchant roads, Mecca's three main functions in ancient days consisted in providing water to passing caravans in an otherwise hot and dry region, offering a merchant bazaar second to none, but most importantly, serving as a religious center, for in it lay the ancient House of Abraham, a cube-shaped shrine whose first prototype was built by the venerable patriarch over two thousand years before.

Mecca lies in a hot and dry valley. The main feature is the Ka'bah, which is at the center of the ringed complex above.

Of the two most important sons of Abraham, Ishmael and Isaac, it was Ishmael who was settled by his father in that valley before it was ever inhabited. Abraham left both Ishmael and his mother there on God's instructions, but they did not perish from thirst, for they soon discovered a bubbling spring that saved them.

This unfailing well also gave them a valuable commodity, which they used to trade for food with passing nomads. Upon a return visit, Abraham saw his family had survived, and in a show of thanks both he and his son built a shrine dedicated to the One True God. Today that shrine is known as the *Ka'bah* or *Cube*. Bedouins eventually began to settle in the valley, and it was Ishmael himself who was their first patriarch and prophetic guide. He instilled within his budding people the importance of monotheism and of pilgrimage to God's shrine in Mecca as a way to rededicate themselves to God. The Jewish Old Testament bears witness to these ancient rites and to Mecca being an age-old center of pilgrimage. In the Psalms of David (84:6), we read about the pilgrimage to *Becca* (the ancient name of the city) and its famed well.

However, something happened along the centuries to the ancient purpose of this town and its shrine. Through evolving customs and the accretion of tribal myths and legends that built up over countless generations, the One God was removed further and further away from the active consciousness of the people of Arabia and was ultimately replaced with an entire pantheon of idols and demigods.

The Arabs came to believe that the One Supreme God, whom they knew as *Allah* (Hebrew: *Eloah*), was remote and disinterested in human affairs and that the idols were the day-to-day maintainers of luck, health, wealth and social stability. They also adopted the view that there was no *afterlife* and certainly no consequences to pay for one's own bad behavior or immorality.

The very notion of God keeping track of their faith and deeds was preposterous to them, for they held that this life was all there was. Although a few brave souls deplored the idolatry of the Arabs, they were drowned out in a sea of superstition and tribal bravado and legend. [1] Thus, one's honor and success were the true measure of a man in his brief life. (Women exerted only a marginal influence on the rough and tumble life of the desert nomads, and they fared only a little better in the dusty settlements that dotted the trade routes.)

Honor, both personal and tribal, was the badge a man wore to showcase his reputation, courage and self-worth. Honor dictated that guests should be treated well - even to excess, but it also held that any small insult or slight could lead to a fight between men and even between entire tribes, a fight that would, more often than not, spiral downward into a generation-wide conflict of revenge and counter revenge, of murder, looting and kidnapping. Add to this the constant inter-tribal raiding that was a fact of life in that visually stunning but desperate land, and one comes away with a picture of a lawless place where chaos could ensue at any moment – a land ruled by longstanding customs and pagan superstitions.

The civilized empires of the day, the Byzantine Romans and the Persians, held little sway in the Arabian Peninsula, though each tried to play the tribes against each other in the north and south of Arabia in their own quest for power and influence. As for religious diversity, only a handful of Christians lived in scattered settlements, some Zoroastrians dwelt in the northeast, while a small number of Jewish tribes were settled in the oasis towns to the north.

---

[1] Men who rejected idolatry as an aberration and insult to the Abrahamic legacy appeared now and again in Arabia, and they were known as hanifs, or dissenters. Before Muhammad was born, four such men of Mecca formed a secret society of sorts, promising to oppose idolatry. Later on, three of them wound up converting to Christianity, and the fourth passed away clinging to the original Abrahamic ideal. (The three who became Christians tried to introduce Christianity to Mecca before Muhammad was born, and the Meccan leadership of the time crushed the movement and forbade the teaching or practice of Christianity in the city.) As a young teenager, Muhammad apparently had brief encounters with two of the four hanifs, namely Zayd ibn Amr and Waraqah ibn Nawfal. In later years, Muhammad explained that Zayd's example had inspired him not to eat of meat sacrificed to idols. As for Waraqah, Muhammad visited his house at least once as a young boy, perhaps out of curiosity about his reclusiveness, though he did not meet Waraqah again until he received his first Qur'anic revelation decades later.

Other than that, the overwhelming majority of Arabs were basically pagans, albeit with a limited sense of an all-powerful God. Arabia, then, was an unspoiled land populated mainly by those who believed in idols. It was a land of contrasts. Even as the oasis towns presented a stark reminder of the cruelties of the desert, the code of honor and bravery added a positive aura to an otherwise warlike and fervently superstitious people.

Mecca was the place where some semblance of a central culture could reign, for the Shrine of Abraham still resided within the Arab imagination. However, it was no longer a center of monotheism. Rather, it was transformed over the centuries into a neutral place where every tribe could store its patron idol in safety.

For religious and trade purposes, the Arabs mutually agreed that four months out of the year were to be truce months, wherein all fighting in Arabia had to cease so people could conduct their business and visit Mecca to venerate their idols. Any violation of these truce months was inconceivable because of the amount of shame it would heap upon the offender's family and tribe (though sometimes various tribes would try to 'bend' the rules on this issue).

The Meccan tribe of Quraysh, which was a collection of loosely related clans that governed the city through a council of elders, ensured that Mecca was more or less an open city for all, though they did so mostly for financial interests. In other words, they exploited the beliefs of their countrymen for their own gain. Yearly trade fairs, like those held in other cities, were especially extravagant and diverse in Mecca due to her special status as the home of the gods. Thus, Mecca was the focal point of nearly the entire Arabian Peninsula, and it was into this world that Muhammad was born.

Muhammad's Youth

Muhammad was born in approximately the year 570 into the clan of Banu Hashim, a weaker and poorer branch of the Quraysh confederation. His young father 'Abdullah died before he was born while away on a trading expedition. His mother Aminah and an African maidservant named Barakah moved themselves and the baby into the house of 'Abdullah's father.

When Muhammad was not yet a year old, he was sent to live with a foster mother in the countryside, as was the custom of Meccan mothers, for about five years, so he could learn the ways of the desert as the basis of his personality. In the care of his bedouin foster mother and her eldest daughter, the boy grew into a healthy specimen who was well-groomed, well-mannered and extremely articulate. When he was finally returned to his mother, he had truly taken on the air of a native son of the desert, which was still the goal of the town-dwellers who were afraid of losing touch with the ways of their ancestors.

Muhammad had the favor of his grandfather, who loved him like he was his own lost son 'Abdullah. The boy would often sit with his grandfather during city council meetings and was even allowed to perch in his lap and on his official rug. When he was about seven years old, his mother Aminah took him on a journey to the northern city of Yathrib. She fervently desired to visit the grave of her departed husband, for that was where he died. She took along Barakah as well, and upon her arrival she spent several weeks mourning at his graveside, while Muhammad played with his distant cousins in the city.

On the return journey, however, Aminah caught a debilitating fever, and her life force slipped away day by day on the harsh caravan trail. When she could travel no longer, the trio abandoned the caravan in which they were a part, and Barakah pitched a tent in which her mistress could rest. Muhammad could do nothing as his mother slowly passed, though before she died she extracted a promise from Barakah never to leave Muhammad and always to care for him. After the pair buried Aminah by the side of the trail, the teenaged girl and small boy returned somberly to Mecca.

Muhammad's frail grandfather felt dearly for the boy, who was now doubly orphaned, but he, himself, was quite advanced in years and knew his time with his grandson would be short. Even as Aminah sought protection for her son with Barakah's promise, so, too, did Muhammad's grandfather make one of his sons, Abu Talib, promise to take the boy in and look after him should he pass away.

When his grandfather finally did pass on a year later, Muhammad soon found himself a boy of about nine years old in his uncle's house. There were quite a number of mouths to feed, and Abu Talib was poor, so Muhammad was given the chore of minding Abu Talib's flock of sheep in the hardscrabble hills outside the city. Thus, Muhammad was a full-time shepherd, often alone in the wilderness for over a decade.

The only real adventure that came into his life was when he was allowed (after much begging) to accompany his uncle on a trading expedition to the city of Bosra in Syria. The twelve-year-old boy was assigned the difficult task of minding the animals, which made for an arduous, though no less rewarding, experience. In the exotic lands of Syria, Muhammad would get to see the wider world for the first time, and it made an impression on him that would last a lifetime.

Muhammad: Citizen of Mecca

When Muhammad became a young man in his early twenties, he developed something of a reputation about town for being honest, generous and well-mannered. He never visited prostitutes or joined the local boys in drinking binges, which were common pastimes for young men at that time. Because of his upright nature, Abu Talib wanted to do something for his nephew to give him a chance to make something of himself, so when he heard about an offer for a caravan manager circulating in the marketplace, he approached the noble lady Khadijah, a rich widow, and offered Muhammad as an employee. Though his nephew was young, he explained, the young man was meticulous and trustworthy.

Khadijah consented, but resolved to send one of her slaves along on the expedition to act as a spy (to make sure that this untried manager was honest and legitimate). Muhammad accepted the job graciously and managed all aspects of his employer's business meticulously. At the age of twenty-four to land such an opportunity was fortuitous indeed!

After making all the necessary preparations, Muhammad joined his heavily laden camels and small crew to the great annual caravan, consisting of thousands of camels sponsored by many different types of investors and merchants, that wound its way northward to Syria. All throughout the journey, Muhammad husbanded Khadijah's trade goods faithfully, and in the markets of southern Syria he conducted himself well and was able to return with a handsome profit.

Khadijah's slave gave a glowing report of Muhammad's manners, managerial style and fair dealing, and when Muhammad, himself, gave a full accounting of the journey and what he accomplished on her behalf, Khadijah found herself falling in love with the man, even though he was fifteen years younger than she. Khadijah later confided in her best friend, who took it upon herself to get the pair married. She succeeded, and Muhammad wed Khadijah some months later.

In addition to finding love, Muhammad was also suddenly lifted from poverty and thrust into affluence, though he never seized

Mecca is the focal point of a Muslim's religious life. The Ka'bah is a shrine originally built by Abraham, and rebuilt many times through the centuries.

control of his wife's wealth, even though it was customary in those days. In fact, it was many years later that Khadijah, herself, publicly declared she was giving control over her wealth to him (after he had privately lamented to her that there were so many poor people he wanted to help, but he didn't have any money to do so).

Muhammad was a model citizen and family man. Over the course of the next fifteen years he and his wife had four daughters and three sons, though each of the boys died as infants. He also regularly gave in charity and was renowned for his honesty. People would often entrust him with their money to hold, as if his house were a safety deposit box, for they knew he would safeguard it and not embezzle it. He even once solved a public dispute that could have thrust the city into civil war.

The Ka'bah had been damaged in a flood, and while it was being rebuilt an argument broke out among the local tribal clans as to who would have the honor of setting the fabled Black Stone back in its mounting on one corner. [2] Muhammad

---

[2] The Black Stone is thought to be a meteorite that fell to earth in the distant past. According to the traditional understanding, Abraham found it in the valley within which Mecca now stands (and perhaps witnessed its fall from afar, guiding him to that particular place). Thus, by this token he knew where to build the original Ka'bah. Legend has it that the stone was originally clear in color, but that it became blackened over time due to the sins of men. It has been a part of Abraham's shrine ever since its beginning and is revered by Muslims as something of a souvenir

was selected by chance to solve the dispute, which threatened to boil over into a fight, as each clan claimed the honor as its own. He devised the ingenious solution of letting the leaders of each clan hold the corner of a blanket, which was then used to carry the Black Stone to its place, then Muhammad lifted it into its setting with his own hands.

As the years wore on, however, Muhammad began to feel restless. From his youth he never believed in the idols. He had heard stories of monotheistic mystics of the desert called *hanifs*, such as Zayd ibn 'Amr ibn Nufayl and others, who rejected idols in favor of the One True God and acted with charity towards all. Muhammad likewise adopted the opinion that man-made idols were patently false, and he, too, felt the urge to stand up for the downtrodden. His time alone in the countryside as a shepherd boy reinforced these views, as he was confronted daily with the vast panorama of the desert and the sky – even as he was an orphan from an early age in a cruel and callous land.

Thus, as he grew older, he found himself frequently lost in thought and looking for answers. The injustice of his people didn't sit well with him, for the poor were treated unjustly by the wealthy, orphaned children were abused and left to starve in many cases, and even the barbaric custom of burying unwanted newborn girls in the sand was accepted as a matter of everyday life in Arabia. How could such injustice happen? Where was God? Was there no way to bring kindness and morality to his people? Muhammad wanted to find answers to these vexing questions that gnawed at his mind. Most of all, he wanted to find God.

The Prophet of God

As he approached forty years of age, Muhammad found himself taking long walks in the hills outside the city. Perhaps it was in reminiscence of his days as a shepherd in the peaceful countryside, or it might have been a way to collect his thoughts in an out of the way place. However, as the days wore on he spent more of his time away from the hustle and bustle of town life.

He also began to have strange dreams that would come true when he was awake. He didn't know what they meant, however, and he used his time alone to ponder and think. One day, he happened upon a tiny cave in the side of a small mountain, and he decided that it would be an excellent place to meditate and pray for guidance. His wife Khadijah understood his restlessness and would often pack food for him when he went out, knowing that he might be gone for the entire day or several days at a time.

One night in the year 610, after several weeks spent in deep thought and reflection, Muhammad happened to fall asleep while in the cave. He was startled awake upon hearing a powerful voice resonating within the very stone itself. *"Read,"* the voice said in a commanding tone.

Bewildered, all Muhammad could manage to say was, *"I can't read."*

---

that connects them to Abraham. Contrary to a grossly misinformed myth in the West, the Black Stone is not an object of worship for Muslims.

Suddenly a heavy weight slammed into his body like a powerful grip squeezing him. He felt the breath being knocked out of him. Just when he felt he couldn't take it anymore, the unseen vice-grip loosened upon him, and he was commanded once more, "*Read.*"

This is the mountain just outside of Mecca where Muhammad used to meditate and pray. It is called the *Mountain of Light* today.

"*But I can't read!*" He stammered, and the squeezing came upon him once more, forcing every molecule of air out of his lungs. He groaned in exasperation. When the grip released itself once more, the command to read came again. Not wanting to risk a third assault, he desperately pleaded, "*What should I read?*"

Then it began, and the voice said:

"*Read in the name of your Lord Who created - created human beings from a clinging thing. Read, for your Lord is Most Generous. He taught with the pen - He taught human beings what they didn't know before.*" [Qur'an 96:1-5]

Muhammad panicked. He did not know what was happening to him. He bolted from the cave, tripped and slid over the rocks outside. He looked up in the brilliant night sky, filled with stars as it was, and he saw the image of a figure, a being surrounded by light, standing as if a giant in the cosmos. "*I am Gabriel,*" it said, "*and you, Muhammad, are the Messenger of God.*" Muhammad felt his heart jump in his throat as he turned and ran all the way back to Mecca, scrambling and tripping in the dark.

"*Cover me! Cover me!*" Muhammad cried as he burst in through his front door, shivering and bedraggled. His wife Khadijah, who was startled out of her bed, took her distraught husband by the hand and led him into the bedroom. She gently laid him down and covered him in a large blanket. He lay there trembling for some time, while she watched over him helplessly.

In halting words he told her what had happened to him, and he lamented that perhaps something bad was going to befall him. She thought for a moment and then told him that because he was always so kind and generous with others, God would never mean him any harm.

Khadijah left him there as he fell into a silent slumber, and she went out of the house seeking the home of her cousin Waraqah. Although he was very old and blind, he had been a closet Christian (for Christianity had been outlawed in Mecca some years before by the pagans) and knew some Gnostic teachings.

Khadijah hoped that with his greater learning and knowledge he might be able to tell her something about the incident. Waraqah listened to her story and said, "*Holy! Holy! Holy! By the One Who has power over my soul, if you would believe me, Khadijah, the one who came to him is the same Holy Spirit who used to go to Moses. He's going to be the prophet of this nation, so tell him to hold on steadfastly. He will be called a liar. He will be persecuted. He will have to fight, and if I'm alive then, God will see that I'll give a good account of myself."*

Khadijah returned home, told her husband of her meeting with Waraqah, and conveyed his advice. She then took him in person to see Waraqah, and after he finished telling his tale, Waraqah forewarned Muhammad that his mission would be fraught with hardship and that his own people would exile him.

When Muhammad expressed his fear at hearing unseen voices, Waraqah counseled him, *"If you hear the hidden voice again, stay and listen to what it says."*

Waraqah passed away a few weeks or months later, but his prophecy would prove to be true. There was a period of about six months when the Prophet received no further communications from God, and this absence distressed Muhammad greatly. One day,

This is the name "Allah" or "God." written in Arabic

however, Khadijah found her husband asleep and noticed he was sweating and shivering slightly. Suddenly, he woke up and said the following words:

You there! The one wrapped up (in a blanket)! Arise and warn! Magnify your Lord! Keep your clothes clean and shun the idols. Don't give (in charity) with the expectation of receiving anything back. For your Lord's sake, be patient. [Qur'an 74:1-7]

Khadijah tried her best to convince Muhammad to lie back down, but he was adamant against it. He said, *"No, Khadijah, the time for sleeping is over. Gabriel has ordered me to warn people and to call them to God. But whom shall I call? Who will listen to me?"* Khadijah confidently told her husband that she believed in him and accepted his message.

And so, the first convert to this new way of life that Muhammad was asked to teach was his wife Khadijah, who trusted him completely. Thus, the ministry of the Prophet Muhammad began with the support of his beloved wife.

The Private Phase

Muhammad kept a low profile for the first three years of his mission. He spent his time meeting privately with friends and relatives, explaining what had happened to him and introducing the teachings of Islam.

Among his first converts were his best friend, Abu Bakr, his young cousin 'Ali, his daughters, his freed maidservant Barakah, and a handful of other men and women. The Qur'an, which began as only a few verses uttered to him in a mountain cave, slowly began to grow as new revelations, some of them quite lengthy, came to him. Sometimes he received the messages while he was dreaming; other times they came upon him when he was awake - which he later described as the ringing of a loud bell in one's ears. Occasionally Angel Gabriel would come to him in person and recite verses to him, give him instructions or answer his questions.

Through his private efforts, Muhammad succeeded in making nearly thirty converts from among his close friends and relatives. Some of his relatives, however, thought Muhammad was impulsive, and they dismissed him as a dreamer or a deluded poet who would soon lose interest in his new endeavor. Little did Muhammad realize how far the rejection of such people would carry.

The Persecution of the Meccans

By the year 613, Muhammad was known to frequent the Ka'bah to pray and meditate. He would also speak privately with small groups about his beliefs and teachings. The Meccan establishment reacted coolly to his presence at first, merely considering Muhammad to be stricken with a fad or passing fancy.

Soon, a few of Muhammad's followers, especially Abu Bakr, were eager to take his message to the general public. It was then that the resolve and strength of the new believers would be truly tested. Abu Bakr gave a speech near the Ka'bah, outlining the main tenets of Islam, and when he had finished, he was attacked and beaten so badly by the idol-worshippers that he had to be helped away from the scene.

At this time, the Prophet also began speaking publicly, though he was from a more influential tribal clan than Abu Bakr, and so wasn't an immediate target of violent persecution. However, as Muhammad continued speaking out for monotheism and attracting more and more followers, the Meccan leaders, including some of Muhammad's own uncles and other relatives, took an increasingly harsher tone with him.

They ordered him to stop his activities, as monotheism, they thought, would ruin the Meccan economy, which was based on the veneration of idols. When he refused, they asked Muhammad's uncle, Abu Talib, to silence him or convince him to take a cash payment to keep quiet. When questioned by Abu Talib, Muhammad said, "*If they were to put the sun in my right hand and the moon in my left, I would not refrain from my mission. I won't give it up until either God proves my cause or I die trying.*" Abu Talib looked upon his nephew thoughtfully and replied, "Do whatever you like, for by the Lord of the Ka'bah, I will not give you up." The Meccans left the room in anger.

As time passed, and the efforts of the Meccans to silence Muhammad failed, they became more violent in their suppression. Soon Muhammad began to endure insults in the streets. His detractors accused him of being possessed, of being a sorcerer or a wizard, of being a fortune-teller or a mere poet looking for fame.

One woman took to throwing garbage in front of his door, while her husband would push the Prophet whenever he saw him praying near the Ka'bah. Worse still, gangs of youths would attack and beat up Muhammad's less connected followers. Converted slaves were beaten savagely by their pagan masters, and in time even Muhammad was often punched and assailed with rocks when he left his house.

To protect his more vulnerable and less well connected followers, Muhammad sent two separate groups across the Red Sea to seek refuge in Christian Abyssinia.

For his part, Muhammad continued to preach, especially to the members of incoming caravans, hoping to find fertile ground for his new faith from outside the city. The Meccans, however, continued to push the notion that Muhammad must have gone mad or had been possessed by a devil, and they warned incoming caravans to be on their guard against his words. The Meccans literally had no other explanation for the eloquent and poetic words of the Qur'an, words that were recited by Muhammad with ever increasing frequency and effect.

Soon the Meccans resorted to murder, and they cruelly killed a man and woman who professed belief in Islam. The situation was nearing a breaking point, and Muhammad's cadre of followers, which now numbered nearly a hundred, were under constant strain, especially as their families disowned them or tried to force them to rejoin paganism.

Muhammad became increasingly vulnerable, and the Meccans succeeded in exiling Muhammad's entire clan and his followers from the city for three years. This cruel 'boycott' was only lifted after visiting Arabs shamed the Meccans into capitulating. Some time afterwards, Muhammad lost his beloved wife Khadijah and then his uncle and protector, Abu Talib. His sorrow was overwhelming.

Muhammad sought refuge in the nearby city of Ta'if but was rebuffed under a barrage of thrown stones. Even though his movement seemed assailed from all sides, he continued to offer Islam to everyone with whom he came into contact. (A large number of verses in the Qur'an even speak to Muhammad personally, telling him to persevere, to ignore the insults and to resist succumbing to depression.)

Eventually, Muhammad's preaching to visitors would soon pay off. Some people from the northern oasis town of Yathrib converted to Islam and returned home only to make more converts. The following year a large group came to the same place just outside of Mecca (a sheltered byway named 'Aqabah) and met Muhammad in secret, pledging themselves to him and inviting him to join them in their city. The Prophet sent a couple of his close companions back with them to their own city to teach them the new faith, and thus Islam took root in Yathrib. A way out for the Muslims had revealed itself.

Muhammad began organizing secret departures of his followers in small groups. Any large scale movement would have attracted the attention of the Meccan authorities who would have been sure to prevent the exodus. When only a few of his followers remained in the city, Muhammad asked his cousin, the teenaged boy 'Ali, to return some funds that some neighbors had entrusted to him, and then Muhammad, accompanied by his trusty friend, Abu Bakr, escaped in the night.

It was good timing, for the Meccans had decided on a plan to assassinate the Prophet while he slept. When the young men chosen for the task found 'Ali sleeping in the Prophet's bed, they sounded the alarm, and soon the hunt was on. The man who could capture or kill Muhammad would receive 100 camels, and so every young man in Mecca who could carry a sword mounted his steed and took to scouring the countryside.

Initially, the fugitives headed south to throw off their foes, and then they took refuge in a cave for three days. (One day they were nearly discovered!) Abu Bakr's teenaged daughter Asma' brought them food and news, while a loyal shepherd pastured his flock in the vicinity of the cave to obliterate all tracks. After playing cat-and-mouse with their pursuers, the Prophet eventually entered Yathrib to the cheers of hundreds of his followers.

This event was known as the *Hijrah*, or migration, and it took place in the year 622. Muhammad had preached for thirteen years in Mecca and now would call Yathrib his home. On account of his prominence, even the name of the city would eventually change, as people took to calling it *the City of the Prophet* or *City*, for short. (*Medina* is the Arabic word for city.)

This is a mosque located in the city of Quba, which lies just outside of Medina. This modern structure sits on the site where Muhammad (p) built the first mosque of Islam. He had stopped here for a few days before entering Medina.

In the City of the Prophet

When the Prophet entered Yathrib, henceforth to be called Medina, there were a lot of challenges from many quarters with which he had to contend. There were two large Arab tribes in the city, the Auws and Khazraj, who were constantly being played against each other by three small Jewish tribes that lived on the outskirts of the town.

The Arab tribes were mainly pagans, but both groups rapidly began to convert to the new faith. The general Muslim community would be made up of two large groups: the Arabs of Medina who converted to Islam, drawn from both the Auws and Khazraj tribes, who became known as the *Ansar*, or Helpers; while the poor immigrant Muslims from Mecca were called the *Muhajireen*, or Immigrants.

Muhammad's status coming in was that of a religious leader, and he quickly moved to become a civic leader as well. His first task was to build a prayer hall, or mosque. Then, with the support of all the various communities of the city, the Prophet arranged the drafting of a constitution, the first in human history, that spelled out the rights and duties of each segment of society. The Arab tribes and the Jewish tribes accepted it, and thus Muhammad's influence brought peace to a city prone to civil war.

For their part, most of the Jews were initially cautious about Muhammad's claim to prophethood. They generally took a wait-and-see attitude and felt that he would eventually join their religion, as they already had a well-established religious tradition stretching back to the days of the patriarchs. Their curiosity, however, turned to skepticism and eventually open hostility, as Muhammad began to preach that God's favor was open to all and that the Jews were not faithfully holding to their trust with God.

To make matters worse for the Prophet, there were a large number of Arab converts who only pretended to accept Islam in order not to appear out of step with the latest trend. The chief among them was a man named 'Abdullah ibn Ubayy, who was slated to be chosen as Medina's first king, but whose ambition was thwarted by the arrival of Muhammad. He and his followers began to be known as the hypocrites, and their activities consisted in conspiring against Muhammad in secret, undermining the confidence of the sincere believers and generally sowing discord and doubt among the community.

Their driving belief was that Muhammad and his followers were merely a passing fad and that one day they would be driven from the city. A large number of verses of the Qur'an speak directly about situations involving both the Jews and the hypocrites, as well as how sincere believers from all backgrounds must behave as brothers toward each other irrespective of their tribal affiliations.

On a personal note, Muhammad, who was alone since his beloved wife Khadijah died, began to marry women to solidify political relationships and also to support older widows whose husbands had passed away.

This process would continue throughout his ministry, and his wives became known as the Mothers of the Believers, a title reflective of the fact that his wives became teachers and resources on Islam for the community. From A'ishah, the daughter of his close companion, Abu Bakr, to the Jewish lady Safiyah, Muhammad's wives were paragons of virtue and are responsible for a great deal of the traditional knowledge we have of him.

The First Desperate Battle

Although the Muslims had escaped from Mecca, the pagans were not content to leave them alone in their new home in the north, especially since Medina lay on one of their main trading routes to Syria. The Immigrants from Mecca, whom Muhammad had ordered not to fight back in the face of the many provocations and assaults heaped upon them by the Meccans, were, in addition, impoverished, as the pagans had seized the land and property the fugitives had left behind.

To alleviate this situation, Muhammad asked the Helpers to each adopt an Immigrant and divide their assets with them. The Medinan Muslims did so with remarkable cooperation, though this had the effect of decreasing their own resources considerably. Many Immigrants felt the unfair seizure of their goods by the pagans must be redressed.

In addition, following typical Arab custom, small groups of young men from Mecca took to raiding the outskirts of Medina and to stealing from small desert tribes that had allied themselves with Muhammad. The constant attacks and murders distressed the Muslims greatly. In the year 624, two years after completing the journey to Medina, a new revelation from the Qur'an exhorted the Muslims finally to fight back. Muhammad planned a daring raid on a large Meccan caravan returning from Syria. With a little over 300 men, he set off to intercept it at an oasis named Badr.

Meccan scouts from the caravan got wind of the movement of Muhammad's forces, and the headmaster of the slow moving camel train, Abu Sufyan, sent word ahead to Mecca for help. The Meccans mustered around a thousand men and headed off at top speed to Badr. The Muslims arrived at the wells of Badr first and prepared themselves to intercept the caravan.

Abu Sufyan, however, wisely guided his charge along another route and avoided Badr altogether. When the Meccan force learned that their caravan was safe, they decided to march on Badr anyway, in order to wipe out Muhammad and his movement forever.

When Muhammad saw the arrival of the much larger force, rather than retreat he ordered his men to bury the water wells, depriving the thirsty enemy of resources, and he organized his men into fighting ranks. He then retreated to a small tent that was erected for him, and he prayed, "*God! I'm asking You for the fulfillment of Your covenant and promise. God, if it's Your will (to let us be defeated), then You may never be worshipped again on this earth.*"

Abu Bakr grabbed his hand and said, "*Messenger of God! You've asked God well enough.*" Then the Prophet left the tent while clad in his armor and began directing his men.

The two sides stood in ranks facing each other and waited for the signal to attack. After some customary individual duals, which the Muslim fighters won handily, the enraged Meccans threw themselves at the Muslim lines. The more disciplined Muslims withheld the assault and actually turned the tide of battle, forcing the more numerous Meccans to flee.

The Muslims won the day and returned to Medina with minimal losses. Captured Meccans were freed upon payment of a fine by their relatives or if they taught Muslim children how to read. The Meccans, for their part, were extremely embarrassed, and the poets of their city immediately began to call for revenge.

Meanwhile, one of the Jewish tribes in Medina challenged the Muslims within days of their return, and open hostilities broke out. The Muslims blockaded the neighborhood of the tribe of Banu Qaynuqa and forced their surrender. The terms were quite generous, considering the fact that the tribe had violated its treaty with Muhammad. They were simply ordered to pack up all of their belongings and leave the city. The tribe eventually settled in Syria.

A Defeat for the Muslims

The Meccans nursed their humiliating defeat with rancor and bitterness. Their poets daily made a great show, in the Arab tradition, of calling for the restoration of honor through proper revenge. Many of Mecca's top leaders had perished at Badr, leaving Abu Sufyan the paramount chief among the tribe of Quraysh. Visiting representatives of the Medinan Jewish tribe of Banu Nadir also made entreaties to the pagans to attack Muhammad and drive him from their city. Finally, in the year 625 a large Meccan force numbering some 3,000 men marched northwards towards Medina.

When Muhammad learned of the impending attack, he mustered about 1,000 men and marched out to meet the foe. The two sides met beside a small mountain named Uhud a few hours march from Medina. However, just before the battle was to begin, 300 men under the command of the hypocrite, 'Abdullah ibn Ubayy, suddenly withdrew, leaving the Muslim side with only 700 men! The Prophet steadied his demoralized men with reminders of God's help to the faithful.

Muhammad knew that the Meccans had brought a powerful cavalry contingent and that it was under the command of one Khalid ibn Walid, a renowned military genius. The cavalry would be unlikely to make a frontal assault, as the lances of the Muslims would decimate their horses, but there was the additional danger that while the outnumbered Muslims were engaged with the foot soldiers, Khalid might swing his troops behind and catch the Muslims in a vice. To guard against this, Muhammad placed fifty archers on a hill to guard the rear of his formation.

When the battle began, the Muslims again proved that superior discipline would win out over the unorganized frontal assaults that were typical of Arab fighters in those days. The Muslims actually succeeded in not only holding off the more numerous forces of their foe, but they actually forced the Meccans into a disorganized retreat. It looked as if the Muslims would win a stunning victory again. As the Muslim foot soldiers pursued their enemies, the archers on the hill began to look longingly on the empty part of the battlefield. The Meccans had dropped many of their weapons and let loose their camels. There was a whole host of goods besides.

Disobeying their orders, around forty of the archers descended from the hill and began to collect the booty off of the battlefield. This was also a well-established Arab tradition, one that Muhammad had already tried to change after Badr. Seeing his opportunity, the Meccan cavalry leader swung his men into action. They disappeared behind a hill and reemerged through a small pass, completely taking the few remaining archers by surprise. After killing them, the Meccans attacked the advancing Muslim line from the rear. It was a complete disaster. The confused Muslims were scattered and dozens were killed.

The Meccan infantry also turned and renewed their attack. The Prophet ordered a hasty retreat up the side of Mount Uhud and narrowly escaped death. Several powerful Meccan warriors surrounded him, and one struck his helmet so forcefully that it drove part of the armor into his cheek. A cordon of Muslim defenders, including a woman with a bow and a sword, quickly made a defensive formation around the Prophet and helped him up the mountain under a withering assault.

By the time the bulk of the Muslims reached the safety of the mountain slope, over seventy of their fellows lay dead on the battlefield. The jubilant Meccans began to celebrate, even as they took up the ghastly chore of mutilating the dead and torturing the wounded, as their traditions dictated. Later, the two sides withdrew back to their respective camps, and the Muslims of Medina took to mourning. When they asked how they could have lost, seeing that they had God's favor, the Qur'an answered their question by telling them God was helping them, but by their own disobedience (i.e., the archers) they failed themselves.

The next day the Prophet gathered as many of his men as he could, a number that was less than five hundred able bodied men (for many men were wounded and could not march again), and he led them back out to Uhud. They made camp and sent messages to the Meccans challenging them once more. The Meccans decided to keep their bragging rights intact rather than risk another confrontation, and they withdrew to Mecca.

Some time after the Muslims returned to Medina, hostilities broke out between the Muslims and the second Jewish tribe of Banu Nadir. A foiled assassination plot against the Prophet was the main catalyst, and soon the Banu Nadir's neighborhood was under siege. The hypocrites had made a secret pact with the Jews to defend them against the Muslims if fighting broke out, but the forces of

'Abdullah ibn Ubayy never materialized. The pattern was similar to that of the previously expelled Banu Qaynuqa tribe: the pressure from the Muslim blockade forced the surrender of the rebels. The Banu Nadir also received the same penalty: packing and leaving the city. The bulk of the tribe went to live in Syria, while a remnant took up residence in the Jewish fortress city of Khaybar, some days march further north.

The defeat at Uhud was a blow to the reputation of the Muslims, and many bedouin raiders boldly began to hammer away at tribes that allied with the Prophet, even brazenly attacking Muhammad's own emissaries and missionaries. In one incident, nearly eighty peaceful men were murdered while encamped in a neighboring territory under a false pledge of safe passage from its chief. Clearly, the mood in Arabia was turning towards greater boldness and hostility.

The Siege of Medina

The Banu Nadir Jews who settled in Khaybar with their Jewish cousins didn't forget their defeat and exile. Representatives of the tribe traveled to Mecca to goad the Quraysh into attacking the Muslims again. They also contacted many other tribes all over central Arabia and succeeded in cobbling together a grand alliance whose purpose would be to invade Medina and wipe out Islam once and for all.

A drawing of Medina done in the year 1541 with the Prophet's mosque in the center.

In the year 627 men from all over Arabia began to assemble, and it would be the largest army of Arabs ever fielded – some ten thousand men. At that time, the total number of Muslim fighters amounted to no more than about two or three thousand, including the women and children.

When word of the impending assault reached Medina, the hypocrites tried to spread panic among the populace. For his part, Muhammad held a meeting to get suggestions from his followers as to what they should do. Some suggested going out to meet the invaders, while others spoke of a strategy of house-to-house fighting.

A Muslim convert from Persia, Salman al Farsi, suggested fortifying the rear of the city while digging a large trench in the open plain from where the Alliance would have to attack. His idea was adopted, and the Muslims set frantically to work. Even Muhammad, a man in his late fifties, went out and dug with the rest, singing songs with the other men as they worked.

The defenses were completed in the nick of time as the fearsome Alliance arrived with the grim determination to slaughter and enslave the Muslims *en masse*. The Arab forces were confused by the trench, however, for it was an unknown stratagem in the peninsula. Their first attempts at an infantry assault were beaten back, as the men struggling to climb through the wide and deep trench were picked off easily by the squads of Muslim archers on the other side. Cavalry was all but useless, as well. After some days of fruitless action, the Alliance leaders decided to lay siege to the city in the hopes of starving it into submission.

After the passage of more than two weeks, the various tribal leaders of the Alliance began to grumble. Their men were getting restless, and it wasn't in the character of Arab bedouins to wait aimlessly for long periods of time. The Meccan leaders under Abu Sufyan's command also began to doubt their strategy. Huyyay, the chief of the Banu Nadir, then took it into his own hands to break the stalemate.

He secretly entered the Jewish fortress of the Banu Qurayzah, whose fortified area made up part of Medina's rear defenses. After heated discussions, he convinced the Banu Qurayzah to betray the Muslims and join in a coordinated assault whose date would be decided upon later. When he returned to the Alliance camp, Huyyay related the news of his success, and the emboldened pagans began to make preparations for the combined assault.

Muhammad found out about the treachery of the Banu Qurayzah and engaged a double agent in a desperate attempt to sow discord among the Alliance members. The agent made the Meccans doubt the sincerity of the Jews, causing the Meccans to order the Jews to attack on a Saturday, which caused the Jews to hesitate. Then Muhammad sent an offer to the powerful tribe of Ghatafan, effectively buying them off. Finally, the secret agent entered among the Banu Qurayzah and made them doubt the loyalty of the Meccans. The bold gambit would soon pay off.

In the days just prior to the Alliance attack, the Banu Qurayzah suddenly cut off all food supplies to the Muslims, as planned by Huyyay, and then the tribe's warriors began to encroach into various parts of the city where the Muslim women and children were quartered. When the Arab forces outside the city were to attack, however, due to their mutual mistrust, their tribal chiefs were paralyzed with inaction as each faction suspected the other of secretly siding with Muhammad.

That night a fierce sandstorm erupted out of the desert, blowing tents and scattering the bedouins. The Alliance crumbled, and all sides returned back to their home territories. The Muslims were overjoyed at their nearly bloodless victory, but the question of the Banu Qurayzah, now barricaded behind their walls, remained.

Muhammad ordered an immediate siege of their fortresses, and the blockade went on for some days, punctuated by bouts of fighting. Eventually, the Banu Qurayzah realized they could not win, but they were fearful of surrendering to the Muslims whom they had betrayed in their most dire hour. Their best hope was in receiving the same punishment of exile that their two fellow Jewish tribes got, but the situation was different this time, and they knew it. The Banu Qurayzah sent a message to Muhammad agreeing to surrender, but only if they could chose the man who was to decide their fate.

Muhammad agreed to the terms, and the Jews selected the chief of the Auws tribe, with whom they had been friendly in the past. Quite unexpectedly for them, the chief asked the leaders of the Banu Qurayzah what the punishment was for betrayal according to their own religion. It was, of course, death. So the Auws chief decreed that the leaders and chief instigators were to be executed, while the rest of the men, women and children were to be taken as bonded servants.

The Prophet acceded to the chief's decision - but added that no mothers were to be separated from their children. Any of the condemned leaders could escape their harsh judgment by converting, though only two men did, and they were thus freed. Of the captives, the civilians of the Banu Qurayzah were parceled out to various Muslim retainers and took on their new roles as bonded servants.

Although individual Jewish families would continue to live freely in Medina for centuries to follow, there would no longer be any organized political force to rival Muslim power in the city. Even the hypocrites stood down and no longer seriously troubled the Muslims as long as the Prophet was alive.

To punish the people of Khaybar, from where the Alliance plot was hatched, the Prophet marched a force there and, after a series of pitched battles, made the residents agree to a peace treaty and the payment of an annual tribute. Other than that, Khaybar would remain a semi-autonomous Jewish settlement until the time of the second caliph, 'Umar ibn al-Khattab, who ordered the Jewish residents of the town to resettle in Syria.

A Bold Move

Late in the year 628, Muhammad saw in a dream that he was going on a pilgrimage to Mecca. This, of course, was an unusual vision, for just one year prior to that the Meccans had marched with a grand alliance of Arabs and Jews to wipe out the Muslims in Medina forever. But Muhammad, who believed that dreams were also a means of divine revelation, announced to his followers that he intended to don pilgrim's clothes and lead a sacred procession to Mecca. It was a truce month in Arabia, a time when all hostilities were supposed to cease to allow religious journeys. The Prophet would be taking advantage of this custom, and the Meccans would be tested in their allegiance to their age-old traditions.

Accordingly, Muhammad set out with 1400 unarmed followers, both male and female, and headed for Mecca. When the Meccans received word that Muhammad was leading a pilgrimage to their city, they were shocked. They attempted to intercept the Muslims with a cavalry expedition, but the Muslim party eluded them and finally made camp in the hills just outside Mecca at a place named Hudaybiyyah. Then the Prophet sent one of his trusted companions into Mecca to begin negotiations.

In time, a delegation from Mecca entered into the Muslim camp, and after heated discussions a deal was hammered out for a ten-year truce. The exact terms of the deal seemed very unfavorable to the Muslim side, and it even stipulated that the Muslims would not be able to complete their pilgrimage that year. However, even with the shortcomings, the Prophet accepted the treaty. His community needed time to recover from all the attacks of the Meccans in the past, and it also gave him room to maneuver and increase the number of tribal alliances he had formed.

Muhammad's companions were despondent, feeling their long journey had been for naught. The Prophet felt their disappointment and ordered them to complete their pilgrimage rites there at Hudaybiyyah. The wisdom of accepting the truce with Mecca, however, would soon became apparent to all.

The Fall of Mecca

One of the terms of the truce deal stipulated that each side was responsible for what its allies did. The Meccans thought this would put the Muslims at a further disadvantage, but it was the Meccans who got caught in the trap. For the first several months of the armistice, the Muslims were succeeding in making more alliances and converts than even they might have imagined.

The Meccans, still living under the illusion of their ascendancy, conspired with a client tribe to attack and murder a group of men from a tribe that was allied with Medina. After the brutal massacre, the Meccans took a hard look at the political map and realized that it was now they who were at a disadvantage.

The Meccans sent a hasty delegation to Medina to plead for the continued observance of the treaty, but Muhammad refused to meet with them. The Meccans had broken the treaty, and they would have to pay the price. The people of Mecca waited for several weeks, constantly hearing rumors of Muhammad's mustering of all his followers to march down upon them. They did not have to wait long.

In the year 630, Muhammad, at the head of an army ten thousand strong, made his way southward towards Mecca. When the massive force, which symbolically equaled the size of the Meccan Alliance that had besieged Medina just two years before, encamped above the hills of Mecca, Abu Sufyan visited the Prophet and surrendered the city to him, even as he pledged himself to Islam.

The next morning, three massive columns of men entered the city from three different sides in a grand procession. The Meccans did not resist, and the Muslims took no offensive action. When Muhammad reached the center of town, he asked the gathered throngs of Mecca what they thought he would do to them. (It must be remembered that the Meccans had engaged in brutality, murder, raiding, torture and all out war against the Prophet and his followers.)

"Only goodness," the people answered hopefully. Muhammad then told everyone that they were forgiven and free. This display of mercy and forgiveness, reminiscent of Abraham Lincoln's line, "...with malice towards none and charity for all," so stunned the Meccans that nearly the entire population converted to Islam within days.

Muhammad's first official act was to order the removal of all of the idols from inside the Ka'bah. Then he asked his trusted companion, Bilal the African, to climb on the roof of the Ka'bah and call the faithful to prayer. (No one has ever had that honor since). Muhammad's victory over idolatry was nearly complete, but the remaining pagans of central Arabia would make one last attempt at defeating the Muslims, and it nearly undid all the progress they had made, as we shall see.

The Battle of Hunayn

Alarmed that Mecca had embraced Muhammad, the leaders of the nearby powerful city of Ta'if organized another grand alliance of bedouins and other pagans to attack the Muslims. Muhammad learned of this and mustered his own forces. The people of Ta'if even decided to bring their women and children with them to the battlefield as a way to encourage their warriors to fight harder. The two armies met in a valley near a place named Hunayn in the middle of the year 630.

The Ta'if forces successfully executed an ambush on the Muslims as they passed through the valley, and for a moment, the Muslims were in retreat. Oddly enough, it was Abu Sufyan, along with a few of Muhammad's most ardent companions, who shielded the Prophet and held off the attackers long enough for the Muslim forces to return. The more disciplined Muslims wound up pushing the enemy forces back, and soon a full-scale rout was in progress. The pagans even ran past their own families and retreated in a panic back into their main fortress at Ta'if. The Muslims captured the women and children and held them while laying siege to the city.

Eventually, Muhammad lifted the siege, and his forces returned to Mecca. The men of Ta'if sent a delegation to the Prophet the following year, beseeching his mercy, and the Prophet then freed their women and children (who were being looked after by the community in Medina). This act of charity caused the remaining pagans in central Arabia to adopt Islam, and thus Muhammad's reputation for compassion became one of his greatest assets in the promotion of his religion.

The Mission Comes to a Close

Muhammad now turned his attention to affairs outside of Arabia. He had been contracting alliances with towns, cities, tribes and settlements all over northern and southern Arabia. In fact, he made it his habit to send ambassadors with personal invitations to join Islam to all the known power centers of the day. He even sent emissaries to the Byzantine Roman Emperor Heraclius and the Persian monarch, inviting them to accept his prophethood and message.

The Persian tyrant ripped up Muhammad's letter, and when he learned of it Muhammad predicted the same would happen to the Persian Empire. Heraclius, for his part, began to make moves against Muslim interests in northern Arabia.

After receiving pleas for help from his northern allies, Muhammad organized an army near the end of the year 630 and marched northward to meet the Byzantine threat. Miraculously, the Byzantines withdrew their forces before Muhammad ever arrived, and thus the Prophet spent a month touring southern Syria completing more alliances. The Muslims arrived back in Medina to great acclaim for the success of the mission.

For the next year and a half, Muhammad spent his time busily organizing his administration in Medina (for he promised the people of that city many years before at 'Aqabah that he would live with them forever) and engaging in diplomatic discussions with the many emissaries who arrived weekly. In the year 632, Muhammad even lead one, last pilgrimage to Mecca on a grand scale. It was in this pilgrimage that people began to see signs that the Prophet would soon take his leave of the world. The Prophet gave a major address during the pilgrimage rites, and an unexpected revelation came to him, which he recited to the gathered crowd of 100,000 men and women:

"This day, those who cover over (the truth of God) have given up all hope of (destroying) your way of life. So don't be afraid of them; rather, fear only Me. This day I have perfected your way of life for you, completed My favor upon you and have chosen for you Islam as your way of life." [Qur'an 5:3]

Abu Bakr and others began to suspect the meaning, and he, for one, wept when he heard these words. Indeed, the Qur'an was declaring it was complete and the victory of Islam was accomplished. The Prophet, who was over sixty years old, began to hint in public and in private that God would soon call him home. In addition, he became increasingly frail and often would need rest from his exertions.

The Passing of a Prophet

One night, the Prophet suffered from insomnia and decided to take a walk in the midnight air of Medina. Accompanied by an attendant, he headed for the graveyard and stared at the silent graves.

When he arrived, Muhammad said, "*Peace be upon you, O people of the graves. You are blessed in your present condition to which you have come, which is not the same condition as the people who still live in the world must endure. Assaults (the effects of aging) are falling one after another (against my health) like waves of darkness, each worse than the one before.*"

After praying for the souls of the dead, the Prophet said to his attendant, "*Abu Muwayhibah! I've been given the keys of this world and eternity in it, and now I'm being offered Paradise and meeting with God. I've been asked to choose between them.*"

His attendant cried out, "*I would give everything for your sake, sir! Isn't it possible to have both? Please take the keys of this world, eternity in it, as well as Paradise.*"

The Prophet answered, "*No, by God, Abu Muwayhibah. I've chosen Paradise and meeting with my Lord.*"

A few days later, the Prophet began to suffer a particularly severe fever, and he found it increasingly arduous to meet with people. When the Prophet's condition worsened, he asked that Abu Bakr take charge of leading the prayers for him. This subtle hint signaled to many Muslims that the Prophet was tapping Abu Bakr to lead after him. Even when he felt strong enough to come into the mosque for prayer, he still allowed Abu Bakr to continue leading the prayers while he himself would pray behind him in the rows.

The Whisper to Fatimah

One day, while his daughter Fatimah was attending to him, the Prophet whispered something into her ear that made her cry. Then he whispered something that made her smile. A'ishah, one of Muhammad's wives, asked her what he said, but Fatimah refused to tell what she regarded as a personal secret. Meanwhile, the fever continued to burn in Muhammad's forehead, and his body shivered with chills. The Prophet overheard Fatimah lamenting, "*Oh, the terrible pain my father is suffering!*"

The Prophet opened his eyes and said to her, *"Your father will suffer no more pain after this day."* The anxious Muslims filed in and out of his apartment throughout the day, some offering medicines and others praying. Everyone felt confused and alarmed for the safety of their beloved Prophet. In his last hour, as his head was resting on A'ishah's lap, the Prophet called out his last words. As A'ishah tells the story:

"The Prophet's head was growing heavier in my lap. I looked at his face and found that his eyes were still. I heard him murmur, 'Rather, God on High and Paradise.' I said to him, 'By Him Who sent you as a prophet to teach the truth, you've been given the choice, and you chose well.'

"The Prophet of God passed away while his head was on my side between my chest and my heart. It was my youth and inexperience that made me let him die in my lap. I then placed his head on the pillow and got up to bemoan my fate and to join the other women in our sadness and sorrow."

It was June 8th in the year 632. He was buried where he passed away.

Later on, Fatimah told A'ishah what was whispered to her. She said, *"The first time he told me that he would not recover from his illness, so I cried. The second time he told me I would be the first from his family to join him, so I smiled."* This prediction would soon come true as Fatimah passed away six months later, leaving behind her grieving husband 'Ali.

A view inside the main mosque in Medina as it appears today. The Prophet's grave is located inside.

With the Prophet having left this world, the new Muslim community had to try to make sense out of what his mission meant and how they were to get along without him. When the Prophet was alive and with them, there were no doubts or uncertainties. All a person had to do was ask for his guidance, and he or she would be sure to receive an answer that was both wise and practical - but now he was gone.

When 'Umar, one of Muhammad's closest companions, heard the news of the Prophet's death, he came running to his front door and drew his sword in anger. He swore that he didn't believe the Prophet was gone and that he'd fight anyone who said otherwise. Obviously, he was overcome with great stress at the thought of losing his beloved friend and guide.

Abu Bakr came on the scene, and when he saw the distraught 'Umar, he went to his friend and announced to the gathered crowd, *"If anyone worships Muhammad, know that Muhammad has died. But if anyone worships God, then know that He is alive and cannot die."* Then Abu Bakr recited the following verse from the Qur'an to drive the point home:

"Muhammad is no more than a messenger. There were many messengers who passed away before him. If he dies or is killed, would you then turn and run away? Anyone who runs away does no harm to God in the least, and God will quickly reward (those who serve Him) in gratitude." [Qur'an 3:144]

33

'Umar accepted the wisdom of his friend's speech, slumped down into his arms and wept at his heart-felt loss. Eventually, Abu Bakr was chosen as the first caliph, or leader of the Muslim community. During his acceptance speech, he addressed the crowds of Muslims as they gathered after his election. His address is one of the most noble ever given by any ruler in all of human history. In it, he spoke of his duties as a leader and the rights of the people. He didn't talk about power or wealth or glory. He spoke as a true Muslim who recognized the huge responsibility that now rested upon his shoulders. Part of his speech is recorded below.

"O people, I've been elected your leader, even though I'm no better than any of you. If I do right, help me. If I do wrong, correct me. Listen well; truth is a trust, and lies are treason. The weak among you shall be strong with me until I secure their rights. The powerful among you shall be weak with me until, if God wills, I've taken what is due from them. Listen well; if people give up striving in the cause of God, He will send disgrace upon them. If a people become wrongdoers, God will send disasters down upon them. Obey me as long as I obey God and His Messenger. If I disobey God and His Messenger, then you are free to disobey me."

Reflections on the Life of the Last Prophet of God

Prophet Muhammad was a truly humane and farsighted man. He exemplified the best virtues of a religious leader and stood for monotheism at a time when much of the world was assailed by darkness and ignorance. He was the best model of a husband, father, leader and friend. He was gracious to all and patient even with those who mocked him and persecuted him. He never laid a hand in anger upon any woman or child and was always compassionate and respectful towards others.

When he finally had the pagans of Mecca in his power, after so many years of living in fear of them, instead of taking the revenge to which we would all say he was entitled, he forgave them and let them go on their way. He was so concerned with the welfare of others that he even forbade people to hurt animals wantonly or use them unjustly. He loved children and counseled people to be affectionate towards them. He also taught people that men and women were equal in the sight of God at a time when women were thought of as mere objects for men's enjoyment.

Even when all of Arabia and some of Syria were completely in his control, he did not behave like a king or a tyrant. He didn't build palaces or wear fancy clothes or make people bow to him. Instead, he wore regular clothes, lived in a small apartment, ate little and treated all men and women as his brothers and sisters. When he died, the sum total of all his worldly possessions consisted of a reed mat for sleeping, a wooden bowl and a handful of barley.

Barakah, his nursemaid from his youth, who was by then over seventy years old, took to visiting his grave every day and crying softly. Once she replied to a person who asked why she went there so often, *"By God, I knew that the Messenger of God would die, but I cry now because the revelation from on high has come to an end for us."*

Even though the Qur'anic revelation came to an end, its power and influence would live on long after, even unto our own times. You have here before you now the Qur'an - the message that was revealed to a prophet over the course of twenty-three long years, in times of sadness and joy, triumph and heartache, but always resonating with the message of hope: surrender yourself to God and you shall achieve eternal life in Paradise. This message, which was revealed 1400 years ago, is here for your consideration today.

How to Approach the Qur'an

The Qur'an is for Muslims the revealed Word of God to His last prophet Muhammad. Therefore, the Qur'an is never thought of as the words of Muhammad, himself. (Muhammad's own words, sayings and doings are called *hadiths*, or traditions, and are collected in separate books apart from the Qur'anic text.) The word "Qur'an" means something that is read or recited, and indeed the Qur'an is more of a collection of impassioned sermons and essays than a dry, legal, historical or theological text.

It has to be understood that Muhammad would suddenly receive Qur'anic revelations at any time, sometimes to address a specific situation or event, and other times to provide guidance, give theological concepts or even offer him words of support when he was feeling depressed or stressed due to the persecution he suffered at the hands of the pagans.

Very few chapters were revealed as a whole. Rather, specific segments or passages would come to him, and Muhammad would tell his followers within which existing chapters to place them. Thus, at any given time, many of the various chapters were constantly growing as new verses were added.

Muhammad arranged everything himself, and he asked his followers not only to write down the verses, but also to memorize them as they came. This was not an unusual custom, for the Arabs, being primarily an unschooled nation, passed on their stories and odes mostly by rote memorization. Thus, when you read the Qur'an, you have to keep in mind that every line of it was spoken publicly to people all throughout the Prophet's mission, often while major (or even minor) events were unfolding, and also that it formed the very foundation of Muhammad's ministry. [3] It was like an interactive Book of Guidance. (If you read the Old or New Testament, you can also see how various teachings came in response to specific situations. Even a casual glance into the life and work of Jesus, for example, shows that the bulk of his teachings were given in response to his interactions with others.)

To get a sense of the tone and style of the Qur'an, especially how it sounds when it is orally recited to an audience that understands what the words mean, imagine mixing the rhythm of traditional American ballads from the nineteenth century with the style and flair of classic Irish songs from days gone by, mixed with exhortations from the great speeches of such figures as Cicero, Thomas Aquinas, Martin Luther King, Jr., or Abraham Lincoln.

The Qur'an tells stories, asks its listeners to ponder over issues, and tries to reach them with a message and a way of looking at life. Imagine taking the best elements of all of these types of sources and coming away with an epic poem that tells the story of humanity and its relationship with God through various episodes, alternating subjects, stories within stories and passages of lyrical, rhythmic song.

---

[3] See 25:32-33 for example, where the Qur'an explains the purpose of the gradual nature of its revelation this way: "Then the faithless ask, "So why isn't the Qur'an revealed to him all at once?" (It's being revealed at this gradual pace) so We can strengthen your heart with it, for We're releasing it in slow, well-ordered stages. They don't bring any issue before you without Us revealing to you the most straightforward and appropriate counterpoint."

Then you'll understand why Muslims are so enamored with the message of the Qur'an in its original Arabic: it's a really unique presentation!

Arabic calligraphy has developed into a highly prized art form, as seen here in the opening verses of chapter two of the Qur'an.

Comparing the Qur'an and the Bible

The Qur'an is completely unlike the Bible in tone, subject arrangement and structure. In fact, other than touching on some familiar topics now and again, the Qur'an cannot be compared to the Bible at all. (Imagine trying to compare Shakespeare's play about Julius Caesar with a book about the history of Rome. The two works would be completely different in nearly every respect, despite having similar subject matter.)

Whereas the Bible is a very linear book, starting with the creation of the world and narrating a continuous story touching upon thousands of people's lives until it ends with prophecies of the End Times, the Qur'an is more like a collection of self-contained mini-lessons that explore very specific issues, sometimes referencing past peoples or prophets for effect, and then it closes its argument before moving on to another topic. It would be like reading a page from the book of Deuteronomy that discusses legal matters, then turning to a page from I Chronicles that contains part of the story of a prophet or other person of interest to emphasize a moral precept, and then turning to a page in the New Testament that discusses forgiveness, a parable or some aspect of salvation.

All these trends are woven together in a coherent way to produce some remarkably powerful literary effects. A further advantage of this approach is that it brings a wide variety of different types of information to the readers' attention, rather than sequestering specific types of information in lengthier (and often disused) sections.

For example, few people prefer to read the long pages of Mosaic law in the Old Testament, rather seeking out the inspirational passages in the Psalms and Gospels. Thus, a large body of important work goes unread. The Qur'an mixes it all together, so the reader gets a dose of each type of spiritual and practical medicine.

The relationship between Muslims and their Qur'an is also different from how Jews and Christians view their Torah and New Testament. For Christians, the Bible is the word of God, but the emphasis is upon the person of Jesus Christ, whom Christians believe is the word of God 'made flesh.' Thus, the Bible is merely a guidebook that points one's attention towards Jesus, where the real salvation lies.

For Jews, who do not accept the New Testament of the Bible, their Torah and related writings are the record of God's interaction with their forefathers, even as it prescribes the path that the Jewish people must follow in order to live in obedience to God. Although the many different sects of Judaism question how far to take the literalness of the text, they all share a common belief that their sacred writings are a central tenet of Jewish cultural life.

For Muslims, the Qur'an is something like the Torah and Jesus combined. They believe that the Qur'an is the last holy book in a long line of scriptures from God to humanity that includes the Torah and the Gospel. Muslims believe that the Qur'an corrects the errors and misinterpretations of previous religious communities such as the Jews and Christians. They further believe that the words of the Qur'an are God's Own speech, and thus it is the very word of God (as opposed to Jesus being 'the word made flesh'). Although some Qur'anic passages came to Muhammad due to external events, Muslims believe that it was God's own revealed guidance to Muhammad in those situations that shaped the verses as they were.

In other words, it doesn't matter if a passage is related to something that Muhammad faced or not, for God's words were revealed to him for specific and general reasons. Given that Muslims believe that God is outside the timeline and can see the future and the past at the same time, His words are eternal even if some of them were revealed at a known point in human history. (In this regard, Muslims believe that the original Torah and Gospel are also God's eternal word. They just question the validity of the scriptures in use today that are labeled by those names, but that don't necessarily carry original or authentic content.)

Because Muslims feel that the Qur'an is so weighty in its status, they take the words of the Qur'an to be both guidance for life and as the binding law of God that humanity should follow. Muslims would never want to disrespect a written copy of the Qur'an, and they are even taught to stop speaking when the Qur'an is being recited aloud, so as not to be disrespectful when God's words are being repeated. (A Muslim is also not allowed to disrespect the religious books of Jews, Christians and others, because, as the belief is, at least some of God's previously revealed words are still contained within them.)

Unique Features of the Qur'an

One of the features that Muslims consider to be miraculous is the fact that the verses are quasi-poetic in nature in that they often follow precise rhyme and meter. One can hear this distinctly when listening to the Qur'an being read aloud in its original Arabic. So not only was the Qur'an conveying a message, but it was also acting as a kind of spellbinding entertainment. [4] It delivered its message and left people in wonderment of its beauty at the same time! This precise poetic flavor is nearly impossible to translate into another language, and that's why this and every other translation in English is more prose-like than poetic.

---

[4] The classical writer al-Jahiz (d. 869) once described the Qur'an and its style thusly, "The Qur'an differs from all known forms of poetry and prose. It is a prose whose rhythm is not modeled on that of standard poetry or rhymed prose, and whose configuration stands as a magnificent evidence and as a great divine proof." (al-Bayan)

The Qur'an has 114 chapters of varying length and comprises approximately 6,236 [5] individual verses. [6] (The invocation of God found at the beginning of every chapter except chapter 9 is not counted as an actual numbered verse, except for with the first chapter.) It is written in what is called classical Arabic (*fus-ha*), and this elegant style of Arabic, derived from the dialect spoken by the Prophet's tribe in Mecca, is the basis for modern, standard Arabic today.

Although there are many dialects and regional differences in how modern-day Arabs speak Arabic, many Arabs still more or less understand Qur'anic Arabic. For an analogy, Qur'anic Arabic to Arabs today is like Shakespearian English to English speakers today. The spoken words can be followed, though many terms or grammatical constructs are no longer familiar to us or take much effort to decipher. Classical Arabic, however, has been well-preserved and is taught in schools all over the world to maintain a link with the original text.

Unlike the classical spoken language, however, Arabic script has undergone some transformations over the centuries. The origin of written Arabic can be traced back to Nabatean script in the fifth century CE. Arabic-speaking traders

Both examples here say, "In the Name of Allah, the Merciful, the Compassionate." Old script is above and newer script below.

took a cursive variety of that script and adapted it to their use as a trade language.

Eventually, it spread among some individuals from the wealthy merchant classes, though the bulk of the Arabs, whether rich or poor, remained largely illiterate. The rudimentary shapes of the letters, which were first introduced to Mecca a generation before the Prophet's birth, were chunky and disconnected and lacked a system of vowels.

After the rise of Islam, the shapes of the letters were gradually streamlined, in much the same way that English letters are no longer written in an ornate Gothic style today. Vowel markers were also added in the early classical period to help in the proper pronunciation of the words of revelation. In our modern world, calligraphic Arabic script is considered among the most beautiful and artistic scripts ever invented.

Another interesting facet of the Qur'an is the way in which it reinterpreted or assigned new meanings to existing Arabic words and literary forms. Although the Arabs of seventh-century Arabia used the word *qasida* for chapter and *bayt* for verse, the Qur'an coined its own terminology. Thus, the Qur'an uses the word

---

[5] Some scribes of written copies of the Qur'an broke up larger verses into smaller ones, resulting in different figures for the total number of verses, though the exact number of words themselves are the same in all editions. (See The Qur'an and Exegesis, by Helmut Gatje, pg. 27.) The Qur'an is made up of 86,430 total words using 323,760 total letters!

[6] There are three main groupings of Qur'anic chapters. The chapters containing more than one hundred verses are called the *ma'in*, or hundreds. Large chapters with less than a hundred verses are called the *mathani*, or frequently repeated ones (due to their often being used in congregational prayer), and the shorter chapters from chapters 50 to 114 are called the *mufasalat*, or the small separated chapters.

surah, which literally means a row, a fence or a step up in progression, for chapter, and the word *ayah*, which literally means a sign, proof or miracle, for verse.

The earliest chapters of the Qur'an were revealed in Mecca during a time when the Prophet had to confront a united bloc of opposition in the form of the pagans who opposed monotheism and championed idolatry and their longstanding customs. These early chapters were mostly short expositions and often took on a dramatic style with powerful rhythms that sometimes mimicked the style of the Arab soothsayers and seers.

This was because the attention span of most Arabs at that time was short, (even as such a condition is common among all peoples even to this day), and if a passage was too esoteric or unfamiliar sounding they might "*thrust their fingers in their ears and turn away.*" Thus, there would literally be only a few moments within which the attention of the public could be captured.

Later Meccan revelations increased in length as the Prophet gained followers, for the new believers had the patience to listen to more detailed expositions of theology and doctrine and could gain inspiration and insight into what exactly Islam was teaching them. As the pagans of the city became more used to Muhammad's preaching, they, too, could listen for longer periods of time and consider what the Prophet was advocating.

After the Prophet migrated to Medina, the length of the chapters dramatically increased, even as the earlier colorful imagery gave way to more practical matters such as legislation, interfaith issues, community relations and other similar topics. The longest chapters of the Qur'an hail from the Medinan period. (Some chapters contain verses revealed from both periods within them.) Ironically, the short Meccan chapters appear near the end of the Qur'an, while the later Medinan chapters appear first in the book.

This is because the Qur'an is not just an historical document charting the growth of Islamic teachings, but rather it is a comprehensive revelation whose verses were arranged according to various related topics and themes within a larger context. All of the arranging was dictated by the Prophet under direction from the angel Gabriel who conveyed God's order in this regard.

The Preservation of the Qur'an

The Qur'an grew slowly and was completed by the end of the Prophet's life. He ordered it to be written down in his lifetime as new passages came to him, and he would always call one or more secretaries to write down the verses while they were fresh in his mind. He also asked his followers to memorize the verses and many companions knew the entire Qur'an by heart. (Everyone else knew varying amounts, and Qur'anic knowledge was widespread.) The various sheets of vellum, leather, tree bark and other materials upon which the verses were written were kept in a large sack in the Prophet's house. Before he passed away, the Prophet recited the entire Qur'an from beginning to end in public two times.

It was in the time of the first successor to the Prophet's rule, Caliph Abu Bakr, that the Qur'an was written on leather scroll sheets in its full, proper format, and many thought this would suffice for preserving the Qur'an, which was still thought of mostly as something to be memorized. A few years later, when new non-Arabic speaking converts in Iraq and Syria began to differ over the proper pronunciation of the Qur'an, [7] and even began to record inaccurate copies reflecting their poor understanding of Qurayshi Arabic, the third caliph Uthman was spurred into action. He ordered the Qur'anic text to be authenticated using the original copy made in Abu Bakr's time. Then he ordered a number of copies of that official tome to be produced and sent to all the major population centers of the expanding Islamic world. All other faulty or incomplete copies were to be destroyed, so as to preserve the original Qur'an as dictated by Muhammad.

This action protected the Muslim world from disunity and scriptural confusion. Due to this farsighted act, there is no alternative body of apocryphal writings or competing editions such as grew up in the first centuries of Christianity when there was no organized Christian scripture. [8]

Even as the central focus of Christianity is Jesus Christ, for Muslims the main link between God and humanity is the Qur'an. It is through the Qur'an that a Muslim learns about God's commands and the tenets of faith. It is in its pages that he or she gains inspiration and learns how to lead a Godly lifestyle. It is a Muslim's bulwark in the storm, a source of guidance and solace, as well as a book of warnings and good news. Muslims repeat portions of the Qur'an every day in

---

[7] Originally, Arabic script was usually written without any vowel marks, and the shapes of some letters were indistinguishable from each other. (Imagine writing English without punctuation, not putting dots on the 'i', writing lines on 'f' or crossing the 't'!) In addition, depending on the dialect of Arabic, the words could be pronounced any number of ways. This was the crux of the resultant problem. Diverse manuscripts with the various readings began to appear in all those areas where Islam spread and in which the Arabic dialect of Mecca was unknown. (The Prophet personally approved of seven different dialects for Qur'an recital, based on permission he received from Gabriel, as quoted in Bukhari and Muslim.) This is why one of Uthman's orders to his team of scholars, who were preparing an authorized edition of the text, was to use the Qurayshi dialect whenever there was a difference of opinion in how a verse could be read, recited or understood. (Bukhari) See the books entitled, Variant Readings of the Qur'an: A Critical Study of Their Historical and Linguistic Origins, by Ahmad 'Ali al-Imam, and The History of the Qur'anic Text from Revelation to Compilation, by M. M. Al-Azami, the latter of which is something of 'the final word' on the subject. Although dots indicating the proper pronunciation of letters existed before Islam, it wasn't until the Umayyad period that Qur'anic manuscripts are written with them.

[8] Some ancient Qur'anic manuscripts that contain minor variations in spelling, synonymous word selections (approved by the prophet in the hadith) and prophetically dropped passages have recently been discovered in an old mosque in Yemen. A closer examination of the manuscripts, which were discarded texts sealed in a hidden chamber behind a wall, most likely will show the effects of copyist errors, accepted synonym usage, preserved historical material and spelling mistakes. (Muslims do not throw used Qur'an pages in the garbage, but rather burn them or bury them when they become worn out. In previous centuries, Muslims have also freely used the margins of Qur'anic pages for writing personal notes and comments!) As written Arabic grammar was not always standardized from region to region in the first few centuries of Islam, as noted in the previous footnote, copyist understandings or errors were bound to occur. In addition, many of the variations made public thus far reflect written examples of the seven approved variations of Qur'anic recitation, which the Prophet allowed. This allowance of synonyms and alternative readings made it easier on different Arab tribes to pronounce the Qur'an, using their own particular dialect and style of Arabic. Apart from this, the first generation of Muslims was aware of a few scattered passages of early revelation that the Prophet ordered not to be included in the official canon, as those early rulings were abrogated by God with later revelations. (See 16:101 and footnote for a more detailed discussion.) Finally, some individual companions had written copies of the Qur'an that contained the entire text, but which had individual chapters in different orders. Apparently, the companions recorded these in the order that they learned them from the Prophet, rather than in the official order the Prophet set later on. 'Abdullah ibn Mas'ud is often mentioned in this regard, and he explained that he kept his manuscript for nostalgic reasons. Even A'ishah, the Prophet's widow, when consulted about this later on, was less concerned about the differing order than one might think. (See An Approach to the Qur'anic Sciences, by Muhammad T. Usmani, for a full discussion.) Consider a situation like this: non-standardized spelling methods, the existence of seven modes of reciting the sacred text and then throw in historical reference material from the evolving years of the Islamic mission, and one can get a glimpse at how alarmed the first generation of Muslims must have been when the problem of preserving a canonical prophetically-sanctioned divine text (as it was finalized at the end of the Prophet's life) first surfaced. Be that as it may, it's been estimated that there are over a quarter of a million surviving ancient Qur'anic manuscripts, both partial and complete, from the first three centuries of Islam, to prove that the Muslim world had a remarkably unified text (as their official canon) from the very beginning. Compare this with the history of the Bible in which the oldest complete manuscripts (such as the Codex Sinaiticus c. 360 A.D.) have entire books, chapters and passages that are different from the contents of modern Bibles today.

their daily prayers. They recite its passages to mark major life events such as marriage and death.

Once a year a public recital of the entire Qur'an (spread out over nearly thirty days) is conducted in mosques and homes all over the world during the fasting month of Ramadan. Muslims revere the Qur'an so much that they would never dare to place a Qur'an on the floor or treat it disrespectfully. For Muslims it is the very speech of God Himself.

Suggested Courses of Study

The Qur'an can be read in three different ways:

* **Reverse Order**. Generally, the shorter chapters were revealed first while Muhammad was conducting his ministry from Mecca and its immediate environs, but they were ultimately placed at the end of the book. Conversely, most of the longer chapters were revealed after the Prophet had migrated to Medina, and most of those appear in the first two-thirds of the book. To gain a sense of how the Qur'anic message unfolded, you can read those chapters labeled as from the Meccan period first. This allows you to observe the growth of the theological foundations of Islam before delving into the Medinan chapters whose main themes shift towards community building, interfaith issues and laws.

* **The Thematic Approach**. A second way to read the Qur'an is by using the index to look up verses by theme. By reading and comparing all of the verses on a particular topic, such as prophethood, interfaith relations, women, revelation, or a particular person, you can gain an overall sense of what the Qur'an stands for on each issue. This approach is particularly useful for those in search of specific information on a narrow topic.

* **In Context**. The third way it can be read is as a biographical aid in exploring the overall history of Muhammad's life and struggle. Using any standard biography of the Prophet's life as a base, such as *Even the Clouds Spread Shade for Him*, by Yahiya Emerick, or *Muhammad: His Life Based on Earliest Sources* by Martin Lings, you can read both the biography and the Qur'an in tandem with each other. We've labeled the chapters as early, middle or late, for both the Meccan and Medinan periods, so you can more easily assign the Qur'anic passages with the major stages of Muhammad's mission. In addition, the index of the Qur'an will help you locate key passages connected with events in Muhammad's life, so you can gain a fuller understanding of how the Qur'anic revelation helped him to respond to the issues at hand.

The Qur'an is what it is. It claims to be of divine origin, and it challenges people to ponder over its verses and to consider the world around them as proof of God's existence. It is a book that has influenced the lives of countless millions of people over the last 1,400 years, even as it continues to do so today for one fifth of the world's population. If approached with respect, it can reveal new insights and interesting nuggets of knowledge to even the most skeptical of readers. The Qur'an is, in its own words, the completion of God's favor to humanity. Whatever way you approach the Qur'an, may your mind be enlightened, may your heart be steadied and may your faith in God grow.

Ameen. Let it be so.

" There is no god but Allah.
Muhammad is the Messenger of Allah"

Bismillahir Rahmanir Raheem

In the Name of Allah,
The Compassionate, the Merciful.

The Opening

1 Al Fatihah
Early Meccan Period

And so the Qur'an *opens* with a condensed summary of its entire message. Thus, following good essay writing format, the opening paragraph of the Qur'an provides a brief summary of what its message was all about. In short, everything begins and ends with God, Who is in control and ready to provide healing, guidance and direction for any who ask.

This chapter offers so many shades of knowledge that it has been said that if the entire Qur'an were lost and only this chapter remained, it would be sufficient guidance for humanity for all time. This is also the first *complete* chapter of the Qur'an revealed to the Prophet, as only partial verses from chapters 96, 73, 68 and 74 preceded it. Therefore, this chapter can be dated to the early part of the year 611.

In the name of Allah, [9]
the Compassionate, the Merciful. [10] [1]

*P*raise be to Allah, Lord of All the Worlds; [2]

the Compassionate, the Merciful [3]
and Master of the Day of Judgment. [11] [4]

---

[9] Muhammad was still frightened of the visions and words he was receiving in the first days of his ministry. Whenever he would walk in the desert, he would sometimes hear the voice of a hidden spirit calling out to him, causing him to run back to the safety of Mecca. When he told his wife's cousin Waraqah about this, he urged Muhammad to stay and listen and report back to him with what he heard. Accordingly, one day Muhammad stood his ground when he heard the voice again during one of his excursions in the countryside. When the voice called out his name, Muhammad said, "Here I am." Then the voice commanded him to repeat that there was only one God and that he, Muhammad, was the Messenger of God. After Muhammad had done so, then the voice commanded him to recite yet further a new set of phrases, which were the verses of this chapter here. *(Wahidi)*

[10] It is said that when the Prophet uttered this phrase from this chapter for the first time in Mecca in public, some pagans shouted at him, "May Allah strike your mouth." *(Wahidi)*

[11] According to a saying of the Prophet, this chapter is divided into two halves: the first part is for a servant to praise Allah, and the second half is for a servant to ask for Allah's help. *(Nisa'i)* 'Umar Ibn 'Abdul-'Aziz (d. 720), a famous Umayyad caliph, used to recite this chapter, one verse after another, with a pause in between each verse. When he was asked why he made those silent pauses, he answered, "To enjoy Allah's reply (to my supplication)." It's no wonder that the Prophet called this chapter, "The Mother of the Book, the Opening of the Book and the Seven Frequently Repeated Verses.' *(At-Tabari.* Also see Qur'an 15:87)

To You alone do we render service [12]
and to You alone do we look for aid. [5]

Guide us on the straight path: [6]
the path of those whom You have favored, [13]
not of those who've earned Your anger, [14]
nor of those who've gone astray. [15] [7]

[12] The Arabic term '*ibadah* means *to be subdued or obedient,* but in a religious context it means *to serve or worship in obedience.* In this translation, we have used either of the two terms *service* or *worship* based upon the context, with the most frequent usage going to the more literal meaning of *service.*

[13] The favored or blessed ones are mentioned in 4:69.

[14] Adi ibn Hatim said, "I asked the Messenger of Allah about the verse of Allah which said, '...*not the path of those who've earned Your anger...,*' and he replied, 'They are the Jews.' And then I asked about the statement, '...*nor of those who've gone astray,*' and he said, 'The Christians are the ones who went astray.'" (*Abu Dawud, Tirmidhi*) It must be remembered that the Jews of the Hijaz, according to the medieval commentator al-Mawardi (d. 1058), were the most hostile to Islam and thus the anger that is mentioned here stems from that. Also see 5:82. As for the Christians, they went astray by taking the Message of Jesus and mixing it with elements of Greek and Roman religion, i.e. the monotheism taught by Jesus became Trinity and religious scholars became 'saints' that could be prayed to for Divine favors. See 5:77 where this is commented on.

[15] The Prophet said, "After the *Imam* (prayer leader) finishes (the last line of *Al Fatihah*), you should say, '*Ameen*' ('Let it be so,') for if your saying of '*Ameen*' coincides with that of the angels, your past sins will be forgiven." (*Muslim*) The Prophet used to say the *Ameen* aloud and used to extend it with his voice, and it is said that the mosque walls would shake from the loud saying of *Ameen* in unison by the people at prayer. (*Ahmad, Abu Dawud, Tirmidhi, Ibn Majah*)

The Cow

2 Al Baqarah
Early to Middle Medinan Period

The focus of this chapter, which takes its name from an incident recounted in verses 66-73, is to give us a sense of the history that exists between God and humanity. Allah created human beings to be the caretakers of the earth. As such, He endowed them with a capacity to learn and know that is far more advanced than any other creature He made. However, due to human weakness, our earliest ancestors lost their fellowship with Allah, and precious few have striven to regain it. Our collective failing is due as much to our own yearning for physical pleasure, as it is to the whisperings of the forces of darkness.

That darkness is embodied in *Shaytan* or Satan, an evil creature who felt he was better than humans were, and thus he set out on a campaign to prove Allah wrong. Allah accepted his challenge, not because He was afraid or in need of amusement, but because, as is His way, He wanted Satan to understand how he went wrong *before* he was going to be vanquished.

Even though humans *could* be corrupted, as Satan proved, he didn't realize that they were also created with an inner nature that constantly prompts them to notice their absence from God. Though Satan continues to try and corrupt as many humans as he can in his foolish quest to somehow best Allah and save himself, some humans still do look for God's truth. Allah constantly holds out the offer of His forgiveness and acceptance into His fellowship, regardless of the direction that human culture or values take.

From the first human beings, Adam and Eve, on through waves of successive civilizations, Allah's message of salvation was renewed through the work of prophets. Therefore, no one can have any excuse when it comes time to face the reality of Judgment Day - when we will all be judged by our faith and life's work and sentenced to either eternal life in Paradise or lengthy (or even permanent) internment in Hellfire.

The Prophet said of this chapter, "The (chapter of the) Cow is the highlight of the Qur'an and its apex. Eighty angels descended with each verse, and it has the Verse of the Throne (2:255), which was extracted from beneath the Divine Throne." (*Ahmad*) He also said, "Don't turn your homes into graveyards. Satan cannot enter a house where (the chapter of) the Cow is recited regularly." (*Muslim, Ahmad, Tirmidhi*)

In the Name of Allah,
the Compassionate, the Merciful

Alif. Lām. Meem. [16] [1]

That is the Book in which there is no doubt.

---

[16] These stand-alone letters are prefixed to some of the chapters of the Qur'an and were a known literary element in pre-Islamic Arabia. Their meaning in the Qur'an is disputed, with some theorizing that they are code letters for hidden messages from Allah. Others think that there is some numerically-based message in them (as in numerology), given that they appear before twenty-nine chapters, and there are twenty-nine letters in the Arabic language (if you count the '*hamza*' as a letter). The most convincing explanation to this writer, however, which is supported by eminent and diverse scholars of

It's a guide for those who are mindful (of their duty to Allah). [2]

(They're the ones) who believe in what's beyond their perception, establish regular prayer and spend in charity out of what We've given to them. [3]

They believe in what's being revealed to you, (Muhammad), even as they believe in what's been revealed before your time, and they're confident of the reality of the next life. [4]

They're living by the guidance of their Lord, and they're the ones who will be successful. [5]

Disbelief and Hypocrisy

*N*ow as for those who (willfully) cover over (their inner awareness of Allah), it doesn't matter if you warn them or not, for they're not going to believe. [6]

Allah [17] has sealed their hearts and ears and placed blinders over their eyes. [18] (On account of their ingratitude) they'll (be made to suffer) a severe punishment. [7]

Among the people (are some) who say, *"We believe in Allah and the Last Day,"* but they have no faith. [8] They try to deceive Allah and those who believe, (by pretending to have faith,) but they deceive no one but themselves – *and they don't even realize it!* [9]

---

the likes of Ibn Kathir, Zamakhshari and Ibn Taymiyyah, is that the letters are a way of communicating to the Arabs that their own language (as represented by the stand-alone letters of the alphabet) is being used to convey a message to them. The Arabs were so proud of their language, and this Qur'an was being revealed in it. However, the idol-worshippers had no explanation for how fantastically poetic and rhythmic the Qur'an was compared with their ordinary poetry. The Qur'an then challenged the Arabs to make a chapter, even a verse like a Qur'anic one (see 17:88, 52:34, 11:13, etc…). The subtext is meant to challenge them thusly: look, here are the letters of your own alphabet – a, b, c – now make something like this book, if you can. If you can't, then accept its message. (See 2:23-24) This view is confirmed by the fact that in almost every instance where these stand-alone letters appear, the very next verse makes some sort of statement about the unique nature of the Qur'an. (See the opening lines of chapters 10-15, for example.) Another addendum to this, which is wholly complimentary, is that the use of disjointed written letters was a common and integral part of the business trade. Individual letters were used to mark the various bundles of trade goods carried by camels, so beginning a Qur'anic chapter with disconnected letters would surely get the attention of the merchant-minded Arabs, who would instantly think of goods and merchandise. (This use of letters as a numerical stock-keeping system was known as the *abjad* system.)

[17] In the Arabic language, the proper name of the One Supreme God is *Allah*. This word usually is taken to mean *the One and Only God,* but there is a deeper history to this word. It is derived, according to the Arabist Fleisher Franz Delitzsch, from the ancient Arabic root *ilah* or *elah*, which means "to be possessed of God." A derivative from that root term, *aliha*, means "to be filled with dread," "perplexed" and "anxious to seek refuge," thus the Qur'an's call is for people to seek refuge with the enigmatic Divine from all that they fear. (*Zamakhshari*) (See 7:200 and 16:98 for example.) The Old Testament Book of Genesis (verses 21:42 & 53) uses the same term where God is called the "fear" or "dread" of Isaac - not in a negative sense, mind you, but in the sense of utter and complete awe. The Hebrew word for God, *Eloah* (or *El*), which occurs 3,350 times in the Old Testament, mostly in its plural 'royal' form of *Elohim*, is linguistically related to the Arabic root *ilah*. Adding the definite article *al* (the) to *ilah* makes it *al-ilah* which is the progenitor of the name *Allah*, or, *The* God. If it is remembered that Ishmael, the son of Abraham who dwelled in Arabia, spoke the same ancient tongue as Isaac, whose descendants became the Hebrews, then it is clear why Arabic and Hebrew both have the same linguistic name for God.

[18] Their hearts (or understanding) are 'sealed' as a sort of punishment for rejecting Allah first. (For the reason see 7:146.) In addition, Allah will let the powers of darkness have their way with such a person, a hypocrite, and he will fall further into error because he rejected the one, true reality in the universe. As Allah said, "*Satan has won them over and made them forget the remembrance of Allah.*" [58:19] Also see 4:79, 10:33, 44 and 10:108. Some commentators think this verse refers to Abu Jahl the pagan. Others say it refers to the Jews who did not accept Muhammad. (*Asbab u-Nuzul*)

There's a sickness in their hearts, so Allah adds to their sickness. [19]

A severe punishment will be theirs on account of their covering over (their innate awareness of the truth). [10]

When they're told, "*Don't cause disorder in the world*," they retort, "*But we're only trying to make it better.*" [20] [11]

Yet, without a doubt they're the ones who are causing the disorder - *without even realizing it!* [12]

When they're told, "*Believe (in Allah), like the (rest of the) people believe*," they sneer, "*Faith is for fools!*"

Yet, they're the fools – *and they just don't know it!* [13]

Hypocrites Think that They're Deceiving Allah

*W*hen they meet the believers they affirm, "*We believe, too*," but when they're alone with their satanic (allies), [21] they take back what they said by saying, "*We're really with you. We were only mocking them.*" [14]

Allah will throw their mocking back at them by letting them fall deeper into error until they're left wandering around, completely lost. [15]

They're the ones who've traded guidance for mistakes, and they gained nothing from the deal. They've lost all sense of direction! [16]

The Parable of the Storm

*T*heir example is like the man (Prophet Muhammad) who lit a torch (of guidance in the darkness of ignorance). [22]

---

[19] The disease or sickness in the hearts of the hypocrites, according to the early commentators, is *perpetual doubt.*

[20] Those who would advance the notion that Muslims must be in a constant state of revolution would do well to listen to these words of the Prophet: "If you're involved in *fitnah* (upheaval or turmoil), then your children will grow up (with it) even as your elders reach old age, and by then *fitnah* will be taken as tradition, and if someone stands up to oppose the *fitnah*, then people will accuse him of doing something wrong." A person in the crowd asked the Prophet when this might occur, and he replied, "When there are fewer honest people and when the number of people seeking power will be rampant. Authentic and sincere students of the religion (*deen*) will decrease, even as the overall number of people learning it will increase. The religion will be studied for worldly gain, and people will do good deeds, but only for their own profit." (*At-Targheeb wa at-Tarheeb*)

[21] 'Abdullah ibn Ubayy of the Khazraj tribe was set to be appointed the king of Medina before the coming of Prophet Muhammad to that city. Ibn Ubayy resented his loss of status after the Prophet arrived, and he made no secret of his associative dislike for Islam, though he pretended to follow Islam because it was on the upward trend. Once when he and some of his followers were about to meet some of Muhammad's companions, he whispered to his friends, "Look how I put those fools off." Then, when he greeted the companions (Abu Bakr, 'Umar and 'Ali), he lavished praise upon them, particularly upon Abu Bakr and 'Umar, two of Muhammad's most trusted confidants. After they left, 'Abdullah told his friends, "Do you see how I was acting? Whenever you see them do the same, and praise them much." When Abu Bakr told the Prophet how Ibn Ubayy was acting, the Prophet informed him that Ibn Ubayy had been mocking them, and this verse was revealed in comment. (*Asbab ul-Nuzul*)

[22] This parable, which according to al-Qurtubi and many others actually references the Prophet's struggles to reach the hypocrites with the truth, is packaged in a real-life issue that had particular resonance with the traveling people of Arabia, for it presented a real fear (that of getting lost in the wilderness at night) with a lesson on how Allah exceeds our capacities and is our true source of guiding light. Verses 19-20 compound that fear of getting lost, adding the imagery of a fierce storm assailing the hapless travelers. The storm is the fear and hardship they face in life without faith in Allah, while the lightning is Allah's flash of guidance, reminding them through sudden events (miracles) and

When it illuminated (the path of right from wrong for both) he (and his people), Allah took away (the) light (of understanding from the hypocrites among them) and left them (lost) in utter darkness, unable to see at all! [17] They're deaf, dumb and blind and won't return to the path! [23] [18]

(Another example) is of a storm cloud seething with (the) darkness (of doubt), thunderous (realizations calling to faith), and the lightning (call of sudden guidance). No matter how much (the hypocrites) cover their ears from the booming thunderclaps (of irresistible Divine Revelation) - *fearing for their very lives* - it doesn't help them, for Allah surrounds those who cover (the light of faith within their hearts)! [19]

When a lightning bolt (of insight or guidance) flashes (deeply within their hearts), it all but blinds them (with its truth), and at the least they grope forward (in its afterglow and understand some of Allah's truth).

However, when the darkness returns (due to their doubting or arrogance), they hesitate (in uncertainty). [24] If Allah had wanted, He could have taken away their hearing and their sight, for Allah has power over all things. [20]

Why are We Here?

O people! Serve your Lord Who created you and those who came before you so you can become mindful (of your duty towards Him). [21]

(He's) the One Who made the earth as your couch and the sky as your canopy. He sends down water from the sky and with it causes many types of plants to grow for your survival. So don't make rivals with Allah, especially when you know better. [22]

If you have any doubts about (the authenticity) of what We're revealing to Our servant (Muhammad), then compose a chapter similar to this. Then call upon your witnesses - *besides Allah* - if you're so certain (of your allegations that he made it all up himself.) [25] [23]

---

unexpected jolts (opportunities to learn a lesson) that the chance to return to the path is always there. Just look around in the brief afterglow of the lightning bolt! If they still chose to go it alone, however, they just get more and more lost.

[23] A person may think he's smart enough to find his way without Allah. He uses his mind to begin to understand the path of life, but he ignores Allah, the One who gave both him and his companions the gift of intelligence to begin with. The haughty people stray off the path of Allah, and at a certain point they've exhausted their natural abilities. When they're so far off the path, the light goes out, and they're utterly lost.

[24] Even people living without guidance have the capacity to think, feel and consider the meaning of things, but because they are often depraved, they see flashes of the truth: that there is really good and evil in the world, that mercy is better than rage, etc. They may ride for a while, blending these truths in their lives, but when their attention is turned aside by some worldly temptation, they forget the guidance and stumble about blindly again, leading an aimless life of consumption and pleasure.

[25] This is a recurring charge leveled against Muhammad and the Qur'an that Muhammad somehow copied from the Bible or was instructed by a reclusive religious figure, possibly Christian or Jewish. No such individuals have been convincingly identified, and the motives of such individuals would be hard to fathom. Muhammad was a semi-retired, part-time trader from a humble background living in a forgotten corner of the world, far removed from civilization. He had no high-ranking status. He could not read or write. He had no appreciable tribal influence. He never attended any school of any kind. He was an orphan from his childhood, and he had no outward or other discernable qualifications for such a grand undertaking. That he would suddenly be 'appropriated' at the age of forty by some shadowy figure(s) to found a world religion borders on pure nonsense. The idol-worshippers of Mecca leveled this charge against Muhammad and even offered suggestions as to who his secret teacher was. However, in the end even they gave up on this angle of attack when the Qur'an kept coming in snippets to Muhammad through the night and through the day, in public, instantaneously and often in response

If in fact you find it impossible (to duplicate this message), *and it is impossible*, [26] then beware of the Fire whose fuel is people and stone - (a blaze) that's been prepared for those who covered over (their innate ability to believe in Allah). [24]

Announce to those who believe and do what's morally right the good news that they shall have gardens beneath which rivers flow. Every time they're furnished with fruit from within, they'll exclaim, *"These look just like what we had before (in our earthly life)."* (That's because) they'll be given (their reward) in the form of what was familiar to them. What's more, they'll be joined by wholesome mates (with whom) to abide for all time. [27] [25]

How does the Lord Use Parables?

Allah won't hesitate to illustrate a point with something as small as a gnat or anything bigger (or smaller) than that. [28]

---

to events as they occurred. Soon, the Meccans began to attack Muhammad from another angle, saying he was possessed by evil spirits or under the influence of sorcery! (See 44:14.) Given that human civilization has never accepted that great literature is the result of demonic influence or magic, we can safely rule out sorcery as an explanation for the Qur'an. Combine this with the fact that for a full 23 years Muhammad received lengthy Qur'anic revelations and was a very public figure with next to no privacy, and the absurdity of the simplistic claim that he was being taught or that he copied the message from somewhere is made clear. Even Einstein needed time to study and think!

[26] The challenge to craft a chapter similar to one found in the Qur'an is meant to make the reader aware of the fact that on many levels, the Qur'anic style of presentation is a marvel. The Qur'an is considered to be the seminal text of erudite and elegant Arabic. Qur'anic grammar is the basis and final authority for the modern standard Arabic that educated people speak throughout the Arabic world. Think of the way in which the King James Bible influenced the development of the English language and multiply its effects manifold. A typical passage from the Qur'an combines the following elements: a rhyme scheme that uses skillful turns of rhythm and meter; a style of grammar that is at once majestic and allegorical; a vocabulary that consists of words that can have multiple, yet complimentary meanings; a thematic structure that links it to other passages, as well as content that, expressed in Arabic prose, reads like the finest Shakespeare to educated speakers of English. So the challenge exists and presents us with many levels of requirements to duplicate. Assuming one would even try, the next level of difficulty would lie in the fact that Qur'anic passages seem to have corollaries and paired passages or chapters found interwoven throughout the work. The task appears both daunting and awe-inspiring.

[27] In Paradise there are *houries*, or mates, who are in the shape of perfect humans, yet without souls or an independent will. They exist only to please our carnal desires, which will be without restriction in heaven. Although males are specifically mentioned as receiving them, it is a matter of debate if females will have them too. Some say that females were not directly mentioned in the Qur'an or hadith literature in connection to them out of modesty and respect for their shyness and reputation, and that they will have them too based on the principle of equity in reward. (See 33:35 and background info, 41:31-32, and 50:35.) In any case, these mates in no way will violate the sanctity of the marriages that were consecrated on the earth (though people who were married on earth are not required to remain married in heaven, if they choose not to be), because houris are not creatures with souls and the people of paradise do not enter into marriage with them. These *houris* are often referred to as the *Virgins* of Paradise, and Jesus, himself, is quoted as likening Paradise to virgins in Matthew 25:1-12. Buddha once showed beautiful *"celestial nymphs"* (who live in the *heaven of the 33 gods)* to his half-brother to talk him out of taking an earthly wife. In heaven, things that were unlawful on earth will be lawful there. For example, wine and other intoxicants are forbidden on earth as the tools of Satan, but in Paradise there will be rivers of wine that will give the most delightful highs but without the discomfort or painful hangovers. See 55:60 where the implication of the verse is to ask, "What did you think you would be doing in Heaven? It's a place of unimaginable reward and pleasure!" (Also see 32:17.) By the way, Meccan revelations emphasize the beauty of the mates of Paradise, perhaps as a way to get the attention of the pagans, while the much later Medinan revelations emphasize their goodness and purity, perhaps signaling to true believers that achieving Paradise is more about righteousness than carnal motivations.

[28] Some Jews of Medina ridiculed the Qur'an because it mentioned things as insignificant as insects in its parables. For example, idols are said to be helpless because they can't protect themselves from a fly, as in 22:73, and spider webs are an example of how weak an argument can be, as in 29:41. Some

Those who believe know that (all scriptural lessons are) the truth from their Lord, while those who cover (their capacity to believe ridicule such things) by saying, "*What can Allah possibly mean by these examples?*"

By them He allows many to fall further into error, and by them He allows many others to be guided.

However, He doesn't allow anyone to be confused by them except for those who've gone beyond the bounds (of morality first). [26]

They're the ones who broke their (natural) bond with Allah after it had been made strong, " and they separated (the family ties) that He's ordered to be joined together.

They behave badly in the world, so in the end they'll be the losers. [27]

How can you suppress (your own natural faith) in Allah, seeing how He gave you life (when you had none)?

Then He's going to take back your life and bring you to life once more, and then you're going to go back to Him. [28]

He's the One Who created everything that's on the earth for your benefit, and then He turned towards the (design of the) sky, making it into seven (layers).

(He was able to do that) for He knows about all things. [29]

On Adam's Creation

*A*nd so it was that your Lord said to the angels, "*I'm going to place a caretaker on the earth.*" 30

However, they asked, "*Are You going to put someone there who's going to cause chaos and disorder and shed blood, while we magnify Your praise and extol Your Holiness?*"

(Allah answered them), saying, "*I know what you don't know.*" [30]

Thereafter, He (brought Adam into being) and taught him the names (and qualities) of everything (in the natural world). 31

Then He placed (the wonders of the natural world) before the angels and said, "*Now tell Me the names (and qualities) of all of these things (you see here before you,) if you're so certain (that I made a mistake).*" [31]

"*All glory belongs to You!*" they exclaimed. "*We know nothing about any of this, other than what You've already taught us, for You are the Knowledgeable and the Wise.*" [32]

Then He said to Adam, "*Tell them the names (and qualities of these things).*"

Jews said, "This doesn't seem like a revelation from Allah." Thus, verses 26-27 were revealed in response. (*Asbab ul-Nuzul*)

[29] Most scholars say this verse refers to people who sever family ties, and the Prophet said of this that, "He will not enter Paradise, the one who severed relationships (with his relatives)." (*Mishkat*)

[30] The Qur'an now begins the tale of humanity literally at its beginning, with the first human being of our species – Adam. Who was he, and where did the fall occur? Readers of the Hebrew Bible will be familiar with this tale, but there are some important differences that have theological implications that will set Islam apart from the teachings of both Judaism and Christianity.

[31] Unlike the Bible, the Qur'an never asserts that humans were made in 'the image' of Allah (see Genesis 1:27). So what gift did Allah give to Adam, if not some divine resemblance? Allah would give Adam the power to understand the environment around him. This is one of the deeper meanings of the term, *ism*, which means 'high point' or 'name.' In other words, Allah gave Adam the ability to know the true (higher) nature of something. Interestingly enough, the root meaning of the word *insan*, which the Qur'an often uses to label human beings, literally means 'to be able to adapt to.' We are one of the only species that can adapt to nearly any physical environment on earth, (as evidenced by our varied sizes, skin colors and metabolisms,) and we possess awareness and understanding through our consciousness about what the significance of nature is.

After he had finished doing so, (Allah) announced to (the angels):

"Didn't I tell you that I know what's beyond perception within the heavens and the earth and that I know what you do openly and in secret?" [33]

The Origin of the Great Rift

So then We gave an order to the angels, saying, *"Bow down (in respect) to Adam."* 32

They all bowed down; however, (a jinn named) Iblis, (who was there watching) didn't bow down. 33

He refused in his arrogant pride and chose to suppress (his awareness of the truth). [34]

We said to Adam:

"Both you and your mate may live in this garden and eat freely of its bounty to your fill, but don't go near this one tree, for it will lead you into corruption." [35]

However, they (were tempted) by Satan and banished (from the home) where they had been.

So then We ordered, *"Get down from here, and live in conflict with each other! Inhabit the expanse of the earth, and fend for yourselves for a while!"* [36]

Thereafter Adam learned words of repentance from his Lord, and He turned towards him in forgiveness, for He's the Acceptor of Repentance, the Merciful. 34 [37]

So We (softened Our attitude towards Adam) and said:

"Get down from here altogether, but if any guidance ever comes to you from Me, whoever follows My guidance will have nothing to fear or regret. [38] *However, those who conceal and deny Our proofs, they shall be companions of the Fire, and that's where they're going to stay!"* [39]

---

32 In verse 30, the angels questioned the wisdom of Allah when He announced that He was about to create a being of flesh with a measure of freewill. The angels assumed they were superior, as they obeyed Allah, the ultimate truth, without question, while the humans would be saddled with the burden of choice. Allah proved to the angels that humans had an edge over them in comprehension and cognitive ability, and His order that they bow was to impress upon them that He, in fact, knew better and that the human being was equipped with superior faculties. In effect, the angels were humbled for making unfounded assumptions against the wisdom of the One Whom they claimed to serve so obediently. Also see 95:4-8.

33 Iblis is a *jinn* and not an angel, and he often kept company with the angels because he was devoted to goodness. He became prejudiced against Adam when he was asked to bow along with the angels to a creature made of *mud*. (*Ibn Kathir*, also see 18:50) *Jinns* (genies) are elemental spirits who often seek to create mischief for physical beings. The term *jinn*, itself, which comes from the root *junna*, literally means *to be hidden* or *concealed*. Thus, the term can be applied to unseen creatures, unknown strangers or to anything that we don't see. The Arabs also referred to babies in the womb as *hidden*, or *jenin*, given that they were not seen. The term for garden is *jennah*, which implies hidden areas behind trees and vines. The name Iblis means *frustrated*. For more details concerning Iblis's challenge to Allah, see 7:12-15 and 7:16-18. Iblis's name was later changed to *Shaytan* (Satan), an Arabic word that means "to separate from" or be rebellious, among other things. This is a reference to the fact that he distanced himself from his Creator in rebellion and also that he seeks to separate people from Allah's fellowship.

34 See 7:23 for words of repentance. In contrast to traditional Western Christian theology, the Qur'an asserts that Allah didn't need to sacrifice *a part* of His Own Being on a cross or be murdered by His creatures before He could forgive them. The first two people merely needed to repent, and then Allah forgave them. Thus, there is also no concept of Original Sin in Islam.

Remembering Allah's Covenant with the Jews

Children of Israel! [35] Remember the favor I bestowed upon you. [36]

Fulfill your covenant with Me, even as I've fulfilled My covenant with you, and fear no one but Me. [37] [40]

Believe in what I'm revealing, which confirms the teachings with you now, and don't be the first to reject it, nor sell My (revealed) verses for a petty gain. [38] *Be mindful of Me!* [39] [41]

Don't confuse the truth with falsehood, nor conceal the truth knowingly. [42]

Be constant in prayer, practice regular charity and bow down to Me, along with those (Muslims) who are already bowing down (in worship). [43]

Don't be Hypocrites

Will you ask other people to be righteous, but then forget your own selves?

---

[35] The use of the term "Children of Israel" is also commonly employed in the Jewish Old Testament (see Numbers 19:2 or II Chronicles 8:2, for example). *Israel* was a nickname of Jacob, who was a grandson of Abraham. The first ethnic name that the descendants of Jacob may have had was the simple term *Hebrew*, which meant *'from the other side,'* seemingly a reference to Abraham being from *the other side* of the Euphrates river (i.e., in Mesopotamia). (Indeed, it has been suggested by some linguists that the Mesopotamian term *hebiru* predates Abraham by many centuries.) After the Hebrews were freed from bondage in Egypt, the term *Children of Israel* came into vogue. Then, after they established a kingdom in Palestine, they become known as *Israelites*. Finally, after they lost their kingdoms their scattered descendants became known simply as *Jews* or the descendants of the tribe of Judah (which was the most prominent surviving tribe for some time).

[36] After presenting a brief summary of the significance of Adam and his fall, the Qur'an now turns our attention to the crucial issues raised when the storied history of the Jewish people is compared with their stated obligations to God. Rather than offering a mere retelling of the many accounts contained in the Old Testament, however, the Qur'an addresses Jews personally and directly and asks them to take an honest look at their relationship to God through the lens of critical self-analysis. This issue is addressed early on in the arranged order of Qur'anic chapters in order to give the reader a sense of the ultimate results of God's favor that was bestowed upon a past nation. This is a logical step to take as a platform for explaining why the Jewish covenant was superseded first by Jesus and then by Muhammad. The Qur'an takes the position that a significant number of Jews in previous ages failed to live up to their end of the covenant that God had established with them at Mount Sinai. Therefore, the Qur'an is calling on Jews to rededicate themselves to God by purifying their faith of the pagan customs and practices that crept into their religion over the centuries, to reflect upon the strengths and weaknesses of the past, and further to perfect their faith by joining the movement brought by Muhammad, God's last prophet to the world.

[37] See Leviticus 26:1-46 where the Jews are addressed similarly about their covenant.

[38] Some Jews of Medina used to write small verses of the Torah on leather scraps and then sell them to the illiterate Arabs as something akin to good luck charms. (*Asbab ul-Nuzul*) Jeremiah 8:8 in the Old Testament levels a similar charge against certain priests in former times.

[39] The term *taqwa* comes from the root word, *waqa*, and it means to protect oneself from harm, to be aware of, mindful of, or conscious of God and His prohibitions, and it has been rendered accordingly throughout this translation, depending upon the context. To pass beyond the limits of what God allows is to invite retribution, but beyond this, falling into sin and personal weakness can make a person feel ashamed of himself. Thus, we can associate righteousness or piety with this term. To *have taqwa* (in Islamic parlance) means to behave in a conscientious and upright manner out of the fear of disobeying our Creator. Once a man named 'Umar ibn al-Khattab (d. 644), who was one of the Prophet's major companions, asked Ubayy ibn Ka'b what *taqwa* meant in practical terms, and he answered by asking, "Have you ever walked on a thorny path?" 'Umar said that he had; then his friend asked, "Then what did you do?" 'Umar explained that he held up the bottom of his clothes and went through it as quickly and carefully as he could. "That is *taqwa*," the scholar said. In other words, living life conscious of the pitfalls all around us, that would plunge us into sin and ruin.

You study the scriptures, so why won't you understand? [40] [44]

Strengthen yourselves through perseverance and prayer, though it isn't easy, save for the truly humble [45] - those who realize that they're going to meet their Lord and that they will return to Him. [46]

Children of Israel! Remember the blessings that I bestowed upon you and how I favored you above all others in the world, [47] so beware of a day when no soul will be able to help another, when no intercession will be accepted, nor any payment (offered) will sway, nor any help come. [41] [48]

Allah Delivered
the Children of Israel

*R*emember that We delivered you from Pharaoh's people, [42] who enslaved you and tormented you, killing your sons while letting your women live. [43] That was an enormous test from your Lord! [49] Then remember that We parted the sea and rescued you, while drowning Pharaoh's people as you stood there watching! [50]

Yet, also recall that while We communed with Moses for forty nights, you took (to worshipping the likeness of) a calf and committed a terrible crime. [44] [51] Even after that We forgave you so you could learn to be truly thankful. [52] Recall that We gave Moses the (revealed) scripture and the *standard* (to judge between right and wrong), so you could be guided. [45] [53]

Remember when Moses (returned to) his people (carrying that revealed message) and declared, "*My people! You've wronged yourselves by taking this calf (as a god). Repent to your Lord, and kill (within) yourselves (all your lowly desires). That's the best thing you can do in*

---

[40] A Jewish man in Medina gave permission to his relatives to consider Muhammad to be a prophet, but he himself refused to accept Muhammad's teachings. This verse was revealed in comment. (*Asbab ul-Nuzul*)

[41] The Children of Israel were chosen to be missionaries for Allah to the nations around them in the Middle East. It is the crossroads of civilization. Therefore, the mission to give God's teachings was extremely important. It was Prophet Abraham who prayed to God to bless his descendants. God said He would bless them, all except the wrong-doers among them. (The Jewish Torah, in Deuteronomy 11:1-7, 19, 27-28 echoes this divine directive to live for God alone or face the wrath of God.) The Qur'an asserts that the Children of Israel failed in their mission due to worldly temptations. Thus, the other descendants of Prophet Abraham, the Arabs, were then chosen to be the message-bearers of God's truth. See Qur'an 2:124, 128 and 130.

[42] Moses was the greatest prophet among the Children of Israel. He is thus given a prominent role all throughout the Qur'an as the focal point upon which Jews may compare what they have now with the pure religion he taught. The varied forms of Judaism extant in the world today are not always in conformity with the teachings of Moses, and many of the regulations of Judaism originated not as a blessing from Allah, but as a means of reprimand to their forbears who often disobeyed Moses and the other prophets. Jesus sought to free the Jewish community from the weight of an oppressive state of legalism, but he was rebuffed. Even still, Allah loves those Jews who would be righteous, and He calls upon them in this book to remember all of His favors and accept His invitation to renew their faith through His last revelation, which confirms what they have from their ancestors. If they insist on remaining loyal to Judaism, then at the least, let them be sincere and faithful to that and not remain inclined to the temptations of the material world.

[43] The Qur'an often gives passing references to events in Jewish tribal history, often relying upon the fact that any Jews who would be hearing the message would know what events were being called into account. This economy of details allows the Qur'an to continue forward in its essential message without having to recount every small detail from past historical periods.

[44] This episode is mentioned in the book of Exodus, chapter 32. That chapter also asserts that Aaron cooperated in the making of the idol (verses 23-24, 35). The Qur'an rejects this account and clears Aaron of any involvement. See 6:84 and 20:90.

[45] The 'standard' is the collected traditions of Moses that are separate from divine revelation.

the sight of your Lord." [46]   And so (Allah) turned to you (in forgiveness), for He's the Acceptor of Repentance, the Merciful. [54]

Allah was Patient with Israel

$\mathcal{R}$emember the time when you said, *"Hey, Moses! We're never going to believe in you until we see Allah face to face!"* [47] For that you were struck down with a thunderous boom, even as you stood there watching! [55]

Yet, even after that We revived you out of your daze so you could have (another chance) to be grateful. [56] We caused the clouds to spread shade over you and sent manna and quails down upon you, (saying), *"Eat of the wholesome things that We've provided for you."* We were never

harmed (when they rebelled); rather, they only harmed themselves. [48] [57]

An Example of Disobedience

$\mathcal{R}$emember (the time when you were approaching a new land) and We issued the following command: *"Enter this town, and eat freely of the abundance you find there, but pass through its gates humbly and preach penitence and forgiveness. (If you act in a noble way,) then We shall forgive you your sins and increase the (fortunes) of those who are good."* [49] [58]

Nonetheless, dishonest people altered the order they received (and behaved poorly towards the inhabitants of the town). And so We sent down upon the offenders an (air-borne) plague from above, for they persisted (in doing wrong). [50] [59]

---

[46] The Old Testament states that the true followers of Moses actually killed 3,000 disobedient Hebrews after he returned down from the mountain, as told in Exodus 32:26-28. Muslim commentators have been divided about the meaning of this verse, with some accepting the Biblical account and other suggesting that because the pronoun 'yourselves' is present, and since suicide was unthinkable, that the verse is suggesting that they were to purge the evil within their own hearts as much as it could mean that Moses had the wrongdoers slain. Both interpretations can be found among the commentators. I have chosen the latter view, given that the same incident, as told in 7:148-156 clearly states that God forgave the disobedient Hebrews when they felt sorry for their sins (while those who remained unmoved were punished with mere shame in this life). Thus, from the Qur'anic perspective, it appears there was no slaughter ordered by Moses of his people, and the Qur'an is best for interpreting itself.

[47] The Qur'an is unequivocal in holding that people are not allowed to see God face to face due to His exalted Majesty being far above that (besides the fact that He created the sun and the stars and we would probably go blind seeing Him!) For the ancient Jews, however, there has been some confusion on this issue, and the call of the Hebrews to Moses to show them God before they would believe is telling. Exodus 24:10-11 states that the nobles and the regular people of Israel "saw God," whereas Exodus 33:20 says that no man can see God and live. Then it says in verse 23 that only His "back parts" can be seen. (Alse dee Deuteronomy 5:4.) The Qur'an does not accept such anthropomorphisms and merely states that the punishment the Jews received for such insolence was to be thunderstruck with terror.

[48] See Exodus 16:12-31 for the particulars of how they rebelled in this regard.

[49] It is thought that the episode mentioned below refers to an incident in which the Israelites entered into a town named Shattim, just east of the Jordan River. Although they were to be the paragons of a godly-oriented people, they failed to be virtuous standard-bearers of Allah's truth on this occasion. Instead, they engaged in idolatry, immorality and sinfulness. See Numbers 25:1-2 and 8-9. Reference to this incident is also made in the Qur'an at 7:161-162. Prophet Muhammad narrated that instead of preaching penitence (*hittatun*), the Hebrews said to the locals, "*Hintatun*," which means, "A grain in a husk." Thus, they were mocking Allah's orders. (*Bukhari*) Also see Jeremiah 9:8-9.

[50] Lit. *from the sky.* Plagues have been a common feature of human civilization for countless centuries, and the Old Testament is full of references to God punishing people with them. The Prophet said of them, "Plagues were a way to chastise the people of the past, so if one of you hears of its spread in the land, then don't approach it, but if the plague should appear in the land in which you are present, then don't leave that land trying to run away from it." (*Bukhari*) This is sound advice to prevent individuals from carrying the plague along with them in their vain attempts to save themselves.

Trials in the Desert

$\mathcal{R}$emember the time when Moses searched for water for his people. [51] We told him, *"Tap the rock with your staff."* [52]

Right away twelve bubbling springs gushed forth, and every clan found its own place. So eat and drink from the resources that Allah provides, and don't cause corruption in the world. [60]

Yet, also recall the time when you complained, *"Hey, Moses! We're tired of eating the same thing (day after day), so call upon your Lord for us to bring us the harvest of the earth: herbs, cucumbers, garlic, lentils and onions."*

"What?" (Moses) cried out. *"Would you trade (the hardship that comes with freedom, and) that's better, for (the regularity of slavery, which) is of far lower value? Go back to some (place like) Egypt, and then you'll get what you're asking for!"*

(As a punishment for their ungratefulness,) they were stricken with humiliation and misery. They brought the wrath of Allah down upon themselves because they rejected His signs and killed His messengers unjustly – and that's because they were a rebellious and defiant (people). [53] [61]

Allah is the Lord of All True Religions

$\mathcal{T}$hose who believe [54] (in Islam) and those who are Jewish, Christian or Sabian [55] - anyone who has faith in Allah and the Last Day and who does what's morally

---

[51] Allah provided abundant help to the Children of Israel after they escaped slavery in Egypt. However, the Children of Israel began to grumble against Moses on account of the harsh, nomadic lifestyle that was thrust upon them. (See Numbers 11:5-6.) In Egypt they lived in houses and had a settled, agrarian lifestyle, albeit with harsh labor quotas and other miseries. The price of freedom was hardship, but they failed to realize this and perhaps still suffered from a form of mental slavery to their old lifestyle.

[52] Why does God refer to Himself in the plural sometimes, using pronouns such as "We" and "Us"? Like most other languages, Arabic can use the term "We" to refer to a single being. By using the pronoun, "We," the majesty *and* power of an individual is magnified. For example, a king may say, "We decree..." instead of saying, "I decree...," (as in 27:16 where Solomon calls himself a "we" while addressing his people). Throughout the Qur'an, God (Allah) will alternately use, "I", "Us", "Me" or "We" to refer to Himself. This technique of language is called the *"Royal We"* and is also employed in Hebrew, English, French and many other languages. (See Genesis 3:22, for example, where God even calls Himself an 'Us'")

[53] Some from among the Israelites murdered their prophets on a number of occasions as recorded in the Bible in II Chronicles 24:21 and Mark 6:17-29. In Matthew 23:29-31, 37, Jesus, himself, accuses his people of murdering the prophets of old. (Also see I Thessalonians 2:15 where Paul makes the same charge.)

[54] This verse was revealed, in particular, to answer the concern of Salman Al Farsi. He was a Persian who was raised as a Zoroastrian, but who then spent a number of years as a Christian, before finally accepting Islam. He asked the Prophet about the fate of all those righteous Christians with whom he lived and studied before he entered into the Prophet's fold. The Prophet casually remarked that those people were going to be in Hellfire, (probably on the assumption that anyone less than a pure monotheist was in trouble with Allah.) Salman describes his inner reaction to the Prophet's words thusly, "The entire earth became gloomy to me." But then this verse was revealed from Allah to correct the Prophet's incorrect assumption. (*Asbab ul-Nuzul*)

[55] The *Sabians* were a semi-monotheistic group of ancient Jewish extraction located primarily in central and southern Iraq in the seventh century, but also in some parts of northeastern Arabia. They were neither Jews nor Christians in the prevailing sense, but had a semi-monotheistic faith that was a blend of primitive Judaism, ancient Sumerian paganism and the messianic teachings of John the Baptist. (They followed many Jewish laws, bathed ritually in the Tigris and Euphrates Rivers, did not allow conversion to the faith, and held that Allah lived in the stars. They prayed to the north instead of towards Jerusalem). The name Sabian itself is thought to derive from their word *masbuta,* which meant *to immerse* or *baptize.* Other names they are known by are Mandaeans, Christians of St. John and Nasoraeans. They are also considered legitimate 'followers of earlier revelation' in Islamic legal

right - their reward will be with their Lord, and they'll have nothing to fear nor regret. [56] [62]

The People Receive the Law

(Children of Israel), remember when We established a covenant with you at the towering heights of Mount Tūr: [57] *"Hold firmly to what We've given to you, and remember what it contains so you can be mindful (of Allah)."* [58] [63]

However, you later turned your backs on it! If it wasn't for Allah's favor and mercy extended towards you, you would've surely been lost. [64]

And so it was that you knew some (of your people) were breaking the Sabbath rules, (you were given, yet, you did nothing). [59] So We said to them, *"Be (like) despised apes!"* [60] [65]

---

parlance and are thus accorded all the rights and privileges of a monotheistic community. Also see 5:69.

[56] So can a person enter heaven if they do not accept Islam? It's generally accepted that any non-Muslim who knows little or nothing about Islam will be judged 'by what they know." In other words, a Christian, a Jew or even a tribesman in the jungle with a primitive religion will be judged by the best of its moral codes. But what of those who learn about Islam to a sufficient degree that they can fairly compare it with what they have currently? Opinion is divided. One commentator named al-Sulami (d. 1106) was of the view that verse 3:85 superseded (abrogated) this verse by declaring that only Islam will be accepted in the Hereafter. On the other hand, al-Qurtubi (d. 1273) said that 3:85 does not abrogate this verse because it directly refers to those people (of different religions) who did in fact leave this life as Christians and did not oppose or reject the Prophet Muhammad. Al-Baydawi (d. 1268) takes this a step further and explains that as long as the Christian, Jew or Sabian does not deny the prophethood of Muhammad, they can still hope for salvation. He offers as proof the Christian visitors from the Abyssinian court who heard the Prophet reciting from the Qur'an (surah 36) and they recognized it as revelation from God with some converting and others not. So to answer the original question, non-Muslims who wish to retain their religion, and who at the same time recognize the Prophet Muhammad as also from God, can perhaps have the hope of salvation in the hereafter as well, and Allah knows best the truth of this.

[57] Without any proof whatsoever, some modern commentators have assumed that Mount Tur is the same as Mount Sinai in the Sinai Peninsula of Egypt. Commentators in the classical period were generally divided on the issue, but many postulated that Mount Tur was somewhere in northern Arabia. Recent archeological explorations in Saudi Arabia have identified a likely mountain at a site known as *Jabal al-Lawz*. See the book entitled, *In Search of the Mountain of Allah: The Discovery of the Real Mt. Sinai*, by Robert Cornuke and David Halbrook.

[58] The Jewish Torah relates the details of the Covenant in Exodus, chapters 19-31. An extremely large number of laws are given – some of them quite difficult – and Moses is commanded to relate them all to the newly freed people. The Hebrews were camped at the mountain for nearly a year.

[59] The practice of doing no work on Saturday, known as the Day of the Sabbath, is so important to Jewish tradition that flouting its rules is punishable by death. (See Exodus 31:12-17.) Although many people assume that the Sabbath is meant to commemorate the day that God 'rested' after the labor of creating the universe, in fact, the Sabbath was instituted only after Moses and the Jews escaped from Egyptian slavery as a way to commemorate Allah's favor. (See Deuteronomy 5:15.) For the Sabbath regulations see Deuteronomy 5:12-14.

[60] The mention of the term *apes* is in recognition that primates often imitate whatever they see. Therefore, Allah, in equating the Sabbath-breakers with apes, is pointing out that they hopelessly copy whatever ignorant ways the cultures and nations around them practice. They will prefer to copy unbelievers and wrongdoers, which is, in fact, what repeatedly happened, if the records in the Bible are to be believed. The same story is mentioned in 7:163-166 where the people are further identified as fishermen who lived in a village by the sea. Some commentators have held that the wrongdoers were actually *physically* turned into apes, (and there is evidence that the Jews of Medina had a legend about it,) though it must be remembered that the Qur'an occasionally uses metaphorical, figurative or allegorical language. Ibn 'Abbas (d. 687) was of the opinion that they were transformed thusly, but that it lasted for only three days. The Jewish Old Testament orders that Sabbath-breakers are to be put to death and that this rule is to be binding upon all Jews for all time (see Exodus 31:14-16, also Deuteronomy 5:12-14). Interestingly enough, there is a tradition from the Prophet, recorded in the

We made an example of them in their own time and for all times to come - a lesson for those who are mindful (of Allah). [66]

The Story of the Spotless Cow

*R*emember when Moses said to his people, *"Allah has commanded that you sacrifice a cow."*

They replied, *"Surely, you're not serious?"*
61

(Moses) answered them, saying, *"Allah forbid (that I would speak) so frivolously."* [67]

So they demanded, *"Call upon your Lord on our behalf to specify exactly what kind of cow."*

Then Moses replied, *"Neither too old nor too young, He says, but somewhere in between. Now do as you're told."* [68]

"Call upon your Lord on our behalf again," they implored, *"to tell us what color it should be."*

So Moses answered, *"A light brown cow, rich in tone and pleasant (to the eye)."* [69]

"Call upon your Lord on our behalf," they pleaded (once more), *"to point out its variety, for all cows look the same to us. If Allah wills, then we'll be rightly guided."* [70]

"He says an unyoked cow," (Moses replied,) *"neither worn out from plowing nor watering the fields. It should be in good condition without any mark or blemish."*

Then they answered, *"Ah! Now you've given us an ample description,"* but even still they offered the sacrifice only grudgingly. [71]

The Torah on Unresolved Murder

*R*emember the time when (some of) you murdered a man and then took to accusing each other (individually)? 62

Allah would soon bring to light what you had concealed. 63 [72]

Bukhari collection, that describes future followers of his who will make lawful things like adultery and liquor and who will be stingy. The Prophet concluded by saying that Allah will turn them into monkeys and pigs and that they'll remain like that until Judgment Day. The commentators, both ancient and modern, understand that report figuratively and not literally, so this principle can legitimately be applied to interpreting this verse, as well.

61 Later on, the Qur'an admonishes Muslims not to question Muhammad endlessly in the same way that Moses was being questioned and stalled. See 2:104-112. The story of the sacrificed cow, albeit without the drama, can be found in the book of Numbers 19:1-4.

62 Ibn 'Abbas (d. 687) explained the details of the incident enumerated in these verses as follows: In one of the encampments of the Children of Israel, there was a man who had no sons but many nephews. They conspired to kill him for his wealth and then dumped the body in front of another encampment. Those people discovered the body and swore to Moses that they did not kill him. Afterwards, Moses gathered the various people, and they tried to point out a single culprit to blame, but then they took to division and bickering. Innocent people might have been killed but for the intervention of Divine guidance, which provided a method, however imperfect, of getting people to accept that some crimes will remain unsolved in this life.

63 Many commentators believe that the priests of the Israelites took some of the sacrificed animal (from verses 2:67-71) and slapped it upon the dead man who then suddenly came to life and told everyone who really killed him. There is no prophetic statement that this happened, nor is there any proof that the man came alive, but this has been the favorite position of classical commentators, even though they have no corroboration in any Islamic or Jewish source documents. Muhammad Asad suggested in his commentary that this verse is really referring to the *application* of group investigation (*apply some of it*) to the situation (*him* or *it*) to resolve the murder. He also proves that when the grammar is deconstructed the old understanding is not tenable. I believe that verses 2:72-73 refer to the practice found in Deuteronomy 21:1-9, for by making a sacrifice and declaring that the culprit cannot be found

We said, "*Apply some of (the principle of absolution) to (this situation)*," and in this way Allah saves lives from being taken (unjustly) and shows you His signs so you can understand. [73] Yet, (in spite of this guidance), your hearts only hardened like stone, even harder!

Though indeed among stones are some from which rivers may flow, others which crack under pressure and let water flow, as well as others that fall down for fear of Allah, and Allah is not unaware of what you're doing. [74]

Dealing with Duplicity

(Muhammad,) how can you hope to convince (the Jews of Medina) to believe in you? Some of them, after hearing and understanding the words of Allah, *changed them on purpose!* [64] [75]

When they meet the believers they affirm, "*We also believe (in Allah)!*"

Though when they're alone among themselves they say, "*We shouldn't let them know what Allah revealed to us (in our scriptures), for they'll only have better arguments to use against us by quoting the words of your Lord.*"

Don't you see (their game)? [76]

Don't they know that Allah is aware of what they hide and of what they bring out in the open? [65] [77]

The Ignorance of the Masses

Now among (the Children of Israel) there are the uneducated (masses) who know nothing of (their) scripture and who believe only in what they want to believe. [66] They follow nothing more than their own fickle whims! [78]

So ruin to those who write (false) scriptures with their own hands (to sell as good luck charms) [67] and say, "*Here, this is from Allah,*" to make a miserable profit with it. [68]

Ruin to them for what their hands fake, and ruin to them for (the gains) they make! [79]

(*applying* the principle of sacrifice-as-absolution to *it*, i.e., the situation), it makes blood feuds, false accusations and misguided revenge less likely, and thus saves lives from being unjustly taken, and Allah knows better. (Also see Leviticus 6: 1-13.) Whatever happened, it became the custom among the Israelites to make a sacrifice in cases of unresolved murder.

[64] Also see the Old Testament Book of Jeremiah 5:20-31.

[65] For a time the Jewish leaders of Medina made a pact among themselves not to reveal their prophecies and predictions about their long awaited messenger from God, fearing that the Muslims would see signs in them that confirmed Muhammad's prophethood. (See Song of Solomon 5:10-16 and Deuteronomy 18:15-22 among others, for example.) When asked for quotes, they would misread from their Torah and other books. On one occasion they hid from the Prophet a verse in their Torah about stoning adulterers. This passage refers to that situation. (*Asbab ul-Nuzul*)

[66] Apparently, some Jewish rabbis of Medina had certain religious writings in which their long awaited prophet was described - *including a description of what he looked like.* When they found that Muhammad resembled this description, it is said that they altered the descriptions in their writings to make it seem as if he did not fit the physical profile. A Jewish rabbi and convert to Islam, 'Abdullah ibn Salam, confirmed that this took place, and when this action of the Jewish scholars was publicly announced, this verse was revealed in response. (*Asbab ul-Nuzul*)

[67] Apostle Paul is even harsher in the Bible by calling Jewish writings nothing more than fables that mislead! See Titus 1:14.

[68] Ibn 'Abbas (d. 687) said that before the coming of Islam some Jews of Medina used to write small passages of the Torah on leather scraps and sell them to the unschooled Arabs, claiming they were holy charms to be used for good luck. That is what this verse is referencing. (*Asbab ul-Nuzul*) Jeremiah 8:8 in the Old Testament levels a similar charge against certain priests in former times.

False Claims of Leniency

They claim, *"Well, our punishment in the Fire will only be temporary."* [69]

Ask (them), *"Did Allah promise you that? If He did, then He won't go back on His word, or are you saying something about Allah that you're not sure of?"* [80]

No way! Whoever earns the wages of sin and is enveloped in evil will be among the companions of the Fire for all time, [81] while those who believe and do what's morally right will be with the companions of the Garden for all time. [82]

The Sworn Duties of the Children of Israel

*R*emember the time when We took an agreement from the Children of Israel, saying, *"Don't serve anything in place of Allah. Honor your parents and relatives. Be kind to orphans and to the poor.* [70] *Speak in wholesome language to others, and lastly, establish regular prayer and practice regular charity."*

However, later on you turned your backs (on these rules), all of you, save for a few, and you backslide even now! [71] [83]

The Sin of Infighting

*R*emember that We took another agreement from you, saying, *"You must not kill or banish each other."* [72] You made a

---

[69] The Jews of Medina had a belief that the world would last no more than 7,000 years and that any Jewish people who go to Hellfire will be punished for seven days only, with each day equaling a thousand years. After that the punishment would be over. This verse was revealed to answer this notion. (*Asbab ul-Nuzul*)

[70] The Islamic religious holiday of '*Eid al-Fitr* was being celebrated in Medina. Young and old alike were pouring forth from the morning prayers to begin the day's festivities. The Prophet was walking towards the exit of the mosque, greeting everyone he saw. Then he saw a thin boy dressed in tattered clothes sitting alone in a corner, crying into his folded arms. The Prophet approached the boy, put his hand on his shoulder and asked him what was wrong. Without lifting his head, the boy pushed the Prophet's hand away and said, "Just leave me alone." The Prophet then rubbed the top of the boy's head and said, "But just tell me, my child, what's the matter with you." At that, the boy sunk his head to his knees and sobbed, "My father was killed in the war against Muhammad. My mother has been married off to someplace else. My property has been taken by others, and when I went to my mother, her new husband drove me away. Today, all the other boys are laughing and celebrating in their nice clothes, but as for me, I have no food to eat, no clothes to wear nor any roof to take shelter under." Tears welled up in the Prophet's eyes, but he tried to smile as he said, "And what of it, my boy? I lost both my mother and my father when I was young." The boy then looked up at Muhammad, and when he recognized who he was, he cringed in embarrassment. The Prophet said to him, "If I became like your father, (my wife) A'ishah became like your mother and (my daughter) Fatimah became like your sister, will this make you happy, my child?" The boy nodded in the affirmative, so the Prophet led the boy by hand at once to his home. Then he called for A'ishah and said to her, "Here is a son for you." A'ishah gave the boy a bath, fed him as much as he wished, and gave him the best clothes she could find. Then she said, "Now go out, my son, and play with the other boys and then come back." He was overjoyed and went out and told the other boys what had happened to him, much to the astonishment of all. (*Anecdotes from Islam*) Though this story may be apocryphal, it illustrates the Islamic attitude towards kindness to orphans.

[71] Jesus, in particular, was very pointed in exposing the hypocrisy of the religious establishment of his people. See Matthew 23:1-7, 13-39, for example. Also Leviticus 19:1-37 lays out a whole host of laws that the Jews promised to follow that are of a high moral character. (Also see I Kings 2:3, 11:33.)

[72] Prior to the coming of Islam to Medina, the three Jewish tribes of Medina would make alliances with one or both of the local Arab tribes of Auws and Khazraj. When the two belligerent tribes would fight, it often happened that Jews would be pitted against other Jews, and they would kidnap each other.

promise to this and can attest to your oath, [84] and yet you're the ones who still kill and banish each other and take sides against each other shamefully in bitter rivalry. [73]

Yet, when some (of your rivals) are brought to you in chains, you ransom them, though it was forbidden for you to drive them off in the first place! [74] Do you believe in only one part of (your) scripture and then ignore the rest? What other fate can there be for people who behave like this, save for utter disgrace in this life?

On the Day of Judgment, however, there's going to be an even steeper price to pay, for Allah is not unaware of what you've been doing. [85] These are the kinds (of people) who buy the life of this world at the cost of the next. Their punishment won't be reduced, nor will they find anyone to help. [75] [86]

We gave scripture to Moses and raised up many messengers after him, and We gave clear evidence to Jesus, the Son of Mary, and strengthened him with the Holy Spirit. [76]

Now do you (Children of Israel) become arrogant whenever a messenger comes to you with something that you don't want to hear? You called some impostors, and others you killed! [87]

The Children of Israel Reject the Last Prophet

*A*mong the (Jews of Medina) are some who say, *"Our hearts are the wrappers (that contain all the knowledge of God)."* Not so! Allah's curse is upon them because they rejected Him, and they only have a tiny remnant of faith. [77] [88]

When a book from Allah does happen to come to them, one that confirms what they already have in their possession, and although they've long prayed for success against those who rejected (faith) and although they recognize (the new book's

---

When the fighting would subside, the Jewish leaders would ransom their fellow Jews amongst themselves, citing scripture as a justification. (*Asbab ul-Nuzul*)

[73] The argument made here is that, as followers of God's revelation, they shouldn't have been fighting each other to begin with – and then to use scripture to justify the freeing of Jewish captives is utter hypocrisy.

[74] See Deuteronomy 24:7.

[75] Does the Qur'an teach that *all* Jews are disobedient and cursed by God? Is it against Jews as a people? Most certainly not! The Qur'an mentions Jews in many different contexts and always to illustrate some specific point. The basic idea is that God gave their ancestors the chance to be His primary ambassadors of faith in the Middle East, but after repeated chances they failed to live up to the mission that was given to them. (See 5:66) The Qur'an then asks Jews to consider accepting Islam as a way to be faithful to the continuing message of the prophets of old. Yes, there are many examples where the disobedience of the Jewish community (as a generalized group) is highlighted in the Qur'an, even in strong language (just as the Old Testament does likewise, see Jeremiah 5:1-2, and 2:32 for example). However, the Qur'an makes full allowance for *individual* Jews to be righteous and faithful to God. It merely asserts that *as a group* they failed in the mission, and so Allah's favor moved on. In verses 7:170-171 and in many other places, the Qur'an plainly states that among Jews there are those who *"hold fast by the Book and do...prayers"* and that *"never will We suffer the reward of the righteous to perish."* Also see verse 5:69 and verses 3:113-115.

[76] Muslims understand the Holy Spirit to be the angel Gabriel, God's main liaison between Himself and His prophets. See 2:97.

[77] Prior to Muhammad's arrival in Medina, the Jews of Khaybar, a settlement some days travel to the north of Medina, had a war with the Arab tribe of Ghatafan. They suffered a defeat in the first battle but then invoked Allah, saying, "O God, we beg in the name of the unlettered prophet that You've promised us to grant us victory over them." On their next engagement they inflicted a great defeat upon their enemies. After Muhammad came to Medina and began preaching, the bulk of Arabia's Jews denied him, claiming that they already had all truth from God. This passage was revealed as a way to remind the Jews of what they had prayed for and now rejected. (*Asbab ul-Nuzul*)

connection with their own), *even still they reject it!* [78]

The very curse of Allah is upon those who cover (the light of faith within their hearts)! [89]

They sold their souls for a miserable price by rejecting - *out of petty jealousy* - what Allah revealed, simply because Allah would bestow His grace (equally) upon His servants, (regardless of race,) as He wills, and so they've earned wrath upon wrath. [79]

There's a humiliating punishment awaiting those who suppress (their awareness of the truth). [90]

When they're told, *"Believe in what Allah has revealed,"* they say, *"We only believe in what He revealed to us (before)."* So then they're rejecting all other revelation, even if it's the truth and confirms (the prophecies) they already have!

So ask (them), *"If you really believe in (God's revelations), then why did you murder the prophets of God in the past?* [91] *Moses came to you with proof; yet, you worshipped a calf, and even after that you continued to do wrong."* [80] [92]

Remember when We took your covenant as the towering heights of Mount Tūr loomed over you. (We had said,) *"Hold firmly to what We've given to you, and listen to it."*

However, (by their actions they showed that) they (might as well have) answered, *"We hear and we disobey."*

Therefore, they were (later) forced to imbibe (a drink made from the shavings of the melted) calf's (dust), precisely because they buried (their inner yearning for Allah). [81]

Say (to them), *"The motivations of your faith are terrible, if you even have any faith!"* [82] [93]

---

[78] Some commentators say that this verse also refers to the habit of the Jews of Medina of telling their Arab neighbors that when their (the Jews) foretold prophet would come, they would be able to get the upper hand over their larger and more belligerent fellows. It has been said that many people in Yathrib (Medina) were primed to accept Muhammad as a prophet, even before ever hearing of him, based on the fact that the Jews of the city spoke so often of a coming messenger from Allah.

[79] Some Jews of Medina were skeptical of Muhammad's claims in part because he was not *Jewish*. In their eyes, all prophets must be of their ethnic group. This was in keeping with their belief that they were the chosen people of God. The Qur'an's contention is that whatever blessings God gave them, they squandered, so God 's favor went somewhere else!

[80] For example, Deuteronomy 18:15-22 prophesizes that one day a prophet *like Moses* will be raised up from the brethren of the Jews. (The Arabs are often referred to as being distantly related 'brothers' to the Jews, as they both trace their ancient roots to the two sons of Abraham.) Christians have long held that this man was actually either Jesus or the Holy Spirit, who for them are two of the three people who make up the Godhead. However, a careful reading of the entire passage reveals that a god, or part of a god, is not being referred to here at all. Jewish theologians, for their part, also hold that an ordinary man is being referenced here, not a divine being. The mystery man is to be a prophet (in other words a human) who obeys God and is like Moses. Muhammad is the only figure that fits the requirements accurately; yet, the majority of the Jews of Medina chose not to apply this prophecy to Muhammad and explained that they would only follow ethnically Jewish prophets.

[81] When Moses found his people worshipping a calf made of gold, he ordered it melted and pulverized, and he forced the people to drink water mixed with its powder. See Exodus 32:19-20.

[82] The Arabic term for faith or belief is *emaan*. *Emaan* comes from the root word *amuna*, which means three main things: to have faith, to confirm or trust in that faith, and finally, to feel safe. Thus, a believer is one who places his or her faith and trust in Allah with the result that he or she is no longer afraid for his or her life or death. This is similar to the Biblical idea contained in Hebrews 11:1 which states that, "Faith is the substance of all things hoped for." The related term to *emaan*, which is *amaanah*, is usually translated as *secure trust*. Someone once asked the Prophet, "What is faith?" He replied, "When doing good makes you feel pleased and when doing wrong makes you feel uneasy, then you're a believer." Then he asked the Prophet, "What's a sin?" He replied, "When something bothers your conscience, give it up." (*Ahmad*)

Who are the Chosen Ones?

$\mathcal{A}$sk them, "*If the home of the next life is yours alone, to the exclusion of all others, then wish for death if you're so certain.*" [94]

Yet, they will never wish for death on account of the sins that their hands have sent on before them. [83] Allah knows all about every wrongdoer! [95]

In fact, you'll find that they crave life more than any other people - *even more than the idol-worshippers!* Every one of them wants to live a thousand years. Yet, longevity won't save them from their due punishment, for Allah is watching everything they do. [96]

Don't Deny Allah's Emissaries

$\mathcal{S}$ay (to them), [84] "*Whoever is an enemy to Gabriel, (the angel) who delivers (revelation) to your heart by Allah's will, reaffirming previous* revelations, and who is the bearer of guidance and good will to the believers -* [97]

Further still, whoever is an enemy to Allah, His angels, His messengers and to both Gabriel and Michael... Then, surely, Allah is an enemy to those who cover over (the awareness of the truth that exists within their hearts)." [98]

And so it is that We're revealing to you self-evident verses that no one can deny save for those who are corrupt. [85] [99]

The Corruption of Babylon

$\mathcal{E}$very time they made a pledge, *some of them pushed it aside*, for without a doubt many of them had no faith. [100]

Even now, when Allah has sent them a messenger confirming their previous revelations, some of those who've received earlier revelation try to hide (their scriptures) behind their backs - *pretending not to know about them!* [101]

---

[83] The Qur'anic concept of good and bad deeds is that you "send them ahead of you." This future place of record holding refers to the Day of Judgment where your record will finally be read. The New Testament echoes a similar concept in I Timothy 5:24.

[84] Some Jews visited the Prophet in his mosque in Medina. A rabbi among them named 'Abdullah ibn Suwriya asked him the name of the angel who was bringing him his revelations. When Muhammad answered that it was Gabriel, the rabbi said, "*Gabriel?* He is our enemy. He's acted against us many times. The worst time was when he sent the news to our prophet that Nebuchadnezzar would destroy Jerusalem. We sent someone to kill Nebuchadnezzar in Babylon; yet, Gabriel steered him away, saying, '*If your God commanded him to destroy you, then He will not help you overcome him. Since no order (of Allah's help) exists, why would you try to kill him?*' (Therefore, Muhammad,) if you would have said Michael, the one who brings rain and mercy, then we would have followed you." (*Baydawi*) At about the same time, 'Umar ibn al Khattab (d. 644) was having a conversation with some Jewish scholars in one of their small schools. ('Umar sometimes went to visit them in their Torah school, so much so that on one occasion one of their scholars remarked to him, "'Umar, you are the most beloved to us." When he asked the reason why, the Jew replied, "Because you come and visit us." 'Umar then said, "I come and am amazed at how Allah's scriptures compliment each other, and how the Torah and the Qur'an are in harmony.") During this particular visit, a Jewish scholar named 'Abdullah ibn Suwriya noticed Muhammad passing by in the street and told 'Umar that he should go out to see him. Before leaving, 'Umar asked the Jews why they didn't follow Muhammad, and they replied that it was because Muhammad was friends with Gabriel, who was their enemy. When 'Umar went out to meet Muhammad, the Prophet immediately recited these new verses (2:97-99) to him before he could tell him about his conversation with the Jews. 'Umar was amazed and exclaimed that he was just coming to tell Muhammad about something the Jews had said about the same issue. In later years, 'Umar said of this incident, "Afterwards, I became rock-solid in my faith." (*Asbab ul-Nuzul*)

[85] The Jewish Rabbi, 'Abdullah ibn Suwriya, said to Muhammad, "You're not bringing anything to us that we don't already know about, and there have been no clear signs revealed about you that should cause us to follow you." Verse 99 here is an answer to that statement. (*Asbab ul-Nuzul*)

They follow the satanic chanting (of their ancestors), [86] even though Solomon strongly disapproved of it. Solomon never rejected (Allah), for only the devilish suppress (their awareness of the truth). [87]

Such people teach others how to do magic and other similar practices, like those that were handed down to two Babylonian [88] leaders (named) Harut and Marut. [89]

Yet, they never taught anyone anything without warning them first, *"We're only here to tempt you, (so don't believe in what we teach) nor renounce your faith."*

So (the occultists) learned from them how to create marital problems between a

---

[86] The Old Testament Book of Isaiah 2:6 also echoes the charge that the Jews became fortunetellers and were involved in the occult. The verses there invite them back to the Godly path. (The Book of Leviticus in verse 19:31 had forbidden them from soothsaying and magic.)

[87] The commentators generally agree that the term devils here is referring to evil men who practice the occult. (*Razi, at-Tabari,* etc…) This verse also defends Solomon against the Biblical charge that he practiced occultism and idolatry, as purported in I Kings 11:1-10.

[88] The Jews were exiled from Palestine in 587 BCE by the Babylonians and forcibly settled in the opulent city of Babylon under a policy designed to weaken their religion and culture through assimilation. (See the biblical book of Jeremiah, chapter 52.) The Jews were, in fact, influenced into following many of the cultural and religious practices of the Babylonians. This was perhaps easy due to the fact that superstition had been creeping into their culture even as far back as the rule of Solomon. Astrology (a Babylonian invention), fortune-telling, black magic, idolatry and the occult were the order of the day, and it was only intensified in the melting pot of Babylon.

[89] Who were Harut and Marut? There are several divergent opinions, and I will summarize each. Some medieval commentators, citing Jewish stories from the Talmud, say they were (possibly fallen?) angels sent to live among mankind. (In the Jewish Talmud, the two fallen angels are named Shamhazai and Azael.) The problem with this position, however, is that from the standpoint of Islamic theology, it would seem strange that (fallen?) angels would be teaching black magic, whose effects were to cause marital discord, and further still, according to the Qur'an, angels never disobey God (see 16:49-50). Thus, this interpretation falls short. Another group of commentators holds that the Arabic word used here to describe those two mysterious figures, which is the plural of *malak* or *malakayn* should not be translated or understood as 'angels' at all. Rather, these commentators propose that Harut and Marut were men – possibly important local *magicians* – who duly warned the Jews who were learning from them that their knowledge would corrupt them away from their cultural values and faith. This is a defensible position given that the root word from which *malakayn* is derived literally means no more than to be in control of something. (The Arabic word for ruler *Malik* is also derived from this word. Also, the three *magi* of Persia who purportedly visited the infant Jesus were *magicians*, not kings, as magicians had king-like status in the East. See Matthew 2:1-3.) You may also see Qur'anic verse 34:42, for example, where the related term *yamlika* or 'they have control' is used merely in the sense of having control over another person's welfare. A third possible interpretation is that Harut and Marut are the names of Babylonian gods (possibly named after real men of antiquity) for whom priests worked magic in their name. Following this line of thought, the Jews were then adopting the religious traditions of Babylon, as represented by these two deities, and learning the spells and incantations commonly associated with devotees of those deities. As evidence we can note that the chief Babylonian god, as mentioned in ancient clay tablets, was Marduk, also known as Marutukku and Marutu. Another prominent deity was Aruru, the goddess of fertility and creator of man, who was also known as Hurarnu. These obviously closely related names could be the Harut and Marut of the Qur'an, and if it could be proved then it would go to support the third possible interpretation of this verse. A fourth possible (though less likely) interpretation that has been offered by non-Muslims is that the Harut and Marut of the Qur'an are Armenian idols of the same name or legendary sorcerers of antiquity known as Iannes and Iambres, in which case those pairs of names would merely replace the names given in the third possible interpretation. Given the distance between Mecca and Armenia, it is unlikely any Arabs or Arabian Jews would be able to make such a connection. What is obvious is that the Jews of Medina knew of these names (Harut and Marut), as evidenced by their being mentioned in this verse directed towards them for their consideration. What is also true is that the Qur'an does not call them 'fallen' nor does it give legitimacy to their actions. As for the spells employed by the ancient Jews, the oldest surviving samples from antiquity are recorded on Egyptian papyri and also from later texts written by Jews in the Greek language. These range from benign spells to more devious ones.

man and his wife, [90] but they could never succeed except by Allah's leave. What they learned only harmed themselves and brought them no gain. They knew that those who practiced (magic) had no share in the next life.

What they've sold themselves to is terrible. *If they only knew!* [102] If they only would've believed (in the truth) and been mindful (of Allah), then they would've earned from Him a far greater reward. *If they had only realized that!* [103]

Learn from the Mistakes of the Past

O you who believe! [91] Don't address (the Prophet in a demanding way by saying), *"Pay attention to us."*

Rather you should say, *"We're ready to listen,"* and then listen (to him), for those who suppress (their ability to attain to sincere faith) will suffer a painful punishment. [104]

Those who suppress (their awareness of Allah's truth) among the Followers of Earlier Revelation [92] and from among the idol-worshippers never want any good to come to you from your Lord, [93] but Allah is the One Who decides who receives His mercy - *and Allah is the master of endless bounty*! [105]

Allah Reveals What He Wills

We don't withdraw any of Our (previously revealed) verses [94] or cancel them out altogether [95] unless We replace it

---

[90] The Prophet once described how the servants of Satan come to him daily with reports of what mischief they've caused among humanity and that Satan is never satisfied unless one of his devils reports that he has caused discord between a husband and a wife. (*Bukhari, Muslim*)

[91] Some Jews used to go to Muhammad and say, *ra'ina*, which was a word in both Arabic and Hebrew. In Arabic, it meant one thing, namely *pay attention to us* or *look after us*, while in the local colloquial language of the Jews it meant *listen, as you hear nothing*. The Jews used to say the word to Muhammad and then snicker among themselves. A local companion named Sa'ad ibn 'Ubadah, who knew what they were doing, threatened some Jews one day for disrespecting the Prophet so. They offered in their defense that it was a word also used by the Arabs, albeit for a different intent. This verse was revealed to the Prophet in response. Thus, Muslims are asked not only *not* to use this word, because some of the Jews were using it to disrespect Muhammad, but they're asked to say something more respectful all together. (*Asbab ul-Nuzul*)

[92] The Qur'an uses a specific term to refer to anyone who follows religious scripture revealed by previous prophets. In Arabic it is *Ahl al-Kitab*, which translates literally as *People of the Book*, i.e., followers of previous scripture. This term gives special recognition to Jews and Christians as being superior in their beliefs to mere idol-worshippers. Although the Qur'an does not accept that they have the original, unedited and uncorrupted revelations of Moses and Jesus, it does accept that some fragments of the ancient prophets' words have survived – and point to the coming of Prophet Muhammad! We have translated this term, *Ahl al-Kitab*, throughout this book as *Followers of Earlier Revelation*, for this is what the title means in practical application.

[93] Whenever Muslims in Medina counseled their Jewish associates to believe in Muhammad, the Jews would reply that what Muhammad brought was good, but they only wished he brought something better than that. This verse references this situation. (*Asbab ul-Nuzul*)

[94] This verse was revealed in response to the charge that some Meccans made that Muhammad would sometimes cancel out or supersede a Qur'anic injunction as the years progressed. They said, "Look at Muhammad, how he commands his companions to do something and then forbids it to them and commands the opposite. He says something today and takes it back tomorrow." (*Asbab ul-Nuzul*)

[95] The Qur'an acknowledges the rare occurrence of 'revelation cancellation' mentioned here, which is called *abrogation* in technical terms, but this verse states that it is part of the process of growth in the evolution of religion. (Even the Bible accepts that Allah can cancel out what He had decreed before. See Jonah 3:9-10 and others.) Early Muslims understood the purpose and mechanism of this process, after all, Muhammad was given the task to change an entire culture in a limited number of years. Some flexibility on the methodology would be a valuable tool in this process. (Also see 16:101.) What does abrogation mean in the practical sense? For one thing, it doesn't mean that Allah has changed His

with a similar one or better. Allah has the power to do all things. [106]

The Faithless Continue to Doubt

Don't you know that Allah has control over the heavens and the earth and that no one can save or protect you apart from Him? [96] [107]

Would you (Muslims, who claim to) believe, question (and doubt) your Messenger (Muhammad), even as Moses was (doubted and questioned) by his followers in the past?

Whoever trades belief for rejection only strays from the middle path. [97] [108]

Beware the Taunting of the Faithless

Many of the Followers of Earlier Revelation will selfishly try to destroy your faith, even after they know the truth. [98] So pardon them, and pay them no mind until Allah fulfills His purpose, for Allah has power over all things. [109]

Establish regular prayer, and give in charity, for the good (deeds) that you send ahead (of you for Judgment Day) are waiting with Allah, and Allah is watching everything you do. [110]

Testing Claims of Immunity

There (are some who) say, *"No one will go to Heaven except Christians and Jews,"*

---

mind. Instead, it recognizes evolution in needs and circumstances. The laws change as people can handle more detailed rules, even though the spirit of the original intent remains. For example, the first chronological mention of alcoholic drinks in the Qur'an appears in 16:67 where it is said that alcoholic drinks come from plants. This was in the late Meccan period. Early in the Medinan period we read in verses 2:219-220 that alcohol can be a blessing and a curse. It was not prohibited it and such a rule would have been hard to implement with so many new and untested converts. Some years later verses 5:90-92 were revealed that did prohibit liquor. Thus, the last group of verses superseded or abrogated all the previous ones. Allah didn't change His mind, but slowly changed peoples' attitudes over time. (Another example is in how inheritance rules were amended before and after the migration to Medina. Before that, Muslims would bequeath to believing friends in favor of pagan relatives. After, Muslims were told to give preference to believing relatives over unrelated friends.) Various scholars have attempted to enumerate the number of verses they feel were abrogated and have come up with figures as low as 4 and as high as a hundred or more! Given that the label of abrogation is applied to both canceled verses and verses that were merely explained in more detail elsewhere, I tend to accept a much lower figure.

[96] Idol-worshippers and visiting Jews used to ask Muhammad for all kinds of miracles to prove his prophethood. One day a crowd went to the Prophet, and one man asked that Muhammad turn a hill into gold. Another man asked for a scripture to descend from the sky, while yet another man, named 'Abdullah ibn Abi Umayyah, asked for a tailor-made revelation addressed to him personally. Some new believers also were beginning to ask such petty questions, as well. This passage was revealed as an answer to that type of petty questioning. (*Asbab ul-Nuzul*)

[97] Honest inquiry is not forbidden in Islam. The Prophet always encouraged questions, and he never shied away from answering them. Questioning can be misused, however, when a person asks questions not to gain knowledge, but to be argumentative or sly in an effort to annoy or trick someone. The Prophet once remarked that a person who questions a scholar merely desiring to trick him and slip him up will go to Hellfire. The only honest question that the Prophet said we should not touch is the question of who made God, for Satan will use that question to sow doubt and dissension. Scholars are exhorted, likewise, not to be afraid of making a mistake in rendering their opinions, for whether correct or incorrect, Allah will reward them, according to the Prophet, for the sake of their honest effort.

[98] A Jewish leader and poet in Medina, Ka'b ibn al Ashraf, was composing poetry to slander Muhammad and his companions and also to incite the Quraysh of Mecca to continue their attacks on the Muslims. Muhammad is counseled in this verse to be patient and calm in the face of the incitement. (*Asbab ul-Nuzul*)

but that's only their wishful thinking. [99] Say to them, *"Prove it, if you're so certain of the truth."* [111]

Not so! Whoever submits his face before Allah and does what's right will be allowed to enter the Garden, and they'll have no reason to fear nor regret. [100] [112]

The Jews say, *"The Christians have no basis (for their teachings),"* and the Christians say, *"The Jews have no basis (for their teachings)."*

Yet, both groups claim to study the same Book! [101] Those who have no knowledge talk like that. Allah will judge between them in their dispute on the Day of Assembly. [113]

Don't Obstruct the Worship of Allah

𝒲ho is more oppressive than the one who forbids the calling of Allah's name in His houses of worship? [102] Those who are eager to ruin them have no right to enter them save in fear (of Allah). They'll have nothing but disgrace in this world and a painful punishment in the next. [114]

Allah is Everywhere

𝒯o Allah belongs
the East and the West;
Wherever you turn,
the Face of Allah is (present). [103]
Truly, Allah is
all-pervading and observant. [104] [115]

---

[99] A group of Christians from Najran visited Medina to interview the Prophet and learn more about him. Some Jewish rabbis came and debated religion with them in a public forum, and their argument became so heated that the rabbis and Christians each accused the other of not understanding religion and having no basis for their positions. This passage was revealed as a comment on this event. (*Asbab ul-Nuzul*)

[100] Islam teaches that human beings achieve salvation, by the grace of Allah, through their faith in Him. Thereafter, a person has to live his or her life as a reflection of that faith by trying to follow Allah's moral way of life to the best of his or her ability. We are not saved by deeds, as some Christians have falsely charged in the past, but by faith. (Christianity also requires deeds *after* faith. See Hebrews 10:24 and James 2:14-16.) If we sin or fall into error, we repent and ask for forgiveness from Allah. (See 40:7, among over a dozen similar verses.) He has promised to forgive the sincere seekers of His mercy. Prophet Muhammad once said, "When you die, all of you should have good expectations of Allah." (*Muslim*)

[101] Note how the point made in this verse further proves the futility of the claim of exclusive salvation made in verse 111. Even in our own time, Jews and Christians will often fake solidarity with each other publicly and further claim that both groups are equally favored of God and united in common cause. In less public forums, however, Orthodox Jews will deride Jesus as an imposter, or bringer of disaster on Jews (like Maimonides in his *Mishneh Torah* and in his *Epistle to Yemen* where he excoriates Jesus), while fundamentalist Christians assert that Jews need to convert to Christianity or burn in Hell. Thus, despite what they say in public, they reach different conclusions about each other from the same holy book!

[102] The mainstream commentators say this reference refers to the pagan Quraysh, who used to prevent the Muslims from praying near the Ka'bah in Mecca, and who later prevented them from coming for pilgrimage after they fled to Medina. (*Asbab ul-Nuzul*)

[103] As the commentators explain, this does not mean He has a *face* like us, but it is an idiom to say that He sees all things open and in secret.

[104] Opinion is divided about the reason this statement was revealed. Some suggest it was a response to some Muslims who were traveling and who couldn't agree on the direction of Mecca when they prayed late in the night. Others hold that it was an answer to the Jews of Medina who were alarmed when the Muslims were asked to turn away from Jerusalem in their prayers, in favor of facing the Ka'bah in Mecca. The second view is more widely accepted.

70

Allah has no Son

𝒯he (Christians) claim that Allah has (given birth) to a son! All glory to Him!

Not so! Everything in the heavens and the earth belongs to Him, and everything is compliant to His will. [116]

He originated the heavens and the earth, and when He gives an order, He only has to say, "*Be,*" and it is! [105] [117]

Don't Disrespect the Majesty of Allah

𝒯hose who have no knowledge ask, "*So why doesn't Allah speak to us or show us proof (of His existence)?*" [106]

That's what those who came before them said, for their hearts are all the same. To those who are firm in their convictions, We've shown Our signs already. [118]

What of the People of the Past?

𝒲e sent you, (Muhammad) with the truth so that you could give good news and also so you could warn. [107] You won't be held responsible for the companions of the raging blaze. [119]

They will never Stop Trying to Turn You to their Ways

𝒯he Jews and the Christians will never be satisfied with you until you adopt their values. [108] Say to them, "*The guidance of Allah is the only true guide.*" If you were to give in to them even after His truth has come to you, then you would have no close ally nor defender who can save you apart from Allah. [120]

Those to whom We've given scripture (in the past,) and who follow it as it should be followed, believe in it sincerely, but

---

[105] Islam categorically denies that Jesus is a god or the literal begotten son of a god (see chapter 112 or 39:67), and the Qur'an asks that Christians look into their own scriptures for proof. Verses such as those contained in John 5:30, 4:34, 5:19, 8:28 and many others clearly show that Jesus did not think of himself as a god *equal* with *the* God in heaven. The Qur'an affirms his prophethood and righteousness and exalts his mother as a righteous believer in God. However, it draws the line at ascribing divinity to either of them. (Some segments of Catholic Christianity, even to this day, hold Mary as part of the godhead. See footnote to 5:116.) If Jesus did use figurative language, calling God his father or calling himself God's son, it must be understood in context. The Jewish Old Testament is full of metaphorical verses in which people are called God's sons (i.e., Psalms 2:7) and in which God is called the father of people (i.e., Jeremiah 31:9), but the Jews never took it in a literal sense. (Psalms 82:6 even calls Jews gods themselves!) Matthew 19:16-17 states the following: "And behold, one came and said unto him (Jesus), 'Good Master, what good thing shall I do, that I may have eternal life?' And he said unto him, 'Why callest thou me good? There is none good but one, that is God: but if thou wilt enter into life, keep the commandments.'" (Matthew 23:9-10 also makes a distinction between God being the father of all and Jesus merely being the master, i.e., a revered teacher.) The preponderance of evidence, even in the Christian New Testament, is that Jesus never claimed to be a supernatural god in the flesh who demanded to be worshipped, but rather he taught that all people, even himself, are subject to God and that he (Jesus) is the supreme guide or master of the age - who was especially anointed (*messiah*) by God. It must be remembered, as well, that the Christian New Testament is not necessarily the Gospel *of* Jesus, but rather a collection of writings *about* Jesus, some of which quote episodes from his life.

[106] A pagan named Rafi' ibn Huraymilah asked the Prophet the question in the verse here. (*At-Tabari*)

[107] Ibn 'Abbas (d. 687) reports that the Prophet wondered aloud one day, "If only I knew what my ancestors have done." This verse was revealed in comment. (*Asbab ul-Nuzul*)

[108] The Jews of Medina and Christians of Najran were trying to influence the Prophet towards their respective positions, sensing perhaps, that as Islam was growing they might be able to influence its course. These verses were revealed in response, informing the Prophet that he should incline to neither side, but rather listen only to God and what He reveals. (*Asbab ul-Nuzul*)

whoever rejects it – they will be the ones who will lose. [121]

Children of Israel! Remember the blessings that I bestowed upon you and how I favored you above all other nations. [122] So then guard yourselves against a day when no soul will be able to help another, when no intercession will be accepted, nor any payment (offered) will sway nor any help come. [123]

Abraham Establishes a Shrine in Mecca

Call to mind that Abraham [109] was tested by his Lord with certain obligations, which he ultimately fulfilled, [110] so (Allah revealed) to him, *"I'm going to make you a leader among the people (of the world)."* [111]

To which he inquired, *"And of my descendants, too?"* (Allah) answered, *"(Yes), but My pledge will not extend to the wrongdoers (among them)."* [124]

And remember that We established the House [112] to be a peaceful place of gathering (for all) people, so take Abraham's place (of worship) as your own. We did indeed arrange for Abraham and (his son) Ishmael to cleanse (and maintain) My House for (the sake of) those who walk around it, who rest by it in contemplation, or who bow down and prostrate themselves (to Allah in adoration). [125]

Remember that Abraham said, *"My Lord, make this settlement a tranquil place, and bless its citizens who have faith in Allah and the Last Day with the fruits (of Your bounty)."*

(Allah) answered, *"I will also provide (prosperity) for a while to its citizens who suppress (their awareness of the truth), before I inflict upon them the punishment of the Fire - the worst destination of all!"* [126]

Remember when Abraham and Ishmael were raising the foundations of the House, Abraham said, *"Accept this from us, Our Lord, for You are indeed the Hearing and the Knowing. [127] Our Lord! Help us to submit (to Your will), and also make our descendants a submissive community towards You. Show us the places where we must perform our rituals, and accept our repentance, for You are indeed the Acceptor of Repentance and the Merciful. [128]*

---

[109] Abraham is a central figure in Judaism, Christianity and Islam. He lived sometime between 2100-1800 BCE in Mesopotamia. (The Old Testament asserts that he was originally from the Mesopotamian city of Ur and then moved to the city of Harran with his family.) After he chose to surrender himself to Allah, he was rewarded with prophethood. Soon he took his family and followers on a meandering journey through the western Fertile Crescent as nomads. He had two primary sons, Ishmael and Isaac. He settled the first son in west-central Arabia while the second son remained with him in southern Syria or Palestine.

[110] Ibn Kathir records the view of several early commentators that the 'certain obligations' referred to covered such things as circumcision and adopting certain elements of good personal hygiene, which would set Abraham apart from the customs of those around him. (See Genesis 17:10 and similar verses.)

[111] The promise made to Abraham is contained in Genesis 17:4-9.

[112] The House is the Ka'bah, or 'Cube.' It is a small square building that stands on the site where Abraham and his son built the world's first place of worship dedicated only to the One Unseen Allah - a place which was meant for all people who believe in the One True God. It must be remembered that Abraham was a nomad at this time, so for him to build a permanent structure was a very sacred and meaningful thing. The Arabic word *maqam* means a place of standing, and it refers to an imprinted stone near the Ka'bah upon which Prophet Muhammad said that Abraham used to stand in worship. One day, the Prophet took hold of the hand of 'Umar ibn al-Khattab and pointed to the imbedded footprint on that stone and said, "That is the station (or 'place') of Abraham." 'Umar replied, "Should we also make it a place of prayer?" The Prophet answered him, saying, "That has not been given to me as a command." Before the sun set that day, this verse came down commanding the Prophet to pray there. Thereafter, the custom of the Prophet was that after he would walk around the Ka'bah seven times praising Allah, he would go to the *maqam* of Abraham and pray a two-unit prayer. (*Zamakhshari*)

"Our Lord! Raise messengers from among our descendants who will convey Your signs. Teach them the scripture, give them wisdom and purify them, for You are indeed the Powerful and the Wise." [113] [129]

Abraham's Tradition Predates Judaism

*W*ho would turn away from the creed of Abraham except for the one who would tarnish his own soul? [114] As it happened, We specifically chose him in this world, and in the next life he's going to be among the righteous. [130]

When his Lord said, *"Submit,"* he replied, *"I submit myself to You, the Lord of All the Worlds."* [131]

Abraham left this legacy to his descendants, as did (his grandson) Jacob, who said, *"My children, Allah has chosen this way of life for you, so don't leave this (earthly) life unless you're surrendered (to Allah)."* [132]

Did you witness Jacob's final moments before death? *"What will you serve after I'm gone?"* he asked his children.

"We're going to serve your God," they answered, *"and the God of your fathers, of Abraham, Ishmael and Isaac, the One True God, and to Him we submit."* [133]

That community has long since passed away. They will be paid back for what they did, as you will be for what you do, and you won't be asked about what they did. [134]

True Religion Predates Judaism and Christianity

*T*hey say, *"Be a Jew,"* or *"Be a Christian, and be saved."* [115]

Say (to them), *"No way! We follow the creed of Abraham, the natural monotheist, and he never made partners (with God)."* [135]

Then say (to them), *"We believe in God and in what He sent down to us and to Abraham, Ishmael, Isaac, Jacob, and the tribes (of Israel).* [116] *(We believe in the message) given to Moses and Jesus and in (the messages) given to all the other prophets from their Lord. We regard each of them*

---

[113] The Prophet said, "I'm the (answer) to the supplication of my father Abraham, the glad tidings (announced by) Jesus, the son of Mary, and my mother saw (in a vision) a light that radiated from her which illuminated the castles of Syria." (*Ahmad*) The last part refers to a dream Muhammad's mother had before he was born in which she reported to her maid Barakah that she saw bright lights radiating from the direction of Syria. Within a few years of the Prophet's passing, the seat of the Islamic Empire was moved to Damascus, Syria, and Syria has remained ever since a destination of choice for those seeking higher learning in the Islamic sciences.

[114] This passage was revealed when some Jews went to the Prophet in Medina and told him that when he was dying, Jacob asked his children to follow religious practices that were equivalent to what they (the Jews of Medina) were practicing in their own times. The witness of the Torah itself disputes this claim, for in Genesis 48:1-28 and 49:1-33 Jacob's dying words are limited to a last meeting with Joseph where he greets Joseph's young sons, and thereafter it recounts a full meeting of all of Jacob's sons where he makes some prophecies about their descendants and then lays out exactly where he would like to be buried and why.

[115] In a public dispute, the leaders of the Jews of Medina and some visiting Christians from Najran tried to convince Muhammad to join their religion. The Jews claimed that Moses was the best prophet and that the Torah was the best book, while the Christians likewise mentioned Jesus and his Gospel. They disagreed with each other and also chose not to accept Muhammad's message. This passage was revealed as a result. (*Asbab ul-Nuzul*)

[116] The Qur'an recognizes and affirms the authenticity of the revelations and inspired messages given to the prophets of old. The Qur'an does not hold 'the Bible' as fully representative of those authentic messages. The Old Testament is a record of the Jewish tribes written long after the ancient prophets passed away. The New Testament is a collection of divergent writings cobbled together from various authors years after the disappearance of Jesus and consists of sketchy biographies, philosophical works, letters to different people and general sermons. It is not considered by Muslims to be the '*revelation*'

73

as equally authentic, and we surrender ourselves to God." [117] [136]

If they come to believe as you do, then they will have found guidance, but if they turn away, (then know) that they're splitting away (from Allah's religion). Even still, Allah is enough protection against them, for He's the Hearing and the Knowing. [137]

Where is the Proof?

(*Say* to the Christians,) *"We've (baptized) ourselves with the color of Allah, and what better color is there? He's the only One we serve."* [118] [138]

Then ask (them), *"Why are you arguing with us about (the nature of) Allah, when He's the Lord of us both? You're responsible for your actions, even as we're responsible for ours, though we're more sincere to Him (than you).* [139] *Or do you claim that Abraham, Ishmael, Isaac, Jacob and the tribes (of Israel) were Jews and Christians?"* [119]

Ask (them), *"Do you know more than Allah?"* Who is more wrong than the one who hides the evidence from Allah that he has with him? Allah is not unaware of what you're doing. [140]

That was a community that has long since passed away. They will be paid back for what they did, as you will be for what you do, and you won't be asked about what they did. [141]

A Change of Focus from Old Religions to Islam

The foolish among the people now ask, *"Why have the faithful now switched their usual direction of prayer (from Jerusalem in the north to Mecca in the south)?"* [120]

---

of Jesus. Further still, the writings of Paul and others are *never* considered by Muslims as revelation from God. According to Islam, they would belong in the category of "...books written with their own hands that are falsely attributed to God." See 2:79. Christian scholars, themselves, from antiquity until today prove that much of the Bible's contents have been edited and altered all throughout the ages in more than a marginal way. The second-century, pagan, Roman author Celsus wrote this concerning what he observed among the new Christian factions arising across the Empire: "Some believers, as though from a drinking bout, go so far as to oppose themselves and alter the original text of the gospel three or four or several times over, and they change its character to enable them to deny difficulties in the face of criticism." In the same vein, an early Church Father, Origen (d. 251), wrote: "The differences among the manuscripts have become great, either through the negligence of some copyists or through the perverse audacity of others...they make additions or deletions as they please." As quoted from the book, *Misquoting Jesus: The Story Behind Who Changed the Bible and Why,* by Bart D. Ehrman, p. 52. The Book of Revelations in 22:18-19 even calls down curses upon those who tamper with God's revelations!

[117] Abu Hurairah reports that he told the Prophet that the Jews of Medina used to recite the Torah in Hebrew and then used to explain it to the Arabs of the city in Arabic. The Prophet then said, "Neither believe nor disbelieve in what the Followers of Earlier Revelation tell you, but rather say to them, 'We believe in God and in what was sent down to us'." (*Bukhari*)

[118] This verse is a reference to the habit of some Arab Christians who used to add a dye to the water they used for baptism. The idea was that the new color signified their new attitude in life. This verse makes a word-play on that practice.

[119] The terms "Jew" and "Christian" were not invented until centuries after the prophets in question, and those ancient prophets and their people certainly didn't have any theology or doctrines like Judaism and Christianity teach today. God is indirectly saying, "*Use your common sense!*" Jesus never heard the terms *trinity* or *Christian,* nor did Abraham or Moses ever hear the terms *Judaism* or *Jew.* See 3:65-68 also.

[120] When the Muslims were living in Mecca, and for about a year after that in Medina, they faced towards Jerusalem (far to the north) whenever they prayed. It may have been a way to make a statement to the Meccans that the Ka'bah shrine, filled with idols as it was, was being misused. In any case, the Prophet always expressed his desire to face the Ka'bah in prayer, and he used to supplicate to Allah about it. Very early in the year 624, the Prophet received a new commandment from Allah (verse 2:144) that directed him to turn away from Jerusalem and thereafter to face towards Mecca in prayer,

Say to them, *"To Allah belongs the East and the West; He guides whomever He wills to the straight path."* [142]

And so it is that We have made you into a moderate community so you can be a witness to all people, even as the Messenger is a witness to you. [121] We first made you pray in the (unusual) direction of (Jerusalem) to test which of you would truly follow the Messenger and which of you would not. (The switch towards Mecca) was indeed a tough (adjustment to make), though not for the ones who were guided by Allah. Allah won't let your (previous expressions of) faith go to waste, for Allah is kind and merciful to all people. [143]

We've seen you look to the sky for guidance, so now We'll turn you towards a more pleasing direction. Now you can turn your face towards the Sacred Mosque (in Mecca), so turn your faces towards it wherever you happen to be.

The Followers of Earlier Revelation can see the proper reasoning in this from their Lord, and Allah is not unaware of what they're doing. [122] [144]

However, even if every convincing proof were presented to them, they still wouldn't join with you in your direction (of prayer), nor you with them. They can't even agree amongst themselves about a direction. If you were to follow their whims, even after everything that's come to you, then you would clearly be in the wrong. [145]

Those to whom We gave revelation (in the past) know the criteria for this, even as they know their own children; yet, some still cover the truth knowingly! [123] [146] (Remember that) truth comes from your Lord alone, so don't be in doubt about it. [147]

Everyone has a goal that they turn towards,
so make your goal the doing
of good wherever you are.

Allah will bring you all together (one day),
for He has power over everything in the end. [148]

---

a change for which the Prophet had been longing for some time. (Note that verses 142 and 143 were revealed *after* verse 144.) As the news spread throughout the neighborhoods of Medina and the surrounding countryside over the following days, people generally obeyed the new dictate, but a small amount of confusion ensued among some of the less fervent Muslims. To the more thoughtful believers, however, this change signified to them that the time to purify the shrine in their old hometown would soon be at hand. Many scholars have also suggested that it was a message to the Jews of Medina that the main city of their religion, Jerusalem, was not as prominent as Abraham's original shrine, the Ka'bah in Mecca.

[121] Some people passed away before the change in the prayer direction was ordered. Their relatives went to the Prophet and asked if their deceased relatives were deficient in their record of good deeds and prayers on account of not having ever prayed facing towards Mecca. This verse was revealed to let them know that Allah will not let their past good deeds go to waste. (*Asbab ul-Nuzul*)

[122] Muhammad said that he was always anxious to turn away from the prayer-direction of the Jews, but that he was waiting on his Lord's command. Angel Gabriel suggested to him to beseech Allah, and this verse was revealed in response. The actual inspiration came to the Prophet while he was leading a congregational prayer in the house of a man named Bishr, and he turned slowly as he recited it, without breaking the prayer, from a northerly direction to a southerly direction. (*Baydawi, Asbab ul-Nuzul*)

[123] The Jews and Christians of west-central Arabia also generally subscribed to the view that the Ka'bah had been originally built by Abraham, and Jewish scripture makes mention of Abraham wandering in the deserts of the region for a time. They didn't want to accept, however, that there was a kind of logic in focusing on the original patriarch's alter to God, rather than Jerusalem, which wasn't dedicated to God's service until the construction of Solomon's Temple many centuries later. (Jerusalem, as a town, had existed as a pagan settlement for many centuries before the descendants of Moses captured it centuries later.) In addition, the Bible supports the idea of praying in the direction of the temple. See Psalm 138:2 and Psalms 84:1-10

No matter from where you start out, face towards the Sacred Mosque (in prayer). It's the honest truth from your Lord, and He's not unaware of what you're doing. [149]

So no matter from where you start out, face the Sacred Mosque (in prayer), and wherever you may be turn your faces willingly to avoid public disagreements. Only wrongdoers will argue further.

Don't be afraid of them; fear Me instead, and I will shower My grace and guidance down upon you, [150] even as We've already sent one of your own kind as a messenger so he could recite Our (revealed) verses to you and purify you, as well as teach you scripture and wisdom and knowledge that you didn't know before. [151]

So remember Me, and I'll remember you. Give thanks, and don't suppress (the faith that dwells within your heart). [152]

You will Certainly be Tested in Your Faith

$\mathcal{O}$ you who believe! [124] Seek courage with perseverance and prayer, [125] for Allah is with the persevering. [153] Don't say that those who've been killed in the path of Allah are dead. No, they're living (in the next realm), though you might not perceive it. [154]

Be sure that We're going to test you in some things like fear, hunger and loss of wealth and self, and also in the fruits (of your labor), but give good news to those who patiently persevere, [155] who say, when stricken with adversity, "*To Allah we belong, and to Him we return.*" [126] [156]

The blessings and mercy of their Lord are upon them, and they're the ones who are truly guided. [157]

---

[124] After the Battle of Badr, which was fought between the Meccans and the Muslims of Medina in 624 CE, some people suggested that the people who died left this world and have no more good coming to them. This passage was revealed in response. (*Asbab ul-Nuzul*)

[125] The term for prayer used in the Qur'an is *salah*. This word literally means in the full sense *to make a connection with Allah,* and it also means *heat* or *burning.* When we pray, or *make salah*, we're metaphorically making a *hot connection* with our Lord. It is linguistically related to and has the same import as the Aramaic word *zelota* and the Hebrew word *tefillah*, both of which mean to stand before God in earnest. As the Prophet Muhammad once said, "A servant of Allah is closest to his Lord when he's bowing down to Him." (*Muslim*) Prayer five times a day is due upon every Muslim who reaches the age of ten, though the Prophet advised we teach children to pray from the age of seven. Such frequent prayer keeps a person focused on Allah and his duty to Him all throughout the day. The Bible also teaches prayer at regular intervals throughout the day, and those who follow Judaism also perform regular, daily prayer. See I Samuel 20:41, Psalms 55:16-17 and Daniel 6:10.

[126] A man named Abu Salamah returned home to his wife, Umm Salamah, and said, "I heard the Messenger of Allah say a statement that made me feel wonderful. He said, 'No Muslim is stricken with an affliction and having said, 'To Allah we belong, and to Him we return,' when the affliction strikes, and then says, 'O Allah! Reward me for my loss and give me something better than it,' but that Allah will do just that." Umm Salamah memorized the words of the supplication in verse 156, and not long afterwards, after her husband passed away from wounds sustained in the Battle of Uhud, Umm Salamah made the same supplication, but she also reported that she wondered aloud if there could be anyone better than her departed husband. After her waiting period had finished, the Prophet paid a visit to her house one day, and she gave him a pillow to sit on. After some pleasantries, the Prophet asked for her hand in marriage. Umm Salamah answered, "Messenger of Allah, it's not that I don't want you; it's just that I'm a very jealous person. I'm afraid that you might suffer some ill manners from me, and then Allah might punish me. I'm also old, and I have children." The Prophet replied, "As for the jealousy you mentioned, may Allah, the Most Exalted, remove it from you. As for your being old, as you mentioned, I also suffer from the same condition, and as for you already having children, they will be as my children, too." She then readily agreed to marry him, and in later years she said, "Allah compensated me with someone who was better than Abu Salamah, and it was none other than Allah's Own Messenger." (*Ahmad*) The quoted phrase in verse 156 is also the standard condolence that one gives to a Muslim who is in mourning over a loved one who has passed on.

Allah Confirms
that which is Valid

(The two hills) of *Safa* and *Marwah* are symbols of Allah. [127] Whoever makes a pilgrimage to the House, or who visits (at other times), is not guilty if he walks between them.

Whoever does good for goodness' sake will always find appreciation with the knowing Allah. [158]

Those who hide the evidence and the guidance that We've sent down - (especially) after it's already been made clear to people in the scripture - are condemned by Allah and those who have the right (to condemn), [159] except for those who repent, reform themselves and proclaim the truth, for in that case they'll be forgiven.

Truly, I am the Acceptor of Repentance and the Merciful. [160] Those who suppress (their awareness of the truth) and then leave this life while actively suppressing it, will bear the condemnation of Allah, the angels and of all people combined. [161]

They will remain in that condition, and their torment will neither lighten nor will it end. [162]

The Signs of Allah

Your god is One God;
there is no god but He,
the Compassionate,
the Source of All Mercy. [128] [163]

Truly, within the creation
of the heavens and the earth.
In the alternation of night and day.

In the sailing of ships through the sea
for people to profit and trade.
In the water sent down by Allah
for the parched land to live.

In the diversity of creatures,
and in the changing patterns
between the earth and sky
of the clouds and winds -
in all of these things
there are signs for the wise. [164]

Yet, even still there are people who would make others equal with Allah. They love them as much as they should love Him, but the love of the faithful for Allah is far stronger.

If only the wrongdoers could glimpse the penalty that awaits them, then they would finally realize that all power belongs to Allah and that Allah is a severe punisher. [165]

---

[127] Thus, we have the Islamic ritual of the *Hajj*, or Pilgrimage to Mecca, introduced. It is a required, once-in-a-lifetime trek for every adult Muslim male and female who can afford it and is physically fit enough to make the journey. There are many elements to the week-long event, and the two hills mentioned are the same hills that Hagar, the mother of Ishmael, ran between seven times in her frantic search for water. The people of Medina, formerly known as Yathrib, used to avoid walking between those hills during pre-Islamic days (when they visited Mecca for pilgrimage), for they thought it was a peculiar tradition of the Quraysh. Some of the Meccan converts, as well, stopped performing rituals concerning the hills after converting to Islam, also thinking they were a relic of the past. There was also some concern about the fact that the pagan Quraysh had erected alters dedicated to two of their deities, *Isaf* and *Na'ilah*, on each hilltop. (The legend was that those two were lovers who fornicated in the Ka'bah and were thus turned into stone pillars.) After the initial peace treaty with the Meccans allowed Muslim pilgrims into the city, the Muslims asked the Prophet about it, and this verse was revealed in response, saying that the ritual of walking was still a valid part of the pilgrimage, even if the idols have to be ignored, and when the Muslims later gained control over Mecca they removed the idols. (*Ibn Kathir*)

[128] When verse 2:163 was revealed, some pagans (in Medina) marveled at it. One of them remarked, "There's only *one* God? Then let Him reveal a verse for us if He's so truthful." Then verse 2:164 came to the Prophet, and he recited it." (*Asbab ul-Nuzul*)

(On the Day of Judgment), those (idols, jinns, false ideologies, and preachers of evil) who were followed will distance themselves from their (hapless) followers.

They'll see the punishment waiting there just for them, and they'll break all bonds with them. [166]

Then their (frightened) followers will cry out (in bewilderment), "*If only we had the chance again, just as they're leaving us now, we would've left them!*"

(However, there's no going back), and so they'll be shown their evil deeds and be filled with utter regret. There will be no escape from the Fire. [167]

Keep Your Food Pure

O people! Eat only what is lawful and wholesome. Don't follow in the footsteps of Satan, for he's clearly your enemy. [168]

He'll order you to indulge in evil and shameful behavior and to speak (lies against) Allah that you can't even imagine. [169]

Old Habits are No Justification

When they're asked to follow what Allah has revealed, they say, "*Not a chance! We'll hold on to the traditions of our ancestors.*" 129

What! Even though their ancestors had no sense, nor any guidance? [170] The example of trying to reach them is like a shepherd shouting (words of wisdom) to sheep. They're deaf, dumb, blind and devoid of sense! [171]

What are the Forbidden Foods?

O you who believe! Eat of the wholesome things that We've provided for you, 130 and give thanks to Allah, that is if you truly serve Him. [172] He's only forbidden you from eating animals that have died by themselves, blood, pork 131 and (anything) that was dedicated to (idols) instead of Allah. 132

However, if one of you has no choice but to eat of these things, without wanting to, nor returning to them (after your desperate situation is over), then he's not

---

129 The reply quoted here in verse 170 was made by a group of Jews to the Prophet after he had invited them to Islam. (*Asbab ul-Nuzul*)

130 The Prophet said, "Allah, the Almighty, is good, and He accepts only that which is good. Allah has commanded the faithful to do the same things that he commanded the messengers to do. The Almighty said, 'O Messengers! Eat only of wholesome things, and do what is morally right.' (23:51) Allah, the Almighty, also said, 'O you who believe! Eat of the wholesome things that We've provided for you.'" (2:172) Then the Prophet mentioned the case of a man who undertook a long and arduous journey. He was disheveled and dusty, and he spread out his hands to the sky saying, "O Lord! O Lord!" Then the Prophet said, "He was calling on Allah while his food was unlawful, his drink was unlawful, his clothing was unlawful, and he nourished himself unlawfully. So how can he expect to be answered?" (*Muslim*)

131 Christians and Jews are also forbidden to eat pork in Leviticus 11:7-8 among other verses of the Old Testament, though Paul (not Jesus – see Matthew 5:17-20) made it permissible for Christians to eat (I Corinthians 8:8, 10:23, Colossians 2:18, I Timothy 4:3-4, etc.) in his quest to make it easier for non-Jews to adopt the new religion he was formulating. See Romans 1:16, 4:15.

132 The Prophet gave the definition of a Muslim thus: "Whoever prays in our manner, facing our prayer-direction, and eats what is slaughtered in our way, that person is a Muslim." (*Bukhari, Muslim*) Would that our modern sectarian-minded fellows adopted such a broad and inclusive definition of who is a real Muslim!

guilty of sin, for Allah is forgiving and merciful. [173]

Those who hide the revelations of Allah and gain a little something by doing it are eating nothing but fire. Allah won't address them on the Day of Assembly, nor will He purify them, for a painful punishment will await. [174]

They're the ones who've bought mistakes instead of guidance and punishment instead of pardon. How eagerly do they seek the Fire! [175] That's because while Allah was revealing the scripture truthfully, they were arguing against the scripture and increasing in their opposition. [176]

What is the Foundation of Faith?

Righteousness isn't turning

towards East or West.
Righteousness is believing in Allah,
the Last Day, the angels,
the scriptures and the prophets.

(Righteousness) is spending of your wealth,
for love of Him, on relatives, orphans,
the poor, travelers,
and on those who ask (for help).

(Righteousness) is freeing slaves, [133]
Establishing regular prayer,
giving in charity, fulfilling your agreements,
and being patient in danger,
hardship, and adversity.
These (people) affirm the truth
and are mindful (of their Lord). [177]

On Murder and the Limits of Retribution

O you who believe! [134] In the event of a murder being committed, fair retribution is in order, (but only the murderer shall be held to account). [135]

Whether a free man is guilty of murdering another free man, or a servant of a servant, or even a woman of a woman, (no one except the one who did the crime may be punished). Though if a relative (of the victim) chooses to pardon the guilty (person), [136] then he should be dealt with

---

[133] The Prophet said, "Allah will free from Hellfire anyone who frees a believing slave." (*Bukhari*) On another occasion the Prophet said, "Whoever builds a mosque, then Allah will build for him a house in Paradise. Whoever frees a slave, then Allah will make that freed slave a ransom for him and save him from Hellfire. Whoever grows old in Islam will have a radiant light on the Day of Resurrection. Whoever shoots an arrow in the cause of Allah, whether it hits its target or not, will receive a reward equal to freeing a slave from one of Ishmael's descendants." (*Ahmad*)

[134] There was a street fight in Medina between some men of different clans, and the stronger group taunted the other, saying that they would kill a free man of their rival in revenge if one of their own slaves were killed or that they would kill a man of them if one of their own women were killed. This was in keeping with the longstanding Arabian custom known as *retaliation* whereby any harm done to one member of one's own tribe or clan would be harshly repaid on the family or associates of the perpetrator. When news of this public challenge reached the Prophet, these verses were revealed that laid out the principle that only the one guilty of a crime should be punished and that going overboard in demanding excessive retribution was wrong. (*Asbab ul-Nuzul*)

[135] The Prophet said, "Whoever aids in the killing of a Muslim, even if by only something he said, then he will have to face Allah with a sign written between his eyes that will say, '*To be left out of the mercy of Allah.*'" (*Ibn Majah*) When one considers the sheer amount of killing that happens among people – even among Muslims - especially the killing of the innocent, one can do nothing but weep for the misguided souls who make a joke of their own religion and follow their own whims and base motivations.

[136] The principle of fair retribution, or *qisas*, that is laid out here means that the penalty for murder is capital punishment, unless the family of the victim forgives the attacker and accepts what is called *blood-money*. Some commentators think these verses refer to the deal made between two of Medina's three Jewish tribes. Before the coming of Islam, the two Jewish tribes of Banu Nadir and Banu Qurayzah had a war with each other, and the Banu Nadir came out the clear winner. They forced the

fairly and should settle a penalty to be paid with gratitude. This is a concession from your Lord and a mercy. [137]

After this, whoever goes beyond the limit (by taking revenge on the innocent, in spite of this clear directive,) will be punished severely. [178] (Innocent) lives are protected through the law of fair retribution, so the sensible among you will restrain themselves. [179]

Making a Will

*I*t's the duty of every believer who owns property to make a will when he (or she) is near death, and he should bequeath fairly to his parents and next of kin. This is binding upon everyone who is mindful (of their duty to Allah). [180]

If anyone changes the will after learning of it, (then know that) they'll be guilty and accountable, and Allah hears and knows all things. [181] However, if someone feels that the deceased was unfair to him, then he may bring about a (legal) settlement, and he won't incur any guilt, for Allah is forgiving and merciful. [182]

The Month of Ramadan

O you who believe! [138] Fasting is prescribed for you, even as it was prescribed upon those before you, so you can increase your mindfulness (of Allah). [183]

(Observe the fast for) a set number of days, but if someone is ill or on a long journey then he can make up the days he missed later. [139] Anyone who would have an exceptional hardship from fasting (has the option) to make up for it by feeding the poor instead, and if someone freely gives more than he must, it's that much better

---

Banu Qurayzah to accept a very unequal concept of justice in which the murder of a person from the Banu Nadir by a person of the Banu Qurayzah would result in the killer's execution, but if a person of the Banu Nadir murdered someone of the Banu Qurayzah, then the Banu Nadir would only have to pay a fine of several pounds of dates in compensation. This was against the Torah, which called for capital punishment equally. (See Genesis 9:6 where capital punishment for murder is required. Also see the Biblical book of Numbers, verse 35:31.)

[137] The Old Testament of the Bible prescribes violent retaliation for a variety of crimes in chapter 21 of Exodus, but only the Qur'an provides a realistic way for the aggrieved family of a murder victim to modify or cancel the prescribed punishments if it so chooses. (Perhaps the relatives want to spare the killer for some reason.) The 'turn the other cheek when wronged' advice of Jesus contained in Matthew 5:38-41, while noble in spirit, is more difficult to implement, and there are few examples in Christian history to point to that would make us confident of its practicality. However, see 5:45 and 41:34. By the way, a murderer is not entitled to inherit from the person he murdered. The Prophet said, "A murderer shall not inherit." (*Mishkat*) This is a great disincentive to many types of murder based on greed and jealousy of one's parents or other relatives.

[138] The Islamic style of fasting is a dawn to dusk abstention from food, liquids and intimate relations. Lying, cheating or fighting can also ruin a person's fast. This month-long training teaches Muslims to maintain those good habits of moral behavior and control over their bodily needs for the rest of the year. Previously revealed religions have also contained a fasting component, and the principle is not new. Mastering the body and its urges is the path to elevating the heart and mind, i.e., the goal of *taqwa*, or mindfulness of Allah.

[139] The jurists of Islam have not been unanimous in deciding what the minimum traveling distance is before a person can be considered a traveler and thus be released from fasting, (though the days must be made up later). Figures have ranged from less than 10 miles to as many as 48 miles. This is due to the fact that there are no unanimous distances given in the prophetic traditions. This is also a challenging question today when a person may drive for a few hours to reach a destination by car – a distance that might have taken two or three days by horse or camel in the old days. The eminent twentieth-century scholar, Abul A'la Maududi, offered a compromise solution: you *know* when you're traveling, rather than merely taking a small day trip. Therefore, when you *feel* you are traveling on a real journey (to another state or country or a far distance in which you are inconvenienced), then you can rightly consider yourself a traveler. The Arabic term used here for traveling, by the way, is *safar*, from which we get the English term *safari*.

for them! [140] Fasting is indeed good for you, if you only knew. [184]

Ramadan is the month in which the Qur'an (began) to be revealed as a source of guidance for all people, as clear evidence of the truth and as the standard of (right and wrong).

So when you see the new moon (signaling the start of Ramadan), fast the entire month, though the very ill and those traveling should fast (later when it's more convenient to do so), for Allah wishes ease and not hardship.

Complete the fast, and praise Allah for His guidance, so you can learn to be thankful. [141] [185]

Despair not of Allah's Notice

When My servants ask you about Me, I am near, and I listen [142] to every suppliant the moment he calls upon Me. [143] So, let them also listen to My call and believe in Me so they can follow the right way. [186]

Allowances after Nightfall

You are allowed to approach your spouses during the *nights* of Ramadan. [144] They're like a garment for you, and you're like a garment for them.

Allah knows what you were doing in secret among yourselves, so He turned to you and forgave you. Now you may approach your wives and seek what Allah has allowed.

(You may) eat and drink until the white thread of dawn appears distinct from

---

[140] If a person is too old or physically unhealthy, or if a woman is nursing her baby or is pregnant, and cannot safely fast, and such a person cannot ever hope to make up the fasts later due to their extreme ill-health or the large number of missed fasts (such as for pregnancy issues), then they can feed one poor person a day for every day of Ramadan that they missed. Women on their monthly courses do not fast on those days, but they must make the missed days up after Ramadan is over, a day for a day. (*Ibn Kathir*) This is called paying *fidyah* or compensation.

[141] A man broke his fast (intentionally) during Ramadan. The Prophet ordered him to either free a slave, fast for two months, or feed sixty poor people (to compensate for his indiscretion). The man said, "I can't manage any of those things." The Prophet then said, "Sit down, and wait." Then a huge basket of dates was brought to the Prophet. He said to the man, "Take these, and give them as charity." The man answered, "Messenger of Allah, there is no one poorer than I." The Prophet then laughed so loudly that his teeth were showing. Then he said, "So eat them yourself." (*Abu Dawud*)

[142] The Prophet said, "Your supplications will be answered, but wait patiently for your Lord to respond. Don't lose hope and begin to complain, saying, 'I called upon my Lord, but He never answered.'" (*Bukhari*) Umar bin al Khattab said, "Go easy on yourself, for the outcome of all affairs is determined by Allah's decree. If something is meant to go elsewhere, it will never come your way, but if it is yours by destiny, from you it cannot flee."

[143] A visitor from a far village went to the Prophet and asked if Allah was far away, thus requiring people to shout loudly in their supplications to be heard by Him, or if He was near, in which case people could whisper to Him. The Prophet remained silent and did not answer. Then this verse came to him, and he recited it aloud. (*Ibn Kathir*)

[144] When fasting was first introduced as a personal obligation, there was some confusion among the community in Medina about what was allowed for them to do after sunset. Some thought that no intimate relations were allowed after the last prayer of the day ('isha). Others used mental gymnastics to justify having intimate relations when they really had misgivings about it. Yet, others were of the understanding that if a person slept after fast-breaking, all eating and such were forbidden for the rest of the night. When 'Umar ibn al-Khattab (d. 644) complained one day about his confusion over the issue, this Qur'anic verse was revealed, clarifying that intimate contact between married people at any time of the night is allowed during the month of Ramadan. (*Ibn Kathir*)

its black thread. [145] Then fast until the night approaches again, but abstain from your wives (even at night) when you're in retreat in the mosques for more intense devotion.

These are the rules set by Allah so keep well within them. He makes His (revealed) verses clear for people so they can (learn to be) mindful (of Him). [187]

Don't Bring Ruin upon Each Other

*D*on't eagerly consume each other's wealth in wasteful pursuits or try to bribe those in authority, hoping to consume unlawfully the property of others. [146] [188]

How do We Use the Moon?

*W*hen they ask you what the new moon signifies, tell them, *"You can use it to calculate the date for people and to regulate the pilgrimage rites."* [147]

There is no Virtue in being Evasive

(*K*now that) there's no virtue in going "through the back door." [148] Virtue comes from listening to Allah, so go "through the front door," (and conduct your affairs openly). Be mindful of Allah so you can prosper. [189]

When Self-Defense becomes Necessary

*F*ight [149] in the way of Allah those who fight you, but don't go beyond the

---

[145] Adi ibn Hatim said, "When the verse: 'Until the white thread of dawn appears distinct from its black thread' was revealed, I took a white rope and a black rope and placed them beneath my pillow. Then I looked at them (in the early dawn), but they were not clear to my eyes, so later I mentioned it to the Messenger of Allah. He laughed and said, 'Your pillow is so gigantic, and long! (That verse is really referring to) the blackness of night and the whiteness of day, (not literally to threads).'" (*Abu Dawud*) The Prophet explained what dawn was by saying: "Eat and drink and do not be rushed by the ascending (white) light. Eat and drink until the redness (of the dawn) appears." (*Ahmad*) Just before the time for the daily fast begins, the Prophet urged his followers to take a small meal called *suhoor* to help them make it through the day.

[146] Two men disputed about the ownership of a strip of land near the outskirts of Medina. One of the men was using unscrupulous means to take possession of the land that he knew was not his. The Prophet asked both men to swear to Allah about their claims, but before the dishonest man swore his oath, the Prophet recited verse 3:77 which reminded him of the dire consequences of dishonesty. The dishonest man then refused to swear to Allah about his claim. The Prophet found in favor of the original owner, and this verse was revealed, warning people not to attempt to seize what was not lawfully theirs. (*Asbab ul-Nuzul*)

[147] Mu'adh ibn Jabal asked the Prophet about crescent moons and why they followed the courses they did. The first part of this verse was revealed in response. (*Asbab ul-Nuzul*)

[148] With regards to the "doors" mentioned here, the pagan Arabs had a strange superstition that held if a person wanted to conduct a religious pilgrimage and consecrated himself for that purpose, then he could not enter his house through the front door. Instead he would jump over a fence, climb in a window, or enter through a back door. This verse addresses this practice and nullifies it. It has even become something of a proverb in the Arab world to the effect that open action is better than secretive schemes. (*Ibn Kathir*)

[149] Here is the first important usage of the Arabic word *qital*, which means *to battle, to kill* or *to fight*. There is a myth among critics of Islam that this verse is ordering Muslims to kill all non-believers. Such a proposition is preposterous and unsubstantiated. Any person with even limited comprehension skills can see that this verse is giving permission to fight back against those who attacked you first.

limits (of decency and humane conduct), [150] for truly Allah has no love for those who go beyond the limits. [151] [190]

Fight the (the idol-worshippers) wherever they're found, and drive them out from where they drove you out, for oppression is worse than killing, but don't engage them at the Sacred Mosque (in Mecca), unless they attack you there first.

If they do, then slay them, for that's the reward of those who suppress (their awareness of the truth and do wrong on account of it). [191]

Though if they cease their aggression, (then remember that) Allah is forgiving and merciful. [192]

If they continue to practice oppression, then fight them until oppression is no more and Allah's way of life prevails.

If they seek peace, then you seek it as well; yet, continue to pursue the (persistent) wrongdoers (among them). [193]

After this, verse 192 clearly defines when the fighting must end – when the enemy isn't threatening or attacking you anymore. There is another myth also, and that is that the related word *jihad* is the Arabic term for *holy war*. Besides the fact that there is no such religious term in Arabic for a *holy war*, the word *jihad* literally means *to struggle* or *strive* in a cause, whether physical, spiritual or even mental. (See 6:109 where the root form of the word *jihad* is used to amplify the strength of a strong oath, or 25:52 where it is specifically used to promote an intellectual defense of Islam.) One must clearly question the motives of the critics of Islam who chose to quote (or misquote) parts of verses or passages without including the surrounding verses that explain the text as a whole. Have they considered passages from the Bible, such as Exodus 22:20, in which it is stated unequivocally that pagans must be killed?

[150] This passage was revealed six years after the Prophet and his followers had left hostile Mecca for the safer refuge of Medina. One night the Prophet had seen himself in a dream leading religious pilgrims back to Mecca to perform a pilgrimage. After a large party of Muslims, led by Muhammad, appeared in the hills outside of Mecca, the alarmed Meccans kept the Muslims from entering the city, even though it was a customary Arab truce month. Some Muslims were concerned that the hostile Meccans might take the opportunity to attack them; however, a Meccan envoy concluded a truce deal with the Prophet. (That pact is known as the Treaty of Hudaybiyyah. See chapter 48.) This treaty stipulated that the Muslims had to turn back and would not be allowed to complete their journey to Mecca that year, but the following year they would be allowed to enter the city for three days to perform their pilgrimage rites. As the following year approached, there was some discussion and concern among the Muslims as to whether or not the pagan Quraysh would continue to uphold their end of the bargain. This passage was revealed about this concern, and it informed the Prophet that if the Meccans reneged on the deal and attacked the pilgrims on their journey, they had prior permission to fight back if necessary. (*Asbab ul-Nuzul*)

[151] Islam accepts the concept of 'the just war.' The commentators are unanimous in saying that this verse allows fighting against an enemy that attacks Muslims unprovoked, but it also stipulates that the Muslim side must exhibit self-control and not go beyond the limits of humane conduct in wartime. The Prophet said, "Fight for the sake of Allah, and fight those who reject Allah, but don't loot, commit treachery, mutilate (the dead or wounded), or kill a child or those who reside in houses of worship." (*Muslim*) On another occasion he explicitly forbade the killing of women and children. (*Bukhari, Muslim*) He also is quoted as forbidding the killing of civilians and animals, and he even forbade the unnecessary destruction of buildings and crops. (*Ibn Kathir*) The utterly *grotesque* interpretations of some modern extremist groups - equating suicide bombing, wanton destruction and the killing of civilians with authentic religiously-recognized martyrdom - is unknown and abhorred in the legal annals of traditional Islam. Modern extremist groups have merely adopted the concept of suicide bombings from non-Muslim, secular movements and have been blinded by their efficiency in expressing anger and revenge. (See the rulings against suicide attacks and wanton mayhem contained in the recent scholarly book entitled, *Defending the Transgressed by Censuring the Reckless Against the Killing of Civilians*, by Shaykh Muhammad Afif al-Akiti.) In several sayings, the Prophet also required a man to get the permission of his parents before he could participate in a physical *jihad*. (*Bukhari, Muslim, Abu Dawud*, as quoted in, *The Lawful and the Prohibited in Islam*, by Yusuf al-Qaradawi.)

On the Sacred Months

*N*ow about the sacred months: for the sacred months and all other restricted things, there is the law of fair retribution. [152] Therefore, if one of (your enemies) goes out of bounds against you (during those truce months), then you may retaliate likewise against him. Be mindful of Allah, and know that He's with those who practice self-restraint. [153] [194]

Don't Abandon Allah's Cause

*D*on't hesitate to use your own resources in the struggle, and don't cause your own destruction from greed. Do what is right, for Allah loves those who do good. [195]

Perform the Pilgrimage to Mecca

*P*erform the major pilgrimage [154] and the minor pilgrimage [155] in the service of Allah, though if you're prevented, then send an affordable offering instead. (Know that no one should) shave their heads until the offering has reached the appointed place. [156]

Indulgences for Special Circumstances

*I*f one of you is sick or suffering from an ailment of the scalp that makes shaving immediately necessary, then in compensation (for completing this part of

---

[152] Arabian custom, purported to trace its roots to Abraham and Ishmael, held that four months of the year were sacred, in which all tribal feuds, wars and hostilities were to cease to allow pilgrims to complete their visits to shrines throughout the land. The Ka'bah in Mecca was the most important of them all. The months of Dhul Qa'dah, Dhul Hijjah and Muharram were reserved for the major pilgrimages to Mecca, which would encompass many days of strict devotion, while the month of Rajab was reserved for minor pilgrimages of a few days.

[153] Self-control was not a hallmark of the pre-Islamic Arabs. Common pagan practices among the pre-Islamic Arabs were quite dramatic. Animals were sacrificed violently, and their blood was washed on the idols posted around the actual Ka'bah structure. Idols inside were prayed to fervently and 'fed' with food offerings; divination occurred in the streets, and wild mystics from the desert were constantly making an appearance. People would also flagellate themselves, and the masses would walk around the Ka'bah, calling upon the names of their idols loudly. It was a common practice for many, especially women, to make this circuit *naked*. (Only people wearing clothes owned by a native Qurayshi could perform this ritual fully dressed.) This is how bizarre the culture was, and it is no wonder that the time before Islam is labeled as the time of *Jahiliyyah* or *Ignorance*.

[154] Thus we are introduced to the Islamic ritual of pilgrimage, or Hajj. This is the famous journey to Mecca that all able-bodied and financially capable Muslims must make at least once in their life. The official pilgrimage is held in the first part of the month named *Hajj*, while pilgrimages performed outside of that month are counted as extra merit. There are a number of religious rites to be performed during the pilgrimage, with the main goals being to gain greater insight into the shortness of this life and also to bring home the reality of our ultimate return to Allah.

[155] There are two types of pilgrimage: the major pilgrimage, or *Hajj*; and the minor pilgrimage, or *'Umrah*. The *Hajj* is the once-in-a-lifetime pilgrimage to Mecca that all Muslims must undertake at least once in his or her life if they are of sound mind, past puberty, fit enough for the journey and financially able. It is performed in the month of Dhul-Hijjah only. The non-binding *'Umrah* can be performed at any time during the year and is counted as a pious act. Most pilgrims combine both types together by arriving in Mecca before the start of the *Hajj,* performing their *'Umrah* and then staying on to complete the *Hajj*. While in Mecca the pilgrims participate in a number of rituals, both within the city and out in the countryside, that enable them to rededicate their lives to Allah through meaningful acts of penance and worship. The Prophet once said of it, "Hurry to go on your pilgrimage if it is due upon you, for none among you knows what will happen to him tomorrow." (*Ahmad*)

[156] As part of the pilgrimage ritual, men must shave all or part of their heads to signify rebirth. Women can merely cut off a lock of hair and are not required to shave their heads bald.

the pilgrimage ritual early), you can either fast, feed the poor, or offer something in sacrifice. [157]

However, when more stable circumstances allow you to perform the pilgrimage and lesser-pilgrimage (rituals as they should normally be done), then offer a sacrifice according to your means.

Whoever doesn't have enough money (to purchase an animal for sacrifice) should fast for three days during the pilgrimage and seven days after he returns (home), completing ten. This is ordained for all those who don't live near the Sacred Mosque. Be mindful (of your duty) to Allah, and know that He's severe in retribution. [196]

Take up the Pilgrim's Garb

The months of pilgrimage are well known (to all). [158] Whoever resolves to fulfill his duty within them, then there should be no sexual relations, immorality or quarreling. Whatever good you do is well known to Allah.

Provide for the journey, (but remember) that mindfulness (of Allah) is the best provision to take, [159] so all you insightful people, be aware of Me! [197]

Furthermore, there's nothing wrong in seeking the bounty of your Lord (through trade) during the pilgrimage. [160] When you pour down into the plain of 'Arafah [161] all together, remember Allah at the Sacred Monument. [162]

Remember Him as He showed you the way, for before this you were (a people) astray. [198] Then move quickly along with the other people at the proper place, [163] and ask Allah's forgiveness for your sins, for Allah is forgiving and merciful! [199]

---

[157] There is an allowance for the person who cannot wait until the end of the week-long *Hajj* to shave his hair due to a medical emergency. A man named Ka'b ibn 'Urja was the catalyst for this part of the verse. He explained his story in the following words: "This (verse) was revealed about my situation in particular, but it is also for all of you in general. I was carried to Allah's Messenger, and the lice were falling in great numbers on my face. The Prophet exclaimed, 'I never thought your struggle (with lice) had become so serious as what I see. Can you afford a sheep?' I answered no, and then the Prophet said, 'Fast for three days or feed six poor people, each with a small measure of food, and now shave your head.'" (*Bukhari*) So the man's pain was relieved, and he offered compensation for having to shave his head early.

[158] The traditional Arabian months of Dhul-Qa'dah, Dhul-Hijjah and Muharram were set aside for pilgrimage, though the actual *Hajj* rites are fixed in the first ten days of Dhul-Hijjah.

[159] Arab pilgrims who went on religious journeys (before Islam) used to take to the road with no supplies. They would beg along the way to their destinations and they considered it a sacred duty. This verse is telling Muslims to bring some supplies on their journeys, as there is no holiness in being a beggar.

[160] Trade, business transactions and shopping are permitted while on the *Hajj* journey, but not while one is engaged in the midst of the holy rituals that are scheduled daily. The pre-Islamic Arabs restricted themselves from engaging in trade during their religious pilgrimages, but when the issue came up after Mecca had become Muslim, the Prophet received this revelation allowing it as long as it didn't interfere with the required rituals. There are many arduous and exhausting rituals in a typical pilgrimage, and taking a break for shopping is a welcome diversion during times of rest or when the day's assigned rituals have ended.

[161] The name for this plain, *'Arafah*, is derived from the word *to know*. The idea is that there, on that barren plain, one can finally *know* the full weight of what Judgment Day will mean and how dependent our lives are upon Allah.

[162] The Sacred Monument is a place located about halfway between 'Arafah and Mina where the Prophet stopped on his pilgrimage to pray. It is known as Muzdalifah.

[163] Some Meccan clans in pre-Islamic times used to stop at Muzdalifah and not continue on towards 'Arafah. This verse tells them that as Muslims now, they must move along swiftly with the rest of the people to 'Arafah, for the rituals there were declared an integral part of the pilgrimage.

Remembrance of Allah in All Places

*W*hen you've finally completed the holy rituals, commemorate Allah - even as you used to commemorate your ancestors (before you were believers) – yet (do it) with far more passion and enthusiasm! [164]

There are some people who pray, *"Our Lord, give us the best in this world,"* though they'll have no share in the next life. [200]

While there are others who pray, *"Our Lord, give us the best in this world, the best in the afterlife, and protect us from the punishment of the Fire."* [201] They will receive their share for their efforts, for Allah is quick to settle accounts! [202]

Remember Allah (during your pilgrimage at the plain of Mina) for the (three) appointed days, [165] but if anyone hurries away after two days, it's not a sin, nor if he stays longer, as long as he guards (his conduct). Be mindful (of Allah) and know that you will all be gathered before Him (in the end). [203]

The Temptations of Earthly Life

*T*here's one kind of person who will try to dazzle you about this worldly life with his words, and he'll swear to Allah that he's sincere at heart, *but he's the most determined enemy!* [204] When he turns his back from you, he looks to make mischief everywhere he can in the world, and he goes around damaging crops and cattle- *and Allah doesn't love disorder!* [166] [205]

When he's told, *"Be mindful of Allah,"* his arrogance causes him to go on sinning even harder. Hellfire is punishment enough for him - *what a terrible place to rest!* [206]

However, there's another kind of person who sells his life to earn Allah's pleasure, and Allah is kind to His servants. [167] [207]

Be Firm in Your Resolve

O you who believe! [168] Surrender yourselves to Allah completely, and avoid

---

[164] At the conclusion of their own pilgrimage rituals, the pagan Arabs used to hold a kind of rally on the plains of Mina in which each clan used to shout and boast about how great its ancestors were. This verse was revealed to ask the Muslims to turn their exuberant focus towards Allah. (*Ibn Kathir*)

[165] The 'appointed days' are the 11th through the 13th day of the month of *Hajj*. (*Ibn Kathir*)

[166] A Meccan pagan named Akhnas ibn Shariq ath-Thaqafi arrived in Medina one day and heaped praises upon the Prophet and Islam. He swore that his aim was to enter into Islam, and he swore to Allah that he was sincere. The Prophet was pleased with his words, but then ath-Thaqafi left the city without converting. Next, ath-Thaqafi began destroying a patch of crops and chopping off the legs of some cattle he found grazing nearby. He had only feigned sincerity and allegiance to the Prophet in order to mock him. This passage was revealed in response. (*Asbab ul-Nuzul*)

[167] The good man being referenced here is Suhayb ar-Rumi, a convert to Islam who wanted to flee Mecca for the safety of Medina. When he was leaving the city, a group of thugs from the Quraysh followed him and tried to seize him. He stood his ground and drew his bow saying, "People of Quraysh! You know well that I'm faster and more accurate than any of you with my bow. By Allah, none of you will be able to reach me before I let loose all my arrows, and I will fight the survivors with my sword. Make a choice: either fight here, or let me go, and I will tell you where I hid my money and property in Mecca." They agreed to let him go in exchange for his wealth, so Suhayb told them and later entered Medina poor and penniless. When the Prophet was informed of this he exclaimed, "The father of Yahiya made a bargain! He made a bargain!" (*At-Tabari*)

[168] Ibn 'Abbas (d. 687) explained that this passage was revealed with regards to some Jewish converts to Islam who tried to harmonize their practice of Islam with what they used to practice of Jewish customs. Thus, they still held the Sabbath in esteem and forbade themselves from eating the milk or meat of certain animals that were forbidden in Judaism. Some other Muslims rebuked them for synthesizing the two faith traditions, but the Jewish converts felt they could do it, and when the matter was brought before the Prophet for resolution, they told him, "The Torah is the Book of God, too, so

the path of Satan, for he's your clear enemy. [208] If you backslide after knowing the truth, (it won't harm Allah in the least), for He's powerful and wise. [209]

So what are they waiting for - for Allah to appear in the billowing clouds with a host of angels to settle the matter once and for all? But all matters will go back to Allah in the end. [210]

Ask the Children of Israel how many evident signs We sent them, though if anyone substitutes (something else for) Allah's (rules) after having received them, know that Allah is a severe punisher. [211]

This world is alluring to those who suppress (their awareness of the truth), and they scoff at those who believe. However, those who were mindful (of their duty to Allah) will be held higher on the Day of Assembly, for Allah will provide unlimited resources to whomever He wants. [212]

All people were once (together) in a single community, and Allah raised messengers among them to give glad tidings (of Paradise) and also warnings (of Hellfire). [169] He also sent the scriptures of truth to be a judge between people in their disputes.

However, after the clear evidence came to them, those who received these (earlier) revealed messages, out of factionalism and pride, fell into disagreement. Yet, by His grace, Allah guided the sincere believers out of their disputes and brought them to the truth, for Allah guides whomever He wants towards a straight path. [213]

Be Prepared for Testing and Trial

𝒟id you think you could enter Paradise without experiencing what those before you did? [170] They were tested through affliction and loss, and (some were) so shaken that even their messenger joined with them in crying, *"When will Allah's help arrive?"* (Remember) that the help of Allah is always near! [214]

What is Good Charity?

𝒯hey ask you what they should spend (in charity). [171] Tell (them), *"Anything you can give to help parents, relatives, orphans,*

---

let us follow it, as well." This passage was revealed telling them that they had to commit to God's last revelation wholeheartedly to be counted among the true believers. (*Asbab ul-Nuzul*)

[169] These would be the prophets from prehistoric times to the dawn of human civilization in the Middle East and elsewhere - men whose names and stories we generally do not and probably can never know, although such names may have survived in the mythology and legends of many cultures. (Were Zeus, Odin, Gilgamesh, Pangku and so many other notable subjects of myth originally true prophets or heroes whose stories were transformed through the ages into grotesque legends?) There is a widely circulated saying of Prophet Muhammad in which he is purported to have said that there were 124,000 prophets raised up in human history and 313 messengers. The messengers were sent with organized bodies of teachings such as could be codified in a book (if writing was available), while the regular prophets were spiritual guides and bringers of prophecy. A few individuals like Abraham, Moses, David, Jesus and Muhammad embodied both offices in one person. Although scholars are of the opinion that the *official* prophets were all male, two women are mentioned in the Qur'an as having received communications from Allah: Mary, the mother of Jesus (see 3:42-43), and Jochebed the mother of Moses (see 20:38, 28:7).

[170] This verse was revealed to console the Muslims who had arrived in Medina, having to leave behind in their hometown all their wealth and property, which were immediately seized by the pagans. Hardship is a way for Allah to help His sincere servants increase in their faith and become worthy of even greater favor and reward later on down the line. (*Asbab ul-Nuzul*) Even the New Testament echoes this principle in II Thessalonians 1:3-6.

[171] This verse was revealed when a wealthy man named Amr ibn al-Jamooh asked the Prophet, "How much should we give in charity, and upon whom should we give it?" (*Asbab ul-Nuzul*)

travelers and the poor is good, and every good you do is known to Allah." [172] [215]

Fight, but Only in the Way of Allah and Only When It is Necessary

𝒥ighting (in the cause of Allah) is a duty laid down upon you, even though it might be unpleasant for you. [173] However, you may hate something that's good for you and love something that's bad for you. Allah knows, and you don't know. [174] [216]

When they ask you about fighting in a sacred month, tell them, *"Fighting in it is indeed wrong, but an even greater wrong in the sight of Allah is to discourage people from His way, to reject Him, and to keep people out of His Sacred Mosque, even driving out those who were already living there!"*

Oppression is worse than killing, (and the oppressors, who will never tolerate your existence), will always seek to wage war against you until they make you renounce your faith, if at all possible. (Just remember) that those who renounce their faith - *and leave this life in a state of rejecting it* - will have wasted their deeds in this world. In the next life, they'll be among the companions of the Fire, *and that's where they're going to stay!* [217]

Those who believe, however, and who suffer exile and strive in the cause of Allah can count on the mercy of Allah, for Allah is forgiving and merciful. [218]

Liquor and Gambling have Greater Harm than Good

𝒲hen they ask you about liquor and gambling, tell them, *"There's both great harm and benefit in them for people, but the harm is greater than the benefit."* [175]

---

[172] On the general issue of charitable giving, the Prophet once said, "No possession is too lowly to be given as charity; Allah gives greater honor to one who forgives, and He elevates the one who humbles himself." (*Muslim*)

[173] About two months before the Battle of Badr (624), the Prophet sent a small scouting party of eight men to gather intelligence about the intentions of the Quraysh. He instructed his men to spy on their caravans and attempt to gain news from them. Two days later, the scouts found a small caravan and pretended to be travelers on the road in order to mingle with them. Some of the scouts suggested to their leader that it would be fortuitous for them to capture the caravan and return it to Medina. Accordingly, they seized two of its four overseers and directed the caravan away from the direction of Mecca. (A third caravan attendant named 'Amr was killed, while a fourth escaped and fled to Mecca.) After the scouting party returned home with the spoils, Muhammad angrily scolded them, saying, "I did not order you to fight during the sacred month." Indeed, the attack might have occurred on the last day of the sacred month of Rajab. The Quraysh in Mecca complained very publicly that Muhammad broke the sacredness of the month, and they sent a delegation to Medina to confront him about it. Meanwhile, Muhammad arranged for the two captives to be freed, and he impounded the goods of the caravan, rather than distributing them to the impoverished immigrant Muslims from Mecca. (One of the ransomed captives decided to accept Islam, and he remained in Medina by choice.) The scouts, for their part, were mortified, and they were ostracized and embarrassed. These verses were revealed as a response to the Quraysh delegation, who had asked why the Muslims would fight in the sacred truce months, and they pointed out that they had no right to claim injury when they had previously murdered and tortured so many Muslims for thirteen years in Mecca, adding insult to injury by seizing their wealth when they fled for their lives. After this passage was revealed, the Prophet ordered the booty to be distributed to the Muslims. (*Asbab ul-Nuzul*) Another report says that he returned the caravan to the Quraysh. (*Baydawi*)

[174] The Prophet was once asked, "Which of three persons carries on a struggle for the cause of Allah: the one who fights to show his bravery, the one who fights for honor or the one who does it to impress others?" The Prophet replied, "The one who struggles to uphold the message of Allah is the person who struggles in the cause of Allah." (*Bukhari, Muslim*)

[175] 'Umar ibn al-Khattab (d. 644) and Mu'adh ibn Jabal asked the Prophet to give the community a definite ruling on intoxicants, pointing out that imbibing them caused drunkenness and debauchery. This verse was revealed to the Prophet, causing 'Umar to ask for more clarification. Later on in

When they ask you how much they should spend in charity, tell (them), *"Whatever you can spare."* This is how Allah clarifies His verses so you can better understand [219] how they relate to this life and the next.

Fairness to Orphans

𝒲hen they ask you about orphans, tell them, *"The best thing you can do is to help them. [176] If you're their guardian, and you happen to mix your affairs with theirs, (never forget) that they're your brothers, (so keep track of their goods faithfully)."* [177]

Allah knows the troublemaker from the morally upright person. If Allah had wanted, He could've put you into as vulnerable a position (as they), for Allah is powerful and wise. [178] [220]

Don't Marry an Idolater

𝑀en), don't marry any women who make partners (with Allah) [179] until they become believers. [180]

A maidservant who has faith is better than an idol-worshipper, even though you may be strongly attracted to her. [181]

(And women), don't marry men who make partners (with Allah) until they believe. A servant who has faith is better than an idol-worshipper, even though you may be fond of him.

Medina, verse 4:43 was revealed forbidding praying while drunk. Sometime after that, 'Umar asked for an even more definitive injunction, and verses 5:90-91 were revealed, forbidding all intoxicants categorically. (*Abu Dawud, Tirmidhi*)

[176] When verses 4:10 and 6:152 were revealed concerning the importance of not squandering or stealing the property of an orphan, those who had orphans and their property under their care became very strict in keeping their possessions separate from the property of the orphans for whom they cared, so much so that they would even prepare meals for the orphans from separately owned ingredients. If the orphan children didn't finish their food, the guardians used to set it aside until the orphan either ate it or it spoiled. Many such people went to the Prophet for they disliked the inconvenience and wastage, and this verse was revealed in response, which said that it wasn't wrong to mix foods that were bought from the two different monetary sources. (*Ibn Kathir*)

[177] Verse 6:152 goes further in admonition, telling guardians not to seize or misuse the property of an orphan.

[178] Islam directs people to have special love and concern for orphans. The Prophet said, "I and the person who looks after an orphan and provides for him will be in Paradise like this," and he put his middle and index fingers together. (*Bukhari*)

[179] The Bible also forbids marriage to idolaters and non-believers in general in Deuteronomy 7:3, Leviticus 18:21, II Corinthians 6:14-18 and Ezra 9:3.

[180] The Prophet sent a man named Abu Murthid Ghanawi to Mecca in order to bargain with the Quraysh for the freedom of some Muslim converts they had captured. While he was in Mecca, Abu Murthid saw an old mistress of his from pre-Islamic days named 'Inaq. She wanted to have relations with him, but he refused her advances, explaining that, "Islam has come between you and me." He did express a willingness to marry her, but wanted to confer with the Prophet first. Then he concluded his business with the Meccans and returned to Medina whereupon he asked the Prophet if he might marry 'Inaq. The Prophet asked about her, and when he was informed that she was an idolater, the first sentence of this verse was revealed forbidding Muslims from marrying those who make partners with Allah. (*Asbab ul-Nuzul*)

[181] As for the remainder of this verse, a man named 'Abdullah ibn Rawaha had an African maidservant whom he slapped in anger one day. He felt remorseful and went to the Prophet for advice. The Prophet asked what her habits were, and 'Abdullah mentioned that she was a very pious Muslim who practiced the faith perfectly. The Prophet answered saying, "'Abdullah, she is a true believer." Whereupon 'Abdullah swore that he would free her and marry her, and he did. Several people went to the Prophet thereafter and, thinking that 'Abdullah had married a *pagan* maidservant, took it as a sign of the permission to marry pagans. They thus beseeched the Prophet to let them marry pagan women to whom they were attracted, as well. This second part of this verse prohibiting marriage with pagan servants was revealed in response. (*Asbab ul-Nuzul*)

The influence (of idol-worshippers) will lead you to the Fire, while Allah calls you to the Garden and to His Own forgiveness. He makes His verses clear to people so they can be reminded. [221]

An Intimate Prohibition

They're asking you about menstruation, so tell (them), [182] *"This is a time of pain and impurity for women, so don't be* *(fully intimate with them) until they're relieved of it.* [183] *Then, after they've purified themselves, you may again go to them as allowed by Allah. Indeed, Allah loves the repentant, and He loves the pure."* [184] [222]

Intimate Permissions

Your women are like your fertile fields, so cultivate them as you wish, [185] but always do something beautiful beforehand (so they know that you love them). [186] Be

---

[182] The Jews of Medina had a general habit of forcing their women to leave their homes when they were menstruating, and neither would they eat nor drink with them. All forms of intimacy were also suspended for this time. Some local Arabs also adopted the custom of not having affection or intercourse during menstruation. (Men from Mecca did not subscribe to this prohibition.) A mixed group of local and immigrant Muslim men, with this issue in mind, asked the Prophet about what was allowed and proper for them to do during women's menses, and this verse was revealed in response, which explained what menses was and then merely forbade actual intercourse but nothing else. When the Jews were told of this, one of their rabbis said, "What's the matter with this man? He never hears of any of our customs without challenging them!" (*Ibn Kathir*)

[183] The Prophet was reported to kiss, hug and caress his wives during their periods. The Prophet said that men could "...do everything you wish, except for intercourse," with their menstruating wives. (*Ahmad*) In later years, a man named Masruq went to visit A'ishah to ask a question, as she was one of the most important scholars among the surviving companions of the Prophet, and he said, "I want to ask you about something, but I feel too shy." She said, "I am (like) your mother, and you are (like) my son." So he said, "What can a man enjoy of his wife when she is having her menses?" A'ishah answered, "Everything except her private part." (*At-Tabari*) A'ishah also reported that while on her menses, she used to wash the Prophet's hair, cradle his head in her lap while he recited the Qur'an, share food with him from the same plate, drink from the same cup and even pass through the mosque if on an errand. (*Bukhari*) On her menses, a woman does not offer the ritual prayers and does not need to make them up when her menses is finished. The Prophet also encouraged menstruating women to attend Islamic festivals and make supplications, even though they can't join in the ritual prayers. They can do all rituals of the *Hajj* except for the march around of the Ka'bah. (*Bukhari*) A woman also does not do any fasting during this time, but she must make up any missed Ramadan fasts later. When the menses days are ended, the woman must take a full bath to attain a state of ritual cleanliness again. Opinion is divided about whether a woman on her menses can touch a Qur'an or recite it aloud, with the common position being 'no' for the first question and 'yes' for the second.

[184] The Prophet once said to a gathering, "The one who repents of his sin is like one who never (did that) sin." Then he recited, "*Indeed, Allah loves the repentant, and He loves the pure.*" [2:222] Then someone asked what the sign of sincere repentance was, and the Prophet replied, "(Having a genuine feeling of) remorse." The last part of this verse is the basis of a supplication to be made after ritual washing for prayer. The supplication is, "O Allah, make me among the repentant, and make me among the pure."

[185] This verse was revealed because of a superstition among the Jews of Medina, which they promoted publicly, that if a man had intercourse with his wife from the back then his newborn children would be cross-eyed. The Immigrants from Mecca, who knew nothing of this belief, were marrying Helper women of Medina, and these women kept refusing to engage in that practice for fear of having deformed children. So one of these women went to the Prophet's wife, Umm Salamah, and asked her to ask the Prophet about what the Jews were saying. The Prophet asked his wife to summon the Helper woman, and he recited this verse, which dispelled that myth and gave a blanket allowance for basically any consensual intimate practice among married couples. (*Tirmidhi*)

[186] With regards to the doing of 'something beautiful' before full intimacy, the Prophet advised men to caress and kiss their wives passionately for some time before going any further. This was to satisfy their wives' legitimate needs, rather than the men merely satisfying only themselves. He referred to such tenderness as sending *ambassadors* ahead. He also said that if anyone said the following words

aware (of your duty to Allah), knowing that you'll have to stand in His presence one day, so convey good news to the faithful. [223]

Fairness during Times of Marital Discord

$\mathcal{D}$on't take the name of Allah as an excuse if the promise is against doing good, acting rightly or making peace among people, for Allah hears and knows (what you're doing). [187] [224]

Allah won't hold you responsible for (unrealistic) promises (or foolish things said) without forethought, but rather for the intentions in your hearts, for Allah is forgiving and forbearing. [188] [225]

Now, those (men) who swear (in anger) to abstain from (having intimate relations) with their wives (cannot prolong their period of abstinence for more than) four months (and must either begin divorce proceedings to set them free or reconcile with them). [189]

If they do (renounce their oath and reconcile with them), Allah is forgiving and merciful. [226] Though if they're determined to initiate the divorce (proceedings, then remember that) Allah hears and knows (all things, so behave in a proper manner). [190] [227]

On Divorce

$\mathcal{D}$ivorced [191] women should wait for three monthly cycles (before seeking

---

before beginning intimacy that their offspring will never be harmed by Satan: "In the Name of Allah. O Allah, protect us from Satan, and also protect from Satan whatever You bestow upon us." (*Bukhari*)
[187] This passage was revealed about the case of a man named 'Abdullah who had sworn an oath to Allah to forsake his friend and refuse to reconcile with his wife. He went to the Prophet and received this ruling from Allah in answer. (*Asbab ul-Nuzul*) It is assumed he then reconciled with both.
[188] Vows made in anger or swearing by Allah's name for small things that should not have even had Allah's name invoked, such as saying, "I swear to Allah that it's my pencil," are reprehensible. Two brothers received an inheritance to share during the rule of 'Umar ibn al-Khattab (d. 644). One brother wanted to divide the property and take his share, while the other brother wanted to keep it intact. The second brother, who was the older and more powerful one, threatened his younger brother, saying, "If you ask me about dividing the inheritance again, then I swear that I'll spend all of it on the Ka'bah's door!" When 'Umar was informed, he told the older brother, "The Ka'bah doesn't need your money, so break your vow, pay the penalty and come to terms with your brother." (*Abu Dawud*)
[189] In pre-Islamic times, if a man wanted to leave his wife but didn't want her to marry another, he would swear to abstain from sleeping with her but then not divorce her no matter how much time passed. This cruel treatment would leave the woman in limbo, neither being released nor taken back. Sometimes the man would abstain from his wife *for years*. A maximum time limit of four months is imposed here, mostly for the purpose of giving the man a defined deadline within which he must either reconcile or lose his wife forever. Thus, this rule forces the recalcitrant or obstinate man to set his wife free so she can get on with her life. (The woman, by the way, is not required to accept offers of reconciliation from the man and may seek a divorce on her own.) Compare with Deuteronomy 24: 1-4.
[190] The Prophet once remarked that the most hateful thing in Allah's sight that He has allowed is divorce. (*Abu Dawud*) The Qur'an, therefore, while providing provisions to regulate it legally, constantly counsels reconciliation and even imposes a three-month waiting period, or *'iddah*, before the divorce can be finalized. This is so the couple can know if the wife is pregnant or not, a mitigating factor that may cause them to reconcile, since the welfare of the new child will be at stake. See 65:1-7 for more details on the waiting period and related matters.
[191] There are four types of marital dissolution recognized in Islamic law: male initiated divorce (*talaq*), in which the female keeps her full dowry; female initiated divorce (*khul'*), in which case the woman may have to give up all or part of her dowry to be released from the marriage tie; annulment (*faskh*), for perhaps an illegal, forced marriage; and finally, cancellation by a judge (*tafriq*), which is usually initiated by a woman who wants to divorce an abusive husband and still get her full dowry from him by court order.

remarriage). [192] If they believe in Allah and the Last Day, then they shouldn't conceal (the news) of anything that Allah may have created in their wombs.

It would be best for their husbands to reconcile with them (in that case), if they were inclined to (reconcile).

(Remember that women) have rights, just as (men) do in all fairness, though men have been given an edge over them, [193] and Allah is powerful and wise. [194] [228]

A divorce (pronouncement) can only be (revoked) twice. (After that) they must either (reconcile once and for all) and stay together lovingly, or (they must) end their relationship (in a spirit of) fairness. [195]

Women are Allowed to Initiate Divorce

*Y*ou (men) are not allowed to take back anything you gave to (your wives), unless both sides fear breaking the rules set by Allah. [196] If so, then there will be no sin

---

[192] Some companions, both male and female, had a variety of issues concerning divorce for which they wanted answers. This passage was revealed in response. (*Ibn Kathir*)

[193] The 'edge' that this verse refers to is the fact that men are obligated to care for women and thus have more responsibility. This translates into a few seemingly inequitable things such as a man receiving twice the inheritance of a woman. However this seeming advantage actually rebounds back upon them for men are responsible to spend of their money on the family, while women are not obligated to do so. Further, men must pay a dowry to their brides and also support their elderly parents and other disadvantaged relatives. See the first clause contained in 4:34 where men are given this responsibility. The edge also may refer to the fact that men are thought to have the first choice at initiating reconciliation talks.

[194] A man once asked the Prophet what the rights of his wife were, and he said, "To feed her when you eat, to buy her clothes when you buy for yourself, not to smack her on her face, not to curse at her, and not to ignore her (in public places, if you're angry with her), but rather only in the house." (*Abu Dawud*) Ibn 'Abbas (d. 687) said, "On account of what Allah said (in this verse), I like to take care of my appearance for my wife, just as I like her to take care of her appearance for me." (*At-Tabari*) The Prophet, by the way, was an exponent of good personal grooming. He bathed daily, brushed his teeth many times a day, kept his hair and beard well-combed and advised people to wear scented oils.

[195] There is a myth that a Muslim man need only say, "I divorce you" to his wife three times, and suddenly she is a penniless divorcee thrown out on the street with no property or rights. Beyond the abuse and fancies of the ignorant masses, there is a prophetically sanctioned procedure that draws a divorce out over three months, thus allowing people time to cool their anger, reassess their decisions, or finalize their separation plans, if necessary. The man who intends to divorce his wife should pronounce his intention while she is off her menses and provided they had no relations since her last menses. Thereafter, the couple should sleep in separate rooms, and the husband is not allowed to force the wife to leave the home. If a month passes and there was no intimacy or reconciliation, the husband pronounces divorce again and the process continues. If the pronouncement is made again in the third month, then the divorce is finalized, and he is not eligible to remarry her unless she were married and divorced by another. See verse 230 below. It is considered bad conduct for a man to pronounce, "I divorce you" three times all at once, and 'Umar ibn al-Khattab (d. 644), one of Muhammad's closest companions, used to order men to be flogged for doing it, for it requires that a man divorce his wife without any chance at reconciliation and prevent them from ever getting back together until she marries and divorces another. By the way, during the three-month waiting period, the man is not allowed to harass his wife, nor may he put her out of the house (unless it is after a third pronouncement and at least one of them must leave the house, depending on who actually owns it). In the male-initiated divorce settlement, the wife keeps all of her own property and wealth – there is no palimony in Islam, and she may put a legal claim on some of the man's property or income as maintenance, as well, and also receive child support. (Chapter 65 also contains supplementary regulations on this topic.)

[196] The last part of this verse is taken as proof that women can initiate divorce against their husbands. It was revealed about the case of a woman named Habeebah bint Sahl who went to the Prophet and waited outside his door early one morning. When he came out of his house to attend the morning prayer, he noticed her and asked who she was. She replied, and then the Prophet asked her, "What's the matter?" She answered, "(My husband) Thabit and I (are the matter). Messenger of Allah, I don't criticize his practice of the religion or his personal habits, but after having accepted Islam, I don't like

on either of them if she returns something (of her dowry) to be free (of her husband). [197] These are the rules set by Allah, so don't go beyond them; whoever (goes beyond) the rules set by Allah, they're truly in the wrong. [229]

Don't Take Marriage and Divorce Lightly

(If a man pronounces) divorce (against his wife the third, irrevocable time), then he cannot remarry her until after she's been married and divorced by another. If this condition is met, then there is nothing wrong for either of them if they reunite, intending to follow the rules of Allah. These are Allah's rules, clarified for those who understand. [198] [230]

When you (men initiate) divorce (proceedings against) women, and they've fulfilled the end of their waiting period, then either reconcile with them fairly and stay together, or let them go fairly. [199] Don't take them back in order to be spiteful and cruel, for whoever does that brings corruption upon his own soul. [200]

Don't take Allah's verses lightly. [201] Remember His favors upon you, and (contemplate the meaning of) what He revealed to you of the Book and the wisdom (that came along with it), as both of them are for your instruction. Be mindful of Allah, and know that Allah is well aware of everything (you do). [231]

Don't Prevent former Wives from Remarriage

When you've divorced women, and they've completed the waiting period, don't prevent them from marrying their former (husbands), [202] if they've agreed

---

being unappreciative (by disliking him, ignoring him and refusing his needs)." The Prophet then allowed her to divorce him upon her returning to him the garden he gave her as her dowry. (*Bukhari, Ibn Kathir*)

[197] In Islam, a woman can seek a divorce from her husband, though she may be required to return either all, or at least a portion, of the dowry, or marriage-gift, that he gave to her to compensate him for his loss as she was breaking the marriage contract with him through no fault of his own. (Also see 4:128 and footnote.) Today, this is usually determined in a divorce court proceeding, and the practice of female-initiated divorce is called *khul'* in Islamic law. If a man divorces his wife, however, he is not entitled to take any of her dowry, and he may have to pay spousal and child support, as well. The Prophet set the waiting period for a woman who initiates divorce at only one month, during which time she moves out of the house (if the husband owns it, or he moves out if she owns it). (*Tirmidhi*)

[198] This provision is for the fickle-minded who can't decide if they want to remain married or not. Perhaps they were not compatible with each other after all, and only by marrying someone else will that be made apparent. The marriage the woman has to another man must be consummated before she can decide to divorce him and get back together with her first husband. (*Bukhari, Muslim, Ahmad*) This makes people think twice about the consequences of their divorce pronouncements.

[199] So if the third monthly course is completed, and the man never pronounced 'divorce' a third time, then the couple can either decide to renew their marriage or go their separate ways in dignity and honor. If the man did pronounce 'divorce' three times by this point, there is no chance for reconciliation, and the divorce is mandatory and irrevocable (unless they both remarry and divorce another).

[200] It is a sin for a man to reconcile with his wife only out of a twisted desire to harass or abuse his wife's peace of mind and perhaps try to gain some advantage over her, financial or otherwise. This deviant, vengeful desire pollutes a person down to his core!

[201] When the Prophet heard of a man who pronounced 'divorce' three times in a row, he got angry and said, "Are you turning the Book of Allah into a joke, even while I'm still here among you!" (*Nisa'i*)

[202] A former maidservant named Barirah (who had been freed by A'ishah) divorced her husband Mughith, who was still a bonded-servant. Mughith was distraught and would publicly trail behind Barirah in tears. The Prophet said to one of his companions, "'Abbas! Aren't you amazed at how much love Mughith has for Barirah and how much hatred Barirah has for Mughith?" The Prophet then asked Barirah, "Why don't you take him back?" Thereupon Barirah asked, "Messenger of Allah, are you ordering me to take him back or only suggesting it?" The Prophet replied, "No, I'm only interceding

with each other in a fair manner. [203] This instruction is for all those among you who believe in Allah and the Last Day. That's the most wholesome course of action, and Allah knows (why), even if you don't know. [232]

On Child Care and Maintenance Issues

$\mathcal{M}$others should nurse their children for two full years. [204]

This (time period) is for the one who can complete this term.

(During this time, the father,) the one to whom the child was born, must support (the expenses of the child) according to his means, though no one will be forced to do more than he is able. [205]

Neither the mother nor the father should be treated unfairly on account of

---

for him." Barirah remarked, "Then I do not accept the suggestion, for I have no need of him." (*Bukhari*) No man can cling to a former wife and seek to reassert his control over her, and no well-wisher can force a couple back together.

[203] The exact reason for the revelation of this verse is as follows. A man named Ma'qil ibn Yasar gave his sister in marriage to a man in the community, but the couple soon divorced. After some time passed, however, both the man and the woman began to miss each other, and they both desired to get married again. (The man had never said '*divorce*' three times, so he was still eligible to remarry her again.) When the man approached Ma'qil and asked to remarry his sister once more, Ma'qil was outraged and said, "You thankless man! I honored you and married her to you, but you divorced her! By Allah! She will never be returned to you!" This verse was revealed to the Prophet concerning this situation, and when it was recited to Ma'qil, he said, "I hear and obey my Lord!" He then let the man remarry his sister, and he paid the compensation for having to break his vow. (*Bukhari, Abu Dawud, Tirmidhi, Bayhaqi*) So, this verse is a warning for family members who may try to obstruct a divorced couple from reuniting.

[204] The suggested amount of time that a baby should be breast fed is two years. The maximum, according to the scholars, is two and a half years. If a woman is unable or averse to doing this, then a wet nurse can be hired to complete the term. In ancient Mecca, upper class women, for example, held a low opinion of breastfeeding, and that's what fueled the custom of sending their newborns to bedouin foster mothers for nursing. Muhammad, himself, was sent to a bedouin lady named Halimah al-Sa'diyya to be nursed and weaned. Even divorced couples must make a definitive decision with regards to this important issue in their baby's development.

[205] If a divorce occurs, the husband will be held financially liable to fully support his divorced wife and their baby through the waiting period months ('*iddah*). After this, during the nursing process of two years, the ex-wife can demand financial support from him for her nursing services. Beyond this rule, the husband can possibly be compelled by a family court to pay full or partial child support for any and all young children he produced, as long as the woman does not remarry, though the man cannot be reduced to poverty by its strictures. If for some reason the mother cannot complete two years of suckling, a wet nurse can be hired to complete the time. Generally, in traditional Islamic law, women get automatic custody of children who are below the age of discretion, which is set at about eight years of age. If a woman is known to be immoral or mentally unfit, then a judge may order custody to be given to the father. The non-custodial parent will, of course, have the right to be consulted on major decisions regarding his or her children's upbringing, and he or she is by no means prevented from seeing them, unless he or she is a known danger to the child's health and a judge forbids contact. If the mother has full custody and she remarries, then support and custody issues are handled in family court. (Also see the book entitled, *Shari'ah: The Islamic Law*, by 'Abdur Rahman I. Doi, p. 214, which contains similar stipulations.) After children reach the age of discretion, they can decide with which parent they want to live, keeping in the mind that the other parent will still be a part of their life. (The idea that a child should have two separate homes that he or she shuttles between weekly is unknown in traditional Islamic family law.) If there are other issues involved that may be beyond the reasoning abilities of the child who is being consulted, such as the fitness of one parent or the other to look after the child properly, again a family court judge (*Qadi*) is to intervene and decide. The practical idea in Islam is that while both parents should have a hand in raising their children, the most tender years are reserved for the mother, while the father must do his duty and support his children. (Also see 65:6-7.)

their child. [206] This also applies to whoever must assume responsibility (in the event of the father's death). If both (parents) discuss and then agree to wean (the child before two years is up), and have consulted upon this, then there is no blame on them for that. [207]

If you wish to hire a wet-nurse for your children, there is no blame on you for that, either, provided that you pay (the wet-nurse) according to the reasonable (amount) that you agree upon. (Above all), be mindful of Allah, and know that Allah is watching whatever you do. [233]

On Widows and Remarriage

𝒪f any of you (husbands) die leaving widows behind, then they must wait for four months and ten days (before they can remarry). [208]

When they've finished that term, then there will be no blame upon you if they honorably do as they please with themselves, and Allah is well-informed of what you do. [234]

There's also no blame on (any of) you (men) if you propose (to a widow), nor (is there anything wrong if you secretly) desire (to marry one while she's still completing her waiting period). Allah already knows if you're thinking about them.

Just don't make secret commitments unless you can speak to them in respectable terms, and don't finalize the marriage details until the appointed waiting period is over. [209]

Know that Allah is already aware of what's on your minds, so be wary of Him, and know that Allah is forgiving and forbearing. [235]

---

[206] The commentators say that this means that the husband is not allowed to seize his child who is living with his ex-wife in order to cause her sorrow, neither is he allowed to force his wife to personally suckle their child if she cannot or is unwilling. At the same time, the mother isn't allowed to harm the child or refuse to see that he is nursed or cared for properly just to spite the father. The heir of the man who has a child to support must also be compelled to fund the financial obligations of the child's departed father. (*Ibn Kathir*)

[207] This verse clearly shows that divorced parents must make mutual decisions with regard to the health and well-being of their child. Thus, the rights of both parties are respected when a child is concerned. (*Ibn Kathir*)

[208] The waiting period for a widow is longer than that of a divorcee to ensure with greater clarity that the widow is, in fact, definitely not pregnant by her departed husband. (It helps dispel any doubts as to paternity.) Islam encourages widows to remarry, unlike some other traditions such as Hinduism, which forbids a widow to remarry, offering her the choice of exile from the family or the travails of the ancient practice of widows leaping onto their husband's funeral pyres. The Prophet led the example in encouraging remarriage for widows in that most of his wives were widows. If a man dies before consummating his marriage to his new bride, his widow gets her full dowry from his estate based upon a ruling from the Prophet who ordered such on behalf of a non-consummated widow named Barwa' bint Washiq. (*Ahmad, Nisa'i, Abu Dawud*) If a woman becomes a widow while she is pregnant, her waiting period ends at the birth of the child based upon the following incident: A woman named Subay'ah al-Aslamiyah was pregnant when her husband Sa'd passed away. She gave birth less than a week later. When her post-natal bleeding ended, she beautified herself whenever she went out in public to attract those who might want to ask for her hand in marriage. A man named Abu Sanabil saw her and said, "Why do I see you beautifying yourself? Are you looking to get married? By Allah, you shouldn't marry until the four months and ten days have passed." Subay'ah recounts what happened next in her own words: "When he said that to me, I got dressed at nightfall and went to the Messenger of Allah and asked him about this matter. He told me that my waiting period ended when I gave birth, and he allowed me to get married whenever I wished." (*Bukhari, Muslim*)

[209] This verse is looking out for the interests of widows. Women who are at their most vulnerable must not be pressured by overly eager men seeking commitments from them. That is why a final decision on remarriage must not be made while the woman is trying to put her life and peace of mind back in order, nor is a marriage contract made during a waiting period valid in an Islamic court of law. (*Ibn Kathir*)

Dowry Details

*T*here's no blame on you in divorcing women before the consummation of marriage or the settling of the dowry, as long as (the bride) is compensated with a gift - the rich and poor as they're able. [210]

A fair gift is a duty upon those who want to do what's most proper. [211] [236]

However, if you divorce (a woman) before the consummation of marriage and after the settling of the dowry, then half of the dowry must be given to her unless she forgives it, or (the groom) in whose hand is the marriage tie chooses (to give her the full dowry).

Giving the whole to her is closer to piety, so don't fail to be generous to each other, for Allah is watching whatever you do. [237]

Don't Neglect the Prayer even in Times of Fear

*G*uard the (times of) prayer, especially the middle prayer, and stand before Allah in a compliant fashion. [212] [238]

If you feel threatened (by an enemy force and cannot pray in the normal way), then pray while standing or riding, but when you're in a secure place once more, then remember Allah in the way He taught you – in the way you didn't know before. [239]

Provide Maintenance for Widows

*T*hose (husbands) who leave widows behind them should provide for them (in their will at least) a year's expenses and a place to stay. [213]

If (any widow) leaves (her home before that), then you won't be blamed for what they reasonably do with themselves. [214]

---

[210] The Prophet married a woman named Umaymah bint Sharahil. After the wedding ceremony was finished, she was escorted to where the Prophet was sitting, and he extended his hand to her. She suddenly changed her mind and decided that she didn't want to be married to the Prophet after all. The Prophet asked a man named Abu Usayd to give her some goods and the gift of two sets of clothes, and then she was released from the marriage bond. (*Bukhari*)

[211] This type of gift, which is not the same as the regular dowry, is given to a woman who is divorced before the consummation of marriage and before the settling of the regular dowry amount. It is called a *mu'tah* gift.

[212] The prayer-time mentioned in this passage is usually assumed to be the late-afternoon prayer, or '*asr* prayer. Usamah ibn Zayd, the son of the Prophet's adopted son, explained the reason for this verse. He said that in Medina very few Muslims would come out to join the Prophet for the afternoon (*zuhr*) and late afternoon ('*asr*) prayers on account of the heat or because of their business activities. This passage was revealed to remind them of the importance of not missing their prayers during the day even if they are apprehensive about their surroundings.

[213] To emphasize the need to care for widows, the Prophet said, "The one who looks after a widow or a poor person is like a struggler (*mujahid*) who struggles in Allah's cause, or like one who offers prayers all night and fasts all day." (*Bukhari*)

[214] The Prophet said, "It is unlawful for a woman who believes in Allah and the Last Day to mourn for more than three days for anyone who has died, except for her husband, for whom she can mourn for four months and ten days." (*Bukhari, Muslim*) In pre-Islamic times, women would mourn the dead in very bizarre ways. According to Zaynab bint Umm Salamah, the stepdaughter of the Prophet, pagan women would remember their husbands by "going into seclusion, wearing the worst clothes and never wearing perfume or any jewelry for a year. She would then come out of seclusion and throw animal dung. Then an animal like a donkey or sheep would be brought. Then she would drain its blood for a time, and this usually caused it to die." (*Ibn Kathir*) Loud weeping and wailing, (even hiring professional 'weepers') were also common, and the Prophet forbade all of these things. He did allow

96

(Remember that) Allah is powerful and wise. [215] [240]

Divorced women should also be given reasonable maintenance. This is a duty for those who are mindful (of Allah). [241] That's Allah making His verses evident for you so you can understand (them better). [242]

Fleeing an Enemy Won't Save You

*H*ave you ever considered those who fled from their homeland in fear, thinking they would be safe? [216] They numbered in the thousands! Therefore, (as a punishment for their cowardice), Allah said to them, "*So die, anyway!*"

Then He restored them to life. Allah grants His favor to people, though most people are thankless. [243] So fight in the cause of Allah (without fear that you might die), and know that Allah hears and knows (all things). [244]

Support Allah's Cause with What He Gave You

*W*ho is it that will lend to Allah a beautiful loan, which He will then redouble and increase many times? [217] Allah is the One Who withholds (resources), and (He is the One Who) grants (bounty to His creatures, so never think you're doing Allah a favor by supporting His cause), for you're (all) going to go back to Him. [245]

The Children of Israel Ask for a King

*H*ave you ever considered the chiefs of Israel who came after (the time of) Moses? [218] They said to a prophet (named

---

and encourage people to visit the graves of their departed ones, though in the early days of his mission he discouraged it because in Arabia it was a cultural practice for people to wail loudly there. A woman went to the Prophet and said her widowed daughter had cried so much for her dead husband that her eyes had become irritated, and she asked if she should put kohl on her eyes. The Prophet exclaimed, "No, (the mourning period) is only four months and ten days. During the days of ignorance, one of you would have mourned for an entire year!" (*Muslim*)

[215] This verse has a colorful history, and its ruling no longer applies in the traditional view of many of the commentators. This verse was revealed before widows were guaranteed by Islam a share of the inheritance of their deceased husbands' estates. (In pre-Islamic custom, a widow was at the mercy of her extended family as to whether or not she would inherit anything – or even be taken in by relatives and cared for!) Thus, a widow was guaranteed a solid year of support through her husband's estate, which was also the length of her traditional mourning period. (This Qur'anic injunction was an improvement in widow's lives, as there was no prescribed safety net for widows before Islam.) Then later on verse 4:12 was revealed, which gave widows from 1/8 to 1/4 of their husband's estates, which was a much better deal for them. Finally, to solidify the reforms for widow welfare, verse 2:234 was revealed, shortening the traditional waiting period (before remarriage) of a widow from one year down to four months and ten days, so she could seek remarriage earlier, if she chose. (She also is fully supported from her husband's estate in his home for the length of the shortened waiting period, and this does not detract from her allotted portion of inheritance.) (*Ibn Kathir*)

[216] There is a story of Talmudic origin that has been passed along in some of the books of Qur'anic commentary that this verse is referring to a group of Israelites who fled the plague in fear, only to die anyway. They were later restored to life upon the supplication of Prophet Ezekiel. It is more probably about a town's militia that attempted to flee from a greater foe, rather than placing faith in God that they would prevail. They were still all but defeated but when they regained their faith, they ultimately prevailed.

[217] After this verse was revealed, the Jews of the tribe of Banu Qaynuqa began to ridicule Islam, saying that Muhammad's God was stricken with poverty. Verse 3:181 was revealed in response. Also see 5:64 and 36:47.

[218] Moses led the Israelites out of Egyptian bondage. His people disobeyed Allah when they were asked to enter Canaan and take possession of it from idol-worshippers. Thus, they were forced to wander in the desert for forty years. (See 5:20-26) When both Moses and that generation of

Samuel), *"Set up a king for us, and then we'll fight in the cause of Allah."*

(Samuel, sensing their duplicity), replied, *"And maybe when you're commanded to fight, you won't fight at all!"*

They (insisted they would, however), by saying, *"Why wouldn't we fight in the cause of Allah? We've been driven from our homes and families."*

Nonetheless, when it came time to fight, they turned back, save for a few among them. Allah knows who the wrongdoers are. [246]

When their prophet told them, *"Allah has chosen Saul to be your king,"* they objected, saying, *"How can he be made our king when we're more qualified than he is to rule? He's not even rich enough!"*

"Allah has selected him over you," he answered, *"and endowed him with knowledge and talent. Allah gives the right to rule to whomever He wants, and Allah is infinitely more knowledgeable (than you)."* [247]

Then their prophet said to them, *"You'll see a sign to prove that leadership is his right in that the Ark of the Covenant will be given back to you. Within it is tranquility from your Lord, for it contains the relics of the families of Moses and Aaron. It will be carried (back to you) by the angels, themselves.* [219] *This will be your sign if you (really) have faith."* [248]

When Saul set out with his army (to face the Philistines), he addressed (his men), saying, *"Allah will test you by that stream. Whoever drinks from it won't be allowed to march any farther with me. Only those who abstain from it will go with me, or who at the very least drink only a sip from their hand."* All of them, save for a few, drank from the stream.

Then after they crossed over (the stream), the (few remaining) faithful (soldiers) lamented, *"We're no match for Goliath and his army today."*

However, those who were certain they would meet Allah one day said, *"How many times has a smaller force defeated a larger one, by Allah's will? Allah is with those who persevere!"* [249]

As they advanced upon Goliath and his forces, they prayed, *"Our Lord, pour determination down upon us, make our stance firm and help us against this nation that rejects (faith)."* [220] [250]

---

disobedient adults passed away, Joshua became the leader of the people. They successfully entered the Promised Land and established their rule. For the next three centuries, however, the Israelites were disunited, often feuded with one another, and adopted many pagan customs in the process. From time to time, leaders called Judges arose who imposed their authority over the wider community. Some of these Judges were even prophets. Samuel was the last great one among these authority figures, and he came at a time (approx. 11th century BCE) when the Israelites demanded a strong monarchy to unite them against their many foes.

[219] The fabled Ark of the Covenant was a decorated wooden box. It was supposedly the repository of sacred items (such as carved religious stones and a magical snake staff, as mentioned in Numbers 21:8-9 and II Kings 18:4). These items were leftovers from the days of Prophets Moses and Aaron. (See Numbers 10:35-36 for the Ark's alleged destructive power.) Interestingly enough, the Qur'an does not ascribe any magical power to the box, but instead holds it a symbol that can improve the morale of the Jewish people. Of late, it had been captured by the Philistines, who were enemies of the Israelites. It was later returned after the Philistines concluded that its possession was causing plagues and pestilence upon their people. It is said that the Philistines put it on a wagon yoked to two oxen and left it alone, and that the angels guided the oxen to bring it back into Israelite territory. (See I Samuel 5:1-12, 6:1-21 and II Chronicles 5:10.) The Ark has been lost since 587 BCE. Muslim popular tradition holds that in the End Times, a leader will arise who will defend Islam from its enemies. This man, who will be called the *Mahdi*, will find the lost Ark near Lake Tiberius, and this symbol will prove his place as an authentic servant of God. (*Al Hawi l'il Fatawa* of Jalaluddin as-Suyuti)

[220] According to I Samuel 17:1-2, the battle took place between Shochoh and Azekah, a place about 14 miles west of Bethlehem. There is a seasonal stream or *wadi* that runs through the valley of Elah (and passes through this area) to the Mediterranean Sea. This is probably the water source being referenced here. Also see Judges 7:4-8.

98

And so by Allah's will they routed them, and David killed Goliath. [221] Allah also gave (David) leadership skills, wisdom and whatever else He wanted to teach him.

If Allah didn't enable one people to deter another, then the world would be filled with turmoil, but Allah is infinitely bountiful to the entire universe. [251]

On Religions of the Past

*T*hese are the revelations of Allah that We're reciting to you in all truth, for you, (Muhammad), are one of the messengers. [252]

Of those messengers, We've favored some above others; Allah spoke directly to one (of them), while others were raised to a higher rank.

To Jesus, the son of Mary, We gave miracles, reinforcing him with the Holy Spirit. [222]

If Allah had wanted to (intervene), the later followers (of all these messengers) would never have fought with each other after receiving the evidence.

Yet, they chose to argue; some believed, and some denied. If Allah had wanted to (intervene), then they would've never fought amongst themselves. Allah does what He wills. [253]

On the Importance of Charity

O you who believe! Spend (in charity) out of what We've supplied to you before the day comes when no bargaining will be accepted, when no friendship will matter nor intercession sway. (That will be the day) when those who rejected (faith) will finally realize that they were in the wrong. [254]

The Verse of the Throne

*A*llah! *There is no god but He:*
the Living, the Everlasting! [223]
No fatigue overcomes Him, nor (does He) rest.

All things within the heavens
and the earth belong to Him;
who can intercede with Him without His behest?

He knows what's ahead of (people after death,)
and (the deeds) they've left behind,
while they know nothing of His knowledge
except for what He allows.

His authority extends over
the heavens and the earth,
and He never tires in their safekeeping.

He alone is the Most High,
the Lord Sovereign Supreme. [255]

---

[221] David was a shepherd boy who happened to come to the battlefield on an errand. The famed Philistine warrior Goliath was striking fear into the hearts of Saul's men. David took up the challenge of meeting him in hand-to-hand combat and slew him with his own sword after knocking him out with a sling thrown stone. (See I Samuel chapters 17 and 18. II Samuel 21:19 claims that an Israelite warrior named Elhanan actually slew Goliath. Note, the words 'the brother of' do not appear in the Hebrew text.) It is said that Saul promised his daughter's hand in marriage to the one who killed Goliath, and this is how David eventually became the king of Israel.

[222] The Holy Spirit is understood by Muslims to be the angel Gabriel.

[223] In a tradition, the Prophet said, "Allah's most magnificent name is sealed within the Verse of the Throne, and whoever calls by it will surely have his prayers answered." *(Abu Dawud)* In another narration, the Prophet said, "Allah's greatest name, the one by which, if He was called upon, would cause Him to answer the supplication, is located in three chapters (then he indicated chapters 2, 3, and 20)." *(At-Tabarani)* One very early scholar named Hisham ibn 'Ammar (d. cir. 887) said that the specific verses within which the greatest name of Allah resides are 2:255, 3:1-2 and 20:111. It is said the exact name or title is *"Al-Hayy al-Qayyum"* which means, *"the Living, the Everlasting."*

Does Islam Allow Freedom of Religion?

*T*here is no (permission) to force (anyone into following this) way of life. [224] The truth stands clear from error. Whoever rejects falsehood and believes in Allah has grasped a firm hand-hold that will never break, for Allah hears and knows (all things). [225] [256]

To those who believe, Allah is a protector Who will lead them out of darkness and into the light. To those who suppress (their awareness of the truth), falsehood is their protector, and it will lead them out of the light and into the darkness.

They'll be the companions of the Fire, *and that's where they're going to stay!* [257]

The Story of Abraham and the Arrogant King

*H*ave you pondered (the tale [226] of the arrogant king) [227] who argued with Abraham about his Lord and the power which Allah allowed him to wield? When Abraham announced, *"My Lord is the One Who gives life and death,"* (the king) cried out, *"I'm the one who (decides) who lives and who dies!"*

Abraham replied, *"Well, Allah makes the sun rise from the East, so can you now make it rise from the West?"* This is how the one who

---

[224] When the conflict between the Muslims and the Jews of the Banu Nadir was settled, with the requirement that the Jews had to leave the city and move elsewhere, it was found that there were a number of Arab children living among the Jews. This was not unusual, as some were adopted, while others were being raised as Jews with their (Arab) parents' consent. The reason why some Arab children were raised as Jews is because of a curious local custom. If a woman was considered to be barren, she would vow that if she ever was able to give birth, she would raise the baby as a Jew in compensation for the miracle. This happened from time to time. The Medinan Muslims did not want these Arab children to leave with the Jews, and they asked the Prophet if they could take custody of them. This verse was revealed in response. The Prophet gave the Arab children the choice of going with the Jews or becoming a part of the wider community in Medina. Some left, and others remained. (*Asbab ul-Nuzul*)

[225] A new Muslim from the tribe of Banu Salim had two sons who had converted to Christianity in the days before Islam came to Medina. They arrived in the city to visit their father who lived there, and when he saw them he told them, "By Allah! I won't let you go until you've both converted (to Islam). The two men refused, and so the father took them before the Prophet with his complaint. The Muslim man said, "Messenger of Allah, shall a part of me go to Hellfire, while I'm watching?" The Prophet, however, recited this passage [2:256-257] and the man's sons were allowed to go and retain their own religion. (*Zamakhshari*)

[226] After Abraham had renounced idolatry and began publicly campaigning against it, he devised a plan to show the people of his city that idolatry was false. That was the incident of destroying the idols (see 21:51-66). When the order came for Abraham to be thrown in a fire pit, (an order apparently given by the priests of the temple,) the famous incident of Abraham surviving the fire unscathed took place (see 21:67-69). After that he was hauled before the royal court, and the exchange recounted below took place. After the king engineered a plot to cause his death, Abraham escaped somehow and left Mesopotamia forever.

[227] Some commentators, following Jewish tradition and an obscure (and weak) prophetic narration that mentions Nimrod's fire being cooled for Abraham, have suggested that the king in question might have been, in fact, Nimrod, a legendary king of Mesopotamia, but the Qur'an is silent on the identity of the king, and it could have been any ruler. Exact identification of a king, given the uncertain time frame of Abraham's birth, is well-nigh impossible today. Interestingly enough, surviving records indicate that no less than five kings who ruled between the years 2225 and 1776 BCE (the window of time within which Abraham lived) had declared themselves to be "Lords of all the world." One of these delusional Mesopotamian kings, who declared himself a god, was Shulgi, (Culgi), who reigned over Ur and the surrounding lands between the years 2047 and 1999 BCE. He completed the great Ziggurat of Ur, whose ruins can still be seen to this day. In typical kingly fashion for his time, he used to boast of his divine abilities and used such legends to influence other cities to ally themselves with him. He wrote of himself, "I am...the god of all the lands."

covered (the knowledge of faith in his heart) was silenced, for Allah gives no guidance to people who are unjust. [258]

Asking Allah for Proof

(*H*ave you learned the lesson) of the one who passed by a ruined city, [228] whose roofs had tumbled down? *"Can even Allah restore this place after so much decay?"* he mused.

So Allah caused him to die for a hundred years, and after that He raised him back to life and asked, *"How long have you been there?"*

"A day, maybe less," was his answer.

"Not so," declared (Allah), *"you were there for a hundred years after, and while your food and drink are preserved, look at your donkey (for it has died and rotted to bones). I'm going to make your example a sign to others, so look closely (as I raise your donkey back to life). Do you see how We knit the bones together and cover them with flesh?"* [229]

When (the man) began to understand, he declared, *"Truly, Allah has power over all that exists!"* [259]

A Demonstration for Abraham

*E*ven Abraham had once asked, *"My Lord, show me how You bring the dead to life."* [230] (Allah) replied, *"Don't you believe (that I can do it)?"*

"Of course!" answered Abraham. *"I'm only asking for my own satisfaction."*

So (Allah) said, *"Take four birds, and train them to come to you (when you call); then divide them up, placing them on separate hills. Call to them, and they'll come swiftly to you.* [231] *(In this*

---

[228] Some commentators have said that the town in this verse is none other than Jerusalem, which had been sacked by the Babylonians and ruined in 586 BCE, and that this verse is really about how Allah restored the Children of Israel to prosperity, even though it looked like they would never regain their power again. (Salman Al-Farsi was of the opinion that the man mentioned here was Prophet Ezekiel. See Nehemiah 2:13-20.)

[229] It is clear from this verse that Ezekiel (d. about 397 BC) is the probable subject of this verse. Verses from Ezekiel 37:1-13 tell of a vision in which God brought Ezekiel to a valley of dry bones, and then told him to speak to bring life back to the scattered bones as a metaphor for the eventual return of the Israelites to their land after being decimated and captured by the Babylonians. Another alternative is that the man is Nehemiah who visited a ruined Jerusalem and wondered how it could be restored. In the end, the identity is not important, for the lesson is that time means nothing to Allah, and that he can change the seemingly impossible at will.

[230] The commentators are of two opinions about the reason for Abraham's question. Some say that during his debate with the king, Abraham felt that the king had scored a point by saying he could control life and death. The king ordered a man executed on the spot and set a captive free to demonstrate his point. Later on Abraham asked for a demonstration from Allah to help him understand the difference between Allah's power and an earthly ruler's power. Other commentators believe Abraham saw a dead animal of some type and marveled over how any dead creature could be restored to life. Given the context of verses 258-260, the first view seems more likely. The Prophet Muhammad commented on our natural affinity for questioning and skepticism when he said, "We're more prone to doubting than Abraham." Then the Prophet quoted this verse. (*Bukhari*)

[231] In other words, Allah can bring the dead to life by merely commanding it to happen in the same way that Abraham called the birds and they came immediately. (Also see 3:47.) Many commentators are of the view that this verse is saying that Abraham was commanded to kill the birds and dismember them and then put random pieces of the birds on the separate hills. Then when he called them, they would miraculously reassemble, come to life and then fly to him. I am not inclined to accept that interpretation for the very reason that Abraham's efforts at 'taming' the birds would have been useless and superfluous. If the demonstration was meant to bring dead birds to life, then there would have been no need to train them to come when called. Therefore, I am of the view, which other commentators espouse, that the purpose of the test was to show the power of command, i.e., Allah can raise the dead with a word of command only. (He only needs to say, *"Be,"* and it is!)

lesson), know that Allah is powerful and wise."
[260]

Charity Multiplies Blessings

The example of those who spend their money in the cause of Allah is like that of a seed grain. From it seven robust stalks rise, and each stalk contains a hundred grains! Allah gives abundantly to whomever He wants, for Allah is enough of a provider and is full of knowledge. [232]
[261]

Charity is not for the Humiliation of Others

Those who spend their money in the cause of Allah, and who neither remind others about what they spent nor humiliate (the poor to whom they give charity), will be rewarded by their Lord. [233]

They'll have no reason to fear or regret. [262] Kind words and forgiveness are much better than charity that hurts. Remember; Allah is self-sufficient and is forbearing. [263]

O you who believe! Don't negate your charity by making others feel they owe you or by humiliating (the poor). This is what the boastful do when they spend to be seen by other people, for they don't really believe in Allah and the Last Day. [234]

They're like a rock covered only by a little soil that a torrent of rain soon washes away, exposing the hard bare stone underneath. They can't do anything with what they've earned, for Allah doesn't guide people who suppress (their awareness of the truth). [264]

The example of those who spend their money seeking only to please Allah and to strengthen their own souls is like a high garden where rain is plentiful and the yields are double. [235] Even if there's no heavy downpour, the dew is enough! Allah is watching everything you do. [265]

Who wants to have an orchard full of date palms and grapevines, with streams flowing underneath and produce of all kinds, but then be stricken with old age while his children are still small, and then have a scorching whirlwind come and destroy it all? That's how Allah makes His revelations clear so you can think carefully. [236] [266]

---

[232] The Prophet said, "When someone gives charity out of lawful earnings, even if it's as little as a date, Almighty Allah will receive it from him with His right hand and will cultivate it for him, just like when one of you plants a field of crops. It will grow until it becomes as high as Mount Uhud." (*Bukhari, Tirmidhi*)

[233] This verse was revealed in response to the willing and cheerful charity that Uthman ibn Affan (d. 656) gave to support Muhammad's mission. He went to the Prophet and said, "I have eight thousand silver coins. I am keeping four thousand for myself and my family, while I am lending to Allah the other four thousand." The Prophet answered, "Allah bless what you kept and what you gave." (*Asbab ul-Nuzul*)

[234] The Prophet said, "There are three kinds of people who won't enter Paradise. The first is someone who (embarrasses his brother by) always reminding him of the favors he did for him. The second is someone who lets his cloak drag on the ground behind him in public (to show he is so rich that he can ruin clothes at will), and the third is a person who sells goods with false claims and then swears to Allah that he's telling the truth." (*Muslim*) Also see Matthew 6:1-18 where Christians are similarly admonished to be sincere in both public and secret, as well.

[235] The Prophet said, "Allah doesn't look at your physical appearance or your money; rather, He looks to your mindfulness (of Him) (*taqwa*) and your actions." (*Muslim*) So a person's physical appearance and financial state matter nothing to Allah, Who only cares about the heart and deeds.

[236] Ibn 'Abbas (d. 687) once explained in a gathering presided over by the second caliph, 'Umar ibn al-Khattab (d. 644), that this verse is also a metaphor for a rich man who does good deeds but then nullifies those good deeds later on by engaging in sinfulness. Thus, he comes to Allah with nothing. (*Fath al Bari*) The Prophet was heard supplicating once, "O Allah! Bestow Your greatest bounty upon me when I'm old and near the end of my life." (*Al-Hakim*)

What is True Charity?

$\mathcal{O}$ you who believe! [237] Spend in charity out of the good things that you've earned and (of the harvest) of the earth that We've allowed to grow for you. Don't choose to spend (in charity) items of inferior quality - *things that you wouldn't even want to receive yourself!* Know that Allah is self-sufficient and is praiseworthy. [267]

Satan scares you with fears of poverty and tempts you to do shameful things, while Allah promises you pardon and grace. [238] Allah is enough of a provider, and He is full of knowledge. [268]

He grants wisdom to whomever He wants, and whoever receives wisdom gains great benefits thereby; yet, only the insightful ever realize this. [269]

Whatever you spend in charity or pledge to give is well-known to Allah. The wrongdoers, (who never give), will have no one to help them, (even as they help none). [270]

So if you donate to charity in public, it isn't wrong, though giving in secret to those in need is much better for you, as this will help to erase some of your sins. Allah is well-informed of everything you do. [271]

Charity is a Sincere Offering to All Who Need It

$\mathcal{I}$t's not required for you to convert the (needy people to your religion before you give to them in charity), for Allah guides whomever He wants. Whatever you spend (in charity) is done for the good of your own soul, for in so doing you've (shown that you're) seeking Allah's face alone. [239] Whatever good you spend will come back to you, and you won't be shortchanged. [272]

(Give to) the needy (missionaries) engaged in the cause of Allah who are prevented from going abroad to support themselves in the world - whom the ignorant consider to be well taken care of because of their modesty. [240] You can recognize them by their faces for they don't ask people persistently. Whatever good you spend, Allah knows about it. [273]

---

[237] Some men of Medina would offer clusters of rotting dates in charity, thinking that they wouldn't be noticed among the piles of date clusters that were often hung on the walls of the mosque to feed the poor. This verse came in response, asking Muslims *not* to donate things to the poor that they themselves wouldn't want. (*At-Tabari*)

[238] The Prophet said, "Both Satan and the angels have an effect upon the son of Adam. Satan's effects consist of his threats about unfortunate consequences (that may result from living the path of faith) and by his call to reject the truth, while the angels' effects consist of promising good results (for faith) and in calling all to believe in the truth. Whoever finds the second thing should know that it's coming from Allah, so he should thank Allah for it. Whoever finds the first thing should seek Allah's protection from Satan." Then the Prophet recited this verse. (*Ibn Abi Hatim*)

[239] Some Muslim converts disliked giving charity to their non-Muslim relatives, and they asked the Prophet about this. This verse was revealed telling them that it was perfectly allowed to give in charity to non-Muslims, as helping another human being is a good act, regardless of the religion of another person. (*Asbab ul-Nuzul*)

[240] Abu Sa'id was sent by his mother to ask the Prophet for some charitable donations. He went to the Prophet and sat down before him, but the Prophet began speaking first and said, "Whoever feels satisfied, Allah will enrich him. Whoever is modest, Allah will give him a decent (standard of living). Whoever is content (with whatever he has), then Allah will be enough for him. Whoever asks people (for more), while he has at least a small amount (of resources), will be counted as a beggar of people." Abu Sa'id recalled that he at least owned a camel, so he went away without asking for anything. (*Abu Dawud, Nisa'i, Ahmad*) Simple living is one of the hallmarks of Islam's advice for this life, and there is a large amount of literature and examples of this philosophical frame of mind throughout Muslim classical civilization. The famous poet, Sa'di Shirazi (d. 1291), once wrote: "Astride a horse I am not, nor camel-like a load. Subjects I have none, nor follow any sultan's code. I worry not for what exists nor fret for what is lost. I breathe with careless ease, and then I live at little cost."

Those who spend their money (in the cause of Allah) through the night and through the day, in secret and in public, will have their reward with their Lord, and they'll have no reason to fear or regret. [241] [274]

The Prohibition of Interest and Other Business Matters

*T*hose who devour interest-money will have no standing except for that of someone who's been knocked down by the touch of Satan – *demented*. That's because they say that business and taking interest-money are the same, *but Allah has made business lawful while forbidding interest!* [242]

Whoever listens to this warning that has come from his Lord and desists (from accepting interest may retain the interest already accrued). Then the matter will rest with Allah. Whoever continues (taking interest after this) will (soon) be among the companions of the Fire, *and that's where they're going to stay!* [275]

Allah cancels out any profits made through interest but adds to acts of charity, for Allah has no love for thankless sinners. [276]

Truly, those who believe and do what's morally right, who establish regular prayer and give the required charity will have their reward with their Lord, and they'll have no reason to fear or regret. [277]

You can Keep Your Principal Investment

O you who believe! [243] Be mindful of Allah, and forego any interest that's owed to you, that is if you really believe. [278] If you don't, then beware of war on the part of Allah and His Messenger. Though if you repent, then you may keep your principal investment. You will do no wrong, and neither will you be wronged. [279]

If a person who owes you money is in financial difficulty, give him time until his circumstances improve, but if you forgive

---

[241] 'Ali ibn Abi Talib, the Prophet's younger cousin, once had four silver coins. He donated one to charity at night, one during the day, one secretly and one in public. The Prophet went to him and said, "This (verse) is for you." Then he recited this new revelation. (*Asbab ul-Nuzul*)

[242] The Prophet cursed those who accepted interest-money, paid it, recorded its contracts, or witnessed to it saying they were all alike. (*Muslim*) On another occasion he said, "A penny of interest knowingly taken by a person is a sin worse than committing unlawful sex thirty-six times." (*Ahmad*) On another occasion he said, "There will come a time when people will live on the income derived from interest." Someone asked him, "Everyone?" He answered, "Those who won't be living on it, will be victimized and clouded by its dust." (*Abu Dawud*) While the wisdom behind the prohibition of interest in Islam is a lengthy one, suffice it to say that the injustice of interest is that it penalizes those who are most in need, while putting creditors in the position of parasites, feeding off the hardship and misery of the less fortunate. While some critics contend that Islam is unique in banning interest, it was long before forbidden by Judaism (which does allow it to be charged to non-Jews) and Christianity (which banned it only until the eighteenth century and then essentially gave up its opposition in the face of the demands of secular governments.) For Biblical evidence see Exodus 22:25, Deuteronomy 23:19-20, Psalms 15:5, Proverbs 28:8, and Ezekiel 18:13, which calls for death upon those who loan on interest! Even Plato, Aristotle, Seneca, Cicero, St. Thomas Aquinas and Martin Luther spoke out against the practice.

[243] This passage was revealed after Mecca capitulated and was under Muslim authority. An Arab tribe in the countryside named the Banu 'Amr was owed money by the tribe of Banu al-Mughirah. The loan also had a certain interest rate attached to it. Verses 278-279 were revealed to the Prophet and he warned the Banu 'Amr that unless they gave up collecting interest on the loan owed to them, (for the Banu 'Amr were insistent about it), he would fight them. The Banu 'Amr agreed to forgo the interest if the principle were repaid immediately, but the Banu al-Mughirah could not afford this stipulation, and the Banu 'Amr would not back down. Verses 280-281 were revealed, and the Banu 'Amr finally agreed to let the debt be repaid slowly. Also, in his treaty with the semi-autonomous Christian community of Najran, the Prophet used this passage to stipulate that they must give up interest-transactions or their treaty of peace would be nullified.

his debt altogether, as an act of charity, that's better for you, if you only knew. [280]

Be mindful of the day when you'll be brought before Allah, for then every soul will be repaid for what it's earned, and no one will be treated unfairly. [244] [281]

The Importance of Business Contracts

O you who believe! [245] When negotiating transactions involving future obligations and (delivery) schedules, finalize any agreement in writing.

Let a legal secretary accurately record the terms between each side. No legal secretary should refuse to write as Allah taught him, so let him record (the contract accurately).

Let the borrower read out the terms (as the secretary writes), and let him fear Allah his Lord, and not leave out any obligation on his part.

If the borrower is mentally deficient, suffering from some illness or (in health too poor) to dictate (the terms) himself, then let his representative dictate the contract faithfully, and have two of your men to act as witnesses.

If two men are not available, then choose a man and two women of whom you approve to be the witnesses, because if one of the (women is not skilled at business) and makes a mistake (in future legal testimony), then the other may remind her. [246] If the witnesses are summoned, then they must not refuse to come.

---

[244] The Prophet said, "Almighty Allah is going to bring a person for judgment and ask him, 'What good did you do in the physical world?' The man will answer, 'Not even one speck of good have I ever done for Your sake, my Lord.' Allah will ask the man the same question two more times, and after the third time the man will say, 'My Lord, You gave me excessive wealth, and I was a businessman. In my deals I used to be generous with my well-off peers; I used to give extra time for the unfortunate ones until they could pay off what they owed me, and I made it easy on them.' Almighty Allah will say, 'I am the One Who is most fit to ease people's suffering, so enter Paradise.'" *(Bukhari, Muslim)* In another tradition, the Prophet said, "Whoever relieves his brother of a burden or forgives his debt will stand in the shade of Allah's throne on the Day of Resurrection." (*Muslim*) In a third saying, he said, "Whoever gives time to a debtor facing hard times will earn charity multiplied two times for each day he gives." (*Ahmad*) Once Imam Abu Hanifa (d. 767) came to know that a certain man would turn back and take a different road if he ever heard that the Imam was coming his way. Abu Hanifa sought the man out and asked him why he always did that. The man replied that he owed him (Abu Hanifa) a large sum of money, and he was ashamed to face him on account of his inability to repay it. Abu Hanifa took pity on the man and forgave him the entire debt. Some eminent authorities, including Ibn 'Abbas, Abu Hurairah and Ibn Jurayj, are of the opinion that this was the very last verse of the Qur'an revealed to the Prophet – just nine days before he passed away on August 8, 632.

[245] This is the longest single verse of the Qur'an. In practical application, there is a story that demonstrates its purpose. The Prophet negotiated with a bedouin to buy his horse. After the price was agreed upon, the Prophet asked the bedouin to follow him to his house so he could get the money to pay him. The bedouin followed after the Prophet at a slower pace, and along the route various people saw the horse and offered to buy it from the bedouin for more money than what he had agreed to with the Prophet. When the bedouin arrived at the Prophet's house the bedouin said, "If you want to buy this horse, then offer a price for it or I'll sell it to someone else." The Prophet, rightly thinking that he had already closed negotiations with the bedouin, said, "Didn't I already arrange to buy the horse from you?" The bedouin said, "By Allah, I haven't sold it to you." Then people gathered while the two were disputing. Eventually the bedouin backed down, but the point was made that in the absence of a written contract for a one-time deal, witnesses are asked to be present. (*Ahmad*)

[246] Does the Qur'an teach that a man's word is worth the word of two women as a matter of principle? No, it does not. The Qur'an does not teach that it takes two women to *equal* one man's testimony, for as evidenced by the Qur'an itself in 24:6-10, a woman's testimony *is equal* to that of a man's and should be accepted *over* the man's if she has been accused of adultery and proclaims her innocence. The reason for two women witnesses *for a business contract* is given right here in this verse. One woman can *remind* the other about the details if she happens to forget, not to mention that many women

Never neglect to draw up a contract for future transactions, whether for large or small sums. That's most fair in the sight of Allah and better for proof and avoiding doubt (concerning your reputations) among yourselves.

If the transaction involves merchandise for only a one-time, face-to-face deal, then there's nothing wrong if you forego a written contract, but have witnesses for commercial contracts.

Ensure that the witnesses and secretaries remain unharmed, for it would be a great sin on your part (if you pressured them unfairly). Be mindful (of Allah), for it's Allah Who is teaching you, and Allah knows about all things. [282]

If you're traveling and a legal secretary is unavailable, then taking a deposit (is good enough to seal the deal). If one of you makes a good-faith deposit with another, then let the trusted one fulfill his duties and fear Allah his Lord.

Never suppress any evidence, for whoever does that will have his heart tarnished with sin, and Allah knows everything you do. [283]

In What shall We Believe?

All things within the heavens and the earth belong to Allah. Whether you reveal what's in your soul or suppress it, Allah will make you answer for it. He'll pardon whom He pleases and punish whom He wills, for Allah has power over all things. [284]

The Messenger believes in what his Lord revealed, as do the faithful. Each of them believes in Allah, His angels, His books and His messengers. (The believers say), *"We don't consider one of His messengers as being better than another."*

(They pray), *"We hear, and we obey, (and we seek) Your forgiveness, Our Lord, for we (know that our) final destination is back with You."* [247] [285]

For What shall We Pray?

Allah will not burden any soul beyond what it can bear. [248] Each will enjoy the good of what it gains, as indeed each (will suffer for the wrong) it has earned by its own efforts. (Pray then these words:)

---

often prefer not to bargain or barter with men over contractual obligations alone and without allies. At that time, and indeed even in our own times, unscrupulous men often attempted to take advantage of women in business affairs. Islam seeks the protection of women from such aggressive males who may try to confuse, bully or cheat women who may be less experienced in business or who may succumb to relentless pressure. The Qur'an recognizes facts of life without implying that women are not as smart as men or any such absurd idea. This is one of those areas that in no way implies superiority of one gender over another. In a court of law or for any other purpose, a woman's testimony is equal to a man's, and the Prophet, himself, demonstrated this numerous times by acting on the testimony of a single woman with no requirement for a second voice to corroborate her story.

[247] A report in the *Muslim* collection of prophetic traditions asserts that this verse was revealed to the Prophet while he was on his ascension to heaven.

[248] When verse 284 was revealed, Abu Bakr, 'Umar, Mu'adh ibn Jabal and others went to the Prophet and knelt down humbly, saying, "Messenger of Allah, we swear by Allah that this is the hardest verse ever revealed for us. All of us speak inwardly of things that we don't like in our hearts, for all of us would desire to own the whole world. If we're condemned for what we think to ourselves, then we're doomed." The Prophet replied, "This is how the verse was revealed." The companions lamented that they couldn't bear such a strict burden, and the Prophet suggested they could either disobey Allah like the people of Moses did or they could obey Allah. They reaffirmed their faith, and a year passed with no further word from Allah on this issue. Then this verse was revealed that gave them relief, saying that Allah would not burden a soul beyond what it could bear; thus, Allah would not hold people to account for what they said within their own thoughts. (*Asbab ul-Nuzul*)

"Forgive us, our Lord, if we forget or sin.
Don't burden us, our Lord,
as those before us have been.

Don't burden us, our Lord,
with something beyond our capacity.

Forgive us our trespasses,
and grant us Your mercy.

You alone are our protector;
so help us against those who are rejecters.   [286]

The Family of Amram

3 Ali 'Imran
Medinan Period

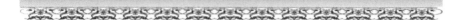

The main focus of this chapter, which is named after a clan of Jewish priests whose lineage stretches back to the time of Moses and Aaron, is to introduce the idea that God has sent an eternal message to the world in a continuous (and evolving) chain of prophethood. Judaism, Christianity and other religions were founded by true prophets who taught monotheism and righteous living, and there has been no corner of the globe that God has not touched with His message. Each successive revealed religion was more advanced than the last, reflecting the corresponding rise in human civilization and cultural development.

If the people that each prophet left behind, however, lost or distorted his teachings, then a later prophet might be raised to correct their descendants. The stories of Mary and Jesus are introduced in this regard, as their example was meant to show how Judaism could be reformed. Prophet Muhammad is offered as the last in a long line of messengers from God who all taught essentially the same basic message of salvation. The Prophet said of this chapter, "Learn and recite the chapters of the Cow and Amram for they are the most radiant lights of the Qur'an." (*Ahmad*)

In the Name of Allah,
the Compassionate, the Merciful

Alif. Lām. Meem. [249] [1]

Allah: there is no god but He, the Living, the Everlasting. [2]

He is revealing this Book gradually to you as a truthful confirmation of previous (revelations), even as He revealed the Torah and the Gospel [3] before this as a guide for all people.

He also revealed to you the (prophetic) standard (of right and wrong). [250]

Those who suppress (their ability to have faith) in these proofs of Allah will suffer the severest punishment, for Allah is powerful and utterly intense in vengeance. [4]

---

[249] The Prophet said, "Recite the Qur'an, for you will be rewarded at the rate of ten good deeds for every letter you read of the Qur'an. Keep in mind that I'm not saying that *alif, lam, meem* is one word, but rather that *alif* is one letter, *lam* is another, and *meem* is another."

[250] Many commentators are of the opinion that this "standard" refers to the life example of the Prophet, known as the *sunnah* in Arabic. The premise is that the Qur'an is Allah's word, while the *sunnah* is the Prophet's living example of how to put that Book's teachings into daily practice. Others are of the opinion that it refers either to another facet of the revealed books, themselves, or to some other area of wisdom. The Prophet said, "A group of my followers will keep on obeying Allah's orders (the Qur'an) and the Prophet's example strictly. They won't be harmed by those who reject them or desert them until Allah's command will come (signaling the Last Day), and they will still be in that state." (*Bukhari*)

Division Leads to Disintegration

*T*here's not a thing on the earth nor in the sky that's hidden from Allah. [5] He's the One Who shapes you in the womb as He wills. [251] There is no god but He, and He's the Powerful, the Wise! [6]

He's the One Who is revealing this scripture to you. Among its verses are some that are plain and clearly understood. They're the foundation of the Book.

There are also other (verses, however, whose meanings) are obscure. Those who have hearts inclined towards dissension dwell upon (the verses) that can be understood in more than one way.

They try to cause division (among the community) by giving them their own (fanciful or misleading) interpretations, [252] but only Allah and insightful people know their true meaning.

They're the ones who proclaim, *"We believe in the (whole of the) Book, because it's all from our Lord."* Only those who think deeply ever truly understand. [7]

"Our Lord," (they pray), *"don't let our hearts go astray, now that You've shown us the way. Shower us with Your mercy, for truly You are the Generous One. [8] Our Lord, You're going to gather all people together one day, and there's no doubt about that, for Allah never breaks His word."* [9]

---

[251] This passage was revealed for a specific reason. An eye-witness narrates, "My brother and I were present in a gathering that is more precious to me than even red camels. My brother and I had arrived and found that some of the leaders of the companions were sitting close to one of the Prophet's doors. We didn't want to be away from them, so we sat near the room also. Then they mentioned a verse and began arguing over it until they were shouting. The Messenger of Allah was so angry that when he came out to them his face was red. He threw sand on them and said, 'Pay attention people! This is how nations before you were destroyed, on account of their arguing with their prophets and contradicting parts of their scriptures with other parts. The Qur'an does not contradict itself, rather it testifies to the truth of itself. Therefore, however much knowledge you have of it then implement it, and whatever you don't know of it, refer the matter to those who have (more) knowledge about it.'" (*Ahmad*)

[252] *Mutashabihat* means something that can be understood in more than one way or interpreted differently or filled with multiple shades of meaning sometimes bordering on the esoteric. Thus, we are cautioned to be careful when interpreting such verses. The Prophet once said, "When you see people busy trying to interpret the *mutashabihat* verses, stay away from them, for they are the people Allah talked about (in the Qur'an)." (*Bukhari*) Does this mean that we can never speculate on their meanings? No, and many companions and later scholars cautiously looked into the possible meaning of such verses. The idea is that no one rigid position can be proclaimed as true above all others. The underlying subtext is that we must be tolerant of other views on these verses, for only Allah knows their true interpretation. There is a tradition in which the Prophet was reported to have said, "Differences in my community are a blessing." This and other sayings have given rise to a rich tradition of divergent scholasticism in Muslim history in which free and open debate among the scholars was often the order of the day. (There have also been bouts of censorship and the like, but a great deal of healthy debate has been possible.) In another saying, the Prophet is reported to have said that a religious scholar gets rewards from Allah for his efforts even if he makes a mistake, for at least he tried. Ibn 'Abbas (d. 687) laid out the order of interpretation generally followed in much of the Muslim world until the medieval period in this way: The first interpretation should be based on other verses of the Qur'an. After that look for a saying of the Prophet. After that look for a report about the verse from a Companion, preferably one from Abu Bakr or 'Umar (generally called *Asbab ul Nuzul* reports that give context stories). If nothing is there after all that, we can use our logic and opinion. (*Ibn Sa'd*) In modern times Muslims have added linguistic studies, accepted medieval authoritative *tafseers* and the rulings of scholars among other techniques. Thankfully most verses are clear and not esoteric so for most of the Qur'an's verses there is little difference of opinion. Abu Darda, the famous Companion once said of this, "You will not be fully knowledgeable until you see different sides of the Qur'an."

Allah's Plan will Prevail

$\mathcal{A}$s for those who suppress (their inner yearning for faith), neither their money nor their children will save them in the least from Allah – *they'll just be more fuel for the flame!* [253] [10] They're no better than the people of Pharaoh and all those (faithless people) before them who denied Our signs. Allah seized them for their sins, *and Allah is a strong punisher.* [11]

Say to those who reject (the truth), *"You'll soon be defeated and gathered together in Hellfire - and how terrible a resting place!"* [12]

You've already been given a sign in the two armies that clashed (at the battle of Badr). [254] One (army) was fighting in the cause of Allah, while the other was resisting Him. With their own eyes (your opponents) saw you to be twice their number, (even though you were outnumbered by them), for Allah reinforces with His help whomever He wants. [255] There's a lesson in this for those who have eyes to see! [13]

Materialism and its Allure

$\mathcal{P}$eople are infatuated with the (worldly) pleasures they so ardently desire, such as women, children, piles of gold and silver, well-bred horses, livestock and productive land. These are the goods of this worldly life, but nearness to Allah is the best investment! [256] [14]

---

[253] After the victorious Muslims returned to Medina following the famous Battle of Badr, in which 313 men overcame a force of approximately 1000 idol-worshippers, the Prophet addressed the leaders of the Jewish tribes of Medina, trying to impress upon them that Islam was a power with which to be reckoned and that they should look again into their scriptures where they would find prophecies about him. It was already a hotly debated topic among the Jews of the city, and a few had already openly joined Islam. The bulk of the Jews, however, were not convinced, and they publicly belittled the Muslim victory at Badr. One of the leaders of the Jewish Banu Qaynuqa tribe said, "Muhammad! Don't be overconfident, for you met the weak (Meccans), who know nothing of war. So what that you defeated them! If you fight us then you would find out how tough we are." This passage was revealed in response. A short while later, fighting broke out between the two sides, and the defeated Banu Qaynuqa were exiled from the city. (*Asbab ul-Nuzul*)

[254] The Battle of Badr is so named after an oasis on a caravan route. The Muslims left Medina hoping to capture a large Meccan caravan that was to make a stop there. This was all part of a low level war that had been simmering ever since the Muslims fled under fire from Mecca. (The Meccans frequently raided the outlying districts of Medina, and Muhammad was finally given permission in a Qur'anic revelation to fight back.) While the caravan got away, the Meccans who came out of their city to intercept the Muslims were sorely defeated, even though they outnumbered the Muslims three-to-one.

[255] When the defeated Meccan idol-worshippers returned home, the only major leader who had not gone out to battle, Abu Lahab, asked his bewildered nephew upon his return what had happened and why they had lost. The young man brought his uncle near to him and replied, "...I couldn't blame our fighters, for we saw white knights on white horses filling the horizon." A slave named Abu Rafi', who had secretly accepted Islam, remarked, "By Allah those must have been angels!" Abu Lahab became angry and started hitting the slave. The slave's owner, Umm al-Fadl, who also was a secret Muslim convert, picked up a stick and hit Abu Lahab on the head, opening a great gash. Abu Lahab looked at her in anger and ran off. Within a few days his wound became infected, and his family deserted him. Within a few more days, this most bitter foe of Islam passed away.

[256] The Prophet said, "Love of the worldly life is the root of all error." (*Ma'ariful Qur'an*) Some may prefer a secular view based on a belief in the superiority and ultimate perfectibility of man (an ideology called secular humanism); yet, this is a flawed ideology in that human beings cannot be perfected in this life, for they do not live long enough to accomplish this goal. Once wisdom begins to sprout in the heart, there are only a few years left before death, and the next generation makes the same mistakes as the previous one. Thus, the activities of each human generation are no more than fragile sandcastles by the shore, destined to be swept away by an endless line of waves. The next generation follows the pattern anew, starting virtually from scratch, and the record of materialism, war, oppression, injustice and ignorance starts all over again. Religion, at the very least, offers the only door for individuals to escape their limitations and have the hope of perfection in an existence that does not end. Is it merely the false promise of fantasy? Consider that religion promises eternal reward in exchange for being

Say (to them), "*Should I tell you about what's far better than (the pleasures of this life)? In their Lord's presence, those who were mindful (of Allah) will have gardens beneath which rivers flow and pure and holy companions to live with forever. (In Paradise) they'll find Allah's good pleasure, and Allah ever watches over His servants.*" [15]

"*They're the ones who used to say, 'Our Lord, we believe, so forgive us our sins and protect us from the punishment of the Fire.'* [16] *They're the patient, sincere, devout and charitable, and they seek forgiveness (for their shortcomings) even at the early light of dawn.*" [17]

The Mistakes of the Past

$\mathcal{A}$llah affirms that there is no god but He, [257] as do the angels and the people of knowledge who are firmly grounded (in scholarship). There is no god but He, the Powerful, the Wise! [18]

The (only valid) way of life in the sight of Allah is surrender (to His will). The Followers of Earlier Revelation didn't take to divergent views except out of jealousy of each other after they received this knowledge. Whoever rejects the proofs of Allah (should remember) that Allah is swift in settling accounts. [19]

If they argue with you, then say to them, "*I've surrendered my whole self to Allah, as have those who follow me.*"

Then ask the Followers of Earlier Revelation and the unschooled (people of Arabia) who've never received (any revelation before), "*Will you now surrender yourselves (to Him)?*" [258]

If they surrender themselves (to Allah), then they will have found guidance. If they turn back, well, your duty was only to convey the message, and Allah is watching His servants. [259] [20]

Those who reject the signs of Allah and who killed the prophets and killed those who called for justice among people, even though it was against all right (to kill them), give them the news of a painful punishment. [260] [21] Any good they do is wasted both in this life and the next, and they'll have no one to help them. [22]

Allah Decides His Response

$\mathcal{H}$ave you ever considered (the case of the Jews of Medina) who received a

---

righteous to one's fellow creatures, while secularism only came up with survival of the fittest and might makes right with no promise for good conduct other than the chance to possibly live in wealth for a brief time – although at the expense of one's fellows.

[257] Two rabbis from Damascus arrived in Medina desiring to meet with the Prophet. When they were in his presence, they asked him his name. They then requested that he answer one question of theirs that, if he answered it correctly, would convince them that he was, in fact, the foretold prophet of which their scriptures had spoken. They asked him, "What is the greatest verse in the Book of Allah?" This particular verse was revealed to the Prophet, and the rabbis, being filled with wonder, accepted Islam. (*Asbab ul-Nuzul*)

[258] Jews and Christians had written religious books, whereas the people of central Arabia had never received any written revelations. They were thus "unschooled." This passage addresses both groups and invites them to accept God's last revelation: a remedy to the religious confusion of the former, and a saving grace for the latter.

[259] Muhammad said, "Prophets were only sent to their particular nations, but I was sent to all people." (*Bukhari*)

[260] II Chronicles 24:20-22 is the immediate reference here. The Christian New Testament echoes a similar sentiment where Jesus is quoted (referencing the incident in II Chronicles) as saying, "Woe to you, teachers of the Law and Pharisees, you hypocrites! You shut the kingdom of heaven in men's faces…You who kill the prophets and stone those sent to you…" (See Matthew 23:15, 25-31, 35, 37.) Also see Jeremiah 7:9-11, 1 Kings 18:13, 19:10, I Thessalonians 2:15 and Lamentations 2:20 for other similar charges.

portion of the scripture in the past? [261] Now they're being called to the (last) Book of Allah to settle their disagreements; yet, some of them turn away and decline (the offer of help)! [23]

That's because their excuse is to say, *"Our punishment (from Allah) will only last a set number of days,"* but they're deceived in their religion by the very (lies) they themselves have fabricated! [262] [24]

How will it be when We gather them all together on that day of which there is no doubt, when every soul will get what it deserves without any unfairness? [25]

The Call of the Lord will Triumph

*P*roclaim (this supplication so they can understand what your beliefs are): [263]

"Lord of All Dominion! You grant authority to whom You please and bring down whom You will. You empower whom You please and weaken whom You will."

"In Your hand is all good, and You have power over all that is. [26] You make the night merge into day and the day merge into night. You bring life from death and death from life, and You grant resources to whomever You want without any limit." [27]

Know a Person by the Company He Keeps

*T*he believers should never take as close allies those who suppress (their awareness of the truth), in preference to

---

[261] There are two different reports to explain why this passage was revealed. The first report is that the Jews asked Muhammad's opinion about a legal judgment regarding adultery committed by two members of the Jewish community. The Prophet asked them what their writings said about it, and they refused to acknowledge the punishment of stoning that their religion prescribed. The Prophet insisted they follow what their tradition said, and they were angry that they had to carry out the sentence. (*Jalaluddin, Ibn Kathir*) The second report says that the Prophet went into a synagogue one day. There he met two Jews named Na'im ibn Amru and Harith ibn Zayd, and they asked the Prophet what religion he was following. When the Prophet replied that he was of the same faith as Abraham, the Jews disputed with him and said, "Abraham was a Jew." The Prophet then proposed that they decide the issue using evidence from the Torah, and the Jews declined to go that route and demurred. (*al-Baydawi*)

[262] Why does the Qur'an sometimes mention Jewish beliefs in a harsh manner? What must be understood is that the Qur'an is not *anti-Jewish*, and it mentions righteous and sincere Jews in a favorable light in several places. Muhammad, himself, had respect for Jews and was never accused by Jews of being unfair with them. (He would even stand in respect whenever a Jewish funeral procession passed by.) He also had liberal business dealings with Jews and respected the Torah. When the Qur'an speaks of Jewish beliefs harshly, for the most part it is only speaking about the form of Judaism that was practiced by the three Jewish tribes of Medina. Those Jewish tribes were not the best example of the noble religion of Judaism. What those tribes practiced was a mixture of authentic Jewish teachings, superstition, political expediency and local assumptions that mainstream Judaism would reject. When the Qur'an addresses one of these issues, it always states what these Jews have *claimed* first, and then it offers a rebuttal. If one were to tabulate the types of beliefs that the Jews of Medina were promoting and compare them with modern Jewish teachings, one would find that the two have very little in common. Thus, the Qur'an is not indicting Judaism as a whole, but rather the perversions of some groups of Jews in Arabia who altered their religion to suit their own personal whims.

[263] When the Muslims were busy digging a trench around Medina just before the Battle of the Trench, a large stone was encountered in one of the digging pits. Some companions called the Prophet over to see what could be done about it, and he came to examine it. Then he took up a pick, struck at it, and it shattered sending sparks in several directions. The Prophet then told his men that in those sparks of light he saw visions of Islam triumphing over Persia, Byzantium and Yemen. The hypocrites and Jews of the city scoffed when they heard about what he said and teased the Muslims about it. This passage was revealed in response. (*Bayhaqi*)

those who believe, unless it's absolutely necessary in order to protect yourselves from them (by keeping them close).

Whoever does that (without that one, valid excuse) will find no help from Allah. [264] Allah personally cautions you (against disobeying Him), for the final destination (of all things) is back to Allah. [28]

Say (to them), "*Whether you hide or reveal your inner-most thoughts, Allah knows them, even as He knows everything within the heavens and on the earth, for Allah has power over all things.*" [29]

A day (will come) when every soul will be confronted with the good that it's done and also with the evil that it's done, and it will wish that its evil were far away! Allah is (personally) warning you (to beware of) Him (and His judgment), though He's kind to His servants. [30]

Say (to them), "*If you truly love Allah, then follow me, so Allah can love you and forgive you your faults, for Allah is forgiving and merciful.*" [31] Then say, "*Now follow Allah and His Messenger.*" If they turn away, (then know that) Allah has no love for those who reject (Him). [32]

The Continuity of Allah's Message

Truly, Allah chose Adam, Noah and the families of Abraham and Amrān above all others in the world. [265] [33] They were

---

[264] Can a Muslim be friends with non-Muslims? Most certainly, yes. Even the Prophet had non-Muslim acquaintances, and he never declined to treat people of other faiths with respect. The confusion is that this passage is often mistranslated to the effect that a Muslim should never have non-Muslim 'friends' - *period*. The Arabic term used in this verse is *wali*, (pl. *awlia'*) which means *protector, best or closest ally* or *close confidant with whom you share secrets.* The standard Arabic word for 'friend' in the regular sense (*khaleel*) is not present here. In other words, a Muslim can have friendships with non-Muslims, but he or she should not make them such close confidants that he or she is unduly influenced by them, for non-Muslims will often try to influence believers to abandon their high moral standards and/or beliefs. (To be fair, in human interaction everyone wants others to be more like them. This is how groups 'norm' themselves.) In another related sense, a Muslim also should not place his safety, well-being or essential survival in a non-Muslim's hands, unless there's no other choice. The Prophet also advised not to make a non-believer one's closest bosom companion when he said, "Don't keep the closest companionship (*tasaahib,* a word related to *sahaba*) with anyone else besides believers, and don't eat with anyone but those who are conscious of Allah." (*Mazhari*) (So we can eat and enjoy company with believers of other faiths – just not with people who care little for any and all spirituality.) By the way, the Christian New Testament has a similar prohibition. In I Corinthians 5:11 we read, "But now I have written unto you not to keep company… (with) an idolater…(and) with such a one not to eat." Also see Qur'an 18:28.

[265] A large number of verses in this chapter (most of those whose content is about Jesus, Judaism or Christianity) were revealed to the Prophet during a series of particularly intense interfaith dialogues in the year 631 with the Jews of Medina, but principally with a visiting delegation of Christians from Najran the following year. Najran was a district in Arabia several hundred miles to the south. The Christians had come (around sixty in number) with their chief priest, al-'Aqib, aka *'Abdul Masih*, and several high officials who had the favor of the Byzantine Roman Emperor. They had received a letter from the Prophet asking for their submission to the Islamic way of life, but they wanted to find out more about this new faith called *Islam,* and the Prophet graciously invited them to Medina. When they arrived some weeks later, their officials and even laymen were dressed in such fine vestments of silk and gold that the people of Medina remarked that a delegation of its like had never been seen before. They entered the main mosque and then held a prayer service, facing towards the East. When the Prophet came out to meet them, he saw their clothes and refused to speak to them and left. The Christians were confused, and so asked what was wrong. 'Ali ibn Abi Talib told them that their clothes were too rich and ostentatious, and he advised them to change into simpler clothes. So they left and then returned to the mosque wearing simple robes, and when the Prophet saw them, he exclaimed, "By Allah! When I saw you at first, I saw Satan among you and he was wearing the same clothes as you, so I didn't look at you." Then the dialogue began. The Prophet invited them to join Islam, but the Christians claimed that they were already submitted to God. Then the Prophet challenged them to a public debate the next day. (*Ibn Hisham & Ibn Is-haq*)When morning came, Salman al Farsi seated the Christians on one side of an open field. The Prophet arrived some moments later carrying his infant

all descended from one line, and Allah hears and knows all (about such) things. [34]

The Story of Mary

A woman of the family of Amrān [266] prayed, *"My Lord, I dedicate my unborn child to Your service. So accept this from me, for You're the Hearing and the Knowing."* [35]

After she gave birth, she cried, *"Oh my Lord, I've delivered a girl!"* [267] Allah knew better (the value of that child) she bore. *"A male is not the same as a female,"* she said, *"and so I will call her Mary, and I commend her and her children to Your protection against Satan, the Outcast."* [36]

Her Lord accepted (the child) graciously, and she grew up healthy and well under the sponsorship of Zachariah to whom she was assigned (as a dependent). [268]

Whenever he would enter her room, he would find her provided with food. *"Mary,"* he would ask, *"where did all this (food) come from?"* *"It's from Allah,"* she would reply, *"and Allah provides to whomever He wants without any limit."* [269] [37]

So Zachariah, (seeing the virtue of Mary), called to his Lord, saying, *"My Lord, give me a pure and virtuous descendant of my own, for You hear all requests."* [38]

Then the angels (appeared before him), even as he was standing there in his room. They said to him, *"Allah sends you the*

---

grandson Husayn, while his other young grandson Hassan held his finger. His daughter Fatimah and her husband 'Ali also sat behind the Prophet. When the discussions began, the Prophet brought up a number of points, including the doctrines of trinity and salvation, along with some lesser issues like the eating of pork, the drinking of alcohol and the use of the cross as a symbol. Among the questions he asked were: "Don't you know that Allah is eternal while Jesus is subject to dying?" "Don't you know that our Lord has control over everything and that He sustains them all. Does Jesus have any of this kind of power?" "Don't you know that nothing is hidden from Allah in the earth and heaven. Does Jesus know any of these things other than what he was taught?" "Don't you know that Allah neither eats, drinks nor eliminates waste, yet the mother of Jesus gave birth to him like other women do, and that he ate and drank and eliminated waste? So how can it be what you claim (that Jesus is God too)?" (*Al-Razi*)Relevant verses from this chapter were revealed sometimes within the meetings and other times during rest breaks. (Verses 33-34 were perhaps the first revelations recited to the crowd.) Surviving accounts indicate that the Prophet got the better in these debates and that some of the visitors even accepted Islam. The remainder, who chose to continue in their religion, concluded an amicable treaty with the Prophet and returned home with a healthy respect for the new faith.

[266] According to the Judeo-Christian tradition, this woman is identified as Hanna.

[267] The widowed mother wanted her child to become a rabbi, but Jewish religious custom forbade female rabbis. The mother amended her supplication after the birth of Mary, merely asking God to protect her from the bad influences of Satan. Little did she know that the guardian Zachariah with whom she would place her was none other than a prophet himself and that he would teach her religious knowledge that even the rabbis did not possess!

[268] Ibn Kathir records the story that when Mary was born her mother took her as a baby to the door of the local temple and told the rabbis that she dedicated her daughter to Allah before birth and that she could not enter the temple herself due to her menstruation. The rabbis were eager that one of them should become the baby's guardian, as the baby's deceased father had been a prominent leader among them. Zechariah, however, insisted on being given the honor to sponsor her, but the other rabbis protested. Finally, they drew lots with the pens they used to copy the Torah to see who would get custody of the girl, and Zachariah won. By the way, scholars deduce from this verse that the mother also has the right to name her daughter and that it is not the exclusive right of the father alone. (*Ma'ariful Qur'an*)

[269] The commentators offer two explanations for how Mary received her regular food deliveries. Some say that the angels caused food to materialize in her room, while others suggest that God put it in the hearts of various people to bring food to her as an act of piety and charity. The food deliveries were significant on two accounts: Zachariah was poor and would have had hardship providing for another mouth; and Mary needed to be healthy for the job God would assign her later, namely to carry and bear Jesus – on her own, in the wilderness!

good news of (a son) named John. [270] *He's going to announce the truth of a word from Allah, and he'll be a disciplined prophet in the tradition of the morally righteous."* [39]

(Zachariah, being astonished,) asked, *"How can I have a son, my Lord, when I'm old and my wife is barren?"*

"So it will be," (the angel) replied. *"Allah does whatever He wills."* [40]

"But my Lord!" (Zachariah) pleaded. *"Give me a sign."*

"Your sign," he replied, *"will be that for three days you will be unable to speak to anyone, except through gestures. Remember your Lord frequently (during this time), and glorify Him in the evening and in the morning."* [271] [41]

The Birth of the Messiah

The angels (appeared) to Mary and said, *"Mary! Allah has chosen you and purified you. He's chosen you above the women of all nations,* [42] *so be compliant to your Lord, prostrate yourself, and bow down with those who bow (before Allah)."* [43]

(This story) that We're revealing to you, (Muhammad), was previously unknown (to you), for you weren't there when the (male relatives) chose reeds randomly to decide who among them must provide (financial support) for Mary, and you certainly weren't there when they argued (over the outcome). [44]

When the angels (again returned to Mary after some time had passed), they said, *"Mary! Allah gives you the good news of a word from Him. He's going to be called the Messiah, Jesus, the son of Mary. He'll be honored in this world, as well as in the next, where he'll be among those nearest (to Allah)."* [45]

"He will speak to people in childhood and also when he's grown, and he's going to be one of the morally righteous." [272] [46]

"But my Lord!" she cried out. *"How can I have a son when no man has touched me?"*

"And so it is that Allah creates whatever He wants," the angels replied. *"When He decides something, He only has to say, 'Be' and it is."* [47]

"He will teach him scripture and fill him with wisdom (by teaching him) the Torah and the Gospel. [48] *(Thereafter He's going to appoint) him as a messenger to the Children of Israel."* [273]

---

[270] John the Baptist was to be the forerunner of Jesus. Jesus is called *a word* (a commanded creation) from Allah and not *the Word* of Allah - an important distinction between Islam and Christianity regarding the status of Jesus. The oft-quoted verse in John 1:1 has been misconstrued by modern Christians to have been something that Jesus uttered, though the words of that verse are not the quoted speech of Jesus, but instead an introduction written by a mystically-oriented, unknown author as something of a prologue for the Book of John.

[271] This account is mentioned in the New Testament in Luke 1:5-25.

[272] Jesus spoke one time as an infant by a special miracle from God in order to defend his mother from the accusations of infidelity hurled at her by her angry relatives. The Prophet said, "No infant spoke from the cradle except for three: Jesus, the boy during Jurayj's time, and one other." (*Bukhari*) For the incident of Jesus speaking as an infant see 19:29-33. The story of Jurayj (George) is told in the prophetic traditions. Jurayj was a righteous man falsely accused of fornication and fathering a child out of wedlock with a prostitute. When Jurayj was being beaten by the people for fornication, the baby boy spoke in his defense and said that his father was a shepherd with whom the prostitute slept. The third baby who spoke did so after his mother made value judgments about two people who had passed by. The mother praised a haughty nobleman and then disparaged a slave girl who was being falsely accused of a crime. The baby told the mother that the man was a tyrant and the slave girl was innocent. In Christian tradition, St. Anthony of Padua (d. 1231) caused a newborn baby to speak in defense of its mother, who was being accused of adultery by her husband.

[273] It appears that Jesus was commissioned as a prophet when he was about thirty years old. A passage from the New Testament book of Luke records that the youthful Jesus, who had not yet begun to preach, went to be baptized by John the Baptist and that it was there that the Holy Spirit (for Muslims this would be the angel Gabriel) came upon him and announced that Allah had chosen him to be His emissary to the people. The key text (which is, by the way, not a quotation of Jesus but the description

"(Jesus) will tell (his people), 'I've come to you with a sign from your Lord. I'm going to breathe life into a lifeless clay bird that I'll create by Allah's command, [274] and I'll heal the blind and the lepers and bring the dead to life, all by Allah's command. I'll tell you what you consume (and waste of the world), as well as what you store away (of good deeds for Judgment Day). [275] (Know that) in all of these things is a great sign if you really have faith. [49]

"I've also come to verify the truth of the Torah that was revealed before me and to make lawful some things that were forbidden to you before. I'm coming to you with proof from your Lord, so be mindful of Allah and obey me. [50] Truly, Allah is my Lord and your Lord, so serve Him. That's a straight way (of life)." [51]

When Jesus (began his mission and) noticed the disbelief (of his people), he (looked for helpers), saying, "Who will help me (call the people) to Allah?"

(Then a group of) disciples (began to follow him, and) they said, "We'll help (you call people) to Allah, for we believe in Allah, and you can be our witness that we're truly surrendered (to His will). [52] Our Lord, We believe in what You've revealed, and we follow this messenger, so record us among those who bear witness." [53]

However, it wasn't long before (the faithless) contrived a plot, though Allah did the same - and Allah is the best planner of all! [54]

(After his people rejected him,) Allah said, "Jesus, I'm going to take you completely and lift you up to Myself. I will purify (your reputation which has been tarnished) by those who reject (the truth). [276] I will make those who follow you superior to those who suppress (their awareness of the truth), even until the Day of Resurrection. Then all of you will come back to Me, and I'll judge between you in those matters in which you differed." [55]

---

of a non-eye-witness) is as follows: "And the Holy Ghost descended in a bodily shape like a dove upon him, and a voice came from heaven, which said, 'Thou art my beloved son; in thee I am well pleased." (Luke 3:22 KJV) Of course, calling someone a 'son' of God was not taken in a literal sense by the Jews of the day, and even Jesus himself once said, "Blessed are the peacemakers, for they shall be called the sons of God." (Matthew 5:9, also see John 10:22-39 where Jesus explains why he's using the metaphorical title of 'son' of God – it was a part of Jewish parlance from as far back as Genesis 6:2!) Muhammad's own moment of being awakened to prophethood happened when he was meditating alone in a mountain redoubt. (See 96:1-5 and footnotes.)

[274] There are two interpretations for the clay bird. Some commentators say that Jesus performed a standard miracle by bringing a clay bird to life in order to astonish his listeners, while others say this is a metaphor for the Jewish nation which was like a lifeless bird. The reformation of Jesus would breathe new life into the community's spiritual practices. There is a report in *Thomas' Gospel of the Infancy of Jesus Christ*, (which was written approximately 150 CE and which was regarded as authoritative by many early Christians, but rejected centuries later), in which we read: "See, your child is at the stream, and has taken clay and molded twelve birds; he has profaned the Sabbath." Joseph came to the place and seeing what Jesus did he cried out, "Why do you do on the Sabbath what it is not lawful to do?" Jesus clapped his hands and cried out to the sparrows, "Be gone." And the sparrows flew off chirping. The Jews saw this and were amazed. They went away and described to their leaders what they had seen Jesus do." (Another early Christian book entitled, *The First Gospel of the Infancy of Jesus Christ* (1:2), also carries the same story.)

[275] This is usually explained to mean that Jesus will expose the waste and greed of his society. Another possible explanation is that this refers to people's deeds that are concealed on earth but 'stored up' on their records in the afterlife. John 8:30-32 has Jesus calling his people to follow his teachings in much the same way that the other prophets said to their people. A third interpretation was that Jesus was set to alter the dietary restrictions of his people, as the next verse suggests.

[276] Jesus was opposed by a faction of the Jewish religious establishment. The Qur'an accepts that his people mostly rejected him. There is even a saying of Prophet Muhammad in which he remarked that one of the previous prophets was beaten so badly that you couldn't even recognize his face. What happened to Jesus? As this verse states, Allah raised him to heaven, mirroring the account in the Gospels that he ascended to the clouds. He will remain there until the End Times, according to the Prophet, at which time he will return to fight the Anti-Christ. Then he will live out his natural life, get married along the way, and pass away and be buried.

"As for those who reject (the truth), I'm going to punish them with a harsh penalty in this world, as well as in the next, and they'll have no one to help them. [56] As for those who believe and do what's morally right, they'll be paid their reward. (Know that) Allah has no love for those who do wrong." [57]

Don't Hold Jesus as a God

$\mathcal{T}$hese are the verses that We're reciting to you, (Muhammad), and they're a wise reminder. [277] [58] The example of Jesus in the sight of Allah is like that of Adam. He created him from dust, saying, *"Be,"* and he was. [59] The truth is from your Lord, so don't be assailed by doubt. [60]

If anyone argues further with you, now that the truth has come to you, (then challenge them,) saying, [278] *"Come, let's meet together: our children and your children, our women and your women, ourselves and yourselves. Then we'll invoke (Allah) and ask Allah to condemn those who lie."* [61]

However, the only true resolution to the debate is affirming that there is no god besides (the One True) God, for He is, without a doubt, the Powerful and the Wise. [62] If they turn aside, (remember that) Allah knows best who the disobedient are. [63]

Say (to them), *"Followers of Earlier Revelation! [279] Let's agree on what we hold in common: that we serve no one other than Allah, that we don't assign divinity to anyone besides Him, and that we don't take one of our own kind to be lord in place of Allah."* [280]

---

[277] One of the Christian priests in the delegation from Najran asked the Prophet who was the father of Jesus. When verse 59 below was revealed in answer, the priest said, "Why are you belittling our sovereign (Jesus)?" The Prophet replied, "What am I saying (to belittle him?)" They answered, "You're saying he's just an (ordinary) servant." The Prophet said, "Yes, he is a servant, but of God, and he is His Messenger, and His word that He bestowed upon the virgin Mary." The Christians became angry and asked, "Have you ever heard of a human being without a father? If you have then point out to us someone like him!" (*Asbab ul-Nuzul*)

[278] After verses 58-60 were recited, then the Prophet recited verse 61 which was a solemn pact based on an Arabian tradition called *mubahala* or *Mula'ana* – a sacred oath taken by five people from each side of a dispute to invoke the punishment of Allah on the side that was lying. The Prophet adjourned the day's dialogue with the Christians and chose five members of his household, including his daughter Fatimah, to be called to participate in the ceremony the following morning. However, in the morning, al-'Aqib, the priest, decided against further participation in these matters, especially the idea of invoking God's wrath against those who lied, and signed a peace treaty with Muhammad before returning home with his party. (*Ibn Is-haq*) They also agreed to pay an annual tax to Medina in lieu of the *mubahala*. The priest also asked the Prophet to send a liaison along with them to be their judge in financial disputes, as they were impressed with Islam's emphasis on absolute fairness at all costs. The Prophet chose a trusted companion named Abu Ubaydah to go with them. (*Ibn Kathir*)

[279] The Christian delegation meeting with Muhammad disagreed amongst themselves concerning the nature of Jesus, much as modern Christian denominations dispute with each other on basic doctrinal issues today. Some in the delegation, who understood Christian assumptions differently, believed Jesus was only the son of God, while others held him to be a co-god in a trinity. A third faction said he was God in the flesh. The Prophet exploited this disunity among them to his advantage, and this verse was revealed as a suggested common statement to which all could agree. (*Ibn Kathir*)

[280] The priests of Najran said sarcastically to Muhammad, "You just want us to say (about you) what the Jews say about Ezra." In other words, the Christians thought that Muhammad wanted them to call him a son of God. (*Razi*) The Jews from long before elevated certain famous rabbis and even Ezra to a near infallible state. This verse decried that and went further, asking them to stop treating their saints and leaders like gods. Hasan al-Basri (d. 728) also affirms that this verse was also asking the Najranites to stop venerating their leaders like they were *holy* men. (*al-Qurtubi*) At-Tabari holds it also refers to abandoning the worship of Jesus as a god. See Qur'an 4:171 & 9:30-31. Al-Razi (d. 1209) said that this verse refers to the belief among Christians that is as follows: "They worship someone other than Allah, and that being is the Messiah (Jesus). They associate others with Him, and that is because they say that Allah is three: Father, Son and Holy Spirit. They have asserted three equal and eternal divine personalities. We say they assert three eternal personalities because they say the underlying substance

If they turn away, then say to them, *"Bear witness that we've surrendered ourselves (to Allah's will)."* [64]

Abraham Was neither a Jew nor a Christian

*F*ollowers of Earlier Revelation! [281] Why do you drag Abraham into your disputes? The Torah and Gospel weren't revealed until long after him. Don't you have any sense? [65]

Aren't you the ones who argue over things you already know? So why argue over things that you know nothing about? Clearly, Allah is the One Who has accurate information, whereas you lack it. [66]

Abraham was neither a Jew nor a Christian. Rather, he was a natural monotheist, submissive (to Allah's will), and he certainly wasn't an idol-worshipper. [67] The first among the people (of this world) who resemble Abraham the most are those who follow (his example), like *this* prophet (Muhammad) and his followers. Allah is

the protector of all who believe (in Him)! [68]

There are some from among the Followers of Earlier Revelation who desperately wish to mislead you, but they wind up only misleading themselves without realizing it. [69]

The Jealousy of the Followers of Earlier Revelation

*F*ollowers of Earlier Revelation! Why do you try to hide the signs of Allah, even after witnessing them yourselves? [70] Followers of Earlier Revelation! Why do you wrap the truth with falsehood and hide the truth on purpose when you know better? [71]

Among the Followers of Earlier Revelation are some who say to each other, *"(Tell the Muslims) you have faith in what the believers received in the early morning, but then denounce it at the end of the day.* [282] *You might be able to cause the weak (in knowledge among them) to return (to their old religions).* [72] *Don't believe anyone (of another religion) unless he believes in yours."* [283]

---

of the Word inserted itself in the humanity of the Messiah. Moreover, the underlying substance of the Holy Spirit inserted itself in the humanity of Mary. Had these two underlying substances not been independent and separate, they could not have separated from the Father and inserted themselves in Jesus and Mary. Thus, because they asserted three independent divine substances, they committed shirk (making partners with Allah)." (*Mafātīḥ al-Ghayb*)

[281] This passage was revealed when a Jewish rabbi in the interfaith gathering said, "Muhammad! You know that we have the best claim to Abraham's religion – more than you or anyone else - *and he was Jewish.* You're just jealous of God." (*Asbab ul-Nuzul*) This shift from Christians to Jews as a topic of address was also noted by Muqatil ibn Sulayman (d. 767), one of the earliest commentators of the Qur'an.

[282] Just after the prayer-direction was changed from Jerusalem to Mecca, a small group from among the Jews hatched a plan in which they would feign allegiance to Islam in the morning and pray towards Mecca. However, in the evening they would switch directions back towards Jerusalem, saying they developed doubts about Islam and thus reverted to their old religion. The idea was to confuse the new Muslim converts in Medina, who were previously used to deferring to the Jews due to their greater knowledge and longstanding traditions. (*Ibn Kathir*) Other commentators suggest the allusion to morning and evening is more general and refers to the Meccan and Medinan phases of the Prophet's ministry, in which case the Jews would have claimed to believe in the early, more general revelations, while disbelieving in the way Islam was shaping up in Medina.

[283] The historian, Ibn Hisham (d. 834), records that one of Muhammad's wives, the Jewish lady Safiyah, told of the time when Muhammad first came to Medina. She noted the response of her community to his arrival. In her own words, she says that she accompanied her father Huyyay and her uncle, Abu Yasir, when they went to meet the Prophet for the first time. After talking with him for some time,

Say to them, *"True guidance is Allah's guidance. (Are you afraid that) someone else might get something similar to what your (ancestors) got in the past or that they might argue with you in the sight of your Lord (with that knowledge?)"* [284] Then say to them, *"All favors are in Allah's hand, and He grants them to whomever He wants, for Allah is caring and knowing.* [73] *He decides who receives His mercy, and Allah is the master of tremendous favor."* [74]

(There are, of course, honest people) among the Followers of Earlier Revelation. They will return a fortune in gold entrusted to them, while others won't give back a single silver coin with which they've been entrusted - *unless you stood there and demanded it!*

That's because they say, *"We're not obligated by our faith (to be fair with those of another religion)."* Yet, how terrible do they lie against Allah, and well they know it! [75]

No way! Whoever maintains his bond (with Allah) and remains aware (of his duty to Him should know that) Allah loves those who are mindful (of Him). [76]

A Little Gain Now at the Cost of Forever

Those who barter away their bond with Allah, along with their faith, making a little profit along the way, will have no share in the next life. [285]

Allah will neither address them nor notice them on the Day of Assembly, nor will He cleanse them (of their sins), for they will have a terrible punishment! [77]

Falsifying the Message of Scripture

There are some from among (the Followers of Earlier Revelation) who distort the meaning of their scriptures when they read them aloud, so much so that even though it sounds like scripture, in fact, it's not! [286]

---

they returned home and agreed that Muhammad just might be the foretold prophet, but then they decided to oppose his mission for they were not fully convinced.

[284] The Prophet said, "The time of your existence compared to that of the previous nations is like the time between the late afternoon and sunset prayers: The people of the Torah were given (the Law). They acted upon it until mid-day, but then they were exhausted and received one measure of reward. The people of the Gospel were given it; they acted upon it until the late afternoon, but then they were exhausted and received one measure of reward. Then we were given the Qur'an, and we will act upon it until sunset when we will be given two measures of reward. The people of the two earlier scriptures will say, 'Our Lord! You have given them two measures and only one to us; yet, we have worked more than they.' Allah will reply, 'Have I stolen a portion of your due?' They will (realize their folly) and answer, 'No.' Then Allah will say, 'This is My blessing, and I bestow it upon whomsoever I please.'" (*Bukhari*)

[285] A man named Al-Ashath disputed with a Jewish man over their joint ownership of a strip of land with a well on it. Al-Ashath claimed he was a part owner but that the Jewish man denied him his right, while the Jewish man said Al-Ashath never owned any of it. When asked by the Prophet, Al-Ashath admitted that he had no evidence to back his claim. Then the Prophet asked the Jew to swear to Allah that the land was all his, and the matter would be settled in his favor. On hearing that, Al-Ashath protested, saying that the Jew would swear falsely, and thus he would lose his fair share of the property. This verse was revealed, and the Prophet, allowing the Jew to keep the land by himself after he swore it was all his, said, "Whoever makes a false oath to deprive a Muslim of his property will meet Allah when He is angry with him." (*Bukhari, Muslim*) The Prophet explained the application of this type of ruling by saying, "An oath will be accepted from a defendant (when there is no physical proof against him)." (*Bukhari*)

[286] The commentators are of two opinions about this verse. Some say that the original Torah and Gospel survive within the Bible but that it is misinterpreted by the priests and rabbis – sometimes intentionally to fit their skewed doctrines. Other commentators say that the original Torah and Gospel were buried and diffused in the holy books of the Jews and Christians by the addition of many writings

Yet they claim, *"This is from Allah's Own presence,"* but it's not from Allah's Own presence! *They knowingly lie against Allah!* [78]

It's not the place of a mere mortal who's been given scripture by Allah, along with sound wisdom and the gift of prophecy, to tell people, *"Worship me instead of Allah."* [287]

Rather, he should say, *"Become people of the Lord as you've learned in the scriptures and as you've studied."* [79]

Neither will a (true prophet) of Allah order you to take angels or prophets as lords (in place of Him). Would he order (the truth to be diluted) after already getting you to surrender (to Allah)? [80]

Allah's Message is Woven into History

Allah took a covenant with the (ancient) prophets (and their followers), saying, *"I've given you the scripture and the (source of) wisdom. If another messenger ever comes to you (after your time), who confirms the truth of what you now possess, then (your descendants) must believe in him and help him."*

(Then Allah) said, *"Do you agree to this pledge?"*

To which they answered, *"Yes, we agree."* [288]

Then (Allah) said, *"So witness (your promise), even as I'm witnessing it along with you.* [81] *Whoever breaks (this pledge) after this will be openly rebellious."* [82]

Are they looking for a way of life other than the Way of Allah? Is this what they do even though all things within the heavens and the earth surrender willingly or unwillingly to Him, and even though all things must return to Him? [83]

Say (to them), *"We believe in Allah and in what was revealed to us, as well as in what was revealed to Abraham, Ishmael, Isaac, Jacob and the tribes (of Israel), and (we believe) in what was given to Moses and Jesus and to all other prophets from their Lord. We don't claim that one of them was better than another, and to Him we surrender."* [84]

Now if anyone looks for a way of life other than submission (to Allah), it will never be accepted of him, and in the next life he'll be among the losers. [85]

---

that are not revelations from Allah, so much so that no one really knows which parts of the Bible are of divine origin and which parts were written by the hands of people. Consider the words of one prominent scholar of the Bible, Richard E. Friedman, who wrote, "The person who assembled the Torah cut it into several parts and then interspersed the parts through the book of Genesis." (From *Who Wrote the Bible,* Harper Collins, 1989, pg. 219.) I tend towards the idea that it may be a combination of both positions that explains the current state of scripture among the Followers of Earlier Revelation.

[287] During the ongoing interfaith meeting that is the subject of many verses in this chapter, a rabbi from Medina, along with the chief priest of the Najrani Christians, asked Muhammad, "Do you want us to worship you and take you as our Lord?" Muhammad replied, "I ask Allah's protection if anyone else besides Him is worshipped or if I were to order you to worship anyone else besides Him. He didn't send me to (ask you to worship me), nor did He order that from me." This passage was then revealed, and Muhammad recited it to them. (*Asbab ul-Nuzul*)

[288] This prophetic covenant is a general summary of what Judaism and Christianity both teach. Both the Old and New Testament make allowance for future prophets and hold that believers in those times must follow them. Muslims who have examined the Bible have identified several passages in which they believe Muhammad (or at the least, Angel Gabriel) was foretold. Deuteronomy 18:15-22 would be the prophecy for the Jews foretelling Muhammad, while John 16:7-14 may be the prophecy for the Christians. In that last passage, a man who extols Jesus as a true sign of God is clearly being mentioned. Verse 13, especially, mirrors exactly the Qur'anic notion that Muhammad merely repeats the revelation that he hears from God. (Also see John 14:30) How can any of these things apply to a *holy ghost,* who, as supposedly part of God himself, would not be so subservient as to merely parrot phrases put in his mouth? Also see Qur'anic verse 2:63.

On Fickle Faith

*H*ow can Allah guide a people who've resolved to cover over (the light of faith within their hearts), [289] even after once having believed and witnessed to the truth of their messenger, and even after proof had come to them? Allah won't guide such corrupted people. [86]

Their reward is the condemnation of Allah, the angels and all of humanity, [87] and that will be their condition for all time. Their punishment will neither lighten nor will they get a break. [88] Exempted are those (among them) who repent and reform themselves, for Allah is forgiving and merciful. [89]

As for those who reject (the truth) after once having believed, and who grow even more stubborn in their rejection, their repentance will never be accepted for they've gone so far astray. [290] [90]

Those who cover over (their ability to see the truth) and who die in that state will never be able to ransom themselves - *no, not for all the gold in the world!* [291] A painful punishment awaits them, and they'll have no one to help them. [91]

Defining Righteousness

*Y*ou'll never achieve virtue until you've (learned) to give to others (in charity) from even your most prized

---

[289] A man from Medina named Mu'adh ibn Afra killed a man named Suwayd for no reason, in the days before Islam came to the city. When the Prophet learned there was a murderer in the city, he sent 'Umar to punish him, but Mu'adh decided to abandon the city and flee. He soon became remorseful and sent his brother Julas to the Prophet to ask him if he could repent and rejoin his family. This passage was then revealed in answer, and when the verses were later read to the man, he said, "I swear by Allah that my people didn't lie about me to the Messenger, nor did the Messenger lie to Allah, and Allah is the truest and most powerful of us three." He then went to the Prophet, and the Prophet accepted him back into the fold. (*Asbab ul-Nuzul*)

[290] The commentators give three possible references here. The first is that this passage applies to the Jews who rejected Jesus and the Gospel (as evidenced by John 13:51-58 and many other passages). The second possibility is that this refers to both the Jews and Christians who disbelieved in Muhammad, even after admitting that what he was saying was true. The third refers to the case of a few people who converted back and forth between paganism and Islam many times, showing their unreliability and lack of integrity.

[291] In the generation before Islam, there lived a famous pagan Arab named 'Abdullah ibn Jud'an who was known for his generosity and good works even long after his death. Some people approached the Prophet and asked him if all the charity work Ibn Jud'an did would benefit him on Judgment Day. The Prophet said, "No, for not even on one day of his life did he say, 'My Lord! Forgive me my sins on the Day of Judgment.'" (*Muslim*) So doing good deeds for an entire lifetime, while notable here on earth, is ultimately without benefit in the Hereafter if a person didn't recognize Allah in some way and ask for forgiveness for his sins. (See the Biblical book of Titus 1:15-16.) However, a person who was not aware of the specific teachings of Allah, as expressed in an authentic expression of His religion, but who did righteousness for Allah's sake, recognizing that there is only one God, such a one has the hope of forgiveness. Before the advent of Islam, there lived in Mecca a *hanif*, or proponent of monotheism, named Zayd ibn 'Amr ibn Nuwfayl. He was righteous by nature and used to campaign against infanticide, idolatry and the worst evils of the Quraysh. He died before Islam came, though his son, Sa'id ibn Zayd, was later a companion of the Prophet. The son asked the Prophet if he could pray for his deceased (and very spiritually and morally-minded) father, even though he never knew Islam. The Prophet allowed him to do so and told him, "He will be raised on the Day of Assembly in a community of his own." (*Ma'ariful Qur'an*) Now the question becomes, does any good come from the meritorious deeds of those who live without faith in Allah at all? Islam teaches that Allah will reward the good deeds done by non-believers by compensating them in this life only. So while a person may do tremendous amounts of charity in this life, if he doesn't believe in Allah, even in a loose, philosophical way, then he will find his reward solely here on earth, perhaps in the form of fame, fortune or enjoyable experiences that bring him some satisfaction. On the Day of Judgment Allah will owe him nothing.

possessions, and whatever you spend in charity is known to Allah. [292] [92]

Reconnecting with Abraham's Religion

The Children of Israel were allowed to eat any type of food before the Torah was revealed, except for what Israel made unlawful for itself. [293]

So challenge them, (when they reject the lifting of some dietary restrictions), *"Come forward and read from the Torah concerning this if you're so honest!"* [294] [93]

Then, whoever invents a lie after this and attributes it to Allah, they're wrongdoers. [94]

Hold Fast to Abraham's Tradition

Say (to them), *"Allah speaks the truth, so follow the creed of Abraham, the natural monotheist, for he didn't make partners (with Allah)."* [295] [95]

The first house (of worship) for people was built in Becca, [296] a blessed place from which emanates clear guidance for all. [96]

There are clear signs (of its sanctity) there, such as the place in which Abraham once stood. (It's a sanctuary) in which anyone can find safety. [297]

Hence, it's a duty laid upon all people from Allah that all who are able should find a way and make a pilgrimage to the House. Whoever still rejects (the truth),

---

[292] Abu Talhah was a man rich in property in Medina, and he had a lovely garden nicknamed Bayruha Garden. Sometimes the Prophet would stop by for a drink from its cool water pool. When verse 92 was revealed one day, Abu Talhah approached the Prophet and offered this garden as a gift for Allah's cause, explaining He only wanted Allah to compensate him for it. The Prophet said, "Excellent! Excellent! It's a valuable property. It's a valuable property. I have heard what you said, and I think it would be best if you were to give it to your near relatives." Abu Talhah then joyfully parceled out ownership of the garden among his relatives and cousins. (*Bukhari, Muslim, Ahmad*) This verse, then, provides a kind of self check for our level of faith. If you are not willing to part with some possession or another in order to help a person in need, then your faith is not yet what it could be.

[293] Apparently, there was a disagreement between some Jews and the Prophet about the eating of camels and rabbits. Islam allowed it while Judaism forbade it. (See Deuteronomy 14:7) This verse here was revealed explaining that before the Torah, the Jews could eat pretty much anything they wanted. Therefore, since the Qur'an now *supersedes* the Torah, the Jews should not object to the lifting of some food restrictions. (*Asbab ul-Nuzul*)

[294] The book of Leviticus (chapters 1-11) contains so many dietary restrictions, peculiar sacrificial rites and odd uses for animal parts that it seems a stretch of the imagination to believe that all of these things originated with Moses. Considering the fact that the Torah was lost for centuries before Ezra wrote a new version, it is not inconceivable that many of these rules were added or invented later on.

[295] When the order came for the Muslims to start facing Mecca in prayer instead of Jerusalem, many Jews in Medina objected, saying there was no basis in the Torah for this. This passage was revealed in response, and it makes the case to the Jews that that city was just as steeped in antiquity as Jerusalem, and thus they should not boast that *their* city is better or more proper. (*Asbab ul-Nuzul, Ibn Kathir*)

[296] *Becca* is an alternative name for Mecca. Mecca, its famed Well of Zamzam, and the practice of regular pilgrimage to the city by throngs annually is even mentioned in the Old Testament of the Bible in Psalm 84:6, giving credence to the ancient nature of the settlement and tradition first begun by Abraham. (The name Becca, itself, means two things: a place where weeping overtakes tyrants, as well as a place of gathering.)

[297] After Islam came and imposed its own rules of conduct in Mecca, the Prophet forbade people from killing any living thing in the city and even forbade people from carrying weapons in Mecca. (*Muslim*) In pre-Islamic times, a criminal could enter the courtyard of the Ka'bah, and even if one of his victims saw him, the aggrieved party wouldn't lay a hand on the criminal for fear of violating the sanctity of the place.

there's nothing that Allah needs from anyone in the entire universe. [97]

Remain True to Your Faith

Say (to them), "*Followers of Earlier Revelation! Why do you refuse to accept (the truth) of Allah's (revealed) verses, especially since Allah witnesses everything you do?*" [98] Then ask them, "*Followers of Earlier Revelation! Why do you try to prevent those who believe from following the path of Allah, attempting to make it seem crooked, while witnessing (that Allah is the truth)? Allah is not unmindful of what you're doing.*" [99]

Don't be Deceived into Disunity

O you who believe! [298] If you listen to some of the Followers of Earlier Revelation, they might (confuse) you into renouncing your faith after you had believed! [100]

How could you reject (your faith) while Allah's verses are being directed towards you and while His Prophet is by your side? Whoever holds firmly to Allah will be guided towards a straight path. [101]

O you who believe! Be mindful (of Allah) as much as you should be mindful (of Him), and don't let death come upon you without being surrendered (to His will). [299] [102] Hold firmly all together to the rope of Allah, and don't be divided. [300]

Remember His favors you received, for when you were enemies, He brought your hearts together in love and made you brothers as a favor from Him. [301] You were on the brink of a fiery pit, but He saved you from it. [302] This is how Allah makes His verses clear so you can be guided. [103]

---

[298] Before Islam came to Medina, the two large, local Arab tribes of Auws and Khazraj were prone to making war upon each other. In times of peace, the two sides would compose poetry belittling the other side and praising their own bravery and courage. After Islam came, both tribes made peace with each other and began to merge into a unified Muslim identity. One day a Jewish man named Shas (Shammas) ibn Qays happened to pass by a gathering of men from both tribes, and he became incensed that these old enemies should be so friendly with each other. He told a young friend of his to join them and start reciting poetry from their old days of conflict, particularly about the day when the Auws nearly wiped out the Khazraj. The young Jew started doing this, and within a short time the men of each tribe began taunting each other like they used to do before Islam. Passions rose so high that men began unsheathing their swords and challenging each other to fight. When the Prophet was informed about what was going on, he rushed to the street where the men were gathered and physically stood between the two mobs, calling for calm, and reciting this newly revealed passage loudly and trying his best to bring the anger of both sides down. The men relented after a while and then felt ashamed and began weeping, reaffirming their ties of religious brotherhood. One of the men later recalled, "On that day we hated no one more than the Messenger (for trying to make us forget our past feuds). Then, he waved his hand to us, we stopped, and Allah brought us together again. Afterwards, we never loved anyone more than we loved the Messenger. I have never seen a day that had such an evil and sad beginning, only to have a good end, like that day had." (*Asbab ul-Nuzul, Ibn Is-haq*)

[299] The Prophet said, "None of you should die except while having sincere trust in Allah, the Exalted and Honorable." (*Muslim*)

[300] The Prophet explained that the rope of Allah is the Qur'an. (*Ibn Kathir*)

[301] The Pre-Islamic Arabs were a collection of warring tribes whose loyalty lay only with their clans. Even Medina (Yathrib) was a fractured society in which civil war was frequent. To this warlike people came a new ideology that set faith in Allah as the binding force in society, rather than tribe or clan. Islam united people who would have ordinarily been at each other's throats. Such is the universally recognized power of Islam to bring brotherhood out of many competing interests, be they tribal, nationalistic, ethnic or racial.

[302] Before engaging in a war, Arab tribes would build a large bonfire to gather their men to rally them. The use of the phrase 'pit of fire' here is thus an idiom to remind the Muslims that before Islam they were always warring with each other. Allah unified them through Islam, and thus they were saved from an endless cycle of war.

So let there arise from among you a community that will invite (people) to the good and command (others to follow) what is known (to be right) while forbidding (them from) what is unfamiliar (to Allah's way of life), for it is these who will be the successful ones. [104]

Don't be like those who divided themselves and took to conflicting views, even after receiving clear evidence of the truth. [303] Tremendous punishment awaits them [105] on the day when some faces will be beaming brightly, while others will be overcast in darkness.

Those whose faces will be overcast (from their shame) will be asked, "*Did you suppress the truth (of Allah in your heart) after having once believed in it? So now experience for yourselves the punishment for your rejection!*" [106]

However, those whose faces will be bright and beaming (with joy) will remain within the mercy of Allah forever. [107] These are the (revealed) verses of Allah that We're conveying to you so that the truth can be established. Allah doesn't want any oppression (to exist) anywhere in the universe. [108] To Him belongs all things within the heavens and the earth, and all issues will go back to Him (for their resolution). [109]

You are the best community brought out from humanity. You encourage what is recognized (as right), and you forbid what is unfamiliar (to Allah's good way), and you believe in Allah. Now if the Followers of Earlier Revelation only had (this kind of sincere) faith, it would have been much better for them. Some of them (truly) believe (and practice their religion sincerely), but most of them are disobedient and wicked. [110]

However, they can do you no real harm, save for some small injuries, and if they ever fought against you, they would most likely turn and flee with no one to save them. [304] [111]

Disgrace overshadows them wherever they're found, except when they cling to Allah or cling to another people, for they've earned the burden of Allah's wrath and utter misery is spread over them. That's on account of their rejecting the signs of Allah and killing the prophets against all right. They did that because they had rebelled and overstepped all bounds. [112]

Jews and Christians are not All the Same

*T*hey're not all the same, for among the Followers of Earlier Revelation is a group that stands throughout the night reciting the revelations of Allah, and they bow themselves (before Him). [305] [113] They believe in Allah and the Last Day

---

[303] The Prophet said, "Whatever I have forbidden you to do, avoid. Whatever I have ordered you to do, do as much of it as you can. It was only their excessive questioning and their disagreeing with their prophets that destroyed those who were before you." (*Bukhari, Muslim*) A casual glance at the Muslim world today and all the sectarian divisions gives one pause for thought. Prophet Muhammad predicted these divisions and remarked that the only group that will attain to Paradise among the many sects is the one that adheres to his example and the example of his companions. All others will be in serious trouble on the Day of Judgment.

[304] A Jewish rabbi, 'Abdullah ibn Salam, converted to Islam along with his family and some associates. The six most powerful leaders of the three Jewish tribes went to him and roughed up him and his family. This verse was revealed in response to their injuries in order to console them. (*Asbab ul-Nuzul*)

[305] Jewish converts to Islam such as Asad ibn 'Ubayd, Tha'labah ibn Sa'yah and 'Abdullah ibn Salam are the immediate reference here. (*Asbab ul-Nuzul*) So this verse is referring to converts to Islam mainly from Judaism. With regards to the practice of night prayer, once the Prophet was delayed and didn't get to the mosque until very late. He saw it filled with Muslims who were waiting for him. Some were already praying while others were sitting or lying around on the floor awaiting his arrival. He smiled and remarked, "Is there anyone from among the (different) religions who pray late at night, besides you?" Then this verse was revealed. (*Ibn Kathir, Ahmad*)

while encouraging what's known (to be good) and forbidding what's unfamiliar (to Allah's good way of life), and they hurry to do acts of righteousness. They're among the morally upright. [114] Nothing will be rejected of the good they did, for Allah knows about those who are mindful (of Him). [115]

As for those who suppress (the knowledge of the truth in their hearts), neither their money nor their children will save them in the least from Allah. They'll be companions of the Fire, *and that's where they're going to stay!* [116]

The example of what they spend in the life of this world is like a chill wind that brings bitter frost. It strikes down the fruit of the harvest of those who've done wrong to their own souls. Allah is not doing any injustice to them; rather, they're bringing it upon their own selves. [306] [117]

Don't Befriend those who would Destroy You

O you who believe! Don't take those from outside your own ranks to be your intimate companions, [307] for they'll try anything to corrupt you, as they only want to ruin you. Stinging hatred issues from their mouths, and what their hearts are hiding is far worse. We're making these verses clear for you, *if you would (only use) your sense!* [118]

Really now! You're ready to love them while they have no love for you - even though you believe in all of (Allah's) scriptures. Whenever they meet you, they spare no effort to say, *"We believe (in Allah), too!"* Yet, when they're away from your presence, they gnaw at their fingertips in rage against you. Say to them, *"Perish in your hatred! Allah knows all the secrets of the heart."* [119]

If you're doing well, it aggravates them, but if some misfortune befalls you, they're delighted. If you would just remain patient (in adversity) and be ever mindful (of Allah), then their scheming won't harm you in the least, for Allah encompasses everything they attempt. [120]

On the Battle of Uhud

*R*emember that morning, [308] (Muhammad), when you left your family

---

[306] The Prophet said, "Renouncing the world doesn't mean that you consider lawful things as unlawful or that you waste the wealth that Allah's given you. Renouncing the world means to have more faith in those things that are in Allah's hands, than what's in your hands." (*Tirmidhi*)

[307] This verse was revealed after the Jews of Medina shed any pretenses of neutrality or goodwill and became openly hostile to the Muslims and their religion. Some Muslims, who had close working relationships with the Jews before Islam, still tried to maintain those close friendships afterwards, even though many of their old friends were now working against the faith. This verse is admonishing them for this. (*Ibn Kathir*)

[308] The famous Battle of Uhud took place in the year 625 near a small cluster of low mountains just outside of Medina. The Meccan idol-worshippers, who wanted to avenge their loss at Badr the year before, organized an army of about 3,000 foot soldiers and cavalry and marched towards the city of their foes. The Prophet (and 'Abdullah ibn Ubayy) wanted to defend from the city, but many of the younger companions were eager to go out and fight, assuming Allah would help them as He had at Badr the year before. Eventually, the Prophet acceded to their desire, and although some companions changed their minds, the Prophet explained that once a Prophet suits up for battle, he doesn't remove his armor until Allah has made a resolution. (*Bukhari*) Accordingly, the Muslims met the pagans in battle with 700 men (and a few women). Originally the Muslims had set out with 1,000 men, but 300 men, following the hypocrite, 'Abdullah ibn Ubayy, left the battlefield and returned to Medina. (Ibn Ubayy claimed he was angry at the Prophet for not heeding his advice to remain behind the city's walls for defense. Later he changed his excuse to saying that he didn't think a real battle would happen, and that's why he returned home with his followers.) The dispirited Muslims were roused to courage by the Prophet's words, and the battle began in earnest. The vastly outnumbered but more disciplined Muslims were winning the fight at first, and the Meccans began to flee. However, some archers that the Prophet placed on a hill to guard a rear pass left their posts against orders to collect booty from the

to assign the believers to their battle stations (at the Mountain of Uhud). Allah was listening, and He knew (all about it). [121]

Remember when two of your regiments almost lost the will to fight. Yet, Allah was their guardian, *and the believers should trust in Allah!* [309] [122] As it happened, Allah had already helped you once before at the (Battle of) Badr when you were only a small force, so be mindful of Allah so you can show your gratitude. [123]

Remember that you (had to rally) the believers, saying, *"Isn't it enough (to know) that your Lord will help you with three thousand angels?* [124] *Really now, if you hold firm (in the face of hardship) and are mindful (of Allah), then even in the face of an onslaught, your Lord will send five thousand angels rushing in a massive blitz!"* [125]

Allah didn't convey this good news for any other reason than to assure your hearts, for there is no help save from Allah, the Powerful and Wise. [126] (Through your efforts, He intended) to vanquish a section of the faithless or steep them in notoriety, [310] so they would have to turn back in unfulfilled frustration. [127]

Now it's not your place to pardon them or punish them, for they're certainly oppressors. [311]

Everything within the heavens and the earth belongs to Allah. [128] He forgives whomever He wants and punishes whomever He wants, and Allah is forgiving and merciful. [129]

Patient Perseverance

O you who believe! Don't consume interest-money, doubled and redoubled! Be mindful of Allah so you can be (truly) successful. [130] Beware of the Fire that's been prepared for those who suppress (their awareness of the truth). [131] Obey Allah and His Messenger so you can receive mercy. [132]

Race together towards your Lord's forgiveness and to a Garden as wide as the heavens and the earth [312] - *reserved only for those who were mindful (of Allah).* [133] They spent (in the cause of Allah) in good times and bad, restrained their temper and overlooked the faults of others. Allah loves those who are good. [134]

---

battlefield. This enabled a surprise rear attack by the Meccan cavalry led by Khalid ibn Waleed, who was not yet a Muslim. After some confusion, the beleaguered Muslims were forced to retreat backwards up the small mountain of Uhud, but then they eventually held their ground, though many Muslims (about 70) had been slain. The Meccan army returned to their camp claiming victory, even though the battle was actually more of a draw, for just as many Meccans lay dead as Muslims. Muhammad brought a contingent of his followers back out for battle again the next day, but the Meccans decided to withdraw in the night, holding on to their narrowly won bragging rights. (*Ibn Hisham*)

[309] Men from the Banu Salamah clan of Khazraj and the Banu Harithah were losing their resolve to fight but were coaxed into regaining their fervor. (*Ibn Kathir*)

[310] After the battle was over, some of the Meccans began to torture the wounded Muslims they found, and even more gruesome than that, they mutilated the bodies of the dead. Abu Sufyan's wife Hind actually cut open the chest of the fallen hero Hamza and chewed on his liver. (She had previously vowed revenge after losing close relatives at Badr.) This barbaric behavior must have given some of the more thoughtful Meccans reason to reconsider the goals for which they were fighting. (Even Abu Sufyan, the pagan leader, tried to distance himself from it). This evil notoriety sullied the reputation of the Meccans in the eyes of many in the region.

[311] Once after a dawn prayer, the Prophet prefaced his usual supplications by asking Allah to curse certain of the most hated Meccan idol-worshippers. He stopped in mid-sentence when this passage was revealed, for it told him it was not his place to call curses down upon anyone. (*Ibn Kathir*)

[312] A man heard this verse, describing Paradise as being as wide as the heavens and the earth, and he asked the Prophet, "So where is the Fire (of Hell), then?" The Prophet replied, "When night comes, it covers everything, so where is the day?" The man answered, "It's where Allah wants it to be." So the Prophet said, "In the same way, the Fire is where Allah wants it to be." (*Ibn Kathir*)

Seek the Forgiveness of Allah

*T*hey were the ones who, when they committed some indiscretion or wrong act against their souls, remembered Allah and sought His forgiveness, [313] and who can pardon except Allah? [314]

Furthermore, they don't consciously recommit those (sins after having repented of them). [135]

Their reward will be forgiveness from their Lord and gardens beneath which rivers flow in which they'll live forever - *what an excellent reward for those who labored (in the world for Allah)!* [315] [136]

Many ways of life have passed away before your time. So travel all over the world, and see how those (former civilizations) that denied (the truth) came to an end. [137]

This is a clear lesson for people and also a source of guidance and admonition for those who are mindful (of Allah). [138]

Explaining the Setback at Uhud

*D*on't lose hope or get despondent, for you must triumph, *that is if you really believe.* [316] [139] Indeed, if you're injured, know that others have been injured likewise. We alternate days (of triumph and defeat) among (nations) so that Allah can make known those who believe and also so that He can take for Himself martyrs from among you.

Allah has no love for oppressors, (and He may use other nations to keep them in check). [140] Even further, Allah (uses such setbacks) as a way to purge the believers (of any impurities) and to erase the gains of those who suppress (their awareness of the truth). [141]

Did you think that you could enter Paradise without first being tested by Allah so He could make known who among you strives hard (in His cause) and (who among you) perseveres (under pressure)? [142]

And so you (said that) you wanted to give your life (in His cause) before you met death, (though that was before you

---

[313] A man named Nabhan saw a beautiful woman in Medina. He wooed her, bought her some food and embraced her. He felt ashamed later and told the Prophet about what happened. This passage was then revealed in comment on the incident. (*Asbab ul-Nuzul*)

[314] The Prophet said, "Allah forgives the person who commits a sin, (then feels ashamed of it), purifies himself, offers a prayer and seeks His forgiveness." Then he recited verse 135 for emphasis. (*Abu Dawud, Ibn Majah*) The repentance procedure in Islam is as follows. When one seeks repentance for a sin, he must have genuine regret for what he did. He must ask for forgiveness from whomever he wronged. He must make up for that sin if possible, such as by a thief returning the stolen goods or their value. He must pray to Allah with heartfelt emotion, seeking His forgiveness. Finally, he must resolve in his heart not to do that sin again. (If he falls into it in the future, he may perform this procedure over, as long as the feelings of remorse are genuine. Allah forgives again and again, but not the crocodile tears of a habitual wrongdoer.)

[315] The Prophet said, "Learn to do without, and you will be the most devout among people. Be content with what you have, and you will be the most thankful to Allah. Desire for others what you desire for yourself, and you will be one of the faithful. Be good to your neighbor, and you will be a true Muslim. Laugh less, for too much laughter deadens the heart." (*Ibn Majah*)

[316] The Muslims were winning at the battle of Uhud until fifty archers the Prophet had set to watch a rear weakness abandoned their posts to collect the goods the fleeing Meccans had left behind. Many Muslims died in the resulting counterattack of the Meccans. When the Prophet returned to Medina with his dispirited forces after the disaster, the women of the city came out beating their faces with their hands in sorrow over their dead husbands and sons. The Prophet lamented to Allah, "Is this what became of your Messenger?" Then this passage was revealed to console him, and he recited it to the people. The resolve of the believers was restored, even if only slowly, and thus many were purged of lingering doubt and weakness of faith. (*Asbab ul-Nuzul*)

actually saw it), *and now you see (death) right in front of you!* [143]

No One will Live Forever

$\mathcal{M}$uhammad is no more than a messenger. [317] There were many messengers who passed away before him. If he dies or is killed, would you then turn and run away? Anyone who runs away does no harm to Allah in the least, and Allah will quickly reward (those who serve Him) in gratitude. [318] [144]

No one can die without Allah's permission, (for every soul has) an appointed time written (for it). So if anyone desires the rewards of this world, We'll give them to him, and if anyone desires the rewards of the next life, We'll give them to him, and We'll swiftly reward those who are thankful. [145]

How many were the prophets who fought alongside men of the Lord? They never lost heart, even after all that befell them in the cause of Allah, nor did they weaken or surrender. And Allah loves those who patiently persevere! [146]

Their words (of strength) were nothing more than this: "*Our Lord!*" they prayed, "*Forgive us our sins, make our stand firm, and help us against the people who suppress (their awareness of You)!*" [147]

Allah gave them a reward in this world, and (they'll receive) an excellent reward in the next life, for Allah loves those who do good. [148]

A Hard Lesson at Uhud

$\mathcal{O}$ you who believe! If you follow (the suggestions of) those who suppress (their faith in Allah), they might cause you to turn away (from faith, yourselves); then your retreat (from faith) would be to your own loss. [149] By no means! Allah is your protector and the best helper of all! [150]

We're soon going to instill panic into the hearts of those who rejected (true faith) in return for their holding others as equals with Allah – (a position for which) He sent no authority! [319] Their home is in the Fire, *and how terrible a place for the wrongdoers!* [151]

---

[317] During the confusion of the Meccan counterattack at Uhud, some Muslims thought Muhammad had been struck down and killed. (Ibn Qami'a, a fierce pagan warrior, even boasted of killing the Prophet to his fellow pagans, though he had succeeded in killing only the Prophet's standard-bearer, Mus'ab ibn Umayr, and he mistook him for the Prophet.) The Muslims then raised their voices in lamentation, and this caused many Muslims to further lose heart and flee. One man called out that he wished 'Abdullah ibn Ubayy would come and cut a deal with Abu Sufyan, while another cried out that the Muslims should abandon Islam and return to the idols, for if Muhammad were a true Prophet, he would not have been killed. Muhammad had only been hit and wounded on his face; he didn't remain down. Instead, he stood and cried out loudly, "Come to me, servants of Allah!" Thus, thirty companions, such as 'Ali, Abu Bakr and a woman named Nusaybah bint K'ab, among others, formed a protective cordon so the Prophet could be whisked away to the slope of Uhud in an expeditious way. Another companion, named Anas ibn an-Nadr, who didn't see the Prophet in the confusion, called to the fleeing Muslims near him, saying, "People! If Muhammad has been killed, surely his Lord is alive and will never die. What would you want to do with your lives after he was no longer here? Fight for what he fought for! O Allah! I ask for Your forgiveness for what they've said, and I have nothing to do with it!" Then he fought on until he was killed. This passage was revealed about that desperate episode and also about men such as Anas who stood firm against all odds. (*Baydawi*)

[318] When the Prophet did, in fact, pass away approximately eight years after the Battle of Uhud, Abu Bakr recited this verse to soothe a distraught 'Umar ibn al-Khattab (d. 644) who couldn't believe that their faithful guide had departed from their midst.

[319] When the victorious Meccans were journeying back home from the Battle of Uhud, their leader, Abu Sufyan, felt that they should have finished the job and wiped out all of the Muslims. He held counsel with his fellow leaders and decided to return to continue the fight. After a few hours riding, however, they were seized with apprehension, changed their minds and returned to Mecca. Many commentators believe that this verse refers to how Allah caused them to change their course of action.

Allah was certainly fulfilling His promise when, by His leave, you were about to vanquish your foes (at the Battle of Uhud), [320] but then you flinched and argued over your orders (to guard the mountain pass). You disobeyed (the Prophet's orders) after (Allah) showed you (the war-prizes) that you coveted.

Some among you desired the things of this world, while others desired the next life. He allowed you to be distracted from your enemy so He could test you (in order to discipline you, and even though you failed in your duty), He's forgiven you, for Allah is limitless in His favor towards those who believe. [152]

When you were scrambling up the slopes (of Mount Uhud in full retreat), not even noticing those around you, the Messenger was behind you, calling you to come back (and face the enemy, but you ignored him).

So Allah brought the disappointment (of shame) upon you, even as you disappointed (the Prophet by running away from him. [321] This added shame) befell you so that you wouldn't feel bad only for the (war-prizes) you missed, but also for what you suffered, as well, and Allah is well-informed of all that you do. [153]

Then, after this time of distress, He allowed a feeling of peace and confidence to descend upon a group of you. [322] Even still, another faction (of your people) took to venting their frustrations and spoke out against Allah, thinking thoughts of pagan ignorance, saying, "*Don't we have any say in the matter?*"

Say to them, "*Surely every command belongs to Allah.*" They try to hide their lack of conviction from you by lamenting, "*If only we were in charge, there would've been far fewer casualties (from the battle).*"

Say to them, "*Even if you had remained in your homes (within the city of Medina, like you had wanted from the beginning), those whose time*

(*Asbab ul-Nuzul*) Other commentators say that this passage refers to the public commentary of the Jews in Medina who questioned the Prophet's credentials as a true messenger of Allah, given that his forces had lost the battle. (*Ma'ariful Qur'an*)

[320] The Prophet had left 'Abdullah ibn Jubayr (d. 625) in charge of 50 archers, and he told them not to move from their place, even if they saw the rest of the army being defeated. When the Meccans began to flee, the archers saw the Meccan women running away over the hills, pulling up their dresses as they ran, exposing their anklets. A cry went up among the archers, "The war booty! The war booty!" Ibn Jubayr ordered the men to stay in position. However, they argued with him, and most abandoned their posts, thinking they could safely start collecting war booty. That disobedience cost the Muslims dearly, as the Meccan cavalry launched a counterattack that caused the deaths of some 70 Muslims. (*Ibn Hisham*) Later on, in Medina, some of Muhammad's followers began complaining, asking how they could have lost the battle when they were assured that they would win. This verse was revealed in response, telling them that Allah was holding up His end of the bargain, while some from among them (the archers) failed to do their part by running after material gains. (*Asbab ul-Nuzul*)

[321] Apparently, many Muslims thought the Prophet had been slain during the Battle of Uhud, and even though he remained facing the enemy and called for them to come back, the people ignored the call. Then the powerful voice of Ka'b ibn Malik rang out, proclaiming that the Prophet was alive and that they should return. This allowed the companions a chance to regroup with new confidence, though tinged with shame at their apparent cowardice. In later years, a man publicly criticized several prominent companions about their having run away from the battlefield at Uhud, and 'Abdullah ibn 'Umar stopped the man, saying, "No one has the right to criticize what Allah has plainly forgiven." Verse 3:155 contains the pardon. (*Bukhari*)

[322] After the Muslims retreated to higher ground, there was a temporary lull in the fighting. This allowed some of the Muslim fighters to rest, while others (especially a hypocrite named Mu'attib ibn Qushayr) began to complain, as this verse quotes his words. Such men had wanted to remain in Medina and defend the city from there, but militarily it made more sense to go out and meet the enemy on ground of their own choosing. Medina was not a fortified city, and allowing an enemy force to assault it might have turned into a rout. The Muslim plan at Uhud worked, in a way, despite the huge loss of about 70 lives, for they succeeded in wearying the Meccans enough to make them want to return home.

it was to die would still have gone forth to their place of death."

This was merely (a test) so Allah could show your true feelings and purge (any impurities) in your hearts, for He knows the secrets of the mind. [154]

Those who deserted (their posts on the battlefield) on the day the two armies clashed (at Uhud) were made to fail by Satan, (who had some influence over them) because of some (sins) they had earned before. However, Allah forgave them, for Allah is forgiving and forbearing. [155]

Affirmation in Death

O you who believe! [323] Don't be like those who cover (their awareness of the truth), and who despair over their brothers (who've died) while traveling the land or in battle, lamenting (loudly), *"If only they would've stayed here with us (safe at home), then they wouldn't have died or been killed."*

Allah brings this regret upon their hearts, for only Allah has the power to preserve life or take it away, and Allah sees everything that you do. [156]

Know that if you're killed, or if you happen to die in the cause of Allah, forgiveness and mercy from Allah are far better than (all the worldly possessions) they can gather. [157] (So remember that) if you happen to die or are killed that you're going to be gathered back to Allah (in the end). [324] [158]

It's only due to Allah's mercy that you're gentle with the (believers in their time of stress), [325] for if you were ever to be harsh with them they would have scattered away from you. So overlook their

---

[323] The Muslim losses from Uhud were high, and their families mourned them greatly in typical Arab fashion. The Prophet sought to curtail some of the more extravagant mourning rituals. He forbade excessive wailing, the hiring of professional wailers, self-cutting, the tearing of one's clothes and killing animals to mourn the dead. This verse was revealed to bolster this change in custom. (*Asbab ul-Nuzul, Ma'ariful Qur'an*)

[324] During the Battle of Uhud, the Muslims were close to being overwhelmed, and for a moment the Prophet was left alone with only a couple of defenders. An idolater named Ibn Qami'a struck down the Prophet's standard-bearer, a man named Mu'sab ibn Umayr, and because Mu'sab resembled the Prophet somewhat, Ibn Qami'a began shouting wildly that he had killed the Prophet. This announcement alarmed many companions. One Muslim woman named Sumayyah rushed through the battlefield trying to locate the Prophet. When she saw him, she said, "Hardships mean nothing to me as long as you're alive, O Messenger." (*Ibn Hisham*) Meanwhile, when Ibn Qami'a realized that the Prophet was still alive, he rushed at the Prophet on a warhorse, struck down fiercely with his sword and hit the Prophet on his shoulder. Then Ibn Qami'a knocked him hard on the face, causing two rings of armor from the Prophet's helmet to become embedded in his cheek. The idolater shouted these words as he attacked the Prophet, *"Take that blow from me! I'm Ibn Qami'a!"* The Prophet was quickly surrounded by a few more defenders, including another Muslim woman, named Nusaybah bint K'ab, and she nearly killed Ibn Qami'a. Then the Prophet sat down to wipe the blood from his cheek. (It must be remembered that he was about fifty-five years old at the time.) He said out loud, "I ask Allah to humiliate you." (The attacker's name, Qami'a, meant 'a humiliated one', so the Prophet was making a play on his name.) Then the Prophet said, "How can a people who will cut their own Prophet's face and break his tooth - when he's only calling them to worship the One God – how can they survive and be successful?" The Prophet then commented, "Allah's wrath is terrible upon those who disfigure their messenger's face." He was silent for a moment, and then he added, "O Allah, forgive my people, for they don't understand." (*Muslim*)

[325] The Prophet was in a difficult position for some months after the debacle at Uhud. On the one hand, he had wanted to defend from the city, but the will of the majority was to go out to fight in the countryside, and then a portion of his followers had disobeyed his orders on the battlefield and this caused the defeat. While on the other hand, many people were now getting emotional due to their losses and ignored those facts. Many Muslims were also stunned and had their faith shaken and were questioning Muhammad's mission, ignoring the fact that it was not his fault that things turned out the way they did. This verse was revealed to the Prophet as general advice that he should not get too frustrated or angry with all that people were saying. (*at-Tabari, Ibn Kathir, Asbab ul-Nuzul*)

shortcomings, pray for their forgiveness and seek their counsel on relevant issues.

When you have come to a mutual decision, then put your trust in Allah, for He loves those who trust in Him. [159]

If Allah is helping you,

who can defeat you?

If He forsakes you,
who can help you after that?

So the believers should
put their trust in Allah. [160]

Trust in the Prophet

No prophet should ever withhold anything, for whoever withholds something will be made to give restitution for what they withheld on the Day of Assembly. [326]

Then every soul will be paid back for what it's earned, and no one will be wronged. [161]

Can someone who follows Allah be equal to someone who has Allah's wrath drawn over them, and whose home is in Hellfire? *How terrible a destination!* [162]

These two types (of people) are on entirely different levels in the sight of Allah, and Allah is watching everything they do. [163]

And so it was that the believers were favored by Allah when He raised up a messenger from among them who recited the verses of Allah to them, purified them, and who taught them scripture and wisdom; they were lost in error before. [164]

There is a Lesson in Failure

What! After a single setback in which you inflicted twice (the damage) that you suffered, (you begin to question Allah), saying, "*How could that (disaster at Uhud) have happened?*"

Say (to them), "*You were the cause of your own (defeat through your own disobedience), for Allah has power over all things.*" [165]

What you experienced on the day when the two armies met (at Uhud) was by Allah's permission so that He could test the believers [166] - *and the hypocrites, too.*

When they were told, "*Come and fight in the cause of Allah, or at the very least defend yourselves,*" (they offered) excuses, saying, "*If we knew a fight was (really) going to happen, then we would've surely followed you (in the battle).*"

They were much closer to disbelief than belief that day. They said with their lips the opposite of what was in their hearts, and Allah knows what they were hiding. [167]

Now they're lamenting, after they've been sitting (in safety all along), "*If only (our slain friends) would've listened to us (and not fought in the Battle of Uhud), then they would not have died.*"

(So then challenge the hypocrites by) saying, "*So save your own selves from death, if you have that power!*" [168]

---

[326] This passage was revealed in response to an incident in which some hypocrites started a rumor that the Prophet had withheld a blanket from the distribution of the captured Badr war booty. This verse reminds the Muslims that unfairly taking anything from the booty is a sin and that it is foolish to accuse the Prophet, who is the least interested in material goods among them all, of withholding something. (*Ibn Kathir*)

The Reward for Ultimate Sacrifice

$\mathcal{D}$on't think that those who are killed in the cause of Allah are dead. [327] No way! They're alive and getting their needs met in the presence of their Lord. [169]

They're rejoicing in His bounty, and also because (they know that through their sacrifice) the ones they left behind are (better) protected from fear and distress. [170]

They're rejoicing in the good pleasure of Allah and in His bounty! Truly, Allah doesn't let the reward of the faithful ever become lost. [171]

The Resolute and the Brave

$\mathcal{T}$hose who responded to the call of Allah and the Messenger (to march to Badr once again, one year after Uhud), even while some of them were still wounded (from Uhud), (should know that) there's a valuable reward for those who do good and remain mindful (of Allah). [328] [172]

Even after people told them, "*A great force (of men) is massed against you, so fear them,*" (instead of wavering), it only increased their conviction and they said, "*Allah is enough for us, and He's the most favorable (One upon Whom) to rely.*" [329] [173]

And so they returned with the grace and bounty of Allah, and no harm

---

[327] A man named Jabir was silently lamenting the loss of his father at the Battle of Uhud. The Prophet saw him and asked, "Why are you looking so glum?" Jabir answered, "My father was killed, and he left behind debts and children." The Prophet replied, "Let me tell you, Allah doesn't speak to anyone except from behind a veil, and He talked to your father (in Paradise) for he had fought (and died). He said to him, 'My servant, ask Me whatever you wish, and I shall grant it.' Your father said, 'Send me back to the world to be killed again fighting in Your cause.' Allah answered, 'I have already given the order that no one can go back to it.' So he answered, 'Lord, then tell those who will come after me (about the reward).'" Then the Prophet announced to his grieving companions that Allah had taken the souls of the martyrs who perished at Uhud and placed them within the bodies of green birds and set them free in Paradise. They get all that they need from the fruit trees and streams of Paradise, and they spend time every day perched beneath the throne of Allah on special branches shaped like candelabras. When they first noticed the endless luxury of Paradise, they asked out loud, "Can someone inform (our relatives and friends in the world) about how well we live here, so they can stop mourning over us and continue to strive like we did?" Allah told them that He would do that, and thus He revealed this passage to Muhammad so all his followers would know. (*Abu Dawud, Asbab ul-Nuzul*)

[328] The day after their debacle at Uhud, many Muslim fighters, including the Prophet, had been wounded. Muhammad, however, called for volunteers to go out and meet the Meccans in the field once more, (as the Meccans were resolving themselves to fight another battle, for their objectives of killing Muhammad and capturing goods and slaves had not been met). About 70 able-bodied men joined the Prophet, though by the time the Muslims left Medina, following the trail of the Meccans, the Meccans had already departed and decided not to fight, preferring to return home. The Prophet went as far as a market town known as Hamra al-Asad before turning back. Before the Meccans withdrew, however, they sent a challenge to the Muslims to meet them again in battle at Badr (the sight of the first Battle of Badr) the following year during a trade fair that was to be held there. Many heeded the Prophet's call to march at that time. Though some hypocrites and an agent of the Meccans named Nu'aym ibn Mas'ud tried to instill fear in the Muslims in both instances (by saying the Meccan army was huge), the conviction that they must follow their leader caused many of the faithful to accompany the Prophet. The Meccans did not show up at Badr in 626 CE. The Muslims joined in the trade fair, and many of the believers made handsome profits. This second trip to Badr is often called *Badr Sughra*, or Little Badr. (*Ibn Kathir*)

[329] The Prophet once decided a dispute between two men, and the losing party accepted the verdict and walked away reciting the phrase in this verse, "Allah is enough for us..." The Prophet called the man back and explained, "Allah does not support inaction, for it is your duty to apply your own effort (to a situation), after which, when you truly find yourself powerless, only then you can say, '*Allah is enough for us, and He's the most favorable (One upon Whom) to rely.*'" (*Ma'ariful Qur'an*) This phrase is a common saying among Muslims in times of crisis or uncertainty.

overcame them (for the Meccans had failed to appear). They were following the pleasure of Allah, and Allah is the master of tremendous bounty. [174]

It's only Satan who instills the fear of his minions in you, so don't fear them. Rather, fear Me if you (really) do believe. [175] Don't worry over those who rush to reject (Allah), because they don't do any harm to Allah at all. Allah wants to exclude them from any share in the next life - *except for suffering a terrible punishment!* [176]

Those who buy rejection (of the truth) at the cost of faith don't do the least bit of harm to Allah. They're going to receive a painful punishment indeed! [177]

Those who suppress (their awareness of the truth) shouldn't think that their (apparent) free reign (and their illusion of power) is to their advantage. We're only giving them more time to increase in their sinfulness, and then a humiliating punishment will await them! [178]

Why does Allah Test Us?

Allah won't leave the believers in the (weak) position that they're now in until He separates what is filthy from what is wholesome, nor will Allah give you insight into what is beyond human perception.

Rather, He chooses from among His messengers as He wills (and assigns each his own level of success). So believe in Allah and His Messenger, for if you believe and remain mindful (of your duty to Allah), then this will secure for you a valuable reward. [179]

Those who greedily hoard what Allah has provided them from out of His bounty shouldn't think that it will be to their advantage.

On the contrary, it's to their detriment, for soon what their greed held back will be tied around their necks on the Day of Assembly. [330] To Allah belongs the inheritance of the heavens and the earth, and Allah is well-informed of everything you do. [180]

No One should Belittle Allah

Allah heard (the boast) of those who said, "*Allah is poor while we are rich!*" [331] We're going to record their statement, along with their unjust murdering of the prophets of old against all right.

We're going to say to them, "*Taste the punishment of the burning agony!* [181] *This is for what you did with your own hands.*" However, Allah will never harm those who (sincerely) served Him. [182]

---

[330] The Prophet said, "Whoever has been granted wealth by Allah and did not pay the required charity on it will find that his wealth will materialize on the Day of Resurrection in the form of a (poisonous) bald snake. The snake will coil all about him on that Day, will catch both sides of his mouth (with his tail and mouth on either side) and will say, 'I am your money. I am your wealth.'" (*Bukhari*)

[331] After verse 2:245 was revealed to the Muslims, Abu Bakr (d. 634), who was the Prophet's closest companion, paid a visit to a rabbinical school in a Jewish neighborhood in Medina. He found one of their scholars, Finhas ibn Azoura', surrounded by students. Abu Bakr addressed him, saying, "Fear Allah and accept Islam, for I swear to Allah that you know Muhammad is the Messenger of Allah who has brought Allah's truth to you. It is written in your Torah, so believe and accept it. Lend a goodly loan to Allah so He will double your reward and admit you into Paradise." Finhas replied, "Abu Bakr, you're suggesting that Allah borrows money from us? However, only the poor borrow from the rich. If what you're saying is true, then Allah is poor, and we are rich. If He were really rich, Himself, then He wouldn't borrow money from us!" Abu Bakr became angry and slapped Finhas, saying, "I swear by the One Who holds my soul, if we didn't have a treaty then I would cut your throat, you enemy of Allah." Later, Finhas went to the Prophet to complain, saying, "Look at what your companion did to me!" The Prophet asked Abu Bakr what happened and why, and after Abu Bakr told the story, this passage was then revealed. (*Asbab ul-Nuzul*)

Yet, they also said, *"Allah made us promise to reject every messenger unless he comes with a sacrifice of burnt offerings."*

Say to them, *"Many messengers came to you before me with clear evidence and even with that for which you're asking. So why did you kill them if you're being so honest?"* [183] Then if they deny you, (Muhammad), so, too, were other messengers denied before who came with clear evidence, sober prophecies and enlightened scripture. [184]

It will be a Hard Road

Every soul will have to experience death, and on the Day of Assembly each of you will receive your full payback. [332] The one who is saved from the Fire and who is admitted into the Garden will have achieved the ultimate goal. The life of this world is nothing more than material gains and illusions. [333] [185]

You're certainly going to be tested through your wealth and your own selves, and you're going to hear much that will distress you from those who received scripture before you, and from those who make partners (with Allah). [334] Yet, if you persevere and remain mindful (of your duty to Allah), then this will determine many results. [186]

Recall that Allah took an agreement from those who received previous revelation. They were (supposed to make the message of Allah) clearly evident to people and not to hide it, but they threw it away behind their backs and made a little profit off of it. What a despicable bargain they made! [187]

Don't think that those who do things and then are smug (in their deceit) or who love to be praised for what they *didn't* do – don't think that they'll escape retribution, for a painful punishment awaits them. [335] [188]

To Allah belongs the control of the heavens and earth, and Allah has power over all things. [189]

---

[332] The Prophet said, "After the faithful are saved from (going to) Hell, they will be stopped at a bridge that passes between Paradise and Hell. There they will take any vengeance for any wrongs they have done to each other in the world. After they are cleansed of (all feelings of injustice), they will be admitted to Paradise. By the One in Whose hand is Muhammad's soul, every one of them will know their own dwelling in Paradise better than he knew his home in this world." (*Bukhari*)

[333] The Prophet said, "People will be resurrected and gathered on the Day of Resurrection barefoot, naked and uncircumcised." His wife A'ishah asked, "Messenger of Allah, will the men and women be standing near each other so they can see each other?" The Prophet answered, "A'ishah, it will be such a terrible time that no one will be able to look upon anyone else." (*Bukhari, Muslim*)

[334] One day, the Prophet tried to preach Islam to a mixed gathering that included 'Abdullah ibn Ubayy, a prominent citizen of Medina who was supposed to have been crowned king of the city, but whose planned ascension to power was thwarted by the arrival of the Prophet and his ascendancy over the city. Ibn Ubayy told the Prophet not to bother him and his friends with his preaching, while one of those gathered spoke up, saying that he wanted to hear more. This caused an uproar, and the gathered Muslims, hypocrites, idol-worshippers and Jews began quarreling with each other. The Prophet tried his best to calm them down and then left. He told a companion named Sa'd ibn 'Ubada, whom he met after the incident, that Ibn Ubayy was disrespectful, whereupon the young man said that the Prophet shouldn't hold hard feelings towards Ibn Ubayy for he had to understand that his coming had deprived him of a crown. He then asked the Prophet to forgive the insolence of Ibn Ubayy. This verse was revealed regarding this incident, and the Prophet resolved to bear with patience the future antics of 'Abdullah ibn Ubayy. (*Bukhari*)

[335] According to Ibn 'Abbas, the first part of this verse is a reference to the Jews of Medina, as they are mentioned in verse 187. Ibn 'Abbas explained that when the Prophet would pose a question to them, they would give wrong answers and be happy about trying to deceive the Prophet. (*al-Qurtubi*) According to Abu Said al-Khudri, the second part of this verse applies to the situation of some hypocrites in Medina who did not join the Prophet when he went out on a campaign, but when he returned, they made excuses and praised themselves for how brave they *would* have been. (*Bukhari, Muslim*)

The Call of Faith in Allah

 Truly, in the creation of the heavens and the earth and in the alternation of night and day are signs for people who think deeply. **336** [190]

They remember Allah while standing, sitting or lying down on their sides, and they contemplate the creation of the heavens and earth, (saying):

"Our Lord! You didn't create all of this for nothing! Glory be to You! Save us from the punishment of the Fire. [191]

"Our Lord, whomever You send into Hellfire is indeed covered in shame, and the wrongdoers will never find anyone to help them. [192]

"Our Lord, we've heard the call of one who calls us to faith. 'Believe in the Lord,' (he said), and we do have faith.

"Our Lord, forgive us our sins, pardon our shortcomings and take our souls back to You in the company of the righteous. [193]

"Our Lord, grant us what You've promised us through Your messengers, and save us from humiliation on the Day of Assembly, for You never break Your word." [194]

Equality in Righteousness before Allah

 Their Lord has accepted them (and will comfort them by) saying, [337] *"I'll never let the efforts of any of you who made an effort (on behalf of Allah) to become lost, be they male or female, for you're equally from each other. Those who left their homes, or who were driven away, or who suffered in My cause, or who fought or were killed, I will pardon their shortcomings and admit them to gardens beneath which rivers flow - and a reward from Allah's Own presence is the best reward of all!"* [195]

Don't be fooled by those who suppress (the light of faith within their hearts) and who seem to do (whatever they please in the land without getting punished). [196] It's only a brief time of pleasure for them - *a time that will be followed by Hellfire* – and oh, how terrible a destination! [197]

However, those who are mindful (of their duty) to their Lord will soon find themselves among gardens beneath which rivers flow, *and there they'll live forever!* (That's) a dispensation from Allah, and what's with Allah is best for the righteous. [198]

---

[336] Years after the Prophet passed away, Ibn 'Umar and 'Ubayd ibn 'Umayr went to visit the Prophet's widow A'ishah. She spoke to them from behind a curtain and said, "'Ubayd, why haven't you come to visit more often?" He answered, "Remember what the poet said, 'Visit every once in a while, and you'll be loved all the more.'" Ibn 'Umar then asked A'ishah, "Tell us about the most unusual thing you ever saw the Messenger of Allah do." A'ishah paused and began to weep. Then she said, "Everything he did was amazing. One night, he came close to me until his skin touched my skin, and he said, 'Let me worship my Lord.' I said to him, 'By Allah, I love your being close to me, and I also love it when you worship your Lord.' Then he used a water skin to perform ablution, without wasting any water, and he stood up in prayer and cried until his beard became wet. Then he prostrated and cried until the floor was wet. Then he laid down on his side and cried. When Bilal came to alert the Prophet about the coming of the dawn prayer, (he saw the Prophet's eyes red from weeping), and he said, 'Messenger of Allah! Why are you crying when Allah has already forgiven your future and past sins?' He answered, 'Bilal, what's keeping you from crying, when this night these verses were revealed to me? Whoever recites them, but then doesn't think deeply upon them, will be ruined.'" (*Ibn Kathir*)

[337] Umm Salamah was the first woman to migrate from Mecca to Medina during the exodus of Muslims from pagan persecution. She once asked the Prophet why Allah didn't mention women specifically when He praised those who migrated for His sake. This verse was revealed to answer her question. (*Bukhari*)

The Sincerity of True Jews and Christians

$\mathcal{A}$mong the Followers of Earlier Revelation are some who believe in Allah and in the revelation sent to both you and to them. [338]

They stand in awe of Allah and don't sell the verses of Allah for a small profit. They'll certainly have their reward waiting with their Lord, for Allah is quick in settling accounts. [199]

O you who believe! Be patient (in adversity), (strive together) in perseverance, and labor on. Be mindful (of your duty) to Allah so you can be truly successful. [200]

---

[338] This verse was revealed when the king of Abyssinia died. He was the Christian king who accepted a number of Muslim refugees who had fled persecution in Mecca, and who refused to hand them over to a visiting delegation of Meccan idol-worshippers who wanted to imprison them. The Prophet asked his community to pray for him, and he beseeched Allah to accept him and forgive him. When the hypocrites of Medina heard about this, they began taunting the Muslims for praying for someone who was not of their religion. This verse was revealed in response. (*Asbab ul-Nuzul*) Some commentators say the king accepted Islam before he died.

The Women

4 An-Nisa'
Medinan Period

The greater part of the various verses of this chapter was revealed during the fourth year after the arrival of the Prophet in Medina at a time when many social issues were being addressed. There were long-standing Arab customs about which the community asked the Prophet with regard to marital life, gender equality and the family. Although traditional Arabian culture held little regard for the rights or status of women, the basic premise taken by the Qur'an was that women were the equals of men before Allah. This was quite a revolutionary concept in a society that devalued women to the point of practicing infanticide against unwanted female newborns.

The Qur'an altered or abolished many such ignorant Arab customs and offered a new compact in the family structure. While men were still given the symbolic leadership role in the family, the rights of women were vastly expanded and documented in scripture. The most noble husband, in the words of Muhammad, is the one who is most kind and dutiful to his family. This chapter also talks about the dangers that hypocrites pose to a morally ordered society. Interfaith issues are also addressed with regard to some of the theological differences among Islam, Judaism and Christianity.

In the Name of Allah,
the Compassionate, the Merciful

O people! Be mindful of your Lord Who created you from a single soul and from her (He) created its mate. [339] From these two were raised all the multitudes of men and women (all over the world).

Be mindful of Allah, the One in Whose name you demand your mutual (rights), and (have respect for women from whose) wombs (you are all born), for Allah is certainly observing you. [340] [1]

---

[339] Males and females are nearly identical in all respects, merely differing in some biological and psychological aspects that form the basis of what are considered to be standard gender differences. In this verse, we are asked to consider how closely related the general physical and mental processes of each gender are. Thus, no believer should oppress someone or look down upon someone simply because he or she is of another gender. The Prophet once remarked, "Truly, women are the twin-halves of men." (*Ahmad, Abu Dawud*) In this verse, it is interesting to note that the term used here for *soul* is feminine, and the word for mate is given the pronoun for belonging to her, i.e., *her* mate. Science has proven that all humans alive in the world today are descended from a single female who lived in remote antiquity. Adam, then, was merely the mate of this woman, whom we know as – *Eve!*

[340] Mothers hold a special status in Islam. Once a man asked the Prophet who was most worthy of his respect and care, and the Prophet replied, "Your mother." The man asked who would be next two more times, and each time the Prophet said, "Your mother." On the fourth time the Prophet said, "Your father." (*Bukhari*) He also remarked once that Paradise lies under the feet of mothers. (*Ahmad*)

The Strong shall not Oppress the Weak

$\mathcal{R}$eturn to the orphans (who are under your care) their rightful property (when they're of mature legal age), and don't substitute your inferior goods for their superior ones. [341] Don't swallow up their possessions by losing track of them in yours, for that's an enormous crime. [342] [2]

Don't Marry Female Orphans to Cheat them or Oppress Them

$\mathcal{I}$f any of you (men) fear that you might not be able to treat orphaned (women) with justice, [343] (by being tempted to marry them for their money while they have no guardian to look after their interests), [344] then marry (other) women of your choice, up to two, three, or four. [345]

---

[341] A man from the large tribe of Ghatafan was the guardian of his orphaned nephew and his property. When the boy came of age, he requested to be given control over his property, but his uncle had mixed all of the boy's property with his own, and he refused to relinquish it to him. The nephew went to the Prophet to complain, and this verse was revealed as a result. When the uncle learned of it, he accepted Allah's judgment and released the property to his nephew. (*Asbab ul-Nuzul*)

[342] It must not be underestimated how cruel and calculating the pre-Islamic Arabs were. When a female child of the clan was orphaned, her guardian would take her in and often take her on as another wife just to get her inheritance, if any was due to her. If she were ugly, he would prevent her from marrying another man and would keep her around in misery until she died so he could take her money. This verse unequivocally required the believers to return an orphan's property – all of it – when they came of age. Also see 2:220.

[343] A'ishah, the Prophet's wife, said this verse was revealed with regards to a man who unscrupulously married an orphan girl who came of age while under his care – a girl who had no one else to look out for her interests - just to keep control of the fruit farm in which they both held an interest. He then seized her share and offered her no dowry. (*Bukhari*)

[344] To rein in the abuse of those would marry rich orphan girls for their money, men were forbidden by this verse from marrying such girls who came of age unless they gave them their due rights and a proper dowry and obtained their consent. If they couldn't be fair and offer premium dowries, then the men were instructed to marry other women. By the way, forced marriage is also prohibited in Islam, and those people who continue to practice it are violating an important Islamic principle. The Prophet said, "A widow and divorcee cannot be married unless she gives her consent, and a virgin shall not be married until her consent is obtained." (*Bukhari, Muslim*) The Prophet actually annulled one marriage when a girl came to him complaining that she had been forced to marry someone against her will. (*Abu Dawud*)

[345] This verse addresses a certain crisis that was facing the Muslim community in Medina. The Muslims had already fought the Meccan idol-worshippers in two major battles at Badr (624) and at Uhud (625), and the population of Muslim men plummeted from approximately 900 down to around 700 due to attrition and other similar reasons. This left a lot of widows, orphans and women of marriageable age who would not be able to find husbands. At that time in history, the surest way for a woman to live within the social safety net was if she were married. Thus, some of the men needed to take on more than one wife for the benefit of these women, and this was the reason for nearly all of Muhammad's marriages, as well. On the flip side, Arabian custom placed no restrictions on the number of wives a man could have, so some men had five, ten or even more wives. The Prophet asked such men to retain only four and divorce the rest. (As the Prophet of Allah, Muhammad was allowed by special dispensation to retain more than four because he had to be free to contract alliances through marriage and his wives became *de facto* instructors of Islam for the entire community.) Polygamy in Islam is not supposed to be the norm, however, nor is it supposed to be about lust, but rather about supporting women who wouldn't otherwise be able to find a spouse. Indeed, the Qur'an, as this verse shows, was putting new restrictions on the pre-existing practice of polygamy to improve the rights of women. Before Islam, a man could marry as many wives as he wanted, and he was under no obligation to treat them equally in any respect. The Qur'an introduced reforms and put an onerous restriction upon the man who wanted to have more than one wife. If he could not be fair, then Allah would hold him accountable. Indeed, the Prophet once said that a man who had more than one wife and was not fair between them would be raised up on Judgment Day with half his body paralyzed! (*Abu Dawud, Mishkat, Nisa'i, Tirmidhi*) Again, it must be remembered that polygamy is not the called for norm in

If you're afraid that you might not be able to treat (multiple wives) equally, then marry only one (woman) or (marry a maid-servant) who is under your authority. [346] This will help keep you from committing injustice. [3]

Give women their rightful dowries in the spirit of an honest gift. [347] However, if

---

Islam, and this passage counsels a man that if he cannot deal fairly with women, then he must confine himself to one. This sentiment is echoed in verse 4:129 where we learn that it is well-nigh impossible to deal fairly between women. The overwhelming majority of Muslim marriages from the beginning of Islam until today have been with one man and one woman. Polygamy is grudgingly allowed only to address a situation like the Muslims faced when this verse was revealed. Bertrand Russell once wrote on this topic, saying, "And in all countries where there is an excess of women, it is an obvious injustice that those women who by arithmetical necessity must remain unmarried should be wholly debarred from sexual experience." (*Marriage and Morals*, p. 47). (It also aids in situations where the wife is barren or otherwise uninterested in sex, and thus a husband with no other options might be inclined to extramarital affairs or divorce.) Judaism, Hinduism and Christianity have also traditionally allowed polygamy. See Deuteronomy 21:15, Exodus 21:10, II Chronicles 11:21 and also I Timothy 3:2, 12, where only a *bishop* or a *deacon* is limited to one wife, for example, (although Jesus allegedly counseled men not to marry at all in Matthew 19:12, and Paul seconded it in I Corinthians 7:27-35). Each of these religions has placed its own regulations upon polygamy, though both Judaism and Christianity have since largely ceased to recognize it as valid alternative due to the influence of persistent Roman cultural values in the Medieval period, save for some sects of Mormonism (though their particular practices are seemingly unregulated when compared to Islam). Benefice, the Confessor of Lower Germany, consulted Pope Gregory in the year 726 in order to know in what cases a husband might be allowed to have two wives. Pope Gregory replied on the 22nd of November of the same year in these words: "If a wife be attacked by a malady which renders her unfit for conjugal intercourse, the husband may marry another, but in that case he must allow his sick wife all necessary support and assistance." One Christian writer summed it up this way: "The New Testament contains no specific injunction against plural marriages. It was commonplace for the nobility among the Christians and Jews to contract plural marriages. Luther spoke of it with toleration." (Caesar E. Farah, *Islam: Beliefs and Observances*, 4th edition, Barron's, U.S. 1987, p. 69) Therefore, neither Christians nor Jews have any basis to criticize Islam for allowing a highly regulated emergency practice that their own religions also technically and historically allow.

[346] The norm in Islam is for a man to have only one wife. Polygamy is allowed with certain restrictions, but is uncommon among Muslims in general, even to this day. Now the question often comes up: can a man marry a second wife without taking the consent of the first? This is an issue that is the subject of serious debate in scholarly circles. The conservative consensus thus far has been that it is not required, (unless the wife writes it into her marriage contract at the time of marriage). It is, at the least, considered good manners on the part of the husband to inform his wife first and get her opinion. It is interesting to note that when 'Ali ibn Abi Talib (d. 661) wanted to take a second wife, Fatimah (d. 633), his only wife and the daughter of the Prophet, was so upset that she went to her father in tears. The Prophet said that whoever makes Fatimah angry makes him angry, and so 'Ali backed down and did not take a second wife. Thus, from this story we can reasonably conclude that although a man might not need his wife's permission, he still must inform her beforehand to see how the issue plays out with her and her family.

[347] In pre-Islamic times, when a man wanted to marry a woman, he would pay a "sale" price to her father or other responsible male relative. Islam changed that custom and instead made the woman the owner of her own freedom and the one who receives her dowry, which would be like an insurance policy for her against future loss, divorce or an opportunity for her to invest to augment her own livelihood. Thus, when a Muslim man desires to marry any woman, he has to gain her consent and then pay the dowry directly to her at the time of the marriage ceremony. (The word for dowry in Arabic is *mahr*, but in this verse it is referred to as *sadaqa*, a word that implies a gift given in honest friendship. See 2:236.) The woman can set the dowry as she likes, and it belongs exclusively to her. If a woman sets a very high dowry and her groom is unable to pay it all, she may defer its payment at a later date. If a man passes away before the payment of the dowry is completed, then its value must come out of his estate and be paid to his widow as a debt owed to her. (In modern times, there has been a curious trend, encouraged by men for obvious reasons, in which women are encouraged to take 'the high road' and ask for only token dowries. There is no shame in Islam, however, for asking for substantial dowries, and many women coupled with such men have later regretted their paltry compensation.)

they return a portion of it to you of their own free will, then accept it and enjoy it as a wholesome pleasure. [348] [4]

When should a Young Orphan's Inheritance be Given to Them?

$\mathcal{D}$on't entrust those who are immature with the property that Allah provided for you as a support. Instead, feed and clothe them (from your resources) and speak to them kindly. [349] [5]

Evaluate (the level of maturity) of orphans when they reach a marriageable age. [350] When you determine that they're able to handle the responsibility (of managing their affairs alone), then release their property to them.

Don't be wasteful with their wealth nor spend it rapidly before they reach maturity. [351] If the guardian is rich, then let him claim no compensation. If he's poor, then he can claim a reasonable portion. When you're prepared to release their goods to them, take witnesses in their presence, though no one can do a better accounting than Allah. [6]

General Inheritance Guidelines

$\mathcal{B}$oth men and women have a share in (the estates) that their parents and nearest relatives leave behind, [352] and

---

[348] This verse counsels men to pay the dowry in a spirit of good cheer, and not grudgingly, which is a kind of unfair pressure on their wife-to-be. A man is not allowed to take back any dowry he gave his wife after he marries her. If the wife later remits some of it of her own free-will, then take it as a double boon. The Prophet said, "Beware! Do not wrong. Remember that a person's property is not lawful (for you to take) unless he gives it to you of his own free will." (*Mishkat*)

[349] This is, at first glance, a general statement of caution: don't let immature or weak-minded youngsters manage their own property, for they will become the victims of unscrupulous vultures. If a young boy or girl is unable to make wise decisions regarding the wealth that's rightfully his or hers by inheritance, then a guardian must be appointed to oversee his or her wealth until such time as he or she becomes able to make sound judgments. Children below the age of puberty and people who are temporarily insane or otherwise mentally challenged fall into this category. (*Ibn Kathir*) The Prophet said, "There is no orphan after the age of puberty, and there is no vowing to be silent throughout the day until the end of the day." (*Abu Dawud*) The Prophet thus set puberty as the dividing line between a child and an adult. (For example, he set the minimum age for a male to join the army at 15 years of age. - *Ibn Kathir*) Clearly, this verse, in context with the surrounding verses, refers to orphans below the age of puberty; yet, in another example of how chauvinism can be used to misuse religion, a handful of ultra-conservative modern scholars have extrapolated this verse to mean that women of any age could be forced to surrender their inherited wealth to a male guardian on the specious claim that women are 'inexperienced' and 'feeble-minded.' The earliest Muslims did not practice such an abominable custom, and did not Khadijah, the Prophet's first wife, spend her money wisely when she spent her inherited wealth to support the mission of the Messenger of Allah? Mainstream schools of Islamic law set the age for maturity (and property-release) as low as fifteen for both boys and girls (*Hanafi*).

[350] Marriageable age is defined for males as the attainment of puberty, with males having the additional requirement of having to achieve the basic financial ability to support a family. For females, the marriageable age is any time after the attainment of puberty, the precise age of which varies greatly among individual females.

[351] The guardian of an orphan who is either underage or undereducated is obligated to withhold his or her property until such time as the orphan can make rational and sound decisions for himself. A man named Ibn Rafa'a died, leaving his infant son behind. The boy's uncle took charge of him and his inheritance. He went to the Prophet and said, "My nephew is an orphan in my lap. When should I give him his property?" This verse, which gives the advice to wait until orphans are of mature mind, was revealed in response. (*Asbab ul-Nuzul*)

[352] A man in Medina named Auws ibn Thabit passed away, leaving behind a widow, a young boy and two daughters. His two cousins, Su'ad and Arfaja, seized his property under the longstanding Arabian custom that women and children do not inherit. The traditional view was that only tough and warlike men deserve each other's property upon death. The widow proposed to the two men that each of them should marry one of her daughters, so they would receive some support from their deceased father's

whether it's a little or a lot, there's a calculated share. [7] If other (more distant) relatives or orphans or the poor are present at the time of the distribution, then give something (of the estate) to them and console them with words of kindness. 353 [8]

Those who are charged (with the distribution of the property) should keep in mind the anxiety of having to leave a helpless family behind. Let them be mindful (of Allah) and speak words of comfort. 354 [9] Those who unjustly

consume the property of orphans only fill their bellies with fire, and for (their callousness they'll soon be made) to roast in a raging blaze! [10]

Who Gets What?

$\mathcal{A}$llah Himself gives you the following directions about your children's (inheritance): 355 the male shall receive a portion equal to what's given to two females. 356 If there are only females, two

---

property, but the pair refused. (This incident happened before the verses guaranteeing women and children's inheritance right were revealed.) The widow went to the Prophet to plead for help, saying, "Messenger of Allah, (my husband) died leaving me and three children, and I am a woman with no resources to spend (on my children). Their father left a valuable piece of land, which is now held by Su'ad and Arfaja, and they are not giving me or my children anything from it. They don't even care about his (orphaned) children at all." The Prophet asked to see the two cousins, and they said, "Messenger of Allah, her children don't ride horses or supply fodder, nor do they battle enemies." The Prophet answered, "Leave until I see what Allah says about them." After they left, this passage was revealed to the Prophet, and the men had to give the woman and her children their rightful inheritance. (*Asbab ul-Nuzul, Ma'ariful Qur'an*)

353 These more distant relatives, who have no overt legal claim to the inheritance, serve another purpose in the inheritance process, as well. If, after all the calculated divisions of the inheritance have been distributed, there is some left over, the remaining wealth will be distributed to them. (*Ma'ariful Qur'an*)

354 The commentators explain this verse to mean that if a terminally ill person has purposely left some people out of his will who might be grieved and feel unfairly treated, he should be counseled gently to amend his will so he can leave this life while doing what is right. The Prophet said, "A man might do the deeds of the righteous for seventy years, but when it comes time to compile his will he commits injustice. So his final act will be his worst, and he will therefore enter the Fire. A man might do the deeds of the wicked for seventy years; yet, he is fair in his will, and so his final act will be his best. Therefore, he enters Paradise." (*Ahmad*)

355 There are two reports about why this verse was revealed. A report in Bukhari says that it was revealed when a dying man asked the Prophet about how he should apportion his estate. A different report in Ahmad, Abu Dawud and Tirmidhi gives the following reason. A widow went to the Prophet with her two daughters and said, "Messenger of Allah, these are the two daughters of Sa'd ibn ar-Rabi' (another version says Thabit ibn Qays) who was killed when he was with you on the Day of Uhud. Their uncle took their property and inheritance and hasn't left anything for them. What is your judgment, Messenger of Allah, for I swear by Allah that they'll never be able to marry unless they have substance." The Prophet replied that he would wait for Allah to decide the matter, which was a way of saying he would wait for a revelation from Allah. A little while later, this verse was revealed. The uncle was summoned to the Prophet and was told to give two-thirds of the estate to the daughters and one-eighth of it to the mother and that he could keep whatever was left. (Either incident could have been the catalyst for this revelation, though the second incident seems more likely given the well-developed background information.)

356 In sixth-century Arabia and in the wider world, women's inheritance rights were nearly non-existent. In those rare places where women could inherit, there were no courts to uphold their rights if greedy men seized their fortune. (The only reason Khadijah had inherited wealth from her two deceased husbands before marrying Muhammad was because her three sons had died very young.) Islam is the first system to enshrine women's right to an inheritance as a religious obligation. Many Western women couldn't inherit property until the late nineteenth century! Why do women inherit half of what men get? Quite simply because men are *required* by Islam to spend their money on their wives and families and even extended relatives (such as orphans), while women are not obligated to do the same. So, as you can see, men need the extra funds to cover their responsibilities, while the women can do what they see fit with their money. In addition, when a man wishes to marry a woman,

or more, then their share is two-thirds of the estate; if only one, her share is half. For parents, a sixth share of the inheritance to each, if the deceased left children. [357]

If the deceased left no children and his parents are the only heirs, then the mother gets a third, unless the deceased left brothers, for in that case the mother will get a sixth. (These distributions will be apportioned only) after the payment of any obligations and debts. [358]

You don't know whether your parents or your children are more deserving (of their share), so (accept) these as the settled amounts that are ordained by Allah, for Allah is knowing and wise. [11]

(Men), in what your wives leave, your share is half if they left no children. If they left children, then you'll receive a fourth, after the payment of any loans and debts. [359] In what you leave, the share (of your widows) is a fourth, if you left no children, but if you left children, then your widows will get an eighth, after the payment of any obligations and debts. [360]

If the person whose inheritance is in question has left neither parents nor children, [361] but has left a single brother or sister, then that sibling will get a sixth of the estate; but if there are more siblings, then they will split a third (of the estate among themselves), after the payment of any obligations and debts, so that no loss is caused to any. This is Allah's decision, and Allah is knowing and forbearing. [12]

These are the rules set by Allah. Whoever obeys Allah and His Messenger will be admitted to gardens beneath which rivers flow, and there they shall remain – *and that's the greatest success!* [13]

Whoever disobeys Allah and His Messenger and goes beyond His rules, then they'll be admitted into Hellfire, and there they shall remain - *a humiliating punishment!* [14]

On Shameful Behavior

𝓘f any of your women are guilty of *shameful behavior,* [362] (then you must) have

---

she is entitled to receive a *mahr,* or marriage-gift, from him, and she sets the amount she desires with no restrictions. A woman doesn't give any such funds to her prospective husband! (Additionally, if a divorce occurs, the man may have to give up some of his wealth to his divorced wife, while the woman's property is not to be touched.)

[357] Also see 4:176, which is supplementary to the provisions of this verse.

[358] Funeral expenses, for example, are to be paid from the estate. Also outstanding debts must be cleared before any calculation of the distribution. (*Ma'ariful Qur'an*)

[359] The lion's share of a deceased woman's property, then, will go to her children, rather than to her husband. Even an unborn child in the womb is entitled, by Islamic law, to have a share of inheritance set aside for it. Because the gender might not be known, it is recommended to postpone settling the estate until after the child is born. (*Ma'ariful Qur'an*)

[360] During the rule of Caliph 'Umar ibn al-Khattab, a man named Ghaylan ibn Aslamah divorced all four of his wives and distributed all his assets to his sons in order to cheat his wives out of their fair share of his estate after he passed away. When 'Umar heard of this, he said, "You've done this to deprive these women from inheriting from you, and that is an enormous injustice. Revoke the divorce pronouncements against them right now and take back the assets you gave to your sons. If you don't do this, then beware of a severe punishment." (*Tirmidhi, Ibn Majah*)

[361] The Arabic term *kalaalah* is usually understood to mean half-siblings or grandparents – in other words someone more distantly related to the deceased in lineage who can claim a share, though they have a weaker level of connection to the estate. In rare instances it happens that a person dies having neither living parents (ascendants) or children (descendants); thus, inheritance rights move up or over in the chain of ascendancy. (Also half-brothers or sisters, etc…) 'Umar ibn al-Khattab was reported to have said that he wished the Prophet had explained this point in more detail before his passing. In general, because of the word *kalaalah* Muslim scholars say this verse is referring to half brothers from the mother's side.

[362] The *shameful behavior (faahisha)* mentioned here most probably refers to lesbianism, and those women who are guilty of it are subject to home confinement until they repent and reform themselves

the evidence of four (honest) witnesses from among you (who will testify) against them.

If they testify (in court against them), [363] then confine them to their homes for life, or at least until Allah provides for them some other way (to reform their behavior). [15]

If two men among you are guilty of *shameful behavior*, punish them both, as well. [364] If they repent and reform, then leave

---

to the satisfaction of the authorities. While many classical commentators have held that the *shameful behavior* can also include adultery and fornication, which carries the punishment of 100 lashes or possibly even capital punishment for adultery (see 24:2), I find that this is debatable given the fact that the punishment of home confinement is outlined here for this specific type of *faahisha*, or shameful behavior, whereas the later verse in chapter 24 is a punishment (lashes) for a specific crime listed there (*zina*, fornication or possibly adultery). In addition, verse 7:80 specifically refers to the crime of Lot's people as *faahisha*, and as is well known, his people were homosexuals. The eminent commentators Mujahid, Qadi Thanaullah and others have also said that these verses [4:15-16] refer to same-sex relations, and I am inclined to agree based on all this evidence. (The crux of the difficulty on this issue is that the Qur'an and *hadith* use the terms *faahisha* and *zina* sometimes interchangeably and other times exclusively, though mostly the two terms are treated as separate crimes.) The legal scholars have generally agreed that beyond this home confinement (until reformation is achieved) there is no specific worldly punishment (*hadd*) for lesbianism. (As explained in *The Kuwaiti Encyclopedia of Islamic Jurisprudence*) During the rule of Abu Bakr, it was also generally agreed that lesbians got home confinement and not execution. (*Ma'ariful Qur'an*)

[363] The four witnesses have to catch the women *in the act* of shameful behavior. Mere accusations are not accepted in an *authentically constituted* Islamic court of law, and this has given rise to the view that it is nearly impossible to prove such charges legally against those who are discreet. This requirement for four witnesses is explained as a safeguard for women, who may be falsely accused by a jealous or unscrupulous relative or acquaintance. Any witnesses who make false or unsubstantiated charges against a woman are themselves to be punished with 80 lashes. (See 24:4)

[364] Many commentators believe that homosexuality is the subject of verse 16. (*Ma'ariful Qur'an*) There is a debate about the punishment for (unrepentant) homosexual men (as none is openly specified here), though their punishment is potentially more severe than the home confinement a lesbian would receive. Since this verse doesn't offer any specific penalty, it is, therefore, the reason that there is a divergence of opinion. (Some early scholars considered the home confinement mentioned previously as applicable to men, also, while most other scholars from early times until today do not.) There is a tradition in which the Prophet is reported to have said, "Allah curses the men who do what the People of Lot did." (*at-Targheeb wa at-Tarheeb*) In another narration he said, "If two men come upon each other, they are both guilty of unlawful sex (*zina*)." The punishment for *zina* is then outlined in 24:2 and it would seem that the matter should rest there. However, there is a report that says that the Prophet called for (unrepentant) homosexuals to be executed, (*Tirmidhi*), but the timing and circumstances of that pronouncement have not been fully documented or explored. (The Bible, of course, prescribes death for homosexuals, see Leviticus 20:13.) In fact, the companions of the Prophet, after his passing, differed over the punishment for homosexuality, and this has led to a divergence of opinion among the legal scholars to this day. Conservative scholars generally adhere to the position that convicted (unrepentant) homosexuals (four witnesses catching them in the act) must be given capital punishment by stoning or some other equally gruesome means, though some legal traditions, such as the Hanafi school of thought, hold that a whipping (as in 24:2) for the first offense is permissible. In most Muslim nations today, where the legal code addresses homosexuality, a combination of fines and/or jail time (home confinement?) is the usually imposed sanction upon unrepentant homosexuals. The key points to remember are that Islam holds that the homosexual is still a human being whom Allah wishes to guide back to Him, (though Islam doesn't consider homosexuality a valid lifestyle, holding that it goes against nature and the purpose of gender differentiation). (See 7:80-81) Further, Islam teaches that the homosexual can ultimately repent of his acts and be "left alone" by society. For those who believe that homosexuality is an innate or preprogrammed identity, there is a report that the Prophet said, "He who has a desire and remains chaste and conceals his secret until his death, dies a martyr." In other words, if one feels that he is born with a certain orientation, if he resists it and keeps it secret, he will get a mighty reward from Allah for surmounting that challenge. No one is given a burden greater than he can bear, so all men and women have the capacity to resist their lower physical desires, whatever they are, for the sake of Allah. Ibn Qayyim al-Jawziyyah (d. 1350) gave this advice: "Repel the thought, for if you don't it

them alone, for Allah is accepting of repentance and merciful. [16]

Allah accepts the repentance of those who engage in immorality in ignorance and who then repent soon afterwards, for Allah will turn to them in mercy, and Allah is knowing and wise. [365] [17]

The repentance of habitual wrongdoers, however, is in vain, even until (the time of) death when one of them says, "*Now I'm ready to repent.*" (Allah also will not accept the repentance) of those who die in a state of rejection (of Allah's truth). They're the ones for whom We've prepared a dreadful punishment! [18]

Don't Treat Women Cruelly

O you who believe! [366] You're not allowed to inherit women against their will, neither should you leave them to languish in the hopes of (forcing them to divorce you) and thus getting back part of the marriage gift that you gave them [367] - except in cases where they're guilty of *shameful behavior*. [368]

Therefore, you (men) should live with (your wives) in kindness and goodwill.

If you become disenchanted with them, it may be that you are disliking something through which Allah will bring much good (for you). [369] [19]

However, if you decide to take one wife in place of another, even if you've given the first one a huge mound of gold as a marriage gift, don't take the least bit of it back.

Would you try to take it by slander and obvious sinfulness? [20]

How could you take it that way when you both have been intimate with each other, and after they've made a solemn agreement with you? [21]

---

becomes an idea. Repel the idea, for if you don't it will become a desire. Fight against the desire, for if you don't it will become an action. If you don't replace it with the opposite course of action, it will become a constant habit, and at that point, it will become difficult to change." (*Al-Fawa'id*)

[365] There is agreement among the classical scholars that every sin committed, even the willfully done ones, is a sign of ignorance. The companions of the Prophet used to say, "Every sin that a servant commits, he commits out of ignorance." (*At-Tabari*) Islam takes into account that there are people who, because of some mental incapacity, are not really responsible consciously for their actions. The Prophet said, "The Pen (that records deeds) is raised for three: a sleeping person until he wakes up, a child until he reaches the age of puberty and an insane person until he becomes sane." (*Abu Dawud, Nisa'i*)

[366] A curious pre-Islamic custom held that if a man died, his son from another wife could claim first rights on her as a wife, in effect *inheriting* his step-mother! He would solidify this claim in public by draping his cloak over her and declaring her to be his. He could also opt to marry her off to someone else that he chose, keeping any dowry she received, or he might keep her around his household to get any inheritance that might be due to her after she died. If he neither treated her as a wife nor married her off, she would be in effective social limbo and would be miserable and destitute. In Medina, one woman named Kubaysha bint Ma'an, whose husband had recently passed away, approached the Prophet complaining that her son-in-law Qays wanted to inherit her as his wife. The revelation of this verse put an end to this practice.

[367] This injunction forbids husbands or other relatives from using tricks or force to get back some of a woman's dowry or other property she owns. In cases where the woman has allowed her husband to defer some of the dowry payments, she is doubly vulnerable, so this verse is protecting her interests. (*Ma'ariful Qur'an*) The Prophet said, "None but a noble man treats women in an honorable manner, and none but a disgraceful man treats women disgracefully." (*Tirmidhi*)

[368] If the wife cheats on her husband, then he has the right to divorce her and claim some of the dowry as compensation. (*Ma'ariful Qur'an*)

[369] The Prophet once made a similar remark in a famous tradition in which he said, "A believing man must not hate a believing woman because for every quality he dislikes, there is another one that he will like." (*Muslim*)

Who are We Forbidden to Marry?

$\mathcal{D}$on't marry those women whom your fathers have married - except for whatever happened in the past, (before this rule was revealed), for it was shameful and despicable and a deplorable custom. [22]

You're also forbidden to marry your mothers, daughters, sisters, paternal and maternal aunts, nieces from your brothers or sisters, foster-mothers who nursed you, foster-sisters (who nursed from the same wet-nurse as you), your step-mothers, your step-daughters in your care, born of a conjugal wife - though there is no sin for you in this if (you divorced the step-daughter's mother) without consummating the marriage, your biological son's wives and also two sisters in wedlock at the same time, except for whatever happened in the past (before this rule was revealed), for Allah is forgiving and merciful. [23]

Conversion to Islam and the Status of Pagan Marriage

$\mathcal{A}$ll women who are already married are forbidden for you (to marry), [370] except for those (pagan women) who come under your control (as maid-servants, and who convert to Islam freely, nullifying their pagan marriage tie).

Allah has ordained (these limits) for you, and except for these (limits) all other (women) are lawful (to marry), provided you court them with gifts from your property, *desiring chastity and not lust.*

Since you gain benefits from them, give them their (marriage gifts) as you're required. However, if after the required (marriage gift) is settled you mutually agree (to modify it), there is no blame upon you, for Allah is knowing and wise. [371] [24]

If any (man) among you doesn't have the means to marry respectable believing women, then he should marry believing women from among those who are under your control, [372] and Allah is fully aware (of the quality) of your faith.

---

[370] This verse was revealed in answer to a question raised by some of Muhammad's companions, who captured a number of women during the Campaign of Hunayn, in which a bitter and aggressive foe (the tribes of the city of Ta'if) declared war on the Muslims of Medina. The people of Ta'if foolishly brought out their entire population and wealth to the battlefield under the odd belief that it would make their warriors fight harder. It didn't work, and the warriors of Ta'if fled away, leaving their families behind to be captured. Soon, some of the companions asked if it was lawful to marry some of those captive women (assuming they would also convert from paganism), but the companions were concerned that some of them were already married to idol-worshippers, whom they knew. The men of Ta'if eventually accepted Islam (after some weeks) and sent representatives to Medina to petition the Prophet to get their goods and families back. He gave them the choice of their families or their captured wealth. They chose their families, and the Prophet asked that all the captured women and children be released.

[371] A Muslim may not marry a woman who is already married. The only exception is for pagan women who happen to be captured in a battlefield situation and then willingly convert to Islam. If they were pagans and then freely convert to Islam, then their previous pagan marriage is considered null and void after the passage of three monthly courses, and Muslim men are free to court them and marry them if the women then choose to accept their offers.

[372] Maidservants (who are not to be confused with hired domestic employees) are allowed for free men to take in marriage, and this option is especially important if it is too expensive (on account of the dowry) to marry a woman of higher status. (See 24:32, also the Old Testament allows it in Deuteronomy 21:10-14.) Conversely, free women are allowed to marry male servants, if they so choose. The scholars generally hold that marrying a servant or a non-Muslim is the less desirable

You (people) are all from each other (so don't judge a potential spouse by his or her lower-class status).

Marry (maidservants) with the permission of their retainers, and give them their marriage gifts according to what is fair. [373]

---

option for an individual, if he or she has the means to marry a free, believing Muslim. (*Ma'ariful Qur'an*) Some early scholars in the Umayyad, and especially in Abbasid, times put forward the view that Islam allows a man to have sexual relations outside of marriage with any and all maidservants he has control over, even as the Bible allows it in Deuteronomy 21:11-14. This was, of course, a gross misinterpretation of the Qur'anic allowance to marry maidservants or captives and have relations with them, and it became a terribly abused practice among some ruling dynasties. Although this egregious misunderstanding is still prevalent in many ultra-conservative circles today, a number of contemporary Muslim scholars are beginning to challenge this view. One of the key understandings is in the progressive nature of the Islamic message. Just as in the case of the prohibition of alcohol, which involved several steps over many years, the Qur'anic revelation was changing the nature of the "master-servant" relationship. In pre-Islamic Arabia, chattel slavery was the norm, and slaves had absolutely no rights. They could be abused and used at the whims of their masters, and this included torture, murder, sexual abuse and forced prostitution. With the coming of Islam, reforms came, though in an evolving fashion, for as in the case of the prohibition of alcohol, a culture cannot be changed overnight. The Prophet was training and redirecting Arab culture away from ruthless barbarity and towards goodness and righteousness, and it is a testament to his efforts that he succeeded in so many respects. In the first ten years of his mission in Mecca, there was no mention of prohibiting sexual relations with slaves. What we do find is that the concept of being a chattel slave was challenged. The Prophet forced his companions to treat their slaves fairly, as human beings, and he also encouraged them to free slaves at every chance they had to seek Allah's pleasure. (Abu Bakr, for example, became an avid purchaser of slaves' freedom.) The Prophet also taught his followers to accept slaves and former slave converts as equals in brotherhood, and this last point was particularly annoying to the Meccan elite, who accused the Prophet of 'upsetting social order.' Later, in Medina, new regulations came, saying that slaves could no longer be called 'slaves' and that masters could no longer be called 'masters.' Indeed, those terms no longer fit within the shifting paradigm between the two states of being. Other new rules were that "those you had control over" had to be clothed and fed like their "retainers" and that "their fellows" could not be beaten, housed poorly, abused, insulted or overworked. (*Bukhari*) Even further, the Qur'an instituted a system whereby such "bonded servants" could arrange to purchase their freedom. (See 24:33) Kidnapping as a way to gain slaves was also prohibited. Prostituting maidservants was also quickly forbidden, and soon the notion that a man could marry maidservants if he couldn't afford to marry a free woman came about. The Prophet said, "Any man who has a maidservant whom he educates, teaches good manners, and then frees and marries will get a double reward." (*Bukhari*) Further reforms after that made the idea of "slavery" virtually no different from enlightened indentured servitude – a temporary position a person may find themselves in due to being captured on the battlefield. (*Ma'ariful Qur'an*)

[373] If a man or woman wants to marry a servant who is under someone else's authority, he or she can, provided he or she asks permission of the retainer. If a person marries a servant of his or her own, then the servant is automatically freed from *bonded servanthood*. Throughout this translation, we specifically refer to servants as servants, and not slaves, for the concept of *slavery* in the Western world is completely out of synch with what has been allowed in Islam. The Qur'an envisions a world in which servanthood is generally a kind of punitive condition for captured enemy combatants – a condition from which they may emerge either through conversion, their own contractual efforts, or the charitable act of their retainer or others. In the Qur'an, we read about people marrying their servants and even that believing servants are superior for one's sons and daughters to marry over free idol-worshippers. [2:221]. In Western-style slavery, there is no concept that a master or mistress can *marry* a slave. Even further, in Western civilization, slaves are considered to be mere property that can be used and abused at will for any purpose. In Islam, by contrast, *servants* are still human beings, and the Prophet forbade abusing them – even a slap is generally forbidden. (Once the Prophet saw 'Abdullah ibn Mas'ud raise his hand to slap his servant, and the Prophet said, "Allah has more power over you than you have over him!" Ibn Mas'ud lowered his hand quickly and then freed the servant.) The Prophet made the following provisions (found throughout the *hadith* books) regarding ownership of a servant: a free person cannot be kidnapped or impressed into servanthood for any other reason than being captured on the field of battle, in a war and while the enemy has not surrendered nor negotiated terms of war conduct. (*Ma'ariful Qur'an*) A debtor cannot be made into a servant on account of his debts. A servant cannot be made to work inordinately long or strenuously. A person must help their

Take them as respectable (wives) and not merely as objects of lust or as secret mistresses. [374]

If they fall into *shameful behavior* after having been taken in marriage then their punishment is half that of higher-class women.

This (provision for reduced punishment) is for those among you who fear giving in (to your lustful impulses with women who are less able to resist you, and who thus should not be held to the same level of accountability as you), though it's better for you that you persevere (against your urges), and Allah is forgiving and merciful. [375] [25]

Allah wants to make (everything) clear for you so He can guide you towards the (same wholesome) example of those (believing people) who came before you, and (He wants) to turn towards you (in mercy with easy-to-follow regulations), for Allah is knowing and wise. [376] [26]

Allah wants to turn towards you, but those who follow their own whims want to turn you far away (from Allah)! [27]

Allah wants to lighten (your burden), for human beings have been created weak (to temptation). [28]

---

servants with arduous tasks. Anyone who has a servant must feed and clothe him or her according to what he or she does for himself. A non-Muslim servant cannot be forcibly converted. A maidservant cannot be used as a prostitute. A servant is not allowed to call his or her retainer their *master,* and a retainer is not allowed to call his or her servant their *slave.* Servants are like our brothers. A maidservant cannot be separated from her children, and a servant has the right to buy his or her freedom by holding down an extra job to buy out his service. If a maidservant marries her retainer and bears a child with him, she is automatically freed. A freed servant is not stigmatized socially, and among the greatest good deeds for a believer is to free a servant from servitude. Thus, as many writers have pointed out, Islam took the existing system of Arab chattel slavery, placed countless restrictions on it, reformed it into bonded servitude and provided a way to eventually eliminate it as a practice all together. Compare this system to the full-fledged chattel slavery such as that practiced in the West until the mid-nineteenth century, (justified by many biblical passages such as Genesis 9:18-27, Leviticus 25:44-45, Exodus 21:20-21 and I Peter 2:18), and eliminated only after lengthy wars and bitter campaigns. Thus, as you can see, there is no concept of slavery in Islam as the West understands it or practiced it. It is more akin to indentured servitude than anything else.

[374] Men are told not to look for mistresses and secret girlfriends, especially among those women whose freedom of choice or available options are more limited. It would be unfair for a man to take advantage of the situation. In Islam, it's either get married or stay single. There is no middle ground.

[375] A bad man may take advantage of a woman who is at a disadvantage economically or in social status. If a man pressures a maidservant into becoming his mistress, he should know that while he has to bear the full punishment of fornication (see 24:2), her punishment is halved, keeping in mind her diminished ability to make empowered choices for herself. Although she could have potentially held firm against his advances, it is unfair to hold her to the same level of culpability given the unequal power dynamics of such a relationship. (Even the Old Testament makes such a provision in Leviticus 19:20.) Even if a maidservant gets married to someone, if she commits a crime of passion, her punishment is still half given her lack of truly free options. As always, the Qur'an advises us to be strong against our urges if it goes against the law of Allah.

[376] Does Islam give parents the right to force their children, particularly their daughters, to marry whom they (the parents) select? Absolutely not! There is the tendency in many traditional cultures, Muslim and non-Muslim, to make arranged matches against the wishes of the children, but this has no sanction in Islam. During the Prophet's time, a young lady named Khansa bint Khidan, who was forced into marrying someone, went and complained of it to the Prophet. The Prophet told her that her marriage was then cancelled if she wished. The lady said she would remain with the man to whom she was married, but she just wanted to make sure that girls had a choice in whom they married. (*Bukhari*) Islamic law stipulates that if a woman is forced into marriage, then that marriage has no legal standing, and she can sue to be free of it. The Prophet said, "A woman should not be given in marriage unless she gives her consent, and a virgin girl should also not be married unless she gives her consent." (*Bukhari*)

Allah's Mercy is Vast

O you who believe! Don't devour each other's possessions recklessly (in wasteful pursuits). Rather, let there be business and trade based upon mutual good will.

Neither should you kill yourselves, for Allah is a source of mercy towards you. [377] [29]

As for the one who does that with malicious intent and a desire to do wrong, We'll soon throw him in a fire, and that's easy for Allah to do. [30]

If you avoid the major sins that you were forbidden to do, then We'll erase your minor faults and admit you through a noble gate (leading into Paradise). [31]

Allah Favors each Differently

Don't be jealous of (the material) things, (such as money or fame,) that Allah has blessed some of you with more than others. [378]

For men there is a share of what they earn, and for women there is a share of what they earn. [379]

---

[377] Suicide and murder are forbidden in Islam. The Prophet once remarked that a person who kills himself with a weapon or poison or by throwing himself off a mountain will be made to repeat that act endlessly in Hell. (*Bukhari, Muslim*) He also said, "Whoever kills himself with something will be punished with it on the Day of Judgment." (*Bukhari, Muslim*) The idea is that by giving up on Allah's plan for our lives, no matter how horrible our lives become or how desperate our struggle becomes, we are essentially denying Allah's power and authority over us and our fate and giving up on His mercy and ability to compensate us for our suffering in this life with a greater reward in the next. A common understanding of the nature of despair among Muslim counselors during the 'Abbasid Dynasty was that the farther away from Allah one was, the greater the extent of stress and anguish that would plague his or her life. Strong faith, if adopted, is something of an antidote for despair, the chief reason for suicide. The Prophet also remarked, "Let none of you desire death, not the one who does good, for he might do more good deeds, and not the one who behaves badly, for he might try to please Allah (one day)." (*Bukhari*) The Prophet also said, "None of you should wish for death because of some misfortune befalling him, but if a person (in despair) feels compelled to wish for death, let him say, 'O Allah! Keep me alive as long as life is better for me, and let me die if death is better for me.'" (Bukhari)

[378] So many verses were being revealed in Medina - verses that gave new and unheard of rights to women - that some jubilant women, seeing true equality for the first time in their lives, wanted to take their newfound liberation all the way to its logical end, so they began demanding the right to go to war alongside of men and to get equal shares in any booty gained. While some women did wind up inadvertently fighting in battle in the Prophet's time, (and they did receive equal shares of booty), it is a principle in Islam that women are not *required* to fight, and thus they should not seek to march out expressly for that purpose. (*at-Tabari*) Umm Salamah, one of the Prophet's wives, said to the Prophet, "Messenger of Allah, men can go out and do *jihad*, (struggle in Allah's cause, sometimes involving war), while we (women) don't, and we only get half of an inheritance." This verse was revealed to remind women that they get what they are entitled to from unrestricted business, inheritance, dowry, etc. and that they should be satisfied with that and not go out of their way to seek what men gain in war. (*Ma'ariful Qur'an*)

[379] A woman went to the Prophet and said, "A man gets a double-share in inheritance, and a woman's testimony (concerning business transactions) is considered half of a man's. Does this mean that we will only get half the reward for our acts of worship?" The Prophet recited this verse and explained that men and women will get equal reward for their worship. Verse 33 then explains that everyone gets a share in inheritance and that the divisions that must be faithfully distributed by the executors (*muwali*) are designed to maximize the benefits for all. (*Ma'ariful Qur'an*) A woman gets half the share of a man, yes, but remember that a man needs to pay a dowry to a woman, and not vice-versa. A man must support his wife financially, and not vice-versa, and a man is obligated to support his family and extended relatives, if need be, and not vice-versa. By the way, the principle of women having the right to earn an income independent of any man, which is in her control exclusively, is

Ask Allah for His bounty, for Allah knows about all things. [32]

Appoint Executors to Distribute the Estate

*F*or (the benefit) of all, We've appointed executors (to distribute the estates) left behind by parents and relatives and those with whom you swore bonds (of brotherhood, and whom you wanted to share in your estate), [380] so give them what is due to them (at the time of distribution), for Allah is a witness to all things. [33]

Dealing with Domestic Disharmony

*M*en are responsible [381] for the welfare of women since Allah has given some (of you) more wherewithal [382] than others, and because they must spend of their wealth (to maintain the family).

Therefore, pious and devout women safeguard the private matters that Allah would have them safeguard. [383]

---

derived from this verse, and Islamic law has upheld this view from the very beginning of Islamic legal scholarship.

[380] In the Meccan period, the Muslims used to make each other heirs in their estates (given that many converts either had no relatives, such as the freed slaves, or they didn't want their unbelieving blood relatives to benefit from their deaths). After the Muslims were settled in Medina, blood-relatives became the focus of inheritance rights, but any leftover agreements from the old days in Mecca had to be honored. A Muslim is still allowed, though, to make bequests to non-relatives.

[381] The word *qawwamun* comes from a root word that literally means 'to stand up.' In this verse, it is used to mean safeguarding another's business, to protect their interests, to preserve and to maintain the safety of women. (Think of the English phrase used to remind men of their implied duties towards their families: 'Stand up and be a man.') This verse, then, does not say that men are the *overlords* of women or are dictators over them. Rather, it states that men must protect and look after women.

[382] The term *fadl*, which is translated here as *given more wherewithal*, can mean more bounty and even excelling in an amount over something. Some commentators say that *fadl* refers to the fact that men get twice the inheritance of a female, (an amount that they then use to spend on the women in their lives). The wording here doesn't mean that women are not *capable* of earning more *money* than men, for even the Prophet's first and only wife for over twenty years (Khadijah) was wealthier than he, nor does it mean men are *better* than women, as some superficial chauvinists have tried to read into this verse. Rather, it is an all-encompassing idea tied to a practical financial reality, and perhaps, if you want to stretch the meaning, it may also suggest that men have been given certain specific *physical* qualities that may better suit them to *protect* and *support* their families in a dangerous world: qualities ranging from more aggressiveness in defense against enemies to extra muscular strength to enable them to labor under more arduous circumstances. (This is similar to the Latin concept of *virtu*, or *manly responsibility*, from which we get the English word *virtue*.) Under this logic, because Allah made men *more suited* to protect and maintain their families in an uncertain and difficult world, men are thus 'appointed' to be officially responsible for caring for the women in their lives. (Contrast this with the words of Paul in the Bible who outright calls women the 'weaker vessel.' See I Peter 3:7.)

There is nothing wrong Islamically if a woman supports herself, especially if she has no other options, nor are women forbidden to work or engage in business, even in classical Islamic theology. (Three of the Prophet's wives, Zaynab bint Jahsh, Umm Salamah and Safiyah, continued to earn their own money while being married to him, and his first and only wife of twenty-five years, Khadijah, had been a successful businesswoman. The wife of 'Abdullah ibn Mas'ud made and sold handcrafts to support herself. Many, many other examples of Muslim women having independent jobs and livelihoods from the Prophet's time until the end of the classical period abound.) The idea is only that if there is a man in her life, then he must shoulder the greater share of the burdens of the family's expenditures and needs both in finances and security. Any money a woman earns is hers to save, invest or spend without any obligation to give it to her husband or spend it on the family.

[383] A believing woman guards her husband's secrets, lawful private business and intimate details, even as she guards her virtue, reputation and fidelity. Men are also expected to do likewise for their wives. This principle of confidentiality and faithfulness is the basis of a successful marriage, and it is also the most important thing that married people owe to each other. The Prophet once asked a group of male

As for those (women) [384] from whom you fear aggressive defiance, [385] caution them (to piety). (If they remain unmoved by your words), then leave them alone in their beds, and finally, (if they continue in their aggressive defiance), then *idribuhunna.* [386]

---

and female followers if they knew of people who talked about their intimate lives in public. The men were afraid to admit it, but a teenage girl raised her hand and said, "Yes, by Allah, the men talk about it, and the women do, too." Thereupon the Prophet said to the group, "Do you know what those people who do that are like? They're like a male and female devil who meet in the street and satisfy their desires in front of an audience." (As quoted in *The Lawful and the Prohibited in Islam* by Yusuf al-Qaradawi.) Also see 30:21 where the Qur'an also exhorts married couples to dwell together in affection and harmony, part of which is the understanding that intimate and private details must remain private.

[384] The women of Mecca were traditionally subservient to their husbands, for Mecca had a harsh and cruel culture, whereas the women of Medina were more used to standing up to their husbands, as it was a more cosmopolitan environment. After the Meccan immigrants were settled in their new homes in Medina, some men began to notice that their wives were starting to challenge them and talk back to them – even in contempt. 'Umar ibn al-Khattab (d. 644) went to the Prophet and complained about this on behalf of himself and his male friends. The Prophet innocently suggested to the men who felt that their families were in turmoil to do *daraba* (a word that can mean either separation or hitting someone, among a dozen other things). However, the next morning around 70 women complained to the Prophet's wives that their husbands had physically abused them. The Prophet became upset when he heard about the complaints, and he declared that any man who beats his wife "is not the best of you," which in prophetic lingo means "they're the worst of you." He also said that any man who beats a woman is not a good man. In other words, the men had misinterpreted or misapplied what the Prophet meant by *daraba.* (*Abu Dawud, Nisa'i,* also see 2:231.) The historian, Ibn Sa'd, includes a quote from the Prophet about this incident in which he addressed his male followers, saying, "I cannot bear the thought of a man with the veins of his neck swollen in anger against his wife while he's fighting against her." (As quoted in *Women of Medina,* trans. by Aisha Bewley.) Then the Prophet awaited a ruling from Allah, and this verse was revealed.

[385] The Arabic term used here for aggressive conflict (*nushooz*) is derived from *nashaza* which means to be elevated (i.e., haughty) or to be in marital discord, though in practical usage this word refers to those who no longer treat their spouses with the respect and kindness that each owes to the other, and instead openly disrespect and treat their spouses in a defiant and contemptuous manner over a period of time. (Some scholars have suggested that it can also include those spouses who make no secret of their attraction to others, as illustrated in a tradition from the *Muslim* collection in which the Prophet said, as part of his farewell pilgrimage, that it's a husband's right that his wife doesn't allow strange men to sit on their marital bed. See footnote below where the narration is quoted in full.) In the case of this verse, if the husband is fulfilling his duty and supports the family in justice and honor, then the wife should be loyal and faithful to her mate. For a wife to betray her husband by treating him with sustained contempt or by cavorting with other men shamefully or by revealing his private affairs maliciously, thereby treating him as an enemy, and further still, to live in open defiance of him – that's a recipe for marital disaster. (*Nushooz,* it should be mentioned, <u>does not</u> apply to simple disagreements, arguments, emotional outbursts, a lack of domestic skill or the daily give and take of marital life.) Although the Qur'an does allow both men and women to initiate divorce, (and Muhammad said it was the most hated thing in Allah's sight, out of all the things that believers are allowed to do), the basic goal is to keep families intact, especially if children are involved. Therefore, this issue of severe marital misconduct is addressed for both males and females. (As for recalcitrant males doing *nushooz,* see 4:128.)

[386] Talking, boycotting intimacy, and then *idribuhunna* (from the verb *daraba*). What does this word mean and what was the intent of its usage in this verse? This word, which means to *"put out or forth, to stretch out or forth or to set out,"* is often translated by male scholars as *beat* or *strike them,* and the abuses of this unfortunate interpretation have given rise to a great amount of unnecessary controversy and caused unconscionable violations of the Islamic rights of women. While the word can be interpreted that way (as in 8:50) in the sense of *stretching forth* (the hand to strike) it can also be used in other ways, and throughout the Qur'an it is often used in those other ways such as in 14:24 and 24:31. When this verse of the Qur'an was revealed to him, (after some men complained to him about their defiant wives,) the Prophet said of it that he had hoped for one thing from Allah but had received another. What did he hope for and what did he receive? While we do not know what he hoped for, as the evidence will show, he neither hoped for a violent *beating,* nor received the command, but something else entirely, which he also disliked. Traditional Islamic jurists have been <u>unanimous</u> in

150

However, if they accede to you (by abandoning their aggressively defiant behavior), then you have no (legitimate) grounds to act against them (any further), and Allah is full of knowledge and greatness. [387] [34]

If any of you notice (that a husband and wife) are about to split up, then

rejecting the idea that this verse gives a man permission to physically assault his wife in order to harm or injure her. Those jurists who have allowed the man to "strike" his defiant wife have insisted that it be done no more than *once* and that it be no more than a light tap to express utter disgust. (See Ibn 'Abbas's ruling of using a *miswak* or toothbrush, for example. Some scholars have even specified how to do the *daraba* as a single symbolic light tap as with the fingers or, as the ancient commentator *Razi* has suggested, a handkerchief.) Other scholars have said that the word *daraba* in this verse is to be understood as *separation* or *set them forth*. (Another form of *daraba* is *yadribuna*, which means to *strike out as a travelor*, or *tap out* as in to leave, or *hit the road*, as in verse 73:20 where people are called to travel.) So according to this interpretation, if a man feels unreasonable hostility from his wife over a long time and after talking and sleeping apart don't work, he must express his anger in a *controlled* way by literally sending her out of the marriage and going on *strike* by leaving the house (possibly leading to a divorce, which may give the wife pause for thought and leave room for reconciliation). Those who favor the second view point out that this is the process that the Prophet followed when he was having trouble with some of his wives (who were disrespecting him over his self-imposed poverty). The Prophet is the model for how to interpret and implement the Qur'an, so we need only look into the three-step process he followed to understand how to apply this verse here in question. (See 33:21.) When he was facing defiance (*nushooz*) from his wives, the Prophet first talked to them; then he boycotted sleeping with them - for an entire month. Finally, when they kept vexing him and treating him in an unreasonable way, he offered to *strike out* on his own and grant them a divorce. (See 33:28-29.) The Prophet went through all three steps outlined in this verse, and he never laid a hand in anger on any of his wives. A'ishah said, "The Prophet never beat any of his wives or servants." (*Ibn Majah, Nisa'i*) The Prophet also said, "No Muslim man should ever hit one of Allah's female servants." (*Abu Dawud, Nisa'i, Ibn Majah*) A man named Mu'awiyah went to the Prophet and later reported this exchange: "I went to the Messenger of Allah and asked him, 'What do you say about (how we must treat) our wives?' He replied, 'Give them food like you have for yourself, and clothe them with what you clothe yourself, **do not smack their faces**, and do not angrily ignore them in public.'" (*Abu Dawud*) So it is clear that both the Qur'an and the Prophet categorically forbid the harming or physical abuse of women. Now looking at this verse even closer, since *daraba* is used here in the singular (one-time) verbal form and not in the intensive (do it repeatedly) verbal form, it's also clear that it could hardly refer to a physical assault. (Who hits somebody once when they're beating them? Yet, a separation or a divorce from a spouse is something that is done usually only once, if ever.) During his last pilgrimage, the Prophet said, "Be mindful of Allah regarding women, for they are your responsibility. You have rights over your spouses, and they have rights over you. It's your right upon them that they not let anyone you dislike enter onto your bed and that they not commit open lewdness. However, if they do that, then Allah has allowed you to ignore them in the bedroom and separate (*daraba*) from them, without committing violence (i.e., by not assaulting your wife)." (*Muslim*) Therefore, when interpreted with the Prophet's application of this verse, coupled with relevant Qur'anic and *hadith* references, this verse actually forbids abusing women at all and instead counsels trial separations (perhaps leading to divorce) as the last resort open to a man who is utterly dissatisfied with an incorrigible situation. A light symbolic tap with a cloth, toothbrush or two fingers is the most allowed for a man to do to signal his frustration and possibility of leaving the marriage. This more defensible and historically appropriate interpretation is now becoming more widely accepted in the Muslim mainstream and has been offered as a legitimate interpretation since the early 1990s in popular Islamic publications such as *Islamic Horizons* and elsewhere. For more on the legal validity of this interpretation, see the book entitled, *Marital Discord*, by Abdul Hamid Abu Sulayman, published by the conservative Sunni Muslim think tank known as the International Institute of Islamic Thought (IIIT), London, 2003.

[387] Muslim women are allowed to argue and disagree with their husbands. The Prophet's own wives used to do this often, and even when he was the caliph, 'Umar ibn al-Khattab commented on this by saying it was their right to do so because they provide the benefits of child care, lawful intimacy and house care. Contrast this with the words of Apostle Paul in I Peter 3:1-2 in which he says that wives must live in subjection to their husbands. (Also see I Corinthians 14: 34-35.) Even the Hindu scriptures assume that a woman is automatically subservient to a man, whether it is to her father, brother or son. (Manusmitri, 5/151)

appoint a mediator from among his family and a mediator from among her family. If they desire to be reconciled, then Allah will bring about harmony between them, for Allah is full of knowledge and is well-informed. [388] [35]

Spend and Allah will Spend on You

Serve Allah and don't associate any partners with Him. Be good to your parents and relatives, and (be good) to orphans, the needy and your neighbors, whether they're near or far, and also to your companions around you and to travelers and to those (servants) over whom you have control. [389] Allah has no love for conceited snobs [36] or for the tightfisted or those who get other people to be tightfisted or who hide the bounty that Allah has given them. [390] We've prepared a degrading punishment for all those who suppress (their awareness of the truth)! [37]

(Allah also has no love) for those who spend their money only so that other people will notice, and who have no faith in Allah and the Last Day. Whoever takes Satan for a confidant – *oh, what an awful confidant is he!* [38]

What hassle would it be for them to believe in Allah and the Last Day and to spend out of what Allah has supplied to them? Allah knows all about them! [39] Allah is never unfair, even by as much as a speck.

If there's any good thing (that's done), He multiplies it and gives a great reward from His Own Self. [40] So how about it then? What if We brought from every community a witness and We brought you, (Muhammad), as a witness against these (people)? [41] On that day, whoever rejected (faith) and disobeyed the Messenger will wish he were made one with the earth, *but they'll never be able to hide any report from Allah!* [42]

Preparing for Worship

O you who believe! Don't come anywhere near (to performing) your prayers while intoxicated until you're able to understand what you're saying. [391]

---

[388] The two mediators are to look into the situation and decide if it is better for the couple to remain married or get divorced. This is the interpretation of their duties that 'Ali ibn Abi Talib advanced in a real dispute that was brought before him. (*Ma'ariful Qur'an*)

[389] The Prophet was adamant about treating servants as equals. He said, "The servant has the right to be fed and clothed and to only be asked to work as he is able." (*Muslim*) The Prophet also said, "When your servant brings any of you a meal, if you don't let him sit and share the meal with you, then at least he should be given a small portion or two of that meal, or a full meal or two, for he's the one who cooked it." (*Bukhari*) Letting the servant sit with you and enjoy the meal, as this saying implies, is the best course of action.

[390] Most commentators are of the view that verse 37 refers to the Jews of Medina who knew that their scripture foretold the coming of Muhammad, but who refused to accept the implications and were thus *tightfisted* (in their faith). (*Ma'ariful Qur'an*) The Song of Solomon in the Old Testament [verse 5:16] actually contains the name *muhammad*, and the preceding verses describe him surprisingly accurately! An alternate explanation advanced by other commentators is that certain Jews were counseling their Arab friends not to make it a habit to give in charity, for it would impoverish them. The Prophet said, "Beware of being tightfisted, for it destroyed those who came before you, even as it encouraged them to cut their family ties, which they did, and it encouraged them to be sinful, which they were." (*Abu Dawud*) He also said, "The generous person is close to Allah, close to Paradise, and close to people. The miser is far from Allah, far from Paradise, far from people and close to the Fire. A generous simpleton is far more loved by Allah than a miserly religious person." (*Tirmidhi*)

[391] The consumption of alcohol was not forbidden in the earliest days of Islam. (See 16:67.) It was a gradual process that took several years to complete. This was no small feat given the love of alcohol that was endemic to Arabian society. Given that Islam was emphasizing self-control and righteousness, it became increasingly clear to the early Muslims that the negative effects of alcohol were hard to overcome. (See 2:219.) Thus, people began to cut back how much they drank on their own. One day

Don't (pray) in a state of ritual impurity, unless you're on the road traveling, until you've washed your whole body. [392] If you're sick or on a journey or one of you has come from using the bathroom or had intimate relations and you can find no water (for your ablutions), then you can take clean sand and wipe your faces and hands with it. [393] Indeed, Allah pardons (sins) and forgives. [43]

The Opposition of the Medinan Jews

*H*aven't you noticed the case of those who already received some portions of scripture (in the past)? They bargain with mistakes and want to sidetrack you away from the path (of Allah). [44] Allah knows all about your enemies! Allah is enough of a protector, and Allah is enough of a helper! [45]

Among the Jews are some who will switch words from their right places and say, "*We hear, and we disobey*," and, "*Listen, may you not hear*," and, "*Lead us to the fields*," – all with a twist of their tongue and a disrespect for faith. [394]

If only they would've said instead, "*We hear, and we obey*," or "*Hear us*," or "*Have consideration for us*," it would've been far better for them and more respectful besides. Yet, Allah has cursed them for their disbelief, and even now only a few of them have any (true) faith. [46]

All you (Jews) who received scripture (in the past)! Believe in what We're sending down (to Muhammad), which confirms (the message of the scripture) that's with you now. (Believe), before We alter the faces of some (of you) beyond all recognition or curse them as We cursed

---

in the Medinan Period, a companion named 'Abdur-Rahman ibn 'Awf invited some friends over for a drinking session. When prayer time came, the inebriated men arose, and the one leading the prayer misquoted a Qur'anic passage, making the verse say the opposite of what it was supposed to say. (Verse 109:2 was recited without the negation.) In a similar report, a man named Sa'd was hit in the nose during a dinner party in which the men were, likewise, inebriated. (*Muslim*) When the Prophet was informed of these things, Allah revealed this verse to him. (*Tirmidhi, Razi*) (Compare with Leviticus 10: 8-10.) After this verse was revealed, a man was appointed to announce after the *adhan* (call to prayer), "Let no drunk person attend the prayers." Later on, alcoholic beverages were completely forbidden, and this multi-year, three-step program was ultimately successful. (See 5:90 and footnotes.) The Prophet also explained that this prohibition from praying while inebriated also extends to those who are very sleepy, and who might not know what they were reciting in their prayers. They should get some rest and then pray. (*Qurtubi*)

[392] A'ishah, the Prophet's wife, told the story of why this part of verse 43 was revealed. She said, "We were traveling with the Messenger of Allah. When we were camped at Al Baida', a necklace of mine broke off, and the Messenger tarried there to look for it. A number of other people also remained with him, and we were far from any source of water. Some people went to (my father), Abu Bakr, and said, 'Do you see what A'ishah has done? She made the Messenger stay with people who have no water.' He came to me while the Messenger was sleeping with his head on my leg and said, 'You made the Messenger stay with people, and there is no source of water.' Then he put his hand on my waist preventing me from moving and said, 'Allah will say whatever He wills.' I remained there all night with the Messenger sleeping while resting his head on my leg. In the morning there was no water (for ablution), and Allah revealed this verse of cleansing with the earth. Sayyid ibn Hudayr said to me, 'This isn't the first blessing you've been given, family of Abu Bakr.' The camel I was to ride was made to rise, and my necklace was found under it." (*Bukhari, Muslim*)

[393] This procedure is called *tayammum*, or dry ablution, and encompasses making symbolic gestures of washing by patting the hands on the sand and wiping the hands over the face and arms. When water is unavailable, this act suffices to purify a person.

[394] The following example of rude discourse directed towards the Prophet is similar to another episode of disrespectful speech that was discussed in verse 2:104. By this time in the Medinan Period, many tribal leaders among the Jews were openly hostile towards Islam and Muhammad, and they made no effort to hide their disdain and ridicule of him with insolent public statements and word-plays to make fun of him. This verse was revealed about such disrespectful comments.

the Sabbath-breakers. Allah's orders will be carried out! [47]

Allah doesn't forgive the assigning of any partner to Him, but He forgives anything else for whomever He wants. If anyone makes another (being) equal with Allah, then he's inventing an enormous sin. [48]

No Racial or Religious Group can Claim Allah as their Own

*H*aven't you noticed the situation of those (Jews of Medina) who claim they're especially pure? [395]

Not so! Only Allah purifies whomever He wants, and no one will ever be wronged by as much as the string of a date seed. [49]

So look at how they've invented lies against Allah, and that's an obvious crime! [50]

Hypocrisy in Alliance with Treason

*H*aven't you noticed the case of those (Jews of Medina) who received a portion of the scripture? [396] Yet, they put their faith in idols and superstition! They told the faithless (idolaters of Mecca) that they (the idolaters) were better guided on the way (of truth) than the believers! [51] They're the ones whom Allah has cursed, and whomever Allah curses - *there shall be no one to help them.* [52]

Do they think they own a share in (Allah's) kingdom? They're (a people who) won't even give a date crumb's (worth of assistance) to their fellows (who are in need). [53] Are they jealous of (other) people because of what Allah gave to them from His bounty?

But We had already given these descendants of Abraham the scripture and the (path of) wisdom and granted them a mighty kingdom (in ancient times). [54] Some of them believed, while some of

---

[395] Some Jewish men went to the Prophet and brought their children with them. They said, "Muhammad, do our children here have any guilt upon them?" The Prophet answered, "No, they don't." The Jews then said, "We swear by the One Whom we swear by that we are just like you: every sin we commit during the day is forgiven during the night, and every sin committed at night is forgiven during the day." This passage was revealed in response. (*Asbab ul-Nuzul*) Also see Isaiah 1:3-8.

[396] One of the most prominent Jewish leaders of Medina, K'ab ibn al-Ashraf, traveled with seventy of his men to pay a visit to the idol-worshippers of Mecca, who were still celebrating their victory over the Muslims at Uhud. His purpose was to engineer a break of his treaty with the Muslims by forging an alliance with the Meccans instead, sensing that the Muslims were in a weakened position. K'ab stayed in the house of Abu Sufyan, the Meccan leader, and a grand meeting was soon held between the men of both sides. At first, the Meccans were wary of K'ab's offer of alliance, citing as proof that they (the Jews) had a religious scripture and that Muhammad had one, as well. Thus, the Meccans insisted that the Muslims had more in common with the Jews and that they must have had more affinity with one another. (The Meccans had no religious books or scriptures, other than long-standing cultural traditions.) In order to prove their good will, the Meccans asked the Jewish leaders to bow to two of their idols, which they did, hence the charge that they *believe* in idols. K'ab proposed that thirty men each from the Jews and the idol-worshippers should touch the Ka'bah and swear a pact against the Muslims in the name of the Lord of that House. After it was done, Abu Sufyan asked Ka'b if he thought they, the idol-worshippers, were better guided in their religion than Muhammad. Ka'b asked Abu Sufyan to summarize Muhammad's beliefs, and Abu Sufyan explained how Islam believes in One God. Then Ka'b listened while Abu Sufyan explained what his own pagan beliefs were, which consisted of a mix of devotion to the idols, maintenance of the Ka'bah and providing guest services to travelers and ransom for captured relatives. Abu Sufyan closed his speech by criticizing Muhammad for abandoning the ways of his ancestors, cutting himself off from his relatives and making up his own religion. Afterwards, K'ab replied to the Meccans, "I swear by Allah that you are better guided than he." When word of these events reached Medina, this passage was revealed in response. (*Asbab ul-Nuzul, Ma'ariful Qur'an*)

them turned their faces from Him. Well, Hellfire is enough of a roasting flame (to punish those who reject Allah)! [55]

We're going to throw all those who rejected Our signs into a fire, and just as their skins are burnt to a crisp, We'll trade (their old skins) for new skins so they can feel the punishment (over and over) again. Truly, Allah is powerful and wise. [56]

We're soon going to admit those who believed and did what was morally right into gardens beneath which rivers flow – *and there they shall remain forever*!

They'll be joined by pure and holy mates. [397] (Even more than that,) We'll enter them into cool shade that stretches forth far and wide! [57]

Don't Take the Right of Another

Allah orders you to return that with which you've been entrusted to those who are owed. [398] When you judge between people, always judge with fairness. Truly, the principles that Allah teaches you are quite excellent! Indeed, Allah listens and observes. [58]

O you who believe! [399] Obey Allah, the Messenger and those who are in authority

---

[397] These are the mates that the righteous will be given in Paradise. They are not like the spouses that were consecrated in marriage on earth, nor do they supersede the earthly marriages in rank. According to many classical writers, these comely creatures are without souls and exist to satisfy carnal desires in Paradise. As explained in Afzalur Rahman's work, *Women in Islam*, both males and females will have them at their disposal.

[398] Before the Muslims had migrated to Medina, the pagan Quraysh allowed the Ka'bah door to be opened for visitors on only two days a week (Mondays and Thursdays). The Prophet had sought entry on one of those days, but the keeper of the door key, Uthman ibn Talhah, rudely tried to keep the Prophet and his friends out. The Prophet said to him, "Uthman, a day will come when you might see the key to the House of Allah in my hand, and then I'll have the power to give it to whomever I wish." Uthman ibn Talhah replied, "If that happens, then the Quraysh would have been dishonored and scattered!" The Prophet then said, "No, they will be established in honor." Then the Prophet entered the Ka'bah. As he later explained it, Uthman Ibn Talhah mused that perhaps what Muhammad said might come to pass. He soon decided to convert to Islam, but his angry family forced him to remain a pagan. In the year 630, the Muslims of Medina arranged the peaceful surrender of Mecca and occupied the city on a day that saw three large columns of Muslim soldiers, ten thousand strong, entering in an orderly and impressive procession. The curious Meccans watched as Muhammad and his close companions ascended to the door of the Ka'bah. As they approached the building, Uthman ibn Talhah shut the door tight and climbed up on the roof. When the Prophet asked for the key to open the door, his men told him that it was with Uthman up on the roof. The Prophet looked up and asked for it, but Uthman called down, "If I knew you were the Messenger of Allah, I would not deny you the key." The Prophet's cousin, 'Ali ibn Abi Talib, climbed up and forcibly snatched the key from his hand and opened the door. The Prophet then went inside and performed a brief prayer. When he came out he saw Uthman ibn Talhah standing there. 'Abbas, the Prophet's faithful uncle, asked if his family could be entrusted with the key and the grand responsibility that went along with it. This verse was immediately revealed, so the Prophet asked 'Ali to return the key to Uthman and to apologize for his rough handling. A surprised Uthman said, "'Ali, first you strong-armed me, and now you're being gentle with me?" 'Ali replied, "Allah, the Most High, has revealed a verse about you." After he repeated it to Uthman, the astonished idolater walked off happily. Suddenly, the Prophet called out to him, asking him to recall the conversation they had had so many years before. Uthman ibn Talhah remembered, and he instantly declared his faith in Islam. Muhammad then announced to the throngs that the right to be custodian of the Ka'bah's key would remain with Uthman ibn Talhah's family permanently and that only an unjust man would deprive them of their right. (*Asbab ul-Nuzul, Ma'ariful Qur'an*)

[399] It is said this verse was revealed because of a man named 'Abdullah ibn Hudhayfah, whom the Prophet had placed in charge of an expedition. 'Abdullah had gotten angry at his men for some reason, and he asked them if the Prophet had told them to obey him. When they replied in the affirmative, he told them to build a fire and jump into it. They built the fire but hesitated to jump into it, especially after one young man said, "You already ran away from the fire (of Hell) when you accepted the Messenger of Allah, so don't rush into it until you return to the Messenger of Allah first. If he

among you. If you have any kind of disagreement among yourselves, refer it to Allah and His Messenger, that is if you (really) believe in Allah and the Last Day. That's the most beneficial way for achieving a settlement. [400] [59]

The Dangers From Within

$\mathcal{H}$aven't you seen the case of the (hypocrites) who declared that they believe (in the revelations) sent down to you and in those sent down to those before you? [401]

(They only make these claims because) they would rather get verdicts (for their disputes) from the flawed (leaders among the Followers of Earlier Revelation), even though they were ordered to reject falsehood.

And so Satan's desire is to lead them further astray into misguidance. [60]

When they're told, "*Come to what Allah has revealed, and come to the Messenger,*" you can see how the hypocrites turn their faces away from you in disgust. [61]

How will it be then when they're trapped with misfortune on account of what their hands have prepared? Then they'll come to you, swearing to Allah, saying, "*We only meant the best and to (help people) reconcile.*" [62]

Allah knows what's in the hearts of those who are like that, so steer clear of them. Yet, still speak words that will touch their souls. [63]

---

commands you to do it, then you can do it." When the expedition returned to Medina, the men went to the Prophet and told him what happened. The Prophet said, "If you would have entered it, you would never have left it. There is only obedience (to a leader) in righteousness." (*Bukhari, Muslim, Ahmad*)

[400] There was a disagreement between two companions, Khalid ibn Waleed and Ammar ibn Yasir. Ammar had promised protection to a convert who belonged to a hostile tribe, but the commander of the expedition, who was Khalid, later captured him and his property. Ammar angrily asked Khalid to release the man, while Khalid felt affronted that his orders and actions were being questioned. Both men brought their dispute to the Prophet upon their return to Medina, and they even engaged in a shouting match in his presence. The Prophet advised Ammar not to take his commander to task in the future without first asking his permission to speak freely. Ammar and Khalid began cursing each other, but Ammar delivered the worst of it. Khalid protested, and the Prophet counseled him to make peace with Ammar, saying that Allah loved Ammar (he was an early and staunch convert committed to justice). Khalid then followed Ammar and begged to make peace with him, and the two reconciled.

[401] The hypocrite, 'Abdullah ibn Ubayy, along with his followers, put up every kind of obstacle they could find to make life difficult for the Muslims. They tried to enflame the Muslim converts to quarrel with each other, and they continually ridiculed, though privately, Islamic teachings to make people doubt the faith. They also encouraged people to go to the Jews for settlements in their disputes, claiming that one religion from Allah was as good as another. A hypocrite named Bishr had a dispute with a Jewish man. Ibn Ubayy wanted K'ab ibn al-Ashraf, the chief of the Banu Nadir tribe, to solve the problem, but the Jew wanted to go to Muhammad for judgment. The Jew forced Bishr to accompany him to see the Prophet. After both sides stated their case, the Prophet ruled in favor of the Jew. Bishr was outraged, and he left to look for 'Umar ibn al-Khattab (d. 644). When he found out where he was, he then dragged the Jewish man along with him to get a 'second opinion.' When they approached 'Umar, Bishr complained to him, saying that Muhammad had found in favor of the Jew against him, and then he challenged 'Umar to give a better ruling. 'Umar replied, "*Is that so?*" and he told the men to wait outside for a moment. 'Umar went into his house and belted a sword around his waist. He emerged and drew his sword in front of the startled men. He began to whack Bishr with the flat side of his weapon until he agreed to back down. 'Umar said, "This is the way I will judge for the one who doesn't agree with the judgment of Allah and His Messenger." Some reports say that 'Umar actually killed Bishr and that the heirs of Bishr brought their case before the Prophet. In either case, 'Umar was absolved for his actions by the revelation of these verses, which all but declared that the hypocrites are *de facto* enemies of Allah. Afterwards people gave 'Umar the nickname of *al-Farooq*, which means that he judged rightly. (*Asbab ul-Nuzul, Ma'ariful Qur'an*)

Messengers are to be Obeyed

$\mathcal{W}$e only sent messengers so they could be obeyed according to the will of Allah. [402] Now if they would've just come to you, (Muhammad), when they were being wrong to their own souls and asked for Allah's forgiveness - *and the Messenger had asked for their forgiveness*, they would've found that Allah accepts repentance and is merciful. [64]

But no, by your Lord, they have no faith unless and until they make you, (Muhammad), the judge between them in all their disagreements. [403]

They must not allow any resistance towards your decisions to appear in their souls, but rather they should accept (your decisions) with the greatest conviction. [65]

If We had ordered them to sacrifice their lives or to leave their homes (and migrate to a new land), [404] very few of them would've done it. [405]

If they just would've done (the little) that they were asked to do, it would've been better for them, and their resolve would've been strengthened. [66] Then We would've given them a great reward from Our presence [67] and guided them towards a straight path. [68]

Whoever obeys Allah and the Messenger will be with those who have the favor of Allah upon them, (among whom are) the prophets, the true (in faith), the witnesses (who sacrificed their lives in Allah's cause) and the righteous.

What a beautiful fellowship! [406] [69] This is the bounty of Allah, and it's enough that Allah knows (about all things). [70]

---

[402] Two Muslims in Medina had a dispute over irrigation rights. The first man (Tha'laba) was a native of the city, while the second man (az-Zubayr) was a cousin of the Prophet who had emigrated from Mecca. The Prophet listened to both men and found in favor of Az-Zubayr. (The settlement essentially was a compromise that said that the men must take turns irrigating their fields.) Tha'laba became angry and accused the Prophet of merely siding with his cousin. That remark upset the Prophet, and he became saddened. This passage was revealed in response. (*Asbab ul-Nuzul*)

[403] In a wider sense, verse 65 is taken as proof that Muslims must obey the injunctions contained in proven *hadiths* or traditions of the Prophet. This is called following the *sunnah*, or way of the Prophet. Also see 33:21 and 33:36.

[404] After the incident involving Bishr and the Jew was made public knowledge (see 4:60-63), the Jews of Medina started taunting the Muslims, saying that they claim to have a prophet, but then they fail to obey his commands. Then the Jews boasted that when their prophet (Moses) told them they had to kill other Jews to get Allah's forgiveness (after the golden calf incident), their forefathers did so. Then the Jews asked the Muslims that if they had received a command like that, would they have obeyed it? This passage was revealed in response. (*Ma'ariful Qur'an*)

[405] This passage states that, at least at that point in history, many Muslims were not strong enough to obey the Prophet unquestioningly. When Abu Bakr heard this verse, though, he said that he *would* have done whatever Allah had commanded. The Prophet mentioned 'Abdullah ibn Mas'ud by name, and declared he would have obeyed any command, likewise.

[406] A man named Thawban, who was very much attached to the Prophet and loved him dearly, once went to him with a particular concern. He explained that he loved him (the Prophet) so much that he hated to be parted from his company – even for an instant. Then he said that he was afraid that he might not see him in Paradise, given that Muhammad would be in the ranks of the prophets up there and would thus be in a higher place than he and also given the fact that he (Thawban) might not even make it into heaven. This passage was revealed to console this concern, pointing out that in Paradise, even the different grades and levels will have occasion to meet and mingle. (*Asbab ul-Nuzul, Ibn Kathir, Tabarani*) On another occasion, addressing the same issue, the Prophet said that on the Day of Judgment, everyone will be with the one they love, i.e., those who loved the Prophet would be with him. (*Bukhari*) He also once said that other categories of people who will be in this beautiful fellowship include honest businessmen, those who are faithful in their worship and those who do a lot of extra praying. (*Ma'ariful Qur'an*)

When in Dangerous Territory

O you who believe! [407] Be cautious and only venture out (into dangerous places) either in groups or all together. [71] Indeed, there are some among you who try to lag behind (when you're on the road).

If misfortune befalls you, they say, *"Allah was gracious to us by not keeping us among them to witness (their misfortune)."* [72] However, if some good fortune befalls you from Allah, he'll say, as if he didn't know you closely, *"Oh, how I wish I could've been there with them because I would've had a great time!"* [73]

What Constitutes a Just War?

Let them fight in the cause of Allah, those who sell the life of this world for the life of the Hereafter. [408] To the one who fights in the cause of Allah, whether he's killed or achieves victory, We're soon going to give him a great reward. [74]

And why *shouldn't* you fight in the cause of Allah and in the cause of those who, being weak, are mistreated: the men, women and children whose only cry is, *"Our Lord! Deliver us from this land whose people are oppressors. Send us someone from You who will protect us, and send us someone from You who will help!"* [409] [75]

Those who have faith (in Allah) fight in the cause of Allah, while those who cover over (their ability to have faith) fight in the cause of falsehood, so fight against the allies of Satan, for truly Satan's plan is weak. [76]

Don't be Cowardly

Haven't you seen the people who were told to restrain their hands (from fighting) and who were counseled instead (to concentrate on) establishing prayer and giving in charity? [410] When the order

---

[407] Due to the constant raiding and attacks of the pagans in the countryside, the Muslims were discouraged from moving about in the land alone. When the Prophet organized patrols or sent out skirmishers to clear an area of raiders, some men of Medina would go absent without leave or otherwise conveniently get "lost" to avoid any potentially dangerous situations. If the patrols were successful and drove off pagan raiders, capturing booty in the process, these laggards would lament their loss of material gains. That is the subject matter of this passage.

[408] Even though the Muslims had migrated to the safe haven of Medina, Muslims were not allowed yet to defend themselves from the Meccans, who harassed, tortured and killed Muslims with impunity both within Mecca and in the countryside. This quoted supplication in verse 75 was what the Muslims were asking of Allah. This passage was then revealed, giving Muslims permission to defend themselves. (*Ma'ariful Qur'an*)

[409] This verse outlines the legal basis for one of the three legitimate causes for a Muslim state to go to war. If there is an evil or repressive regime, the Muslims are obligated to fight it. (Exodus 22:21-24 addresses the cries of the oppressed in even stronger terms!) The other two causes are self-defense when the Muslim state is attacked and when a foreign government unfairly restricts or forbids the free practice and preaching of Islam. In other words, if freedom of religion is denied, then the Muslims are obligated to rectify the situation. As has been discussed elsewhere, traditional Islamic legal theories do not recognize vigilante action by rogue elements, even if they claim to be advancing Muslim interests or defending Muslims. There is no concept in traditional Islamic Law of people circumventing Islamic rules of war (such as intentionally harming non-combatants) in order to achieve their aims.

[410] This passage was revealed with regards to several of Muhammad's followers who were severely persecuted in the early days of the Meccan period. At that time they were begging Muhammad to let them fight back against the idol-worshippers who would daily assault them in the streets and vandalize their property. Muhammad always refused their request and counseled them to be patient and engage in more religious activity. After the Migration to Medina, the order finally came to fight the Meccans, and many of these same men became reluctant to go to war. The Prophet said, "Allah has guaranteed

finally came for them to fight, a bunch of them became more scared of people than they were scared of Allah!

"Our Lord!" they cried out. *"Why have You ordered us to fight? Won't you postpone it for us, at least for a while longer?"*

Say (to them), *"The enjoyment of this world is indeed short. The next life is better for the one who is mindful (of Allah). You won't be wronged by as much as the string of a date seed!* [77] *Wherever you are, death will find you, even if you lodge yourselves in mighty towers!"*

Whenever good fortune befalls them, they say, *"This is from Allah,"* but if they're ever hit with misfortune they say, *"This is all your fault, (Muhammad)."*

Say to them, *"Every (outcome) is from Allah."*

So what is it with these people that they don't understand a single phrase? [78] Any good that comes your way is from Allah, while any misfortune that befalls you is your own fault. We sent a messenger to people, and Allah is enough of a witness for that! [79]

Whoever obeys the Messenger obeys Allah, while whoever turns away (from you, Muhammad,) well, We didn't send you to be their caretaker. [80] They say, *"We obey,"* but when they leave you a bunch of them brood through the night on the opposite of what you've taught them, though Allah is keeping a record of their nightly tirades, so steer clear of them. Place your reliance upon Allah, for Allah is enough to take care of things. [81]

Haven't they considered the Qur'an with care? If it were from any other (source) besides Allah, then they would've found many matters of disagreement within it. [82]

Whenever the (hypocrites hear) rumors about safety or impending danger, they announce it publicly (without checking on it first). [411] If they would only refer the matter to the Messenger or to the proper authorities among them, then investigators could check on the incidents with them. If it wasn't for Allah's grace and mercy towards you, all save for a few of you would've followed Satan. [83]

Fight in the Cause of Allah

(Muhammad,) fight in the cause of Allah, though you're only responsible for your own self. [412] Rally the believers. Allah will surely restrain the power of the faithless, for Allah is the strongest power and the strongest punisher. [84] Whoever makes a recommendation in a good cause becomes a part of it. Whoever makes a recommendation in an evil cause shares responsibility in it. Allah has the power to direct all things. [85]

Spread Goodwill for the Sake of Allah

When someone gives you a greeting, reciprocate with a nicer greeting than that or one equally as nice, [413] for

the struggler in His cause that He will either bring him death and admit him to Paradise, or He will help him return home safely with whatever rewards and war booty he has gained." (*Bukhari*)

[411] The hypocrites often raised false alarms about attacking Meccan raiding parties, and they spread every rumor of impending doom that they could in order to unsettle the sincere Muslims. (*Ibn Kathir*)

[412] This passage was revealed about the appointment to fight once again at Badr, an appointment that the elated Meccans made with the Prophet after they prevailed at Uhud. (See 3:172 and footnotes.) Some Muslims hesitated to follow the Prophet when he began making preparations for this march. So this verse is saying, in other words, if no one else follows the Prophet in opposing evil, it won't be his fault. The Meccans wound up not appearing at all.

[413] Pre-Islamic greetings included such phrases as, "May Allah keep you alive for a thousand years," "May Allah shower good fortune upon you," and "May fortune rise over you." (*Ma'ariful Qur'an*) The Islamic greeting of, "Peace be upon you," by way of contrast, rather than calling to long life or good fortune, informs us that we, as people, will respect each other's rights. In other words, "You

Allah is keeping track of all things. [86] Allah! There is no god but He. He's going to gather you all together on the Day of Assembly, and there's no doubt about that! Now whose word can be more honest than Allah's? [87]

Don't Let the Hypocrites Corrupt You

So what's wrong with you that you've split into two groups (of opinion) about the hypocrites? [414] Allah has thrown them by the wayside because of what they've earned.

Do you want to try and guide one whom Allah has left astray? Whomever Allah leaves astray will never discover a way (out of darkness)! [88]

The (hypocrites) only want you to cover over (the truth of Allah in your hearts) like they've covered it over (in their hearts), for then you'll be on the same level. [415] So, don't take close allies from among them until they migrate, for Allah's sake, (to Medina). If they become rebels (and make war against you), then capture them or kill them (in battle) wherever you find them. [416]

Don't take close allies or advocates from among them, [89] unless it's with those who join a faction with which you have a treaty (of peace), or those who come to you

---

have nothing to fear from me, and I will respect your rights as a human being." (As explained by Ibn 'Arabi in his book, *Ahkam ul-Qur'an*) Islam teaches that both life and fortune will pass away, but goodness that comes from doing good to your fellows is a reward accumulating in Allah's presence. As for particulars about offering the greetings, the Prophet instituted the following points: Allah is closer to the person who greets first; failing to offer the greetings is a sign of being a miser; a returning family member should greet those in his or her house; a smaller group should greet a larger one first; one who arrives to a group should greet it first; when one is greeted with peace, he or she must reply with the same; and the young should greet the old first. (*Ma'ariful Qur'an*)

[414] A constant cause of concern for the authentic Muslims in Medina was the issue of the hypocrites. They were a large faction of people who pretended to enter Islam, but who conspired against it. They were the proverbial *fifth column*. Just before the Battle of Uhud was to begin, the one thousand-strong Muslim force was reduced by three hundred men when a contingent of hypocrites suddenly withdrew back to Medina. When the battle was over, the beleaguered, though not destroyed, Muslim veterans were disputing over what to do about them. Some wanted them punished, while others wanted them left alone in the hope that they would reform themselves. Another group of hypocrites were Meccans who had migrated to Medina, but who then later reneged on their faith and returned to Mecca. Thus, the true believers were divided into *two opinions* about these kinds of people. This verse was revealed pointing out that there was little hope of salvaging those whom Allah has abandoned. (*Ma'ariful Qur'an*)

[415] Suraqah ibn Malik visited Medina after the battles of Badr and Uhud had passed. He asked the Prophet for a peace treaty between the Muslims and his tribe, the Banu Mudlaj. The Prophet sent Khalid ibn Waleed, who had become a Muslim by that time, to return with Suraqah to seal the peace treaty. The main points of the treaty were that: the Banu Mudlaj would not support the Quraysh of Mecca any further; anyone who allies with the Banu Mudlaj becomes a party to this treaty's terms; and finally, if the Quraysh ever come to accept Islam, the Banu Mudlaj would do so likewise. This passage was then revealed about their case. (*Asbab ul-Nuzul*)

[416] This only applies to those who make themselves your enemies. The idea that you must fight your enemies with all your might and attack them before they attack you is not a new one in human history, and armies everywhere train their soldiers to kill enemies on command before they themselves are annihilated. The famous American general, General Geroge S. Patton, said in his autobiography that: "...as you attack them they cannot find the time to plan how to attack you..." (From *War As I Knew It*, p .135.) Even though swift and lethal action in war is to be expected, be that as it may, a Muslim is not allowed to harm the innocent civilians of his enemy, nor is he allowed to initiate hostilities without probable cause or prior provocation. Even further, he must take care to prevent collateral damage as much as possible. Ibn 'Umar remarked that there was a time when a woman was found dead on a battlefield. Thereupon the Prophet ordered that it was forbidden to kill women and children in war. (*Bukhari*) This is a statement of the Prophet that indicts the evil actions of extremists from all religions, including from the Islam milieu.

with hearts that hold them back from fighting you - and fighting their own people!

If Allah had wanted, He could've given them an advantage over you, and they would've fought you. If they stay back and don't try to fight you and instead send you (offers) of peace, then Allah hasn't given you any legitimate reason (to fight against them). [417] [90]

You'll find other (hypocrites) who want to gain your confidence and the confidence of their own people. [418] However, every time they're tempted (by their twisted desires), they fall into them.

[419] If they neither leave you (to openly join your enemy) nor give you any peace (while remaining among you), other than merely not (attacking you at the moment), then you may capture them and kill them wherever you encounter them. [420] In their case, We've given you clear permission (to fight) against them. [421] [91]

The Penalties for Homicide

$\mathcal{A}$ believer should never kill another believer, though if it happens by mistake, (then a penalty must still be paid). [422] If someone kills a believer

---

[417] There is a myth that a Muslim only makes peace to prepare for another attack against his enemy in the future. Islam requires that a peace treaty be honored. The Prophet never broke his treaties unless the other side either broke them first, or was clearly about to do so. A Muslim is not supposed to seek a life of perpetual war. Islam envisions a society of families, communities and mutual trade both within and without the boundaries of the sphere of faith. No soldier wants to die for a useless or unjust cause. A famous general named Douglass MacArthur once said, "'The soldier, above all other people, prays for peace, for he must suffer and bear the deepest wounds and scars of war." The Prophet advised, "The best person is the one who has a long life and does good deeds." (*Ahmad, Tirmidhi*) Thus, peace is the desired state of a Muslim community.

[418] It is said that this verse is specifically about the two desert tribes of Asad and Ghatafan, who sent representatives claiming allegiance to Islam, but then who worked against Islam behind the scenes. (*Ma'ariful Qur'an*)

[419] The Prophet said, "There are three clear signs of a hypocrite: whenever he speaks, he lies; whenever he promises, he breaks his promise; and when he is trusted, he betrays that trust, even though he fasts and prays and claims he is a Muslim." (*Bukhari, Muslim*) 'Umar ibn al-Khattab once remarked, "The thing I fear most for the safety of this community is the learned hypocrite." When asked how one could be both learned and hypocritical, he replied, "When his learning does not go beyond verbal knowledge, while his heart remains untouched."

[420] Some critics of Islam look upon these two verses (89 & 91) and their ominous-seeming repetition of the phrase "kill them" as some kind of proof that Islam is violent by nature or that the Qur'an requires non-believers to convert or die. This nonsense could be assumed if one were to merely take that phrase out of context. The same could be done with the many passages of the Bible that also could be construed to be some sort of proof that Judaism or Christianity requires non-believers to be killed. However, in context, this passage (89-91) does not say unbelievers must be killed for no other reason than they are non-believers. It doesn't even talk about non-believers at all! This passage is about hypocrites among the Muslims or hypocrites who live among non-Muslims who are waiting to attack or engage in treason against their professed faith, and who refuse to back down from that stance. To show that this passage is even still interested in maintaining peace, verse 90 forbids fighting them as long as they sincerely desire to make peace, as well.

[421] If an enemy is living in or around your midst and refrains from attacking you merely because they're not strong enough yet to do so, then it would be foolish to take the future threat lightly. This verse references such a faction in Medina that would neither leave to join the pagans nor make peace with the Prophet. Those hypocrites were just waiting for the chance to attack the Muslims. This verse gives the Muslims permission to attack such a fifth column when their hostile intentions become known. Pre-emption is allowed in cases where there is clear evidence of a looming threat. The Muslims of Medina, as it turned out, didn't need to exercise this clause, as the hypocrite faction eventually crumbled.

[422] A man in Mecca named Ayyash accepted Islam but kept it a secret in fear for his safety. He eventually escaped to Medina and remained there for some time. Meanwhile, his idolatrous mother back in Mecca told her two sons that she wouldn't eat, drink or go in her house until her son was brought back to her. The two men, accompanied by a friend named Harith ibn Zayd, went to Medina,

(accidentally), then they must free a believing servant and pay monetary damages to the family of the deceased, unless they decline it freely. [423]

If the deceased belonged to a community that is hostile to you and that person was a believer, the freeing of a believing servant (is enough). [424] If they belonged to a community with which you have a treaty, then again monetary-damages must be paid to their family, and a believing servant must be freed.

If someone cannot procure (a servant to free because of a financial hardship or some other reason), then a fast of two consecutive months must be observed by them, and this is a concession from Allah, for Allah has all knowledge and wisdom. [92]

If someone kills a believer on purpose, then their reward is in Hellfire, *and that's where they're going to stay!* The wrath and curse of Allah will be upon them, and a harsh punishment will be prepared for them. [93]

It's not for You to Judge Another's Sincerity

O you who believe! [425] When you go abroad (to fight) in the cause of Allah,

---

located Ayyash, and kidnapped him, bringing him back to Mecca bound and shackled. His mother and brothers berated him and beat him, ordering him to give up Islam. They left him tied up under the blazing sun, and Harith ibn Zayd succeeded in making Ayyash, under torture, renounce his faith in Islam. After they let him free, Ayyash began to feel angry at having been abused and forced to give up his faith. He swore to Harith ibn Zayd that if he ever found him alone he would kill him. Sometime later, Ayyash again escaped to Medina and renewed his commitment to Islam. After the Conquest of Mecca, Ayyash found Harith walking in the street and set upon him and killed him. The people around him began shouting that Harith had become a Muslim. Ayyash, who didn't know he had recently converted, was filled with remorse. He immediately went to the Prophet and said, "Messenger of Allah! You know about my situation with Harith, and I didn't know he had entered into Islam when I killed him." This passage was revealed in response. (*Ibn Kathir*)
[423] If a Muslim accidentally kills a *dhimmi*, or non-Muslim whose rights are guaranteed by the state, then the monetary damages are equal to that of a Muslim victim. (*Ma'ariful Qur'an*) There is also a penalty to be paid on behalf of a fetus who dies when its mother is harmed. Two women from the tribe of Hudhayl were quarreling, and one of them threw a stone at the other causing her to have a miscarriage. The Prophet decided that the compensation for killing a fetus was to free a bonded servant. (*Bukhari*)
[424] The fines for wrongful (unintentional) death were fixed at a certain number of camels (or the value of them) to be paid by the killer's family. The killer still has to free the servant or fast on his own.
[425] The Prophet had sent out a patrol into the countryside to guard against Meccan or bedouin raiders. The patrol came upon a lone bedouin named 'Amr who gave the Islamic greeting of peace. The Muslims didn't take any action against him, but one man from among them named Muhallam, who had previous quarrels with 'Amr in the days before Islam, killed him and took his camel. When the patrol returned to Mecca, the Prophet scolded Muhallam harshly. In another incident, the Prophet sent out a patrol under the command of a man named Miqdad, and he came upon a district where some enemy pagan bedouins were. They all fled, except for one wealthy man who declared his faith in Islam. Miqdad decided not to believe him, and he struck him down. Another member of the patrol was horrified and said, "You killed a man after he said there was no god other than Allah! By Allah, I'm going to tell what you did to the Prophet." When the patrol returned and the Prophet was informed, he ordered Miqdad to be summoned and said, "Miqdad! Did you kill a man who declared there is no god other than Allah? What will you do tomorrow when you face (someone else) who says the same thing?" Miqdad explained to the Prophet his reasons for doing what he did, and he further postulated that the man was only saying what he did to spare his life and keep his valuables. The Prophet became livid and said, "Were you able to look into his heart to see if he was truthful or not?" The man said he was sure, but the Prophet remarked, "What will happen to you if he complains against you on Judgment Day? Did you kill a man who said there was no god but Allah? You're ruined because you don't know what he was really saying." Then verse 94 was revealed, and the Prophet said, "He was a believer who hid his faith among his disbelieving people. He declared his faith to you, but you killed him, even though you used to hide your faith before in Mecca." (*Bazzar*) Miqdad passed away some years after

check carefully (before taking action against those whom you meet on the battlefield, and about whose intentions you're uncertain).

Don't say to an (enemy soldier) who (seems to pause) to offer you the greetings of peace, *"You aren't a believer,"* (wanting to kill him) in your greed for the temporary riches of this life. There's plenty of profits and gains with Allah. You used to (kill for profit) like that before (accepting Islam), until Allah placed His favor upon you. So check carefully (whom it is you're confronting), for Allah is aware of everything you do. [426] [94]

Some Earn More than Others in Allah's Cause

The believers who sit (at home) without a valid excuse and who never get hurt are not equal to those who struggle in the cause of Allah with their money [427] and their persons. [428] Allah has granted a higher grade to those who struggle and use their money and their persons over those who sit (at home). [429]

Allah has promised good to both, but those who struggle are distinguished by Him with a valuable reward above those who remain (at home). [430] [95] That's a special designation given especially by Him, along with His forgiveness and mercy, for Allah is forgiving and merciful. [96]

Migrating away from an Evil Land

When the angels take the souls of those who died while in a state of injustice against their own selves (on account of their not leaving the hostile people who

---

that, but when he was buried in the earth his body was found exhumed the next day. He was reburied and found exhumed two more times. Finally, the body was thrown into a wooded area after the Prophet remarked that the earth was not accepting his body because it was tainted with sin. This verse was revealed about this affair. (*Asbab ul-Nuzul*)

[426] The view of modern extremists that the killing of innocent Muslims is allowed if it is a by-product of their so called "*jihads*" is shown to be a false and evil notion, as this verse categorically prohibits killing any believer. As further proof, verse 48:25 clearly states that the Muslims were not allowed to attack hostile Mecca given that secret believers living there would have been unintentionally harmed in the process. The Prophet once said, "I am your predecessor at the fountain of *kawthar*, and some men amongst you will be brought to me, and when I will try to hand them some water, they will be pulled away from me by force whereupon I will say, 'O Lord, my companions!' Then the Almighty will say, 'You do not know what they did after you left, they introduced new things into the religion after you.'" (*Bukhari*)

[427] The Prophet once said, "You can learn whatever you like, though your knowledge will never benefit you until you put it into action." (Quoted from *Al-Muwafaqat* of Imam al-Shatibi.)

[428] After these two verses were revealed, the Prophet's main secretary, Zayd ibn Thabit, said that he was sitting with the Prophet in a gathering when the old blind man, Ibn Umm Maktoum, came and asked about his case, since he was handicapped by his blindness and unable to join the Prophet when he summoned the men to fight the idol-worshippers, even though he wished he could help. Zayd remarked that the Prophet leaned over on his (Zayd's) thigh and that the weight of the Prophet's leaning became extraordinarily heavy. The Prophet was sweating as the revelation was coming to him, and the crushing weight on Zayd's leg only eased when the revelation was finished. Then verse 95 was amended by revelation to say that a valid excuse absolved a person from having to serve. The Prophet asked Zayd to write down what he was reciting afresh on a parchment. (*Bukhari*)

[429] The Prophet said, "The one who provides equipment to a warrior in the way of Allah, the one who actually goes and fights and the one who remains behind to look after the family of a warrior who is fighting in the way of Allah, all of these three are counted as having fought in the way of Allah." (*Bukhari, Muslim*)

[430] A'ishah, the wife of Muhammad, once asked the Prophet, "Since we hold that striving in Allah's cause (physically) is the best action, shouldn't we (women) also struggle (do *jihad*) in Allah's cause?" The Prophet answered, "The best (physical) struggle (for women) to undertake is a pilgrimage (to Mecca), which is done according to my example." (*Bukhari*)

163

oppress them, when they could leave if they wanted to), [431] they're going to ask (the sinful souls), "*What was your situation in the world?*" [432]

They'll answer by saying, "*We were weak and oppressed in the land, (and that's why we hid our faith and never left the enemy's territory when we should have done so.)*"

The (angels will answer them,) saying, "*Wasn't Allah's earth big enough for you to move yourselves away (to some place safer)?*" They're the ones who will find their resting place in Hellfire, and oh what an evil destination it is! [97]

However, those who were (truly) weak and oppressed, the men, women and children who had neither the means nor the ability (to flee) nor (who found a leader) to direct their way [98] (are not to blame), for Allah shall forgive them, [433] for Allah pardons and forgives. [434] [99]

Whoever forsakes his home in the cause of Allah can find in the world many safe hideouts, for it's a wide and spacious place. If he dies as a refugee far away from home for (the sake) of Allah and His Messenger, his reward is due with Allah, and Allah is forgiving and merciful. [100]

Prayer in Dangerous Places

*W*hen you travel through the open countryside, [435] it isn't wrong if you shorten your prayers out of the fear that the faithless might ambush you, for those

---

[431] Mingling or living among non-Muslims is not the problem being addressed here. The problem is consorting with those who hate Islam and/or Allah in general, or compromising your faith out of fear when migration is an option, and supporting, even just by your quiet participation as one among them, those who want to fight against those who believe in Him. How can a person justify being around such people who are dedicated to destroying faith in God?

[432] This verse was revealed concerning the case of some secret converts to Islam who chose to remain in Mecca among the idol-worshippers, even though they could have easily escaped to Medina and lived by their convictions openly. They were trying to play both sides of the game, as it were, and their situation was known to the Muslims in Medina. Some of these lukewarm converts marched alongside of their fellow Meccans to the Battle of Badr and lost their lives in the battle as they fought against the Muslims of Medina. The Prophet also said of them that when the angels were taking their souls, they were berating them harshly for their poor choices and asking them the questions presented here in this passage. (*Bukhari*)

[433] According to the sayings of the Prophet, if a person migrates to another place for the sake of preserving his or her religion or to remove him or herself from evil influences, then that person is counted as an immigrant in Allah's cause. All the person's sins are then forgiven. (*Ma'ariful Qur'an*) Also see 16:41.

[434] When word of verse 97 reached the secret converts who remained in Mecca after the Battle of Badr, one old man named Habib al-Laythi told his sons, "Carry me (to Medina), for I'm a weak old man, and I don't know the way." His children began the two-week journey northward, carrying him on a stretcher. Eventually, they had to stop just shy of their goal, as their father was near death. He clasped his hands together, and his last words were, "O Allah, this is for You, and this is for Your Messenger. I choose You even as the Messenger of Allah chose You with his own hand." When news of his death reached Medina, the Prophet said that had he reached the city, his reward would have been more complete. This passage was revealed in response, saying that Allah will give a full reward, even to refugees who die on their journey towards the sanctuary of faith. (*Asbab ul-Nuzul*)

[435] The Prophet led a group of Muslims on patrol near a place named Asafan. The time for the early afternoon prayer arrived, and the Muslims were praying in congregation when a party of Meccan raiders (led by Khalid ibn Waleed) appeared in the distance. One of the pagans counseled that this was the best time to attack the Muslims, while another suggested that there was a second prayer (the late afternoon) in which the Muslims took even more interest, and the man suggested that that would be a better time to strike. While the idol-worshippers were debating when to strike, the Prophet concluded the group prayer and recited this newly revealed passage, explaining what the idol-worshippers were plotting. When the next prayer time came, the Prophet ordered his men to pray while holding their weapons, and the two rows of men alternated standing and bowing, so there would always be one line able to respond to the enemy if need be. (*Abu Dawud*)

who cover over (their ability to have faith) are clearly your enemies. [101]

When you're with (other Muslims on a journey, Muhammad), and you stand up to lead them in prayer, assign one group of the (believers) to stand (for prayer) with you, taking their weapons with them, (while the others stand guard).

When they finish their prostrations, let them set up (their guard-positions) in the rear, and let the other group which didn't pray yet come forward and pray with you - taking all precautions and holding their weapons.

The faithless would eagerly attack you in a single rush, if they (saw that) you were without your weapons or away from your gear.

It isn't wrong, however, if you pack your weapons away when it's raining or if you're too ill to carry them, but even still take every precaution for yourselves.

Truly, Allah has prepared a humiliating punishment for those who suppress (their awareness of the truth). [102]

When you've concluded the prayer, remember Allah while standing, sitting or lying down on your sides, and when you're free from danger, perform the prayer-ritual (in the normal way), for prayers are a duty upon the faithful at set times. [436] [103]

Don't hesitate in pursuing the enemy. If you're suffering from hardship, (know that) they're suffering similar hardships, too. (Remember that) you have hope in Allah, while they have hope in nothing. Allah is full of knowledge and wisdom. [104]

Hypocrites may Try to Use You

$\mathcal{W}$e sent the Book down to you in all truth, so you can judge between people as directed by Allah. [437] Therefore, don't

---

[436] The Prophet explained the manner of prayer in his own words, and a believer is bound to follow the method he taught. The Prophet said, "Pray as you have seen me praying." (*Bukhari*) See 33:21 and 2:151.

[437] This entire passage was revealed in response to a situation that occurred due to a theft. A suspected hypocrite named Ta'ma ibn Ubayrak (aka Bashir) had a neighbor named Rifa'ah. Ta'ma came to know that Rifa'ah had a bag of flour in his house, and at that time early in the Medinan Period, many Muslims were suffering from deprivation, so Ta'ma broke into Rifa'ah's house, took the big bag of flour and proceeded to walk home with it, not realizing that the bag had a small hole in it and was leaking a trail of flour after him. When he reached his home and understood what had happened, he became frightened, ran to the house of a Jewish neighbor named Zayd, and gave him the bag to hold, not telling him that it was stolen property. The owner of the flour, following the trail to Ta'ma's house, demanded his property. Then Ta'ma swore to the crowd of his relatives (that was quickly gathering) that he didn't take it and that he knew nothing about it. Rifa'ah swore that he knew Ta'ma took the bag, and he pointed to the trail of flour that led to his door. Then Ta'ma pointed out that the flour trail led away from there to the house of a Jew, and Ta'ma promptly swore that the Jew stole the flour. (Another version of the story has Rifa'ah being told that a cooking fire was seen in Ta'ma's house, causing him to go there to investigate, with Ta'ma claiming he got the bag from a hapless companion named Labid, with the charge eventually being craftily shifted by Ta'ma's family to the Jew in question.) The crowd proceeded to the home of the Jew, and he produced the bag, claiming that Ta'ma asked him to hold it and that he didn't know it was stolen. Other Jews also corroborated his story. The identity of the thief was uncertain then, with both Ta'ma and the Jew accusing each other (and an indignant Labid fuming in their midst). Ta'ma's relatives came up with the idea that they should ask the Prophet to come and argue for their side, and they went to him and tried to convince him that Ta'ma was innocent. Rifa'ah and his family, on the other hand, were convinced that Ta'ma was the real culprit and that he was trying to mask his crime by framing an innocent person. The relatives of Ta'ma, however, were so persuasive and passionate in their defense, that the Prophet was nearly convinced of their position, even to the point of suggesting that Rifa'ah and his family were falsely accusing a Muslim family of theft. The Prophet decided to wait for a resolution from Allah. After only a few days at most, this passage was revealed to the Prophet. The Jew was thus declared innocent of the crime. Ta'ma then fled the city and renounced Islam in favor of idolatry. He found no peace in Mecca among the pagans, however,

let yourself be (used) as an advocate by traitors. [105] Rather, seek the forgiveness of Allah, for Allah is forgiving and merciful. [106] Offer no defense on behalf of those who've betrayed their own souls, for truly Allah has no love for underhanded sinners. [107]

They may hide (their intentions) from other people, but they can't hide (them) from Allah, for He's in their midst when they plot in the night - using the kinds (of vile) words that He detests! *Allah surrounds them in everything they do!* [108]

They're the kind of people on whose behalf you may offer a defense in this world, but who is going to defend them against Allah on the Day of Assembly, and who will take care of things for them then? 438 [109]

If anyone commits an offense or otherwise wrongs his own soul, but then later seeks Allah's forgiveness, he will find Allah to be forgiving and merciful. [110] If anyone earns a sin, he earns it against his own soul. Allah is full of knowledge and wisdom. [111] If anyone earns a fault or a sin and then blames it on someone else who is innocent, he will carry (upon himself both) the lie and an obvious sin. [112]

If it wasn't for Allah's favor and mercy towards you, a group of (the hypocrites)

would've certainly schemed to lead you astray, but they've only succeeded in leading their own souls astray. They're incapable of causing you any real harm, for Allah has sent down the Book to you and (the standard of prophetic) wisdom, 439 and (He taught you) what you didn't know (before). Allah's favor is powerfully inclined towards you. [113]

In most of their secret discussions there's nothing good (being said or planned). However, if someone is encouraging a charitable deed, (planning) an exemplary (act that will help many) or (devising ways to) make peace between people, (then being secretive is allowed). Whoever engages (in secret discussions) for these (ends), while looking only for the pleasure of Allah, soon shall We give him a valuable reward. [114]

Enemies of Allah shall be Vanquished

If anyone works against the Messenger, even after guidance has been clearly conveyed to him, and follows a path other than that of a believer, We'll leave him on the path he's chosen and then lead him into Hellfire - *what a terrible destination!* 440 [115]

---

for when the woman he had taken up lodging with in Mecca found out about his criminal past, she threw him out of the house. Penniless and hungry, he eventually broke into a house in Mecca by tunneling through a wall. The wall collapsed on him, however, and killed him. (*Asbab ul-Nuzul, Ma'ariful Qur'an*)

438 The Prophet said, "Hellfire is surrounded by desires and passions, while Paradise is surrounded by hardships and trials." (*Bukhari*)

439 This 'wisdom' is understood by the commentators to be the Prophet's rulings and teachings – as a separate body of knowledge apart from the divine Qur'anic revelation. Collectively, this is called the Prophet's way or *sunnah*. This is further proof of the validity and importance of the *hadith* literature in properly understanding how to live and implement the Islamic way of life.

440 The brother of a man named Maqees ibn Dubabah was killed in the countryside in a district known as an-Najjar, and Maqees went to the Prophet seeking justice. The Prophet sent him along with a representative to the tribe of Fihr to ask them to produce the murderer, so he could be brought to justice. The tribal elders said they didn't know who killed Maqees's brother, but they would pay the penalty or blood-money to him to compensate him for his loss. Maqees was given one hundred camels. As he was riding back with them towards Medina, he thought that it wouldn't look honorable in the eyes of the Arabs to accept the blood-money and that someone had to die for the killing of his brother. He looked at the Prophet's representative who was riding with him and concluded that since he was also a man of the Fihr tribe, he could revenge himself upon him. So, he beat the man to death with a rock

What Kind of a Friend is Satan?

Allah doesn't forgive (the sin of) making others equal with Him, but He forgives any other sins besides this for whomever He wants. [441] Whoever makes others equal with Allah has made a huge mistake and gone far off into error. [116] (The idol-worshippers) call upon goddesses (for favors) in place of Him, but they're really calling upon a relentless devil! [117]

Allah had cursed Satan, but he (was defiant and challenged Allah), saying, "*I will ensnare a certain number of Your servants.* [118] *I'll mislead them and urge them (to sin). I'll order them to slit the ears of cattle (for the sake of mindless superstition) and to disfigure what Allah created.*" [442] Whoever takes Satan for a protector in place of Allah is clearly lost in bewilderment! [119]

Satan makes them promises and urges them (to commit sins), but Satan's promises are nothing more than deception. [120] (His followers) will have their dwelling in Hellfire, and they'll find no way out. [121] However, We're soon going to admit those who believed and did what was morally right into gardens beneath which rivers flow – *and there they shall remain forever*! Allah's promise is true, and whose word can be more honest than Allah's? [122]

What is the Best Way?

*N*either your desires nor the desires of the Followers of Earlier Revelation (can prevail). [443] Whoever does wrong will be repaid accordingly, and he'll find neither a best friend nor helper besides Allah. [444] [123] Whether they're male or female, whoever does what's morally right and has faith will enter the Garden, and not the least bit of injustice will be done to them. [124]

Whose way of life can be better than the one who submits himself to Allah, does

---

and took his camels to Mecca where he renounced Islam and boasted of his exploits to the approving idol-worshippers. Some years later, when the Muslims compelled the bloodless surrender of Mecca, Maqees was found, arrested and executed for the brazen murder. This verse references that man and his actions. (*Asbab ul-Nuzul*)

[441] A man named 'Abdullah once asked the Prophet, "What's the greatest sin in Allah's sight?" The Prophet replied, "To set up a partner with Allah, even though He created you by Himself." The man then asked what the next two greatest sins were, and the Prophet said, "To kill your children for fear of sharing food with them and to commit adultery with the wife of your neighbor." (*Bukhari*)

[442] Some commentators say this refers to the practice of castration, while others say is refers to people tattooing their bodies. The Prophet forbade people from doing both activities. (Getting a tattoo was a common pre-Islamic custom.) The idea behind prohibiting tattoos is that a tattoo defaces the physical appearance with which Allah graced a person, as if somehow the appearance Allah gave a person isn't good enough and must be masked over. Those who had tattoos when they converted were not sanctioned for it upon conversion, as conversion causes a person's record of deeds to be wiped clean.

[443] Ibn 'Abbas (d. 687) explained that this passage was revealed in response to a claim made by a group of Jews who told the Muslim listeners, "We're better guided than you. Our prophet came before your prophet. Our book came before your book, and we're more worthy of Allah than you." The Muslims offered that their prophet came last and was thus the best of all due to his superseding all others. (*Ibn Kathir, Asbab ul-Nuzul*)

[444] Every bad deed a person does will come back to him as retribution from Allah, either in this life or in the next, unless Allah forgives it. When the second sentence of verse 123 became known to them, the companions became distressed. When the Prophet asked Abu Bakr why he and others were so despondent, he explained, "Messenger of Allah, there's hardly anyone among us who hasn't committed at least a small sin in his life. Now if every wrong has to be paid back, who among us can ever hope to escape unharmed?" The Prophet replied, "Abu Bakr, you and your believing brothers don't need to worry about that because the hardships you face in the world will be the compensation for your sins." (*Tirmidhi*) In another report about the same incident, the Prophet explained that the punishments in retribution a person may receive on account of sins are not always a payback that will come from Hellfire. Small hardships, even stepping on thorns or getting pinched, will pay back one's sins. (*Muslim*)

167

what's morally right and follows the creed of Abraham, the natural monotheist? Indeed, Allah even took Abraham as a friend. [125] Everything in the heavens and on the earth belongs to Allah, and He embraces all things. [126]

Don't Oppress Widows and Orphans

$\mathcal{T}$hey're asking you for instructions (on how to treat) women, [445] so tell them:

"Allah (Himself) gives you (men) instructions on (how to treat) them. (Follow) what's been recited to you in (this) book concerning women who have orphaned children, [446] and from whom you're withholding their rightful property - and yet you seek to marry them (to get at their wealth or you avoid marrying them without letting them marry others in order to keep control of their property)!

"And also (follow the rules that you have been given concerning) the helpless children (in your midst). Your (duty) is to do justice to orphans, (so you must be fair and give widowed women and their orphaned children their inheritance)! There's not any good deed that you can do, without Allah knowing all about it." [127]

Treat Women with Fairness

$\mathcal{I}$f a wife fears aggressively defiant behavior [447] from her husband or is afraid

---

[445] Islam granted automatic inheritance rights to women and to orphans. Pre-Islamic Arab traditions did allow inheritance for these two groups, but the usual practice was for unscrupulous men to seize the inheritance or otherwise play games to keep control of it. Even worse, male relatives could assume control of that inheritance by either "inheriting" the widow or forcibly marrying the orphan girl. One man complained openly in Medina about this change in custom, saying, "How can women and children have the right to inherit when they neither work nor earn a living? Are they going to start inheriting now as if they were men, even though they did not earn that wealth?" After the revelation of verse 4:3, another man, who resented the changing of longstanding Arab customs regarding the permissibility of taking advantage of orphan girls to get at their inheritances, went to the Prophet for clarification. This man, a clan leader named Jabir ibn 'Abdullah, had an unattractive, blind female cousin under his care, (who had also happened to have inherited a fortune from her deceased father). His plan was to keep her around and prevent her from marrying another so as to keep control of her inheritance. He exclaimed to the Prophet, "Does an ugly, blind girl have the right to inherit?" The Prophet replied, "Yes, most definitely." Then he recited this verse of the Qur'an. (*at-Tabari*)

[446] There are three opinions about this part of the verse, which was revealed a short time after the Battle of Uhud, a battle in which many Muslim men lost their lives, leaving many widows and orphans behind. The first opinion is that it refers to grown women with dependent children who lost their husbands and whose estates were then supervised for them by male relatives. Some of those men were interested in marrying them but were withholding their lawful property from them or failing to offer an adequate dowry, putting the women (and their dependent orphans) at a disadvantage. The other interpretation is that this verse refers to the teenaged daughters of widows who had not received their fair share of their inheritance from the males who took over management of their fathers' estates. If a man, then, desired to marry her, again she would be at a disadvantage. The third interpretation is that it refers to orphaned teenaged girls who were under the care of men who mixed their property so closely together with the that of the orphans that they wanted to marry them merely to maintain their new augmented prosperity. If the young ladies refused to marry them, the men would obstruct them from marrying anyone else, not wanting their wealth to decrease. This second and third interpretations are the weakest due to the fact that the Arabic word used for orphan here is in the masculine gender, meaning orphans - boys or girls. In addition, the Arabic word for women (*nisa'*) is also present. Thus, despite some commentators' insistence, it probably doesn't refer to men marrying orphaned young girls, but rather means that men who were thinking of taking advantage of women with orphans should back down and be fair. In either case, however, the meaning of the verse is the same: a man who wants to marry a female whose interests he is looking after must first do justice by releasing her property to her and giving her a proper dowry. Pre-Islamic abuses of orphans and their property were legendary.

[447] *Nushooz*, i.e., aggressive defiance or disloyal conduct on the part of the husband, such as becoming unreasonably overbearing, abusive, uncaring, or cavorting with women he is not supposed to see or shamelessly acting contemptuously towards his wife. Also see 4:34 and the Biblical book of Deuteronomy 22:13-19 where a woman is *forced* to remain married to a bad husband if he dishonored

he will abandon her, it isn't wrong for them if they arrange a fair settlement between themselves (to mutually alter the stipulations of the marriage contract or initiate a divorce). [448]

A (fair) settlement is best, even though people's souls are swayed by greed. [449] If you do good and guard yourselves (against committing injustice, remember that) Allah is well-informed of whatever you do. [128]

You'll never be able to achieve fairness between women, (if you happen to have more than one wife), no matter how hard you try, though don't turn away (from one wife) altogether, as if you were leaving her to languish. [450] If you come to a friendly understanding and remain aware (of your duty to Allah, know that) He's forgiving and merciful. [129]

However, if (a married couple) has irreconcilable differences (and must separate), Allah will provide for all concerned from His abundance, for Allah is the One Who cares for all things and is wise. [451] [130]

Allah is in Control

*A*ll that is within the heavens and on the earth belongs to Allah. And so it was that We directed those who received revelation before you that they should be mindful of Allah, just as We've also directed you (Muslims) to do likewise. If you reject (Him, just remember) that all things within the heavens and on the earth belong to Allah and that Allah is free of all needs and (is the only One) worthy of being praised. [131] Again, everything in the heavens and on the earth belongs to Allah,

---

her reputation unjustly. The Prophet once said that among the first cases to be judged on Judgment Day will be those in which the hands and feet of a man will be forced to testify against their owner for all the physical pain he caused his wife. (*Tabarani, Ma'ariful Qur'an*)

[448] Here is the background story for the revelation of the 'abandon' part of this passage. A man named Ibn Abi as-Sa'ib wanted to divorce his wife because she had grown old and he was disenchanted with her. The woman didn't want a divorce, and so she suggested an alternative. She said, "Don't divorce me. Let me look after my children and set aside a few nights each month for me." The man accepted this arrangement. (*Asbab ul-Nuzul*)

[449] There is a myth that Muslim women are not allowed to divorce their husbands. Besides the fact that this verse says otherwise, the Prophet, himself, affirmed for women the right to divorce and even granted a few divorces to women who sought to divorce their husbands. One woman named Jamilah went to the Prophet and asked to divorce her husband, Qays ibn Thabit, for no other reason than she thought he was so ugly to look at that she could not stand the sight of him. The Prophet granted her request for a divorce. (*Bukhari*) Female initiated divorce is called *khul'* in Islamic law. (Also see 2:229.) There is another myth that an Imam's permission is required before divorce. This is not true as any civil court with witnesses can be the vehicle for a mutually agreed upon settlement. The key is in public disclosure with the binding finality that goes along with it. A third myth is that a woman must have a husband's permission to divorce him. This is patently not true. If he refuses to make a settlement with her, then she is free to take him to court for a settlement. Finally, a fourth myth is that marriage is a religious sacrament in Islam, like it is in most Christian sects. On the contrary, it is a civil contract, which is merely regulated by religious injunctions.

[450] The Prophet said, "Whoever has two wives but then inclines to one of them (more than the other) will come on the Day of Judgment paralyzed on one half of his body." (*Abu Dawud*)

[451] Divorce and remarriage are a natural part of any community's life. Islam addresses these issues squarely and allows for incompatible couples to separate and find new life partners. The meaning of Allah providing bounty to divorced couples is that both sides get their lawful property and the woman has her dowry to help support her until she finds another spouse. If there are children involved, the ex-husband also may be required to pay child support. Compare the Islamic view on the subject with other faith traditions. Divorce is allowed in Christianity, but Jesus allegedly forbade remarriage for divorcees in Matthew 5:32 and 19:9 except in the case of adultery and fornication, (Paul also commented on it in I Corinthians 7:39 and Romans 7:2-3). Traditional Judaism allows only men to divorce (Deuteronomy 24:1-4), though a divorced woman is allowed to remarry, though never to the man who divorced her. The Qur'an provides, without question, the most generous terms for divorced women out of all three religious traditions.

and Allah is enough to take care of all affairs! [132]

If He ever wanted to, He could destroy all you people and create another species, because Allah has the power to do that. If anyone desires a reward in this life, (remember) that in Allah's (hands) are the rewards [133] both of this life and of the next, and Allah hears and watches (over all things). [134]

Stand up For Justice

O you who believe! Stand up firmly for justice as witnesses before Allah, and (be fair witnesses even if it's) against your own selves, your parents or your relatives, as well. (Also, be fair), whether it's (against) the rich or the poor, for Allah can best protect (the legitimate interests) of both sides. Don't follow your own whims, for only then can you (judge) with fairness. If you distort (the truth) or fail to do justice, then know that Allah is well-informed of whatever you do. [452] [135]

Don't be Unreliable in Your Faith

O you who believe! Believe in Allah and His Messenger and in the Book that He sent down to His Messenger, and believe in the books that He sent down to

those who came before (your time, as well.) Whoever rejects Allah, His angels, His books, His messengers or the Last Day has made a huge mistake and gone far off into error. [453] [136]

Those who believe, but who then suppress (their faith), then believe again, and then *again* suppress (their faith) - *and go on increasing in their rejection*, Allah won't forgive them nor will He guide them on the path (of truth). [137]

Inform the hypocrites that there's (nothing) for them to look forward to (in the next life other than) painful punishment. [138] So those who take as their close allies (people) who've rejected (Allah) in preference to the believers - *are they looking for high status among them?* Yet, all high status belongs to Allah! [139]

He's already sent down to you (the instructions) in the Book that when you hear the (revealed) verses of Allah being mocked and ridiculed, you're not allowed to sit with (such people) until they turn to a different topic. [454]

If you did (stay there, while insults were being hurled against Allah's revelations), then you would be no better than they. (Know that) Allah will collect the hypocrites and all those who suppressed (their faith, and He will throw them) all together into Hellfire. [455] [140]

---

[452] The Prophet sent 'Abdullah ibn Rawahah to the Jewish settlement of Khaybar to collect the tax on agricultural produce. The Jews offered 'Abdullah a bribe if he would go easy on them. He became angry and declared that he would not be unfair even one bit. On that the Jews said, "This (kind of justice) is the basis upon which the heavens and the earth were created." Then they paid their taxes in full. (*Ibn Kathir*)

[453] Imam Abu Hamid al-Ghazali (d. 1111) once wrote: "Don't be like the deceived fools who are happy because their wealth increases every day while their life shortens. What good is added wealth when your life span dwindles? Only get happy if you've increased in knowledge or done good deeds, for they are the two companions that will be with you in your grave after your family, wealth, children and friends walk away." (*Ihya 'Uloom ud-Deen*)

[454] Verse 6:68, which was revealed in Mecca long before this verse was revealed, is what is being referenced here in the opening sentence.

[455] A person who claims to be a believer but then sits with those who insult Allah is showing him or herself to be a hypocrite. Ibn Kathir, in his monumental work of commentary, offered the following saying of the Prophet to show that this ban can theoretically be extended to sitting with those who disobey Allah's laws, and who thus mock the revelations of Allah indirectly. "One who believes in Allah and the Last Day should not sit down to eat in a place where liquor is being served."

They're the ones who bide their time and watch you, (looking for any signs of weakness). If you gain a victory from Allah, they say, *"Weren't we on your side all along?"* but if the faithless gain (the upper hand), they say (to their allies), *"Aren't we more valuable to you now, because we protected you from the believers?"* Allah will judge among all of you on the Day of Assembly, and Allah will never give those who suppress (their faith) a way (to succeed completely) over the believers. [141]

The hypocrites think that they're out-smarting Allah, *but He's the One out-smarting them!* When they stand up to pray, they stand sluggishly, only wanting to have people see them. [456] They don't remember Allah very much at all! [142] (They're) distracted all throughout (their prayer), not being (completely loyal) to one side or the other. You'll never find the way for someone whom Allah leaves astray. [143]

O you who believe! Don't take those who suppress (their faith) as close allies in preference to other believers. Do you want to give Allah the very evidence to use against you? [144] The hypocrites will be in the lowest depths of the Fire, and you'll find no one to help them. [145]

(They're all doomed) except for those who repent and reform themselves and who then hold firmly to Allah and purify their way of life in Allah's sight. If they do all of that, then they'll be (counted) among the believers, and Allah will soon grant a valuable reward to the believers. [146]

(All you people,) what would it do for Allah to punish you if you're thankful and you believe? (Know that) Allah is appreciative (of the good you do) and that He knows (about all things). [147]

Don't Eagerly Spread Bad News

Allah doesn't like for bad news to be announced in public, except where injustice has been done, for Allah hears and knows (all things). [457] [148] Whether you publicize a good deed or hide it or pardon a (personal) offense (done against you), know that Allah has the power to pardon (all sins). [458] [149]

Allah and the Israelites

Those who seek to suppress (the true knowledge of) Allah and His messengers and who want to separate Allah from His messengers by saying:

"We believe in some but reject the rest," and those who try to take a (compromising) middle course [150] - they're all equally

---

[456] The Prophet said, "It is the prayer of a hypocrite. It is the prayer of a hypocrite. It is the prayer of a hypocrite, who keeps sitting until the sun is about to set and is about to pass behind the horns of Satan, then he rushes to stand and offer four quick units of prayer (like a chicken) pecking, and he only remembers Allah a little in each of them." (*Muslim*) This refers to the *'asr*, or late afternoon prayer, whose time ends when the sun is about to begin its setting on the horizon. ("The Horns of Satan" is an Arabic figure of speech for the place of the setting of the sun – nighttime being the time when people get a bit foolish in their behavior, if they're not careful!) The Prophet also said, "The hardest prayers upon the hypocrite are the night (*'isha*) and dawn (*fajr*) prayers. If they knew the rewards for them, they would attend them, even if they had to crawl." (*Bukhari*)

[457] A disgruntled dinner guest was complaining in public that his hosts did not feed him well. When the Prophet learned of this, he received this revelation in response that tells believers not to complain in public about anything they don't like unless it is concerning some injustice. (*Asbab ul-Nuzul*) The Prophet said, "Allah, the Exalted, has forgiven my community for what they talk about to themselves, as long as they don't talk about it in public or implement it." (*Bukhari*)

[458] The Prophet said, "Whatever words are uttered by those who curse each other, the one who started it will carry its burden, unless the one who was wronged goes out of all bounds (in retaliation)." (*Abu Dawud*) The Prophet also said, "Giving in charity never decreases wealth, and Allah will increase the honor of a servant who pardons and who is humble for Allah's sake, so that Allah will increase his rank." (*Muslim*)

suppressing (the light of faith within their hearts). We've prepared a humiliating punishment for those who suppress (their faith)! [151]

To those who believe in Allah and His messengers and who make no distinction between any of the messengers, We will soon give them their reward, for Allah is forgiving and merciful. [152]

The (Jewish leaders among) the Followers of Earlier Revelation (in Medina) are asking you to bring down a (holy) book from the sky for them (to see, before they will accept you as a true prophet). [459] (Their forefathers) asked Moses for an even greater (miracle than that) when they demanded of him, "*Show us Allah in the flesh!*"

They were seized by thunder (and rendered unconscious) for their unjust presumption! Yet, they worshipped the calf even after all the clear proofs that had come to them! Even still We forgave them, and We also gave Moses a clear mandate (to lead them). [153]

For their covenant [460] We (brought them) to the raised heights of the mountain, (and afterwards, while they were traveling,) We had commanded them, "*Enter this (city's) gate with humility.*" [461] We also commanded them, "*Don't violate the Sabbath,*" and We took from them a solemn promise. [154]

True Knowledge is not Inborn

$\mathcal{H}$owever, they broke their promise, rejected the signs of Allah, killed the prophets against all right, and now they're saying, "*Our hearts are the covers (within which are written Allah's truth, so we don't need any other revelations).*" [462]

Certainly not! Allah has set a seal upon (their hearts) on account of their rejection, and they have only a little faith. [463] [155]

(Furthermore, they're in such a state because) they suppressed (Allah's truth), made unfounded accusations against Mary, [464] [156] and boasted, "*We killed Jesus, the Messiah, the son of Mary.*" However, they didn't kill him, nor did they crucify him, but it was made to appear to them that they did. [465] Those who argue about it are

---

[459] A group of Jews in Medina challenged Muhammad to bring down a scripture from the sky, even as Moses received his revelation on Mount Tūr from the hand of Allah. Only then, they said, would they believe he was a true prophet. This verse references this challenge. (*Asbab ul-Nuzul*)

[460] See 2:63.

[461] The story is mentioned in 2:58.

[462] A rabbi of Medina felt that Allah's truth was already written in the hearts of his people as in the pages of a book. Thus, their hearts were the 'covers' of that divine understanding. He made the quote that is answered in the following verse. (*Asbab ul-Nuzul*)

[463] The commentators explain that it's not that a Jewish person cannot believe fervently in Allah through the path of Judaism. Rather, the context of this passage clearly shows that because most Jewish people deny the missions of both Jesus and Muhammad, the overall 'quantity' of their faith and belief is 'smaller' in scope by having that much *less* to believe in. (*Zamakhshari*)

[464] The followers of Judaism do not believe in the virgin birth of Jesus and hold that a man, possibly a paramour, must have impregnated his mother Mary. However, both Islam and Christianity hold that God caused her pregnancy miraculously. Mention of the charge made against Mary is found in 19:27-28.

[465] European Christians have long persecuted Jews on the grounds that they killed their *god* Jesus. Muslims do not believe that Jesus was killed or crucified; thus, Muslims have never held a religious 'grudge' against the Jews. Most Muslim scholars put forward the view that Jesus somehow escaped the entire scene on the Hill of Golgotha and was later bodily raised to God. If someone did die on a cross that afternoon, two thousand years ago, it might have been Judas Iscariot or someone the Romans thought *looked* like Jesus, who perhaps was even mistakenly pulled out of the crowd in the confusion of a mob. Only Allah knows, of course, the truth. Records from some early Christian sects (like the Basilidians) reveal that some believers thought Jesus did, in fact, escape to safety before being raised

full of doubts and have no (concrete) information. On the contrary, they only follow theories, for they certainly didn't kill him. [157]

Certainly not! Allah raised (Jesus) up to Himself, for Allah is powerful and wise. [158] Each of the Followers of Earlier Revelation must believe in (Jesus) before they die, for on the Day of Assembly, (Jesus) will be a witness against them. [466] [159]

For the misbehavior of the Jews, We made certain (foods) forbidden to them that were (otherwise) good and wholesome - (food) that was allowed to them (before), but they had hindered too many people from Allah's path, (and were thus given these harsh dietary guidelines as a punishment). [467] [160]

They took interest money, even though they were forbidden to, and they used up people's wealth foolishly. [468] We've prepared a terrible punishment for those among them who reject (the truth). [161]

However, those (Jews) who are firmly educated and who have (true) faith - they believe in what's been revealed to you, as do those who pray and give in charity to the poor and who believe in Allah and the Last Day. Soon We will grant them a valuable reward. [469] [162]

---

to Allah. (Early Christian theologians such as Ignatius, Tertullian and Irenaeus also noted that some of their compatriots in fact questioned the validity of the crucifixion. Several early Christian books such The Apocalypse of Peter and the Acts of John also say the crucifixion was in realty an illusion.) The way Jesus escaped being killed, however, is all speculation. The clear statement of the Qur'an, as presented here, is that he was not killed or crucified. This is, of course, unacceptable to modern Christian theology whose entire world view is based on the idea that a man-god died to assuage the anger of the father-god, and then a ghost-god entered the world to save humans from their sins thereafter. If there were no death and resurrection, then Christianity would have to develop an alternative theology. As a suggestion, perhaps they could begin with what Jesus said when he stated: "The first of all commandments is, 'Hear, O Israel, the Lord our God is One Lord.'" (Mark 12:29)

[466] Jesus, himself, said something similar in John 12:44-50. In addition, in verse 44 of that chapter he makes a clear distinction between a person believing in him and believing in God. So from the Qur'anic point of view, a belief in the truth of Jesus is required of all. The caveat is that the truth of Jesus was that he was God's messenger, not His biological son. The saying of a son or child of God was never understood by Jesus or his people to mean that someone was a biological son of a god. Jesus said in John 1:12: "Yet to all who received Him, to those who believed in His name, he gave the right to become children of God." It was only a beautiful metaphor that later people took too literally! The Prophet said, "Don't overly praise me like the Christians exaggerated Jesus, the son of Mary, for I am only a servant, so say, 'God's servant and messenger.'" (Bukhari) The Prophet also said, "Whoever testifies that there is no god but God, alone with no partners, that Muhammad is His servant and messenger, that Jesus is God's servant and messenger and His word bestowed upon Mary and spirit created by Him, and that Paradise is true and Hellfire is real, then God will admit him into Paradise with whatever deeds he performed." (Bukhari)

[467] This refers to the extremely large number of dietary guidelines that Jews were ordered to follow. (See Leviticus 6:14-23, 8:23-33, 11:1-44 and many others, for example.) By way of contrast, the dietary guidelines in Islam are much lighter and reflect direct concerns of human welfare such as the prohibitions against pork and alcohol, both of which contain grave dangers to health.

[468] Jews were forbidden to charge interest on loans. This injunction might have been tampered with and was possibly reworded to say that Jews were only forbidden to charge interest to other Jews, but that they could charge interest to non-Jews. (See Exodus 22:24, Deuteronomy 23:19-20 and Ezekiel 18:8-9, 13, 17) Besides being an exceptional example of injustice, many Jews (even to this day) have also continued to charge interest to other Jews, thus making them guilty of disobeying their own (possibly doctored) law. (See Exodus 22:12 where God makes this very same charge against them.) The description used here in this verse - of 'eating' the property of others - is especially apt given that the Hebrew word for interest is *neshek*, which literally means "a biting."

[469] This is a reference to the small but steady stream of Jewish converts to Islam as a result of Muhammad's preaching. (Notably, the rabbi 'Abdullah ibn Salam and men such as Tha'labah and Usayd.) By entering Islam the Qur'an was making the case that they were *returning* to their forefathers' covenant with Allah.

All Prophets Taught the Same Message

$\mathcal{W}$e've sent revelation to you, (Muhammad), in the same way that We sent revelation to Noah and to the messengers who came after him. We sent revelations to Abraham, Ishmael, Isaac, Jacob and the tribes (of Israel), as well as to Jesus, [470] Job, Jonah, Aaron and Solomon, and We gave the Psalms to David. [163]

We've already told you the story of some of the messengers, but of others We haven't. [471] *Allah even spoke directly to Moses.* [164] The messengers gave good news, as well as warnings, so that people (who lived generations) after (the time) of each messenger would have no plea (of ignorance) against Allah, for Allah is powerful and wise. [165]

This Message is from Allah

$\mathcal{A}$llah testifies that what He sent down to you was sent from His Own knowledge, and the angels testify as well, though Allah is enough of a witness Himself! [472] [166] Those who cover (the light of faith within their hearts) and keep others away from the path of Allah have strayed far away in error. [167]

Allah won't forgive those who cover over (their ability to have faith in Him) and who do wrong, neither will He guide them towards any pathway, [168] *save for the pathway to Hellfire,* and there they shall remain forever, and that's easy for Allah. [169]

O people! The Messenger has come to you in all truth from Allah, so believe! It's in your best interest to do so. However, if you reject (the truth, know that) everything in the heavens and on the earth belongs to Allah, and Allah is full of knowledge and wisdom. [170]

A Call to Christians to Abandon False Doctrines

$\mathcal{F}$ollowers of Earlier Revelation! Don't go to extremes in your religious (doctrines), and don't make statements about Allah that aren't true. [473] Jesus, the son of Mary, was a messenger from Allah and His (creative) word bestowed upon (the virgin) Mary and a spirit sent from Him. [474] So believe in Allah and His messengers (who were mortal men).

---

[470] Jesus is reported to have said in the Bible: "Most assuredly, I say to you, he who hears my word and believes in Him who sent Me has everlasting life, and shall not come into judgment, but has passed from death into life." (John 5:24) Is this not identical with the message of Prophet Muhammad? Thus, all prophets taught the same truth from God.

[471] The Qur'an was not meant to be a history book, listing the names and stories of every prophet who ever lived. It only mentions the names of twenty-five, and only in conjunction with teaching some specific lesson or principle.

[472] Some prominent Meccans visited Muhammad in Medina and said, "We asked the Jews about you, and they said they didn't know anything about you (and your authenticity as a prophet). So show us who is corroborating your claim that Allah sent you as a messenger." This passage was revealed in response. (*Asbab ul-Nuzul*)

[473] Christians went too far in their doctrines by elevating a man (Jesus) to the status of a god, while Jews went in the opposite direction, completely denying Jesus as a messenger from God and further denigrating him as a false rabbi and an illegitimate son of Mary.

[474] Christianity and Islam have different understandings of what Jesus being a "word" from God actually implies. For Christians it signifies a part of God, Himself, entering into earthly flesh, whereas for Muslims it is simply the verbal command of God to create something new, in this case a baby with no earthly father. See Qur'an 3:47-51. This verse is sometimes used by Christians to assert that the Qur'an accepts Jesus as a part of God, especially in the phrase that says Jesus is "a spirit sent from Him." In the court of the fabled 'Abbasid caliph Harun ar-Rashid, a Christian physician cited this verse as proof that the Qur'an was teaching that Jesus was part of God. The Muslim scholar to whom he was speaking, 'Ali al-Waqidi, then read verse 45:13 which stated that everything in the heavens and

Don't say, "*Trinity.*" [475] Don't do it, as that would be best for you. Truly, Allah is just one God, *glory be to Him!* He's (far above) having a child! He owns everything in the heavens and on the earth, and Allah is quite enough to take care of matters (for Himself)! [476] [171]

The Messiah never refused to be Allah's servant, [477] nor have the angels, nor the nearest (people devoted to Him). Whoever arrogantly refuses to serve Him will be gathered back to Him (for judgment). [172]

Those who believed and did what was morally right will be given their due reward by Him, *and even more out of His bounty!* [173]

But those who were hesitant and arrogant will be punished by Him with a painful punishment, *and they'll find no one to help them or protect them besides Allah!* [173]

O people! Absolute proof has now come to you from your Lord in that We've sent you a clear light. [174]

So those who believe in Allah and hold firmly to Him will soon be admitted to (a state of) mercy and grace from Him, and

---

the earth "came from" Allah, and he challenged the Christian to extrapolate from that statement that everything everywhere was a part of God. The Christian had no answer and instead converted to Islam. (*Ma'ariful Qur'an*)

[475] The New Testament proclaims that God is a trinity in I John 5:7, but is this the pronouncement of Jesus, or of any prophet? No, Jesus is not the one who spoke or wrote these words. This is the statement of an anonymous writer who wrote this letter, which was later attributed to a man named John, decades after Jesus left the world, and at a time when Christians were of diverse opinions about the nature and person of Jesus. (Paul, a Jewish convert to the Christian movement, was the biggest proponent of the evolving trinity theory, but even he sometimes hinted that Allah is more powerful than Jesus. See II Corinthians 11:31.) The people who saw Jesus alive thought that he was only a prophet - none thought of him as a god, as evidenced by the fact that no one fell flat on their faces, worshipping him as the creator of the universe. Instead, they walked with him, talked with him, argued with him, doubted him and even had dinner with him! (Matthew 28:19 does have Jesus mentioning the names of the father, son and holy ghost, but modern Christian scholars recognize that this trinitarian phrase was inserted in the text at a later date by an unknown writer, and Biblical translations often delete or footnote this passage. This is proven by the fact that the Gospel of Mark, which was written earlier than Matthew, has the same incident, with no trinity of beings being mentioned by Jesus. See Mark 16:15.) So why did many Christians three centuries later decide that Jesus was God? (Indeed, the first use of the word 'trinity' only came in the third century and was coined by a Carthaginian lawyer named Tertullian.) With the help of the imperial power of the Roman emperor Constantine, who himself was well-versed in man-gods and mystical philosophy, the doctrine of the trinity gained ascendancy and was favored dogma by the year 325. The main details of this theory were mainly formulated by a church bishop named Athanasius, and later by another bishop named Alexander. Those Christians who dissented, after the official doctrine was adopted by the Catholic Church in the year 451, were either persecuted or silenced - permanently. (Those who held that the trinity was false were known as followers of Arius, and they suffered greatly.) Athanasius himself is reported to have confessed that the more he tried to explain the trinity, the more unclear his arguments became! (See John 14:28 and 8:42 where Jesus affirms he is not equal with God.)

[476] Ibn 'Abbas said this verse directly references four different Christian groups of the time who had various views on Jesus and his status. The four groups were the Jacobites (who believed Jesus was God), the Marcusites (who believed Allah was in a trinity), the Melkites (who believed Jesus and Allah were partners)and the Nestorians of Najran (who believed Allah had a son). Also see 5:17, 72-73.

[477] Muslims believe that Jesus will return during the End Times. The Prophet said, "The prophets are paternal brothers (in religion). Though their mothers are different, their way of life is the same. I, more than anyone else in the world, have more of a right to Jesus, the son of Mary, for there was no prophet between him and me. He will descend (from heaven), and if you get to see him you will recognize him. He is a well-built man with skin between a red and white complexion. He will descend wearing two long yellow garments, and his hair will appear to be wet even though there is no water in it. He will break the cross, kill pigs and cancel the *jizyah* tax on non-Muslims, even as he calls people to submit (to God)...Jesus will remain for forty years and then will die, and Muslims will offer his funeral prayer." (*Ahmad, Abu Dawud*)

He will guide them to Himself along a straight path. [175]

More on Inheritance Law

$\mathcal{N}$ow they're asking you for (an additional) legal decision (concerning inheritance in cases in which there are no descendants or ascendants). [478]

Say (to them), *"Allah gives you the following instructions for people who leave neither descendants nor ascendants as heirs. If it's a man who dies and he leaves a sister, but no children, she will get half the estate he leaves. If (the deceased was) a woman who left no children, her brother gets her estate. If there are two sisters (or more, left as heirs), they will get two-thirds of the estate (to share between them). If there are brothers and sisters, males and females, (then they will share the entire inheritance, with) the male receiving twice the share of the female."*

And so Allah makes things clear to you so you won't do anything in error, (and remember that) Allah knows about all things. [176]

---

[478] A man named Jabir ibn 'Abdullah was on his deathbed, and he asked to see the Prophet. He had no parents or children to whom he could give his estate, but he did have seven sisters. He was unsure about how much inheritance he should leave for them to split amongst themselves, whether a half or two-thirds. He was vexed greatly for he didn't want to give the wrong amount and be accountable to Allah. The Prophet told him to ease his mind, and this verse was revealed in answer. Thus, the sisters received two-thirds of the estate to divide amongst themselves. (*Asbab ul-Nuzul*)

The Banquet Table

5 Al Ma'idah
Late Medinan Period

This chapter was revealed over many months in Medina near the later days of the Prophet's mission. Thus, it addresses a wide variety of issues, many of them reflecting the intense interfaith dialogues going on within the city. The memorable lines contained in the middle of verse three, which speak of the completing of Islam as a way of life, were revealed during the Prophet's last pilgrimage in the year 632. Some believe that that passage may have been the last Qur'anic revelation the Prophet received. It was this passage that led many of Muhammad's closest followers to conclude that the ministry of their beloved guide was coming to a close. The Prophet reportedly said of this chapter: "The chapter of the Banquet Table has been revealed as the last stage in the revelation of the Qur'an. Therefore, take what has been pronounced as lawful within it as lawful forever, and take what has been pronounced unlawful in it as unlawful forever." (*Ma'ariful Qur'an*)

In the Name of Allah, the Compassionate, the Merciful

O you who believe! Fulfill your obligations! You're allowed (to eat) all domestic livestock, except for (the animals) that have been forbidden to you by mention (of their names or categories). You're also forbidden to hunt (wild animals) while you're under (pilgrimage) restrictions, and Allah certainly makes rules that He wants. [479] [1]

O you who believe! Don't violate (the holiness) of the symbols of Allah, nor violate the holy month (of *Hajj*) nor (the animals) brought for sacrifice nor the garlands that identify them [480] nor the safety (of those who visit) the Sacred House looking for the bounty and approval of their Lord. [481] However, when you're freed from the restrictions of the holy places and

---

[479] When a Muslim undertakes to perform the pilgrimage to Mecca, he or she must observe certain rules that are designed to teach them to consider the reality of their own insignificance. In addition to the fact that no living thing can be hunted or killed, the harsh desert climate, the rough traveling conditions to and from the ritual sites and the constant exhortations to remember Allah impress upon the pilgrims their utter dependence on Allah.

[480] Animals brought for the ritual sacrifice are often decorated with garlands for their journey to Mecca. Pagans used to decorate themselves with garlands during months outside of the truce months to gain safe passage through hostile territories. This verse is asking people not to treat such markers so loosely.

[481] A pagan Bedouin raider from the dry Najd region named Hutam ibn Hind wanted to see the Prophet and hear about his teachings face-to-face. After the Prophet told him about the teachings of the faith and also the new rules about pilgrimage that the Qur'an mentioned in verse 5:1, he accepted Islam. Then he told the Prophet that he would tell his tribe about Islam, and if they accepted Islam, he would return, but if the tribe rejected Islam, he would stay with them. He also mentioned that he thought it would be hard to convince his tribe. After Hutam left, the Prophet said: "This man came in with the face of an unbeliever and went out with the face of a deceiver." As Hutam passed through the pasturelands outside Medina, he decided to rustle some cattle and escaped. The next

pilgrim's clothes, you may go hunting (animals for food) once more.

Don't let (your) hatred for some people, who once kept you out of the Sacred Mosque, lead you into being spitefully wrong in return. [482]

Help each other in righteousness and mindfulness (of Allah), but don't help each other in sinfulness or aggression. Be mindful of Allah, for Allah is strict in the final outcome. [2]

Ordained Dietary Guidelines

*Y*ou're forbidden to (eat the following things): meat from animals that died by themselves; [483] blood; [484] pork; anything that was dedicated to any other name besides Allah's name; anything that was killed by strangling, a blunt strike, [485] falling or by being slashed to death, as well as anything that's been (partly) eaten by a wild animal - unless you're able to slaughter it (properly); and anything that was sacrificed on stone (altars). You're also (forbidden) to divide (up meat portions among people) by drawing marked

---

year Hutam was making his way to Mecca in full pilgrim gear, and some of the Prophet's companions wanted to waylay him because of all the trouble he had caused them with his theft, but the Prophet refused to give permission as the man was in pilgrim's clothes. That is why verse 5:2 was revealed. (*At-Tabari*) Later, when the Muslims were attempting to make their first pilgrimage to Mecca in the year 628, the idolaters prevented them from entering, and the negotiations at Hudaybiyyah began. Some companions observed a caravan of pagan pilgrims going to Mecca at the same time and wanted to stop them out of spite. The Prophet forbade them, citing this verse. Verse 9:28 made it forbidden for pagans to enter Mecca ever afterward. (*Ibn Jarir*)

[482] This verse is a reminder to the Muslims at the Prophet's time not to hold a grudge against any people from Mecca who used to fight and persecute them. By this time, Mecca was under Muslim control, and the last of the idol-worshippers were gradually accepting Islam. Islam teaches brotherhood, and conversion to Islam erases offenses and slights done before that. In the wider sense, if we are angry with anybody, we still must do right by them. Once 'Umar ibn al-Khattab (d. 644), who had ascended to the office of caliph, saw a man he did not like, and (being the bold man that he was) he told him that he disliked him. The man replied, "Are you going to take away my rights?" 'Umar answered, "I do not like you, but I will respect your rights."

[483] The Prophet made an exception for fish and locusts, which do not need any special slaughtering rituals and which can be eaten even if found dead (as long as they're edible, of course). (*Ahmad*)

[484] Many societies, even into modern times, consume cow or horse blood (sometimes by tapping into the veins of living animals) to supplement their diets. However, blood carries many dangerous pathogens and is absolutely unsafe for human consumption. For this reason, even after an animal is slaughtered, the carcass is drained of as much blood as possible before butchering. (Any blood that does not drain and cannot flow out from the meat is exempted.) This requirement to drain the blood is also a law in the Bible in Leviticus 7:27. This, along with giving the animal a painless death and pronouncing Allah's name at the time of slaughter, makes meat *halal* or allowed for a Muslim. The Prophet did allow the consumption of the liver and spleen.

[485] The Prophet forbade slaughtering animals by beating them to death with sticks, which was a common pre-Islamic practice among the Arabs. (*Ibn Kathir*) If an animal is pierced by a spear or arrow while hunting, then one is allowed to eat of it, but if the arrow does not penetrate the skin, and rather kills the animal merely by blunt force, then the animal is not allowed to be eaten. By extrapolation, some Muslim legal scholars have ruled that animals killed by gunshot are also not allowed to be eaten, as the *purpose* of the bullet is to kill by blunt trauma. (*Ma'ariful Qur'an*) The difference is that an animal that is pierced by an arrow will bleed relatively cleanly from the cut as it dies, while an animal killed by blunt force will not release any blood, and thus toxins will remain that would have been otherwise released. While a bullet pierces the skin and causes blood to flow, the resulting wound is often not *clean* and the internal structure of the animal (organs, blood vessels, etc.) is greatly damaged causing a vast amount of chaotic internal bleeding and thus, *contamination* of the meat.

(arrowheads) to make random selections, for that method is immoral. [486]

This day, those who cover over (the truth of Allah) have given up all hope of (destroying) your way of life. So don't be afraid of them; rather, fear only Me. This day, I have perfected your way of life for you, completed My favor upon you and have chosen for you Islam as your way of life. [487]

If anyone is forced by desperate hunger (to eat the forbidden things that were mentioned before), with no desire to do wrong, (then they may eat the forbidden foods for survival purposes only), for Allah is forgiving and merciful. [488] [3]

Now they're asking you what else is allowed for them (to eat), so tell them, *"You're allowed to (eat) anything that's healthy and pure* [489] *and also what you've taught your trained hunting animals (to catch), as you were already directed by Allah.* [490] *(You may) eat what*

---

[486] The Arabs used to dole out meat portions by essentially drawing straws, or in this case, reaching into a bag of marked arrowheads to see who got the best shares. People who might have needed a larger share of the meat to feed their family might find themselves consistently unlucky and receive only small portions, or even nothing if they drew an unmarked arrow! Likewise, those who didn't need the larger cuts might be overly fortunate.

[487] This was one of the last passages revealed to Prophet Muhammad, indicating that his ministry was coming at an end. The name of the religion, *Islam*, or surrender to Allah's will, is given in this verse. It was revealed on a Friday during the Prophet's Farewell Pilgrimage in the year 632 and recited to the gathered throng of 100,000 people on what is known as the Day of Arafat. While many Muslims were elated at this confident statement from Allah, 'Umar ibn al-Khattab began to weep openly. When the Prophet asked him why he was weeping, 'Umar replied, "This verse seems to signal that your time in this world is drawing to a close. With the perfection of Islam, the need for a messenger has been fulfilled." The Prophet replied in the affirmative. Eighty days later, the Prophet passed away, leaving 'Umar distraught and despondent. Some years later, after 'Umar had been elevated to the office of caliph, a Jewish man in Medina approached 'Umar and said, "Leader of the Muslims, you recite a verse in your book that, if it were revealed to us, would have caused us to make that day a holiday." Umar replied, "Which verse is that?" Then the Jew read this verse. 'Umar exclaimed, "I swear to Allah that I know the day in which it was revealed to the Messenger and its hour. It was late in the daytime on the day of 'Arafat on a Friday." (*Bukhari, Muslim*)

[488] Some people from a land prone to famine once asked the Prophet what circumstances of desperation would make eating unlawful things lawful, he said, "When you can't find food for lunch and dinner, and you have nothing harvested with which you can eat, then eat from it." (*Ahmad*)

[489] All permitted or *halal* meats, as well as produce such as fruits, legumes, nuts, vegetables and grains, are considered "good and pure." The Prophet specifically forbade the eating of animals that hunt and kill other animals with their teeth, such as lions, wolves, snakes or lizards, and he also prohibited eating birds that hunt and kill others with their claws, such as falcons and hawks. (*Ma'ariful Qur'an*)

[490] Angel Gabriel appeared to Muhammad, and the Prophet wanted him to enter his house. The angel refused, saying that he would not enter any house that contained a (realistic) representation (of an animal or human) or that contained a dog. Muhammad became concerned for he had none of those things in his house. When he mentioned this in a gathering, one of his female companions named Khawlah thought that maybe his house needed cleaning to satisfy the angel's objection. Accordingly, she volunteered to clean his house for him, and while sweeping she found a dead puppy that had died while hiding under a bed. Afterwards, Muhammad honestly thought that dogs must be unclean so he ordered that all dogs in Medina should be killed or driven off. A man named Abu Rafi' was sent out to perform this grim task, but he first came upon an old woman who had a guard dog that helped her. Feeling pity for her, Abu Rafi' left her dog alone. He returned to the Prophet and told him about it, the Prophet ordered him back out to do the deed, but then many people converged on Muhammad's house and asked why he wanted dogs to be killed, as they were useful for hunting and protection. Muhammad remained silent, awaiting a ruling from Allah, and this verse was then revealed. Thereafter, Muhammad allowed the keeping of dogs, but stipulated that they had to be used for hunting or protection and kept outside the house. Unfortunately, later generations of Muslims have taken this as a kind of taboo against owning dogs at all. The wisdom of not keeping dogs in the house is that they are not 'house pets,' but are built to exist in the free, outside world. Locking a dog in a house is akin to locking a bird in a cage. As much as the bird wants to fly, the dog wants to roam, and thus should be kept outdoors. Of the five surviving *madh-habs*, or schools of legal thought, the Maliki branch allows dogs in the house as long as the intention is that they are guard dogs. The other schools

they capture for you, but be sure to declare the name of Allah over it. Be mindful of Allah, for Allah is quick in taking account." [4]

This day, everything healthy and pure has been made lawful for you. The (ritually slaughtered) food of those who received scripture in the past is also lawful for you, and your food is lawful for them. [491]

(With regards to marriage, you're allowed to marry) virtuous believing women, and (you may also marry) virtuous women from among those who received scripture before your time, but only if you give them their required marriage gifts and only if you desire decency and not lustful behavior or secret affairs. [492]

If someone rejects (faith in Allah), then his deeds will be rendered useless, and in the next life he'll be among the losers. [5]

Preparing for Prayer

O you who believe! When you prepare yourselves for prayer, wash your faces and your hands up to the elbows. Wipe the top of your heads (with water), and (wash) your feet to the ankles. If you're in a state of greater impurity, then bathe your whole body.

However, if you're sick, on a journey, answered the call of nature or were intimate with the opposite sex and you can't find any water (to wash yourselves), then you can take either clean sand or earth and use it to wipe your faces and hands.

Allah doesn't want to put you into any hardship; rather, (He wants to) purify you and complete His favor towards you, so you can be thankful. [6]

---

also allow dogs but with more requirements. The Prophet did allow cats to be kept indoors, and he was fond of them. One oft-repeated story, perhaps spurious but indicative of his love of cats, is that once a cat fell asleep on the corner of his robe, and rather than disturb the cat from its restful slumber, the Prophet cut off the corner of his robe upon which the cat slept.

[491] This verse is understood by Muslim scholars to mean that meat *properly prepared* by *observant* Jews or Christians is allowed for Muslims to eat. (*Qurtubi, Ibn Kathir, Ma'ariful Qur'an*) In the Prophet's time, most Jews and Christians in Arabia observed some basic slaughtering standards that included mentioning Allah's name before felling the animal, cutting the jugular vein swiftly, thus minimizing the pain felt by the animals, and then draining the excess blood from the animal. (See Acts 15:29, 21:25 and I Corinthians 10:20-21) While Orthodox Judaism retained this practice, as the centuries progressed, Christian culture has largely abandoned such methods of meat preparation in favor of methods that are cruel, brutal and often laced with a near total disregard to animal welfare. (Even a brief look into the methodology of so-called 'factory farming' would give any person with a conscience pause for thought.) Muslim scholars are virtually unanimous in their verdict that meat prepared in such a manner does not meet the minimum requirements of the *halal* (Muslim kosher) standard, and thus they advise that the only meat of the Followers of Earlier Revelation that is still allowed for a Muslim to eat is actual *kosher* meat prepared by observant Jews (or by Christians who slaughter similarly, if any can still be found). That the meat prepared by non-observant Christians is forbidden to eat is an issue that was decided in the first generation of Islam. During the rule of caliph 'Ali ibn Abi Talib, the caliph expressly prohibited Muslims from eating the meat of a particular Arab Christian tribe on the grounds that that tribe did not practice the dictates of their professed religion and that their religious habits consisted of no more than the drinking of wine, which Christianity allowed. (*Ma'ariful Qur'an*)

[492] Muslim men are allowed to marry moral (*muhsanat*) women from among the Jews and the Christians, as long as they (the Muslim men) desire a wholesome relationship based on justice and fairness. The non-Muslim wife must be given her due marriage gift, even as a Muslim woman would receive it. It is part of honesty that the concept of a marriage gift be fully explained to them beforehand, so they can decide what they would like to receive with full knowledge. Islamic law stipulates that the husband is not allowed to interfere with the wife's practice of her own religion, nor can he force her to convert, though the children are to be raised as Muslims.

Remember the Favors of Allah

$\mathcal{R}$emember the favors of Allah that have been bestowed upon you, and remember His covenant that He concluded with you when you said, "*We hear, and we obey*." [493] Be mindful (of Allah) for Allah knows what you're thinking. [7]

O you who believe! Stand forth firmly for Allah as witnesses to fair dealing. Don't let the hatred of others towards you make you swerve towards injustice or towards being unfair (to them in return). Be fair, for that's the closest to being mindful (of Allah). So be mindful then, for Allah is well-informed of everything you do. [8]

Allah made a promise to those who believed and who did what was morally right that they'll receive forgiveness and a great reward. [494] [9] Whoever rejects (their natural faith in Allah) and denies Our (revealed) verses will be among the companions of the raging blaze. [10]

Allah Protected the Prophet from Harm

$\mathcal{O}$ you who believe! [495] Remember the favor of Allah that He bestowed upon

---

[493] This refers to the two famous Pledges of 'Aqabah, in which visitors from Yathrib (curious about the Prophet) came to listen to him and then converted to Islam. They pledged allegiance to Muhammad while he was still under persecution in Mecca. The first Pledge of 'Aqabah took place in the year 621, while the second took place in the year 622. By the middle of the same year, the Prophet escaped Mecca and took refuge in Yathrib, which was thereafter named Al Medina, or The City (of the Prophet). An eyewitness to the first pledge reported the following: "We pledged our allegiance to the Messenger of Allah on the night of the first Pledge of 'Aqabah, promising that we would not make others equal with God and that we would not steal, commit fornication, kill our (unwanted female) children or engage in slander. We agreed to obey the Messenger in all that is right. He said to us, 'If you fulfill this pledge, then Paradise is yours. If you commit one of these sins and receive punishment for it in this world, then that will serve as its restitution. If you hide it until the Day of Judgment, then it will be for Allah to decide if he will punish or forgive you." At the second Pledge, the chief of the Khazraj tribe of Yathrib said to the Prophet: "By the One who has sent you with the truth, we swear that we will protect you as we protect them. Accept our pledge of allegiance, Messenger of Allah, for we are a people who know how to fight, a knowledge that has been passed down among us from father to son."

[494] No one is perfect, and Islam does not expect people to be perfect. The Prophet said that if no one sinned, then Allah *would* destroy us and create a people who would sin and then seek forgiveness from Allah and He would forgive them. (Muslim) In this regard, Ibn al-Qayim al-Jawziyyah (d. 1350) once wrote: "Do you think the righteous don't commit sins? They simply hide them and don't expose them. They seek forgiveness for them and do not insist on engaging in them. They admit to them and don't justify them, and they do good deeds after they have wronged themselves (by sinning)." As an aside, a Muslim who sins does not need to broadcast his or her sin publicly if there is no need to rectify a public harm or make whole a specific victim. Allah knows about it, and repentance done sincerely sets the record straight with Allah.

[495] A man named Ghawrath met with the leaders of the hostile tribes of the desert, namely the Muhareb and Ghatafan tribes, and asked if they wanted him to kill Muhammad. They agreed and asked him how he could possibly accomplish that. He replied that he would take Muhammad by surprise. Ghawrath bided his time and kept an eye out for an opportunity to approach his prey. One day, he saw Muhammad sitting alone under the shade of a tree with his sword on his lap. He approached him and casually asked if he could have a look at the blade. The Prophet handed it to him, and Ghawrath drew it and immediately pointed it at the Prophet menacingly, though he couldn't bring himself to thrust it in for the kill. Finally, he asked him, "Muhammad, aren't you afraid?" Muhammad replied that he was not. Then Ghawrath said two or three times, "Who will protect you from me now?" Muhammad answered, "Allah will." Ghawrath hesitated and then suddenly dropped the sword. Muhammad picked it up and called to his nearby companions. While the assailant was still sitting there, Muhammad narrated the incident and then Ghawrath was allowed to go free. Sometime later, Muhammad was visiting the Jewish neighborhood of the Banu Nadir, seeking their assistance in settling a blood-money suit brought by a desert tribe against one of the companions who had killed two of their men. Ka'b ibn Ashraf, the Jewish leader, invited the Prophet into his courtyard and bade him and his companions

you when certain people made plans to move their hands against you, but He restrained their hands from ever reaching you. Therefore, be mindful of Allah, and the believers should trust in Allah. [11]

An Appeal to Jews and Christians

*A*nd so it was that Allah made a covenant with the Children of Israel. We appointed twelve scouts from among them (to go into the land of Canaan to gather intelligence in preparation for their entry). 496

Allah had already told (the Children of Israel), *"I'll be with you as long as you establish regular prayer, give in charity, believe in My messengers, respect them, and loan to Allah a beautiful loan. Indeed, I'll erase your shortcomings and admit you into gardens beneath which rivers flow. If any of you cover over (your ability to have faith) after this, then he's truly wandered far from the even path."* [12]

However, because (the Children of Israel) broke their agreement, We cursed them and allowed their hearts to grow hard. (They manipulated the words of revelation) by rearranging them from their (proper) places, and they forgot a good part of the message that was sent to them. Even still you'll find many of them

engaged in new trickery, *but forgive them and try to overlook (their shortcomings), for Allah loves those who are good.* [497] [13]

We also took a covenant from those who call themselves Christians, but they forgot most of the message that was sent to them. That's why We've let them become disunited in mutual envy and hatred of each other, even until the Day of Assembly. Allah will soon inform them (of the true meaning) of that in which they were engaged. [498] [14]

Followers of Earlier Revelation! Our Messenger has come to you revealing many things that you used to hide in (your religious) scriptures and passing over many (practices of the past that are now unnecessary). A (new) light and a clear scripture have come to you from Allah. [15] With these Allah will guide any who seek His good pleasure towards the pathways of peace and safety. Furthermore, He'll lead them out of darkness and into a light, by His will, and lead them to a straight path. [16]

---

to sit under the shade of a wall while he ostensibly went to order food to be made. Ka'b then retreated into another room and told a man named 'Amr ibn Jahsh ibn Ka'b to drop a heavy stone from the roof down upon Muhammad to kill him. Just before the man could do the deed, however, Angel Gabriel came and warned the Prophet, who promptly got up and left. This verse was revealed soon afterwards, referencing both incidents, and was meant to emphasize that Allah would protect this prophet until the end of his mission. (*Asbab ul-Nuzul, Ibn Kathir*)

[496] The story of the twelve scouts is recounted in the Old Testament in the Book of Numbers 13:1-16.
[497] The Prophet said, "Allah loves kindness and compensates (you) for it in a way that He doesn't compensate (you) for harshness or anything else." (*Muslim*) In other words, Allah rewards kindness and goodness, while punishing those who are harsh and mean.
[498] From almost the beginning, the Christians of the world have been disunited into many competing sects. They also managed to lose most of the teachings of Jesus, as evidenced by the scant amount of his sayings that have survived. The first four generations of Christians simply failed to preserve adequately the full record of Jesus' teachings, and later generations suppressed what remained even further if it didn't fit their evolving doctrines, labeling such records as Apocrypha and such. See the books entitled, *Beyond Belief: the Secret Gospel of Thomas*, by Elaine Pagels or, *The Lost Gospel of Q*, by Marcus Berg, (Ulysses P., 1996) for fascinating discussions into how modern Christians are using rediscovered ancient Christian writings to try and identify and even reconstruct the actual and accurate teachings of Jesus.

On Judeo-Christian Claims

$\mathcal{T}$hose who say that God is Jesus, the Messiah, the son of Mary, are covering over (the real truth). [499]

Say (to them), "*Who has the power to hold back Allah if He wanted to destroy the Messiah, the son of Mary, his mother and everyone else on earth? To Allah belongs the control of the heavens and the earth and everything in between. He creates whatever He wants, for Allah has power over all things.*" [17]

The Jews and the Christians say, "*We're the sons of God,* [500] *and He loves us (above all others).*"

Then ask (them), "*So, why will He punish you for your sins (if you don't repent of them)? By no means! You're only mortals from among the (many peoples) that He's created. He forgives whomever He wants, and He punishes whomever He wants. The control of the heavens and the earth and all that's in between them belongs to Allah, and back to Him is the final destination.*" [18]

Followers of Earlier Revelation! Now Our Messenger has come to you making (things) clear for you after a pause in (the chain of) Our messengers.

That way you won't be able to say, "*No bearer (of good news) or warner ever came to us!*"

Now a bearer (of good news) and a warner has come to you, and Allah has power over all things. [19]

The Children of Israel and the Promised Land

$\mathcal{R}$ecall when Moses said to his people, "*My people! Remember Allah's favor towards you when He placed prophets within your midst, and when He placed you in charge (of your own destiny after you were enslaved in Egypt) and how He gave you what He hadn't given to any other nation.* [20] *My people! Enter the holy land, which Allah has assigned to you, and don't turn back, for then you'll be among the losers.*" [21]

"*But Moses!*" they cried. "*There's a powerful nation already here in this land, and We'll never be able to enter it unless they leave. If they go away, then, and only then, can we go in!*" [501] [22]

However, two God-fearing men - upon whom Allah had granted His favor - came forward and (boldly) suggested, "*Enter (their main stronghold) through a certain entrance (that we discovered on our scouting mission). When you're inside (the walls of the city), victory will be yours, so trust in Allah if you really have faith.*" [502] [23]

---

[499] This verse is referring to the Christians of Najran and/or to the Jacobite Christian sect, according to many early commentators such as al-Jawzi (d. 1200) and Ibn 'Abbas (d. 687).

[500] Traditionally, Jewish writers and prophets have made the metaphorical statement about righteous people as being God's sons. No Jew ever took this statement literally, and Jesus, himself, used the device as a part of his poetic heritage. The Bible is replete with many verses where the righteous are called the sons of God. See Job 38:7, Genesis 6:2 and Matthew 5:9.

[501] A short time after freeing the Hebrews and other believers from Egypt, Moses was given the mission to settle them in a new land where they could become a nation. He quickly sent 12 scouts to reconnoiter the area (see Numbers chapter 13), and they returned with glowing reports of a bountiful region. In the land of Canaan there were many areas in which the weary refugees could settle. All that stood in the way were several war-like peoples, chief among whom were fearsome natives often called the Canaanites, who would never let the people of Moses settle in their territory without a fight. The Old Testament records God promising Canaan to the seed of Abraham forever, i.e., the Jews and the Arabs. See Genesis 15:18.

[502] The Old Testament identifies these two stalwart men as Joshua and a Midianite ally named Caleb, whom Moses had sent ahead as scouts in Canaan. (See Numbers 14:6-9 and 26:65.) They were unable to sway the frightened Hebrews with their tactical suggestion, however, and thus God forbade the entry of the Hebrews into their newly designated homeland for forty years (see Numbers 2:7). During their wandering in the desert, Moses passed away, and Joshua succeeded him as the leader.

(Yet, many of the people persisted in their cowardice) and said, "*Moses! As long as they're present we'll never be able to enter this land - even until the end of time! You and your Lord can go and fight while we sit here (and watch).*" [24]

(Moses) called out, "*My Lord! I only have power over myself and my brother, so separate us from these rebellious people!*" [25] (Allah) answered, "*So indeed it shall be. This land will be forbidden for them for forty years. Until then, they'll wander aimlessly in the wilderness, but don't feel depressed on account of these rebellious people.*" [26]

The Story of Cain and Abel

$\mathcal{R}$elate to them the story of the two sons of Adam in all accuracy. [503] They both presented an offering (to Allah), but it was accepted from one, though not from the other. (In a jealous rage, Cain) said to his brother, "*I'm going to kill you!*"

"*Allah (only) accepts offerings,*" (Abel) replied, "*from those who are mindful (and sincere to Him).*" [504] [27] (Then he tried to reason with his angry brother), saying, "*If you raise your hand against me to kill me, I won't raise my hand against you to kill you, for I fear Allah, the Lord of All the Worlds. [28] As for me, I want you to take my sins upon yourself to add them with yours, for then you'll become a companion of the Fire, and that's the payback of all those who do wrong.*" [29]

(Cain's jealous) soul incited him to murder his brother, and so he killed him and became hopelessly lost. [30] Then Allah sent a raven, scratching on the ground, to show him a way to hide the body of his brother. "*I'm ruined!*" he cried out. "*Couldn't I (at least have been) like that raven over there and buried my brother's body?*" Then sorrowful regret began to well up within him. [31]

It was for the sake (of that crime) that We made it a principle for the Children of Israel that if anyone took a life, unless it be (to punish) a murder or to prevent the spread of chaos in the land, that it would be as if he had murdered the whole of humanity.

Conversely, if anyone saved a life, it would be as if he had saved the life of the whole of humanity. However, even though Our messengers came to them with clear evidence (of the truth) - even after that many of them continued to commit abuses in the land. [32]

The Most Severe of Punishments

$\mathcal{T}$he punishment for those who wage war against Allah and His Messenger, and who strive hard to cause chaos and murder throughout the land, is execution or crucifixion or the cutting off of their hands and feet from opposite sides or (at the very least) exile from the land. [505]

---

[503] According to early Jewish scholars, Adam apparently had to allow his children to marry each other, given that there were no other people around for that purpose (a logical conclusion). One of Adam's daughters, however, was very beautiful and desirable, thus setting up a potentially tense competition between his two eldest sons. (See Jubilees 4:1-12 and Enoch 85:1-10.) Many early Muslim commentators have also adopted this view and repeated this explanation in their commentaries, including Ibn Kathir. According to the story, Cain and Abel both desired to be married to her, and they quarreled about it. To settle the dispute, both men had to offer something to Allah in sacrifice. Abel's sacrifice was accepted, while Cain's was not, (as evidenced by it not catching fire,) and that's the reason why Cain was so driven by anger that he would take the life of his brother. It was, then, the first crime of passion.

[504] Apparently, Cain offered grain on his alter while Abel offered a young goat for his sacrifice. When a fire was lit under their respective offerings, Cain's would not burn. He grew angry on account of it.

[505] Apparently, a group of eight Arab bedouins led by a man named Abu Burda Aslami went into Medina, pretending to be interested in Islam and seeking the hospitality of the Prophet. At the time, the Muslims were being pressured from all sides and were in constant fear of attack from the Meccans in the south and hostile tribes in the north, west and east. These bedouin visitors were treated honorably

That's the humiliation that they'll receive in this world, but an even more painful punishment awaits them in the next, [33] except for those who repent before they fall into your power, for in that case know that Allah is forgiving and merciful. [34]

The Best Goal to Seek

$\mathcal{O}$ you who believe! Be mindful of Allah. Aspire to get closer to Him, and exert your utmost in His cause so you can be successful. [35]

As for those who cover over (their inner knowledge of the truth), even if they had everything in the whole wide world, *and even double that*, and offered it as a ransom on the Day of Assembly, no offer to avoid punishment will be accepted - and their punishment will be painful! [506] [36]

Their only wish will be to get out of the Fire, but they'll never be able to escape from it, for their punishment will endure. [37]

Punishment for Theft

$\mathcal{A}$s for the thief, male or female, cut off the hand of both by way of payback, for this is a fitting (example of poetic justice) from Allah as a consequence for (the sin) they earned, and Allah is powerful and wise. [507] [38] Though, if (the thief) repents after his crime and reforms himself, then Allah will turn to him (in forgiveness), for Allah is forgiving and merciful. [508] [39] Don't you know that the

---

and graciously, and a non-aggression treaty between their tribe and the Muslims was established. When the visitors asked for some cattle to be brought to them so they could milk them for their daily food needs, some cows was promptly procured for them. Then, one night they murdered the assigned cowherd, stole the cattle, killed some people on their way to Medina to embrace Islam and then tried to escape with the loot. They were caught before they could melt away into the countryside. For the heinous murder and resultant terrorism, for the theft, for cruelly abusing the hospitality of the Muslims, and to discourage others from such terrorism, the men were staked to the ground in the desert with their hands and feet cut off on opposite sides. (*Asbab ul-Nuzul*)

[506] The Prophet said, "An inmate of the Fire will be brought out of it (for questioning) and will be asked, 'Son of Adam, what do you think of your dwelling place?' He will say, 'It's the worst dwelling place!' Then he will be asked, 'Would you try to bribe your way out with an entire earth full of gold?' He will answer, 'Yes! O Lord! Yes!' Then Allah will say to him, 'You're a liar, for I asked you for far less than that (in the world), and you didn't do it.' Then he will be returned to the Fire." (*Muslim, Nisa'i*)

[507] The hand that steals is the hand that has to pay. That is what is meant by a fitting or *poetic* punishment. Although it might seem like an odd and even barbaric punishment for theft, especially by the standards of the modern world, it must be remembered that it is a powerful deterrent. In those places where this rule is enforced, theft is nearly unheard of, even as the punishment is rarely if ever meted out. Spending years and years in jail seems to do little to reform the habits of thieves (and may make such criminals worse!) and is a high expense for the public to pay for so little return. On a more technical note, in Islamic legal theory, this punishment is not automatic. In the first instance, Islamically-speaking, anyone accused of a major crime has the right to a fair trial with at least two eye-witnesses who are willing to testify against him. Then if the guilt of theft is proved, the judge must decide whether to apply the punishment or not. For example, if a person stole to feed himself or his family, then he must be let off with mercy and given Islamic welfare money, which is known as *zakah*. Secondly, the value of the stolen goods must exceed a certain minimum amount (more than the value of 25% of a gold *dinar*, according to the Prophet as quoted in *Bukhari*) in the same way that modern legal systems make a distinction between petty theft and grand larceny. (An Islamic gold *dinar* is 22k gold weighing 4.25 grams.) If petty theft, then a lesser punishment or fine is to be imposed. Thirdly, this punishment is all the convicted thief has to endure, not endless years languishing in a prison cell, as criminals must face in modern penal systems.

[508] After Mecca was occupied by the Muslims in a peaceful takeover, a local woman named Fatimah was caught stealing from some people. She was brought before the Prophet, and he ordered her hand to be cut off. Her relatives offered to pay a heavy fine instead, but the Prophet repeated his order. Some people among the Quraysh contacted Usamah ibn Zayd, the son of Barakah and Zayd ibn Harith,

control of the heavens and the earth belongs to Allah? He punishes whomever He wants, and He forgives whomever He wants, for Allah has power over all things. [40]

Facing Down
the Hypocrites of Medina

$\mathcal{M}$essenger! Don't lose yourself in grief over those who race each other into rejection, (whether it be from) among those (Arab hypocrites) who say, '*We believe*' with their lips, but whose hearts are devoid of faith, or it be among the Jews (of Medina), who will listen to any lie and accept (any slander) told to them by people who never even met you! [509]

They switch words from their proper sequence, and they say, "*If (Muhammad) gives you (what you like to hear,) then take it, but if not, then beware.*"

---

and asked him to go and get a different verdict from the Prophet. When he went to the Prophet and tried to talk to him about it, the Prophet told him, "Don't intercede in a punishment ordained by Allah." Zayd asked the Prophet to beseech Allah to forgive him. That night the Prophet gave a speech in which he said, "Those who came before you were ruined because when an honorable person among them stole, they would leave him alone, but when a weak person among them stole, they would punish him according to the full extent of the law. By the One Who holds my soul in His hand, if Fatimah, the daughter of Muhammad stole, I would still order her hand to be cut off." Thereafter the thief had her hand cut off. Then she later came to the Prophet and asked if Allah would forgive her, and the Prophet said, "Yes, this day you are free from your sin just as the day your mother gave birth to you." (*Bukhari*) A'ishah said of her that her repentance was accepted and that she later got married and used to visit her when she wanted a question conveyed to the Prophet on some matter or another. (*Bukhari*) Also see footnote to 5:49.

[509] Muhammad could not read or write Arabic, and he certainly did not know how to read or understand Hebrew. When the rabbis of Medina would quote from the Torah in their discussions with Muhammad, some of them would purposely leave out some lines as they translated from Hebrew into Arabic in order to keep some information secret. Jewish converts to Islam would often point this out to the Prophet. (See 2:100-103.) A Jewish man of Khaybar committed adultery, and based upon his high status his fellow Jews were reluctant to apply any harsh punishment to him. They resolved to send him to Muhammad for judgment on the pretence that if he ruled in favor of the flogging that the Qur'an called for [24:2], then he would be a secular leader in their eyes, and they could follow him. However, if he ruled in favor of stoning, as the Torah prescribed, then he was an actual force to be reckoned with, and the Jews must be on their guard against him. They then went to the Prophet who was sitting with some companions in the mosque and asked what they should do about this adulterer. Muhammad remained silent and either called for some rabbinical students to be brought to him or he himself accompanied them to one of their small yeshivas, or religious schools (the reports do not specify). The Prophet said to the Jewish scholars, "I appeal to you by God who revealed the Torah to Moses. What punishment does the Torah prescribe for an adulterer?" One of the rabbis answered, "They are rubbed with ash, defamed and whipped, and the defamation comes by placing both guilty parties back to back on a donkey that is led around the streets." The others present affirmed their agreement, but the Prophet noticed that one man among them was keeping silent. The Prophet was told that his name was Ibn Surya, and then he appealed to him for his answer to the question, making him swear an oath to God to be truthful. When Ibn Surya replied that the actual punishment was death, the Prophet further questioned him, saying, "When is the first time in which you disobeyed the order of Almighty God?" Ibn Surya replied, "One of our ancient king's relatives committed adultery, and the stoning was put off. Then a lesser noble also was found to have been adulterous, and the king wanted him stoned. However, his family objected, saying that they wouldn't let their relative be stoned unless the king's relative was stoned first. It was then that they compromised on the punishment among themselves (and lessened it)." The Prophet then asked a rabbi to read from the Torah about adultery, and the man began to read the appropriate section from a scroll, but he kept his finger over the verse calling for stoning and read the verses before and after it. The Jewish convert to Islam, 'Abdullah ibn Salam, (also a former rabbi) informed the Prophet that the first rabbi had skipped a line, and he asked the man to remove his finger and read the verse. When he did, the Prophet then answered, "I judge by what is in the Torah." Then he ruled that the adulterers were to be stoned. The adulterous couple was then taken out and stoned, but the Prophet did not take part in it. This verse was revealed concerning this and other similar affairs in which the Jews asked for Muhammad's rulings on various issues. (*Asbab ul-Nuzul*)

186

If Allah wants to put someone into utter turmoil, you can do nothing for them against Allah (and His plan). (The ones to whom He does that) are those whose hearts Allah has no desire to purify. They'll have nothing but disgrace in this world, and in the next life they'll have a severe penalty to pay. [41]

The (Jews of Medina) listen to lies and devour anything that's been prohibited to them. If they do happen to come to you and ask you to solve their internal disputes, you can either render a verdict or decline to hear the case altogether.

If you decline (to get involved), they can't do any harm to you at all (in their spite). [510] If you choose to adjudicate, then judge fairly between them, for Allah loves fair judges. [42] However, why are they coming to you for decisions at all when they have their own Torah right there with them? It already contains Allah's commandments. Yet, they turn away from it even still, for they're not really all that faithful. [43]

We revealed the Torah, and it contained both guidance and enlightenment (within its pages). The prophets (of old), who surrendered (themselves to Allah's command), used it to judge among the Jews, and the rabbis and legal scholars (also used it to render their judgments, as well). (They were charged with safeguarding and living by) the portion of Allah's Book that was entrusted to them, and they witnessed to their duty.

Therefore, (you Jews of Medina), don't be afraid of (disappointing mere) people. Rather, be afraid of (disappointing) *Me*, and don't sell My (revealed) verses for a petty price.

If anyone judges by any other standard than what Allah has revealed, then they're truly covering over (the truth). [44]

We decreed for them in (the Torah): *"A life for a life, an eye for an eye, a nose for a nose, an ear for an ear, a tooth for a tooth, and a wound in exchange for a wound."*

Now (this principle has been amended,) so if anyone chooses to refrain from retaliating, for (the sake of) charity, [511] then it's an act of atonement for himself.

---

[510] Before the Prophet had entered Medina, the Banu Nadir and the Banu Qurayzah Jewish tribes made war on one another in the context of a wider war between the Arab Auws and Khazraj tribes. When the hostilities were over, the two Jewish tribes settled on a system of blood-money fines to prevent future all-out war, with the victorious tribe (the Banu Nadir) receiving twice the payments for lives lost as the Banu Qurayzah. Thereafter, if one tribesman murdered someone from the other tribe, the Banu Qurayzah would have to pay double the fine in blood of the Banu Nadir. (Therefore, if a man of the Banu Qurayzah murdered a man of the Banu Nadir, two Banu Qurayzah men would be killed in compensation, and so on.) After the Prophet arrived, the Banu Qurayzah, who had been forced to settle under those humiliating terms, were faced with a case of murder and refused to cooperate with the Banu Nadir any further, wishing to refer the matter to Muhammad's judgment. (That is what this passage is about.) This almost rekindled the war between the two Jewish tribes, as the Banu Nadir refused to renegotiate on the Banu Qurayzah's appeal to religious fraternity with their Jewish cousins. The Prophet mediated, saying that the blood-money fine must be equal for both. This earned him enmity from the Banu Nadir and explains some of their intense hostility. It also explains why the Banu Qurayzah were the last (and most reluctant) Jewish tribe to betray him of the three Jewish tribes that lived in Medina. (They only betrayed the Muslims at the insistence of a secret agent from the previously exiled Banu Nadir during the Siege of Medina!) (*Ahmad*)

[511] A man stabbed another man in the leg with an animal horn, and the wounded man went to the Prophet seeking to retaliate against the offender by doing the same to him. The Prophet forbade him from doing anything until his leg healed. (This would've also given the man time to cool his anger and either forgive his attacker or accept a payment of money in compensation.) The injured man didn't wait as ordered, and he stabbed the original assailant in his leg. Later on, the man who had retaliated impatiently developed a limp, and the Prophet blamed him for not waiting until he was healed. The Prophet once said, "Anyone who suffers a wound on his body and forfeits his right to retaliation as an act of charity, then Allah will pardon him that which is similar to what he forfeited." (*Nisa'i*)

⁵¹² If anyone judges by any standard other than what Allah has revealed, then they're truly wrongdoers. [45]

We sent Jesus, the son of Mary, following in their footsteps, to affirm the (truth of the) Torah that had come before him, and We gave him the Gospel, in which there was both guidance and enlightenment, as an affirmation of the Torah that had come before him.

(The Gospel) was a source of guidance and also admonition for those who were mindful (of Allah). [46] And so, let the people of the Gospel judge by what Allah revealed in it. If anyone judges by any standard other than what Allah has revealed, then they're truly rebellious. [47]

Scriptures are the Standard of Judgment

*N*ow We've sent the Book to you, (Muhammad), in all truthfulness, affirming the scriptures that came before you and safeguarding within it (the truth of the previous revelations), so judge between (the Jews and Christians) according to what Allah has revealed (to you). ⁵¹³ Don't follow their petty whims and thus swerve away from the truth that's come to you.

We've given to each one of you (differing religious groups) a legal tradition and a clear method (for dealing with legal issues).

If Allah had wanted, He could've made you all into one community, but He tests you in what He's given you, so forge ahead as if you were racing towards everything virtuous. Your ultimate return is back to Allah, and He's going to show you (the truth) of those things about which you argued. [48]

Therefore, judge between them according to what Allah has revealed, and don't follow their petty whims. Be wary of them so they won't seduce you away from what Allah has sent down to you. If they turn away (and ignore your rulings), then know that Allah wants to punish them for some of their sins. ⁵¹⁴ As it is, most people are disobedient! [49]

Are they looking for a (flawed) ruling (that's similar to how people used to judge) in the ignorant (days before Islam?) For those who are convinced (of the truth in their hearts), who can be a better judge than Allah? [50]

Don't Look to Enemies for Alliance

O you who believe! Don't take Jews and Christians as your close allies, ⁵¹⁵ for

---

⁵¹² This statement about charity resulting in atonement is not part of Jewish Law and is inserted here by divine prescription as a way to supersede the principle of retaliation. The Mosaic principle is given but then modified by the Qur'an, the revelation Allah sent to replace all other previous scriptures. In the Prophet's time, a man became angry at Bilal ibn Rabah, who was of African ancestry, and he called him racist insults. Afterwards he felt bad, went to Bilal, put his face on the ground and then told Bilal to step on his head in retribution. Bilal picked the man up and forgave him.

⁵¹³ Four leading Jewish men of Medina, including K'ab ibn Asad and Shas ibn Qays, wanted to see if they could corrupt the Prophet away from being sincere in his religion. They went to him and told him that they were the leaders of the Jews, and if they converted then all the Jews would follow them. Their only requirement was that he render a biased judgment in favor of them in a dispute they had with some men of their community. This verse was revealed concerning this incident. (*Asbab ul-Nuzul*)

⁵¹⁴ The Prophet said, "Whoever sinned in this life and was punished for it, then Allah is far more just than to combine two punishments on His servant. Whoever commits a mistake in this life and Allah hides that mistake and pardons him, then Allah is far more generous than to punish the servant for something that He has already pardoned." (*Ahmad, Ibn Majah, Tirmidhi*)

⁵¹⁵ The Arabic term used here, *awlia*, is often translated as 'friends;' yet, this is not the Arabic word one uses when referring to a *friend*. This word (sing. *wali*) implies a deep alliance based on mutual interests with one party acting in the role of protector over the other. If the person with whom you

they're only the close allies of each other. [516] Whoever among you turns to them (for alliances, in place of a believer,) is one of them, for Allah doesn't guide corrupt people. [517] [51]

Do you see those who have a sickness in their hearts? They run eagerly to them after exclaiming, "*We're afraid that changing times might bring disaster down upon us!*" Allah will grant a victory or a decisive result, as He wills, and then they'll be sorry for what they've been hiding within themselves. [52]

Then the believers will be the ones to say, "*Are these (hypocrites) the same ones who swore their strongest oaths by Allah that they were on your side?*" Whatever they do is of no use, and they're going to be the ones who will lose. [53]

O you who believe! Whoever among you falls away (from following) his (Islamic) way of life should know that Allah will soon produce a people whom He will love - *and who will love Him back!*

They'll be easygoing with other believers, yet stern against the faithless, striving in Allah's way and paying no mind to all the blame that accusers may heap upon them. That's Allah's favor, which He grants to whomsoever He wills, and Allah embraces all things and is full of knowledge. [54]

Who is Your True Ally?

*Y*our (true) closest allies are Allah, His Messenger and those who believe. [518] They're the ones who establish prayer, give in charity and who bow down (in sincere worship). [55] Whoever turns towards Allah, His Messenger and the

---

would make such a relationship has some ulterior motive or conflict of interest that would eventually cause him to seek your destruction, then what would be the sense of building such a close tie of protection to begin with? Also see 2 Corinthians 6:14 where the Apostle Paul says: "Do not be unequally yoked with unbelievers."

[516] In his first days in Medina, the Prophet had concluded treaties of mutual security with the three Jewish tribes of the city. After some months it was learned that the Banu Qurayzah Jews were playing both sides of the fence, so to speak. While publicly appearing to be friendly with the Muslims, they had also invited a delegation of Meccan leaders to a secret summit in their fortress just outside Medina proper. A group of Muslim riders was sent out to turn the Meccan delegation back, while the senior companions debated what to do about this obvious betrayal. The Muslim patrol was unable to intercept the Meccans, and thus they got through. This particular passage concerns the case of two men who were present among the Muslims as they debated what to do, and it concerns their alliances with the Jews of Medina. The first man, 'Ubadah ibn as-Samat, said, "Messenger of Allah, I have many Jewish allies. They appear to be ascendant, but I will turn to Allah and His Messenger and abandon the protection of the Jews. I will look for refuge in Allah and in His Messenger." Then the hypocrite, 'Abdullah ibn Ubayy, told Muhammad, "I'm a man who's afraid that changing times might bring disaster down upon us. I will keep the Jews as my allies." Muhammad replied, "O Father of Hibab, whatever protection you get from the Jews that exceeds what 'Ubadah ibn as-Samat had is only for your own sake." 'Abdullah ibn Ubayy answered, "Then I accept that." Then these three verses were revealed. No action was taken against the Banu Qurayzah other than to warn Muslims not to get too close with them, as verse 51 suggests. (*Asbab ul-Nuzul, Ma'ariful Qur'an*)

[517] Friendships and amiable relationships with Jews and Christians are not forbidden in Islam. The warning here is only to not make them your closest bosom allies in preference to those who share your faith and allegiance to Allah. The Bible is even more strict about relationships with unbelievers. In I Corinthians 5:11 we read, "But now I have written unto you not to keep company... (with) an idolater...(and) with such a one not to eat." In the Qur'an in verses 60:8-9 Muslims are explicitly allowed to have relationships built on mutual respect with non-Muslim friends and relatives.

[518] 'Abdullah ibn Salam, the Jewish rabbi who converted to Islam, along with his family, went to the Prophet one day and said, "Messenger of Allah. Our house is far from here. We have no place to sit and talk, for our people, having seen us believing in Allah and His Messenger, have disowned us and pledged not to talk to us or marry with us, and we're finding it hard on us." This verse was revealed in response. (*Asbab ul-Nuzul*)

believers – *that's the fellowship of Allah* - and they shall be victorious! [519] [56]

Don't Ally with those Who Disrespect You

O you who believe! [520] Don't take those who mock and belittle your way of life as close allies, whether from among those who received a scripture before you or from among those who reject (the truth). Be mindful of Allah if you're true believers. [57]

When you announce your call to prayer, they mock and belittle it, for they're a people who have no understanding. [521] [58]

Say (to them), *"You Followers of Earlier Revelation, are you ridiculing us for no other reason than that we believe in Allah and in the revelation that came down to us, as well as in the revelations that came before us? (It may just be) that most of you are rebellious (against Allah)."* [59]

Say (to them), *"Should I tell you about something worse than those (whose religion you're ridiculing), and for which Allah took (your ancestors) to task?* [522] *Those who had Allah's curse and wrath drawn over them,* [523] *some of whom were like apes* [524] *and pigs, and they were the servants of falsehood. They're much worse in status and that much farther astray from the even path!"* [60]

When they come to you, they say, *"We believe (in Allah), too,"* but they're really coming with rejection (of your teachings) on their mind, and when they leave you, they go out with the same (sentiment), and Allah knows all about what they're hiding. [61]

You see most of them rushing into sin and misbehavior and eating whatever they've been prohibited to eat. *What they're doing is pure evil!* [62] Why aren't their rabbis and legal scholars admonishing them against using sinful language and eating what they've been prohibited to eat? *(The*

---

[519] After talking to 'Abdullah ibn Salam, as mentioned in the previous background note, the Prophet walked out of the mosque while people were still inside praying and kneeling. He saw a beggar who appeared to be happy. "Has anyone given you anything?" he asked him. The beggar replied in the affirmative and showed the Prophet a gold ring. When the Prophet asked who gave it to him, the beggar pointed to the Prophet's cousin, 'Ali ibn Abi Talib. "How did he give it to you?" The Prophet asked. The beggar replied that 'Ali had shoved it in his hand while the former was in the process of bowing down in prayer. The Prophet said, "Allah is the greatest," and then this verse was revealed to him. (*Asbab ul-Nuzul*)

[520] This verse was revealed about two men named Rifa'a and Suwayd, who faked their allegiance to Islam, while working behind the scenes to undermine the believers through gossip, plotting, and sowing doubts. Even still, some sincere believers maintained friendly relations with them. This verse warned them to avoid hypocrites such as these.

[521] For a time, whenever the Muslim call to prayer was announced in Medina, some Jews made it a point to tease the Muslims on their way to the mosque by mocking the prayer positions and laughing. This passage was revealed in response. (*Asbab ul-Nuzul*)

[522] A number of Jews went to Muhammad and asked him in which prophets he believed. He began his reply by reciting verse 2:285, which mentions that Muslims must accept all true prophets from Allah When Muhammad then mentioned that he believed in Jesus, the Jews rejected his answer saying, "We swear to Allah that we've never heard of a more unfortunate religion both in this life and in the afterlife than yours, and we don't know any religion more evil than yours." This verse was revealed in response. (*Asbab ul-Nuzul*)

[523] Those who were disobedient among the Jews were condemned in the harshest words in the Old Testament, and the statement of guilt is being repeated here. Deuteronomy 11:28 pronounces the curse for following falsehood. Hosea chapters 8-11 are replete with verses showing God's anger upon the Children of Israel for their disobedience. Jeremiah 16:11-13 condemns them to wander aimlessly through the land, 'aping' every ignorant custom of the heathens. The book of Amos is also very indicative of God's wrath upon the disobedient and how they will be utterly destroyed.

[524] Sabbath-breakers were equated with apes because they aped the customs of the idolaters. (See 2:65) Those who are equated with swine are those who devoured every unwholesome and forbidden practice such as eating forbidden foods or taking interest-money.

immoral things) they're promoting are pure evil!
[63]

Don't Hold Allah as Miserly

𝒯he Jews (of Medina) have said, *"Allah's hand is tied up."* 525 Well, let *their* hands be tied up, and let them be cursed for what they've said.

Not so! Both of His hands are stretched out wide, and He expends as He wills. The revelation that's coming to you from your Lord causes belligerency and rejection to grow in most of them!

As it is, We've instilled antagonism and hatred among them that will last even until the Day of Assembly. Every time they stoke the fires of war, Allah extinguishes them, though they persist in trying to cause chaos in the land. Allah has no love for those who cause chaos. [64]

If only the Followers of Earlier Revelation would've believed and been mindful (of their duty to Allah), then We would've glossed over their shortcomings and admitted them into gardens of delight. [65]

If only they would've held firmly to the Torah, the Gospel and all the revelation that was sent to them from their Lord, then they would've enjoyed themselves from every side. Although there are men from among them who are on the right track, most of them participate in sinful conduct. [66]

An Appeal to the Jews and Christians

ℳessenger! 526 Proclaim what's been revealed to you from your Lord, for if you don't, then you will have failed to deliver the message.

Allah will defend you from the people (who seek to harm you), for Allah doesn't guide those who reject (His message.) 527 [67]

Say (to them), *"Followers of Earlier Revelation! You have no (legitimacy) unless you hold firmly by the Torah, the Gospel and all the revelation that has come to you from your Lord."*

(Sadly), it's the very revelation itself that you've been receiving from your Lord that's making most of them increase in belligerency and rejection, but don't be worried over people who reject (Allah). [68]

---

525 A Jewish man of Medina named Nabbash was ridiculing the Prophet for asking for donations to support his cause. Another Jew named Finhas bin Azura often chided Muslims by saying, "God's hands are tied up," in effect, suggesting that Allah was a miser Who didn't spend of His bounty for the benefit of humanity (and his own tribe's falling fortunes). This verse is a reply to that statement. (*Asbab ul-Nuzul*)

526 The Prophet explained why the first half of this verse came to him, saying, "When Allah, the Exalted, sent me with my message, I was overwhelmed with it, and I knew that many people were against me." This exhortation to action reiterated to him the importance of fulfilling the duty that Allah had laid upon him. A'ishah said that anyone who says that Muhammad ever hid anything from the revelation was a liar and that if he ever were to hide a verse, it would have been this one. (*Bukhari, Muslim*) (Paul echoes a similar sentiment in I Corinthians 9:16-17 with the message he felt compelled to preach.)

527 The second half of this verse was revealed to alleviate the Prophet's fear of being murdered by assassins in his sleep. He was with his wife A'ishah one night, but he remained awake and uneasy. When she asked him why he wasn't sleeping, he said, "I wish there was a good man to watch over us tonight." A'ishah then narrated that while they were talking, they heard a noise outside their door that sounded like weapons being clanked together. The Prophet called to the unknown people outside of his door, and two trusted men, Sa'ad and Hudhayfah, answered that they were coming to stand guard over his house. The Prophet then slept for a time but then woke up and recited this new verse, "Allah will defend you..." He then called out to his volunteer guardians and asked them to go home, for Allah would look after him. (*Tirmidhi*)

Those (Muslims) who believe, along with the Jews, the Sabians [528] and the Christians, anyone who believes in Allah and the Last Day and who does what's morally right, they'll have no cause for sorrow or regret. [69]

And so it was that We made a covenant with the Children of Israel and sent them messengers. However, every time a messenger came to them with what they didn't want (to hear) - *they called some of them imposters, and others they killed!* [529] [70]

They didn't think there would be any dangerous repercussions from it, so they became blind and deaf (to faith). Yet, even then, Allah kept turning towards them (to give them more chances), though many of them remained blind and deaf (to faith). Allah was watching what they were doing. [71]

On the Trinity

$\mathcal{T}$hose who say that Allah is the Messiah, the son of Mary – they're covering over (the truth)! The Messiah, himself, said, "*Children of Israel! Serve Allah, the One Who is my Lord and your Lord.*" [530]

Whoever makes partners with Allah, well, Allah will forbid him entry into the Garden, and instead the Fire will be his home – and the corrupt will have no one to help them. [72]

Those who say that Allah is one of three (in a trinity) are covering over (the truth, as well), for there is no god but the *One* God. If they don't stop what they're saying, then a painful punishment will overtake those among them who suppress (their awareness of the truth). [73] So why don't they turn to Allah and ask for His forgiveness? Allah is forgiving and merciful! [74]

The Messiah, the son of Mary, was no more than a messenger, and *many messengers passed away before him*. His mother was an honest woman - *they both had to eat food (like any other mortal human being)*. Do you see how Allah is making His evidence clear for them? Yet, look how they're deceived away (from the truth)! [75]

Ask (them), "*Are you going to serve something besides Allah - something that has no power to bring you any harm or benefit? (Well, then remember that) Allah is the Hearing and the Knowing.*" [531] [76]

---

[528] The Sabians are a religious group whose roots go back to a form of ancient Judaism blended with Sumerian paganism, but then later incorporated the messianic fervor of John the Baptist. They are also called Mandaeans. There is another group of people in Mesopotamia who claimed the title of Sabians, but their claim is a hoax. Before Christianity arrived in upper Mesopotamia, the people of Harran and the surrounding areas worshipped a trinity of old goddesses: Nanna-Sin (the moon-goddess), Ishtar (the fertility goddess from which the name Easter comes), and Shamash (the sun goddess). After Alexander the Great conquered the area, Harran became a center of learning and knowledge, fusing together Greek philosophy and local beliefs. This type of learning is labeled as Hermetic knowledge after one of the Greek thinkers whose methodology was adopted there. Hermetic knowledge combines elements of paganism, Platonism, Stoicism and Zoroastrianism. These false-Sabians did not include Adam or Abraham in their cosmology. When Islam came, the Muslims left the odd cultists of Harran alone for many decades. One caliph named al-Marwan, after noting that the people of Harran were star worshippers and such, ordered the people of Harran to convert to Islam, but they successfully argued that they were the Sabians mentioned in this verse, thus al-Marwan left them alone, and they survive as a community to this day. The true Sabians, or Mandaeans, also still exist in scattered places throughout Mesopotamia.

[529] See the Old Testament Book of II Kings 17:13-15.

[530] The New Testament affirms that Jesus was not a god born on earth. In John 20:17, we read that Jesus told Mary Magdalene, "Go unto my brethren, and say unto them, I ascend unto my father and your father; and to my God and your God." (Also see Mark 12:29 and Luke 18:19.) All of these and similar statements from Jesus' own mouth reflect his poetic use of the terms 'father' and 'son' in reference to God, a practice that was present in Jewish religious discourse for centuries.

[531] The common practice among the non-Protestant Christians of the world, with slight variations by sect, is to pray to Jesus, his mother or to a pantheon of hundreds of "saints" for favors and intercession

Then say to them, *"Followers of Earlier Revelation! Don't go beyond the boundaries in your way of life without any justification, nor should you follow the fickle whims of the peoples who went astray before you, for they've misled many from the even way."* [532] [77]

Jews must not Ally with those Opposed to Allah

Those who suppressed (Allah's truth) from among the Children of Israel were cursed by David's own tongue and also by Jesus, the son of Mary, for their disobedience [533] and constant violation (of Allah's law). [78] They rarely discouraged each other from the immorality in which they themselves used to indulge, and their actions were quite evil! [79]

Now you see many of (the Jews of Medina) turning towards the faithless (idol-worshippers for alliances), and the deeds that they're sending ahead for themselves are quite evil, indeed! [534] Allah's wrath is upon them, and they will linger in eternal damnation. [80]

If only they would've put their faith in Allah and in the Prophet and in what was revealed to him, then they would've never taken (idol-worshippers) for allies. However, most of them are disobedient. [535] [81]

How do True Christians View Islam?

(Muhammad,) you're going to find that out of all the people who hate the believers, the Jews (of Medina) and the

---

with God. The Qur'an would suggest that it would be better to direct prayers to the source, namely, to God. See 12:40 for the most definitive statement on this subject.

[532] Ibn 'Abbas said this entire passage (72-77) was a call to the Christians of Najran to not continue in beliefs and practices that had diluted the message of Jesus, simply because they were used to them. Jesus taught monotheism. However, Apostle Paul introduced Greco-Roman trinitarianism without any authority into the young but expanding Christian world. In fact, there are so many pagan customs that have been incorporated into Christian culture as to be almost unbelievable. The Roman holiday celebrating the god of the sun was transformed into Christmas. The theology of God being born on earth was lifted from prevalent Greek and Roman mythology. Greek mysticism was melded into the early Gnostic sect, which had an influence on the Book of John. The idea of redemption by the suffering or death of a god goes back to the stories of Heracles, who suffered madness after killing his children, before salvation was allowed (Greek) and the Descent of Inanna, who entered the underworld as was made to suffer and die before coming back to life (Sumer). Cultural trappings such as festive mistletoe, Easter eggs, decorated Christmas trees (which are actually forbidden in Jeremiah 10:1-5), Halloween, the significance of the number twelve, choosing Sunday over Saturday for a Sabbath, the celebration of Christmas on December 25th which was a Roman celebration of the Sun god, saint veneration, and such - all of these have their roots in the paganism of the Babylonians, Phoenicians, Greeks, Romans, Germanic tribes, Vikings and Egyptians. Christian scholars know and affirm this knowledge (and write criticisms on the subject, a tradition that goes back to the early church fathers). Nonetheless, these pagan practices and influences are accepted by lay Christians without question. The Qur'an, then, is asking Christians to go back to their simpler, more monotheistic roots, to go back to Jesus and what he stood for and actually taught, and to abandon the accretions and additions that have been made to his simple yet expansive message.

[533] The relevant angry pronouncements of David and Jesus can be found in the Bible in Psalms 109:17-20, 78:21-22, 69:27-28 and in Matthew 23:33 and 12:34. (Even Paul commented similarly in I Thessalonians 2:14-16.)

[534] The Jews of Medina were used to making tribal alliances of convenience with the pagan Arabs around them. The Old Testament, however, is very clear and categorically forbids Jews from having such alliances, let alone friends, from the ranks of idolaters. Yet, the Jews of Medina, particularly the Banu Nadir and the Banu Qaynuqa, forged these alliances of mutual protection and friendship with the pagan tribes and with the Quraysh of Mecca, culminating in the grand alliance of Jews and pagans that resulted in the Siege of Medina. Islam barely survived, and this desperate time provides the context for the serious tone in this passage. (*Ibn Kathir*)

[535] See Deuteronomy 6:1-7, 17 where Jews are commanded to obey the laws of Moses for all time.

193

idol-worshippers (of Mecca) are the strongest (in their hostility).

However, those whom you'll find to be nearest to the believers in love are those who say, "*We are Christians*," for among them are priests devoted to learning and monks who have renounced the world, [536] and they're not arrogant. [82]

When they hear what was revealed to the Messenger, you see their eyes overflow with tears for they recognize the truth of it. Then they pray, "*Our Lord! We believe! Record us among the witnesses.* [83] *What can hold us back from believing in Allah and in the truth that has come to us, since we've been constantly yearning for our Lord to admit us to the company of the righteous?*" [84]

Allah will reward them for what they've said with gardens beneath which rivers flow – *and there they shall remain* - and that's how Allah rewards (those who do) good! [85] However, those who reject (the truth) and call Our (revealed) verses nothing more than lies will be companions of the raging blaze. [86]

All Things in Moderation

O you who believe! Don't forbid the good things that Allah has allowed for you. Just don't overindulge (in lawful things), for Allah has no love for the overindulgent. [537] [87]

How to Pay for a Broken Promise

*E*at from the wholesome resources that have been provided for you by Allah, and be mindful of Allah - *the One in Whom you believe.* [538] [88]

---

[536] It was St. Basil (d. 379) who enumerated the qualities of a true Christian. In his collected works, entitled *The Letters*, he wrote, "The Christian should not be ostentatious in clothing or sandals for all this is idle boasting. He should wear cheap clothes...He should consume nothing beyond what is necessary or which tends to extravagance...He should not strive for honor nor always seek first place. Each one should hold all men above himself. He should not covet money nor horde unnecessary things...He who approaches God should embrace poverty in all things and be pierced with the fear of God." That is the type of Christian who recognizes the good qualities of Islam. Also see Luke 20:46.

[537] In the early Medinan period, whenever the Prophet took men out on patrol or to engage in a skirmish, the men would leave their wives behind. Some men asked the Prophet, "Should we castrate ourselves?" (They were wondering how they could survive for weeks with no female companionship.) It was then that this verse was revealed, and the Prophet allowed men to make temporary marriages with women in the bedouin camps and towns they passed along the way. This was a common custom in Arabia at that time, and women used it for their economic benefit. (For a fee a woman would marry a man for a fixed time period after which the marriage was dissolved.) Near the end of his life, the Prophet forbade such temporary marriages, as men were better trained by Islamic teachings in how to control their needs away from their wives. (*Bukhari*)

[538] During one of his speeches, Muhammad reminded people about the seriousness of the Day of Judgment, and many left the gathering in tears. Ten men gathered in a home. Among them were Abu Bakr, 'Ali ibn Abi Talib, 'Abdullah ibn Mas'ud and Salman al-Farsi, and they swore that they would fast every day, pray all night, never sleep in a bed, never eat meat, and dedicate their swords to Allah's cause. When the Prophet heard about this, he called them together and said, "Do you think it's right that you made the oath that you did?" They replied that they did it for the sake of righteousness. The Prophet then said, "I didn't command you to do like that. Your bodies have rights upon you, so fast but then eat, pray but then sleep, and also eat meat. Whoever objects to my way is not of me." Then the Prophet went out and delivered a speech in which he said, "What's wrong with some people? They forbid sex, food, perfume, sleep and the pleasures of this world. I have not ordered you to be priests or monks, for it is foreign to my faith to give up meat and sex, as it is also foreign to renounce the world and live like a hermit. The trial for my people is fasting, and the renunciation of the world for them is *jihad* (struggling in Allah's cause), so serve Allah and never make any partners with Him, for the people who came before you were ruined by extremism. They were hard on themselves, and so Allah became hard on them, You see the ruins of their monasteries and hermit caves." This verse was revealed to reinforce that legitimate needs must not be curtailed in extreme ways out of a misguided sense of austere righteousness. (*Asbab ul-Nuzul*)

Allah won't hold you to any unreasonable things that you (foolishly) swear (to do), but He will hold you to account for your serious pledges (that you make and then fail to fulfill). [539] So to atone for breaking (an unreasonable or foolish) pledge, you must feed ten poor people with what you would normally feed your family, or you may clothe them, instead, or free a bonded servant.

If all of these options are too difficult for you, then fast for three days. That will make up for the (foolish) promises (you made but cannot keep) - but safeguard (all) your (solemn) promises! This is how Allah explains His verses clearly for you so you can be thankful. [89]

Liquor and Gambling are Now Forbidden

O you who believe! [540] Truly, liquor [541] and gambling, stone altars (dedicated to idols) [542] and (making random choices to decide distributions of goods by blindly picking marked) arrowheads (from a bag) [543] are all the disgraceful works of Satan, so forsake them so you can be successful! [90]

Satan wants to stir up hostility and hatred among you with liquor and gambling, so as to hinder you from remembering Allah and (also to hinder

---

[539] In a direct continuation of the events surrounding the previous background note, the ten men who made such an austere oath to worship non-stop then asked the Prophet what they should do about their previously made pledge, and this verse was revealed giving them a way to absolve themselves of it, though with a penalty to pay. (*Asbab ul-Nuzul*)

[540] Very early in the Medinan period, 'Umar ibn al-Khattab (d. 644) had asked the Prophet for a definitive ruling on alcohol, and verses 2:219-220 were revealed, which called it more harmful than good. On another occasion, Umar asked again, and 4:43 came in response, which forbade people to offer prayers while drunk. The final prohibition in this verse came about due to a drunken rampage of the Prophet's uncle Hamza. 'Ali' ibn Abi Talib was making preparations for his marriage to the Prophet's daughter Fatimah. He went out to saddle his two camels and was intending to go to some Jewish goldsmiths to buy some jewelry to present to his bride-to-be at the wedding banquet, but when he came upon his camels, he found they were hacked to death. He cried out in anguish and asked those near the stable who had done such a thing. He was told that Hamza was at a drinking party with some friends of his from Medina and that a singer with them had sang, "Hamza, there are some old camels tied up out in the yard. Go and drive your sword in their flesh." Hamza staggered out and hacked the camels up and took some meat back to the party. In distress, 'Ali ran straight to the Prophet to tell him what had happened. When he was informed, the Prophet went immediately to the house where the party was taking place. He began to berate Hamza for his violent act, but Hamza, who had swollen eyes from his binge drinking, told the Prophet, "You're nothing but the slave of my father." The Prophet knew he was drunk and left. This passage was revealed making liquor forbidden, and it is said that when the people heard it, they were dumping their wine jugs in the streets of Medina, causing it to collect in great puddles. (*Ibn Kathir*)

[541] This is the final verse in a three-step progression leading to the ultimate ban upon intoxicants. The Arabs were addicted to liquor as much as any other nation. Just as Prohibition failed in the United States of America for its abruptness, so, too, would an all out ban fail for the Arabs who considered alcohol an essential part of life. 'Umar ibn al-Khattab said that *khamr* (liquor or intoxicants) includes anything that alters the mind (*Ibn Kathir*), and thus the scholars are unanimous that mind-altering drugs and narcotics are also forbidden in Islam.

[542] The pre-Islamic Arabs would choose a large rock or stone pillar and dedicate it as an alter to one of their idols. They would place portions of meat atop it to 'feed' their gods. Is it any wonder that both Islam and Christianity forbid offerings to idols. (See I Corinthians 10:20.)

[543] The Arabs used to employ chance and luck in the distribution of slaughtered meat portions. A group would purchase an animal to slaughter, and instead of sharing the meat equally, they would draw marked arrowheads with different proportions marked on them. Some would get double or triple portions by chance, and others would get nothing at all! Random drawings to decide specific shares are permissible if the value of each random share received is equal or, in the case when there is a limited number of goods, if everyone has an equal chance to get some by lot or to decide who goes first in a game. (*Ma'ariful Qur'an*)

you) from prayer. 544 Won't you give up (those bad habits)? [91] Obey Allah and obey the Messenger, and be wary (of what will do you harm). If you turn back, then know that Our Messenger must only proclaim (the message) clearly. [92]

Your Past Vices are Forgiven

*T*hose who believe and who do what's morally right won't be held responsible for (the alcohol or gambling proceeds) they've consumed (in the past), just so long as they're mindful (of Allah) and believe, *while doing what's morally right.* 545 Again, so long as they're mindful (of Allah) *while holding to faith.* And again, so long as they're mindful (of Allah), *and then do what's right,* for Allah loves those who are virtuous. [93]

Hunting Restrictions in Mecca

O you who believe! Allah is going to test you with the hunting prey that comes within reach of your hands and spears, so He can distinguish who (among you) fears Him sight unseen. Whoever breaks (the following prohibition) after this will have a painful punishment. [94]

O you who believe! Don't kill any hunted prey while under (pilgrimage) restrictions. 546 If anyone does that on purpose, then to make up for it a domestic animal equal in value to the one he killed must be brought in offering to the Ka'bah, overseen by two fair people among you.

(He can also make up for it) by feeding poor people or fasting according to the calculated equivalent (of that many meals), so in this way he can feel the seriousness of his action. Allah forgives what happened in the past, but whoever does it again will find that Allah will exact a penalty from him, for Allah is powerful and a master of reprisal. [95]

However, you are allowed to hunt any prey that lives in or on the sea and to use it for food, as a benefit for yourselves and for those who are traveling, but again, you're forbidden to hunt game animals on land so long as you're consecrated under

---

544 The Prophet said, "Ten things related to liquor were cursed: the liquor itself was cursed, as well as the drinker, the server, the seller, the buyer, the brewer, the one who asks for it to be brewed, the one who transports it, the one who receives it, and whoever makes a living off of profits connected with it." (*Abu Dawud, Ibn Majah*)

545 When the Muslims of Medina were pouring their wine and other liquor in the streets, a barkeeper named Abu Talha also began to empty his flasks as well. Some people outside his home began to question whether Muslims who had died before this prohibition would be forgiven for having drunk liquor or gotten rich off gambling. This verse was revealed absolving them of sin, and the general principle in Islam has been that a sin done in ignorance is forgiven or at least mitigated by Allah. (*Ibn Kathir*)

546 No hunting, killing of animals or cutting of plants (other than scorpions, rats, wild wolves or other dangerous animals that may attack, crows, kites and a specific type of grass called lemon-grass used for feeding herd animals) is allowed in Mecca's city limits. (These exceptions were enumerated personally by the Prophet.) This is the test mentioned in verse 94 above. For a people who were used to hunting for food, to see a rabbit or some other animal within easy reach, but then to restrain one's hand from hunting it, was a very trying test. However, as verse 97 states: Mecca is a place of peace and security where all harm (even to animals) is forbidden. There is an interesting episode in which the Prophet was leading a group of pilgrims on the road to Mecca. One of the men, by the name of Abu Qatadah, was accompanying the party, but he wasn't going to Mecca to perform the pilgrimage and thus was not under pilgrimage restrictions. He fell behind the main group with a few others and eventually saw a wild animal and killed it for food. His friends, who were under pilgrimage restrictions, were terrified and thought he did wrong due to this passage above [5:94-95]. When they went to the Prophet, he approved of Abu Qatadah's hunting, for he was not consecrated as a pilgrim, and he allowed the pilgrims to eat of the meat. (*al-Muwatta*) By the way, the Prophet also forbade carrying unsheathed weapons in all mosques everywhere. Even arrowheads must be wrapped or covered to avoid accidentally injuring another person.

(pilgrimage) restrictions. Be mindful of Allah for He's the One to Whom you'll be gathered back. [96]

Allah made the Ka'bah, the Sacred House, to be a stable refuge for people. (He also sanctified) the sacred (truce) months, the offered animals, and the garlands that identify them, so you can know (by seeing them) that Allah has knowledge of whatever is in the heavens and on the earth and that Allah knows all about everything. [97]

Know that Allah is strict in punishment but also that Allah is forgiving and merciful. [98] There is no other duty laid upon the Messenger than to proclaim (the message), and Allah knows what you show and what you hide. [99]

Say (to them), "*Evil is not equal to what's wholesome, even though evil is so widespread that it seems normal and good to you. Be mindful of Allah, you people of understanding, so you may prosper.*" [547] [100]

Learning to Trust in Allah's Wisdom

O you who believe! [548] Don't ask questions about (trivial) things that would be difficult for you if they were explained to you in detail. [549] However, if you ask

(about religious stipulations) when the Qur'an is being revealed, then they'll be clarified for you.

Allah pardons that (kind of honest inquiry), for Allah is forgiving and forbearing. [101] Some people before you questioned (their messengers) incessantly like that, and eventually they fell into rejection (of Allah). [102]

Allah didn't set up (such superstitions as slitting the ears of she-camels) to mark them (and their milk) as reserved (only for idols), sending (animals) to roam in pastures (as especially blessed by idols), dedicating male-camels if they had a certain number of copulations, or reserving she-camels (because they give birth only to female calves).

It's only those who reject (the truth) that have invented such lies against Allah, and most of them have no reasoning ability. [103]

When they're told, "*Come to what Allah has revealed, and come to the Messenger,*" they say, "*The customs of our ancestors are good enough for us.*" [550] However, their (ancestors) had no sense, nor did they have any guidance! [104]

O you who believe! Look after your own souls, for no harm can come to you from the wayward people if you cling to guidance. [551]

---

[547] The Prophet was giving a speech in which he said that Allah has cursed those who drink liquor, make it, serve it, sell it or buy it. A bedouin stood up and asked, "Messenger of Allah, I was a merchant in this trade, and I made a lot of money from selling liquor, so will it be to my benefit if I spend those profits in obedience to Allah?" The Prophet replied, "Even if you spend it during a pilgrimage, in *jihad* or through charity, it won't make any difference to Allah, for Allah accepts nothing but what is wholesome." Then this verse was revealed. (*Asbab ul-Nuzul*)

[548] One day, the Prophet gave such a stirring sermon in the mosque that the people in general were weeping. In the midst of this outpouring of emotion, a man came forward and asked, "Who is my father?" Obviously, the man's question was totally inappropriate to the mood of the venue! The Prophet told the man his father's name, and then this passage was revealed. (*Bukhari*)

[549] The Prophet once said, "Leave me as I have left you, those before you were ruined because of asking too many (trivial) questions and arguing with their prophets." (*Muslim*) (See 2:108.)

[550] If a person converted to Islam, the Meccans tried to shame him (or her) by accusing him of turning his back on his ancestors and insulting their longstanding family traditions and memory. This verse was revealed in response. (*Ma'ariful Qur'an*)

[551] One day the Prophet was asked about this verse (5:105), and he said, "Indeed, promote what is right, and forbid what is wrong, until (there comes a time when) you see greed being obeyed, passions followed (over logic), this worldly life preferred, and every person charmed by his own opinion. At

You're all going to return to Allah, and then He'll explain to you (the true meaning) of all that you did. [105]

Choosing Witnesses for a Will

O you who believe! [552] Appoint witnesses among yourselves whenever death comes near to one of you (in order to witness the recording of) your will. (Choose) two just people from among you, either from among your own (family) or from outside of it.

If you're traveling through the land and death is about to overtake you, and if you have doubts about (the emergency witnesses you must choose), then stop them after the ritual prayer has ended and ask them to swear an oath to Allah, saying, *"We don't want any worldly gain in this affair, even if one of our close (relatives stands to gain), nor will we hide any testimony before Allah. If we did that, then we would be acting sinfully."* [106]

If it becomes known that those two committed the sin (of perjury), then let two others stand up in their place who are (close relatives of the deceased) and thus have a more rightful claim.

Let them swear to Allah, saying, *"We swear that our testimony is more accurate than these other two and that we haven't stretched (the truth), for if we did so then we would be acting wrongfully."* [107]

That's the most appropriate (thing to say) so they can (be influenced) to give their testimony in the way it was supposed to be done, or (at the very least) so they might fear that the testimony of others might contradict their own testimony.

Be mindful of Allah and listen, for Allah doesn't guide the disobedient. [108]

What will Jesus Say on Judgment Day?

*O*ne day, Allah will gather the messengers together and ask them:

"How (did people) respond (to your preaching)?"

They will answer, *"We don't have any information about that, for You're the One Who knows what's beyond perception."* [109]

---

that time, it will be your duty to care for your own soul, and to leave the rest (of the world to itself). There are days coming after you, when patience will be like clutching a live coal. The one who does a (good) thing in those days will have a reward similar to that of fifty people who do as you do." Then the Prophet was asked, "Messenger of Allah, fifty men from among us or among them?" He replied, "Indeed, fifty of you." (*Tirmidhi*)

[552] Two Christian men named Tameem and Adiyy used to make frequent trips between Medina and Mecca. On one journey a new Muslim from the Quraysh tribe named Budayl accompanied them, but he became gravely ill along the way in a region that contained no Muslims. Before he died he secretly wrote a will and put it in his luggage. Then he called his two Christian companions and put all of his property into their custody and made them agree to distribute it to his family upon their reaching Medina. When the two men returned to Medina, they gave all the property to the man's relatives, but they concealed a prized silver drinking bowl decorated with gold. When the man's family found the written will (that mentioned the bowl in the luggage,) they asked the two men about it, but they swore they never saw it. They were brought to the Prophet who asked them to swear to Allah that they didn't have it, and they swore that they did not, and a ruling was given in their favor. Sometime later, the expensive bowl turned up in Mecca with a goldsmith, and the man who had it said he had bought it from Tameem and Adiyy. Some friends of the deceased took the bowl to Medina and swore by Allah that it had belonged to their dead friend and was a part of his estate; they also claimed that their witness was more reliable than that of the other two men. When summoned once more, the two Christians said that Budayl had sold it to them before his death, that there were no witnesses to the transaction, and that was why they didn't mention it in the previous hearing. The Prophet ruled in favor of Budayl's relatives, and the Christians had to pay for the value of the bowl. This passage was then revealed to give guidance for people who find themselves in similar circumstances. (*Asbab ul-Nuzul*)

Allah will then say:

"Jesus, son of Mary! Recall My favors upon you and your mother. I supported you with the Holy Spirit. [553] *(I allowed) you to speak to people in infancy, as well as when you were fully grown. I taught you the scripture and gave you wisdom, along with the Torah and the Gospel. You made a bird out of clay by My leave that you breathed to life, and it became a (real) bird by My leave."*

"You also healed the blind and the lepers by My leave, and you revived the dead by My leave. I prevented the Children of Israel (from harming) you while you were showing them the clear evidence, though the faithless among them said, 'This is nothing more than some kind of magic.' [110] *I also inspired the disciples to believe in Me and in My messenger, and they said (to you), 'We believe, and you be (our) witness that we're surrendered (to Allah's will).'"* [111]

The Doubting Disciples

$\mathcal{O}$nce the disciples said, (in a moment of doubt), *"Jesus, son of Mary! Can your Lord send down upon us a banquet table from heaven?"* [554]

"Be mindful of Allah," Jesus answered, *"if you're really (true) believers."* [112]

They replied, *"We only want to eat from it to satisfy (the doubts) in our hearts, so we can know (for certain) that you're truthful and also to witness a miracle for ourselves."* [555] [113]

Jesus, the son of Mary, prayed, *"O Allah, our Lord! Send down upon us a banquet table from the sky so there will be a joyous occasion for the first and the last of us, and also as a sign from You. Provide for us, because You're the best provider."* [114]

"I will send it down to you," Allah said, *"but if any of you cover over (your ability to have faith) after this, then I'll punish him like I haven't punished anyone else in all the worlds!"* [115]

Jesus' Testimony Continues

$\mathcal{A}$llah will ask (on Judgment Day): *"Jesus, son of Mary! Did you tell people, 'Worship me and my mother as gods in place of (the One True) God?"* [556]

---

[553] Archangel Gabriel is known as the Holy Spirit in Islamic theology, for he is the one who brings God's revelations to His chosen messengers. Neither the Qur'an nor the Torah accepts the common Christian definition of the Holy Spirit as a part of a three-person godhead.

[554] Some commentators believe this refers to the famed Last Supper in which Jesus and his disciples sat down to share a sumptuous meal together. Others say it refers to a different time when a table came down from the sky with seven fishes and seven loaves of bread and that some of the disciples stole food from it, saying it might not descend to feed them the next day. Thus, the table immediately ascended. (At-Tabari) It could also refer to the miracle of the loaves and fishes in which the disciples asked Jesus how they were to feed a multitude of thousands with only a few fish and loaves. Then Jesus handed out the food and the supply was never exhausted. (See Mark 6:33-44.) Finally, it could have been a situation like that of his mother Mary whom her uncle Zachariah always found supplied with food, possibly by a well-wisher who was moved by God to give it to her. Jesus prayed for the food and a well-wisher provided for them. In this case, it could, in fact, refer to the Last Supper, though Allah knows better. (See Mark 14:12-17.) Other commentators say that the Disciples were asking for a festive banquet table so they could turn that day into an annual feast day, such as the Jews had other feast days. (at-Tabari)

[555] The disciples of Jesus sometimes questioned or doubted him and wanted to see miracles to reaffirm their faith. (For an example, see Mark 7:45-52.) As for his miracles, Jesus performed many miracles involving food, such as in turning water into wine (John 2:1-11), feeding a multitude with a basket of loaves and fish that never emptied (John 6:5-13) and helping fishermen pull in a huge harvest (Luke 5:4-11).

[556] Some early Christian sects and writers, even until our own time among certain non-mainstream Catholic factions, hold that Mary is a part of the godhead (a holy quartet!) or at the least she is a *co-redemptrix*, or instrument of salvation, along with Jesus. In the year 2001, a petition was sent to the Vatican calling for Mary to be declared co-redemptrix, and it was signed by 42 cardinals, 500 bishops

"Glory be to you!" he'll reply. *"I could never have said what I had no right (to say), and if I ever said something like that, then You would've known about it. You know what's in my heart, while I don't know what's in Yours, and You know all hidden mysteries."* [116]

"I never said anything to them except what You commanded me to say: 'Worship Allah, my Lord and your Lord.' I was their witness while I lived among them. When You took me up (to Heaven), You became their Watcher, and You're a witness over all things." [117] *If You choose to punish them, well, they're Your servants (to treat as You please), though if You choose to forgive them, (then of course You can because) You're the Powerful and the Wise."* [557] [118]

Allah will declare, *"This is a day in which the truthful will benefit from their honesty, for they shall (be rewarded with) gardens beneath which rivers flow - and there they shall remain forever!"*

Allah will be pleased with them and they with Him – and that's the greatest success! [119] To Allah belongs the control of the heavens and the earth and whatever is within them, and He has power over all things. [120]

---

and even the famed Mother Theresa. Both St. Irenaeus who lived in the second century and St. Cyril of Alexandria who lived in the fifth century advanced the view that Mary was a primary cause of salvation. St. Cyril wrote of Mary: "Hail Mary *Theotokos* (Mother of God), venerable treasure of the whole world...it is you through whom the Holy Trinity is glorified and adored,...through whom the tempter, the devil is cast down from heaven, through whom the fallen creature is raised up to heaven, through whom all creation, once imprisoned by idolatry, has reached knowledge of the truth, through whom holy baptism has come to believers...through whom nations are brought to repentance...." (St. Cyril of Alexandria, *Hom in Deiparam,* PG 65, p.681; c. 431 CE). In the Eastern Orthodox church, Mary is regarded as perpetually sinless, eternally a virgin and the 'Queen of Heaven.' The Catholic Church designated her the "Mother of God" in the year 431 at the Council of Ephesus.

[557] The Prophet gave a speech one day, saying, "People! You will be gathered back to Allah while you're barefooted, naked and uncircumcised. The first among all creation who will receive clothing (during the proceedings on Judgment Day) will be Abraham. Some people from my community will be taken and brought to the left side (from where people will be thrown in the Fire), and I will cry out, 'But they're my followers!' I will be told, 'You don't know what they invented (in your religion) after you,' So I will then say as Jesus said..." (Then the Prophet quoted this verse.) Then the Prophet said, "I will be told, 'These people kept turning on their heels after you left them.'" (*Bukhari, Abu Dawud*) On another occasion, a companion named Abu Dharr said that there was a night when the Prophet recited this verse over and over again. (*Ibn Kathir*)

The Livestock

6 Al An'am
Late Meccan Period

This chapter, which is largely from the late Meccan period, gets its name from the large number of verses discussing pagan superstitions about their livestock animals. The Qur'an mentions quite a few of them and refutes them one at a time. Owing to its overall time frame, set in the final years of the worst of the Meccan persecution, we can also detect a large amount of passionate debate, with the statements of pagans recorded along with the answers Allah is telling Muhammad to give in response. The issue of idolatry and its falseness is attacked from many angles, including the story of Abraham's father who opposed his own son. Even as that particular tale has Abraham abandoning his homeland for the sake of Allah, the foreshadowing of the Prophet's own migration to another city is clearly evident.

In the Name of Allah,
the Compassionate, the Merciful

*P*raise be to Allah, the One Who created the heavens and the earth and (Who) made both the darkness and the light. Even still, those who suppress (their faith) continue to hold others as equals with their Lord! [1]

He's the One Who created you from clay and then decided the length (of your lives). There's yet another deadline with Him, as well, though you're in doubt about it. [558] [2]

He's (the only) God within the heavens and on the earth. He knows what you conceal and what you reveal, and He knows what you're earning (on your record of deeds). [3]

Yet, no sign from their Lord ever reaches them without their turning away from it, [4] and now they're denying the truth when it comes to them (this time, as well). Soon they'll be given more prophecies about what they've been ridiculing! [5]

Don't they see how many generations We destroyed before them, (peoples) whom We had established in the land more firmly than you (people of Mecca are established today)?

We sent abundant rain down upon them from the sky and provided them with streams of flowing water beneath them. Yet, We destroyed them for their sins and let new generations arise after them. [6]

In Answer to the Faithless

*I*f We sent a written page down to you that they could touch with their very own hands, those who cover over (their

---

[558] The second 'deadline' with Allah is the coming of the Day of Judgment. The first is our own individual death date.

ability to have faith) would be sure to say, *"This is clearly no more than magic!"* 559 [7]

They also say, *"So why isn't an angel being sent down to him?"* 560 Though if We *did* send an angel, then the issue would be settled at once, and they would have no more time to delay! [8]

And if We *were* to send down an angel, We would send him (in the form) of a man, and that would cause them to be confused about something they're already confused by! [9]

And so it was (Muhammad) that many messengers before you were ridiculed by their critics, but they were (eventually) surrounded by the very thing at which they laughed. 561 [10] Say (to them), *"Travel throughout the world, and see how those who denied (the truth) were brought to an end."* [11]

Then ask (them), *"To whom does the contents of the heavens and the earth belong?"*

Say (to them), *"(It all belongs) to Allah. He wrote down (the rule) of mercy for Himself, and He's going to gather all of you together for the Day of Assembly.* 562 *There's no doubt about that! Those who don't believe will lose their own souls,* [12] *for any (and all creatures) that rest within the night or the day belong to Him, and He's the Hearing and the Knowing."* [13]

Ask (them), *"Should I take someone other than Allah for my protector, when He's the Originator of the heavens and the earth? He feeds others but is never (in need of being) fed!"*

Say (to them), *"I've been ordered to be among the first of those who surrender (to Him), so don't you be among those who make partners (with Allah)."* [14]

Tell (them), *"If I were ever to disobey my Lord, then I would be in utter fear of the punishment of a momentous day.* [15] *On that day, whoever has (the punishment) turned away from him, it will be due only to His mercy, and that will be the clearest success of all."* [16]

If Allah touches you with some setback (in your life), there's no one who can remove it but He, and if He touches you with something positive, (know that) He has power over all things! [17] He is the Irresistible One Who towers over His servants, and He's the Wise and Well-informed. [18]

You Know this Message is the Truth

Ask (them), *"So what's the most compelling evidence?"* 563 Then say (to them),

---

559 A Meccan pagan named 'Abdullah ibn Umayyah told the Prophet that he wouldn't believe in him unless he (Muhammad) climbed up to heaven and brought him back a book that mentioned him ('Abdullah) by name and that commanded him to believe in Muhammad as a messenger. Then 'Abdullah further said that even if this happened, he still wouldn't believe. This verse was revealed in response. (*Asbab ul-Nuzul*) Also see 24:40.

560 'Abdullah ibn Umayyah, accompanied by an-Nadr ibn al-Harith and Nawfal ibn Khalid, approached the Prophet sometime after the revelation of verse 6:7, and the group reiterated that they wouldn't believe unless Muhammad brought a book from the sky for them, but this time they added that it should be carried by four angels who would swear that they were from Allah. This passage was revealed in response. Later on, 'Abdullah did accept Islam, and he was martyred in the Battle of Ta'if. (*Ma'ariful Qur'an*)

561 Muhammad was walking one day, when he passed by al-Walid ibn al-Mughirah, Abu Jahl and Umayyah ibn Khalaf. When they saw him, they started ridiculing him and being verbally abusive. This verse was revealed to console the Prophet. (*Ibn Hisham*)

562 The Prophet said that Allah, Himself, said, "Before I decreed the Creation, I wrote down in My ledger, that I keep with Me: 'Truly, My mercy will be stronger than My wrath.'" (*Bukhari, Muslim*. Also see 6:12.)

563 The Meccan leaders approached the Prophet one day and said, "We don't see anyone (important) believing in your message. We asked the Jews and Christians about you, and they said they have no mention or descriptions of you (in their scriptures), so tell us who is testifying to the idea that you're a messenger, as you claim." This passage was revealed in response. (*Asbab ul-Nuzul*) Other reports

"Allah is the witness between you and me that this Qur'an has been revealed to me by inspiration, so I can warn you and all who come into contact with it (of Allah's coming judgment). [564] *So can you really testify that there are other gods equal with Allah?"*

Say (to them), *"No! I don't testify that (there are many gods besides Him)!"* Then say, *"Truly, He's only One God, and I disown whatever you join with Him."* [19]

Those to Whom We've given (previous) scripture also recognize (the truth of) this (doctrine of monotheism), even as they know their own children, but those who've lost their own souls refuse to believe. [565] [20]

The Evil Fate of Idolaters

 $\mathcal{W}$ ho's more wrong than the one who invents a lie against Allah or who denies His (revealed) verses? The unjust will definitely never succeed! [21] One day, We're going to gather them all together and say to those who made partners (with Allah), *"Where are all the partners you claimed (existed and worshipped in place of Allah)?"* [22]

There won't be any commotion they can use (as a distraction) other than to say, *"We swear to Allah, our Lord, we never made partners (with Allah)!"* [23]

See how they're going to lie against their own souls! However, (the excuses) they made up will only put them further into trouble! [24]

The Punishment for Feigned Interest

 $\mathcal{A}$ mong them are some who pretend to listen to you; [566] (therefore, as a punishment) We've cast a veil over their hearts to prevent them from understanding, as well as put a deafening silence in their ears. Even if they saw every one of the proofs (of Allah), they would never believe in them, even to the point that they come to you and debate.

As it is, those who cover over (their ability to have faith) are already saying, *"These (verses) are nothing more than ancient tales!"* [25]

Others just keep themselves away from (hearing the Qur'an) and are thus kept away, but they're only destroying

---

suggest this passage was revealed in response to the challenge of three idolaters named al-Nahham, Qardam, and Bahri, who tried to convince the Prophet to accept that there are many gods.

[564] The Prophet said, "To whomever the Qur'an has come, I am his warner." (*Ma'ariful Qur'an*)

[565] 'Abdullah ibn Salam, the Jewish rabbi who converted to Islam, was asked about this verse, and he explained it by saying, "We knew about the qualities of the blessed Prophet through the revelation Allah gave to us in the Torah. In this way, our knowledge was certain and beyond doubt. This is on a higher level than our recognizing of our own children, among whom it is possible to doubt their legitimacy." A Christian convert named Zayd ibn Sa'nah explained that he tested the Prophet's legitimacy by observing how he controlled his emotions and did not become angry when provoked. Zayd explained that this was the sign in both the Torah and Gospel of Allah's last messenger. (*Ma'ariful Qur'an*) Later on in Medina, 'Umar ibn al-Khattab had a conversation with 'Abdullah ibn Salam, and 'Umar asked him, "Do you recognize Muhammad (as having been foretold in the Torah) just as you recognize your own son?" 'Abdullah replied, "Yes, and even more so. The Truthful One (Angel Gabriel) descended from heaven upon the Truthful One on the earth (Muhammad) with his description (as it was in the Torah), and I recognized him, although I knew nothing of the story of his mother." (*Qurtubi*)

[566] The most important Meccan leaders stopped to listen to what the Prophet was saying one day. Among them was a widely traveled man named an-Nadr ibn al-Harith, who often told the Quraysh stories from the lands in which he had sojourned. After a few minutes they asked an-Nadr, "What is Muhammad talking about?" An-Nadr answered, "By the One Who made the Ka'bah, I don't know what he's saying, but I see him moving his lips and talking about nothing more than tales of past peoples, just like the ones I used to tell you about." This verse was revealed in response. (*Asbab ul-Nuzul*)

their own souls without their even realizing it! [567] [26]

If you could just see it, when they're placed before the Fire! They're going to cry out, *"If only we could be sent back (for another chance), then we would never deny the proofs of our Lord! We would for sure be on the side of the faithful!"* [27]

But no! (The reality) that they used to conceal (from their conscious minds) will become crystal clear to them, and even if they were returned (to life), they would still fall into forbidden things, for they're truly a bunch of liars! [28]

Then they say, *"There's nothing beyond our lives here on earth, nor will we ever be raised to life again."* [29] Oh, if you could just see it when they're brought before their Lord!

He's going to tell them, *"Isn't this real enough now?"* They'll answer, *"Of course it is, by our Lord!"* Then He'll say, *"So now taste the punishment for rejecting (Me)!"* [30]

Those who deny their meeting with Allah are truly lost, even until the Hour (of Judgment) comes upon them suddenly. That's when they'll cry out, *"Oh no! We never thought this (would happen)!"* They will have to bear their own burdens on their backs, and evil are the burdens they're going to bear! [31]

So just what is the life of this world save for entertainment and distraction? The best home (of all) is the home of the next life, (which has been reserved) for those who were mindful (of their ultimate return), so won't you think deeply on it? [32]

Words of Solace to a Beleaguered Prophet

$\mathcal{W}$e know all about the stress that their words are causing you, (Muhammad,) but it's not *you* that they're rejecting. It's the (revealed) verses of Allah that the wrongdoers are condemning. [568] [33]

Even so, other messengers were rejected before you, and they were patient against the criticism they faced, even until Our help finally reached them.

No one can change the (commanding) words of Allah. (That's why) some of the stories of previous messengers have come to you (to give you strength and inspiration). [34]

If their aversion to you is stressful, (you must realize) that even if you (opened) a tunnel in the ground or raised a ladder to the sky and brought them a miraculous sign, (they would still never believe in you).

If Allah had wanted, He could've brought them all together into guidance, so don't be affected by (their) ignorance. [35]

The ones who listen will readily accept (your message), but as for the dead (at heart), well, Allah is going to resurrect them and bring them all back to Him anyway. [36]

They ask, *"So why isn't a miracle being sent down to him from his Lord?"* Answer them by saying, *"Allah is able to send down (miracles if He so chooses),"* but most of them don't understand. [37]

---

[567] This verse concerns the Prophet's pagan uncle, Abu Talib, who offered his nephew protection but refused to accept Islam no matter how much the Prophet tried to reason with him. This was painful for the Prophet, as his uncle had been his guardian ever since he was around eight or nine years old. Other commentators say it also extends to the Meccans in general who tried to prevent people from listening to Muhammad recite Qur'anic verses. (*Qatadah, Ma'ariful Qur'an*)

[568] The Prophet's foe, Abu Jahl, who was one of his biggest enemies (and his father's cousin), passed by him one day and said, "Muhammad, we're not calling you a liar, because we've always known you to be honest. However, we're calling what you've brought a lie." This passage was revealed in response. (*Asbab ul-Nuzul*)

There isn't a creature on the earth nor anything that flies on wings without its being organized into communities just like you. We haven't left anything out of the Book!

All (those creatures) are going to be brought back to their Lord (in the end). [569] [38]

Those who deny Our proofs are deaf and dumb in (self-inflicted) darkness. Whomever Allah leaves to wander (will remain lost), while whomever He wants (to guide) will be placed on a straight path. [39]

Say (to them), *"Think about it. If Allah's wrath suddenly overtook you or the Hour (of Judgment) came, would you call upon any other besides Allah? Answer me if you're so honest.* [40]

"Without a doubt! You would definitely call upon Him! Then, if He so desired, He could take away (the situation) that made you call upon Him in the first place! In that case, you would utterly forget (the idols) that you so often join with Him!" [41]

The Nations that Turned Away

And so it was that We sent other (prophets) before you to the nations (of the world), and We inflicted (upon those nations) suffering and hardship so they could learn to be humble. [42] So why didn't they learn to be humble, when the suffering that We sent came upon them? On the contrary, their hearts became harder, and Satan made their deeds seem proper and good to them. [43]

When they finally forgot the reminder they had received, We opened the doors to them of every (material blessing), and while they were in the middle of boasting about all (of Our gifts) they were given, *We suddenly seized them*, leaving them (in utter ruin) and despair! [44] And so the corrupted people were cut off at the root! So praise be to Allah, the Lord of All the Worlds! [45]

Allah's Proofs are Self-Evident

Now ask them, [570] *"Do you think that if Allah took away your hearing and your sight and*

---

[569] The question is often asked about the fate of animals in the next life. This verse could be construed to mean that Allah will gather them all back together in the next life, even as He gathers humans, as well, but it is not conclusive. All animals are considered to be surrendered to Allah's will (i.e., they are Muslims), but they have not been granted free will or a *ruh*, or spirit from Allah, and are thus not in need of a code of morality or system of guidance – they have instinct instead. The Prophet said of animals, "All the animals and insects keep glorifying Allah, but when their glorification ceases, then Allah takes their spirit. The death of animals has not been entrusted to the Angel of Death." (*Qurtubi*) Muslim scholars generally assume that when an animal dies its existence comes to an end. However, there are several reports from the Prophet that suggest that at least some animals will be present on Judgment Day. For example, any animals we hurt for no good reason will be there and will be allowed to take revenge on us. The Prophet specifically mentioned the case of a woman who starved a cat to death and who will have her face scratched repeatedly by that cat in reprisal. The Prophet also emphasized on another occasion that justice will be so complete on Judgment Day that even a horned ram that butted another one for no good reason will be taken to task. (*Tirmidhi*) Will there be animals in Paradise? Undoubtedly, for some reports from the Prophet, and even some Qur'anic verses [such as 56:21] – mention the presence of animals. Will the animals we knew and loved on earth as pets join us in Paradise? There is no clear answer other than to note the many Qur'anic verses that describe Paradise as a place where everyone will have whatever they wish for, and more besides. See 41:31, for example.

[570] This passage was an answer to the pagans of Mecca who insisted that if Muhammad was a true prophet of Allah, then Allah would have made him rich and given him magical powers. The logic employed to respond to this charge is simply that Allah has all the power and treasure and that it's not

sealed up your hearts that any other god besides Allah could restore them to you?" Do you see how We explain the proofs in differing ways? Yet, still they turn away! [46]

So then say (to them), *"Do you think that if Allah's punishment came upon you suddenly or with fair warning, that anyone else would be destroyed except the unjust?"* [47]

We don't send messengers with any other purpose than to give good news and to warn so that the believers can improve themselves, and, indeed, they'll have nothing to fear nor regret (on the Day of Judgment). [48]

However, those who deny Our proofs will have punishment descend upon them because they never prevented themselves from doing wrong. [49]

Say (to them), *"I'm not telling you that I have Allah's treasures with me, nor do I know what's being kept hidden, and I'm not telling you that I'm an angel, either. I'm only following what's been revealed to me."* Then ask them, *"Are the blind and the seeing the same? Won't you think it over?"* [50]

Warn those who have the apprehension within themselves of being brought back before their Lord that they won't have anyone to help them nor vouch for them except Him, and for that reason they should be mindful (of Him). [51]

A Society of Equals

Don't send away (the common people) who call upon their Lord in the morning and evening, seeking His approving gaze. [571] You're not responsible for anything they (think or do), nor are they responsible for you. (Therefore, there's no reason for) you to turn (the common people) away, (just because the pretentious people want you to,) for if you did that, then you would become a tyrant yourself! [52]

This is how We test some of them by letting them compare (their social status) with others, so they might say, *"Are these (commoners) the ones whom Allah has favored among us?"* Doesn't Allah know best who the thankful are? [53]

When the (people) who believe in Our (revealed) verses come to you, say to them, *"Peace be upon you."*

Your Lord has written it upon His (Own nature) to be merciful, so if any of you did sinful deeds in ignorance but then repented and improved (his conduct), then He is forgiving and merciful. [54] That's Our explanation of the verses (of this Qur'an) so the (self-destructive) path of the wicked can be exposed. [55]

---

necessary to give those things to a prophet just to prove his claim. When has wealth or magic been a proof of holiness or truth? Where was the wealth of Buddha or Jesus, and how great were they? What miracle did Noah perform; yet, we speak his name with reverence today? Does a prophet always need supernatural miracles, or can the truth and logic of Allah's Own words and creation be enough of a proof? (*Ma'ariful Qur'an*)

[571] One day some chiefs of the Quraysh approached the Prophet's uncle, Abu Talib, and explained that they couldn't be seen in Muhammad's gatherings, as low class people and former slaves were always in attendance. When Abu Talib told the Prophet, 'Umar ibn al-Khattab, who was present, suggested that perhaps if the Meccan nobles came to attend, the rest of the people would move aside. Sometime later, the Prophet was sitting in a gathering of his followers, and a group of Meccan nobles including 'Utbah, Harith ibn Nawfal and others happened by. They saw Bilal the African, Suhayb the freed Byzantine slave, Salman the freed Persian slave and various other men of mixed races and social classes. The Meccan nobles didn't want to listen to Muhammad in the company of those whom they thought of as commoners, slaves and unworthy poor people, so they asked the Prophet to send them away so they could meet with him alone. Verse 52 was revealed immediately, telling Muhammad not to turn the commoners and others away just to please the rich and arrogant nobles of his city. (*Asbab ul-Nuzul*) After this verse was revealed, 'Umar feared he had erred and begged forgiveness from the Prophet. Verse 53 was revealed to comfort 'Umar and explain that this was Allah's way of testing and thus reforming people. (*Ma'ariful Qur'an*)

Believe in the One True God

Say (to them), *"I'm forbidden to serve those whom you call upon besides Allah."* [572] Then say (to them), *"I'm not going to follow your foolish whims, for if I did, then I would be going far off the path, and I wouldn't be among the guided."* [56]

Then say, *"I'm following the clear evidence of my Lord, but you're denying Him. (The punishment that) you (dare) to be hurried on isn't in my power to bring. The command belongs to Allah alone. He speaks the truth and is the best of all Deciders."* [57]

(Finally,) tell (them), *"If (the punishment) that you (dare) to bring on sooner were in my power to bring, then the issue would be solved right away between me and all of you, for Allah knows who the wrongdoers are."* [58]

The keys to what is beyond (human) perception, the treasures of which are known to no one save Him, are His alone. He knows what's in the earth and in the sea. Not even a leaf falls without Him knowing it, nor a single grain is lodged in the darkness of the earth, nor is there anything fresh or withered without it already being recorded in a clear ledger. [59]

He's the One Who (temporarily) takes hold of your souls (while you sleep) in the night, and He knows all about what you do in the day. At dawn He causes you to rise up (from your sleep), so a set number (of days consisting of your life span) can be marked off. In the end, you're going to go back to Him, and then He's going to show you the meaning of all that you did. [60]

He's the Irresistible, towering high over His servants! He's appointed guardians to watch over you even until the time when death comes upon one of you. Our messenger (angels) take each individual soul, and they never fail in their task. [61] Then (those souls) are brought back to Allah, their true protector. It's in His power to judge, and He's swift in reviewing (their records). [62]

Ask them, *"Who's the One Who can save you from the dark (dangers) of both land and sea, when you're (forced to) call upon Him trembling and in fear, saying, 'If only He would save us, then we would ever be grateful'?"* [63] Say to them, *"Allah is the One Who can save you from these and from all other miseries – and yet you're still making others equal (with Him)!"* [64]

Say (to them), *"He has the power to send disasters upon you from above you and from under your feet, and (He has the power) to confuse you (and divide you into opposing) factions so you can experience violence from each other."*

Do you see how We explain the verses in different ways so they can understand? [65]

Yet, your people are denying this (message) even though it's the truth. Say to them, *"I'm not responsible for taking care of your affairs."* [66] Every message has a set duration, and soon you will know (the truth)! [67]

Don't Sit with those who Disrespect the Qur'an

Whenever you see people wading into (pointless arguments) about our (revealed) verses, you must turn away from

---

[572] The Meccans used to taunt the Prophet, saying, "So bring down upon us the suffering that you're promising us." It was a way to mock him and show that he was powerless to do it. However, as the Qur'an points out in many places, Allah can punish, but He gives people time for a while so they can come to repent. After a particularly tense exchange with some Meccans who mocked him greatly, the Prophet was distressed, and he walked alone in a field pensively. He looked up and saw Angel Gabriel in a cloud, and the angel asked him if he wanted him to make two mountains fall upon Mecca to destroy the people. The Prophet replied that he didn't, and his only desire was for the Meccans to have children who would serve none but Allah. This passage was revealed in response to their mocking and daring. (*Muslim*)

them until they change to a new topic. If Satan ever makes you forget this, you can leave the gathering of the wrongdoers the moment you remember. [68]

Those who are mindful (of Allah) will have no account in this regard, for their only duty is to remind them so that perhaps they can (gain an) awareness (of Allah's truth). 573 [69]

However, you must forsake (the company of) those who treat their way of life as a joke or a game, and who are deceived about the nature of this world's life. Remind them that every soul destroys itself by its own course of action and that it won't find any close ally nor defender besides Allah. Though it may offer every kind of bribe (to avoid the penalty it will have to pay,) none will be accepted.

That's the fate of those who destroy themselves through their own actions. They'll have nothing to drink but scalding water, and a terrible punishment (awaits them) on account of their covering over (the truth they should have accepted). [70]

Calling to Allah's Guidance

Say (to them), "*Should we call upon others besides Allah when they can't do us any good or harm? If we did that then we would be turning back on our heels after having been guided by Allah! (We would be) like the one who's been made into a fool by devils: wandering around in the world aimlessly - all the while his companions try to guide him back, saying, 'Look over here!'"*

Then say (to them), "*The only true guidance is Allah's guidance, and we've been commanded to surrender ourselves to the Lord of All the Worlds* [71] *and to establish prayers, being mindful (of Him), for He's the One to Whom we're going to be gathered back.*" [72]

He's the One Who created the heavens and the earth for a true purpose. The day when He says, "*Be*" is (the day) something is.

His word is the truth, and all dominion is His on the day when the trumpet will be blown. He knows what's beyond human perception, as well as what's plainly evident, for He's the Wise and Well-informed. [73]

Abraham and His Noble Legacy

It happened once that Abraham 574 said to his father Azar, "*Are you taking idols for gods? It seems to me that you're a people making an obvious mistake.*" 575 [74] That's the

---

573 Some companions approached the Prophet and asked him about verse 68, for they were afraid that since people always end up disagreeing or arguing about something, the mere act of getting together might become a source of sinfulness since argumentative people are always present and eventually start disrespecting Allah or His way of life. Verses 69-70 were then revealed, explaining that people can go to gatherings and not be held accountable for the vain arguments and useless quibbling of others that may suddenly come out, as long as they have no intention of joining in except to stand up for truth and goodness. If the foolish persist, then leave their company. (*Ma'ariful Qur'an*)

574 Abraham lived in Mesopotamia nearly four thousand years ago. His people were idol-worshippers, and his own father was an ardent idolater and possibly a maker of idols. There is a great amount of Jewish lore concerning Abraham's father Azar, whom they know as Terah. (Some Muslim scholars of antiquity such as Razi have held that Azar is just a title, with the true name of Abraham's father being Tarakh.) If it is true that Abraham's father was a carver of idols, as this lore suggests, then this would have given the young man insight into the futility of idols.

575 There is an old Jewish story that states that Abraham's father used to make his son carry small idols in the streets to sell. One day, Abraham was tired and sat by a river to rest. On a whim, he threw one of the idols into the water to see what would happen. He instantly became terrified at the thought of being struck down by lightning or suffering some other horrible fate, but then nothing happened to him. He mused that the idol couldn't even save itself from drowning or punish someone who had disrespected it, and thus he disbelieved in the idols that were made by men's hands. Another Jewish story has Abraham smashing the idols in his father's workshop and then arguing with him about the

result (of Our demonstration) to Abraham, when We showed him that We have all dominion over the heavens and the earth, and thus he was convinced (that the idols were false). [75]

When the night had overshadowed him, he looked up and saw a (bright) planet. *"This is my Lord,"* he had exclaimed, but when (the planet) set (below the horizon), he said, *"I don't like things that disappear."* [76]

Then he saw the moon rising, and he exclaimed, *"That's my Lord!"* However, when the moon also vanished (below the horizon), he said, *"Unless my Lord gives me guidance, then I'll be mistaken like the rest of the people."* [576] [77]

Then he saw the sun rising (in all its glory), and he exclaimed, *"Now that's my Lord! That's the greatest!"*

However, when the sun also vanished (below the horizon), he proclaimed, *"My people! Now I'm truly free of your making partners (with Allah)! [78] I've set my face upon the One Who initiated (the creation of the) heavens and the earth, and I'll never make partners (with Him)."* [79]

His people began to argue with him, so he told them, *"Are you arguing with me about Allah, after He's guided me? I'm not afraid of the partners you've made with Him, for nothing happens without My Lord's permission. My Lord encompasses everything within His knowledge, so won't you take a reminder?"* [80]

"How can I be afraid of those partners you've made in place of Him, when you're not even afraid to make partners with Allah without any authority at all? So which of our two sides should feel safer then? (Tell me if you think) you know!" [81]

"It's only those who believe and who don't confuse their faith with something wrong that are secure, for they're the ones who've been guided." [577] [82]

That was the kind of logic concerning Us that We gave to Abraham to use against his people. We raise up whomever We want in increments, for your Lord is full of wisdom and knowledge. [83]

(In time,) We granted him (a son named) Isaac and (a grandson named) Jacob, and We guided each of them. Even before them we had guided Noah, and among (Noah's) descendants were David, Solomon, Job, Joseph, Moses and Aaron. That's how We reward those who do good. [84]

(Also among his descendants were) Zachariah, John the Baptist, Jesus and

---

idols. (See the book entitled, *Legends of the Jews*, by Louis Ginzberg, *et al.*) This would be a logical segue into how the young Abraham began the search for his true Lord by disproving that the stars (and the light of the planets, which are called morning stars,) the moon and the sun his people worshipped, were also false gods. This is an important detail, given that the ancient people of Mesopotamia worshipped the sun, the moon, the stars and even the planets, among other assorted deities. (The chief 'morning star' goddess, representing the planet Venus or Jupiter, in Abraham's time was named Inanna; the moon god was Nanna-Sin; and the sun god was Utu.) Some classical commentators have suggested that the name Azar is not to be taken as a proper name and that it means instead "foolish one" in an obscure dialect. Thus, the verse would read, "It happened that Abraham said to his father, "Foolish one, are you taking idols for gods?" (*Razi*)

[576] The chief deity in Abraham's town of origin was the moon god Nanna-Sin. He was depicted as an old man with a long beard and four horns. On the summit of the great ziggurat of Ur was a single small alter upon which a different woman was placed each night with whom the god (represented by a priest) could 'cohabit.' We know then that Abraham's people were chiefly worshippers of a moon god by the fact that this verse specifically has him stating that if guidance from the real Lord wasn't accepted by the people, after he had shown the people that the moon was merely an object, then the people would remain mistaken (in their veneration of the moon).

[577] When they heard this verse, the companions were afraid and asked the Prophet how anyone can possibly go to heaven, since all have done wrong against their souls (i.e., sinned), even sometimes after having become believers. The Prophet explained that the word *zulm* here, which usually means oppression, darkness or wrongdoing, is to be equated with the sin of *shirk*, or idolatry. (*Ma'ariful Qur'an*) Also see verse 31:13 for the background and result of this verse's message.

209

Elijah. They were all among the righteous, [85] as were Ishmael, Elisha, Jonah and Lot.

We favored each of them above (anyone else in) all the worlds, [86] along with their parents, children and brethren. We chose them and guided them to a straight path. [87]

This is Allah's guidance, and He uses it to guide whomever He wants among His servants. If any of them make partners with Him (after knowing the truth), then all their efforts will go to waste. [88]

They were the ones to whom We gave the scriptures, sound judgment and the gift of prophecy.

If any (of their descendants) disbelieve in these things, then We'll transfer their obligation to another people who won't reject them. [89]

They were the ones who received Allah's guidance (in the past), so emulate them in guidance.

Then say to (the skeptical Meccans), *"I'm not asking you for any reward for all of this. This is no less than a reminder to all the worlds!"* [90]

The Reality before Allah

*T*hey're not thinking highly enough about Allah when they say, *"Allah never sends anything down to mortal men."* [578]

Then ask (them), *"So who sent down the scripture that Moses brought? It was a light and a guidepost for people, but you've turned it into an odd collection of pages for show,* [579] *while still holding back much of it. Were you taught things that neither you nor your ancestors knew?"*

Say (to them), *"Allah (knows the truth);"* then leave them alone to guess and speculate. [91]

This (Qur'an) is the Book that We've sent down to bring blessings and also to confirm whatever came before it, so you can warn (Mecca,) the mother of all cities [580] and all those around it (of Allah's coming judgment). Those who believe in the next life will believe in this, and they'll guard their prayers strictly. [92]

Who's more wrong than the one who invents a lie against Allah and who says, *"I've been inspired,"* when he hasn't been, or who says, *"I can reveal something just like Allah reveals"?* [581]

---

[578] Muhammad was speaking with a visiting Jewish rabbi named Malik ibn as-Sayf, and the rabbi became angry when the Prophet pointed out that Allah did not like for a religious leader to be gluttonous. (The man had the appearance of one well-fed to the extreme.) Thus, the rabbi swore angrily that Allah never revealed any scripture from heaven. This verse was revealed in response. (*Asbab ul-Nuzul*)

[579] Although the Torah was a very lengthy book, the Jews of the city used to write small passages on leather vellum and sell them to the illiterate Arabs as something akin to good luck charms. Thus, they turned the Torah into 'an odd collection of pages' while holding back the rest from the people. This practice of theirs (making money off the scripture) was also commented on in 2:41 and elsewhere.

[580] The chief or *mother* of all cities in Arabia is Mecca. It was the religious and cultural center of Arabia in the Prophet's time. Even today, it is the one city of the world that receives more diverse visitors in greater numbers than any other.

[581] This verse was revealed about the following situation. One of the Prophet's followers was a literate man named 'Abdullah ibn Sa'd ibn Abi Sarh. One day, the Prophet summoned him to write down some new verses that had been revealed to him. So 'Abdullah came and began to write as the Prophet dictated verses from chapter 23 (verses 12-16). The scribe became amazed at the detailed description of the creation of human beings about which he was writing, but the Prophet assured him that this was what Allah had revealed to him. When 'Abdullah left he began to doubt the Prophet's honesty (as people in those days had no knowledge of the process involved in the formation of a fetus), and he said to his friends, "If Muhammad is truthful, then I'm inspired, too, just like he is, and if he's lying, then I'm merely saying things like he is." Then he converted back to paganism, though he never carried arms against the Muslim cause. Later, when the Prophet returned to Mecca at the head of an army,

If you could only see how the corrupt will be during the confusion of their death throes. The angels will reach out with their hands (and say), *"Away with your souls. This day you'll get your payment – a humiliating punishment on account of your saying things about Allah against all right and because you arrogantly (rejected) His signs!"* [93]

And so you'll come back to Us - naked and alone – just as We created you the first time. You'll leave behind everything We ever granted you, and We won't see any of the intercessors accompanying you that you thought were your partners. All relations between you and them will be severed, and all your delusions will have merely led you astray. [582] [94]

Note the Many Signs of Allah in Nature

Allah causes grains and seeds to split and sprout, for He brings life from death and death from life. That's how Allah is to you, so how is it that you're so deceived (about His nature)?" [95]

He splits the dawn (from the night) and made the night for rejuvenation and rest, while the sun and the moon are for counting the passage of time. That's how He's arranged (for your world to work, for He's) the Powerful and the Knowing. [96]

He's the One Who made the stars (as reference points) to guide you on your way through the unknown regions of land and sea, and this is how We explain Our signs for people who know. [97]

He's the One Who produced you all from a single soul. (So understand that this world that you inhabit) is a place to linger, and it's also a point of departure. This is how We explain Our verses for people who understand. [98] He's the One Who sends down water from the sky and uses it to produce plants of every kind. From them, We grow lush green vegetation bringing forth grain piled high.

From date palms, clusters of dates hang within easy reach, and there are vineyards of grapes and olives and pomegranates, as well! (They're all) similar (in form) but different (in variety), and when they start to bear fruit - just look at their fruit when they ripen! In all these things are signs for people who believe. [99]

Allah is Above all Definitions

Yet, they're turning the jinns into (Allah's) partners, [583] even though *He* created *them*, and they're assigning sons and daughters to Him without any knowledge! All glory be to Him in the highest! (He's high) above what they make Him out to be! [100]

The original cause (for the creation) of the heavens and the earth is due to Him, so how can He have a son when He has no female consort? He created everything, and He knows about all things. [101]

That's Allah for you, your Lord; there is no god but He, the Creator of everything, so serve Him (alone), for He has power over every affair. [102] No vision can comprehend Him; yet, His

---

Uthman ibn Affan (d. 656) brought 'Abdullah to the Prophet under a guarantee of safety. He repented and converted back to Islam.

[582] A man named 'Abdullah ibn Shakhir once approached the Prophet while he was reciting this passage. When he was done, the Prophet said, "The son of Adam says, 'This is my wealth. This is my property,' but his real property consists of only three things: (the food) that he consumes, (the clothes) that he has worn and torn, and (the money) that he gives away (in charity) and so acquires (as good deeds). Everything else is left to others when he departs." (*Muslim*) The Prophet also said, "A person will not be questioned about three things: the clothes he uses to cover his body, the food with which he satisfies himself, and the house he uses for shelter." (*At-Tabari*)

[583] Some pagans believed that Allah and Satan were brothers and that Allah created people and animals while Satan created snakes, lions and scorpions. This verse comments on that belief. (*Ibn Kathir*)

comprehension is over all vision, for He's the Subtle and Well-informed. [584] [103]

Proof has now come to you from your Lord. If anyone will allow their reason to see it, then it will be to his own (benefit). If anyone chooses to remain blind to it, (then it will be to his own detriment, so tell them,) "*I'm not your guardian.*" [104]

That's how We explain the verses in various ways so they can say, "*You've learned it well*," and so We can clarify things for those who know (how to recognize the truth). [105]

On Tolerance

(*M*uhammad), follow what's being revealed to you from your Lord, for there is no god but He, and turn away from those who make partners (with Allah). [106]

If it would've been Allah's will, then none of them would've ever (taken idols) as partners (with Allah).   However, We didn't send you to be their guardian, nor are you the one who has to arrange their affairs. [107]

Don't insult those (idols) that they call upon besides Allah, [585] for they might insult Allah in their ignorance, out of spite. [586] We've made each community's actions seem appropriate and good to itself, but in the end they're all going to go back to their Lord. Then We're going to tell them the meaning of everything they ever did. [108]

The False Oaths of the Faithless

*T*hey swear to Allah with their strongest oaths that if only a miracle came to them, then they would believe on account of it. [587] Say (to them), "*Miracles*

---

[584] The Prophet said, "Allah doesn't sleep, and it's not fitting for His majesty for Him to do so. He raises and lowers the scale of everything. The deeds of the day ascend to him before nightfall, and the deeds of the night ascend to Him before daybreak. His screen is made of light or fire, and if He removes it, the light of His face will scorch every created thing that His sight reaches." (*Muslim*) However, this prohibition extends only to mortal, material things. In the next world, the world of light, energy and spirit matter, Allah can be seen, and the Prophet explained that people will be able to see Him from Paradise, much to their eternal delight. (*Tirmidhi, Ahmad*)

[585] Islam teaches that paganism is wrong. However, the Qur'an doesn't allow a believer to ridicule and insult the beliefs of a non-believer, even a pagan, lest the person, in his anger, insult Allah ignorantly out of spite. A believer can use every tool of logic to confront the false beliefs of another, but if they begin to feel insulted, then it's time to rethink strategies. As an example, a Muslim may prove that the Trinity is illogical, but if Christians begin taking it as an attack on Jesus himself, then the Muslim must apologize and try another approach.

[586] The revelation of this verse came about when the Prophet was attending to his uncle, Abu Talib, who was very ill. A delegation of Meccan chiefs came to make a last ditch effort to persuade Muhammad to compromise before the influential, yet elderly, Abu Talib passed on. When Abu Talib asked Muhammad what he wanted of the Meccans, he explained that he would only accept the truth of the One God from them. Then he made the famous statement that "even if they put the sun in my right hand and the moon in my left, neither will I desist nor compromise in this message." The pagans, oddly enough, felt their religion was being insulted, and they warned Muhammad that they would begin insulting his God if he didn't desist from his stubbornness. This verse then came cautioning the Prophet to be more sensitive to the unbelievers when engaging in dialogue.

[587] One of the Meccan leaders said to the Prophet, "Muhammad, you're telling us that Moses tapped a rock with a stick and that twelve springs gushed out, that Jesus raised the dead to life, and that the Thamud had a miracle camel. Well, then bring us some of those miracles, and then we'll believe in you." The Prophet asked them what kind of a miracle they wanted, and they said, "Turn that hill named Safa into gold." The Prophet answered, "If I did that, would you believe in me?" The gathered crowd answered in the affirmative. Then the Prophet walked away and invoked Angel Gabriel, who came to him invisibly and said, "If you want, I will transform that hill into gold, but (Allah) doesn't make such a miracle unless He would follow it up with punishment, so do you want to leave them alone until they

are in Allah's presence (and they come only by His command)," but how can you be made to understand that even if (such miracles) came, they would still not believe? [109]

We're going to steer their hearts and eyes away, even as they refused to believe in the first instance, and We're going to leave them in their disobedience to wander blindly. [110]

Even if We *did* send angels to them or caused the dead to speak to them or gathered every (other kind of proof) before their very eyes, they still wouldn't believe, save for Allah's will, as most of them are ignorant. [111]

Every Prophet had Enemies

*A*nd so it is that We've made a diabolical enemy to oppose every prophet, drawn from among both jinns and men, who would inspire each other with dazzling words of deception. If your Lord had wanted, then they would've never been able to do it, so leave them and what they're inventing alone. [112]

Let those who don't believe in the next life indulge in (their lies) to their heart's content, let them feel pleased about it and let them get whatever they can out of it. [113] Say (to them), "*Should I look for a judge other than Allah, when He's the One Who sent you a fully explained scripture?*"

Those who've been given a scripture (before you) know that it's been sent down by your Lord in all truth, so don't be among those who doubt. [114]

The pronouncements of your Lord are fulfilled with truth and justice, and no one can change His pronouncements, for He's the Hearing and the Knowing. [115]

If you were to follow what most (people say) here on earth, then they would lead you away from the path of Allah, for they do nothing but guess, and they do nothing but speculate. [116] Your Lord knows better who is straying from His path, and He knows better who is being guided. [117]

A Reminder of the Forbidden Foods

*Y*ou can eat whatever (meat) that's had Allah's name pronounced over it (at the time of slaughter), if you believe in His (revealed) verses. [118] And why shouldn't you eat of those things that have had Allah's name pronounced over them? He's already explained for you in detail what's forbidden, unless you're forced to eat it (out of desperation).

However, (when it comes to issues of food,) many (thoughtless people) mislead others for their own selfish reasons and without any knowledge. Your Lord knows best who's going beyond the boundaries. [119]

Leave off all sinning, whether done in the open or in secret, [588] for those who indulge in sin will be repaid with the consequences of whatever they did. [589] [120] Therefore, don't eat of (any meat) that hasn't had Allah's name pronounced over it (at the time of slaughter), for that would be an act of disobedience. Truly, devils

---

repent?" The Prophet said, "Leave them alone then until they repent." Then this passage was revealed, and the Prophet recited it to the crowd. (*Asbab ul-Nuzul*)

[588] A man named an-Nawwas asked the Prophet the meaning of the word 'sin' (*ithm*), and the Prophet replied, "A sin is what you find in your heart, and you would hate for people to know about it." (*Muslim*)

[589] Some idol-worshippers were objecting to the Prophet's teaching that animals found dead by themselves should not be eaten. One of them said, "Muhammad, tell us about a sheep. If it died by itself, then who killed it?" The Prophet said, "Allah caused it to die." Then the pagan, thinking he was being clever, said, "So, you're claiming that what you and your followers kill is lawful and what the dog and the hawk kill is lawful, while what Allah kills is unlawful?" This verse was revealed in response. (*Asbab ul-Nuzul*)

try to inspire their associates (among people) to argue with you, and if you obeyed them, then you would be no better than an idol-worshipper. [121]

The Arrogance of the Proud Ones

Can someone who was dead (to faith), and then whom We brought back to life with the light (of truth) that guides his steps among people, be equal to someone who is lost in darkness from which he can never come out? 590 As it is, those who suppress (their awareness of the truth) are pleased with what they're doing, (even though it's wrong). [122]

And so We've placed wicked leaders in every town, drawn from among its most influential citizens, so they can weave their schemes, but in the end they're only scheming against their own souls, even though they don't realize it! [123]

When a verse (is revealed from Allah) and then presented to them, they say, *"We won't believe (in it) until we see (a miracle) like Allah's (other) messengers got."* 591

Allah knows best how to send down His message! Those wicked ones will soon be humiliated in Allah's presence, and they will be severely punished on account of their scheming! [124]

If Allah wants to guide someone, He opens up his heart to *Peaceful Surrender*, 592 and if Allah wants to leave someone astray, He tightens his chest until it's so constricted that *he feels as if he's climbing high up into the sky!*

That's how Allah penalizes those who won't believe. [125]

This is the way of your Lord, and it leads straight (to the truth). We've explained the verses (of this Book) for people who accept reminders. [126] For them is the realm of peace in the presence of their Lord, and He will be their protector on account of what they did. [127]

Both Humans and Jinn will be Questioned

One day, He will gather everyone together (and say), *"You gathered assembly of jinns! You were very hard on those human beings."*

Their human associates will answer, *"Our Lord! We benefited from each other*

---

590 This passage is a reference to the conversion of the Prophet's uncle, Hamza ibn 'Abdel-Muttalib. The Prophet was walking one day, and his cruel enemy, Abu Jahl, threw dung on him. The Prophet saw Hamza coming into town, returning from a hunt while he was carrying a bow in his hand. He complained to him of what Abu Jahl had done, and Hamza became angry and confronted Abu Jahl with his bow raised high. Abu Jahl began to tremble, but he defended himself saying, "Father of Ya'la, don't you see what he's brought? He's brought confusion to our minds, insulted our gods and left the ways of our forefathers." Hamza replied, "And who's more ridiculous than you? You worship stones instead of Allah, so I testify that there's no god but the One God, that He has no partners, and that Muhammad is His servant and Messenger." This passage was revealed in response. (*Asbab ul-Nuzul*)
591 The Prophet said, "There wasn't a single prophet among the prophets who didn't get some kind of miracle that saved people or made them believe. What I was given from Allah was the divine revelation. So I hope my followers will be more numerous than those of any other prophet on the Day of Resurrection." (*Bukhari*)
592 *Islam* means surrender/submission and peace. When a person surrenders their pride and arrogance and loves Allah for the sake of pure love, they submit to His will and follow His teachings. Doing this brings a person inner peace because they are aligned with the very purpose of the universe and life itself. People spend a lifetime looking for that treasure, never realizing it is so easy to gain! When we take a step towards our Lord, He comes to us running, as the saying of the Prophet tells us. The famous poet, Jalaluddin Rumi (d. 1273), once wrote, "That which Allah said to the rose, causing it to blossom in splendorous beauty, He also said to my heart, making it a hundred times more delightful." (*Mathnawi* III, 4129)

(immensely), but now we've reached our deadline, the one that You decided for us." 593

(Allah) will then say, *"Your home will be in the Fire, and you're going to remain there, except as Allah wills, for your Lord is full of knowledge and wisdom."* 594 [128]

Therefore, We let the wrongdoers (turn towards each other) for close support, (and because of their unholy alliances We will cast them all into Hellfire, irrespective of rank, race or status), on account of what they've earned. [129]

(Allah will then say to them all,) *"You gathered assembly of jinns and human beings! Didn't any messengers from among you ever come to you and relate My (revealed) verses to you and warn you of the meeting of this day of yours?"* (The crowds will sadly answer,) saying, *"We testify against our own selves."*

The life of the world deceived them, and that's why they'll be made to testify against their own selves, (admitting) that they had rejected (faith). 595 [130] (Indeed, messengers were sent to them for) that (very purpose), because their Lord would never destroy any civilization for its bad conduct while its people were unaware (that they should turn towards Allah). [131]

Everyone is ranked according to what they do, and your Lord is not unaware of what (each of you) is doing. [132] Your Lord is Self-sufficient, and He's a master of mercy. If it were ever His desire, He could destroy you all and put in your place whomever else He wanted to succeed you, even as He let you arise from the descendants (of previous civilizations) of old. [133] Everything that you've been

promised will come to pass, and there's no way you can steer it away. [134]

Say (to them), *"My people! Do whatever you can, for I'm going to do likewise. Soon you're going to know who will have the (best) outcome in the afterlife, and the wrongdoers will never be successful."* [135]

Addressing the Superstitions of the Pagans

𝒯he (idol-worshippers) assign to Allah a share of the harvest and the livestock that He (has caused to be) produced. They say on their own (whim), *"This much is for Allah, and this much is for our idols."* However, the *share* of their idols never gets back to Allah, while the *share* of Allah just goes to support their idolatry! That's an appalling distribution! [136]

Even further, their 'partners' have made the practice of killing their own children seem appropriate and good to most of the idol-worshippers, so much so that it leads to their own destruction and causes confusion in their way of life. 596 If Allah had wanted to prevent this, then they would've never done that, but leave them alone with what they've invented. [137]

Then they say on their own that certain livestock (animals) and crops are taboo and that no one should eat of them except whomever We (supposedly) allowed to do so. (They also say) that some livestock (animals) are not meant to be harnessed for labor or that some are not to have Allah's name pronounced over them (when they're slaughtered). These are all

---

593 Pagan travelers in the desert, upon entering an unknown valley, used to proclaim, "I seek the protection of the master (jinn) of this valley." Thus, humans and jinns 'benefited' from each other. (*At-Tabari*)

594 Hellfire is not forever for everybody. Some will enter Hellfire and get their due punishment. When their limit is reached, the angels will retrieve them from the pit, restore their bodies and usher them into Paradise. The Prophet once said (in a very famous narration) that if anyone has even a speck of faith in his heart, he'll eventually be taken out of Hell, reconstituted afresh and admitted into Heaven. (*Bukhari*)

595 Ibn 'Abbas (d. 687) said, "If you really want to know how ignorant the Arabs were, then read all the verses in chapter 6 beyond verse 130." (*Ibn Kathir*)

596 The widespread practice of female infanticide is being referenced here. Also see 81:8-9.

inventions made in Allah's name! He's soon going to pay them back for their invented (superstitions). [138]

Superstition is not Equal to Divine Principles

They also say, "*What's in the wombs of certain livestock (animals) will be reserved for our men (to eat) and forbidden for our women, but if it's a stillborn (calf) then everyone can share in it.*" 597

Well, He's going to repay them soon enough for their (generous) interpretation (of the so-called rules). He's full of wisdom and knowledge (and would never have invented such things). [139]

Those who foolishly and ignorantly kill their own children are lost! (They're lost even further because) they've made restrictions on the food that Allah has provided for them by inventing (superstitions) against Allah. They've gone astray and have no guidance. [140]

He's the One Who brought about gardens of plants that grow on climbing vines and plants that don't grow high, orchards of date palms, cultivated fields with vegetables of every kind, and olives and pomegranates, (which are) similar (in form) but different (in variety). So eat their fruits when they're in season, but give what is due upon them (to the poor) on the day of harvest. 598 Don't let any of it go to waste, for Allah has no love for those who waste. [141]

Some types of livestock were made for labor, while others were made for providing meat. So eat from what Allah provided for you, and don't follow in Satan's footsteps, for he's your obvious enemy. [142]

Take (a look) at these eight livestock (animals) that come in pairs: (first examine) a pair of (male and female) sheep, and then a pair of (male and female) goats. Then ask them, "*Has (Allah) forbidden the two males or the two females or what's in the two females' wombs? Give me a convincing answer if you're so honest!*" [143]

(Now consider the status of) a pair of camels and a pair of oxen. Ask (the idol-worshippers), "*Has (Allah) forbidden (you to eat of) the two males or the two females or what's in the two females' wombs? Were you there when Allah commanded you about that? Who's more wrong than the one who invents a lie against Allah in order to lead unknowing people astray? Truly, Allah doesn't guide wrongdoers.*" [144]

Say (to them), "*I haven't found anything in what's been revealed to me that would restrict a person from eating something if they wanted to eat it, unless it's a dead carcass or flowing blood or pork – and that's an abomination – or what's impure because it was dedicated to other names besides Allah. Although if someone is forced by desperation (to eat forbidden foods) and is not trying to be disobedient or seeking to go beyond the bounds, (know that) your Lord is forgiving and merciful.*" [145]

---

597 This practice mentioned below was a peculiar pagan custom in which calves born to cows marked for sacrifice were specially reserved as food only for the priests of certain idols. Women were forbidden to eat of these calves, unless they were stillborn calves found within the animals after slaughter. This verse pokes fun at this practice and calls it a mindless superstition to be discarded. (*Ibn Kathir*)

598 The required tax on harvests is part of the *zakat* or annual charity duty of a Muslim, though some commentators believe that this verse was revealed before the *zakat* amount was made official, so by the time of this Meccan revelation, poor people could come by on harvest day and collect free seeds and hay from Muslim land owners. (*Zakat* (required charity) is one of the five pillars of Islam. The proceeds go to feed the poor, orphans, widows, stranded travelers, impoverished preachers, etc… Also see 70:24.) While the valley of Mecca was not suited for growing things, there were small areas in the countryside around western Arabia that did support some limited agriculture, and by this time the Prophet had made converts among many desert tribes. At-Tabari wrote that this verse is referencing a man named Thabit ibn Qays who vowed one day to feed anyone with free dates who came to him. So many people came that day that he didn't have any dates left!

On the Arcane Dietary Restrictions of the Jews

$\mathcal{W}$e made it forbidden for the followers of Judaism (to eat) everything with an undivided hoof, [599] and We also forbade them to eat the fat of oxen and sheep, except for the fat on their backs, entrails and bones.

These (restrictions) were on account of their brazen disobedience, and We're certainly correct (in what We say). [146] If they accuse you of lying, then say to them, *"Your Lord is the master of mercy and embraces all things, though His wrath will never be turned away from wicked people."* [147]

Can You Blame Allah for Your Foolish Customs?

$\mathcal{T}$hose who make partners (with Allah) say, *"If Allah had wanted to (prevent us from worshipping idols), then neither ourselves nor our ancestors would've ever made partners with Him, nor would we have had any taboos."*

Now those are the same types of fraudulent arguments that their own ancestors used to employ - *until they felt Our wrath!*

Say (to them), *"Do you have some kind of knowledge (to back that claim)? If you do, then show us! You're just guessing, and you're just speculating."* [148] Then say, *"Allah has the most convincing arguments, and if He really had wanted, He could've guided you all."* [149]

Say (to them), *"Produce your witnesses to prove that Allah made such restrictions (on food, as*

you're claiming)." If they bring some witnesses (who will falsely testify), then don't remain in such a gathering, nor should you follow the fickle whims of those who treat our (revealed) verses as lies and who don't believe in the next life, given that they make others as equals with their Lord. [150]

The Ten Commandments of Islam

$\mathcal{S}$ay (to them), *"Come here, and I'll announce the (real) restrictions of Allah. They are as follows:* [600]

- Do not take any other as His equal;

- Be kind to your parents;

- Do not kill your children for fear of poverty, as We provide resources for you and for them;

- Do not go near shameful deeds, whether in public or in secret;

- Do not take a life, which Allah has made sacred, except for a just cause (under the law), and that's His command so you can reflect; [151]

- Do not touch an orphan's property, unless you're going

---

[599] As mentioned in the book of Leviticus 11:3-6.

[600] A group of visitors came to the Prophet one day to determine if he was a real messenger of God. During the course of the conversation he recited verses 6:151-153 and 16:90 to them. One of the listeners was a man named al-Mafruq ibn Amr, who was the chief of the large Shayban tribe. He was amazed at how different the verses were in comparison to common Arabic poetry, and he exclaimed, "What you have recited are the not the words of a human being. If they were the words of a human being we would have been able to recognize it." (As quoted in Syed Qutb's seminal work, *Artistic Imagery in the Qur'an*, page 34.)

to improve it, until they attain their full maturity;

- Measure (goods and amounts honestly); [601]

- And balance justly, and We don't burden any soul beyond what it can bear;

- When you speak, stand out for justice, even if it concerns a close relative;

- And fulfill the Covenant of Allah. [602]

This is what He's commanded of you, so you can take heed. [152] This is My straight path, so follow it. [603] Don't follow other paths, for they'll only divert you away from His path. This is what He's commanded of you, so you can be mindful (of your duty to Him). [153]

This is the Book of Guidance

*W*e then gave the Book to Moses, completed it and explained it thoroughly for those who would be good, so it could be a source of guidance and mercy and so they could believe in the meeting with their Lord. [154] This (Qur'an) is (a new) scripture that We've revealed as a source of blessing, so follow it and be mindful (of what it says) so you can be worthy of mercy. [155]

(You've been given this new scripture) so that you'll never be able to say, "*Scripture was given to two groups before us, but what they learned from was never introduced to us!*" [156]

Likewise, you'll never be able to say, "*Oh, if only a book had been sent down to us, then we would've followed its guidance better than they did.*"

Now clear evidence has come to you from your Lord, and a source of guidance and mercy. Who is more wrong than the one who rejects Allah's signs and turns away from them? Soon We're going to repay those who turned away from Our signs with a terrible punishment on account of their avoidance. [157]

Are they waiting to see the angels coming for them, or your Lord, or the unmistakable signs of your Lord's (coming)? [604] On the day when the signs of your Lord do arrive, it won't do any good

---

[601] The Prophet said, "Measuring and weighing (fairly) is a required duty that has brought about the downfall of many nations before you that were destroyed with divine punishment (because they failed in their duty to be fair)." (*Ibn Kathir*) Also see chapter 83. The Prophet's advice was to give a little extra to the customer when measuring. (*Ahmad, Tirmidhi*) He also counseled us not to ask for more than what is due when extracting payment or taking delivery and also not to be overly concerned if the measured amount you receive is slightly less than the full amount you are due. Rather, we should be happy that we received the full amount, or at least nearly the full amount that we were owed. (*Bukhari*) This slight generosity on both sides promotes good will in business, rather than a cut-throat attitude. (*Ma'ariful Qur'an*)

[602] The *Covenant of Allah* is the promise to struggle in His cause – even if it costs you your life – as is the duty of every faithful servant of the Living God. See 9:111 where this covenant is mentioned. Also see 61:10-13.

[603] A group of people were sitting with the Prophet when he drew a straight line in front of him and said, "This is Allah's path." Then he drew two other lines, one to the right and one to the left, and said, "These are the paths of Satan." He then placed his hand on the middle line and recited verse 153. (*Ahmad*) Another report adds that the Prophet also said on this occasion, "There is a devil on every path (other than Allah's straight path), and it entices people away from the straight path and welcomes them to the other paths." (*Darimi*)

[604] These are some of the foretold portents signaling the coming of the End Times. When these come to pass, then belief will not be accepted. Among these, the most significant one will be the appearance of a wicked leader known as the *Dajjal*, or Anti-Christ, who will dupe people into believing in him instead of Allah. The Prophet said, "When the following three signs appear, it won't do anyone any

for a soul to believe in them, if it hadn't already believed in them or made a good account (of its sincerity) through (acts of) true faith. Say (to them), *"Wait, because we'll be waiting, too."* [158]

Remain Firm on the Truth

*T*hose who break up their way of life into sects and competing factions – *you must have nothing to do with them!* [605] Their affair lies with Allah, and in the end He's going to tell them the meaning of everything they ever did. [159]

Whoever does something good will be given ten times as much to his credit, while whoever does an evil thing will be credited with one bad deed, and no one will ever be treated unfairly. [606] [160]

Say (to them), *"My Lord has truly guided me to a straight way, the established way of life,* *the creed of Abraham, the natural (monotheist), and he was never an idol-worshipper."* [161]

Then say, *"Truly, my prayers and my sacrifice, my life and my death, are all for Allah, the Lord of All the Worlds.* [162] *He has no partners, and this is my order, that I must be the first to submit (to His will)."* [607] [163]

Ask (them), *"Should I look for another lord besides Allah, when He's the Lord of all things? Every soul brings its own results upon none other than itself, and no bearer of burdens can bear the burden of another. In the end your return is with Allah, and He's going to tell you the meaning of all those things about which you argued."* [164]

He's the One Who made you successors in the earth, and He's placed some of you in higher positions than others so He can test you with (the varying gifts) that He's given you. Your Lord is quick to punish, though He's also (quick to show) forgiveness and mercy. [165]

---

good to believe unless they had already believed before. They are the rising of the sun from the West, the *Dajjal*, and the rising of a beast from the earth." (*Muslim*) The first sign has been interpreted to mean that the West becomes more powerful than the Eastern (or Islamic) world, while the third sign remains enigmatic and is steeped in mysterious symbolism. See 27:82 and footnote for more on the beast.

[605] The Prophet explained this verse by saying, "These are the people who invent new doctrines (*bid'ah*) in their religion, and the ones who follow such vain desires in this Muslim nation will not have their repentance accepted by Allah."

[606] The Prophet said, "Whoever intends to do something good is rewarded by Allah with one good deed for having intended it. If he actually does that good deed, then Allah rewards him from ten to seven hundred times. Whoever intends to do something wrong but doesn't do it is also rewarded by Allah with one good deed (for having not done it). If he does that bad deed, then he is credited with only one sin." (*Bukhari, Muslim*)

[607] A companion of the Prophet named Abu Musa al-Ash'ari once said of verses 162-163, "I wish that every Muslim would keep reciting this passage over and over until they make it their motto for life." (*Ma'ariful Qur'an*)

The Heights

7 Al A'raf
Late Meccan Period

This chapter, much like the last one, was revealed in the very last days of the Prophet's stay in Mecca. It also addresses new concerns such as budding interfaith relations with Jews. Even though there weren't any Jews living in Mecca, it was, nonetheless, a hub of trading activity that saw visitors of many faiths. The Meccan leaders used to ask the Jews questions pertaining to Muhammad and what their religion might have to say about him. Thus, this chapter addresses both pagans and Jews, even as it lays out new theological concepts for the believers. One such new concept was the place between Heaven and Hell known as the Heights, reserved for those whose records are so finely balanced between good and evil that they don't deserve Heaven or Hell. Eventually, they will all be admitted into Paradise.

In the Name of Allah,
the Compassionate, the Merciful

Alif. Lām. Meem. Sâd. [1]

(This is) a book that's being revealed to you (from Allah), so don't let your heart be troubled any more over (how people may respond to it), for with (this Book) you can give warnings and reminders to the believers. [2]

(All you people!) Follow what's been revealed to you from your Lord. Don't follow (the whims) of others or take others besides Him as protectors. How few are the warnings that you take! [3] Just how many settlements have We destroyed? Our punishment came upon them suddenly by night or while they were taking their afternoon rest. 608 [4]

Regardless, when Our punishment finally came upon them, they cried out, saying no more than, *"We were so wrong!"* [5] We're going to question those who had Our message sent to them, even as We're going to question the bearers (of all those messages). [6] We'll narrate their complete story to them with full accuracy, for We were never absent (from their midst). [7]

The weighing (of all the evidence) on that day will be fair and just. Those whose scales are heavy (with good) will be successful. 609 [8] Meanwhile, those whose

---

608 Many cities have been destroyed suddenly and with little warning, such as Sodom, Iram (Ubar), Pompeii and Herculaneum. Some were buried under the sudden eruption of nearby volcanoes or blasted with earthquakes or sandstorms, sometimes even preserving the bodies of many a startled resident!

609 The Prophet said, "There are two sayings that are dear to the Merciful (God). They're easy on the tongue but weighty on the scale (that will weigh your good deeds). They are to say, 'Glory be to Allah, and His is all Praise', (*Subhanullah wa bihamdihi*) and 'Glory be to Allah, the Most Great.'" (*Subhanullahil 'owdheem*) (*Bukhari*) In addition, there is another tradition in which the Prophet said that a man will come on Judgment Day and find 99 scrolls worth of bad deeds facing him on the scale of deeds. Then a small paper will be given to him upon which will be the phrase, *"There is no god but Allah,"* for the man had said it often while alive. The man will be incredulous and will ask what good

scales are scarce (of good) will find that they've lost their own souls because they treated Our signs wrongly. [610] [9]

The Fall of Iblis

*A*nd so it was that We settled you on the earth, and We provided for you the resources that you need to survive; *yet, how little thanks you give!* [611] [10]

And so it was that We created you and gave you your shape. We then ordered the angels to bow down to (your original ancestor) Adam, and they all bowed down, except for (a *jinn* named) Iblis, who didn't join those who bowed. [612] [11] (Allah) said to him, *"What's preventing you from bowing down, when I've commanded it?"*

"I'm better than he is," (Iblis) replied, *"for You made me from fire, while You made him from clay."* [12]

"Get down and away from here!" (Allah) ordered. *"You can't be arrogant here! Get out of here, for you're the least (of all creatures)!"* [13]

"Give me time!" (Iblis) cried out. *"(Give me time) until the day when they're all resurrected."* [14]

"You shall have your time," (Allah) answered. [15] Then Iblis said, *"And since it was You Who made me slip up, I'll lie in wait for them on Your 'straight path.'* [16] *I'll attack them from their front and their back and from their right and their left, and in the end You'll see that most of them are thankless (towards You)."* [17]

"Get out of here!" (Allah) ordered, *"You're banished! If any of them follow you, then I'll fill Hellfire with you all!"* [613] [18]

In the Garden of Eden

*"A*dam," (Allah said), *"You may live in the garden with your mate and eat whatever you like, but don't go near this one tree, for it will lead you into corruption."* [614] [19]

---

that little scrap will do on the good deed side of the scale. The paper will be placed on it, and it will grow heavier and heavier, lifting his over-weighted bad-deed side right up! (*Tirmidhi*) In another report, the Prophet explained that the ink used by a scholar will be of more value than the blood of martyrs. (*Ma'ariful Qur'an*)

[610] As Ibn 'Abbas (d. 687) explained it, even though a person's deeds are an immaterial thing, on the Day of Judgment, Allah is going to give them solid form and then weigh them. (*Ibn Kathir*) (See 18:49) Chapter 101 echoes the same principle in a short, yet poetic, way.

[611] The Prophet said, "He among you who wakes up while healthy in body, safe in his family and having enough provisions to live on that day, it's as if the world and all that was in it were collected for him." (*Ibn Kathir*)

[612] As has been mentioned in the footnote to 2:34-35, Iblis was a *jinn* (elemental spirit) and *not* an angel. When Allah commands that those before Him should bow, even if He seems to address only one type of creature, all are bound to obey. Iblis did not obey and thus didn't join the angels who were bowing down, as this verse specifies. Why didn't he bow down? The scholars explain that when pride first entered Iblis's heart, Allah's anger emboldened the growing blindness in his inner understanding, and he could no longer comprehend or fear the majesty of Allah. Thus, he became bold and combative, as this passage shows. Also see 2:34 and footnote.

[613] This is another in a multitude of instances where 'the sentence' or decree of Allah that will be proved true against humans is mentioned.

[614] Genesis chapter 3 contains the ancient (but corrupted) version of this story, and there are some parallels here. However, there are also important differences. The first difference is in assigning blame. The Bible has Adam immaturely placing the blame for eating from the tree on the woman, and God accepts Adam's excuse and then curses the woman with subordination to men and painful childbearing as a punishment for 'fooling' the man (Genesis 3:12, 16, also I Timothy 2:12-15). The Qur'anic version, however, lays the blame on them both equally, and the woman is not singled out specifically. (Also painful birthing is considered by the Qur'an to be a kind of noble suffering that a woman bears for her children's sake. See 46:15.) The second main difference is in the nature of the tree from which the pair were forbidden to eat. The Biblical narrative implies that the tree *did* have power, while the Qur'an only quotes Satan *as claiming* that it did. In reality, it was perhaps merely a

Then Satan began to whisper suggestions to them both, for he wanted to cause them to see their nakedness, which was hidden (from their sensibilities). 615 *"The only reason your Lord has forbidden this tree to you,"* (he) told them, *"is because (He's afraid that) you might transform into angels or some other immortal being."* [20] Then he swore to them both that he was giving them good advice. [21]

In this way, he orchestrated (their fall) through deception. When they tasted (the fruit) of the tree, then their nakedness became clearly evident to them, and they began to sew leaves together from the garden to cover their bodies. Then their Lord called out to them, *"Didn't I forbid you from that tree, and didn't I tell you that Satan is your clear enemy?"* [22]

"Our Lord!" they cried. *"We've done wrong against our own souls! If You don't forgive*

us and show us mercy, then we'll be utterly lost!" [23]

"Go down away from here," (Allah) said, *"and live in the world, (struggling) in competition with each other. It'll be your home and your place of livelihood for a while."* [24] Then He added, *"You shall dwell in (the earth), and there you shall die, and from it you will be taken out again (for judgment)."* [25]

To the Children of Adam

Children of Adam! We've bestowed upon you clothing to hide the shame (of your nakedness), as well as to adorn you. (Remember, however, that) the robe of *mindfulness* 616 is the best (with which to clothe yourself). These are some of the verses of Allah (that are being revealed to you, Muhammad,) so they can be reminded. [26]

---

test for the humans. (When they realized they had failed God, they felt the sensation of shame for the first time.) The third difference is that the book of Genesis states that God had a *second* tree in the garden, one that grants eternal life to the one who eats from it. God is said to have been afraid that if Adam ate from that *second* tree, then Adam would become an immortal like God, Himself (Genesis 3:22-23). The Qur'an makes no mention of any second tree, nor would it ever claim that God would be afraid of anything. Finally, the fourth significant difference is in the aftereffects for human nature. Western Christianity (and to some extent Judaism) teaches that Adam and Eve's fall caused a shift in the psychological makeup of the human species, making them automatically prone to sin and preordained to suffer God's punishment from their birth. (Psalms 51:5) While Jews were to sacrifice animals to please the Lord, the specifically Christian doctrine of *Original Sin* provides that the only way God could forgive the sins of people would be if He gave birth to a *part* of Himself on earth and let humans kill Him. Then, when that part of God was sent to Hell for three days (as some Protestant sects assert, or at the least, preaching in Hell, as the Catholic church counters,) a *third* part of God, which was a *ghost*, could come into the world and fill the hearts of the faithful with God's love. This theology requires a belief that God is three separate people who act in *unison* for the common good. This grouping is known as the Trinity. There is no doctrine of Original Sin accepted in the Qur'an. (See Qur'an 4:171-172.) People are only presented as being weak to temptation, gullible and hasty, but not automatically inclined to being *sinful*, because we are born with the counterforce of an inner nature that seeks to have our interrupted fellowship with God restored (a concept known as *fitrah,* or the primordial attraction to Allah). Thus, the interplay of these inner struggles are influenced by the outer forces of Satan and God, and it's up to each individual to hearken to one side or the other.

615 Adam and Eve lived naked in the garden. They did not feel any shame, for that emotional sensation was foreign to them. If Satan could make the pair disobey Allah regarding the tree, then he could also succeed in making them feel ashamed about their own bodies. This would be the door through which Satan could gain influence over their other emotions, such as greed, hatred and jealousy. According to a tradition of the Prophet, Satan, himself, said, "I got people to indulge in sin, and thus I ruined them, but they ruin me back whenever they recite that there is no god but Allah. Therefore, I get them busy with false notions and useless ideas that they think are true, proper and right; thus, they feel no need to repent of their innovations." (*Ma'ariful Qur'an*)

616 *Taqwa,* in religious terms, is mindfulness of Allah's presence and of our responsibility to try never to disobey Him. In other words, we should not get filled with pride over how beautiful or trendy our clothing is, for whatever we are wearing, the important thing is working for Allah's pleasure because He is the One we will all have to face in the end.

Children of Adam! Don't let Satan deceive you like he did when he got your ancestors expelled from the Garden (of Eden), stripping them of their facade (of innocence) to expose their shame.

Both he and his band (of devils) see you from a place where you can't see them, and We've made devils the allies of those who suppress (their ability to see the truth). [27]

Answering those Who Blame Allah

*W*hen (the faithless) do shameful things, they say, "*These are the customs that we received from our ancestors,*" or they say, "*Allah told us to do it.*" [617]

Say (to them), "*Allah never commanded shameful things. Are you saying something about Allah without knowing (any better)?*" [28]

Say (to them), "*My Lord commands justice and that you dedicate your whole self (to Him) in every act of worship and that you call upon Him with complete sincerity, for all religion belongs to Him.* [618] *Even as He started you in the beginning, so shall you return.*" [29]

A section of them are guided by Him, while another section has rightfully gone astray because they took devils for their protectors instead of Allah, all the while thinking they were being guided! [30] Therefore, Children of Adam! Wear your good clothes at every place of prayer, and eat and drink (as you like). [619] However, don't overindulge, for Allah has no love for those who overindulge. [31]

Don't Renounce the World

*N*ow ask them, "*Who has forbidden the exquisite (gifts) of Allah, which He has made*

---

[617] The pagans of Mecca required visitors to wear special clothes to walk around the Ka'bah. If they did not have such clothes, they could walk around the structure naked. If they wanted to wear clothing, and it was not sacred, they had to throw the clothes away afterward so no one could use them again. (*Ibn Hisham*) This is what the 'shameful thing' in this verse refers to. The Quraysh also forbade visitors from bringing their own food to Mecca while on pilgrimage. When the Prophet spoke out against these customs, the pagans offered the excuse quoted in verse 28. Verses 29-33 were revealed in response. (*Ibn Kathir*)

[618] There is a misconception among many that Islamic salvation is dependent on a person's deeds. This misconception has given rise to the false notion, particularly among Christians (who fault Judaism's emphasis on works,) that Muslims 'buy' or 'earn' their salvation (whereas Christians boast that heaven is free for them upon mere acceptance of the death of a man-god). The fact, however, is that although Islam places a great deal of importance on deeds as a sign of faith, it is not deeds that gain a person salvation in the next life. The Qur'an repeats the following phrase: "Those who believe and do what's morally right" so many times it becomes patently obvious that faith comes first before deeds. Now if all that were required to go to heaven were good deeds, then even the most embittered atheist would go to heaven if he gave charity and was kind to those around him for the span of his life. Without faith there is no salvation. The Prophet said, "Know that the good deeds done by any of you will not admit him into Paradise." When the people near to him asked, "Not even for you, Messenger of Allah?" the Prophet replied, "Not even for me, unless my Lord grants (Paradise) me out of His favor and mercy." (*Bukhari*) The New Testament of the Bible quotes an activist named James as saying, "*Faith without works is dead.*" (James 2:26. Also see I Kings 8:32 and I Timothy 2:10.) This is exactly what a Muslim would say to explain why Islam promotes good behavior as a proof of faith. It is precisely the Christian confusion about the status of good works that has led many churches to deemphasize good works in favor of a murky and sensationalist-based faith built upon emotional experiences rather than practical, thoughtful modifications to daily behavior. Doesn't the last chapter of the New Testament quote God as saying, "Behold, I am coming soon! My reward is with Me, and I will give to everyone according to what he has done"? (Revelations 22:12)

[619] The part about the eating and drinking in this verse refers to the pagan habit of restricting their food intake while on their religious pilgrimages. Muslim pilgrims are allowed to eat normally as long as they aren't wasteful. The Prophet once counseled that when people eat they should reserve one third of their stomachs for food, one third for drink and one third for air. 'Umar ibn al-Khattab said, "Eat in moderation…for it is good for your health and gives you more stamina for your worship."

available to His servants, and (who has forbidden) the wholesome (things He has) provided?"

Say (to them), "*In the life of this world, (the natural gifts of the earth) belong to the believers, and they will be the only ones on the Day of Assembly who will have them.*"

This is how We clearly explain the verses (of this Book) for people who understand. [32]

Then say (to them), "*My Lord has forbidden all shameful deeds, whether done in the open or in secret, (and He's forbidden) sinfulness, flagrant injustice, joining partners with Allah for which He's sent down no authority, and saying things about Allah of which you know nothing.*" [33]

Each Nation is Given a Chance

Every community has been given its own (predetermined) time limit, and when their deadline is due, they can't prolong it even for an hour, nor can they delay it. [34]

Therefore, Children of Adam! Whenever a messenger comes to you from your own kind conveying My verses to you, whoever is mindful (of that message) and reforms himself will have no cause for fear or sorrow. [35]

Those who suppress (their ability to recognize the truth of) Our (revealed) verses and (even worse) treat them in a haughty manner will be companions of the Fire, *and that's where they're going to stay!* [36]

The Fate of Those Who Deny Allah

Who's more wrong than the one who invents a lie against Allah or who denies His (revealed) verses? They're the ones whose due punishment must come back to them from the book (of deeds), [620] even up to the point when our (angelic) messengers arrive and take their souls, saying, "*Where are all those (false gods) that you used to call upon besides Allah?*"

(The doomed souls will answer), "*They've left us to languish!*" And so they will testify against their own souls that they had indeed buried (their ability to recognize the truth of Allah). [37]

(Allah will say to them), "*Enter into the companionship of all those jinns and humans who have passed away before you - (all of whom) are in the Fire!*"

Every time a new community will enter into (Hell), it will curse its sister-communities that preceded it, so much so that after they've all followed each other into it, the last one will say of the first, "*Our Lord! They're the ones who misled us, so double their punishment in the Fire.*"

Then He'll say, "*The punishment is doubled for all!*" They just don't understand! [38]

Finally, the first (community that entered Hellfire) will say to the last (one that entered it), "*So, you're no better than we are after all! Now suffer the punishment for your deeds, (just as we have to)!*" [621] [39]

---

[620] Whatever evil they did is recorded in a ledger, and it will come back to haunt them one day when they'll have to answer for what they've done. Alternatively, this verse can be understood to mean that the recorded fate of doomed sinners will overtake them eventually.

[621] The Prophet once told the following story: Paradise and Hellfire had an argument. Hell said, "I've been favored with arrogant people and tyrants." Paradise said, "What's wrong with me that only the poor and humble people enter me?" Allah, the Exalted, said to Paradise, "You are My mercy with which I grant mercy to those among My servants that I want." Then He said to Hell, "You are My punishment with which I inflict punishment upon whomever of My servants that I want, and I'm going to fill both of you!" (*Bukhari*)

Those who suppress (their ability to recognize the truth of) Our (revealed) verses and (even worse) treat them in a haughty manner will find no opening in the gates of the sky, [622] nor will they ever enter Paradise – *no, not until a twisted rope can pass through the eye of a needle!* [623]

That's Our way of paying back the wicked! [40] Their resting place will be under layers and layers of Hellfire, and that's how We pay back wrongdoers! [624] [41]

A Conversation between Heaven and Hell

*T*hose who believe and do what's morally right - *and We don't place upon any soul a burden greater than it can bear* – they'll be the companions of the Garden, *and in it they shall remain!* [625] [42]

We're going to erase from their hearts any hidden sense of unease, even as rivers are flowing beneath them! *"Praise be to Allah,"* they'll exclaim, *"Who guided us to this,*

for we never could have guided ourselves, save for the guidance of Allah. And so it was that messengers from our Lord came to us with the truth!"

(When they finish their joyous exclamations,) they'll hear the call (of welcome): *"The Garden is right there before you! You've inherited it on account of all that you did!"* [43]

(Now before each group is entered into its respective place), the companions of the Garden will call over to the companions of the Fire, saying, *"We've found our Lord's promise to be true. Have you found your Lord's promise to be true, as well?"* [626]

"Yes," they'll answer, but then an announcer (will interrupt them), saying, *"Allah's curse be upon the wrongdoers!* [44] *They're the ones who turned others away from the path of Allah, trying to make it seem crooked, and they were the ones who rejected the next life."* [45]

There will be a screen erected between them, and on high places (in between the two groups) there will be men whose (scales of deeds had balanced perfectly in between good and evil). [627] They'll clearly

---

[622] 'Abdullah ibn 'Abbas explained that this means their prayers will not be answered, their souls will not enter Paradise, and moreover their record of good deeds will not be recorded in the place where the records of the righteous are kept. (*Ma'ariful Qur'an*) See 83:18-21.

[623] The term *jamal*, which is often translated as *camel*, was understood by many early commentators, including Razi (d. 1209) and Zamakhshari (d. 1144), by an alternative definition, which is *twisted rope*. Ibn 'Abbas (d. 687) also held that twisted rope is the appropriate meaning of the term *jamal* used here, and it was widely accepted among many companions of the Prophet, as pointed out by the Muslim scholar, Muhammad Asad (d. 1992), in his more recent commentary.

[624] The Prophet said, "There is a deep valley in Hell from which even Hellfire itself seeks refuge 400 times a day. This valley has been prepared for those of (my) community who pretend (to be righteous believers), who (pretend) to uphold the Book of Allah, and for those who spend in causes other than in the cause of Allah, and who make pilgrimage and engage in struggle (or *jihad*, for all the wrong reasons)." (*Ibn Majah*)

[625] The Prophet said, "No believer is required to humiliate himself." Someone asked what he meant, and the Prophet answered, "By taking on challenges that he can't handle." (*Ahmad*)

[626] After the Battle of Badr in the year 624, a battle in which the Muslims were victorious over the Meccans, the Prophet walked to the freshly dug graves of the pagan leaders who had fallen in battle and said, "Abu Jahl ibn Hisham! 'Utbah ibn Rabi'ah! Shaybah ibn Rabi'ah! Have you found your Lord's promise to be true? I certainly found my Lord's promise to be true!" 'Umar ibn al-Khattab (d. 644) asked the Prophet if the dead could hear, and the Prophet replied, "By the One Who holds my soul in His hand, you're not hearing my words better than they are, but they cannot respond." (*Muslim*) Islam teaches that the dead souls in the grave have a limited amount of awareness of the world around them and can hear the living for a short time. After the angels come to them and begin interrogating them, their awareness of the outside world ends, and they either dream peacefully or have nightmares until the Day of Judgment, depending on their state of belief when they died.

[627] On the Day of Judgment, after the judgments are over, a screen will be erected between the saved and the doomed so they can no longer see each other. There will be a high place called the Heights

recognize (both the people of Paradise and Hell) by their features.

(The people in the high places) will call out to the companions of the Garden, *"Peace be upon you,"* and even though they haven't entered into it yet, they'll feel confident of doing so. [46]

When they turn and gaze upon the companions of the Fire, they'll cry out, *"Our Lord! Don't send us among the wrongdoers!"* [47]

The companions of the Heights will recognize familiar men (down in Hellfire) by their features and will ask them, *"What has all your hoarding and arrogance done for you now?* [48] *Aren't those (people over there, heading into Paradise,) the same ones that you swore would never receive Allah's mercy? (On the contrary, they're the ones who are now being told), 'Enter the Garden – never more shall you fear nor shall you regret.'"* [49]

The companions of the Fire will call over to the companions of the Garden, saying, *"Pour down some water upon us or anything else with which Allah has provided you!"*

(The companions of the Garden) will answer, *"Allah has truly forbidden those things to those who rejected (Him)* [50] *- those who took their way of life as a joke and a game, and who were deceived by the life of the world."*

That day We're going to forget them, even as they forgot their meeting of this day of theirs. *Oh, how eagerly they snubbed Our (revealed) verses!* [51]

And so it was that We had sent a book to them filled with knowledge and explained in every detail, as a guide and mercy to people who believe. [52] So are they just going to wait for (its predictions) to be fulfilled?

On the day, when (its predictions) are fulfilled, those who ignored it before will cry, *"Our Lord's messengers really did come with the truth! Isn't there anyone now who can intercede for us? Can we be sent back (to earth for another chance), for then we would act differently than how we used to act?"*

They're going to lose their own souls, and all the lies they invented will leave them to languish. [53]

It is Allah's Right to Command

Truly, your Lord is Allah, the One Who created the heavens and the earth in six stages. [628] Then He established Himself upon the throne (of power). He draws the night like a veil over the day, and each chases the other swiftly.

He created the sun, the moon and the stars, and they're all governed (by laws) under His command. Isn't it His right to create and command? Blessed be Allah, the Lord of All the Worlds! [54]

---

which will contain those who believed in Allah, but whose good and evil deeds were too closely balanced to send them in one direction or the other. (The Prophet also said those who went to war in a *jihad* without their parent's permission, and who died as a result, will also be there.) Eventually, they will all get into Heaven, but they are made to wait to bring home to them how close they came to perdition. (*Ma'ariful Qur'an*)

[628] The Arabic word *yawm*, which usually means *day*, is also used for *stages, segments* or *time periods*. Muslim commentators such as Baydawi have never assumed that the use of the term *day* in the Qur'an, when referring to the creation of the world, meant a literal 24-hour day like ours, for such small segments of time did not exist at the moment of creation. The sixteenth-century scientist, Abu as-Su'ud, even proposed that the use of the term *yawm* in the Qur'an really should be understood in terms of creation 'events.' That the Qur'an understands that God's 'days' are different from earthly days is clearly shown in verses like 70:4 where one time period or day (the Day of Judgment) is compared to 50,000 of our years. Could Allah have created it all in one day, as 36:82 says Allah can create in an instant? Undoubtedly, but as the Prophet declared, "To labor patiently is from Allah; to be hasty is from Satan." (*Bayhaqi*) Allah creates what He wills according to His Own wisdom and timetable.

How You Should Call upon Your Lord

Call upon your Lord (in public) with heartfelt pleading, and (also call upon Him) when you're alone, (but in both cases do it in a dignified manner,) [629] for Allah has no love for those who are unruly (in their supplications). [630] [55]

Don't create disorder in the land after it's been made right. Call upon Him with fear and longing, for Allah's mercy is near to those who do good. [631] [56]

He's the One Who sends the winds like heralds of good news ahead of His mercy. When (the winds) have heaped together the moisture-laden clouds, We push them to barren lands and cause water to fall upon it. Then We use it to grow every kind of lush vegetation. Now that's also how We're going to raise you from the dead, so perhaps you might remember it. [57]

From good, clean earth, plants spring up in their Lord's presence. However, from polluted soil, nothing grows save for meager (weeds), and this is how We explain the verses in so many ways, so you can learn to be thankful. [58]

The People of Noah Reject Him

We sent Noah to his people, and he said, "*My people! Serve Allah! You have no other god than Him.* [632] *I fear for you the punishment of an awful day!*" [59] The leading men among his people answered him, saying, "*We see that you're clearly mistaken.*" [60]

"*My people!*" he replied. " *I'm not mistaken. Rather, I'm a messenger from the Lord of All the Worlds!* [61] *I'm only expressing the message of my Lord and advising you, for I know things from Allah that you don't.* [62] *Is it so strange for you that a message has come to you from your Lord, carried by a man from among your own people as a warning? (This is how it is) so you can be mindful (of Allah) and have His mercy (sent down upon you).*" [63]

Yet, they denied him, and so We saved him and those who were with him in the boat. We overwhelmed all those who rejected Our signs in the great flood. They were a people who were blind (to the truth)! [64]

---

[629] Some people, based upon customs from pre-Islamic times, used to shout and beseech to Allah in loud and noisy voices. This passage was revealed to counsel people to behave maturely when they call upon Allah. (*Asbab ul-Nuzul*)

[630] The Prophet said, "People! Be easy on yourselves! Truly you're not calling to One Who is deaf or absent, for the One you're calling on is the Hearing and the Near." (*Bukhari*)

[631] A man named 'Abdullah ibn Mughaffal once heard his son supplicating and asking Allah for a white castle on a hill in Paradise. The man told his son, "Ask Allah for Paradise and ask for His protection from the Fire, for I once heard the Messenger of Allah say, 'There will come some people who will transgress in supplication and cleansing.'" (*Ahmad*) Also see 39:3 and footnote.

[632] When and how did the flood of Noah occur, and did it engulf the entire world or merely the region in which Noah lived? These have been recurring questions that have some intriguing answers. Stories of the flood and how a blessed man survived it by floating his family on a boat have come down to us from ancient Mesopotamia. The unknown writers of the Jewish Torah also adopted this account and went a step further in claiming that the flood of Noah was an event that covered the entire world in water for more than seven months, killing everything on earth save for Noah's family and whatever animals he had gathered with him in his boat. (See Genesis 8:4-5.) Modern science disputes this claim, pointing out that there is no geological evidence for a world-wide flood that would have covered over the tallest mountains with sustained depth (besides the fact that there isn't enough water on the planet to do that). The Qur'an never states openly that the entire world was covered in water. Verse 25:37 and others specifically state that it was Noah's people who were destroyed in the flood, while all other verses that refer to the size and scope of the flood describe it as terrible, having waves like mountains, destroying Noah's people, etc., but never saying the *entire* world was submerged. So the Qur'an is ambiguous on this point (of whether the flood was global or more localized).

The People of 'Ad Reject their Prophet

$\mathcal{W}$e sent to the people of 'Ad their brother Hūd, and he said, "*My people!* [633] *Serve Allah! You have no other god than Him, so won't you be mindful?*" [65] The leaders of the faithless among his people answered him, saying, "*We see that you're naïve*," and, "*We think you're a liar.*" [66]

"*My people!*" he said. "*I'm not naïve; rather, I'm a messenger from the Lord of All the Worlds!* [67] *I'm only expressing the message of my Lord, and I'm a trustworthy advisor.* [68] *Is it so strange for you that a message has come to you from your Lord, carried by a man from among your own people as a warning? Recall that He made you inherit (this land) after the people of Noah and gave you a high reputation in the eyes of other nations. Recall (all the blessings) that you've received from Allah, so you can be truly successful.*" [69]

"*Have you come to us,*" they asked, "*to have us worship only one God and to give up what our ancestors worshipped? So bring down upon us (all those punishments from your God) with which you've been threatening us, if you're being so honest!*" [70]

"*You've had affliction and wrath from your Lord come upon you already,*" [634] *(*Hūd) replied, "*(because of your arrogant rejection of the truth). Are you going to argue with me about the names that you've made up (for your idols), both you and your ancestors, without any permission from Allah? So wait and see, for I'll be waiting with you.*" [71]

Then We saved him and those who were with him through (an act of) mercy from Our Own self, and We cut out the roots of those who denied Our signs and who didn't believe. [72]

The People of Thamud Reject their Prophet

$\mathcal{W}$e sent to the people of Thamud their brother Salih, and he said, "*My people!* [635] *Serve Allah! You have no other god than Him. Clear evidence has come to you from your Lord! This camel (that's been especially sanctified by Allah) is your sign, so leave her to graze on Allah's earth.* [636] *Do her no harm, or you'll be seized with terrible punishment.*" [73]

"*Remember that He let you inherit (the earth) after the people of 'Ad and gave you dwellings*

---

[633] The people of 'Ad were an ancient civilization that existed over four thousand years ago in present-day Oman and the surrounding area. Their ruined city of Iram was rediscovered by archeologists in 1992. The Qur'an described it as a city of tall towers. When the city was unearthed, it was found to have quite a few tall towers around its outer walls as giant watch towers. Although the Arabs knew nothing of the 'Ad and their lost city of Iram but faint legends, (it was known as Ubar to the Greeks and Sishur to other civilizations), archeologists excavating the ancient city of Elba in Syria came upon a hidden, four-thousand-year-old library in which the names of all the cities with which it conducted trade were listed. Iram was one of the names recorded.

[634] According to many commentators, apparently a famine or some other natural disaster had afflicted the region already, and the people were being warned to expect more if they didn't reform themselves.

[635] The Thamud were a tribal group that existed in an area known as Al-Hijr, today located in southern Jordan and Northern Arabia. They were known to the Babylonians, Assyrians and the Greeks, the latter of whom referred to them as the *Thamudaei*. The ruins of their towns and cities were scattered all throughout the area, and the Arabs were well aware of their existence. Although the area was not well-suited for a large population, income from trade allowed their civilization to thrive from about 2400 BCE to around the fifth century of the common era when their power failed. In their later years, their descendants became known as the Nabateans. The Thamud were also mentioned in the annals of Sargon the Great (d. 2279 BCE).

[636] Some commentators say that the people of Thamud asked their messenger Salih to turn a big boulder into a pregnant camel, and by that miracle they would believe in him. When Salih allegedly did so, this camel was their sign, and they had to allow it to drink freely from the wells. It was a test for them, for the leaders of the tribe monopolized the wells and charged people high fees to get water for themselves and their animals. Needless to say, the elite members of the tribe did not accept the message of their prophet. (*Ibn Kathir*)

within the earth out of which you build palaces and fortresses for yourselves, both in the plains and in the mountains, where you carve them (from the mountainsides). [637] *Remember (all the blessings) that you've received from Allah, and cause no harm or chaos in the earth."* [74]

The leaders of the arrogant faction among his people said to the ones whom they thought were weak and powerless, and who had come to believe (in the teachings of Salih), *"Are you really certain that Salih is a genuine messenger from his Lord?"* Then they answered them, saying, *"Indeed, we do believe in what was sent to him."* [75]

The arrogant ones then said, *"Well, we reject what you believe in!"* [76] Then they (cut the legs of the camel,) crippling her, and brazenly defied the order of their Lord. They (boasted about it) and said, *"Salih! Bring on your threats, if you're really a messenger (of Allah)!"* [77]

Then the mighty quake took them by surprise, and by morning they were left cowering in their homes. [78] Salih (saw the damage and then) left them, saying, *"My people! I conveyed to you the message that was sent to me from my Lord. I gave you good advice, but you had no love for advisors."* [638] [79]

The People of Lot Reject Him

$\mathcal{L}$ot said to his people, [639] *"Are you engaging in a shameful and perverted act),* [640] *a practice unlike anything (any other nation) ever did in the entire world?* [80] *You're using other men instead of women for your passions? No way! You're a people who've gone out of control!"* [81]

His people offered no other response than to say, *"Drive them out of your city, these people who want to be so moral and pure!"* [82]

Then We saved him and his family, except for his wife, for she was one of those who remained behind. [641] [83]

Thereafter, We rained down upon (the city) a shower (of blasted stone), and you can see how those wicked people were ended! [84]

---

[637] Although the core region of 'Ad civilization was in southern Arabia and the core region of the Thamud civilization was in central and northern Arabia, the Thamud, who arose centuries after the 'Ad, did push into lands formerly held by the 'Ad before their cultural group collapsed. Inscriptions in the Thamudic style of writing have been found in ruins all over southern Arabia and as far north as Jordan.

[638] When the Prophet was leading an expedition towards Syria at the request of some allied tribes who were being harassed by the Byzantine Romans, the Muslims stopped to camp near the ancient territory of the Thamud people, at the place called Al-Hijr (the Stony Ground). Some people found a well and began filling their pots with water and making dough for bread. When the Prophet noticed what they were doing, he ordered them to spill the water from their pots and give the dough to their camels. He then led the group away to another area. They found another well, and he allowed the people to use that one. When he was asked about the area from which he took them away, he forbade the companions from entering a place where previous peoples had been destroyed, and then he said, "I'm afraid that what happened to them may happen to you, so don't enter (those places)." (*Ahmad*) He also said that no one should pass through such areas unless they were weeping.

[639] Lot was Abraham's nephew, and he had followed his uncle out of Mesopotamia many years before. While Abraham continued a bedouin kind of lifestyle, Lot took his family and servants to the ancient city of Sodom. While he was there, he tried to spread Allah's word among the people of that city, but they were given over to worldly pleasures.

[640] The word used here to describe the sinful acts of the people of that place is *faahishah*, which means unlawful sexual activity. Thus, homosexuality is included in the definition of this word. This is an important distinction when differentiating between the penalties for adultery/fornication and sodomy for they are not the same. See 4:16 and 24:2. In former times, the name *sodomy* was synonymous with homosexuality.

[641] The Qur'an does not make any mention of Lot's wife escaping with her family and looking back only to be turned into a pillar of salt. The Qur'an only affirms that she remained behind in the city and was destroyed.

The People of Madyan Reject their Prophet

*T*o (the people of) Madyan We sent their brother Shu'ayb, [642] who said, *"My people! Serve Allah! You have no other god than Him. Clear evidence has come to you from your Lord! So measure and balance honestly (in your trading activities), and don't withhold from people what they're owed. Don't cause disorder in the world after it's been made right. That will be to your good if you really have any faith."* [85]

"Don't stake out every road and intimidate the people who believe in Him away from the path of Allah, trying to imply that there's something wrong with it. Remember how you were so few in number and then He multiplied you, so keep in mind how the disobedient are ultimately (vanquished). [86] If there's a section among you who believes in that with which I've been sent and a section that doesn't believe, then just be patient until Allah decides the matter between us, for He's the best One to judge." [87]

The leaders of the arrogant faction among his people said, *"Shu'ayb! We're going to drive you out of our settlement, both you and those who believe with you, unless all of you return to our traditions."*

(Shu'ayb) answered them, saying, *"What! Even though we would hate it! [88] We would be lying against Allah if we returned to your traditions, especially since Allah has saved us from them. There's no way we would ever return to them unless our Lord Allah allowed (or planned) for it. Our Lord comprehends everything in His knowledge, and we trust in Allah. Our Lord! Decide between us and our people in all truth, for You're the best of all who open (matters for decision)."* [89]

The faithless leaders among his people said, *"If any of you follow Shu'ayb, then you'll all be losers!"* [90] And then the earthquake took them without warning, and they lay cowering in their homes by morning. [91]

Those who denied Shu'ayb were reduced (in power), as much as if they never even had a vibrant civilization! It was those who denied Shu'ayb who were the losers! [92] Shu'ayb (saw the devastation and then) left them, saying, *"My people! I conveyed to you the message that was sent to me from my Lord, and I gave you good advice. So how can I mourn over a people who refused to believe?"* [93]

Arrogant Nations Always Respond the Same Way

*W*e never sent any prophet to any settlement without plunging its people into hardship and extreme adversity so they could learn to be humble. [94] Then We would transform their hardship into prosperity until they advanced and multiplied, so much so that they (inevitably) began to say, *"Our ancestors were also affected by cycles of hardship and prosperity."* Then We would suddenly seize them when they least expected it! [643] [95]

If the people of those settlements had only believed and been mindful (of Allah in good times and bad), then We would've opened for them blessings from both the sky and the earth. [644] However, they denied (Allah), so We took hold of them on account of what they earned. [96]

Did the people of those settlements feel so safe from Our wrath, even though it might have come (upon them) in the night

---

[642] Shu'ayb was a prophet sent to the people of Madyan, (*aka* the People of the Thicket), a land in northern Arabia near the city of Tabuk. The original land of Madyan is an old land stretching in an arc across northern Arabia towards the Sinai, and it has been settled with various peoples who have come and gone.

[643] The Prophet said, "A believer will continue to be tested with afflictions until he ends up purified from sins, whereas the example of a hypocrite is that of a donkey that doesn't know why its owners tied it up or released it." (*Ahmad*)

[644] These blessings include rain and good weather, as well as fertile soil and abundant crops.

while they slept? 645 [97] Did they feel so safe against its coming in broad daylight while they frolicked about? [98] Did they feel so safe against Allah's plan? No one can feel safe against Allah's plan except people who lose! [99]

Isn't it clear enough to those who eventually inherit the land (after previous nations collapsed) that if We wanted, We could punish them for their sins and seal up their hearts so they can no longer hear, as well? [100]

Those were the settlements whose stories We're telling you. Messengers went to them with clear evidence (of Allah's truth), but they were not the ones who would believe in what they had already rejected before.

That's how Allah seals up the hearts of those who (willfully) suppress (their obligation to believe in Him). [101] We didn't find most of them (living up) to their promise, and We found most of them rebellious and disobedient. 646 [102]

The Meeting of Moses and Pharaoh

*T*hen after (their time) We sent Moses with Our signs to Pharaoh and his nobles, but they treated them wrongfully.

647 Just see how the disobedient scoundrels were defeated! [103]

Moses said, *"Pharaoh! I'm a messenger from the Lord of All the Worlds,* [104] *and I'm bound to say only what's truthful about Allah. Now I've come to you with clear evidence from your Lord, so let the Children of Israel depart with me."* [105]

"If you've really come with a (miraculous) sign," (Pharaoh) replied, *"then show it (to me), if you're really being so honest!"* [106]

Then Moses threw his staff (down on the floor), and suddenly it became a serpent in plain sight! [107] Next, he drew his hand sharply (from his side), and suddenly it was glowing white for all who saw it! [108]

Moses and the Sorcerers

*"T*his is some kind of skilled sorcerer,"* Pharaoh's nobles began saying (to each other), [109] *"but he just wants to drive you from your land. So now what do you advise?"* [110]

The (other nobles) said, *"Keep him and his brother occupied and waiting. Meanwhile, send word to all the cities to gather* [111] *the most skilled sorcerers (we have) back here to you."* [112]

---

645 The Prophet said, "A sudden death is a mercy for a believer, but it's a grievous punishment for the disbeliever." (*Ahmad*)

646 This refers to the promise made by our spiritual, primordial matter before we were even created. See 33:72-73.

647 It has long been assumed that there were two different pharaohs in the story of Moses, one during Moses' youth and another whom he confronts many years later as a prophet. The pharaoh who ruled Egypt when Moses was a youth was long thought to be Ramses II (d. cir. 1235 BCE), though recent scholarship has suggested that it was an earlier ruler, Khenephres *aka* Sobekhotep IV (d. cir, 1470 BCE), rather than Ramses II. Given the number of years that passes between Moses' youth and his later return, a two-pharaoh theory is much more likely. After Moses escaped Egypt and spent some years in Midian (Madyan), the older pharaoh died and was succeeded by his son. The son of Khenephres was a pharaoh named Dudimose (d. cir. 1445 BCE). Under the rule of Dudimose, Egypt sank into ruin. An ancient Egyptian scribe named Mentho describes the disastrous results of Dudimos' reign this way: "In his reign, for what cause I know not, a chastisement from Allah smote us, and unexpectedly from the regions of the East, invaders of obscure race marched in confidence of victory against our land (Egypt). By determined force they easily seized it without striking a blow, and having overpowered the rulers of the land, they then burned our cities ruthlessly, razed to the ground the temples of the gods and treated all our natives with cruel hostility, massacring some and leading into slavery the wives and children of others." The invaders who easily took over a weakened Egypt upon the death of Dudimose were the Amalakites of the Middle East.

231

When Pharaoh's sorcerers arrived, they first said (to their master), *"Of course, we'll be amply rewarded if we win?"* [113]

(Pharaoh) replied, *"Yes, (you'll be rewarded), for you'll be brought near (to my circle of power)."* [114]

(Then Pharaoh's sorcerers confronted Moses,) saying, *"Moses, will you cast first, or should we go first?"* 648 [115]

"You cast first," Moses answered, and when they threw (their ropes and sticks to the floor and chanted their spells,) they bewitched the eyes of the people and terrified them, for they employed powerful magic. [116]

Then We inspired Moses, saying, *"Now throw down your staff,"* and just like that - it swallowed up all the lies they faked! [117] That's how the truth was proven and their actions were shown to be false. [118]

What did the Sorcerers Say?

$\mathcal{A}$nd in this way (the sorcerers of Pharaoh) were defeated - and right there (in public)! They were made to look so feeble! [119]

Then, the sorcerers fell flat on the floor and prostrated, [120] saying, *"We believe in the Lord of All the Worlds,* [121] *the Lord of Moses and Aaron!"* [122]

Pharaoh (eyed them angrily) and said, *"Are you accepting Him without my permission? This is all just a hoax that you devised back in the city to drive out (its ruling class)! You're going to know straightaway (who's really in charge)!* [123] *To be sure, I'm going to cut off your hands and your feet from opposite sides and stake you all on wooden posts (until you die)!"* [124]

"As for us," (the sorcerers) replied, *"we'll be sent back to our Lord.* [125] *You're just taking your revenge out on us because we believed in the signs of our Lord when they came to us. Our Lord!"* (they then implored,) *"Pour patience down upon us, and take our souls back to You as ones who have submitted!"* [126]

Pharaoh's nobles, (looking on in shock,) said (to him), *"Are you going to just leave Moses and his people alone to cause unrest in the land, while they leave you and forsake your gods?"*

(Pharaoh became enraged) and said, *"We'll kill their male children and leave their females alive, for we have total power over them!"* 649 [127]

(After Moses left and returned to his people,) he said to them, *"Pray to Allah for help and wait patiently, for the earth belongs to Allah, and He gives it as an inheritance to whichever of His servants that He wills. The final result will be for those who were mindful (of Him)."* [128]

(As they suffered under the yoke of Pharaoh, however, his people began to complain,) saying, *"We've had nothing but trouble both before and after you came to us."*

(Moses chided them,) saying, *"Your Lord will destroy your enemy and make you the inheritors of the earth in order to test you in your actions."* [129]

---

648 According to a report in Qurtubi, Moses had a short exchange of words with the chief of the sorcerers before the match began in which the sorcerer told Moses and Aaron that there was no way they could win. He even boasted that if his side lost, he would declare his conversion to the beliefs of Moses right in front of Pharaoh.

649 The previous pharaoh of Egypt (Kenephres?) had ordered the male infants born to the Hebrews to be killed. That was the reason that Moses wound up in a basket on the Nile and was taken into the pharaoh's household. Now this new pharaoh (Dudimose?) would repeat the same cruel order, seeking to wipe out all Hebrew men and leaving the more easily controlled females as dependent slaves of the state. The order would have no expiration date, as the previous one did, and thus the Hebrews would disappear as a race. The order was never put in force because of the appearance of strange signs in nature, which gave the pharaoh and his nobles pause for reflection, and these are four of the nine plagues that followed.

How did the Egyptians Respond to the Plagues?

*A*nd so it was that We took hold of Pharaoh and his people (and punished them) with years (of drought) and poor harvests so they could perhaps be reminded. [650] [130]

Whenever things got better, however, they said, "*This is due to our own (diligent) efforts,*" though when stricken with hardship they said it was because of the evil omens of Moses and those who were with him. Their 'evil omens' were nothing more than their (own inventions), as far as Allah's view (was concerned,) but most of them didn't understand. [131]

They said, "*It doesn't matter what miracles you bring out in order to work your magic on us, (Moses,) for we're never going to believe in you!*" [132]

So We sent upon them a disastrous (flood), [651] locusts, lice, frogs and a red-stain: signs that were self-explanatory, but they were arrogant, and they were a wicked people. [652] [133]

Every time a disaster would befall them, they would cry, "*Moses! Call upon your Lord for us, invoking His promise to you. If you relieve us of this torment, then we'll truly believe in you and send the Children of Israel away with you.*" [134]

And yet, every time We relieved them of the torment, after it's due course was completed, they broke their word! [135] So We got them back by drowning them in the sea, for they had (willfully) denied Our signs and were unconcerned about them. [136]

We made a people who were thought of as weak inherit lands in both the two Easts and the two Wests, and they were the lands that We had blessed. [653] The fine

---

[650] This verse suggests that it might have taken years for Moses to convince the Pharaoh to release the Hebrews to him, rather than the much shorter period the Biblical narrative offers.

[651] This perhaps included floods, storms or epidemics of disease in which many people lost their lives.

[652] The Qur'an mentions a total of nine separate *signs* that the Egyptians received (see 17:101). They are 1) the staff that turned into a snake [7:107]; 2) the glowing hand [7:108]; 3) the years of drought [7:130]; 4) the poor harvests [7:130]; and then the five mentioned in this verse which are: 5) *tufan*, or a natural disaster, most probably a flood or perhaps dust storms; 6) swarms of locusts (to humiliate Min, the Egyptian god of crops); 7) an epidemic of lice and sores (to humiliate the Egyptian god of healing Thoth); 8) an inundation by frogs leaving the swamps and invading peoples' homes (as a way to humiliate the Egyptian concept of the god of frogs, of Heqt); and 9) *dama*, or a tainted bloody-colored thing (perhaps the water or some period of civil strife leading to bloodshed). The Arabic word *dama* can mean either blood or a smeared, tainted red color. If we assume from the narrative contained in the book of Exodus, chapter 7 that the Nile river ran red for some days, (as a way to humiliate the Egyptian belief in the god of the Nile, Hapi,) we have to question whether or not the details of the Hebrew Bible must be accepted at face value, where we read that the Nile turned into *actual* blood for seven days (Exodus 7:15-25) and everything in the river died. Given that this is the only real mention of this particular plague in the whole of the Qur'an and since it is not mentioned _what_ was turned bloody-colored or if it was actual blood in the water (or bloodletting from fighting or strife) or merely a stained red color to the Nile, which is one of *dama's* meanings, we can speculate about extreme sediments from Upper Egypt that flowed downriver by the command of Allah and colored the Nile River red to impress upon Pharaoh that Allah's power is potent, or we can speak of the phenomenon of "red tides," which are a common enough occurrence for the body of water next to Egypt to be called the "Red" Sea. (In the ancient Egyptian legend of their god Ra, the deity used red clay from upper Egypt mixed with beer to trick his daughter into thinking that the water was blood!) By the way, in the Qur'an there is no mention of every first-born Egyptian being killed by the Angel of Death as there is written in the Bible in Exodus 12:12.

[653] The kingdom of Israel, especially at its height, exerted its power and influence on lands to its northeast, southeast, northwest and southwest. As for the 'two easts,' the various non-Jewish tribes were subdued in an ever-expanding zone of influence, and as for the 'two wests,' ancient Israel encompassed part of the Sinai peninsula, and also Solomon married a daughter of the Egyptian pharaoh

saying of your Lord was fulfilled for the Children of Israel, because they had been patient. We (eventually) brought down to ruin all the great works and structures that Pharaoh and his people built. [137]

The Children of Israel Begin to Waver

𝒲e led the Children of Israel across the sea, and soon they came upon a people who were devoted to some idols they had with them. (The Israelites) said, *"Moses! Make a god for us like the gods they have."* (Moses) answered, *"You're an ignorant people!"* [138]

"As for these (people you've encountered), their (superstitions) are doomed to extinction, and what they're doing is foolish." [139] Then he said, *"Should I look for a god other than Allah, when Allah is the One Who's given you more favors than any other people in all the universe?"* [140]

So remember, (all you Children of Israel), that We saved you from Pharaoh's people, the ones who afflicted you with the worst punishments and who killed your male children while letting your females live. That was an enormous test from your Lord. [141]

Moses Receives the Tablets

𝒲e ordained that Moses (should spend) thirty nights plus ten more (upon

Mount Tūr), and so the full term of forty nights was completed with his Lord.

Moses left his brother Aaron in charge (of the encampment) and had said to him, *"Be my representative with my people. Do what's morally right, and don't follow the way of the morally depraved."* [142]

When Moses arrived at the place that We decided for him, his Lord addressed him. Moses replied by saying, *"My Lord! Show Yourself to me, so that I may look upon You."*

(Allah) replied, *"No, you cannot see Me, but look upon the side of that peak (over there). If it remains in place, then you will have seen Me."* 654

When his Lord materialized His glory upon the mountainside, it crumbled into dust, and Moses fell down and fainted. 655

When he came back to his senses, he said, *"All glory be to You! I turn to You in repentance, and I'm the first to believe!"* [143]

"Moses!" (Allah) said. *"I've chosen you above other people with the message (I've sent to you) and the words (I've spoken to you). Take (the revelation) that I'm giving you, and be thankful."* [144]

We recorded for him on the Tablets everything having to do with instructions,

---

of his day and held influence there on account of it. Israel also extended its influence to Lebanon and up into the lower reaches of Anatolia (thus influencing the northwest of Israel).

[654] The Prophet explained this verse by saying that less than the equivalent of a fingertip of Allah's power was made manifest on that mountain slope, and still it shook and crumbled. (*Tirmidhi, Ahmad*) This story is contained in Exodus 33:17-23, though it mentions (strangely) that Moses saw God's "back parts."

[655] A Jew went to the Prophet and complained, saying, "Muhammad! One of your Helpers just smacked me in the face!" The Prophet ordered the man to be summoned, and he asked him why he did that. The man answered, "Messenger of Allah, I passed by that Jewish man and heard him swearing, 'No way, by the One Who chose Moses over all humanity!' I asked him, 'Over Muhammad, too?' and then I got angry and smacked his face." The Prophet said, "Don't prefer me above the other prophets. On the Day of Resurrection, people will be struck unconscious, and I will be the first to wake up. When I look around I'll see that Moses is holding onto a pillar of the throne (of Allah). I won't know if he woke up before me or if he received (that honor) on account of his being struck unconscious on Mount Tur." (*Bukhari*)

along with their explanations. [656] *"Take hold of these (laws) firmly, and order your people to take hold of the best within them, for soon will I show you the (ruined) dwellings of the rebellious (nations that came before you, so you can learn from their examples).* [657] [145]

"And I shall steer away from My signs those who act arrogantly in the earth against all right. Even if they see the signs, they're not going to believe in them, and even if they see the path of common sense, they're not going to adopt the way. Rather, if they see any way to go astray, that's the path they'll choose. That's because they denied Our signs (when they first heard of them) and were unconcerned about them." [146]

"Those who deny Our (revealed) verses and the meeting of the next life – their life's work is for nothing. How can they expect to be rewarded by anything other than what they've done?" [147]

The Children of Israel and the Golden Calf

The people of Moses took a golden calf (for an idol). (They made) it with their own jewelry after he had left them. (The statue even) seemed as if it were making a sound, but didn't they see that it couldn't speak to them nor guide them on a path?

They took it (as an object of worship), and they were in the wrong. [148] When they later regretted what they had done and saw that they had made a mistake, they said, *"If our Lord doesn't have mercy on us and doesn't forgive us, then we'll truly be lost."* [149]

When Moses returned to his people, he was angry and upset. *"You've done evil in my stead while I was gone!"* (he cried.) *"Are you so eager to bring Allah's command down upon you so quickly!"*

Then he put down the Tablets, grabbed his brother by his head and dragged him down.

(Aaron) cried out, *"Son of my mother! The people thought nothing of me, and they almost killed me! Don't make (our) enemies celebrate over my predicament, and don't include me among the corrupt!"* [150]

(Then Moses) prayed, *"My Lord! Forgive me and my brother! Admit us to Your mercy, for You're the most merciful of the merciful."* [151]

Those who took the calf (as an idol) will be engulfed with wrath from their Lord and also with humiliation in this life. That's how We repay those who craft (nothing but lies). [152]

However, those who do wrong, but then repent of it and believe, (should know) that your Lord is forgiving and merciful. [153]

When Moses' anger subsided, he picked up the Tablets, for there was guidance and mercy inscribed upon them for those who revere their Lord. [658] [154]

---

[656] These Tablets would form the basis of the Torah, which would grow in size as the years passed. (The revelation would eventually be written on leather scrolls and other materials.) According to Exodus 24:12, the Ten Commandments were written on these small stone Tablets.

[657] The Hebrews had been in Egypt for several generations when Moses led them out. They were going to pass through many regions of the Middle East and see many ruins. They were supposed to take lessons from those sights. Indeed, the Qur'an encourages the preservation of ancient ruins as a source of lessons. Even though some misguided extremists destroyed the ancient Buddhist ruins in Afghanistan in the Bamiyan valley in 2001, precious few other Muslim rulers, either classical or modern, have ever made war upon the huge monuments of the past. Muhammad, also, never ordered old ruins to be destroyed. The Prophet once warned Muslims in general, repeating himself three times, "Extremism destroyed those who came before you. Those who are rigid shall perish." (*Al-'Etisam of Imam al-Shatibi*) See verses such as 6:11, 22:46, 27:69, 35:44 and many others that encourage the preservation of the ruins of past civilizations in order to learn lessons.

[658] The Prophet said, "Being told something is not the same as seeing it for oneself. Allah told Moses that his people were doing this and that; yet, he had no reaction. It was only when he saw what they

Then Moses chose seventy of his people (to come) to Our meeting place (to beg for forgiveness.) [659] When they were caught up in a violent earth tremor (on the mountain), Moses cried out, "*My Lord! If You had wanted, You could've destroyed both them and me long before! Would You destroy all of us for the actions of the foolish among us? This (whole affair) is no more than a test from You.*"

"*You use (Your tests as a means) to send astray whomever You want and guide whomever You want! You are our protector, so forgive us and be merciful to us, for You're the best of all forgivers!* [155] *Stipulate for us what's best in this life, as well as in the next life, for we've turned to You (for guidance).*"

Then (Allah) replied, "*I bring My punishment to bear upon whomever I want, but My mercy extends over all things. I prescribe it for those who are mindful (of Me), who give in charity and who believe in Our signs.*" [156]

To Whom will Allah Show Mercy?

(Who are the ones to whom My mercy will extend? It is for) those (Jews and Christians) who follow the Messenger,

the unschooled prophet, [660] whom they will find mentioned in their own (scriptures) - in the Torah and the Gospel – for he'll command them to do what's recognized (as right) and forbid them from doing what's unfamiliar (to Allah's good way of life).

(The Messenger of Allah) will allow them (to partake of) what is pure and forbid them from what is unclean. He will release them from the heavy burdens (of their religious law) and from the shackles (of burdensome religious injunctions) that were upon their (necks). [661]

So it shall be that those who believe in (the Messenger of Allah), hold him in the highest regard, help him and follow the light that will be sent down with him, they are the ones who will be successful. [662] [157]

(Muhammad, now) say (to them), "*O people! I'm the Messenger of Allah who's been sent to you all. He's the One to Whom the control of the heavens and the earth belongs. There is no god besides Him. He brings life, and He brings death, so believe in Allah and in His Messenger, the unschooled prophet, who himself believes in Allah*

---

were doing that he put the Tablets down." (*Ahmad, Tabarani*) The Qur'an does not hold that Moses broke the tablets, as the Old Testament asserts.

[659] The seventy men were ordered to fast, pray and beg for forgiveness for their people. When Moses then led them upon the mountain to seek Allah's renewed favor, a dark cloud covered the mountain, and Moses ordered them to remain in one spot and wait for him. The people heard Allah speaking to Moses but couldn't see anything through the haze. When Moses returned to them, they said to him that they wouldn't believe he was really talking to Allah unless they saw Him face to face. That's when they were struck dumb with a loud thunderclap. The seventy men died from it, and that's why Moses prayed, "My Lord! If You had wanted, You could have destroyed both them and me long before! Would You destroy all of us for the actions of the foolish among us?" (*Ibn Is-haq*)

[660] This refers to Prophet Muhammad, who never learned to read and write.

[661] Mosaic Law, as the body of laws that Judaism teaches is called, is loaded with many burdensome restrictions, minute details and oddities that make it an arduous path to follow for those who try to follow it faithfully. Islam releases the Jews from nearly all of these restrictive laws that were imposed upon their ancestors.

[662] The Prophet's companions used to respect him with the highest reverence, especially in the last years of his life when the miracle of Islam was apparent for all to see. They used to lower their eyes in his presence and speak softly to him. Once a Meccan spy named 'Urwah ibn Mas'ud infiltrated Medina to gather intelligence for his masters, and when he returned to Mecca, he had this to say about how the Prophet's men loved him. "I've observed the courts of great kings like the Roman and Persian emperors, and I once met the Negus, king (of Abyssinia), but the respect and reverence I saw in the hearts of the Muslims towards their prophet was unique, unlike any place else in the world. I don't think you'll ever succeed against them." (*Ma'ariful Qur'an*)

and in His words. *Follow Him so you can be guided.*" [663] [158]

The Disobedient Eventually Lose

$\mathcal{A}$mong the people of Moses there is a community who guides truthfully and does justice. [664] [159] (In the past), We had divided (the Children of Israel) into twelve tribes.

When his people asked him for water, We inspired (Moses), saying, "*Tap the rock with your staff.*" Twelve springs gushed out of it, and every group knew its own place to drink.

We shaded them with clouds and sent down manna and quails, saying, "*Eat of the good things that We've provided for you.*" They never did Us any harm (when they disobeyed); rather, they only harmed themselves. [160]

Recall how they were told, "*Reside within this town and eat whatever you want, but speak of humbleness when you enter its gates and walk in humility, for then We'll forgive you your sins and increase (the fortunes) of those who are good.*" [161]

Then unscrupulous people among them altered the order they had received (and they behaved poorly towards the inhabitants of the town). Therefore, We sent upon them a plague from the sky, for they persisted in doing wrong. [665] [162]

Who were the Sabbath-Breakers?

$\mathcal{Q}$uestion them about (the fate of the people of) the seaside town. [666] They broke (the sanctity) of the Sabbath, for whenever it was their Sabbath day, the fish (of the sea) would come to them clearly ready to be caught. However, on days other than the Sabbath, they were nowhere to be found! This is how We tested them, for they were prone to disobedience. [163]

Then a group of (the disobedient people who ignored the issue) protested (to the preachers among them), saying, "*Why are you preaching to (them), when Allah will*

---

[663] Apparently, Abu Bakr and 'Umar had some sort of a disagreement, and 'Umar stormed off to his home in anger. Abu Bakr trailed after him, trying to calm 'Umar down, but when 'Umar entered his house, he closed the door angrily and locked it. Abu Bakr went to the Prophet to apprise him of the situation, and when 'Umar calmed down, he too, went to the Prophet to tell him what had happened. The Prophet looked upset by 'Umar's loss of temper before, and when Abu Bakr noticed that 'Umar was about to be scolded, Abu Bakr stepped forward and nobly took the blame for the incident. The Prophet thereupon exclaimed, "Can't you people leave (this) one of my companions alone and leave him free of your bothering? Don't you people recall that when I had first declared by Allah's will, "*O you people! I'm the Messenger of Allah who's been sent to you all,*" that you all had called me a liar? Only Abu Bakr affirmed my truth as a prophet!" (*Bukhari*) Thus, the Prophet used a reference to this verse to extol the virtue of Abu Bakr.

[664] The Qur'an specifically states that there is a section of the Jewish people who are sincere and faithful to the truth of Allah. This is important to remember when other verses are read that take backsliders and hypocrites to task among them. Also see 2:113.

[665] A plague from the sky can mean a plague that was carried through the air, like some infectious diseases are. The plague they suffered from and the city in which they behaved badly is mentioned in the book of Numbers 25:1-9.

[666] It is said that on the Sabbath day the fish would come close to the shore and nearly bob their heads out of the water, daring the Jews to catch them. The men gave in to these temptations. They tried to circumvent the injunction by laying their fishing nets and traps out in the water on Fridays, but then waiting until Sunday to harvest them. They willfully disobeyed the laws of Moses that had come down to them. (Tabari) (All work, including fishing, is forbidden on Saturdays under Mosaic Law.) The villagers who did not participate divided into two groups, with some preaching against the deceit, while the rest chose to ignore it. The ones who were overlooking the sin asked the question in verse 164. The name of the town mentioned in this verse is said to have been Aylah, and it was supposed to have been situated on the Red Sea.

eventually destroy them anyway or bring a terrible punishment down upon (them for their disobedience)?"

The (preachers) replied, *"We're doing our duty to your Lord, for you just might become mindful (of Him) yet."* [164]

When they forgot the reminders that had been given to them, We saved those who had spoken out against evil and severely punished the corrupt for their disobedience. [165] When they boldly went beyond what they were allowed, We said to them, *"Be like rejected apes!"* [667] [166]

Allah's Punishment Came upon Them

*Y*our Lord declared that He would send (other nations) against (the Children of Israel,) who would afflict them with humiliating tyranny, even until the Day of Assembly, for your Lord is swift in bringing conclusions; yet, He's also forgiving and merciful. [668] [167]

And so We scattered them throughout the world in a Diaspora. [669] Among them are some who are righteous and also others who are far less (virtuous) than that. We've tested them both in prosperity and hardship so they might return (to the path of Allah). [168]

Later generations came after them, and the scriptures became their responsibility, but they chose the worldly possessions of this life, justifying their choice by saying, *"We're going to be forgiven anyway."* [670]

If similar material possessions ever came their way, they would take hold of them yet again.

Wasn't the scriptural covenant taken from them, (in which they agreed) that they wouldn't say anything about Allah but the truth? Yet, they're the ones who are studying what's in (the scripture and then misapplying it)!

The realm of the next life is better for those who are mindful (of Allah), so won't you understand? [169] Those who hold firmly to the scripture and who establish prayer – We'll never let the reward of the righteous be lost! [170]

When We brought the towering heights of the mountain above them - like it was a raised canopy, so much so that they thought it might fall over on top of them, (We said), *"Hold firmly to what We've given you, and remember what it says so you can be mindful (of your duty to Allah)."* [671] [171]

---

[667] See 2:65 and accompanying footnote.

[668] Given their disobedience to Moses, and given the disobedience of succeeding generations even though they had so many prophets raised among them, the Children of Israel were cursed with having enemies continually besetting them with persecution and calamity. (The Old Testament books of Lamentations and Amos particularly record the suffering of later generations.) God warned them in Deuteronomy 11:28, I Kings 9:6-7 and elsewhere not to disobey Him or else, and they earned His wrath. The end of this verse, however, reminds Jews that God is forgiving and merciful. Thus, all they must do to get this sentence removed is to return to fellowship with God and repent of their disobedience. Then they can take their rightful place in the vanguard of righteousness to be a light among the peoples of the world showing the way back to God's good favor. Also see 7:159.

[669] The tragic Jewish Diaspora, which was accomplished in two phases, first by the Babylonians and later by the Romans, caused Jewish populations to be scattered over the known world. Some of those communities held on to God's religion, while others either assimilated completely or transformed their religion into an irrelevant cultural fixture, and thus they took to sinfulness.

[670] The Old Testament seems to suggest that God will forgive all Jews in the end. (See Jeremiah 50:20.) Of course, the Qur'an disputes the assertion that a whole people will be forgiven wholesale. See 2:78-82.

[671] This verse (along with 2:63, which mentions the same incident) has been interpreted in various ways. Some commentators say that it means that God caused the mountain to grow in size when the Children of Israel arrived. Others say God caused it to shake, as in an earthquake, thus giving them fear. Indeed, the Arabic terms used here can mean either to raise something or to shake. It seems to

Humans are Duty Bound to Accept Faith in Allah

*W*hen your Lord brings offspring from out of the loins of the children of Adam, He makes them (first) bear witness about themselves by asking them, "*Am I not your Lord?*"

They say, "*Of course, and we are a witness to that!*"

(We do that) so you won't be able to say on the Day of Assembly, "*We had no clue about any of this,*" 672 [172] and also so you won't be able to say, "*Our ancestors took other gods besides Allah in the past, but we're only their descendants, (and it's not our fault that we've followed them without knowing any better). Are You then going to destroy us for the inventions of people who were dishonest?*" [173] That's how We explain the verses in detail so they might return (to Allah's path). [174]

About the People who Deny Allah

*R*ecite for them the story of the man to whom We sent Our (revealed) verses, but then he slipped right by them (without even a care), enabling Satan to follow him.

Thus, he went far off the (moral) way. 673 [175]

If We had wanted, We could've elevated him with the (revelations), but he (stubbornly) clung to the earth and followed his own fickle whims.

His example is that of a dog. If you make a move against him, he just rolls out his tongue, and if you leave him alone, he still just rolls out his tongue!

That's the example of those people who deny Our (revealed) verses, so repeat this story so they might be mindful (of its message). [176] Despicable is the caricature of those who deny Our signs and who do harm to their own souls! [177]

Whoever is guided by Allah, he's truly guided. Whomever He leaves astray, they're in a state of loss! [178] And so it is that We've made many jinns and human beings for Hellfire. They have hearts, but they don't understand with them.

They have eyes, but they don't see with them. They have ears, but they don't hear with them.

They're like cattle – *No! They're even more mistaken than that!* They're completely unconcerned (about Allah's warnings)! [179]

---

me that a synthesis of the two ideas can be found if we assume that the Children of Israel came right to the base of the mountain and saw it looming up high above them like a canopy, and then God caused it to rumble and shake to let them know His power was real and that they should prepare themselves to be obedient.

672 This is a very deep passage, and it has been interpreted several ways. Most commentators say that it means that the imprint of Allah is upon us collectively as human beings even before birth, causing us to seek Him after our birth when we reach the age of reason. Indeed, the Prophet once said, "Every child is born directed towards its true disposition (to worship Allah), and its parents make it a Jew, Christian or Zoroastrian." (Then the Prophet recited verse 30:30 for emphasis.) (*Bukhari*)

673 While a minority of commentators hold that this verse should be understood as a general reference to any person who disregards Allah's revelations, most of the commentators assert that the man referred to here was named Bal'aam the son of Bo'er. He lived during the time of Moses, and he was an inhabitant of southern Palestine at the time when the Jews were beginning to enter the area. The local people were afraid of the coming of the Jews, and they beseeched Bal'aam to ask Allah to help them destroy the Children of Israel. After bribing him, Bal'aam tried to utter an invocation against the Children of Israel, but his words came out with the opposite import. Because he had disregarded the orders of Allah, He was chastised spiritually. Allah then revealed verses to him and used him to utter a warning to the people of Moab. (See Numbers 24:13.) A very full and lengthy story about him is recounted in Numbers, chapters 22-24. Only Allah knows which interpretation is correct.

Don't Sit with those who Take Allah's Name in Vain

*T*he most beautiful names belong to Allah, so call upon Him using them, but shun the company of those who use His names improperly, for they're soon going to be paid back for what they've done. [674] [180]

They must Pay Heed before Disaster Strikes

*A*mong those whom We've created is a community that guides (others) to the truth and that does justice by it. [675] [181] However, We're gradually going to bring ruin upon those who deny Our signs – *in ways they can't even detect!* [182] I'm going to give them some time, for My plan is unchangeable. [183]

Don't (the Meccans) ever consider that their companion (Muhammad) just might *not* be possessed by a jinn and that he just might *indeed* be a clear warner? [184]

Don't they see anything in the functioning of the heavens and the earth and in all that Allah has created that might give them an inkling that their time might just be drawing to a close? So what message will they believe in after this? [185]

Whomever Allah leaves astray, there can be no one to guide him, for He will leave them wandering aimlessly in their overconfidence. [186]

When will the Hour Come to Pass?

*N*ow they're asking you about the Hour (of Judgment) [676] – "*When will it come to pass?*" [677]

Say (to them), "*Its knowledge is in the presence of my Lord, and no one can predict when it will occur save Him. It weighs heavily upon the heavens and the earth, and it will come upon you out of nowhere.*"

Really now, they're asking you as if you were somehow eagerly in search of it! So tell them, "*Its knowledge is in the presence of Allah,*" though most people don't know (anything about it). [187]

On Petty Fortune-telling

*S*ay (to them), "*I have no power to bring either benefit or harm upon myself, except for what Allah allows.* [678] *If I had knowledge of what's beyond perception, then I would've had tremendous good fortune, and no misfortune would have ever come upon me. I'm just a warner and an announcer of good news to those who believe.*" [188]

---

[674] This is an echo of the traditional Jewish and Christian advice not to take the name of Allah in vain. (Also see Exodus 20:7) II Corinthians 6:13-15 also advises against being with people who do not believe in God. Also see I Corinthians 15:33.

[675] The Prophet recited this verse and then said, "The people who are being referenced in this passage are my people who will take to deciding their disputes truthfully and with justice in all circumstances." (*at-Tabari*)

[676] Some Jews who were visiting Mecca approached the Prophet and said, "Muhammad, inform us when the Hour (of Judgment) will take place, if you're truly a prophet, for we know when it will be." This verse was revealed in response. (*Asbab ul-Nuzul*)

[677] The Prophet left us with some signs of the Last Day's coming, and among these are the following: There will be much bloodshed on earth. People won't care much for others. People will not know each other very well anymore. Scholars will be banished, and people will be so weak in their faith that they won't know right from wrong, nor will they speak out against evil deeds. The Prophet once described the End Times thusly: "Isolation and loneliness will be common among people, and few people will be able to recognize each other." (*Ahmad*)

[678] Some Meccans asked the Prophet if Allah ever revealed to him what future market prices would be, because they wanted to know when they should buy and when they should sell in order to make money. Others asked him if Allah ever told him which pastures would be fertile and which would be barren. This verse was revealed in response. (*Asbab ul-Nuzul*)

How do People Belittle Allah's Blessings?

*H*e's the One Who created you from a single soul, and He made from it her mate, so she could dwell with her (husband as a family).

After they've gone into each other, she soon comes to bear a light burden and carries it around, though when she grows heavy, they both pray to Allah, their Lord, saying, *"If You grant us a perfect and healthy child, we promise that we'll be thankful."* [189]

However, when He grants them a perfect and healthy child, they let other (gods) share in the gift that they received, *even though Allah is so high above the partners they make with Him!* [190]

So are they taking (inanimate objects) to be partners with Him, (things that) cannot create anything and that are just created things themselves? [191]

(Those inanimate objects) can't help them, nor can they even help themselves! [192] (But alas,) even if you show (those idol-worshippers true) guidance, they won't follow you, for it's all the same to them whether you call to them or keep quiet! [193]

Those upon whom you call besides Allah are merely (created) servants like yourselves. So go ahead and call upon them, and see if they listen to your prayers, that is, if you're really being so honest! [194]

Do they have feet with which to walk, or hands with which to hold, or eyes with which to see, or ears with which to hear?

Say to those (who believe in idols), *"Call your 'partners,' and plan (your worst) against me, and don't give me any break!* [195] *My protector is Allah, the One Who revealed the Book, and He protects those who are moral and upright.* [196] *All those whom you call upon besides Him can't help you, nor can they help themselves!* [197] *If you call them to guidance, they won't hear you, and even though you may see their eyes staring at you, they don't see anything."* [198]

Commit yourself to forgiving (others by overlooking their shortcomings and actions against you), order good conduct, and turn away from the ignorant. [679] [199]

If any suggestion from Satan assails you, then seek Allah's protection, for He hears and knows (all things). [200] Those who bring (Allah) to mind when an evil thought from Satan assails them are reminded (of their allegiance to Allah), and suddenly they can see clearly again! [201]

However, their (evil) 'brothers' will always seek to plunge them into error, and they never pause. [680] [202]

Allah Reveals in His Own Time

*W*henever you don't bring them a (new) verse (when they expect to hear one), they say, *"Why don't you have your (material) ready yet?"* [681]

---

[679] When this verse was revealed, the Prophet asked Angel Gabriel about it. The Prophet later said of this discussion that he was commanded to forgive those who did wrong to him, to be generous to the one who gives him nothing, and to keep relations alive with those who break them with him. (*at-Tabari*) Many scholars also say it counsels the Prophet to accept what his followers sincerely offer and not to be critical or overly harsh if they fail to measure up due to weakness. (*Ma'ariful Qur'an*)

[680] The common phrase for banishing evil thoughts is to say, "I seek the protection of Allah from Satan, the Rejected." The 'evil brothers' referred to here can mean either evil jinn in whom people believe or other people who are a bad influence on their friends.

[681] Sometimes the Prophet would receive a whole chapter of the Qur'an at once. Other times he would get only a verse or two. More often than not, he would get a small passage, then affix it to existing passages and thus have a full chapter whose various parts might have been revealed over weeks, months or years. It happened sometimes, however, that the Prophet wouldn't receive any revealed verses at all, and at such times, the idol-worshippers taunted Muhammad, assuming that he was the author of

Say to them, *"I only follow what's been revealed to me from my Lord, and it's no less than insight from your Lord and a source of guidance and mercy for all who believe."* [203]

How should We Recite the Qur'an?

*W*hen the Qur'an is being read, listen to it attentively and keep quiet, so you can receive mercy. [682] [204] Remember your Lord inwardly with humility and awe.

Don't speak too loudly (when you repeat His praises) in the morning and evening. Don't be careless (about Allah)! [205]

Those (angels) who are the nearest to your Lord aren't too proud to serve Him. So glorify Him, and bow yourselves down before Him. [683] [206]

the revelations and that he was merely unprepared with his material. This verse instructs Muhammad to tell those people that Allah gives verses when He wants to, and not when people demand them from the Prophet. (*Ma'ariful Qur'an*)

[682] While in Mecca, the Prophet would lead clandestine group prayers with his followers – sometimes in peoples' homes and other times out in the countryside. Some of the worshippers would repeat whatever the Prophet said in prayer, which annoyed him, while others would sometimes talk among themselves when they were supposed to be praising Allah. This passage was revealed to let the believers know they were to keep silent in prayers and maintain a spiritual focus meditating upon Allah. (*Ma'ariful Qur'an*)

[683] After reading this verse it is customary for the one who has faith in Allah to prostrate himself on the floor and praise Allah.

The Spoils of War

8 Al Anfal
Early Medinan Period

~~~

This chapter was revealed shortly after the Battle of Badr and deals with a number of issues related to the conduct of war and its aftermath. The title of the chapter comes from the discussion over the division of captured goods. One fifth of all booty goes to the Prophet so he can fund the Islamic movement. (He usually gave everything he received away, so much so that there was often never even any food in his apartment.) The concept of the Just War is discussed, and the believers are exhorted not to be timid if they are called upon to fight a foe. A key phrase is contained in verse 38, which sums up the Qur'anic attitude towards those who make war upon Allah's community: if you stop your attacks and repent, Allah will forgive you your past actions. If you don't, you will be vanquished.

In the Name of Allah,
the Compassionate, the Merciful

They're asking you [684] about the captured goods (collected after a battle). [685]

Say (to them), "*The goods (seized on the battlefield) belong to Allah and His Messenger, so be mindful of Allah and maintain good relations among you. [686] Obey Allah and His Messenger if you're (really true) believers.*" [687] [1]

---

[684] After the Battle of Badr, a lot of goods and materials were collected from the battlefield. The fleeing pagans of Mecca left weapons, horses, tents and other miscellany. In the evening after the battle, some factions of the Muslims began arguing over how to divide the war booty. The group that collected it thought it should be theirs (finders keepers), while the groups that either guarded the Prophet after the battle or who kept on pursuing the enemy felt they should have the most for their extra efforts. This verse told the believers to let the Prophet decide what to do with the war booty, and he distributed it evenly. (*Ibn Kathir*)

[685] A man named Sa'd ibn Abi Waqqas saw his brother become a martyr during the battle. He slew the fierce Meccan warrior who killed his sibling and then picked up the man's sword from the battlefield. Given all that happened that day, Sa'd desired to keep that sword as a memento. The Prophet said to him, "The sword is neither yours nor mine, so put it down (in the pile of booty). Sa'd was apprehensive that the Prophet might distribute the sword to someone else, but a little while later a man came to him and told him to go see the Prophet. The Prophet told him, "You asked me to give you the sword, but it's not for me to decide about. However, Allah has allowed me to give it to you."

[686] One companion named 'Ubadah ibn Samit later explained that when this verse was revealed, it relieved the companions of having to squabble over material things. (*Ahmad*) Tirmidhi and Ibn Majah report that the Prophet used to dislike war booty and that he would encourage the bravest fighters (who got the most) to share some of it with the weaker fighters. Verse 8:41 takes up this issue again and specifies the exact amounts that are to be used by the Islamic government and what is to be distributed to the participants in the war. Chapter 59 (verses 7-8) discusses a different classification of property that comes under Muslim control without fighting, and its use is completely at the discretion of the Islamic government.

[687] The Prophet said, "I've been given five things which were not given to any prophet before me, and I'm not saying it out of pride. I was sent to all the people of the world, both the black and the white (races). Allah made me victorious by casting fear (into the hearts of my enemies) for one month's

Indeed, believers are those who, when they're reminded of Allah, feel a tremor in their hearts, and when they hear His verses being recited, their faith is increased.

They let their Lord take care of their affairs. [2] (They're the ones) who establish prayer and spend out of the resources that We've provided for them. [3]

The Battle of Badr

*T*hese are the true believers, and they have varying degrees of status, (depending upon their efforts), in their Lord's sight, 688 as well as forgiveness and a generous share of resources (awaiting them in the next life). [4]

(These different grades in status in Allah's sight) are evidenced by the fact that when your Lord had ordered you to leave your home, 689 (Muhammad, to make a stand at the wells of Badr) for a true purpose, 690 a segment of the believers

---

journey (in all directions). War booty has been made lawful for me; yet, it wasn't lawful for any before me. The entire earth has been made a place on which to pray and a source for purification. I've been given the right of intercession, and I'm saving it for my community on the Day of Resurrection. Therefore, the intercession will cover all those who don't make partners with Allah." (*Ahmad*) The Old Testament book of Numbers asserts that Moses had permission to distribute war booty (Numbers 31:6-54). However, no Muslim would ever accept that the terrible and heartless war crimes mentioned in that same passage could ever be a truthful representation of Moses or his mission. This is not to mention the fact that the first five books of the Torah as they exist today were largely penned many centuries later by people other than Moses. Thus, from the Muslim point of view, that would be another example of how tribal history was incorrectly passed on through the generations. Given that the Torah was lost for centuries and only rewritten in the time of Ezra, it is easy to assert that much of what is considered to be the Torah today may very well be at best embellished.

688 The Prophet said that the people in Paradise can see the people on the other levels of Paradise "...*just as you see a distant planet in the horizon of the sky.*" He then said that Abu Bakr and 'Umar will be in the highest level. (*Ahmad, Abu Dawud, Tirmidhi*)

689 Some people said to the Prophet, "You marched us here (to Badr) to capture the caravan. You never told us there would be any fighting, otherwise we could have prepared for it." This verse was revealed in comment on that. (*Ibn Kathir*)

690 The Prophet was ordered by Allah to leave his home and rally the believers to engage either the Meccan caravan returning from Syria or the Meccan army that was sure to be mobilized to protect it. There is a misconception among some quarters that the Prophet somehow was in the habit of raiding caravans like a common brigand. This is an unfortunate slander, and those who perpetuate this myth either willfully hide the historical facts or are honestly ignorant of the laws of war. A state of war existed between the Muslims of Medina and Mecca from the moment the Prophet escaped from Mecca and migrated as a refugee to Medina. (He narrowly escaped being murdered by the pagans the very night he fled!) The Meccans spent the next two years, from 622 to 624, raiding Medina and outlying settlements, capturing Muslim travelers and torturing and murdering them and encouraging local pagan bedouins to do the same (all the while the Muslims were barely able to look after themselves). In addition, the pagans seized the property the Meccan Muslims had left behind in Mecca, which impoverished the refugees immediately. (This money was also invested in the Meccan trading empire.) What Muhammad did was to begin to fight back gradually. Since he didn't have vast forces at his disposal, he had to send out small expeditions and patrols to engage the frequent Meccan raiders. (There were many small engagements between armed groups of ten to twenty men in the countryside, and these fights were called *ghazwahs*, or skirmishes.) After two years of weak defense, a different tactic came to the fore: if a Meccan caravan could be seized, it would harm the enemy economically, and this conduct is allowed under the laws of war under any nation or religion It was never the Prophet's aim or desire to enrich himself or the community, as evidenced by the fact that he did not make it a policy to capture non-Meccan caravans that passed through his territory, and of the handful of captured Meccan ones, he sometimes let them go (if the men who were operating them were of good character - such as the case of Abu al-As). Any goods that were captured and held, as part of the war effort, were distributed in such a way as to leave him (the Prophet) with nothing. (This particular

didn't like it, [5] and they argued with you (about it), even after the reality (of the situation) was made evidently clear. *(Indeed, they made it seem as if) they were being marched off to their own deaths right before their own eyes!* [6]

Allah had promised that one of the two (enemy) groups would fall to you.

Although you were hoping that it would be the thornless (caravan returning to Mecca from Syria), Allah wanted to have the truth of His words demonstrated. 691

He also wanted to cut off the root of those who suppressed (the light of faith within their hearts) [7] so He could demonstrate that the truth is true and falsehood is a lie, no matter how much the wicked hate it. 692 [8]

Allah Helped the Faithful at the Battle of Badr

(Remember) how you had fervently asked for the help of your Lord (at the Battle of Badr), and He answered you, saying, *"I will help you with a regiment of a thousand angels."* [9]

This announcement wasn't made for any other purpose than to assure your hearts, for there is no help except from Allah's presence, and Allah is powerful and wise. [10]

(Remember) how He covered you in a state of rest (just before the eve of battle) to calm your anxiety (as a gift) from Himself, and He made water fall from the sky to cleanse you, to remove the taint of Satan, to strengthen your hearts and to make your stance firm. 693 [11]

Meccan caravan, which was the first the Prophet attempted to take, was invested in by every tribe of the Quraysh, and it was also escorted by 40 armed Meccan chieftains along with their men.) It must be remembered that the Prophet never accumulated any wealth, himself, and that he lived a very spartan lifestyle. He didn't let his wives accumulate wealth, either. (A fact that led some of them to complain of their abject poverty. See 33:28-29.) Any skirmishes or seizures that did occur were all a part of the ongoing war between Mecca and Medina. After the Treaty of Hudaybiyyah, there was no further hostilities, except from the Meccan side, and this is what led to their downfall.

691 When the Muslim force of some 313 men and a few women, (who would be the medical and support staff), set out in the year 624, their stated goal was to intercept the easy, unprotected (hence *thornless*) Meccan caravan returning from Syria. This was the large, annual caravan that included an enormous amount of wealth. If it could be captured, it would set back the Meccan war effort and raise the status of the Muslims among the pagan bedouins. The caravan was set to arrive at an oasis known as Badr, which also had a small settlement of the same name. There were several important wells there that would provide water for the thousands of animals that made up the caravan. However, it wasn't meant to be so easy for the Muslim side, and this was the in the plan of Allah, for instead of intercepting the caravan, the Muslims were directed to engage a Meccan army made up of over a thousand men that would arrive some days later. The outnumbered Muslims achieved some important successes in that battle that were actually more advantageous than merely capturing the Meccans' goods. Nearly all the top Meccan leaders were killed in the battle; the Meccans were humiliated in the eyes of the Arabs; the Muslims gained a tremendous boost of confidence, and the Meccan raids were more infrequent for some time.

692 Prior to marching out to the battle, the Prophet consulted his men about what to do, and a man named Al-Miqdad said, "Messenger of Allah! March to what Allah commanded you, for we are with you. By Allah, we will never say to you what the Children of Israel said to Moses: 'You and your Lord can go fight while we sit here (and watch).'" (See 5:24.)

693 Before the battle, the Muslims were tense and filled with anxiety, for they had reports of the immensity of the Meccan force, which was soon to arrive the next morning. The men fell into a relaxed slumber after some time, and a cool rain fell, which didn't happen often in that sandy patch of desert, giving the men confidence and courage. This enabled them to keep the influence of Satan away from their hearts, for he assailed them with thoughts of fear and retreat. 'Ali ibn Abi Talib reported that on the night before battle was joined, everyone had fallen asleep at Badr, save for the Prophet who remained up all night in prayer and supplication. (*Abu Ya'la*)

245

(Muhammad,) remember also that your Lord inspired the angels (to bring a message of hope to your heart that said), *"I'm with you, so steady the believers. I'm going to put fear into the hearts of the faithless, so raise (your weapons and aim) towards their necks, and raise (your weapons to strike) at their fingertips, (as they brandish their weapons against you)!"* 694 [12]

That's (what they deserve) because they (dared) to oppose Allah and His Messenger. Whoever opposes Allah and His Messenger (should know that) Allah is severe in administering punishment. [13]

"This (defeat at Badr) is for you, (all you enemies of Allah), so taste it!"

Indeed, all those who suppress (their natural faith in Allah) will be punished in the Fire! [14]

O you who believe! When you go forth and engage the faithless in battle, never turn your backs to them. [15] If anyone turns his back (and runs away) – unless it's part of a strategy (to defeat the enemy through a trick) or to rejoin a battalion – then he's going to bring Allah's wrath down upon him, and his home will be in Hellfire – *the worst destination!* 695 [16]

It wasn't you who struck them down (at the Battle of Badr); it was Allah. When you threw (a symbolic handful of pebbles at the idol-worshippers as the battle commenced, Muhammad), it wasn't something you did, but Allah Who did it, so He could test the believers with a fine test from Himself, for Allah hears and knows (all things). 696 [17]

That's (why the battle took place). Truly, Allah thwarts the plans of those who suppress (the light of faith within their hearts). [18]

(All you faithless Meccans!) If you had ever looked for a definitive resolution (in your struggles with the believers), then there you have it! 697 The resolution has come to you, so if you would just stop (opposing Allah), it would be better for you. 698

---

694 In other words, be men, be strong and fight your enemy with all your might, for Allah will put the conviction in you to prevail.

695 According to the early commentators, the rule is that if a Muslim is outnumbered only by two-to-one, he may not flee, but any odds greater than that are grounds for fleeing to regroup later. (*Ma'ariful Qur'an*) See 8:66.

696 When the battle was about to begin, the Prophet told his men, "By the One Who holds power over Muhammad's soul, the man who fights them today, firmly and persevering, Allah will let him into Paradise." Then he prayed to Allah, saying, "O Allah! Here come those who deny You – the Quraysh of Mecca – all proud and arrogant. You promised me victory, so let that promise be fulfilled as soon as possible!" Then the Prophet scooped up a handful of pebbles and threw them in a symbolic gesture towards the Meccan army. He did this three times – one shot to the Meccan left, to the right and then to the center. Some commentators say that this gesture had the miraculous effect of making the pagans see poorly as they rushed at the Muslim lines. In later years, some of the men who had been pagans at Badr, but who had converted later on to Islam, reported that the Prophet's symbolic action did have an effect on their performance that day.

697 While some commentators hold that this passage is directed towards the Muslims, other commentators are of the view that this passage is actually directed towards the pagans, and this seems likely given the shift in focus at the end of verse 18. The commentators who hold this view base it on the supplication of Abu Jahl, a prominent pagan, who, along with his friends, are reported to have taken hold of the curtain that hangs over the Ka'bah, just before leaving for Badr, and to have prayed for a clear resolution between their idolatry and Islam. Abu Jahl declared: "*Our Lord, whichever of the two parties was less kind to his relatives, and brought us what we do not know, then destroy him tomorrow.*" The Muslim victory at the Battle of Badr was then that definitive ruling from Allah – a sign that He favors Islam. (*Asbab ul-Nuzul*)

698 In traditional Arab culture, captured enemies were either tortured to death or sold into slavery. After the Battle of Badr, Muhammad exhorted his followers to treat the captured Meccans well. In later years, a Meccan said of this episode, "Blessed be the men of Medina. They let us ride while they walked. They gave us bread when it was scarce and contented themselves with only dates."

If you ever return (to fight against the believers,) then We'll bring about more of the same. The forces under your command are of no use to you, no matter how numerous they become, for Allah is with the believers, (and He helps them to achieve victory). [19]

Obey the Messenger of Allah

O you who believe! Obey Allah and His Messenger. Don't turn away from him when you hear (him speaking), [699] [20] nor be like those who say, "*We hear*," but then they don't listen. [21]

Truly, the worst creatures in Allah's sight are those who (intentionally refuse) to hear (when they really can hear) and who (refuse to) respond (when they really can respond, for they don't use) their reason! [22]

If Allah would've known of any good (qualities) within them, He would've made them listen. However, even if He did make them listen, (owing to their current state), they would've merely turned away and refused (to believe)! [23]

O you who believe! Respond to Allah and His Messenger when He calls you to what will give you life. Know that Allah can come between a person and his heart [700] and that you'll all be gathered back to Him. [24]

Be mindful of the chaos and trials that affect more than just the sinners among you, and know that Allah is severe in punishment. [701] [25]

Remember how you (Muslims) used to be such a small group (in the early days of

---

[699] Ibn Majah narrated from al-Miqdaam ibn Ma'di Yakrib that the Messenger of Allah said: "Soon there will come a time when a man will be reclining on his pillow, and when one of my sayings (hadiths) is narrated to him, he will say, 'The Book of Allah is (sufficient) between us and you. Whatever it states is permissible we will take as permissible, and whatever it states is forbidden, we will take as forbidden.' Truly, whatever the Messenger of Allah has forbidden is like that which Allah has forbidden."

[700] Some commentators say that this phrase means that Allah has more power than a wicked person who, although he may be planning some devious scheme, cannot frustrate Allah's plan in the end. Other commentators explain that it means that Allah brings faith to the heart of those who show some inner desire for it, and He extinguishes it from whomever willfully blinds himself to faith. The Prophet said, "The heart is like a feather in the desert: the wind blows it all around." He also used to pray, "O Turner of Hearts, keep my heart firm in Your religion." (*Ahmad*)

[701] The person who thinks that he will be shielded from the troubles of the world simply because he lives faithfully to Allah is not taking into account that the ebb and flow of life's tide can wash over anyone's happy home and swamp him under a load of stress and challenges. Although living a lifestyle dedicated to Allah can help people cope better with the pain and suffering that are natural parts of life, it by no means guarantees that they won't have moments that try their faith. The Prophet explained that a believer who undergoes hardships and bears them with patience is actually getting sins removed from his record on account of it. There is another source of hardship, however, that comes upon us from our inaction and silence. Think of the person who remains aloof, refusing to speak out for justice or against injustice. When evil spreads, it touches all, even those who do not indulge in it. The Prophet said, "By the One Who holds my soul in His hand, you must promote what is recognized as (good in Allah's religion) and forbid what is outside the norms, or Allah might send a punishment from Himself down upon you, and you'll be supplicating to Him, but He won't answer your call." (*Ahmad*) This tradition was explained by a companion named Hudhayfah, who said in the years after the Prophet's passing, "…someone would say one word during the time of the Messenger of Allah and become a hypocrite on account of it. I now hear the same kinds of words from some of you four times in one sitting. Truly, you must either enjoin that which is recognized (as good), forbid the strange and unfamiliar and encourage each other to do good, or Allah will surround you all with trials or make the wicked among you become your leaders. The righteous will then supplicate, but their supplication will not be accepted." (*Ahmad*) Finally, the Prophet said, "If sins become evident in my community, Allah will surround them with punishment from Him." When someone asked what would happen to the righteous among them, the Prophet replied that they would also suffer from the trials but that Allah would forgive them in the next life. (*Ahmad*)

the Prophet's mission). Everyone in the land thought you were so weak; you were constantly afraid of people robbing or kidnapping you, but He found a place of refuge for you (in Medina) and gave you strength with His help. He also provided wholesome resources for you, as well, so you could be thankful. [26]

Let not Material Concerns Destroy Loyalty

O you who believe! [702] Don't betray the trust of Allah and the Messenger, and don't knowingly take things that don't belong to you. [27]

Know that your property and your children are no more than a source of testing for you and that with Allah lies your most substantial reward. [28]

Appreciate All that Allah did for You

O you who believe! If you're mindful of Allah, then He'll give you a standard (to judge between right and wrong). He'll erase your shortcomings from (your record) and forgive you, as well, for Allah is the master of tremendous favor. [703] [29]

Recall how the faithless (idol-worshippers of Mecca) plotted against you, (Muhammad,) either to imprison you, murder you or drive you out (of the city). They were making plans, and Allah was making plans, and Allah is the best planner of all! [704] [30]

---

[702] When the Banu Qurayzah were on the verge of surrendering to the Muslims after the Meccan siege of Medina was lifted, they asked to see an old friend of theirs named Abu Lubaba to get his opinion about what they should do. They had demanded that the Prophet merely exile them for their betrayal of the Muslims, but the Prophet would only accept their unconditional surrender. The leaders of the Banu Qurayzah knew they had no choice but to do so, but they sent the counter demand that they wanted to pick the one who would judge them. They were inclined to pick the chief of the Auws tribe, Sa'd ibn Mu'adh, as he had been friendly with them before Islam. So they asked Abu Lubaba his opinion about what might befall them if they surrendered. Abu Lubaba, who was swayed by the fact that some of his family and property were located in the district of the Banu Qurayzah, put his finger over his throat and made a cutting motion, implying that they shouldn't accept any deal because any judgment they would receive would be severe. Abu Lubaba immediately felt ashamed, for he knew he had betrayed the Prophet by attempting to taint the negotiations. When he left the fortress of the Banu Qurayzah, he immediately went to the mosque and tied himself to a pillar, vowing not to eat or drink anything until Allah forgave him, even if it meant his death. After several days he passed out in delirium, but then he was revived and told that Allah accepted his repentance. He then said he would not leave the pillar unless the Prophet came and untied him with his own hands. The Prophet came and did so. Abu Lubaba offered to give all his money and property away to compensate for his mistake, but the Prophet told him to give away only one third and that would be sufficient. This passage was revealed about this situation. (*Asbab ul-Nuzul*)

[703] The Prophet said, "There are three qualities and whoever has them has tasted the sweetness of faith: whoever holds Allah and His Messenger dearer to their heart than their own selves; whoever loves a person for the sake of Allah alone; and whoever would rather be thrown in a fire than ever go back to disbelief after Allah has saved him from it (i.e., the fire of Hell)." (*Muslim*)

[704] By the year 622, things had become untenable for the Muslims in Mecca and for the Prophet in particular. The pagans of the city were murdering Muslims, torturing believing slaves and their own relatives who had converted, and assaulting random Muslims in the street. The leaders of the Quraysh met in their meeting hall, called the *Darul Nadwa*, and were making suggestions for a final solution to their problem with Muhammad. Imprisonment and banishment were considered, but Abu Jahl ibn Hisham proposed outright assassination, and the council adopted the plan. His scheme was to select young men representing every clan under the umbrella of the Quraysh so that when they struck him down in the night, the Prophet's own clan, the Banu Hashim, would be powerless to take revenge against so many other clans. Angel Gabriel went to the Prophet and warned him to flee for his life that very night. The Prophet snuck out of town under the cover of darkness with his trusty friend, Abu Bakr. He had already sent nearly all the rest of his followers northward to Medina in a carefully

When Our (revealed) verses were recited to them, they said, "*We heard this kind of stuff before. If we ever wanted to, we could say things just like this, for these (verses) are nothing more than old legends.*" [31]

Allah will Punish Evil in His Own Time

*A*lso remember how they said, "*O Allah, if all of this is really the truth from You, then (we dare You) to send a shower of stones down upon us from the sky. Punish us as hard (as You can)!*" [705] [32]

However, Allah wasn't going to punish them as long as you were still living there among them, nor was He going to do it while they still had time to repent. [33]

So what reason is there for Allah not to punish them now, [706] since they're keeping people away from the Sacred Mosque, even though they're not its (legitimate) guardians?

No one but the mindful can be its guardians, but most of them don't understand. [34] Their prayers at the House (of Allah) are no more than whistling and the clapping of hands. [707] (The only answer such foolish prayers can receive is,) "*Suffer the punishment for your rejection (of Allah's truth)!*" [35]

Those who cover over (the truth of Allah in their hearts) only spend their money to hold people back from the path of Allah, and that's how they're going to keep on spending it. [708] In the end, they'll have nothing more than regrets, and they'll be overwhelmed (in despair).

Then the faithless will be gathered together at (the edge of) Hellfire [36] so Allah can separate the tainted from the pure and also so He can pile the tainted (sinners) in a heap and throw them all into Hellfire. They're the ones who will be utterly lost! [37]

Making Peace With Your Enemies

*T*ell all those who suppress (their ability to believe) that if they stop (their opposition to Allah's cause), then their past (sins) will be forgiven for them, [709] but if they persist, then the example of the ancients is there (for all to see as a warning). [38]

Go on fighting them until chaos and disorder have ceased and until Allah's way of life prevails, but if (the faithless) end (their attacks upon you, then know that) Allah sees everything that they're doing.

---

managed exodus over many weeks. After eluding Meccan scouting parties for three days, the Prophet entered Medina to a chorus of cheering people. (*Ibn Kathir, Tabari*)

[705] An-Nadr ibn al-Harith, a vile poet of the Quraysh, had said the things mentioned in this verse to the Prophet in the days when the Prophet was still living in Mecca. In effect, an-Nadr denied revelation and even dared Allah to punish him. This was originally commented upon by the Qur'an (in a Meccan revelation) in verses 70:1-3, and now the punishment he asked for befell him, as an-Nadr was one of those captured and later killed after Badr. (Some reports say he was killed in the battle itself.) (*Nisa'i, Ma'ariful Qur'an*)

[706] The Meccans were punished after all with the Battle of Badr where every important clan leader who attended fell in battle.

[707] When the pagan Arabs used to perform religious rites around the Ka'bah, they literally would clap, whistle, shout and act in every wild manner, thinking that Allah and their idols were *pleased.*

[708] After the Battle of Badr was over, the pagan Meccans were distraught with grief over their losses of both men and honor. Abu Sufyan, who had safely guided the precious Meccan caravan in from Syria, was called upon by his people to donate money from the trading enterprise to raise a new army to fight the Muslims once more. He made a public call for the other investors to do likewise. When news of this reached Medina, this passage was revealed in response. (*Asbab ul-Nuzul*)

[709] The Prophet said, "Whoever becomes good in Islam won't be punished for what he did during his days of ignorance (before Islam). Whoever becomes bad in his Islam will face the punishment for his previous and later deeds." (*Bukhari*)

If they refuse (to make peace), then know that Allah is your close ally, and He's the protector of all and the best source of aid! [711] [40]

How Allah Helped the Believers in the Battle

$\mathcal{K}$now that out of all the captured goods you gain, a fifth of it is reserved for Allah and for the Messenger *and* for close relatives (who are in need), [712] as well as for orphans and (stranded) travelers. (So believers, do not be upset when that amount is deducted from the total distribution of goods,) if you really have faith in Allah and in (the victory) We sent down to Our servant on a Decisive Day, the day when the two forces met (at battle at Badr), for Allah has power over all things. [713] [41]

---

[710] The concept of a just war in Islam boils down to three principles. Unless one of the conditions is present, then warfare is not permissible for a Muslim state. The three times when war is allowed are: 1) when the Muslims in Islamically-controlled territories have been attacked, 2) when a tyrant is oppressing his people or a nation is waging unjust aggression and oppression against another people and 3) when a nation forbids the free preaching or practice of Islam. For example, Muslims have no grounds for rebellion or aggression against a non-Muslim nation if there is religious freedom and no unjust oppression against them or any other minority group. Conversely, if the Muslims are being ruled by a tyrant who suppresses the free practice of Islam, then Muslims are not obligated to defend such a regime if it gets into a war with foreign powers. What if a non-Muslim nation attacks an Islamically-governed state without provocation and war results, when can a Muslim state declare victory and cease hostilities? Either the military capabilities of the enemy are subdued and can no longer fight, or the enemy sues for peace, and in that case the Muslim state is obligated to enter peace talks leading to a just settlement. (War criminals are to be pursued, however, until they are captured and brought to justice.) Theoretically, a Muslim state, ruled by Islamic principles alone, (which can be manifested through a wide variety of political philosophies,) should never initiate hostilities against any other entity except for the three cases mentioned previously. Furthermore, the conduct of the war must be tempered with self-control, as civilians and the innocent are not to be harmed. All of these principles are derived from the verses of the Qur'an and the sayings of the Prophet. The misconception in the West, often promoted by fear-mongers, that Islam is somehow warlike or prone to militarism is not supported by either the two main sources of Islam or the facts of history, which if examined quantitatively show that it has been the Western world that has been the most consistently warlike of any civilization in the last five hundred years. (From the mid-1400s to the early 1900s, Europeans conquered every continent on earth and destroyed nearly every longstanding culture it encountered.) Modern, mostly secular states that happen to have Muslim populations are not the yardstick by which to judge Islam as a religion or as a cultural experience, for modern states in the Muslim world are generally not ruled by traditional Islamic principles, but rather by the secular ones that former European colonial masters left behind. Until the era of European Colonialism, the '*Ulema,* or Islamic scholars, were generally an independent force in society that could temper the actions of the rulers using the power of religious authority. Today, the small remnants of this institution are largely ignored and/or manipulated by secular and/or highly illiterate leaders and movements.

[711] Ibn 'Umar was once asked his view of warfare and turmoil, and he replied, "Do you know what chaos and oppression are? Muhammad used to fight against the idolaters, and his fighting with them was (to end) chaos and oppression. (His fighting) was not like your fighting (today), which is done merely for the sake of power." (*Bukhari*)

[712] The immediate reference is to the clans of Banu Hashim and Banu al-Muttalib, the Prophet's extended relatives, who suffered at every stage from Meccan persecution on account of Muhammad being a member of those two groups. So the Prophet used to distribute charity to them after the migration to relieve their poverty and reward them for their perseverance. The Prophet said, "When a Muslim spends on his family expecting only Allah's reward, then it will be recorded as charity on his part." (*Ahmad*) Surprisingly enough, when his own daughter Fatimah asked for a servant to help her with the household chores, he pointed out to her that the poor people living in the mosque were more in need of help than she. (*Bukhari, Muslim*)

[713] From the Battle of Badr onwards, the principle is that one-fifth of all captured war material and goods must be reserved for Allah's work, i.e., for helping weak or poor people, freeing slaves, supporting orphans, education, etc... The rest is to be distributed to the soldiers who fought in the battle at the discretion of the commander or other authority figure. The Prophet never enriched himself with that one-fifth he was charged with distributing, but rather he always gave it all away to help his

(Remember) how you were on one edge of the valley and (the enemy) was on the other, and (remember) how the caravan was located on lower ground than you. Even if you had made an appointment in advance, you couldn't have timed it so well. [714]

However, it was a foregone conclusion in Allah's (plan) so that those who lived and died (that day) could do so knowing full well (that Allah had arranged this). [715] Allah is indeed the Hearing and the Knowing! [42]

(Remember) that in your dream Allah made it seem to you that they were few in number. If He had shown you how large a force they really were, you would've been discouraged, and you would've certainly second-guessed yourself, but Allah preserved you in your decision, for He knows (how your) hearts (work). [716] [43]

(Remember) that when you met (the enemy in battle), He made them seem to you like a much smaller force than they actually were, and He made you seem fewer in number, likewise. [717] That was so Allah could bring to a conclusion something that was already determined, for all issues go back to Allah. [44]

O you who believe! When you meet an (enemy) force, be firm and remember Allah often so you can be successful. [718] [45] Obey Allah and His Messenger, and don't argue with each other, for you might lose your resolve and diminish your strength. Persevere, for Allah is with those who persevere. [46]

community. After the Battle of Badr was over, the Prophet gave a speech exhorting the Muslims to put in the collective pile of war booty every small thing they found and not to secretly withhold anything. He also told them, "I have no share in it except for my own share, the fifth designated to me, and even that fifth will be given to you. Therefore, surrender even a needle and thread or anything bigger or smaller than that." (*Ahmad*) Women who accompany a Muslim army to act as nurses, support personnel and the like also get an equal share in the booty. (A report in Abu Dawud has the Prophet distributing an equal share to the women who marched with the Muslim army to subdue Khaybar.)

[714] Think of the way in which the famous Battle of Badr came about. The Meccan caravan was on the road somewhere returning from Syria. The Meccan army was on the road heading northward, not knowing where the Muslims were, and the Muslim force was on the road from Medina, not knowing for some time that the Meccan army was on the move. None of the parties knew where the others were. Yet, the Muslims and Meccans found each other at the Wells of Badr while the caravan got away by a hair's breadth. In those days, before GPS satellites, maps and accurate time pieces, let alone phones to coordinate groups of men hundreds of miles apart, all three parties converged in a small area at the same time. Thus, the battle was brought together by Allah's plan.

[715] Both our lives and deaths – and how we die – have consequences for now and the future. A righteous person does not seek death, but there are times when fighting is necessary, such as during the decisive battle of which this passage speaks. Not all lived to enjoy the victory, as a few tragically perished. As the verse here points out, there are some deaths that do have meaning and were for a true cause. We protect those whom we love, and the causes we believe in, when we make the ultimate sacrifice of ourselves. An ancient Roman writer named Publilius Syrus (d. 43 BCE) once noted, "Man's life is short; so therefore an honorable death is his immortality." Allah guides the universe and has an ultimate plan, and He does not let our sincere sacrifices, whatever they may be, be forgotten. That is His promise to us.

[716] Contrary to the odd notions of modern extremists, to be a Muslim is not to be constantly in search of war or conflict. The Prophet gave a sermon after one battle in which he said, "My people! Don't look forward to fighting the enemy in combat. Instead, you should pray that Allah keeps you in a state of peace and security. However, if the inevitable happens and you have to confront them, then stand firm, be patient, and remember that Paradise is under the shade of swords." (*Muslim*) In other words, be strong in war, but don't go looking for it or hope for it.

[717] 'Abdullah ibn Mas'ud explained that on that day at Badr, the enemy appeared to be smaller in number than it actually was. He said to a man near him that day, "They look about to be ninety in number." The man replied, "No, they must be about a hundred." (*Ma'ariful Qur'an*) In fact they were a thousand!

[718] 'Remembering Allah' in battle means to shout, "Allahu Akbar" or "Allah is Great," and other such phrases.

Don't be like those (pagans of Mecca) who started from their homes puffed up with pride only so other people would see them. (Their goal) was to hinder others from the path of Allah, but Allah surrounds whatever they do! [47]

How a 'Satan' was Defeated

(*R*emember) how *Satan* made their actions seem good to them [719] and how he told them, "*No people can ever beat you today as long as I'm near you.*" [720] However, when the two forces came in full view of each other, (Satan) turned on his heels and said, "*I'm free of you! I see what you don't see. I'm afraid of Allah, and Allah is harsh in punishment!*" [721] [48]

The Worst of All Creatures

*T*he hypocrites and the weak at heart [722] say, "*These people are being misled by their religion!*" However, if someone trusts in Allah, (that's the best thing to do), for Allah is powerful and wise! [49]

If you could just see it - when the angels take the souls of those who rejected (faith) - how they're going to raise up (their hands to strike) towards their faces and their backs (to punish them). [723] (And then when they enter Hellfire, they'll be told,) "*Suffer the punishment of the raging flame!* [50] *That's (the punishment you deserve) because of what your own hands have sent ahead - and Allah is never unfair to His servants!*" [724] [51]

---

[719] The 'satan' referred to here in this verse was a powerful desert chieftain named Suraqah ibn Malik through whom Satan made false promises to the Meccans. When the army of the Quraysh was mustering and preparing to leave Mecca, the Meccans were more than a little apprehensive about marching out and leaving their city undefended. (The Quraysh had a rivalry with a bedouin tribe called the Banu Bakr, who might take the opportunity to raid Mecca.) Suraqah, who lived in the vicinity of the Banu Bakr, came riding into Mecca, flanked by strong warriors of his own, and promised the Meccans that he would restrain the ill-will of the Banu Bakr. Then he told the Meccans that no people would ever beat them that day, as long as he was on their side. (As recorded in this verse.) During the battle, however, when it looked like the Meccans were about to be routed, Suraqah said what the ending of this verse quotes him as saying, and then he fled from the battlefield, much to the astonishment of the Quraysh. (*Ma'ariful Qur'an*)

[720] When the Meccan army learned that their caravan had gotten away and had escaped the Muslims, it was suggested that the army could turn back. However, Abu Jahl said to the leaders of the Quraysh, "No, by Allah! We will not turn back until after we've arrived at the Wells of Badr, slaughtered camels, gotten drunk and listened to women singing to us. That way the Arabs will always talk about our brave stance and what we did on that day." (The Meccans brought along drums and some female singers to celebrate their expected victory.)

[721] After the battle of Badr was over, seventy Meccans lay dead, including nearly every major clan leader. The Prophet ordered their bodies stuffed down a dry well and buried over.

[722] The 'weak at heart' are thought to be the hypocrites in Medina and those believers who were weak in faith and who could be turned away from faith.

[723] According to the Prophet, when the Angel of Death comes to retrieve the soul of the wicked, he appears to that soul looking terrifying and scary. Then he says, "Get out, wicked soul, to scorching heat, boiling muck and the shade of black smoke." Then the soul of the wicked disintegrates throughout his body, but the angels retrieve it and tear it out (of the throat) like a needle being ripped out of wet wool. (*Ahmad*) This dreadful time mentioned in the first sentence of this verse refers to the shadowy existence in between death and resurrection when the soul of a dead person is tied to the grave. (This is a state known as *Barzakh*, or the Partition.) Evildoers will have their souls punished by visiting angels daily. The souls of the righteous are suspended in a pleasant, dream-like state and do not feel the passage of time. The Prophet said, "When death approaches the believer, angels with white faces and white clothes come to him and say, 'You good soul! Come out to comfort and sustenance and to a Lord Who is not angry.' The soul then comes out of his mouth like a drop of water is poured out of a water jug." (*Ahmad*)

[724] The Prophet said that Allah, Himself, said, "My servants! I have prohibited injustice for Myself, and I've prohibited it to you in your dealings with each other. Therefore, don't commit injustice against each other. My servants! I'm keeping track of your deeds, so whoever found something good, then

(Their deeds) are like those of Pharaoh's people and those who went before them. They rejected the signs of their Lord, so Allah seized them for their sins, and Allah is strong and harsh in punishment. [52] That's because Allah will never (suddenly withdraw) the favors that He's granted to a people unless they change their souls (for the worst), and Allah listens and knows. [53]

As for Pharaoh's people and those who went before them, they denied the signs of their Lord, so We destroyed them for their sins. We even drowned Pharaoh's (army), for they were indeed corrupt. [54]

Who is the Most Despicable?

*T*ruly, the worst creatures in the sight of Allah are those who suppress (their awareness of His truth) and who have no faith. [725] [55] They're the ones with whom you may make a treaty, but who then break their treaties every time. They literally have no concern for Allah! [56]

Therefore, if you ever gain ascendancy over them on the battlefield, scatter them completely, so that those who come after them will have a lesson to consider. [57] If you fear treachery from any group, then throw back (their treaty at them) so you'll at least be on an even level with them, for Allah has no love for the treacherous. [726] [58]

Prefer Peace but be Prepared for War

*D*on't let those who suppress (their inner awareness of the truth) think that they can make progress (against Allah), for they can't escape (the punishment they deserve). [59] Keep yourselves prepared against them to the best of your ability, especially with a strong mobile force that can strike fear into Allah's enemies and your enemies and also other (potential enemies) about whom you know nothing, but about whom Allah knows. [727]

---

let him praise Allah for it, while whoever found something besides good, he has only himself to blame." (*Muslim*)

[725] These verses were revealed about the Banu Qurayzah tribe of Medina that was obligated by treaty to help the Muslims repel the Meccans' grand alliance that came to attack Medina during the Battle of the Trench. Instead, when representatives from the previously expelled Banu Nadir secretly approached the Banu Qurayzah to defect, the chief of the Banu Qurayzah tribe caved in under pressure and agreed to betray the Muslims.

[726] If a Muslim leader is truly convinced that his community is going to be betrayed by another group with whom they have a treaty, then the Muslim leader can cancel the treaty, so at least they can prepare themselves and not be obligated to be docile and friendly with those who are about to stab them in the back. The Prophet said, "Whoever has a treaty of peace with a people, then he should not untie any part of it or tie it harder until the treaty reaches its appointed term, or he can (publicly) declare the treaty cancelled (in cases of treachery), so they can be on equal terms again." (*Abu Dawud, Tirmidhi, Nisa'i*) Islam also forbids that we make false or fake treaties to deceive an enemy. The eminent scholar An-Nawawi confirmed this when he wrote, "The scholars are agreed that it is permissible to deceive the unbelievers in a war (through battlefield strategies), expect if it means the breaking of a treaty or a trust, in which case it is not permitted." The Prophet said, "There is no people who betray their trusts except that Allah gives their enemies power over them." (*Al Muwatta'*) So even though some non-Muslims falsely accuse Islam of having the ability to make treaties based on deception, the truth is that we must make all treaties in good faith and have the intention to follow them. We can only break a treaty if it is clear that the other side is about to do so, and we must publicly announce that the treaty is void before taking any action against an opponent.

[727] During the days of conflict with the Meccan idol-worshippers, the Muslims had a shortage of warhorses, wagons, platforms and other materials of war. This verse counsels them to acquire such things to make them more formidable in battle or at least to provide deterrence effect. The modern equivalents, of course, are tanks, battleships and the like. Some enthusiastic modern Muslim activists have suggested that Muslims must acquire nuclear capability in order to fulfill the requirements of this verse in a contemporary context. Although Muslim scholars have not considered this issue in depth, I

Whatever you spend in the cause of Allah will be repaid to you, and you won't be treated unfairly. [60] (Remember) that if the enemy leans towards peace, then you also must pursue the path of peace. Trust in Allah, for He's the Hearing and the Knowing. [61]

Be Wary of False Intentions

$\mathcal{I}$f (you detect) that they're really attempting to deceive you (through false peace negotiations,) then Allah is enough for you (against them). He's the One Who strengthened your hand by His help and (with the aid) of the (faithful) believers. [62]

He united the hearts of the believers (in brotherhood, even though they came from so many diverse backgrounds).

Even if you spent everything on earth, you never could've produced that kind of heartfelt (unity by your own efforts), but Allah brought them together, for He is powerful and wise. [728] [63]

You can Overcome Twice Your Number

$\mathcal{O}$ Prophet! [729] Allah is enough for you and for those who follow you among the believers. [64]

---

would venture to say that nuclear weapons are forbidden in Islam given that their use would violate so many Islamic dictates for the proper conduct of war, including the indiscriminate killings of civilians, women, children, animals, the resultant radiation that would harm the environment for wide distances (and centuries) and the unnecessary destruction of property not directly related to a battlefield. Thus, in my humble understanding, a properly constituted Islamic government, guided by authentic Islamic principles, has no choice but to work for the banning of such weapons from every nation on earth. See 2:190 and footnote.

[728] The Prophet united together in faith many different groups that would have been, but for the sake of Islam, at each other's throats. The Meccan migrants to Medina had no natural love for the citizens of Yathrib (Medina). The people of Yathrib, itself, were divided into two tribes, the Auws and the Khazraj, which had often warred with each other. The miscellaneous converts represented many races, colors and ethnic groups, which included both free people and former slaves, as well as Arabs, Asians, Africans and Jews. They would not have naturally flocked together in brotherhood in any other circumstance. Islam brought all of these people together, and it is this multicultural blending power of Islam that is often praised as the answer to racism. The Prophet said during his farewell sermon that there is no superiority based upon race and that all people are merely the children of Adam, and he was made from dust. Then he said the best person is the one who is the most thoughtful about Allah (and this is independent of race, class, gender or any other standard).

[729] The Prophet's uncle 'Abbas was one of those Meccans taken prisoner. He had in his possession twenty ounces of gold, as he was one of the quartermasters of the Meccan army who was charged with procuring food for the men. When the Prophet came to see him, 'Abbas said he had been a secret Muslim in Mecca. Then he asked if he could be freed and if that gold could be used to pay for his ransom. The Prophet declined, saying that only Allah knew if he was a true Muslim, for he had marched against the Muslims. This verse was revealed to the Prophet in answer to 'Abbas' question. Then the Prophet said that the gold in question was part of the funds used to fight against the Muslims and was thus forfeit. The Prophet then made 'Abbas responsible for ransoming his nephew 'Aqeel, as well. 'Abbas began to plead poverty, but then the Prophet asked him about the gold he had left with his wife for her and her sons' upkeep should anything happen to him at Badr. 'Abbas was astonished and asked how the Prophet knew about his secret savings and its purpose. The Prophet replied, "Allah told me about it." 'Abbas declared that no one knew what he had done except himself and Allah, and then he declared himself a true and sincere Muslim. Later on, when the Prophet was distributing the spoils of Badr in Medina, 'Abbas came and asked for some, too. The Prophet said he could take some, and 'Abbas stuffed his robe full of whatever he could fit in its folds. He asked for help to carry everything, but the Prophet refused to help him. So 'Abbas dropped several things and hobbled away clutching as much treasure as he could manage, leaving an astonished Prophet puzzling over his uncle's greediness. In later years, after his fortunes had risen twenty-fold, 'Abbas used to say that Allah repaid him that twenty ounces of gold he lost by increasing his wealth twenty times – a prophecy in this verse for him that came true! (*Ma'ariful Qur'an*)

O Prophet! Rally the believers to battle. [730]

If there are twenty among you who persevere, they can beat two hundred; if a hundred, they can beat a thousand of the faithless, for those who cover over (their ability to have faith) are devoid of reason. [65]

For the moment, Allah has eased (your burden), because He knows you're at a disadvantage (in men and material).

As it is now, if there are a hundred persevering people among you, they can beat two hundred. If a thousand, they can beat two thousand by Allah's leave, for Allah is with the persevering. [66]

Prisoners of War

It's not right for a prophet to start taking prisoners of war (wholesale, just in order to collect their ransoms,) when he hasn't even subdued the land.

You (believers) want the temporary goods of this lower world, while Allah wants (to give you the rewards) of the next life, and Allah is powerful and wise. [731] [67]

If it wasn't for prior permission granted by Allah, [732] you would've been punished severely for (the ransoms) you took, [68] but go ahead and lawfully enjoy (the profits) you previously made from the war (through prisoner release payments),

---

[730] On the day of Badr, the Prophet told his men, "Get ready to march forth towards a Paradise as wide as the heavens and the earth." A man named 'Umayr asked if it was truly that big, and the Prophet said it was. Then 'Umayr said, "Excellent. Excellent." When the Prophet asked him why he said it, the man replied that he wanted to live in it. The Prophet said he would indeed get to enter it. Then 'Umayr threw the dates he was eating on the ground and said, "If I've lived until I finished eating those dates, then it will indeed be a long life." He fought vigorously until he lost his life that day.

[731] The Arabs had a custom whereby a captured enemy could be freed if his people paid a ransom or fine to those who had captured him. There was no concept of holding enemy prisoners for long periods of time, unless they were made into slaves or objects of torture. Thus, many Arabs looked upon war as a way to enrich themselves, as the more prisoners they captured, the more money they received in slave sales, ransoms or release payments. During the Battle of Badr, when the Muslims routed a superior force of idol-worshippers, some seventy pagans were taken into custody. A report in Tirmidhi states that Angel Gabriel came to the Prophet and said that if the Muslims ransomed the 70 men, instead of executing them, then in the next battle with the pagans, an equal number of Muslims would fall. When the Prophet told the companions a great debate ensued. 'Umar wanted to kill the prisoners, while Abu Bakr wanted to free them either without ransom as a gesture of good-will to the people of Mecca or with ransoms to fund the Cause. The Prophet inclined towards mercy and took the middle position (at the urging of the majority) of allowing his followers to ransom the prisoners back to the Meccans. (Some of the Meccan prisoners, who were literate, and whose families couldn't afford the release payment were granted parole if they taught Muslim children in Medina how to read and write.) There are numerous other *hadith* reports in which the Prophet counsels good treatment of prisoners of war, and verses 70-71 in this chapter seem to require that POWs be treated kindly, for they one day might convert. 'Umar's objection about the focus on ransoms was addressed in this verse chastising the Prophet for the ransoms. The Prophet exclaimed, after this verse was revealed, "If a punishment came down from the sky, nonoe of us would be spared except for 'Umar. Truly he forbade me and I didn't listen." (*al-Muqatil*)

[732] Before the Battle of Badr, the Prophet told his men that some people from his own tribe of Banu Hashim were in the pagan army and that they had no desire to fight the Muslims, but they had been compelled to join the Meccan force. He, therefore, asked the Muslims that if they recognized any men from his own clan to spare them in the battle. (*Ibn Is-haq*) They could then ransom them later. That's what this 'permission' probably refers to. In normal circumstances, no commander should tell his men in advance of a battle to be on the lookout for specific people to spare among the enemy. Another interpretation of this verse is that before Badr, taking war booty or ransoms was not explicitly allowed, but the command to allow it did exist in Allah's book of knowledge and was thus revealed to allow it.

but be mindful of Allah, for Allah is forgiving and merciful. [733] [69]

The Case of 'Abbas, One Captive of Badr

O Prophet! Say to the captives that you're holding, "*If Allah finds any good in your hearts, then He'll give you something better than what's been taken from you, and He'll forgive you, for Allah is forgiving and merciful.*" [70]

If any of them intend to betray you, then (know that) they've already betrayed Allah. That's why He gave you power over them, for Allah is full of knowledge and wisdom. [71]

Walking on the Path to Allah

*T*hose who believe and migrate and who struggle with their wealth and their lives in the cause of Allah, as well as those who give them refuge and help – they're the close allies of each other. [734]

As for those who believe but who don't migrate (from a hostile land), you're not obligated to protect them until they migrate (to an Islamic territory).

Though if they seek your help in religious matters, then it's your duty to help them, unless it would be against a people with whom you've made a treaty.

---

[733] Some commentators have taken an extreme view and are of the opinion that this verse is rebuking the Prophet for having taken prisoners at all, and they feel that this verse is saying that the Prophet should have executed the prisoners captured at Badr, as 'Umar ibn al-Khattab had urged. What is more likely is that this verse was revealed to rebuke the Muslims for being so interested in making money off of captured prisoners when the foe (the Meccans) was still a threat. Thus, the Muslims are exhorted to focus on achieving victory rather than focusing on profiteering. The Prophet reportedly said later on, "A severe punishment from Allah for our policy was very close, and if it would have befallen us, only 'Umar ibn al-Khattab and Sa'd ibn Mu'adh would have been spared." (Those two objected most forcefully to the ransoming.) Despite the background story, it is an untenable position to say that this verse is calling for the automatic execution of prisoners of war, especially given the fact that the Prophet was given two choices, and Abu Bakr even proposed a third. Such an extreme position (calling for mandatory execution of prisoners of war) is not directly deducible by what is said in this verse, nor is it borne out by later actions of the Prophet (for he took prisoners of war in all later battles, as well, and forbade the killing or mutilating of them). This verse doesn't say it's wrong to take captives *as a principle,* for there are always those who will surrender, and if taking prisoners were forbidden or executing prisoners were mandatory, then what purpose would verse 70 of this chapter serve, which counsels talking about faith and Allah's mercy with prisoners of war? Again, this verse is merely cautioning against eager war-profiteering before final victory is achieved. The issue was soon settled by the revelation of verse 47:4, which gives Muslims the choice to either free prisoners for goodwill or ransom them. (Proven war criminals can be tried and executed, however.) The next two verses that follow allow the Muslims to keep what they earned from the ransom payments they received at that time, but they also caution them to be careful in the future so they can remain focused. The fact that the Prophet always treated prisoners well and exhorted others to do so is a greater testament against the views of extremists who let harshness overshadow their understanding. Muslims (and Christians) universally hold that part of the mission of Jesus was to moderate the harshness of the Jewish legal scholars; yet, these same Muslims never believe they could ever be guilty of the same shortcoming themselves! Think of how many Meccan prisoners from Badr accepted Islam later on and became companions of the Prophet, including 'Ikrimah, the son of Abu Jahl, and Abu Al-As, the husband of the Prophet's own daughter Zaynab! Contrary to how this verse is usually translated into English, the Arabic word *ithkhan* (to subdue utterly) does not automatically mean bloodshed or slaughter, but comes from the root that means to thoroughly subjugate, subdue or negate the power of another. (*Ma'ariful Qur'an*)

[734] Ostensibly, this verse is speaking about the Muslims in Mecca who were ordered to migrate to Medina. After Mecca was captured, the Prophet said there was no more need for Meccan Muslims to flee to Medina, so this injunction was superseded by circumstances. There is, of course, a wider principle here, and the commentators have suggested the meaning as I have rendered it.

Remember that Allah is watching everything you do. [735] [72]

Those who cover over (their ability to believe) are the supporters of each other. Unless you (trust each other) likewise, then there will be turmoil throughout the earth and great corruption besides. [73]

Those who believe, who migrate and who strive in the cause of Allah, along with those who give them refuge and help them – they're the real believers!

They'll have forgiveness and a generous share of resources (in Paradise). [74]

Those who believe later on, who migrate and strive hard alongside of you, are one with you, as well, but ties of familial relationship have precedence (in legal matters) in the Book of Allah, [736] and Allah knows about all things. [75]

---

[735] Whenever the Prophet would send an expedition of men to face an enemy in the countryside, (and there were many bedouin tribes intent on raiding Medina), he used to counsel the commander in the following words: "Fight in the Name of Allah, and in Allah's cause. Fight those who reject Allah. When you meet your pagan enemy, then call out to them to accept one of three choices, and whichever they agree to, accept it and turn away from them. First, call them to embrace Islam. If they agree, accept it from them and turn away from them. (If they do accept Islam,) then further ask them to leave their (pagan) land and come to where the Migrants (who fled persecution) live. Tell them that if they do this, they'll have both the rights and the duties of a Migrant. If they (accept Islam but) refuse (to migrate) and want to stay in their own land, then tell them that they'll be considered just like any other Muslim bedouins and that Allah's law will still apply to them just as it does to all believers, though they won't have any share in war booty or seized goods, unless they perform *jihad* with the other Muslims. If they refuse all of this, then ask them to pay the exemption tax. If they accept, then take it from them and turn away from them. If they refuse all of these options, then trust in Allah and fight them." (*Muslim*) (Compare this with Deuteronomy. 20: 10-15.) The compensation tax, or *jizyah*, is a form of annual tax that an able-bodied non-Muslim man pays to the Muslim government under whose protection he is living. It entitles both he and his family to the rights of a citizen, as well as entitles them to protection from enemies, without requiring any men among them to be drafted into the army in times of war. When a Muslim army under the command of the prominent companion, Abu 'Ubaydah, was forced to retreat from the city of Homms in Syria in the face of powerful Byzantine attacks, the Muslim commander gathered all the leaders of the city before abandoning it and returned their *jizyah* payment to them. He explained that since the Muslim government could not protect them, it had no right to their tax money. On a related issue, the Christians of Najran joined the Muslim army and fought under the banner of 'Umar ibn al-Khattab at the Battle of Buwayb in 636; thus, he exempted them from paying the *jizyah*. They later offered to pay the *zakah* tax to the Muslim government, which was double the amount of the *jizyah* rate, and 'Umar accepted their noble offer. The Islamic government is also required to spend funds on its non-Muslim subjects, such as in maintenance of their churches and synagogues, free healthcare, and even welfare payments to the needy. These principles were carried out more or less by most Islamically minded governments from the classical period up until the demise of the Ottoman Empire in the twentieth century. Non-Muslim women, children, the aged, handicapped and infirm, priests, rabbis and monks are exempted from all *jizyah* obligations.
[736] The bonds of brotherhood in Islam are based on mutual faith in Allah, but for legal matters such as inheritance and custody, blood-ties take precedence over faith bonds. When the Muslims from Mecca immigrated to Medina, for a few years the Meccan Muslims and Medinan Muslims would let each other inherit property from each other, because all their other relatives were pagans. Later on, when Muslim families were reuniting and the fabric of Arabia was turning to Islam, the law reverted to a normal lineage-based system. It is forbidden for a Muslim to bequeath anything to a non-Muslim relative. The Prophet said, "No followers of two religions inherit from each other. Therefore, a Muslim doesn't inherit from a disbeliever, nor does a disbeliever inherit from a Muslim." (*Al-Hakim*, with nearly identical reports in *Bukhari* and *Muslim*)

Repentance
9 At-Tawbah
aka Al-Bara'ah
Late Medinan Period

This is the only chapter of the Qur'an that does not begin with an invocation of Allah's mercy. There have been various explanations as to why the traditional phrase of "In the Name of Allah" was left off. Many early Muslims were under the impression that it might be something of a continuation of the last chapter, (and this was the opinion of Caliph Uthman,) while the complimentary view in modern times is that this chapter is unlike all other chapters both in initial tone and content, in that it seems from the outset to be stern and full of warnings to both the remaining pagans of Arabia and the hypocrites. 'Ali ibn Abi Talib explained it exactly in this way by saying that to begin in Allah's name is to have the assurance of His protection, but in this chapter, the opening lines are a revocation of Allah's protection, and thus the introductory invocation of Allah is left off. (*Ma'ariful Qur'an*)

The hidden subtext in this chapter is that Islam was now unstoppable and was clearly on track to ultimate victory. If that weren't a good enough sign for the remaining pagans of Arabia (some of whom had violated their previously signed treaties with the Prophet) and the hypocrites (who still foolishly thought they could stop the progress of Islam), then they truly were as twisted as the Qur'an made them out to be and were, by extension, unworthy of fellowship or entry into Mecca – Allah's holy sanctuary. Thus, verses 1-37 were revealed soon after the conquest of Mecca with a clear purpose: to cancel all treaties made between the treacherous pagans and the Muslim state - only guarantying the peace for the remainder of the traditional truce months. The Muslims were commanded, however, to continue to honor the treaties they had with those pagan tribes that adhered faithfully to their end of the bargain until the treaty durations expired, even as they were reminded of the looming Byzantine threat to the north.

Here is the background for the remaining verses in this chapter. Verses 38-72 were revealed in the middle part of the year 629, and they concern the Prophet's efforts to organize an army for the journey to Tabuk, a border town that was located at the northernmost reaches of Arabia. Here are the events that led up to the Prophet's call to arms. Local client rulers of the Byzantines (the Ghassanids) had murdered some of the Prophet's envoys. Thus, the Prophet felt obligated to organize a military response. Late in the year 629, he sent a force of three thousand men (under the command of his adopted son, Zayd ibn Harith) to Syria, to show that such brutality would not go unanswered. After receiving a call for help from Suhrabil ibn Amr, the king of Basra, the Byzantine Emperor Heraclius sent an army of his own, commanded by his brother Theophanous (Theodore), which, drawing upon many local allied Arab tribes, swelled the defenders to anywhere from 10,000 to 100,000 men. (The reports differ and are sometimes greatly exaggerated.) The two armies met in Syria at the famous Battle of Mu'tah.

Regardless of the true number of enemy troops, the odds against the Muslims were bad, and by all rights the Muslims should have been vanquished handily. On the eve of battle, one companion named 'Abdullah ibn Ruwahah said to the uneasy Muslims: "Men, what you're disliking is the same thing that you've come out in search of, in other words, martyrdom. We're not fighting the enemy with numbers or the strength of multitudes, but we're confronting them with this religion that Allah has honored us with. So come on! Both prospects are fine: victory or martyrdom." Then the men said, "By Allah, Ibn Ruwahah is right."

When the battle commenced, the Byzantine's massive numbers threatened to drown out the Muslims. However, the Muslims used stunningly unorthodox cavalry tactics and were able to avoid being swallowed up by the endless sea of Byzantines. Zayd eventually fell in the battle, however, and his lieutenant, Ja'far ibn Abi Talib, took command. When he, too, fell, the third man to take control of the Muslim force, 'Abdullah ibn Ruwahah, said aloud to those around him, "O my soul! If you're not killed, you're bound to die anyway. This is the fate of death overtaking you. What you wished for, you've been granted. If you do what they (Zayd and Ja'far) have done, then you're guided aright!" He fell in the battle shortly thereafter. (Meanwhile, back in Medina, the Prophet sorrowfully informed the people about the death of those prominent companions, before news had ever reached the city. When Ja'far's family was informed of what the Prophet had foreseen, they began to weep uncontrollably, and the Prophet asked them not to weep, for Ja'far was, he explained, now in Paradise.)

After fierce and desperate fighting, Khalid ibn Walid was given command and led a fighting retreat complete with a clever ruse to make it seem as if he were receiving fresh troops. The Byzantines, being stunned by the fierce bravado of the Muslims, also withdrew, but not before claiming victory. When Khalid led the beleaguered survivors back to Medina, some people actually started berating the men as cowards who should have died on the battlefield (citing verses 8:15-16). However, the Prophet came out and stopped the people from saying this, telling them, "No, they're strugglers in Allah's cause who will fight again another day." (Verses 8:65-66 were revealed allowing Muslims to retreat if the odds were more than two to one against them.)

The bold gambit of the Muslims did impress many southern Syrian and southern Iraqi tribes, and thousands of people from these semi-independent tribes (who were previously allied to either the Byzantines or Persians) accepted Islam. According to the historian Nicephorus, Heraclius was aware of this problem and traveled to Antioch to plan his next move. His strategy would involve, not surprisingly, brute force. The Byzantines sought to crush the progress of Islam by harassing and oppressing any tribes that converted. (Eventually they began to position troops for a proposed assault on Medina, itself!) After the Byzantines began executing some tribal chieftains who had accepted Islam, and with scattered reports that the Byzantines were organizing Syrian Arabs for an invasion of the south, the Prophet had no choice but to organize an army to meet this northern threat.

Thus, in September of the year 630, the Prophet himself marched an army of 30,000 people (including many women volunteers) northward to Tabuk in response to the threat of the Byzantines. (Many hypocrites sought exemptions from service, however, and feared leaving Medina due to the fact that the Muslims were so poorly equipped. There was also a heat wave afflicting the region, dampening the enthusiasm of the weak at heart.) The Byzantines, however, still smarting from their experience at Mu'tah, wound up withdrawing all their forces from northern Arabia, and no actual fighting took place.

The Prophet used his time in the region (about twenty days) to cement further alliances and also to extract promises of tribute from those tribes that had previously helped the Byzantines, particularly the Ghassanid tribe. (Some local chieftains, impressed with the Muslims, began to convert, as well.) This successful expedition by the Prophet resulted in offers of allegiance from rulers and chiefs all over the Arabian Peninsula, southern Syria and southern Iraq. And so, the Prophet returned to Medina at the head of a triumphant mission.

Then, verses 73-129 were revealed after the Prophet returned home, and they address a variety of issues related mostly to this campaign and also to the hypocrites.

(This is a declaration) of exemption [737] from Allah and His Messenger to those pagan tribes with whom you've made treaties, (and who've been unfaithful to them). [1]

You (pagans) may travel (safely) anywhere you wish throughout the land during the (next) four months, but know that your (treacherous) deeds will never frustrate Allah, for Allah is certainly going to bring humiliation down upon those who reject (the truth). [2]

(This is) an announcement from Allah and His Messenger to all the people gathered on the day of the Great Pilgrimage (in Mecca) that Allah and His Messenger are dissolving all (treaty) obligations with the idol-worshippers.

If you (treacherous idol-worshippers) would only repent, it would be best for you, but if you turn away, then know that you can't frustrate Allah, so give the news of a painful punishment to those who suppress (their faith). [3]

(However, those treaties) that you've made with those idol-worshippers who *have been* faithful to the terms, and who *didn't* give aid to any of your enemies, are not cancelled, so fulfill your obligations with them to the end of (each treaty's) term. [738] Indeed, Allah loves those who are mindful (of their obligations). [739] [4]

Now when the sacred (truce) months have passed, [740] fight the (double-crossing) idol-worshippers wherever you find them. [741] Capture them, besiege their

---

[737] The Prophet had peace treaties with many pagan bedouin tribes, and some honored them while others continued to raid Muslim interests. After the fall of Mecca, the Muslim situation became more secure, and the shaky treaties that provided at least a semblance of security for the Muslims in Medina could be reevaluated based on current conditions. Those bedouins who honored their treaties would continue to enjoy them, but those bedouins who used their treaties as a shield to hide behind, striking out when they pleased, were put on notice that their treaties were being cancelled after the passage of the sacred months. Thus, the Prophet was "exempted" from honoring treaties with those who did not honor them with him. This revelation gave fair warning to all of Arabia, and thus the scholars conclude that any Muslim government is required to make public its repudiation of any treaties before taking any action against its enemies.

[738] This verse refers to the tribes of Banu Kinanah, Banu Damurah and Banu Mudlaj who were still honoring the terms of the treaties they agreed to with the Prophet and affirmed in the precincts of Mecca. (There were nine months left on those treaties.)

[739] Among the many slanderous and false charges made by some critics against Islam is the mistaken notion that a Muslim government can cancel any treaty it makes at a whim. They cite this chapter as proof and make all kinds of insinuations about the alleged untrustworthy nature of treaties any Muslim would sign. Their lack of understanding is pitiful, and their hypocrisy is enormous. Verses 1-4 contain principles that any modern government or international institution – even the common sense of the masses – would accept. Obey treaty obligations strictly. However, if the other side is clearly violating their end of the bargain, then such a treaty is no treaty at all and should be discarded *with fair notice.* The Prophet never broke the terms of any treaty he signed. Rather, it was the other side that would always break the deal first, and then the Prophet was free to act, such as in the case of the Meccans breaking the terms of the Treaty of Hudaybiyyah, when they supported their allies in an attack on a tribe allied with Medina.

[740] Even if individual treaties expired before the coming of the next pilgrimage season, an extension was given to each hostile tribe until the end of the truce months, so public announcements could reach all over Arabia that their day of reckoning for their treachery was due. (*Ma'ariful Qur'an*)

[741] After the customary truce months were over, the Prophet's plan was to subdue the pagan tribes who had used their treaties as a cover to create further mischief. This verse has been misinterpreted, however, by both religious extremists and critics of Islam to somehow mean that a Muslim state is meant to be in *perpetual war* against all non-Muslims all around it. Despite the fact that this is a

(settlements) and ambush them at every outpost.

However, if they repent, establish prayers and give in charity, then leave them to their way, for Allah is forgiving and merciful. [5]

If an individual idol-worshipper asks you for security, then grant safe passage to them so they can have the opportunity to hear the word of Allah.

Then escort them to a place where they can be safe. (They deserve this gracious treatment), for they're a people who don't know (about Allah's way of life). [742] [6]

Those Who Break Treaties willfully must be Opposed

*H*ow can there be a treaty with idol-worshippers in the sight of Allah and His Messenger, other than with those with whom you've made a treaty near the Sacred Mosque?

As long as they're true (in their word) to you, then stay true (in your word) to them, for Allah loves those who are mindful (of their honest obligations). [7] Again, how can (there be treaties with idol-worshippers), [743] especially given the fact that if they overpowered you, they would neither respect family ties nor treaty obligations? [744]

---

fallacious leap of meaning, both parties fail to realize that this verse, in historical context, is directed squarely against a particular group of idol-worshippers who were guilty of a specific crime, that of betraying their treaties. If there is any wider lesson in this verse for Muslims in later times, it's that permission is given to cancel the treaties and fight against those who make treaties with you but then betray the terms of those treaties first. By the way, after the Prophet's passing, the first caliph, Abu Bakr, used this verse to justify declaring war on some southern tribes who were Muslims, but who refused to pay the required charity any longer. These were called the Wars of the *Ridda*, or Apostasy.
[742] Even though a group may be an enemy, it doesn't mean that every individual among them desires to fight or work against you. An allowance must be made for such people who come to you and ask for safe passage, information or asylum. They can also have the opportunity to see Muslims firsthand and hear and experience the reality of their beliefs. Perhaps they were filled with misconceptions before. In any case, they cannot be forced to convert (see 2:256). If they desire to remain pagans, then see them to a safe land where they can dwell. The scholars say that this verse also means that non-Muslim ambassadors and emissaries are guaranteed safety during their journeys to and from the seat of the Muslim government. The Prophet always granted ambassadors and message carriers diplomatic immunity. After the conquest of Mecca, the Prophet also granted four months of immunity to those few hostile Meccans who decided to flee the Muslim advance. Later on, nearly all of them accepted Islam, even 'Ikrimah, the son of Abu Jahl!
[743] How can you contract a treaty with a people who will betray the terms of the treaty, work against you and then overpower you? How can you do it when they'll disregard all social and political norms and work to oppress you, even though you might be related to some of them by blood and even though their sworn treaties are supposed to prevent them from harming you? Think of all the international treaties that have been signed among nations in modern times from the Geneva Convention and Nuclear Non-Proliferation Accords to the Universal Declaration of Human Rights and the numerous conventions against torture; yet, these have been flouted by many signatory governments with impunity and hubris! When only one side keeps a promise, it is best to scrap your agreement and start over.
[744] The word *dhimmah* means contractual obligations. It's the same term used to describe the relationship between an Islamic government and the non-Muslims living under its authority and protection. In exchange for the payment of an annual tax known as the *jizyah* (which is usually slightly higher than the *zakah* rate for Muslims), Christians and Jews become *dhimmis*, or contractual citizens of the state. They are free to practice their own religion and choose their own local leaders. They are afforded all legal rights under civil law and are not obligated to be drafted into the army in times of war. For its time, this concept of legal multiculturalism was far more advanced than any other system of the day, where the usual policy of any government back then was either to kill or banish those of another religion or to convert them forcibly. (The Bible also has a system for dealing with subject peoples, though it seems very politically incorrect to discuss it. See Deuteronomy 20:10-16 for example.) It must be noted that despite the alarmist claims of some critics of Islam, the function of an Islamic state is not to subjugate non-Muslims and make them pay taxes until they convert. If non-

They say what you want to hear, but their hearts are filled with loathing towards you, for most of them are disobedient wrongdoers. [8]

They've sold the signs of Allah for a miserable price and have hindered people from His way.

What they've done is utterly criminal! [9] Indeed, when it comes to a believer, they neither respect family ties nor obligations, and thus they'll go beyond all bounds! [10]

Yet, despite all of that, if they repent, establish prayer and give in charity, then they'll become your brothers in religion. That's how We explain the verses for people who understand. [11]

However, if they betray their agreements after giving their word and then taunt you about your religion, [745] then fight the leaders of rejection, [746] for they have no beliefs that would constrain them. [12]

And *shouldn't* you fight against people who betray their agreements and plot to drive away the Messenger and who take aggressive action against you first? Are you scared of them? By all rights, you should fear Allah, if you truly believe. [13]

So fight against them, and Allah will punish them by your hands and humiliate them.

(He'll) help you against them and heal the (bruised) feelings of the believers [14] by calming the sense of outrage within their hearts.

Allah turns toward whomever He wants, and Allah is full of knowledge and wisdom. [15]

Did you think you were just going to be left alone before Allah could distinguish who among you has striven hard (in His cause) and who has restrained himself from taking others as close intimates in preference to Allah, His Messenger and (the community of) believers? Allah is well-informed of all that you do. [16]

Muslims migrate into an Islamic state to settle down, they become *dhimmis*. If a non-Muslim state makes war on the Islamic state and if the Islamic state begins to achieve victory, then when the non-Muslim state calls for a negotiated peace, the Islamic state is obligated to enter peace negotiations [2:193]. If the non-Muslim state that attacked the Islamic state does not sue for peace and is instead vanquished in the war, its citizens become *dhimmis* and are thereafter protected by the Islamic state. An Islamic state can exist side-by-side with non-Muslim states, as long as peace and good relations are maintained [2:190]. (It must be noted that Muslim countries today, with their secular leaders, kings, dictators, and odd mixtures of culture, Western political trappings and pseudo-religion do not generally qualify as *Islamic* states in the traditional sense.) Remember that the treaties that the Prophet made with the Jews of Medina were treaties between equal parties; they were not *dhimmi* contracts, and the Prophet never broke any treaty he made with Jewish or Christian entities. The Prophet once said, "Beware! Whoever is cruel and hard on (a non-Muslim) with whom you have a treaty, or who curtails his rights, burdens him in more than he can bear, or takes anything away from him against his will, I shall be his prosecutor on the Day of Judgment." (*Abu Dawud*) He also said, "My Lord has prohibited me from wronging anyone protected by a treaty or anyone even besides that." (*Ma'ariful Qur'an*)

[745] This is the verse that Muslims use to justify fighting against those who mock and belittle Islam or its Prophet. Libel against revered religious figures is a crime in Islamic law. This is not the same as criticism of the *misapplication* of that figure's teachings, it must be remembered, nor can this principle be used to stifle healthy religious diversity. It covers mocking and taunting of the sacred, and in this Islam would also extend such protections to the reputation of all other prophets such as Jesus and Moses. Western cultures used to have strong laws against the mocking of their sacred symbols, though militant secularism has made the ridicule of religion and holy figures a praiseworthy activity in modern times. (*Ibn Kathir*)

[746] In other words, don't bother with ordinary people who are being misled by their leaders, propagandists and hate-mongers. Fight against the head of the snake, for the ignorant masses don't know what they're doing or what's being done to them most of the time.

Only the Faithful should Control Places of Worship

𝒥t's not the place of idol-worshippers [747] to maintain the prayer-houses [748] of Allah, for they've given proof against themselves that they reject (Him). Their efforts are useless, and they're going to dwell in the Fire. [749] [17]

Allah's prayer-houses must be maintained only by those who believe in Allah and the Last Day and who establish prayer, give in charity and fear none but Allah. [750] They're the ones who (can be considered) to be rightly guided; (thus, they'll treat those places of worship with proper reverence). [18]

Are you (of the opinion) that merely giving water to pilgrims and maintaining the Sacred Mosque (in Mecca) is somehow equal to (the sacrifices made for Allah's sake) by those who (truly) believe in Allah and the Last Day and who struggled in the cause of Allah? They're not equal in Allah's sight, and Allah doesn't guide an oppressive people. [751] [19]

Those who believed (in Allah), who migrated and who struggled in the cause of Allah with their wealth and their lives, are more valuable in the sight of Allah, and they are the ones who will be successful. [20]

Their Lord has given them the good news of mercy from His Own Self, of His satisfaction and of gardens filled with everlasting delights that will (be theirs) forever! [21] They will live within them forever, and with Allah are the greatest rewards! [22]

Making the Choice

𝒪 you who believe! [752] Don't take your fathers or your brothers as close allies

---

[747] It is said that this passage was revealed in response to the ongoing contention of many pagan Meccans that they were sincere custodians of Allah's holy shrine in Mecca. The words of the Prophet's uncle 'Abbas, who was captured several years before this revelation at the Battle of Badr, are indicative of this viewpoint. When he was brought to Medina, many of his relatives who had become Muslim and who had migrated with the Prophet began scolding him for believing in idols and cutting off family ties. 'Ali ibn Abi Talib was especially hard in his accusations. 'Abbas said in his defense, "What's wrong with you, for you're only mentioning our shortcomings and not our strong points?" When 'Ali asked what those were, 'Abbas replied, "We (pagans) fill the sacred shrine with pilgrims; we serve the Ka'bah, and we give water to the pilgrims while freeing those in debt." (*Asbab ul-Nuzul*)

[748] The term *masjid* is usually translated as mosque. Yet, the word means a place of prostration or worship. It is used in a general sense in this verse and can apply to any type of religious temple devoted to the One God, be it a church, synagogue or a mosque, and therefore I've translated it in the generic sense of a prayer-house, i.e., place of worship. Idol-worshippers have no business maintaining any of them.

[749] This passage points out to the pagans that those who rejected the supremacy of Allah in favor of man-made idols had no business operating a shrine dedicated to Allah – no matter how they tried to justify it. Would anyone imagine idolaters maintaining St. Peter's Basilica in Rome or any other church, mosque or synagogue? It is thoroughly illogical, and this verse points out that only those who believe in Allah sincerely, and in no other false gods or idols, have the right to be in charge of holy places dedicated solely to the One God.

[750] The Prophet once said, "If you notice that a person is at the mosque on time (for prayer,) then be assured of his true faith, for Allah the Most High said..." And then he quoted this verse [9:18]. (*Tirmidhi*)

[751] Later on, after 'Abbas had accepted Islam, he had a discussion with 'Ali ibn Abi Talib and Talhah ibn Shaybah in which he and Talhah boasted of their services to the Ka'bah and how after Islam that was all they needed to do. 'Ali replied that he had been praying facing the Ka'bah six months before any of them, and he also was striving with the Prophet all along, and thus his service to Allah was more valuable than their services to the Ka'bah. They asked the Prophet about it and verses 19-22 were revealed. (*Ma'ariful Qur'an, Muslim*)

[752] When new converts to Islam in Mecca were asked to migrate to Medina, they were often inundated with requests from their non-Muslim relatives to stay where they were. Even after the Conquest of

if they love concealing (the truth of Allah) more than having faith (in Him). Anyone who does that is doing wrong. [23]

Say (to the believers, who may be inclined to remain among their pagan relatives,) *"If your fathers, brothers, spouses, relatives, financial gains, trade deals that you're afraid will suffer or the lovely homes you live in are more beloved to you than Allah, His Messenger or in struggling in His cause, then you just wait until Allah's command comes to pass.* [753] *Allah doesn't guide people who are rebellious."* [24]

Allah Helps the Righteous

*A*s it is, Allah has already helped you on many battlefields. On the day of (the Battle of) Hunayn, however, when your great numbers made you feel overconfident - *that by itself did nothing for you.* [754]

The wide earth hemmed you in (as you passed through the narrow valley and were suddenly taken by surprise in ambush). Thus, you turned back in retreat. [25]

Mecca, converts from the pagan tribes of the countryside continued to face this familial pressure to remain at home. This passage asks such converts to make a choice: either remain with the pagans for worldly reasons or migrate for the sake of Allah. (*Ma'ariful Qur'an*)

[753] The 'command' is thought to be Allah's decision of judgment against those who disobeyed the order to migrate. It could either be misfortune in this life or punishment in the next. (*Ma'ariful Qur'an*)

[754] In the year 630, just after Mecca surrendered to the Prophet, the nearby city of Ta'if organized an army to fight against the Muslims under the command of one Malik ibn 'Awf an-Nadri. The two powerful tribes of Hawazin and Thaqif, who were the nucleus of the new enemy, were so confident of victory that they ordered all their women, children, camels and sheep to accompany them to the battlefield, thinking it would make them that much more earnest to win the fight. When the Prophet received news of the march of this new foe, he organized an army that numbered over twelve thousand men and set out from Mecca to meet this new enemy. (He asked the people of Mecca, his former foes, for the loan of weapons to equip his army. They were pleased that he asked, rather than took, and provided many weapons.) When the Muslims entered into a narrow valley named Hunayn, they were suddenly ambushed by the enemy – almost 20,000 strong - with a rain of arrows followed by an infantry charge, and the startled Muslims retreated in utter confusion. The Prophet and a few faithful companions not only stood their ground, however, but they continued to advance, and even Abu Sufyan, the recent convert, stood by the Prophet and helped defend him from the rushing assault of the enemy. (He later remarked that he would rather be ruled by a Qurayshi man than by a man of Ta'if!) The Prophet called for the Muslims to return and asked his uncle 'Abbas to shout loudly to them. 'Abbas cried out, "Companions of the Tree (from the Pledge of Ridwan), Companions of the Chapter of the Calf!" (This was a reference to chapter two of the Qur'an and it's special place in the hearts of many.) Feeling ashamed at their cowardice, the Muslims returned and drove the forces of Ta'if back. Even some embittered Meccans who had come, secretly desiring to kill the Prophet in the confusion, found faith in Allah and instead helped the Prophet! Soon the pagans were on the run. They abandoned their women, children and goods in their camp and ran all the way back to the secure walls of their city. The Muslims took some 6,000 men, women and children captive and then laid siege to the city. The companions asked the Prophet to pray for the ruin of Ta'if, but the Prophet instead prayed for their conversion. Siege engines and catapults were soon brought by the recently converted Muslim tribe of Banu Daws from the south, but after a little less than a month, the Prophet lifted the siege, realizing that a sacred truce month had just arrived. However, he vowed to the beleaguered men of Ta'if that he would return with a new force the following year unless they capitulated. Some days passed, and a delegation of men from Ta'if arrived at the Prophet's camp even before he returned to Mecca. They made offers of peace and then declared their conversion to Islam. They begged for the return of their families and goods. An-Nadri even sent word that both he and his nobles had converted. The Prophet asked the delegation to choose what they wanted returned: their captured men, women and children or their captured goods. They chose their people, and, after calling upon his men to consider freeing the captured people as a gesture of goodwill towards their new brothers-in-faith, the Prophet succeeded in getting the 6,000 captives freed. He also gave a hundred camels to an-Nadri and confirmed him as chief of the city of Ta'if. An-Nadri, who was surprised by the Prophet's generosity, then composed a poem to praise the Prophet and his graciousness. (*At-Tabari*)

Then Allah sent His tranquility down upon the Messenger and upon the believers, and He sent forces (of angels) you couldn't even see. [755] Thus, He punished the faithless, and that's how He repays those who cover (the light of faith within their hearts). [26]

Then after that, Allah accepted the repentance of whomever He wanted to from among those (who fled after the initial ambush), for Allah is the forgiving and merciful. [27]

O you who believe! [756] The idol-worshippers are impure, so don't let them come near the Sacred Mosque after this year of theirs has passed. [757] If you're afraid of becoming poor (on account of the financial losses that this ban might cause),

then Allah will enrich you as He wills from His Own bounty, for Allah is full of knowledge and wisdom. [28]

Be Prepared to Defend Yourselves

(Don't be afraid to) fight against those who don't believe in Allah and the Last Day, who don't forbid what Allah and His Messenger have forbidden, and who don't accept the true way of life. [758]

(If) those who received the scripture (before you make war upon you, then fight them) until they (agree) to pay (an annual) tax from their own hand, [759]

---

[755] One of the Hawazin tribesmen later narrated how angels had routed them, saying, "When we met the Messenger of Allah and his companions on the Day of Hunayn, they didn't remain on the battlefield for more than the time it takes to milk a sheep! (The Muslims fled after the ambush.) When we routed them we chased them until we came upon the rider of the white mule, who was the Messenger of Allah. Suddenly, men with glowing and handsome faces intercepted us and said, 'Disgrace their faces! Go back!' So we ran away, but (the returning Muslims) followed us, and that was the end for us." (*At-Tabari*)

[756] After the conquest of Mecca, pagan pilgrims continued to enter Mecca, and they continued to perform their religious rites, sometimes naked, often clapping and whistling, as they were wont to do. Thus, after a short time had passed, the Prophet forbade the future entry of idolaters into Mecca, and this verse was the source for his ruling. (*Ma'ariful Qur'an*)

[757] This verse mentions specifically that only pagans are prohibited from entering Mecca. In the years immediately following the Prophet's passing, Jews and Christians were still allowed to enter the city. The early scholar, Jabir ibn 'Abdullah, said this verse does not apply to non-Muslim servants nor to *dhimmis* (Jews and Christians under contractual relationship to the Muslim government). (*Ibn Kathir*) Later on, during the rule of 'Umar ibn 'Abdul-'Aziz (d. 720), the famed Umayyad caliph, the order was given (by his decree) to extend the ban for entering Mecca to Jews and Christians, as well. Since that time Muslim orthodoxy has enshrined this principle, leaving only the Hanafi school of Islamic Law holding that Jews and Christians are allowed to enter Mecca. (There has never been any bar on Jews and Christians (or Zoroastrians) from living elsewhere in the Arabian Peninsula.) However, all schools of law agree that no non-Muslims are allowed to preach or build houses of worship in Arabia, based upon the saying of the Prophet that Arabia cannot be home to two religions. There is no prohibition for other Muslim countries to have the presence of churches, synagogues and other non-Muslim houses of worship.

[758] In historical context, this verse was revealed after the Byzantine Empire had already become openly hostile to the Muslims of Medina and a war footing was in place. The purpose of this verse is as a rousing call for the Muslims to face a declared enemy that happened to be culturally Christian (the Byzantines).

[759] There is a generally accepted rate for the *jizyah* tax, which is the tax that non-Muslim male wage-earners pay to an Islamic government to exempt them from certain duties and Islamic financial taxes and that also guarantees their people the rights of citizenship and protection. The Prophet had made a *jizyah* deal with the Christian tribe of Najran that they should forward two thousand articles of clothing to Medina annually. (Considering the large size of the Najrani Christian tribe, this amounted to about 5% of their gross domestic product. This general amount was further enshrined and confirmed by Caliph 'Umar ibn al-Khattab when he made a *jizyah* deal with the Christian tribe of Bani Taghlib and pegged the rate of annual payment to be twice the rate of the *zakat* that Muslims pay on their yearly accumulated savings and assets. Muslims pay 2.5% annually.) (*Ma'ariful Qur'an*) This prophetic practice also means that *jizyah* arrangements are to be made with the recognized leadership of non-

acknowledging that they've been subdued. [760] [29]

When a Holy Man is Overly Magnified

$\mathcal{T}$he Jews call Ezra a son of God, [761] and the Christians call the Messiah a son of God, but those are just phrases from their mouths.

They do nothing more than copy what the faithless in ancient times used to say. Allah's curse is upon them, and they're greatly deceived! [30]

They've taken their theologians and saints as lords in place of Allah, and also the Messiah, the son of Mary, as well, even though they were ordered to serve none but the One God alone [762] – *there is no god besides Him!* [763]

Muslim entities, and not with individuals. The expression here referencing 'from their hand' means that only those of means can be taxed, and those who 'have nothing in their hand,' are not to be taxed. (*Baydawi*) Those non-Muslims who are categorically exempted from *jizyah* include women, children, the disabled, the handicapped, religious leaders and the very old. (*Ma'ariful Qur'an*)

[760] This verse is not suggesting that Muslims must fight against Jews and Christians for all time until they submit to taxation, as some extremists (and critics of Islam) might believe, and there are ample other verses that make it clear that in Islam war is defensive in nature. When Muslims are at peace with a Jewish or Christian entity, then there is no cause for the Muslims to fight any further or make any attempt to conquer them. This is proven by the following verses: 22:39 (where permission to fight is given only to those who have been wronged); and 2:192-193 (where the establishment of a peace treaty obligates the Muslims to stop fighting - except against evil tyrants). The Prophet concluded a peace treaty with the Christians of Najran, and the Islamic state never fought them. Likewise, the Prophet made treaties with Zoroastrians, Jews and some Christian tribes of southern Syria with no military action involved. It is only the general war with the Byzantines that this verse is referencing.

[761] Not all seventh-century Jews called Ezra, the hero of the Babylonian Return, a 'son' of God. (Though it must be remembered that to Jews, calling someone a 'son' of God implied no biological connection, and the Old Testament labels many people as 'sons' of God to emphasize their holiness and righteousness.) At the Prophet's time, however, there was apparently a sect of Jews living in Yemen who labeled Ezra a 'son' of God, though perhaps only metaphorically. (*Encyclopedia Judaica,* vol. 6.) In addition, the ancient Jewish books of I and II Esdras do describe Ezra in fairly miraculous terms, even going so far as to assert that he was entered into heaven without having to die first.

[762] An Arab pagan named 'Adi ibn Hatim, the son of the legendary chief, Hatim Tai, of whom many stories of chivalry and generosity abound, accepted Christianity in the days before Islam came. During the war between the Meccans and the Muslims in Medina, 'Adi ibn Hatim's tribe, the Banu Tai, fought against the Muslims. Some of his family members were captured, and he felt compelled to resettle in Syria. The Prophet, however, quickly freed 'Adi's relatives, including his sister, and he even gave her generous gifts. Thereafter, she traveled to Syria to meet her brother, and she exhorted him to accept Islam and pay a visit to the Prophet in Medina. He threw caution to the wind and made the two-week journey to Medina. When he finally met the Prophet, he ('Adi) was wearing a silver cross around his neck. The Prophet saw this and recited this verse, but then 'Adi interjected, saying, "They didn't worship (their scholars and saints)!" Thereupon the Prophet replied, "Yes, they did. (Their theologians and saints) used to prohibit what was allowed (for Jews and Christians), and they allowed what was prohibited, and (their followers) obeyed them. This is how they 'worshipped' them." Then the Prophet said, "'Adi, what do you say? Did you run away (to Syria to keep from hearing,) '*Allah is the Greatest,*' proclaimed? Do you know of anything greater than Allah? What made you run away? Did you run away so (you wouldn't have to hear,) '*There is no god other than Allah,*' being proclaimed? Do you know of any god who is more worthy of worship than the One God?" Then the Prophet invited 'Adi to embrace Islam, and he eagerly accepted. Thereafter, the Prophet said, "Truly, the Jews have earned (Allah's) anger, while the Christians are (merely) mistaken." (*Ahmad, Tirmidhi*) See Deuteronomy 6:4-9 or Mark 12:29-30 for related points.

[763] The issue is not that they listened to their scholars, for scholars are important in learning God's religion. (See 16:43) The problem is that the Jews and Christians would ignore or bypass what their scriptures said and ask the scholars directly without bothering to read the scriptures for themselves. Thus, any scholar, priest or rabbi was free to give whatever opinion he wished without worrying that his flock would check on the truth of his ruling. Many examples of this abound, such as the priests of the Middle Ages selling 'indulgences,' which were basically tickets purchased to lessen one's stay in purgatory. Among Jewish rabbis there are also many such practices, such as the writing of spells, good

He is far more glorified than the partners they ascribe to Him! [764] [31]

This is the True Religion and it will Prevail

*T*hey want to put out the light of Allah's (truth) with their mouths, but Allah won't allow anything but the perfection of His light to be completed, no matter how much the faithless hate it. [32]

He's the One Who sent His Messenger with guidance and the true way of life so that it can prevail over all other ways of life, no matter how much the idol-worshippers hate it. [765] [33]

Beware the Corruption of "Men of God"

O you who believe! Truly, there are many theologians and saints who deceptively eat up the wealth of the people, and thus they divert them from Allah's path. [766]

There are those who stow away (untaxed) gold and silver without spending it in Allah's way, so give them the news of a painful punishment. [767] [34]

(That will be) a day when (their wealth) will be made burning hot in the fires of Hell, and it will be used to brand their foreheads, their sides and their backs. [768]

"This is what you stowed away for yourselves! Now experience (the value) of what you stowed away!" [35]

Don't Alter the Calendar to Gain an Advantage

*T*here are twelve numbered months in Allah's sight, [769] and this was recorded

---

luck charms and incantations for sale to the gullible public, of which many examples have been unearthed by archeologists throughout the Middle East. Muslim *imams* and scholars, by the way, are also sometimes guilty of these types of practices.

[764] As in Deuteronomy 6:4-9 or Mark 12:29-30.

[765] The Prophet said, "Allah made the eastern and western regions of the earth come close for me (to see), and the rule of my community will extend as far as I saw." (*Muslim*) The Islamic world grew and expanded continually until the fifteenth century and eventually stretched from Spain and Morocco in the west to Indonesia in the east. Thereafter, it began to shrink, and it continues to crumble around the edges as various non-Muslim powers chip away at it and absorb chunks of it into their nations, a development that the Prophet also foretold in numerous reports.

[766] Most commentators are of the opinion that this verse is a general warning for all religious leaders and that this warning also applies to Muslim religious leaders. The Prophet said, "The slaves of the dollar (*dinar*) are losers. The slaves of the silver coin (*dirham*) are losers." (*Ibn Kathir*)

[767] The famous companion of the Prophet, Salman al-Farsi, had been a Christian for a time and served various priests in Syria. He commented on seeing both honest and dishonest men of the cloth and even once witnessed a priest's hidden stash of gold being uncovered, much to the consternation of his congregation. When this verse was revealed, the Prophet exclaimed, "Perish, all gold! Perish, all silver!" He repeated this phrase three times, and then someone asked him, "Then what kind of wealth should we work towards?" Thereupon he answered him, saying, "A tongue that remembers (Allah), a submissive heart, and a spouse who supports (you) in practicing your religion." (*Zamakhshari*)

[768] The Prophet said of this verse that wealth accumulated by Muslims from which the *zakah* tax was not paid is also included as a source of condemnation on the Day of Judgment. (*Abu Dawud, Ahmad*)

[769] Of the twelve months, the pagan Arabs set aside four as holy or truce months. During those months, people were encouraged to travel for religious purposes and for trade, and hostilities were supposed to be suspended. This was the custom since time immemorial in the Arabian Peninsula, but the various pagan groups played with this sanctity by arbitrarily postponing holy month restrictions as it suited them by changing the date or inserting an extra month at will. Thus, one side in a war between cities or tribes might stop their own offensive activities, while another might continue theirs, saying they're delaying the start of the holy month's restrictions upon them. This was, of course, a chaotic mockery

by Him on the day He created the heavens and the earth. [770]

Four of them have sacred restrictions, and that's the established custom, so do no wrong against yourselves within them (by violating this rule). [771]

Fight against the idol-worshippers in a united front, even as they fight against you in a united front (even during the restricted months,) but know that Allah is with those who are mindful (of Him). [36]

Arbitrarily postponing (restricted months) is an added degree of suppression (of Allah's truth), and those who suppress (their awareness of the truth) are led into doing wrong on account of it. They make it lawful one year (to violate a restricted month) and forbidden another year.

They adjust the number of months restricted by Allah, so (in their eyes) restricted months become lawful! The wickedness of their actions seems good to them, but Allah won't guide a people who suppress (their faith). [37]

Answer the Call to Fight

O you who believe! [772] What's wrong with you? When you're called to go out and fight in the cause of Allah, suddenly you hold tightly to the earth? Do you prefer the life of this world more than the next life? But the life of this world provides such little comfort when compared to the next life! [773] [38]

---

of the concept of truce months. Therefore, in their ongoing struggle with the pagans of Arabia, the Muslims were often at a disadvantage, for the pagans would postpone or advance the restrictions of the truce months at their whim. Meanwhile the Muslims would be divided about what to do when attacked in a holy month, with some wanting to defend themselves and others hesitant to respond and violate the sanctity of the truce month. This passage was revealed to inform the Muslims that if the pagans violate the truce months, then they should be united together in confronting them. (*Ibn Kathir*)

[770] There are two systems in use in our world today to keep track of the passage of the years: the lunar calendar, based on the cycle of the moon; and the solar calendar, which is based on the movement of the earth around the sun. Both of them are built on the principle of twelve months consisting of around thirty days each, though the solar calendar is less accurate and requires periodic adjustment (leap years etc). The early Muslims knew of both systems, and the medieval writer, Ibn al-'Arabi, commented on the utility of both in these words: "The solar calendar is for the benefit of worldly matters, while the lunar calendar is for religious observances." So while modern Muslims (and Jews) often regulate their religious festivals by the lunar cycle, they have generally also made use of the solar calendar currently in ascendancy in this materialistically oriented world.

[771] During the Prophet's last pilgrimage to Mecca, he actually fixed the correct start for the month of Hajj, as among the Arab tribes no one could agree on exactly what day that month started. (*Ma'ariful Qur'an*) The four sacred months are *Dhul Qa'dah, Dhul Hijjah, Muharram* and *Rajab*, and Islam retains only the emphasis that those months are times for increased worship and devotion. The first three months are contiguous in the calendar. As a note of interest, the Arabic word for month, *shahr*, is used exactly twelve times throughout the Qur'an. The word for day, *yawm*, is used 365 times. The plural term for days, *ayyam* and *yawmayn*, are used exactly 30 times. (There are usually thirty days in each month in the Islamic calendar.)

[772] In the year 630, the Prophet received word from visiting Syrian olive traders that the Byzantines had amassed an army and were preparing an attack on Medina. Apparently, word of the success of Islam had reached the Byzantine emperor Heraclius, and he was not one to allow a new power to rise, especially since he had recently concluded a terrible war with the Persians in the year 627. Thus, the Byzantines mobilized and began operations against any Arab tribes that were inclined towards Islam in southern Iraq and Syria. The Prophet organized his followers to march northward to meet this new challenge. The Expedition to Tabuk, as it came to be called, saw no combat, as the Byzantines withdrew unexpectedly. Yet, the Prophet's hand was strengthened in southern Syria and Iraq when he contracted alliances with local rulers all over the area. A faction of hypocrites decided to remain in Medina and thus weakened the potential size and resources of the expedition. Their cowardice is what this passage is referencing.

[773] When the Islamic governor of Egypt, 'Abdul-'Aziz ibn Marwan (the man who married 'Umar ibn al-Khattab's granddaughter and who was the father of the Umayyad Caliph, 'Umar ibn Abdul-'Aziz) was near death, he said to his assistants, "Bring the burial shroud that I will be covered in to me so I

If you don't go out, then He'll punish you severely, and then He'll just replace you with another people. You bring no harm upon Him at all (by refusing to answer His call), for He has power over all things. [39] If you don't help (the Prophet against the Byzantine Romans,) then (you should know that) Allah helped him when the faithless drove him away (from Mecca and tried to hunt him down).

He was just one of two (men hiding out) in a cave when he said to his companion, (Abu Bakr, who was afraid that the Meccans would capture them), *"Don't be afraid, for Allah is with us."* 774

Then Allah sent His tranquility down upon him, and (later, at the Battle of Badr,) He strengthened him with forces (of angels) that you couldn't even see. He brought down utterly the (boasting) claims of the faithless, for Allah's word is the highest of all. 775 Allah is indeed powerful and wise. [40]

March out, whether lightly or heavily equipped, and strive with your wealth and your persons in the cause of Allah. That's best for you if you only knew. [41]

If there would be a guaranteed profit and an easy journey, then they all would follow you, but it's going to be a far distance, (and it will be hard) on them, so much so that (many of them are now falsely) swearing, *"If only we could make it, then we would certainly accompany you."* They're destroying themselves (with their false assertions), for Allah knows that they're lying. [42]

On those Who Made Excuses and Remained at Home

*M*ay Allah forgive you (Muhammad)! 776 Why did you grant anyone exemptions (from joining the Expedition to Tabuk) before you even had the opportunity to see clearly which of them were honest (in their petitions) and which of them were liars? [43]

Those who (really) believe in Allah and the Last Day would never ask to be excused from striving with their wealth and their persons, and Allah knows best who's mindful (of their duty to Him). [44] The only ones who ever ask to be excused are those who don't believe in Allah and the Last Day and whose hearts are filled with doubts - leaving them hesitant in their misgivings. [45]

---

can inspect it." When it was brought before him, he looked at it and said, "Is this all that I'm going to have from this life?" He then turned his back and cried while saying, "Damn you, life! Your abundance is meager; your meagerness is short lived, and you tricked us." (*Ibn Kathir*)

774 The Prophet and Abu Bakr hid out in a cave for three days after they fled their hometown in 622 CE, trying to escape from a Meccan assassination plot. The Meccans sent out patrols and offered a handsome reward for the one who would bring Muhammad back - *dead or alive*. One such patrol came near the cave, and its men dismounted and approached the small opening. Abu Bakr whispered to the Prophet, "If any one of them looks down by his feet, he will see us." The Prophet replied, "Abu Bakr, what do you think about two people who have Allah as their third?" The Meccan bounty hunters found a cobweb covering the cave entrance and also a pigeon's nest. They concluded that the cave had been undisturbed for some time, and they left. (*Ibn Hisham*)

775 When the Prophet and his followers were living under persecution in Mecca, the pagans often boasted of their strength and promised that they would prevail. Now after their defeat, their boasts were brought down to nothingness, and Allah's word prevailed.

776 The Prophet, being soft-hearted, began granting exemptions to people from the general mobilization he had called for earlier for the two-week march northward to Syria. (Many of these exemptions were granted to people who were otherwise fit for service.) Similar to the reason for the revelation of chapter 80, this passage contains an admonition from Allah to the Prophet for such honest errors in judgment. Allah wanted to expose for the believers what was really in their hearts, so each could understand if he was truly obedient or merely paying lip service. This is a prime example of how the Qur'an was an interactive revelation among Allah, the Prophet and those around him, both believers and unbelievers. Through this lively dialogue, if you will, between Allah and the community He was nurturing, one can more easily understand how to apply the Qur'an's guidance in his life.

If they had really intended to march out, then they would've made some kind of preparations for it. Therefore, Allah didn't like that they should march out (anyway, due to the mischief they would've caused along the way), so He hindered them further, and they lagged behind. Thus, they were told, *"Sit with those who stay and sit (at home)."* [46]

If they would've marched out with you, they wouldn't have augmented (your strength). Rather, they would've caused indiscipline (among your men) as they scurried about in your midst, sowing seeds of sedition among you. Some of you would have listened to them, and Allah knows who the corrupt ones are. [47]

As it is, they had already plotted sedition before, and had made your situation unsettled (in the past), even until the truth arrived and the order of Allah became clear, though they hated it. [777] [48]

Hypocrites are Unreliable

*A*mong them are some who said, *"Grant me an exemption, and don't give me a hard trial to face,"* but hadn't they already been tried before (during previous battles)! [778]

Truly, Hellfire surrounds all those who suppress (their faith)! [49]

If something good happens to you, it bothers them, but if some disaster strikes you, they say, *"We prepared ourselves (for this setback) beforehand,"* and then they turn away self-satisfied. [50]

Say (to them), *"Nothing happens to us except what Allah has already recorded for us, and He's our Protector."* So let the believers trust in Allah! [51]

Then tell (them), *"Are you expecting anything else for us other than one of two good possibilities, (either victory or martyrdom)? All the while we're expecting that you'll receive a punishment from Allah, either from His Own Self or from our hands. Just wait and see, and we'll be waiting, too."* [52]

Tell (them), *"Spend whatever you want or whatever you feel compelled to (spend to support the northern expedition,) but it won't be accepted (as a good deed by Allah), for you're a rebelliously disobedient people."* [53]

Their contributions won't be accepted because they rejected Allah and His Messenger. They come to prayers lacking motivation, and they spend (in charity) only reluctantly. [54] So don't be impressed by their money or their sons.

---

[777] During his early days in Medina, the Prophet had to deal with a faction of hypocrites, led by 'Abdullah ibn Ubayy, who stirred up trouble at every turn. Ibn Ubayy later passed away from old age, and the Prophet buried him graciously with respect. However, the hypocrites Ibn Ubayy helped to cultivate remained and continued to work against the Prophet from behind the scenes. Even after Mecca was vanquished without a fight, making Allah's "order" clear, they still tried to create sedition at every turn. It was a faction of these hypocrites who caused two opposing Muslim forces to fight in later years during the rule of 'Ali ibn Abi Talib (the fourth caliph) at the Battle of the Camel in Iraq (656 CE). Ironically, 'Ali commanded one army, and the Prophet's widow A'ishah commanded the other. She led a coalition seeking justice against the killers of Uthman ibn Affan (d. 656), who had been the third caliph, and she and her group thought 'Ali was moving too slowly in this regard. The two groups were preparing to mediate their dispute with negotiations, but the hypocrites, who had placed men in both camps, suddenly rushed out at each other to make it seem as if a battle had been ordered. The unsuspecting men on both sides then flew at each other in a mad rush and chaos broke out. Such was the reach and devious nature of the hypocrites of Medina.

[778] The quotation below that begins this passage was the statement of Jadd ibn Qays, who was a leader among the Banu Salamah tribe. The Prophet had asked him, "Would you like to go and fight the yellow ones (the Romans) this year?" Ibn Qays replied, "Messenger of Allah! Grant me an exemption, and don't put me in turmoil, for by Allah, my people know that there isn't a man who is more attracted to women than I, and I'm afraid that if see the women (of the Romans) that I wouldn't have any patience (to control myself)." So the Prophet granted him an exemption on such a flimsy excuse. Then the Prophet advised the rest of the Banu Salamah tribe to choose another chief. 'Abdullah ibn Ubayy of the Auws tribe also (predictably) asked for an exemption. (*Asbab ul-Nuzul*)

Allah wants to punish them with these things in the life of this world, so they'll leave (this life) with souls that have rejected (Allah). [55]

They swear to Allah that they're on your side, but they're not on your side. They're constantly nervous (that they might be singled out)! [56] If they could find some place to escape to, either a cave or a hideout, they would turn towards it straightaway in a rush. [57]

Hypocrites are Never Satisfied

$\mathcal{A}$mong them [779] are some who talk against you with regards to (how you're distributing) charity. If they're given some, then they're happy, but if they're not (given any), *then they're upset!* [58]

If only they would've been satisfied with what Allah and His Messenger had given them and had said, "*Allah is enough for us! Allah and His Messenger will give us something from His bounty soon enough, and we place our hopes (for material blessings) in Allah.*" [59]

Those Deserving of Charity

$\mathcal{C}$harity is meant for the poor, for the needy, [780] for those whose profession it is to distribute it, [781] for encouraging (recent converts), [782] for the (freeing) of bonded servants, [783] for those (straining under a

---

[779] When the Prophet was distributing some charity, a recent convert from among the bedouins named Hurqoos ibn Zuhayr (*aka* Dhul Huwaysira) was unsatisfied with his share, and he said, "Be fair! Be fair!" 'Umar got angry and asked the Prophet for permission to kill the disrespectful man, but the Prophet stopped him and replied to Hurqoos, "Woe to you! Who is fairer than I am?" Then the Prophet said, "If I weren't fair, then I'd be truly lost!" After Hurqoos left, the Prophet told his companions, "Among this man's descendants will be some whose prayer, when one of you sees it, would make his own prayer seem lacking, and his fast will seem the same as compared to their fast, but they will be rebels in religion, just like an arrow goes through the body of a hunted animal. Wherever you find them, fight them, for truly they're the worst (spiritually) dead people under the cover of the sky." (*Bukhari*) This passage was then revealed about Hurqoos. Years after the Prophet's passing, Hurqoos joined an extremist group of ultra-purists known as the *Kharajites*, and he fell in the Battle of Nahrawan against the caliph's forces. Extremist groups to this day generally follow this deviant ideology, which is based on the notion that all Muslims besides themselves are hopeless sinners in need of correction, though they've renamed themselves in recent years with a nod, ironically, towards the pious ancestors.

[780] The difference between the poor (*fuqara*) and the needy (*miskeen*) is that the poor are people with self-respect who don't beg, whereas the needy are those who are so desperate that they feel they have no choice but to beg. Another way of looking at it is that the poor are those who have a legitimate reason for their condition, such as illness that prevents them from working, whereas the needy are able-bodied people who suffer sudden disaster. The Prophet gave the three cases when an able-bodied person can lawfully beg. These are a debtor who can no longer handle his debts, a person afflicted with disaster that impoverished him, and a man who was stricken with poverty beyond his control, so much so that three of his relatives come to know of it. (*Muslim*) What of an able-bodied person who is under no strain but who chooses to beg? The Prophet said, "Charity should not be given to a rich person or to a person who is physically fit." (*Ahmad, Abu Dawud, Tirmidhi*)

[781] People hired to supervise and distribute charity to the needy can be paid their salaries from the general charity fund.

[782] This stipulation has two purposes. The first is to help indigent or struggling converts. The second is to use cash to further solidify the loyalty of those converts whose influence or skills are useful to the Islamic movement, and for whom financial rewards would be a strong motivation to commit wholeheartedly to the cause. The Prophet employed this strategy with some notables, such as with the chief of Ta'if after he converted to Islam (though he was given gifts from the war booty), and some men received sustained payments throughout Abu Bakr's reign. During the tenure of 'Umar ibn al-Khattab, he cancelled such payments, saying, "Allah has uplifted Islam and is no longer in need of their support."

[783] Slavery, as the Western world understands it, is not a part of Islam. Captives of war can be (but do not have to be) turned into indentured or bonded servants as a consequence of being enemies of Allah's religion, but they have the same basic *human* rights in Islam as any free person and can even petition

load) of debt, for use in the cause of Allah, [784] and also (to help stranded) travelers. These are the stipulations set by Allah, and Allah is full of knowledge and wisdom. [785] [60]

Don't Annoy the Prophet

*A*mong them [786] are some who upset the Prophet when they say, *"He'll listen to anybody."*

Reply to them, saying, *"He listens to what's best for you. He believes in Allah. He believes in the (integrity of) the faithful, and he's a mercy for those who believe."* Whoever upsets the Prophet will have a painful punishment. [61]

They swear to Allah in front of you to impress you, but it would be more appropriate for them to impress (both) Allah and His Messenger, if they're (sincere) believers. [787] [62] Don't they know that the fire of Hell is reserved for all who oppose Allah and His Messenger and that that's where they'll have to stay? That's the worst humiliation of all! [63]

The Apprehension of the Hypocrites

*T*he hypocrites [788] are afraid that a chapter might be revealed about them, exposing what's really in their hearts. Say to them, *"Go ahead and make fun of (this message)! Allah will bring out whatever you're worried about (and make it known)!"* [64]

If you ask them (what they were talking about), [789] they say, *"We were just

---

their retainer for a contract whereby they can buy their freedom. Contrary to popular misconceptions about Islam in some circles, and despite abuses that may have occurred in some eras of Muslim history, the simple fact remains that from its sources, Islam does not promote the capture or holding of bonded laborers. (The Prophet said that it is forbidden to enslave a free person, so going out to kidnap people to make them slaves is forbidden in Islam, as well.) Indeed, Islam employs a mechanism to encourage, and sometimes even require, people to free their bonded servants, and the companions were well-known to free people *en masse*. A man once asked the Prophet, "Messenger of Allah, direct me to an action that will draw me closer to Paradise and keep me away from the Fire." The Prophet replied, "Emancipate a person and free the neck (of a servant)." The man asked, "Messenger of Allah, aren't they both the same thing?" The Prophet answered, "No, when you emancipate a person, you're doing it on your own, but you free a neck (from servanthood) when you help in the price (required to free someone)." (*Ahmad*) Once, when the Prophet was told that a man got angry, slapped his maidservant and then freed her out of fear of Allah, he remarked that if he hadn't have freed her, then he would have been punished by Allah.

[784] The *cause of Allah* is a general theme that early scholars unanimously understood to mean either *zakah* or *jihad*.

[785] This verse was revealed after a man had approached the Prophet, asking for some goods to be given to him out of the funds for distribution. The Prophet replied, "Allah, the Most High, never allowed any prophet to distribute the *sadaqah* by his own decision, nor did He give this power to anyone who was not a prophet. He determined from His Own Self eight categories (of people who are to receive it.) If you fall under one of those eight categories, then I can let you have some." (*Abu Dawud*)

[786] Some hypocrites were slandering the Prophet, and when they were told to stop, one of them said, "He'll listen to anybody." This meant that they felt they could lie to the Prophet's face and convince him that they didn't say anything wrong. This verse references that. (*Ibn Kathir*)

[787] The commentators explain that by pleasing the Prophet, one is also pleasing Allah, for the Prophet is the instrument of Allah's will on earth.

[788] During the Expedition to Tabuk, some hypocrites were ridiculing the Prophet for daring to march an army northward, saying, "This man wants to conquer all of Syria – its palaces and fortresses, and it's just not possible." Others took to belittling the sincere believers and making fun of them. This verse was revealed in response. (*Asbab ul-Nuzul*)

[789] A hypocrite said in a gathering while encamped during the Expedition to Tabuk, "I've never seen any (oral) reciters like ours! They have the hungriest stomachs, the most deceitful tongues, and they're the most cowardly in battle." A sincere Muslim spoke out, saying, "You lie! You're a hypocrite, and I'm going to tell the Messenger of Allah." When the Prophet was informed, he summoned the man who said it. The man kept saying he was only joking. Then this verse was revealed. (*Ibn Kathir*)

talking nonsense, all in good fun." Ask them, "Were you poking fun at Allah, His verses and His Messenger?" [65]

Make no more excuses, you people who rejected (faith) after (supposedly) having accepted it! [790] Although We may forgive some of you, We're still going to punish others among you on account of their wickedness. [66]

Hypocrites Protect Each Other

$\mathcal{H}$ypocrites, both males and females, are all alike with each other. They call (people) towards bad conduct and discourage good behavior, while closing their hands tight (to avoid giving in charity). They've forgotten Allah, so He's forgotten them.   The hypocrites are certainly rebellious wrongdoers. [791] [67]

Allah has made a promise to the hypocrites, both male and female, and to those who suppress (their faith in Him), that they will have the fires of Hell in which to dwell. [792] That will be enough for them, for Allah's curse and a relentless punishment are what they're going to get! [68]

"(All you hypocrites!) You're just like those who came before you. Yet, (the ancient peoples)

had more (worldly) power, wealth and sons than you. They had their time to enjoy their share, even as you and those who came before you did, also. You even speak the same kind of nonsense that they did! Yet, their actions were useless, both in this world and the next, and they're going to be the losers (in the end, just as you will be, if you don't repent)." [793] [69]

Haven't they heard the stories of those who went before them, of the people of Noah, the (tribes) of 'Ad and Thamud, the people of Abraham, the companions of Madyan, and of the overthrown (towns of Sodom and Gomorrah)? Messengers went to all of them with clear evidence (of the truth). It wasn't Allah who did them any wrong, for they wronged their own souls. [70]

The Unbreakable Bonds of Brotherhood

$\mathcal{T}$he believers, both male and female, are the close protectors of one another.   They command what is recognized (as good) and forbid what is unfamiliar (to Allah's way of life). They establish prayer, give in charity, and obey Allah and His Messenger. Allah will pour His mercy down upon them, for Allah is powerful and wise. [71]

---

[790] The Prophet said, "The example of a hypocrite is that of a sheep wandering between two herds. Sometimes he goes to one of them and sometimes to the other, and he's confused over whom he should follow." (*Muslim*)

[791] Conscious hypocrisy is considered one of the gravest shortcomings in the pantheon of sins in Islam. The two-faced liar is on a much lower scale than the person who is sinful in ignorance of morality or the truth. As such, the Qur'an often speaks of hypocrites as receiving punishments far in excess of the ignorantly sinful.

[792] 'Umar ibn al-Khattab went to the main mosque in Medina and found Mu'adh ibn Jabal sitting by the Prophet's grave, weeping. 'Umar asked him why he was crying, and Mu'adh replied that it was something that he had heard from the Messenger of Allah so many years before. He said that the Prophet had said, "A little bit of hypocrisy is like making partners with Allah. Anyone who is hostile to a friend of Allah is on his way to opposing Allah. Allah loves the fair, pious and secluded people whom no one notices are absent. (They're the) people who don't receive invitations (to parties) and who are not treated with honor when they're present. Their hearts are the lamps of guidance, and they come out from every dusty and obscure place." (*Ibn Majah, Bayhaqi*)

[793] The Prophet warned Muslims, saying, "You will adopt the ways of communities that came before you, and you will copy them in everything, so much so that if you were to see one of them crawling into a lizard's hole, you would follow him." When Ibn 'Abbas heard about this saying, he mused, "How similar is our night (century) to last night (former centuries). They are the Children of Israel, and we've been likened to them." (*Qurtubi*)

273

Allah has made a promise to the believers, both male and female, of gardens beneath which rivers flow in which to dwell, and beautiful mansions in everlasting gardens of delight. [794] However, the greatest delight of all is to please Allah, and that's also the greatest success! [72]

Be Firm against Hypocrites and their Wily Ways

 Prophet!

Strive hard against the faithless and the hypocrites. Be firm with them, for their dwelling place is in Hellfire – *the worst destination!* [73]

They swear to Allah that they've never said anything (against you), [795] but indeed they've uttered words of rejection, and they're rejecting (Allah) even after (they claimed) to have submitted (to Him).

They tried to (assassinate the Prophet), though they were unable to carry it out. [796] *This was their response to the bounty with which Allah and His Messenger had enriched them!*

If they repent, it would be the best for them, but if they persist (in their rebellious ways,) then Allah will punish them with a painful penalty, both in this life and in the

---

[794] A group of companions said to the Prophet, "Messenger of Allah, talk to us about Paradise; of what is it made?" He replied, "Bricks of gold and bricks of silver. Its cement is made of musk; its gravel is of pearls and rubies, and its sand is of saffron. Whoever enters it will enjoy its delights and will never get depressed, and they will live forever and will never die. Their clothes will never wear out, nor will their youth ever fade." (*Ahmad*)

[795] The first part of this verse references what a hypocrite named Julas said while on the expedition. Julas had just finished hearing a speech by the Prophet in which he had warned the hypocrites that their opposition to Allah was tearing them apart inside and that Allah would punish them in the next life. Julas then returned to his friends and said, "By Allah! If what Muhammad says is true, then we're worse than donkeys." A dependent of his named 'Amr ibn Qays retorted, saying, "What Muhammad says *is* true, and so you are worse than donkeys." Then he told Julas, "By Allah! Julas, you're the closest person to me; you've been the most favorable to me, and I would never want any harm to touch you more than anyone else! But you've said something that, if I told on you, then you would be exposed (as a hypocrite), but if I hid it, it would destroy me. One of them is the lesser of the two evils." After the Muslims returned to Medina from Tabuk, 'Amr went and told the Prophet what Julas had said. The Prophet summoned him to the mosque and asked him why he said what he did. Julas invoked the curse of Allah upon himself if he was lying, and then he swore to Allah facing the pulpit of the mosque that he never said anything like that. 'Amr swore he was truthful, as well, and then said, "O Allah! Prove the truth of the honest and expose the lies of the liar." Then this verse was revealed to the Prophet, and he recited it. Thereafter, Julas repented of his words, and it is said that his repentance was sincere. He was never known to indulge in hypocrisy again (*Ibn Kathir*)

[796] On the journey back from the Tabuk expedition, a faction of hypocrites who had wanted 'Abdullah ibn Ubayy to be crowned king plotted to assassinate the Prophet by surrounding him slowly with their numbers and then pushing him off his mount down a cliff, if ever one appeared on the trail. However, their plot unraveled due to the vigilance of two companions who never left the Prophet's side and warned him when the men began to converge on his intended path. The Prophet shouted at them, and they fled. He asked the two men who had been watching over him, Hudhayfah and 'Ammar, if they knew who the men were. Hudhayfah replied, "No, Messenger of Allah. They were wearing masks, but we do recognize their horses." The Prophet then said, "They're going to be hypocrites until the Day of Judgment. Do you know what they wanted to do?" The two men answered in the negative, and the Prophet said, "They wanted to surround the Messenger of Allah and throw him (down into) the valley." Hudhayfah said, "Messenger of Allah! Should you ask their tribes to send their heads to you?" The Prophet answered, "No, for I wouldn't want it to be said by the Arabs that Muhammad used some people for fighting and, after Allah gave him victory with their help, that he commanded them to be killed." Then he said, "O Allah, throw a *dubaylah* at them." The men asked the Prophet what that was, and he replied, "It's a fiery dart that falls into the heart of one of them and brings about his end." Later on someone asked Hudhayfah about those assassins, and Hudhayfah mentioned that the Prophet told him the names of all of them, and he told no one else. Thus, Hudhayfah had the nickname, "*The Holder of the Secret.*" (*At-Tabari*)

next. In that case, no one on earth would be able to protect them or help them! [74]

On Those Who Betray their Pledge

$\mathcal{A}$mong them are some who made a deal with Allah that if He gave them (great riches) from His Own bounty, then they would (reciprocate) by giving (richly) in charity (in the cause of Allah), and further that they would be among the righteous. [797] [75]

Yet, when He *did* give them (riches) from His bounty, they became greedy and turned back, reluctant (to support the cause). [76]

So He let hypocrisy grow in their hearts (as a result,) and it will remain there until the day when they're going to meet Him (for judgment), and that's because they broke their deal with Allah and also because they lied. [77]

Don't they realize that Allah knows all their secrets and their veiled schemes and that Allah knows what's hidden (in the deep recesses of their hearts)? [78]

Don't Belittle the Donations of the Poor

$\mathcal{T}$hose who ridicule the believers [798] when they give in charity from their own convictions, [799] or who (ridicule those who have) nothing more to give than their own labor due to their poverty, and then who

---

[797] A man named Tha'labah went to the Prophet and asked for him to beseech Allah to make him rich. The Prophet said to him, "Woe to you, Tha'labah, a little thanks that you can give is much better than what you won't be able to handle." Then the Prophet told him that if he really wanted riches, then he could invoke Allah to give them to him. Thereupon, Tha'labah swore the oath that is contained in verse 75. The Prophet then gave Tha'labah a herd of sheep, and within a short amount of time the herd expanded greatly, causing Tha'labah to become very wealthy. Because of the size of his herds, though, he also had to move progressively farther from Medina, resulting in his more and more infrequent visits to worship in the mosque. Later on, when the Prophet sent people to collect the charity tax from Tha'labah, he put off the tax collectors on two separate occasions. This passage was then revealed about him, and someone went to him and told him, "You're ruined! A passage has been revealed about you!" So Tha'labah hurried to the Prophet and begged him to accept his charitable contribution, but the Prophet told him that Allah has forbidden him from accepting his charity. Then Tha'labah began throwing dust on his own head in sorrow, and the Prophet told him, "It's because of what you did. I gave you an order, and you disobeyed it." After the Prophet's passing, Tha'labah went to Caliph Abu Bakr and begged him to accept his charity, and Abu Bakr refused, saying the Prophet never accepted it. The same thing happened during the rule of 'Umar ibn al-Khattab and Uthman ibn Affan (d. 656), and Tha'labah passed away in despair during Uthman's reign. (*Ibn Kathir*) It is said that Allah did not accept his repentance because he harbored hypocrisy in his heart. (*Ma'ariful Qur'an*)

[798] The Prophet made a public call one day for donations to support the cause. A poor man named Abu 'Aqil came and donated a small amount of dates, explaining that he worked all night drawing water, earned two measures of dates for his pay and was thus donating half of what he earned. Some hypocrites laughed and said, "Allah and His Messenger don't need this (small amount), for what benefit could it bring." The Prophet then picked up the dates with his own hands and placed it atop the pile of donated money and goods. Then a man named 'Abdurrahman ibn 'Awf came forward and asked if anyone else was going to give in charity, and the Prophet replied, "No one except you." Thereupon 'Abdurrahman declared he was donating a huge sum of gold in charity. 'Umar ibn al-Khattab said, "Are you crazy?" 'Abdurrahman said that he wasn't and explained that he really did have that much money, and he donated it. The hypocrites defamed him and said he just wanted to show off. This verse was revealed regarding this incident and is meant to show that even a little given sincerely can mean a great deal in Allah's sight and that a lot given in Allah's cause should be praised and not ridiculed. (*Asbab ul-Nuzul*)

[799] The hypocrites were never satisfied and took every opportunity to belittle those who gave to support the Islamic cause. According to Abu Mas'ud: "If a person brought a large donation, (the hypocrites) would say, 'He is only showing off for the benefit of others,' but if a person brought a small donation, they would say, 'Allah doesn't need such (a small) donation.'" (*Bukhari, Muslim*)

further tease them (for donating huge sums of their resources to Allah's cause, should know) that Allah will throw their ridicule back upon them and that they're going to have a painful punishment. [79]

Whether you ask for their forgiveness or not – even if you asked seventy times for their forgiveness, Allah won't forgive them because they rejected Allah and His Messenger. [800] Allah will not guide a people who are rebellious and corrupt. [80]

About Those Who Remained behind in Medina

*T*hose who remained behind (in Medina) rejoiced in their inaction behind the back of the Messenger of Allah. [801] They hated (even the mere thought) of striving in the cause of Allah with their wealth and their persons, and they said, *"Don't go out (on the Expedition to Tabuk) because it's far too hot (in the desert)!"*

Say (to them), *"The fires of Hell are even hotter!"* If they would only realize it! [81]

So let them laugh a little now, for soon they will cry much more as a payback for what they've earned (for themselves on their record of deeds.) [82]

If Allah brings you back to any of them and they ask you for (permission) to venture out (with you on some future expedition), tell them, *"You're never going to venture out with me, nor will you ever fight an enemy by my side, for you chose to sit and be inactive the first time, so now keep sitting with those who get left behind."* [83]

Don't Honor a Hypocrite

*N*ever offer a (funeral) prayer for any of them that dies, nor stand by their grave (as they're being lowered down into it), for they rejected Allah and His Messenger, and thus died in a state of defiant rebellion. [802] [84]

So neither be impressed by their money nor their (numerous) sons, for Allah wants to punish them through these things in this world so that they'll leave this life

---

[800] In Semitic parlance the number seventy is synonymous with 'a lot' of something.

[801] There was a heat wave and famine in Medina, and the journey north to Syria was going to be a long, hard trek of two weeks. The Prophet warned his followers of this and asked for donations to cover the expenses of the mission. Many Muslims came forward, men and women, and huge sums of money were donated. However, some others warned against the discomfort of the hot journey and tried to dissuade their friends from going. This passage was revealed about them. (*Ibn Kathir*)

[802] This passage (84-85) was revealed concerning 'Abdullah ibn Ubayy, the leader of the hypocrites of Medina. He passed away, and his son, who was a committed believer, went to the Prophet and asked if he could bury his father in one of the Prophet's robes. The Prophet gave it to him, and then the son asked the Prophet to pray for his departed father. The Prophet was about to pray for him when 'Umar ibn al-Khattab objected, saying that the dead man had been a hypocrite and an enemy of Allah. The Prophet replied, "I've been given the choice of whether to pray for him or not. I know that if I pray for the forgiveness of (a hypocrite) seventy times, he won't be forgiven. Yet, if I knew that he'd be forgiven if I prayed for forgiveness more than that, then I'd do it." (*Bukhari*) The reports differ as to whether the Prophet actually offered a funeral prayer for him or merely a supplication, but this passage was revealed sometime later, forbidding funeral prayers for known hypocrites. Why did the Prophet give his robe for the funeral? After the Battle of Badr, many years before, one of the prisoners taken was the Prophet's pagan uncle 'Abbas. He had no shirt, and because he was a tall man, the Prophet asked for the equally tall 'Abdullah ibn Ubayy to give one of his shirts to clothe 'Abbas. He did so. The Prophet then was returning the favor. (*Qurtubi*) The Prophet said of the robe that was used to bury Ibn Ubayy: "What good will my clothes or my prayers do for him against Allah? I swear to Allah that I hope he is saved more than a thousand of his people." (*Asbab ul-Nuzul*) He also later remarked that he hoped by his action that thousands of Ibn Ubayy's followers would become Muslims. (*Ma'ariful Qur'an*) Even though he caused the Prophet much grief, the Prophet knew why 'Ibn Ubayy was a hypocrite, (he would have been made king of Yathrib, but for the coming of Islam). Thus, the Prophet always treated him as a special case and with compassion, even though Ibn Ubayy clearly didn't deserve it. (A stance that was ordered of the Prophet in verse 3:186.)

with souls that have lost (their ability to believe in Allah). [85]

When a chapter came down (asking them) to believe in Allah and to strive alongside His Messenger, the eligible ones from among them came to you and asked for exemptions, saying, *"Leave us, for we'd rather stay with those who sit (at home)."* [86] They preferred to be with those who stayed behind! Their hearts are sealed shut, and they understand nothing! [87]

However, the Messenger and the believers with him strive with their wealth and their persons. Therefore, they shall have the best (reward), even as they'll be the most successful. [88] Allah has prepared gardens for them beneath which rivers flow, and there they shall remain - *and that's the ultimate success!* [89]

The Bedouins Offered their Excuses

$\mathcal{S}$ome of the (bedouin) Arabs also came to you in order to offer their excuses and to claim exemptions. [803] And so, those who were dishonest to Allah and His Messenger sat idly by.

It won't be long before a painful punishment overtakes those among them who suppressed (their awareness of the truth). [90]

There's no blame, however, on those who were too weak or ill or who couldn't find the resources to spend (for the journey), [804] as long as they're sincere to Allah and His Messenger. There are no grounds of complaint against the good (people who wanted to come, but who couldn't find a way), for Allah is forgiving and merciful. [91]

No Blame for those who could not be Accommodated

$(\mathcal{T}$here are also no grounds of complaint) against those who came to you for transportation and to whom you had to say, *"I have no transportation for you."* [805] They turned back with tears overflowing from their eyes at their inability to spend (money to arrange their own way). [92]

There are, however, legitimate grounds (for complaint) against those who claimed exemption even though they were independently wealthy. They preferred to remain with those who stayed behind. Therefore, their hearts were sealed shut, and they understood nothing. [93]

They're going to make their excuses to you when you return to them, but say to them, *"Don't make any excuses (for your cowardice), because we're not going to believe you. Allah already told us about your situation, and it's what you do that Allah and His Messenger will consider. In the end, you're going to be brought back to the One Who knows the hidden and the clear, and then He's going to show you the true meaning of all that you did."* [94]

When you return back to them, they're going to swear to you in Allah's

---

[803] Many newly converted bedouins still had the tribal mentality of self-defense of the clan above all other considerations. Some bedouins felt that if their isolated camps were short of men, hostile tribes would take that as an opportunity to strike. (*Razi*) Muhammad was trying to change that mentality, and if enough bedouins of different groups joined him, those who remained behind would be more reluctant to attack the defenseless camps of their rivals. This coming together of all bedouins represented a sea change in the lifestyle of the desert nomads.

[804] At this time there was no established public treasury in the community. Any goods that had come into the control of the Muslims up to that point had been immediately spent on charity, supporting widows, etc.

[805] A group of men volunteered for the Expedition to Tabuk, but when the Prophet explained he had insufficient resources to equip any more men, they left weeping bitterly. The Prophet later told his companions after they returned from the journey, "Some people were left behind in Medina, but it was like they were with us all the time in every valley and every mountain pass we crossed. They were left behind only for legitimate reasons." (*Bukhari, Abu Dawud*)

(name) that you should leave them alone - so go ahead and leave them alone (by shunning them), for they're stained (by their very own sins), and Hellfire is their destination.   That's the reward they deserve for what they've done. [95]

They're also going to swear to you (as to the validity of their excuses), trying to make you pleased with them. If you do become pleased with them, (then you should know) that Allah is not pleased with those who were rebelliously disobedient. [96]

The (bedouin) Arabs are the worst when it comes to rejection and hypocrisy and are thus more likely to be ignorant of the command that Allah has sent down to His Messenger. [806] Allah is full of knowledge and wisdom. [97]

Some of the (bedouin) Arabs consider what they spend (in charity) to be a financial penalty. They keep looking for disasters to come upon you, but let the worst disasters fall upon them, for Allah listens and knows (all about their treachery). [98]

Some of the (bedouin) Arabs, however, do believe in Allah and the Last Day. They look upon what they spend (in charity) as a way to bring themselves closer to Allah's presence and to (be worthy) of the Prophet's prayers (for their forgiveness and success.)

They truly are brought closer (to Allah by their charity and sincerity), and soon Allah will admit them to His mercy, for Allah is forgiving and merciful. [99]

Forgiveness is Offered Freely to those who Seek It

The forerunners (in faith) are those who were the first to migrate (from Mecca), then those who helped them (in Medina) and finally those who followed (closely behind) them in doing what was good. [807]

Allah is pleased with them and they with Him, and He's prepared for them gardens beneath which rivers flow to live within forever.   That's the ultimate success! [100]

Some of the (bedouin) Arabs (that live) around you (in the countryside) are hypocrites, even as there are (hypocrites) among the people of Medina. They're persistent in hypocrisy, and although you don't know (who they are), We know who they are.

We're going to punish them twice (through fear and humiliation), and then they're going to be sent into an even more severe punishment after that! [101]

---

[806] The two bedouin tribes of Ghatafan and Asad are the main tribes referenced here. They were so wily and without honor that the Muslims were incredulous as to their wild ways and lack of sophistication and common sense. Once the Prophet was dealing with a bedouin from one of those tribes who brought a small gift to him – but then the man demanded a large one from the Prophet in exchange. The bedouin was so uncouth and uncivilized as to defy patience, causing the Prophet to remark later, "I almost decided never to accept any gift except from people of Quraysh, Thaqif, the Ansar or the tribe of Daws." (Nisa'i)   The groups mentioned were either urban to semi-urban village dwellers with a sense of manners.   The Prophet once remarked, "The one who lives in the desert becomes hard-hearted; the one who hunts game becomes careless, and the one who associates with rulers falls into controversies." (Ahmad)

[807] The three groups who are praised as being in the forefront of faith are the Immigrants (Muhajireen) from Mecca, the Helpers (Ansar) of Yathrib who welcomed the Immigrants in and supported them, and finally the general body of believers who consistently do the right thing and support Allah's cause. The Prophet was particularly fond of the Ansar, and he later lamented that their numbers were thinning every year while the numbers of general converts were swelling. He exhorted the rest of the Muslim community to be kind to them, for they helped him when no one else did. He also said that none of his faithful companions will enter Hell. (Tirmidhi)

Conflicted Actions

(There are) some other (people) who've admitted to their sins. [808] They had mixed moral deeds with evil ones, but Allah will turn to them (in forgiveness), for Allah is forgiving and merciful. [809] [102] Take charity from their wealth so you can cleanse and purify them, and pray for them, for your prayers are truly a source of tranquility for them. Allah hears and knows (about all things). [103]

Don't they know that Allah accepts the repentance of His servants and that He accepts their charitable contributions? Allah is the One Who Accepts Repentance, and (He truly is) the Merciful. [104]

Say (to the people who want to repent of their sins), "Do (good deeds), for Allah will soon see the results of your efforts, even as the Messenger and the believers (will see them, as well). Soon you're going to be brought back to the One Who knows the hidden and the plainly seen, and He's going to show you the meaning of all that you did." [105]

(Indeed, among this group of people) are some who are waiting nervously for Allah's command, so they can know whether He's going to punish them or turn towards them (in forgiveness). Allah is full of knowledge and wisdom. [106]

The Mosque of Mischief

There are those who built a mosque (for no other purpose) than to promote mischief and rejection (of Allah), seeking to divide the believers and to set up a rallying place for those who previously made war on Allah and His Messenger. [810] They're

---

[808] Ten men who failed to respond to the mustering of the militia to march toward Tabuk felt ashamed. Sometime after the army left, seven of them swore to their wives that they would tie themselves to their fence posts or to pillars in the mosque until the Prophet forgave them. When the Prophet returned about a month later, he asked about the men he saw tied to posts and poles. When he was told about their situation, he swore he would not call for them to be released until Allah forgave them. This passage of forgiveness was revealed, and the Prophet ordered them to give money in charity to atone for their cowardice. (*Asbab ul-Nuzul*) One of these men, a man named Abu Lubabah, remained at his pillar - wanting the Prophet himself to untie him. He did.

[809] The Prophet said, "Last night two (angels) came to me (in my dreams) and took me to a town built with gold and silver bricks. We met two men there, and one half of their bodies resembled the most handsome human beings you ever could see, but their other halves were of the most hideous human beings you ever could see. The two (angels) told those men, 'Go and submerge yourselves in that river.' So they submerged themselves in it. When they returned to us their hideousness disappeared, and they were in the most pleasing condition. The (angels) said (to me), 'The first garden (over there) is the Garden of Eden, and that's your dwelling place.' Then they said, 'As for those men who were half ugly and half handsome, they were those who mixed good deeds with bad deeds, but Allah forgave them.'" (*Bukhari*)

[810] After the Prophet and Abu Bakr fled Mecca for the safety of Medina in 622 CE, they stopped in the small town of Quba, which was just outside the city limits of Yathrib (Medina), and stayed for a number of days. There they dedicated the first mosque of Islam, and the Prophet would often visit it thereafter. When the full might of the hypocrites of Medina came to bear upon the Prophet and his followers in subsequent years, a faction of the hypocritical tribe of Banu Ghanam built a mosque of their own in a nearby neighborhood of Quba named Dhu Awan. They used it as a base of opposition to the Prophet, while pretending to be pious Muslims. They were also allied with a notorious Christian man from Yathrib named Abu Amir, who was one of those who left Medina to join the Meccans and then fought against the Muslims at Uhud. (Abu Amir had a heated argument with the Prophet and vowed that whichever of the two men was wrong, he should die alone far from home. His son Hanzalah, by way of contrast, was a faithful supporter of the Prophet.) In addition, the mosque was partly financed by the Christian Ghassanid king of southern Syria, who wanted to use it as an intelligence gathering installation. Before he even returned from the Expedition to Tabuk, the Prophet came to know of the linkage and also for what the mosque was being used. Several letters from Abu Amir to the hypocrites were also intercepted – letters that encouraged sedition and rebellion! When some of the hypocrites invited the Prophet to enter Quba first before Medina and to pray in their mosque, this passage was

going to swear that they meant nothing but good by it, but Allah declares that they're all liars. [107]

Never set foot within (their mosque), for there's (another) mosque (nearby in the town of Quba) whose foundations were laid from the first day upon mindfulness (of Allah). It's far more appropriate for you to stand within that one, for there are people inside of it who love to be purified, and Allah loves those who make themselves pure! [108]

Whose (place of worship) is better: the one who lays his foundation upon mindfulness of Allah and the seeking of His pleasure, or the one who lays his foundation upon a weak sand dune that's ready to crumble at any moment? It will crumble – *along with him* – and topple into

the fires of Hell. Allah doesn't guide people who are wrong! [109]

Such a (weak) building foundation could never be anything more than a cause for nervousness in their hearts - even until their hearts are shattered (by stress)! Allah is full of knowledge and wisdom. [110]

This is Allah's Deal

*A*llah has bought from the believers their lives and their wealth, and in return (He'll give them) Paradise. [811]

They will fight in His cause; they will kill and be killed – and this is a promise that He's bound by in the Torah, the Gospel and the Qur'an. Who is more faithful to his agreement than Allah? [812]

---

revealed. The Prophet then ordered some of his companions to go to the *Mosque of Mischief,* as it was called, and have it torn down. One man named Thabit ibn Arqam later built a house on the site, but he had no children survive him – ever - and thus the seemingly cursed plot fell into disuse. Thereafter, the site became a garbage dump. Abu Amir did die far from home in southern Syria among strangers. (*Ma'ariful Qur'an*) Only a mosque built for sincere devotion to Allah can be called a mosque of Allah. No house of worship should be used to plot against the religion to which it is supposed to be dedicated.

[811] These two verses (111-112) were revealed in the Meccan Period after the last Pledge of 'Aqabah, in which some seventy visitors from Medina pledged themselves to the Prophet and invited him to resettle in their city. (There were two prior such pledges by smaller groups of six and then twelve persons respectively.) At this last pledge, taken some months before the Prophet left Mecca for the safety of Medina, one of the new converts asked the Prophet, "Messenger of Allah, we're making a deal right now. If there are any requirements from either your Lord or you, let them be enumerated at this time clearly." The Prophet said, "As for Allah, I lay down the condition that you all shall worship Him and only Him. As for myself, the condition is that you should protect me as you protect your selves, wealth, property and children." Someone asked him, "If we fulfill these two conditions, what will we get in return?" The Prophet replied, "Paradise." The people exclaimed then that they accepted that deal and that they would never cancel this agreement. Then these two verses were revealed, and the Prophet recited them. The people then lined up to place their hands in his to make their solemn oaths. (*Ma'ariful Qur'an*)

[812] It has been a principle enshrined in all divinely revealed scriptures that the righteous have to fight against the wicked. If they don't, then wickedness spreads, and innocent men, women and children suffer under the yoke of evil and oppression. The Torah is full of instances where the righteous were exhorted to fight against evil, while the New Testament echoes this theme in Hebrews 11:32-34 and also when Jesus famously stated, "Do not think that I came to bring peace on the earth; I did not come to bring peace, but a sword. For I came to set a man against his father, and a daughter against her mother, and a daughter-in-law against her mother-in-law; and a man's enemies will be the members of his household." (Matthew 10:34-36) The caveat, however, that sets apart war for Allah's sake and distinguishes it from mere war for conquest or loot is that a just war in the name of Allah is to stop oppression, so that all people may live in peace and security with regard to their lives and property. All other causes for war are fueled by greed, and men fighting for such causes know no limits and conduct themselves like barbarians. The war for Allah's sake envisions peace at the end for both the conquered and the conqueror, while war for greed envisions nothing but the destruction and subjugation of one's enemies. The Prophet was once asked who fought for Allah: the one who fights for fame, fortune or adventure, and the Prophet replied that the only one who is counted as fighting for Allah is the one who fights only to uphold His religion and for His sake alone. (*Bukhari, Muslim*)

So be pleased with the bargain you've made, for that's the ultimate success! [111]

(The true believers are those who) turn (to Allah) in repentance, serve Him, praise Him, wander abroad (in His cause), [813] bow down in prostration before Him, command what is recognized (as good), and forbid what is unfamiliar (to Allah's way of life). They're the ones who observe Allah's limits, so now give good news to the believers! [112]

Faith and Falsehood have a Clear Divide

𝒥t's not right for the Prophet and the believers to pray for the forgiveness of idol-worshippers, [814] even if they're close relatives, after it's been made clear to them that they're going to be companions of the raging blaze. [815] [113]

Abraham only prayed for his father's forgiveness because of a promise he had made to him. [816]

However, when it became clear to him that (his father) was an enemy of Allah, he distanced himself from him. It was just that Abraham was accustomed to invoking (Allah frequently), and he was forbearing. [114]

Allah will never let a people go astray after He's (begun to invite them to) guidance, until after He's made clear to them that of which they should be aware, for Allah knows all about everything. [115]

The control of the heavens and the earth belongs to Allah. He gives life, and He brings death. You have neither any protector nor helper apart from Him. [116]

---

[813] Early scholars such as 'Ikrimah say that this wandering consists of traveling to seek education about the religion.

[814] After the Prophet's beloved uncle, Abu Talib, passed away, affirming his allegiance to idolatry even as he breathed his last, the distraught Prophet vowed to continue to pray for his forgiveness. Later on, in the early Medinan Period, 'Ali heard a man loudly praying for his deceased pagan parents to be forgiven. When 'Ali asked the man why he was praying for his pagan parents, he explained that Abraham also prayed for his pagan father. (Based on verse 19:47.) 'Ali informed the Prophet about this, and sometime later, this verse was revealed prohibiting Muslims from praying for relatives who had died while still believing in idols. (*Tirmidhi, Bukhari, Muslim*)

[815] Even into the Medinan Period, many Muslims had pagan relatives, and when their relatives would pass away, they were torn about what to do for a eulogy. One companion bemoaned his pagan father's passing to the Prophet, and the Prophet tearfully replied that even his own mother might be destined for Hellfire, as she might have died an idolater. (*Muslim*) Even though Islam was not extant in her time, she might have had thoughts that idolatry was wrong and rejected it, as many *hanifs* or Arab monotheists of the time already had. Only Allah knows if she did, and Muslim scholars generally feel that she died as a believer in the one God. (*Ibn Kathir*) This verse sets forth the principle for Muslims not to pray for the forgiveness of those who died willingly as pagans, for they died in a state of defiance to Allah's religion. There is no prohibition, however, for praying for the forgiveness and guidance of non-Muslims while they are alive. (*Qurtubi, Ibn Kathir*)

[816] Verses 6:74-83 tell the basic story of how Abraham came to disobey his father in matters of religion. 19:41-50 adds more details of the family conflict and contains the crucial passage where Abraham promises his father he'll pray for him. The following *hadith* supplements the overall story. The Prophet said, "On the Day of Resurrection, Abraham will meet his father Azar (Terah) whose face will be overcast and dusty, and he'll say to his (father), 'Didn't I tell you not to disobey me?' His father will reply, 'This day I will not disobey you any further.' Abraham will then beseech Allah, saying, 'Lord! You promised me that you wouldn't disgrace me on the Day of Judgment, but what can be more disgraceful for me than to curse or dishonor my own father?' (See 26:87 for the promise.) Then Allah will say, 'I've forbidden Paradise for those who rejected (faith). Look at what's beneath you.' Then he will look and see a blood-stained hyena being caught by the legs and thrown into the Fire." (His father was transformed into a representation of his true nature, and so Abraham wouldn't see the form of his father being cast into Hell and would thus not be overtly shamed.) (*Bukhari*) This was to emphasize to Abraham that Allah's justice is absolute and applies across the board to all. Thus, He would not show unfair favoritism to Azar when He wouldn't show it to others.

Allah Tested the Believers

*A*nd so it was that Allah turned towards the Prophet, the Immigrants, and the Helpers who followed Him during a difficult time (on the Expedition to Tabuk, for the journey was long and hard). 817

However, a segment of them let their hearts become crooked, (influencing them away from their duty,) but He turned towards them, as well, for He was kind and merciful towards them. [117]

The Case of the Three Who were Forgiven

(*H*e also turned in mercy) to the three (men) who remained behind (without a valid excuse). 818 (They were so remorseful) that the vast earth, itself, seemed to close in upon them, and their souls seemed to strangle them (with guilt), as well.

They understood that there was no running away from Allah, unless (it was on a path) that led back to Him. So He turned towards them so they could repent, for Allah is the Acceptor of Repentance and the Merciful. [118]

Reflections on the Lessons of Tabuk

O you who believe! Be mindful of Allah, and be among those who are truthful (to their vows). [119] It wasn't right for (some of) the people of Medina and the local desert Arabs to refuse to follow the Messenger of Allah, nor was it right that they preferred their own lives over his.

That's because there was (no sacrifice) they could've made, whether it was thirst, fatigue or hunger in the cause of Allah, nor any step (they could've taken) to raise the ire of the faithless, nor any injury they could've received from the enemy, (without being generously repaid for it by Allah). Indeed, Allah never lets the reward of those who do good become lost. [120]

They also could not have spent anything, whether a little or a lot, or trekked across a valley without having that deed recorded to their credit, and that was so Allah could reward their actions with good (in return). 819 [121]

---

817 The journey northward towards Syria was so difficult in the full heat of the desert sun that even the water ran out for the army of 30,000. The men became so desperate that Abu Bakr asked the Prophet to pray for rain for them, citing the fact that Allah always listened to his call. The Prophet prayed for rain and didn't lower his hands until rain fell some hours later. Repeated rain showers fell in intervals for days after that, and the men had sufficient water to drink and wash themselves.

818 There were three men named Ka'b ibn Malik, Hilal ibn Umayyah and Murarah ibn ar-Rabi' who were otherwise perfectly able-bodied and fit to answer the call for the Tabuk Expedition. They had been among the earliest converts, but they failed to muster with the rest of the militia when it was time to march northward. (Murarah was dissuaded from participation by, among other things, the fact that it was harvest time, and he became somewhat inclined to comfort and prosperity. Hilal was having a family reunion. K'ab was wealthy and couldn't bear to leave his fortune behind!) When the Prophet returned, these men were shunned for about fifty days, and they felt miserable, so much so that it seemed (as one of them later described it) that the earth and their own souls were closing in upon them. The Christian king of the Ghassanid tribe in Syria, Suhrabil ibn Amr, received reports of the shunning of these men, and he sent a letter to Ka'b offering to take him in to his kingdom if Ka'b would renounce Islam, but Ka'b threw the letter in his cooking fire. In time, the Prophet accepted the remorse of these men, and they were welcomed back into the community upon the revelation of this verse. Ka'b left a rather lengthy account of his experience and recounted how joyful both he and the community were when it was all over. (*Bukhari, Muslim*)

819 When the Prophet was raising funds for the Tabuk Expedition, 'Umar ibn al-Khattab came forward and donated one hundred fully equipped camels. Uthman ibn Affan (d. 656) then came and donated the same measure, and when Uthman laid a thousand gold coins in the Prophet's lap, the Prophet

The believers, however, should not march out all together (leaving no one behind to guard the home front). If a certain number remains behind during every expedition, then they could exert themselves in learning the religion. [820]

Thus, they could remind the people when they return (home) that they should be on their guard (against immorality). [122]

O you who believe! Fight the faithless who are all around you, (ready to strike at you). Be resolute against them, and know that Allah is with those who are mindful (of Him). [123]

Be Firmly Committed to the Cause

*W*henever a chapter comes down, some (of the hypocrites) say, *"So who among you feels their faith has been strengthened by it?"* Oh, but those who (truly) believe *do* have their faith strengthened by it, and they rejoice besides! [124] Those who are weak at heart [821] find that (newly revealed verses) add nothing but doubts to their doubts; thus, they're going to die in a state of rejection. [125]

Don't they see that they're being tested at least once or twice every year. [822] Yet, not only *do they not repent;* they don't even pay attention to the reminders! [126] Whenever a chapter comes down, they look at each other (and say), *"Is anyone looking at you?"* [823] Then they turn away, even as Allah has turned their hearts away, for they're a people who don't understand at all. [127]

Now a messenger has come to you from among yourselves, and he's worried sick that you might be harmed (in the cause of Allah). In fact, he's distraught over (your welfare), for he's truly kind and merciful to the believers. [128] If they turn away, just tell them:

*"Allah is enough for me.
There is no god but He.*

*On Him do I trust;
He's Lord of the throne supreme."* [824] [129]

---

fingered them and said, "It doesn't matter what (potential bad deeds) Uthman may do after this." (*Ahmad*) In other words, he is guaranteed Paradise for his generosity to Allah's cause.

[820] This chapter speaks very harshly of the people who remained behind and failed to participate in the Expedition to Tabuk. In order to mitigate the fears of Muslims who feel compelled to go out to fight an enemy, leaving no one behind to protect their families or keep society functioning, this verse was revealed to affirm that there are some who have to remain behind for legitimate reasons. (*Ibn Kathir*)

[821] Hypocrites and believers whose faith was always assailed by doubts.

[822] Ever since the Prophet migrated to Medina, the Muslim community had to face at least one major challenge per year, whether it was fighting off pagans, having missionaries ambushed or suffering from famines or civil disunity. Thus, the opportunity to stand up for truth in a meaningful way was a frequent occurrence. Didn't the hypocrites ever stop and think that all their slinking and cowardice were getting tired and pathetic?

[823] The hypocrites were constantly afraid that new Qur'anic revelations might mention them or expose their activities, so when they heard of new verses, they would ask each other if anyone was looking at them suspiciously. (*Ibn Kathir*)

[824] Some reports claim that these last two verses [128-129] were the last ones revealed to the Prophet, just before he passed away. (*Qurtubi*)

Jonah

10 Yunus
Late Meccan Period

This chapter is the first in a series of six late Meccan chapters that continue to address the core theological concepts of Islam. Nature and its complexity are proof of Allah's handiwork for those who care to look into it deeply. Allah communicates with humanity through messengers who receive His messages and teach them to their fellows. The reality of life is that it's a short time filled with temptations, tests and trials that we must weather. In the end, if we are successful in negotiating the storms of this world, with full faith in Allah, then we can achieve permanent success in the Hereafter, or if we succumb to immorality, vice and corruption, we may suffer punishment in Hellfire. Like a high stakes test, our conduct in this world ultimately decides our fate. Allah will punish injustice, though He is more merciful to us than we could ever deserve.

In the Name of Allah, the Compassionate, the Merciful

*A*lif. Lām. Rā. [825]

These are the verses of the Book of Wisdom. [1] Is it so strange to people that We've sent Our inspiration to a man from among themselves, so he could warn people (of Allah's judgment) and give the good news to the believers that they can achieve confirmed status in the sight of their Lord? Yet, the faithless say (of it), *"This is obviously just magic!"* [2]

Your Lord is Allah, the One Who created the heavens and the earth in six time periods. Then He established Himself upon the throne (of power) and began issuing commands. There are no intercessors other than those whom He allows. That's your Lord Allah, so serve Him. Won't you take a reminder? [3]

All of you will return back to Him, and Allah's promise is true. He's the One Who began the process of creation and then repeats it, so that He can justly reward those who believe and do what's morally right. Those who reject Him will be forced to drink boiling muck, and they'll have a painful punishment on account of their rejection. [4]

He's the One Who caused the sun to glow brightly with multiple (colors in splendor) and the moon to be illuminated. He measured out (the moon's) stations, so you could keep track of the years and the passage (of time). Allah didn't create (all of these things) except for a true purpose, and He explains His verses to people who understand. [5]

Truly, in the alternation of night and day and in everything that Allah created in

---

[825] Ibn 'Abbas (d. 687) explained the pagan position alluded to in this verse by saying, "When Allah sent Muhammad as a messenger, most of the Arabs denied him and his message, saying, 'Allah is too exalted to send a mere human being like Muhammad.'" Thus, this passage was revealed, commenting upon their objection. (*Ibn Kathir*)

the heavens and the earth are proofs for those who are mindful (of Him). [6] Those who don't look forward to their meeting with Us, who are satisfied with the life of this world and who disregard Our (revealed) verses [7] - they're going to have their home in the Fire on account of what they've earned for themselves. [8]

However, those who believe and do what's morally right will be guided by their Lord on account of their faith – rivers will flow beneath them in gardens of delight! [9] Their supplication within (the garden) will be, *"Glory be to You, O Allah!"* [826] Their greeting within will be, *"Peace,"* [827] and they'll end their supplications by saying, *"Praise be to Allah, the Lord of All the Worlds!"* [828] [10]

The Fickle Nature of Humanity

If Allah were to rush forward for people the evil consequences (of their deeds) in the same way that they (want) Him to rush forward the good (things that they think they deserve), then their (time) would come to an end immediately, but We leave those who don't look forward to their meeting with Us wandering in their willful blindness. [11]

When misfortune comes upon a human being, he cries out to Us while lying down on his side, sitting or standing. However, when We've removed his misfortune, he passes on his way as if he had never cried out to Us when hardship assailed him before! That's why the extravagant think their (pointless) deeds are beneficial for them. [12]

And so it was that We destroyed generations that came before you when (their people) turned into oppressors. Their messengers went to them with clear evidence; yet, they still wouldn't believe! That's how We repay the wicked. [13] Now We've caused you (Arabs) to inherit the land after them to see how you would act. [14]

Yet, when Our clear verses are recited to them, [829] those who don't look forward to their meeting with Us say, *"Bring us some other Qur'an, or change this one (to suit us)."*

Say (to them), *"It's not my place to change it, for I follow only what's being revealed to me. If I ever disobeyed my Lord (by making up verses on my own), then I would be in utter fear of the punishment of a momentous day."* [15]

Then say (to them), *"If Allah had wanted, then I wouldn't be reciting (this message) to you, nor would He have made it known to you. I've lived with you for a whole lifetime before this (message came to me, and I've never spoken of religious issues before), so won't you realize (that it came suddenly and that it must be from Allah)?"* [16]

Who's more wrong than the one who invents a forgery and then attributes it to Allah or who denies (the truth of) His (authentic) verses? The wicked will never succeed! [17] They serve in place of Allah things that can neither harm them nor

---

[826] The Prophet said, "The people of Paradise will be inspired to glorify Allah and praise Him as naturally as their very breathing." (*Muslim*)

[827] 'Abdullah ibn Salam was a rabbi in Medina before the coming of Islam. He later said, "When the Messenger of Allah first arrived in Medina, people were scared away, and I was one of them. Then when I saw him, I realized that his face was not the face of a liar. The first thing I heard from him was his saying, 'People! Spread the greetings of peace, feed others, be dutiful to your relatives and pray at night while others are sleeping so you can enter Paradise in peace.'" (*Ahmad*)

[828] The Prophet said that Allah Himself said, "A servant of Mine who is always busy glorifying Me, so much so that he hasn't the time to ask for what he should ask for, then I will grant to him the best of what anyone asks for, and that is to have his needs taken care of without his even asking for it." (*Hadith Qudsi*)

[829] Five leaders among the Quraysh went to the Prophet and asked him to alter the teachings of the Qur'an so that they could keep worshipping their idols. This verse references their request. (*Asbab ul-Nuzul*)

benefit them, but then they (try to justify their idol-worship by) saying, *"These (idols) intercede for us with Allah."*

So ask (them), *"Are you really informing Allah about something in the heavens and the earth about which He doesn't know?"* Glory be to Him! He's so high above the partners they're assigning to Him! [18]

And what were people other than one community (in the beginning); yet, they fell into disputes (with each other and scattered away all over the world). If it wasn't for a word (of command) that your Lord previously issued (to let people have free will and then be judged by what they chose), then their differences would've been settled between them (immediately). [19]

Then they ask, *"So why isn't a miracle being sent down to him from his Lord?"*

Answer (them), saying, *"The unseen (realm of the supernatural) belongs to Allah, so wait (and see), for I'll be waiting with you."* [20]

Many don't Understand the Reality of their Lives

*W*hen We give people a taste of mercy after they had been suffering from some hardship – then look - they start plotting against Our signs straightaway! Say to them, *"Allah's plan is even faster than that! Our (angelic) envoys are keeping track of whatever you're planning."* [21]

He's the One Who makes it easy for you to travel over the land and sea. You board ships and sail along on them with favorable winds, and (the sailors) are pleased with their (progress).

However, when a storm arises and the waves begin to assault them from all sides, they feel as if they're going to perish. Then (they realize) that all religion belongs to Allah, so they cry out to Him, (pledging to serve Him) sincerely, saying, *"If You save us from this, then we'll be forever grateful!"* [22]

Then, when He saves them, they act outrageously throughout the earth (once more) against all right! O people! Your rebellion is against your own souls! (There's only a) short time to enjoy the life of this world – and then you're going to come back to Us, and that's when We're going to tell you the meaning of everything you ever did. [830] [23]

The example of the life of this world is like the water that We send down from the sky. It mingles with the various plants of the earth and causes them to sprout (to life). (These plants) then provide food for both people and animals. (The plants keep on growing) until the earth is clothed with their (blossoms and flowers), and then it's made (beautiful).

The people who own (the land around them) think that they're in control of it, but then Our command comes upon it by night or by day. Then We reduce it to dry stubble, as if there had never been any luxurious growth there just the day before! That's how We fully explain (Allah's) signs for those who think. [831] [24]

---

[830] The Prophet said, "A person who had lived a prosperous life in the world will be brought forward (on Judgment Day) and dipped once in the Fire. Then he will be asked, 'Have you ever experienced any goodness or felt any comfort?' The person will cry, 'No!' Then a person who had experienced terrible deprivation in the world will be brought forward and dipped once in the ecstasy (of Paradise). Then he will be asked, 'Have you ever faced any deprivation or misery before?' The person will cry out, 'No!'" (*Muslim*) Such will be the difference between what we experience in our earthly lives, in comparison to the magnitude of what is to come, that we will forget about everything that ever happened to us before.

[831] The Prophet said, "The one who makes this world his focus, Allah will deprive him of contentment and heartfelt satisfaction. He will remain ever in greedy pursuit of wealth and unattainable desires, and he will never receive more than the share that Allah has ordained for him. Whoever makes their focus the next life, Allah will bestow contentment and heartfelt satisfaction on them. He will also

The Final End is Where the Outcome will Be Decided

*A*llah is calling (you) to the Realm of Peace, and He guides whomever He wants towards a straight path. [25] Those who do good will have good (in return) – *and even more than that!* [832] There will be neither darkness nor shame upon their faces, for they're the companions of the Garden, and there they shall remain! [26]

Those who've earned evil against themselves will be rewarded similarly with evil, and they'll further be covered in disgrace.

They'll have no one to defend them against Allah, and their faces will be shrouded in the darkest shades of night. They're the companions of the Fire, *and that's where they're going to stay!* [27]

One day, We're going to gather them all together, and We'll say to those who made partners (with Us), *"Go to your places! You and the idols you've made!"*

Then We're going to separate them, and their partners will say, *"It wasn't us you were worshipping!* [28] *Allah is enough of a witness between you and us that we knew nothing of your worship of us."* [29]

Then and there every soul will be tried for what it had earned (in its life) before, and they'll be turned over to Allah, their rightful guardian. Whatever they invented will leave them to languish! [30]

The Sentence is Proven True against Them

*A*sk them, *"Who provides resources for you from the sky and the earth? Who has power over hearing and sight? Who brings life out of death and death out of life, and who governs the course of all matters?"* (After they've thought about it), they'll be sure to say, *"Allah."* Then ask them, *"So won't you then be mindful (of Him)?"* [31]

That's Allah for you, your true Lord. What is there after truth except mistakes? So how is it that you're turning away? [32]

And so it is that the pronouncement (that evil will be defeated) will be proven true against those who rebel, for they won't believe. [833] [33] Ask them, *"Is there any (idol) from among your (false gods) that can begin creation and then renew it?"*

Say (to them), *"Allah began the creation, and He renews it. So how are you deceived away (from the truth)?"* [34]

Ask them, *"Are there any among your (idols) that can guide someone to the truth?"* Then say to them, *"Allah guides to the truth. So isn't the One Who guides to the truth more worthy of being followed than (an idol or false god) that will remain lost unless it's guided (itself)?"*

Just how do you figure things? [35] Most of them follow nothing but conjecture; yet, conjecture can never win out over the truth, and Allah knows what they're doing. [36]

---

protect them from being greedy for wealth, and they will get their allotted share in this world." (*At-Targheeb wa at-Tarheeb*)

[832] The Prophet said, "When the people of Paradise enter into it, a caller will say, 'People of Paradise! Allah has made a promise to you that He wishes to fulfill.' They will reply, 'What can it be? Didn't He already make our scales heavy? Didn't He already brighten our faces and save us from the Fire?' Then Allah will remove the veil (that shrouds Him), and they will see Him. By Allah, they will never have been given anything more beloved by them or more delightful to them than looking at Him (directly)." (*Muslim*)

[833] The decree, sentence, or word against them is the general prediction that Allah made that most people will be thankless and will disbelieve in Him and thus be punished by Him. See 38:84-85, 11:119, and 32:13.

About those who Say the Prophet Invented It

This Qur'an isn't something that could've been produced by any other besides Allah. On the contrary, it confirms (the truth of those revelations) that came before it, and it's a detailed explanation of the Book (of Allah). [834] There's nothing doubtful within it, (for it's a scripture revealed) from the Lord of All the Worlds! [37]

Are they saying, "*He made it all up?*" Then (challenge them by) saying, "*So bring a chapter just like it, and then call upon anyone you can besides Allah (to compare the two), if you're being so honest.*" [38]

But no! They're denying what they can't even comprehend even before it's been fully clarified for them. In the same way, those who came before them also denied (the truth of their revelations,) but just see how the wrongdoers came to an end! [39]

Among them are some who believed in (their scriptures), while others did not, and your Lord knows best who the immoral are. [40]

If they accuse you of lying, then tell them, "*My deeds belong to me, even as your deeds belong to you. You're not responsible for what I'm doing, nor am I responsible for what you're doing.*" [41]

Now among them are some who merely pretend to listen to you, but can you force the deaf to hear, even while (those uncaring people) have no intellect? [42] There are others among them who stare at you, but can you guide the blind, even as they refuse to see? [43] Allah is never unjust to people in the least. Rather, it's people who are unjust to their own souls. [44]

One day, He's going to gather them all together, and it'll seem (to them) as if they had passed only a single hour of a day (in their earthly lives). They're going to recognize each other's (faces), and so it will be that those who denied their meeting with Allah and who refused guidance will be lost. [45]

Whether We show you now some of what We've promised them or We take your soul (before that), they're all going to come back to Us (in the end). Then Allah will be the witness over what they've done. [46]

A messenger was sent to every community (in the world). When their messenger comes before them (as a witness on the Day of Judgment), the issue will be decided between them with justice, and they won't be treated unfairly. [47]

(Now your people are) asking you, "*So when will this promise come to pass, if you're being so honest?*" [48]

Say (to them), "*I have no power to bring harm or benefit to myself, except as Allah wills. Every community has its own (predetermined) time limit. And when its deadline is reached, it can neither prolong it by an hour nor accelerate it.*" [49]

Ask (them), "*Do you see? If His punishment were to come upon you (suddenly) during the night or during the day, which part of it would the wicked want to hurry on? [50] Would you then finally believe in it at last?*"

"*What! Will you now (believe it's real when it happens), even though you wanted to hurry it on!* [51] *Then the wrongdoers will be told, 'Suffer the unending punishment! You're only getting what you deserve!'*" [52]

Now they're asking you to confirm it by saying, "*Is that the truth?*"

Tell (them), "*Absolutely! By my Lord, it's the truth, and you can't escape from it!*" [53]

---

[834] Even Paul recognized that all religiously-based scripture was useful for learning, and thus Christians and Jews might find much in the Qur'an that will help them better understand God and the purpose of their lives. (See II Timothy 3:16.)

Answer Allah's Call and be Saved

For every soul that sinned, if it had everything on earth to offer as a ransom (to save itself), it would offer it. (Nonetheless, such bribes won't be accepted,) so they're going to be filled with regret when they see the punishment. They'll be judged with justice, however, and they won't be treated unfairly. [54]

Isn't it (a fact) that whatever is in the heavens and on the earth belongs to Allah? Isn't it (a fact) that Allah's promise is a true one? Yet, most of them don't understand. [55] He's the One Who gives life and death, and you're going to return back to Him. [56]

O people! An earnest appeal has now come to you from your Lord, as well as a healing for your hearts and guidance and mercy for the believers. [57] Say to them, "*Let them celebrate in Allah's bounty and in His mercy.*" [835] That's better than (all the money) that they stow away. [58]

Ask them, "*Have you seen (and considered) all the resources that Allah sends down for you, (so you can survive in this world)? [836] Yet, you make some of those things forbidden (to eat) and other things lawful (to eat, for no logical reason)."* Then ask them, "*Has Allah given you permission (to do that), or are you making things up and assigning them to Allah?*" [59]

So what do those who invent lies against Allah think about the Day of Assembly? Allah is the master of endless favor towards the people (of earth); yet, most of them are thankless. [60]

Allah is always Watching Over You

There isn't a single thing that you're involved with, nor any portion of the Qur'an that you recite, nor any deed that you do without Us being there to see it, even while you're still in the middle of it!

There's nothing on the earth nor in the heavens that's hidden from your Lord – *nothing even as small as a speck* - and nothing smaller or greater than that exists without its being recorded in a clear record. [61]

Without a doubt, the closest allies of Allah will have neither fear nor sorrow! [837] [62] They're the ones who believed and who were mindful (of their duty to Him). [63] So there's good news for them in the life of this world, as well as (good news for them) in the next - *Allah's words (of prophecy) never change* - and that (promise which is from Him is indeed the signifier of) the greatest success! [64]

Don't let what (the faithless) are saying bother you, for all combined powers belong to Allah. He's the Hearing and the Knowing. [65] Without a doubt, (all creatures) within the heavens and the earth belong to Allah.

So what are they following, those who call upon 'partners' in place of Allah?

---

[835] The Prophet explained this verse by saying that the bounty is the Qur'an, and the mercy is our ability to recite it and to act according to its teachings (and thus win Allah's favor). (*Ma'ariful Qur'an*) Thus, this verse is telling the pagans that they should be happy with Allah more than they are with material possessions and worldly concerns.

[836] The 'resources' in this verse refer to the Arab superstitions regarding what cows, camels or goats they could eat depending on how they were birthed, what time of year, whether they were twin births or not and other such arbitrary things. Chapter six also contains lengthy discussions on this issue. See 6: 138-144.

[837] The Prophet said, "Among Allah's servants will be some whom the prophets and martyrs will consider fortunate." When the people asked him who they were, the Prophet replied, "They are the people who loved each other for the sake of Allah without any other considerations, such as money or kinship. Their faces will be lit up by layers of light. They won't experience any fear when others will be afraid, nor will they feel sorrow when others are grieving (on the Day of Judgment)." Then he recited this verse. (*Abu Dawud*)

They're following no more than conjecture and inventing lies. [66] He's the One Who made the night for you to rest in and the day to make things clearly seen. There's evidence in these things for any who care to listen. [67]

Addressing an Outrageous Claim

Now they're claiming, *"Allah has begotten a son!"* Glory be to Him! He's the Self-Sufficient! Everything in the heavens and on the earth belongs to Him! You have no basis to make such a claim! Are you saying things about Allah about which you know nothing? [68]

Say (to them), *"Those who invent a lie against Allah will never succeed."* [69] Just a bit of fun in the world (for them) - *and then they'll come back to Us!* Then We'll make them suffer a terrible punishment on account of their covering (over the truth). [70]

All Prophets had to Struggle

Recite for them the story of Noah, when he said to his people, *"My people! If my continued presence among you is a burden for you, even as I've been reminding you of the signs of Allah, (it doesn't matter) for I'm depending on Allah. So join together, both you and your idols, and gather your plans (against me). Don't second guess your plans. Then sentence me (to death), and give me no chances. [71]*

"If you (do decide) to turn away (from my preaching, then consider this): I haven't been asking you for any reward (for my efforts). My reward is due from none other than Allah, and I've been commanded to be with those who submit (to His will)." [72]

(His people ultimately) rejected him, but We saved him and whoever was with him in the boat. We let them inherit (the land), even as We overwhelmed in the flood those who rejected Our signs. [838] Now go and see how those who were warned were brought to an end! [73]

Then after him We sent messengers (all over the world) to their individual nations. They brought clear signs to them, but their (people) wouldn't believe in what they had already (decided to reject) beforehand. That's how We seal the hearts of the defiant. [74]

Moses and the Sorcerers

Then after them We sent Moses and Aaron with Our signs to Pharaoh and his nobles, but (the Egyptians) were an arrogant and wicked people. [75] When the truth came to them from Us, they said of it, *"This is obviously magic!"* [76]

Moses said to them, *"Are you saying this about the truth when it's come to you? Is this what magic is like? Mere sorcerers are never successful!"* [77]

(The Egyptians responded,) saying, *"Have you come to turn us away from the traditions of our ancestors, so you and your brother can become powerful in the land? (Well, it won't work) because we're never going to believe in you!"* [78] Then Pharaoh commanded, *"Bring me every skilled sorcerer (that we have)!"* [79]

When the sorcerers arrived, Moses said to them, *"Cast down whatever (spell) you wish to cast!"* [80] After they had their turn to cast, Moses said, *"What you've brought is wizardry, but Allah will render it useless, for Allah never lets the work of the immoral triumph. [81] By His words, Allah will prove the truth, no matter how much the wicked hate it!"* [82]

---

[838] There is no mention in the Qur'an concerning the duration of time that the flood lasted. The Bible claims it lasted for almost a year and covered the entire world under water before gradually receding. The oldest Mesopotamian records record the flood that occurred there to have been only six or seven days.

None of (the Egyptians) believed in Moses except for some of the offspring of (Pharaoh's) people, for they feared persecution from Pharaoh and his nobles. Pharaoh certainly was a tyrant in the land whose cruelty knew no bounds. [839] [83]

The Children of Israel Believe in Moses

$\mathcal{M}$oses announced (to the Hebrews), *"My people! If you believe in Allah, then trust in Him, if you're truly submissive (to His will)."* [84]

"We trust in Allah," they answered. (Then they prayed,) *"Our Lord! Don't make us a test for the oppressors.* [85] *Save us, through Your mercy, from those who reject (You)."* [86]

Then We inspired Moses and his brother, saying, *"Make homes for your people in Egypt, and turn your homes into centers (of worship). Establish prayers, and give good news to the believers."* [87]

Moses prayed, *"Our Lord! You've given Pharaoh and his nobles fancy trinkets and wealth in the life of this world. Our Lord, they've misled (many) away from Your path, so obliterate their wealth and harden their hearts so much so that they won't believe until they see the painful punishment."* [88]

"Your prayer is accepted," came the answer. *"So stand by the straight (path), and don't follow the path of those who have no knowledge."* [89]

The Children of Israel Escape from Egypt

$\mathcal{W}$e led the Children of Israel across the sea. Then Pharaoh and his hordes brazenly followed after them in (their blind) rage, even until he was overwhelmed and about to be drowned, at which time he said, *"Now I believe - there's no god save for the One in Whom the Children of Israel believe! Now I submit!"* [90]

"What! Now (you want to submit)?" (it was said to him.) *"Just a little while ago you were the cause of great turmoil!* [91] *We're going to save your body today, so you can become an example to those who will come after you. Yet, still most people are unconcerned with Our signs!"* [92]

And so it was that We settled the Children of Israel in an appropriate place and provided them with wholesome resources.

It was only *after* they were given knowledge that they fell into rival groups, but Allah will judge between them as to their differences on the Day of Assembly. [93]

Ask those who came Before You

$\mathcal{I}$f you're ever in doubt about what We're revealing to you, (Muhammad,) then just ask those who've been reading the scripture before you. [840]

---

[839] The Prophet said, "There are three types of people who will not have their supplications rejected: a just leader; a fasting person until he breaks his fast; and the supplication of an oppressed person, for Allah will raise (his supplications) above the clouds on the Day of Judgment. The doors of the sky will be opened for it, and Allah will say, 'By My grace! I will certainly grant it for you, even if only after some time has passed.'" (*Ahmad, Ibn Majah*)

[840] The Prophet suffered from so many insults and accusations at the hands of his idol-worshipping critics that he, too, being only human, sometimes felt moments of weakness and uncertainty while in Mecca. Keep in mind that the message he was bringing was also new to him and completely different from what he had experienced in his cultural background living in central Arabia. This is something that many Muslims and non-Muslims fail to appreciate. We take it for granted today that people talk of prophets, monotheism, good manners, theology, an afterlife and all the rest, but Muhammad did not grow up in such an environment. Islam was as new to him as it was to his pagan critics. Here he is told that if his own heart wavers under the assault of the pagans, he can ask the people who already had a scripture if what he is bringing is, indeed, similar to what the prophets of old brought. Mecca,

The truth has indeed come to you from your Lord, so don't be among the doubtful, [94] nor be among those who deny Allah's (revealed) verses, for then you'll be among the losers. [95]

Those who've had the sentence of your Lord proven against them won't believe, [96] even if every proof were presented to them – *that is until they see the painful punishment (right before their eyes)!* [97]

Of All the Cities, Who Believed?

𝒲hy hasn't there been a single settlement that believed, so that by its faith it could have prospered, other than the people of Jonah? [841] When they believed We removed the punishment of disgrace from them in the life of this world, and We allowed them to enjoy themselves for a (little) while longer. [98]

If Allah had wanted, He could've made everyone on earth into believers, (but He didn't). So how can you make people believe when they don't want to? [99] No soul can believe except by Allah's leave, and He brings dire consequences down upon those who don't use their reason. [100]

Say (to them), *"Look around at all (the wonderful signs) throughout the heavens and on the earth,"* though neither proofs nor warners are of any use to a people who have decided not to believe. [101]

Do they really expect any (other fate) than what befell those who passed away before them in former days? Then say (to them), *"You just wait then, for I'll be waiting with you, as well."* [102]

In the end, We saved Our messengers and those who believed, and it was entirely appropriate for Us to save those who believed. [842] [103]

A Call to those in Doubt

𝒮ay (to them), *"O People! If you have any doubts about my way of life, (then know that) I don't serve what you're serving in place of Allah. Moreover, I serve Allah, the One Who will take your souls (at death), and I've been commanded to be among the faithful.* [104]

"(I've also been told), 'Set your face upon the pure natural way. Never be an idol-worshipper,

---

being a trading town, did see Christian and Jewish merchants passing through from time to time. Some of them actually converted to Islam after the Prophet shared his message with them, proclaiming it to be the completion of their own religions.

[841] Jonah was sent to dwell among the people of Nineveh sometime between the years 793-753 BCE, during the reign of King Jeroboam II of Israel, (according to II Kings 14:23-25). Jonah was sent to preach in that foreign city, perhaps because the land of Israel was rife with idolatry, even into the royal house where the worship of a golden calf was (once again!) in full favor. Apparently, Nineveh, the city to which Jonah was sent, which was an early capital of the ruthless Assyrian Empire, is the only major city on earth that heard a prophet's preaching and then repented from the lowest of its people up to the ruling classes. Whereas the usual pattern in all other instances has been that the poor respond to a prophet, while most of the rich people and rulers fight against him, fearing a loss in their wasteful and extravagant lifestyles. Then Allah's just punishment comes in either the form of a natural calamity or invasion from outside invaders. The name of the Assyrian king that Jonah convinced was most likely Ashur-Dan III (772-755 BCE). This king ruled over an empire in flux, with restless nobles, rebellions, and strange portents that appeared, such as a total eclipse of the sun and two separate plagues that struck the land. This had the probable effect of making the people ready to listen to the preaching of a prophet, and it fits precisely with the pattern of divine intervention so often mentioned in the Qur'an (see 6:42-45). Unfortunately, the subsequent generations of the people of Nineveh soon forgot the teachings of Jonah. The city eventually fell in 612 BCE to an invading coalition of Medes, Babylonians and Susians. Thus, they enjoyed themselves *"for a (little) while longer."*

[842] 'Abdullah ibn 'Umar relates that one night after the Prophet had led the night prayers, he turned to the congregation and said, "Do you see this night you have? One hundred years after this night, none of those who are here in this land will be alive." (*Muslim*)

[105] *nor call upon any other besides Allah, for they're just (material) things that can neither benefit nor harm you. If you did, then you would truly be wrongdoers.'"* [106]

If Allah touches you with some harm, no one can remove it besides Him, and if He intends for any good to come your way, then no one can withhold His favor. [843] He causes it to reach whichever of His servants that He wills, for He's the Forgiving and the Merciful. [107]

Say (to them), *"People! Now the truth has come to you from your Lord! Whoever is guided is guided for the good of his own soul, and whoever goes astray does so to his own loss. It's not my place to manage your affairs."* [108]

Now follow the revelation that's being sent to you, (Muhammad,) and be patient until Allah decides the matter, for He's the best one to decide. [844] [109]

---

[843] The Prophet said, "No Muslim supplicates to Allah with a supplication that does not involve sinfulness or the severing of relations of the womb, but Allah will grant him one of three things: He will either respond to his supplication quickly, save it for him until the next life, or He will turn away from him an equal amount of harm." Some people asked, "What if we supplicate more?" He replied, "There is more with Allah." (*Ahmad*)

[844] Some years later, after the Muslims had fled to Medina, the Meccans and the Muslims met in the year 624 and did battle at the Wells of Badr. The outnumbered Muslims won a stunning victory, despite having odds of three-to-one against them. This battle has often been called the first distinctive 'decision' of Allah, which was meant to show the people of the region that His favor was upon the Prophet and his followers.

Hud

11 Hud
Late Meccan Period

This chapter is similar to the last in theme, and it continues the veiled subtext of separation. In other words, it prepares the Prophet and his followers for the possibility of abandoning their hometown. This is hard for anyone to do, let alone large groups of people. Late Meccan chapters like this continually mentioned episodes from the lives of prophets such as Noah and Moses who had to make a clean break from their people and past lives for the sake of a brighter future. When the order finally came to the Prophet to lead his followers to Medina, they would've already been well-versed in the principle of migrating for the sake of Allah's faith. Such was the tense atmosphere in the late Meccan period that it even began to show upon the appearance of the Prophet. Abu Bakr, noting that the Prophet seemed to be getting worn down, asked him, "It seems that you've been aging. Why is that?" The Prophet answered, "The chapter of Hud and others like it have aged me." (*Tirmidhi*)

In the Name of Allah,
the Compassionate, the Merciful

*A*lif. Lām. Rā.

(This) Book contains clear injunctions that have been categorically explained by One Who is wise and well-informed. [1] Therefore, you should serve none other than Allah.

(Muhammad, say to all people,) *"I've (been sent) to you from Him both to warn and to give good news. [2] Therefore, seek the forgiveness of your Lord, and repent to Him, so He can provide you with good things to satisfy you (here on earth)* for a while [845] *and ultimately grant His favor upon those who are worthy of merit.* [846] *If you turn away, then I'm afraid that you'll be punished on a momentous day.* [3] *All of you will go back to Allah, and He has power over all things."* [4]

As it is, they close up their hearts and try to hide from Him! [847] However, even though they wrap themselves up in their cloaks, He still knows what they hide and what they show, for He knows (all the secrets) of the heart. [5]

---

[845] The good things that cause satisfaction do not refer to obtaining riches and material goods. As the commentators explain, they refer to Allah making a person content with what they have in this life so they no longer covet or feel ashamed on account of possessions or the lack thereof.

[846] A man named 'Uqbah ibn 'Âmr once asked the Prophet, "What is (the best way to attain) safety (on the Day of Judgment)?" The Prophet replied, "Control your tongue, let (the walls of) your house surround you, and weep for your shortcomings." (*Tirmidhi*) This is a snapshot of the qualities of a true believer.

[847] Ibn 'Abbas (d. 687) was asked about this verse. He explained that it was about a superstition the pagans had in which they were afraid to expose themselves to the sky if they had to remove any of their clothes, either for answering the call of nature or from sleeping with their wives. (*Ibn Kathir*) This verse is telling them that Allah sees them no matter how much they try to hide.

The Faithless can't Hide in their Denials

*T*here isn't a creature that moves on the earth without its being dependent upon Allah for its provisions. [848] He knows where its usual resting place is, even as He knows where it lurks for a while, for everything is recorded in a distinctive ledger. [849] [6]

He's the One Who created the heavens and the earth in six time periods, and His throne was over the water. (He created you) so that He could test (you in order to bring out) which of you is most noble in conduct. However, (Muhammad), even if you told them, *"You really are going to be resurrected after death,"* those who suppress (the light of faith in their hearts) would be sure to say, *"This is obviously just magic."* [7]

Then if We delayed the punishment for some time, they would be sure to say, *"So what's holding it back?"* Oh, but on the day when it actually comes upon them - *nothing will hold it back from them then* - and they'll be completely surrounded by what they used to laugh at! [8]

Beware the Fickle Heart

*I*f We let a human being have a taste of Our mercy, but then withdraw it from him, he becomes despondent and thankless. [9] If We then let him experience good fortune after a bout of hardship has befallen him, he merely says, *"My streak of bad luck is over,"* and then he becomes proud and overconfident. [10] Although that's not the case with those who persevere and do what's morally right, for they're going to be forgiven, and they'll have a great reward. [11]

Stay the Course

*P*erhaps you've been tempted to abandon some of what's been revealed to you, or perhaps your heart has become filled with anxiety (at the prospect that) they might say, *"Why aren't any treasures being sent down to him, or why aren't there any angels coming along with him?"* You're only a warner, and Allah is the One Who manages all affairs! [12]

(Perhaps you're afraid) they might say, *"He made it all up!"* (If they do say that, then) tell them, *"So bring ten chapters like it, and call whomever you can other than Allah (to judge them as to their similarity), if you're really so honest! [13] And if your (idols) don't answer you, then know that this revelation is being sent down with Allah's knowledge and that there's no god besides Him. So now will you submit (to Him)?"* [14]

Those who desire the life of this world *and all its glitter* will be repaid by Us for the deeds they did within it, and (they) won't be shortchanged. [15] They're the ones who will have nothing in the next life - *other than the Fire!* All the plans they made will be useless there, even as all that they did will come to nothing! [850] [16]

---

[848] The Prophet said, "Allah's hand is full, and it is not diminished by spending throughout the night and the day." (*Bukhari*)

[849] That is Allah's Own record of what occurs in the universe. Nothing is left out.

[850] The Prophet told the following story: "Surely, the first person who will be judged on the Day of Resurrection will be a martyr. He will be brought before (Allah) Who will then list all the favors that were bestowed upon him (in the world), and he will recognize them. Then (Allah) will ask, 'What did you do with them?' He will say, 'I fought in Your cause and died a martyr.' Whereupon (Allah) will say, 'You're lying. You fought so people would call you brave, and so they said it.' Then the command will be issued, and he will be dragged on his face and thrown into Hellfire. Then, a person who acquired and taught knowledge and recited the Qur'an will be brought before (Allah) Who will remind him of the blessings (he received), and he would recognize them. (Allah) will then ask, 'What did you do with them?' He will reply, 'I acquired and taught knowledge and recited the Qur'an for Your sake.' Whereupon (Allah) will say, 'You're lying. You acquired knowledge so people would call you a

Are (such evil people the same as) those who accepted the (revealed scriptural) proof [851] of their Lord, which was taught by a witness sent from Him, even as the Book of Moses (was also sent) before it, as a source of guidance and mercy?

(The believers) put their faith in it, but those factions (from days gone by) who abandoned (their revelations) will have nothing but the Fire as their promised meeting place. Have no doubt about that, for it's the truth from your Lord, though most people don't believe. [17]

Who can be more wrong than the one who invents a lie against Allah? They're going to be brought back before their Lord, and then the witnessing (angels) will say, *"These are the ones who lied against their Lord!"* [852]

Without a doubt, Allah's curse will befall the corrupt! [18] They're the ones who hinder others from following the path of Allah, trying to make it seem crooked - *all the while they're the ones who are rejecting (the concept) of the next life!* [19]

There's no way they can obstruct Allah (and His purpose) in this world, nor will they find anyone to protect them besides Allah. Their punishment will be doubled, for they (couldn't bring themselves) to hear (the message) or notice (the signs of Allah). [20] They're the ones who've lost their own souls, and whatever

they invented will leave them to languish. [21] Without a doubt, they're going to be the biggest losers in the next life! [22]

Those who believed, who did what was morally right and who humbled themselves before their Lord, they'll be the companions of the Garden, *and there they shall remain!* [23] The two classes (of people, both the faithless and the believer), can be compared to the blind and deaf and the seeing and hearing. Are they the same in comparison? So won't you take a reminder? [24]

Noah's People Rejected Him

*A*nd so it was that We sent Noah to his people, (and he announced), *"I'm a clear warner (who's been sent) to you* [25] *(to teach you) that you should serve no one else besides Allah. I'm afraid that you might be punished on a terrible day."* [26]

The leaders of the faithless among his people said, *"We don't see anything in you more than a mortal man like ourselves, nor do we see anyone following you except the weakest and least sophisticated among us, nor do we see you as any better than the rest of us. No way (are you a messenger of Allah)! We think you (and your followers) are liars!"* [27]

(Noah) replied, *"My people! Have you considered that I (just might have) been given clear evidence from my Lord and that He might have indeed sent His mercy down upon me from His*

---

scholar; you recited the Qur'an so they would call you a reader, and so you were.' Then the command will be issued, and he will be dragged on his face and thrown into Hellfire. Then a person whom Allah made affluent and who was given riches will be brought forth and informed about the favors he received, and he will recognize them. Then (Allah) will ask, 'What did you do with them?' He will reply, 'I donated to every cause that You would have wanted me to support.' (Allah) will say, 'You're lying. You donated so that people would call you generous, and so it was said.' Then the command will be issued, and he will be dragged on his face and thrown into Hell." (*Muslim*)

[851] The 'proof' is the Qur'an.

[852] The Prophet said, "Allah, the Most Exalted and Sublime, will come near to a believer and conceal him in His shade, and He will screen him from other people and make him confess his sins. 'Do you remember this sin?' He will ask. 'Do remember that sin? Do you remember the other sin?' This will go on until He makes him admit to all of his sins, so much so that the believer will think he's about to be doomed. Then Allah will say, 'I have concealed these sins for you in the life of the world, and I've forgiven them for you today.' Then the believer will be given his record of good deeds. As for the faithless and the hypocrites, the witnesses will say, *'These are the ones who lied against their Lord! Without a doubt, Allah's curse will befall the corrupt!'*" (From verse 11:18) (*Bukhari, Muslim*)

Own presence? However, if (those things) are unclear to you, then should we force you to accept (Allah's truth) when you're dead set against it?" [28]

"My people! I'm not asking you for any money in return (for my preaching). My reward is due from none other than Allah, and I'm not going to push away (the poor people) who believe, (just because you look down upon them). They're going to meet their Lord, (even as you will). It's just that I've (come to the conclusion) that you're an ignorant people." [29]

"My people! Who would help me against Allah if I pushed the (poor) away? So won't you take a reminder? [30] *I'm not telling you that I have the treasures of Allah, nor do I know what's hidden, nor do I claim to be an angel. And I won't say about the ones whom you look down upon that Allah won't grant them something good, for Allah knows what's in their souls, and if I ever were to (push the poor away), then I would be acting like a tyrant."* [31]

They answered, *"Noah! You've argued with us and carried on the argument for a long time, so now bring down upon us that with which you've threatened us - that is if you're really telling the truth!"* [32]

"Allah will certainly bring it down upon you," (Noah) replied, *"but only when He wants to do it, and then you won't be able to stop it!* [33] *If Allah wants to leave you astray, then my advice won't do you any good, even though I want to advise you, for He is your Lord, and you're going to return back to Him."* [34]

(So now are the idol-worshippers of Mecca) saying, *"(Muhammad) has just made (this story) all up"?*

(Answer them), saying, *"If I made up (the story of Noah), then it would be my fault alone, but I'm free of all your (kinds of) corruption.* [853] [35]

The Great Flood

Noah received an inspiration (from Allah) that said, *"No more of your people will believe, except for those who've already believed. Therefore, don't feel any more sadness over what they're doing.* [36] *Build a boat under Our watchful eye and by Our inspiration, and don't petition Me any further about those who do wrong, for they're going to be drowned."* [854] [37]

So (Noah) began to build the boat, but every time the leaders of his people passed by him they would ridicule him. [855] He would say to them in answer, *"If you're ridiculing us now, (know that) we're (soon) going to be ridiculing you.* [38] *Soon you're going to know who it is that has a humiliating penalty in store, and who it is that will have a lasting punishment."* [39]

Then Our command arrived, and the heated banks (of the rivers) began to overflow! *"Board (the boat),"* We said, *"and take a pair of male and female from every kind (of useful livestock).* [856] *Load up your family, all*

---

[853] In addition to the rampant sin and debauchery of Arabia, the Meccans also practiced idolatry and mindless superstition, *and they had the nerve to accuse Muhammad of inventing the story of Noah?* Muhammad had the well-earned reputation, from an early age, of being completely honest. So how could they accuse him of blatant lying or forgery? He was free of their kind of corruption by their own witness. As the Meccans would find out later, such stories were known to other communities - even those living thousands of miles away.

[854] Noah preached to his people for many years. After he was finally and completely rejected by his people, as evidenced by his speech contained in chapter 71, Allah decreed that he should build a boat and save the few who believed. This is perhaps the world's oldest story, and we remember it to this day for the many lessons it yields.

[855] Noah lived in Mesopotamia in a city that was far from any large body of water (other than the nearby Euphrates river), so for him to build a large boat, in an open field away from the river, must have seemed doubly ludicrous.

[856] The commentators are divided as to which category of animals Noah was asked to take. Those who follow the Biblical line of thought view the flood as a world-wide event, and they say he took a pair of every animal, and even plants. Those commentators who believe that it was a local flood that devastated only Noah's own people say that Noah brought pairs of livestock animals that his people

except for those against whom the sentence has already been given, and (load) the believers." However, only a few had ever believed along with him. [40]

(Noah) said to (his followers), "*Set out upon (the boat), for its course and its coming to anchor will be in the name of Allah, and my Lord is truly forgiving and merciful.*" [41]

(Thereafter, the boat) floated with them upon waves (that towered over them) like mountains. Noah called out to his son, who had become separated from the rest (of the faithless), "*My son! Come on board with us, and don't (share the same fate) as the faithless!*" [42]

"*I'll climb upon some mountain,*" he called back, "*and that will save me from the (rushing) water!*" (Noah looked away in sadness and) said, "*Today, no one is safe from the command of Allah, unless He decides to be merciful to him.*"

Then the waves came between them, and (his son) was just another one of those who had been drowned. [43]

Then the saying went out: "*Earth! Swallow your water! Sky! Clear (yourself of clouds)!*" Then the water diminished, and the matter was fulfilled.

The boat came to rest upon Mount Judi, and the saying went out: "*The wrongdoing people have passed away!*" [44]

Then Noah called upon his Lord and said, "*My Lord! My son was of my own family. Even still, Your promise is true, and You're the fairest judge of all.*" [45]

"*Noah!*" (Allah) replied. "*He was no longer part of your family, for his actions were other than moral, so don't ask Me about things you may know nothing about. This is a word of caution that I'm giving to you so you won't be one of the ignorant.*" [46]

"*My Lord!*" (Noah) answered. "*I seek Your protection so that I won't ask You about things I may know nothing about. Unless You forgive me and show me mercy, then I would surely be among the losers.*" [47]

The call went forth: "*O Noah! Come down (out of the boat) with peace from Us and also with blessings upon you and upon the people who are with you, (and also upon the communities that will descend) from them – peoples to whom We'll give enjoyment, even though in the end a terrible punishment from Us will befall them.*" [48]

These are some of the hidden stories (that were unknown) to you (Muhammad) and that We're revealing (to you). Neither you nor your people knew them before. So bear patiently (the persecution of the Meccans), for the final (victory) is only for those who were mindful (of their duty to Allah). [49]

Hūd Calls to His People

$\mathcal{W}$e sent to the (people of) 'Ad their brother Hūd. He said (to them), "*My people! Serve Allah! You have no other god than Him. You've been doing nothing but inventing (false gods).* [50] *My people! I'm not asking you for any reward for this, for my reward is due from none other than the One Who created me. So won't you understand?*" [51]

"*My people! Ask your Lord to forgive you, and turn to Him (in repentance).* [857] *Then He'll send abundant rain down upon you and add strength to your strength. Don't turn away in wickedness!*" [52]

"*Hūd!*" they answered. "*You haven't brought us any convincing proof. We're not about to abandon our gods on your word alone, nor will we ever believe in you.* [53] *We'll admit to no more*

---

would need after they disembarked from the boat (to build their society anew). Today, many commentators assume it was a local flood, as nowhere in the Qur'an does it say the entire world was underwater.

[857] The Prophet said, "If a person accepts Islam sincerely, then Allah will forgive all his past sins, and from that moment the record of deeds begins again. His good deeds will be rewarded from ten to seven hundred times. A sin will be recorded as it is, unless Allah forgives it. (*Bukhari*)

than to say that maybe some of our gods have afflicted you with insanity."

(Hūd) replied, "*I call upon Allah as my witness, even as you are witnesses, as well, that I'm free of your making partners* [54] *in place of Him, so plot against me all you want, and give me no chance.* [55] *I'm going to trust in Allah, the One Who is my Lord and your Lord. There isn't a creature that moves without Him having a hold on its forelock, and my Lord is on a straight path."* [56]

"*If you turn away, then (at least) I've conveyed the message to you with which I was sent. (Now it just might happen that) my Lord will cause another people to rise up in your place. (No matter how much you resist Allah,) you can't harm Him in the least. My Lord is the guardian of all things."* [57]

And so when Our command came We saved Hūd and those who believed along with him by an act of Our Own mercy, and We saved them from a tremendous punishment. [58]

And so that was the (people of) 'Ad. They renounced the signs of their Lord, disobeyed His messengers, and obeyed the commands of every arrogant enemy (of faith). [59]

They were pursued by a curse in this life, and on the Day of Assembly, (oh, how they'll be punished), for the 'Ad rejected their Lord, and so - *away with the 'Ad, the people of Hūd!* [60]

The Thamud Suffer a Similar Fate

𝒲e sent to (the people of) Thamud their brother Salih. He said (to them), "*My people! Serve Allah! You have no other god than Him. He's the One Who produced you from the earth and settled you upon it. Ask for His forgiveness, and turn to Him (in repentance), for my Lord is always near and ready to respond."* [61]

(His people) said, "*Salih! You were one of us, and we had always placed our best hopes in you (that you might one day be our leader). Are you now forbidding us from worshipping what our ancestors worshipped? We have serious doubts about what you're calling us towards."* [62]

"*My people!*" (Salih) answered. "*What do you think? If I have evidence from my Lord and if He's given me mercy from His Own Self, then who could help me against Allah if I ever disobeyed Him (by giving up this mission)? So (the bribes) you're offering me (to quit) are no more than the instruments of my own ruin.* [63]

"*My people! This camel (you see here is specially blessed) by Allah and is a sign for you. Therefore, leave her to graze on Allah's land, and do her no harm, or a swift punishment will befall you."* [64]

(Then the arrogant people among them) cut (her legs) and crippled her, so (Salih) told them, "*Enjoy yourselves in your homes for the next three days, (after which you're going to be destroyed), and that's a promise that won't be proven false."* [65]

When Our command came, We saved Salih and those who believed along with him from the humiliation of that day through an act of Our Own mercy. Your Lord is Capable and Powerful! [66]

The mighty blast overtook the wrongdoers, and they lay cowering in their homes by the morning. [67] (It looked) as if they had never lived or flourished there before! And so it was (their fate), for the Thamud rejected their Lord, and so - *away with the Thamud!* [68]

The Ruin of Lot's People

𝒪ur emissaries went to Abraham with good news. They said, "*Peace,*" and "*Peace,*" he answered back.

Then he hurried to serve them a roasted calf. [69] However, when he noticed that their hands never moved to partake of (the meal), he became suspicious of them and grew afraid. "*Don't be afraid," they said, "for we're being sent against the people of Lot." [858] [70]

His wife just stood there and laughed when We gave her the good news of (a son named) Isaac and (a grandson named) Jacob. [71] "*Misfortune is mine!*" she sighed. "*How could I bear a child now, seeing that I'm an old woman and my husband here is an old man? That would be something amazing, indeed!*" [72]

"*Are you amazed at Allah's command?*" they asked. "*Allah's mercy and blessings are (invested in) you, the people of (this) house, and He is indeed praiseworthy and full of glory.*" [73]

When Abraham's sense of unease had left him, and after he had heard the good news (of a son), he began to plead with Us on behalf of Lot's people, [74] for Abraham was (by nature) forbearing and prone to beseeching (his Lord as a matter of habit). [75]

"*Abraham!*" (the angels said.) "*Put an end (to your pleading). The command of your Lord has already gone out. They're going to receive a punishment that cannot be turned away.*" [76]

When Our emissaries arrived (in the district of Sodom and Gomorrah and met with) Lot, he became worried about their (safety), for he felt powerless (to protect) them (from his wicked people). [859] "*Oh, what a stressful day!*" he cried out, [77] (as he noticed) his people rushing towards his (house), eager (to seize his guests), for they had long been engaged in perverted ways.

"*My people!*" he beseeched them. "*My daughters are here, and they're more appropriate for you!* [860] *Be mindful of Allah, and don't disgrace me with regards to my guests. Isn't there a single man among you with good sense?*" [78]

"*You know we want nothing from your daughters,*" they answered, "*and you know quite well what we want (to do with your guests)!*" [79]

"*If only I had the strength to keep you at bay,*" (Lot) cried out, "*or some strong force to call upon!*" [80]

"*Lot!*" (the angels) said. "*We are emissaries from your Lord! They won't reach you, (for we're going to hold them back). Flee (this city) with your family while some of the night still remains, and don't let anyone look back. However, your wife (is not going to leave with you). Thus, she's going to suffer the same fate that they're going to suffer. Their time will be up by the morning, and isn't the morning near at hand?*" [81]

When Our command came, We turned (their towns) inside out and rained shower upon shower of hard-packed brimstone down upon them [82] – (each blow being) imposed by your Lord, and such (punishments) are never far from those who do wrong. [83]

---

[858] The angels mentioned here were disguised as humans, so as not to arouse alarm or undue adulation. 'Abdullah ibn 'Abbas said that they were three in number and that they were the angels Gabriel, Michael and Israfil. (*Qurtubi*) According to reports mentioned in Ma'ariful Qur'an, the guests were acting strangely. They had arrow heads and were poking the food with them. Other reports derived from Jewish sources say that the angels were being evasive in their answers to Ibrahim's queries about their identity. At-Tabari reports that the angels refused the meal unless they could pay Abraham for it. Abraham asked only that they begin the meal by mentioning Allah's name and that that would be payment enough. The angels turned to one another and said that it truly is appropriate that Allah calls this man a friend.

[859] It was Lot's wife who informed her wicked friends of her husband's secret guests, no doubt telling them how handsome they were. Lot's wife became completely engaged in the ways of the locals and forgot about Allah. In addition, she used to tell the people about what Lot was doing, as well as inform them whenever he had guests from out of town. The riotous crowds would then come and dishonor Lot's guests in the most shameful and deplorable manner. (*Ibn Kathir*)

[860] Some commentators are of the opinion that Lot's call to offer his *daughters* should not be taken literally and that through this line of reasoning he was telling the men gathered before his door that they should give up their homosexuality, (or he was possibly using this appeal as a stalling tactic), knowing full well that the crowd would have never considered his daughters seriously at all. (See Genesis 19:8 where Lot is also quoted as offering his daughters to appease the wild mob.)

Madyan was also Tested

$\mathcal{W}$e sent to (the people of) Madyan their brother Shu'ayb. He said, "My people! Serve Allah! You have no other god than Him! Don't cheat when you measure or weigh (in your business dealings). I see that you're in prosperity now, but I'm afraid that you'll be punished on an overpowering day." [84]

"My people! Weigh and measure fairly, and don't withhold from people what rightfully belongs to them. Don't spread corruption in the land with a desire to cause chaos. [861] [85] (The fairly earned profits) that Allah has left for you are the best for you, if you only had faith! However, I haven't been given the task of watching over you." [86]

"Shu'ayb!" they answered. "Are the prayers that you're making (to your God) telling you that we should give up worshipping what our ancestors did or give up using our property as we see fit? Oh, aren't you the one who is so forbearing and filled with common sense, (especially when you're telling others what to do)!" [87]

"My people!" (Shu'ayb) replied. "Now you just see if I have clear evidence from my Lord (to back up my claim. Here, take a look at my own business dealings), for (Allah) has given me good returns (through honest trade as a bounty) from His Own Self. I don't want to engage in what I've been forbidden to do, unlike your own practices. My only desire is to improve (your lives) to the best of my ability. My success will come only from

Allah! I trust in Him and turn to Him (in repentance)." [88]

"My people! Don't let my opposition (to your longstanding practices) cause you to do (more) wrong (in response), for you might suffer a fate similar to that of the peoples of Noah, Hūd or Salih, and the people of Lot are not so far away from you (that you should claim ignorance). [862] [89] Ask your Lord to forgive you, and turn towards Him (in repentance and obedience), for my Lord is full of forgiveness and loving tenderness." [90]

"Shu'ayb!" they answered. "We don't even understand most of what you're telling us! In fact, we think you're the weakest among us. If it wasn't for your family (connections), we would've stoned you already, because you don't have any power to prevent us." [863] [91]

"My people!" he replied. "Is my family's (influence) the most important factor for you to consider (in deciding whether to harm me or not), even more than (your fear of) Allah? Are you casting Him aside behind your backs (so easily)? My Lord completely surrounds whatever you're doing!" [92]

"My people! Do whatever you can, and I'll do whatever I can, likewise. You're soon going to know who will have a humiliating punishment befall them and who is lying, so keep on watching, for I'll be watching with you." [93]

When Our command came, We saved Shu'ayb and those who believed along with him through an act of Our Own

---

[861] This refers to the highway robbery and raiding that some from his tribe commonly practiced. (*Ibn Kathir*) They also shaved the edges of gold and silver coins to steal wealth, even as the coins appeared mostly normal. Thus, cutting or shaving coins has been made a crime in Islamic law. (*Ma'ariful Qur'an*)

[862] The lands of Salih's people were only a short journey's south/southeast of the area where the people of Lot used to dwell. Even as Sodom and Gomorrah were destroyed by an earthquake and resultant shower of stones, Salih's people were likewise obliterated in a cataclysm. It is said that the main city in question was located in southern Jordan in a place now named Ma'an.

[863] The Prophet once asked a group of his companions, "Do you know who is really poor?" The companions replied that in their estimation a poor person was someone who had no money or possessions. Thereupon the Prophet said, "The real poor person from my community is the one who will come on Judgment Day with tremendous good deeds and a good record of prayer, fasting, charity and the like; yet, (while he was alive in the world) he had insulted people, falsely accused people, devoured people's property unjustly and had someone killed, beaten or harassed. All those oppressed people will take their complaints to Allah, and the good deeds of the oppressor will be distributed to the oppressed. Finally, when there are no good deeds left, and there are still more complaints to be settled, then the sins of the oppressed people will be transferred to the oppressor, and thus he'll be thrown into Hellfire." (*Muslim*)

mercy, but the mighty blast took hold of the corrupt, and they lay cowering in their homes by morning. [94] (It looked) as if they had never lived and flourished there before! And so it was that the (people of) Madyan were removed - *just like the people of Thamud!* [95]

Take Heed of the Pattern of History

*A*nd so it was that We also sent Moses with Our signs - and also with a clear mandate [96] - to Pharaoh and his nobles. However, (his nobles) obeyed Pharaoh's orders, and (obeying) Pharaoh's orders was not the most rational (thing for them to do). [97]

He's going to stand before his people on the Day of Assembly and then lead them into the Fire - *and oh, how terrible is the place into which they'll be led!* [98] They're followed by a curse in this (life), and on the Day of Assembly they're going to get an awful gift (in exchange for their awful deeds). [99]

These are some of the stories of the nations (of the past) that We're narrating to you. Some of them still exist, while others have been mowed down. [100]

It wasn't We Who did them any wrong. Rather, they did wrong against their own souls. All those idols that they used to call upon besides Allah were of no use to them when Allah's command went out, nor did they add anything (to their plight) except for more destruction. [101]

That's what being seized by your Lord is like when He seizes towns steeped in the midst of their own corruption, and His grasp is exceedingly firm! [864] [102]

There is a sign in this for those who fear the penalty of the next life. That will be a day when all people will be gathered together, and that will be a day of giving testimony. [103] We won't delay it any more than the time that's set for it. [104]

On the day when it arrives, no soul will be allowed to speak unless it's been granted His permission. Some of those (assembled) there will be wretched, and others will be esteemed. [865] [105]

The wretched will be in the midst of the Fire, and they'll have nothing but moaning and wailing, [106] and they'll remain there for as long as the heavens and the earth endure, except as your Lord wills, and your Lord does whatever He wants. [107]

Meanwhile, those who are held in high esteem will be in the midst of the Garden, and they'll remain there for as long as the heavens and the earth endure, except as Allah wills, and it will be an unending gift. [108]

Have no doubts (about the true nature) of what these (Meccans) are worshipping, for they're worshipping nothing more than what their ancestors worshipped before them (out of blind habit). We're going to pay them back what is due to them without withholding anything. [109]

And so it was that We gave the scripture to Moses, but (later generations) differed about it. If it wasn't for the statement (of principle) that went out before from your Lord (that people will

---

[864] The Prophet said, "Allah gives some time to a wrongdoer until He seizes him, and then he cannot escape." Then the Prophet recited this verse. (*Bukhari, Muslim*)

[865] When this verse was revealed, 'Umar ibn al-Khattab asked the Prophet, "Messenger of Allah, is there some sign for us to know (of which group we will be a part)? Will it be because of something a person did or didn't do?" The Prophet replied, "'Umar, it will be due to something that he did and that was recorded by the pens (of the guardian angels), but every easy deed was created for its purpose." (*Tirmidhi*) The last part of the tradition means, as explained by another tradition, that people who are inclined towards good find the doing of good deeds easy, while those who are inclined towards evil find evil deeds easy.

302

have time to make their choice as to whether or not to believe), then the matter would've been decided between them. However, they persist in doubts and misgivings about it. [110]

What is a Sincere Believer?

*A*ll shall be repaid by your Lord for the result of their deeds, for He's well-informed about everything they're doing. [111]

Therefore, stand up firmly (for the truth) as you've been ordered to do, both you and those who are with you who turn (to Allah for guidance).

Don't overstep (Allah's laws). Indeed, He's watching everything you do. [112]

Don't lean towards (being on the side of) wrongdoers, or else the Fire will take hold of you. You have no other protector than Allah, and you won't be helped (by anyone else if you cross Him). [113]

Establish prayer at the two ends of the day and during some hours of the night, for good deeds remove evil deeds. [866]

This is a reminder for those who would be reminded. [114] Bear with patience (any hardships that befall you), for Allah will never allow the reward of the righteous to be lost. [115]

Parting Thoughts on the Path of Truth

*S*o now why weren't there - in all the generations that went before you - people with sense enough to prevent others from spreading chaos and disorder in the earth, save for the very few whom We saved (from harm)?

The wrongdoers followed after nothing more than what pleased them, and they were truly wicked. [116] However, your Lord never destroys a settlement unjustly, (that is) as long as its people are behaving well. [117]

If your Lord had wanted, He could've made all people into a single community. However, they never cease to argue, [118] except for the ones who've been graced with your Lord's mercy, and this is the purpose for which We created them. [867]

The sentence of your Lord will be fulfilled: "*I will fill Hellfire with jinn and people all together!*" [119]

(The purpose) of all of these stories of (the ancient) messengers that We're relating to you is to strengthen your heart. These (stories) that are coming to you contain the truth, as well as warnings and reminders for those who believe. [120]

So say to those who don't believe, "*Do whatever you can, and we'll do whatever we can.* [121] *Wait for some time, and we'll be waiting, also.*" [122]

---

[866] A man had kissed a woman to whom he was neither married nor related, and he went to the Prophet in repentance and asked how the sin could be erased. This verse was then revealed. After the Prophet recited it, the grateful man asked, "Messenger of Allah, is this verse just for me?" The Prophet replied, "This is for all of my community." (*Bukhari*)

[867] The Qur'an offers the reason why Allah created living creatures. It was so that He could extend mercy towards them. Allah is love [85:14], and He extends that love to all. In the contest of free will, however, the Qur'an makes it abundantly clear that Allah does not love those who do evil on earth and harm their fellow creatures. Even in that condition, however, Allah continues to hold out the gift of repentance and forgiveness. Even an evil person can regain fellowship with Allah. The way is open for each person's entire life up until just before their death throes begin. The material world is in some ways our nemesis, however, for our flesh desires it greatly at the expense of our spiritual and intellectual well-being. It is so much easier to give in to bodily urges than to be self-controlled and thoughtful. In this the Prophet left us with this warning, "Hell is surrounded by delights, while Paradise is surrounded by hardships." (*Bukhari, Muslim*)

The (knowledge) of unseen things within the heavens and the earth belongs only to Allah, and all matters will go back to Him (for their resolution), so serve Him, and trust in Him. Your Lord is not unaware of what you're doing. [123]

Joseph

12 Yusuf
Late Meccan Period

The story of Joseph has long been considered one of the most engaging and heart-warming accounts in the Qur'an. It is also the single longest chapter with only one continuous theme and story line. It was revealed near the last days of the Prophet's stay in Mecca, at a time when the pagans and enemies of Islam were closing the noose of public enmity around the Muslims from all sides. A group of visiting Jews from the northern city of Yathrib (later to be called Medina) had doubts about the validity of Muhammad's prophethood.

Hoping to expose him as a possible fraud, they suggested to the pagans that they should ask him to narrate a Jewish story that the Arabs knew nothing about. In the main square of Mecca, a pagan man asked him, "What happened to Joseph and his brothers? How did they come to live in a far-away land among strange people?"

If Muhammad failed to answer, then it could've been said that he was a fake and not a true prophet. Muhammad exclaimed that he would wait for revelation from his Lord. A short while later, Muhammad stood out in the public forum and proceeded to recite the entire story of Joseph and his brothers - without a pause or break - until the entire length of this chapter was finished. (Verses 1-3 were revealed and added later.)

As Muhammad recited the story, the crowd fell silent. When he had finished, the Jewish visitors who witnessed the event left without saying a word. A few weeks later, several more visitors came from Yathrib, this time Arabs, and they accepted Islam at a site called 'Aqabah. The Muslim community now had two great lights to give them hope: the addition of new believers from another city; and *the most beautiful of all stories*, as the Qur'an described the story of Joseph.

In the Name of Allah,
the Compassionate, the Merciful

*A*lif. Lām. Rā.

These are the verses of the clear Book. [1] We've sent it (in the form of) an Arabic Qur'an so you can think (on it) deeply. [868] [2]

---

[868] In other words, this chapter is the retelling of a Hebrew story in the Arabic language, so the Arabs who asked the Prophet about the story of Joseph could understand it. The deep reflection and pondering comes in when people consider that the Prophet could not have known this story, for he couldn't read or speak Hebrew, nor could he read or write in any language. How then could he narrate the entire story in one sitting in a public square and fill it full of rhyme, passion and drama? (We must also remember that there were no translations of the Old Testament in Arabic at that time. This was not done until the tenth century by a Jewish scholar in Egypt named Said bin Youssuf al Fayyumi.)

Now We're going to narrate to you the most beautiful story in Our revealing this portion of the Qur'an to you. [869] You didn't know (this story) before. [3]

The Dream

Joseph said to his father, "*O Father! I saw (in a dream) that eleven stars, the sun and the moon were all bowing themselves to me!*" [870] [4]

"*My little son,*" his father answered. "*Don't mention this vision to your brothers for they might plot against you (out of jealousy). Satan is the clear enemy of all of humanity!*" [5]

"*(It's my feeling) that your Lord is going to choose you (to be a prophet) and teach you how to interpret (the meaning of passing events).* [871] *(By this gift), He will complete His favor upon you and upon the descendants of Jacob, even as He had already completed it upon your forefathers, Abraham and Isaac. Indeed, your Lord has all knowledge and wisdom.*" [6]

And it just so happens that in (the story of) Joseph and his brothers, there are definitely lessons for (those) people who asked! [7]

The Brothers Plot against Joseph

(Joseph's older brothers complained among themselves,) saying, "*Our father loves Joseph and his (younger) brother (Benjamin) more than he loves us, even though we're just as good! Our father is obviously mistaken!*" [8]

(Then one of the brothers suggested), "*So then let's kill Joseph or send him away to some far off place. Then our father will give us all his attention. There'll be plenty of time for all of you to reform yourselves later on.*" [9]

However, one of the other (brothers) said, "*Don't kill Joseph! Why don't you throw him down in the bottom of a well? Then some passing caravan can find him (and take him away).*" [872] [10]

(Later, the brothers approached their father and said,) "*Father! Why don't you entrust Joseph with us, since (you know) we have his best interests at heart?* [11] *Send him with us tomorrow to enjoy himself and play. We'll protect him (from any danger).*" [12]

"*I'm uneasy,*" their father replied, "*about your desire to take him (along with you). I'm afraid that a wolf might eat him while you're not paying attention.*" [13]

"*If a wolf were to eat him,*" they answered, "*while there's so many of us (there to protect him), then we would have perished (first)!*" [14]

So, they took Joseph out with them, (after assuring their father he would be

---

[869] The classical writer, Nouruddin Jami' (d. 1492), crafted a dramatic retelling of this entire story in his book entitled, *Yusuf and Zulaikhah*. It has since been regarded as a highly spiritual exploration into the complicated lives of the two main characters, the unspoken details of which make this tale so fascinating. The tragic Arabian story of *Layla and Majnoun*, collected and assembled by Nizamuddin (d. 1209), also echoes a similar theme of romantic/spiritual tension and ultimate redemption.

[870] Verse 100 of this chapter reveals the meaning of this dream of Joseph. Dreams that come true are from Allah and are real, according to Islam. The Prophet once said, "Nothing is left of prophethood (after I pass away) except glad tidings." The people asked, "What are the glad tidings?" He replied, "True good dreams (that convey glad tidings)." (*Bukhari*) He also said, "The dream of a believer is a dialogue in which he has the honor of talking to his Lord." (*Tabarani*) In other words, the only supernatural communication between Allah and humanity after Allah's last prophet to the world passed away will be in the form of dreams that may come true, which any individual can have.

[871] *Taweeli al-ahadith* can mean understanding passing events or interpreting the true meaning of things that occur in sequence. In other words, Joseph would one day gain the wisdom to interpret events and explain their meaning. This ability would also extend to visions and dreams.

[872] The Old Testament names this more high-minded brother as Reuben. See Genesis 37:20-22.

fine), but secretly they had all agreed to throw him down a well. [873]

(Then, as they seized Joseph and were about to throw him into the deep pit,) We revealed (this message to) his (heart), *"One day you're going to tell them about their affair when they won't even know (who you are)!"* [15]

Then (the brothers) returned home at nightfall in tears. [16] *"Oh, Father!"* they cried. *"We went racing with each other and left Joseph all alone (to watch) our things. Then a huge wolf (came and) ate him up! Yet, you'll probably never believe us, even though we're telling the honest truth!"* [17]

(Then they pulled out his shirt,) which they had secretly stained with false blood. *"It can't be!"* Jacob cried. *"You must have made (some kind of plan) amongst yourselves! As for me, I can only wait with gracious patience. Only Allah can (help me) bear (the pain) of what you've described."* [18]

Then a caravan of travelers passed by, and when they sent their (water boy) to the well, he let down his bucket and shouted, *"Hey! (Look at this!) What a lucky break! Here's a fine young boy!"* [874]

Then they stowed him away like a treasure, though Allah knew what they were doing. [19] (Joseph's brothers) sold him (to the caravan) for the measly price of (a handful) of silver. That's how low of an opinion they had of him! [20] [875]

Joseph in Egypt

The Egyptian who bought (Joseph) said to his wife, *"Treat him honorably, for he might bring us some benefit, or we could even adopt him as a son."* [876]

This is how We settled Joseph in the land so We could teach him how to interpret passing events. Allah has complete proficiency over His affairs; yet, most people never realize it. [21]

---

[873] When the brothers had Joseph out of sight of their father, they began slapping him and abusing him all the way to the well where they intended to imprison him until he either starved to death or was found by passing nomads. Joseph was begging them to let him go, but they tied him with ropes and beat him into silence. They taunted him, telling him to call on those 'eleven stars' for help. When they threw him down the deep well, he would have drowned, except he found a stone to stand upon and was able to keep his head above water. (*At-Tabari*) The commentators say that Joseph was a young teenager at the time and that he spent three horrible days in the well. (*Ma'ariful Qur'an*)

[874] Some commentators hold that the name of the young man who discovered Joseph in the well was Malik ibn Du'bar. (*Ma'ariful Qur'an*) The caravan in question was an Arab caravan. The Arabs were traders linking Africa, Arabia, Syria and Asia from time immemorial. To find a lone young boy they can sell into slavery was considered by such people as a lucky break indeed.

[875] Some commentators say that the brothers went back to the well when Joseph was taken out and demanded money from the caravan owners to buy the boy (as also mentioned in the Old Testament in Genesis 37:25-28). Other commentators suggest that the brothers had no more contact with Joseph and that the caravan merely found him and took the boy away. Based on the context of these two verses [12:19-20], it seems the first view is more likely, as it was the brothers who held Joseph in contempt. According to reports in al-Qurtubi and Ibn Kathir, this type of language used here indicates, in common merchant parlance of the day, that the selling price for Joseph was under 40 silver coins and thus a 'measly' sum to well-established mobile merchants. (The Bible claims that Joseph's selling price was a mere twenty pieces of silver. See Genesis 37:28.) Although official government-stamped coinage was not yet invented, the use of gold and silver as a trade medium had long been established throughout the Middle East from as far back as 2500 BCE.

[876] Traditionally, the man who bought Joseph is known as Potiphar (Qitfir or Itfir in Arabic), while his title of *al-'Aziz*, which means powerful official, is how the Qur'an refers to him. It is thought that he served in the government of the Amalikite (Hyksos) ruler Rayyan ibn al-Walid as priest of the god named On. This king led a dynasty of foreign origin that had subjugated northern Egypt some years before. (*Zamakhshari*) Others date him earlier to the reign of the two pharaohs Sesostris the I and III. The name of Potiphar's wife has traditionally been known as Zulaikhah. Some commentators say she was also known as Ra'eel. Joseph lived in her house for about ten years, and he was approximately 17 at the time he was brought into the service of her family. (*Zamakhshari*)

In time, as Joseph became fully mature, We endowed him with sound judgment and intelligence, and that's how We reward those who are good. [22]

However, she in whose house he lived (began to feel attracted to him), and she sought to seduce him against his (moral) nature. She bolted the doors and said to him, *"I'm ready for you now, (so come to me)!"*

"Allah forbid!" Joseph exclaimed. *"Your husband is my master! He's the one who made my life here tolerable! No good comes to people who do wrong!"* [23]

The fact was, however, that she desired him greatly, and he would've desired her, except that he remembered the proof of his Lord. Thus, We turned him away from decadence and (the desire to do) shameful deeds, for He was one of Our sincere servants. [877] [24]

Then they raced each other to the door, and she tore his shirt from behind (as he attempted to get away). When they reached the door they found her noble (husband) standing right there! (Thinking quickly,) she said, *"What other punishment can there be for someone who wickedly (tried to seduce) your wife) except prison or a painful beating!"* [25]

"But she's the one who tried to seduce me away from my own nature!" (Joseph) protested.

Just then, a member of her household who witnessed (the scene as it unfolded),

suggested, *"If his shirt is torn from the front, then she's telling the truth, and he's the liar!* [26] *But if his shirt is torn from the back, then she's the liar, and he's telling the truth!"* [27]

When he saw that Joseph's shirt was, indeed, torn from the back, (he turned to his wife and scolded her), saying, *"Truly, this is your ploy, and your ploy is formidable!* [878] [28] *Joseph, forget any of this ever happened!"* (Turning back to his wife), he said, *"Apologize for your offense, for you're clearly at fault!"* [879] [29]

The Women of the City Find Out

(When news of the event became known), the (upper class) women of the city (began to gossip), saying, *"The wife of the great minister wants to seduce her own houseboy. He must have stricken her with passionate desire. We can see that she's clearly losing her mind!"* [30]

When she heard of their malicious gossiping, she invited them and prepared a banquet for them. (After they all arrived and were seated,) she gave each of them a (fruit-cutting) knife.

(While they were cutting their food), she called out to Joseph, saying, *"Come out (Joseph, and stand here) before them."*

When they saw him, (his handsome features) astounded them, and they cut right through (their fruit) to their hands! [880]

---

[877] In classical Muslim literature, it was surmised in popular writings that Zulaikhah had portraits of herself painted all over her room, so that even if Joseph turned away from her, he would see images of her wherever he turned. The Prophet said that when Joseph was faced with the temptation to be with Zulaikhah, the angels reported to Allah that Joseph was thinking a bad thought. Allah told them to only record it as sin if he acted on it, but if he resisted the sin, then they should record it as a good deed, for he restrained himself for Allah's sake. (*Muslim*)

[878] Potiphar is quoted here using the plural form of the pronoun 'you.' Thus, he is blaming women in general for their considerable talent in ensnaring men's hearts. As the commentators have pointed out, this is just Potiphar's opinion, based on perhaps his own moment of anger, and it in no way applies to all women. (*Ma'ariful Qur'an*)

[879] This wealthy and powerful man was easy going by nature, and he did not think to revenge himself upon either Joseph or his wife, which was fortunate for them both.

[880] Apparently, Joseph was extremely good looking. During his journey into heaven on his Ascension, the Prophet Muhammad passed by Joseph in the third layer of heaven, and he commented about him,

"*Allah save us!*" they cried. "*He's no mere mortal! This is no less than an angelic being!*" [31]

"*There before you now,*" she said, "*is the one you blamed me for! (Yes,) I did try to seduce his very soul, but he eluded me and resisted me in order to preserve his innocence! Now if he doesn't do what I command, he'll surely be thrown into prison and be with the most contemptible!*" [32]

"*My Lord!*" (Joseph) cried. "*I desire prison far more than what they're calling me towards, and unless You steer their ploy away from me, I might become attracted to them and act like an ignorant fool.*" [33]

Then his Lord heard (his plea) and turned their ploy away from him, for truly He is the Hearing and the Knowing. [881] [34] Then, after they saw the evidence (of what was going on), it occurred to (the husbands of the women) that it would be best to put him in prison for a while. [35]

The Two Prisoners

*N*ow along with Joseph there were two other men who were put in (the prison). [882]

The first one said, "*I saw myself (in a dream) pressing wine.*"

The second one said, "*I saw myself (in a dream) carrying bread on my head with a swarm of birds eating off it.*"

(Then they said to Joseph), "*Tell us the meaning of these (strange dreams), for we can tell that you're a good one (to ask).*" [36]

(Joseph) answered, "*Even before your next meal comes, I'll explain to you the meaning of (your dreams that will predict) events before they even happen to you. This is part of what my Lord has taught me. I've abandoned the customs of (these) people who disbelieve in Allah and reject the (punishment) of the next life.* [37] *I follow the customs of my fathers, Abraham, Isaac and Jacob, and none of us ever made any partners with Allah. This comes from the grace of Allah that's been bestowed upon us and upon people (in general), though most people are thankless.*" [38]

Then he said, "*My fellow inmates! Which is better: many lords arguing among themselves, or the One, Irresistible Allah?* [39] *If you don't serve Him, then you're serving nothing more than names that you and your ancestors made up, and Allah gave no one permission to do that. The right to command is for none save Allah, and He has commanded that you serve nothing besides Him. That's the straight way of life, but most people don't understand.*" [40]

"*My fellow inmates,*" he continued. "*As for the first of you, he will again pour out the wine for his master to drink. As for the other, he will be*

---

saying, "He was given half of all beauty, and the rest was spread throughout the rest of creation." (*Muslim*)

[881] Zulaikhah wanted to turn her handsome young slave into nothing more than a plaything for her and her girlfriends' pleasure. Joseph, however, being a Godly-oriented man, cried to Allah for deliverance, for he knew the weakness of mortal man in the face of determined female charms. How did he escape the women at the banquet? What were the proofs of Allah that reminded him to be righteous? These questions were the subject of a small but persistent body of speculation in the classical period, and the great commentator at-Tabari offers several different hypotheses culled from many writers. Some early commentators have suggested he ran out of a door; others have said that the women felt powerless to take him due to the look of resoluteness on his face; yet, others have suggested that the banquet was interrupted by some of the women's husbands who arrived unexpectedly, leading into the events of verse 35. Here in the Qur'anic text, there is no clear explanation for either question offered, though this hasn't stopped Muslim writers from delving into the deeper issues raised by this tale.

[882] Ibn Kathir records that when Joseph was placed in prison, the officer in charge of him came to admire him and told him so. Joseph protested that no one should love him, because anytime someone came to love him, he suffered for it. Then he gave the example of how he was loved by a paternal aunt of his, and then he was falsely accused of stealing from her as a boy. When his father loved him, he found himself thrown in a well and then sold as a slave in a foreign country. When Zulaikhah loved him, he was thrown in prison. As much as Jacob grieved for his lost Joseph, one can imagine the grief of Joseph in this, his most desperate hour.

309

hung from a stake, and the birds will eat off his head. The matter you two asked me about has been decided." [41]

(Then Joseph) whispered to the one whom he thought would be released, "Mention me to your master." However, Satan made (the man) forget all about it, so Joseph lingered in prison for a few more years. [42]

The Mysterious Dream

$\mathcal{T}$he king [883] (of Egypt called out to his nobles) and said, "I saw (in a dream) seven fat cows being eaten by seven skinny ones and seven green shafts of grain and seven others withered. My nobles! Tell me what my vision means if you can explain the meaning of visions." [43]

"Just a confused bunch of symbols," they replied. "We're not experts at figuring out the meaning (of such cryptic dreams)." [44]

However, the one who had been released (from prison), and who now remembered (Joseph) after so long, said, "I'll tell you what it really means. Send me (to the one who can solve this riddle)." [45]

(When the wine-server arrived at the prison, he went to Joseph's cell) and said, "Joseph, the one (who predicted the) truth (for me so long before)! Explain for us the meaning of (this new vision): seven fat cows being eaten by seven skinny ones; seven green shafts of grain followed by seven withered ones. Tell me, so I can return to the people (at the royal court) so they can know." [46]

(Joseph) replied, "For seven years you'll diligently grow crops like you always do, but when you harvest them leave all the grains in the stalk except for the little that you must eat. [47] Then after this will come seven dreadful years (of bad harvests), in which you will have to live off of what you had stored up in advance, saving only small, guarded supplies. [48] Then after that, a year will come in which the people will be delivered (from the drought), and they'll press (wine and oil once more)." [49]

Joseph in the Court of the King

($\mathcal{W}$hen the man returned with the meaning of the dream), the king (was impressed), and said, "Bring him to me."

However, when the herald (of the king) went (to the prison to release Joseph, he refused to leave his cell), saying, "Go back to your master and ask him, 'How is it with the women who cut their hands?' My Lord is aware of their trap." [884] [50]

(The king then ordered the women who were involved in the affair to be gathered before him.)

Then he asked them, "What were your intentions when you tried to seduce Joseph's very being?"

The women answered, "God save us! We don't know anything bad about him!" Then the wife of the great minister said, "The truth has now become clear, for it was I who tried

---

[883] Many commentators in modern times have noticed that the ruler of Egypt in this tale is called a king, while in the stories of Moses, the ruler of Egypt is called a pharaoh. It was during the beginning of the 18th Dynasty in the 16th century BCE that the title of pharaoh began to be applied to the foreign kings of Egypt. As such, the Qur'an provides some dating for both Joseph (prior to the 18th Dynasty) and Moses (after the beginning of the 18th Dynasty). This dating is consistent with Biblical dating, which places Joseph being born circa 1914 BCE and Moses leading the Exodus circa 1446 BCE. (Biblical dating is based on Solomon beginning the Temple in 966 BCE, the Temple being started 480 years after the Exodus (see I Kings 6:1), the Israelites spending 430 years in Egypt (see Exodus 12:40), and the story of Joseph in Genesis. Of note, Genesis anachronistically refers to the king of Egypt during the time of Joseph as "Pharaoh.") To Muslim scholars of the medieval period, the Egyptian king in the story of Joseph has traditionally been known as Rayyan ibn al Walid (and sometimes as Ruiyyan ibn al Usayd). (Ma'ariful Qur'an)

[884] The commentators explain that Joseph did not mention Zulaikhah by name, for he wanted to save Potiphar's household from embarrassment. (Ma'ariful Qur'an)

to seduce him, but he indeed remained honorable." [51]

(When Joseph was informed of the proceedings, he exclaimed,) *"So there it is – (I desired the truth to come to light so that my master) would know that I was never unfaithful to him in his absence, and Allah never guides the plans of betrayers!* [52] *I don't deny my guilt, for the soul can descend into depravity unless my Lord is merciful. Certainly, my Lord is forgiving and merciful."* [885] [53]

Then the king commanded, *"Bring him to me; I'm going to take him into my personal service."*

When (Joseph arrived at court, the king reassured him), saying, *"Feel confident today in my presence, for your position is secure and established."* [886] [54]

(Joseph) said, *"Put me in charge of all the granaries in the land. I'll guard them knowing (their full importance)."* [55]

And so it was in this manner that We established Joseph in the position that he could take anything in the land in whatever quantity he willed.

We parcel out Our Mercy to whomever We want, and We never lose the reward of those who do good. [56] The reward of the next life is much better for those who believe and who are mindful (of Allah). [57]

The Brothers Go to Egypt

(When the foretold famine struck the region), Joseph's brothers arrived in his presence (to buy food), but they didn't recognize him, although he knew immediately who they were. [58]

After he had provisioned them with what they needed, he told them, *"Bring me (the youngest) brother you have from the same father as yourselves. Don't you see that I give full measure and that I provide the best hospitality?* [59] *Now, if you don't bring him to me, you won't get any more (grain) from me, nor shall you ever come near me again."* [887] [60]

They answered, *"We'll certainly get our way from his father. Surely we'll do it."* [61]

Then (Joseph quietly) told his servants, "Put their trade goods back into their saddlebags, (and do it in such a way) that they won't find out until after they've returned to their families, for that may spur them into returning (for more supplies)." [62]

---

[885] Some commentators believe that verses 12:52-53 are a continuation of Zulaikhah's confessional speech, while others feel that these words are the compassionate reply of Joseph who was told about Zulaikhah's heartfelt remorse. Either interpretation is equally defensible, though I have chosen to render it as the relieved words of Joseph, following the majority of commentators. Note how Joseph acknowledges that he could have fallen into sin and temptation, if Allah had not strengthened his spirit.

[886] According to reports cited in Zamakhshari, when Joseph was brought before the king, he (Joseph) greeted him in Hebrew. The king, who knew many languages, was astonished to hear a language he did not know. After enquiring about it, he began to speak to Joseph in many different languages, and Joseph was able to respond in them all. This impressed the king, and he asked to hear Joseph's interpretation of his dream from his own mouth. After Joseph had finished, the king was so impressed with his character that he asked Joseph what he wanted to have. Thus, Joseph asked for a position in the government overseeing the grain harvests.

[887] According to the eminent commentator Baydawi, Joseph accused the brothers of being spies and asked them detailed questions about their families in the process of his interrogation. The brothers told Joseph they were a family of twelve brothers, but that one of them had died before in the desert. (This had the effect of making Joseph fear for the safety of Benjamin.) When Joseph pointed out that they were ten and the last one was not present, that was when the brothers revealed that their youngest sibling remained at home to console their elderly father. Joseph then demanded that one of the ten remain as a hostage, while the others would return to their people to fetch their youngest brother to prove that they were not spies. Other commentators suggest that the brothers had asked for an extra load of grain for an absent brother of theirs, and Joseph agreed as long as they would return with that absent brother to prove they were truthful.

(When the brothers) returned to their father, they said, *"Father! We won't get any more grain (unless we take our youngest brother with us next time), so send our brother (Benjamin) with us so we can get more (supplies). We'll certainly protect him."* [63]

"Should I trust you with him," (Jacob) replied, *"when I had already trusted you with his brother (Joseph) so long before? Even still, Allah is the best guardian. He's the most merciful of the merciful."* [64]

Then, when they were unpacking their supplies, they found their trade goods (hidden in the grain). They said, *"Father! For what more can we ask? Our trade goods have been returned to us so we can go and get more food for our families. We'll protect our brother and get a full load of grain (extra from our host in Egypt). That's like nothing (for him to give)."* [65]

Jacob said, *"I'll never send him with you unless you swear a special promise to me in Allah's name that you'll be sure to bring him back, unless you, yourselves, are trapped."*

After they swore their oath, he said, *"Allah, You be the One Who guarantees what we've said!"* [66]

(Then he gave his sons the following instructions), saying, *"My sons, don't enter the city all from the same entrance, but rather each of you should pick a different entrance, not that I can help you against Allah with my advice. No one can decide (the outcome of events) except Allah. I'll trust in Him, and let everyone who would trust (in something) trust in Him."* [67]

When they entered the city in the way their father had instructed, it didn't help them in the least against (the plan of) Allah. It was just something Jacob felt he had to say, for he was - *by Our instruction* - very intelligent (and experienced), but most people don't know that. [68]

Who Took the King's Cup?

(When the brothers arrived and) were admitted back into Joseph's presence, he took his (younger) brother (Benjamin) aside and insisted that he stay with him. [888] He told him, *"(Benjamin,) surely I'm your own brother, so don't be worried over what the (other brothers) may do."* [69]

Then after Joseph had given them the supplies they needed, he (secretly) put a drinking cup into his (youngest) brother's saddlebag.

(When the brothers began to leave for the return journey,) an announcer shouted out after them, *"Hey, you there! In the caravan! You're surely thieves!"* [70]

(The brothers turned towards the guards) and said, *"Just what is it that you're missing?"* [71]

"We're missing the great cup of the king," they replied, *"and whoever brings it back will get a camel's load (worth of valuables)."*

(Then the captain of the guard said,) *"I can assure you of that!"* [72]

(The brothers protested), saying, *"By Allah! You know we didn't come here to make trouble in this land, and we're certainly not thieves!"* [73]

"So then what should the penalty be (for this crime)," the (Egyptians) asked, *"if you're found to be liars?"* [74]

"The penalty" they answered, *"should be that the owner of the saddlebag in whose possession you find the item should be held (as a slave) to pay for the crime. This is how we penalize criminals (in our country)."* [75]

---

[888] Joseph and Benjamin were from a different mother than the other brothers. This is why it was so easy for the elder brothers to discriminate against them – petty jealousy. After they did away with Joseph (or so they thought), it was only natural for them to begin persecuting Joseph's younger brother, who naturally was elevated to Jacob's favorite. Joseph sensed that Benjamin was being treated badly by his older brothers and reassured him, even as he removed him into 'protective custody' straightaway.

Then (Joseph came and) began to search their baggage first, before coming to his brother's (bag). When (he opened) the bag of his brother (Benjamin, he held up the cup), and there it was! That's how We planned it for Joseph.

He couldn't hold his brother, according to the law of the king, except that Allah willed it. We increase the status of whomever We want, but above all learned masters is a more knowledgeable One. [76]

(The brothers) cried out, *"If he stole something, then you should know that he had another brother who used to steal before!"* Joseph kept his feelings to himself, so as not to give the secret away to them. Instead, he said, *"You're in the worst position, and Allah knows best the truth of what you claim!"* [77]

They begged, *"Great one! He has an old and respected father! Take one of us in his place, instead. We see that you're fair (in your decisions)."* [78]

(Joseph) replied, *"Allah forbid that we should take anyone besides the one who had our property. If we did that, then we would be acting unjustly."* [79]

What will the Brothers Tell their Father?

*W*hen (the brothers) saw no chance of him changing his mind, they discussed the matter among themselves privately. The most senior one among them said, *"Don't you know that you made a promise to your father in Allah's name and that even before this you failed in your duty to Joseph? As for me, I won't leave this land until my father allows me or Allah*

makes a decision about me, and He's the best to decide." [889] [80]

"Go back to your father and tell (him), 'Father! Your son stole something. We report only what we know, and we couldn't guard against what we didn't expect! [81] *Ask at the town we passed through and in the caravan in which we returned, and you'll see that we're telling the honest truth.'"* [82]

(When Jacob was informed), he cried out, *"Not so! You've made up a story to cover yourselves! I can do no more than endure this (tragedy) with dignity. Allah will bring them all back to me (somehow), for He's full of knowledge and wisdom."* [83]

Then he turned away from them and cried, *"How sad I feel for Joseph!"*

Then his eyes glazed over and became white. Blinded by his sorrow, he became increasingly despondent. [84]

(The brothers) shouted, *"By Allah! You'll never stop remembering Joseph until you exhaust yourself or die!"* [85]

(Jacob answered them), saying, *"I'm only complaining about my sorrow and sadness to Allah, and I know things from Allah that you don't.* [86] *My sons! Go back to Egypt, and ask about Joseph and his brother! Never give up hope of Allah's compassion. Truly, no one despairs of Allah's compassion except for those who suppress (their awareness of His power over them)."* [87]

(When the brothers returned to Egypt) and entered (Joseph's presence once again), they said, *"Great one! Grief has come upon our family and us. We only have a few goods left (to trade), so grant us full rations as an act of charity for us. Allah rewards the charitable."* [890] [88]

---

[889] It is thought that this more influential brother was Reuben (or Judah?), who also spoke out against killing Joseph so many years before. He was the one who suggested leaving Joseph in the well to be found by others or sold to travelers and taken away. Thus, it shows that the brothers were not all equal in their sinfulness. (See 12:10)

[890] Why did Joseph carry on the charade that he did in front of his brothers? Perhaps he wanted them to realize their mistake for themselves. This would have been far more valuable a teaching tool than merely revealing himself at the outset. In a similar way, when the Prophet's two young grandsons, Hassan and Husayn, saw an elderly man performing his ablution improperly, rather than pointing out his mistake and embarrassing him, they asked the man to watch them make ablution, under the guise

(Then Joseph spoke), saying *"Do you remember how you dealt with Joseph and his youngest brother in your ignorance?"* [89]

(When they realized who the man before them was,) they asked, *"Are you really Joseph?"*

"(Yes), I am Joseph," he replied, *"and this is my brother (Benjamin)! Allah has brought the gift (of this reunion) to all of us. Truly, whoever is mindful (of Allah) and who patiently perseveres (through any hardships), Allah will never let the reward of those who were good become lost."* [90]

(The brothers) cried out, *"By Allah! Allah has indeed preferred you over us, and we're guilty of a crime!"* [91]

"Let there be no blame upon you this day," Joseph replied. *"Allah will forgive you, and He's the most merciful of the merciful.* [92] *Now, go and take my shirt with you; cast it over my father's face, and he will see again. Then return here all together with your families."* [93]

Jacob's Premonition

$\mathcal{E}$ven as the caravan departed (from Egypt, Joseph's) father exclaimed (to the people around him in his encampment), *"I smell the scent of Joseph, even though you may think I'm senile."* [94]

"By Allah!" they replied. *"But you have an old, wandering mind."* [95]

However, when the herald of good news arrived and put the shirt over (Jacob's) face, he immediately regained his ability to see. Then he exclaimed (to those around him), *"Didn't I say to you that I know things from Allah that you don't?"* [96]

(Then the brothers) cried out, *"Father! Ask forgiveness for our sins; we were truly in the wrong."* [891] [97]

"Very soon will I ask my Lord to forgive you," he replied, *"for He is indeed the Forgiving and the Merciful."* [892] [98]

The Fulfillment of the Dream

$(\mathcal{W}$hen Jacob and all the rest of his family) entered into Joseph's presence, he provided a home for his parents with himself, saying, *"Enter safely into Egypt, if it pleases Allah."* [99]

He exalted his parents onto a high place (of honor), but they all fell down prostrate before him. (Joseph) exclaimed (in wonder), *"My Father! This is the completion of the vision I had so long before.* [893] *Allah has made it all come true! He was good to me when He got me out of prison and then brought all of you here from out of the desert - even after Satan had*

---

that they wanted an elder to check them to make sure they were doing it right. When the man saw them do it properly, he realized his own mistake and ever after performed his own ablutions in a correct manner.

[891] The Prophet said that the following conversation took place between Allah and Satan. Satan said, "By Your power, Lord, I will keep luring Your servants (into sin) as long as their souls are in their bodies." Allah said, "By My power and majesty, I will keep on forgiving them as long as they keep asking Me for forgiveness." (*Ahmad*)

[892] The commentators suggest that Jacob delayed his supplication for forgiveness either to look for the right moment when it might be more likely to be accepted by Allah, or to see Joseph first and get his opinion on the matter, for forgiveness sometimes also depends on the wronged person feeling vindicated. (*Baydawi*)

[893] Verse 12:4 contains the vision of the sun, the moon and eleven stars bowing before Joseph. These would be his father and mother (or step-mother) and eleven brothers. It is interesting to note that in Genesis 37:9-11, the same interpretation of the dream is given, yet, in verses 35:16-21 (of Genesis), Joseph's biological mother Rachel is said to have died while giving birth to Benjamin. This means that "the moon" could not have been Rachel bowing to her son Joseph in the climactic scene of the story. The Qur'an makes a veiled assumption in verse 100 that it was Joseph's own mother whom he exalted, though the ambiguity in the term 'parents' can go either way.

caused conflict between me and my brothers. My Lord is subtle in what He wills, for He is the Knowing and the Wise." [100]

(Joseph prayed), "My Lord! You've indeed given me some power and taught me how to interpret passing events. Originator of the heavens and the earth! You're my protector in this world and in the next. Take me as one surrendering (to Your will), and join me with the righteous!" [101]

This is one of the hidden stories that We're revealing to you by inspiration. [894] You weren't there among (Joseph's brothers) when they agreed on their affair and made a plot. [102] Yet, most people won't believe, no matter how hard you wish them to. [103]

The Natural Signs of Allah

You're not asking (the faithless) for any reward for this - *this is no less than a reminder for all the worlds.* [104] Then how many signs in the heavens and on the earth do they pass by? Yet, they turn (their faces) away from them! [105] Most of them don't believe in Allah without making (others as partners) with Him! [106]

Do they feel safe against the overwhelming nature of Allah's wrath coming down upon them or of the sudden arrival of the (final) Hour without their even noticing it? [107]

Say (to them), "*This is my way. I'm inviting (you) to (believe in) Allah with evidence as clear as sight. (This is) my (way, and the way of) whoever follows me. Glory be to Allah! I'll never be an idolater!*" [108]

We didn't send before you any beings other than men whom We inspired, and they lived in human communities. Don't they travel through the earth and see what became of those (disbelieving nations) before them? (Regardless of what people acquire), the home of the next life is the best for those who are mindful (of Allah). So won't you understand? [109]

(The forces of darkness will be granted a period of ascendancy), even up to the point when the messengers begin to lose hope (of the success of their mission) and feel they've been denied (utterly by their people).

Then, (without any advance warning), Our help will come and reach them, and We'll save whomever We want, but Our punishment will never be averted from the wicked. [110]

And so it is that there are lessons in the stories (of past civilizations) for people of understanding. (This tale of Joseph) is not a fictional account, but a confirmation of (the message that came) before it. [895] It's a detailed account of all things and a guide and mercy to a believing nation. [111]

---

[894] What happened to Joseph after the events of this story? According to some Jewish traditions, after Potiphar passed away, the king of Egypt arranged the marriage of Joseph to Potiphar's widow Zulaikhah, and they had three children. (*Ma'ariful Qur'an*) Genesis 41:50 offers an alternative view for consideration.

[895] The Hebrew story of Joseph, though embellished with many extraneous details, is still a true story in its basic form, as the Qur'an affirms. By clearing the story of additions made through the centuries, as the Qur'an implies, the basic lesson to be learned from this tale of a family's redemption can once again be appreciated.

Thunder

13 Ar-Ra'd
Late Meccan to Early Medinan Period

This chapter was mostly revealed in the later portion of the Meccan period, although a few verses date from Medina. It summarizes many of the ongoing themes touched upon in other chapters and introduces some dramatic imagery and unique doctrines related to the next life. The name of the chapter is derived from verse 13 where the very thunder itself is said to resonate with the praise of Allah.

In the Name of Allah,
the Compassionate, the Merciful

Alif. Lām. Meem. Rā.

These are the verses of the Book, the very one that's being revealed to you from your Lord, and it's the truth. Yet, most people don't believe. [1]

Allah is the One Who raised the skies without any supports that you can see. Then He established Himself upon the throne (of power). He tamed the sun and the moon, (causing) each to complete its orbit in a precise amount of time. And in this way He regulates all matters. (The reason why) He explains the proof (of His power) in such detail is so that you can believe confidently in the meeting with your Lord. [2]

He's the One Who spread the earth out wide and placed firm mountains within it and (flowing) rivers, as well. (He also placed upon the earth) all types of fruit in pairs, two by two, and He draws the night like a veil over the day. In these things are signs for people who think. [3]

There are (distinct) regions adjoining each other on the earth,   as well as vineyards, fields of grain and date palms growing from either (multiple root systems) or from only one (root).   They're all watered with the same water; yet, some of them (produce fruits that) are better for eating than others. In these there are signs for those who reflect. [4]

If you're amazed (at how they can deny Allah, after seeing how complex the world He made is), even more amazing still is their saying, *"When we're reduced to dust, are we really going to be created as good as new?"*

They're the ones who are blatantly denying their Lord, so they're the ones around whose necks will be shackles! They'll be the companions of the Fire, *and that's where they're going to stay!* [5]

They're asking you to hurry on something awful in preference to something good. Yet, there have been many humiliating punishments (that struck previous peoples) before them. However, your Lord is full of forgiveness towards people, even in their corruption, just as He's also harsh in punishment. [6]

And then the faithless ask, *"So why isn't a miracle being sent down to him from his Lord?"* Yet, you're only a warner and a guide for all nations. [7]

Allah Encompasses All Things

*A*llah knows what every female bears and how much the wombs are early or late, for everything is measured in His sight. [8]

He knows what's beyond perception, as well as what's clearly seen, for He's the Great One, the Highest of All! [9]

So it's all the same whether one of you hides his words or says them openly or whether you lay hidden by night or walk about in broad daylight. [10]

(Every person has angels) following him, both before him and behind him. [896] They guard him by the command of Allah.

Truly, Allah will never change the condition of a people unless they change what's in themselves.

Whenever Allah wants to bring misfortune down upon a people, there can be no averting it, nor will they find any protector besides Him. [11]

Thunder is a Reminder

*H*e's the One Who shows you the lightning as a source of both fear and hope, and He's the One Who raises up the heavily laden clouds (bursting with rain). [897] [12]

The very thunder, itself, glorifies His praises, as do the angels - wonderstruck (by His power). He sends booming thunderbolts and strikes whomever He wants. Yet, these (people) are still arguing about Allah, though He's extremely cunning (in His planning). [13]

Supplications are honestly due to Him alone. Those (idols) whom they call upon besides Him don't hear them any more than if they brought their empty hands to their mouths to take a sip of water and nothing reached them. The supplications of those who cover (the light of faith within their hearts) are nothing more than blunders. [14]

All who reside within the heavens and the earth bow down before Allah, either willingly or unwillingly, as do their

---

[896] The Prophet said, "Every one of you has a companion from the jinn and a companion from the angels." The people said, "Even you, too, Messenger of Allah?" He replied, "Even I, as well, except that Allah has helped me against (the jinn), so he only influences me to do good." (*Muslim*)

[897] There is a story that two pagan men from Mecca approached the Prophet just after he arrived in Medina and asked about Islam. One of them named 'Amr ibn at-Tufayl asked what he would get if he accepted Islam, and the Prophet replied that he would have all the rights and duties of an ordinary Muslim. 'Amr then asked if he could be made the ruler of the Muslims after the Prophet passed away, and the Prophet answered him, saying, "That's not your right or your people's right; however, I could appoint you as a cavalry leader." 'Amr said, "I'm already a cavalry leader in the land of Najd. What if you rule the cities and I rule the countryside?" The Prophet refused this offer, and 'Amr and his friend, a man named Arbad, left in anger, vowing to bring an army back with them to destroy the Muslims. Before leaving town, however, they hatched a plot to kill the Prophet. While 'Amr was to engage the Prophet in conversation, Arbad would sneak up from behind the Prophet and strike him down. 'Amr returned to the Prophet and accordingly began to distract him. Arbad came from behind, but for some reason he couldn't pull his sword from its sheath. The Prophet saw Arbad behind him, trying to unsheathe his sword, and he realized what was going on, so he left them in haste. The two men fled the city, but two companions named Sa'd and Usayd came upon them and ordered them to surrender. The pair fled again, and Arbad was struck by a stray lightning bolt in the desert and died. 'Amr took refuge in a woman's house (she belonged to the tribe of the hypocrite, 'Abdullah ibn Ubayy,) and she noticed he had an ulcer growing on his leg. On his return journey to Najd, he died from that ulcer. This passage was revealed in comment on this situation. (*Ibn Kathir*)

shadows in the mornings and the evenings. [898] [15]

Ask them, "*Who is the lord of the heavens and the earth?*" (Answer for them by) saying, "*Allah.*" Then say to them, "*So are you taking protectors other than Him, things that have no power to bring either benefit or harm to themselves?*" Ask them, "*Are the blind and the seeing the same, or is the darkness the same as the light?*"

Are they making partners with Allah – partners who (somehow managed to) create (things by themselves) that are just like what He created, so much so that (the two) creations seem the same? Say to them, "*Allah created everything, and He's the One and the Irresistible.*" [16]

He sends down water from the sky. The resulting channels flow in a measured way, and the rushing (rapids) carry away the foam that forms on its surface. Likewise, a similar kind of foam also arises when they heat (ore) in the fire to make jewelry or tools. That's how Allah distinguishes the truth from falsehood, for the foam is discarded while what is useful for people remains on the earth. That's how Allah lays out His examples. [17]

Two Ways of Life, Two Results

Good things will come to those who respond to their Lord. However, those who ignore Him – even if they had everything in the heavens and on the earth and much more besides to offer as a bribe, (it would be of no use), for a strict accounting will be made of them. Their ultimate home will be in Hellfire, and what a terrible place to rest! [18]

Is the one who knows that what's been revealed to you from your Lord is the truth the same as someone who's blind (to that fact)? Only the thoughtful ever take

reminders. [19] They're the ones who fulfill their agreement with Allah, and they don't break their word. [20]

They (have respect for the family ties) that Allah has commanded to be joined, and they fear both their Lord and the strict accounting (to come). [21] They're patient and seek Allah's (approving) gaze, even as they establish prayers and spend (in charity) out of what We've supplied to them, both in secret and in public. They also ward off evil with good.

They're the ones who will gain the final home [22] – everlasting gardens that they'll be allowed to enter, along with the righteous among their parents, spouses and descendants. Angels will enter (upon their presence) from every gate, [23] (saying), "*Peace be upon you on account of your patient perseverance! How delightful is the final home!*" [24]

However, those who break their agreement with Allah after having given their word, who separate what Allah has ordered to be joined, and who cause chaos and disorder in the land – they'll be far removed (from Allah's mercy), and they'll have the most miserable home! [25]

Allah increases or restricts the resources of whomever He wants. (Those who only love this life) revel in the life of this world, but the life of this world is nothing but a passing pleasure compared to the next life. [26]

Believers Know the Truth

Those who suppress (their awareness of the truth) ask, "*So why isn't a miracle coming down to him from his Lord?*"

Say (to them), "*Allah leaves astray whomever He wants, and He guides those who repent (of their sins towards the path leading back) to Him.*" [27]

---

[898] After reading this verse it is customary for the one who has faith in Allah to prostrate himself on the floor and praise Allah.

"(They're the ones) who believe and whose hearts find relief in the remembrance of Allah, for without a doubt, in the remembrance of Allah hearts can find relief. [28] *Those who believe and do what's morally right will find the deepest satisfaction and the finest homecoming."* [29]

And so We've sent you to a community that has had many other (civilizations) pass away before it, in order for you to recite to them what We're revealing to you. [899]

Yet, they're rejecting the Compassionate! Tell them, *"He is my Lord; there is no god but He. I trust in Him, and to Him I turn."* [30]

This Qur'an is a Serious Message

$\mathcal{I}$f there ever was a recital (of scripture) that could move mountains or crack the earth or cause the dead to speak, [900] (then this would be it)!

But no! The command over all things rests with Allah. Don't the believers realize that if Allah had wanted, He could've guided all people together?

As for those who suppress (their faith), misfortune will continue to befall them because of their (misguided) actions, or it will settle in near their homes even until Allah's promise comes to pass. Indeed, Allah never fails in His word! [31]

And so it was that messengers who came before you were ridiculed, but I gave the faithless some time before I finally seized them, *and oh how (terrible) was My conclusion!* [32]

The Final Destination

$\mathcal{I}$s the One Who stands over every soul and what it records for itself (the same as any other)? Yet, they've made partners with Allah! Ask them, *"So name them! Are you going to tell Him about something that He doesn't know on the earth, or are you just saying something (with no truth to it)?"*

No way! Those who suppress (their understanding of the truth) are pleased with their posturing, but they're really being kept away from the path (by it). For those whom Allah leaves astray, there can be no one to guide them. [33] They're going to be punished in this worldly life, but the punishment of the next life is so much more severe, and they'll have no defender against Allah. [34]

(What's the) likeness of the Garden that's been promised to those who were mindful (of Allah)? Rivers will flow beneath (its trees)! There'll be no end to eating, nor will its shade ever cease!

This is the final (destination) for those who were mindful (of Allah), while the final (destination) of those who covered up (their faith) is in the Fire. [35]

---

[899] The Prophet had asked some Meccans to bow down in the name of the Compassionate Allah, and they said, "Who is *the Compassionate*, and why should we bow down just because you ask us to?" That is what this verse is referencing. (*Asbab ul-Nuzul*)

[900] A Meccan named 'Abdullah ibn Umayyah approached the Prophet and said, "You're pretending that you're a prophet and that you get prophecies. Yet, Solomon was given power over the wind, Moses over the sea, and Jesus raised the dead to life. So call on your God to make the mountains move, make rivers flow in this land for irrigating fields, bring the dead body of (our legendary ancestor) Qusayy to life and make him talk and confirm whether Islam is valid or not, or turn the stones underneath you into gold so we can have enough money to last us through summer and winter - that is if you're not just pretending to be among (the ranks of the prophets)." This passage was revealed to the Prophet immediately, and he recited it. Then the Prophet said, "I swear by the One Who holds my soul that I would be given that if I wished for it. However, (the angel) asked me to choose between two things: either to enter (Paradise) through the gate of mercy, or to leave you alone so you can choose (your fate) by yourselves and thus be misguided. So I chose the gate of mercy, knowing that he told me that if you reject faith that you'll be punished more than anyone else ever was." (*Asbab ul-Nuzul*)

Those to whom We've given the scripture (in the past) rejoice in what We've revealed to you, but among the factions (of other religions) are some who reject a part of it.

Say (to them), *"I'm commanded to serve Allah and not to join partners with Him. I call to Him, and back to Him is my final goal."* [36]

Thus, We've revealed (the Qur'an) as an authoritative (book) in the Arabic (language). [901] If you were to follow their whims after already receiving knowledge, then you would find neither any close ally nor defender (to help you) against Allah. [37]

The Prophet will be Victorious over His Foes

$\mathcal{W}$e sent messengers before you and arranged for them to have wives and children. [902] It was never the place of a messenger to bring a miracle unless Allah allowed it, and for every age (of history) there has been a scripture. [38] Allah rescinds or confirms whatever He wants,

for He has the Mother of the Book (with Him). [39]

Whether We show you now part of the (punishment) that We've promised them or take your soul back to Us (before it befalls them), your duty is only to proclaim (the message) to them. It's Our task to call them to account. [40] Don't (the Meccans) see how We're gradually reducing the lands (over which they hold influence) from their outlying borders? Allah commands, and no one can hinder His command, and He is quick to settle accounts. [41]

The (faithless) who came before (these people) also made plans, though Allah is the ultimate planner over everything at once! He knows what every soul earns for itself, and the faithless will soon know who will have the final home (of Paradise). [42]

The faithless may say, *"You're not a messenger (from Allah),"* but say to them, *"Allah is enough of a witness between you and me, even as is anyone who knows (of Allah's previously revealed) scriptures."* [43]

Abraham

14 Ibrahim
Late Meccan Period

This chapter, which is something of a continuation of the arguments introduced at the conclusion of the last, was revealed during the late Meccan period when it seemed inevitable that some sort of break or separation had to occur between the pagans and the Muslims.

Indeed, verses 13-15 foreshadow the ultimate action that the Meccans would take, that of threatening to drive the Prophet and his followers away. Unbeknownst to them, however, the Muslims were soon to leave on their own to a sanctuary far to the north known as Yathrib, and later as *Medinat-un-Nabi*, or the *City of the Prophet* (*Medina* for short).

In the Name of Allah,
the Compassionate, the Merciful

Alif. Lām. Rā.

(This is) a book that We've revealed to you so you can lead people out of every type of darkness and into light, by Allah's leave, towards the path of the Powerful and Praiseworthy. [1]

Allah is the One to Whom belongs whatever is in the heavens and whatever is on the earth. Those who suppress (their awareness of the truth) are doomed to a harsh punishment! [2]

Those who love the life of this world more than the next life, and who try to hinder others from the way of Allah - *wishing to make it seem crooked* – they're the ones who are far off in error. 903 [3]

The Messengers and Their Missions

We never sent any messenger unless he spoke the language of his own people, so that he could explain things to them clearly. 904 Allah allows whomever

---

903 Debates and public speeches were common in the Prophet's time, and he engaged in them freely, sometimes scoring points and getting people to consider new ideas, other times finding his message falling on deaf ears. It was when, for example, prominent pagans twisted the Prophet's words to make them seem like something else or told outright lies or forcibly prevented the Muslim side from having its voice heard that a problem arose. Even today, the message of Islam is often misrepresented, both by non-Muslim critics and even some people with Muslim-sounding names who believe in extremist ideologies never before found in Islam. This verse addresses the general phenomenon of misrepresenting the faith and trying to keep people from it in a cunning and dishonest fashion.

904 The Qur'an was revealed to Muhammad in Arabic and specifically in the dialect of the Quraysh tribe of Mecca. Other Arab tribes in the far corners of Arabia spoke Arabic, but with regional accents, and the Prophet beseeched Allah to allow the Qur'an to be recited in the various dialects of the Arabs. Gabriel informed the Prophet that the Qur'an could be recited in the seven major dialects of the Arabian peninsula, though the official dialect decided by the companions after the Prophet's passing is the Qurayshi dialect, based on the fact that Muhammad was from the Quraysh. (*Bukhari*) Also see 41:44

He wills to go astray, [905] and He allows whomever He wills to be guided, for He's the Powerful and Wise. [4]

And so it was that We sent Moses with Our signs (and told him), "*Lead your people out of darkness and into light, and teach them to remember the days of Allah.*" [906]

Truly, there are signs (in this story) for every extraordinarily patient and thankful person. [907] [5]

Remember when Moses said to his people, "*Recall Allah's favors upon you when He saved you from Pharaoh's people. They mistreated you greatly - butchering your sons while leaving your daughters alive. That was an enormous test from your Lord.*" [6]

And remember when your Lord proclaimed (His promise to you, saying), "*If you're thankful, then I'll grant you even more (than just your freedom), and if you're ungrateful, then (know that) My punishment is harsh.*" [7]

Even Moses had told them, "*If you ever became ungrateful, and if everyone else on the earth likewise became ungrateful, even then Allah would have no need (for any of you), for He would still be praised (by other beings).*" [8]

Ignoring the Messengers

*H*aven't you heard the stories of those who lived before you – the people of Noah and 'Ad and Thamud and all those who came after them? No one knows about them more than Allah.

Messengers went to each of them with clear evidence. However, their (people) invariably put their hands up over their mouths and said, "*We reject whatever you've been sent with, and we're doubtful of the value of what you're calling us towards.*" [9]

Their messengers would ask them, "*Do you have any doubts about (the existence of) Allah, the Creator of the heavens and the earth? He's calling you so He can forgive you your sins and give you an extension on your time limit.*"

(The people would always answer,) saying, "*You're no more than a mortal man like us! You just want to turn us away from what our ancestors worshipped. So bring us a clear and decisive (miracle to prove your mission is true!)*" [10]

Their messengers would answer them, saying, "*While it's true that we're no more than mortals like yourselves, Allah favors whichever of His servants that He wants. It's not our place to

---

where the explanation is given as to why the Qur'an was revealed in the Arabic language. No prophet was sent to a nation unless he either grew up with their language or at least learned it well enough to preach in it, such as in the cases of Lot and Jonah who both preached in languages they had to acquire.
[905] Some critics have accused the Qur'an of suggesting that God willfully misleads people in a capricious or malicious way for no other reason than He is 'mean.' This is a gross mis-understanding of the situations when God would 'allow' a person to go astray or fall further into error. When a person declares themselves a rebel against God *first*, and then takes actions to oppose God, goodness and justice, then God lets them fall further into their delusions. His Message is still there for them to see, but if they continue to ignore, is it right to stop someone who refuses all offers of help and seeks to fight against you? The Bible contains the exact same sentiment in 2 Thessalonians 2:11 where we read: "For this reason, God sends them a powerful delusion so that they will believe the lie..." Also see Romans 1:24, II Chronicles 18:7 and 18:22. The New Testament commentator Heinrich Meyer writes of this verse: "For according to the Pauline view it is a holy ordinance of God that the wicked by their wickedness should lose themselves always the more in wickedness, and thus sin is punished by sin. But what is an ordinance of God is also accomplished by God Himself." (Meyer's New Testament Commentary, 1980 Alpha Publications edition)
[906] The *days of Allah* that are mentioned here can mean one of two things. The first is that the Children of Israel were being asked to recall their righteous ancestors who lived by Allah's commands. The second interpretation could mean that they were being asked to remember that all time belongs to Allah, and in the end there will be a final day when people will be brought for judgment.
[907] The Prophet said, "Faith is composed of two parts: half of it is patience, and the other half is gratitude." (*Bayhaqi*)

bring a clear and decisive (miracle) without Allah's permission.

"(True) believers should trust in Allah, (rather than in miracles)! [11] *We have no reason not to trust in Allah, for He's guided us on our pathways. Therefore, we're going to patiently endure all of your abuse. Those who would trust (in something) should trust in Allah."* [12]

Then the rejecters (of truth) would tell their messengers, *"We're going to drive you out of our land, unless you return to our traditions!"*

Thereupon, their Lord would inspire (the messengers), telling them, *"We're going to destroy the wrongdoers,* [13] *though We'll lodge your (bodies) in the earth, (and you shall remain there) long after (they're gone). That's how it is for anyone who fears his meeting (with Me) and who takes My threat (of punishment) seriously."* [14]

(Even though the wrongdoers) wanted to have victory (over the righteous), each and every stubborn tyrant failed in frustration. [908] [15]

Hellfire is coming up ahead of each one of them. Therein he'll (be forced to) drink boiling, disgusting muck [16] in huge gulps, but he'll never be able to get it past his throat!

Death will confront him from every side; *yet, he'll never die,* for a relentless punishment is what he'll have to face. [17]

The Price of Evil

The example of those who reject their Lord is that their deeds are like ashes that are blown around by a strong gust of wind on a stormy day. They have no power at all over what they've earned for themselves, and that's by far the worst mistake! [18]

Don't you see that Allah created the heavens and the earth for a true purpose? If it were ever His desire, He could remove you and bring about some new kind of creation, [19] and that's not too hard for Allah. [20]

(The faithless) will be marched all together before Allah. Then the weak-minded will say to (the influential) and self-assured, *"We were only following whatever you suggested, so can you do anything for us now against Allah's wrath?"*

"If Allah had guided us," they'll reply, *"then we would've guided you. It doesn't matter now whether we're outraged or resigned to our fate, for there's no way for us to escape."* [21]

Once the issue has been decided, Satan will say, *"Allah made a true promise to you, but I broke my promise to you, and I had no power over you other than through suggestion.* [909] *You listened to me, so don't blame me. You only have yourselves to blame. I can no more hear your cries than you can hear mine. I don't accept the blame for what you previously did when you joined*

---

[908] The Prophet said, "If you see my community being afraid of telling a tyrant that he is, in fact, a tyrant, then it may be the end of my community." (*Ahmad, Bayhaqi, Tabarani*)

[909] Jinns are creatures made of a type of energy that is drawn from fire. (They are not fire, itself, but merely made of a part of that type of energy. See 15:27.) Thus, they operate on a specific plane of energy and are outside the power of our vision. Given that all of our thoughts in our brains are merely bursts of electrical energy, it is not unreasonable to understand how demonic influence assails us. Satan and his minions "whisper" or implant "suggestions" in our thoughts, and so we see our brainpower getting influenced by outside energy. One way to measure the effect of the jinn on the mind is to consider those times in which it seemed a powerful negative thought was popping into your head, seemingly out of nowhere and without your active permission. That may have been a jinn "whispering" his dark motivations in your mind. To be sure, people are perfectly capable of thinking up sinful things themselves. Yet, there are other times when our bodily urges and negative thoughts seem to coalesce without any rational explanation. As Satan said, "*I'm going to mislead them and create in them false desires.*" [4:119] After the thought is placed, it is our choice either to act upon it or to call upon Allah to banish the evil thought. Depending upon our choice we either sinned or passed a test of faith.

me (in Allah's power)." Truly, wrongdoers have a terrible punishment prepared for them! [22]

However, those who believed and did what was morally right will be admitted into gardens beneath which rivers flow, and there they shall remain, by their Lord's leave. They'll be greeted with the word, *"Peace!"* [23]

The Parable of the Two Trees

Don't you see how Allah sets out the example of a good word? It's like a good tree whose roots are strong and stable, with branches jutting up into the sky. [910] [24] It bears fruit at all times, by its Lord's permission.

Allah offers such examples for people so they can be reminded. [25] Now the example of a rotten word is like a rotten tree that's been torn out of the earth by its roots. It has no way to hold itself up! [26]

Allah will support and uphold those who believe in the good word, both in this life and in the next, [911] while Allah will let the wrongdoers go astray, and Allah does whatever He wants. [27]

The Unstinting Bounty of Allah

Haven't you seen those who paid Allah back for His favor by suppressing (accurate knowledge of Him), and who have thus brought their people into the realm of doom [28] – *Hellfire?* [912] They're going to burn in it, - *and how terrible a place to settle!* [29]

They were the ones who set up rivals with Allah, in order to steer others away from the path. So say to them, *"Enjoy yourselves now, but you're headed straight for the Fire!"* [30]

Tell My servants who believe to establish prayer and to spend (in charity) out of the resources that We've given to them, both in secret and in public, before a day arrives in which there will be neither bargaining nor friendship. [913] [31]

---

[910] The 'good word' mentioned here is understood to refer to the basic statement of faith, or *kalimah*, which is the phrase, "There is no god except Allah." The Prophet once said of it, "Whoever declares that there is no god but Allah will go to Paradise." Someone asked him how the sincerity of that statement could be measured, and the Prophet replied, "By accepting this phrase, you should refrain from what Allah has forbidden." (*At-Targheeb wa at-Tarheeb*) The Prophet said that the good tree mentioned in the Qur'an is the date tree and that the rotten tree is the colocynth, a kind of vine-like bush known as the vine of Sodom (which is also mentioned in the Bible in II Kings 4:39-40 as a 'wild gourd'). (*Tirmidhi, Nisa'i*)

[911] The Prophet explained that the reference to the next life here is specifically the time in the grave when souls will be waiting for the Day of Judgment, a time known as *barzakh*. When the angels come to the deceased person's soul the first time, they will ask it what it worshipped in the world. If it answers with the statement of faith (the 'good word' or *kalimah*), then it will sleep peacefully until resurrection. (*Ma'ariful Qur'an*)

[912] This passage refers to the pagan Arabs of old who transformed Abraham's shrine in Mecca over many generations into a house of idolatry and superstition. The Prophet once identified the man who instituted idolatry in Mecca. He said it was a man named Abu Khuza'ah. Tribal oral history records that he was the son of Luhay ibn Qam'ah of the tribe of Jurhum, which was the ruling tribe of Mecca before the Quraysh invaded the city and drove the Jurhumites away several centuries before the birth of Muhammad. (*Ahmad, Ibn Kathir*)

[913] The Prophet told the following story: "A man once vowed to give charity to a prostitute, so he went out one night, found one and gave her charity. The next day when people found out, they grumbled and ridiculed him for giving his charity to a prostitute. When he heard about their disapproval, he said, 'Thank you, Allah, for leading me to give charity to a prostitute.' Then he vowed to give charity to a rich man, and that night he found one and gave him charity. Again, the next day the people mocked him, this time for giving charity to a rich man. When the man heard of their disapproval, he said,

Allah is the One Who created the heavens and the earth. He sends down water from the sky and uses it to produce the fruits that sustain you. He put at your service the ships that sail through the sea by His command, and He also put rivers at your service, as well. [32] Likewise, He put the sun and the moon at your service; they both follow their orbits without fail, even as He made the very night and day useful for you. [914] [33]

He gives you everything for which you could ask! If you ever tried to count Allah's favors, you would never be able to enumerate them all! [915] Yet, still humanity is lost in corruption and ingratitude! [34]

The Prayer of Abraham

*R*ecall when Abraham said, "*My Lord! Make this settlement (of Mecca) tranquil and secure, and keep me and my descendants away from idol-worship. [916] [35] My Lord! So many people have been led astray by them. Whoever follows me is of the same mind as me, and whoever*

'Thank you, Allah, for leading me to give charity to a rich man.' Then he vowed to give charity to a thief, so that night he went out in search of a thief, found one and gave him charity. This also outraged the community, but the man kept on thanking Allah for guiding him to give charity to a prostitute, a rich man and a thief. Shortly afterwards the man passed away, and he was told, 'Your charity was accepted, for it may be that the prostitute will discontinue her shameful business and turn to Allah for forgiveness; it may be that the rich man will start thinking about giving in charity himself, and it may be that the thief will repent of his stealing and give it up.'" (*Muslim*)

[914] The sun and the moon are used by human beings to calculate time, and their orbits are so regular that we can rely upon their witness for our own planning.

[915] The Prophet was overheard supplicating, "O Allah! All praise belongs to You. (I will never) be able to thank You enough, nor do I ever wish to be cut off from You, nor do I ever (wish to arrogantly) feel too rich (to know I must) rely upon You, O Lord." (*Bukhari*)

[916] Ibn 'Abbas (d. 687) narrated the following story from the Prophet that fills in missing details from this Qur'anic episode in the story of Abraham. The story goes as follows: The first lady to use a waist strap (a kind of pocket/belt) was (Hagar), the mother of Ishmael. She used it to brush the dirt to hide her tracks from Sarah, (who was Abraham's first wife and who bullied Hagar out of jealousy. So Abraham took Hagar and Ishmael to an empty valley in Arabia (which is the place where the Ka'bah would later be built). He sat them under a large tree that was near to where the well of *Zamzam* would later sprout. At that time Mecca did not exist, and there was no water there. Abraham left them there with a bag of dates and a jug of water. When Abraham began to depart, Hagar ran after him crying, "Abraham! Where are you going? Why are you leaving us in this valley where there's no people or water?" She said this several times, but he ignored her as he rode away. Finally she called out to him, "Did Allah command you to do this?" Abraham answered, "Yes." Hagar replied, "Then He certainly won't abandon us." She then went back to the tree and sat down as Abraham made his way out of the valley. When he was out of sight, Abraham prayed for them (and then returned to Palestine). Hagar took care of her son Ishmael, who was barely more than an infant, but then the water ran out, and they became wracked with thirst. Hagar saw her son dehydrating on the ground, and she frantically ran back and forth between two hills that were later named Safa and Marwa, searching in vain for any sign of other people. She had to raise her sleeve (over her eyes to shield them from the hot sun). She ran back and forth to the top of each hill seven times but saw no one… On the fourth circuit, however, she heard a sudden voice out of nowhere that said, "Shush." She craned her head to listen for the source of the sound but then gave up, saying, "I heard you! Do you have anything to help us?" Then she looked and saw an angel poking the ground with his wing, and water began to flow, so much so that she cried, "Enough! Enough! (*Zam! Zam!*)" That's the Well of *Zamzam* today. She ran to the water spout and began cupping it in her hands. Then she began digging around it to make it a small pool. She filled up her water jug, and the water didn't stop flowing…The angel then said to her, "Don't fear abandonment, for the House of Allah will be built in this place by this boy and his father, and Allah never abandons His people." (*Bukhari*) Sometime later, a group of bedouins from the tribe of Jurhum saw birds circling over a distant valley. Thinking there might be water there, they came upon the well and noticed the mother and her son. They decided to settle there, and Ishmael later married one of their women, thus mingling the seed of Abraham with the bedouins to form a new ethnic group: the northern Arabs. When Abraham returned to visit some years later, he saw the beginnings of a settlement that would one day grow into Mecca. (The prayer contained in verses 35-41 is what Abraham then said in thanks.)

disobeys me – well, You're forgiving and merciful." [36]

"Our Lord!" (he continued,) *"I've settled some of my descendants in this barren valley next to Your Sacred House, so they can, our Lord, establish prayer. So make some people sympathetic towards them, and supply them with fruits so they can learn to be thankful."* [37]

"Our Lord! You know what we conceal and what we reveal, for nothing at all can ever be hidden from Allah, neither on the earth nor in the sky. [38] *Praise be to Allah Who has given me my sons, Ishmael and Isaac, even in my old age, for My Lord hears all requests!* [39] *My Lord! Make me a prayerful person, and make my descendants prayerful, as well. Our Lord! Hear my request.* [40] *Our Lord! Forgive me and my parents and all those who believe on the Day of Account."* [41]

Allah Delays Punishment for a Reason

$\mathcal{D}$on't think for a moment that Allah ignores the actions of the wrongdoers. He's only giving them a break until the day comes when eyes will stare unblinking, [42] when they'll run around in a frenzy with heads raised, not looking at themselves, and feeling a void in their guts! [43]

So warn people of the day when the punishment will come upon them, when the wrongdoers will cry, *"Our Lord! Give us more time, even just a little! We'll surely answer Your call and follow the messengers then!"*

(However, they'll be told,) *"Weren't you the ones who swore before that you would never be brought down (from your powerful positions)?* [44] *You lived (near the ruins of past civilizations) who had done wrong against their own souls! You clearly saw how We dealt with them, and We offered so many examples to you!"* [45]

They wove their mighty schemes, but their schemes were in Allah's full view (and thus could never succeed) - *even though (their plans) seemed strong enough to shake the mountains!* [46] So don't ever think that Allah will fail in what He's promised to His messengers, for Allah is Powerful and a master of retribution. [47]

The Promise of a Day of Justice

$\mathcal{A}$ day will come when the earth will be transformed into a different earth, even as the skies will be transformed, as well, and then everyone will be marched before Allah, the One, the Irresistible. [48]

That day you'll see the sinners all tied together in chains; [49] their only clothing will be burning, oozing tar, even as their faces will be enveloped in fire. [50] (That'll be their fate), so that Allah can repay every soul with what it deserves, for Allah is swift in settling accounts. [51]

This announcement (is a message) for all humanity, so let them be warned by it, and let them know that He is only One God. Let thoughtful people then be reminded. [52]

The Stony Ground

15 Al Hijr
Late Meccan Period

By the late Meccan period the Prophet was feeling continuously fatigued. The constant persecution that he and his followers were facing, the daily insults, the stories of woe that his followers brought to him of their own travails and suffering, and the fact that, despite all the logical arguments he brought to prove that idolatry was false, the majority of his people still clung to ignorant traditions – all of these things began to take a toll on the Prophet. This chapter was revealed to the Prophet partly to console him and partly to convince him to remain steadfast, hoping upon the favor of Allah to change his circumstances and those of his followers who believed in his message and suffered on account of it.

*In the Name of Allah,
the Compassionate, the Merciful*

Alif. Lām. Rā.

These are the verses of the Book and a clear recitation. [1] It just may happen that (one day) those who covered (the light of faith within their hearts) will wish that they had surrendered (to Allah), [2] but leave them alone to eat and make merry – preoccupied in their false hopes, for soon they'll know (the truth)! [3]

We've never destroyed any settlement without setting their time limit in advance, [4] nor can any community know when its term is up, nor can they delay it. [5]

The Mocking of the Faithless

(The Meccans) say, "*Hey you, the one who's getting this 'revealed message.' (We think) you're crazy!* [6] *So why aren't you bringing angels down to show us if you're really so honest?*" [7] However, We never send angels down except for a compelling reason, and (if they did happen to come), then the (faithless) would get no relief! [917] [8]

We're sending the message down to you, (Muhammad,) and We're going to protect it. [9] We sent messengers before your time among the religious sects of the past, [10] but no messenger ever came to them without them mocking him. [11]

---

[917] The Prophet said, "How will you react when five (types of disaster) befall you? I seek Allah's refuge that you'll never have to experience them and that you'll never have (the sins) within you (that would bring those disasters upon you). Whenever public wickedness prevails in a community, they're struck with plagues and diseases that were unknown to their ancestors. Whenever a segment of society stops paying charity, then they're deprived of rain from the sky. It's only on account of the animals (that live in that region that any rain would fall on them at all). Whenever a segment of society cheats people in measuring amounts accurately, then they'll surely be stricken with drought, famine and oppression from a tyrant leader. Any time the leaders of a nation rule by other than what Allah revealed, then they're afflicted with enemies who will deprive them of some of their power. When they stop ruling themselves altogether by (revealed scripture) and the example of their prophet, then they seek to overpower each other (through civil war and strife)." (*Ahmad, Ibn Majah*)

That's how We (allow the notion) to seep into the hearts of the wicked [12] that they can disbelieve in (the message because it's so easy to insult Allah's prophets). However, the customs of the ancients have passed away! [13]

Even if We opened up a door to the sky for them and they climbed ever farther up into it, [14] they would still say, *"Our eyes are just blurry – no, wait! We've been (the victims) of some kind of sorcery!"* [15]

The Signs of Allah

*A*nd so it was that We placed the constellations in the sky and made them as decorations for all who see them. [16] We're also guarding them from every outcast devil. [17] If any of them secretly tries to hear something, he's chased away by a brilliant shooting star. [918] [18]

We spread the earth out (wide like a carpet) and placed within it steady mountains. We developed everything on earth in a balanced way [19] and provided resources for the survival of both you and the (many creatures) that are not your responsibility. [20]

There's nothing (that exists) without its proper resources being (arranged for it) in Our sight, and We release nothing (of those resources) unless it's measured out accordingly. [21]

We send the fertilizing winds and cause water to fall from the sky to provide you with water, even though you're not in charge of its supply. [22] We're responsible for bringing life and death, and We're going to inherit (all things after they die). [23]

As it is, We know who [919] among you moves ahead and who falls behind. [920] [24]

---

[918] The idea, as understood by traditional scholars, is that the next realm of Heaven lies beyond the veil of physical existence, i.e., space. Between the earth and the unseen realm lies the rest of the physical universe, including the stars and other planets. The angels approach the earth and sometimes remain in the sky and discuss what will happen on earth. The evil jinn try to approach them to hear the secrets spoken by the angels. This is in keeping with the chief devil's goal (i.e., Satan) to corrupt humanity (to prove to Allah that jinns are superior to humans). These evil jinns, or devils, then seek to rush back to the surface of the earth to whisper what they heard into the hearts of fortune-tellers, astrologers and other people engaged in predicting the future. [72:8-10] The people make their predictions, and some of them come true. Thus, people become dazzled, are misled away from Allah and come to rely upon fortune-tellers and the like for guidance in worldly affairs. (The Prophet did say that for every truth the fortune-tellers say, there are 99 lies.) To guard against the devils doing this with impunity, flaming fireballs, i.e., shooting stars, chase the devils away from the upper atmosphere. This doesn't mean that every shooting star we see throughout the year is chasing a devil, but traditionally Muslim scholars have held that this is the technique Allah uses to guard the secrets of the angels from the evil jinns that seek to destroy us humans. The Prophet did tell his companions that shooting stars have nothing to do with predicting events on earth, a belief that pre-Islamic Arabs held. (*Muslim*) Also see 37:6-10.

[919] Ibn 'Abbas (d. 687) explained the reason for the revelation of these two verses. He said, "A beautiful woman, among the most beautiful of women, used to come (to the mosque) and pray behind the Prophet. Some of the men used to intentionally seek out the rows closest to the front so they wouldn't be able to see her (by making furtive glances back at the women's prayer lines). Other men would pray in the last row (of the men's lines) so they could peek back under their raised arms (when they were prostrating) and look at her. Because of this, Allah revealed this passage." (*Ibn Majah, Abu Dawud, Ahmad, Tirmidhi, Nisa'i*)

[920] As the background commentary explained, this verse was revealed with regards to gender locations during congregational prayers. There are many points of etiquette for the spiritual maintenance of a mosque vis-à-vis the presence of mixed genders. To begin with, there was no partition of any kind separating the men and the women in the Prophet's mosque. There was a women's section in the rear and a men's section in the front. Thus, if both genders are going to be present in the same room, then they had better focus on prayer and not on each other. Indeed, this verse is telling the Muslims that Allah knows if they're thinking of Him or of something else. The Prophet once said that the prayer lines that are best for men are in the very front and best for women in the very back, and this utterance is probably connected to this episode. This is a practical arrangement and is in no way sexist or

Your Lord is the One Who will gather them all together, for He's full of wisdom and knowledge. [25]

The Fall of Satan

$\mathcal{A}$nd so it was that We created human beings from pliable clay - from mere molded mud, [26] and We created the jinns, even before (human beings), from the intense heat (of pure energy). [921] [27]

Your Lord said to the angels, *"I'm going to create mortal man from mineral-rich clay, from molded mud. [28] After I've constructed him and breathed into him (something of) My spirit, [922] you must all bow down to him (out of respect)."* [29]

The angels fell down in prostration all together, [30] but Iblis didn't (join with the angels), for he refused to be one of those who bowed. [923] [31] Then Allah asked, *"Iblis! What's wrong with you that you didn't join those who bowed down?"* [32]

"I'm not going to bow down to a mortal man," Iblis answered, *"for You created him from mineral-rich clay, from mere molded mud!"* [33]

"Then get out of here!" Allah ordered. *"You're an outcast, [34] and you'll be cursed all the way to the Day of Judgment!"* [35]

"My Lord!" Iblis cried out. *"Give me some time (to prove my case) up until they're resurrected."* [36]

---

suggestive of a lower status for women. This arrangement is just to insure that the attention of men is solely upon Allah, so that is why they are asked to sit in the front and keep their eyes forward. (Also see 24:30-31.)

[921] Jinns are elemental creatures made from a component of fire. However, they are not 'fire' as we know it, for the Arabic term, *samoum*, used here, means that part of the fire that is above the tip of the visible flame where no color is seen, but the burning heat is still felt. Think of invisible white-hot fire. (Some translators render this word as scorching wind from a smokeless fire.) Thus, jinns exist on something of an infrared or even more intense plane of being – almost electrical in nature. They communicate with human beings by 'whispering' in our minds. Since our thoughts are nothing more than impulses of energy, the jinns merely attempt to alter the course of our thoughts slightly or try to bend them to their will. It is up to us, when we feel such negative influences in our thoughts, either to follow through with them or to seek Allah's protection. If we do the latter, Allah promised that it will cancel the Satanic influence.

[922] What is meant by 'His spirit?' There are mixed views on this issue, with some scholars postulating that the soul that we humans are endowed with is a small sample taken from the same spirit-matter that makes up Allah. This in no way means that we are gods ourselves, and no scholar has ever assumed such. Instead, it is akin to taking a cup of water from the sea. Is the water in the cup still the sea? No, it is separated and disconnected. It may be consumed, cycled through the environment, bottled and even used to create electricity, but eventually it may find itself back in the sea from whence it came, but until then, it's just water. Likewise, when the child in the womb has reached 120 days of development (according to the explanation of the Prophet), an angel comes and breathes a *spirit from Allah* into the baby. Assuming the child is born and lives its life (for good or evil), one day he or she will die, releasing that spirit back into the universe where it rejoins its master essence. (See 2:28) This *ruh* (spirit or divine gift) is what sets us apart from all other life forms that we know about. From this we can conceive of morality, justice and truth, even as we can use our hyper-expanded imagination to peer into the recesses of the very meaning of the universe itself. Our use (or misuse) of this *spirit* will determine whether our unique personality (called a *nafs* or individual self) enters Paradise or is doomed to Hell. (See 33:72-73) The Sufis often take this concept (of having a spirit on loan from Allah) as the basis for their poetry and philosophy. To achieve union with Allah, in their view, is not *becoming* Allah, but rather returning your soul back to its rightful master (a state they equate with being drunk with ecstasy, no less!) The Day of Judgment is when our *nafs*, or individual essence, is judged on how well we took care of the spirit that was loaned to us. (See 16:111, 29:57-59 and 21:35, for example.) Other scholars contend that the 'spirit' was specially created matter from Allah's creative will and implanted in human beings to give us our essential quality and unique nature.

[923] Remember that Iblis was a jinn who was often in the company of the angels, and he did not bow down when the angels did 'all together.' Verse 7:12 specifically mentions that Allah included more than just the angels in His command to bow down. Also see 2:34 and footnote.

"You'll have your time," (Allah said), [37] "until a day whose arrival is appointed." [38]

"My Lord!" (Iblis) said. "Since You made me slip up, I'm going to make (immorality and wickedness) seem proper and good to those on earth, and I'm going to deviate all of them (morally) [39] - except, (of course), for Your sincere servants among them." [40]

"The path (that they follow) will be the straight one that leads back to Me," (Allah) answered, [41] "and you'll have no power over My servants, except for the ones who put themselves in the wrong and follow you." [924] [42]

Hellfire is the promised destination of them all! [43] There will be seven gates (leading within it) – one gate for each class (of sinners). [925] [44]

Now as for those who were mindful (of their duty to Allah), they will be among gardens and springs. [45] (They'll be told,) "Enter within in peace and safety!" [46] Then We're going to cleanse their hearts of any lurking sense of bitterness (so they'll truly) be brothers as they face each other, (relaxing) on couches. [47]

They'll feel no exhaustion, nor will they ever be asked to leave. [48] So announce to My servants that I am *indeed* the Forgiving and the Merciful [49] and that My punishment will be a terrible punishment. [50]

Who were the Guests of Abraham?

*T*ell them about the guests of Abraham. [51] When they came before him and said, "*Peace*," he answered them back, saying, "*We're uneasy about you.*" [52] They said, "*Don't feel uneasy, for we're here to give you the good news of a son who will be exceedingly perceptive.*" [53]

(Abraham) asked, "*Are you coming here to give me this good news now that I'm an old man? So what kind of good news is that!*" [54]

"*We're bringing you this good news in all truth, so don't be discouraged!*" (they replied). [55]

(Then Abraham realized he had been hasty and) said, "*Who can be discouraged at Allah's mercy except for those who are astray?*" [56]

Then he asked, "*So what's the errand that's brought you here, emissaries (of Allah)?*" [57]

"*We're being sent (to destroy) a wicked people,*" they answered, [58] "*except for the family of Lot, whom we're supposed to save all together, [59] though not his wife, whom we've determined will remain behind.*" [926] [60]

---

[924] The Prophet said (in a lengthy tradition) that Satan puts doubts in the mind of a son of Adam when he considers accepting Islam and that if he is thwarted and the person becomes a believer in Allah, then Satan merely moves to another perch from which to strike. When the believer feels he must migrate to a safer place to preserve his religion and family, Satan puts more doubts in his head about it. If the believer ignores Satan, then Satan merely moves to an even newer perch down the line. If a believer is asked to fight evil, then Satan assails him with thoughts of death, his widow marrying someone else or of losing all his wealth. If a believer resists and ignores Satan, then Allah will send such a staunch believer to Paradise if any of the following four things ever happen to him: if he dies naturally, if he's killed in a just cause, if he drowns, or if an animal breaks his neck. (*Ahmad*)

[925] The commentators differ as to whether the seven gates represent the main general entrance to Hell or if they are the names of the seven distinct levels of Hellfire. The names of each of the seven levels of Hell are as follows: (1) *Jaheem*, (2) *Jahannam*, (3) *Sa'ir*, (4) *Saqar*, (5) *Nata*, (6) *Hawiya* and (7) *Hutama*. (From *The Spectacle of Death and Glimpses of the Life Hereafter* by K.M. Islam)

[926] Abraham was the uncle of Lot and they had parted ways some years before. While Lot was still clinging to faith, his wife was a sinner, having become influenced by the ways of the evil people in her city. She would betray her husband by informing the masses whenever her husband had guests in the house. The wicked people would then come and violate his guests. On account of that, Allah had no interest in saving her.

In the Cities of the Plain

*W*hen the messenger (angels) came to Lot's family, [61] (Lot) said, *"You seem to be strangers (to this city)."* [62]

"Yes," they answered, *"and we've come to you to bring about (the order of destruction from Allah that the faithless) have been doubting.* [63] *Thus, we've come here to bring the reality home to you, and we're honest in what we say.* [64] *So travel by night with your family when there's only a little of the night left, and you, yourself, must be the one (who guards) the rear. Let no one look back, and keep going onward to where you're told to go."* [65]

And so, We let him know about the command that the roots of (the wicked) were going to be cut off by the morning. [66]

The local people of the city came running excitedly (when they learned there were strange men in Lot's house). [67] (Lot) said to them, *"These are my guests, so don't disgrace me.* [68] *Rather, be mindful of Allah, and don't dishonor me!"* [69]

"Didn't we forbid you from (hiding) anyone at all (from us!)" they shouted. [70]

"My daughters are here," (Lot) pleaded, *"if you have to do something."* [927] [71]

By your very life, (Muhammad), they were milling about wildly in their drunkenness! [72] Then the powerful blast overtook them before morning. [73] We turned (their city) upside down and rained down upon them a shower of hardened stones! [74]

Truly, there are signs in this (incident) for those who consider. [75] Even though the (city) was located on a highly (traveled) road, (now it can no longer be found)! [76] So truly, there are signs in this for those who believe. [77]

Destroyed Nations

*T*he Companions of the Thicket [928] were also wrongdoers, [78] and likewise We took vengeance upon them. They were located on a clearly marked route, (but their prominence did nothing to save them). [79]

The Companions of the Stony Ground also denied their messengers. [929] [80] We sent Our signs to them, but they kept turning away from them. [81] They used to carve their dwellings out of mountain cliffs, (thinking they were) secure. [82] Then the powerful blast seized them one morning, [83] and nothing they prepared was of any use to them. [84]

Don't Lose Heart

*W*e didn't create the heavens and the earth and everything in between them except for a true purpose. The Hour (of Judgment) is certainly drawing near, so

---

[927] The mob wanted to seize the strangers who were with Lot for the mob's lowly passions, but Lot couldn't conceive that angels from the Lord should be so treated, that's why he offered his daughters to them for their lusts. It may seem like a callous act on the part of the father, but remember his options: let the crowd rape an angel or his daughter. He was scared, confused and certainly didn't want to have a messenger from Allah, under his care, treated so. What Lot didn't realize was that the angels could take care of themselves. In addition, perhaps Lot wasn't so callous after all, because he knew the men wouldn't be interested in his daughters anyway. They said as much in verse 11:79!

[928] The Companions of the Thicket were the ancient people of Madyan, who worshipped a thicket of trees.

[929] The Companions of the Stony Ground refers to the people of a region of northern Arabia, where the land is rocky and somewhat craggy. There are ruins of an ancient people there in the hills. Those ruins are carved dwellings in rock faces.

excuse (the shortcomings) of others with gracious detachment. [930] [85]

Your Lord is the Most Knowledgeable Creator! [86] And so it is that We've given you the seven frequently repeated verses, (so you can gain inspiration and strength), and a majestic Qur'an. [931] [87]

Don't strain your eyes longingly at what We've given certain classes (of people in power and wealth,) nor should you feel sorry for them (because they're blinded by those things). Rather, you should (focus yourself) on lowering your wing (in kindness) to the believers. [88] (All you need to) say (to the arrogant ones is), *"I'm the one who's warning you plainly."* [932] [89]

(And thus, you must continue your preaching,) even as We're directing (Our revelations) to those who are dividing themselves (up into different camps concerning the truth of this message), [90] and who also try to slice this Qur'an up into disjointed sections (by quoting it out of context in order to ridicule it). [933] [91] And so, by your Lord, We're going to question all of them together [92] about what they've done. [934] [93] So call to them openly with whatever you're commanded, and turn away from those who make partners (with Allah). [94]

We're enough (of a protector) for you against those who ridicule you [95] and against those who set up a rival god with Allah. Soon they're going to know (the truth)! [96] We know how your heart aches at what they're saying, [97] but glorify and praise your Lord, be among those who bow down prostrate, [98] and serve your Lord until what is certain comes to you. [99]

---

[930] The Prophet said, "Bring good news, and don't drive people away. Make things easy, and don't make them hard. Obey each other, and don't differ among yourselves." (*Bukhari*)

[931] This passage refers to the first chapter of the Qur'an, which has seven verses and is recited (at the minimum) seventeen times a day in an individual's ritual prayers. The reminder of this essential chapter, coming as it is after the exhortation to be gracious with people, is quite appropriate given that the opening chapter reminds us that Allah is the ultimate source of our well being. Who can be overly cross or angry with people when we desire that Allah overlooks our own mistakes! For Muslims, the first chapter of the Qur'an is akin to the Lord's prayer for Christians. The Prophet said of chapter one of the Qur'an: "By the One Who holds my soul in His hands, Allah did not reveal in the Torah, in the Gospel, in the Psalms or in the (rest of the) Qur'an anything like [this chapter]; it is the seven frequently repeated verses." (*Bukhari*)

[932] The Prophet said, "The example of both me and that with which Allah sent me is that of a man who went to his people and said, 'People! I've seen an (invading) army with my own eyes! I'm clearly warning you! Flee! Flee!' Some of his people believed him, and they left by nightfall at a slow pace and escaped. Others didn't believe him and remained where they were until the morning when the army overtook them and utterly destroyed them. This is the example of the one who obeys me and follows what I've brought and the example of the one who disobeys me and rejects the truth that I've brought." (*Bukhari, Muslim*)

[933] The pagans would go out and meet incoming caravans to warn the new visitors not to believe in the call of a man among them named Muhammad, and they also warned that he was a sorcerer. They would recite scattered phrases of the Qur'an to the visitors and ridicule its message, (without reciting anything in context); thus, they 'sectioned' it up. (*Ibn Kathir*) Strangely enough, this seems to be the same practice of modern critics of Islam.

[934] After the incident mentioned in verse 6:10, the particularly intense bullying of the Meccans continued for several days more. The following passage was revealed. (*Ibn Hisham*)When the companions asked the Prophet about this passage and asked what they will be questioned about, the Prophet replied that people will be questioned about whether they believed in the one God or not and their commitment to Him. (*Qurtubi*)

The Bee

16 An-Nahl
(aka An-Ni'am)
Late Meccan Period

This chapter was revealed after the migrations of some of the Prophet's followers to Abyssinia. Although the migrants eventually returned after hearing false reports that Meccan persecution had eased, the situation of the fledgling religious sect was uncertain and seemingly grim. The mention of plots against the believers of ancient days is also a clear reference to the ongoing schemes and plots that the idolaters were continually hatching against the followers of the Prophet.

No greater example is there of the ability of otherwise normal people to become oppressors and mean-spirited purveyors of cruelty than in the way that the Meccans, who thought so highly of themselves, became so wicked and gratuitously violent against those who disagreed with the backward superstitions that held sway in that culture. The Muslims were not calling for a violent overthrow of the society. Rather, they called for reforming personal conduct, establishing a social safety net to support the weak and poverty-stricken, and considering abandoning idolatry and the many invented superstitions that had no basis in logic or reason.

In the Name of Allah,
the Compassionate, the Merciful

*A*llah's command will come to pass, so don't seek to rush it. [935] *All glory be to Him!* He's so high above the partners they assign to Him! [1]

He sends the angels with the spirit of His command and bestows it upon whichever of His servants that He wants, (saying): *"Warn (people) that there is no god but I, so be mindful of Me."* [936] [2]

He created the heavens and the earth for a true purpose. He's so high above the partners they assign to Him! [3] He created human beings from a drop of mingled fluids, and look how that same (human) becomes openly quarrelsome! [4]

---

[935] Some of the pagans used to ridicule the Prophet because the foretold punishment from Allah wasn't materializing upon them. A pagan poet named an-Nadr ibn al-Harith even taunted the Prophet, saying, "O Allah! If it's within Your power, then throw stones down upon us to hasten our suffering!" This passage was revealed in response to their ridicule, promising that the punishment would come one day, but not when they wanted. (*Asbab ul-Nuzul*)

[936] About two or three years after this verse was revealed, the entire leadership of the Meccan pagans fell in the Battle of Badr, save for Abu Lahab, who remained in Mecca but died soon thereafter from an infection. (See chapter 111. Within approximately six years after that, the Prophet returned to Mecca at the head of an army, ten thousand strong, and forced the peaceful surrender of the city. When all the Meccan pagans were in his power on that day of victory, he pardoned them and left them alone, causing them to convert *en masse* in wonder over his noble generosity.

What has Allah Provided for Us?

$\mathcal{H}$e created livestock (animals) for you. You use (their hides) for warmth and make other useful products, even as you eat them, as well. [937] [5] You feel delighted at their sight as you corral them (in the evening) and when you lead them out to pasture (in the morning). [6]

They carry your heavy loads to places that you couldn't get to (by yourselves), unless you were to exhaust yourself on the journey! (Allah provided you with these beasts of burden), for your Lord is kind and merciful. [7]

(He also created) fancy horses, mules and donkeys for you to ride, and for you to parade about in exhibitions. He will create other (modes of transportation) that you (currently) know nothing about. [8]

It's Allah's (prerogative) to point out the right path, because there are other paths that swerve aside. If Allah had wanted, He could've guided you all (by giving you no choice but to be believers). [9]

He's the One Who sends water down from the sky. You drink from it, and from it grows the bushes upon which you graze your cattle. [10] He also uses (the same water) to produce for you the grains, olives, dates, grapes and all the other types of fruit. There is a sign in this for those who reflect. [11]

He made the night and the day, the sun and the moon and the very stars themselves useful for you by His command. There are signs in these (things), as well, for those who use their reason. [12]

There is also, in all the things that He's multiplied for you in the earth and that encompass every shade of color, a sign for people who remember (the favors of Allah). [938] [13]

He's the One Who tamed the sea for you, so you could eat fresh meat from it and also so that you could harvest (the pearls and shells) that you wear as ornaments.

You see the ships sailing through the waves that allow you to seek out Allah's bounty. (Thus, the many resources that you gain should) give you (further reason) to be grateful. [14]

He set up firm highlands in the earth to minimize the effects of earthquakes upon you, and (He laid out) rivers and

---

[937] People are allowed to eat all types of domesticated livestock, except for donkeys, mules and pigs.

[938] What is the position of the Qur'an on evolution? In general, the Qur'an is fairly ambiguous and can be interpreted to reflect both creationist or evolutionary ideas. Modern-day Islamic scholars take divergent views on this issue, and sometimes argue one position or the other, oftentimes with great passion. (Compare the views on evolution of Palestinian scholar Adnan Ibrahim and the Pakistani American scholar Yasir Qadhi, for example.) Earlier generations of Muslim scientists were not troubled by this science vs faith argument that modern Muslims unwittingly inherited from fundamentalist Christians. Indeed, ten centuries before Darwin's theories, Muslims were already speculating on the effects of natural selection and evolution. For example, the ninth-century social commentator and zoologist, al-Jahiz, observed the following phenomena concerning natural selection: "Animals engage in a struggle for existence; for resources, to avoid being eaten and to breed. Environmental factors influence organisms to develop new characteristics to ensure survival, thus transforming them into new species. Animals that survive to breed can pass on their successful characteristics to offspring." (Kitab al-Hayawan) This is proven science, though science cannot explain the rise of life itself from lifeless matter and it is especially helpless in explaining human consciousness in a world where no other example exists. Rather than hold to arguments defined by modern passions and outside forces, it may be that the Qur'an presents something of a compromise between science and religion, and this middle ground is found precisely in its ambiguity. A Muslim can choose to believe in both science and God (or intelligent design) and not feel any unease about it. See 7:185 for the Qur'an's practical and poetic take on this subject. Also see 35:27-28 where variation within species is clearly laid out.

334

passes (in the world), so that you could be guided on your travels. [15]

(He also provided the many natural) landmarks and even the stars above by which (travelers) may orient themselves. [16] So is the One Who can create (such) things equal to the one who can create nothing at all? Won't you take a reminder? [17]

If you ever tried to add up all of Allah's favors, you would never be able to count them all! Indeed, Allah is forgiving and merciful! [18]

Allah knows what you conceal and what you reveal. [19] The (statues) that they call upon besides Allah can create nothing, for they themselves are merely created (things) [20] - *dead and lifeless*! They don't even know (if or) when they'll be resurrected! [21]

The Two Potential Results

Your god is One God. Those who have no faith in the next life have stubborn hearts, and they're arrogant besides! [22]

Without a doubt Allah knows what they're (doing both) in secret, as well as out in the open, and He has no love for the arrogant. [23]

When they're asked, "*What has your Lord revealed?*" They answer, "*Tales from long ago!*" [24]

On the Day of Assembly they can bear their own burdens in full, as well as the burden (of the crime they committed against) the unsuspecting (people) whom they misled! *Oh, how terrible the burdens they will bear!* [25]

And so it was that those who came before (these Meccans) also schemed (against Allah), but Allah knocked out the foundation of their structure, and the roof caved in upon them!

The wrath (of Allah) took hold of them from directions they never even expected! [26]

On the Day of Assembly, He's going to cover them in shame and say, "*So where are all My partners about which you used to argue?*"

The people of knowledge will remark, "*Today, those who covered (the light of faith within their hearts) are truly covered in shame and misery.* [27] *They're the ones who had their souls taken by the angels while they were in a state of corruption against their own selves.*" [939]

---

[939] The Prophet once told a group of people waiting for a funeral, "When a believer is about to leave this world and go forward to the next world, angels with faces white as the sun come down to him from heaven with one of the shrouds of Paradise - and some of the perfume of Paradise. They sit away from him as far as the eye can see. Then the angel of death comes and sits at his head and says, 'Good soul, come out to forgiveness and acceptance from Allah.' (The soul) then comes out as a drop flows from a water-skin, and he seizes it. When he does so, (the other angels) don't leave it in his hand for an instant but take it and place it in that perfumed shroud, and from it there comes forth a fragrance like that of the sweetest musk found on the face of the earth. They then take it up and do not bring it past a company of angels without their asking, 'Who is this good soul?' To which they reply, 'So and so, the child of so and so', using the best names by which people called him on the earth. They then bring him to the lowest heaven and ask that the gate should be opened for him. This is done, and from every heaven its archangels escort him to the next heaven until he is brought to the seventh heaven, and Allah Who is great and glorious says, 'Record the book of My servant in the vault and take him back to earth, for I created humanity from it, I shall return them into it, and from it I shall bring them forth another time.' His soul is then restored to his body, and two angels come to him, making him sit up, and say to him, 'Who is your Lord?' He replies, 'My Lord is Allah.' They ask, 'What is your religion?' He replies, 'My religion is Islam.' They ask, 'Who is this man who was sent among you?' He replies, 'He is Allah's Messenger.' They ask, 'What is your (source of) knowledge?' He replies, 'I have read Allah's Book, believed in it and declared it to be true.' Then a voice cries from heaven, 'My servant has spoken the truth, so spread out carpets for him from Paradise, and open a gate for him into Paradise.' Then some of its joy and its fragrance comes to him; his grave is made spacious for him as far as the eye can

(Then the doomed sinners) will offer their abject submission, saying, "*We didn't do anything wrong (intentionally).*"

(However, it will be said to them), "*That's not true, for Allah knows what you were doing.* [28] *So enter into the gates of Hellfire, and stay in there!*" The home of the arrogant is an awful one indeed! [29]

When those who are mindful (of Allah) are asked, "*What has your Lord revealed?*" they say, "*Only the best!*" For those who do good, there will be good in this world, and the home of the next life is even better! How excellent is the home of those who were mindful! [30]

They'll be admitted into eternal gardens beneath which rivers flow! They'll have everything there they ever wished for, and that's how Allah rewards those who were mindful (of Him). [31] They're the ones who will be taken by the angels (at death) in a state of purity, and who will be told, "*Peace be upon you. Enter the Garden on account of what you did (in the world).*" [32]

Are (the faithless) just waiting (for the time when) the angels come for them, or (are they waiting) for the arrival of the command of your Lord? That's what those who went before them did, but Allah never did any injustice to them (when He punished them), for they had been doing injustice against their own souls. [33]

The evil of their deeds overtook them, and the very thing at which they used to laugh closed in upon them from all sides! [34]

Allah Keeps His Promises

*T*hose who make partners (with Allah) say, "*If Allah had wanted to (prevent us), then we would've never worshipped anything besides Him - neither ourselves nor our ancestors - and we would never have prohibited anything in preference to His (laws).*" That's how others

---

see, and a man with a beautiful face, beautiful garments and a sweet odor comes to him and says, 'Rejoice in what pleases you for this is your day, which you have been promised.' He asks, 'Who are you, for your face is perfectly beautiful and brings good?' He replies, 'I am your good deeds.' He then says, 'My Lord, bring the last hour; my Lord, bring the last hour, so I can return to my people and my property.' On the other hand, when a faithless person is about to leave the world and proceed to the next world, angels with dark faces come down to him from heaven with woolen cloth and sit away from him as far as the eye can see. Then the angel of death comes and sits at his head and says, 'Wicked soul, come out to displeasure from Allah.' Then it becomes dissipated in his body, and he draws it out as a prickly stick is drawn out from moistened wool. He then seizes (the soul), and when he does so (the other angels) do not leave it in his hand for an instant but put it in that woolen cloth and from it comes forth a stench like the most offensive corpse found on the face of the earth. They then take it up and do not bring it past a company of angels without their saying, 'Who is this wicked soul?' To which they reply, 'So and so, the child of so and so', using the worst names that he was called in the world. When he is brought to the lowest heaven, a request is made that the gate be opened for him, but it is not opened for him." (The Prophet then recited the verse, "The gates of heaven will not be opened for them, and they will not enter Paradise until a twisted rope can pass through the eye of a needle." Then the Prophet continued his story, saying, "Allah, Who is the most Great and Glorious, then says, 'Record his book in the pit in the lowest part of the earth,' and his soul is thrown down." (Then the Prophet recited the verse, "He who assigns partners to Allah – it's as if he had fallen down from the sky and been snatched up by the birds or made to fall by the wind in a far off place." Then the Prophet continued his story, saying,) "His soul is then restored to his body, and two angels come to him, make him sit up, and say to him, 'Who is your Lord?' He replies, 'Alas, alas, I do not know.' They ask, 'What is your religion?' He replies, 'Alas, alas, I do not know.' They ask 'Who is this man who was sent among you?' He replies, 'Alas, alas, I do not know.' Then one cries out from the sky, 'He has lied, so spread out carpets from Hell for him, and open a gate for him into Hell.' Then some of its heat and hot air comes to him. His grave is made narrow for him up until his ribs are pressed together in it, and a man with an ugly face, ugly garments and a bad smell comes to him and says, 'Be grieved with what displeases you, for this is your day which you have been promised.' He asks 'Who are you, for your face is ugly and it brings evil?' He replies, 'I'm your wicked deeds.' The (unfortunate soul) then says, 'O My Lord, don't bring the last hour.'"

before them behaved. What else is there for the messengers to do other than to convey the message clearly? [35]

And so it was that We sent to every community a messenger (who said), "*Serve Allah, and shun falsehood.*"

Among them were some who were guided by Allah, while others among them had (the consequences of) their mistaken ways proven true against them.

So travel all over the world, and see what happened to those who denied (Allah). [36] If you're anxious for them to be guided, (know that) Allah doesn't guide those whom He leaves astray, and there will be no one to help them. [37]

They swear by Allah – *using their strongest oaths* – that Allah will never raise the dead to life.

But no! It's a promise He's going to keep, though most people don't know it, [38] so that He can present to them the meaning of those things in which they differed, and so that those who covered (the light of faith within their hearts) can finally know that they were indeed liars. [39]

When We want something to happen, We only need to say, "*Be,*" - and there it is! [40]

Migration for Faith will be Rewarded

$\mathcal{W}$e're going to give a fine (reward) in this world to those who migrated (from their homes in the cause of Allah) after suffering under persecution. [940]

However, the reward of the next life will be even greater, if they only knew! [41] (They were the ones) who persevered patiently and who placed their trust in their Lord. [42]

Muhammad, You are One of the Chosen

$\mathcal{T}$he messengers that We sent before you, (Muhammad), were no more than (mortal) men (like yourself) to whom We granted revelation. [941]

Just ask the people who received the message before you, if you don't know about it. [43]

(We sent them) clear evidence and scripture, just as We're also sending the message down to you, so you can convey clearly to people what's been sent for them, and so they can also think about it. [44]

So do those who make evil schemes feel so safe that Allah won't cause the earth to swallow them up or that the punishment won't come upon them suddenly from where they least expect it? [45]

(Do they feel so safe that they don't think) He'll take a hold of them while they're in the middle of their affairs, having no chance to prevent it, [46] or that He won't take a hold of them by gradually eroding (their power)?

---

[940] This verse refers to the nearly eighty men, women and children who fled Meccan persecution to Abyssinia in the year 615. Later on, the Muslims were settled in lush Medina, a "fine" homeland indeed!

[941] The pagan Meccans disbelieved in the Prophet, saying that if Allah was truly powerful, then He would've sent an angel to warn them. This verse, which references the ancient human prophets that were revered by the Jews and Christians, was revealed in response to reassure Muhammad that Allah had really chosen him, even though he was only a man, because it's what Allah has always done. It is thought that after this passage was revealed and made known to the Meccan public, that the pagans of Mecca were motivated to send emissaries to the Jews of Medina to ask them about the validity of Muhammad's teachings. Thereafter, passages in both chapters 17 and 18 were revealed to address some of the issues about which the Jews told the pagans to ask Muhammad.

Your Lord is kind and merciful, (and He may take that slower route in order to give them time to repent). [47]

Don't they look at what Allah has created, even (at the small) things, like the way in which their shadows bend to the right and the left, prostrating themselves before Allah in the most humble way? [48]

Whatever is in the heavens and whatever is on the earth bows down to Allah, from crawling creatures all the way up to the angels.

None of them are too proud (to submit to His will). [49]

(The angels) stand in awe of their Lord Who towers over them, and they do everything they're commanded to do. [942] [50]

On Dual Gods

Allah has said, "*Don't take gods in pairs, (saying there is one god of good and another god of evil), for He is only One God, so be in awe of Me.*" [943] [51]

Whatever is in the heavens and the earth belongs to Him, and sincere obedience is due only to Him. *So should you be mindful of any other besides Allah?* [52]

How do People Disobey Their Lord?

Nothing good ever comes to you except that it comes from Allah. Whenever you're stricken with hardship, you cry out to Him in desperation. [53] Yet, when He removes your hardship, some of you make partners with their Lord, [54] as if to show their ingratitude for the favors We've granted them. *So enjoy yourselves now, but soon you'll know (the truth)!* [55]

The Foolish Tenets of Paganism

The (Meccans) set aside a portion of the resources that We've provided to them for their survival. [944] (Then they offer that portion) to (their idols), *not even knowing (if they're real or not)!* By Allah! You're going to be questioned about all of your superstitions! [56]

The Shameful Choices of the Pagans

Then they assign daughters (as offspring) to Allah - *all glory belongs to Him!* - even as they keep for themselves (the sons) that they desire! [57] When the news is brought to one of them of (the birth) of a female (child), his face darkens, and he's filled with anguish. [945] [58] He hides himself

---

[942] After reading this verse it is customary for the one who has faith in Allah to prostrate himself on the floor and praise Allah.

[943] The Zoroastrians of Persia held that there were two, coequal gods: one of light and the other of darkness or evil. Some Gnostic Christian groups also held similar ideas. The pagan Arabs were inclined towards these dualistic ideas and sometimes made pairs of gods themselves to represent different extremes. This is what this verse is referencing.

[944] The pagans of Arabia used to reserve a portion of their produce for their idols, in the same way that Hinduism and even some forms of Buddhism reserve a share of food to "feed" their idols. (Also see 6:136.)

[945] Pagan Arab men believed that women were inferior to them in all respects. Daughters were seen as burdens because they couldn't fight, hunt or labor as hard as men, and when they married they went to live with their husbands' families and thus took resources away from their own family. For this daughters were looked down upon, and fathers would sometimes take their newborn baby girls and

from his fellows in shame, on account of the bad news he's received.

Should he keep (the baby girl) in contempt or bury her in the sand? *Oh, what a terrible predicament on which they must decide!* [59] This is the vile example of those who don't believe in the next life, while the highest example belongs to Allah, for He's the Powerful and the Wise. [946] [60]

If Allah were to seize people (and punish them) for their corruption (according to what they deserve), then He wouldn't leave a single creature alive (on the earth)! However, He gives them a break for a set amount of time. When that time limit expires, then they have no way to delay (their due punishment) - no, not even for an hour, just as they have no way to advance it. [947] [61]

They attribute to Allah what they hate (for themselves), even as their tongues express the lie that they deserve everything that's good for themselves. Yet, without a doubt the Fire (is all that) they're going to get, and they're going to be among the first to be ushered into it! [62]

By Allah! We sent (prophets) to those nations that went before you, but Satan made their (evil) actions seem appropriate and good to them. He's also the patron (of these Meccans) here today, but they're going to receive a painful punishment. [63]

We didn't send the Book to you for any other purpose than for you to explain to them clearly those things about which they've been arguing, and also so it could be a guide and a mercy for those who believe. [64]

Ponder these Signs of Allah

Allah sends water down from the sky, and He uses it to give life to the earth after it was dead. There is a sign in this for people who listen. [65] There is another sign in livestock (animals), for We produce (milk) for you to drink from a place within their bodies between the contents of their intestines and blood, a drink pure and tasty for any who drink it! [66]

And from the fruit of the date palm and from grapevines you get alcoholic beverages and wholesome (non-alcoholic) products, as well. [948] In this is a sign for people who are wise. [67]

---

bury them alive in the sand. As verse 59 points out, the pagans have set up for themselves an evil choice on account of their disregard for the value of females, and so their example is one of evil upon evil, whereas Allah's way takes the high road. If they only believed in the true God, then they wouldn't have put themselves in such a bad position when daughters were born. The Prophet said, "When a daughter is born in a house, Allah sends angels to that house who say, 'All you who live in the house! Peace be upon you!' After they have said that, they take the daughter under the protection of their wings, and moving their hands softly upon her head, they say, 'Here is a frail being, born to another frail being.' Allah will extend His support to whomever will look after her and bring her up." (*Tabarani*) The Qur'an brought unheard of reforms to the status and well-being of women that one writer remarked, "Among the Quran's most detailed legislation is that designed to improve the status of women. The Quran is the only major religious text to acknowledge misogyny and enjoin correctives." (Tamara Sonn, *The Blackwell Companion to the Qur'an*, 2006)

[946] The scholars explain that the import of the mention of Allah's wisdom here is to emphasize to the pagans that in Allah's wisdom both male and female children must be valued equally. The pagan custom of killing unwanted infant girls goes against the order that Allah created, as evidenced in verse 4:1. The Prophet promised Paradise to any man who had at least two daughters and then raised them properly, educated them and treated them right. He, himself, had four daughters.

[947] 'Ali ibn Abi Talib was once speaking to some people about the magnitude of the Day of Judgment. Then he remarked, "By Allah! If I'm forced to spend from dawn to dusk lying on a bed of thorns, with my hands and feet in chains, and if I were dragged through the streets and markets like that, it would be better for me than to present myself in the court of Allah if I have committed an oppression against any one of His creatures or if I have usurped the rights of another." (*Nahjul-Balaghah*)

[948] This verse, mentioning that alcoholic drinks are a by-product of some fruits, was revealed before intoxicants were made forbidden. In any case, it's not telling anyone to drink them, for the Arabs of

Your Lord inspired the bee to build its nests in hillsides, on trees, and in (the structures that people) erect. [68] Then (He inspired it) to eat of the many (flowering) fruits and to follow humbly the wide paths of its Lord. They produce from within their bodies a drink of varying shades of color that is a source of healing for humanity. In this is a sign for those who reflect. [69]

Allah creates you, and then He causes you to die. Among you are some who are reduced to a state of senility (in your old age), so much so that you know nothing, even though you had known much before. [949] (Allah can do this) for Allah is full of knowledge and power. [70]

The Folly of Idolatry

Allah has favored some (of you) with more (material) blessings than others. [950] Those who've been favored with more resources aren't going to cast them at those whom they control to make them equal with them. Would they so eagerly scorn Allah's bounty like that? [71]

Allah has given you mates of your own kind, and from your mates He's produced for you sons, daughters and grandchildren, even as He's given you so many wholesome resources besides.

Would it then be right for (your descendants) to believe in falsehood and be thankless towards Allah's bounty [72] and

to worship others in place of Allah - beings who have no power to provide them with resources from the heavens or the earth, and who could never gain the ability to do so? [73]

So then don't invent (false) representations of Allah, for Allah knows (what He's really like), and you don't know. [74]

Allah lays out the example of a slave under the control of another. He has no power at all, while another (person) to whom We've given Our favors (freely) spends (of his wealth without restriction) in private and in public. Are the two equal? Then praise be to Allah, but most of them don't understand. [75]

Allah lays out the further example of two men. One of them is dumb and has no ability to do anything. He's a constant headache to his guardian. No matter where he sends him, he does nothing right. Is this kind of man equal with someone who commands justice (with full confidence) and is on a straight path? [951] [76]

What has Allah Done for You?

To Allah belongs whatever is beyond human perception in the heavens and the earth. What is the command of the Hour (of Judgment) but the twinkling of an eye or even quicker? Truly, Allah has power over all things! [77]

Mecca were already regular drinkers. It merely points out the many uses humans have in the things that Allah created. Grape juice, dried date cakes and vinegar, which are useful and wholesome, also come from those sources. (*Ma'ariful Qur'an*)

[949] A man went to the Prophet and said, "Messenger of Allah, the commandments of Islam have become too hard for me, and I'm now old, so tell me of something that I can keep doing." The Prophet answered, "Keep your tongue moist with the remembrance of Allah." The early scholar of the Qur'an, 'Ikrimah ibn Abi Jahl, once said of this verse that senility will not affect the one who has the habit of reciting the Qur'an often. (*Ma'ariful Qur'an*) Modern research has concluded that those whose minds are more active are, in fact, less affected by the degeneration of mental capacity.

[950] This verse is cited as proof that Islam allows people to have differing levels of wealth, and thus Islam is opposed to communism. (*Ma'ariful Qur'an*)

[951] This next example is of a person who is an aimless unbeliever who lives without guidance and makes sins and mistakes everywhere he goes, while the second person is the believer in Allah who lives by a definite code of conduct. Thus, the latter person avoids most sins and calls people to justice.

He's the One Who brought you out of the wombs of your mothers when you didn't know a single thing. Then He placed within you the abilities of hearing and sight, as well as intelligence and affection, so you could learn to be grateful. [78]

Haven't they seen the birds held aloft in the midst of the sky? Nothing holds them in place save Allah, and that is a sign for those who believe. [79]

Allah provided you homes as places of rest and tranquility. He provided for you (the knowledge of how to make) tents out of animal skins, which you find so light (and easy to handle) when you travel, as well as when you stop (to make camp).

Out of their wool, their fur and their hair, (you make) things (like clothing and blankets) that you can use for a while for your comfort. [80]

Allah has also provided for you, out of what He's created, things (like trees) that can give you shade. He provided the mountains wherein you can find shelter.

He produced clothing for you to protect yourselves from the heat and armored vests to protect you from violence against each other (in warfare). That's how He completes His favors upon you, so you can submit (to His will in thanks). [81]

However, if they turn away, (know that) your only duty is to convey the message clearly. [82]

They recognize Allah's favors; yet, then they deny them (by denying the One Who provided them). Thus, most of them are thankless. [83]

The Witnesses Testify

*O*ne day We're going to raise a witness from every community. Then there won't be any more excuses accepted from those who covered (the light of faith within their hearts), nor will they be allowed to make up (for their sins). [84] When the wrongdoers see the punishment (right there before them), it won't be lessened, nor will they receive any break (from it). [85]

When those who associated partners with Allah actually see their partners, they're going to say, "*Our Lord! These are our (idols) whom we used to call upon besides You.*" However, (the idols) will throw their statement back at them, saying, "*You're all liars!*" [86]

On that day they're going to validate their utter dependence on Allah, and all their inventions will leave them to languish. [87] Those who rejected (Allah) and who hindered (people) from the path of Allah will have punishment upon punishment, for they used to cause trouble. [88]

One day We're going to raise a witness out of every community drawn from among their own, and We'll bring you out as a witness against these (people of Mecca). We've sent down to you the Book that explains everything. It's a guide, a mercy and a source of good news for those who've submitted (to Allah). [89]

Fulfill Your Agreement with Allah

*A*llah commands that justice be done, that good be implemented and that relatives be treated with generosity. [952] He

---

[952] The Prophet invited a passing acquaintance named Uthman ibn Madh'un into his courtyard one day. As the two men were sitting and conversing, the Prophet suddenly gazed up into the sky and fell silent for a while. Then he looked at the ground and shook his head as if to remember something, and then he looked up into the sky once more. After some time passed, Uthman asked him what he was doing and noted that he had never seen him act that way before. The Prophet replied that the angel Gabriel

forbids all shameful acts, as well as criminal behavior and rebellion. This is how He's instructing you so you can be warned. [90]

Fulfill the agreement of Allah after you've agreed to it, and don't break your oaths after you've sworn upon them. [953] You've made Allah your guarantee, and Allah knows everything that you do. [91]

Don't be like a woman who pulls apart the yarn she's just spun, even after it became strong, nor use your oaths to deceive each other, just so that one group can have an advantage over the others (through making temporary alliances).

Allah will test you in this, and on the Day of Assembly He's going to clear up for you the matters about which you argued. [92]

If Allah had wanted, He could've made you all into one unified community, but He leaves astray whomever He wants, and He guides whomever He wants, though you will all be questioned about what you've done. [93]

So don't use your oaths to deceive each other, for the foot that was firmly planted might begin to slip, causing you to suffer the evil (consequences) of having hindered others from the path of Allah.

You would then have a severe punishment befall you. [94]

Don't sell the agreement of Allah for a miserable price, for there's (a reward) with Allah that's far better for you if you only knew. [954] [95] Whatever (material goods) you have will vanish, but whatever lies with Allah will last forever. We're going to compensate those who patiently persevered by rewarding them according to the best of their deeds. [955] [96]

Whoever does what's morally right, whether male or female, and has faith, We're going to give him a new life that's a life of purity. We're going to reward them according to the best of their deeds. [97]

Allah is in Control of What He Reveals

*W*henever you read the Qur'an, ask for Allah's protection against Satan, the outcast. [98] He has no authority over those who believe and who place their trust in their Lord. [99] He only has authority over those who take him as their patron and who make partners (with Allah). [100]

When We substitute one verse for another, [956] and Allah knows what He's

had come to him while they were sitting. Uthman asked the Prophet what Gabriel had told him, and the Prophet recited this verse. Uthman later remarked that on account of this experience, his faith was made rock solid and his love for the Prophet was settled in his heart for good. (*Ma'ariful Qur'an*)

[953] It was common for the Arabs to ally with one another, through swearing an oath of loyalty, for the gain of a temporary advantage. If they thought they would be more powerful by canceling their current alliance and allying with another group, they would. Thus, they made their oaths a joke. This verse forbids this misuse of oaths in making alliances. In fact, the Prophet eventually forbade the making of oaths for any other purpose than personal goals. He said, "There is no oath-making (for political alliances) in Islam, and any oaths made in the days of ignorance are only reinforced in Islam." (*Ahmad*) In other words, making personal pacts between non-governmental groups is forbidden, unless they were made before Islam's coming, in which case they must be honestly observed. Personal vows and formal political treaties between governments are, of course, exempted from this ban.

[954] This is against those who would betray their principles for some bribe. The classical scholar, Ibn 'Atiyyah, defined an illegal bribe as: doing something for a fee that a person was supposed to do for his religion's sake for free, or not doing something for a fee that he was supposed to do for his religion's sake. (*Ma'ariful Qur'an*)

[955] The Prophet said, "He will have achieved success, the one who submits (to Allah), and who is then given enough resources, and who is content with Allah for what He has given him." (*Muslim, Ahmad*)

[956] The Qur'an was a growing body of verses all throughout the Prophet's mission. Occasionally, the Prophet would be given new verses that would supersede the rulings of previously revealed ones, (as

gradually revealing, they (object) by saying, *"You're just a lying fraud."* Certainly not! Yet, most of them don't understand. [101]

Tell them, *"The Holy Spirit* [957] *is bringing the revelation from your Lord in all truth, in order to strengthen (the faith) of the believers, and as a source of guidance and good news to those who've submitted themselves (to Allah)."* [102]

No One is Teaching Muhammad Anything

We know that they're saying, *"It's a man who's teaching him,"* but the tongue of the (foreign slave) to whom they're pointing is not fluent (in Arabic), [958] while this (Qur'an) is in the purest and most precise Arabic. [959] [103]   Those who don't

---

the times and circumstances of his movement changed). This only happened a handful of times during the twenty-three year history of revelation. In most cases, the superseded verses remained part of the preserved text and the first generation of Muslims knew which verses were the most up-to-date rulings from Allah. Only in a few reported instances were some older verses ordered by the Prophet to be removed from the official canon. He would explain that Allah had ordered such verses to be *forgotten*, *lifted* or *dropped*. (*at-Tabari, as-Suyuti, Abu Ubayd,* etc…) The technical terms are *unsiya, rufi'a* and *usqita*, respectively. As an example, Anas bin Malik claimed to have known about a verse that was revealed after some Muslims had perished in a skirmish, but then that verse was later dropped. That report is found with *at-Tabari*. In another instance, 'Umar recalled that there was an early dropped verse that talked about proper manners while respecting parents, which had addressed a peculiar Arab shortcoming. When the minor issue was corrected in the culture, it was no longer an issue of importance. While early Muslims were aware of this revelatory process and took it as a natural part of the evolution of Allah's scripture in the first Islamic community (*Bayhaqi*), nevertheless the Prophet's pagan critics would seize upon this issue with the charge that Muhammad himself was the author of the message, and not Allah, given that in a few instances a new revelation would abrogate (or eliminate) an old one. This is the issue that this passage is referencing. However, such a charge is without standing when, for example, you consider all of the gradual changes that Islam was making in Arabian culture. Should every minor revelation correcting every bad pagan habit remain in the final canon, when Allah has the power to keep the Qur'an in its most current and relevant form until the end of the Prophet's mission? Given that only a handful of verses met this fate, is the issue even that relevant? Furthermore, such was the nature of the Prophet's ministry: fluid change and evolution in the complexity of Islam and its scripture as circumstances evolved. Asking the Arabs to change their culture in an instant and then constantly reminding them of each and every small change in an ever-growing compendium would have been counter-productive (not to mention the fact that the length of the Qur'an might have been much longer and its relevance and majesty diluted. Are there no Biblical verses that abrogate each other? Is there no evidence of Biblical verses being dropped, especially when different ancient manuscripts are compared? Don't we know so little about the actual process of the recording and editing of the laws and teachings of Moses? Don't Christians claim that Jesus' teachings trump the laws of Moses? Aren't there writings of Paul that abrogate other verses in the Bible? Didn't Paul make up some laws on his own?) Evolutionary change in the revelation - stretched out over many years - made the process of Quranic growth and regrowth seem relatively unobtrusive and organic. By the time Islam was a firmly-rooted tradition at the end of the Prophet's mission, its holy book was complete, finalized by prophetic edict and ready to take on the ideologies of the wider world and beyond. Muslims believe that Allah designed it to be so, and Muslims have never had a problem with this knowledge.

[957] i.e., Angel Gabriel.

[958] There were several young foreign slaves in Mecca who were originally from Persian or Byzantine-controlled lands. Two of these young slaves, named Jabr and Yasar, worked as blacksmiths, and it is said that they knew some passages from the Bible and used to say them. The Prophet sometimes stopped at the young men's workshop to talk to them, perhaps hoping to have an affinity with others who believed in one God, but this made the tongues of the Meccans begin to wag. Since they couldn't find any other plausible explanation for the Prophet's constant revelations, they began to insinuate that these teenage slaves were teaching Muhammad about religion and that somehow those boys were the source of Islam! When one of those boys was asked if he were teaching Muhammad, the boy replied, "No, Muhammad is teaching me!" This passage was revealed in response. (*Zamakhshari*)

[959] Could any random person, such as the two slave boys (or any other foreign slave) being referenced here, be the source for the thousands of verses of the Qur'an? The Qur'an itself points out that the young man/men in question only spoke broken, rudimentary Arabic, whereas the Qur'an was in

343

believe in Allah's (revealed) verses will not be guided by Allah, and they're going to have a painful punishment. [104] It's those who don't believe in Allah's verses who are frauds, and they're all liars! [105]

Faith Renounced Under Duress is Still Valid

*W*hoever rejects Allah after having accepted faith in Him - unless he's been forced to (renounce it) while his heart remains committed - and who has opened his heart to rejection, Allah's wrath is upon (all such people). [960]

They're going to have a severe punishment, [106] and that's because they love the life of this world more than the next life. Allah will never guide people who reject (Him by choice). [107]

They're the ones who've had their hearts, ears and eyes sealed up by Allah, and they're unconcerned (about it). [108] Without a doubt, they're going to be losers in the next life. [109]

However, your Lord – for those who migrated (from their homes) after having been persecuted and who then struggled and persevered – after all of this, your Lord is forgiving and merciful. [110]

One day every soul will come forward to plead for itself. Every soul will then be repaid for what it has done, and none of them will be treated unfairly. [111]

The Example of a Prophet to His People

*A*llah lays out the example of a society enjoying peace and security, even as it was amply supplied with resources from every quarter. Yet, it was thankless towards Allah's favors.

Therefore, Allah caused it to experience both hunger and panic. (It encircled them) like a cloak (wrapped around them), all on account of (the evil in

---

flawless Arabic prose and diction. On account of the baseless allegations of the pagans, however, the Prophet stopped visiting those young men in order to silence his critics. (Meanwhile, the revelations kept on coming to the tune of thousands of more verses.) There is also another interesting point to ponder. The foreign slaves such as Jabr, Yasar, Ya'ish, Qays and Addas, who are so often suggested as 'the source' of Muhammad's teachings, were all cultural Christians (and most probably not of the fiery evangelist kind, which did not exist yet). Even further, the Qur'an does not reflect any form of Christian doctrines or theology, such as it was in Byzantine Orthodox lands. (Even the person of Jesus is given less coverage than Moses, and there is no mention of Paul, the trinity, cryptic signs of the apocalypse, the four Gospels, atonement, Joseph, carpentry, Roman and Greek cities, Pontius Pilate, etc...) If Muhammad were somehow making the rounds among busy, illiterate young slaves to get source material for "his" scripture, then it would have certainly reflected the beliefs of the purported religion of those slaves. (In addition, when the Prophet was later in Medina, surrounded by eager - and often nosy - followers for ten years, who was supposedly teaching him then?) Such an idea is preposterous! Sadly, even to this day critics of Islam keep searching for 'the human source' of Muhammad's revelation. Many of these critics react in horror when asked if Jesus or Moses had any human 'sources' or 'influences'. (And we know so precious little historically about both men!) Why not let Allah be the source of them all?

[960] When Meccan persecution against the Muslims mutated into murder, some Muslims felt compelled to recant their faith to save their lives, even though they secretly held onto faith. The worst incident was when the pagans seized a man named Ammar, along with his father Yasir and his mother Sumayah and some others, and took them to a field to be tortured. They tied Sumayah and Yasir to the ground and speared them to death. They then roughed up Ammar and threatened to kill him, like his parents, if he didn't renounce his faith. Ammar did so weeping and out of fear and then later went to the Prophet in mortal fear of displeasing Allah. The Prophet accepted that Ammar never really gave up Islam, and he counseled the young man to tell the pagans the exact same thing that he said before if they ever threatened him again. This passage was revealed in response, giving hope to those whose fear of pain would make them say anything to avoid it. (*Asbab ul-Nuzul*)

which its people) used to indulge. [961] [112] Then a messenger came to them, who arose from among themselves, but they denied him. Thus, the punishment seized them even as they were still busy in their corruption. [113]

Some Dietary Restrictions

*E*at from the resources that Allah has provided for you that are lawful and pure, and be thankful for Allah's favor, if it's Him you really serve. [114] He's only forbidden you (to eat) dead carcasses, blood, pork, and anything that's had a name other than Allah's name invoked over it.

However, if someone is forced by necessity (to eat of these forbidden things in order to avoid starvation) and does so only reluctantly, without indulging in it more than necessary, then Allah is forgiving and merciful. [115]

(All you people!) Make no statements in support of the lies that your tongues may promote, arbitrarily declaring, "*This is lawful, while that's forbidden*," in order to somehow attribute fraudulent lies to Allah. Those who invent fraudulent claims and assign them to Allah will never succeed. [116] There's only a slight profit (to be made in promoting such lies), but then they'll have a painful punishment. [117]

We prohibited for the followers of Judaism what We already told you about before, and We were never unfair to them. Rather, they were unjust against their own selves. [118]

However, your Lord - to those who do wrong in ignorance and who then thereafter repent and reform (themselves) - after all of that, your Lord is indeed forgiving and merciful. [119]

Follow the Path of Abraham

*A*braham was a model of devotion to Allah, for he was a natural monotheist, and he never made partners (with Allah). [120] He was thankful for Allah's favors, for He chose him and guided him to a straight way. [121]

We gave him good in this world, and in the next life he's going to be among the righteous. [122] Then We inspired you, (Muhammad,) with the message that you should follow the creed of Abraham, the natural monotheist, and he never made partners (with Allah). [123]

Wisdom in Dialogue

*T*he (restrictions) of the Sabbath were only imposed upon (the Jews) who argued (about Allah's commands), but Allah will judge between them in what they've been arguing about. [962] [124]

---

[961] This is an interesting verse on account of all the various interpretations the commentators have offered, and it is an excellent example of the diversity of opinion about the meaning of unclear or obscure references that arose in the classical age of commentary. Some say it refers to Mecca, and thus to the famine of which 44:10-12 speaks, while others say it is a general reference to any society or town that rejects its Prophet, while a third opinion is that it is about the return of the Prophet *after* the conquest of Mecca. One of the keys to understanding verses of this type is to try and pin down the historical context and chronology of the passage in question, coupled with the internal textual references. Since this passage speaks of famine *before* a messenger was sent to the people, it cannot be a reference to the famine that the Qur'an foretold in chapter 44. It also cannot refer to the return of the Prophet during the conquest of Mecca given that these verses were revealed before that event. Thus, if Mecca is really being referenced here, then the famine would have to have been something the Meccans experienced *before* Prophet Muhammad began his message. Thus, this reference is a reminder to them of how Allah controls their ultimate fate, no matter how well off they are at any given time.

[962] Although this is a Meccan chapter, these last verses [124-128] were revealed in Medina and were tacked on at the end of this chapter by the Prophet's order. These few verses in particular make mention

Invite (others) to the way of your Lord with wisdom and beautiful preaching, and reason with them in ways that are best. Your Lord knows best who is straying from His path and who is being guided (towards it). [125]

Take the High Road

$\mathcal{I}$f you can bring consequences against them, then don't bring any consequences against them that are worse than what you've suffered. [963] However, if you persevere patiently instead (and suppress the urge to retaliate), then that's the best for those who are patient. [126]

Therefore, be patient, for your patience is due to none other than Allah. Don't feel sorry for them, and don't be worried on account of their scheming. [127] Allah is with those who are mindful (of Him), and He's with those who (promote) what's good. [128]

---

of one of the many issues that were coming out in the growing interfaith dialogue between the Muslims and the Jews. From the context of verses 118-125 we can deduce that the Arab converts in Medina had probably asked if there was a Sabbath for them as there was for the Jews (or perhaps the Jews had suggested to them that they should have one). This passage points out that in Abraham's original religion there was no Sabbath and that the Jews were given harsh dietary requirements and difficult Sabbath regulations on account of their disobedience to Moses. Verse 16:125 advises the Muslims to talk rationally and politely when these kinds of issues are raised.

[963] This passage is sometimes understood to be a continuation of verses 118-125, in that an interfaith issue involving the status of the Sabbath came up in Medina, and an argument might have ensued, save for the patience of the Muslim side. Under that line of reasoning, this passage is telling the Prophet to keep on preaching and to be high-minded about it, even if the listeners, who in this case would be Jews, have some objections to his views on the subject. Then verse 126 would say that if the preacher could score a point, as it were, in the interfaith debate, that he shouldn't go overboard in pressing his advantage, for it would only put the listener on the defensive. When you score a point of logic, be patient and resist the urge to pounce too eagerly on the weakness in your opponent, that is if you want to make him feel respected and welcomed enough so you can perhaps one day open his heart to faith and not just tear him down. Other commentators say this passage is not connected with the preceding verses [118-125] at all and that it was revealed after the Battle of Uhud, when the Muslims, who had narrowly escaped destruction, returned to the battlefield the next day to find that the pagans had mutilated the dead Muslim fighters. When the Prophet saw the body of his beloved uncle Hamza badly cut up, he became very distraught and called for revenge upon the pagans many times beyond what they did to Hamza. This verse, then, would be telling the Prophet not to go beyond the limits of what was done to him. After he recited it, the Prophet said, "We will be patient. We will not take revenge out on anyone." Then the Prophet made up for his thoughtless oath as outlined in 5:89. (*Ma'ariful Qur'an*) Given the change of tone in verses 126-128, the second view seems more likely, i.e., that this passage is referring to self-restraint in the face of atrocity, and Allah knows best.

The Night Journey

17 Al Isra'
aka *Bani Isra'il*
Late Meccan Period

This chapter was revealed mainly in the year 621, with a few portions being revealed earlier. This was about one year before the migration to Medina, and the unmistakable tone of closure presented in this chapter clearly shows that the Muslims were expecting that they would soon abandon Mecca for a safer place. Already Islam was growing in the northern city of Yathrib, due to the efforts of some very dedicated new converts there, and the Muslims in Mecca were restive as they chafed under Meccan persecution. Some Muslim converts had already been murdered by the pagans, and the tension was apparent and palpable.

With regards to the Night Journey and Ascension, the Prophet's cousin, Hind bint Abi Talib (aka Umm Hani), said, "The Messenger of Allah spent the night in my house. He said his night prayers and went to sleep. Just before dawn, he woke us up, and we all prayed the dawn prayer together. When the prayer was finished, he said, 'Umm Hani. I prayed with you the night prayer in this place, then I went to (Jerusalem) and prayed there, and as you can see, I've just finished praying the dawn prayer here with you.' I said, 'Messenger of Allah, don't tell people about this for they'll ridicule you and hurt you.' He replied, 'By Allah, I'm going to tell them.'" (*At-Tabari*)

Then the Prophet went out of her family home and told people the following account: "While I was in Mecca, the roof of the house was opened, and Gabriel descended. He opened my chest and washed it with Zamzam water. Then he brought a golden tray full of wisdom and faith, and having poured its contents into my chest, he closed it. Then a creature that was all white was brought, which was smaller than a mule but bigger than a donkey. The creature's stride was so wide that it reached the farthest point of its eyesight in just one step. I was carried on it."

The Prophet then explained that he was taken to Jerusalem on that mount, which flew at a dazzling rate of speed, and that he was deposited on the Temple Mount. There the spirits of the prophets of old materialized behind him, and he led them in prayer. Then the Prophet continued his account, saying: "Gabriel then took my hand and ascended with me to the nearest heaven." The Prophet was then taken into the otherworldly dimension of the *Akhirah*, or Hereafter.

As he passed further through its levels, he saw various prophets from ancient days, including Adam, Abraham, Moses and Jesus. Each of them welcomed him with warm greetings as he went by them. When he was taken into the seventh and highest layer of Paradise, he saw innumerable wondrous sights, including the delights of Paradise and the coming and going of multitudes of angels. The Prophet continued his story, saying, "Then (Gabriel) took me until we reached the *Sidrat-il-Muntaha* (the Lote Tree of the Furthest Boundary), which was shrouded in colors I can hardly describe." (See Qur'an 53:1-18]

"Then I was (brought close) to the *House of Ma'moor* (in which 70,000 angels visit everyday), and three containers were offered to me. One had wine, the other milk and the third honey. I took the milk. Gabriel said, 'This is the Islamic way of life, which you and your followers are following.'"

Next, Gabriel brought Muhammad closer to the highest boundary of Paradise, beyond which the full manifestation of Allah's power exists. The Prophet described that he couldn't even comprehend the wonders of creation that he was witnessing. In later years when someone asked the Prophet what he saw at that point and if he, in fact, saw Allah, he said, "Only blinding light, how could I then see Him?" (*Ahmad*) It was during this part of the journey that Muhammad received the direct command from Allah that his followers were to offer prayers *fifty* times in a day.

When the Prophet was being taken back down through the seventh layer of Paradise, Moses stopped him and convinced him to go back to Allah and ask for a reduction. Moses pointed out that he had had a hard enough time with the Children of Israel and that fifty prayers upon his followers would be too much. The Prophet did accordingly, and Moses convinced him to ask for further reductions. Eventually the prayers were reduced to five times a day, and the Prophet told Moses he was too shy to ask for any further reductions after that. Muhammad was then brought back down to the Temple Mount in Jerusalem, and from there the mysterious steed carried him back to Mecca, where he was finally deposited back in his bed.

Predictably, when the Prophet told his story, the Meccans ridiculed him fiercely. A few converts to Islam actually renounced their faith, thinking that the Prophet was saying something totally preposterous. *How could a man go to Jerusalem and back in one night?* Some people went to Abu Bakr and told him what had happened, and they asked him if he believed it was true. He replied, "By Allah! If Muhammad, himself, has said it, then it's true. He tells us that the word of Allah comes to him directly from Heaven to Earth at any hour of the night or day, and we believe him. Isn't this a greater miracle than what we're questioning here today."

Then Abu Bakr led a crowd to the Prophet, and they all listened to his story directly. When the Prophet finished describing Jerusalem, a city to which he had never been, and recounted what he had seen of its streets and buildings, those who were present, and who had been to Jerusalem before, agreed that it was an accurate description of the city.

Abu Bakr, who had himself visited Jerusalem many times, declared, "You spoke the truth, Messenger of Allah." Then the Prophet announced that on his way back to Mecca from Jerusalem, he saw a caravan on the road leading towards Mecca. He said that he had called to the leaders of that caravan to point out to them where one of their animals had wandered off in the desert and that he drank from a water jar on the back of one of those camels. He also predicted when that caravan would return (at sunrise on such-and-such day) and that a gray camel would be in the front of the line.

On the appointed day, a caravan did enter Mecca at sunrise, led by a gray camel, and when the leaders of that caravan were questioned, they described how they were led by a stranger's voice to their lost animal in the desert. It was also found that one of their camels was carrying a water jar on its back that had a broken seal. Due to his affirming the truth of the Prophet's story, Abu Bakr earned the nickname, *As-Sadeeq*, which means the one who affirms the truth.

Glory be to the One Who took His servant on a journey by night from the sacred place of prostration (in Mecca) to the faraway place of prostration (in Jerusalem) - *to an area that We've specially blessed* - so We could show him some of Our signs. [964] Indeed, He's the One Who Hears and Observes (all things). [965] [1]

The Children of Israel Were Punished for their Sins

We gave the scripture to Moses and made it a source of guidance for the Children of Israel. [966] So don't take anyone other than Me as your keeper, [2] all you (Jews) who are descended from those whom We carried with Noah! He was a truly thankful servant! [3]

We warned the Children of Israel in (their) scripture that they would twice cause corruption in the earth and be filled with conceited arrogance, (and thus they would be punished twice). [4]

When the first warning came to pass, We sent Our servants, (the Babylonians), against you, *and they were greatly skilled in warfare.* [967] They rampaged through every

---

[964] The Prophet was taken from his bed one evening on a fantastic journey so that Allah could show him what the next realm actually was like. The first part of his journey (the *Isra'*, or Night Journey) was when the angel Gabriel came to him at night and took him on a winged steed called the *Buraq* all the way to Jerusalem at a very fast rate of speed. The second part of his journey consisted of rising from the Temple Mount up to Heaven to see what the next life was like and to have his faith strengthened. (This is called the *Mir'aj*, or Ascension to Heaven.)

[965] The Prophet said, "On the night when I was taken on the Night Journey, I awoke back in Mecca the next morning filled with anxiety, for I knew that my people wouldn't believe me." He sat outside pensively, and then his biggest critic, his foe Abu Jahl, came by and asked him with a sneer, "Is there anything new?" The Prophet then told of his Night Journey and Ascension to Heaven, and Abu Jahl excitedly called for a crowd to come and hear Muhammad speak, hoping it would prove once and for all that his nephew was crazy. The crowd became astonished at his tale, and they began to laugh. Then some of the people asked him to describe Jerusalem, for Muhammad had never been there before. He described it accurately, causing some to say, "By Allah, he got the description right." (*Ahmad*) In accepted Catholic tradition, a woman named Mary of Jesus of Agreda (d. 1665) also claimed to be mystically transported to a far distant place, the deserts of New Mexico to be exact, where she preached to Jumano Indians. This doctrine in the Catholic Church is called "bilocation." Among Mormons, Prophet Jesus also was said to have been transported to the New World to preach the message of God after he was taken up to heaven from the Middle East. Other famous Christian Saints who are also said to have experienced bilocation are: Anthony of Padua, Ambrose of Milan, Severus of Ravenna, Padre Pio of Italy and Alphonsus Maria d'Ligouri. Tantric Buddhism also accepts this doctrine of bilocation and instantaneous mystical travel. The Qur'an does not assert that Muhammad was in two locations at once however, but that he was taken from one place to another and then returned through mystical means. Many scholars hold that it was his spirit that was taken, and not his physical body.

[966] The Prophet said, "Convey these teachings to people, even if it's only one verse. Discuss with others the stories of the Children of Israel, for it's not wrong to do so. Whoever tells a lie concerning me intentionally, then let him take his seat in the Fire." (*Bukhari*)

[967] The Jewish prophets are recorded in the Old Testament issuing scathing words of warning to their people for their constant backsliding into idolatry and corruption. (See II Kings 22:16-17) Isaiah, in particular, warned of the coming judgments of Allah against his people. See Isaiah 3:16-26, 5:20-30 and 8:3-4, for example. The first 'overwhelming punishment' was the invasion of the Babylonians (586 BCE), who wiped what remained of Israel off the map and forced many of the Jews into exile in Babylon. The Biblical book of Lamentations is a sorrowful reflection on their plight. (The Assyrians had already attacked and subsumed northern Israel in 721 BCE but had not completely destroyed the independence of the rest of the Jews of the south in Judea.) After the Babylonians were defeated by a new rising empire, the new Persian king, Cyrus the Great, allowed the Jews to return home in about

part of your homes, and thus it was a warning fulfilled! [5]

Then We allowed you to return (to the land of Israel, after your captivity in Babylon), as a kind of (victory for you) over them. We also added to your wealth and sons and allowed your population to increase. [6]

If you were any good at all, you were good for the benefit of your own souls, and if you were evil, it was to the detriment of your own souls. Then later, when the second warning came to pass, (after you had become disobedient once more), your faces were framed in disgrace as (the Romans) entered into your temple of prayer, even as (the Babylonians) had done so (long before), and they destroyed whatever they laid their hands on. [968] [7]

Your Lord will show you mercy (yet again, by allowing you to recover and rebuild), but if you return (to sinful ways), then We'll return (with a third penalty). We established Hellfire as a prison for those who cover (the light of faith within their hearts). [8]

The Reality of History

This Qur'an certainly guides (people) towards stability (in their lives and societies) and gives good news to the believers who do what's morally right that they shall have a great reward. [969] [9]

Those who don't believe in the next life (should know) that We've prepared a painful punishment for them. [10] A person (inadvertently) cries out for evil when his cry should be for good, but people are impatient by nature. [11]

We made the night and the day as two (of Our) signs. We darkened the sign of the night, even as We illuminated the sign of the day, so you can go out and look for the bounty of your Lord, and also so you can keep track of and count the passage of years. Thus, We explain everything in detail. [12]

We All Have to Make Choices

We've tied the bird (of his fortune) around the neck of every human being, and on the Day of Assembly We're going to bring out a record that he'll see laid out in the open. [970] [13] *"Read your record! Today your own soul is enough to account against you!"* [14]

Whoever finds guidance is guided for the benefit of his own soul, while whoever goes astray does so to the detriment of his own soul. No bearer of burdens can bear the burden of another. We never brought Our punishment down upon any nation unless We raised for them a messenger (to warn them first). [15]

---

520 BCE. The Jews then tried to resurrect Judaism and owe the most to the efforts of their great scholar Ezra, who tried to recreate all the knowledge that was lost. Also see Leviticus 26:14-39, which contains dire threats from Allah against the Jews if they disobey Him further.

[968] The second major catastrophe that befell the Jews came after they rejected Jesus as God's messenger. (See the book entitled *Jesus in the Talmud* by Peter Schafer for a more thorough discussion of this issue.) Even though Jewish nationalists rose in revolt against their Roman overlords in the first century CE, the important point was not the mere gaining of independence – they had rejected God's chosen messenger! So the second cataclysmic event was the resultant destruction of Jerusalem by the Romans in the year 70 CE and the forced dispersal of the Jews throughout the Roman world, i.e., the *Diaspora*.

[969] Some commentators believe this passage is referring to the taunting of an-Nadr ibn al-Harith, when he dared Allah to send down destruction upon him and his fellow pagans. (*Ma'ariful Qur'an*)

[970] The pagan Arabs used to try and predict the future by looking at which way the birds flew (similar to what the ancient Romans did). This passage is making a play on that by saying that a person's fortune is with them and their own deeds, rather than being determined by something external to them like bird patterns. (*Asbab ul-Nuzul*)

When We decide that a nation is to be destroyed, We send Our command to those who are lost in the pursuit of pleasure, (telling them that they must reform or else face the consequences), so the sentence can be proven true against them (that they deserve their punishment). [971] *Then We destroy them completely!* [16]

How many generations have We destroyed after Noah? It's a fact that your Lord is well-informed and observant of the sins of His servants. [17]

Whoever desires the temporary things (of this world) will have them in whatever quantity We wish to give, but afterwards We're going to give them Hellfire so they can burn within it in humiliation and disgrace. [18] Whoever desires the next life, *who makes an effort to achieve it as is required,* and who has faith, their efforts will be appreciated (by Allah). [19]

Both (the believers and the faithless) have Our bounty showered down upon them, for the bounties of your Lord are not withheld. [20] Have you noticed how We've given more to some than to others? However, the next life is where the higher status and greater bounty awaits. [21]

Your Lord Commands Kindness to Parents

Don't set up other gods alongside of Allah, or you'll end up humiliated and forsaken. [22] Your Lord has decided that you must serve no one else but Him and that you should be kind to your parents. Whether one or both of them becomes old in your lifetime, never speak to them disrespectfully nor scold them, but rather speak to them in generous terms. [23]

Kindly lower the wing of humility towards them and say, "*My Lord! Be merciful to them even as they cherished me when I was small.*" [972] [24] Your Lord knows what's in your heart, so if you behave in a moral fashion, then He's forgiving to those who repent (of their sins). [25]

Sharing the Wealth

Give what's rightly due to your relatives, the needy and (stranded) travelers. Don't waste your money like a squanderer. [26] Squanderers are like the brothers of devils, and Satan was ungrateful to his Lord. [27]

If you (don't have any money to give to the poor) and are forced to turn away from them, though in the expectant hope that some mercy might come to you from your Lord (that you can later share with them), [973] at the very least say something to put them at ease. [974] [28]

Don't tie your hand to your neck (like a miser), nor extend it out so far (in donating) that you become guilty (of

---

[971] The Prophet narrated that on the Day of Judgment four types of people will come forward and rightfully claim that they truly had no way to hear Allah's message. They are the deaf, the insane, the senile old person and a person who lived at a time when there was no active revelation coming in among his people. Allah will accept their pledge of obedience, but they will still have to go into Hell, though the Fire will be forbidden to harm them. They will live in coolness (until Allah sends them into Paradise). (*Ahmad*) Children who die below the age of puberty also automatically go to Heaven, regardless of the religion in which their parents raised them.

[972] The Prophet said, "Treat the elderly with respect, for being respectful to the elderly is honoring Allah. Whoever does not treat them with respect is not one of us." (*Mishkat*)

[973] The Prophet once said, "To smile in your brother's company is charity. To command good deeds and to prevent others from doing wrong is charity. To guide a person who is in a place where he might go astray is charity. To remove dangers from the road like thorns or sharp objects is charity. To pour water from your jug into your brother's jug is charity. To guide a person on his way who has defective eyesight is charity." (*Bukhari*)

[974] Some people asked the Prophet for a share in some cloth that had been donated, but he had none left to give. This verse was revealed to tell the Prophet what to do in their case. (*Ma'ariful Qur'an*)

causing your own) poverty. [975] [29] Your Lord provides abundant resources to whomever He wants, and He measures (out slimmer resources to whomever He wants, as well). Indeed, He is well-informed and watchful (over the needs) of His servants. [30]

Seven Pillars of Righteousness

Don't kill your children because you're afraid of becoming poor. We'll provide resources for them, as well as for you. Indeed, killing them is an enormous crime. [31]

Don't go anywhere near any unlawful sexual activity [976] for it's a shameful practice [977] and opens the way (to even greater sins and dangers.) [32]

Don't take the life of anyone (whose life) Allah has forbidden (to be taken), except for a just cause (under the law). If anyone is killed wrongfully, then We've given his heir the power (to either demand punishment, take monetary restitution or forgive).

However, don't let him go beyond the limits (in his legal right) to take a life, (as he might bring harm to the innocent), for he's already being supported (by the law and should be satisfied with his options). [33]

Don't (tamper with) an orphan's property before he reaches the age of full strength (at maturity), unless you plan to improve it. Fulfill every agreement, for every agreement (that you make) will be asked about (on the Day of Judgment). [34]

Give full measure (to your customers) when you measure (for them), and weigh with an accurate scale, for that's best for achieving a good result. [35]

Don't get involved with things about which you know nothing, for every act of hearing, seeing or (feeling in) the heart will be asked about (on the Day of Judgment). [36]

Don't strut through the earth acting like you're so great, for (you're not strong enough) to rip the earth apart, nor can you grow as tall as the mountains. [37]

All sinful practices like those are despicable in the sight of your Lord. [38] These are among the (pillars of) wisdom that your Lord has revealed to you, so don't take any other god alongside of Allah, or you just might find yourself being cast into Hellfire in disgrace - with (only yourself) to blame! [39]

Pagans don't Understand the Use of Reason

Has your Lord chosen to give you sons, while taking daughters for Himself among the angels? You're making an outrageous assertion! [978] [40]

---

[975] There is a story told that a poor boy went to the Prophet and asked for a shirt and that the Prophet gave his only good shirt to him, leaving him with nothing to wear. As such, he remained in his home without a shirt until someone gave one to him. This passage was then revealed. (*Ma'ariful Qur'an, Asbab ul-Nuzul*)

[976] Unlawful sexual activity (*zina*) consists of adultery and fornication. When a person breaches the barrier of what is proper, he becomes open to depravity, and an avalanche of sins beset him or her, leading to his or her own ruin.

[977] This verse labels adultery and fornication (*zina*) generically as *faahisha*, or shameful behavior. Elsewhere, however, the Qur'an separates the particulars of each sin and gives differing penalties to each. See 24:2 for the penalty for adultery and fornication (*zina*) and 4:15 for the penalty for shameful behavior (*faahisha*), which is thought by some to be the Qur'an's way of referring to homosexuality and lesbianism (as suggested by verse 7:80).

[978] The pagans believed that the angels were the female daughters of Allah, while they (the pagans) valued sons for themselves above daughters. Thus, by attributing to Allah what they didn't want for themselves, they were making Allah seem shortchanged.

And so it is that We've explained (the issues in) various (ways) in this Qur'an, so they can be reminded, but it only seems to make them distance themselves from it even more! [41]

Say to them, *"If there were (other, lesser) gods (existing) alongside of Him,"* - as they claim – *"then they would surely (be working hard to do those things) that would bring them closer to the Lord of the throne, (in their efforts to win His favor.)"* [979] [42]

Glory be to Him! He is high above all the things that they're saying (about Him) – infinitely higher! [43]

The seven heavens, the very earth and all who (live) within them glorify Him! There isn't anything that exists that doesn't glorify His praise, even if you don't understand how they glorify Him. He is indeed forbearing and forgiving. [980] [44]

What do the Faithless Seek in the Qur'an?

When you recite the Qur'an, (Muhammad), We put an invisible screen between you and those who don't believe in the next life. [45]

We put wrappings over their hearts to prevent them from understanding the Qur'an and also a deafness in their ears.

When you're remembering your one Lord in the Qur'an, they just turn their backs in disgust. [46]

We know what they're really listening for when they listen to you, (for they merely wish to find something to criticize) so they can talk about it in their private conversations, saying, *"You (Muslims) are following nothing more than a man who's been bewitched!"* [981] [47]

---

[979] This verse has been interpreted in two different ways. The basic premise is that for the pagans of Arabia, their idols were subordinate gods that people could pray to for favors and such, while the supreme God *Allah* was remote and disinterested in human affairs. So these demigods were, like in Greek mythology, the link between human beings and the Great Originator, (which for the Greeks was Chaos). The first opinion about the meaning of this verse is that it is posing the simple question: "If there were mini-gods, then wouldn't they try to unseat the top god and steal his throne, such as Zeus and the gods of Olympus did in unseating the Titans?" The second opinion, which has much more merit, is that this verse is saying that if there were mini-gods, wouldn't they themselves be trying outdo each other to please the top god, just like human beings should be doing? The subtext is simply this: if your gods are subordinate and seeking to please God, then shouldn't you do so likewise?

[980] There are countless verses of the Qur'an that mention some type of sin or shortcoming into which a person can fall. The amazing thing is that nearly all of them end with some type of refrain or reminder that even after all their bad behavior, Allah is still forbearing (patient with us), forgiving, merciful, kind, compassionate, etc… The way Allah portrays Himself in the Qur'an, which some people foolishly believe is as a harsh and angry God, is actually the most loving Being of all. We do every foolish and sinful thing, but He constantly reminds us that His forgiveness and mercy are always waiting. The Prophet said that Allah, Himself, said, "O son of Adam, even if you came to me with an earth full of sins, and you met me not holding any other as My equal, then I would meet you with forgiveness equal to that." (*Hadith Qudsi*)

[981] The Prophet would often recite the Qur'an aloud in his house at night. Even though the Meccan leadership officially disavowed and scorned him, still the verses themselves were often mesmerizing, giving rise to their charges that he was a sorcerer who bewitched men with his verses. One night three prominent idolaters snuck near the windows of the Prophet's house, but each came alone and wasn't aware of the others. These three men, Abu Jahl, Abu Sufyan and Al-Akhnas ibn Shurayq, stayed listening until the dawn. They noticed each other when they were leaving, and when they each admitted to stealthily listening to the Qur'an, they swore they wouldn't do it again, lest the young men of the tribe start to do the same. The next night, however, each of the three returned, thinking that he alone would not keep his word. When they noticed each other again, they took to swearing and vowing to keep their word this time, but the same incident occurred the next night, as well. In the morning Al-Akhnas went to Abu Sufyan and asked his opinion about what Muhammad was saying. Abu Sufyan replied, "By Allah, I heard some things I recognized and knew what they were about, but I heard other things whose meaning and import I didn't know." Al-Akhnas nodded his agreement and left. Later

Do you see what kind of an example they're making of you! However, they're the ones who've gone astray, and they'll never find a way (out of their mistaken beliefs). [48]

The Faithless Object to the Resurrection

"*What!*" they exclaim. "*When we've rotted away to dust and bones, are we really going to be made like new?*" [49]

Say (to them), "*(Yes, indeed), even if you were made of stone or iron, [50] or some other created material that's even harder than (the hearts) in your chests!*" Then they ask, "*So who's going to bring us back (to life)?*"

Tell (them), "*The One Who created (you) the first time!*"

However, they just bob their heads towards you (condescendingly) and say, "*So when will all this come to pass?*"

So say (to them), "*The time might be close at hand, [51] and it will be a day when He calls you, and you'll (be forced to) answer with His praise, even as you'll think you only stayed (in the world) for a little while.*" [52]

Beware of Your Constant Enemy

Tell My servants that they should only speak of good things, for Satan tries to make divisions among them. [982]

Satan is the obvious enemy of humanity! [53] Your Lord knows you best. If He wants to be merciful to you, then He'll do so, and if He wants to punish you, then He'll do so. We haven't sent you to be their warden. [54]

Your Lord knows (all about every creature) that (exists) within the heavens and the earth. We gave some prophets more gifts than others, even as We gave the Psalms to David. [983] [55]

There is no Escaping the True Conclusion

Say (to them), "*(Go ahead and) call upon all those whom you pretend (to be gods) besides Him! They have no power to solve your troubles, nor can they ward them off.*" [56]

Those upon whom they're calling (for favors) are themselves trying to find their own way to their Lord, even if they're already close (to Him)! [984]

---

on, he went to Abu Jahl and asked his opinion, and Abu Jahl answered, "We've always been in competition with the Bani 'Abd Manaf, (the Prophet's sub-clan). We fed (the poor) when they did, and we gave away (in charity) as they did. So when we were running neck and neck with them like in a horserace, they said, 'There's a Prophet among us to whom revelation comes from Heaven.' So how can we compete with that? By Allah we will never believe in him nor accept what he says." Then Al-Akhnas left. (*Ibn Hisham*) This passage is a reference to this kind of behavior on the part of the Meccans. They would also look for snippets of the Qur'an that could be willfully misinterpreted or ridiculed publicly to make Islam seem like something it was not.

[982] It is said that this verse was revealed after some of the Prophet's companions asked him how they should respond to the insults of the pagans. (*Asbab ul-Nuzul*)

[983] Every prophet had different circumstances with which to deal, and some got greater miracles (*lit.* Allah's favors) and such than others. Some prophets, like David, received beautiful words of praise and thanks as their revelations (see I Chronicles 16:7-36 for an example of one of David's psalms). Others didn't get any scriptural material at all but rather received only commandments, prophecies or the mission to preach only general things without any legal specifics.

[984] Many commentators say this verse is referencing not only the pagan idols, but the personages of Jesus, Mary, Ezra and other famous, saintly people whom later followers took to be gods or god-like

They ardently desire to receive His mercy, even as they're in mortal fear of His punishment, *for your Lord's punishment is truly something to think about!* [57]

There's not a single settlement that will escape Our annihilation, or at the very least (have a taste of) a strong punishment, before the Day of Assembly (arrives), and that (statement has been) recorded in the Book (of Decrees). [985] [58]

We never withhold sending miracles for any other reason than the fact that ancient peoples (so frequently) called them lies. We sent a (special) camel [986] to the (people of) Thamud for them to see, but they treated her badly. And so it is that We only send miracles (in order to make people) afraid (of the coming punishment). [59]

(Remember) when We told you, *"Your Lord surrounds people (in His power)!"* We didn't send the vision (of the next life) down upon you for any other purpose than to be a test for people. (The mention of) the cursed tree (of Zaqqum) in the Qur'an (was for the same purpose), as well. [987] We (only use such symbols) to instill fear in them (so that they'll perhaps be inclined to listen), but it only adds to their immense suppression (of faith). [60]

Satan's Challenge to Allah

*W*hen We told the angels, *"Bow down (in respect) to Adam,"* they all bowed down. Iblis, however, (who was a jinn in their company), did not bow along with them).

"How can I bow down to a creature that You made from mud?" he asked. [61] *"Look at that!"* he continued. *"This (human) is the one whom You're honoring over me! If You give me a chance until the Day of Assembly, I'll make his descendants blindly obedient (to me), all but (maybe) a few!"* [62]

"Get away from here," (Allah) replied, *"and if any of them follow you, then Hellfire will be enough of a reward for you all! [63] Mesmerize any of them that you can with your (alluring) voice (of temptation). Assail them with your cavalry and with your infantry. [988] Share in their wealth and children, [989] and make promises to them - even though the promises of Satan are nothing more than deception. [64] As for My servants, however, you will have no power over them. Your Lord is quite enough to take care (of them)."* [65]

---

in their own right. This verse is pointing out that even all of the people who have been elevated to the status of gods or who are deemed god-like are, themselves, merely striving to get close to God.

[985] This is Allah's rule book, which He wrote Himself and in which is every rule and principle by which the universe will be governed. He began this ledger, even before the creation, by inscribing it with the rule: My mercy will prevail over My wrath. (*Bukhari*) See 6:12.

[986] See 7:73.

[987] Supernatural things like the Prophet's journey to Jerusalem and Paradise, and then back again in one night, and the mention of things like a cursed tree in Hell make doubtful people even more doubtful. This is what happens even though by all rights they should be afraid, especially given all the other proofs and logic of Islam. Indeed, they must realize that they just might really have to face some very dire consequences one day if they continue to reject the One Who created them. Verses 37:62 and 44:43 also mention the cursed tree of which the residents of Hellfire will partake, and those verses predate the revelation of this chapter. When Abu Jahl first heard of the tree of *Zaqqum*, he ordered dates and butter to be brought to him, and he ate them, saying, "Let us have some more *zaqqum*, for we don't know of any other *zaqqum* than this." (*Ibn Kathir*) He thus increased in his suppression of faith, as this verse notes. Also see 37:62.

[988] Satan's followers among the jinn are known as the *shayateen*, or the devils (lit. the *separators*). Human beings also become the obedient slaves of Satan, and they ever try to drag their fellows down into corruption; thus, they're 'devils' themselves.

[989] Satan will tempt people to mix corruption with wealth through gambling, theft, living extravagantly, sinful trade and miserliness. He will tempt people to take too much pride in their children, spoiling them, or he may use their children to bring about anxiety and fear within them, or he may make them adulterous and thus have broken families, or he may tempt them to harm their children through infanticide of female offspring (in their desire for sons). (*At-Tabari*).

Your only Safety Lies with Allah

*Y*our Lord is the One Who makes ships sail smoothly through the sea so you can seek of His bounty (through fishing or trade), for He is merciful to you. [66]

When a calamity seizes you at sea, however, all those (false gods) that you call upon besides Him leave you to languish! Though when (Allah) returns you safely to land once more, you turn away (from Him), for human beings are thankless! [67]

Do you feel so safe then that He won't make a part of the earth swallow you up when you're back on (dry) land? (Do you feel so safe) that He won't send a windstorm against you that'll leave you helpless to take care of yourself? [68]

Do you feel so safe that He won't send you back out to sea (on a subsequent voyage) and then send a heavy gale against you to drown you on account of your ingratitude? Even still, you won't have anyone to avenge yourself against Us! [69]

(So be grateful), for We've been generous to the sons of Adam by providing them with transportation on both land and sea, by giving them resources that are wholesome and by granting them favors more advantageous than most of the rest of creation ever received. [70]

The Record will be Complete

*O*ne day, We're going to call out the leaders of every people. Those who receive their records in their right hand will read their records, and they won't be wronged in the least. [71] However, those who were blind (to the truth) in this world will be blind (to it) in the next life, [990] for they had veered off the path. [72]

Their plan was to tempt you away from what We were revealing to you and to get you to substitute in Our name (principles) that were quite different. [991] (If you had done so), then (those evil people) would've become your closest friends! [73]

If We hadn't given you strength, then you probably would've inclined a little towards (their requests). [74] In that case, We would've made you suffer equal amounts (of punishment), both in this life and after death, and you wouldn't have had anyone to help you against Us! [75]

Their (ultimate) plan was to try and frighten you into fleeing from (your) hometown, so they could keep you away in exile. If they (had succeeded in driving you away), then they would've remained (safe in their homes) only a little while longer

---

[990] The 'blindness' on the Day of Judgment, as explained by the commentators, means they will be unable to acquire or obtain any faith or forgiveness at that time, for they will *see* no way to do it. It doesn't mean they will lose the ability to see with their eyes. This interpretation is confirmed by relevant prophetic traditions. (*Ma'ariful Qur'an*)

[991] This passage was revealed in response to some pagans who asked the Prophet to give them special treatment in exchange for their conversion. One report says that it refers to the leaders of Mecca who told the Prophet they would be more inclined to follow him if he drove away his poor underclass followers. (*Ma'ariful Qur'an*) Another report says that members from the tribe of Thaqif visited the Prophet and offered conversion if he would exempt them from charity and prayer, exempt them from having to cancel the interest owed to them, even as they could continue to charge interest, and that their sacred trees would be protected and inviolate. According to this report, the Prophet was in the midst of having his secretary write this contract for the tribe, when this verse was revealed telling him not to cave in to their demands. (*Zamakhshari*) Yet, a third incident attributed to this revelation is that the Quraysh asked Muhammad to alter a verse of the Qur'an to their liking. In desperation he almost agreed with them, but this passage told him to stand firm and warned him to be on his guard against the subtle suggestions of those who would have him compromise. (*Zamakhshari*)

after you (left, before We destroyed them). [992] [76]

This has been our mode of operation with the messengers We sent before you, and you will never find any change in how We operate. [77]

Strengthen Yourselves for What Lies Ahead

*E*stablish prayers after the sun begins to decline (at noon) until the onset of nightfall, and recite (the Qur'an) at dawn, for reciting (the Qur'an) at dawn is witnessed (by the angels). [993] [78]

Pray in the late hours of the night, as well, as an extra bonus for you (above and beyond what's required), [994] for your Lord will shortly raise you to a highly regarded position. [995] [79]

Now utter (this supplication, and then prepare yourself to migrate to Medina), *"My Lord! Let my entrance be an honest entrance, let my exit be an honest exit, and bestow upon me power from You to help me."* [80]

And also declare (this phrase in order to strengthen your resolve for the coming migration), *"The truth has arrived, and falsehood will vanish, for falsehood always vanishes!"* [996] [81]

We're sending down in this Qur'an that which is a source of healing and mercy for the believers, even as it causes nothing but loss to the wrongdoers. [997] [82]

Each will Act according to His Nature

*W*henever We bestow Our favors upon a human being, he turns away and becomes aloof, but when calamity strikes him, he descends into deep despair. [83]

---

[992] One of the alternative plans of the Meccans was to capture the Prophet in the street, tie him up, deposit him in a faraway land, and then prevent him from returning for fear of his life.

[993] According to a saying of the Prophet, the angels work in two shifts, and they change their shifts at *fajr* time, or the prayer just before dawn, and at '*asr* time or the late afternoon prayer. Thus, if we are praying, they will tell Allah we were praying when they came upon us and praying when they left us. (*Bukhari, Muslim*) What a wonderful report to be given to our Lord!

[994] This bonus prayer is known as *tahajjud* prayer. It is not obligatory, but it is highly praised in Allah's sight. After people go to bed and sleep for most of the night, they get up to pray a two-unit prayer an hour or two before the first light of dawn appears. They can pray additional times as they wish. The Prophet made it his habit to pray the *tahajjud* prayer, and in time many other people began to join him. Later on in Medina, he skipped doing it in the mosque one night, and this confused some people who had always looked forward to joining him. When they asked him about it the next morning, the Prophet explained that he skipped doing it in the mosque one night, because he was afraid it would be made an obligatory prayer on the community, (given how its practice was rising in popularity). He also counseled people to make *tahajjud* a regular habit or not to do it at all, rather than doing it only haphazardly with no regularity. A person who goes to bed with the intention of praying *tahajjud* later, but then sleeps through it inadvertently, still gets the reward of having done it. (*Nisa'i, Ibn Majah*)

[995] This is thought to be the Prophet's exalted status on the Day of Judgment when he will be given the right to intercede on behalf of people to save them from Hellfire.

[996] This verse is something of a "throwing down the gauntlet" phrase to let the pagans know that the next phase of the Prophet's mission, that of fighting back, is coming near to hand. Ironically, eight years after this verse was revealed, in the year 630 when the Prophet returned triumphantly to Mecca at the head of ten thousand followers, he recited this very ending phrase from this verse as he began toppling the 360 idols that were in and around the Ka'bah.

[997] Most commentators say that this passage [80-82] was the actual command for the Prophet that informed him that he would have to exit from Mecca and enter into Yathrib (later to be called Medina). It counseled him to remember that he was migrating for pure motives to assuage any latent fears or misgivings. The predictions here proved true. The Prophet returned any money with which he was entrusted to their rightful owners before he left Mecca, and when he entered Medina, people lined up in throngs, welcoming him, singing songs and begging for the honor of housing him.

Say to them, *"Everyone acts according to his own disposition, but your Lord knows best who is being guided on the way."* [84]

What is the Nature of the Human Spirit?

*N*ow they're asking you about the spirit. [998] Tell them, *"The spirit [999] is under the command of my Lord, and no knowledge of it has ever come to you except for a little." [1000]* [85]

If We ever wanted, We could take away (this message) with which We've been inspiring you, and then you wouldn't have anyone to represent you in your claim against Us. [86] However, (the extent of) your Lord's mercy and His favor towards you is indeed tremendous! [87]

Say to them, *"If the whole of humanity and all the jinns were to gather together to produce something similar to this Qur'an, they could never produce the like of it, even if they all worked together and pooled their resources."* [88]

And so it is that We've explained for people in this Qur'an every type of example (so they can ponder over them).

Yet, most people are unwilling to accept it and are thankless. [89]

Answering a Flurry of Objections

*T*hey say, *"We're never going to believe in you until you make a spring gush forth for us from the earth,* [90] *or until you have a garden filled with date palms and grapevines and rushing streams flowing abundantly in their midst,* [91] *or until you make the sky shatter and fall down upon us, as you pretend will happen, or until you bring Allah and the angels here in front of us,* [92] *or until you have a house decorated with gold, or until you have a ladder that can reach right up into the sky! Even then, we won't believe you ever climbed up there, unless you send a book down to us that we can read (for ourselves)." [1001]*

Say (to them), *"Glory be to my Lord! Am I not a messenger who's just a mortal man?"* [93]

Nothing prevented the people (of former nations) from believing when guidance came to them, except for their saying, *"Has Allah really sent a mortal man as a messenger?"* [94]

Say (to them), *"If the earth were populated by angels, going about their business quietly, then*

---

[998] 'Abdullah ibn Mas'ud (d. 653) reported the following incident that caused the revelation of this verse: "While I was strolling with the Prophet through a desolate patch, he stopped to rest on a palm leaf stalk. Some Jews passed by, and one of them said to the others, 'Ask him about the spirit.' Another one said, 'Why do you want to ask him about that?' A third man among them said, 'Don't ask him, or you might get an answer you won't like.' Finally they agreed on: 'Let's all ask him.' Then they asked the Prophet, but he didn't answer, and then I knew he was receiving revelation, so I stayed where I was. Then the new revelation was received, and the Prophet recited (this verse)." (*Bukhari*) The "spirit" is thought to be Angel Gabriel. Others have said it is the spirit or soul that resides within each person.

[999] The "spirit" is thought to be Angel Gabriel. Others have said it is the spirit or soul that resides within each person. The scholars differ as to whether this verse was revealed in the late Meccan or early Medinan periods.

[1000] The scholars differ as to whether this verse was revealed in the late Meccan or early Medinan periods.

[1001] This passage recounts a relentless assault from the pagans, who said all of these things to the Prophet in a huge outdoor gathering that they arranged. (The entire incident is recounted in *at-Tabari*.) After they asked for many miracles to benefit their city and themselves, the Prophet told them, "I won't do any of that, and I won't ask my Lord for these things. I wasn't sent for this reason; rather, Allah sent me to you to bring you good news and warnings. If you accept what I've brought you, then it will be good fortune for you in this world and in the next, but if you reject it, then I will wait patiently for the command of Allah until Allah judges between me and you." So that's when they asked the Prophet to make the sky fall upon them. The Prophet then said, "That's for Allah to decide, and if He wants to, He will do that to you." These verses were revealed about that incident. (*Asbab ul-Nuzul*)

We would've certainly sent an angel down from the sky to be a messenger for them." [95] Then say, *"Allah is enough of a witness between you and me, for He's well-informed and watchful over His servants."* [96]

For the one who is guided by Allah, such a one is truly guided, but for the one whom He leaves astray – *you won't find any protector for him in place of (Allah)!*

On the Day of Assembly, We're going to gather them together, flat on their faces – *blind, mute and deaf* - and then their destination will be in Hellfire. Every time (the heat of the fire) seems to wane, *We'll stoke the fire back to its full intensity!* [97]

That's the compensation that they're going to receive because they rejected Our (revealed) verses and said, *"What! When we've rotted away to dust and bones, are we really going to be made like new once more?"* [98]

Don't they see that Allah, the One Who created the heavens and the earth, has the power to create them as they were (before)?

It's only because He's set a specific time-limit for them - *and there's no doubt about that* - but still the wrongdoers do nothing more than thanklessly refuse (the invitation of salvation). [99]

Say (to them), *"If you had control over all the treasures that (emanate from) the mercy of my Lord, you would be unwilling to share them (with others) out of the fear of spending too much, for human beings are tightfisted!"* [100]

Take the Example of Moses

*A*nd so it was that We gave nine evident miracles to Moses when he came (before Pharaoh and his nobles) [1002] – just ask the Children of Israel! Pharaoh said to him, *"Moses! I think you've been bewitched!"* [101]

"You know full well," (Moses) replied, *"that these (miracles) have been sent down by none other than the Lord of the heavens and the earth, as clear evidence for all to see. I think that you, Pharaoh, are doomed to perish!"* [102]

Thus, (Pharaoh) resolved to wipe (the Hebrews) off the face of the earth, but We drowned him and all those who were with him, [103] and We said to the Children of Israel, *"Dwell upon the earth, but when the final promise comes to pass, We're going to gather you in a mixed crowd (on the Day of Judgment)."* [104]

The Qur'an is the Truth

*W*e sent (the Qur'an) down for a true purpose, and it has, indeed, been sent down for that true purpose. We didn't send it to you for any other reason than to give good news and also to warn. [105]

We divided this Qur'an (into sections) so you could recite it to people in intervals, and (that's why) We've been revealing it in successive stages. [1003] [106]

Tell (the idol-worshippers of Mecca):

"Whether you believe in it or not, the (Jews and Christians) who were given knowledge (of Allah's revelations) before you fall down on their faces humbly when they hear it being recited to them, [107] and they say, 'Glory be to our Lord! Our Lord's promise has been fulfilled!' [108] *They*

[1002] See 7:133.

[1003] The Qur'an is designed for easy reading. The entire book is divided up into thirty divisions (each is called a *juz*) so that it can be read in a month's time. It also has seven larger divisions (each called a *manzil*) so the more ambitious can read it in a week. On a more merciful level, it has divisions (called *hizb,* quarters or groupings) that comprise groups of 20 or more lines for even easier reading. All of this is in addition to the standard division of 114 chapters. Take your pick - set reading portions are already tailor-made for you so you can read it at your own pace!

fall down on their faces weeping, [1004] *and it increases their humble (submission)."* [1005] [109]

Also tell (them), *"Call upon Allah, or call upon the Compassionate,* [1006] *for regardless of whatever name you use to invoke Him, the most beautiful names belong to Him."* [1007]

How should We Recite the Qur'an?

(*M*uhammad!) [1008] Don't recite (the Qur'an) in your prayers too loudly or too softly, but recite in an even tone in between the two extremes. [110]

Then say, *"Praise be to Allah, Who doesn't give birth to children, nor does He have any partner in His kingdom, nor does He need anyone to protect Him from weakness, so magnify Him greatly!"* [111]

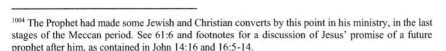

[1004] The Prophet had made some Jewish and Christian converts by this point in his ministry, in the last stages of the Meccan period. See 61:6 and footnotes for a discussion of Jesus' promise of a future prophet after him, as contained in John 14:16 and 16:5-14.

[1005] After reading this verse it is customary for the one who has faith in Allah to prostrate himself on the floor and praise Allah.

[1006] In Yemen, which lies at the extreme southwest of Arabia, ancient Himyaritic inscriptions that predate Islam by centuries have been discovered that show that ancient Jews and at least some Christian and pagan Yemenis there called upon Allah by the name of *Rachman.* This term also can be found in Talmudic literature as a reference to Allah. Thus, this verse is emphasizing that Allah can be called upon by many titles, as long as those titles are befitting the majesty of Allah. It's not, then, the exact name that is so important, but the faith of the one who is calling upon his Lord. (See: *The Himyarite-Ethiopian War and the Ethiopian Occupation of South Arabia in the Acts of Gregentuius,* Vassilios Christides, 1972)

[1007] The Prophet was prostrating and calling upon Allah, saying, "O Compassionate, O Merciful," when a pagan man happened by. The ignorant pagan said out loud, "He claims to pray to one (Allah), but he's praying to two!" Then this verse was revealed mentioning that Allah has many holy names by which He can be invoked. (*Ibn Kathir*)

[1008] This verse was revealed in Mecca at a time when the pagans would ridicule the Qur'an whenever they heard it being recited. The Prophet used to recite it in a strong and clear voice, but it would often attract needless heckling from the pagans. However, if he recited it too softly, his companions and also interested pagans wouldn't be able to hear it from him and learn it, so this verse tells him to take a middle ground. After the migration to Medina, these restrictions were no longer as essential and didn't apply, though the commentators say it remains as a general principle for the believers not to shout or whisper in their prayers, but to take a middle course. (*Ibn Kathir, Bukhari*)

The Cave

18 Al Kahf
Late Meccan Period

This chapter holds a special place in the imagination of Muslims. The Prophet once said of this chapter: "Whoever recites the Chapter of the Cave on Friday, it will illuminate him with light from one Friday to the next." (*Al-Hakim*) On another occasion he said, "Whoever memorizes ten verses from the beginning of the Chapter of the Cave will be protected from the Anti-Christ." (*Ahmad*) Finally, he also once said of this chapter, "Whoever recites the first and last verses of this chapter, there will be a (spiritual) light from his feet to his head, and if he were to recite the entire chapter, for him there is light from the earth to the sky." (*Ahmad*)

This portion of revelation came during a particularly difficult time. Due to relentless Meccan persecution, a large number of Muslims had migrated to Abyssinia for safety. Meanwhile, back in Mecca, the leaders of the Quraysh sent two messengers (an-Nadr ibn al-Harith and 'Uqbah ibn Abi Mu'ayt) to Yathrib (Medina) to ask the Jews about Muhammad and to get their opinion as to whether he was a true prophet or not.

The Jews sent back a suggested list of three topics about which they could ask him. "Ask him," the rabbis said, "about the reason for why the young men left their city and sought refuge in a cave and then what happened next, for this is a unique event. Ask him about the man who traveled both to the east and the west of the earth and what happened to him. Finally, ask him about the spirit and what it was." (*at-Tabari*) Those three questions are the reason for revelation of some of the portions of this chapter. When the Meccan messengers returned, they asked the Prophet about these issues. At first Muhammad said that he would have the answer right away, but he forgot to say, "As Allah wills." To teach him a lesson - that he could not order Allah to reveal things - no new revelation came for fifteen days. The Prophet realized his mistake and repented. Then verses 18:23-24 were revealed to explain the reason for the delay, and then finally the answers came.

Be that as it may, the Meccans were unfazed by the fine answers given in this chapter. They decided to punish Muhammad and the two clans to which he was most closely related, and from which many of his followers came, by forcibly ejecting them from the city and isolating them in a barren desert valley. They wrote their decree on vellum and hung it in the Ka'bah for effect. This was known as the Boycott, and for three years the Meccans refused to trade with the exiles, sell them food or allow them to leave the valley. The Muslims suffered deprivation on an appalling scale. If it wasn't for secret food deliveries smuggled in by sympathetic Meccans in the night, the Muslims would surely have perished.

Visiting Arab chieftains from the countryside eventually shamed the Meccans into lifting their cruel policy. When the document hung within the Ka'bah, wherein was written the decree, was examined, it was found that ants had eaten away all the ink, leaving the sheet blank. It was little consolation for the Prophet, however, for in the same year the Boycott was lifted, his beloved wife and soul-mate Khadijah passed away, a death no doubt hastened by the many years of suffering in the open desert during the Boycott. The Prophet's uncle and only political protection, Abu Talib, also passed away, leaving the Prophet more vulnerable to violence than ever before. Perhaps the story of the Sleepers of the Cave contained within this chapter is a veiled note of hope for the Prophet that persecution doesn't last forever and that eventually the truth will prevail over ignorance.

In the Name of Allah,
the Compassionate, the Merciful

*P*raise be to Allah, the One Who sent down to His servant a Book in which He allowed no crookedness. [1]

(It's a Book that's) straightforward (and clear), so He can warn (all people) of a terrible penalty from Him, and so that He can give good news to the believers who do what's morally right that they're going to have an excellent reward [2] - (a reward) that will stay with them forever. [3]

(It's also a message that's been revealed) so He can warn those who say, *"Allah has begotten a son."* [4] They have no knowledge (that could justify their claim), nor did their forefathers (have any certain proof), either.

It's such an outrageous statement that's coming from their mouths, for what they're saying is no more than a lie! [5]

Perhaps you'll worry yourself to death as you follow after them, distressed that they're not believing in this narration. [6]

Whatever (riches and distractions) that We've placed in the earth are but a dazzling display by which We test them, in order to bring out those whose conduct is the best. [7] (In the end), We're going to reduce whatever is upon (the earth) to dry dust. [8]

The Companions of the Cave

*H*ave you ever considered that the Companions of the Cave [1009] and the inscribed writings might be among Our wondrous signs? [1010] [9] When the young men fled (from persecution) to the cave,

---

[1009] Jewish visitors from Yathrib (Medina) were trying to help the Meccan idol-worshippers expose Muhammad as a fraud by providing them with questions that they could ask him, hoping he would stumble. They told the Meccans to ask Muhammad about the Companions of the Cave, and this story contained in verses 9-22 was revealed in response.

[1010] Who were the Companions of the Cave? Most of the classical commentators usually say this story refers to the Christian legend of the Seven Sleepers of Ephesus, and they take all the details from early Christian sources and repeat them. Basically, a group of Christian young men fled persecution from the Roman emperor Decius in approximately the year 250 CE and slept in a cave in some kind of a coma until sometime in the early fifth century, when they awoke to find their religion was now the law of the land under the converted emperor Theodosius. An inscription written in lead was placed by the cave to let people know who was in there. All of this is according to Jacob of Serugh (d. 521) who wrote about them in a poem. Other Muslim commentators offer a whole host of supernatural "sleeper" events from Spain to Iraq, and they include convoluted and very suspect narratives culled from unreliable sources. A handful of more discerning commentators suggest that this story is really about an earlier group of Jews who fled persecution under Roman rule, and this is what Ibn Kathir postulates in his commentary on verse 13. Is there a possible identification for this earlier episode? During the years 66-70 CE, a faction of puritanical Jews in Palestine rose up in revolt against the Roman occupation. It was a foolish gamble, and the Jews were all but routed. As the Romans were near achieving total victory, a group of these purists (sometimes known as Essenes and other times known as the renegade sons of the priest Zadok, who were banished by the Greek rulers of Jerusalem) fled to the desert and stowed their holy writings away in some caves at Qumran, even as they lived in them for a time. This group, which labeled itself as the 'Sons of Light' or 'Men of Holiness,' was faithful to the Torah and refused to compromise with the assimilated rabbis of the cities who allowed elements of pagan superstition to seep into their religion. This group of Jews remained apart from society for a number of years - *completely isolated* - and later left their caves and rejoined their countrymen when they said, *"Our Lord! Be merciful to us, and resolve our situation in the most appropriate way."* [10]

Then We boxed up their ears for a number of years in the cave, (so they would have no news of the outside world). [1011] [11] Then, (after some time had passed), We awakened them to test which of the two sides (among them) would be better able to calculate the length of their stay. [12]

We're telling you their story truthfully, for they were young men who believed in their Lord. Therefore, We increased them in guidance. [13]

Indeed, We fortified their hearts when they had confronted (their people), saying to them, *"Our Lord is the Lord of the heavens and the earth, and we're never going to call upon any god besides Him. If we did that, then we would be saying something blasphemous.* [14] *These people of ours have taken other gods in place of Him, so why don't they bring some clear authority to justify what they've done? Who can*

be more wrong than the one who invents a lie against Allah?" [15]

(Then they made a plan to escape the wrath of their people, saying to each other), *"After you've turned away from them and all that they serve besides Allah, then seek refuge in the cave. Your Lord will shower His mercy upon you and make your situation easy to bear."* [16]

The World Transforms

(If you were looking out from) the cave's entrance, you would've seen the sun as it rose away leaning to the right. When it set, it would move away from them and then down to the left, all the while they remained there, lying in the middle of the cave. These are among the signs of Allah. Whomever Allah guides is guided (to the straight path), while whomever Allah leaves astray – *you won't find any right-minded supporter for him!* [17]

---

open persecution had ended. The writings they left behind were discovered only in 1947 and are known as the Dead Sea Scrolls. Those who favor the opinion that a group of these Jewish purists were the Companions of the Cave offer as evidence the fact that the challenge to the Prophet on this topic came from the Jews, who would seemingly have had no interest in maintaining or circulating Christian legends whose locus was hundreds of miles away in the Greek and Syriac speaking Anatolian Peninsula and Levant. In addition, the Arabic term *ar-raqeem* that is used here means 'inscribed or imprinted writings,' which could be a reference to the Dead Sea Scrolls, which were written between 200 BCE and 68 CE. At least one of them was imprinted on copper and is known as a treasure map today! (The scrolls have been called the most spectacular discovery of ancient manuscripts in history - *perhaps a wondrous sign of Allah.*) For these reasons it just may be that the story in this chapter is referring to a righteous group of Jewish young men of a puritanical sect. This view is further strengthened by this description of the Essenes (or the sons of Rabbi Zadok, who was a spiritual leader from David's time) left by an early Church father named Hippolytus (d. 235). He wrote, "These (purists) practice a more devotional life (than the Pharisees and Sadducees), being filled with mutual love…they turn away from every act of inordinate desire…they renounce matrimony, but they take the boys of others, (to raise as their own). They lead these adoptive children into an observance of their own peculiar customs…they despise wealth, and do not turn away from sharing their goods with those that are destitute. When an individual joins the sect he must sell his possessions and present the proceeds to the community…the head of the order distributes it to all (members) according to their needs." (As quoted in Vol. V of *The Anti-Nicene Fathers*, ed. by Rev. Alexander Roberts and James Donaldson. Wm. B. Eerdmans Publishing Co., Grand Rapids, 1951.) In this Qur'anic telling of the story, it is teenage boys, seemingly unconnected to any parents, who flee as a group. They are deeply religious, an obvious sign of sustained indoctrination. They take only coins with them, a sign of the habit of their sect to distribute coins to all members. Finally, their leader freely distributes the coins to the one charged with finding food for them all.

[1011] Literally it says that Allah "boxed their ears up" as in a boxer landing a blow on an opponent so he is knocked out cold. What does this colorful idiom mean? Were they lulled into a deep stasis-like condition and slept for many years, or did they live in such isolation for years that it was as good as being *dead* and *deafened* to the outside world? Were they constantly in prayer and so people who peered in their caves saw them prone on the ground all the time? The choice of meaning is yours, for either interpretation is possible, depending on how you wish to look at this episode.

You would have thought they were awake (if you saw them), but they were asleep! We turned them on their right sides and their left, while their dog stretched out his two forelegs at the entrance.

If you would have come upon them, you would have run away in abject terror of them! [18] That's (how they were) when We awakened them, so they could ask each other (about their situation.) One of them asked, *"How long have you all been here?"*

"We've been here a day or maybe part of a day at most," (they answered, but after a long discussion), they (all agreed that they weren't sure), and so they said, *"Allah knows best how long you've been here. Let's send one of you with his money to the city to see which is the best kind of food he can bring, so you can at least satisfy (your hunger) with it. Let him be discreet, and let him not talk to anyone about (the rest of us),* [19] *because if they come upon (you), then they'll stone you or force you to return to their traditions. Then you'll never succeed."* [20]

It was (on account of his antique coins and dress) that We made people aware of their situation. (This was so) they could know that Allah's promise is true and that there can be no doubt about the Hour. Later on, (after the youths grew old and died, the people) disagreed among themselves about how (best to commemorate) their case.

"Let's construct a (monumental) structure over (their graves)," (some people suggested), but their Lord knew about them (and their less than honest intentions). However, those who won the decision said, *"We're going to build a house of prayer over (their graves)."* [1012] [21]

(The people who know about this story differ over the details, with some) saying that there were three (young people in the cave) and that their dog was the fourth among them. (Others) said they were five, with their dog being the sixth, but they're just guessing about what they haven't seen. (Others even assert that) they were seven, with their dog being the eighth. [1013]

Say (to them), *"My Lord knows best what their exact number was, and only a few (people) know for sure (how many they were)."* [1014]

So don't get drawn into arguments with them (on such speculative issues), but rather (talk to them) only on topics that have clear resolutions, and don't consult any of them at all about (such obscure topics). [22]

[1012] If the Companions of the Cave were the Seven Sleepers of Ephesus, there is a cave there today that is purported to be the cave used by those youth. Both the cave and a nearby shrine dedicated to them have been a tourist trap for centuries. If the cave in question was a hideout of the Essenes and is somewhere in Palestine, then that location would have been remembered for a time as a holy place, before being lost to the recesses of time. In addition to the Qumran site, in nearby Jordan there is another cave at Abu 'Alanda which locals claim is the one mentioned in this chapter. There was a shrine built over it, though it has fallen into disrepair in modern times. (In 2011, 70 metal-plate books with imprinted Judeo-Christian writings were discovered in a cave not far from there.) Only Allah knows which location is correct.

[1013] While the issue of the Companions of the Cave was still being discussed publicly, visiting Christians from Najran (who would have presumably preferred the Ephesus connection) were divided amongst themselves as to how many young men went into the cave to escape persecution. Their various answers are quoted here. The verse advises the Prophet not to dwell on speculation, and that Allah alone knows the true number. This information was (wisely) not revealed, as it was unnecessary, and the argumentative people would have disputed the figure anyway.

[1014] When the clumsy Meccans, egged on by the Jews, asked the Prophet to tell them about the Companions of the Cave, you can imagine how they would throw out questions in a disorganized manner. "Who were they?" "The people say they were four. Is that true?" "No, they say they were five!" "No, were they seven?" "What about their dog, what color was it?" The Meccans didn't care about the story or its lessons. They only desired to trip the Prophet's tongue and find something, anything, to catch him up on.

Don't Forget to Account for the Will of Allah

$\mathcal{N}$ever say of anything, *"I'll do it tomorrow,"* [1015] [23] without adding, *"If Allah wills."* If you forget (to add this phrase), then remember your Lord (when you recall your lapse) and say, *"I hope that my Lord guides me closer to the rightly guided way."* [1016] [24]

(Some people say that the Companions of the Cave) stayed in their cave for three hundred years, and (others) add nine (more years to that figure). [25]

Tell them, *"Allah knows better how long they stayed, for the unseen (secrets) of the heavens and the earth belong to Him. He sees them and listens (to all things). (Nothing that exists) has any protector besides Him, and He never shares His rule with anyone."* [26]

Choose Your Side

$\mathcal{R}$ecite what's been revealed to you of the Book of your Lord. No one can change His words (of command), [1017] and you'll never find anyone who can save you besides Him. [27]

Keep your soul content with those who call upon their Lord in the morning and in the evening, seeking His face. [1018]

[1015] When the Prophet was first asked about the Companions of the Cave, he said he would have the answer the next day by the latest, but he failed to add the required addendum for future plans, "If Allah wills." Thus, as a penalty, the answer to the question was delayed for over two weeks. Then, along with the revelation of the Sleeper's story, verses 23-26 also came to admonish the Prophet about this. (*Asbab ul-Nuzul, Ibn Kathir*)

[1016] This seemingly divergent passage is not a random insertion of unrelated text within the larger surrounding narrative. (See textual background note above.) In Arabic this passage [18:23-24] is completely part of the surrounding rhythm and rhyme scheme, and in the context of the larger story it can also emphasize that Allah's will is paramount, for even as the Companions of the Cave fled in fear of their lives, Allah's will changed their fear into a new day of security. Thus, we must always make an allowance for the will of Allah both in small things and in large ones. He knows the future, and we do not. It also skillfully foreshadows the coming story in verses 18:32-44, causing the reader to make connections between different areas of the same chapter. (*Ibn Kathir*)

[1017] All commentators have understood "words" here to mean the decreed commands of Allah. Some ill-informed critics of Islam have suggested that the Muslim position - that the previous revelations of the Torah and the Gospel have been tampered with - is incompatible with verses like this, which seem to say that no one can change Allah's 'revelations.' But this verse is not referring to whether or not people can tamper with written texts, but to the uttered *commands* that Allah gives. Anyone can erase a word on a page, but Allah's spoken commands will endure. In addition, His revelations will always remain in pristine form with Him, no matter what people do to books on earth. An identical understanding is contained in I Peter 1:25 of the New Testament! (Compare a KJV, NIV or RSV of the Bible, and one will find many alterations, but it's not the written text that is Allah's 'word' but the commands!) The term used here for words is *kalimat*. This term is not usually equated with prophetic revelation in Islamic parlance. Rather, words such as *dhikr, nuzul, kitab, qur'an, zabur* and the like are used for organized and collected scriptures or bodies of teachings. This verse is in effect saying, "Recite the Qur'an, for no one can stop you from succeeding in your mission because no one can change Allah's *word of command* that His side will be the winner in the end." As for protecting books recorded by human scribes, Islam makes no claim that they cannot be changed. The Prophet used to forbid his followers from taking written pages of the Qur'an into enemy territories for fear that 'unbelievers' would deface, destroy or disrespect the revelation of Allah. So if he knew that people could manipulate a written page for good or ill, then the Muslim position still stands that the Torah and the Gospel of today are not the originals given to the ancient prophets, even though the originals still survive with Allah. (For example, see the book entitled, *Who Wrote the Bible?* by Richard Elliot Friedman for an objective, scholarly study into how the scriptures have been manipulated and edited for a variety of reasons in ancient times.)

[1018] Some of the Prophet's companions in Mecca were poor and wore tattered clothing. One day a group of pagans went to the Prophet, and one of them, Uyaynah ibn Hisn, asked Muhammad to exclude such coarse and rough people from his gatherings if he wanted to join them in the meetings. Another

Don't let your eyes pass beyond them, desiring the flashy glitter of this world's life. [1019] Don't obey anyone whose heart We've allowed to become careless of Our remembrance, who follows his own whims and whose purpose (in life) is lost. [28]

Say to them, *"The truth (has now come to you) from your Lord."* Whoever wants to believe (in it), will do so. Whoever wants to reject it, will do so. We've prepared for the wrongdoers a fire whose (flames) will surround them like walls. Every time they ask for relief (from the heat), they'll have scalding water poured over them as hot as molten brass! It'll sear their faces! *Oh, how awful a drink and how horrible a place to rest!* [29]

As for those who believed and did what was morally right, *We're never going to lose track of the reward of anyone who did good!* [30] For them are everlasting gardens beneath which rivers flow. They'll be adorned with gold bracelets while wearing embroidered robes of green silk. They'll relax on couches within (the garden) - *oh, how wonderful a payment and how excellent a place to rest!* [31]

The Story of the Boastful Gardener

*L*ay out for them the example of two men. We gave one of them two gardens of grapevines, surrounded them with date palms, and then placed grain fields in between. [32] Both of the gardens produced abundantly, and there was never a bad harvest, and in their midst We let a gentle stream flow. [33]

His harvests were truly grand, so (one day) he had a tense conversation with his companion during which he boasted, *"I have more wealth than you, and I have more (influence in society than you on account of my) many followers!"* [34]

Then he went into his garden in a state of injustice against his own soul. (Looking around, he then said to himself,) *"I don't think any of this will ever perish, [35] nor do I think the Hour (of Judgment) will ever come. Even if I was brought back to my Lord, I'm sure I'll find something there even better in exchange."* [36]

His companion had told him, when they had talked before, *"Are you going to reject the One Who made you from dust, then from mingled fluids, and then crafted you into a man? [37] As for me, (I believe) that He's my Lord Allah, and I'll never make any partners with Him."* [38]

"Whenever you go into your garden, why don't you say, 'It is as Allah wills,' and 'There is no strength except with Allah?' If you've noticed that I have less money and fewer children than you, [39] it's because my Lord will give me something better (in the afterlife) than your (earthly) garden. Perhaps He might send thunderbolts from the sky (down upon you) and turn (your garden) into shifting sand, [40] or maybe your water supply will sink in the earth so deep that you'll never be able to recover it." [41]

And so it came to pass that the fruits (of his labor) were encompassed (in utter destruction). He just stood there, wringing his hands in worry over what he had invested on his property, which was now destroyed down to its very foundations!

All he could say was, *"I'm ruined! If only I had never made partners with my Lord!"* [1020] [42]

---

prominent pagan named Umayyah ibn Khalaf had also advised the Prophet in this regard. This verse was revealed in response, directing the Prophet to prefer the company of the sincere, no matter their socio-economic status. (*Muslim*)

[1019] The Prophet said, "Whoever adopts a simple mode of dress, in spite of his (vast) wealth and affluence, only for the sake of humbleness and modesty, Allah, the Exalted, will dress him in the clothes of nobility and wisdom." (*Abu Dawud*) 'Umar ibn al-Khattab said in later years: "Get used to rough living, for luxury doesn't last forever."

[1020] His making 'partners' with Allah doesn't necessarily mean that he was an idol-worshipper. The Prophet defined two levels of doing *shirk*, or making partners in Allah's divinity and power. The first level is in the obvious worship of idols or elevating any creature into a divine role besides Allah. The

He had no group of supporters (to help him) against Allah, nor was he even able to save himself! [43]

(On the Day of Judgment), the only protection that will be available will be from Allah, the Ultimate Reality. He's the best One to reward and the best One to bring matters to a close. [44]

What is this World Really About?

*L*ay out for them the example of what this world is really like. It's like the water that We send down from the sky. The plants of the earth absorb it, but soon afterwards they become as dry stubble to be blown about by the winds. Allah is the only One Who prevails over all things! [45]

Wealth and sons are merely the glitter of the life of this world, but the moral deeds that endure are the best in the sight of your Lord, and the best on which to hope (for the future). [1021] [46]

One day We're going to send the mountains away, and you're going to see the land as a level plain. Then We're going to gather all of them together, leaving no one behind. [47] They'll all be standing at attention before your Lord in rows, (and they'll be told), *"So now you've come back to Us (as naked) as (the day) We created you the first time. But no! You never thought We would bring about your appointed meeting!"* [1022] [48]

(Each person's) record (of deeds) will be placed (before him), and you'll see the wrongdoers in a state of panic on account of what (their records) contain. [1023] *"We're doomed!"* they'll cry out. *"What kind of book is this! It leaves out nothing small or great, and it makes mention of everything!"*

Thus, they'll find out about everything they ever did, for it will all be right there, laid out before them, and your Lord won't treat anyone unfairly. [49]

When We are Questioned

*W*e told the angels, *"Bow down to Adam,"* and they all bowed down, except for Iblis, who was one of the jinns. He broke away from his Lord's command. So are you now going to take him and his descendants as protectors besides Me? They're your enemies, so it's a truly bad deal that the wrongdoers are making! [50] I didn't let them witness the creation of the heavens and the earth - *no, not even their own*

---

second level is in what the Prophet coined as *al-riya'*, or showing off. In other words, when we think we're so great and mighty, we're placing ourselves in competition with Allah's power. The Prophet said, "I'm most afraid for you about little *shirk*." When he was asked what that was, he replied, "Showing off. Allah will say on the Day of Judgment, as people are being rewarded or punished for their deeds, 'Go to the one for whom you were showing off in the world, and see if you will get any rewards from him.'" (*Ahmad*) Also see 17:37 for the perfect statement against ever feeling arrogant.
[1021] The Prophet said, "Well done! Well done for doing five things that will weigh (heavily) in the balance: (saying), 'There is no god besides Allah,' 'Allah is greater,' 'Glory be to Allah,' and 'Praise be to Allah'; and finally a righteous child who dies and his parents seek Allah's reward (by not becoming bitter or despairing overly much)." (*Ahmad*)
[1022] The Prophet said, "Allah will gather people on the Day of Judgment naked, uncircumcised and *buhman*." When the Prophet was asked what *buhman* meant, he replied, "They will have nothing at all with them. Then a voice will call out to them that could be easily heard by all those near or far, saying, 'I am the King. I am the Judge. None of the people of Hell will enter Hell if he is owed something by one of the people of Paradise, until I have settled the matter, and none of the people of Paradise will enter Paradise if he is owed something by one of the people of Hellfire, until I have settled the matter, even if it's only as small as a slap.'" When people asked the Prophet how people could be recompensed from each other when they came with nothing, the Prophet replied, "By good deeds and evil deeds." (*Ahmad*)
[1023] The Prophet said, "On the Day of Judgment, everyone who betrayed something will have a banner (behind him) by which he will be known." (*Ahmad*)

creation - nor would I take such misleaders as assistants. [51]

One day (Allah) will say, *"Call upon those whom you assumed were My partners."* They'll call out to them, but they won't answer back. Then We'll erect a dreadful prison wall between them. [52] The wicked will see the Fire and feel themselves falling into it, and they'll find no way out. [53]

Many will Turn Away

$\mathcal{W}$e've given detailed explanations in this Qur'an, using every kind of example for people (to ponder). Yet, human beings argue over most things. [1024] [54] There's nothing to prevent people from believing – especially now since guidance has come to them - nor from asking for their Lord's forgiveness, except that they've followed the pattern of ancient peoples (who denied that Allah would ever send His revelations to a mortal man) or that they would suffer from the onslaught of (Allah's) punishment. [55]

We only send messengers to give good news and to warn, but the faithless argue over foolish points in an effort to weaken the truth (in the eyes of their fellows). They take My (revealed) verses and what they've been warned with as a joke. [56]

Who's more wrong than the one who's reminded of the signs of his Lord but then turns away from them in forgetfulness because of what his hands have done? (As a penalty), We've wrapped veils over their hearts to prevent them from understanding and placed a deafness in their ears. Even if you called them to guidance, they'd never agree to be guided. [57]

Even still, your Lord is the Forgiving and a master at showing mercy. If He were to take a hold of them (immediately and punish them) for what they've earned for themselves (on their record of deeds), then He would've certainly hurried their punishment forward.

However, they have their time limit, and after that they'll have no place to be safe. [58] (This is the pattern of previous) generations that We destroyed. When they were immersed in corruption, We fixed a final date for their destruction. [59]

Moses Seeks a Teacher

$\mathcal{B}$y Allah's command, Moses (set out on a journey to seek a man wiser than himself). He said to his servant, [1025] *"I won't give up until I've reached the junction of the two seas or until I've spent years traveling."* [1026] [60]

When they finally did reach the junction, (they made camp for the night), but they forgot all about their fish, (which then leapt out of its container) and made

---

[1024] The Prophet went to visit his daughter Fatimah and her husband 'Ali one night in Medina. They were about to go to bed and hadn't prayed any further that night. The Prophet asked them, "Aren't you going to pray?" 'Ali replied, "Messenger of Allah, our souls are in the hand of Allah. If He wants to wake us, He will." The Prophet chuckled and then walked away slapping his thigh as he recited the ending of this verse, "…*human beings argue over most things.*" (*Ahmad*)
[1025] Some commentators think his assistant might have been none other than a young Joshua, who would later lead the Israelites into the promised land.
[1026] Moses was often disobeyed by his people, and they were prone to arguing with him. After one such episode, Moses lost his temper and said, "Who's the smartest man among the people? It's me - I'm the smartest!" Because Moses didn't say Allah was the most knowledgeable of all, Allah made him go on a quest to learn patience. Allah told him to go to the coast (of the Red Sea) where the Gulf (of 'Aqabah) and the Gulf (of the Suez) meet at the bottom tip of the Sinai Peninsula and look for a person there who was more learned than even he. Moses asked Allah, "How can I find him?" Allah inspired him with the following instructions: "Take a fish in a container, and you will find him where you lose that fish." So Moses set out with his servant, bringing a fish in a container, on the journey to find the wisest man in the world. (Condensed from *Bukhari*)

its way into the sea through a tunnel. [1027]
[61]

After they (arose the next morning and) traveled (some distance farther), Moses said to his assistant, *"Bring us our breakfast, for as it is we've endured so much fatigue on our journey."* [62]

"Did you see (what happened) when we were resting on that boulder (the night before)?" (the servant exclaimed). *"I forgot (to tell you about) the fish, and only Satan could've made me forget to mention it. It (leapt out of the container) and made its way back into the sea in an amazing way!"* [63]

"That was it!" Moses cried. *"That was (the sign) for which we were looking!"* Then they retraced their footsteps [64] and found one of Our servants upon whom We had granted mercy from Our Own presence and whom We had taught from Our Own knowledge. [1028] [65]

"Can I follow you," Moses asked, *"so you can teach me something of the good sense that you've been taught?"* [66]

"You won't be able to have patience enough (to learn) from me," (Khidr) replied, [67] *"for how could you have patience in situations where your knowledge is incomplete?"* [1029] [68]

"Allah willing, you'll find me patient," (Moses) replied, *"and I won't disobey your commands."* [69]

"If you really want to follow me," (Khidr) said, *"then don't ask me about anything until I've spoken about its meaning first."* [70]

The Mysterious Journey

Then they proceeded on (and took passage on a ship), but then (Khidr) damaged (the boat and caused it to take on water). [1030] (Moses) cried out, *"Have you damaged it in order to drown those within it? What an awful thing you've done!"* [71]

"Didn't I tell you," (Khidr) intoned, *"that you would have no patience with me?"* [72]

"Don't hold my forgetfulness against me," (Moses) cried, *"nor be hard on me in my position."* [73]

So then they proceeded on until they met a young man, but then (Khidr) killed him. *"Have you killed an innocent person,"* (Moses) cried out, *"who hasn't murdered anyone! What a horrible thing you've done!"* [74]

"Didn't I tell you," (Khidr) answered, *"that you would have no patience with me?"* [75]

[1027] The commentators explain this part of the episode thusly: the pair traveled down the coast to the tip of the Sinai Peninsula, and the servant was charged with carrying the container in which the fish was kept. At some point, the two travelers stopped to sleep near the junction of the two seas by a spring named *al-Hayat* (the life giving), which (unbeknownst to them) was reputed to be a miraculous spring that brought any dead animal to life. Accordingly, the fish came to life, flipped out of the container and landed in a crevice, perhaps between the rocks near the shore. It swam through the water-filled tunnel it found out into the sea. The servant saw what happened, but he was too tired to stop it. He then forgot to tell his master. (Perhaps he thought it was a dream.) (*Ibn Kathir, Bukhari*)

[1028] The man Moses found was a wise sage named Khidr. His name means *green* in Arabic, and the Prophet said he had that name, because he once sat on a patch of pale, withered vegetation, and it turned green with new plant growth. (*Bukhari*)

[1029] The Prophet said, "A strong believer is better than a weak believer, though there is good in both, so work for things that will be to your benefit, and (avoid) things that you're not able to handle. If you're ever overcome by some situation, then say, 'Allah has planned as Allah willed.' Beware of saying, 'What if,' for, 'What if,' begins the work of Satan." (*Ibn Majah*)

[1030] The Prophet's narration adds that the sailors mentioned in this verse had let Khidr and Moses aboard for free and that he damaged a bottom part of the hull by prying up a plank with an ax. After Moses objected, Khidr stood by the railing and watched as a bird came near the side of the boat. It dipped its beak once or twice in the water. Then Khidr turned to Moses and said to him, "My knowledge and your knowledge, in comparison to Allah's knowledge, is like what this bird took out of the sea." (*Bukhari*)

Then (Moses) beseeched him, saying, *"If I ever ask you about anything after this, then you have every right to part ways with me, and you would be fully justified as far as I'm concerned (to make me leave)."* [1031] [76]

Then they traveled farther until they came to some people in a town. They asked them for food, but the (townspeople) refused to give them any hospitality. (As they passed through the town,) they came upon a wall that was about to collapse, but then (Khidr) repaired it. *"If you want,"* (Moses) remarked, *"you could ask them for some payment for (your labor)."* [77]

"This is where you and I will go our separate ways," (Khidr) announced, *"but first let me tell you the full meaning of those things for which you had no patience."* [78]

"As for the boat, it belonged to some poor (sailors) who used it on the sea, and I only desired to make it (temporarily) unserviceable, for there was a certain king coming up ahead of them, seizing every boat by force." [1032] [79]

"As for the young man, his parents were believers, and we were afraid that he was going to bring sorrow down upon them due to his rebellious and thankless nature. [80] Therefore, we only desired that their Lord give them (a better son) in exchange, one who would be purer and nearer to a merciful disposition." [1033] [81]

"As for the wall, it belonged to two young orphans of the town. Below it was a buried treasure that was their due right. Their father had been a moral man, so your Lord desired that they should reach maturity and find their treasure, as a mercy and favor from your Lord. [1034] I didn't (do all those things) from my own motivations. This is the meaning of (all of those things) for which you had no patience." [1035] [82]

The Master of Two Horns

*N*ow they're asking you about the Master of the Two Horns. [1036] Say to them, *"I'll narrate for you something of his story."* [1037] [83] We established him in the

---

[1031] The Prophet said, "May Allah's mercy be upon us and upon Moses! If he had stayed with his companion, he would have seen amazing sights, but he said, 'If I ever ask you about anything after this, then you have every right to part ways with me, and you would be fully justified as far as I'm concerned (to make me leave).'" (*At-Tabari*)

[1032] Apparently, the boat was owned by ten brothers, half of whom were handicapped. The able-bodied brothers used the boat and its produce to support their needy relatives. (*Ma'ariful Qur'an*)

[1033] The Prophet said, "The boy that Khidr killed was on the path to becoming a rejecter (of Allah) from the day he was born." (*Muslim*) The Qur'an, of course, is not offering murder as a way to deal with children who are on the road to evil behavior, and there are no Qur'anic verses or prophetic traditions that advocate such a doctrine. Remember that the Qur'an is recounting a journey that Moses made and things he saw in the company of a kind of guru. The principle of killing a bad child is, however, enshrined in the Old Testament, in a passage supposedly written by Moses. In Deuteronomy 21:18-21, parents of a bad son are counseled to denounce him publicly and have him stoned to death. (Also see Exodus 21:15, 17.) Islam has no such provision. (See 16:125)

[1034] The Prophet said that the treasure was a chest full of gold and silver. (*Tirmidhi*)

[1035] When Moses realized that his own people were impatient with him just as he was with Khidr, he became a wiser and better leader. Thus, the management principle is offered in the Qur'an that a true leader never loses touch with the perspective of his or her underlings.

[1036] The following subject, that of the story of the "Master of the Two Horns," is one of the topics that visiting Jews from Medina told the Meccans to ask Muhammad about. Who was the Master of Two Horns? It was hoped by the Arabs and Jews that Muhammad would stumble on this issue and expose his lack of knowledge. Yet, when the revelation of this story came to him, the Jews realized that Muhammad was a man with which to be reckoned, and the pagans were further dumbfounded. The Master of Two Horns refers to King Cyrus the Great of Persia, who was spoken about in glowing terms in the Jewish scriptures in the book of Daniel (8:20) and also in the book of Isaiah (verse 45:1), where he is called (in Hebrew) the *Messiah*.

[1037] No record or opinion as to the identity of this figure has survived from the time of the Prophet and his companions. Early commentators were divided among themselves as to which historical figure *Dhul Quarnayn* could be. However, by the end of the classical period, many commentators, after

earth and gave him the means to reach every (place he wanted). [1038] [84] He followed one way [85] until he reached the setting of the sun, and it appeared to him to set (behind) a murky body of water. [1039] Near it he found a people (who were given

having been exposed to the stories and legends of Alexander the Great (d. 323 BCE), applied the title to him and were elated that such 'a great man' was mentioned in their holy book. Those who still subscribe to this opinion, that Alexander is being spoken of here in verses 83-101, point out that Alexander traveled widely and often wore a pair of ram's horns on his helmet, a decoration commemorating the Egyptian god Ammon-Ra, which even found its way onto coins minted during the ill-fated ruler's reign. However, putting these two inconclusive and incidental details aside, could *Dhul Quarnayn* really be Alexander of Macedon? That question can only be answered by first defining the character of the man mentioned in this chapter and then comparing it with all the available historical accounts that we have of Alexander. *Dhul Quarnayn* is presented as a pious man who ruled with justice. He also traveled generally west, then generally east and then generally north. Alexander the Great traveled east *first*, then north, and finally south before going back west, so the chronology of travel doesn't fit here. This is not the only thing that disqualifies him, however, for Alexander was a polytheist who thought of himself as the son of Zeus! He was also fond of wine, murdered some of his friends and conquered for no other purpose than to be famous forever. (He got what he wanted!) So Alexander doesn't fit very well with the description of *Dhul Quarnayn*. So who was *Dhul Quarnayn*, or the *Master of the Two Horns*? It was the Jews of Medina who had suggested to the Meccans that they ask Muhammad this question. This story was revealed in response. A Persian king named Cyrus the Great (d. 529 BCE) is the definitive candidate, and the proof is very convincing. If we remember the origin of the question that the Meccans put to the Prophet, that it came from the Jews of Medina, and if we also remember that every other similar question the Jews proposed originated from their religion, historical experience and their scripture, then we need do no more than look to the Jewish scriptures for the source of the reference. The Jewish prophet Daniel, who was living in captivity in Babylon, saw a vision of a ram with two horns of different heights (Daniel 8:20). (Thousands of Jews, including Daniel, had been forcibly relocated from Israel to Babylon by the Babylonian tyrant Nebuchadnezzar many years before.) Then Daniel saw a goat (in his vision) with one small horn breaking the two horns of the ram, and then the goat's horn broke into four pieces in turn. According to Daniel, Angel Gabriel came and explained the meaning of the vision. It was that the nations of the Medes and the Persians (symbolized as two horns) would unite to make a great empire spanning a huge territory (under Cyrus's rule) and further that a Greek king, (Alexander the Great,) would then vanquish that empire, and in turn his kingdom would break up into four smaller kingdoms. (See Daniel 8:1-22) In Daniel's lifetime, the Babylonians were in fact defeated by Cyrus the Great, the first king and uniter of the Medes and the Persians (see Daniel 5:30-31), and on a map Cyrus's empire looks roughly like two horns arcing up to the east and west with Persia as the epicenter, while the eastern half of his empire arcs up further north than the western half. (As Biblical scholars admit, the book of Daniel erroneously rearranges the chronology of the two Persian kings, Cyrus and Darius I and mistakenly identifies Darius I, the third reigning Persian king, as the *first* Persian king and conqueror of the Babylonians. Ezra 4:3-5, however, gets the chronology right.) Cyrus the Great has been beloved of Jews ever since that time on account of the fact that he let the Jewish captives return home to Israel. He is also revered by Jews as having been a righteous man, devoted to Allah, (see Daniel 6:26-28) and the renovator of many holy places in Jerusalem. Thus, *Dhul Quarnayn* can be none other than Cyrus the Great of Persia, as the Jews knew him to be the meaning of the vision of the master of the two ram's horns. (*Ma'ariful Qur'an, Tafhimul Qur'an*)

[1038] Daniel 8:4 specifically says the king of the two-horned empire could go wherever he wanted, unimpeded by anyone. Cyrus never lost a battle (save for his last with a Central Asian warrior queen in which he died), nor was he deterred by any obstacle. He even bridged impassable rivers with pontoon floats! The Persians, by the way, were great road builders, and one of Cyrus's successors, Darius I (d. 486 BCE), would eventually build the world's first transnational highway called the Royal Road.

[1039] Some critics of Islam, who seem to have no imagination for literary devices, have charged that the Qur'an somehow promotes the idea that the sun sets *inside* a *murky pool*! Besides the fact that the Arabic words don't give that exact impression, if you get to the actual meanings of the words used, for anyone who has ever witnessed a sunset behind a body of water, without ever believing the sun touches the water, doesn't it look like it's setting *in* it? Such critics who advance literalisms seem to contend that Allah has no license for imagination or for a sense of literary flourish. (No Muslim scholar to the best of my knowledge has ever interpreted this verse to say that the sun sinks in a well! Even Ibn Kathir pointed out that this phrase was an idiom that meant Cyrus conquered as much as he wanted until he came to the limits of the land, bounded by the sea. In Medina, the Prophet himself once said that the sun sets between the horns of Satan – another romantic flourish that means that nightfall is a

to misbehavior, but who had no power to resist him). We said, *"Master of the Two Horns! Either punish them or treat them well."* [1040] [86]

"The one who does wrong shall be punished," he announced. *"Then he'll be sent back to his Lord, and He'll punish him with a harsh penalty.* [87] *However, the one who has faith and does what's morally right will be well rewarded, and we'll issue easy commands to him."* [1041] [88]

Then he followed another way [89] until he came upon the rising of the sun. He found it rising upon a people who had not been provided by Us with secure shelter. [90] (He left them alone) as they were, for We knew better what he had there before him. [1042] [91]

---

time when people become more prone to risky behavior, - as some modern studies have confirmed.) Unfortunately for such critics, the Qur'an is full of such charming descriptions. The commentators from the very beginning (Ibn Kathir, etc…) have understood this verse as it is, that it means the king reached a dark-hued shallow body of water or inland sea of some sort (but less than an ocean) and saw the sun go down on the other side of it.

[1040] With the help of ancient historians (Herodotus, Xenophon, etc.), we can definitively place the travels of Cyrus the Great and match them with those of *Dhul Quarnayn*. (The fact that Cyrus's expeditions match the order given in the Qur'an is quite astounding!) After uniting the Medes and the Persians (the two horns of Daniel's vision), Cyrus led his army westward into Asia Minor (present-day Turkey) in the year 547 BCE. Even a cursory glance at a map of Cyrus's travels to the west shows that he passed through what is today known as Turkey. In central Turkey there is a 580 square mile salt lake known as Tuz Golu, which is shallow and muddy, due to the high rate of annual evaporation it experiences for much of the year. The empire of Lydia was located in this region, and its eastern border lay right on the western shore of this lake. (Some have suggested that Cyrus went straight to the Aegean Sea, and beheld the sun setting in its murky darkness, and the Arabic word used here is not bahr (ocean) but 'Ain or Sea, though there is scant historical evidence that Cyrus personally went to the shores of the Aegean Sea.) Thus, when Cyrus's forces reached the border of Lydia, Cyrus would have seen the sun setting beyond this dark, shallow lake to the west. Cyrus passed around this lake on his way into Lydia to take its capital city of Sardis. He waged war on the people of Lydia because their despotic ruler Croesus had attacked the city of Pteria and enslaved its people against all right. (Pteria was a part of Cyrus's grandfather's possessions, against whose corrupt rule Cyrus was first encouraged to revolt. Indeed, the reason Cyrus traveled so widely was that he was securing the far flung provinces of his grandfather's realm.) The Lydian army was nearly bested at the battle of Pteria and withdrew into the walls of its fortress at Sardis.

[1041] Cyrus laid siege to the Lydian capital of Sardis. The Lydians tried one last effort to oppose Cyrus on the battlefield but were forced to withdraw. After Cyrus' men secretly gained entrance into Sardis, Croesus was forced to surrender. After taking possession of the city in 546 BCE, Cyrus ordered that Croesus and his band of corrupt nobles be executed. According to Herodotus, at the last minute, Cyrus changed his mind and spared the life of Croesus and his men. (Croesus, about to be publicly thrown in a fire, repented of his evils, remembering the words of an old Athenian acquaintance named Solon, who had chastised him for his arrogance and greed.) Cyrus even befriended Croesus after that display of remorse! Then Cyrus established just laws among the people of western Anatolia so they would not fall under the spell of corruption again. The grateful Greeks of the Anatolian coast, for example, even labeled Cyrus as the 'Law Giver.' (An original clay cylinder inscribed with the tolerant and humane principles of Cyrus has survived to this day.) After Cyrus departed from Lydia, a local strongman named Pactyas revolted, promising riches to his people, but he was soon captured by a Persian general and sent in chains to Cyrus for punishment. Thus, verses 84-88 are fully identified. In summary, Cyrus traveled west to a land containing a murky body of water, uprooted a despot, had the choice to forgive him or not, forgave him, rewarded righteousness, reformed the laws of the land, and punished someone (the rebel) who did wrong.

[1042] Historical records tell us that Cyrus then traveled in an easterly direction out of Asia Minor. He mopped up the last remnants of resistance to his rule along the way, including taking the city of Babylon without a fight. It was then that he earned the eternal favor of the Jews by letting them return home to Palestine (See Ezra 1:1-8). Some commentators believe that the 'people who had no shelter' were the captured Jews of Israel who had been sent there in exile. There is also an alternative view that puts Cyrus even further East. From Babylon Cyrus then continued in an easterly direction and entered into the wilds of the easternmost reaches of the empire that he was trying to solidify. He traveled deep into such uncivilized northeastern lands as Arochosia, Bactriana (southern Afghanistan), Sattagydia and Mardiania. Here we find Cyrus in the shadow of the Hindu Kush mountains in a region

Then he followed another way [92] until he came upon (a land) between two mountain (ranges). He found beneath them a people who could barely understand a word (of his language). [1043] [93] They told him, *"Master of the Two Horns!* [1044] *The Yajuj and Majuj (tribes) cause great destruction in the land. Could we pay tribute to you so you can build a strong barrier between us and them?"* [94]

"(The wealth and power) that my Lord has granted me is better (than any tribute you could give). Help me instead with your strength (and labor), and I will build a barrier between you and them. [95] *Now bring me pieces of iron!"*

(Then he ordered the people to build) until he had filled the space between the steep mountains (with strong fortifications). [1045] *"Blow (with your bellows!"* he then commanded), and when he had made it as hot as fire, he said, *"Now bring me molten copper so I can pour some of it over (the iron to reinforce the defenses)."* [1046] [96]

---

collectively known as Greater Khurasan, which is Persian for 'the place of the rising sun.' Thus, the metaphor of the 'rising of the sun,' for it would have certainly looked like the sun arose from behind the mountains. (Ibn Kathir, among others, explain that verses 86 and 90 mean that *Dhul Quarnayn* traveled from one end of his empire to the other, an idea which fits here splendidly.) This region was, indeed, an area inhabited by uncivilized nomads such as the Paktyan and Rhoplutae tribes of Arachosia, peoples who were not worth trying to subjugate. Cyrus left such peoples alone as he was more interested in subjugating settled towns and cities. Thus, by way of summary again, the Qur'an tells us that *Dhul Quarnayn* traveled east to the farthest point that he could reach, into a land inhabited by uncivilized nomads, and that he did not oppress nor subjugate the uncivilized peoples he encountered there. This is exactly the course of action that Cyrus followed and it may hold more weight as an interpretation rather than holding that the people mentioned in this verse were the exiled Jews, and Allah knows best.

[1043] Again we find that the route of Cyrus and *Dhul Quarnayn* match each other. He had already gone west as far as he could, then he had gone east as far as he could. Now he went *another way*, in this case, northeast through Bactria into Central Asia and the lush Ferghana Valley. The 'two mountains' mentioned in verse 93 are the Himalayas to the north and the tip of the Hindu Kush (known as the Pamirs) to the south. This new land that Cyrus entered, Sogdiana by name, was a settled and fertile valley between the mountains whose people were under constant threat of attack from barbarian nomads who flooded in through a narrow pass from time to time. (Modern-day Samarqand was the capital city of Sogdiana.) The Sogdians, being only distantly related to Cyrus's own people (the Medes and Persians), could *barely understand a word* of his language. Thus, communication would have been very difficult at first, *but not impossible,* until some common way of harmonizing the different dialects could be devised. When they could communicate with each other, the Sogdians told Cyrus of their great nemesis to the north.

[1044] The two nomadic tribes whose violent raiding struck fear in the hearts of people from Europe to China were called the Sacae (Scythians) and the Massagetes by the Greeks. (The Persians called them the Apa Saka and the Ma Saka.) Ibn Kathir was also of the opinion that the *Yajuj* and *Majuj* were tribes from somewhere north of the Black Sea. Unfortunately, many modern translators identify the Yajuj and Majuj with the Biblical Gog and Magog, though the two have nothing to do with each other, as the Gog and Magog of the Bible are described quite differently and serve a different purpose in Biblical theology than the Yajuj and Majuj of the Qur'anic story, and Allah knows better.

[1045] Cyrus is credited with building a string of fortifications throughout Sogdiana up to and along the Jaxartes (Syr Darya) river to protect the people of the region from the barbarian raiders, who were being led by a warrior queen named Thamaris. The crowning jewel of these fortifications was the fortress of Kurushkatha (Cyropolis to the Greeks, or City of Cyrus). Cyrus built it in 530 BCE to protect the entrance to the heavily populated Ferghana Valley. Indeed, the narrow Khudjand Pass, which Cyrus's main fort was meant to guard, has been the traditional invasion route for the nomads of the steppe for ages. Sadly, Thamaris was able to draw Cyrus out into the wilds of Central Asia, and after he had pursued her tribe for some miles, she surrounded his army and slaughtered them. His fortresses, however, still stood and prevented the worst of the raids. Today, the ruins of this fortress are located in the country of Tajikistan, in an area known as Kurkath. The ruins are just south of a later fortress built by Alexander the Great for a similar purpose.

[1046] While it is obvious that the major building material for the fortress in question would have been stone and brick, metals at key points such as gate jambs would have added strength and stability. Sadly,

And so the (enemy) was rendered helpless to climb over (the walls of the forts), nor could they penetrate them from below. [1047] [97]   (When he saw that the enemy was powerless to invade the valley,) he remarked, *"This is a mercy from my Lord,* [1048] *but when my Lord's promise comes to pass, then He'll reduce (the deterrent) to dust, and my Lord's promise is a true one."* [98]

On that day, We're going to let (the barbarians) surge forward like waves, one after the other. [1049] Then the trumpet will be blown, and We'll collect them all together. [99] We'll present the full expanse of Hellfire for the faithless to see [100] - *those whose eyes had been under a veil against remembering Me* - moreover they were (unwilling) even to listen (to the message)! [101]

A Day of Winners and Losers

$\mathcal{D}$o the faithless think that they can take My (created) servants as protectors besides Me? Well then, We've made Hellfire ready to entertain all those who suppressed (their ability to believe)! [102]

Say (to them), *"Should we tell you about those who are going to lose the most in their deeds?* [103] *(It's) those whose life's work has been wasted, even as they thought they were getting something good for their efforts."* [104]

---

any metals used in the construction of the fortress would have rusted away long ago. Some classical and even modern commentators such as 'Abdullah Yusuf Ali have proposed that Dhul Quarnayn built a gate made of iron to keep the invaders out. As proof they note that an iron gate in the Caucasus mountains was written about by early travelers, both Arab and Chinese, between the seventh and ninth centuries. The problem with this theory, besides the fact that neither Cyrus nor Alexander ever traveled in the Caucasus mountains, is that the Arabic text here in this verse says the king erected a *sudda*, or barrier (fortification, deterrent, fort, line of control, etc…) and not a *baab*, or gate. Thus, it is a strong fortress or string of such deterrents that must be identified. I personally am of the opinion that the walled fortress of Cyropolis, which is the crowing jewel of a string of forts, is the *sudda* or barrier in question. I base my position on the following points: on the prominent strategic location of Cyropolis and its sister forts, which together guarded the pass into the valley; the fact that it was meant to deter the Scythians and Massagetes (Yajuj and Majuj?) and succeeded in doing so; because of the barrier's location in between two mountain ranges and because the barrier protected a valley; the Jews who asked the question of Muhammad took a direct reference to Cyrus from their scriptures (the book of Daniel); and also because of the fact that this fortress was built in a land whose inhabitants had some (but very little) knowledge of Cyrus's own language. Couple these points with the fact that Cyrus is, as many modern commentators (including Maulana Maududi) have shown, the most like *Dhul Quarnayn* in all respects, though Allah knows better.

[1047] The Arabic word used here (*naqba*) is usually translated as dig or tunnel, perhaps in the sense that the invaders could not tunnel under the walls of the fortifications. Since it was a string of hilltop forts at intervals that Cyrus built, then the alternative meaning of the word can be used here, namely, that the invaders could not pass through or penetrate the line of defenses from below.

[1048] Cyrus apparently did believe in One God. Daniel 6:26 records this in witness (even as the previous verse in that book incorrectly names the king as Darius. Ezra 4:3-5 gets the right chronology.)

[1049] The Prophet once had a nightmare, and he woke up his wife Zaynab and said, "There is no god other than Allah! The Arabs are ruined on account of a misfortune that is approaching: a little gap has been opened today in the barrier of Yajuj and Majuj!" Then he made a circle with his index finger and thumb. Zaynab asked him, "Messenger of Allah, will we be destroyed even though there will be righteous people among us?" The Prophet replied, "Yes, if sinfulness increases." (*Bukhari, Muslim*) Some classical commentators say that this doom upon the Arabs probably refers to the devastating Tartar and Mongol invasions that brought Arab rule in the Middle East to an end in the thirteenth century and wiped out the last vestige of the Abbasid Caliphate in 1258. (Those two groups were the loose descendants of the Central Asian Scythians.) The Mongols, in particular, were so savage that they massacred millions of Muslims all across Persia, Iraq and Syria. Eventually, the descendants of the Tartars and Mongols accepted Islam, but they were never fully Islamized, and this has been a thorn in the side of the Muslim world even to this day. If that is what happens when a small gap is opened in the barrier, how will it be when the barrier is crumbled to dust just before the Day of Judgment, and barbarian hordes are once again released upon the world!

They're the ones who denied the (revealed) verses of their Lord and their meeting with Him. Their works will be rendered void, and on the Day of Assembly We'll give them no weight (in the balance of deeds). [1050] [105]

That's their reward – *Hellfire* – because they rejected (their Lord) and took My (revealed) verses and messengers as a joke. [106]

Those who had faith, however, and did what was morally right will be entertained in an exclusive garden in Paradise. [1051] [107] There they shall remain, never wishing for anything to change! [108]

Allah is without Limit

$\mathcal{S}$ay (to them): [1052]

"If the ocean were made of ink

(and it was used to write out) the words of my Lord,

the ocean would run dry first before the words of my Lord would be exhausted, even if we added another ocean just like it to help!" [109]

Muhammad is no More than a Man

$\mathcal{S}$ay (to them), "I'm just a man like yourselves. [1053] I've received inspiration (that commands me to inform) you that your God is One God and that whoever expects to meet his Lord, let him do moral deeds and let him not join any partners at all in the service of his Lord." [1054] [110]

[1050] The Prophet said, "A very fat man will come forward on the Day of Judgment, and he will weigh no more than a gnat's wing to Allah. So recite if you will, *'...on the Day of Judgment We will give them no weight.'*" (*Bukhari, Muslim*) In other words, those who had the power on earth to stuff themselves and live a life of leisure will have no power on the Day of Judgment.

[1051] *Firdaws* is considered the most exclusive garden in Paradise. The Prophet said, "If you ask Allah for Paradise, then ask Him for *Firdaws*, as it is the highest part of Paradise, in the midst of Paradise, and from it spring the rivers of Paradise." (*Bukhari*)

[1052] This verse was revealed in response to a Jewish man who boasted to the Prophet that the Old Testament was a lengthy text; thus, his people could claim a greater amount of knowledge and legitimacy on account of its massive size. (*Asbab ul-Nuzul*)

[1053] Apparently this verse was revealed in the Medinan Period in response to a Muslim man who told the Prophet that he did good deeds for the sake of both Allah and his reputation and that this dual purpose of his was good enough for him to satisfy his own sense of duty. (*Ma'ariful Qur'an*) This verse warns against adding any 'partners' in one's service to Allah, even if that 'partner' is one's own sense of self-satisfaction or pride in one's reputation.

[1054] In a narration, the Prophet explained that if a person does a good deed and he has any other goal in mind besides pleasing Allah, even slightly, then Allah will reject the entire good deed. In another, longer narration, he said, in part, that Allah will say on the Day of Judgment, "Whoever used to associate anyone with Allah in the deeds that he did, let him seek his reward from someone else besides Allah, for Allah is the least in needing any partner or associate." (*Ahmad*) Abu Hurayrah was concerned about the implication of this verse. He told the Prophet that when people call on him while he is at home, if he happens to be praying, he gets happy that people found him at prayer. So he wanted to know: was that showing off? The Prophet replied in the negative and explained that it was the source of two rewards: one for praying in secret and the other for setting a good public example. The Prophet also explained that if people praise a good deed that it is merely good news for a believer. (*Ma'ariful Qur'an*)

Mary
19 Maryam
Middle Meccan Period

This chapter was revealed in approximately the year 614. By that time, the Meccan leaders had failed in their initial efforts to break the will of the Prophet and his followers. Their next major policy initiative involved open persecution and economic pressure. After some months passed, and the travails and suffering of the Muslims of Mecca became unbearable, the Prophet told his followers that they could migrate to Abyssinia if they chose, that the government there was overseen by a just king, a Christian king, and that they could stay there until Allah had made a better situation for them in their homeland.

The first migration was of eleven men and four women, who narrowly eluded capture. A few months later, in the year 615, a much larger group of refugees, consisting of over eighty men and eleven women, escaped Mecca, leaving only about forty or fifty Muslims behind in Mecca with the Prophet. The migration of so many people caused a great amount of consternation in Mecca, as every family had at least one member who left, even close relatives of Abu Jahl, Abu Lahab and Abu Sufyan had migrated.

The leaders of the Quraysh decided to send a delegation to Abyssinia to petition the king to return the refugees to Mecca. The two men they chose soon arrived at the court of the king of Abyssinia, bearing expensive gifts. At first they lavished offerings upon the king's officials, and then they met with the king in person and asked for the return of the Meccans who had taken refuge in his kingdom. They explained the refugees were religious rebels who gave up the religion of their people and didn't embrace Christianity, either.

The king, being a fair man, decided to let the Muslims plead their case, saying, "I'm not going to give them back without a proper hearing, for these people have put their trust in my country, rather than in any other country. They've come here to seek shelter, and I won't betray them. Thus, I'll send for them first and investigate the charges that these people have made against them. Then I'll make my final decision."

The leaders of the Muslim migrants were brought to the king, and their spokesman was Ja'far ibn Abi Talib, who said, "O King! We were a people lost in ignorance and had become very corrupt. Then Muhammad came to us as a Messenger of Allah. He did his best to reform us, but the Quraysh began to persecute his followers, so we've come to your country in the hope that here we will be free from persecution." Then Ja'far was asked to recite some of the Qur'an, and he recited verses from this chapter that relate to Mary, Jesus and John the Baptist. The king began to weep, and he said, "Most surely this revelation and the revelation of Jesus have come from the same source. By Allah, I will not give you up into the hands of these people."

The Meccans weren't about to give up so easily, however, and the next day they met with the king once more to press him to turn over the Muslims. They told the king that the Muslims denied the divinity of Christ and thus hoped to inflame hatred in his heart towards the Muslims. When the king summoned Ja'far again and asked him what the Qur'an said about Jesus, Ja'far answered, "He was a servant of Allah and His Messenger. He was a spirit and a word of Allah, which had been sent to the virgin Mary." The King then traced a line on the floor with his staff and said, "By Allah, the difference between us and you is no thicker than this line." Then he returned the gifts of the Quraysh, saying, "I can't be bribed." He then sent them away, while giving permission to the Muslims to remain in his kingdom in peace.

In the Name of Allah,
the Compassionate, the Merciful

Kāf. Hā. Yā. 'Ayn. Sād. [1]

(This is) a reminder of the mercy of your Lord to His servant Zachariah [1055] [2] when he called out to his Lord in private supplication, [3] saying, "*My Lord! My bones are weak, and my head is sparkly grey. However, I've never been left without blessings when I've called upon You, my Lord.*" [4]

"*Now I'm worried about what my relatives (will do) after me, and my wife is barren, so grant me an heir from Yourself,* [5] *one who will inherit (the mantle of righteousness) from me and from the family of Jacob. Make him, My Lord, someone with whom You'll be pleased.*" [6]

"*Zachariah,*" (a voice called out to him), "*we've come to give you the good news of a son who shall be called John.* [1056] *We've never called anyone else by that name before.*" [7]

"*My Lord!*" (Zachariah) replied. "*How can I have a son, seeing that my wife is barren and I'm weakened by old age?*" [8]

"*And so it shall be,*" (the voice) answered, "*for your Lord says, 'That's easy for Me, for I already created you before when you were nothing.'*" [9]

"*My Lord,*" (Zachariah) implored, "*give me a sign!*"

(The voice) replied, "*Your sign shall be that for three nights you won't be able to speak to anyone, even though you're not mute.*" [10]

Then Zachariah left his private chamber and came out among his people, inspiring them (through hand motions) that they should glorify Allah in the morning and at night. [1057] [11]

The Nature of John the Baptist

"*John! Take hold of the scripture firmly!*" [1058] We made him wise, even from his youth, [12] and (gave him) sympathy from Us towards (every living thing), for he was pure-hearted and mindful (of Allah). [13]

He was also kind to his parents and was neither aggressive nor rebellious. [14] So peace be upon him the day he was born, the day that he died and the day that he's raised to life again. [15]

[1055] Zachariah was a family elder and religious leader. He held his fractious relatives together on the path of faith by sheer force of his personality. Like parents everywhere, when he became old he began to look down the path of the future and worry about all those generations who would come after him. Since he had no son of his own whom he could groom to be a leader after him, he called upon Allah to bless him with one. The knowledge he inherited from his forefathers, going all the way back to Jacob, could then be passed on to his satisfaction. The Prophet said that Zachariah was a carpenter by trade and that he used to eat from what his own earnings provided him. (*Muslim*)

[1056] The name John (*Johanan*) literally means in Hebrew *a gift of God.* He is John the Baptist, and was a gift from God to his father. In Arabic, his name is *Yahiya*, and it means *to be made alive.*

[1057] The Prophet said, "O people! Spread peace (to all), feed others, care for relatives, and pray at night while others are sleeping, for then you will enter Paradise in peace." (*Tirmidhi*)

[1058] According to the Qur'anic commentary of Abu Nasir al Haddadi (d. abt 1009), this verse is saying, in other words, for John to be faithful to the Torah and live by it, as his father Zachariah, taught him. (*Tafsir-Munir*)

Mary Receives Her News

$\mathcal{M}$ention in the Book (the story of) Mary when she withdrew from her family to a place in the east. [16]

She erected a curtain (to screen herself) off from (her family), and then We sent Our angel to her, who appeared like a mortal man in all respects. [1059] [17]

"I seek the protection of the Compassionate from you!" she cried out (when she saw the stranger approaching). "If you're wary (of Allah, then you'll leave me alone)!" [18]

"Truly, I am a messenger from your Lord," he answered, "(sent to tell) you about the gift of a pure boy." [19]

"But how can I have a son," she asked (in surprise), "when no man has ever touched me, and I'm not a loose woman?" [20]

"And so it will be," he answered, "for your Lord says, 'That's easy for Me.' (Your son) will be appointed as a sign for people, as well as a (source of) mercy from Us, and thus it's been decided!" [21]

Then she conceived him [1060] and withdrew with him to a far off place (outside the city). [1061] [22]

The labor pains soon drove her to the trunk of a palm tree, and she cried out, "Oh! If only I had died before this and become something forgotten or lost to sight!" [1062] [23]

"Don't be distressed!" a voice called out from under her. [1063]

"Your Lord has provided a spring for you. [24] Now shake the palm tree towards you, and it will shower ripe dates upon you. [25] So eat, drink and rest your eye, and if you happen to see any man, tell him, 'I've vowed a fast for the Compassionate, and I won't talk to any person at all today.'" [26]

[1059] When Mary became a teenager, it became more difficult for her to continue her religious studies publicly, as girls weren't allowed to study rabbinical knowledge in those days. This may have been the reason she moved to the eastern side of either the town or her family's compound and then set up a private area for herself, enclosing it with a curtain. Indeed, there is value in privacy for more sincere religious devotions. Ibn Taymiyyah (d. 1328) once wrote of solitude thusly: "It's important for the worshipper to be isolated from others at the time for (personal) prayers, remembering Allah, reciting the Qur'an and evaluating himself and his actions. Also, isolation allows a person to supplicate, seek forgiveness, avoid evil, and more besides."

[1060] According to Ibn 'Abbas, when the angel had put Mary at ease, he approached and blew his breath through her robe and into her womb, causing the start of her pregnancy. (*Zamakhshari*)

[1061] Notice how the character of Joseph, whom Christians claim was Mary's husband, plays no role in the Qur'anic story. (The New Testament asserts that Mary went to a village named Bethlehem with a new husband named Joseph, but the Qur'an makes no mention of this and merely intimates that the birth was performed some distance from her hometown.) Some scholars of Christianity have even asserted that Joseph was a fictional character added to the story later on to give legitimacy to the pregnant Mary, who in those days would have been considered scandalous if she were pregnant and unmarried – even in a written story. Interestingly enough, some segments of Christianity have held that Mary was a "perpetual virgin" her whole life, but Matthew 1:25 asserts that Joseph "knew her" after her firstborn son Jesus was born. Having a firstborn also implies *"other borns,"* and it has long been assumed that Jesus had siblings, (with at least one brother).

[1062] When Mary began to show her pregnancy, she knew she couldn't remain in her hometown, surrounded by people who might accuse her of promiscuity. She packed up some belongings and left the village. When her food ran out and the pain of her pregnancy got to her, she cried out in desperation at the trunk of a tree. Allah answered her prayer.

[1063] The commentators usually explain that this was the voice of an angel sent to calm Mary in her frightened moment of pain and distress. Food and water would be provided for her in her last stage of pregnancy, and she was given a convincing statement to use to ward off any strangers who might wonder about the young woman sitting under a tree in the middle of nowhere. Her statement that she was fasting was not a lie, however, for fasting (*sawm*) in Islam doesn't mean to fast from food exclusively. It can be applied to other aspects of self-denial, such as giving up arguing, talking, drinking or any other thing for a set time period.

Jesus Spoke as an Infant

In time, she went back to her people, carrying (the baby, but when they saw her) they cried out, "*Mary! You've come to us with something bizarre!* [1064] [27] *O Sister of Aaron!* [1065] *Your father wasn't a bad man, and your mother wasn't a loose woman!*" [28]

(Mary was speechless and frightened), and she merely pointed to the baby. (Her family looked surprised) and asked, "*How can we talk to a baby in a cradle?*" [1066] [29]

(Then the baby Jesus spoke out), saying, "*I am a servant of Allah. He's given me (knowledge of) the scripture and made me a prophet.* [30] *He's placed blessings upon me wherever I may be and has made me prayerful and charitable for as long as I live.* [31]

"*(He also) made me gentle towards my mother, being neither aggressive nor rude.* [1067] [32] *So peace be upon me the day that I was born, the day that I die* [1068] *and the day that I'll be raised to life again.*" [33]

This was Jesus, the son of Mary, and that's an exposition of the truth about which they're arguing. [34]

It's not right (to say) that Allah has taken a son. All glory be to Him! Whenever He decides something, all He has to do is say, "*Be,*" and it is! [1069] [35]

[1064] Mary's relatives thought she had committed fornication, and they berated her, reminding her that she was descended from the House of Aaron and that her parents had been fine, upstanding people. How could she have dishonored her status and parents?

[1065] Some critics of Islam assert that verse 28 inaccurately calls Mary the 'sister' of Aaron, a man who lived many centuries before. Such critics must be forgiven for their ignorance of how language is used in human cultures, for a person can be associated with a noble ancestor as a sister or son or daughter, even though they are not immediately related to that distant ancestor. (In a tradition the Prophet explained this verse in this very same way.) Even the Christian New Testament calls Elizabeth, the wife of Zachariah, one of Aaron's daughters, even though Aaron was from the distant past (Luke 1:5). Also see 66:12 and footnote about the use of ancestor references in Semitic parlance.

[1066] Jesus spoke one time as an infant by a special miracle from Allah in order to defend his mother from the accusations of infidelity hurled at her by her angry relatives. The Prophet said, "No infant spoke from the cradle except for three: Jesus, the boy during Jurayj's time, and one other." (*Bukhari*) The story of Jurayj (George) is told in the prophetic traditions. Jurayj was a righteous man falsely accused of fornication and fathering a child out of wedlock with a prostitute. When Jurayj was being beaten by the people for fornication, the baby boy spoke in his defense and said that his father was a shepherd with whom the prostitute slept. The third baby who spoke did so, according to an obscure prophetic tradition, after his mother made value judgments about two people who had passed by. The mother praised a haughty nobleman and then disparaged a slave girl who was being falsely accused of a crime. The baby told the mother that the man was a tyrant and the slave girl was innocent. In Christian tradition, St. Anthony of Padua (d. 1231) caused a newborn baby to speak in defense of its mother, who was being accused of adultery by her husband.

[1067] A child must be gentle and respectful to his mother for life. The Prophet once said, "May his nose be rubbed in dust." He repeated saying this two more times and then added, "the one who finds that one or both of his parents became old, and he failed to enter Paradise because he didn't serve them." (*Ahmad*)

[1068] Jesus was not crucified or killed, but rather Allah saved him and took him into the next realm to await the End Times when he will be returned to earth to fight the Anti-Christ. (A second century Gnostic Christian text found at *Nag Hammadi*, known as the Second Treatise of the Great Seth, also makes this claim.) After winning the battle, Jesus will marry, have a family and then die of old age. This information is all culled from the traditions of the Prophet Muhammad. This verse [19:33] and the earlier verse about John the Baptist of a similar type [19:15] are interesting because they use a different tense for the verb "to die." In the verse about John, it says, "the day that he died" (*yawma yamutu*) whereas in the verse about Jesus it says, "the day that I die" (*yawma amutu* which is implied future tense).

[1069] The Prophet said, "Whoever testifies that there is no god besides Allah, alone, Who has no partners, that Muhammad is His servant and Messenger, that Jesus was Allah's servant and Messenger, and a

(Jesus, himself, said), *"Allah is my Lord and your Lord, so serve Him, for that's the straight path."* [1070] [36]

However, the various factions (among the Christians) differed amongst themselves (about the true nature of Jesus).

Those who cover up (the truth) will be doomed at the sight of a momentous day. [1071] [37] Oh, how they're going to hear and see (the truth) on the day when they appear before Us.

As of today the wrongdoers are clearly mistaken, [38] but warn them still of the stressful day when the issue is going to be decided once and for all. They're careless, and they don't believe (in the truth). [1072] [39]

(In the end, however,) We're going to inherit the earth, as well as whoever's upon it, and then they're all going to come back to Us. [40]

Abraham and His Father

*M*ention in the Book (something about) Abraham, for he was an honest man and a prophet. [41] He said to his father:

"My father! Why are you worshipping things that can neither hear nor see nor bring you any benefit at all? [42] My father! Some teachings have come to me that haven't reached you, so follow me, and I'll guide you to an even path. [43] My father! Don't be in the service of Satan, for Satan is a rebel against the Compassionate. [44] My father! I'm afraid that a punishment might befall you from the Compassionate that might cause you to be included among Satan's allies." [1073] [45]

"Are you talking against my gods?" (his father) demanded. *"Abraham! If you don't back off, then I'll stone you! Now get yourself away from me!"* [46]

"So peace (and good bye) to you then," (Abraham) answered. *"However, I'm still*

---

word that He bestowed upon Mary and a spirit from Him, and that Paradise and Hell are both real, then Allah will admit him into Paradise regardless of anything else they did." (*Bukhari, Muslim*)

[1070] John 14:12 and 24 quotes Jesus as saying people must obey what he (Jesus) is telling them to do, and if they don't listen to and implement his sayings, then they are not of him. Thus, the words of a true prophet. John 12:49 clearly lays out how Jesus thought of himself: "For I have not spoken of myself; but the Father which sent me, He gave me a commandment, what I should say, and what I should speak." (KJV) Can anyone read this, and numerous others sayings attributed to Jesus, and come away with any other conclusion than that he, himself, felt subordinate to God?

[1071] Muslims must believe in Jesus, but they must also hold the line against turning him into another god alongside of God. Christians were divided as to the nature of Jesus in the first four centuries of their religious movement, with different groups holding different opinions about his nature. Unfortunately, the most successful group was the Trinitarian party (three gods in one), whereas the Unitarians (who believed that Jesus was not Allah) and the Gnostics (who were like Christian Sufis) lost the battle. Christians today say that the Trinitarians won because it was planned so by God. This is a shaky position upon which to base the crux of their entire movement, for then anything can be attributed to God, even idol-worship, which the pagans offered as proof of God's will for them! Trinitarianism prevailed because it was adopted by literate Greeks and Romans who had the will and power both to propagate their views widely and to suppress those who differed with them. The Unitarians, who were mostly concentrated in North Africa and the Middle East (Jesus' home turf), were weaker, less organized, less literate and had no imperial power to back up their views. When Islam came many centuries later, the bulk of the Unitarian Christians, tiring of persecution from Trinitarian Europe, gradually (and freely) converted to Islam over the course of two hundred years.

[1072] The Prophet said that on Judgment Day, the very institution of death will be given the shape of a black and white ram. Then Allah will call the attention of both the saved and the damned to it, and the ram will be slaughtered. (In other words, death will be dead and no one will ever die again.) Then an angel will say to everyone, "People of Paradise! Forever for you and no more dying. People of Hell! Forever for you and no more dying." Then the Prophet recited this verse [19:39] for emphasis. (*Bukhari*)

[1073] In other words, he was afraid that his father might die while being a sinner and that in the next life he would be grouped with the followers of Satan.

going to pray to my Lord for your forgiveness, because He's always been kind to me." [1074] [47]

"Now I'm going to turn away from you and from those whom you call upon besides Allah. All I can do is call upon my Lord and hope my prayer to my Lord doesn't go unanswered." [48]

And so he turned away from (his people) and from those (false gods) that they worshipped besides Allah. (In time), We granted him Isaac and then Jacob, and We made each one a prophet. [49]

We granted Our mercy to them and gave them high honors that are (still spoken of by the) honest tongues (of those in later generations). [50]

Other Prophets also had their Commission from Allah

$\mathcal{M}$ention in the Book (something about) Moses, for he was selected (by Allah) and was both a messenger and a prophet. [51] We called out to him from the right side of the mountain and brought him close to Us for an intimate conversation. [52]

Out of Our mercy, We granted (him the help of) his brother Aaron, and he was made a prophet (alongside of him). [1075] [53]

Also mention in the Book (something about) Ishmael, for he was true to his word, and he was a messenger and also a prophet. [1076] [54]

He used to order his people to pray and to give in charity, and his Lord was pleased with him. [55] Mention further in the Book (something about) Idrís. [1077] He was an honest man and a prophet [56] whom We exalted to a high place. [1078] [57]

Those were some of the prophets from Adam's offspring who were favored by Allah. (Some of them were descended) from those whom We carried (in the boat) with Noah, and some of them (were descended) from Abraham and from

---

[1074] See 9:113-114 where the result of this prayer is discussed.

[1075] Moses was apprehensive about possibly stuttering in front of Pharaoh, so out of His mercy Allah elevated his more eloquent older brother Aaron to prophethood to reassure him and strengthen him. See 28:34.

[1076] Generally, a messenger is the next level in status above a prophet. A messenger has all the abilities of a prophet, such as prophecy and leadership capacity, along with the added benefit of getting some type of codified scripture or body of organized teachings. Of course, Abraham still had contact with his son Ishmael even after he set him and his mother in the wilderness of central and northern Arabia (see Genesis 25:9), so what then was the message of Ishmael? Consider the many customs from time immemorial that were practiced by the Arabs of northern and central Arabia. Many of the rituals of the pilgrimage to Mecca predated Muhammad's mission by millennia, and the pagan Arabs still had some ideas about angels, the Supreme God and some legends from the days of Ishmael. Thus, something of his message survived, though it had been horribly mutated by the time of Muhammad's mission.

[1077] Some early commentators, have held that Idrís is the same person as the Biblical Enoch mentioned in Genesis 5:21. Early Islamic scholars have also said that he is synonymous with Hermes Trismegistus, a mythological composite of an ancient Greek philosopher and the Egyptian god Thoth whose purported scripture is the 'Emerald Tablet.' Some others have suggested that Idrís could have been a prophet completely out of the Biblical sphere of influence, from any known land, from anywhere in the world. So who was he? Speculation can go in any direction, so the most logical position is to assert that he was one of the ancient prophets with whom Allah was pleased, and his exact identity may have been lost to us. His name, itself, is related to the Arabic verb, *darasa*, which simply means *to study or teach*. Thus, Idrís was a purveyor of knowledge or someone who taught. Muhammad said, "Idrís was the first person who made a pen and used it to write." The world's first writing instrument that is in the form of what we would call a pen was a simple reed, the use of which was first invented in the fourth millennium BCE in the vicinity of Egypt. Therefore, this early prophet was from extremely ancient days and most assuredly outside of the Hebrew tradition!

[1078] During his night journey to Jerusalem and subsequent ascension to Heaven, Prophet Muhammad saw Idrís in the fourth level of Paradise.

Israel. [1079] They were among those whom We guided and selected. Whenever verses (revealed from) the Compassionate were recited to them, they would bow down prostrate in tears. [1080] [58]

After them came generations (of people) who missed their prayers [1081] and followed their own whims. Soon enough they're going to be lost in disillusion, [59] but that's not the case with those who repent and believe and who do what's morally right.

They're going to enter the Garden, and they won't be wronged in the least. [60] (For them) are gardens of delight - the same ones that the Compassionate promised to His servants in the realm beyond human perception. His promise will surely come to pass! [61]

They'll hear no useless chatter (in Paradise), but rather the greetings of peace. They'll have whatever they need there for their survival every morning and evening. [62]

That's what the Garden will be like, and that's the place We're going to give as an inheritance to those servants of Ours who were mindful (of their duty to Allah). [63]

The Statement of the Angels

(Angel Gabriel told Muhammad),

[1082] *"We don't descend (down to the earth) without your Lord's command. Whatever is in front of us and behind us and all things in between belong to Him, and your Lord never forgets* [1083] [64] *- the Lord of the heavens and the earth and everything in between! So serve Him, and be constant in your service to Him! Do you know of any other who can be named (as an equal) with Him?"* [65]

The Bridge over Hellfire

The human being says, *"So then when I'm dead, am I really going to be raised back to life again?"* [1084] [66] Doesn't the human being recall that We created him from nothing already once before? [67]

By your Lord, We're certainly going to gather them back together, along with all the devilish (jinns). Then We'll bring them forward on their knees and gather them all around Hellfire. [68] We'll then drag out from every faction all those who were the most rebellious against the Compassionate. [69] *We know best who deserves to be burnt in (the fire)!* [70]

[1079] *Israel* was a nickname for Jacob, Abraham's grandson.

[1080] After reading this verse, it is customary for the one who has faith in Allah to prostrate himself on the floor and praise Allah.

[1081] The Prophet said, "May Allah have mercy upon the man who gets up at night to pray and awakens his wife. If she refuses to get up, he sprinkles water on her face. May Allah have mercy upon the woman who gets up at night to pray and awakens her husband. If he refuses to get up, she sprinkles water on his face." (*Abu Dawud, Ibn Majah*)

[1082] When the pagans were asking the Prophet questions about the Companions of the Cave, the Master of the Two Horns and other topics, the Prophet said that he would answer them the next day, but he failed to say, "As Allah wills", (hence the reminder in 18:23-24). A full fifteen days passed, during which the pagans began taunting the Prophet for his lack of response from Allah to their questions. When Gabriel finally did go to the Prophet with the new revelations of most of chapter 18, the Prophet expressed his gratitude at finally seeing him. He also asked why he didn't come sooner. This passage here was revealed to him to explain that the angels only go where they are commanded and serve at Allah's pleasure – not at the pleasure of a mere human being. (*Asbab ul-Nuzul*)

[1083] The majority of commentators explain that this refers to the beginning of time, the end of time and everything in between.

[1084] This passage was revealed in response to Ubayy ibn Khalaf, a pagan leader who picked up an old bone in his hand and said, "Muhammad is pretending that we're going to be raised up after death!" (*Asbab ul-Nuzul*)

There's not one among you except that you're going to have to pass over (the bridge that spans over Hellfire). [1085] This is an outcome that your Lord will bring about, [71] but We're going to save those who were mindful (of their Lord), even as We're going to leave the wrongdoers on their knees. [1086] [72]

Allah Gives Us All a Chance

*W*hen Our clear verses are recited to them, the (well-to-do among) the faithless say to the (common) believers, *"Which of these two sides is in a better position? Which group seems more impressive in the public forum?"* [1087] [73]

Yet, how many generations before them have We destroyed who were better equipped and more impressive in their appearance (than they)? [74]

Say to them, *"If anyone goes astray, the Compassionate will hold out (the rope of salvation) to them, up until the point they see the promised (penalty of Allah coming to pass), whether it be the punishment (of destruction) or the coming of the*

Hour. Then they're going to realize who it was that was in the worst position and who it was that had the weakest influence (among men)!" [75]

Allah increases the guidance of those who seek to be guided. Moral deeds that endure are the best in your Lord's sight for repayment and the best for profitable returns. [76]

Allah Records Everything

*H*ave you seen the type (of person) who rejects Our (revealed) verses; yet, he has (the audacity) to say, *"I'm certainly going to be blessed with abundant wealth and children."* [1088] [77]

Has he peered into what's beyond human perception or made a deal with the Compassionate? [78] Absolutely not! For We're going to record what he's said, and We're going to increase his allotted share of punishment! [79] Everything that he's said will come back to Us, and he's going to appear before Us bare and alone. [80]

They've taken other gods in place of Allah and expect to get power (from

---

[1085] This refers to a razor thin bridge that spans the chasm of Hellfire. All people will be made to approach this bridge after the judging by Allah is completed. The wicked will get snagged on jagged edges straightaway and tumble in (or be pushed in by the angels if they were particularly bad), while those who are destined for Paradise will pass over it (with some being cut along the way as payback for some sins). This bridge is called the *sirat*.

[1086] There will be some people who fall off the bridge and tumble into Hellfire, perhaps due to some unfulfilled oath, even though they were believers. (*Bukhari, Muslim*) After they've served their sentence, the angels will enter Hellfire and look for them, only recognizing them by the marks of ablution on their bodies that the Fire is not allowed to burn off. They will be removed from Hellfire, then reformed anew in perfect bodies and will thus enter Paradise fully cleansed of their shortcomings. The Prophet remarked that even if someone has faith in their hearts equal to a mustard seed, they will be eventually taken out of Hellfire. Hell is forever only for certain categories of hopelessly wicked people, such as brazen hypocrites, the most morally depraved wrongdoers, the open enemies of Allah and His prophets and those who never gave up idolatry, even though they heard or felt that there might be something wrong with it.

[1087] These verses echo the common Meccan objection to the Prophet's preaching. Muhammad was attracting converts mostly from the lower classes in society, and the wealthy Meccan leaders mocked this trend, pointing out that they dressed better and looked more refined due to their affluence.

[1088] A follower of the Prophet named Khabab ibn al-Aratt, who was a blacksmith, went to a pagan named Al-As ibn Wa'il to collect payment for a sword he had made for him, but Ibn Wa'il refused to pay him what he owed unless Khabab renounced his faith in the Prophet first. Khabab refused, saying he would never do that even until the day Ibn Wa'il died and was raised to life again. Ibn Wa'il then asked Khabab if he really believed that there would be a heaven filled with gold and silver after death. When Khabab nodded in the affirmative, Ibn Wa'il then boasted, "And so after I've been brought back to life and been given wealth and children, then I'll repay you your money!" This passage was revealed in comment on this episode. (*Bukhari, Muslim*)

them)? [81] Absolutely not! Those (false gods) are going to reject the service they offer to them, and they're going to be their opponents (on the Day of Judgment)! [82]

Haven't you seen how We've riled up the devils against the faithless to make them furious with anger? [83] So don't be in a hurry against them, for We're merely counting down (the days they have left before We punish them). [84]

One day We're going to gather the righteous before the Compassionate like an honored delegation, [85] even as We're going to drive the wicked into Hellfire like a thirsty herd (of cattle) being driven to a well. [86]

No one will have any power to intercede, except for the one who has permission from the Compassionate. [87]

Ascribing Children to Allah

They're claiming that the Compassionate has taken a son! [88] They've uttered an outrageous statement! [89] It's as if the skies are ready to explode, as if the earth is ready to crack apart, as if the mountains are ready to crumble to pieces [90] that they should call for the Compassionate to take a son! [91] It's not conceivable for the Compassionate to take a son! [92]

There isn't a single being in the heavens nor on the earth except that it must come as a (humble) servant to the Compassionate. [1089] [93] He's counted them and numbered them all precisely! [94] Each one of them will come before Him alone on the Day of Assembly, [95] and He'll bestow His love upon those who believed and did what was morally right. [1090] [96]

Thus, We've made (this Qur'an) easy on your tongue, so you can use it to give good news to those who are mindful (of their duty to Allah), as well as warn those people who are given to senseless opposition. [1091] [97]

How many generations before them have We destroyed? Can you find a single one of them (still surviving) or hear so much as a whisper from them? [98]

[1089] Islam is a way of life based on faith and good conduct, though faith is more important, and good conduct is not sufficient to enter Paradise. The Prophet said, "None of you will enter Paradise by their good deeds alone, nor will you be rescued from Hellfire, not even myself, save for the Mercy of Allah." (*Muslim*) So faith is more important than works, though works are a proof of faith, as the Qur'an emphasizes. The old phrase, "Put your money where your mouth is," exists for a reason.

[1090] The Prophet said that Allah, Himself, said, "My servant draws closer to Me through the religious duties I placed upon him. My servant then continues to draw closer to Me with voluntary (good actions) until I love him. When I love him, I become his ears that he uses to hear, his eyes that he uses to see, his hand that he uses to strike and his foot that he uses for walking. If he then asks Me for anything, I would surely grant it to him, and when he asks for My protection, I will surely give it to him. I don't hesitate in anything I have to do as much as I hesitate in taking the life of My believing servant. He hates death, and I hate to hurt him." (*Hadith Qudsi*)

[1091] Some critics of Islam argue for no other reason than out of a desire to confuse others. For example, there are those critics of Islam who spend a great amount of time trying to "prove" that the God of the Qur'an is not the same God as in the Judeo-Christian tradition. (They assert that "Allah" is an Arabian moon goddess and other such nonsense!) It's a futile point, however, for the Qur'an says that Allah is the same monotheistic and unseen God that spoke to Abraham, Moses and Jesus. It even argues tirelessly against idol-worship, anthropomorphism and such. Still these critics try to tie people up in circles over a moot point to keep them from ever delving into the real heart of Islamic teachings. (*Allah* is merely the Arabic word for *God*, like *Dios* is the Spanish word for *God*, whose origin is from the old name *Zeus*, and Arabic speaking Christians say 'Allah,' even as translations of the Bible into Arabic use 'Allah' for God.) Talking in circles does nothing more than confuse the ones doing the talking, thus carrying them farther and farther away from ever understanding the truth! Let such critics tackle the question of whether the God of Judaism and the God of Christianity are the same! The theologies are completely opposed to each other to an even greater degree than the ideology of Islam! (Even the Hebrew word for God is *Elah*, which is linguistically the same word as *Allah*!)

Ta Ha

20 Ta Ha
Middle Meccan Period

This chapter was revealed in approximately the year 615. This was near the time of the migration of over eighty Muslim refugees to Abyssinia. They were desperate people who sought protection from the violent Meccan persecution. The city of Mecca was so torn by upheaval with the introduction of Islam that one pagan named 'Umar ibn al-Khattab decided to end the problem once and for all. He vowed to his fellows that he would go and kill the Prophet right away.

Accordingly, he drew his sword and stormed through the streets of Mecca, looking for Muhammad. As he passed by one street, an acquaintance of his named Nu'aym saw him and asked him what he was going to do. When 'Umar mentioned his grim purpose, Nu'aym told him, "You should look to your own first, for your own sister and brother-in-law have embraced Islam." 'Umar became enraged, and he set off towards his sister's house in a fuss.

When he arrived, he heard some chanting coming from inside the front door. He burst inside and found one of Muhammad's followers, Khabab ibn al-Arat, sitting with 'Umar's sister Fatimah and her husband Sa'eed. Fatimah was holding a leather scroll. She tried to hide it, but 'Umar had already heard them reading from it, and he started shouting at them. Khabab ran into another room to hide (for 'Umar was something of a tough and fearsome man), while 'Umar began beating Sa'eed.

Fatimah rushed to shield her husband, and 'Umar swung his fist at her in his madness and struck her across the face, causing her to bleed. 'Umar froze when he saw his sister on the floor in pain, and he surveyed the scene of destruction he had just caused with his own hands. He cooled down and asked Fatimah for the scroll. She made him promise not to tear it up, and then she asked him to go home and take a quick bath before she would let him touch it.

When he returned, he read the scroll, which contained chapter 20 of the Qur'an. After reading only a few lines, he exclaimed, "This is something amazing." Khabab came out of hiding (for he had hidden again when he heard 'Umar returning), and said, "By Allah, I have high expectations that Allah will get great service from you to propagate the message of His Prophet, for just yesterday I heard the Prophet praying to Allah saying, 'My Lord, make Abul Hikam ibn Hisham (Abu Jahl) or 'Umar ibn al-Khattab a supporter of Islam.' In that case then, 'Umar, you should turn to Allah. Turn to Allah!"

'Umar was persuaded by these words, and he immediately accompanied Khabab to see the Prophet, and there 'Umar embraced the faith.

Ţā. Hā. [1092] [1]

We didn't send this Qur'an down to you in order to give you a hard time, [2] but only as a reminder for those who fear (Allah). [3] It's a revelation from the One Who created the earth and the heavens on high. [4]

The Compassionate [1093] is firmly set upon the throne (of power), [1094] [5] and to Him belongs whatever is in the heavens, whatever is on the earth, as well as everything in between and even under the ground! [6]

(It doesn't matter) if you talk out loud (or keep your thoughts to yourself), for He knows every secret - *even what's concealed (in your hearts!)* [7] Allah! There is no god but He! The most beautiful names belong to Him! [8]

The Story of Moses

*H*as the story of Moses reached you? [9] He saw a fire (in the distance) and said to his family, *"Wait here for I see a fire. Maybe I can bring you back a burning branch or perhaps find some kind of useful news."* [1095] [10]

When he went to the fire, a voice called out (to him, saying), *"Moses!* [11] *I am your Lord! Remove your shoes, for you're in the valley twice sanctified.* [12] *I have indeed chosen you, so listen to the inspiration."* [13]

"I am Allah. There is no other god than I, so serve Me (alone) and establish prayer, so you can remember Me." [14]

"The Hour (of Judgment) is coming, though I plan to make its (arrival) obscure, so that every soul can be repaid according to what it has earned. [15] *Don't let those who have no faith in it, who merely follow their own whims, steer you away from it, or you'll be ruined."* [16] *Now, Moses, what's that in your right hand?"* [17]

"It's my staff," (Moses) replied, *"and I use it to lean on and to beat down fodder for my flocks to eat, and it has other uses, as well."* [18]

"Throw it down!" (Allah) commanded. [19]

When (Moses) threw it (on the ground, suddenly) it became a slithering serpent!

[1092] The pagans used to tease the Muslim converts about their frequent prayers – even into the late night – saying that the Qur'an only brought them hardship and difficulty. This passage was revealed to answer this taunt. (*Ma'ariful Qur'an*)

[1093] *Ar-Rahman* is a frequently used attribute and name of Allah in the Qur'an. The Prophet explained the significance of this name, which when translated means '*The Compassionate.*' He said that Allah, himself, said, "I am the Compassionate (*ar-Rahman*). I created the womb (*raham*) and derived My Own Name out of it. Thus, whoever keeps relations with it, I will keep relations with him, while whoever severs it, I will sever ties with him." (*Tirmidhi*) Therefore, the believers don't sever their ties with their families, especially their mothers.

[1094] What does it mean that God is sitting on a 'throne?' Since Islam is very strict about not ascribing to the Divine human qualities, such as sitting down somewhere, this verse was the subject of much debate in the early days of *tafseer* development. Some traditional commentators held that the Lord indeed has some type of Throne, but we do not know what it is, whereas others, particularly those identified as 'Rationalists' or *Mu'tazili*, have suggested that the Arabic term '*arsh* is figurative only and is meant for people to understand that God is in control, using the imagery of a throne, for that is how we understand the position of leadership. In later centuries, a compromise position was reached between the Traditionalists and Rationalists which basically said that "the servant knows that, just as God the Lord says, He alone sits on the throne, how this is we do not know, for more than this He did not say." (*Hadaddi, Tafseer-i Munir*)

[1095] Keeping in mind the life of nomadic people, a lifestyle which Moses was living at the time, when a fire is seen in the distance, it means the possibility of meeting others and either learning some news (*lit.* guidance) or at the very least getting a burning branch to light one's own campfire more easily.

[20] *"Now pick it up,"* (Allah) commanded, *"and don't be afraid, for We're going to transform it back to what it was before.* [21] *Now place your hand in your shirt. It will come away (glowing) white, though causing no pain. (This is) a further token (of Our power) that We're showing to you,* [22] *so We can show you (two of) Our mighty miracles.* [23] *Now go to Pharaoh, for he's (a tyrant who's) out of control."* [24]

Moses Makes a Request

"$\mathcal{I}$*ncrease me in my intelligence,"* (Moses) prayed. [25] *"Make my task easy for me,* [1096] [26] *and remove the stutter from my speech,* [27] *so they can understand what I'm saying to them.* [28] *Give me an assistant from my family* [29] *– my brother Aaron -* [30] *and strengthen my resolve through him.* [31] *Let him share in my task,* [32] *so we can glorify You often* [33] *and remember You often,* [34] *for You're the One Who watches over us."* [35]

"So that's how it will be, Moses, just as you've requested," (Allah) replied. [36] *"We were already favorable to you, even before this,* [37] *when We directed your mother with inspiration,* [1097] *(saying,)* [38] *'Put (your baby) in the box, and drop it in the river. The river will deposit him on the shore, and he'll be found by someone who is an enemy to both him and Me.' I covered you in love from Myself so you could be raised under My watchful eye."* [39]

"Then your sister went forward and said (to the people of Pharaoh's house), 'Would you like me to show you someone who can nurse him?' [1098] *Thus, We returned you back to your mother, so that her (anxious) eye might be cooled, and also so she wouldn't be stricken with grief. Then, you later*

killed a man, [1099] *but We saved you from distress, and then We tested you in many different ways. You stayed a number of years with the people of Madyan, and finally you arrived here as you were supposed to, Moses."* [40]

"And so have I prepared you for My Own (service). [41] *So go now, you and your brother, with My miraculous signs. Never falter in your remembrance of Me.* [42] *Go to Pharaoh, for he's (a tyrant who's) gone out of control.* [43] *Speak mildly to him, however, for he might heed the reminder or fear (Allah)."* [44]

In the Land of the Pharaohs

($\mathcal{J}$ust before they met with the pharaoh, Moses and Aaron prayed), *"Our Lord! We're afraid that he might mistreat us or that he might get out of control!"* [45]

"Don't be afraid," (Allah) replied to them, *"for I'm with you, and I hear and see (everything).* [46] *Go before him and say, 'We are indeed messengers sent by your Lord, so release the Children of Israel to us, and oppress them no further. We've come here before you with proof from your Lord. Peace be upon the one who follows (His) guidance.* [47] *Truly, it's been revealed to us that punishment will befall all those who deny (their Lord) and turn away.'"* [48]

(When they said these things to Pharaoh), he asked, *"Moses! Who is this Lord of yours?"* [1100] [49]

[1096] The Prophet said, "Religion is very easy, and whoever overburdens himself in it will not be able to continue in that way. So you should try not to be extremists but try to be near to perfection and accept these good tidings that you may be rewarded. Gain strength by worshiping in the mornings, afternoons and during the last hours of the night." (*Bukhari*)

[1097] Two women are mentioned in the Qur'an as receiving communication from Allah. Although they are not considered prophets, it does advance the point of view that Allah has communicated to both males and females, as exemplified in His communications with Mary, the mother of Jesus, and here with the mother of Moses.

[1098] The new found baby wouldn't take milk from any of the palace nursemaids, and Pharaoh's wife was afraid the baby would die. It was then that Moses' sister Miriam sent word to the palace servants (that she might know) of a good nursemaid who was in need of employment.

[1099] See 28:15-21 for this incident.

[1100] The plural form of 'yours' is used here in the Arabic text to include Aaron in the address of Pharaoh.

"*Our Lord,*" (Moses) replied, "*is the One Who gave everything its basic nature and then guides (all things to their ultimate end).*" [1101] [50]

"*So what about (our) previous generations (who didn't serve your Lord alone)?*" [1102] (Pharaoh) asked. [51]

"*That knowledge is recorded in my Lord's presence,*" (Moses) answered, "*and my Lord never makes a mistake, nor does He forget.* [52] *He's the One Who spread the earth out wide for you. He opened roads for you upon it, and He sends water down from the sky.*"

As a General Comment for All

(Know then, all you people), that We use that (very same water) to produce every kind of diverse vegetation (which you find so useful). [53] So eat (of those plants as you like), and pasture your herd animals, also, and there are signs in this for people of reason. [1103] [54]

We created you from (the earth), and We will surely return you to it; then We shall draw you out from it once again (at the resurrection)! [55]

Pharaoh Reacts

And so it was that We showed each of Our miracles to Pharaoh, but he denied them all and refused (to believe). [56]

"*Moses!*" he said. "*Have you come to drive us away from our land with your magic?* [57] *(If so), then we can produce magic that will match yours! Let's schedule a match between us, and it will be binding upon us both to attend. We'll even hold it on neutral ground.*" [58]

"*The date of your match, then, will be during the great festival,*" (Moses) answered, "*so*

[1101] Being well aware of Egyptian religious beliefs, Moses took the issue directly to the heart of the matter by asserting that the 'unseen' Allah is the One Who began creation and guided it to fruition, and not the idols decorating the temples of the land. Indeed, in the pantheon of gods of ancient Egypt, there was, in fact, an all-powerful god who was considered to be the hidden force behind all of creation. This deity, known as Âmen, was an ancient god - even in the days of Moses - and Egyptologists believe that knowledge of this deity was handed down from the most ancient of days preceding the formation of Egyptian civilization proper. In hieroglyphic texts, Âmen is described as "hidden," "unseen," "the creator of all things," "of unknown form," "the one who speaks and things come into being" and other such epithets which clearly point the way, as far as the Islamic theory of the corruption of religion over time goes, to the probability that Âmen is the name of God for the Egyptians of the most ancient days. Following this line of reasoning, even as the Arabs after the time of Abraham added idols, a wife, children and other false attributes to God, the Egyptians did so likewise. Given that Islam teaches that prophets were sent to all nations in antiquity, it is not preposterous to assume that Moses called to the original unseen god of the Egyptians to make the point that they were steeped in an idolatry of their own making that has nothing to do with the ultimate and ancient truths of the unseen God of all the worlds.
[1102] At the time of Moses, Egyptian civilization was already old, with many previous dynasties having already passed away. Pharaoh, who was being confronted by an upstart Hebrew, must have mused over the longstanding line of pharaohs that preceded him and how this line of continuity seemed more concrete to rely upon than the words of a man who was raised as an orphan child in his own palace. He also was questioning the fate of those previous generations, for Egyptians believed that the dead continued to live in an afterlife that was something of a mirror image of this life. If Moses was claiming that Egyptian gods were false and that there was only One True God, then what happened to all the rulers of the past? Did they have some other fate in the afterlife than they had expected?
[1103] Humans eat plant foods such as vegetables and grains but cannot eat most of the grasses that herd animals do. However, humans can eat the meat that was grown from those inedible plants and that was deposited on the frames of so many types of domesticated and wild animals. Is there not a miraculous sign in this from the Creator?

gather the public (there) after the sun has risen." [1104] [59]

Then Pharaoh withdrew (for private consultations with his advisors). He gathered together the details of his plan, and then he returned (to address Moses). [60]

"You're doomed!" Moses said to them, *"Don't craft a lie against Allah, or He might destroy you completely with (His) punishment, for the one who crafts (a secret plan against Allah) will fail in frustration."* [61]

So the (pharaoh and his nobles) argued over what they had been arranging, but they kept their discussions a secret. [1105] [62]

(Pharaoh's nobles) said, *"These two are just sorcerers. Their goal is to drive you out of your land with their magic and also to abolish your honored traditions.* [1106] [63] *So finalize your plan, and assemble (your people) in rows (to watch). Whoever wins that day will have the advantage."* [64]

The Great Showdown

When the appointed day arrived, Pharaoh's sorcerers) said, *"Moses! Will you cast (your spell) first, or should we be the first to cast?"* [65]

"No!" (Moses) replied. *"You cast first!"* Then, after (they had cast down) their ropes and rods, it seemed to him that, due

to their magic, they really had come to life! [66] Moses began to feel afraid inside himself. [67]

"Don't be afraid," We said, *"for you have the advantage!* [68] *Throw down what's in your right hand, and it will quickly swallow up all that they've faked.* [1107] *What they've faked is nothing more than a sorcerer's trick, and a sorcerer is never successful anywhere he goes."* [69]

Then the sorcerers fell down prostrate (in wonder), saying, *"We believe in the Lord of Aaron and Moses!"* [70]

"Are you believing in him without my permission!" (Pharaoh) exclaimed. *"He must have been your leader all along! (He's) the one who taught you your magic! I'll order your hands and feet to be cut off on opposite sides, and then I'll hang you on tree trunks. That way, you'll know for certain who it is that can give a more brutal and conclusive punishment!"* [71]

"We'll never hold you as more important than the evident proofs that have come to us, nor will you ever be more important (to us) than the One Who originated us," they cried. *"Order whatever you want to order, for your orders can only affect what's part of the life of this world.* [72] *As for us, we now believe in our Lord, and we (hope) He forgives us for our mistakes and for the magic that you made us do. Allah is far better (than you) and more lasting."* [73]

Indeed, whoever comes before his Lord in a state of wickedness will have Hellfire, within which he'll neither die nor live. [1108] [74] The one who comes to Him

---

[1104] The Egyptians, being a very religious people, had numerous festivals and solemn ceremonies throughout the year, both to honor their gods and celebrate the harvests.

[1105] Being a prophet has its advantages. Moses was intuitive enough to realize that Pharaoh and his officials were concocting a plan. He warned them not to try and put one over on Allah, for Allah would then punish them.

[1106] The ancient Egyptians believed that a balance had to be maintained between heaven and earth, and this delicate balance was embodied by the goddess *Mott*. If imbalance came due to a lack of devotion to the ancient rituals of Egyptian religion, then disaster would strike the land. Thus, the officials were appealing to Pharaoh with the greatest thing in their belief system: these two foreign men want to upset the balance of all things by abolishing our way of life!

[1107] The serpent that Moses produced swallowed up all the wiggling ropes and sticks of the court magicians.

[1108] The Prophet said, "The people of Hellfire – the ones who deserve it – will not die in it, nor will they be alive. Instead, they'll be people who will be justly punished by the Fire for their sins. It will only gradually kill them and devour them until they become like burnt charcoal. Then intercession will be allowed. They will be brought out (of Hellfire) group by group, and they'll be spread upon the

as a believer, however, and who did what was morally right – they're the ones who will be ranked highly! [75] For them are everlasting gardens beneath which rivers flow, and there they shall remain. That's the reward of those who kept themselves pure! [76]

The Escape from Egypt

*A*nd so it was that We sent a revelation to Moses that said, *"Travel by night with My servants, and strike a dry path for them through the sea. Have no fear of being overtaken (by Pharaoh's army), and don't be terrified (of him), either."* [77]

Then Pharaoh pursued them with his forces, but they were completely overwhelmed and smothered under the sea. [1109] [78] Thus, Pharaoh led his people astray instead of guiding them. [79]

Children of Israel! We saved you from your enemy and made an agreement with you on the right side of the mountain. We even sent manna and quails for you (to help you survive your flight from Egypt). [80] So eat of the wholesome things that We've provided for you.

Don't go beyond (what you've been allowed), or My condemnation might befall you. Whoever has My condemnation descend upon him, thus shall he perish! [81] Even still, I forgive anyone who repents, believes, behaves morally and then accepts guidance. [82]

The Plot of the Storyteller

*"W*hat made you hurry back here (to the mountain) ahead of the rest of your people, Moses?"* (Allah asked). [1110] [83]

"They're following in my tracks," (Moses) replied. *"I only hurried back to You, My Lord, to please You."* [84]

"We have given your people a test in your absence," [1111] (Allah) said, *"and the Storyteller* [1112] *has led them astray."* [85]

---

rivers of Paradise. Then it will be said, 'People of Paradise! Pour (water) over them.' Then they'll start to regenerate like a seed growing on the muddy banks of a flowing river." A man listening nearby said of the Prophet and how he described the scene, "It's like the Messenger of Allah had lived in the desert (and been as eloquent a narrator as the desert folk)." (*Ahmad*)

[1109] See Exodus 15:1-21 where the Hebrews are shown celebrating just after Pharaoh and his legions were drowned.

[1110] Moses left his people encamped near the sacred mountain, which was located somewhere in northwestern Arabia. Then he went up the slopes alone for forty days to commune with Allah.

[1111] Exodus chapter 32 mentions this story, though with significant differences from the Qur'anic rendition.

[1112] Who was the Storyteller, or *as-Saamiri* mentioned here? To begin, the term *saamiri* is probably not being used here, as some people claim, as a reference to a person from Samaria, (i.e., a *Samaritan*,) which was a later territory near historical Israel. (Though Jewish sources point out that the term for *samaritan* used in the Bible in II Kings 17 is actually a title for a religious group among Jews (*shomronim*) that predates the actual founding of Samaria - and even Moses. See entry for *samaritan* in the Encyclopaedia Judaica.) The Qur'an generally refrains from assigning a title to a person based solely on his country of origin, and it is highly unlikely that obscure place names in Palestine were known to most Meccans, who did most of their travels in Syria and Iraq. When we look into the actual meaning of the Arabic term *saamiri* we must first look at its root which is *samara*. From this root, a variety of meanings are formed, including the terms *brown*, *pleasant nightly chat*, *to be nailed down*, *entertainer* and *teller of fictitious tales*. It can also mean a *watcher* or *lookout*. The actual designation of *saamir*, according to the common Arabic usage, is conversationalist, storyteller or entertainer, and this is what the unnamed man in this verse engaged in. (Verse 23:67 uses the exact same word in a slightly different grammatical form for the same purpose.) The tenth-century scholar, Muhammad ibn Is-haq ibn al-Nadim, using the definition of *saamir* in the same way, noted that the fictitious tales of a storyteller (*al-asmar*) are fit only for nightly entertainment! (From *al-Fihrist*) Do we know the name or true identity of this Storyteller? Many commentators, going back to Ibn 'Abbas (d. 687), have held that he was either an Egyptian (who followed Moses out of Egypt) or he was a Hebrew who had been

Then Moses angrily returned to his people and said, *"My people! Didn't your Lord make a good enough promise to you? Did you think the promise wouldn't be fulfilled for a long time? Were you looking for your Lord's wrath to come down upon you? Is that why you broke your promise to me?"* [86]

"We didn't break our promise to you of our own accord," they answered. *"We were forced to carry the heavy ornaments of the nation (of Egypt when we left that land.* [1113] *It was for this reason that) we threw them in (the bonfire), and that's what the Storyteller suggested we do.* [87] *Then he brought out (of the fire) the image of a calf, and it seemed as if it were making a sound.* [1114] *It was then that (some people) said, 'This is your god and the god of Moses, but Moses has just forgotten.'"* [88]

Couldn't they see that (the statue) had no power to reply to any word (they spoke to it) and that it had no power to do them any harm or benefit? [89]

Aaron had already said to them before (they started worshipping it), *"My people! You're being tested in this (situation). Your Lord is Compassionate, so follow me and obey my orders!"* [90]

However, they replied to him, *"We're not going to give this (idol) up, and we'll keep on (worshipping) it until Moses comes back to us."* [91]

"Aaron!" (Moses) shouted, (when he returned). *"What stopped you from (opposing them) when you saw them going astray?* [92] *Were you disobeying my orders?"* [93]

"Son of my mother!" (Aaron) cried out. *"Don't grab me by my beard nor by my head! I was afraid that you might say to me, 'You caused a split among the Children of Israel and didn't respect my word.'"* [94]

(Moses turned towards the man who crafted the idol) and said, *"So, Storyteller, what (do you have to say) about yourself?"* [95]

"I saw (something) that they couldn't see," he replied. *"So I took a handful of the traces that the messenger left behind and tossed it in.* [1115] *That's what I felt that I should do."* [96]

"Get out of here!" (Moses) ordered. *"Your (curse) in this life is that (you'll be an outcast) and will have to say, 'Don't touch me,' (for you'll be stricken with an affliction).* [1116]

---

living completely according to Egyptian culture while the Hebrews were still in bondage. One classical commentator, al-Baydawi, even assigned a name to this man, calling him Musa ibn Zafar, though the source for this name is most probably spurious. When Moses was away receiving Allah's commands, the Storyteller convinced the Hebrews through his stories and persuasive arguments that they needed to make a god they could see – a god of gold!

[1113] Some scholars are of the opinion that in Moses' absence, the Hebrews debated whether it was right for them to take the property of the Egyptians. Aaron (or the Storyteller) ordered all the gold to be thrown in a pit, and they would await the return of Moses for a decision. The Storyteller then suggested to make the gold into an idol and somehow got the figure to make a sound, causing the people to think it was a real god. (*Ma'ariful Qur'an*) See Exodus 12:35 where the Hebrews "borrowed" the gold of Egypt as they left.

[1114] Ibn 'Abbas (d. 687) said that the sound came from wind passing through a hollow part of the idol, and the foolish people took it as the actual mooing of a calf. (*Ibn Kathir*) Such devices (idols with special noise-making holes for wind to pass through) were used in antiquity in later Egyptian and even some Greek temples.

[1115] There are two interpretations of this verse. The first is that the Storyteller tried to defend himself by saying that he mixed some traces of the teachings left behind by Moses with some ideas of his own and influenced people that way. Other commentators have explained this enigmatic verse by saying that the Storyteller took some dirt from a footprint, either left behind by Moses or an angel, and threw it on the golden cow, (dramatically, no doubt,) causing it to make a sound. The Arabic word used here is *athar*. It means many things, including relics, marks, tracks, teachings, reports, sources, influence and also exclusive knowledge, among a dozen other things. Only Allah knows which interpretation is right.

[1116] What was the sign of his being an outcast? Some have suggested that the Storyteller was stricken with leprosy. Others have suggested it was a self-imposed exile from social contact brought about by

Beyond that, you'll have the unbroken promise (of punishment in the next life waiting for you). Now look at your 'god,' the thing to which you've become a devoted worshipper. We're going to melt it in a bonfire and scatter its particles to oblivion!" [1117] [97]

Our Lives will Seem Like Nothing on that Day

*T*ruly, your only god is Allah, the One before Whom there are no other gods. He is expansive and fully aware of all things. [98] And so We've narrated to you some stories of what happened in days that have passed away. We've sent a message to you from Our Own presence. [99]

Whoever turns away from it will bear a heavy burden on the Day of Assembly. [100] They'll remain in that (condition), and their burden that day will be awful, indeed! [101]

On the day when the trumpet is blown, that day We'll gather the sinful, bleary-eyed (with fright). [102] They'll be whispering to one another, saying *"You stayed (in the world) no more than ten (days at the most)."* [103]

We will certainly know better (than they) what they're talking about, and then the best behaved among them will say, *"You stayed (on the earth) for no more than a day!"* [104]

Understand the Magnitude of Judgment Day

*N*ow they're asking you about the mountains - (will they really be crumbled to nothing)? Say to them, *"My Lord will pull them out from their roots and scatter them like dust,* [105] *leaving a smooth, level plain behind.* [1118] [106] *Nothing bumpy will you see, nor anything uneven remaining there."* [1119] [107]

On that day, (all people) will follow (the voice of) the caller without deviation. All noise will be hushed in the presence of the Compassionate, and you'll hear no more than the sounds of shuffling feet. [108]

On that day, no one's intercession will do any good, save for those who were given permission (to intercede) by the Compassionate, and whose speech is acceptable to Him. [109]

He knows what lies before them, as well as what lies behind them. Yet, they can't comprehend Him at all in their knowledge! [1120] [110]

Faces will be lowered in humility before (Him) – the Living, the Everlasting!

Whoever carries the burden of evil (on his back that day) will be in utter failure, [111] while the one who behaved morally and who believed will have no fear of

---

shame. Only Allah knows the truth of this matter, though it seems likely to me that since the Old Testament is full of examples of Allah throwing plagues on the people of Moses that this would be the most likely reason for the Storyteller to become an outcast.

[1117] Moses ordered the calf to be melted and pulverized. He forced some of the guilty people to drink water mixed with the powder of it. See 2:93 and footnote.

[1118] It's interesting that the Qur'an puts forward the notion that mountains have roots. This was not something that was known in the ancient world and is an accurate description of actual geologic structures found deep under mountain ranges and rooted in the activities of plate tectonics.

[1119] The Prophet said, "On the Day of Judgment, all people will be gathered on a white (featureless), flat land that looks just like a piece of wheat bread, for it will have no landmarks anyone can recognize." (*Bukhari, Muslim*)

[1120] The Prophet said, "The Exalted (Allah) will say, 'Bring out of the Fire anyone who has a seed's weight of faith in his heart.' So a large number of people will be brought out. Then He will say, 'Bring out of the Fire anyone who has half a seed's weight of faith in his heart. Bring out anyone who has the weight of a speck of dust's worth of faith in his heart. Bring out anyone who has the weight of an atom of faith in his heart.'" (*Bukhari*)

being wronged nor of having anything (due to him) withheld. [112]

And so We've revealed (this scripture) as an Arabic recital. We've mentioned within it some of what's been forewarned, so that perhaps they can be mindful (of Allah) - or at the least they can be reminded (of the truth)! [113]

Allah is high above all others – the Ruler, the Reality! [121] So don't be hasty with the Qur'an before its revelation is completed to you, (Muhammad). Rather, you should say, *"My Lord! Help me to know more!"* [122] [114]

The Fall of Adam

*A*nd so it was that We had made a covenant with Adam, but he was careless about it, and thus We found no firmness in his resolve. [115] When We said to the angels, *"Bow down to Adam,"* they all bowed down. However, (a jinn named) Iblis didn't bow down, for he refused. [123] [116]

Therefore, We (warned him,) saying, *"Adam! This is an enemy to both you and your wife, so don't let him get you thrown out of the garden, for then you'll be miserable.* [117] *There are enough (comforts) for you here to keep you from starving or feeling naked,* [118] *nor will you suffer from thirst or sunburn."* [119]

Then Satan whispered to him, saying, *"Adam! Should I lead you to a tree of eternity and to a kingdom that will never pass away?"* [120]

Then both (Adam and his wife) ate from it together, and the awareness of their nakedness came to their senses.

They began to sew leaves together from the garden to wear as clothes. Adam had disobeyed his Lord and let himself be deceived! [121]

Later on, his Lord chose him, turned to him (in forgiveness) and guided him. [122] He said, *"Both of you go down and away from here, though (your descendants will be) enemies of one another. However, if there ever comes any guidance from Me, (and it will surely come), whoever follows My guidance will never lose his way nor fall into misery.* [123] *Although, the one who turns away from My message will have a constricted life,* [124] *and We'll raise him up blind (to faith) on the Day of Assembly."* [124]

---

[121] Whenever the Prophet used to receive revelation, he used to try to memorize it as quickly as possible for fear of forgetting it. This verse is telling him to slow down and ask Allah to help him remember it. Also see 75:16-19.

[122] This short supplication (*"Rabbee zidni 'ilma."*) is popular among Muslims in their private devotions.

[123] This story (of the angels being made to bow down to Adam and Satan refusing to follow suit) was also known to the Jews and is contained in a section of ancient Jewish writings that are called the Old Testament Pseudepigrapha. The Midrashic literature, which was written by ancient rabbis to supplement Jewish teachings, also makes mention of these events. One piece of literature from these sources is entitled, "The Life of Adam and Eve." The Midrashic account reads as follows. "(How did) Adam the protoplast (do so)? The day when he was endowed with his knowledge, the Holy One, blessed be He, commanded the ministering angels: 'Enter and bow down to him!' The ministering angels entered to perform the will of the Holy One, blessed be He. (However,) Satan, who was the mightiest of all the angels in heaven, said to the Holy One, blessed be He, 'Master of the universe! You created us from the Divine Glory, and now You say to us, 'Bow yourselves down!' before one whom You created from the dirt of the earth??!?' The Holy One, blessed be He, answered him: 'This one who originates (from) the dirt of the earth possesses some wisdom and intelligence which is not in you!'" (Albeck H (ed.): *Midrash Bereshit Rabbati*. Jerusalem, Mekize Nirdamim, 1940.) In this story from the Midrash, Satan (or Iblis) is identified as an angel, while in the Qur'an he is labeled as a jinn.

[124] Despite whatever worldly success they achieve, their horizons will become narrower and narrower. No matter how rich and successful they become, their focus will literally be squeezed so that even wealth will no longer bring them joy and satisfaction – and they'll be unable to see anything beyond it. Oh, what a cursed way to live!

"My Lord!" he'll cry. *"Why have You raised me up blind (to faith) when I used to be able to recognize (things clearly)?"* [1125] [125]

"Wasn't it the case that whenever Our (revelations) came to you, that you ignored them? So today you're going to be ignored!" [126]

That's how We're going to compensate the one who went out of control and who didn't believe in the (revealed) verses of his Lord. *Yet, the punishment of the next life is even more serious and lasting!* [127]

Isn't it guidance enough for them to consider how many generations before them We destroyed and in whose ruins they now move about? There are signs in this for reasonable people. [128]

If it wasn't for the fact that their Lord (had already decreed) the verdict (that all nations will have a specific deadline, then their punishment) would've come upon them already. However, there is a set time limit. [129]

Prayer Strengthens Resolve

So be patient with what they're saying. Glorify the praises of your Lord before the rising of the sun, before it sets and during some hours of the night. Glorify (Him) at the two ends of the day, as well, so you can have (even more spiritual) satisfaction. [1126] [130]

Don't let your eyes gaze longingly at those (material goods) that We've given to some groups among them to enjoy, (for it's only) the splendor of this world through which We test them. The provisions that are with your Lord are better and more lasting. [1127] [131]

(Muhammad,) command your family to pray, and (ask them to) commit themselves to it. [1128] We're not asking you to procure any resources (for Us), for We're going to provide them to you, and the final destination is for the mindful. [132]

They may ask, *"So why isn't he bringing us some kind of miracle from his Lord?"* [1129] But

---

[1125] As the commentators explain, it is not their eyesight that will be blinded, but rather their capacity to understand and accept faith. (This is clarified in verse 20:126 where the blindness is essentially that they will be ignored by Allah's light and grace.) They will, in effect, be spiritually blind on Judgment Day, almost as if they've had the light of their souls put out. This makes Hellfire the only option they have left to them. There is a prophetic tradition that confirms this interpretation, as well.

[1126] Some commentators say that this verse mentions the five daily prayers that were first enjoined upon the Prophet and that were later made obligatory upon all Muslims. The prayers are 1) *fajr* i.e., before sunrise; 2) *'asr*, i.e., before sunset; 3) *'isha'* i.e., the hours of the night; 4) *zuhr*; and finally 5) *maghrib*. The last two are what are called the prayers at the two sides of the day. *Zuhr* is the first prayer after the sun has come up and is performed in the early afternoon, while *maghrib* is the prayer performed when the ball of the sun disappears. Other commentators regard this verse as more general and assert it mentions suggested times for prayer and contemplation without being specific as to prayers that became required later on.

[1127] 'Umar ibn al-Khattab once went into a small upper floor apartment in which the Prophet was staying after he had begun a boycott of his wives. He noticed the Prophet had nothing with him other than a rough straw mat, a few implements hanging on the wall and a pile of edible tree pods. 'Umar took in the scene, and then his eyes filled with tears. When the Prophet asked him why he was crying, 'Umar replied, "Messenger of Allah! Khosroes (of Persia) and Caesar (of Byzantium) are living in luxury; yet, you're the One that Allah chose for a friend among all of creation?" The Prophet then said, "Are you in doubt, O son of al-Khattab? Those people have merely had their good fortune hurried on for them in the life of this world." (*Bukhari*)

[1128] Several members of Muhammad's extended family had accepted Islam by the time of this revelation. This verse is asking him to institute prayers as a habit among them. (*Ibn Kathir*)

[1129] The pagans of Mecca already knew there were Jews and Christians in the world who spoke of one God, prophets, a life after death and such. Didn't the pagans realize the miraculous nature of those earlier revelations, which were also messages carried by mortal men? People don't always have to be

hasn't enough clear evidence already come to them in the ancient scrolls of revelation? [133]

If We *would* have inflicted punishment upon them before this, then they would surely have cried out, *"Our Lord! If only You would've sent us a messenger, then we would've followed Your (revealed) verses long before we would've ever needed to be humbled or disgraced!"* [134]

Say (to them), *"Each of us is waiting, so you just wait, and soon you'll know who were the companions of a straight way and who were truly guided."* [135]

---

dazzled with supernatural miracles. At some point, they have to use their reason and consider a message based on its own merits.

The Prophets

21 Al Anbiya'
Middle Meccan Period

This chapter presents a series of arguments for Prophet Muhammad to employ against the pagans who questioned that Allah would actually choose prophets from among human beings to deliver His messages. It must be remembered that the idol-worshippers had no concept of divine revelation, let alone of it coming to a human being. Their culture was filled with superstition and idolatry. The only value that any man could have in the eyes of his fellows was in the raw courage and reputation for bravery that he could amass through the rough and tumble world of the desert. The pagans knew that Jews and Christians claimed something similar to what Muhammad was bringing, but those beliefs held little sway in most of Arabia where animism was the religion of prominence. The Qur'an, however, was a challenge coming from within their own society. Thus, their rejection of it was more pointed and even desperate. The many stories of the various prophets mentioned in this chapter were a way for the pagans to open their imagination and thoughts to the prospect that Allah did, indeed, communicate His messages to human beings many times in the past and that He was doing it once again!

In the Name of Allah,
the Compassionate, the Merciful

*P*eople are getting closer and closer to their reckoning; yet, they're careless about it and just turn away. [1]

No fresh message ever comes to them from their Lord without them listening to it as if it were a joke [2] – all the while their hearts are occupied (with trivial things).

The wrongdoers hide their secret discussions (in which they say), *"Is this (man) any different from the rest of you? Are you going to fall for (his) magic while you see it (for what it is)?"* [3]

Say (to them), *"My Lord knows (everything) that's spoken within the heavens and* on the earth, for He's the Hearing and the Knowing." [4]

"No way!" they say. *"It's just a bunch of jumbled dreams! No way! He made it up! No way! He's just a poet! So let him bring us a miracle like the ones that were sent down in ancient times!"* [5]

The (people of) those previous settlements that We destroyed didn't believe, so will these (people) ever believe? [6]

Before you, We sent messengers who were (ordinary) men whom We inspired (with revelation). [1130] If you're not sure about it, then ask those who (already)

[1130] Prophets of Allah have special missions and divine support. As far as miracles are concerned, the overwhelming majority of prophets were not granted spectacular miracles, and those who were given such needed them for their daunting task. Prophet Muhammad had Allah's favor, and as his story

possess (previously revealed) messages. [1131] [7] We didn't give (any prophets before you) bodies that could go without food, nor were they immortal. [8]

In the end, We fulfilled Our promise to them and saved them, along with whomever else We wanted to save, and We destroyed those who went out of control (in their wickedness). [9] And so it is that We've revealed a book to all of you that contains a message directed towards you. Won't you at least reflect (upon it)?" [10]

History is Proof of Allah's Will

*H*ow many settlements have We destroyed completely on account of their corruption and then established other people in their place? [1132] [11] Whenever they sensed Our punishment (coming for them), they tried to run away from it! [12]

Oh, don't run away now! Go back to your luxuries and your dwellings, so you can be questioned (about them)! [13] They would cry out, *"We're doomed! We were truly wrong!"* [14] and their cry never ceased until We cut them down to dry stubble. [15]

We didn't create the heavens and the earth and everything in between them for a mere diversion. [16] If We had wanted to be entertained, then We could've chosen (Our entertainment) from that which is with Us – that is if We were ever so inclined! [17]

But no! We hurl the truth against falsehood and knock out its brains! Thus, falsehood passes away. (If you don't stop making incorrect statements about Allah,) then you'll be destroyed on account of how you're (falsely) defining (Him). [18]

All those (who reside) within the heavens and the earth belong to Him. Even those (angels) who are closest to Him are not too proud or weary (to serve him). [19] They glorify Him throughout the night and the day, and they never pause or falter (in their praise)! [20]

There are No Equals With Allah

*H*ave they taken gods from the earth who can raise (the dead to life)? [1133] [21] If there were other gods in (the heavens and on the earth) besides Allah, then there would've been chaos in both!

Glory be to Allah, the Lord of the throne, for He's high above what they

---

bears witness, his miracle was the fact that an orphan boy in the desert brought a scripture and religion that triumphed against all odds and created a world civilization that spanned from Spain to China in only about a hundred years.

[1131] The pagans objected to Muhammad's claims of prophecy, saying that he was just a man like themselves. This verse is asking them to talk to Jews and Christians and find out from them if previous prophets were men or some kind of supernatural beings.

[1132] 'Abdul Rahman ibn Khaldun (d. 1408) wrote extensively on the cyclical nature of history. He penned an exhaustive treatise on the causes of the rise and fall of nations entitled *Kitab al-'Ibar*. In his prologue volume, which is an often separately published book entitled *al-Muqaddimah*, Ibn Khaldun lays out a cyclical pattern that goes something like this: less advanced people, whether driven by religious zeal or the ambitions of powerful personalities, overthrow more advanced nations that had become weak with the passage of time. Then those conquerors settle down and eventually become civilized enough to become soft themselves one day – only to be overthrown by a new rising tide of less developed, though intensely focused invaders. No doubt verses like this one inspired Ibn Khaldun in the formulation of his theories! A recent book by Gregory Clark entitled, *"A Farewell to Alms,"* (Princeton University P., 2007) also complements Ibn Khaldun's many economic theories quite well.

[1133] This is possibly a reference to the Christians having taken Jesus, a man, to be their god. He did not raise the dead to life by his own power, but it was a miracle that Allah granted to him, just as the prophet Elisha allegedly did the same (see II Kings 8:1; also see Qur'an 3:49 and 5:112-115).

attribute to Him! [1134] [22] He can't be questioned for what He does, but they'll be questioned (for what they do). [23]

Have they taken other gods for worship besides Him? Say (to them), *"Bring me your evidence. This (Qur'an) is the (proven) message of those with me and the (proven) message of those who came before me."* [1135] But no! Most of them don't know the truth, and so they just turn away. [24]

We never sent any messenger before you without giving him this inspired message: *'There is no god besides Me, so serve Me.'* [25] Yet, they say, *"The Compassionate has taken children for Himself."* Glory be to Him!

Not so! The (beings that you call His children) are only honored servants. [26] They don't speak before He speaks, and they do what He commands. [1136] [27]

He knows what's (coming) ahead of them and what's (happened) behind them. They can't intercede at all unless they're acceptable to Him, and they hold Him in fear and reverence. [28]

If any of them should ever say, *"I'm a god in place of Him,'* then We would reward him with Hellfire, and that's how We reward the wrongdoers! [29]

[1134] If people have a theological view of the world that involves an entire pantheon of gods, such as can be found in Greek mythology, with many gods, half-gods and the like, and further still if they make their gods out to be nothing more than humans with super powers, then it is entirely plausible to assume that such gods would never work together and would always be trying to undermine each other, even as the myths of the Greek, Roman, Oriental and Hindu gods attest. (Think about the war between the Greek gods and the Titans, for instance.) If there were many gods, then the chaos would be evident and would engulf the natural world, as each god strives to gain power over the regions controlled by other gods.

[1135] In other words, the pagans claim their gods are real, but they cannot bring any proof or corroboration from any other religious group, nor can they produce any ancient scripture or obvious signs. The revealed message of the Qur'an, however, is the proof that Allah is One, even as it is a continuation of that tradition of revelation from God that included messages to Abraham, Moses and Jesus.

[1136] This verse mainly refers to the pagans who thought Allah had daughters from among the angels, but it also answers the doctrine of the Christians, who said God had a baby boy who was carried in the womb of a human girl named Mary. It is an inescapable fact that even when one reads the four Gospels in the Bible, the distinct impression is given that Jesus is not equal to God and that he is subservient to Him. It is unfortunate that the rest of the New Testament spends much of its time trying not only to overlook this fact, but also to turn the situation on its head and make it seem as if Jesus and the separate 'Father' are co-equals (see Philippians 2:5-11), with a holy *ghost* to round out the three-in-one equation. This is like the Roman Triumvirate of Julius Caesar, Pompey and Marcus Crassus or the later one of Octavian *aka* Caesar Augustus, Marcus Lepidus and Mark Antony, which was a known political structure in the first century CE when early Christian doctrines were being formulated. Perhaps this notion of the trinity of co-equals was a mere extension of this Roman political concept, and it allowed non-Jews to understand and find familiar ground with the new religion when Paul and his followers began to spread their version of Christianity outward from its Jewish roots. (Also note the contemporary triumvirate of the Greek religion in Zeus and his two brothers, Hades and Poseidon.) The idea of God having children was also a known and accepted concept among the Greeks and Romans of that time, making them undoubtedly even more comfortable with the new faith, as it was presented to them. In John 8:42-47, during a lengthy exhortation to the Jews to follow him, Jesus is purported to have said, "If God were really your Father, then you would love me. I came from God, and now I am here. I did not come by my own authority. God sent me. You don't understand these things I say. Why? Because you cannot accept my teaching. Your father is the devil. You belong to him. You want to do what he wants. The devil was a murderer from the beginning. He was always against the truth. There is no truth in him. He is like the lies he tells. Yes, the devil is a liar. He is the father of lies. I speak the truth. That is why you don't believe me. Can any of you prove that I am guilty of sin? If I tell the truth, then why don't you believe me? The person that belongs to God accepts what God says. But you don't accept what God says, because you don't belong to God." After reading a passage like this, can anyone doubt that Jesus and Muhammad have the same status as created beings before God? (Also see Mark 12:29.)

Isn't Nature Proof Enough of Allah?

Don't those who suppress (their awareness of the truth) see that the heavens and the earth were once fused together in a single piece, and then We split them apart? (Don't they see) that We made every living thing from water? So won't they believe? [1137] [30]

We placed firmly rooted highlands in the earth so it wouldn't shake along with them, and We made broad passes (between them) for them to travel through, so that (through these landmarks) they could be guided (in their travels). [31]

We made the sky as a sheltering canopy, as well. [1138] Yet, they turn away from these miraculous signs (in nature that point to an intelligent Creator). [32] Moreover, He's the One Who created the night and the day and the sun and the moon; each of them swims gently along in its rounded (orbit). [33]

We didn't grant immortality to any mortal being before you, so if you died all of a sudden, (Muhammad), would they get to live forever? [1139] [34]

Every soul will experience death, and We're testing you through both disaster and good fortune, and (in the end) you'll all be brought back to Us. [1140] [35]

The Foolish Reject Faith

When the faithless see you, (Muhammad,) they treat you with nothing but contempt, saying, *"Is this the one who's talking (against) your gods?"*

(Worse still), they reject the Compassionate whenever He's mentioned! [36] Human beings are indeed impulsive from their very creation! Soon will I show you My signs, and then you won't ask Me to hurry them on anymore! [37]

"So when will all of this come to pass," they ask, *"if you're really being so honest?"* [38] Oh, if only the faithless knew (for sure about the time) when they'll be powerless to keep the fire off their faces and their backs, and when they'll be quite beyond help! [39]

But no! It'll come upon them all of a sudden, leaving them perplexed! They'll have no power to keep it away, nor will they be given a break! [40]

Many messengers were ridiculed before you, but their critics were

---

[1137] Previous generations of commentators have not fully known how to interpret this line. Many modern commentators hold that it is a clear reference to the Big Bang theory, which asserts that all matter, including the earth, was once fused together in a compact unit that suddenly split apart, eventually resulting in the galaxies, planets, stars and other heavenly bodies over billions of years. This is a plausible interpretation as the plural word *samawat* (heavens) is used here, which is usually used in Qur'anic parlance to refer to all the zones of space outside the earth. (Compare with verse 21:32 where earth's specific 'sky' is mentioned in the singular.)

[1138] The sky, including the ozone layer, protects the earth from harmful radiation and the like, as well as mitigating the effects of small meteorites, which often burn up in the atmosphere. Were it not for the sky as it is, life could not exist on the planet. The Prophet has said: "The sky is stretched over the earth like a canopy, and therefore it is the earth's roof" (Ibn Jarir)

[1139] The pagans wanted to see Muhammad dead so they wouldn't have to hear his message of monotheism and accountability before Allah, and they often told him so. However, even that wouldn't save them from still having to face their Lord one day. That is the reason for the revelation of this verse.

[1140] The Prophet said, "A person will be tested according to his level of religious commitment. The stronger his religion, the harder he'll be tested." (*Ahmad*) The second caliph, 'Umar ibn al-Khattab, once said, "We were tested through hardships, and we bore them with patience; yet, when we were tested with pleasures, we were impatient (in enjoying them and were thus thankless to Allah.)" (*Ma'ariful Qur'an*)

eventually surrounded by the very thing at which they scoffed! [41]

Heed the Warning Before It's Too Late

*A*sk them, *"Who can keep you safe throughout the night and the day from (the command) of the Compassionate?"* Yet, still they turn away from the remembrance of their Lord. [42] Is it because they have gods that can protect them from Us? They don't even have the power to help themselves, nor can anyone protect them from Us! [43]

Oh, but no! [1141] We've certainly given the luxuries of this life to these (people) and to their ancestors, until their time seemed to extend indefinitely. Indeed, don't they see that We're gradually reducing the land (that they hold influence over) from its outlying borders? (Do they still think) they're going to win? [44]

Say to them, *"I'm only warning you as the revelation (dictates me to do)."* However, the deaf can't hear the call, even when they're issued a warning! [45] If only a slight breath of your Lord's punishment were to touch them, they would surely cry out, *"We're doomed! We were truly in the wrong!"* [46]

On the Day of Assembly, We're going to set up the scales of justice, so that no soul will be treated unfairly in the least. If there's something even as light as a mustard seed, We're going to bring it (to the scale). We're sufficient enough to take an account (of all things). [47]

And so it was that We gave the standard (of judgment) to Moses and Aaron, as well as a light (called the Torah,) and a reminder for those who would be mindful (of Allah). [1142] [48]

They were the ones who feared their Lord sight unseen and who were in awe of the Hour (of Judgment). [49] Now this (Qur'an) is a blessed message that We're sending down (to all of you), so are you just going to dismiss it? [50]

Abraham had a Similar Challenge

*A*nd so it was that We gave clarity of thought to Abraham, and We knew everything about him. [51] He had said to his father and his people, *"What are these images to which you're so devoted?"* [1143] [52]

"We found our ancestors worshipping them," they replied. [53]

"Well, both you and your ancestors have been clearly mistaken!" (Abraham) declared. [54]

"Have you really brought 'the truth' to us," they asked, *"or are you only joking?"* [55]

"Certainly not!" he answered. *"Your Lord is the Lord of the heavens and the earth, and He's the One Who brought them into being! I'm just a*

[1141] Even though this chapter was revealed in Mecca during a time when the Muslims were suffering from pagan persecution, the pagans were, nevertheless, losing some control and influence around them. Within Mecca, people were converting to Islam, mostly from the poor classes. Thus, they no longer obeyed the tribal chiefs of the city. Outside of Mecca, Muhammad was making converts from tribes both distant and near. This, as this verse suggests, was slowly resetting the strategic map in favor of Islam.

[1142] The bright light and reminder given to Moses was the Torah.

[1143] There are other versions of this story in Jewish and Christian lore, but the Qur'anic version is different in many important details and includes dialogue not to be found in any other source. In the many competing Jewish versions, Abraham first destroys the idols in his father's workshop before taking on the temple idols. It is also said that he was thrown in the fire pit with a whole crowd of relatives and other people, though only he survived, and that over 900,000 people came to watch him burn, though he remained unharmed for three days. A Muslim would hold that the Qur'anic narrative is a correction of previous versions of the tale that were corrupted over the long centuries of transmission. See 2:258 and footnote.

witness to this (truth). [56] *By Allah! I have a plan for your idols after you've turned your backs!"* [57]

And so he broke them to pieces, all except the big one, so (the priests) could return (and find it standing alone, unscathed amidst the rubble). [1144] [58]

(When the priests returned and saw what had happened), they said, *"Who did this to our gods? He must have been a criminal!"* [59]

(Someone in the crowd) said, *"We heard a young man named Abraham talking out against them."* [60] The (priests) said, *"Then bring him before the eyes of the people, so they can witness (his confession)."* [61]

(When he was brought), they asked him, *"Are you the one who did this to our gods, Abraham?"* [62]

"What!" (Abraham) answered. *"Someone must have done it – ah, there's the big one. Just ask (all the broken idols about it), that is if they're able to speak."* [63]

Then (the people) turned towards each other (to discuss the matter amongst) themselves, and they said, *"You were all truly wrong (because idols really cannot speak or save themselves)."* [1145] [64]

Then their thoughts became muddled, and they reversed course saying (to Abraham), *"You know full well that they can't speak (so why are you trying to distract us?)"* [65]

"So are you worshipping besides Allah," (Abraham) asked, *"things that can neither benefit you nor harm you?* [66] *Shame on you and the things that you're worshipping besides Allah! Don't you have any sense?"* [67]

"Burn him!" they shouted. *"Protect your gods if you must do something!"* [68]

We said, *"Fire, cool down and be a place of safety for Abraham!"* [69] But then (the nobles) made a plan against him, but We caused them to fail. [1146] [70] We saved (Abraham) and Lot (and directed them) towards the land that We blessed for (all the nations) of the world. [1147] [71]

We granted (Abraham a son named) Isaac and (a grandson named) Jacob as an extra gift, and We made each of them righteous. [72] We also made them into leaders to guide (their people) by Our command. We inspired them to do good, to establish prayer and to give in charity, and they always served Us. [73]

We also gave discernment and knowledge to Lot and saved him from the city that was steeped in filthy behavior. [1148]

[1144] Abraham entered the temple when the priests were away for festivities; then he broke all the smaller idols with a hammer or an axe. He hung the tool he used to break the idols hanging around the neck of the biggest idol, which was left unscathed. (The largest idol was probably Nanna-Sin, the ubiquitous moon god of much of Mesopotamia.)

[1145] Most commentators suggest that verse 64 should be understood to mean that the people *almost* realized that their idolatry was indeed false. (One old Jewish tale quotes the king as admitting, "Idols neither speak nor eat nor move.") At the last moment, however, the idolaters snapped back into defending their beliefs. There is an alternative view that Abraham confused the people into admitting their idols were lifeless and dead. That was why they were so angry that they wanted to burn him alive on the spot.

[1146] After Abraham escaped the fire unhurt, the stunned crowd let him go. He was soon taken in front of the king and interrogated. Why did the king want him killed? During his meeting with the king, Abraham had dumbfounded him with the logic mentioned in verse 2:258, so the king ordered Abraham to be punished, though he escaped, as this verse asserts. The young Abraham had a small window of opportunity to escape. The book of Genesis says that Abraham's father moved his family out of Ur to a northern city named Harran, possibly to protect him. Abraham eventually left his father and moved into Palestine.

[1147] This refers to the Holy Land which encompasses the modern nations of Jordan, Israel and greater Palestine. These lands were specially blessed by Allah. Due to their significance and strategic value, they have been fought over for thousands of years.

[1148] Although he lived in the wicked city of Sodom, Lot never became corrupted.

They really were an evil and rebellious people! [74] We admitted him into Our mercy, for he was one of the righteous. [75]

On Noah, David, and Solomon

*W*hen Noah called to (Us) in the past, We listened to him and saved him and his family from the great anguish. [76] We helped him against the people who denied Our signs. They really were an evil people, so We drowned them all together! [77]

When David and Solomon rendered their verdict concerning the case of some people's sheep that had wandered by night into the field (of someone else, causing crop loss), We (were there), witnessing their verdict. [1149] [78]

We endowed Solomon with a clear understanding of the matter, and to each of them We gave discernment and knowledge. We caused both the mountains and the birds, along with David, to glorify Us, [1150] and We made it happen. [1151] [79]

We also taught (David) how to make coats of armor for your benefit, so you could be protected from each other's violence in combat. Won't you then be thankful? [80]

Solomon had the very winds themselves at his disposal, and he used them (to propel his ships) towards the land that We had blessed, and We knew all about everything (he did). [1152] [81] (Solomon also had control) over some of the devilish ones who (were forced) to dive (in the sea to collect pearls) for him, and who did other work, besides. We were guarding them (so they couldn't do mischief or flee). [1153] [82]

There were Other Prophets Who were Blessed

*W*hen Job cried out to his Lord, saying, *"Misery has come upon me, but You're the most merciful of the merciful,"* [83]

We listened to him, took away his misery, restored his family to him and doubled their number – all as a mercy from Our presence and a reminder for those who serve Us. [84]

Ishmael, Idrís and Ezekiel – each of them was patient, [1154] [85] so We admitted

---

[1149] There was a very interesting court case in Solomon's time which is the subject of this Qur'anic verse. Some sheep wandered into another man's fields by night and ate up all the young shoots, causing the farmer's crops to be ruined. David ruled that the farmer should be allowed to keep the sheep in compensation, but his young son Solomon, who was not yet a teenager, suggested that the farmer should be allowed to keep the sheep and use them only until he recouped his losses (by taking their milk, wool and young lambs). This way the farmer could be compensated, and the shepherd wouldn't be ruined for something he never intended to happen. David accepted his son's suggestion, and it was a very wise ruling, indeed.

[1150] This is a reference to what is reported in Psalm 148:1-14 where the order is given to everything living and non-living to praise God. The birds, mountains, etc. are all mentioned there.

[1151] The Prophet was passing by a home at night when he heard a man named Abu Musa al-'Ashari reciting the Qur'an in an exceptionally beautiful voice. He remarked about it, "That man has been given one of the flutes of the people of David." Abu Musa heard what the Prophet said and came out, saying, "If I knew you were listening, then I would've done my best for you!" (*Fath al-Bari*)

[1152] There have been two opinions about this power of Solomon. Some have said it means that Solomon could order the wind to move at his command. Others have said it refers to Solomon's fleet of ships, which plied the region under favorable winds and brought him vast riches through trade (see I Kings 9:26-28). (See 34:12 where the purpose of the wind for Solomon is mentioned.) The land that Allah had blessed, by the way, refers to the land of Palestine, which was known as Israel in Solomon's day.

[1153] See 34:12-14 for an explanation of Solomon's control over these *hidden ones*.

[1154] Ishmael was patient due to his having to endure possibly being sacrificed by his father. (At-Tabari thought it was Isaac who was to be sacrificed, though Muslim scholars generally believe is was Ishmael

them into Our mercy, for they were among the righteous. [86]

And the fish master, (Jonah) [1155] - he left in anger and thought We wouldn't try to stop him, but he had to cry out in the darkened (belly of the fish), *"There is no god besides You! Glory be to You! I was truly wrong!"* [1156] [87]

We listened to him and saved him from his distress. That's how We save those who have faith! [88]

When Zachariah called upon his Lord, saying, *"My Lord! Don't leave me childless, though You're the best inheritor (of the future),"* [89]

We listened to him, too, and granted him (a son named) John. And so We cured his wife's (infertility!) These prophets were quick to do good. They used to call upon Us in hope and trepidation, and they were humble towards Us. [90]

And (Mary), the one who had maintained her virginity - We breathed Our spirit into her and made her and her son a sign for all the worlds. [91]

Truly, this community of yours is one community, and I am your Lord, so serve me. [92] (It will come to pass that later generations will) divide their affairs amongst themselves (by breaking up into sects), but they're all going to return to Us. [1157] [93]

Whoever does a moral deed and has faith, his effort won't be rejected, for We're going to record it. [94]

A Sign of the End Times

$\mathcal{I}$t's forbidden for any settlement that We destroyed to ever return (to life) [1158] [95] until (the people of) *Yajuj* and *Majuj* are unleashed and they swoop down from every hill. [1159] [96]

---

and not Isaac who was in that incident, as explained by Ibn Taymiyyah and Ibn Kathir.) Idrís taught for many years and was not always listened to, while Ezekiel, according to Biblical sources, had to tell the people of Jerusalem they were going to be conquered, without being too specific as God warned him the people would ignore him (Ezekiel 3:26-27), and his wife also died of the plague and he was told not to mourn her in the traditional way, but use her example as a sign of what was to come from the Babylonians. (Ezekiel 24:15-24)

[1155] Jonah was originally from a small town in Nazareth named Gath-heper. He was sent to dwell among the Assyrians in their capital at Nineveh in order to preach to them. The Assyrians were a ruthless and cruel warrior race, and the prospect of living among them must have been abhorrent to a man like Jonah. Therefore, he turned back in anger (possibly mixed with fear) and tried to flee Allah's command. He took passage on a boat to Tarshish, but wound up being thrown overboard by frightened sailors seeking to placate the sea during a storm. He was quickly swallowed up by a large fish instead of drowning! Jonah survived and later convinced the people of Nineveh to repent, and he dwelt among them to guide them for a time. (See 10:98 and footnote for more information concerning his story.)

[1156] The Prophet once remarked that any supplication made by a person, coupled with the cry of Jonah, would surely be accepted by Allah Who would then remove his distress and misfortune. (*Ahmad, Tirmidhi*) The Biblical book of Jonah records the lament of our hero of the same name in Jonah 2:2.

[1157] Verses 91-92 here are both a statement of principle and a prediction of what eventually came to pass. The Muslim community is meant to be united, and the standard of membership in the fellowship of Islam is very simple. The Prophet once remarked that any person who says that there is no god but Allah and who eats halal meat is a Muslim. Variations after that are acceptable (within some well-defined yet generous limits). Yet, within a generation of the Prophet's passing, new sects arose that claimed exclusive truth, and dissension arose in the Muslim world that has remained to this day. Allah will bring all people back to Him, and He will tell them the truth of all that they did. Also see 6:159, 23:53-54 and 30:32.

[1158] This refers to cities specifically destroyed by an act of Allah's will. Normal natural disasters or other calamities can strike a land and its people can rebuild.

[1159] The *Yajuj* and *Majuj* are invaders who will invade and conquer much of the Middle East. Translators usually label them as the Biblical Gog and Magog, but this may not be a valid linkage. These two tribes (at least their ancestors) are mentioned in chapter 18, verses 83-101, along with the

When the true promise draws near, that's when the eyes of those who covered (the light of faith within their hearts) will be staring – unblinking in horror. *"We're doomed! We never thought about any of this! We were truly wrong!"* [97]

The Fate of False Gods

$\mathcal{T}$o be sure, both you and (the false idols) that you worship besides Allah will be no more than fuel for Hellfire, *and you're going to reach it!* [1160] [98] If those (idols) were really gods, then they would never even have to go near it, but each of them will be made to stay in it! [99] For them there will be nothing more inside than weeping and crushing silence. [100]

However, those who already had a good (record) with Us will be far removed from that place. [1161] [101] They won't hear even the faintest sound of Hellfire, for they're going to be in the place for which their souls had hoped. [102]

The Great Distress won't bother them at all, for instead they'll be met by angels (who will say), *"This is your day that you've been promised!"* [103]

This is a Message for People to Consider

$\mathcal{O}$ne day We're going to roll up the sky like a written scroll. [1162] Even as We began creation in the beginning, so shall We produce a new one. That's a promise

---

story of Cyrus the Great, and were originally most likely two bands of fierce nomadic warriors of Central Asia: the Scythians and Massagetes, as the Greeks knew them. Later invaders from the same region were the Mongols and the Tartars who between them devastated much of the world from Europe to China. Interestingly enough, many scholars of the thirteenth and fourteenth centuries considered those two tragic depredations the fulfillment of this Qur'anic prophecy. It may be possible.

[1160] The Prophet was sitting with some prominent pagans near the Ka'bah and preaching to them one day, when the eloquent speaker, an-Nadr ibn al-Harith, came to the gathering and started disputing with him. The Prophet won the argument and then recited this newly revealed passage to the gathering. Then he got up and went to sit with some other people. (*Asbab ul-Nuzul*)

[1161] After the Prophet had left the gathering (see background for verses 98-100), one of the pagans remaining in that group, al-Waleed ibn al-Mughirah, said, "By Allah, an-Nadr ibn al-Harith couldn't beat the son of 'Abdel Muttalib in an argument. Muhammad even claims that both we and these gods that we worship are fuel for Hellfire." Another man named 'Abdullah ibn az-Zab'ari, who had some knowledge of Christian and Jewish doctrines, said, "By Allah, if I met with him, I'd beat him in an argument. Ask Muhammad whether everyone who is worshipped instead of God will be in Hellfire along with those who worshipped them, because we worship the angels, the Jews worship Ezra, and the Christians worship the Messiah, Jesus the son of Mary." Al-Waleed and the other men in the group were impressed with his tactics and thought he had made some good points. Then the pagans approached the Prophet, who was still with the new gathering, and asked him about this. The Prophet replied, "Everyone who desires to worship something other than God will be with the one who is worshipped, for indeed they're worshipping Satan and whoever told them to worship that object." Just before the pagans could object that this would also put Jesus in Hell, the Prophet recited these new verses [101-103], which made the caveat that good people who were worshipped against their will would be exempted from going to Hell along with those who worshipped them. Then verse 21:26 was revealed, which called the idea of assigning children to Allah ludicrous. Az-Zab'ari then accused Muhammad of wanting to be worshipped as a part of God, like the Christians called Jesus a part of God. Thereafter, to the amazement of al-Waleed, who had accompanied az-Zab'ari to watch, the Prophet recited the following additional verses: 43:57-61. (*Ibn Kathir*)

[1162] Some modern commentators have postulated that this phrase, '*roll up the sky like a written scroll*' is a veiled reference to the antithesis of the Big Bang, a phenomenon known as the Big Crunch. According to this theory, even as all the matter of the universe has been steadily moving away from the epicenter of the Big Bang, one day the acceleration will slow and then reverse itself until all matter comes together and recompacts itself. Besides the fact that this theory is only a hypothesis, the word used in this verse is the singular *as-sama'* or sky, which is usually indicative of the immediate zone around the earth. Thus, this verse speaks only of the destruction of the earth's atmosphere, at the most.

binding upon Us, and We can certainly fulfill it! [104]

And so it was that We wrote in the Psalms, which came after the message (of Moses): *"The land shall be inherited by My righteous servants."* [1163] [105] There's a lesson in this for people who serve (Allah). [106]

(Muhammad,) We didn't send you except to be a mercy to all the worlds. [107] So say to them, *"It's been revealed to me that your God is One God. So will you now submit (to Him)?"* [108]

If they turn back, then tell them, *"I've expressed the message to you evenly and fairly, and I don't know if what you've been promised is near or far.* [109] *He knows what's being uttered openly and what's being held in private.* [110] *I don't know if (the delay in punishment) is meant to be a test for you or merely a time for you to live for a while."* [1164] [111]

Then say (to them), *"My Lord! Judge truthfully (between us). Our Compassionate Lord is the One to Whom We should look for help against all (the false things) you attribute (to Him)."* [112]

[1163] See Psalms 37:29 where Allah is reported to have said, "The righteous shall inherit the land and dwell therein forever." Most commentators have suggested that the 'land' in question here in this verse is really a reference to Paradise. Thus, only the righteous will inherit the eternal home. See 39:74 and 23:10-11. (*Ma'ariful Qur'an*)

[1164] The Prophet said, "Indeed, the immensity of the reward is commensurate with the immensity of the test. Truly, if Allah loves a people, He tests them. Whoever then is contented (after hardship), he shall have joy, while whoever gets angry (at his misfortune), anger will come down upon him." (*Tirmidhi*)

405

The Pilgrimage

22 Al Hajj

Late Meccan to Early Medinan Period

This is a transitional chapter. Verses 1-18 were most likely revealed in the Prophet's last months in Mecca. The remaining verses are definitely Medinan in their tone and structure and were probably revealed within the first year or two after the Migration to Medina in the year 622. The name of this chapter indicates that after the Muslims had migrated to Medina, they had begun to grow nostalgic for their hometown of Mecca, especially when the month of *Hajj* had arrived. Many wondered what the future held and about relations with the Meccan pagans they had left behind. The point is also made in this chapter that the Quraysh had no right to prevent people from visiting the public shrine, known as the Ka'bah, located within their city. It was also during this first two years in Medina that Meccan raids on the Muslims in Medina began in earnest, and many Muslims wondered when they would be given permission to fight back. Verse 39 of this chapter is universally recognized as the first verse to authorize self-defense. Shortly after it was revealed, the Prophet authorized the first Muslim expedition to quell some bedouin raiders near the coast of the Red Sea early in the year 624.

In the Name of Allah,
the Compassionate, the Merciful

O people! Be mindful of your Lord! The convulsions of the Hour (of Judgment) will be a terrible thing! [1]

On the day when you see it, every nursing mother will forget her suckling babe, and every pregnant woman will have a miscarriage.

You'll see people (stumbling about) as if they were drunk; yet, they won't be drunk! Allah's punishment will be that intense! [2]

Even still, there are some people who have no knowledge; yet, they continue to argue about Allah, and they follow every rebellious devil. [1165] [3]

It's (a principle that's) already been recorded that whoever inclines towards (Satan) will be misled by him and guided by him towards the punishment of the raging blaze. [4]

Consider the Origin of Humanity

O people! If you have any doubts about the resurrection, then (consider how We brought you into being the first time). We created you from dust, then from a

---

[1165] The commentators say that this is a reference to wicked human beings who goad their people into endless and futile theological debates about Allah, resulting in widespread confusion and disillusionment among the masses. By extension, the blame goes ultimately back to the real Satan, and the next verse gives his fate.

drop of mingled fluids, then from a clinging (leech-like) thing, and then from a chunk of partially formed and partially unformed flesh, so that We could make (the course of your development) obvious to you. We cause whomever We want to reside within the womb for a set time period. [1166]

Then We bring you out as infants (and allow you to grow until) you reach your age of full strength. Some of you are made to die (young), [1167] while others are propelled into a feeble old age with the result that they lose all knowledge even though they had known so much before.

You also see the earth, how it's barren and lifeless. Yet, when We shower rain down upon it, it stirs (to life) and bursts forth with every kind of beautiful growth in paired (plant organs). [1168] [5] That's because Allah is the true Reality. He gives life to the dead, and He has power over all things. [6]

The Arrogant will Perish

The Hour (of Judgment) will come to pass. There is no doubt about it, and neither is there (any doubt) that Allah will resurrect those who are in their graves. [7]

Yet, there are some people who argue about Allah without any knowledge or guidance or even an enlightened book! [8]

Such (a person then) cocks his head (arrogantly) to the side and distracts others away from the path of Allah. Well, he's going to have nothing but disgrace in this life, and on the Day of Assembly We're going to make him taste the burning punishment! [9]

"This is (what you deserve) because of what your hands sent ahead of you!"

Allah is never unfair to (His) servants. [10]

When Faith is Fickle

There are some people who serve Allah as if they were standing squarely (on the edge of fickle whims). [1169] If something good happens to them, they're content with it, but if some misfortune befalls them, they turn their faces away (in disappointment). They're going to lose both this world and the next, and that's a loss for all to see! [11]

They call upon others in place of Allah (for good luck and fortune). Yet, (those idols) can do them no real harm nor bring them any benefit at all! (Believing in idols) is the most obvious loss! [12]

[1166] 'Abdullah ibn Mas'ud (d. 653) said, "The Messenger of Allah, who is the honest and inspired one, told us, 'Every one of you is collected in the womb of his mother for the first forty days, then he becomes a clinging (leech-like) thing for another forty days and then a lump of flesh for another forty days. Then Allah sends an angel to write four statements. He writes what his provision will be, (the nature) of his deeds, the length of his life, and whether he will be blessed or miserable. Then (the angel) blows a spirit (*ruh*) into him." (*Bukhari, Muslim*) Based on this narration, the traditional view has been that after 120 days the fetus is to be considered a full-fledged human being.

[1167] Babies and small children sometimes tragically die, as do people in the prime of their lives. This is the way of things, even as the same happens all throughout the web of life that makes up our world. For those who bear with patience the loss of those whose time seemed to be inadvertently shortened, they can still hope for rewards from Allah and an eventual reunion with their dearly departed ones. The Prophet once promised Paradise to those women who lose their babies and then bear the loss with patience.

[1168] This reference to beauty and paired growth is to flowers which have paired organs.

[1169] Ibn 'Abbas (d. 687) explained the reason for this verse by saying, "People would come to Medina (to declare their conversion to Islam). If their wives bore sons and their mares gave birth to foals, then they would say, 'This is a good religion,' but if their wives or mares didn't give birth, they would say, 'This is a bad religion.'" (*Bukhari*)

In fact, it may be the case that (such a person) is really calling upon something that will harm him even more than it could ever possibly benefit him! That's the worst kind of patron to have and the worst kind of follower, as well! [13]

Allah's Plan will Prevail

$\mathcal{A}$llah will allow those who believed and did what was morally right to enter into gardens beneath which rivers flow, for Allah fulfills what He plans. [14]

If anyone thinks that Allah's not going to help (His Prophet) in this world and in the next, then he should stretch a rope up to the sky and (climb up there so he) can cut off (Allah's help) by himself, (if he thinks he can stop it). [1170]

Then let him see if this scheme of his will do away with the source of his tension! [15] This is the way in which We send down verses with precise (challenges so they can be warned), and Allah guides whomever He wants! [16]

Truly, the believing (Muslims), (the followers of) Judaism, (the followers of) the Sabian faith, the Christians, the Magi (who follow Zoroaster) and the idol-worshippers - Allah will judge among them on the Day of Assembly, for Allah is a witness over all things. [17]

Don't you see that everything within the heavens and the earth bows (in submission to His will) - the sun, the moon, the stars, the hills, the trees, the animals and a large number of people, as well?

At the same time, there's another large number (of human beings) who have had due punishment justified against them. Whomever Allah humiliates, there can be no one to honor him, for Allah does whatever He wants. [1171] [18]

The Faithless have No Chance of a Final Victory

$\mathcal{T}$here were) two opposing groups who argued with each other about their Lord (at the Battle of Badr). [1172] Those who rejected (faith in Him) will have clothes made of fire tailored just for them and (buckets) of boiling muck poured over their heads! [19] It will melt their guts away, as well as their skins! [20]

They'll also have iron hammers (used against them to drive them on), besides! [21] Every time they'll wish to get away from it - *from their torment* – they'll be forced back into it, (and they'll be told), *"Suffer the burning punishment!"* [22]

(On the other hand,) Allah will allow those who believed and did what was morally right to enter into gardens beneath which rivers flow. They'll wear bracelets

---

[1170] The pagans were complaining that Muhammad's preaching was causing stress and dissension in the city. This verse dares them to prevent Allah from helping His Prophet, if they can. Some commentators think this verse is saying that if they really want to stop the Prophet, then the faithless should hang a rope from the sky and hang themselves with it, if they think it will bring them peace of mind. (*Asbab ul-Nuzul*)

[1171] It is customary that when this verse is recited, the reader or listener should bow down humbly and prostrate to Allah for a moment. The Prophet said, "When the son of Adam recites the verses containing (required) prostrations, Satan runs away weeping and says, 'Oh! I'm ruined! The son of Adam was commanded to prostrate, and he prostrated, so he will be given Paradise. When I was commanded to prostrate, I refused, so I'm doomed to Hellfire.'" (*Muslim*)

[1172] This passage refers to the Prophet's uncle Hamza, who along with 'Ali and 'Ubaydah, were arguing with the pagan leader 'Utbah and two of his friends, Shaybah and Al-Walid, just before the two trios engaged in single combat before the Battle of Badr began. 'Ali finished the argument saying, "I'm going to be the first one to kneel down before the Compassionate so that the dispute can be settled on the Day of Judgment." The three Muslim fighters killed the three pagans in the duel, and then the full battle got under way. (*Bukhari*)

of gold and pearls, and adorn themselves with clothes made of silk! [23]

They had been guided towards the purest speech of all, [1173] and thus they were guided towards the path of the Praised One. [24]

The Meccans Prevented the Pilgrims

Those who reject (Allah) and who've been holding others back from the way of Allah and from the Sacred Mosque (in Mecca), which We had (intended to be) open for all people *– both the resident and the visitor are equal there –* and those who want to do (any type of) evil or injustice there - *We're going to make them all suffer a painful punishment!* [25]

The Origin of the Pilgrimage

When We showed Abraham where to build the (Sacred) House, [1174] (We told him), *"Don't take anything as a partner in My divinity. Purify My House for those who walk around it, stand (near it) or bow down in prostration."* [26]

"Declare the pilgrimage ritual to all people. They're going to come to you on foot and on every type of well-worn transportation, traveling from every deep canyon (on earth), [27] *so they can bear witness to things that will benefit them, and so they can remember the name of Allah during the appointed days."* [1175]

"Then after they've (slaughtered) the livestock that He's allowed for them, you can eat from them and feed those who are in desperate need. [28] *Thereafter, let them clean themselves up, fulfill their vows and then walk around the Ancient House."* [29]

This is (the origin and purpose of the Pilgrimage to Mecca). Whoever honors the sacred rituals of Allah will have the best (reward waiting for him) in the presence of his Lord.

You're allowed to eat any type of livestock (during the Pilgrimage), except for (the forbidden things) that have already been mentioned to you. So shun the abomination of idols, and shun false doctrines. [30]

Follow the natural (monotheistic) way of life for Allah's sake, and never make any partners with Him. If anyone makes partners with Allah, it'll be as if he fell from the sky and was snatched up by birds or as if he were carried away by the wind and

---

[1173] What is the 'purest speech?' The Prophet said, "They will be inspired (to say) words of glorification and praise, just as they are inspired to breath." (*Muslim*) Some scholars think this verse also refers to the *kalimah*, or essential statement of 'There is no god but Allah.' (*Ma'ariful Qur'an*)

[1174] The Ka'bah is the oldest continuously used religious shrine in the world. Its history goes back nearly four thousand years to the time of Abraham. Since that time, it has been built and rebuilt as necessary. How did Allah show Abraham where to build the Ka'bah? Here is one possible explanation. A very small meteorite fell from the sky and landed in the valley of Becca, which would later be the site of the city of Mecca. Abraham saw this sign from afar and thus knew that that valley was the place where he had to leave his second wife Hagar and his son Ishmael. Later, he would build a religious shrine there when he came back for a visit and saw his son had survived. Abraham recovered the meteorite and placed it as a decoration in the side of his shrine. That is the Black Stone, which still sits in one corner of the Ka'bah shrine in Mecca to this day. Muslims do not worship this stone, nor do they ascribe any special significance to it other than as a revered link back to Abraham. During the pilgrimage season, devout people try to touch or kiss the stone in respect to Abraham. Those who cannot reach it point to it when they pass by it.

[1175] The *appointed days* are the first ten days of the Islamic month of *Dhul-Hijjah*, during which all the rituals of the Pilgrimage are performed. The Prophet said, "There are no days that are more important in the sight of Allah or in which deeds are more loved by Him than these ten days, so increase your (saying of the testimony of faith), your extolling of Allah's greatness and your praising (of Him)." (*Ahmad*)

thrown in a faraway place! [1176] [31] That's (exactly what his situation would be like)!

Now whoever truly wishes to honor the symbolic (ritual of sacrifice ordained) by Allah (should know) that it can only (be done properly) by a (person who has a) heart that's mindful (of its duty towards Him). [32]

There are certain benefits for you to enjoy for a while in the (animals that you raise and then dedicate to Allah for the Pilgrimage). Then they're to be brought (near the vicinity) of the Ancient House (for sacrifice). [33]

The Purpose of the Sacrifice during the Pilgrimage

$\mathcal{W}$e've appointed religious rituals for every community (on earth), so they could commemorate the name of Allah over the resources He gave them from among (the many types of) livestock (animals).

Your God is One God, so submit yourselves to Him and give good news to the meek [34] whose hearts are filled with awe whenever Allah is mentioned, who are patient with what troubles them, who maintain their prayers and who spend in charity out of the resources that We've provided for them. [35]

The sacrificial animals that We've made for you are symbols of (obedience) to Allah. There are benefits in them for you,

so pronounce the name of Allah over them as they're lined up and also when they've been laid down on their sides (after slaughter).

Then you may eat from them and feed those poor people who are quietly enduring (their misfortune), as well as those poor people who come begging in desperation. This is why We've placed the animals under your control, so you can be thankful. [36]

It's not their meat nor their blood that reaches Allah, but rather your mindfulness (of your duty to Him) that reaches Him. That's why He placed them under your control, so you could extol Allah's greatness for the guidance He gave to you, and also so you could give good news to those who do good. [37]

Permission is Given to Fight Back Against Oppression

$\mathcal{A}$llah will defend those who believe, for Allah has no love for thankless traitors. [1177] [38] Those who've been attacked now have permission (to fight back) because they've been wronged, and Allah can provide them with powerful aid. [39]

They're the ones who've been driven from their homes against all right and for no other reason than that they've said, *"Our Lord is Allah."*

[1176] The Prophet said, "When the angels of death take the soul of a faithless person at death, they take his soul up to the sky, but the gates of heaven are not open for him. Instead, his soul is thrown down from there." (*Ahmad*)

[1177] After enduring persecution for thirteen years in Mecca, the Muslims finally fled from the city for the safer city of Yathrib (Medina) to the north in the year 622. Then they endured two years of Meccan and bedouin raids that kept them in a constant state of fear. During these many years the Muslims were not allowed to fight back or defend themselves. This approach of non-violence, even though by all rights they would have been justified to fight back earlier, helped to test the believers and solidify their resolve. (The theory is that non-violence only works for so long and only against an opponent with a conscience to which you can reasonably appeal.) Finally, in the year 624, this passage was revealed, giving the Muslims permission to fight against their oppressors. The Prophet immediately began organizing patrols to curtail the bedouin raiders. Later in the same year, the Battle of Badr took place, which showed the Muslims that they could achieve victory with Allah's help against superior odds.

If Allah didn't use one set of people to check (the ambitions) of another, then there would've been many monasteries, churches, synagogues and mosques, which are used to commemorate the name of Allah abundantly, pulled down and ruined. Allah will definitely help those who help Him, for Allah is strong and powerful! [40]

(He helps) those who would establish prayer and spend in charity and who would encourage what is recognized (as right) and forbid what is unfamiliar (to Allah's way of life) – (these things they would do) if We ever made them dominant in the land. Indeed, all final results are with Allah! [41]

If You are Rejected, Others Were Before You

$\mathcal{I}$f they deny you, (Muhammad,) well then it was the same with other peoples before them who also denied (their prophets), such as the peoples of Noah, 'Ad and Thamud, [42] as well as the peoples of Abraham and Lot [1178] [43] and the companions of Madyan. *Even Moses was denied (by his people), too!* I gave a break to those who suppressed (the light of faith within their hearts), but then I seized them, *and oh, how terrible was my repudiation (of them)!* [44]

How many settlements did We destroy (in the past) that were given to practicing oppression (and wrongdoing)? Now they lie in ruins under shattered roofs! How many wells and mighty castles now lie deserted, crumbling and abandoned? [45]

Why don't they travel through the world, so that their hearts can gain insight from the (relics of the past) and so that their ears can hear (the tales of days gone by)? Truly, it's not their eyes that are blind, but the hearts within their chests! [46]

Yet, they're asking you to hurry the punishment forward! Even still, Allah won't fail in His promise, for a day in the sight of your Lord can be like a thousand years of your estimation. [47] How many settlements were there that were given to oppression but to which I gave a break? In the end, I seized them all, and the final destination (of all things) is back to Me. [48]

Satan Brings Opposition to the Messengers

$\mathcal{S}$ay (to them), *"People! I'm a clear warner for you!* [49] *Those who believe and do what's morally right will get forgiveness and a generous share!* [50] *However, those who campaign against Our (revealed) verses, trying to prevent them (from achieving their purpose), shall be companions of the raging blaze!"* [51]

We never sent any messenger or prophet before you that didn't have Satan try to disrupt his plans when he formulated them. [1179] However, Allah erases whatever Satan throws in, and Allah will confirm His verses, for Allah is full of knowledge and wisdom. [52]

(He allows) Satan to instill doubts (in people's hearts) so He can make it a test for those who have a sickness in their hearts or who have hardened hearts. The wrongdoers are in extreme opposition (to the truth)! [53] (He allows doubts to exist)

[1178] The people of Abraham were his community in Mesopotamia, while the people of Lot were the people of Sodom, the city in which he and his family and retainers eventually settled and assimilated.
[1179] Satan tries his best to dash the inner hopes of prophets and messengers by sowing doubts and fears in their minds. The men that Allah chooses to be His message-bearers are only human, and they're subject to the normal range of human emotions. If people don't listen to them, if they reject them and hurl insults at them, they're going to feel it. Satan or satanically-minded people use these human emotions to disrupt people's hopes that they can ever succeed. The forces of evil also continually tempt the prophets and try to make them go astray. Even Jesus was tested by the devil in a relentless contest of wills! (Matthew 11:1-4 and Luke 4:1-14. See 6:112 also.) In addition, Satan also tries to sow confusion among the followers of the prophets.

so that those who have deep knowledge can come to realize that (the Qur'an) is the truth from your Lord, and also so they can believe in it and have their hearts softened towards it. Indeed, Allah guides those who believe towards a straight way. [54]

The faithless will never stop doubting (the truth of the Qur'an), even until the Hour (of Judgment) comes upon them all of a sudden, or until some punishment overtakes them on a gloomy day. [55] The right to rule on that (final) day will belong to Allah, and He's going to judge between them.

Those who believed and did what was morally right will be in gardens of delight! [56] Meanwhile, those who rejected and denied Our (revealed) verses will have a humiliating punishment. [57]

Allah will Reward the Martyrs

*T*hose who migrate (from their homes as refugees) in the cause of Allah, and then who are subsequently killed or die – they're going to have a wonderful share of resources granted to them by Allah, for Allah is the best provider of resources! [58]

He'll admit them to a place that will bring them complete satisfaction, for Allah is full of knowledge and is forbearing. [59] That's (going to be their reward)!

The one who doesn't retaliate more than he's been injured, and who is further attacked without warning, then Allah will help him, for Allah erases (sins) and forgives. [60] That's (within His power to do) because Allah merges the night into

the day, and He merges the day into the night.

Allah listens and watches (over all things). [61] Moreover, (it's within His power to help you, for He is) Allah, the ultimate Reality. Whatever they call upon besides Him is nothing more than falsehood, and Allah is the Highest and the Greatest. [62]

Don't you (people) see that it's Allah Who sends down water from the sky, and thereafter the earth blossoms forth with green (plants)? Allah understands (the details of) every type of intricate arrangement. [63] Whatever is within the heavens and on the earth belongs to Him, for Allah is the Self-sufficient and the Praiseworthy. [64]

Don't you (people) see that Allah has tamed whatever is on the earth for your use, even the ships that sail through the sea by His command? He prevents the sky from falling on the earth, except for whatever He allows (to fall from it, such as rain), for Allah is kind and merciful to people. [65] He's the One Who brought you to life, and then He causes you to die - only to bring you to life once more! Yet, human beings are thankless! [66]

Allah Made many Ways of Life over the World

*W*e appointed religious rituals for every community (on earth) to follow, so don't let them argue with you on this point. [1180] Rather, keep on calling them to your Lord, for you're definitely following the correct guidance. [67]

If they keep arguing with you, tell them, "*Allah knows best about whatever you're*

[1180] The pagans were disputing with Muhammad about whether it was allowed to eat animals that died by themselves, for, as they reasoned, Allah caused their death, and they should be as fine to eat as the animals that had been slaughtered in the ritual way. It was the pagan custom, after all, to kill animals as they pleased (even by beating them to death with clubs) or to eat dead carcasses they found. This passage here is telling them that Allah always established methods of correct slaughtering and that the pagan method was not correct by any standard of Allah. Islam forbids eating animals that died by themselves, nor can animals be cruelly killed. (*Asbab ul-Nuzul*)

doing." [68] Then Allah will judge between you on the Day of Assembly (and solve) your disagreements. [69]

Don't you know that Allah knows about all things within the sky and the earth? (Every event) is recorded in a ledger, and that's easy for Allah. [70] Even still, they worship (idols) in place of Allah, having no clear mandate to do so nor any accurate knowledge. Those who are corrupt will have no one to help them! [71]

When Our clear verses are read out to them, you can clearly see the defiance on the faces of those who suppress (their awareness of the truth), as if they were about to pounce on those who are reading Our verses to them!

Say to them, "*Should I tell you about something that you'll dislike far more than these verses? It's the Fire that Allah has promised to the faithless, and that's the worst destination!*" [72]

Idol Worship is Foolish and Illogical

O people! Here is a comparison, so listen to it! Those (idols) that you call upon besides Allah can't create as much as a fly, even if they all got together to do it. Further still, if a fly were ever to take something away from them, they wouldn't have any power to get it back from that fly! How weak is the one who seeks (knowledge from idols), and how weak are (the idols) from whom he seeks (to learn)! [73]

They haven't thought highly enough of Allah, for Allah is strong and powerful! [74] Allah chooses messengers from among both angels and people, and Allah hears and sees (all things). [75] He knows what's in front of them and what's behind them, and all decisions go back to Allah (for their resolution). [76]

O you who believe! Bow down, and prostrate yourselves (in prayer). Serve your Lord. Do what's best so you can be successful. [77]

Strive in His cause with honest effort, for He's chosen you and hasn't made any difficult (regulations) for you to follow. This way of life is no less than the creed of your forefather Abraham.

(Allah) is the One Who has named you *Submitters,* [118] both before and in this (revelation), so that the Messenger could be a witness for you, and so you could be witnesses (to your faith) before all people.

Establish prayer, give in charity, and hold firmly to Allah. He is your protector, and (He's) the best for defense and the best for giving help! [78]

---

[118] This is the translation of the word *Muslim*. Thus, the Qur'an has coined this term to describe the followers of Allah. Abraham called people to become submissive or compliant to Allah, and so it is perfectly fine to say he labeled his followers as Muslims, as well. See 2:128 where the meaning of Muslim is explained in Abraham's speech.

The Faithful

23 Al Mu'minun
Late Meccan Period

This chapter was revealed during the days of famine in Mecca that chapter 44 had foretold. It goes over the familiar themes of Allah's signs and the need for people to recognize Allah as their Creator and ultimate judge. It also contains some words of advice to the Prophet to help him cope with the persecution of the Meccans. 'Umar ibn al-Khattab said of this chapter: "This chapter was revealed in my presence, and I, myself, saw the condition of the Prophet during its revelation. When the revelation was finished, the Prophet (turned to us and) said, 'On this occasion, ten verses have been sent down to me that, for the one who measures up to them, will most surely make him enter Paradise.' Then he recited the first verses of this chapter." (*Ahmad, Tirmidhi, Nisa'i, Hakim*) In later years, a man named Yazid ibn Babnus asked the Prophet's widow A'ishah to describe for him the habits and behavior of the Prophet. She replied to him that he followed the message as it was revealed in the Qur'an. Then she recited the first ten verses of this chapter. Afterwards she said, "These verses describe his behavior." (*Nisa'i*)

In the Name of Allah,
the Compassionate, the Merciful

So it will be that the believers will succeed [1] – those who are humble in their prayers, [1182] [2] who avoid useless chatter, [1183] [3] who engage in charity, [4] who guard their modesty [5] - except with their spouses and those (maidservants) under their authority (whom they've married), [1184] for there's no blame for them in this. [6] Whoever goes beyond (these limits), they're indeed going out of bounds. [7]

[1182] The Prophet said, "Allah keeps watch over His servant while he's praying as long as he is concentrating on Allah, but when he turns his attention elsewhere, Allah turns away from him, likewise." (*Ma'ariful Qur'an*) In another incident, the Prophet was observing a man at prayer, but the man was fiddling with his clothes and playing with his beard. The Prophet remarked that if that man had any humbleness in his heart, it would have been clearly shown in his body. In other words, he would have stood still and respectfully while at prayer.

[1183] Mindless gossip and pointless conversations lead people into sin. How many people have been hurt by the idle wagging of a careless tongue! The Prophet Muhammad once said, "Allah doesn't like foul language nor the use of it." He also said, "A person who believes in Allah and the next life should speak about good things, or else he should keep silent." (*Bukhari*) Thus, a Muslim is not allowed to speak badly or use profanity.

[1184] The servants they marry are also lawful for them, and this is pointed out specifically so there can be no doubt that former bonded-servants have equal status with people who were always free, lest some people look down upon others. The Prophet said, "There are three types of people who will be given their reward twice: a person from among the Followers of Earlier Revelation who believed in his prophet and then believed in me; a servant who performs his duty well towards Allah and for whomever he works; and a man who has a maidservant and then educates her, teaches her refined manners, frees her and then marries her." (*Bukhari*) Also see 24:32 and 70:30 and footnote.

(True believers) are those who faithfully discharge their trusts and agreements, [8] and they guard their prayers strictly. [9] They'll be the inheritors [10] who will inherit an exclusive garden in Paradise, and there they shall remain! [1185] [11]

The Reality of a Temporary Life for Human Beings

$\mathcal{W}$e created (each) human being from minerals extracted from clay, [12] and then We placed him as a mingled drop, securely held in place. [13] Then we transformed that drop into a clinging thing. Then out of that clinging thing, We formed a chewed up lump. Out of that chewed up lump, We fashioned bones and clothed them in flesh.

So then out of (that initial tiny drop), We made another creature! So blessed be Allah, the best of all creators! [14] Then after (your life span has passed), you're going to die. [15] Then after that, you're going to be raised to life again for the Day of Assembly! [16]

The Fruits of the Earth

$\mathcal{A}$bove you We made seven layered tracts, and We're not unmindful of Our creation. [17] We send a measured amount of water down from the sky and lodge it in the earth. We can drain it off, as well. [18]

We use (that water) to grow gardens of date palms and vineyards for you, in which you can find abundant fruit that you can eat. [19] (We also grow a type of olive) tree, (the best of which) sprouts near Mount Tur, from which you get olive oil and relish for your meals. [20]

You can even find a lesson in domesticated livestock, for We produce (milk) from within their bodies for you to drink. There are many other benefits in them for you, as well, such as their meat that you can eat, [21] and also in the fact that you can ride upon them like ships (traversing the land). [22]

The Saga of Noah

$\mathcal{A}$nd so it was that We sent Noah to his people. He said (to them), "*My people! Serve Allah! You have no other god than Him! Won't you be mindful (of Him)?*" [23]

The chiefs of the faithless among his people said, "*He's no more than a mortal man just like the rest of you! He only wants to have an advantage over you! If Allah really wanted to send someone to us, then He could've sent down angels. Really now, we've never heard anything like this coming (down to us from the traditions) of our ancestors! [24] He's just a man who's been possessed (by evil spirits), so wait a while (for him to go away).*" [25]

"*My Lord!*" Noah cried out. "*Help me against their lies!*" [26]

And so We revealed to him: "*Build a boat under Our sight and inspiration. When Our command arrives and the heated banks (of the river) give way (and cause a flood) upon the land, take on board a pair of every (kind of useful livestock animal), both male and female. [1186] Also bring your family aboard, except for those who will have*

[1185] The Prophet explained what this passage was about when said, "There are none of you except that you have two homes, a home in Paradise and a home in Hellfire. If he dies and enters Hell, the people of Paradise will inherit his home. This is what Allah meant by, 'They'll be the inheritors...'" (*Ibn Majah*)

[1186] Muslim commentators have always assumed that the animals that Noah was to take were from his local area – animals that he would need to rely upon for rebuilding his community after the flood, such as sheep, goats and other similar things. Muslim theologians have generally never promoted the idea that a pair of every animal *on earth* went in the boat with Noah. It has been the general trend in Muslim scholarship to assume that only the people of Noah's region were destroyed by great flooding. Noah's descendants then went on to repopulate the region.

the sentence proven true against them. [1187] *Don't appeal to Me any further on behalf of the wrongdoers, for they're going to be drowned."* [27]

"When you and everyone with you have gone on board the boat, then say, 'Praise be to Allah, the One Who has saved us from these corrupted people.' [28] *Then pray, 'My Lord! Let me also leave this boat (at a future date) with Your blessings, for You're the best One to allow (us) to leave.'"* [29]

There are signs (in this story for people to consider), for We're always testing (people in their faith). [30]

The Cycle of History Continues Unabated

*T*hen We raised another generation (of people) after them, [31] and We sent them a messenger (drawn) from among their own, (who said), *"Serve Allah! You have no other god than Him! Won't you be mindful (of Allah)?"* [32]

The leaders among his people who rejected and denied their rendezvous in the next life, and upon whom We had showered the luxuries of this world, said, *"He's no more than a mortal man just like the rest of you. He eats the same food that you eat and drinks the same liquids that you drink.* [33] *If you were to obey a mere mortal who's no different than the rest of you, then you'd truly be lost.* [34] *Is he promising you that after you've died and become rotten bones that you'll be brought (to life) again?* [35] *That's a far off prospect that you've been promised!"* [36]

"There's nothing else (for us) other than our lives here in this world! We (humans) die, and (new generations are then given) life, but we'll never (individually) be raised to life again!" [37]

(This) is just a man who's made up a lie about Allah, and we're never going to believe him." [38]

(Their prophet) cried out, *"My Lord! Help me, for they're accusing me of a lie!"* [39]

"They're going to be sorry in just a little while," (Allah) replied. [40] Then the blast rightly overtook them, and thus We reduced them to nothing more than scattered debris. *So away with the wrongdoers!* [41]

Then We raised other generations after them. [42] No community can advance its final time limit, nor can it delay it. [43]

And then We sent Our messengers one after another, and every time a messenger went to his community, they accused him of lying.

So We made them follow one after another (in destruction), reducing them to mere historical accounts. *So away with the people who won't believe!* [44]

Then We sent Moses and his brother Aaron with Our signs and a clear mandate [45] to Pharaoh and his nobles, but they acted arrogantly and were quite a conceited people. [46] (Pharaoh and his nobles) said, *"Should we believe in two mortal men who are just like us, especially since their people are our slaves?"* [47]

So they denied them and were thus plunged into destruction. [48] And so it was that We gave Moses the Book, in order for (his people) to be guided. [49]

We also made the son of Mary and his mother a sign, as well, and We sheltered them securely on high ground in comfort and with flowing streams. [1188] [50] *"All you*

[1187] Noah's own wife and son did not believe in his prophethood and refused to board the boat. See 38:84-85 for the proverbial 'sentence' or verdict of Allah.

[1188] Some commentators say that this refers to the place where Mary bore Jesus - that it was on a safe, dry hill near a spring (see 19:22-26), while others think that this refers to Jesus and Mary being in a beautiful place in Paradise. Yet a third interpretation is that Jesus had enemies who wanted to kill him as a child, but Allah gave him and his mother a safe place to live so he could grow into manhood. Any of these interpretations could be subscribed to, though the first makes more sense in the context of what is actually stated in this verse.

messengers! Eat only wholesome (foods), and do morally upright deeds, for I know what you're doing." [1189] [51]

Be United for the Truth

(O you who believe!) Truly, this community of yours is one community, and I am your Lord, so be mindful of Me. [52] (People) have divided their way of life into sects among them, with each faction satisfied with its own doctrines. [53]

Leave them alone in their confusion for a while. [54] Do they think that just because We've granted them wealth and children [55] that We're (always) going to rush every type of good (fortune) their way?

Certainly not! They just don't understand. [56]

Without a doubt, those who anxiously fear their Lord, [57] who believe in the signs of their Lord, [58] who don't make partners with their Lord [59] and who give whatever they give (in charity) with nervous hearts, (knowing that) they're going to return to their Lord, [60] they're the ones who rush forward (to do) every type of good deed. [1190]

They're foremost (in doing what's pleasing to Allah). [1191] [61]

You have no More Excuses with Allah

We don't place a burden upon any soul that's greater than it can bear. [1192] We have a record before Us that shows the truth, and they won't be treated unfairly. [62]

But no! Their hearts are overwhelmed in confusion about this. More than that, there's still some (sinful) things that they're doing - and that they'll keep on doing - [63] even until the moment comes when We seize in punishment all those who had the luxuries of this world (and who were thus heedless). *Oh, how they'll cry out (for mercy) then!* [64]

"Don't cry out (for mercy) today!" (they'll be told,) *"for you'll find no help from Us!* [65] *My (revealed) verses were read out to you, but you used to turn back on your heels* [66] *arrogantly, saying bad things about them like a storyteller in the night."* [67]

Haven't they thought seriously about the word (of Allah), or has something come to them that's never come to their ancient ancestors? [68]

Is it that they don't recognize their messenger? Is that why they're refusing him? [69] Do they say, *"He's possessed"?* Certainly not! (On the contrary), he's

---

[1189] The Prophet said, "O people! Allah is wholesome, and He only accepts what is wholesome. Allah commands the believers just like He commanded the messengers by saying, 'All you messengers! Eat only wholesome (foods)...'" Then the Prophet also recited verse 2:172, which has a similar message. Finally, the Prophet mentioned a man who was dirty, dusty and disheveled from traveling, and he said, "...his food, drink and clothes are impure, and he's fed himself with what's forbidden. If he extends his hands towards the sky and says, 'Lord! Lord!' How can his prayer be answered?" (*Muslim*)

[1190] The Prophet's wife A'ishah asked the Prophet about this passage [57-61], wanting to know if the people who had fearful hearts were fearful because they were committing sins like drinking alcohol or stealing. The Prophet replied, "No, O daughter of the Truth-confirmer (Abu Bakr), it's not like that. They're the ones who pray and fast and give in charity while being afraid that their deeds won't be accepted by Allah because of their own shortcomings. They rush forward to do good deeds, and they're in the forefront in doing them." Then the Prophet recited verse 61. (*Ahmad, Ibn Kathir*)

[1191] For a further description of the reward of this type of sincere believer, see 56:19-26.

[1192] Ibn 'Abbas was of the opinion that this passage is a reference to the leaders of the Quraysh tribe of Mecca and that this was a veiled threat to them that because they were persecuting Allah's Prophet, they were in for trouble at a later date. Their downfall at Badr, then, would be the fulfillment of this threat. (*Ma'ariful Qur'an*)

bringing them the truth, but most of them hate (to hear) the truth! [70]

If the truth were shaped according to what they would like it to be, then the very heavens and the earth and every (creature) within them would've been warped (out of all recognition)!

But no! We're giving them their reminder, but they're turning away from their reminder! [71]

Is it that you're asking them for some kind of reward? Your Lord's reward is far better (than anything they can give), for He's the best One to provide. [1193] [72]

You're calling them to a straight path, [73] and those who don't believe in the next life are veering away from that path. [74]

If We were merciful to (the idol-worshippers of Mecca) and relieved them of the agonizing (famine) from which they've been suffering, then they would still eagerly persist in their rebelliousness, wandering all around in distraction. [1194] [75]

We punished them with this (famine so they could learn a lesson), but they've neither humbled themselves before their Lord, nor have they begged Him (for relief). [76] (Their arrogance will continue) - even until We open a door for them that will lead to a painful punishment. Then they'll be in abject despair within (their place of doom)! [77]

Our Senses Tell Us the Truth

*H*e's the One Who endowed you with hearing, sight, sensitivity and self-awareness. Yet, you're hardly thankful at all! [78] He also multiplied you throughout the earth, and in the end you'll (all) be gathered back to Him. [79] He's the One Who gives life and death. The alternation of the night and the day is His (doing), so won't you understand? [80]

But no! They repeat the same kinds (of denials) that the ancients said! [81] They say, *"When we've died and become rotten bones, are we really going to be raised to life again?* [82] *These things were promised to us and our ancestors before, but they're no more than the tales of the ancients!"* [83]

Ask (them), *"To whom belongs the earth and all beings upon it? (Speak) if you know!"* [84] They'll (be sure) to say, *"To Allah!"* Then say to them, *"So won't you take a reminder?"* [85]

Then ask (them), *"Who is the Lord of the seven heavens and the Lord of the great throne (of power)?"* [1195] [86] They'll (be sure) to say, *"Allah is!"*

Then say (to them), *"So won't you be mindful (of your duty to Him)?"* [87]

Now ask (them), *"In whose hands is the control of everything, and who protects all and doesn't need protecting? (Speak) if you know!"* [88]

[1193] Compare this with 18:94-95 where even a king refuses payment because he appreciates what Allah has given him.

[1194] See the introduction to chapter 44 and 44:10-12 and commentary for the details of this foretold famine that eventually struck Mecca. The Prophet had beseeched Allah saying, "Allah! Help me against them by sending on them seven years (of famine) like the seven years of Joseph's (famine in Egypt)." (*Bukhari*) Abu Sufyan, the *de facto* leader of the pagans in Mecca, eventually approached the Prophet when he was settled in Medina and begged him to ask Allah to lift the famine and drought. The Prophet prayed for relief, and the heat wave abated soon thereafter. (*Ma'ariful Qur'an*)

[1195] In Arabic idiom, the seat or throne of a king was synonymous with and symbolic of his power. Thus, when the Qur'an mentions that Allah has a throne, it doesn't necessarily mean that Allah literally *sits on a chair*, and no Muslim scholar would ascribe such literal imagery to Allah, even though we sometimes talk in these anthropomorphic terms. Rather, Muslim theologians have usually understood that this is a reference to Allah's *power*, and at least some of the pagans of Mecca would have understood this in the same way, as well. Muslims also don't believe that when Allah's 'hand' or 'eye' is mentioned that He has a *hand* or *eye* like us created creatures.

They'll (be sure) to say, *"Allah!"*

Then say (to them), *"So how can you be so deceived (into worshipping idols)?"* [89] By no means! We've sent them the truth (which they affirm with their own tongues); yet, they practice lies (in spite of it)! [90]

Allah never took any son, nor is there any other god with Him. (If there were many gods), then each god would've taken (control) over what it had created, and some of them would've tried to dominate the others!

Glory be to Allah (above all) they're making Him out to be! [91] He knows what's beyond human perception and what's plain to see, and He's high above what they're joining with Him! [92]

Be Strong, Prophet of Allah

(Pray to your Lord), saying, *"My Lord! If you're going to show me (the punishment) that they've been promised,* [93] *then, my Lord, don't place me among the people who do wrong!"* [1196] [94] Oh, indeed, it's entirely possible for

Us to show you (the punishment) about which they've been warned! [95]

So ward off the evil (things they say) with (a state of) goodness, for We know what they're describing (you to be). [1197] [96]

Say, *"My Lord! I seek Your protection from the incitement of devils,* [97] *and I seek Your protection, My Lord, from them ever coming near me."* [1198] [98]

There are no Confessions accepted when Life is Over

(The faithless will remain blind to the truth) - even until death comes upon one of them, and he cries out (in his grave), *"My Lord! Send me back (to life)* [99] *so I can act righteously in those things that I neglected!"*

(However, he's going to be told), *"No way! It's just something he's saying!"* Then a barrier will be raised before them until the day they're resurrected. [1199] [100]

When the trumpet will be blown, all relations between them will cease, nor will

---

[1196] The Prophet sometimes made this supplication: "Allah! I seek Your protection from old age. I seek Your protection from being crushed or drowned, and I seek Your protection from being assailed by Satan at the time of death." (*Abu Dawud*)

[1197] The Prophet said, "Among the manners of a believer are these: when he speaks, he speaks nicely; when someone speaks to him, he listens attentively; when he meets others, he welcomes them with a smiling face; and when he makes a promise, he fulfills it." (*Ad-Daylami*)

[1198] This passage addresses the Prophet and how he should handle all the horrible insults he was receiving. The "devils" mentioned here refer to both the Prophet's human detractors, as well as possibly the doubts and gnawing misgivings that can come from having to bear insults on a daily basis. In that, there is a wide lesson for all people here. Verse 97 specifically is a plea to Allah to help a person overcome his anger when being insulted by someone who wants to get a rise out of him.

[1199] Here we have mention of the Islamic doctrine of *barzakh*, or the barrier. When a person dies, the angels draw his soul out of his throat. The soul hovers near the body until it's buried or otherwise disposed of. Then the soul sinks in the earth and remains in a state of suspended animation until the Day of Judgment when the soul is brought out and used to recreate the human being anew. The Prophet said, "When the coffin is ready and people lift it above their shoulders, if the body is that of a virtuous person, it urges, 'Take me ahead; take me ahead.' If it is the body of a wrong-doer, it says, 'Curses! Where are you taking me?' Its screams are heard by everything except humans, and if they could hear it, they would faint." (*Bukhari*) When first laid to rest, two angels will come to the dead soul and ask it three questions. (Who is your Lord? What was your religion? Who was your prophet?) Our answers will determine what happens next. The barrier is the partition between life and death. No soul may cross it and return to life. Good souls will rest peacefully and not feel the passage of time, while the souls of the wicked will be quite awake. The wicked will be tormented every day by angels who will come and beat them and berate them for their wickedness. The Prophet often prayed to Allah for protection from the punishment of the grave.

anyone (even think to) ask about anyone else that day! [101]

Then those whose scales are heavy (with good) will be successful, [1200] [102] while those whose scales are scarce (of good) will have lost their own souls and be relegated to Hellfire. [1201] [103] The fire will burn their faces, and they'll scowl horribly (in pain). [104]

"Weren't My verses read out to you?" (they'll be asked). *"Didn't you treat them as lies?"* [105]

"Our Lord!" they'll cry. *"Our own misfortune overtook us, and we were a people who went off course.* [106] *Our Lord, take us out of this. If we ever return (to sinful ways after this), then we would really be wrongdoers (and would deserve this punishment)!"* [107]

"Get back into it even further!" (Allah) will reply, *"Speak no more to Me!* [108] *There was a group of My servants who used to pray, 'Our Lord! We believe, so forgive us and have mercy on us, for You're the best One to show mercy!'* [109] *Yet, you laughed at them, even until your ridicule of them made you forget My message!* [110] *I've rewarded them this day for their patience, and they're the ones who've triumphed."* [111]

Then (Allah) will ask them, *"How many years did you stay on earth?"* [112]

"We stayed for a day or part of a day," they'll reply. *"Just ask those who keep track."* [113]

"You stayed only for a little while," He'll exclaim, *"if only you would've known!* [114] *Did you think that We created you just for fun and that you wouldn't be returned to Us?"* [115]

Glorify Allah in the Highest

(*O* you who believe!) Extol (the glory of) Allah! The Ruler, the Reality! There is no god besides Him, the Lord of the throne of honor! [1202] [116]

If someone calls upon any other god alongside of Allah, he doesn't have any right to do so! His account will stand in the sight of his Lord, and the faithless will never be successful! [117]

So pray then, *"My Lord! Forgive and show mercy, for You are the best One to show mercy!"* [118]

[1200] Interestingly enough, the Prophet once said that on the scales set up on Judgment Day, the ink used by scholars will weigh more than the blood of martyrs. (*Ma'ariful Qur'an*) This tradition has been one of many prompts that has made the desire to be a learned scholar a common goal of Muslims throughout the ages.

[1201] According to numerous prophetic traditions and the concurring consensus of all major scholars, even a person who claims to be a Muslim can go to Hellfire if his sins are more numerous than his acts of goodness. For such a one, Hellfire is a time of purging and purification, and he may eventually be released and admitted to Paradise (unless, of course, he was a die-hard hypocrite, in which case he may never get out). (*Ma'ariful Qur'an*)

[1202] 'Abdullah ibn Mas'ud recited this verse in the ears of a person who was ill. The man recovered in record time, and when the Prophet heard about it, he asked Ibn Mas'ud about it. When Ibn Mas'ud confirmed what he had done, the Prophet said, "I swear by the One Who has power over my life, if a true believer were to recite these verses on a mountain, the mountain itself might even move from its place." (*Qurtubi*)

The Light

24 An-Noor
Middle Medinan Period

This chapter was revealed in approximately the year 627. It was a tense time for the Muslims who had lost face among the tribes of the desert, due to their being defeated at Uhud. Hostilities arose from every quarter. Indeed, seeing that the Muslims were not invincible after the Battle of Uhud in 626, Abu Sufyan left a challenge for the Muslims to fight the Quraysh once again at the Wells of Badr the following year (no doubt wanting to erase their earlier defeat there).

Accordingly, the Prophet marched a force of some 1500 fighters there at the appointed date, but the Quraysh failed to show up. Instead, Abu Sufyan tried to break the Muslim resolve by sending a man to spread rumors in Medina about how fearsome the Quraysh army would be, hoping to prevent the Muslims from accepting his challenge! The Prophet camped with his men at Badr for eight days and then marched his men back home.

A few weeks later, the Prophet received reports that two bedouin tribes were preparing to launch an attack on Medina, so the Prophet again assembled a force (this time of 400 men) and marched out to prevent their assault. Finding the bedouins had fled rather than risking a fight, the Prophet once again returned to Medina with his men. Then word of a new threat from the powerful Banu Mustaliq tribe reached Medina, and the Prophet assembled yet another force (this time of 700 men) to meet the foe before it could strike. He came upon the tribe's encampment while they were unaware of his march.

The tribe was defeated, and its people taken into custody. (It was a pre-emptive attack, and this is allowed in Islam if it is clearly known that an enemy is already making preparations to attack you first.) The Prophet was assigned Juwayriyyah, the daughter of the Banu Mustaliq chief, as his share of the booty, but he freed her and married her. Then all the other captives were freed by the enthusiastic companions. Due to his gracious treatment, the tribe accepted Islam.

On the return trip from the campaign, the Prophet's wife A'ishah was inadvertently left behind in one of the campsites when she went looking for a lost piece of jewelry. A companion of the Prophet, finding her there, escorted her to Medina, arriving a day behind the main body of the army. Hypocrites immediately seized upon this to spread rumors and slander that A'ishah had been unfaithful with her escort. This grieved the Prophet, A'ishah and many others, as baseless accusations tend to take on a life of their own.

This chapter was eventually revealed to the Prophet from Allah, absolving A'ishah of any guilt. In addition, harsh words are directed against slanderers and those who falsely question a woman's honor without proof or sincerity. Other miscellaneous matters of social interaction are also addressed.

This is a chapter containing Our regulations that We're sending down. [1203] We've included self-evident verses within it so you can be reminded. [1] Any woman or man who is guilty of adultery or fornication [1204] is to be whipped with a hundred lashes each. [1205]

[1203] The Qur'an was not revealed in a blank cultural context. The Arabs were renowned for their poetry, and it was the main vehicle for passing on news, challenges, boasts, warnings, viewpoints on life, and entertainment. So important was poetry in the society, that the seven best poems of the day were written on vellum and hung within the Ka'bah itself. Those poems were called the Seven Hanging Odes, or the *Mu'allaqat*. One of the most beloved of those was the poem by one Imru'l-Qays, whose work was flush with boasts about his exploits with women, how he invaded their private rooms, seduced married women into adultery and exposed them shamelessly. This chapter is almost point-for-point a refutation of those kinds of immoral values, with regards to exploiting women, that were cherished by the men of Arabia. Therefore, the Qur'an was trying to put limitations on the behavior of men, who had assumed, through their cultural heritage, that they could do as they pleased with women and their reputations.

[1204] The term used here (*zina*) is a generic term for any unlawful sexual relations outside of marriage and is commonly applied to both adultery and fornication. (*Ma'ariful Qur'an*)

[1205] Although no one disputes that a fornicator would get a whipping, after the Prophet's passing there was some confusion among his companions and their students about the punishment for adultery. Based on this verse, some said it was lashes, while others, citing *hadith* reports, said the punishment was elevated to stoning by prophetic injunction (or divine revelation). (*Bukhari, Muslim*) This second position was strongly advanced by 'Umar ibn al-Khattab, among others. The latter position eventually rose to prominence in the succeeding years, (with some dissenters), and it became the common legal position in the classical period of Islamic scholarship that a married adulterer is to be stoned to death, while an unmarried fornicator is to be whipped with a hundred lashes (administered in such a way that it causes no bleeding or permanent scarring) and banishment for a year. (The latter punishment being outlined in the Bukhari collection.) The proponents of stoning base their position on several *hadith* reports in which it appears that the Prophet called for this more drastic punishment. Other commentators assert that the Qur'anic punishment of whipping is to be applied to both the adulterer and the fornicator in preference to the stoning that is contained in the *hadith* reports. Their argument is based on the common position that the Qur'an trumps what the Prophet may (or may not) have said and that no *hadith* report can abrogate a Qur'anic injunction. Why would there exist *hadith* reports that suggest that the Prophet called for the stoning of adulterers rather than a whipping? It must be remembered that the injunction for stoning adulterers is from the Torah, that no such verse appears in the Qur'an, and that the Prophet recommended to the Jews who came to him with at least two adultery cases that they must follow what's in *their* scripture, the Torah. (See Qur'an 5:41 and footnote where one of these cases is recounted.) The Qur'an, which abrogated or superseded both the Torah and the Gospel, has its own outlined punishment of whipping. It cannot be abrogated, opponents of stoning assert, by any human source. Some pro-stoning scholars take the position that the Qur'an does say to flog adulterers, but that it's *really* calling for stoning them. They justify this by saying that there is an 'uncollected' or 'forgotten' verse of the Qur'an that ordered stoning that the Prophet at some point stopped reciting out of dislike for it. There is also an odd mention in the Ibn Majah and Ahmad collections that the so-called 'stoning verse' was written on a leather parchment and kept in A'ishah's house and that a goat came in and ate the leather piece while the Prophet's funeral was being performed, resulting in the verse being lost forever! Besides that report sounding a bit whimsical, the untenable nature of such a position is in the fact that staunch Muslims readily charge that the Jews of Medina had hidden a verse of their Torah that called for stoning (Deuteronomy 22:22), dishonestly reducing the penalty for adultery from death to flogging, while at the same time, these same Muslims are saying they want to eliminate the ruling of the existing Qur'anic verse that calls for adulterers to be flogged in favor of the harsher penalty of stoning, based on a verse that *doesn't even appear* in their own book. When the Jews of Medina asked the Prophet for a ruling on this issue, he *did* order them to follow their religious law to the letter. Thus, the Prophet technically did call for stoning. Yet, in later years, he actually refused to repeat the order for stoning, even though 'Umar wished to hear it from him. *Could it be that the ruling on stoning was never a Qur'anic verse, but was instead the Prophet's opinion based on his respect for the law of Moses, and that he later received direction from Allah to drop that idea, with that divine commandment being backed up by an actual Qur'anic verse that outlines flogging*

Don't let compassion sway you regarding their case, for it's part of Allah's way of life - that is if you're (sincere) believers in Allah and the Last Day. Also arrange for some believing witnesses to observe their punishment. [2]

Don't Match the Pure with the Tainted

*T*hereafter, don't let any man guilty of adultery or fornication marry anyone except a woman who is also guilty of the same crime, or (he can marry) a pagan. [1206]

Likewise, let no woman who is guilty of adultery or fornication marry anyone except a man who is guilty of the same crime, or (she may marry) a pagan. (Marrying someone guilty of unlawful sex) is forbidden for the believers. [3]

Don't Slander Respectable Women

*T*hose who make an accusation against a respectable woman, and who don't produce four witnesses (who caught her in the act of adultery or fornication), then whip (the ones who brought the unsubstantiated charge) with eighty lashes, and never accept any testimony from them ever again, for they're disobedient troublemakers. [4] If they repent afterwards and reform themselves, then Allah is forgiving and merciful. [1207] [5]

---

as the punishment Allah decrees? (Thus, the issue of the existence of a stoning report supposedly left out of the Qur'an can be reconciled.) Allah only knows and only He knows which legal position is right. I take no firm stance either way other than to say that there is a serious punishment to be suffered for this serious crime. By the way, four witnesses must catch the person in the act of adultery or fornication for the punishment to be due, and if a spouse accuses another of it on his or her sole testimony, the accused can swear to Allah that he or she is innocent and have the guarantee to be found not guilty in a court of law. Thus, the only practical way anyone would get either of these punishments (whipping or stoning) is if they volunteered for it! Now about "uncollected" verses, would any of the companions willfully let any verse go unrecorded in the official text if they knew it existed and was supposed to be preserved? Could a verse be 'lost' because a goat ate it, when there were so many companions who had the entire Qur'an memorized? When Uthman ibn Affan (d. 656) was asked by his nephew, Ibn az-Zubayr, why he included a particular verse in the finalized edition of the Qur'an that he had ordered to be compiled - a verse that some people at the time thought was abrogated by another verse (2:240 was abrogated, some say, by verse 2:234), he replied, "My nephew, I shall not change any part of the Qur'an from its place." Thus, Uthman, one of the Prophet's closest companions and a member of his inner-circle, testified from his own mouth that he collected the Qur'an in its full form as the Prophet envisioned it, regardless of what others would think about the continued validity of individual verses. *(Fath al-Bari, Ibn Kathir)*

[1206] The exact reports differ slightly, but the basic issue surrounding the revelation of this verse is that some poor believer(s) asked about marrying prostitutes. Either they wanted them to keep plying their trade and thus have money coming into their coffers, or the women themselves wanted to keep doing it so they would be financially independent. This verse forbids chaste people from marrying people who did *zina*, or adultery and fornication, and those who led that lifestyle can only marry others like them or (converted) pagans (who had no prohibition against committing adultery or fornication, and who may presumably fall into it again or be jaded by their past).

[1207] If they publicly repent for slandering a woman and thereafter lead a righteous life in the eyes of their fellows, then such people can, at least in theory, regain Allah's favor and perhaps the right to have testimony accepted again, provided they admit to having lied. (There is no way, however, to avoid the whipping.) The reputation of a woman is her honor. If anyone questions it without foundation or makes false charges, they've done tremendous harm to a potential mother, wife, sister or daughter. By the way, the culturally-based practice of so-called *honor killing*, in which a family member kills a female relative for fear she has *dishonored* the family, a practice that is prevalent in some backward countries in the Middle East, Asia and Africa, has absolutely no legal basis in Islamic Law (though it is in the Bible in Deuteronomy 22:21). 'Honor' killing is routinely spoken against by Islamic legal scholars, and it falls under the crime of murder. Those who practice this unnatural and extra-legal custom are blameworthy and will have to answer for it on the Day of Judgment, that is if they escape

Addressing Accusations of Adultery

$\mathcal{A}$s for those who make an accusation (of adultery) against their spouses, and who don't have any witness other than themselves, their sole testimony (can be accepted) if they swear to Allah four times that they're telling the truth [6] and then swear a fifth time [1208] that the curse of Allah should come upon them if they're lying. [1209] [7]

However, (the spouse) can avert the punishment if they swear to Allah four times that (the accuser) is telling a lie [8] and then swears a fifth time that Allah's wrath should come down upon them if (the accuser) was telling the truth. [1210] [9]

If it wasn't for Allah's favor and His mercy towards you, (then you would've committed injustice in disputes involving infidelity), but Allah accepts repentance and is wise. [10]

The False Charge against A'ishah

$\mathcal{T}$hose who brought out the slanderous (charge of adultery against the Prophet's wife A'ishah) are nothing more than a gang [1211] among you (who tried to stir up trouble). [1212] Don't think of it as a

---

prosecution in this life. Verse 24:2 is the only legally-sanctioned punishment, and it can only be applied if four witnesses catch the people in the act and testify before a judge in a court, and the penalty must be applied equally to both the male and the female.

[1208] The process works the same way whether the accuser is the husband or the wife.

[1209] Ibn 'Abbas (d. 687) related that some companions had been discussing what should happen if they were by themselves and they caught their spouse in the act of adultery with someone else. Would they themselves get the 80 lashes because they could not produce four witnesses? Who would ever report a case of adultery then? Their concern was soon answered. A man named Hilal ibn Umayyah went to the Prophet and swore that he found his own wife cheating on him with a man named Sharik ibn Sahma. The Prophet disliked hearing such an accusation, since the Qur'an had already laid down the rule that four witnesses must be brought if someone wants to lodge a charge of infidelity against someone, so he asked Hilal if he were prepared to accept 80 lashes because he lacked corroborating witnesses. Another companion nearby named S'ad ibn 'Ubadah mused to his friends that he thought the Prophet would declare all the future testimony of Hilal to be unreliable and void. Hilal was very upset, and he beseeched the Prophet for some ruling from Allah. The Prophet was about to order the man whipped (based on the previously revealed verses 4-5 of this chapter), but then he suddenly froze and began to look as if he were under great strain, (signaling to those around him that he was receiving a new revelation). When he became relaxed again, the Prophet recited verses 6-10, and he said to Hilal, "A bargain for you, since Allah found a solution for you and absolved you, and I hoped for that from my God." Later that day, Hilal and his wife went before the Prophet in the mosque, and the Prophet made each of them swear to Allah about their statements and invoke His curse upon them if they were lying, and both sides did so as this passage [24:6-9] outlines, thus canceling each other's accusations. (Hilal's wife did hesitate before taking the fifth oath as to her innocence, but then she said, "I will not dishonor my family today.") With that done, the wife escaped the accusation and the punishment for adultery. Then the Prophet predicted that she was pregnant, and then he annulled their marriage and forbade anyone from ever accusing her of adultery or accusing the child of being illegitimate. Next, he said that if the child was born with reddish hair, then it was Hilal's child, but if it were born with curly hair, dark eyes and was heavy-set (like Sharik looked), then it was not Hilal's child. Later she gave birth to a child that fit the second description, and the Prophet said, "If it wasn't for the oath that she swore, I would have dealt with her." Her son took his mother's family name and was never attributed to any father. He eventually grew up to be a governor of Egypt. (*Ibn Kathir*)

[1210] Accusations of infidelity are grounds for automatic divorce, and the couple can never remarry.

[1211] This 'gang' is a reference to 'Abdullah ibn Ubayy (and his henchmen) who did the most to keep the scandal alive and in constant circulation.

[1212] Whenever the Prophet led a large expedition, one of his wives would usually accompany him to look after him. When the Prophet set out at the head of several hundred men to attack the Banu Mustaliq tribe, which was secretly preparing to attack the Muslims first, A'ishah was the one who

bad thing, however, for it was ultimately a good thing for you (that this issue was dealt with openly). [1213]

Every man among them will have his sin recorded, and the one who was the most involved among them will have a terrible punishment (from Allah). [11]

When you first heard of the situation, why didn't the men and women of faith think better (of A'ishah) to themselves and say, "*This is obviously a false charge*"? [1214] [12]

---

came along. On the return journey, the Muslims made camp, and it was there that A'ishah noticed that one of her prized pieces of jewelry was missing. As the men prepared their mounts to resume the journey home, A'ishah, not realizing the pace of packing, walked back along the trail hoping to spot her gold necklace. When she returned to camp after finding her necklace, she found that the men had all gone and moved on. Her palanquin, or camel mounted chamber, was always covered in a curtain, so no one noticed that she wasn't inside when the party set out once again. A'ishah remained in the abandoned camp, confident that her absence would soon be noticed and that someone would be sent to look for her. One Muslim man named Safwan ibn al-Mu'attal, who had been given the chore of collecting any lost baggage, came upon A'ishah and found her sitting in the campsite. He placed her on his camel and set off immediately after the main body of the army. They reached Medina about a day behind the army. When people saw the young man leading A'ishah into the city, the tongues of the hypocrites began to wag. 'Abdullah ibn Ubayy, in particular, began avidly spreading the rumor of adultery, and even some sincere believers got caught up in the rumor-mongering. The Prophet immediately defended A'ishah and Safwan as honest and trustworthy in a public speech, and when he asked for help against the gossip campaign from Ibn Ubayy, the Muslims in the mosque broke up into two factions along tribal lines and began quarrelling. The Prophet was stunned, and A'ishah was heartbroken over the accusations. A'ishah soon moved back in with her parents and stayed with them for a month to rest, and the Prophet checked in on her from time to time as he consulted with his companions about the rumor-mongering that was going on. The issue continued to divide the Auws and Khazraj companions who continued to argue over the matter. A'ishah described her heartache as the worst thing she ever felt in her life, saying, "I cried continuously every day and couldn't sleep, so that my parents expected me to die from my extreme sorrow." Safwan was equally in despair and protested his innocence profusely. Then, after one month passed, the Prophet visited A'ishah and said, "There is no god but Allah. I've been told (rumors) about you, but if you're innocent, then Allah will prove it (today), though if you've committed a sin, then ask forgiveness of Allah and repent to Him, for if a servant of Allah admits his sin, then his repentance will be accepted." A'ishah began to feel better, and she motioned for her parents to answer for her, but they declined, citing the fact that they didn't know what they were to say. Then A'ishah said, "Even though I'm still young and I haven't read much of the Qur'an, I do know what you've heard and thought about me. Even if I said that I'm innocent, and Allah knows it, you probably wouldn't believe me, and if I admitted to something of which Allah knows I'm innocent, then you'd probably believe me then. So I haven't found for you and me any other saying than what the father of Joseph said." Then she recited Joseph's quote from verse 12:18, and afterwards she turned away and laid down on her bed. The Prophet went out into another room, and a few moments later this passage was revealed [24:11-26], which proved A'ishah's and Safwan's innocence and exposed the plotting of the hypocrites. The Prophet laughed joyfully and announced first, before reciting the verses, "A'ishah! Good news for you! Allah has proven your innocence!" A'ishah was overjoyed when she heard the news, and she soon moved back into her own apartment fully exonerated.

[1213] Gossip is one of the most natural things for any group of people to engage in, and it is also one of the most destructive behaviors out of the many in which people indulge. The Prophet was sensitive to people's tongue-wagging, for he understood well how idle chatter can divide people and create scandals and hatreds in society. One night he was walking his wife Safiyah to her home after a late night of worship in the mosque. Two men were passing by in the street. When they saw the Prophet in the dim light walking with a woman, they hurried on, not wanting to bother him. The Prophet, fearing the men might think something bad about him, (that he was with a woman to whom he was not married), called out to them and said, "I am here walking with my wife Safiya." The men said they thought nothing bad, and the Prophet explained that he wanted to make sure no one would be plagued with thoughts from Satan. (*Ibn Kathir*)

[1214] When the gossip began to spread around Medina, Umm Ayyoub, the wife of Abu Ayyoub al-Ansari, said to her husband, "Have you heard what the people are saying about A'ishah?" He replied, "Yes, and it's all lies. Would you ever do that, mother of Ayyoub?" She answered, "No, by Allah! I would never do that!" Then Abu Ayyoub said, "A'ishah is even better than you." (*Ibn Kathir*) It is

Why didn't they bring four witnesses to prove it? When they failed to bring witnesses, they were (proven) to be liars in the sight of Allah. [13]

If it wasn't for Allah's favor towards all of you and His mercy - *both in this world and in the next* - then a terrible punishment would've certainly befallen you on account of your indulgence in this affair. [14] While you (people) were eagerly passing (this lie along) with your tongues and saying with your mouths things you knew nothing about, you thought it was just a trivial matter, but in Allah's sight it was a serious issue. [15]

When you (first) heard about it, why didn't you say, "*It's not right for us to talk about this. Glory to You, (Our Lord), this is an awful rumor!*" [16]

Allah is warning you seriously not to repeat this (vicious rumor-mongering), that is if you're (sincere) believers. [1215] [17] Allah makes His verses clear for you, for Allah is full of knowledge and wisdom. [18]

Those who love to spread scandalous accusations among the believers will have a painful punishment in this life, as well as in the next life. Allah knows (all about their evil intentions), even though you don't know. [19] If it wasn't for Allah's favor towards you and His mercy, (then you believers would've been punished for your participation, too), but Allah is kind and merciful. [20]

Maintain Good Relations

O you who believe! Don't follow in the footsteps of Satan. If anyone follows in Satan's footsteps, then he'll order (them to do) what's shameful and despicable. If it wasn't for Allah's favor towards you and His mercy, then none of you would've ever been sanctified. Allah sanctifies whomever He wants, and Allah listens and knows (all things). [21]

Don't Hold a Grudge Against Family

*D*on't let those who've been endowed (with great wealth and status) among you swear that they're no longer going to help their relatives, the needy or those who've migrated in the cause of Allah (simply because those people might have behaved poorly). [1216] Forgive them, and overlook (their faults). Don't you want Allah to forgive you, too? Allah is forgiving and merciful! [22]

---

also important to note in this case that Safwan brought A'ishah into Medina openly, in front of everybody, while she was mounted on his camel. If something shameful had occurred, then they would have come into town at night in a sneaky way. So the question remains, "Why didn't people think more highly? Why were some people's minds so intent on thinking the worst?"

[1215] The Prophet said, "Don't annoy Allah's servants or abuse them or look for their hidden faults. Whoever seeks out the faults of his Muslim brother, Allah will expose his faults and embarrass him, even if he's hiding in his house!" (*Ahmad*)

[1216] Abu Bakr found out that one of the men who kept the false charges against his daughter A'ishah circulating was none other than his poverty-stricken cousin, Mistah ibn Uthathah, to whom he had always given money in the past. Thus, Abu Bakr vowed to cut off any support for him. A'ishah learned of her relative's slandering of her one night from Mistah's own mother, who said, "Mistah should be ruined!" A'ishah incredulously asked, "Are you abusing someone who was present at the Battle of Badr?" Mistah's mother replied, "Oh my, haven't you heard what he's been saying?" Then she told A'ishah about his part in the rumors and gossip, causing her to feel even more terrible. This passage asks Abu Bakr, and by extension anyone else with wayward relatives, to forgive their faults out of a spirit of charity and generosity. When the line was read to him, "Don't you want Allah to forgive you," Abu Bakr replied, "Of course, we would love, Our Lord, for You to forgive us." (*Ibn Kathir*) The Prophet reiterated this Qur'anic concept by saying that the real test of kindness towards relatives is not just by helping them when they are friendly towards you, but by helping them still after they've cut you off. (*Ma'ariful Qur'an*)

The Punishment of Slanderers

*T*hose who make false charges against naive, yet respectable, believing women, are cursed in this life, and in the next life they're going to have a terrible punishment [23] on the day when their tongues, their hands, and their feet will testify against them as to what they've done. [24]

On that day, Allah will repay them for the genuine results of their way of life. Then they'll (finally) realize that Allah is the Obvious Truth. [25]

Tainted women are for tainted men, and tainted men are for tainted women. Wholesome women are for wholesome men, and wholesome men are for wholesome women.

(Respectable people) are not affected by what (slanderers) say (about them), and they're going to have forgiveness and a generous share (in Paradise). [26]

Asking Permission to Enter a Home

O you who believe! [1217] Don't go into anyone's homes other than your own unless you've asked permission first and greeted those who (live) within them.

That's the best (practice) for you (to follow) so you can be reminded (of the importance of respecting the privacy of others). [27]

If you find no one in the house, (or if no one answers you), then still refrain from entering until you've been given permission.

If you're asked to leave, then leave, for that's the purest course of action for you (to follow), and Allah knows what you're doing. [28]

It's not wrong for you to enter buildings (without permission) if they're not used for habitation, and which serve some other (public) purpose for you. [1218] Allah knows what you reveal and what you (try to) hide. [29]

Modesty Begins With the Eyes

*T*ell the believing men that they should lower their gaze (and not stare lustfully at women) and that they should guard their modesty.

That's the purest course of action for them to follow. Allah is well-informed of everything they do. [30]

Likewise, tell the believing women that they should lower their gaze (and not stare lustfully at men), that they should guard their modesty, and that they shouldn't display their attractions - other than what must ordinarily show.

They should also draw forth their headscarves (to cover) their bosoms and not let their curves be seen except by their husbands, their fathers, their husbands' fathers, their sons, their husbands' sons,

---

[1217] A woman went to the Prophet and said, "Sometimes when I'm in the privacy of my own home, I don't want to be seen by either my father or my son, but my father still enters while I'm (not fully dressed). So what can I do?" (Pre-Islamic Arab culture had previously no restrictions on entering another person's home at will.) This passage was revealed in answer and lays down the principle that people's privacy must be respected. (*Asbab ul-Nuzul*)

[1218] Abu Bakr, when he heard verses 24:27-28 being recited, asked the Prophet about the abandoned homes people would sometimes find and sleep in on their trading trips to Syria. This verse was revealed in response. (*Asbab ul-Nuzul*) It also covers going into stores and other places of business. Obviously, if the store or office is closed, the visitor will have to wait for normal business hours before entering.

their brothers, their brothers' sons, their sisters' sons, their female (relatives and acquaintances), their bonded maidservants, their menservants who have little interest in intimacy (such as the very old), and children who are innocent of intimate attraction.

(Also tell them) that they shouldn't stamp their feet in order to draw attention to their hidden (charms and jewelry).

O you who believe! Turn together towards Allah so you can be successful! [31]

Get Married when You Can

Single people among you should get married, and the morally upright among your bonded servants and maids (should get married, as well).

If any of them are too poor (to support a family), then Allah will enrich them from His bounty, for Allah pervades all things and has knowledge. [32]

Those who don't yet have the financial means to marry [1219] should keep themselves chaste until Allah enriches them from His bounty.

Don't Prevent Bonded Servants from Working for Their Freedom

Also, if any of your bonded servants ask you for a written contract (to buy their freedom), then give them one. [1220] If you've found them to be good (in character), then give them some money yourselves out of what Allah's provided you (to aid them in buying out their contracts).

Don't Send Women into Prostitution

Don't turn your maid-servants into prostitutes just so you can make some money off the goods of this world, [1221] especially since they desire to be chaste, though if any (unscrupulous man unlawfully) forces them (to be prostitutes), then even after (they've been) forced, Allah (will forgive those maid-servants), for Allah is forgiving and merciful. [1222] [33]

And so We've sent down to you evident verses and examples from (the lives of) those who came before you, as a way of forewarning those who are mindful (of Allah). [34]

[1219] When a man asks a woman to marry him, he must pay her a marriage gift or dowry, and the bride sets the amount. This verse refers to those men who cannot afford to give what the woman asks and she is unwilling to accept a down payment.

[1220] Suba'ih, the servant of a man named Huwaytib, asked for an emancipation contract, but Huwaytib refused. This verse was revealed in response. (Asbab ul-Nuzul)

[1221] 'Abdullah ibn 'Ubayy had several slave girls, including two women named Mu'adhah and Musaykhah. In pre-Islamic days, he had forced them to become prostitutes to make money off of them. After Islam came to Medina, the women converted to Islam and were sincere in their conversions. They wanted to know if what they were being made to do was allowed in Islam, so Musaykhah, accompanied by her mother, went to the Prophet and asked about it. This verse was revealed forbidding the evil practice, and thus they were able to stop being a part of that unwholesome lifestyle. (Asbab ul-Nuzul)

[1222] Thus, with this ruling we find that prostituting one's maid-servants (or any women) is forbidden in Islam. This verse is also a message of hope to those two women and to all women everywhere who are forced into prostitution that Allah will not hold them accountable for what they've been forced to do, even as the evil-doers who force them will be punished either in this life, the next or both. Forced prostitution is so prevalent in today's world that all governments would do well to enact the total Islamic ban on prostitution.

Allah is the Light...

Allah is the Light of the
heavens and the earth.
The example of His Light is like a nook.
Within that nook is a lamp,
and the lamp is encased in crystal.

The crystal resembles a star,
glittering (like a pearl)
whose (flame is) lit from a blessed tree –
an olive (tree) - neither from the
East nor the West,
whose oil is glistening and glowing,
even before it's been lit!

Light upon Light!

Allah guides whomever He wants towards His Light, [1223] and (this is how) Allah gives examples to people, for Allah knows about all things. [1224] [35]

(His Light shines forth) in houses (of worship) that He's allowed to be built and sanctified, [1225] and in which His name is remembered and His glorification is done, both in the mornings and the evenings, [36] by men who let neither business nor trade divert them from the remembrance of Allah, nor from establishing prayer nor from giving in charity.

They fear the day when hearts and eyes will be all aflutter (at the horrors of Judgment Day). [37]

And so, Allah will reward them according to the best of their deeds, *and He's going to add even more for them besides out of His bounty*, for Allah gives resources to whomever He wills without limitation. [38]

The Futile Works of this World

The deeds of those who suppress (their faith) are like a mirage in the desert, which a thirsty man mistakes for water, until he comes up to it and finds it to be nothing at all!

He will, however, find Allah there with Him, and He's going to pay him back what is due to him, for Allah is quick to settle accounts. [39]

(Their example is also) like (that of a man, trapped under) the darkness of a deep ocean, overwhelmed under a great wave, topped by another great wave, topped by a dark cloudiness - darkness in layers one above another!

If he stretches out his hand (before his face), he can hardly see it! [1226] For the one who has not been granted any light from Allah, there can be no light! [40]

[1223] In the immoral poem of Imru'l-Qays, which hung in the Ka'bah and called for men to be out-of-control with women, he describes his beloved as a shining light, before tumbling into a dark night of isolation and suffering. By contrast, this verse shows Allah to be the true source of radiance, while the "great waves of darkness" in verse 40 symbolize the doom of those who went astray.

[1224] The Prophet said, "Allah, the Exalted One, created His creation in darkness, and then later that day He sent His Light upon them. Whoever was touched by His Light on that day will be guided, and whoever was missed will go astray. Therefore I declare, 'The pens have dried in accordance with the knowledge of Allah, may He be glorified!'" (*Ahmad*)

[1225] It is said that this passage is a reference to a blacksmith and a sword maker, both of whom literally used to drop everything and rush to the mosque when the call to prayer was announced. (*Qurtubi*)

[1226] There is a well-known modern anecdote connected to this verse about a man who was a sailor by trade. He read this verse and asked a Muslim he knew if Muhammad had ever sailed on the ocean before. The Muslim said that he hadn't. Then the sailor asked if Muhammad had ever seen the ocean before, and again the Muslim replied that he hadn't. Then the sailor remarked that only someone who had been deep under the sea, such as in a deep sea diving suit or submarine, would have known that that's how the environment appears there if one were deep under water and looking up – waves under waves of current, with darkness in layers, one above the other with a cloudiness beyond. Then the sailor accepted Islam. Also see 6:25.

All Things Praise Allah's Glory in their Own Way

Don't you see that all creatures within the heavens and the earth glorify Allah, even the birds as they fly with their wings spread out wide?

Every (creature) knows how to make its own kind of prayer and glorification, and Allah knows what they're all doing. [41] The control of the heavens and the earth belongs to Allah, and back to Allah is the final destination (of all things). [42]

Don't you see that it's Allah Who moves the clouds gently, then joins them together and then piles them up in a heap? Then you see raindrops issuing from within them. (Don't you see that) He sends *mountains of clouds* down from the sky?

Hailstones come from within them, and He uses them to pelt whomever He wants, and He turns them away from whomever He wants.

(Indeed,) the blinding flash of (one of) His lightning bolts can blind (your very) sight! [43] Allah alternates the night and the day, and in these (signs) are lessons for those who are perceptive. [44]

Allah created every creature from water. Among them are some that crawl on their bellies, some that walk on two legs and others that walk on four.

Allah creates whatever He wants, for Allah has power over all things. [45] And so it is that We've sent down evident signs, and Allah guides whomever He wants towards a straight path. [46]

The Problem of False Obedience

(The hypocrites) say, "*We believe in Allah and in the Messenger, and we obey*," but even after (saying all of that), some of them turn away, for they're not (really) believers. [1227] [47]

When they're called (to appear before) Allah and His Messenger, so He can judge between them, some of them refuse (to come)! [48] However, if the truth is on their side, then they'll come to (the Prophet), acting all cooperative and compliant. [49]

Is it because there's a sickness in their hearts, or are they just uncertain, or are they afraid that Allah and His Messenger will treat them unfairly? No way! They're the ones in the wrong! [50]

The reply of the believers, when they're called (to appear) before Allah and His Messenger so He can judge between them, is nothing else besides, "*We hear, and we obey*." They're the ones who will be successful! [51] Whoever obeys Allah and His Messenger and fears Allah, while being mindful of Him, will be among the winners. [52]

(The hypocrites) swear to Allah adamantly, claiming that if you but gave the command, they would leave (their homes and march with the militia in times of war). Tell them, "*Don't just swear on it, for actual obedience is a more fitting (way to prove your sincerity), and Allah is well-informed about what you're doing.*" [53]

Say to them, "*Obey Allah, and obey the Messenger, but if you turn away, then (the Prophet) is only responsible for his own duty, even as you're (only responsible) for what's been placed upon you. If you obey him, then you will be guided*

[1227] A hypocrite named Bishr was disputing with a Jewish man over ownership of some land. The Jew wanted to go to Muhammad for a settlement, but the hypocrite wanted to go to another man for judgment, saying that Muhammad would not judge fairly. (Bishr knew he was in the wrong, and he wanted to go to K'ab ibn Ashraf, a Jewish chief, for a ruling.) This passage was revealed concerning this issue. (*Asbab ul-Nuzul*)

rightly, for the Messenger's only duty is to convey (the message) clearly." [54]

Allah's Promise of Relief will come to Pass

$\mathcal{A}$llah has promised to those among you who believe and who do what's morally right that they'll inherit the land, [1228] even as He had granted it to those who came before them.

(He's also promised) that He'll firmly establish the way of life that He's chosen for them and that He'll transform the fear that they've been living under into a sense of security. [1229]

(In order for this to happen), they must serve only Me and not make any partners at all with Me. If anyone thanklessly suppresses (their awareness of faith) after this, then they're rebellious and disobedient. [55]

Be constant in prayer, and give in charity, as well. Obey the Messenger so you can receive (Allah's) mercy. [56] Never assume that the faithless are going to hold back (Allah's plan) in the land, for their resting place is in the Fire. *Oh, how awful a place in which to reside!* [57]

Teaching People to Respect Your Privacy

$\mathcal{O}$ you who believe! [1230] Make your bonded servants and the young (children) among you ask your permission (before coming in a private room to see you) at these three times: before the pre-dawn prayer, when you've disrobed for an afternoon rest, [1231] and after the time of the late-night prayer has ended. These are the three times when (people are likely) to be undressed.

Outside of these times, it isn't wrong for you or for them to move around and interact with each other (in the home). This is how Allah clearly (explains) the verses to you, for Allah is full of knowledge and wisdom. [58]

After those young children among you reach puberty, they still must ask for permission, even as those older than they must, and (again) this is how Allah clearly (explains) His verses to you, for Allah is (indeed) full of knowledge and wisdom. [59]

[1228] In the early years of Islam, the Muslims were beleaguered and under fire from all sides. Some companions asked the Prophet, "Will there ever come a time when we can live in peace and put down our weapons?" The Prophet replied, "Yes, and that time is coming very soon." Then this verse was revealed. (*Qurtubi*) The Prophet also told his companions, "You won't stay like this for long, and then each of you will sit in dignified meetings where there will be no (need for) weapons (at hand's reach) anywhere." (*Ibn Kathir*)

[1229] These three predictions of the Qur'an came to pass in the Prophet's lifetime. 1) The Muslims eventually had complete control in Arabia, even though they were only a small, weak community. 2) Islam became so spectacularly successful that the Islamic world expanded faster than any empire in history; thus, Islam became firmly rooted. Finally, 3) the Muslims, who had been living under a constant state of fear from the Meccans, the bedouins and others, eventually tasted the fruits of peace in their land. When this verse was revealed, all of these three predictions seemed unattainable. Indeed, ever since they had fled from Mecca, the Immigrants used to keep their weapons close by their beds at night, fearing a sudden attack from the pagans in the dark.

[1230] A woman named Asma' bint Marthid went to the Prophet and complained about how sometimes young children or servants were coming in upon her at home when she wasn't decently dressed. 'Umar ibn al-Khattab also came to him with a similar complaint, and he asked if Allah could make a ruling about this situation, so people could have their privacy at home respected. This verse came in answer to this problem. (*Asbab ul-Nuzul*)

[1231] The cultural pattern in Arabia at the Prophet's time included taking an afternoon rest or siesta, even as many cultures today still retain such a custom. Taking a nap at mid-day has recently been shown by preliminary medical studies to be effective in reducing stress and also in reducing the rate of heart problems. Thus, many in our modern world are looking into reestablishing this refreshing habit (which the Qur'an assumes people will be prone to indulge in as a matter of course.)

Elderly Women Have Fewer Dress Restrictions

𝒥t isn't wrong for elderly women who are past the prime age of marriage to abandon wearing their outer cloak, as long as they don't display their beauty in an obvious manner. However, it's still best for them to be modest, for Allah listens and knows (about all things). [60]

Accept all Regardless of Ability

𝒥t isn't wrong for the blind, the handicapped, the ill, [1232] or yourselves if you eat (your meals) in your own homes, or in those of your fathers, your mothers, your brothers, your sisters, your father's or mother's brothers and sisters, or in homes to which you have the keys [1233] or in the homes of your close friends. [1234]

It isn't wrong if you eat together or separately, but if you enter a home, then greet each other (with the words) of peace, blessings and goodness, (which are a greeting) from Allah. [1235] This is how Allah (explains) the verses for you, so you can understand (what proper manners are). [61]

How to Behave in the Presence of the Prophet

𝒯rue believers are those who believe in Allah and His Messenger. [1236] When they're with (the Prophet in the midst of important) communal affairs, they don't leave until they've asked him if they could be excused.

Those who ask you to be excused are those who (have shown that) they believe in Allah and His Messenger, so when they ask you to be excused for some business of theirs, then excuse whomever you want, and ask Allah to forgive them, for Allah is forgiving and merciful. [62]

[1232] It had been the custom in pre-Islamic times for people to forbid the blind, the handicapped and the ill from coming to their dinner parties, on the belief that the misfortune of those people would befall the hosts, too. Also, handicapped people in those days would often feel embarrassed at their condition and usually refrained from going out to peoples' houses for dinner parties, even if their relatives wanted to take them along with them. This verse forbids such disdain for the handicapped and encourages people to invite those with disabilities to their tables, even as it tells handicapped people not to be ashamed of their state. In addition, dinner parties that are segregated by social status or wealth are also forbidden. A prominent companion, 'Abdullah ibn Mas'ud (d. 653), once said, "If only the rich are invited and the poor are left out, we have been ordered (by the Prophet) not to respond to such an invitation."

[1233] This refers to house-sitters who might be afraid of eating the food in the house they've been asked to look after, even after they've been expressly told that they can. When the companions used to go out on military campaigns, they would give the keys to their homes to the ill and lame and would tell them they could eat what they liked in return for looking after their property. The handicapped people used to hesitate eating any food out of shyness. (*Ma'ariful Qur'an*)

[1234] Dinner parties in the homes of friends are an integral part of life. Once the Prophet was invited to the wedding feast of one of his companions, Abu Usayd as-Sa'idi. Abu Usayd's own new wife was serving a drink to the Prophet made of water that had been sweetened with dates. (*Bukhari*) Although traditional Muslim cultures today often observe strict separation of the genders at social gatherings, such was not the case in the Prophet's time or in the immediate centuries thereafter.

[1235] Some people of Medina wondered if it was allowed to eat alone, as was their habit before Islam. They felt guilty about it, thinking that since Islam emphasized community so much that it might also require communal family dinners. This part of the verse addresses that concern. (*Asbab ul-Nuzul*)

[1236] This verse was revealed while the Muslims were digging a trench in front of the city of Medina just before the Battle of the Trench in the year 626. Everyone was assigned a quota of digging – even the Prophet fulfilled his share – but some hypocrites would dig a little and then slink away. This verse was revealed about them. (*Bayhaqi, Ibn Is-haq*)

Don't consider the call (to attend a meeting) with the Messenger like any ordinary call from each other. Allah knows those among you who slip away (from his meetings without asking permission), holding to some (lame) excuse.

Let those who oppose the Messenger's command beware, for some chaotic situation might befall them, or a terrible punishment might afflict them. [63]

There's no doubt that whatever is in the heavens and on the earth belongs to Allah. He knows what you're up to, and one day you're going to be brought back to Him. Then He's going to tell you the meaning of all that you did, for Allah knows about all things. [1237] [64]

[1237] The eighth-century scholar, Hasan al-Basri (d. 737), once wrote, "The Muslim takes an account of himself more vigorously than a businessman does of his partner."

The Standard

25 Al Furqan
Middle Meccan Period

This chapter was revealed in response to the many challenges the Prophet was receiving from the Meccan pagans who were adamant in their belief that there were many gods, not just one. They pointed to their idols made of wood, sticks and stone and challenged the Prophet to bring them proof more convincing than that physical evidence there before them. They also called into question the fact that the Prophet was not endowed with supernatural powers and lived as any other human being did. The Prophet was well into the public phase of his ministry and oftentimes found himself overwhelmed with questions, accusations and taunts. Through this chapter he was able both to steady his resolve and to answer many of the issues raised by his critics. Although the bulk of this chapter dates from the middle Meccan period, many scholars feel that verses 68-70 were revealed in Medina.

In the Name of Allah,
the Compassionate, the Merciful

Blessed be the One Who sent down the *Standard* to His servant, so it could be a warning to all the worlds. [1]

He's the One Who controls the heavens and the earth. He hasn't taken any son, nor does He have any partners in His dominion. He created everything and measured their proportion exactly. [2]

Yet, still they've taken in His place other gods that can't create anything at all and that were themselves created!

They have no control over the harm or good that befalls them, nor do they have any power over death, life or resurrection! [3]

The Accusations of the Critics

The faithless say, [1238] *"This is all just a pack of lies that he's made up, and some people helped him do it!"*

They're the ones who've brought an unfair charge and an unsubstantiated accusation. [4] Then they say, *"It's all just tales from long ago that he's ordered to be written down. They're being dictated to him in the morning and at night."* [5]

Say (to them), *"This (message) was sent down by the One Who knows the mysteries of the heavens and the earth, and He's forgiving and merciful."* [6]

[1238] This passage was revealed in response to the taunting of the popular Meccan poet, an-Nadr ibn al-Harith. He told his fellow Meccans one day, "By Allah, Muhammad cannot tell a better story than I, and his speech is only of old fables that he has copied, as have I." He also said the quotes that are reproduced in verses 4-5. (*Asbab ul-Nuzul*)

Now they're saying, *"What kind of a 'messenger' is this? He eats food (just like we do) and walks around in the markets! Why hasn't an angel been sent down to him to warn us alongside of him?* [7] *Why hasn't he been given a treasure or a nice garden in which to have his meals?"* 1239

Then these same corrupt (critics) say (to the believers), *"You're following some kind of lunatic."* [8] Do you see, (Muhammad,) how they're making you out to be? However, they're the mistaken ones, and they'll never be able to find a path (to salvation). [9]

Blessed be the One Who could grant you far better things than those if He so desired: *gardens beneath which rivers flow and lofty palaces!* [10] But no! They're just denying the Hour (of Judgment). We've prepared a raging blaze for all those who deny the Hour! [11]

When (Hellfire) sees them in the distance, they'll hear its fury and overwhelming roar, [12] and when they're tied up together and cast into a tight crevice within, they'll beg to be obliterated at once! [13] *"Don't beg for just one obliteration today! Beg for endless obliteration!"* [14]

Ask them, *"Is that (fate) better or the Eternal Garden that's been promised to the mindful?"* That'll be their reward and also their final destination. [15] They'll have everything within for which they ever wished, and they can dwell within it forever. Now that's a promise from your Lord for which to pray! [16]

On the day when He's going to gather them all together - *they and the things they used to worship besides Allah* - He's going to ask (those objects of worship), *"Are you the ones who led My servants astray, or did they veer off the path by themselves?"* [17]

"Glory be to You!" they'll cry. *"It wasn't our right to take any protectors besides You. You provided them with abundance, and their ancestors, too, until they finally forgot the message. Thus, they were (proven to be) a worthless bunch of people!"* [18]

(Then Allah will say to the sinners), *"Now (your idols have testified) that what you've been saying is a lie! Now you can no longer avoid (the punishment you deserve), nor will you (find anyone) to help you. Anyone among you who did wrong will now suffer a massive punishment."* [19]

The messengers that We sent before you, (Muhammad), were no more than (ordinary men) who ate food and walked through the markets, and that's how We've made some of you (people) to be a test for others. Won't you be patient then, for your Lord is watching? [20]

They do Nothing but Deny

*T*hose who think that they're never going to meet Us say, *"So why aren't any angels being sent down to us? Why aren't we seeing our Lord (face to face)?"* They think so highly of themselves, and their audacity is enormous! 1240 [21]

When the day comes that they finally do see the angels, the sinners won't have any good news at all that day! They'll cry out (in fear), *"(Where can we hide) to be safe?"* 1241 [22]

Then We'll turn towards whatever (good) deeds they (accumulated in this life) and transform them into mere scattered dust! [23] On that same day, however, the companions of the Garden will have the best place of rest and the finest sanctuary! [24]

1239 The pagans mentioned a garden here to mock the idea of a garden paradise in the next life.

1240 The Prophet said that Allah, Himself, said, "Glory is My robe, and pride is My garment; whoever rivals Me in either of them, I will make him dwell in the Fire." (*Abu Dawud*)

1241 There is an alternative interpretation to the ending quotation in this verse, and that is that instead of the sinners crying out for a safe place to hide, the angels will be telling them that Paradise is a refuge they cannot ever hope to enter. (*Ma'ariful Qur'an*)

The Remorse of an Apostate

$\mathcal{T}$he day when the sky will be shredded by a (descending) cloud, 1242 angels will descend (from within it) in ranks! 1243 [25] That will be the day when ultimate control will rightfully belong to the Compassionate. It's going to be a sore day for those who suppressed (their ability to believe). [26]

That's the day when the one who did wrong will bite his hands and say, "*If only I would've joined with the Messenger on a path (to truth)!* [27] *I'm doomed! If only I would've never taken (Satan) for a friend!* [28] *He led me away from the message after it had come to me! Satan is a traitor to all humanity!*" [29]

Then the Messenger 1244 will say, "*My Lord! My people took this Qur'an as a joke.*" [30] And so We've set up an adversary for every prophet from among the wicked (among his people, whom he must confront), 1245 but your Lord is (powerful) enough to guide and to help. [31]

Then the faithless ask, "*So why isn't the Qur'an revealed to him all at once?*" (It's being revealed at this gradual pace) so We can strengthen your heart with it, for We're releasing it in slow, well-ordered stages. [32]

They don't bring any issue before you without Us revealing to you the most straightforward and appropriate counterpoint. [33] Those who will be cast down prone on their faces as they're being gathered together for Hellfire will be in the worst position and the furthest off the way! [34]

Other Messengers have been Opposed

$\mathcal{A}$nd so it was that We sent the Book to Moses and set up his brother Aaron to be his assistant. [35] We told them, "*Go, both of you, to the people who've denied Our signs.*"

Then We destroyed (those people) completely! [36] Likewise Noah's people – when they denied the messengers, We drowned them all and made (their story a lasting) legacy for people (to remember). We've prepared a painful punishment for the wrongdoers! [37]

1242 This verse is interpreted to mean that after the first blast of the horn, signaling the end, and after the second blast of the horn, signaling the start of Judgment Day, on the plain of judgment, the clouds will part due to the descent of some cloud-like object in which Allah's power will be made manifest. It will be borne by the angels. (*Ma'ariful Qur'an*)

1243 This passage was revealed with regards to 'Uqbah ibn Mu'ayt. 'Uqbah used to be friendly with Muhammad and often invited him over to dinner. When Muhammad became a prophet, he told 'Uqbah that he would no longer be able to dine with him unless he stated that there was only one God and that Muhammad was His messenger. 'Uqbah repeated the words forthwith. The next day, Ubayy ibn Khalaf, a severe critic of the Prophet, found out about 'Uqbah's apparent conversion, and he was very angry with him. Ubayy confronted 'Uqbah about it, and even though 'Uqbah protested that he only said what he said to please Muhammad, Ubayy wasn't convinced. After a lot of arguing, Ubayy got 'Uqbah to renounce Islam. To confirm his rejection of Islam, Ubayy told him to disrespect Muhammad publicly. Thus, 'Uqbah went out and either spit in the Prophet's face or threw animal guts on him in the street. The predicted lamentations of men such as 'Uqbah on Judgment Day are contained in verses 27-29. (*Qurtubi, Asbab ul-Nuzul*)

1244 The Messenger is Prophet Muhammad.

1245 This is an answer to the Prophet as to why he had to face such bitter and wicked foes: it strengthens the resolve of the Prophet, gets every issue out in the open for the masses to consider and enables the patient to acquire good deeds on account of their perseverance. The most prominent enemy for Muhammad during his days in Mecca was his indirect paternal uncle, Abu Jahl. (The Prophet's father was a cousin of Abu Jahl's father.) In Medina it would be the hypocrite, 'Abdullah ibn Ubayy.

And (what of) the 'Ad, Thamud, and the Companions of the Shallow Pool, [1246] and the many generations that passed between them! [38] We sent examples to each of them (to convince them to believe), but then We ruined them completely (on account of their sins). [39]

Already (these pagans of Mecca) must have passed by the (remnants of) the nation (of Sodom and Gomorrah), which (was destroyed) under an awful shower (of brimstone and fire). Haven't they seen (that broken land)! But no! They never expect that they'll be raised to life again! [40]

When they see you, they treat you with scorn, saying, "*Is 'this' the one whom Allah sent as a messenger?* [41] *He almost got us to abandon our gods, except we were so stable (in our devotion to them)."*

Soon enough, when they see the punishment before them, they'll know who was the furthest off the path! [42]

Have you seen the one who takes his own whims for a god? Could you ever manage his affairs? [1247] [43] Do you think that most of them are listening to you or understanding you? They're nothing more than cattle! Even more than that, they're the furthest astray! [44]

Take Note of the Signs of Allah's Power

*H*ave you ever noticed how your Lord lengthens the shadow, (as the afternoon progresses)? If He had wanted, He could've made it stand still, but We've made the sun to be its guide, [45] and then We draw it in towards Us in slow, easy stages. [46]

He's the One Who made the night as a cloak for you and sleep as your manner of rejuvenation, even as He made the daylight for going abroad once more. [47]

He's the One Who sends the winds as heralds of good news going forth from the hands of His mercy. We send cleansing water pouring down from the sky [48] and use it to give life to the barren land, and also to quench the thirst of the herd animals and the many peoples that We've created. [49] And so We distribute it among them so they can remember (the gifts We give to them), but most people are thankless. [50]

If We had wanted, We could've sent a warner to every town (in the world). [51] So don't pay attention to those who suppress (their faith), but rather strive against them using (the logic) of this (Qur'an) with your utmost capacity. [1248] [52]

He's the One Who let loose the two types of flowing waters: one is fresh and sweet, while the other is salty and bitter. Yet, He made a firm barrier between them. [53] He's the One Who created mortals from water, (and then He) established ties of lineage and marriage, for your Lord has also measured (the form of human society). [54]

Yet, still they're worshipping things besides Allah that can bring them neither

---

[1246] Who were the Companions of the Shallow Pool? The commentators differ in their views, but a majority think it refers to a tribe that lived along a trading route in Yemen and that had abundant wells and oasis pools. They are thought to have been a remnant of the previously destroyed tribe of Thamud from the far north of Arabia. Thus, their land is called *Hadramawt*, or "After the Death."

[1247] There was a poor man among the pagans of Mecca who could not afford to purchase an idol of his own. He was forlorn on account of this, as it was the custom that every family would have their own "house idol" to worship. So he took a date that he had, carved a face on it, and then proceeded to worship it as his god. Later in the day, however, he became hungry. After some thought, he popped his "god" in his mouth and ate it. How can you reach a person so fickle as that! These were the kinds of people that the Prophet was trying to reach.

[1248] This verse was revealed in Mecca, long before any order to fight back was given. Therefore, it refers to the mental, logical, theological and verbal struggle that the Muslims were locked into with the pagans.

benefit nor harm! The rejecter (of truth) is ever a collaborator against his Lord! [55] We didn't send you for any other purpose than to give good news and warnings, [56] so say to them, "*I'm not asking you for any reward (for this choice I lay before you) that each of you should choose whether or not he would like to take a path towards his Lord.*" [57]

Put your trust in the One Who's always alive and never dies. Glorify His praise, for He's capable enough to know the shortcomings of His servants. [58]

He's the One Who created the heavens and the earth and everything in between them in six stages, and then He mounted the throne (of power). (He's) the Compassionate! Just ask anyone who has information (about Him)! [59]

When they're told, "*Bow down and prostrate yourselves to the Compassionate,*" they say, "*Who's the Compassionate?* [1249] *Are we really supposed to bow down prostrate to what you're ordering us?*" Thus, their aversion (to Allah) grows! [1250] [60]

Blessed be the One Who placed constellations in the sky and Who placed therein a lamp and a lighted moon. [61] He's the One Who made the night and the day to follow each other (as a sign) for any who wish to be reminded or who wish to be thankful. [62]

Walking the Path of Salvation

The (true) servants of the Compassionate are those who walk humbly through the earth. Whenever the ignorant try to engage them (in futile argument), they say to them, "*Peace.*" [63]

(Allah's true servants) are those who pass the night in worship, prostrating and standing (obediently). [64]

They're the ones who pray, "*Our Lord! Steer the punishment of Hellfire away from us, for its punishment is horrible. [65] Oh, what an awful place in which to reside, and (what an awful place in which) to rest.*" [66]

When they spend (in charity), they're neither extravagant nor stingy but maintain a position in between. [1251] [67] They never call upon anyone else besides Allah, nor do they ever take any life that Allah made sacred, except for a just cause, nor do they commit adultery or fornication.

Anyone who does those things will have to pay the price, [68] and the punishment (he'll face) on the Day of Assembly will be doubled for him.

He'll remain there in disgrace [69] unless he repents, believes and does what's morally right (before he leaves this life), for then Allah will transform his evil (nature) into goodness, for Allah is forgiving and merciful. [70] Whoever repents and does what's morally right has genuinely repented to Allah. [71]

(Allah's true servants) are those who (keep themselves away from situations) where they would witness fraud or corruption. If they pass by foolishness, they pass by it with dignity. [72]

Whenever (Allah's true servants) are admonished with their Lord's (revealed) verses, they don't act as if they're deaf or blind to them. [73] They're the ones who pray, "*Our Lord! Grant us spouses and children*

[1249] The Arabs had never known *Allah*, or the Supreme God, by the name of *Compassionate*. Therefore, when the Qur'an started calling Allah by that designation, the Meccans were resistant to adopt that new title for Allah.

[1250] After reading this verse, it is customary for the one who has faith in Allah to prostrate himself on the floor and praise Allah.

[1251] The Prophet said, "The thoughtful man adopts a middle course in his spending habits." In a related saying he explained that a person who is moderate in his spending would never become destitute. (*Ma'ariful Qur'an*)

who will be a comfort to our eyes, and make us leaders in righteousness." [74]

These are the ones who will be rewarded with a lofty place (in Paradise) on account of their perseverance, and they're the ones who will be met with welcome and peace. [75] They'll remain there, *and* oh, what a beautiful place in which to reside, and (what a beautiful place in which) to rest! [1252] [76]

(So now say to the faithless), "*My Lord won't have any regard for you unless you call upon Him, but you're denying (Him), so soon your (lack of faith) will keep you tied (to an awful doom).*" [77]

[1252] Critics of Islam sometimes point out the sensual and very material nature of the Islamic conception of Paradise, suggesting that Islam promises its followers a very pleasurable rather than spiritual afterlife. Besides the fact that no other promise would capture the imagination of large numbers of people and make them willing to forgo pleasure in this world for the sake of the next, the Qur'an emphasizes that spiritual concerns will reign supreme there. People will be praising Allah and interacting with each other in righteousness. Doesn't the New Testament of the Bible contain tantalizing hints of a sensual and material afterlife, with references to pearly gates, streets paved with gold, and banquets prepared for the faithful?

The Poets

26 Ash Shu'ara'
Middle Meccan Period

The idol-worshippers of Mecca persistently denied the message of the Prophet. They made up one excuse after another for rejecting it. These ranged from denying that their idols were false inventions to complaints that Muhammad wasn't showing them spectacular miracles. This chapter opens with words of encouragement to the Prophet that he shouldn't let grief and sorrow over the disbelief of his people weigh down too heavily upon him. Thereafter, it discusses, in various ways and through various stories of the past, that Allah's signs are evident both in nature and in the course of human history.

It must be remembered that Muhammad *was* given powerful miracles, as well, such as the Qur'an, itself (a nearly illiterate man from Arabia suddenly spouting literature and poetry of the highest order, whose message was more than mere poetry), to more concrete things such as making true predictions, making the moon appear to split, and preaching a message that brought out the very best in its followers. However, the pagans made excuses for those things, as well. (Not finding any human explanation for the Qur'an, they took to saying Muhammad was possessed by a jinn who gave him the words. For the moon, they said Muhammad had cast a spell over them and bewitched their eyes. For the good conduct of his followers, they said his followers were just low common people who didn't know any better.)

In the Name of Allah,
the Compassionate, the Merciful

Tā. Seen. Meem. [1]

These are the verses of the clear Book. [2] Maybe you'll worry yourself to death because they won't believe. [3]

If We had wanted, We could've sent a miracle from the sky down upon them that would've definitely made them bow their necks in humility! [4]

However, a fresh reminder from the Compassionate never comes to them without their turning away from it. [5]

And so it is that they've denied (this message). Yet, (the effects) of the prophecy at which they're laughing will soon come down upon them! [6]

Haven't they looked at the earth and how many wonderful pairs of things We've grown upon it? [1253] [7]

These are indeed miracles, but most of them put no faith (in them). [8] Yet, even still, your Lord is the Powerful and the Merciful! [9]

[1253] This is a reference to the pairs of males and females among nearly most creatures. Even most plants have pairs of organs of different genders that are fertilized by the actions of insects and other creatures.

Moses and Aaron are Sent to Pharaoh

*W*hen your Lord called out to Moses, He said, "*Go to the people of corruption!* [10] *Go to the people of Pharaoh. Won't they be mindful (of Allah)?*" [11]

(Moses) said, "*My Lord! I'm afraid they're going to call me a liar!* [12] *(I'm afraid) that I might be stricken with fright and that I might stammer in my words! So send (my brother) Aaron (along with me to help).* [13] *What's more, I've been charged with a crime (in that land), and I'm afraid they're going to kill me.*" [1254] [14]

"*By no means!*" (Allah) replied. "*Both of you go forth with Our signs, for We're going to be with you, and We're going to listen (to your prayers).* [15] *Go then to Pharaoh and say to him, 'We've been sent by the Lord of All the Worlds,* [16] *so send the Children of Israel with us!'*" [17]

The Showdown

(*W*hen Moses arrived in Egypt and delivered his message to Pharaoh), the (Pharaoh) said (to Moses), "*Didn't we take care of you as a child, and didn't you live among us for many years of your life?* [18] *Then you (killed a man) like you did, and you were thankless (for all our kindness towards you)!*" [19]

"*I did do it,*" (Moses) answered, "*but it was a mistake,* [20] *and I ran away from you because I feared you. Since then my Lord has granted me sound judgment and has chosen me to be one of the messengers.* [21] *What's more, for what 'favor' are you scolding me? You're keeping the Children of Israel in bondage!*" [22]

"*And just who is this 'Lord of All the Worlds' (of whom you speak)?*" (Pharaoh) asked. [23]

"*The Lord of the heavens and the earth,*" (Moses) answered, "*and everything in between, if you really want to be sure.*" [24]

"*Do you hear that?*" (Pharaoh) said to those around him. [25]

"*(He's) your Lord and the Lord of your ancestors from the very beginning,*" (Moses) continued. [26]

"*This 'messenger' who's been sent to you (Hebrews) is crazy!*" (Pharaoh) exclaimed. [27]

"*(He's) the Lord of the East and the West and all points in between,*" (Moses) intoned, "*if you only understood!*" [28]

(Then Pharaoh addressed his court), saying, "*If any of you choose a god other than me, then I'll put you in prison!*" [29]

"*Even if I was able to bring you something that clearly (proves the truth of what I'm saying)?*" (Moses) asked. [30]

"*Then bring it on, if you're really so honest!*" (Pharaoh) replied. [31]

So (Moses) threw his staff down, and suddenly it became a serpent, clear (as day)! [32] Then he drew out his hand, and it radiated white (light) for all to see! [33]

Moses Duels With the Sorcerers

(*P*haraoh whispered) to his nobles around him, "*Now that's one skilled sorcerer,* [34] *but his aim is to drive you (and me) out of the country with his magic, so what do you suggest (we do)?*" [1255] [35]

"*Keep him and his brother preoccupied,*" (his nobles replied), "*and then send couriers to every*

[1254] Moses got involved in a fight between a Hebrew slave and an Egyptian. Moses punched the Egyptian and accidentally killed him. That's why he fled Egypt in fear of his life so many years previously. See 28:15-21.

[1255] Being a materialistic man, Pharaoh automatically assumed that Moses and Aaron were merely trying to supplant him in his rule and take over the country. Given that Moses, according to the historian Josephus, had military experience in his younger years, this was a very real possibility.

settlement to collect [36] *back to you all of our most skilled sorcerers."* [37]

Then the sorcerers were gathered in due course for the reserved day (of the showdown). [38] The spectators were asked, *"Are you all gathered here (and ready to watch),* [39] *so we can all (reaffirm our faith) in the ways (of our master Pharaoh) if the sorcerers win?"* [40]

When the sorcerers arrived, they (first) addressed Pharaoh, saying. *"Of course, (we assume) we're going to be well rewarded if we win?"* [41]

"Of course," (Pharaoh answered), *"and when you (do win), you're going to be (promoted) to my inner (council)."* [42]

Moses said to them, *"Cast whatever you're going to cast!"* [43]

So they threw down their ropes and their rods and chanted, *"By the power of Pharaoh, we shall be victorious."* [44]

Then Moses threw down his staff, and (suddenly it became a huge serpent). It swallowed up all the tricks they had devised! [45] Then (the stunned) sorcerers fell down and lay prostrate (on their faces.) [46] *"We believe in the Lord of All the Worlds,"* (they cried), [47] *"the Lord of Moses and Aaron!"* [48]

(Pharaoh was shocked, and) said, *"Have you believed in him before you have my permission? He must have been your leader all along - the one who taught you magic! Well, soon you'll know (who has the real power), for I'm going to cut your hands and feet off from opposite sides, and then I'll hang you all from wooden stakes (to die)!"* [49]

"It doesn't matter (what you do to us)," they replied, *"for we're going back to our Lord (after*

we die). [50] *We only hope that our Lord will forgive us for our mistakes, given that we were (among) the first (of our people) to believe."* [1256] [51]

The Great Escape

We inspired Moses, saying, *"Travel with My servants by night, for you're certainly going to be pursued."* [52] Then Pharaoh sent heralds to every city (to gather his forces.) [53]

(When the army was assembled, he said to them), *"Those (Hebrews) are only a small group,* [54] *and they've brazenly enraged us.* [55] *Now we're gathered in our multitudes, and we were warned well enough in advance (of their plots)."* [56]

And so We lured them (from their land) and from their gardens and springs [57] and opulent wealth. (And in this way they were deprived of) their noble position! [58]

Well there it is, but We made the Children of Israel inherit those (very same things when We established them in the fertile land of Palestine). [59] Meanwhile, (the hordes of Pharaoh) pursued (the Hebrews) at dawn, [60] and when the two groups saw each other, Moses' people cried out, *"Surely we're going to be overtaken!"* [61]

"By no means!" (Moses) cried out, *"for My Lord is with me, and He will guide me (in what to do next)!"* [62] Then We inspired Moses: *"Now strike the sea with your staff!"* Then it divided in two, and each of the sides became as solid as cliffs! [63]

We made (the pursuers) come close (to the center of the path as they pursued the

---

[1256] The medieval poet, Abul A'la of Ma'arri (d. 1057), summed up this very Islamic attitude succinctly when he wrote, "There's a tower of silence; ah! the bell has swung high - another man is meant to be! For some years the song of the bell and the man's life will move in harmony. But alas, when your song ends, so shall your life end, as well! There is no sword necessary for Death to arrive, for he's already here and waiting to strike. Neither helm nor shield will save you from his sudden, fateful swing, for we're all no more than letters, the crooked alphabet of Allah, and He will read us well, before He wipes us all away."

Hebrews in their blind rage). [1257] [64] And then We saved Moses and everyone else who was with him, [65] while We drowned all the rest! [66]

There is indeed a sign in this (story), but most of them don't believe (enough to see it). [67] Your Lord is the Powerful and the Merciful. [68]

Abraham and His Father Speak

$\mathcal{N}$arrate for them (something of) Abraham's (story). [69] He said to his father [1258] and people, "*What are you worshipping?*" [70]

"*We're worshipping idols,*" they replied, "*and we're utterly devoted to them.*" [71]

"*But do they hear you when you call (on them)?*" (Abraham) asked. [72] "*Do they bring you any good (when you worship them) or cause you any harm (if you neglect them)?*" [1259] [73]

"*Not at all!*" they replied. "*However, we found our ancestors doing like this, also.*" [74]

"*Have you taken a good look at what you've been worshipping,*" (Abraham) asked, [75] "*both you and your ancestors before you? [76] (All those things) are my enemies except for the Lord of All the Worlds. [77] (He's) the One Who created me, Who's guiding me [78] and Who provides my food and drink. [79] When I'm sick, He cures me. [80] (He's the) One Who will cause me to die and bring me back to life, [81] and He's the One Who,*

I hope, will forgive my faults on the Day of Judgment." [82]

(Abraham then prayed), "*My Lord! Endow me with wisdom, and make me one of the righteous. [83] Let (my reputation be carried) on the tongues of honest (people) in coming (generations). [84] Make me one of those who inherit the Garden of Delight.*" [85]

"*Forgive my father, for he's among the mistaken. [86] Don't let me suffer any disgrace on the Day of Resurrection, [87] the day when no amount of wealth or children will do any good, [88] (and when everyone will lose) except for the one who presents a submissive heart to Allah.*" [89]

There will be Regrets for Sinfulness

$\mathcal{T}$he Garden will be brought near to those who were mindful (of Allah), [90] while the Fire will come in full view of those who were hopelessly lost. [91]

Then they'll be asked, "*Where are those things you used to worship [92] besides Allah? Can they help you now? Can they even help themselves?*" [93]

Then they'll be thrown inside of it, both the (idols) and those who were hopelessly lost, [94] along with the hordes of Iblis all together! [95]

After they're inside (of Hell), they're going to argue (with their lifeless idols), saying, [96] "*By Allah we were clearly mistaken [97] when we thought you were equal with the Lord*

[1257] Different routes out of Egypt have been proposed by historians. Some suggest that the Hebrews crossed into northern Sinai through an area of shallow lakes and that Pharaoh's army was overtaken there. Others suggest that the Hebrews crossed from Egypt into a shallow area of the Red Sea that was miraculously (or plausibly) open for them and that this path led from Egypt into the southernmost tip of the Sinai Peninsula or even northwest Arabia. We may never know for sure the exact route, but the story of this great escape has captivated the imagination of countless generations.

[1258] The Prophet said, "On the Day of Judgment, Abraham will see his father covered with dust and darkness." (*Bukhari*) See 9:113-114 for more discussion about the meaning and result of Abraham's request for forgiveness for his father.

[1259] The Prophet was walking near the Ka'bah one day when he saw a group of pagans worshipping their idols. They set them up and adorned them with ostrich eggs and earrings. Then they started bowing to them. Muhammad exclaimed, "People of Quraysh! You're going against the creed of your fathers, Abraham and Ishmael, who both submitted (to Allah)." The pagans replied, "Muhammad, we're only worshipping them so they bring us closer to Allah." (*Asbab ul-Nuzul*)

443

of All the Worlds. [98] *What were they, those (people) who seduced us (into idol-worship), except for wicked (liars)!* [99] *Now we have no one to speak out for us* [100] *nor a single friend to feel (sympathy for us).* [101] *If only we had the chance to go back (to our former lives), then we would surely be among the believers!"* [102]

There is a sign in this (realization of theirs); yet, most of them don't believe. [103] Yet, even still, your Lord is the Powerful and Merciful One. [104]

The People of Noah Denied

$\mathcal{N}$oah's people denied the messengers. [105] Noah, their brother, said to them, *"Won't you be mindful (of Allah)?* [106] *I'm a trustworthy messenger for you,* [107] *so be mindful of Allah and obey me.* [108] *I'm not asking you for any reward for this (preaching), because my reward is due from none other than the Lord of All the Worlds,* [109] *so be mindful of Allah and obey me!"* [110]

"Should we believe in you," they asked, *"seeing that only low class people are following you?"* [1260] [111]

"Just what do I know about what they're doing?" he replied. [112] *"Their account is with none other than my Lord, if you only understood.* [113] *I'm not going to drive away those who believe,* [114] *for I'm no more than a clear warner!"* [115]

"If you don't stop (what you're doing)," they threatened, *"then we're going to stone you!"* [116]

"My Lord!" (Noah) cried. *"My people have denied me,* [117] *so make an open decision*

between us, and save me and those believers who are with me!"* [118]

And so We saved him and those who were with him in a crowded boat, [119] and then We drowned all those who remained behind. [120]

There is a sign in this; yet, most of them don't believe. [121] Yet, even still, your Lord is the Powerful and Merciful One. [122]

The People of 'Ad Denied

$\mathcal{T}$he (people of) 'Ad denied the messengers. [123] Hūd, their brother, said to them, *"Won't you be mindful (of Allah)?* [124] *I'm a trustworthy messenger for you,* [125] *so be mindful of Allah and obey me.* [126] *I'm not asking you for any reward for this (preaching), because my reward is due from none other than the Lord of All the Worlds."* [127]

"Are you erecting monuments on every high place just to amuse yourselves? [128] *Are you constructing buildings for yourselves that will last forever?* [129] *When you exercise your power, will you do it with more force than necessary?* [130] *Be mindful of Allah, and obey me!* [131] *Be mindful of the One Who taught you everything you know* [132] *and Who gave you livestock and children* [133] *and gardens and springs.* [134] *I fear for you the punishment of an awful day."* [135]

"It's all the same to us," they said, *"whether you inform us or don't inform us,* [136] *for (your teachings) are no more than the invention of the ancients.* [137] *We're certainly never going to get any kind of punishment!"* [138]

Then they denied him, so We destroyed them. There is a sign in this; yet,

---

[1260] There was a poor bedouin named Zahir ibn Haram who used to bring small presents to the Prophet whenever he came to Medina to trade. The Prophet used to praise him and called him, "...our bedouin and our villager." Zahir was a very unattractive, ugly-looking man, however, and he had always been teased when he was younger. Thus, he had very low self-esteem. One day, the Prophet saw him in the marketplace, and he approached Zahir from the back and gave him a hug. Zahir didn't recognize who was hugging him, so he said angrily, "Let me go. Who is this?" When he turned around and saw the Prophet, he felt ashamed at his gruff reply, and he turned back around in sorrow, leaning on the Prophet's chest. Zahir then cried out somberly, "Who will buy me as a slave? O Messenger of Allah, you can see that I'm worthless, by Allah!" The Prophet answered him, saying, "But in Allah's sight you are not worthless." (*Sharh as-Sunnah*)

most of them don't believe. [139] Yet, even still, your Lord is the Powerful and Merciful One. [140]

The People of Thamud Denied

*T*he (people of) Thamud denied the messengers. [1261] [141] Salih, their brother, said to them, *"Won't you be mindful (of Allah)?* [142] *I'm a trustworthy messenger for you,* [143] *so be mindful of Allah and obey me.* [144] *I'm not asking you for any reward for this (preaching), because my reward is due from none other than the Lord of All the Worlds."* [145]

"(Do you think) you're just going to be left alone in safety with all that you have here, [146] *with (your) gardens and springs* [147] *and crops and fruitful date palms?* [148] *You confidently carve your homes out of mountain sides,* [149] *(but that won't keep you safe from Allah's wrath), so be mindful of Allah and obey me.* [150] *Don't obey (the ways) of the high and mighty* [151] *who cause chaos and disorder in the land and improve nothing."* [152]

"You've been bewitched!" they cried. [153] *"You're no more than a mortal man like the rest of us. So bring us a miracle if you're telling the truth!"* [154]

"Here's a camel," he replied. *"She has her turn to drink (water from the well), and you'll have your turn to water (your animals) on your reserved day.* [155] *Don't let any harm come to her, or* *punishment will take hold of you on an awful day."* [156]

Then they crippled her, and although they came to regret it, [157] the punishment seized them nonetheless. There is a sign in this; yet, most of them don't believe. [158] Yet, even still, your Lord is the Powerful and Merciful One. [159]

The People of Lot Denied

*T*he people of Lot denied the messengers. [160] Lot, their brother, [1262] said to them, *"Won't you be mindful (of Allah)?* [161] *I'm a trustworthy messenger for you,* [162] *so be mindful of Allah and obey me."* [163]

"I'm not asking you for any reward for this (preaching), because my reward is due from none other than the Lord of All the Worlds. [164] *Out of (everyone available to you) in the whole world, are you approaching (other) men (for your lusts)* [165] *and leaving behind the ones whom your Lord created for you to be your mates? No way! You're a people who are completely out of control!"* [166]

"If you don't stop (what you're saying)," they threatened, *"then we're going to drive you away!"* [167]

"I detest what you're doing!" he replied. [168] *"My Lord! Save me and my family from what they're doing!"* [169] So we saved him

---

[1261] The Thamud are a people who lived centuries before the time of the Prophet in an area that encompasses part of northern Arabia and southern Jordan. Their homes, which were carved in the sides of cliffs and small mountains, can still be seen today.

[1262] Lot settled in Sodom (Sadum), which (is generally believed) to have been located somewhere near the present-day Dead Sea. His extended family, friends and servants assimilated into the culture of the locals, and he dwelt among them for many years. This is why he is also called 'their brother,' which is a term in Arabic (and English) that can be used in the sense of a companion, a citizen of a place, an ideological convert or compatriot, or someone who becomes part of the people they live among by virtue of time. The Qur'an affirms that Lot was the blood relation of Abraham and that they both left their homeland to flee idol-worship and then parted ways at some point, with Lot going to the city and Abraham living as a bedouin. The use of 'brother' in the Qur'an doesn't always mean a direct blood relation, and the other prophets mentioned in this chapter, such as Salih, Hud and Shu'ayb, who are also called 'brothers' to their people, are not technically being called the blood relative of everyone in their tribe. The Meccan Muslims and Medinan Muslims were called 'brothers' in the Qur'an, as well, even though they were often unrelated, simply on account of the fact that they dwelt in each other's company and developed a strong bond of solidarity. Further still, all Muslims are called the brothers (and sisters) of every other Muslim by virtue of group identity.

and his family all together, [170] save for an old woman who remained behind. [1263] [171]

Then We destroyed (the others) to the last (man)! [172] We rained a shower (of brimstone) down upon them, and it was a terrible downpour upon those who had been warned! [173] There is a sign in this; yet, most of them don't believe. [174] Yet, even still, your Lord is the Powerful and Merciful One. [175]

The People of Madyan Denied

𝒯he Companions of the Thicket denied the messengers. [176] Shu'ayb [1264] said to them, *"Won't you be mindful (of Allah)? [177] I'm a trustworthy messenger for you, [178] so be mindful of Allah and obey me. [179] I'm not asking you for any reward for this (preaching), because my reward is due from none other than the Lord of All the Worlds."* [180]

"Measure (what you sell) fairly, and don't shortchange, [181] and weigh with accurate scales. [182] Don't withhold what people are owed, and don't cause chaos and disorder in the land. [183] Be mindful of the One Who created you and the people of old." [184]

"You've been bewitched!" they cried. [185] *"You're no more than a mortal man like the rest us, and we think you're a liar. [186] So make a piece of the sky fall down upon us if you're really telling the truth!"* [187]

"My Lord knows best about what you're doing." he replied. [188] And so they denied him and thus were seized with punishment on a dark and gloomy day - *and that was a tremendous day of punishment!* [189] There is a sign in this; yet, most of them don't believe. [190] Yet, even still, your Lord is the Powerful and Merciful One. [191]

So Now Listen to Your Lord

𝒯ruly, this revelation is from the Lord of All the Worlds. [192] It was revealed by the Trusted Spirit [1265] [193] to your heart, so you could become a warner [194] in the plain Arabic language. [195] Truly, it was (foretold) in (the scriptures) of old, [196] so isn't it proof enough for them that the scholars among the Children of Israel knew about it? [1266] [197]

If We would've revealed it to a non-Arabic speaker, [198] and if he would've (tried to) recite it (with an accent) to them, then they would never have believed in it. [199]

That's how We've caused the wicked to (reject it) in their hearts (of their own accord, after hearing its message recited clearly). [200] They're not going to believe in it until they see the painful punishment. [201] Even still, it's going to come upon them suddenly when they're not expecting it, [202] and then they're going to cry, *"Won't we get any break?"* [203]

[1263] Lot's wife didn't want to leave, as she was enamored of the culture of the people. She was a traitor to her husband and used to tell the men of the street whenever Lot had visitors. (See 66:10.)

[1264] This time, the pattern of this chapter is broken in that Shu'ayb is not called 'their brother.' According to Ibn Kathir, it is because this group of people, who were the people of Madyan, are given the title here of the idol they worshipped, which was a unique tangle of twisted trees in a single formation. Their 'goddess' resided within the thicket, or *aykah*. Neither Prophet Shu'ayb nor any other prophet should be called the 'brother' of a people if their idol's name is given in their specified title. (In 7:85 he is called 'their brother', but the nation is referred to as the 'People of Madyan.' This is a very fascinating and often overlooked aspect of the precise nature of many Qur'anic details.)

[1265] This refers to the archangel Gabriel, who carries the divine revelation from Allah to Allah's chosen prophets. He is also sometimes called the Holy Spirit in the Qur'an (see 2:87).

[1266] This is an apparent reference to some Jewish scholars who had come to Mecca to investigate the man who was claiming revelation from God, namely, Muhammad. From the context it is clear that they publicly endorsed that it was at least similar to what they had. The details of this encounter have not survived, however. Perhaps verses 198-199 are an answer to the issue of why the Qur'an was being revealed in Arabic, when the book of Moses was revealed in Hebrew, and Allah knows best.

So are they asking for Our punishment to be hurried on? [204] What do you think? (Should We) let them enjoy themselves for a few years longer [205] and then bring down upon them what they've been promised? [206]

Oh, but nothing they enjoyed will do them any good then! [207] We never destroyed any town without (sending) warners [208] to remind (them about Allah) first, and We were never unfair (to any of them). [209]

Evil Cannot Produce Good

This (Qur'an) is not being revealed by any devils, [210] for it's not in agreement with (their values), nor could they ever (make something like this). [211] On the contrary, they're far removed from ever even hearing (anything like this from their own kind)! [212]

Don't call upon any other deity besides Allah, for if you do, then you'll be punished. [213] Warn your nearest relatives, [1267] [214] and lower your wing (in kindness) to the believers who follow you. [215] If they ever disobey you, then say, *"I'm not responsible for what you've done."* [216]

Trust in the Powerful and Merciful, [217] Who sees you standing upright (when you pray), [218] even as He sees your movements when you're among (people) who are prostrating (to Allah in unison). [219] He is the Hearing and the Knowing. [220]

Poetry can be Positive or Negative

Should I inform you about those upon whom the devils really descend? [221] They descend upon every lying, sinful (fortune-teller), [222] who listens to (the evil things) that they're told, and most of them are liars. [1268] [223]

As (for the slanderous words) of (hostile) poets, only the hopelessly lost follow them. [224] Haven't you seen how they wander aimlessly in every valley [225] and how they speak about things they don't even do? [1269] [226]

Exempted (from this blanket condemnation) are those (poets) who believe and do what's morally right, and who remember Allah often and defend themselves (in verse) only after they've been unfairly attacked. Soon enough those who are wrong will know by what kind of damage they're going to be vanquished! [227]

[1267] The Prophet was commanded to warn his clan, the Banu Hashim, and other related clans. Once he approached the people of a clan near to his own and said to them, "O Banu Abd' Munaf! I'm a warner. My example is that of a man who sees the enemy, so he rushes to save his family, fearing that the enemy will reach them before he does." (*Muslim, Nisa'i*)

[1268] Devils or evil jinns descend upon fortune-tellers and whisper secrets into their minds. Once some people asked the Prophet about fortune-tellers, and the Prophet answered, "They're nothing." Then the people pointed out that sometimes they made true predictions, whereupon the Prophet said, "That's just a true report that the jinn snatched (by spying on the angels), then he babbles it like the clucking of a chicken into the ear of his friend, but he mixes it with more than a hundred lies." (*Bukhari*) In another narration the Prophet said that people hear one true prediction from a fortune-teller, and based on that they decide to believe everything he says, just because he got something right once. (*Bukhari*)

[1269] The poets of Arabia were essentially the wandering comedians, propagandists and entertainers of their age. Many pagan poets turned their verbal talents against the Muslims and viciously ridiculed them at every turn with great venom. The Muslims had their own poets, as well, and they were sometimes employed in answering the enemy poets in the ongoing propaganda wars. See 49:5 for one such episode when there were dueling poets. One famous poet named 'Abdullah ibn az-Zab'ari told the Prophet upon his conversion, "Messenger of Allah! My tongue will surely try to make up for the things it said when I was bad - when I used to go along with Satan during my years astray." (*Ibn Kathir*) The Prophet himself explained that verses 221-226 apply only to poets who use their talents for evil, while verse 227 applies to poets who use their talents for good. (*Ma'ariful Qur'an*)

The Ant

27 An-Naml
Middle Meccan Period

This chapter presents a series of dramatic episodes in the lives of several previous prophets. There are various lessons that can be gleaned from this chapter. Thus, it is something of a "teachable moment" for those who listen to it and ponder over its meanings. The chapter also introduces the concept that non-human creatures also communicate with each other and that human beings can also learn to communicate with some of them.

In the Name of Allah,
the Compassionate, the Merciful

Tā. Seen.

These are the verses of the Qur'an and the clear Book. [1] (It's) a guide and a source of good news for the believers. [2] They're the ones who establish prayers, 1270 give in charity, and have full confidence of the next life. [3]

We're going to make the deeds of those who don't believe in the next life appear dazzling to them so they can wander around confused. [4] They're the ones who will have a painful punishment, and in the next life they're going to be losers. [5] As for you, (Muhammad,) you're receiving the Qur'an from the very presence of a wise and knowing Being. [6]

The Day Moses was Chosen

*M*oses said to his family, *"I noticed a fire (on the mountain). I'll (go there) and bring you some news (if it's from a traveler's campfire), or (if not,) then I'll at least bring you a burning*

branch to light our campfire so you can be warm." [7]

When he approached the fire, a voice called out, *"Blessed be whoever is within this fire, and whoever is around it, and all glory be to Allah, the Lord of All the Worlds. [8] Moses! I am Allah, the Powerful and the Wise. [9] Now throw your staff down (on the ground)!"* (So Moses did as he was told), but when he saw it start to move and wiggle like a snake, he turned to run away.

"Moses! Don't be afraid, for in My presence those who are messengers need not fear, [10] but if any commit injustice and then afterwards trade their evil ways for good; yet, still, I'm forgiving and merciful. [11] Now put your hand in your cloak, and it will come away blazing white (even though you won't be burned). (These are but two) of the nine (miraculous) signs for Pharaoh and his people, for they're a rebellious people." [12]

When Our signs reached (the court of Pharaoh), so they might open their eyes, they said instead, *"This is obviously magic!"* [13] Thus, they arrogantly scoffed at them, even though they were convinced of them deep down in their souls. Then just see how We defeat the disobedient! [14]

1270 Ibn Sina (aka *Avicenna*, d. 1037) wrote: "Prayer is the thing that allows the soul to realize its connection with the Divine. Through prayers, human beings worship the truth and look forward to an everlasting reward. Prayer is the cornerstone of the religion, and the religion is the means by which a soul is cleansed of all that defiles it. Prayer is the worship of the Originator of all things, the Supreme Ruler of the World, the Source of All Strength. Prayer is the adoration of the One Whose existence is needed." (*Kitabul Najat*)

Solomon and the Hoopoe

$\mathcal{A}$nd so it was that We gave knowledge to David and Solomon, and they both declared, "*Praise be to Allah, Who favored us above so many of His believing servants!*" [15]

Solomon was David's heir, and he announced, "*O people! We've been taught the language of the birds,* [1271] *and we've been given (knowledge) of so many things.* [1272] *This is clearly a favor (from Allah)."* [16]

The crowds of jinns and men were lined up at attention before Solomon, along with the birds, and they were all kept in ranks. [17]

(He marched with them) until they came to a valley full of ants. One of the ants (was alarmed), and she said, "*All you ants! Get in your homes, or Solomon and his huge (army) might crush you without even knowing it!*" [18]

(Solomon) smiled, amused at what she said, and he exclaimed, "*My Lord! Grant me the capacity to be grateful for all Your favors, which You've bestowed upon me and my parents, so I can do what's right and pleasing to You. Admit me, through Your mercy, into the company of Your righteous servants."* [19]

(One day) he was taking a roll call of the birds and said, "*Why don't I see the hoopoe? Is he absent without leave?* [20] *I'll definitely punish him severely or even slaughter him, unless he brings me a good excuse."* [21]

The hoopoe wasn't long in coming, though, and he gave his report, saying, "*I'm coming to you with a report about something of which you're unaware. I've just come back from (the land of) Sheba, and I have an accurate report.* [22] *I found a woman there who was ruling over them with every necessary resource of authority, and she also had a magnificent throne."* [1273] [23]

"*I found her and her people worshipping the sun in place of Allah. Satan has truly made their actions seem dazzling to their eyes. He's kept them away from the path, so they're without the guidance* [24] *that would prompt them to worship Allah alone, the One Who brings to light what's hidden within the heavens and the earth and Who knows what you hide and show.* [25] *Allah! There is no god but He, the Lord of the throne of glory!"* [1274] [26]

(Solomon) said, "*We'll soon see whether you told the truth or not.* [27] *Go and carry this letter of mine, and deliver it to them. Then stand back, and wait (for the reply) that they'll send back with you."* [28]

[1271] How was the bird able to *speak* to Solomon? Solomon kept a number of birds in his service for sending messages, such as carrier pigeons, which were also used in many other cultures. He may have also had a number of hunting birds such as falcons and eagles. The hoopoe is a bird common to the Middle East. Returning to the original question, could a man ever 'speak' to an animal, or could an animal ever 'speak' to a man? Allah gave Solomon this ability to converse with animals. It is not an unheard of concept, for the Bible records a man having a conversation with a donkey, by Allah's command. See Numbers 22:28-32. In addition, modern researchers have taught certain apes how to communicate with sign language, and some of them have developed quite impressive communication skills.

[1272] Solomon is using the 'royal we' in his speech. Referring to himself in the plural to emphasize his royal being and his authority. The vehicle of talking birds was the inspiration for the famous Muslim fable, *The Conference of Birds*, by Fariduddin 'Attar (d. c. 1220). It is sort of like a Muslim *Canterbury Tales*. The hoopoe bird is the main character and guide for all the other birds who were searching for their king (which was a metaphor for people seeking Allah).

[1273] This female ruler is traditionally called Bilquis and she was the Queen of Sheba, which was located in modern-day Yemen. The Old Testament and even the Jewish apocrypha (II Targum of Esther) record a similar tale as found here, though with some significant differences. See I Kings 10:1-13 or II Chronicles 9:1-12.

[1274] After reading this verse, it is customary for the one who has faith in Allah to prostrate himself on the floor and praise Allah.

The Queen of Sheba

*T*he Queen of Sheba, addressed her court), saying, *"All you nobles! A regal letter has been delivered to me.* [29] *It's from Solomon, and it reads as follows:*

'In the Name of Allah, the Compassionate, the Merciful. [30]

Don't be too proud to (heed my request), so come to me submissively.' [31]

"All you nobles," she then asked, *"counsel me what I should do about this situation, for I've never decided any issue without your advice."* [32]

"We're a powerful nation," they said, *"and we can wage fierce warfare, but it's your decision, so think deeply on what you will command."* [33]

"When kings enter a land," she mused, *"they ruin it and turn the best of its people into the worst, and that's just what they do."* [34]

(Then she said), *"I will send him a gift, and then I'll see with what (response) my ambassadors will return."* [35]

When (the ambassadors bearing gifts) came to Solomon, he said to them, *"Are you going to bring me mere treasure, when what Allah has already given me is far better than what He's given to you!* [1275] *Not so! You're the ones who are pleased with your gifts!* [36] *Return (home) to (your kingdom), and mark my word that I'll be coming to (your people) with such forces that they'll never be able to withstand, and (unless your queen comes here to meet me), we'll drive them away from there in disgrace, and they'll be humiliated!"* [37]

Solomon and the Queen

*S*olomon) said, *"All you nobles! Which of you can bring her throne to me before she arrives here to submit?"* [38]

A powerful, yet cunning, jinn [1276] said, *"I'll have it brought to you before you even stand up from your meeting, for I'm strong enough to do that, and you can surely trust me (with this task)!"* [39]

(However, another jinn) who was well-versed in knowledge of the scripture said, *"I'll bring it to you in the twinkling of an eye."*

Then when Solomon saw it appear right there in front of him, he said, *"This is by the favor of my Lord as a test to see whether I'm thankful or not. Whoever is thankful (for the blessings that Allah gave him), then his gratitude is for (the good of) his own soul. Whoever is thankless, well, My Lord is self-sufficient and noble."* [40]

Then he commanded, *"Disguise her throne so she won't even recognize it. Let's see whether she (is capable) of being guided (to the truth) or if she's one of those who can't be guided."* [41]

So when she arrived, she was asked, *"Is this your throne?"*

She exclaimed, *"It looked just like this! We knew about this before, and we hereby submit (to Allah)."* [42] She had only been diverted from (true faith before) by what she used to

---

[1275] The Prophet joined some of his companions after he had bathed and dressed himself. 'Umar ibn al-Khattab remarked, "You're looking happy today, Messenger of Allah." The Prophet replied, "Yes, I am." Then people in the gathering started talking about affluence, and the Prophet said, "Affluence is not a bad thing for someone who has the fear of Allah in his heart, but remember, for a righteous person, good health is even better than affluence, and being cheerful is a bounty bestowed by Allah." (*Ahmad*)

[1276] An *ifrit* is a powerful and cunning type of jinn that is ever bent on creating mischief. Solomon chose the second jinn to bring Bilquis's throne because he didn't boast when he offered his services. Perhaps the first one was planning to embarrass Solomon or do some act of mischief. Perhaps this is the jinn of whom fables speak, who was imprisoned in the lamp later found by Aladdin! Thus, Qur'anic stories even informed the fiction and fantasy literature of Muslim civilization.

serve in place of Allah, for she was (raised among) a people who had no faith. [43]

She was asked to enter within (the main hall) of the palace, but when she saw the floor (and how it sparkled translucently), she thought it was a pool (of water).

She lifted up the ends of her dress, exposing her legs, (and was about to walk into the room like that), when (Solomon) said, *"This floor is reflective, for it's been polished to a clear shine!"*

(The queen) exclaimed, *"My Lord! I truly did wrong against my own soul. I submit, along with Solomon, to the Lord of All the Worlds."* [44]

The Trials of the Thamud

$\mathcal{A}$nd so it was that We sent Salih, their brother, to the (people of) Thamud, and he said, *"Serve Allah!"* Thereafter, (his people) divided into two competing factions. [45]

(Salih) said, *"My people! Why are you asking for something dreadful to be hurried on instead of something good? If you would just ask Allah to forgive you, you might receive mercy."* [46]

"We see a bad omen in you," [1277] they answered, *"and in those with you."*

(Salih) responded to them, saying, *"Your bad omen is with Allah. No way! You're a people who are being tested."* [47]

The Plot of the Nine Assassins

$\mathcal{N}$ow in the city there lived nine men from one clan who often caused trouble in the land, and furthermore they made no effort to reform themselves. [1278] [48] They said to each other, *"Let's swear together in Allah's name that we'll ambush him and his followers by night, then we can (lie) to his patrons later on, saying, 'We never saw any attack on his people, and we're telling the truth!'"* [49]

Thus, they plotted and planned, but We were planning, too, even though they didn't realize it. [50] So see how their plot was foiled! [1279] Then We destroyed them and their people all together! [51] Their houses were left in ruins because of their corruption, and in this is a sign for people who know. [52] We saved those who believed, however, and who were mindful (of Allah). [53]

The Example of Prophet Lot

$\mathcal{L}$ot said to his people, *"Will you do something so perverted, even watching it (in public)! [54] Are you really using men instead of*

[1277] Bad omens or signs are a kind of superstition. For the Arabs (and the Romans before them), they were sometimes represented in the erratic habits of birds. The Prophet said, "(Believing in) omens is like making partners (with Allah). People may see a glimpse of their (portents), but Allah dispels (omens when people) put their reliance (on Him)." (*Ahmad, Abu Dawud*)

[1278] The story is told that the nine men mentioned in this passage were noblemen of the tribe. Two pagan women, one who divorced a follower of Salih and an old woman with several beautiful daughters, held a bitter grudge against Salih. The two women publicly offered a reward to anyone who would kill the camel. Finally the two women each recruited a man to do the job. The divorcee promised her assassin money, while the old woman promised her most beautiful daughter to the killer she hired. Seven other men of the clan were also recruited. The nine men ambushed the camel and shot its leg with an arrow. To encourage them, the beautiful daughter of the old woman accompanied the men and showed her face to them. The men set upon the camel and savagely killed it with their swords. When Salih was informed of what had happened, he told the people of his tribe, "*Enjoy yourselves in your homes for three days.*" (See 11:65) (*Ibn Kathir*)

[1279] The nine men plotted to kill Salih before the threatened three-day limit was up. They knew where he used to pray in solitude in the countryside, and they waited to ambush him in a grotto. However, a rock slide covered the plotters in their hiding place, and they were never heard from again. (*Ibn Kathir*)

women for your passions? That's not right! You're an ignorant people!" [55]

His people gave him no other answer than to say, "*Drive them out! Drive out the followers of Lot from the city - these people who want to be so clean and pure!*" [56]

We saved him and his family, except for his wife, for We determined that she would remain behind. [57] Then We rained down upon them a shower (of brimstone), and it was a terrible downpour upon the warned. [58]

Which is Better?

Say (to them), "*Praise be to Allah, and peace be upon His servants whom He has chosen!*" So who's better - Allah or the 'partners' they make with Him? [59] (Which of them) created the heavens and the earth and sends down water from the sky?

In fact, We use it to produce the lovely orchards (in which you find so much delight). It's not in *your* power to make the trees within them grow (without Allah's help. So can there be another) god with Allah? No way! (Those who think otherwise) are people with no sense of justice! [60]

Who made the earth a stable place on which to live with rivers flowing in its midst, and (who) placed firm highlands upon it? (Who) settled a boundary between the two bodies of water, (salty and fresh,) so they don't mingle? (Can there be another) god with Allah? No way! Yet, most of them don't know. [61]

Who answers the call of a distressed person when he calls upon Him? [1280] Who

relieves his suffering and makes you inherit the earth? (Can there be another) god with Allah? *Oh, how few reminders you accept!* [62]

Who guides you through the darkness of both land and sea, and who sends the winds as bearers of good news ahead of His mercy? (Can there be another) god with Allah? Allah is high above what they associate with Him! [63]

Who initiated the creation (of all things) and then renews it, and who gives you resources from both the sky and the earth? (Can there be another) god with Allah? So say to them, "*Bring out your evidence if you're really so honest!*" [64]

Then tell them, "*None in the heavens nor on the earth, besides Allah, knows the unseen, nor can they be aware of when they're going to be resurrected.*" [65] No way! They can neither understand nor comprehend the (magnitude) of the next life. No way! They're confused about it, and they can never be anything but blind to it! [66]

The Faithless Deny

The faithless ask, "*After we've crumbled to dust, are we really going to be raised (from the dead) – both ourselves and our ancestors?* [67] *Well, both ourselves and our ancestors were already promised this in the past, but it's all no more than ancient fables.*" [68]

Say (to them), "*Go abroad in the world, and see how the wicked (civilizations of the past) came to an end.*" [69] Then feel no sadness for them, (Muhammad,) nor worry yourself over their plots. [70]

They ask, "*So when will this promise (come to pass), if you're really so honest?*" [71] Tell

---

[1280] The Prophet said, "Anyone who is overcome by sadness or grief and supplicates in the following words, surely Allah will remove his grief and sadness and exchange them for delight: 'O Allah! I am your servant and the child of your female servant. My forelock is in your hand. Your decision regarding me will surely come to pass. Your judgment is fair towards me. I invoke You by every name You have and by which You call Yourself, as they're sent down in Your Book, taught to any of Your creatures, or kept with You in the knowledge of the unseen that's there with You. Make the Glorious Qur'an the springtime of my heart, the light of my chest, the remover of my grief and the dissolver of my concerns.'" (*Ahmad*)

them, *"It just might be that some of what you want to hurry on could be close behind you!"* [72] Your Lord is favorable towards people, but most of them are thankless. [73]

Your Lord knows what's hidden in (people's) hearts, even as He knows what they reveal. [74] There's nothing hidden in the heavens or on earth without it being recorded in a clear record. [75]

The Solution to Jewish Doctrinal Disputes

This Qur'an addresses most of that over which the Children of Israel disagree, [76] and it's a guide and a mercy for those who believe. [77]

Your Lord will decide between them according to His judgment, for He's the Powerful and the Knowing. [78] So trust (your affairs) to Allah, for you're on (the path) of clear truth. [79]

You can't make the dead listen, nor can you force the deaf to hear your call - *especially since they're running away in retreat.* [80]

You can't guide the blind, either, nor can you prevent them from swerving aside. You can only make those listen who believe in Our signs, and who then submit (voluntarily). 1281 [81]

The Judgment cannot be Denied

When the sentence (of Allah's judgment) is fulfilled against (the faithless), We're going to produce a thing creeping from the earth, 1282 and it will speak to them, for humanity has never been convinced of Our miraculous signs. [82]

And one day We're going to collect from every community a group of those who denied Our signs, and they'll (be made to stand) at attention [83] until they come (before Allah for judgment). He'll ask them, *"Did you deny My signs, even though you weren't sure (if you should have done that or not), or were you doing something else?"* [84]

And so the sentence will be fulfilled against them on account of their corruption, and they won't be able to offer a defense. [85]

The Final Word

Don't they see that We made the night for them to rest in and the day for them to see? There are signs in this for people who believe! [86]

On the day when the trumpet will blow, all beings within the heavens and the

---

1281 A man named Amr went to the Prophet and said, "Give me your right hand so that I may give you my pledge of loyalty." The Prophet stretched out his right hand, but then Amr withdrew his hand abruptly. The Prophet said, "What has happened to you, O Amr?" He replied, "I need to lay down one condition." The Prophet asked, "What condition do you intend to put forward?" Amr said, "That Allah forgives my sins." The Prophet said, "Didn't you know that converting to Islam erases all previous sins?" (*Muslim, Ahmad*)

1282 The thing *that will creep from the earth and speak* has always been an enigmatic subject for the commentators. The Arabic word *dâbatan* is usually translated as a *beast*, and the Prophet predicted that in the End Times a *dâbatan* will rise from the earth and speak. What does this mean? Is a monster of some sort going to wake up underground and emerge and speak to people? There are a variety of interpretations on this issue. What we can add is that it must be remembered that Arabic words oftentimes have multiple and widely varied meanings. The root word of this term, which is *daba*, means anything from a crawling reptile or a horse or mule to a rushing outpouring of something. Other meanings include vitality, to gain ascendancy and even a sand hill. This verse is saying that in the End Times, when Allah's judgment is about to overshadow the earth and the wicked upon it, that something will come out of the earth and will communicate some type of message to humanity, as something of a final sign to humanity that they never believed in Allah's other signs. What will the *dabatan* actually be? Only Allah knows.

earth will be struck with terror, save for those whom Allah wills, and everyone will come forth in utter humility. [87]

You see the mountains now and assume them to be solid, but they'll drift away (on the Last Day), even as the clouds drift by. That will be Allah's handiwork, for He's the One Who perfects everything, and He's well-informed of all that you do. [88]

If anyone does good, then good will come to him from it, and he'll be safe from terror on that day. [89] If anyone does evil, he'll be thrown on his face in the Fire. Can you ever be rewarded with other than what you did? [90]

(Say to them, Muhammad,) *"As for me, I've been commanded to serve the Lord of this city (of Mecca), the One Who made it holy and Who owns all things. I've been commanded to be among those who submit (to Allah)* [91] *and to recite the Qur'an."* 1283

Whoever is guided is guided for the good of his own soul, while if anyone goes astray, just tell him, *"I'm no more than a warner."* [92]

Then say, *"Praise be to Allah, the One Who will soon show you His signs so you can recognize them, and your Lord is not unaware of what you're doing."* [93]

1283 The Prophet said, "The one who reads the Qur'an aloud is like someone who gives news of charity, while the one who conceals the Qur'an (by not reciting it aloud) is like someone who conceals acts of charity." (*Abu Dawud*) This means that if someone recites the Qur'an to themselves, even though no one knows what they're doing besides Allah, they will be counted as having given charity in secret. If they recite it aloud for all to hear, they are still rewarded, but at a different scale. See 2:271.

The Tales

28 Al Qasas
Late Meccan Period

This is one of the very last Meccan revelations. While some of it was revealed to Muhammad while he was still residing within the city of Mecca, the first 50 and last 4 verses were revealed later, while the Prophet was on the run in the desert during his migration to Yathrib (Medina) in the year 622. Indeed, the pursuing pagans were difficult to elude, and the Prophet, along with Abu Bakr and a trusty guide, were feeling worn down from the journey. Once, while they were encamped, Angel Gabriel came and asked Muhammad if he was feeling homesick. The Prophet replied that he was, and so the story of Moses contained in this chapter was revealed to him to comfort him and strengthen his resolve (verses 1-50). (*Ma'ariful Qur'an*) In the main, this chapter concentrates on the story of Prophet Moses. It is a metaphor for Prophet Muhammad's own experience and offers the promise of eventual triumph (see verse 5, for example). In fact, many parallels can be drawn between the two prophets, most notably in the way each is presented with a seemingly insurmountable task, which results in their eventually having to depart from their iniquitous people.

In the Name of Allah,
the Compassionate, the Merciful

Ṭā. Seen. Meem. [1]

These are the verses of the clear Book. [2] Now We're going to recite to you some of the story of Moses and Pharaoh in all its truthfulness, for people who believe. [3] Indeed, Pharaoh exalted himself in the land.

He divided his people into different social classes, causing the downfall of some of them [1284] – *even killing their sons but not their daughters,* [1285] for he was truly evil. [4]

We wanted to empower those who were being oppressed in the land, to make them leaders, to give them an inheritance (in the earth), [5] to establish their nation firmly in the world, and to use them to show Pharaoh, Haman, and their hordes that they couldn't (hold back) the very things they were trying to prevent. [6]

[1284] He reduced the Hebrews to slavery, even though their ancestors came into Egypt during the time of Prophet Joseph as free people. This oppression was caused by both his xenophobia and the general hatred of the Egyptian ruling class for Semitic peoples, especially since Egypt had been conquered and ruled for a time by other Semites known as the Hyksos. Perhaps after native rule was restored, the Hebrews became prime targets for racial discrimination. See note for verse 12:49.

[1285] This Pharaoh sought to control the population growth of the Hebrews by infanticide: ordering the death of baby boys from time to time. By not ordering the death of baby girls, he ensured generations of population imbalance, which would further serve the interests of the Egyptian government.

Allah Inspired
the Mother of Moses

We directed the mother of Moses by telling her, *"Suckle him as usual, but when you're afraid for his safety, set him adrift in the river (Nile). Don't be afraid or feel sad, for We're going to restore him to you and then make him one of Our messengers."* [1286] [7]

(When Pharaoh's men were close, she did as she was commanded and set the baby adrift in the river.) Later on, Pharaoh's own family fished him out, (not realizing that) Moses would one day become their enemy and also a source of regret for Pharaoh, Haman and all their hordes. They were grossly mistaken! [8]

The Pharaoh's wife [1287] exclaimed delightedly, *"A joy to the eye for you and me! Don't kill him, (my husband), for he might be useful to us, or we might adopt him as a son."* They had no idea (what they were doing). [9]

(When the news reached her that her baby was taken into Pharaoh's house,) Moses' mother felt a great emptiness in her heart. [1288] She would've revealed the secret, but We strengthened her heart so she could remain faithful. [10]

She had told (the baby's older) sister, *"Follow him (as he floats down the river)."* She had watched him discreetly, and the (Egyptians) didn't catch on. [11]

We forbade (the baby) to suckle (from any of the wet nurses of the palace,) until (Moses' sister approached them) and said, *"Do you want me to show you a family home where (the baby) can be fed and looked after for you by those who will care diligently?"* [1289] [12]

This is how We restored him to his mother so her eyes could be comforted, so her worry could be abated, and so she could know that Allah's promise is true, but most (people) don't understand. [13]

[1286] The Egyptians had a policy of killing Hebrew baby boys in alternate years. This was to ensure that there were at least some male slaves to do the work that the Egyptians, themselves, didn't want to do. Aaron was born before Moses in one of those alternate years and was allowed to live. Moses was born in a year of death, however, but his mother Jochebed concealed her pregnancy from the local midwives whose task it was to monitor births. Moses' mother would suckle her baby and keep him hidden in the house. Whenever someone she feared would come near her home, she would put the baby in a box-like basket and put the basket in a thicket of reeds by the side of the river Nile, tied to a rope. One day she was so spooked by coming visitors that she forgot to tie the rope, and the basket floated away with the baby inside. She sent her daughter to see where the basket went to, and it drifted right towards one of the riverside palaces of the Pharaoh. (*Ibn Kathir*)

[1287] The noblewoman mentioned here would be the wife of the pharaoh who ruled when Moses was very young. If this story took place during the rule of Pharaoh Kenephres, then his wife is identified in historical records as Merris. The new, second pharaoh, who ruled Egypt many years later (when Moses was much older and had become a prophet) would have been Kenephres's son, Dudimose. Muslim tradition states that his wife was named 'Asiyah. It has long been discussed as to whether 'Asiyah was present both when Moses was found and later when he was a prophet many decades later. There is no reason to assume that she was or wasn't, for as a member of a royal family, or at least well-connected enough to have later married a pharaoh, she most probably would have known of Moses as he grew into manhood. Also see 66:11.

[1288] The mother of Moses had sent her daughter to follow the basket. When the daughter saw it pass before one of Pharaoh's palaces and get retrieved, she told her mother, who would have petitioned for the return of her baby, but Allah strengthened her heart, and she held her tongue.

[1289] After refusing all offers of milk, Pharaoh's wife, who had become attached to the baby, was in a state of alarm. She sent her servants carrying the baby out in the city and searched for a wet nurse for hire. It was at this moment that the sister of Moses recognized the baby one of them was carrying and approached her, suggesting that she knew of a wet nurse where the baby could be raised and fed. Thus Moses would spend a part of each day in the company of his real mother and another part of the day with his adoptive mother, but no one could reveal the secret that Moses was being raised by his biological mother. (*Ibn Kathir*)

The Young Prince

*W*hen (Moses) grew into manhood and his character was settled, We bestowed wisdom and knowledge upon him, [1290] for that's how We reward the good. [14] (Then one night) he ventured out into the city, unnoticed by others, (and explored its streets) until he came upon two men having a fight. One of them was (a Hebrew), and the other (was an Egyptian) and thus his enemy. [1291]

The (Hebrew) man called out to him for help against his opponent, so Moses punched (the Egyptian) with his clenched fist and (accidentally) killed him. (Moses) cried out, "*This is Satan's doing, for he's an enemy who clearly leads (his victims) towards mistakes.* [15] *My Lord,*" he then prayed, "*I've been wrong, so forgive me.*" Thus, Allah forgave him, for He's the Forgiving and Merciful. [16]

"*My Lord,*" he prayed once more, "*Since You've favored me, I swear I'll never help any immoral person (again).*" [1292] [17]

So he spent (the night hiding) fearfully in the city until the morning broke. Then he saw the same (Hebrew) man who had asked for his help the day before calling for his help yet again! Moses told him, "*You're clearly some kind of troublemaker!*" [18]

However, when (Moses) resolved to restrain the man who was an enemy to both him and the (other Hebrew, the Egyptian attacker) shouted, "*Hey, Moses! Do you want to kill me like you killed a man yesterday? You just want to be a tough guy in the land and not a reformer.*" [19]

Suddenly, (a friend) came running from the other side of the city and warned Moses, saying, "*Moses! The nobles are meeting to decide your fate. They plan to kill you, so run away. That's the best advice!*" [1293] [20] So he fled the scene in guarded fear and prayed, "*O my Lord! Save me from the tyrants.*" [1294] [21]

The Fugitive Finds a Home

*A*nd so he (fled Egypt) and set out towards (the land of) Madyan, saying, "*My Lord will guide me towards the right path.*" [22] Then he arrived at a watering hole in Madyan and found a large group of people gathered there, (watering their flocks).

Meanwhile, two ladies, who sat nearby, were kept waiting (with their sheep). He asked them, "*What's the problem here?*"

"*We can't get a turn at the watering hole,*" the (women) replied, "*until the shepherds leave, and our father is too old (to stand up for us).*" [23]

So he, himself, watered their flocks, (and when he had finished) he went back to rest in the shade. "*My Lord,*" he prayed, "*I could use whatever good You send me.*" [24]

A little while later, one of the ladies came back to him, walking bashfully, and said, "*My father has invited you (to a banquet) to

---

[1290] The *knowledge* was that he was really a Hebrew, and the wisdom he received was his beginning to question his identity and what it meant.

[1291] Moses learned who he really was while being raised in the house of his own mother, but he had to feign dual loyalties to the royal household. Thus, he knew that the Egyptians were not really his friends or allies.

[1292] Moses didn't mean to kill the Egyptian, but by letting the heat of the moment get to him, he joined in the fight when it would have been more prudent to have first found out what the problem was. Here he promises not to help anyone ever again who may be engaged in wrongdoing, for he realized that automatically siding with someone just because they were of the same ethnic group was not a wise thing to do. See 4:135.

[1293] This probably would have been one of Moses' friends from the royal court.

[1294] Moses was guilty of unintentional homicide, but he knew he would not get a fair hearing or trial, for it was well known that Hebrews guilty of killing Egyptians were automatically put to death, no matter what the mitigating circumstances were. .

reward you for watering (our flock) for us." [1295] (When Moses arrived at their father's camp), he told him his whole story. (The old man reassured him), saying, *"Don't worry about it. You've escaped from an oppressive people."* [25]

(One of the ladies) said, *"My father, why don't you give him a job, for the best worker is a strong and trustworthy one."* [26]

(Her father) then said (to Moses), *"In fact, I want to marry one of these two daughters of mine to you, but on one condition: that you work for me for eight years. However, if you finish ten years in total, it would be a favor from you, but I don't want to put a burden on you. You'll find that I am, Allah-willing, a morally upright man."* [27]

(Moses) answered, *"Then that's how it will be between you and me. Whichever of the two time periods I (choose to) fulfill, don't let it be held against me. Let Allah's guarantee be on what I say."* [1296] [28]

The Burning Bush

*A*fter Moses had completed his term of service, (he struck out on his own) and journeyed with his family (in search of opportunity.) [1297] (One day, while they were camped in the desert), he saw a fire burning on the slopes of Mount Tur. *"Wait here,"* he said to them. *"I see a fire. I want to bring you some news from it, or at least a burning branch that you (can use to start your campfire) to warm yourselves."* [29]

(When he finally) reached (the fire, he heard) a voice coming from the right side of the valley, emanating from a tree on blessed ground. *"Moses! I am Allah. The Lord of All the Worlds. Now throw your staff to the ground!"* [30] After he did it, he saw it

wiggling like a snake, so he turned to escape and was hesitant to venture back.

"Moses!" (the voice commanded.) *"Come closer, and don't be afraid, for no harm will come to you.* [31] *Now slip your hand in your shirt, and it will come away blazing in perfect whiteness. Then fold your limb to your side again without fear (of being burned). These are two miracles (that you've been given) from your Lord (to impress) Pharaoh and his nobles, for they've become a rebellious people."* [32]

(Moses) cried out, *"My Lord! I killed one of their men, and I'm afraid they're going to kill me.* [33] *My brother Aaron is a better speaker than I, so send him as my partner to back me up, though I'm still afraid that they'll call me a liar."* [34]

"We'll strengthen your arm with your brother and grant power to you both that will keep them from harming you. (If you employ) Our signs, that will ensure that both of you, as well as any who follow you, will succeed." [35]

Pharaoh

*M*oses (returned to Egypt) and went to (its leaders) with clear proofs, but they said, *"This is no more than invented sorcery, and We've never heard anything like this (message) from our ancient ancestors!"* [36]

"My Lord knows best," (Moses answered), *"who is coming with guidance from Him and who will have the (best) result in the realm of the next life. Tyrants will certainly never succeed!"* [37]

"O Nobles!" Pharaoh said. *"I don't know of any other god for you than myself. Haman! Fire up the (furnaces to make) bricks of clay, and build me a towering palace so I can climb up to the God of Moses. As for me, I think he's a liar!"* [38]

[1295] Without any textual justification whatsoever, some classical commentators have identified the old father of these ladies as Prophet Shu'ayb. As most modern commentators have shown, this is probably not a correct linkage.

[1296] Ibn 'Abbas (d. 687) said that Moses fulfilled the longer term out of his generosity. (*Ibn Kathir*)

[1297] Some commentators are of the opinion that Moses missed his home and family and wanted to visit Egypt in secret. Enough years had passed, and his appearance as a bedouin might just have enabled him to envision successfully pulling off such a bold visit.

Against all right he was arrogant throughout the land, both he and his hordes. They never thought they would come back to Us! [39]

So we seized him, along with his hordes, and threw them into the sea! So just look at how wrongdoers are finished off! [40]

We made (their conduct) the pinnacle of all invitations to the Fire, and they'll find no one to help them on the Day of Assembly. [41] A curse will follow them in this world, and on the Day of Assembly they're going to be hideous (to behold, on account of how they're going to be disfigured). [42]

Moses and Muhammad

*A*nd so it was that We revealed the Book to Moses, following a time in which We destroyed (many) earlier generations, so that people could be given insight, guidance and mercy and also so they could be reminded. [1298] [43]

You weren't there, (Muhammad,) when We gave the commission to Moses on the western side (of the mountain), nor did you witness (his exploits). [44] We raised up other generations that lasted for many ages, and you weren't living among the people of Madyan either, nor were you reciting Our (revealed) verses to them. Yet, We always kept sending (reminders to humanity). [45]

You also weren't there on the side of (Mount) Tūr when We called out (to Moses), but (now here you are:) a mercy from your Lord to warn a people who've

never had a warner before you. *So now let them have their reminder!* [46]

If (you) were never (sent to them), and a disaster befell them on account of what they did with their own hands, then they might be (within their rights) to say, "*Our Lord! Why didn't you send us any messenger, for then We would've followed Your (revealed) verses and believed?*" [47]

So now, when We're sending Our own truth to them, they (have the audacity to) say, "*Why hasn't he brought any (miracles) like Moses brought?*"

But haven't they already rejected (the miracles) that Moses was given?

They said, "*Those are just two kinds of sorcery backing each other up!*" Then they said, "*We reject them both!*" [48]

So say to them, "*Then bring a book from Allah that's a better guide than both (the Torah and the Qur'an), so I can follow it, if you're really so honest!*" [49]

If they don't listen to you, it's because they're following nothing but their own whims.

Who can be more wrong than the one who follows his own whims, lacking any guidance from Allah? Allah certainly won't guide people who do wrong. [50]

Accepting the Book

*A*nd so it is that We've reinforced (Our cascading revelations) by sending the spoken words (of scripture) to them so they

---

[1298] Muslims are taught to accept the Torah, Psalms and Gospel as true expressions of divine revelation. As such, a Muslim is not allowed to disrespect a Bible or copy of the Torah. Even though Muslims believe that the original revelations of the former prophets have been edited, added to and otherwise tampered with, they do believe that some portion of those original revelations is still contained within the modern versions of those books of the same name. Muslims are even allowed to research the scriptures of Jews and Christians and quote them for examples of Allah's earlier injunctions, as companions of Muhammad such as 'Abdullah ibn Salam and K'ab al-Ahbar (converts from Judaism) did, and they were never censured by any of their contemporaries. The Qur'an gives permission for this in practice also in verse 3:93.

can be reminded. [1299] [51] Those to whom We sent scripture in the past believe in this one, too. [52]

When it's recited to them, they exclaim, "*We believe in it, for it's the truth from our Lord, and we were already submissive (to Allah's will before.)*" [53]

They're going to be rewarded twice, for they persevered, used good to ward off evil and spent (in charity) out of what We gave to them. [54]

When they hear useless talk, they turn away from it and say, "*Our actions count for us, and yours count for you. Peace be upon you; we're not looking (to associate with) ignorant people.*" [55]

When Loved Ones don't Believe

*Y*ou'll never be able to guide all those whom you love, though Allah guides whomever He wants, and He knows better who it is that accepts guidance. [1300] [56]

Belief in Allah is not a Hindrance

*T*hey say, "*If we followed this 'guidance' along with you, then we would surely be swept away from this land!*" [1301] However, didn't We already establish them in a secure sanctuary where all kinds of fruits are brought (in trade) as a bounty from Us? Yet, most of them don't understand. [57]

How many towns have We destroyed that took pleasure in their (wealthy) lifestyles? Their ruins are deserted, and their remnants are few, and thus We were the inheritors (of their wealth and power). [58]

And your Lord never destroyed any town unless He first sent a messenger among its main public places who would recite Our (revealed) verses to them. And We never destroyed any town unless its people were wrongdoers. [59]

What you've been given (in this life) is only useful for this life. It's (no more than) dazzling trinkets, but (the rewards) that are with Allah are far better and longer

---

[1299] Some commentators believe that this passage was revealed in Medina in the year 628. At that time, forty emissaries from the Christian king of Abyssinia arrived in Medina to extend their king's greetings to Muhammad. The Prophet was in the midst of setting off for the fortress town of Khaybar to subdue it, and these men joined in the campaign. Some were wounded, but none were killed. Before they set off for their return journey to Africa, the ambassadors offered to send some funds to help the economically strapped Muslims, and they affirmed their belief that Islam and Christianity were compatible and complimentary. (*Tabarani, Ma'ariful Qur'an*)

[1300] This particular verse was revealed to console the Prophet concerning his beloved uncle, Abu Talib, who had just passed away while still unwilling to forsake his idols. (*Muslim*) The Prophet had approached him on his deathbed just before his demise and asked him to recite the testimony of faith. The Prophet's main foe, Abu Jahl, was there also, and he kept trying hard to convince Abu Talib to die an idolater. Eventually Abu Talib agreed with Abu Jahl and said he would not forsake the religion of his father, who was an idolater. The Prophet told Abu Talib he would pray for his forgiveness anyway, but then another verse was revealed forbidding a Muslim from praying for forgiveness for an idolater. Some scholars have debated whether prayers for Christian and Jewish relatives are permissible, as they are not in the category of idolaters. (See 9:113) (*Bukhari, Muslim*)

[1301] The pagan tribe of Quraysh were the masters of Mecca, a major trading city and religious site of pilgrimage for people all over the peninsula. They were afraid that if they rejected idolatry, the hundreds of tribal groups that housed their idols in the city would revolt and drive the Quraysh from their favored position. Al-Harith ibn Uthman ibn 'Abd Munaf said the statement recounted in the verse below, and it refers to this situation. This passage was revealed to point out to him, and to the Quraysh in general, that their tribe was in power only by Allah's permission and that it was He Who could protect or destroy any nation. (*Nisa'i, Asbab ul-Nuzul*)

lasting, so won't you think about that? [1302] [60]

The Plight of the Doomed

*A*re they the same: [1303] the one to whom We've made a good promise and who will receive it; and the one to whom We've given the good things of this life, but who will then be dragged back for (harsh judgment on) the Day of Assembly? [61]

On that day, (Allah) will call out to (the sinners), asking, "*Where are My 'partners' that you've been imagining?*" [62] Those whose sentence of guilt will be proven true against them will say, "*Our Lord! These are all the people whom we led astray, but we only led them astray because we, ourselves, were astray. We renounce them right here in front of You, for they weren't really worshipping us.*" [63]

Then it will be said to (their sinful followers), "*So call on your 'partners' now!*" But even though they'll try to call upon them, their (heroes and false gods) won't listen. Then they're going to see the punishment that awaits them. *If only they would've listened to the guidance!* [64]

(Allah) will call to them that day, saying, "*How did you respond to your messengers?*" [65]

However, all their arguments and excuses will get jumbled (in their minds), leaving them unable even to ask each other anything. [66]

However, those who repented, believed and did what was morally right can hold out the hope that they'll be among the successful. [67]

All will Return to Allah Regardless

*Y*our Lord creates whatever He wants and selects the best for (all creatures). Glory be to Allah! He's high above what they join with Him. [1304] [68] Your Lord knows everything that their hearts hide and what they show. [69]

He is Allah. There is no other god besides Him. All praise belongs to Him in the beginning and the end. The power to command belongs only to Him, and you're all going to go back to Him. [70]

Day and Night are Blessings from Allah

*T*ell them, "*Don't you see it? If Allah made the night last forever, all the way to the Day of Assembly, then what other god besides Allah could bring you any form of light? Won't you listen?*" [71]

Then ask them, "*Don't you see it? If Allah made the daytime last forever, all the way to the Day of Assembly, then what other god besides Allah could bring the darkness of night upon you so you could rest? Won't you see it?*" [72]

It's from His mercy that He's established the (alternating pattern) of night and day, so you can have a rest cycle, and so you can go out in search of His bounty. This is (a reason) for you to be thankful. [73]

He'll call upon them one day, asking, "*Where are My 'partners' that you've been imagining?*" [74] Then We'll bring out a witness from every community and say,

---

[1302] The Prophet said, "By Allah, this life compared to the next life is like one of you dipping his fingertip into the sea; let him consider what he brings out." (*Ahmad*)

[1303] Most commentators say this verse refers to Hamza (the Prophet's uncle) and/or 'Ali ibn Abi Talib (the Prophet's cousin), both of whom were on the good side, and Abu Jahl (another uncle of the Prophet and an ardent foe), who was on the side of evil. (*Ibn Kathir*)

[1304] A man named Walid ibn Mughirah told the Prophet that Allah didn't have any say in the matter of who was a prophet or not. Thus, he would disbelieve in Muhammad's mission. This passage was revealed in response. (*Asbab ul-Nuzul*)

"Now show your proof (that Allah has partners)." That's when they'll know the truth of Allah, and whatever they invented will leave them to languish. [75]

Korah, the Arrogant

$\mathscr{K}$orah [1305] was from among Moses' people, but he behaved contemptuously towards his fellows. [1306] We bestowed upon him so much wealth that the very keys to (his treasure chests) weighed down a group of strong men.

One day his people told him, *"Stop gloating, for Allah has no love for people who gloat.* [76] *Instead, use (the wealth) that Allah has given you to secure a home in the next life, without having to neglect your own needs in this world. Be good (to others), even as Allah has been good to you. Don't cause disorder in the earth, for Allah has no love for troublemakers."* [77]

However, he answered them, saying, *"All this is mine from my own efforts and knowledge."* Didn't he know that Allah had already destroyed before him many generations that were far stronger and wealthier than whatever he amassed? However, the wicked are not always made to answer for their sins (in this life). [78]

So (Korah) strutted around among his people in all his finery, and those who only desire what this physical life contains (saw him and) said, *"If only we had (the wealth) that Korah has! He's the master of tremendous good fortune!"* [79]

However, the truly learned people said, *"(We feel) sorry for you. Allah's reward is the best for those who believe and do what's morally right, though no one receives it except the patient."* [80]

We made the earth open wide, and it swallowed both him and his entourage. He didn't have any supporters who could help him against Allah – *he couldn't even help himself!* [1307] [81]

Those who had envied his position just the day before were saying the very next morning, *"Allah increases or restricts the resources of any of His servants as He wills. If Allah's favor weren't upon us, He could've made the earth swallow us up, too! Those who reject Him are never successful."* [82]

We're going to grant the realm of the next life to those who have no desire to gloat nor cause trouble throughout the earth. The ultimate conclusion (is the best one) for those who are aware (of their duty to Allah). [83] Whoever does good will be rewarded better than the value of what he did, but whoever does wrong will be punished only according to the value of his deeds. [84]

Continue to Strive despite the Odds

$\mathscr{T}$he One Who bestowed the Qur'an upon you will surely bring you back to the destination. [1308] So say to them, *"My Lord knows better who is coming with guidance and who is clearly wrong."* [85]

[1305] Many commentators are of the view that Korah (Qarun) was a cousin of Moses, though there is no proof for this position. The story of Korah is also contained in the Bible in Numbers 16:1-35.

[1306] Korah had been favored under the rule of Pharaoh, even though he was a Hebrew, and he had enriched himself so mightily at their expense that the keys to his strongboxes were metaphorically so numerous it took strong men to carry them all!"

[1307] The Prophet once made mention of Korah, saying, "When a man from among the people who came before your time went out wearing two green garments, walking proudly and arrogantly, Allah commanded the earth to swallow him up, and he will remain sunk in the earth until the Day of Resurrection." (*Ahmad*)

[1308] Ibn 'Abbas said that this passage was revealed to the Prophet when he emerged from the cave he was hiding in while on the run from the Meccans during his migration to Medina in the year 622. The Prophet had looked back in the direction of Mecca and felt sadness, and the angel put these words in his heart to console him. (*Ibn Kathir*)

You never expected that a Book would be sent down to you, but it was a mercy from your Lord, so do nothing that will help the faithless (against you). [86]

Let nothing turn you away from the (revealed) verses of Allah after they've been revealed to you. Invite all to your Lord, and don't mingle with idol-worshippers. [1309] [87]

Don't call upon any god other than Allah, for there is no other god besides Him. Everything will pass away except His face. The power to command is His, and you'll all be brought back to Him. [88]

[1309] Even though a believer is not supposed to mingle freely with idolaters, nevertheless, they are not supposed to shun them insolently or rudely. The basic attitude of a Muslim is that all people are potential believers, and thus we must keep the door of invitation open. Many a convert came into Islam after experiencing the warmth and generosity of a sincere believer. Jalaluddin Rumi once commented on this in one of his teaching stories, saying, "The Jewish man told of his dream (in which he saw Moses) – oh, there are many Jews who have had a praiseworthy end. Don't spurn any unbeliever, for isn't there the hope that he may die as a Muslim? What do you know of his dying day, that you should forever turn your face from him?" *Mathnawi* VI, 2450.

The Spider

29 Al 'Ankabut
Middle Meccan Period

This chapter was revealed just prior to the immigration of vulnerable Muslims to Abyssinia in the year 615. The grave tone in the first three verses is a clear indication that some of the Prophet's followers began to second guess their decision to join Islam in the face of the relentless persecution they faced at the hands of the Meccan pagans. Using the examples of past nations who were also put to the test, this chapter closes with a direct appeal from Allah to the beleaguered faithful to stand firm for Allah's sake.

In the Name of Allah,
the Compassionate, the Merciful

Alif. Lām. Meem. [1]

Do people think they're going to be left alone [1310] by just saying, "*We believe,*" and that they won't be tested? [1311] [2]

We tested those who came before them, and Allah will make known who is true (in their belief), and He will make known who the liars are. [3]

Do those who do evil assume they can beat Us? [1312] Well, their assumption is plain wicked! [4] Whoever places their hope in their meeting with Allah (should hold firm), for the deadline set by Allah is fast approaching, and He's the Hearing and the Knowing. [5]

Whoever strives (in the cause of Allah) is striving for (the good of) his own soul. Allah doesn't need anything from any part of the universe. [6] Those who believe and do what's morally right will have all their

---

[1310] Even after the Prophet had left Mecca for the safer environment of Medina, people back in Mecca were still accepting Islam. The Prophet sent messages to them telling them they wouldn't be accepted as true Muslims until they immigrated to Medina. They replied that others who had attempted to leave suffered from the depredations of the idol-worshippers, and they were afraid of being harmed. This passage was revealed to strengthen their resolve, and the slow trickle of emigration resumed. (*Asbab ul-Nuzul*)

[1311] The Prophet said, "The people who are tested the most are the prophets, then the righteous, then the next best and the next best. A person will be tested in accordance with the degree of his religious commitment – the stronger the religious commitment, the stronger his test." (*Tirmidhi*)

[1312] During the height of Meccan persecution, one Muslim tradesman, a blacksmith named Khabab ibn Aratt, related the following story: "I used to be a blacksmith in Mecca, and once I did some work for Al-As ibn Wa'il. When I went to collect my payment, he told me, 'I won't pay you unless you renounce Muhammad.'" Later, according to Khabab, while he was sitting with the Prophet near the Ka'bah, he said to him, "Messenger of Allah, now the persecution is out of control, so why don't you pray to Allah (for help)?" The Prophet became distraught and said, "The believers before your time were persecuted much more than you. Their bones were scraped with iron combs, and their heads were cut with saws. Still they didn't give up their faith. I assure you that Allah will fulfill this mission. There will come a time of such peace that someone could travel from Sana to Hadramawt, and he'll have no fear from anyone, save Allah. However, you people have already become impatient." (*Bukhari*)

past sins erased, so We can reward them according to the best of what they did. [7]

When *not* to Obey Parents

We have made it a duty upon every human being that he should show kindness to his parents. [1313] However, if (your parents) ever strive to make you set up partners with Me after everything you've learned, then don't obey them. [1314]

All of you will return to Me, and I will tell you the meaning of all that you did. [8] Those who believed and did what was morally right will be admitted among the righteous. [1315] [9]

The Weak in Spirit

Among people there are some who say, *"We believe in Allah."* However, if they undergo any hardship in Allah's (cause), they act as if the people who were oppressing them were somehow the very punishment of Allah laid upon them!

Then, if your Lord provides you with some kind of help, they're quick to say, *"We've always been on your side!"* Doesn't Allah know better what's in the hearts of (all beings) in the universe? [10] Allah knows who the true believers are, and He knows who the hypocrites are. [11]

All are Responsible for Themselves

The faithless say to the believers, [1316] *"Follow our way, and we'll pay for your sins ourselves,"* but they'll never be able to pay for anyone else's sins in the least - and they're all liars! [12] They'll have to bear their own load, with much more added besides. Then, on the Day of Assembly, they'll have to answer for all their false assertions. [1317] [13]

[1313] This passage was revealed about a companion named Sa'ad ibn Abi Waqqas, who converted to Islam against the wishes of his mother, yet remained with her, trying to care for her, despite her self-imposed hunger strike to protest his actions. In his own words, Sa'ad recounts: "When my mother heard the news of my conversion to Islam, she flew into a rage. She approached me and said, 'O Sa'ad! What is this religion that you've embraced that has taken you away from the religion of your mother and father? By Allah, either you forsake your new religion, or I will not eat or drink until I die. Your heart will be broken with grief for me and remorse will consume you on account of the deed you've done - people will blame you forever.' 'Don't do (such a thing), my mother,' I said, 'for I won't give up my religion for anything.' However, she went on with her threat... For days she neither ate nor drank. She became emaciated and weak. Hour after hour, I went to her, asking whether I should bring her some food or drink, but she stubbornly refused, insisting that she would neither eat nor drink until she died or until I abandoned my religion. So I said to her, 'O my Mother! In spite of my strong love for you, my love for Allah and His Messenger is indeed stronger. By Allah, if you had a thousand souls and each one departed one after another, I would not abandon this religion for anything.' When she saw that I was determined, she relented unwillingly and then ate and drank." (*Muslim, Tirmidhi, Ahmad*)

[1314] Also see 31:14-15.

[1315] The scholars are generally of the opinion that verses 8-9 were revealed in the Medinan Period.

[1316] Muhammad publicly asserted on many occasions that people will have to answer to Allah for the evil that they do. Some of the idol-worshippers actually taunted the small cadre of Muslims, saying that if they would only rededicate themselves to the idols, then their pagan neighbors would take their sins upon themselves. Since the idol-worshippers didn't believe in sins anyway, they were really being sarcastic. This verse was revealed in response to that situation. (*Asbab ul-Nuzul*)

[1317] The Prophet said, "Beware of doing injustice, for on the Day of Resurrection, Allah will swear an oath, saying, 'By My glory and majesty, no injustice will be overlooked today.' Then a voice will call out, 'Where is so-and-so, the son of so-and-so?' He will be brought forward, followed by his good deeds which will seem like mountains, so much so that the gathered throngs will gaze at them in wonderment, until that person is standing before the Compassionate (Allah). Then the voice will be commanded to say, 'Whoever is owed something by so-and-so or was wronged by him, let him come forward now.' So they will come forward and gather before the Compassionate. Then the

The Call of the Prophets is often Ignored

*A*nd so it was that We sent Noah to his people. He dwelt among them fifty years shy of a thousand. [1318] Yet, (even after all his preaching), the flood overwhelmed those who persisted in wrongdoing. [14] We saved him and his followers in the boat, and We made it a sign for all (people) everywhere. [1319] [15]

Abraham (was also sent to his people), and he told them, *"Serve Allah, and be mindful of Him! That's the best thing for you if you only knew! [16] You're worshipping idols besides Allah, and you're making up nothing but myths. Those things you worship besides Allah have no power to provide you with resources (for your survival).*

"So look for your necessities of life from Allah. Serve Him, and give Him thanks, for you're all going to go back to Him. [17] If you deny this, well, generations before you denied it, as well. The duty of a messenger is only to convey the teachings clearly." [1320] [18]

Haven't they seen how Allah initiated the creation and then repeats it? That's easy for Allah to do. [19] So say (to them):

"Travel all over the world, and see how Allah initiated the creation.

In the same way will He recreate (it all) once more, for Allah has power over all things. [20]

He punishes whom He pleases and is merciful to whom He wills, and back to Him will you all return. [21]

Whether you flee through the earth or fly through the sky, you won't be able to elude Him, for you have no one else to protect you or help you besides Allah." [22]

Those who reject the signs of Allah and their coming appointment with Him, they're the ones who have no hope of My mercy. They're the ones who will suffer a painful punishment. [23]

Compassionate will say, 'Settle the accounts for My servant.' The (angels) will ask, 'How can we settle the account?' He will say, 'Take from his good deeds and give it to them.' They will keep taking from his good deeds until there is nothing left, and there will still be people with scores to settle. Allah will say, 'Settle the accounts for My servant.' The (angels) will say, 'He doesn't even have one good deed left.' Allah will say, 'Take from their evil deeds and give them to him.'" Then the Prophet recited this verse. (*Ibn Kathir,* with a similar report in *Muslim*)

[1318] The Qur'an states that Noah lived 950 years. According to Genesis 5:3-32, many people in ancient times lived for centuries. (Adam lived for 930 years!) Genesis 9:29 states that Noah was 950 years old when he died. (He was 600 years old when the flood began, according to Genesis 7:6.) In modern times, a select few have lived for 120 years or more. If Noah lived as long as he did, then it can be assumed he married and was a widower many times over. In the ancient Sumerian accounts of the survivor of the flood, the name for Noah is Ziasudra. (His father is the author of one of the oldest texts in the world called the Instructions of Shurupak, in which moral precepts are listed.) In later Akkadian and Babylonian versions the name is Utnapishtim. These names mean, "He of long life," and "He found life" respectively.

[1319] The commentators differ over what this means. Some hold that it means that Noah's boat will remain on the side of the mountain for future generations to discover and take a lesson from it. Others say that Noah, who might have lived as long as six thousand years ago, was the first to develop the concept of a large cargo vessel and that the memory and knowledge of ship building would remain after him. Still a third group believes it is merely the story of Noah and the flood that has remained and enlivened the imaginations of peoples everywhere. Indeed, ancient Sumerian and Babylonian records also make mention of a time of floods, even as the Hebrews carried this story with them for ages.

[1320] The messenger conveys the message, but it is up to the people to choose to listen or not. The messenger will not be blamed if he is ignored.

The Blessings of Abraham

The only answer Abraham's people gave to him was to say, "*Kill him! Burn him alive!*" However, Allah saved him from the flames, and there are signs in this for people who believe. [24]

(Abraham) said to them, "*You've taken idols for yourselves in place of Allah, just because it makes you feel a close bond in this life.* [1321] *On the Day of Assembly you're all going to disown each other and curse at each other. Your final destination will be in the Fire, and there will be no one to help you!*" [25]

The Story of Lot

Lot believed (in what) his (uncle Abraham taught), and he said, "*I'll forsake my home for my Lord, for He's the Powerful and the Wise.*" [26]

We (further blessed Abraham) with a line of descendants through Isaac and Jacob and instituted prophethood and scripture among them. We rewarded him in this life, and in the next life he's going to be with the righteous. [27]

Lot said to his people, "*You're more perverted than any other people that existed in all the universe!* [28] *Are you approaching other men (for intimacy) and even accosting them on the roads (for your lusts)? You do such abomination in your clubs, as well!*"

His people gave him no other answer but to say, "*So bring Allah's punishment down upon us, if you're really so honest!*" [29]

"*My Lord!*" he cried. "*Help me against these depraved people!*" [30]

Then Our (angelic) messengers went to Abraham with the awaited news and told him, "*We're going to destroy the people of this place, for they're wrongdoers.*" [31]

"*But Lot is there!*" (Abraham) interjected.

"*We know who's there,*" they answered, "*and we're going to save him and his followers, but not his wife, for she will remain behind.*" [32]

When our messengers went to Lot, he became worried (for their safety). He felt powerless (to protect) them (from his wicked people).

(The angels) told him, "*Don't be afraid or worried, for we're here to save you and your followers, though your wife will remain behind.* [33] *We're going to bring (Allah's) punishment down from the sky upon the people of this settlement, for they're in a state of evil rebellion.*" [34]

And so it was that We left (the destruction of their land) as an evident sign for people who think. [35]

Madyan and Pharaoh Perish

To (the land of) Madyan went their brother Shu'ayb, and he said, "*My people! Serve Allah, and be mindful of the Last Day. Don't spread the evil of corruption in the land.*" [36] Yet, they denied him and were seized by a blast that left them cowering in their homes by the morning. [37]

And (the people of) 'Ad and of Thamud - the ruins of their settlements are laid out clearly for your inspection. [1322]

[1321] The practice of idolatry in Mesopotamia was elaborate, and the tight rituals lent a certain kind of community spirit to the society. Idolatry became the glue that held the community together. Thus, it was the foundation for their communal love and loyalty.

[1322] The ruins of ancient cities dot northern Arabia on into Jordan. Some of these are associated with the Thamud people. Where are the ruins of the city that the 'Ad used to inhabit? Muslim commentators in the past were unsure of the identity of their capital city of Iram, which was known to the Greeks as Ubar, but the first definitive proof of a city named Iram came in 1975 when archeologists unearthed

Satan made their (evil) deeds seem right to them, and he steered them all away from the path (of Allah), even though they were very far-sighted peoples. [38]

And Korah, Pharaoh and Haman - Moses went to them in the past with clear evidence (of the truth). Yet, they acted outrageously in the land, *but they couldn't get away from Us!* [39]

We seized each of (those wrongdoers) for their sins. Among them were some who suffered from deadly sandstorms; some were shattered with deadly blasts; some were swallowed up by the earth, while others were drowned (in the sea). Allah wasn't the author of their harm, however, for they brought harm to their own souls. [40]

The Example of the Spider

*T*he example of those who take protectors other than Allah is that of a spider that builds its dwelling (out of delicate webs), for the flimsiest of homes is the home of the spider, if they only knew. [41]

Allah knows what they're calling upon besides Him, for He's the Powerful and the Wise. [42] These are the kinds of metaphors that We lay out for people; yet, no one understands them save for those who have knowledge. [1323] [43] Allah created the heavens and the earth for a truthful

purpose, and there are signs in this for the believers. [44]

Stay the Course with Allah's Support

*R*ecite what is being inspired to you of the Book, and establish prayer, for prayer discourages shameful behavior and bad deeds. The remembrance of Allah is even greater, and Allah knows what you're doing. [45]

Don't argue with the Followers of Earlier Revelation except in a better way, unless it's with those who are corrupt among them. Say to them, *"We believe in the revelation that's come down to us and also in what's come down to you. Our God and your God are the same, and we surrender to His will."* [46]

And so We've sent the Book to you, (Muhammad). (Some of) those to whom We've already given scripture in the past have faith in it, as do some of these (former pagans of Arabia). [1324] No one repudiates Our (revealed) verses save for those who suppress (their faith). [47]

You were never able to recite a book (of scripture) before this, nor could you have ever written one with your right hand. If you would've (been known to recite verse in public or write) before, then the babblers would have had a valid reason to doubt. [1325] [48] But no! The (fact

---

the ancient city of Ebla in northwestern Syria. There amid the ruins, which were over 4,500 years old, was a huge cache of ancient tablets, which recorded the dealings of Ebla and other cities. One of the cities mentioned was Iram. In the year 1992, archeologists discovered the ancient city of the 'Ad in present day Oman, and its physical description matched that found in the Qur'an. It is also probable that the name of this city survived in legends throughout some parts of Arabia, given that when it thrived it was an important trade center and land of expensive incense cultivation. See 50:13 and footnote.

[1323] The Prophet once recited this verse to a group of people, and then he said, "That person is knowledgeable, the one who ponders over the message of Allah, acts obediently to Him, and keeps away from those actions that He does not like." (*Baghawi*)

[1324] While in Mecca, Muhammad would sometimes preach to visiting Jews and Christians who came for trade and business. Some of them converted to Islam, just as some of the pagan Arabs did, as this verse references.

[1325] Although Mecca held regular poetry contests, and there were even renowned public podiums for people to display their talent daily, Muhammad was never a participant in these forums. He was not known among his peers as a man of rhymed language, nor did he know how to write. (After

that you never did these things before) is a sign for the insightful. No one repudiates Our (revealed) verses but the corrupt. [49]

Then they say, "*So why are no miracles being sent down to him from His Lord?*" Tell them, "*Miracles are indeed with Allah, but I'm only a plain warner.*" [50]

Isn't it enough for them that We've sent down a book to you that's recited in front of them? There are merciful (teachings) within it and reminders for the believers. [51]

Say (to them), "*Allah is witness enough between you and me. He knows what's in the heavens and the earth. Those who believe in falsehood and reject Allah – they're going to be the losers.*" [52]

They're asking you to bring on the punishment (about which you've warned them). If it wasn't for the fact that there's a fixed time limit (for their civilization to exist), then the punishment would've surely come upon them (already) - *and it will come upon them, when they won't even (see it) coming!* [53] So are they really asking you to bring on the punishment?

Without a doubt, Hellfire will surround those who covered up (their ability to believe)! [54] On the day when punishment will overshadow them from above and below, they'll be told, "*Suffer the results of your actions!*" [55]

A Direct Appeal from Allah

*M*y believing servants! [1326] My earth is wide, so serve Me, (even if it means migrating to a safer place). [56] Every soul will experience death, and in the end you'll be brought back to Us. [57] Those who believed and did what was morally right will be given a home in the Garden.

They'll live within mansions beneath which rivers flow, and there they'll get to stay (forever)! How excellent a reward for doing (good)! [58] They were patient, and they put their trust in their Lord. [59]

The Contributions of Allah cannot be Discounted

*H*ow many creatures are out there that aren't equipped with the resources they need to survive? [1327] Allah provides for both them and you, and He's the Hearing and the Knowing. [60]

If you asked them who created the heavens and the earth and who subjected the sun and the moon (to natural laws),

---

prophethood, he employed dozens of scribes to do this for him.) The Qur'an is pointing that fact out here, primarily as a way to remind the Meccans of what has occurred: a man who never recited or wrote before is suddenly blazing with elegant verse and expounding upon organized essays and sermons that are being recorded and distributed. As the next verse offers, there is a sign in this inexplicable phenomenon. If Muhammad were a known poet or writer before the beginning of his ministry at forty years of age, then the people could have fairly accused him of being overly creative or delusional in his own talent.

[1326] This verse was revealed before the migration to Medina. As you can see, the Prophet and his followers were being primed for their coming abandonment of their hometown. As hard as it is to move, remaining in an evil city is worse. Medina was going to be much better for Islam to grow and be safe. The Prophet once said, "All cities belong to Allah, and all people are His servants. Therefore, wherever you find goodness, you live there." (*Ahmad*)

[1327] The Prophet and Ibn 'Umar, the son of his dear friend, were visiting the home of one of the Helpers, or Medinan converts, and the Prophet began to eat some dates. He saw that Ibn 'Umar wasn't eating. He offered him some, but Ibn 'Umar refused to eat, saying he had no appetite for them. The Prophet then said, "I've got an appetite for them since I've just passed four days without really eating anything, knowing that if I asked my God, He would provide for me like Caesar or the Emperor of Persia. So what do you think about people who earn their own living?" Then this verse was revealed, and the Prophet recited it. (*Asbab ul-Nuzul*)

they would surely answer, *"Allah."* So why are they so confused? [61]

Allah increases the resources of whichever of His servants that He wills, and He likewise restricts them (for whichever of them He wills), for Allah knows about all things. [62]

If you asked them who it was who sends down water from the sky and uses it to bring life to the barren earth, they would surely answer, *"Allah."* Then say (to them), *"So praise be to Allah!"* However, most of them don't reason well. [63]

What is there in this world except distractions and games? The realm of the next life is where the real living is, if they only knew. [64]

Now if they were to set sail on a boat, they would call upon Allah (for safe passage) with sincere conviction, for (in that case they would recognize) that He owns all religion.

Then, after He deposited them safely back on the shore, they would go and make partners with Him, [65] thanklessly snubbing what He gave them and plunging themselves into endless diversions! Soon they're going to know (the truth)! [1328] [66]

Don't (the Meccans) see that although We've granted them a secure sanctuary (in their midst), yet even still people are being swept up (into Islam) all around them? [1329] Even so, they're still believing in false things and rejecting Allah's favors! [67]

Who does more wrong than the one who invents a lie against Allah or denies the truth when it comes to him? Isn't there a home in Hellfire reserved for those who (willfully) suppress (their awareness of the truth)? [68]

As for those who strive in Our (cause), We're going to guide them to the paths [1330] (that will lead them back to) Us, for Allah is with those who are good. [69]

[1328] After the Muslims successfully occupied Mecca in a peaceful surrender, a handful of pagans fled, thinking that the Prophet would take vengeance upon them for their criminal deeds during the long years of persecution and conflict that the Muslims endured at their hands. 'Ikrimah, the son of Abu Jahl (who was a bitter foe of the Prophet), journeyed to the Red Sea and booked passage on a ship bound for Abyssinia. During the voyage, a sudden squall overtook the boat, and it began to rock violently in the waves. The crew of the boat began to ask the passengers to pray to Allah for deliverance, for no one could save them except Him. (The sailors were probably Christians.) As 'Ikrimah reports, he said to himself, "By Allah, if there is no one who can save us on the sea except Him, then there is no one who can save us on land except Him, either." Then 'Ikrimah made a vow: "O Allah, I vow to you that if I come out of this, I will go and put my hand in the hand of Muhammad, and I will find him kind and merciful." The boat made it to shore, and 'Ikrimah reversed his journey and returned to Mecca, where he repented to Allah and declared himself a Muslim at the Prophet's hand. In later years, he became a scholar of religious knowledge. (*At-Tabarani*)

[1329] Even though the Quraysh tribe of Mecca lived in a city with a shrine that, by their own admission was built by Abraham and dedicated to the One God, and even though, despite their best efforts to persecute Muhammad and the Muslims, the peoples of surrounding territories were converting to the faith with ever greater frequency, these same 'custodians' of Mecca continued bowing to idols made of wood, stone and even animal bones. They just didn't get it!

[1330] There are many different roads that people may take before they reach the path of Allah. Some people must travel through a variety of roads in life, both good and bad, before their hearts ultimately open to the one path of Allah. It is for this reason that Allah gives people (and nations) some time in their lives to make choices, learn and then reassess what they've been doing. Our time limits are all different, and none of us knows how long we have. Therefore, the sooner we stop being deluded by this temporary life of pleasure and get on with the task of learning about the truth, purpose, usefulness and meaning of our lives, the better!

The Romans

30 Ar-Rum
Middle Meccan Period

Starting in the year 612, the Persian Empire launched a series of devastating attacks against the Byzantine Romans in Syria, Egypt and even into Anatolia itself. With barbarian invaders to the west, governors revolting in the north, east and south and the mighty Persians rampaging through their eastern lands, the Byzantines looked as if they might be wiped out - even their capital city of Constantinople was put briefly under siege.

These events were set in motion within the first two or three years of the Prophet's ministry in Mecca, and as the years passed with greater Persian success, these events had propaganda value for the pagans.

The Byzantines were Christians who believed more or less in one God, while the Persians presided over an empire filled with idolatry and who themselves subscribed to the dualistic religion of Zoroastrianism.

The Meccans taunted the Muslims, telling them that this was a sign that their One God was defeated and fleeing. The Muslims were despondent and unable to respond until this chapter was revealed in about the year 620. The opening verses boldly predicted that the Romans would recover and move on to defeat their enemy within three to nine years.

When the significance of this revelation became clear, Abu Bakr cheerfully went through the streets of Mecca telling everyone about it. One of the leaders of the Quraysh, Ubayy ibn Khalaf, offered to make a bet with Abu Bakr about this.

Abu Bakr agreed, but Ibn Khalaf made him agree to the middle figure of six years, which is in between the three to nine years that the word *bid'* implies in Arabic. (This was before betting was made illegal in Islam.) If the Byzantines were not victorious within six years, then Abu Bakr would have to pay.

Six years passed with no clear Roman victory, and Abu Bakr had to pay up. Early the following year, however, the Byzantines inflicted a crushing defeat upon the Persians at Nineveh (in 627) and forced them to flee back to their home territory, and many Muslims told Abu Bakr he was wrong for settling on a single year when *bid'* meant from three to nine years.

Because this unlikely prediction made by the Qur'an came true, many new converts entered the fold of Islam. [1331] *(Tirmidhi)*

In the Name of Allah, the Compassionate, the Merciful

Alif. Lām. Meem. [1]

The Romans have been defeated [2] in the lowest place on earth, [1332] but they'll be victorious (over their Persian enemies), in spite of this defeat, [3] in three to nine years' time. [1333]

Command over the past and the future belongs to Allah, and when that day (of victory arrives), the believers will be the ones celebrating [4] with Allah's help. [1334]

He helps whomever He wants, for He's the Powerful and the Merciful. [1335] [5] (This is) Allah's promise, and Allah never backs away from His promise, but most people don't understand. [6]

They only understand the outward aspects of the life of this world, while they're unconcerned with the next life. [7] Haven't they pondered (this question) within themselves, that perhaps Allah didn't create the heavens and the earth and everything in between them except for a valid reason and a limited time? Even so, there are still many people who deny the meeting they have with their Lord. [8]

Haven't they traveled throughout the earth and seen what happened to all those (civilizations) that came before them? They were stronger than (these people here today) and worked the land and populated it in far greater numbers than they ever could've done.

[1331] Some versions of the story have the Prophet asking Abu Bakr to hold to the full nine years as his bet, and thus he won a hundred camels from the heirs of the recently deceased Ibn Khalaf. The Prophet told Abu Bakr to donate them to charity, as he did not approve of gains made by gambling, even though the Qur'an had not officially prohibited it yet. *(Ma'ariful Qur'an.)*

[1332] The Persians defeated the Byzantine Romans on a battlefield by the Dead Sea in about 613, which is a region that has the lowest elevation on earth (approx. 395 meters below sea level). Although many translators usually translate the Arabic term *adna* as *nearest*, the root word *dani* literally means the *lowest*. Besides, northern Palestine is nowhere 'near' to Mecca, being several weeks' worth of journeying away by caravan, so the true meaning of *adna* - which is *lowest* - has to be presented as it is. Where is the internal evidence to support the use of the word this way? The Qur'an uses a related form of the word frequently in the phrase *hayat ad-dunya*, which means the life of the *lower* (world), i.e., the life of this physical world as opposed to the Next Life *up* in Heaven. This is a fascinating detail about the geographic lay of the land that would have been completely unknown to anyone alive at that time. News of this decisive battle reached into Arabia, and the pagans of Mecca taunted the Muslims, saying that a monotheistic power (the Byzantine Romans) was defeated by a pagan one (the Persians).

[1333] In Arabic parlance, the amount of time mentioned in this verse *(bid'i sineen)* is any number between three to nine years. The Persians began their assaults on the Byzantine lands in the year 612. This chapter was revealed in approximately 620, when the Persians were on the verge of total victory. The Byzantines, however, snatched victory back after almost certain defeat a few years later in 627 and turned the tide against the Persians who steadily had to give ground thereafter. Thus, the prediction of the Qur'an was fulfilled in approximately seven years. The Persians were forced to sign a humiliating peace treaty in December of the year 628.

[1334] When the Byzantines did achieve victory, the Muslims were elated, and the idol-worshippers were now despondent, as the forces of monotheism triumphed over the forces of theistic dualism. This swayed some people in Mecca to convert to Islam.

[1335] One of the Meccan idol-worshippers had boasted to the Muslims, "You have a scripture, and the Christians also have a scripture, but we are without any scripture. Our Persian brothers have overcome your Roman brothers, and so shall we overcome you if you ever try to fight us." This passage was revealed in response. *(Asbab ul-Nuzul)*

Messengers went to them with clear evidence (of Allah's truth; yet, they rejected them). It wasn't Allah Who did them any wrong; rather, they wronged their own souls. [9] In the end, the final result for evil is greater evil in return, for they denied the signs of Allah and treated them as a joke! [10]

The Verdict is for Allah Alone

Allah is the One Who initiates the creation and then repeats it, [1336] and then all of you will go back to Him. [11]

On the day when the Hour (of Judgment) is established, the guilty will stagger along in despair. [12] They'll have no one to intercede for them among their 'partners,' and what's more they're going to reject their 'partners' (as false friends). [13]

On the day when the Hour is established, that will be the day when they'll be divided into categories. [14] Those who had faith and did what was morally right will rejoice in ecstasy, [15] while those who rejected faith and denied Our signs and their meeting in the next life will be taken in for punishment. [16]

So glorify Allah in the evening and when you rise up in the morning [17] - *all praise within the heavens and the earth belongs to Him* - (glorify Him) in the late afternoon and at midday, as well. [18]

He brings life from death and death from life, and He gives life to the earth after it was dead. [1337] *And that's how you're going to be brought out (of your graves at the resurrection)!* [1338] [19]

Evidence of Allah's Hand in Human Society

Among His signs is the fact that He created you from dust. Then from that (simple substance), you became widely scattered mortals! [20] And among His signs is the fact that He created spouses for you from among your own kind so you can dwell with them in harmony. [1339]

Indeed, He put love and mercy between you, [1340] and there are signs in this for people who think. [1341] [21]

[1336] This refers to the original creation of the material universe and then to the second recreation when the dead are raised to life for judgment.

[1337] The Prophet once said, "Remember death, the destroyer of pleasures, for not a day passes upon the grave except it says 'I am the house of remoteness; I am the house of loneliness; I am the house of dirt; I am the house of worms.'" (*Tirmidhi*)

[1338] The Prophet said that whoever recites these verses [17-19] in the morning, then all the deficiencies in his deeds during the day will be repaired, and if one recites them at night, then all the deeds of the night will be repaired of deficiencies, as well. (*Tabarani, Abu Dawud*)

[1339] Marriage is a civil partnership in the Islamic worldview. It is not a dictatorship of the husband, despite what some rustics seek to promote. The wife is not even responsible for doing the housework, as Islamic scholars often point out. If she does it and other domestic chores, it is a favor for the husband for which Allah will reward her. Otherwise he has to hire a housekeeper! (In Islamic law, the wife can have her own job, property and income independent of the man and can use it as she wills without his permission, in addition to getting the benefit of being supported by him in her daily needs for food and shelter.) There is no verse in the Qur'an that tells women that they must 'obey' their husbands blindly, such as one finds in the New Testament in Ephesians 5:22-24, Colossians 3:18, I Peter 3:1-6 and I Corinthians 11:3.

[1340] The Prophet said, "Allah has divided mercy into one hundred parts, out of which he retained ninety-nine parts with Him and has sent the one remaining to earth. From this one part emanates all the compassion that the whole of creation shows towards each other. So much so that an animal will lift her hoof above her young lest it should get hurt." (*Bukhari*) Also see footnote to 2:24.

[1341] The Prophet once remarked that when a husband and wife look upon each other with love, then Allah looks upon them in mercy. Muhammad demonstrated how affection and love are expressed in daily life with his own wives. He used to hold hands openly with whichever wife he was walking in

Among His signs are the creation of the heavens and the earth and the differences in your languages and skin colors. There are indeed signs in this for people who know. [22]

Among His signs are the occasions during the night and day when you sleep, and also your daily search for the resources that His bounty provides. There are signs in this for those who listen. [23]

Among His signs that He exhibits to you is the lightning that causes you to hope (for rain), as well as to fear (for your lives). He sends down water from the sky and uses it to revive the earth after it was barren. There are indeed signs in this for the thoughtful. [24]

Among His signs is the fact that the sky and the earth stand firmly by His command. However, when He calls to you with a single shout, you'll emerge from (your graves) in the earth! [25]

All (creatures) that reside within the heavens and the earth belong to Him, and they're all devoted to Him. [26] He's the One Who initiates the creation and then repeats it. That's easy for Him to do.

All throughout the heavens and the earth, the most stunning examples are His, for He's the Powerful and the Wise. [27]

Use Your Common Sense

*N*ow He's going to set out for you an example taken from your own selves. Do you take partners from among your servants to share *equally* in the wealth We've given you?

Do you feel the same kind of fear towards them as you would feel fear towards each other? [1342] This is how we explain the verses precisely for people who use their reason. [28]

But no! The wrongdoers follow their own whims instead of knowledge. So who can guide those whom Allah leaves astray? They'll have no one to help them (escape from the punishment they deserve). [29]

So set your face firmly upon the natural religion (of monotheism). [1343] Allah instilled this instinctive nature upon all of humanity, and Allah never changes what

---

public, and sometimes he would walk arm-in-arm with her. He was very patient in his demeanor and would compliment his wives. He also lent a hand in the household chores, washing and mending his own clothes, for example. He once advised people that the best man is the one who is the kindest to his wife.

[1342] This is an obvious address to the pagans, who thought slaves were nothing more than property. Would they take a slave as their equal? Would they ever fear displeasing one, as they would fear displeasing one whom they considered an equal? Then why would Allah make idols of wood or stone His equal?

[1343] In modern times, certain fundamentalist Christian groups have advanced the odd idea that the God of the Qur'an is not the same as the Judeo-Christian God. They have done this in an effort to sow suspicion among their flocks towards Islam. While undoubtedly the conception of God in the Qur'an is more monotheistic than the Christian trinity, the Qur'an repeats over and over that it is a message from the same God that spoke to Abraham, Moses and Jesus (see 29:46). Ironically, Islam and Judaism have more in common in terms of conceptualizing God than either has with Trinitarian Christianity. One modern Jewish activist, Eliezer Abrahamson, gave this response on the status of Islam in Jewish law: "According to Jewish law, Islam is a true form of worship of Allah (*Shu"t HaRamba'm,* 160). It recognizes the One indivisible God as the Creator and Ruler of the Universe. For this reason, a non-Jew who follows Islam is not considered an idolater according to Jewish law." Thus, Judaism accepts that the God of Islam is the same God as its own. Those Christians who try to drive a wedge between the three Abrahamic faiths don't realize that the wedge would put Islam and Judaism on one side and their own faith on the other!

He creates. [1344] This is the straight religion; yet, most people don't understand. [1345] [30]

Turn back to Him (in repentance), and be mindful of Him. Establish prayer, and don't be among those who make partners (with Allah). [31] Those who split their religion up into competing factions – *each side happily assumes it has (the truth)*. [1346] [32]

Our Lack of Appreciation for Allah's Favor

𝒲hen misfortune comes upon people, they cry out to their Lord, turning back to Him (in sincere repentance). Yet, when He gives them a taste of mercy from His Own Self, some of them make partners with their Lord [33] - (as if to show) how really thankless they can be for what We've given them. So enjoy yourselves now – *oh, but soon you'll know!* [34]

Have We sent down to them some kind of authority that tells them all about the 'partners' they have? [35]

When We give people a taste of mercy, they rejoice in it. However, when hardship comes upon them, because (of mistakes) they made with their own hands, they're plunged into despair! [36] Don't they see that Allah increases or restricts the resources of whomever He wants? There are signs in this for those who believe. [37]

(So don't be afraid to) give what is due to your relatives, the poor and stranded

---

[1344] The commentators explain that this verse refers to Allah's revealed religion and our natural affinity towards it. If we avoid our own shortcomings of disbelief, temptation, materialism or arrogance, then we gravitate towards Allah and feel at peace. Even if environmental influences or personal flaws lead us astray, the seed of faith remains within each of us, albeit in a dormant state that ever awaits the rain of insight to cause it to grow. Thus, what Allah created does not change, but we change, at least on the surface. Regarding religion, the basis of most of the world's religions shows some degree of uniformity in spiritual practice, regardless of the particular worship methods, and this is a further sign of the original origin of all religions - from a Being that knows how to touch our hearts. Is there any religion with no form of prayer or meditation directed towards personal growth and the eternal truth? Thus, even the principles of divine religion do not change, even if we alter the forms and invent new doctrines on our own. The Prophet explained that Allah created everyone as a natural monotheist but that Satan messes them up in their religion as they grow and mature. (*Muslim*)

[1345] The Qur'an advances the concept that all human beings are endowed with a spirit (*ruh*) from Allah while still in their mothers' wombs. If we have something from Allah within each of us, then it stands to reason that that part of us will always recognize, in a vague sort of way, where it belongs. Thus, the concept of *fitrah*, as it is mentioned here in this verse. Our *fitrah*, or inborn inclination towards Allah, is that feeling within all of us that prompts us to be religious. Science today has even identified such a "Allah gene" within us that prompts us to believe in the supernatural. It is this inner nature that logically causes us to doubt the validity of idols, even as it causes us to question the reason for our existence in this world. Those who don't listen to their *fitrah* and who reject Allah's proofs warp their souls and become prone to immorality. Allah lets them sink further into error as a punishment for their willful lack of common sense, though He makes His signs continually available for them to consider anew. He even lets greater tests befall them so they have the chance to break out of their negative thinking pattern and embrace their Creator. On the flip side, those who listen to their *fitrah* seek out Allah's truth and may travel the world in search of knowledge, perhaps changing religions along the way, until they are fully satisfied they have found Allah's truth. The innate predisposition to seek spiritual meaning is often thought of in scientific circles today as some sort of 'Allah gene.'

[1346] This is a prescient warning to the followers of Islam not to break up into sects, for each will assume it has the truth, when it may very well be only partially right. The criticism here, however, is a direct reference to the habit among Christians and Jews to break up into competing sects. Although Muslims, too, eventually split up into sects, the Prophet said that the correct one could be identified by seeing which one followed his example and that of his companions. The Prophet also said that his community would never unite on an error. Therefore, we should look for the largest sect that adheres closely to what the Prophet and his companions practiced, without historical or theological oddities or practices that developed centuries later and that can be proven to be invented practices.

travelers. [1347] This is the best course of action for those who seek Allah's face, and they're the ones who will be successful. [38]

Remember Where the Best Returns Lie

The (false) *gifts* that you give out to other people, (in the hopes) of making a profit (in return) off their property, doesn't get you any increase (in value) with Allah. [1348] However, what you give in charity, seeking only Allah's face, (will increase your value with Him). They're the ones who will get multiplied returns. [39]

Allah is the One Who created you and gave you your resources. Then He'll cause you to die and then bring you back to life again. Can any of your 'partners' do anything like that?

Glory be to Him! He's high above the partners they make with Him. [40]

The World is Your Example

Corruption has appeared on land and at sea because of what the hands of people have done. [1349] (Allah allows it to go forward) so they can suffer the (bad consequences) of their actions and thus have a chance to return (to Him). [41]

Say (to them), *"Travel all over the world, and see the end result of all those (civilizations) that came before you, and most of them made partners (with Allah).* [42] *So set your face towards the straight religion before a day comes from Allah that can't be put off, a day when people will be divided (into different categories)."* [43]

Whoever rejected faith will suffer from that rejection, while the one who did what was morally right will have prepared a fine resting place for himself. [44] (That's so) He can reward those who believed and did what was morally right from His bounty. Truly, He has no love for those who suppress (their awareness of the truth). [45]

Signs in Nature are to be Pondered

Among His signs are the winds that He sends as welcome news (for sailors), and also so you can have a taste of His mercy. (Those same winds) propel ships (through the sea) by His command, allowing you to search for His bounty, and also so you can be thankful. [46]

And so it was that We sent messengers before you, (Muhammad,) to their respective nations, and they brought clear evidence. We took retribution upon those who were wicked, and it was Our task to help those who believed. [1350] [47]

[1347] The Prophet once said, "Whoever seeks Allah's protection, give that person protection. Whoever asks in the name of Allah, give him a place of safety. Whoever does something nice for you, reward him, and if you don't have anything, at least call upon Allah's blessings on his behalf until you know he has been rewarded (by Allah)." (*Fiqh-us-Sunnah*)

[1348] This verse describes a practice in which a person gives a gift in the hopes that he will receive a reciprocal gift of equal or greater value than what he gave. This is giving without good intentions, for the giver wants to hedge his or her bets and hope for a greater return later. So it is like a loan almost. As such, the term that is used in this verse is *riba*, or increase, which later became equated with interest money. We could translate the word as investment money, reflecting the goal of the false-gift transaction, and also because of the fact that at this time in the Meccan Period, charging interest on loans was not forbidden yet. (*Ma'ariful Qur'an*)

[1349] Some commentators held that this line also encompasses pollution and humanity's ruining of the environment. The Prophet said, "When an evildoer dies, it is a relief for people, the land, the trees and the animals." (*Tirmidhi*)

[1350] The Prophet said, "No Muslim defends the honor of his brother except that there would be a right upon Allah to defend him from Hellfire on the Day of Resurrection." Then the Prophet recited this verse. (*Ibn Abi Hatim*)

Allah is the One Who sends the winds that form the clouds. Then He spreads them in the sky as He wills and breaks them into fragments until you see water coming out from within them.

Then after He's caused (the rain) to fall upon whichever of His servants that He wills, you see them celebrating, [48] even though they were in abject desperation just a moment before. [49]

So examine the results of Allah's mercy: how He gives life to the earth after it was barren. This is how life will come to the dead, for He has power over all things. [50]

On the other hand, if We happened to send a whirlwind that damaged their crops, leaving them withered and yellow, they would become thankless once more! [1351] [51]

What will it Take for Them to Listen?

*Y*ou can't make the dead listen, nor can you force the deaf to hear the call, especially once they've turned their backs on it, [52] and neither can you lead the blind back from their wandering. [1352] You can only convince the faithful to listen, for they've believed in Our (revealed) verses, and they've surrendered (their wills) to Us. [53]

Allah is the One Who created you weak (at birth), and Who gave you your strength after that weakness. Then after that strength, (He will) give you weakness once more and grey hair, as well. He creates whatever He wants, for He's the Knowing and the Determiner. [54]

On the day when the Hour (of Judgment) is established, the wrongdoers will swear that they hadn't lived but an hour - *that's how used to being deceived they were!* [55]

Then the learned people who believed will say (to them), *"You were just passing time within Allah's recorded (plan), all the way up to the Day of Resurrection. Now this is the Day of Resurrection, but you weren't paying attention!"* [56]

So no excuses the wrongdoers offer that day will do them any good, nor will they be allowed to make amends. [57]

And so We've laid out in this Qur'an every kind of example for people (to learn from), but even if you brought them a miracle (that they couldn't deny), the faithless would say of it, *"You're only talking nonsense."* [58]

That's how Allah seals the hearts of those who won't understand. [59] Have patience with them, for Allah's promise is real, and don't let the faithless shake your resolve. [60]

[1351] The hidden subtext is that people should not tie their faith in Allah to the fact of being in good or bad times. Whether the wind blows one way or the other, our faith should be independent of our life's circumstances. The famous Umayyad caliph, 'Umar ibn 'Abdul-Aziz, once wrote, "Whenever Allah gives a blessing to a servant, then takes it back from him, and the servant endures the loss patiently, then He may reward him with a blessing that's better than the one He took away."

[1352] Jesus is quoted as saying something similar in Matthew 13:13, when his disciples asked why he always told parables or stories.

Luqmān

31 Luqman
Late Meccan Period

This chapter takes its name after a legendary wise man Luqman whose ultimate identity is unknown. The example of the sage, who was virtually unknown to Arabian lore, is meant to create further connections between the past and the contemporary preaching of the Prophet, in order to show that Allah is ultimately the source for all wise and noble teachings. The remainder of the chapter is dedicated to highlighting more proofs of Allah's power, as well as the reality of the next life.

In the Name of Allah,
the Compassionate, the Merciful

Alif. Lām. Meem. [1]

These are the verses of the Book of wisdom. [2] (It's a source of) guidance and a mercy to the righteous. [3]

They're the ones who establish prayer, give in charity and have the full confidence in their hearts of the next life. [4] They're being guided by their Lord, and they'll be successful. [1353] [5]

There are some among people who buy useless tales that are devoid of knowledge, in order to mislead others from the path of Allah by making a mockery of (knowledge). [1354] They'll have a humiliating punishment. [1355] [6]

[1353] The Prophet said, "The height of wisdom is the fear of Allah. The best thing that can dwell in the heart is certainty (of the truth of Allah). Doubt comes from disbelief. Youth is one branch of insanity. The happiest person is the one who learns a lesson from someone else. The saddest person is one who was sad from his mother's womb. The end is near." (*Bayhaqi*)

[1354] There are two references as to the reason for this verse. They both revolve around a man named an-Nadr ibn al-Harith, who had traveled frequently to Persia. He offered the Quraysh his tales of Persian heroes as an alternative to listening to the Qur'an. He also tried to use music to take people's attention away from the Qur'an. He used to bring out a foreign slave girl he owned to sing when Muhammad was preaching. He used to say, "Muhammad makes you listen to the Qur'an; then he asks you to pray and fast, and he makes life hard for you. Come and listen to this music instead, and have some fun." (*Ma'ariful Qur'an*)

[1355] Some conservative scholars have used this verse to rule that all music and singing is forbidden. This extreme position, however, is not supported by the wider *hadith* literature, which contains several references to incidents of singing that were approved of by the Prophet. In addition, this verse and the background describes to what the *useless tales* refer, in that they are for the purpose of making a mockery of knowledge by using music to *compete* with intelligent conversation when it is being offered. The Prophet specifically allowed women and girls to sing and play drums during times of celebration, such as at weddings and other events. See reports in Tirmidhi, Tabarani and Bukhari. He also sang with his companions when they were digging the trench around Medina. When the Muslims used to travel long distances, drums would be played to lessen the monotony of the road, and songs would be sung, as well. (Drums or small tambourines seem to be the only instruments specifically allowed in the traditions.) The Prophet also composed a suggested wedding song of celebration for

When Our (revealed) verses are read out to someone like that, he turns away arrogantly, acting like he didn't hear anything – almost like he was deaf in both ears! Give him the news of a terrible punishment! [7]

Those who believe and do what's morally right will have gardens of delight, [8] and there they shall remain! Allah's promise is true, for He's the Powerful and the Wise. [9]

He created the heavens without any supports that you can see. He rooted firm highlands in the earth so it wouldn't shake with you, and He raised up all kinds of animals throughout (the earth).

We send down water from the sky and produce every type of beneficial species (of plant) in pairs. [10] That's the creation of Allah!

Now show Me something that anyone else besides Him has created - it's just not possible! Therefore, the wrongdoers are clearly mistaken. [11]

The Wisdom of Luqmān

*A*nd so it was that We bestowed wisdom upon Luqmān, (telling him), *"Be thankful to Allah. [1356] Whoever is thankful, then it's to the good of his own soul, but whoever is ungrateful, (know that) Allah doesn't need anything and is (already being) praised."* [12]

"My son," Luqmān said to his child during a lesson, *"don't make any partners with Allah, for making partners is the worst offense (against Allah)."* [1357] [13]

(On account of the sacrifices that parents make for their children), We made it a duty upon every human being (to be respectful) to his parents. After enduring wave upon wave of pain, his mother finally gives birth to him, and then he's (totally dependent on her) for two years of weaning. So be thankful to Me and to your parents, for the final destination (of you all) is back (to Me). [1358] [14]

---

girls to sing as they clapped their hands and played tambourines. That song is recorded in Tabarani and goes as follows: "To you we have come! To you we have come! So welcome us, as we welcome you!" (Also recorded in *Ibn Majah.*) Some commentators have attempted to extrapolate even further and have forbidden hobbies and pastimes, in general, on the spurious notion that they distract one from religion. This is an untenable position, for as the *hadith* literature shows, the Prophet engaged in or approved of many different types of sports and pastimes from wrestling and archery to foot races, swimming, horseback riding, target practice, poetry and storytelling. (There are obscure traditions that forbid the playing of backgammon and chess, but these are obviously spurious reports, as those two games were not invented yet in the Prophet's time.) The Prophet said, "Let your heart rest sometimes," and many scholars take this as the permission to engage in recreational activity. (*Ma'ariful Qur'an*)

[1356] Luqmān was not a prophet, but he was a very wise man. It is said that he was offered the choice to become either a prophet or a very wise man. He chose the latter on the reasoning that the office of prophethood carries too much responsibility. He is often thought of as something of an Aesop of the Middle East, if you will. Though it is uncertain when and where he lived, some have suggested he was a citizen of the ancient city of Iram (Ubar), which was a major trading center in present-day Oman nearly a thousand years before the lifetime of the Prophet. Others have placed him outside of Arabia altogether and have suggested that he was an African wise man, a carpenter by trade, who lived in the era of Prophet David. Most commentators seem to favor the latter view. Ibn Kathir records that Luqmān's son's name was Thārān.

[1357] When verse 6:82 was revealed, many of the companions became distressed, for it said that believers are those who don't confuse their faith with oppression and wrong. Some people asked the Prophet the meaning of the Arabic word *zulm*, which means any type of wrong, injustice or offense, and they exclaimed that everyone has done it, so how can there be hope for them? The Prophet said, "That's not what *zulm* means (in this verse). Haven't you heard what Luqman said?" The prophet then recited this verse. (*Muslim*) Thus, the *zulm* mentioned in 6:82 is talking about the practice of offending Allah by making partners with Him.

[1358] One of the Prophet's companions was man named Sa'ad ibn Abi Waqqas. He was a cousin of his mother Aminah so they were related through that venue. He was an early convert and the Prophet

However, if (your parents) try to force you to set up partners with Me, offering (deities) about which you know nothing, then don't obey them. Yet, still keep company with them in this world in a fair manner. [1359]

Keep yourself on the path of those who turn towards Me, for all of you will return to Me, and I'm going to tell you the meaning of everything you did. [1360] [15]

"My son," (Luqmān said,) *"even if there were a tiny speck of mustard seed lodged within a rock or anywhere else in the heavens or the earth, Allah can bring it out, for Allah is aware of all subtleties.* [1361] [16] *My son, establish prayer, encourage what's known (to be right in Allah's sight) and forbid what's strange (or unfamiliar to Allah's good way).*

"Persevere with whatever happens to you, for that shows determination in dealing with matters. [17] *Don't puff up your cheek (arrogantly) at other people nor strut around through the earth, for Allah has no love for conceited snobs.* [18] *Walk moderately, and speak softly, for the most annoying noise of all is the shrill of a donkey."* [1362] [19]

Asking People to Believe

$\mathcal{D}$on't you see that Allah has tamed everything in the heavens and on earth for you and that He's showered His favors down upon you - *favors that you can recognize and others that you can't even fathom?*

Still there are some people who argue about (the existence) of Allah without knowledge, without guidance and without a scripture to enlighten them! [20]

When they're asked to follow what Allah has sent down, they say, *"No way! We're going to follow what we found our ancestors doing."*

What! Even if it's Satan calling them to the punishment of the raging flame? [21]

Whoever submits his face to Allah and is good, then he's taken hold of the most secure handhold, for the final outcome rests with Allah. [22]

Whoever rejects faith, however - don't let their rejection bother you, for they're going to come back to Us, and then We're going to tell them the meaning of all that they did.

---

was delighted to welcome him into the fold. However, Sa'ad's mother was angry at him for leaving idolatry and she vowed to starve herself until he abandoned Islam. Days went by, and Sa'ad begged his mother to eat. She refused until the day came when Sa'ad told her, "O my mother! In spite of the love I bear for you, my love for Allah and His Messenger are indeed stronger. By Allah, if you had a thousand souls and one soul after another would depart, I would still not abandon this religion for anything." She then relented and ate again. This verse was revealed commenting on Sa'ad's devotion to both his mother and his faith.

[1359] A follower of Islam still must maintain kind relations with his or her parents, even if they are of a different religion. This is the importance that the Qur'an places on respecting the ones who carried you and raised you while you were helpless. The commentators say this verse is making reference to an actual situation where a pagan mother tried to force her son to renounce Islam, and he refused. Eventually she gave up her efforts.

[1360] It is said that this last line of this verse was revealed for the sake of the Prophet's best friend, Abu Bakr. After he had accepted Islam, being one of the first persons to do so, five of his close friends asked him if his conversion was sincere. When Abu Bakr affirmed his choice to follow Muhammad, each of his friends, who included Uthman ibn Affan and Az-Zubayr, also declared that they believed in Muhammad, as well.

[1361] The Prophet said, "Luqman the Wise used to say, 'When something is given into the care of Allah, He looks after it.'" (*Ahmad*)

[1362] Among the several nuggets of wisdom that have survived the ages among the Arabs, there is a report that Luqman was once asked how he gained his wisdom. He replied, "By watching ignorant people. Any time I saw faults in such a one, I avoided doing the same."

Allah knows all the secrets of the heart! [23] We give them time to enjoy themselves for a while, but in the end We're going to drive them ever deeper into relentless punishment. [24]

If you asked them who created the heavens and the earth, they would be sure to say, *"Allah."*

So say (to them), *"Praise be to Allah."*

Yet, even still most of them don't understand! [25] To Allah belongs whatever is in the heavens and the earth. Allah is the Self-Sufficient and Praiseworthy. [26]

If all the trees of the earth were pens, and the ocean (was made of ink) - even backed up by seven more oceans - still the words of Allah would not be exhausted, for Allah is strong and wise. 1363 [27]

The creation and resurrection of you all isn't (any more difficult for Allah than doing both) to a single soul by itself, for Allah hears and sees (everything all at once). 1364 [28]

Don't you see that Allah merges the night into the day and merges the day into the night and that He's the One Who tamed the sun and the moon, each following its own set trajectory?

Allah is well-informed about all that you do, [29] and that's because Allah is the True Reality.

Whatever they're calling upon besides Him is falsehood, for Allah is the Highest and the Greatest. 1365 [30]

Our Last Hope is with Allah

Don't you see the ships sailing through the sea by Allah's favor, in order for Him to show you some of His signs? In this (example), there are signs for every patient and thankful person. [31]

If an overshadowing wave climbs up over (the bow of the ship), the (sailors) cry out to Allah, offering to devote themselves to Him (if He saves them). 1366

Yet, when He brings them safely back to the shore, some of them stop halfway (in between faith and rejection). Yet, no one rejects Our signs except for deceitful betrayers. [32]

O people! Be mindful of your Lord, and fear the day when no parent will be able to do anything for his own child, nor any child for his parent.

Allah's promise is indeed the truth, so don't let the life of this world fool you, nor let the Great Deceiver trick you into (rejecting) Allah. [33]

Allah has Knowledge of the Unseen

The knowledge of the Hour (of Judgment) is with Allah. 1367 He's the One

---

1363 The "words" of Allah are often interpreted as being His commands for the creation and functioning of things. There is an entire universe to oversee, and Allah is capable of running it all, and more besides.

1364 Allah's powers are so vast, and His abilities so limitless, that He can keep track of all life *forms - as if He were watching only one!*

1365 The Prophet said, "The truest word of any poet was the saying of Labid: 'Truly, everything besides Allah is false.'" (*Bukhari*)

1366 This refers to the phenomenon known today as "rogue waves" in which an unusually high wave (up to eight stories tall) comes from an unknown source and suddenly towers over a ship, threatening to swamp it. If Allah saves people from such unnatural things, they are usually thankless in the end.

1367 A bedouin came in from the desert with a horse and a colt to sell in the market. He saw Muhammad and asked, "Who are you?" He replied, "I'm the Prophet of Allah." The bedouin asked, "*Who is the*

481

Who sends down the rain, and He knows what's in the wombs (of pregnant women). No one knows what he'll earn tomorrow, nor does anyone know in what land he'll die, [1368] though Allah is full of knowledge and is well-informed (about all these things). [34]

---

prophet of Allah?" When Muhammad reaffirmed to him that he was, the man then asked him, "So when will the Hour come to pass?" "It's part of the unseen, and no one can know it save Allah," answered the Prophet. Then the man asked, "So when is it going to rain?" "It's not known except by Allah." "So with what is my horse pregnant?" he asked. "It's not known except by Allah," the Prophet intoned. Then this verse was revealed in response. (*Asbab ul Nuzul*)

[1368] The Prophet said, "If Allah wants to take a person's soul in a particular land, He gives him a reason to go there." (*Al-Hakim*)

The Prostration

32 As-Sajdah
Middle Meccan Period

The tone of this chapter reflects the fact that when it was revealed, the Meccan persecution had not yet reached its height. It answers a number of objections posed by the pagans, as well as emphasizing the utter 'rightness' of submitting to Allah. The Meccans are also asked to consider the fate of previous civilizations who rejected the call of Allah.

In the Name of Allah,
the Compassionate, the Merciful

Alif. Lām. Meem. [1]

The revelation of this Book is from the Lord of All the Worlds; there's nothing doubtful within it! [2] So are they saying, *"He must have made it all up"*?

Certainly not! It's the truth from your Lord, so you can warn a nation that never had any warner before you, and also so they can be guided. [3]

Allah is the One Who created the heavens and the earth and everything in between them in six stages; then He established Himself upon the throne (of power). [1369] There's no one who can protect you nor vouch for you other than He, so won't you be reminded? [4]

He regulates all commands within the sky and the earth, and then after (the end has come, all affairs and matters) will ascend back to Him (for resolution) in a day that is like a thousand years of your estimation. [1370] [5] That's what He's like –

[1369] The commentators explain this *taking control of the throne* to mean that after Allah created the universe in six stages, or *days*, He affirmed it to be under His law, thus the symbol of the *throne*, which is the traditional symbol of power for a ruler.

[1370] Some critics have suggested that there is a contradiction between the following three verses: 22:47, 32:5 and 70:4. The first two verses [22:47 and 32:5] are often interpreted to mean that a day to Allah is like a thousand years of our time, while the last verse [70:4] is often said to mean that a day to Allah is like fifty thousand years. This misunderstanding is easily dispelled upon a close examination of what each of these verses is *specifically* referencing, for the verses in question apply to completely different things. Verse 22:47 states (in general terms) that a day to Allah *can be like* a thousand years of our own time. So verse 22:47 is a general statement that is unrelated to the subject matter of the remaining two verses. Verse 32:5 states that Allah rules the universe, and then *after that* (i.e., after He shuts down humanity's term) it will take a day that is like a thousand years (refer to 22:47) for all the *affairs* (records) to be assembled in the place on high. Now what is verse 70:4 referencing? Verse 70:4 is saying that *the angels* and *spirit* (Gabriel) will ascend to Allah (for the Day of Judgment, as verses 70:1-3 imply) which itself is a 'day' (or time period) that will last for *fifty thousand years*. This figure is confirmed in a tradition of the Prophet when he said that the Day of Judgment (where punishment will be meted out) will, in fact, last for fifty thousand years. In addition, verse 32:5 ends with the phrase, *of your estimation*, while verse 70:4 does not reference human timekeeping, so the number in 70:4 is a specially fixed duration from Allah (confirmed by prophetic tradition). Thus, the Prophet confirmed that this one 'day' (of Judgment) will last a lot longer than any other time period. Thus, there is no contradiction among these three verses on account of what each is referencing.

the knower of the hidden and the clear – the Powerful and the Merciful! [6]

He's the One Who created everything superbly! He initially created the human being from (nothing more) than clay. [7] Then He made his descendants from the extract of lowly mixed fluids. [8]

Then He constructs (each of them in his mother's womb) and then breathes into him something of His spirit. Then He endows you with (the faculties of awareness): hearing, sight and feeling. (Yet, for all of these gifts), you're hardly thankful at all! [9]

Accepting the Concept of an Afterlife

*T*hey say, "*What! When we're deep underground (and rotted away), are we really going to be made again like new?*"

But no! (They're) rejecting their appointment with their Lord. [10] Tell them, "*The Angel of Death* [1371] *will be put in charge of you, and he's going to collect your souls and take you back to your Lord.*" [11]

If only you could see how the guilty will be hanging their heads dejectedly before their Lord. "*Our Lord!*" (they'll cry out in despair). "*Now we see it, and now we've heard (our records read out to us). Please, send us back (to earth), and then we'll reform ourselves, for now we really do believe!*" [12]

If We had wanted, We could've guided every soul, but the truth of My sentence will come to pass: "*I will fill Hellfire with jinns and people all together!* [13] *So suffer it! You forgot this appointed day of yours, so now We're going to forget you! Suffer the eternal punishment for your deeds!*" [14]

The true believers are those who, when they hear Our verses being read out to them, fall down in adoration and praise of their Lord. They're never too proud (to bow down before their Lord). [1372] [15]

Their bodies propel them to rise restlessly from their beds (at night) so they can call upon their Lord earnestly in hope and fear, [1373] and they spend (in charity)

[1371] According to a saying of the Prophet, when Angel Azra'il was chosen to be the Angel of Death, he complained to Allah, saying, "O My Lord! You've given me such a task that the entire race of the children of Adam - *throughout the entire world* - will think badly of me on account of this, so much so, that every time I am mentioned, I'll be considered an evil thing." Allah replied to him, saying, "We've taken care of that by implementing such clearly recognizable diseases and other causes of death in the world that everyone will attribute death to those causes and diseases, and thus you will be shielded from their remarks." (*Qurtubi*)

[1372] It is customary that those who believe in Allah will stop reading after this verse and prostrate themselves in awe of Allah.

[1373] This verse refers to those who give up sleep in favor of prayer, whether by getting up early for the predawn prayer, not napping before the night prayer, or getting up in the darkness of the night to perform the late night, optional prayer known as *tahajjud*. A famous companion named Mu'adh ibn Jabal once asked the Prophet, "Prophet of Allah, tell me of a deed that will grant me admittance into Paradise and save me from Hellfire." The Prophet said, "You've asked about something of great importance, and it's easy for the one who has it made easy for him by Allah. Serve Allah, don't make 'partners' with Him, establish prayer, pay the required charity, fast in the month of Ramadan and perform a pilgrimage to the House." Then he said, "Shouldn't I tell you about the gates of goodness? Fasting is a shield; charity wipes out sin, and the prayer of a person in the middle of the night (brings forgiveness)." Then he recited this passage. Afterwards he said, "Shouldn't I tell you of the greatest of all things and its pillars and highest peak?" Mu'adh answered, "Of course, Messenger of Allah." Then the Prophet said, "The greatest of all things is Islam; its pillars are the prayers, and its highest peak is *jihad* for the sake of Allah." Then he said, "Shouldn't I tell you upon what all of these things depend?" Mu'adh again answered, "Of course, Messenger of Allah." Then the Prophet took hold of his tongue and said, "Control this." Then Mu'adh asked, "Messenger of Allah, are we going to be held accountable for what we say?" The Prophet answered, "May your mother lose you, Mu'adh! Will people ever be thrown into Hellfire for any other reason than because of what their tongues say?" (*Ahmad*)

out of the resources that We've given them. [1374] [16]

No soul knows what delights of the eye are kept hidden from it as a reward for the (good) they have (all) done (during their time in the world). [1375] [17]

The Twisted are not Equal to the Righteous

*A*nd so is the one who believes no better than the one who is a twisted deviant? No, they're not equal at all! [1376] [18]

Those who believe and do what's morally right will be given gardens for their welcoming place as a reward for what they used to do (in the world). [19]

Twisted deviants will have for their place of welcome (nothing else save) the Fire, and every time they want to get out of it, they'll be pushed back into it.

They'll be told, "*Suffer the punishment of the Fire – (the punishment) that you used to call a lie!*" [20]

However, before We condemn them to that (dreaded) punishment, We let them experience some (lesser) forms of punishment here (in the) lower (life of this world), so they can at least have (a chance to repent of their evil) and return (to the path of Allah). [21]

So who's more wrong than the one who is reminded of the signs of his Lord but then turns away from them? We're indeed going to get retribution from the wicked! [22]

Take the Lesson for What it Is

*A*nd so it was that We gave a scripture to Moses; therefore, (Muhammad,) have no doubt (that a scripture is coming to you, too).

We made (the Torah) to be a guide for the Children of Israel, [23] and We set up leaders from among them who guided them by Our command.

(We favored them) for as long as they patiently persevered and believed in Our signs, [24] but your Lord will judge between them and their points of difference on the Day of Assembly. [25]

Haven't they learned any lessons from all those generations that We've destroyed before them, and among whose ruins they now explore?

There are signs in this, so aren't they listening? [26] Don't they see how We drive the water to barren land and use it to grow plants for their cattle to eat, and for them, as well? [1377] Don't they see (any of those things)? [27]

They just ask, "*So when will this all come out in the open, if you're really so honest?*" [28]

[1374] The Prophet once remarked that faith lies in between hope and fear. We fear disobeying Allah's limits and laws, more so than we would fear disobeying our own parents for the utter shame with which it would fill us. Then we hope in Allah's immense forgiveness and mercy, thus giving us the courage to continue in this life of testing, for Allah has promised in this Book that salvation is for the *sincere*, not necessarily the *perfect*.

[1375] The Prophet said, "Whoever enters Paradise, he will enjoy a life of luxury and never feel deprivation. His clothes will never wear out, and his youth will never fade. In Paradise there are things that no eye has ever seen, no ear has ever heard and no person has ever conceived of." (*Muslim*)

[1376] This passage was revealed concerning the case of 'Ali ibn Abi Talib and Walid ibn 'Uqbah ibn Abi Mu'it. Walid boasted to 'Ali, "I'm stronger than you, more eloquent and a more powerful fighter than you." 'Ali said, "Shut up, you twisted deviant." (*Asbab ul-Nuzul*)

[1377] Since this verse mentions water specifically and not rain, the commentators explain that this refers to rivers that flow through deserts as well as underground water sources that can flow and bubble up through the earth even in dry regions. (*Ma'ariful Qur'an*)

Say (to them), *"When the Day of Victory (arrives), believing then won't do any (good) for the faithless, and they won't be given any break, either."* [1378] [29]

So turn away from them and wait, for they'll be waiting, as well. [30]

[1378] Some commentators hold that this verse refers to the Judgment Day; others feel it is a prophecy about the Battle of Badr, when Islam was finally settled on a solid footing, and many pagans were vanquished on that day of victory.

The Allied Forces

33 Al Ahzab
Middle Medinan Period

Early in the year 627 CE, the largest Arab army that had ever been assembled marched on Medina to destroy Islam and the Muslim community forever. In preparation for this impending assault, the vastly outnumbered Muslims hastily dug a large trench along the exposed outskirts of the city. (This was the suggestion of the Persian convert, Salman al-Farsi.) The rear of the city, which contained many walled houses, was fortified together, and the disjointed walls were sealed with heavy brickwork.

The twelve-thousand strong allied army, cobbled together by the leaders of the banished Banu Nadir Jews, was a formidable coalition made up of well-armed Meccans and men from five large bedouin tribes. When the jubilant horde approached the city and found a wide trench laid out before them, they scoffed and hesitated, for traditional battles among the Arabs had always involved simple frontal assaults of armed men against each other.

The trench made their cavalry useless, and the attackers were thus forced to order a series of infantry charges. Their men were unable to cross the deep ravine in sufficient numbers, however, to overwhelm the defenders on the other side, who assailed them with arrows. Thus, the Allies settled in upon a strategy of blockading the city. It would be only a matter of time before Medina would be starved into submission, they reasoned.

After some relatively uneventful weeks, one of the organizers of the coalition, Huyyay ibn Akhtab, persuaded the one remaining Jewish tribe in Medina, the Banu Qurayzah, to repudiate their treaty with the Muslims and join in a coordinated assault to overwhelm the Muslims from all sides. The situation for the Muslims was truly bleak. To make matters worse, a large number of hypocrites within the city were counseling their fellows either to break with the Prophet and join the enemy or, at the very least, to escape and flee into the desert.

The Muslims had never faced such a dire situation. However, through the skillful use of a double agent and an understanding of the fragile nature of the coalition facing him, the Prophet was able to split the resolve of the Allies and cause them to doubt each other's intentions. A sudden desert storm that arose one night convinced the demoralized attackers to lift the siege and flee - almost one month to the day after the attack began.

In the Name of Allah,
the Compassionate, the Merciful

O Prophet! Be mindful (of Allah). [1379] Pay no mind to those who suppress (their awareness of the truth) nor to the hypocrites, for Allah is full of knowledge and wisdom. [1]

[1379] There are several different, yet complimentary, reports as to the references for the revelation of this passage. The most common of them is as follows. Some months after the Battle of Uhud, a delegation

487

Instead, follow the inspiration that's coming to you from your Lord, for Allah knows exactly what you're doing. [2] Put your trust in Allah, for Allah is enough to look after (your) affairs. [3]

Adopted Children must Retain their Own Surnames

*A*llah hasn't placed two hearts in any man's chest, nor has He made the wives whom (some of) you (have wrongfully) divorced [1380] by (saying they're like your mothers), *equivalent* to your mothers, [1381] nor has He made your

adopted children your actual (biological) children. [1382]

All these pronouncements are merely phrases from your mouths. Allah explains (how it's really meant to be) in all truth, and thus He guides you on the path. [4]

Call (your adopted children) by the surnames of their fathers, for that's the right thing to do in the sight of Allah. [1383] However, if you don't know (the surnames) of their fathers, then call them your brothers in faith and your protected ones.

There is no blame if you make a mistake in this, for it's your heart's intentions (that matter). Truly, Allah is forgiving and merciful. [1384] [5]

---

of Meccan pagans was allowed to enter Medina to parlay with the Prophet under a guarantee of safety. They included Abu Sufyan, 'Ikrimah, the son of the slain Abu Jahl (at Badr), and Abdul A'war as-Sulaymi. The delegation met first with 'Abdullah ibn Ubayy and some of his hypocrites. Then the Meccans, accompanied by two hypocrites named 'Abdullah ibn Sa'd and Ta'ma ibn Ubayrak (who is mentioned in the background to verses 4:105-112), went to hold a meeting with Muhammad. Abu Sufyan began his address, exclaiming, "Don't say anything about our gods Lat, 'Uzza and Manat, except that they have the power to advocate and that they bring benefits for their worshippers, and then we'll leave you alone with your Lord." The Prophet didn't agree, and 'Umar ibn al Khattab (d. 644), who was also present, asked for permission to kill them. "But I have guaranteed their safety," the Prophet objected. So 'Umar told the delegation, "Go with Allah's curse and anger upon you." The Prophet then asked the delegation to depart the city. These three verses were then revealed. (*Ma'ariful Qur'an*)

[1380] See 58:1-2 and introduction to the chapter for an explanation of the odd pre-Islamic custom of *zihar*, whereby a man could say that he had the same feelings towards his wife that he has for his mother and thus he won't sleep with his wife any further, while not fully divorcing her so she can marry someone else.

[1381] One day when the Prophet was praying in congregation he trembled momentarily. Some hypocrites then said (oddly enough) that the Prophet was wavering between his adopted home of Medina and his love of his hometown, and thus they said, 'He has two hearts.' The first part of verse four was revealed to affirm that the Prophet has a single heart and a single purpose. (*Ibn Kathir*) The remainder of this passage was revealed to settle the status of actual blood relationships versus adoptive ones.

[1382] There is a misconception that Islam does not allow adoption. This is untrue. What Islam doesn't allow is taking a child and giving it one's own family name, so that the child grows up not knowing who he or she really is. An extreme danger is that such a person may wind up unknowingly marrying his own sibling who was adopted by someone else, or at the very least, when an adoptee finds out they were adopted, they begin to long for their real parents and seek them out. Islam is very insistent that taking orphans into one's home and raising them with love is praiseworthy and of the highest good. It merely stipulates that their identity should not be hidden from them.

[1383] This passage was revealed a short time before the Prophet's adopted son, Zayd ibn Harith, had divorced his wife Zaynab, and the continuation of this issue is taken up in verses 36-40 of this same chapter. In the past, people had always called Muhammad's adopted son Zayd ibn Muhammad, but after verse 5 was revealed, people began calling him by his real surname, Zayd ibn Harith. (Zayd later married Muhammad's childhood caretaker, an African lady named Barakah!)

[1384] The Prophet said, "If a judge uses independent reasoning (*ijtehad*) and reaches the right decision, he will have two rewards. If he uses independent reasoning and reaches the wrong decision, he will have one reward." (*Bukhari*) The meaning is that a judge is still rewarded by Allah, even if he makes an honest mistake, because he at least tried to think a problem through with logic when the Qur'an and sayings of the Prophet didn't exactly cover an issue or dilemma.

The Prophet is closer to the believers than they are to themselves, and his wives are like their mothers. [1385] Blood-relatives have closer ties to each other (in inheritance rights) than (the wider fellowship) of believers and immigrants (who fled oppression), according to the decree of Allah. [1386]

However, continue to do the right thing for your close associates, as that's decreed in the Book (of Allah). [1387] [6]

All Prophets were the Same in Purpose

*R*ecall that We took an agreement from (all the prophets), even as We (took such an agreement) from you, (Muhammad,) and from Noah, Abraham, Moses and Jesus, the son of Mary. We took from them a formal agreement [7] (that stipulated that Allah) would question the honest (messengers) about their sincerity (in conveying the messages to their peoples).

He's prepared a painful punishment for those who (ungratefully) suppress (their natural disposition to believe in Him). [8]

The Great Siege of Medina

O you who believe! [1388] Remember the favor of Allah upon you when an overwhelming horde (of enemies) came down upon you (to attack you right at Medina). We let loose against them a fierce desert sandstorm and other forces you couldn't even see, for Allah is watching everything you do! [9]

The (enemy) came upon you from above you and below you [1389] - eyes lost

---

[1385] The wives of the Prophet were given the honored title of "Mothers of the Believers" or "*Ummahat al Mu'mineen*," and their status required them to set the best example. They served as teachers, resource people for questions and also as community leaders.

[1386] After the Treaty of Hudaybiyyah was signed in the year 628, in which the Meccans agreed to a ten-year truce with the Muslims, the Muslims were allowed to perform a pilgrimage the following year. When the Muslims arrived the next year and performed their pilgrimage, they were making ready to leave when suddenly the very young daughter of the Prophet's uncle Hamza (who was killed in the Battle of Uhud in 625) followed after the Prophet, saying, "Uncle! Uncle!" (She wanted to leave Mecca and go to Medina where all her father's friends and close relatives had settled.) 'Ali took her by the hand and led her to Fatimah and said to her, "Take care of your uncle's daughter." So Fatimah picked her up, but then two other men came (Zayd and Ja'far) and disputed as to who should have custody of her. 'Ali said, "I have more right because she's the daughter of my paternal uncle." Zayd said, "But she's the daughter of my brother (in faith)." Ja'far said, "She's the daughter of my paternal uncle, and I'm married to her maternal aunt, Asma' bint 'Umays." The Prophet came and settled the dispute, saying the girl should be in the custody of her maternal aunt. Then he said, "The maternal aunt has the same status as the mother's." (*Bukhari*)

[1387] When the immigrants from Mecca settled in Medina, they began to share inheritance rights with the Medinan Muslims, or *Helpers* (as they were forbidden to leave their property to their non-Muslim relatives back in Mecca). After Mecca and Medina were united, this verse stopped this practice, as inheritance, in normal circumstances, is based only on blood-relations. The Prophet said, "There is no believer except that I'm the closest of all people to him in this world and in the hereafter. Recite, if you like, 'The Prophet is closer to the believers than themselves.' If any believer leaves behind any wealth, let his own relatives inherit it. If he leaves any debt or orphans, bring them to me and I will take care of them." (*Bukhari*) Some scholars have suggested that the last portion of this saying obligates a Muslim government to support orphans and debt relief for the destitute who left their families with debt.

[1388] The Great Siege of Medina was the most harrowing time for the Muslims. The pagans expected a speedy victory. Instead, due to the many defenses erected by the Muslims, especially a five-yard deep trench across the exposed front of the city, the Allies had to settle in for a blockade. After a month the alliance collapsed, and a fierce sandstorm drove the hoard away.

[1389] The pagan Ghatafan tribe attacked the trench from the eastern high ground while the Quraysh and their allies concentrated their efforts on the western side of the trench which was at a lower elevation..

hope, and hearts leapt up to their throats, (as some of you) imagined all sorts of (treasonous) thoughts against Allah. [1390] [10] That was traumatic for the faithful, and they were shaken with intense trembling. [11]

The hypocrites and the (believers who are) weak at heart (panicked and) cried out, "*Allah and His Messenger have promised us nothing more than a fantasy.*" [12]

Some of them said, "*People of Yathrib! You can't withstand (this assault)! Pull back now, (and protect your own homes)!*" [1391]

A group of them even went to the Prophet and asked to be excused from the defense (of the city), saying, "*Our homes are exposed and undefended.*"

Their homes were not exposed, nor were they without defense. They only wanted to run away (from the front lines). [13]

If there had, in fact, been a way (for the enemy to slip through) from the sides (of the city), and if (those infiltrators) called to (the hypocrites) to betray (the believers) and join them, then (know that) they wouldn't have hesitated for an instant to do it! [14]

(Surely, they would've turned on you), even though they had already made an agreement with Allah not to turn their backs on you, and an agreement with Allah must be answered for! [15]

Say (to them), "*Running away won't do you any good if you're just trying to escape death or*

(a fierce) battle, for even if you did (get away), you wouldn't enjoy more than a moment's rest." [16]

Then ask (them), "*Who could shield you from Allah if it were His desire to punish you or to show you mercy?*" They'll find neither any supporter nor any helper apart from Allah! [17]

Surely, Allah knows about those among you who tried to discourage (people from joining in the defense of Medina) and also about those who said to their brothers, "*Come over here with us,*" but who then participated in the fighting for only a short while. [18]

They held back from (committing fully) to you. When they're terrified, you'll see (people like that) looking to you (for help), with their eyes swiveling around like someone about to die!

When the fear is past, however, they'll stab at you with their sharp tongues and stretch themselves out to grab whatever goods they can. These kinds of people have no faith, so Allah has cancelled the value of their deeds, and that's easy for Allah to do. [19]

They think that the Allied Forces are still lurking (in the countryside somewhere). Well, if the Allied Forces did happen to appear (before the walls of Medina once more), then (the hypocrites) would (once again) wish they were wandering around in the deserts with the bedouins, asking for the latest news (from a safe place). However, if they did stay in your company, they would hardly aid in the battle. [20]

(*Zamakhshari*) Seeing these assaults, some Muslims, especially the hypocrites, were greatly alarmed and fearful, and their penchant for panic caused them to spread discord in public at every turn.

[1390] When the pagan forces, over twelve thousand strong, arrived, some of the pagans made camp on low ground in the plain, while others made their camps in the hills overlooking Medina. The sight of their many campfires must have been frightening indeed to those mere 3,000 Muslim fighters within the city walls! One man named Mu'attib even publicly shouted, "Muhammad promised us the treasures of Khosroes and Caesar, but look. We can't even (go out of the city gates) to go to the bathroom!" A more faithful man named Abu Sa'eed asked the Prophet, "O Messenger of Allah, is there anything we can say, for our hearts are in our throats?" The Prophet replied, "Yes, say, 'O Allah, cover our weaknesses and calm our fears.'" This passage was revealed in comment. (*Ibn Kathir*)

[1391] It was a man named Auws ibn Qayzi of the tribe of Banu Harithah who said the following statement on behalf of his clan, but his people were really more interested in fleeing a potentially catastrophic battle. (*Ibn Kathir*)

Courage and Faith

The Messenger of Allah provides you with a beautiful example (to follow), for anyone who longs for Allah and the Last Day and who remembers Allah often. [1392] [21]

Indeed, when the believers (in the city of Medina) saw the Allied Forces (approaching in the distance to attack), they said, *"This is what Allah and His Messenger promised us (would happen), and Allah and His Messenger told us the truth."* [1393]

(The prospect of desperate battle) did no more than increase their faith and submission (to Allah). [1394] [22]

Those Who were True to their Oath

There are some men from among the faithful who've been true to their promise with Allah.

Some have completed their oath (by sacrificing their lives in Allah's cause), while others are still waiting (to prove themselves), and they've never swerved (in their determination) at all. [1395] [23]

[1392] This is one of the verses used to justify following the prophetic traditions, or *hadiths*, as this verse says to follow the Prophet's example. Since we learn about his example from the voluminous *hadith* reports that have come down to us, we must, therefore, follow the example of his conduct as outlined in those traditions (as long as they're well-proved as authentic, of course). Imam ash-Shafi'i once asked a group of people to ask him any question, and he would answer from the Qur'an. Then a man asked about the case of a person who killed a wasp while under pilgrimage restrictions. The Imam recited verse 59:7, which states that we must take whatever the Prophet gives us, and then the Imam narrated a *hadith* in which the Prophet talked about the permissibility of killing certain creatures, such as stinging insects if they attack you, even though during the pilgrimage no killing of living creatures is otherwise allowed. (*Qurtubi*) Thus, the common phrase is said among Muslims that a believer must follow the Qur'an and the *Sunnah*, or Prophet's example. The Prophet said, "I am leaving two things with you. You will never go astray as long as you hold to them tightly: the Book of Allah, and the example (*Sunnah*) of His Messenger." (*Muwatta*) He also said, "...whatever the Messenger of Allah has declared to be forbidden, it is the same as being forbidden by Allah." (*Abu Dawud, Ibn Majah*)
[1393] This is precisely the meaning of 2:214 where the Qur'an explains that believers will be tested with tremendous trials to purify their hearts and bring them closer to Allah and to purity.
[1394] When the two opposing sides drew up for the first day of battle, the Muslim fighters, who numbered less than three thousand, took up positions in front of Medina, while the pagans formed ranks in the plain outside the city. Only the wide trench separated the two sides. The trench made cavalry charges useless, and infantry charges were repelled by squads of Muslim archers in foxholes. The women and children were holed up in fortified sections of the city, and the fortress of the Jewish tribe of Banu Qurayzah protected the rear approaches of the city with its 800 fighting men. (After being swayed by secret promises of victory, the Banu Qurayzah switched sides and the Muslims were faced with a two-front war!) When the Prophet initially saw the horde of Arabs approaching the city, he invoked Allah, saying, "O Allah, Who revealed the Book and is quick in calling to account, defeat the Allies. O Allah, defeat them and shake them up!" The only serious incident of hand-to-hand fighting happened midway through the siege when a fearsome pagan warrior named 'Amr led a small cavalry charge that actually made it over the trench by forcing the horses to leap further than they should have been able to under normal circumstances. The Prophet called for volunteers to mount horses and repel the threat, and no one answered the call due to their fear. Then 'Ali ibn Abi Talib came forward and challenged 'Amr to a duel, which was a common Arab custom. 'Ali wound up winning, rallying his men and causing the remaining cavalrymen to flee.
[1395] A man named Anas ibn al-Nadir was unable to participate in the Battle of Badr, and he made an oath, saying, "I swear that if I have another chance, I'll make people notice what I'll do." When the Battle of Uhud was at hand, he prayed for forgiveness from Allah and declared he was free of what pagans believe. He entered the battle and told one of the companions, "I swore by the One Who owns my soul that I'll be the first one to enter Paradise." Then he fought without hesitation until he was killed. The companions later reported that when they found his body it had over 80 wounds on it, and they didn't know if it was him for certain until his sister was able to identify the shape of his fingertips.

(They know that) Allah will reward the truthful for their truthfulness and punish the hypocrites, if He so desires, though He may be merciful to them, for Allah is forgiving and merciful. [24]

Allah turned back the faithless in all their fury, and they gained no advantage at all! Allah is enough (of an ally) for the believers in their battles, for Allah is strong and powerful. [25]

He brought the Followers of Previous Revelation who had joined the (enemy's) side down from their strongholds and caused their hearts to panic.

You killed a portion of the (Banu Qurayzah) [1396] and took another portion (as bonded-servants). [1397] [26]

This passage was revealed concerning his case and the case of others who were likewise martyred. (*Bukhari*)

[1396] The betrayal of the Banu Qurayzah could not be overlooked. No sooner had the Allies left than the Muslims laid siege to the fortress of the Banu Qurayzah. The siege lasted about twenty-five days. At the end, the Banu Qurayzah agreed to surrender only if they could choose the one who would judge them. The Prophet agreed, and the Banu Qurayzah chose their old friend, the chief of the Auws tribe to decide their fate. The Auws chief, Sa'd ibn Mu'adh, had been wounded during the siege from the Allies and was recovering in a tent when he was brought on a specially outfitted donkey to give his verdict. The Prophet said to him, "(These people)," and he pointed to the gathered leaders of the Banu Qurayzah, "have agreed to accept your judgment, so pass judgment on them as you wish." Sa'd asked, "My judgment will be carried out?" The Prophet said, "Yes." Then Sa'd asked the leaders of the Banu Qurayzah what the punishment for treachery was in the Torah. The Banu Qurayzah hung their heads in shame, for they knew that it was death. Then Sa'd decreed that the leaders were to be executed and the non-combatants, women and children were to be taken as bonded servants. (Is this an unreasonable verdict against those who betrayed and almost caused the downfall of their former allies? Remember that after World War II was over, the victorious powers of the United States, Britain, France and the Soviet Union held public trials of the leaders and war criminals of Germany and Japan, and thereafter they executed many of them.) The Prophet did intervene in the parceling out of the civilians as bonded servants, ordering that no mothers should be separated from their children. He also offered to spare the life of any of the condemned men who agreed to convert to Islam, returning their property in the bargain. Only two of the leading men of the Banu Qurayzah took up the offer.

[1397] It has long been assumed that the fighting men of the Banu Qurayzah were executed as traitors after the tribe surrendered to the Muslims, (upon the ruling of Sa'd ibn Mu'adh,) and that the elderly, the women and their children were given over to bonded servitude. New research into the sources for these reports has shown that there was no wholesale execution of the men of the tribe, and the Qur'an, itself, bears witness to it in the choice of grammar used. The verse here uses the masculine gender when referring to those who were taken into servanthood (*tasiroun fariqan,* literally: 'a portion (of them) you took into custody (to be servants).' In Arabic, the masculine gender would not have been used if only (or mostly) women and children were taken into servanthood. Furthermore, there are no mass graves anywhere in or around Medina (especially not in the main market where the unsubstantiated report incredulously asserts that up to 700 men were beheaded and then buried – the Prophet would have never buried anyone in so public a square). Thus, we are forced to look at the sources of the report that claims *all* the men were killed for treason. As it turns out, that report is traced to descendants of the Banu Qurayzah, and it was incorporated by one of the earliest historians of Islam, Ibn Is-haq (d. 783), without question or verification, into his monumental work of biography. He even named each of the Jewish men to whom he spoke, as well as their sources, going back to two men of the Banu Qurayzah tribe (giving further evidence that the men were not killed wholesale). It must be remembered that some of the compilers of the Prophet's biography, such as Ibn Is-haq, were not always as strict as the scholars of *hadith* in verifying the truth of all the reports they received. (In his introduction, Ibn Is-haq said of the information he collected, "Only Allah knows which of these narrations are true or not.") This is a small blemish on the otherwise exemplary efforts of such men. Scholars in Ibn Is-haq's own time and afterwards, such as Imam Malik and Ibn Hajar, denounced Ibn Is-haq for including such spurious tales as this one that were not investigated properly. (Unfortunately, other writers, who did their work centuries later, such as Ibn Kathir and at-Tabari, merely parroted this particular story without trying to ascertain if the facts were right.) It was never the precedent in the Prophet's policies to kill wholesale the men of his enemies, and both Jewish tribes he fought earlier were merely exiled – and they took their wealth with them. Even after the final episode with the Banu

He caused you to inherit their lands, houses and goods. (Then, later on), you also (gained control) over (the distant city of Khaybar), a place where you had never been before, for Allah has power over all things. [1398] [27]

An Option for the Wives of the Prophet

 O Prophet! [1399] Say to your wives: *"If you want the life of this world and all its glitter, then come on! I'll set you up in style and then set you free in a fine manner.* [28] *However, if you're longing for Allah and His Messenger and the home of the next life, (know that) Allah has prepared a tremendous reward for the good among you."* [1400] [29]

Qurayzah, Muhammad thereafter continued his strict policy of merely exiling or subduing any other Jewish tribes who made war against him. When the northern Jewish settlement of Khaybar was taken the following year, (from which the plot to invade Medina was hatched,) the Muslims found a remnant of the previously exiled Jewish clan of the Banu Nadir residing there among the Khaybari Jews. Even though they were guilty of inciting great enmity against the Muslims, the Prophet merely told them, "Sons of Abu al-Huqayq! I have known the extent of your hostility to Allah and to His Messenger; yet, that does not prevent me from treating you as I treated your brethren." In other words their punishment was *exile*, and that expedition was *after* the surrender of the Banu Qurayzah. (The original Khaybari Jews, incidentally, were allowed to remain on their land with the payment of tribute.) Therefore, most probably only a handful of men of the Banu Qurayzah, known to have been the leaders of the betrayal, were executed. (Ibn Kathir even records how during the rule of 'Umar ibn al-Khattab, the caliph had a religious conversation with a former rabbi *of the Banu Qurayzah*, who had recently converted to Islam! This account is taken from his commentary of chapter 37 of the Qur'an.) In addition, the report in Bukhari of S'ad ibn Mu'adh's verdict specifically says only the 'warriors' or 'fighting men' were to be executed for treason. (*Bukhari*, 5, 58, 148) So we can conclude that after the traitors were taken into custody, their leaders and warriors were killed, with the rest of the non-combatant men, elderly and women and children taken into bonded servitude, and thereafter their descendants carried the grudge and told the tale in an exaggerated way to make it look like their forebears were punished more harshly than they were, and Allah knows best.

[1398] About ten or twenty days after the conclusion of the Treaty of Hudaybiyyah with the Meccans, the Prophet marched his followers northward to subdue the hostile Jewish settlement of Khaybar. This was where the previously exiled Banu Nadir had settled and from where the entire grand alliance of Jews and pagans against Medina was forged. The settlement capitulated after some days of fighting, and the local Jews were allowed to remain on their land upon the payment of a yearly tribute to Medina. The Banu Nadir were exiled yet again and moved to Syria.

[1399] The Prophet's wives were upset and annoyed that they had to live an austere life of poverty. The Prophet, himself, owned practically nothing, for he constantly gave whatever came into his possession away to charity. It often happened that his wives had barely enough food for a proper diet. Thus, they began to grumble and ask for a material lifestyle that would seem more appropriate to their higher status as wives of the Prophet of Allah. Even as another family crisis was solved through a Qur'anic dispensation (see 66:1-5) that offered his wives the choice to divorce him and have a nice and enriching settlement, here also the same offer is given.

[1400] The Prophet was completely dedicated to a life of prayer and charity. As some commentators have noted, after his only wife Khadijah died, he might not have ever married again, but for the practical purposes of alliance building and supporting widows. This verse tries to make an important point clear to his nine wives of the time: if they want more material wealth and comfort, then they don't belong with the Prophet. If they can bear with patience their straightened circumstances in this life, Allah will give them a great reward in the Afterlife. When these verses were revealed to confirm that choice, the Prophet went to A'ishah first and said, "I'm going to tell you something, and you don't have to be quick in your answer until you talk with your parents." Then he recited this passage. A'ishah answered, "What do I need to talk to them about? I choose Allah and His Messenger and the home of the next life." (*Bukhari*) A'ishah then asked the Prophet not to tell his other wives about her decision to stay with him, but he said, "Allah didn't send me to be harsh; rather, He sent me to teach in a gentle and easy manner. If any of them asks me what your decision was, I will tell her." (*Ahmad*) Later, Abu Bakr and 'Umar ibn al-Khattab went to visit the Prophet when he was sitting with all his wives.

Women of the Prophet! If any of you were ever proven guilty of outrageous acts, then the punishment would be doubled for her, and that's easy for Allah. [30]

If any of you are devoted to the service of Allah and His Messenger and do what's morally right, then We'll double her reward and provide her with a generous amount of benefits. [31]

Special Regulations for the Prophet's Household

$\mathcal{W}$omen of the Prophet! [1401]

You're not in the same category as other women.

If you have the awareness (of Allah in your hearts), then don't be too soft spoken when you speak (with men in public), otherwise a person with a warped heart might become (infatuated) with you. [1402]

So speak firmly and forthrightly. [32] Stay quietly in your homes, [1403] and don't make a dazzling spectacle (of yourselves)

They began berating the women saying, "You're asking the Prophet for what he doesn't have!" The Prophet stopped the two men, and then his wives said, "By Allah, after this we will not ask the Messenger of Allah for anything that he doesn't have." (*Ahmad*)

[1401] The Prophet was having a meal at the home of one of his wives named Umm Salamah, when she brought out a particularly tasty dish. He asked her to go and invite his daughter Fatimah, her husband 'Ali and their two small sons, Hassan and Husayn, to share in the meal. After they arrived and began to eat, Husayn began to play with a cloak in the back of the room. Suddenly, this passage came to the Prophet, and he recited the verses. Then he asked the four guests to gather close to him. He wrapped the cloak around them and lifted his hands heavenward saying, "My Lord! These are my family, and they're special to me, so remove all shortcomings from them and make them pure and spotless." Umm Salamah came closer and said, "And me among them, too!" The Prophet said to her, "Truly, the best for you. Truly, the best for you." (*Asbab ul-Nuzul*)

[1402] The Prophet's wives lived in private apartments attached to the mosque in Medina. Several of them conducted women's study circles, while the remainder devoted their lives to acts of piety and charity. Both men and women often approached them with questions regarding Islam. To forestall any possibility of causing infidelity in some men's minds, these women were asked to live humbly and modestly and not to speak to men in soft feminine voices, but rather in an even tone.

[1403] Some very conservative commentators have extrapolated from this verse that *all* women are forbidden to leave their homes as a general rule and, furthermore, that the very voice of a woman is not to be heard in public places. Thus, the adoption of the practice of *purdah*, or female seclusion, that became widespread throughout the Middle East and parts of Asia during the last five centuries. But is this what the Qur'an is calling for? To begin with, the term *purdah* is of Persian origin and appears nowhere in the Qur'an or *hadith* literature. (*Purdah* describes a pre-Islamic Persian custom in which well-to-do women were kept at home at all times to emphasize the fact that they were wealthy enough not to have to work in the fields and thus to be browned by the sun.) This position, that women are forbidden to leave their homes save for the direst of needs, is a fallacious leap of doctrine. First of all, this verse is addressed specifically to the wives of the Prophet, and even still it does not categorically forbid them from ever leaving their homes, for the Prophet's wives <u>did</u> continue to go out and move about in society (with the Prophet's approval), only more discreetly and infrequently than before. Ordinary women in the Prophet's time and for many centuries beyond did not remain in their homes as a matter of policy, for many needed to work (and they were frequently in the public sphere – even in the mosques), and there is voluminous evidence from the traditions, biographical literature and history books to demonstrate this. (Compare this verse with the biblical verses of I Timothy 2:11-12 or I Corinthians 14:33-35!) Save for the harsh rulings of some modern extremists and the assumptions of certain rustics, who mistake long-standing cultural practices for religion, the general opinion of most mainstream scholars is that women can hold jobs, go to the mosque and go to school, even as they can go out for other needs. (*Ma'ariful Qur'an*) The Prophet said, "You (women) have been allowed to go out for your needs." (*Muslim*) Furthermore, what gives men the right to determine what the specific needs of individual women are?

494

like (women used to do) in the backward days before (Islam). [1404]

Establish prayer, give in charity, and obey Allah and His Messenger.

Allah wants nothing more than to cleanse you of any blemishes (in your character), O you people of the (Prophet's) household, and to make you pure and spotless. [33]

Meditate on what is recited to you in your homes of the verses of Allah's (Book) and His wisdom, for Allah is well-informed of the deepest mysteries (of the soul). [34]

Men and Women have Equal Status before Allah

$\mathcal{F}$or men and women
who have surrendered (to Allah),
for men and women [1405]
who believe,
for men and women

who are devout,
for men and women
who are honest,
for men and women
who are patient,
for men and women
who are humble,
for men and women
who donate to charity,
for men and women who fast,
for men and women
who guard their chastity,
and for men and women
who remember Allah often…

For them Allah has prepared forgiveness and a great reward. [35]

The Case of Zayd ibn Harith

$\mathcal{I}$t's not right for a believer, whether male or female, to second guess a decision about a matter that's been decided by Allah and His Messenger. [1406]

[1404] Is there a principle that all women can glean from this verse? The commentators say that in pre-Islamic times some women used to flirt with men shamelessly, and that's what this verse is seeking to bring to peoples' attention. The famous commentator Mujahid said, "Some women used to go out purposefully walking in front of men (to attract their attention), and this was from the days of ignorance." Another commentator named Qatadah wrote, "When they went out of their homes, (some women in pre-Islamic times) used to walk in a shameless and flirtatious manner, and Allah, the Exalted, forbade that." (*At-Tabari*) The Prophet allowed women to leave their homes for their legitimate needs and tasks. Despite the illogical position of some extreme conservatives, women cannot be excluded from the social and religious life of the community. The Prophet said, "Do not prevent the female servants of Allah from (attending) the mosques of Allah, just let them go there wearing no perfume." (*Abu Dawud*) By the way, there were no partitions of any kind separating men from women in the mosques in the Prophet's time or in the time of the caliphs, even into Umayyad and early 'Abbasid times. Both sexes prayed and listened to speeches in the same space, with men sitting in the front and women sitting in the back. (The practical effect of this seating arrangement is so that men, who are universally recognized as more susceptible to *distraction*, can keep focused on the proceedings there before them.) According to a *fatwa*, or legal ruling by Islamic scholars, contained in the book *Majalat al-Buhuth al-Islamiyah*, erecting a partition in the mosque to separate men from women is an innovation in religion and is thus forbidden. (pub. 1979, *fatwa* #2611.)
[1405] The Muslims who had fled to Abyssinia during the worst days of Meccan persecution gradually began to migrate to Medina to join the Muslims who had already settled there. Among these latecomers was a woman named Asma', who was wife of Ja'far ibn Abi Talib. She went to some of the Prophet's wives and asked, "Is there anything revealed in the Qur'an with regards to us (women)?" When they told her that there was not, she then went to the Prophet and lamented, "Why are women always hopeless and shortchanged?" When the Prophet asked her what she meant, she explained, "Because (women) haven't been mentioned in righteousness the same as men." Umm Salamah, the Prophet's wife, also asked something similar. The Prophet waited for guidance from Allah, and soon this verse was revealed to assuage and assure women of Allah's equal estimation of both. (*Asbab ul-Nuzul*)
[1406] Only the Arabs had a taboo against marrying the divorced spouses of adoptees. Judaism, Christianity and even modern legal traditions have no such restriction. This action of the Prophet

495

Whoever disobeys Allah and His Messenger is clearly mistaken in error. [1407] [36]

(Muhammad, when Zayd wanted to divorce his wife Zaynab,) you had said to (your adopted son Zayd, a man) who had received Allah's grace and your favor, *"Stay (married) to your wife and be mindful of Allah."*

However, you were hiding something in your heart that Allah was about to disclose. [1408] You were afraid of (what) people (would think if you were to marry the woman that Zayd divorced, but it's more appropriate) for you to fear Allah.

Then, after Zayd dissolved (his marriage) to her, following all the proper procedures, We joined her in marriage to you, so that there wouldn't be any more (confusion) among the faithful about (the permissibility) of marrying the ex-spouses of their adopted children, after all the proper procedures (of divorce) have been followed, for Allah's command must be fulfilled. [37]

There shouldn't be any obstacles for the Prophet in discharging the duty that Allah has laid upon him. This principle of Allah was practiced by those who passed before, and the command of Allah is an irresistible decree. [38] (The principle outlined above is accepted by) those who convey the messages of Allah and who fear Him. So fear no one besides Allah, for Allah is enough to make an accounting (of what people do). [39]

Muhammad is not the father of any of your men, [1409] but he is the Messenger of Allah and the Seal of the Prophets. [1410] Indeed, Allah knows about all things. [40]

---

abolished this pagan taboo among the Arabs. The Qur'an affirms this right, for the adopted and the adopter have no immediate blood ties whatsoever.

[1407] Long before he had become a prophet, Muhammad had adopted a son named Zayd ibn Harith while he was living in Mecca. Originally, the boy was a Syrian slave that his wife Khadijah had given to him, but Muhammad had freed him and taken him as his own. Thus, he was known as Zayd ibn Muhammad. Zayd's Syrian father later came in search of his son and found him living safely in Mecca. Zayd, who had grown up from boyhood in Mecca in Muhammad's household, politely told his father he wanted to remain where he was. Years later, after the commencement of the prophethood of Muhammad and after the Muslims were settled in Medina, the Prophet brokered a marriage between his distant cousin, Zaynab bint Jahsh (d. 642), and Zayd. The marriage didn't work out, however, for the upper class Zaynab was not content to be married to a common man who was a former slave, and she treated him with veiled contempt (in her belief that he was beneath her nobility). As time passed, Zayd did not like how he was being treated by the haughty Zaynab, and he asked the Prophet about divorcing her. The Prophet counseled him to remain married, but the love was gone in that marriage. Thus, despite Muhammad's efforts to preserve the marriage, Zayd wound up divorcing Zaynab. A short time later, the Prophet proposed to her, and she readily accepted the offer. This situation, however, created a minor scandal - with the Jews and hypocrites of Medina accusing Muhammad of marrying his own son's former wife. This passage was revealed after verses 4-6 of this chapter, clarifying that there is no harm in marrying someone who was married to an adopted person, as the adopted person is not a biological relative, and thus the usual restrictions do not apply.

[1408] Before Zayd divorced Zaynab, the Prophet knew that their marriage was about to end. He felt that Allah would use this situation to make a point; yet, he had to suppress his feeling that he might be married to Zaynab later on, and he continued to counsel to Zayd to stay married to Zaynab. (*Zamakhshari*)

[1409] Although the Prophet had several sons, all of them died in early childhood. Thus, he was the father 'of no men' in the community.

[1410] Muhammad is the "Seal of the Prophets." In other word he is the cap on the bottle of divine revelation. He once said, "My example in relation to the prophets who came before me is that of a man who built a house beautifully and well, except that one brick in its corner was missing. The people went around it and wondered at its beauty, but said, 'If only that final brick were put in its place!' I *am* that brick, and I am the last of the Prophets." (*Bukhari*, also see Matthew 21:42-44 for an interesting statement from Prophet Jesus.) Thus, Muhammad is the conclusion of all of Allah's direct communication with man. Therefore, any person who claims to be a prophet after Muhammad is not accepted as authentic by the mainstream majority of Muslims. (*Ma'ariful Qur'an, Ibn Kathir*)

Allah's Message of Hope in Tough Times

𝒪 you who believe! Remember Allah with great remembrance. [41] Glorify Him in the morning and at night. [42] He's the One Who sends down blessings upon you, and the angels do so as well, in order that He can bring you out of darkness into the light, and He's merciful to the believers. [43]

On the day when they're going to meet Him, they'll greet each other by saying, "*Peace.*" He has indeed prepared a generous reward for them. [44]

Instructions for the Prophet

𝒪 Prophet! We've sent you to be a witness, a bringer of good news, a warner [45] and also a caller to Allah's (path), by His leave, like a lamp shining light in dark places. [46] So give good news to the faithful that they'll have great favor from Allah (waiting for them). [47]

Don't obey those who suppress (their faith) nor the hypocrites, and pay no mind to their pestering ways. Rather, put your trust in Allah, for Allah is enough to take care of all matters. [48]

Divorce before Consummation

𝒪 you who believe! When any of you marries a believing woman, but then divorces her without ever having had intimate relations with her, then there's no need for you to keep track of her waiting period. Give her a gift, and then set her free graciously. [49]

The Prophet's Defined Marriage Rules

𝒪 Prophet! We've made lawful for you your wives to whom you've given their dowries, [1411] as well as those (maidservants) under your control who've been acquired through spoils and were assigned to you by Allah.

(Also lawful for you in marriage are) the daughters of your paternal and maternal aunts and uncles, (as long as they've demonstrated their loyalty to Islam) by migrating (from Mecca to Medina) with you, [1412] and any believing woman who offers herself (in marriage) to the Prophet, if the Prophet wishes to marry her. [1413]

[1411] This verse was revealed to the Prophet to lay out specifically what sort of women he was allowed to take as wives. It is said that Maymunah bint al-Harith, who proposed marriage to the Prophet and whom he accepted, is especially referenced here.

[1412] While Muhammad was still living in Mecca, he had asked for the hand of his cousin, Umm Hani bint Abi Talib, in marriage, but she politely declined, and he accepted her excuse. This verse was later revealed in the Medinan Period, and Umm Hani explained that she was now forever forbidden in marriage to the Prophet, as she had not migrated to Medina and was still a pagan at the time that Mecca was liberated. (*Zamakhshari*)

[1413] A'ishah said, "I often felt jealous of those women who offered themselves (in marriage) to the Prophet." (*Bukhari*) (There is no stigma or prohibition in Islam for a woman to propose to a man, according to *Fath al-Bari* 2/219.) A woman named Khawlah bint Hakim walked into the mosque one day and proposed to the Prophet, offering herself in marriage. The Prophet remained silent for a few moments, and then a man stood up and said, "Messenger of Allah, marry her to me." The Prophet asked the man about the potential dowry he could offer her, and it turned out he had no possessions, so the woman accepted for her dowry that the man teach her what he knew of the Qur'an. On another occasion, a woman named Umm Sharik entered the mosque and also offered herself in marriage to the Prophet. The Prophet again declined the offer. A'ishah, who was present, remarked (out of jealousy) that she thought any woman who so brashly offered herself in marriage to a man was something of a lowlife. This verse was revealed to the Prophet to lay out specifically what sort of women he was

These (specific marriage regulations) are only for you, (Muhammad), and not for any other believers. [1414] We know what regulations We've already stipulated for them with regards to their wives and (the maidservants) under their control.

(We've spelled out your allowances specifically here) so that you won't have any difficulty (in knowing what you're allowed to do), for Allah is forgiving and merciful. [50]

A Dispensation for the Prophet

*Y*ou can postpone any of (your wives' turns to be with you), as you like, or you can see whichever one of them as you like. [1415]

You won't be blamed in either case if you call upon one of them whose turn you had postponed.

(Your exemption from having to follow a rigid, fixed schedule among your wives) is so that their eyes may be cooled, that their anxious feelings (may be answered), and that they can be satisfied with whatever you can offer them. Allah knows what's in your hearts, and Allah is full of knowledge and forbearance. [51]

(Now that some time has passed, Muhammad,) you're forbidden to marry any more women after this (new verse revealed here now), nor can you substitute any of them for (other) wives, even though you might be attracted by their beauty, except for any (maidservant you wish to marry) who may be under your authority. [1416] Allah watches over all things. [52]

Etiquette in the Prophet's Household

O you who believe! When you're coming for a meal, don't enter the Prophet's house without permission, and don't arrive so early that you're waiting

---

allowed to take as wives. It is said that Maymunah bint al-Harith, whom the Prophet did accept after she offered herself, is especially referenced here.

[1414] The Prophet received specific instructions and allowances for his own personal life. He was allowed to have more than the maximum legal limit of four wives, due to his status, which made it possible to broker alliances through marriage, support widows and also marry those who were unwilling to marry others, such as Zaynab, who had very high standards regarding who her husband would be. The Prophet married a total of eleven women (after his first wife died) while in Mecca and Medina, (though he was monogamous with his first wife Khadijah for over twenty-three years in Mecca until she died, bringing the total number of women he married in his lifetime to twelve). He never had more than nine living wives at one time, for he had married several older widows, and some of them passed away before he did. All of his marriages after Khadijah passed away were to support widows, demonstrate legal rulings, or cement alliances.

[1415] The Prophet had been dividing up his scant free time equally among his wives, and this was a hardship for him for two reasons: he was generally busy with worship and community work and found it hard to keep a regular family schedule, and he also had more fondness for some of his wives and preferred to spend more of his free time with them in their apartments. A'ishah reports that he said in exasperation one day, "O Allah, I've done as much as I can with regard to what's under my control, so don't blame me for what's under Your control and not mine." (*Ahmad*) In other words, he had no control over his feelings and heart. The Prophet, therefore, desired to be granted flexibility with regard to his scheduling, for he had to ask permission from the wife whose turn it was to see him if he wanted to spend time with another, and this new verse was revealed to give that flexibility to him.

[1416] This verse, which was revealed about seven years after the migration to Medina, forbade the Prophet from marrying any other free women, except for maidservants whom he could marry. He eventually married Maria the Copt, (according to *at-Tabari* & hadith 6819 in *al-Hakim*,) who was a gift from the ruler of Egypt, and she bore him a son named Ibrahim (who tragically died in infancy). Some sources state she was a concubine before the Prophet freed her after the birth of the baby. (*Ibn Is-haq*)

around for (the food to) finish (cooking). [1417]

When you're invited inside, come in. Then, when the meal is over, leave in a timely fashion without trying to engage in small talk.

This upsets the Prophet, but he's too shy to ask you to leave - though Allah isn't too shy to tell you the truth. [1418] When you ask (his wives) for something, ask them through a *hijab*. [1419] This is more wholesome for the sake of both your hearts and theirs.

(Know that) it's not right for any of you to annoy the Messenger of Allah, nor should you marry any of his widows after he has passed away. That would be going too far in the sight of Allah. [53] Whether you show something or hide it, (remember that) Allah knows about all things. [54]

There is no blame on the (wives of the Prophet if they see and converse with the following categories of men, without a partition between them): their fathers, their sons, their brothers, their brothers' sons, their sisters' sons, their female (friends and relatives) and the servants under their authority. Be mindful of Allah, for Allah is a witness to all things. [55]

Allah and His angels send blessings down upon the Prophet. O you who believe! Call for blessings to be sent down upon him, and wish him peace with due respect. [56]

Those who (deliberately) annoy Allah and His Messenger are cursed by Allah in this world, while in the next life, He has prepared a humiliating punishment (especially) for them. [57]

Further still, those who (deliberately) annoy the believing men and believing women, without a valid reason, take upon

---

[1417] The Prophet was a human being and had his own particular habits. He was generous and friendly with everyone, but all of us have our limits. He used to see and talk to so many people throughout each day that at times he longed for some peace and quiet. When he gave a dinner party to celebrate his marriage to Zaynab bint Jahsh in the year 626, his many guests ate their fill and then departed, but three men remained sitting and didn't leave for a long time. Zaynab, herself, felt embarrassed at these men who couldn't take the hint to leave, so she turned her back to them and faced the wall. Eventually, they left. The Prophet was too shy to tell those people that they had tarried in his home for too long after the meal, so after they left, Allah, Himself, Who promised to look after the Prophet's peace of mind, revealed this passage to ask the faithful to give the Prophet some personal space. (*Bukhari*)

[1418] The faithful were so eager to observe everything that they could about the Prophet that they would peek into his keyhole, climb up on his roof to see into his courtyard and wait outside his door to get a glimpse of him or to get some advice. This is how much they loved him. Sometimes they forgot that he had only the endurance of a single man.

[1419] There are various stories to explain why this verse was revealed, and all of them revolve around 'Umar, who was apparently concerned that the Prophet's wives were free to go out in society without a head covering and looked upon by all. In one instance, he accidentally touched A'ishah's finger while a food bowl was passed to him, and this caused him great consternation. Ever concerned that the Prophet's family be protected from strange men and false accusations, it seems he was lobbying for a ruling from Allah to govern public interactions between the Prophet's wives and the general male public. When this verse was revealed, the Prophet's wives were asked to conduct their public business dealings with unrelated men through a *hijab* (a screen divider in a room or a face veil. (*Ibn Ati Hatim, al-Tabarani*, et al) Certain rustic cultures have assumed that the regulations laid out here (and in verse 55) that ask the Prophet's wives to speak to unrelated men from behind a face veil or curtain apply, by extrapolation, to all women. This is an extreme view, as the general lot of women in the community of Medina did not implement this for themselves. They still went out with faces uncovered (though with hair covered), and spoke to men in public places as the need dictated, such as in the bazaar, the mosque and other, similar public places, without being segregated into all female zones in every place. (Even into the times of the caliphs, how could there have been all those heroic Muslim female warriors at such battles as Qadisiyya and Hattin if they were hiding behind screens or in a full face veil?) In a narration of A'ishah, she said that the ordinary women of Medina, when they heard this verse, made head scarves for themselves by cutting up curtains, and that was all they did. (Not all women covered their hair fully in public before the revelation of this verse.) (*Abu Dawud*)

themselves the crime of slander and also an obvious sin. [58]

Dress Code for Women in Public

O Prophet! [1420]

Tell your wives and daughters and the believing women that they should draw their outer garments [1421] closely over their bodies (when they go out in public).

That's the easiest way for them to be known (as respectable), so that they won't be accosted (by strange men). Allah is forgiving and merciful. [1422] [59]

Warning the Hypocrites of Medina

In all seriousness, if the hypocrites, the (believers who are) weak at heart, and the rabble-rousers who try to stir up sedition in the city don't stop (their treasonous activities), then We'll certainly stir you up against them! Then they won't be able to remain (in the city) as your neighbors for very long! [60]

They'll be cursed, and wherever they'll be found they'll be captured and slain completely. [61] This is the same practice of Allah (that's always been) enforced by those who lived in the past, and you won't find any change in the practice of Allah. [62]

The Coming of the Hour

*P*eople ask you (when) the Hour (of Judgment will come to pass). Tell them, *"Only Allah knows the answer (to that question)."* How can you be made to understand? *The Hour could be very near!* [1423] [63]

Allah has truly cursed the faithless and prepared for them a blazing fire, [64] and there they shall remain forever – and they'll neither find any supporter nor any defender (to aid them)! [65]

The day when (the haughty expressions on) their faces will be turned upside down (by the humiliation of the) fire (is the day) when they'll cry out, *"We're*

[1420] Although the Prophet and his followers had migrated to Yathrib, soon to be known as Medina, and established themselves there from the year 622, the Muslims did not rule over the whole city as if it were their own city-state. It wasn't until the year 628 that Muslim sway over the city was fully cemented. Prior to this, Muhammad and his followers had to maintain a delicate balance between many competing interests, such as the Jewish tribes, the hypocrites, and the large number of pagans that remained among the local bedouin population. Thus, not every vice could be eliminated or policed right away. One of these vices was prostitution. Although it was forbidden to Muslims, the many non-Muslim residents and visitors in the city still sought out prostitutes for their services. If a woman walked outside in the streets at night and her hair was unveiled and her clothes were loosely draped, it was taken as a sign that she was "available-for-hire." Thus, to help Muslim women avoid being accosted by such lecherous men, this verse was revealed, advising them how to dress so the non-Muslims seeking prostitutes wouldn't molest them.

[1421] The outer garments or *jilbab* mentioned here is often considered to be an outer cloak, coat, robe, long shawl or an over shirt. It is not synonymous with an all-enveloping tent-like structure called a *burka*, which is a later cultural invention of Persia and India. (Also see 24:30-31)

[1422] It is not commonly known in the West that Muslim men also have a dress code and that it is nearly identical to the requirements for women in that the body must be covered. (Proper public dress is a fully covered body, though men who need to work or dive in the sea and such can wear shorts, as long as the area between the navel and below the knees is fully covered.) Men's clothes must be loose, and a turban or cap is preferable too.

[1423] The Prophet said, "From among the signs of the (final) Hour are the following: religious knowledge will be taken away, ignorance will increase, fornication will be widespread, the consumption of alcohol will be common, the population of men will decrease and the population of women will increase, so much so that fifty women will be looked after by one man." (*Bukhari*)

doomed! If only we had obeyed Allah and obeyed His Messenger!" [66]

They'll also say, *"Our Lord! We obeyed our leaders and our heroes, and they misled us on the path.* [67] *Our Lord! Give them twice the punishment, and curse them terribly!"* [68]

Follow Allah's Command

O you who believe! Don't be like those who troubled Moses – *even Allah had to clear him of all the things they said of him* - for he was honorable in Allah's sight. [1424] [69]

O you who believe! Be mindful (of Allah), and always speak in a straightforward manner, [70] so He can reform your behavior and forgive you your sins. Whoever obeys Allah and His Messenger has already achieved the greatest success! [1425] [71]

We offered the commitment (of self-awareness) to the heavens, the earth and the mountains, but they all refused to accept it out of fear (of the consequences).

Humanity agreed to undertake it, *though it overstepped and was foolish,* [72] so much so that Allah now has to punish hypocrites, both male and female, and also the faithless, both male and female. Allah turns in mercy, however, to the believers, both male and female, for Allah is forgiving and merciful. [73]

[1424] The Israelites were disobedient to Moses because they had lived in Egypt for generations and picked up many bad habits, along with a skeptical and disobedient attitude. The pure faith of their ancestors, Jacob and Isaac, was all but gone. After Moses led them to freedom, he had to endure their ignorance, even as he had to try and teach them to be faithful and obedient to Allah again. The following story, related by the Prophet Muhammad, illustrates the extent of Moses' predicament: The Israelites used to bathe naked together in communal places. Moses used to take his baths alone (for he was very shy and meek, as Numbers 12:3 asserts). Some of the Israelites started spreading the following rumor: "The only thing that's keeping Moses from bathing with the rest of us is that he has a defect on his body." Once, when Moses went out to take a bath, he put his clothes over a stone. (When he had finished bathing and went to retrieve his clothes), the stone miraculously bounced away with his clothes still on top of it! Moses ran after that stone yelling, "My clothes! Hey, stone! My clothes! Hey, stone!" He ran past the Israelite camp, and when they saw him they exclaimed, "By Allah, Moses doesn't have any defect on his body." The stone abruptly stopped, and Moses quickly grabbed his clothes. Then he took up a big stick and began to beat the stone so hard that it made deep marks in it. (*Bukhari*)

[1425] The Prophet said, "Allah will bring a servant close (to Him) on the Day of Judgment and make him confess all of his sins. This will go on until the servant thinks that he's about to be destroyed. Then Allah will say, 'I've hidden these sins for you in the worldly life, and I'm forgiving them for you today.' Then he will be given his book of good deeds in his right hand. For the rejecter and the hypocrite, the witnesses will say, 'These are the ones who lied against their Lord, and the curse of Allah is upon the corrupt.'" (References verses 7:44-45, with reports from *Bukhari, Muslim, Ahmad*)

Sheba

34 Saba'
Early Meccan Period

This is one of the earlier chapters in the Meccan period. We can clearly detect through the style and tone of this revelation that the Qur'anic dialogue with the pagans was still on a much more philosophical level. Outright public persecution of the believers had not yet begun in earnest, and the Prophet was engrossed in his ministry with the task of getting across to his people that Allah really did take an interest in human affairs and that this message was a sign from Him. The example of the ancient people of Sheba (from the land of Yemen) serves as a metaphor for the Prophet's own struggle with the Meccans.

In the Name of Allah,
the Compassionate, the Merciful

Praise be to Allah, the One to Whom belongs whatever is in the heavens and whatever is on the earth. All praise belongs to Him in the next life, and He's the Wise and Well-informed. [1]

He knows what sinks into the earth and what comes out of it, as well as what descends from the sky and what ascends up into it. [1426] He's the Merciful and Forgiving! [2]

Those who suppress (the truth) say, "*The (final) Hour will never come upon us!*"

So tell them, "*Surely it will! By my Lord, it will indeed overtake you! He knows what's beyond human perception. There's nothing even as small as an atom [1427] that's hidden from Him in the heavens or in the earth, nor anything bigger or smaller than that, except that it's being written about in a clear book.* [3] *(He keeps track of everything), so He can reward those who believe and do what's morally right. They're the ones who'll have forgiveness and a generous reward.*" [4]

Those who try to thwart Our signs, attempting to stall their progress, will receive a humiliating punishment. [5] Those who have been given knowledge [1428]

[1426] The four things mentioned here are commonly understood to be 1) the grave, 2) the resurrected souls, 3) the angels and/or revelation and finally 4) the records of people that go back to Allah (carried by angels).

[1427] The term *zarrah* is the Arabic word for the smallest thing possible that is known. Thus, most translators render it as *atom*. It is interesting to note that this verse suggests that there are things even smaller than that, and thus even the atom can be split into smaller parts.

[1428] The reference to "intelligent people" is not only limited to those who are educated in the traditional sense, but also to anyone who uses his mind effectively regardless of educational level. With that said, Islam places a great emphasis on the acquisition of knowledge and learning. The Prophet said, "Learning is a duty upon every man and woman who has submitted to Allah." (*Ibn Majah*) Although some intellectually impoverished cultures in the Muslim world have the bizarre idea that females should not learn or go to school, such a position is not supported by the Qur'an, the sayings of the Prophet, or by the example of the first thousand years of Islamic civilization where women were often educated to the same degree as men (and sometimes more so). It is reported in several classical

can see that what's been sent down to you from your Lord is the truth and that it guides (people) to the path of the Powerful and the Praiseworthy. [6]

Yet, the faithless just sneer (to each other), saying *"Should we show you a man who claims that when you're all rotted away that you'll be made again like new?* [7] *Has he forged a lie against Allah, or has a jinn gotten into him?"*

No way! Rather, it's those who don't believe in the next life who are in for (a stiff) punishment, and they're the ones who are the most mistaken. [8]

Don't they see what's right in front of them and behind them all throughout the sky and the earth?

If We wanted, We could make the earth swallow them up or cause a piece of the sky to fall down upon them. [1429] There are surely signs in this for every responsive [1430] servant. [9]

The Power of David and Solomon

*A*nd so it was that We granted abundant favor from Ourselves to David: *"O Mountains! (Join with him as he sings the praises of Allah) by echoing (his songs), and, all you birds, join with him, as well!"* [1431]

We (taught him how) to make iron soft and pliable (and told him), [10] *"Make coats of armor!* [1432] *Set the rings of chain mail in proper order, and do what's morally right, for I see all that you do."* [11]

(Furthermore, We placed) the wind (under) Solomon's (command). Its morning gust (would propel his ships) on a month's (journey), and its evening gust (would bring them back) a month's (journey). [1433] We also caused a veritable fountain of copper to flow for him.

Among the obscure ones there were some who were made to work in his

---

accounts that in the Muslim city of Cordoba, during the many centuries of Muslim rule there, that certain districts were so lighted at night by the many lamps of female Qur'an copyists that the night seemed as if it were day. The names of literally thousands of female scholars from the classical period of Islam have survived to this day. Sadly, after the disastrous Mongol invasions of the 13th century, the Muslim world was transformed from a place of relative equal opportunity in education into a dogmatic and conservative relic of its former self.

[1429] Some commentators say this refers to meteorites, the descent of which was well known to the Arabs.

[1430] The term *muneeb* means to respond to Allah, to repent and to turn back to Him.

[1431] The Prophet said, "The most beloved prayer in the sight of Allah is the prayer habit of David. He used to sleep for nearly half the night, stand in prayer for nearly a third of it and then sleep for a sixth more of it. The most beloved of fasting in the sight of Allah is the fasting habit of David. He used to fast every other day, and he never fled from the battlefield." (*Muslim*)

[1432] The Bronze Age gave way to the Iron Age sometime between the years 1500 and 1200 BCE. Thus, iron work was a technology that was available to the ancient Israelites. Under David's rule (1010-970 BCE), Israelite armor made dramatic improvements.

[1433] There are two existing interpretations of what the wind being like a month means. The first (and most fantastic) suggests that Solomon could travel while literally riding the wind and could go anywhere in half a day's journey that would take anyone else a full month. The second (and more practical) interpretation is that Solomon's trade ships were propelled by the wind much faster than other nation's ships, and this added to his wealth and prestige. (See I Kings 9:26-28.) A third interpretation could simply be that Solomon's kingdom benefited from abundant trade. Solomon was historically known as an exporter of vast quantities of copper and bronze products in the ancient world and was quite possibly the most prolific exporter on the international market! (Recent archeological evidence has even identified an ancient copper mine in southern Jordan that was in operation during the rule of King Solomon. The site, just south of the Dead Sea, is called *Khirbat an-Nahas* today.) Thus, ore issued forth from Solomon's mines and his smelting operations produced metal in abundance. I Kings 7:13-47 describes some of Solomon's brass work and also names his chief metallurgist, the foreigner called Hiram of Tyre.

presence by his Lord's leave. [1434] If any of them disobeyed Our orders, We punished him with a scorching fire. [12]

And so, they labored for him, (building) whatever he desired, such as battlements, decorative friezes, huge wash basins and hefty cauldrons in fixed stands. [1435] *"Labor on, O family of David, with thanks."* Yet, few of My servants are thankful. [1436] [13]

Later, when We ordained his death, there were no clues to be seen to suggest (to the workers) that he was dead, (for he remained seated upon his throne), other than a tiny crawling (insect) that kept gnawing away at his staff.

When (the staff that his body was leaning on) toppled over, the obscure ones realized that if they had known what was unknown to them, they would never have remained (at work) in their humiliating and punishing (servitude). [1437] [14]

The People of Sheba

*A*nd so it was that there was a sign for the people of Sheba in their vicinity. [1438] There were two expansive gardens to

---

[1434] Who were the 'obscure ones' (Arabic: *jinns*) who worked for Solomon? The word *jinn* itself merely means hidden, covered, unknown or concealed, and it is sometimes applied in the Arabic language to describe unknown people or foreigners. If that is the intent of this verse, then it can easily match up with the description given in II Chronicles 2:17-18 where we read that Solomon took a census of all the unknown *strangers* in his kingdom (non-Jews), and then he set them to work building his palace and the main temple in Jerusalem. If we follow the more traditional interpretation of this verse and assume that the invisible elemental spirits are being spoken of, then we can also find support in Hebrew records for that position, as well. Ecclesiastes 2:8 contains two Hebrew words *shiddah we shiddoth,* which according to some Jews means male and female demons, of which Solomon acquired many, as the verse would read if translated properly. Biblical translators, however, have usually rendered these two words as 'musical instruments' or as 'many female concubines.' (The words have nothing to do with music so it is a patent mistranslation.) The two terms come from the Hebrew root word, *shadad,* which means to be burly, powerful and utterly destructive. This is why some Jews consider it to be a reference to powerful demons (as the singular form of the word, *shad,* is commonly used as such). (See b.Yoma 75a; b. Gitten 68b from the Midrash Tehillim 78:12.) Using this logic, those Jewish commentators hold that all the many women who seduced Solomon were female demons sent to tempt and trick him away from Allah. I am inclined to understand that the *jinns* spoken of here are the *strangers* mentioned in II Chronicles, though Allah knows better.

[1435] The Old Testament mentions many of the fantastic furnishings and other objects that were made for Solomon's palace and capital city. See II Chronicles, chapters three and four or I Kings, chapters 6 and 7.

[1436] When this verse was revealed, the Prophet explained it by saying, "There are three actions, and whoever does them will achieve similar success as the house of David." When the companions asked what those three acts were the Prophet replied, "Act with justice whether you're feeling angry or pleased; be moderate in times of both prosperity and difficulty; and be mindful of Allah both in public and private." (*Tirmidhi*)

[1437] Solomon died upon his throne, and his body was propped up by his royal scepter. The *jinns* thus remained on task completing his work projects, all the while not knowing that they could have escaped, seeing that their master had died. When a wood-boring worm caused the staff to fail, the jinns scattered in frustration.

[1438] This story takes place in southwestern Yemen, which was known in those days as the land of Saba' or Sheba. (This is also the land from which Bilquis, the queen of Sheba, arose during the time of King Solomon. The countryside at the time of this particular group of people was irrigated through a series of well-maintained channels and canals fed by a dam trapping water from a chain of three mountains. This structure was called the Ma'arib Dam. The dam initially flooded in the second or third century due to weakened foundations, and this caused massive flooding and damage to the district of Ma'arib. The Auws and the Khazraj tribe of Yathrib (Medina) were the descendants of refugees from that time who fled north. Subsequent rulers repaired the dam, but then corruption in society led to poor maintenance of the structure for hundreds of years. Around the time the Prophet was born, a final collapse of the dam occurred due to weakened timbers, (brought on by rats that had eaten away at the supports), and this devastation - and the resultant

the right and to their left (along every canal). *"Eat of the bounty of your Lord, and be thankful to Him! (Your) land is a fine one, and (your) Lord is a forgiving One."* [15]

However, they turned away (from their Lord), so We sent a flood against them that breached their dams and transformed their two (luxurious) gardens into gardens (of ruin), where only mustard trees, tamarisks and thorny bushes grew. [16] That was what they deserved, for they were utterly thankless (for Our favors and did wrong). Would We ever bring such a payback against anyone else besides the thankless? [17]

We had placed many prominent towns between them and the towns that We had blessed (in Syria), and We had measured out appropriate traveling intervals, (saying), *"Travel along (the caravan routes) safely by night and by day."* [18]

But they said, *"Our Lord! Make the distances between our intervals longer, (so we can inflate prices and make more money)!"* Thus, they wronged themselves, and in time We made them the subject of old legends, for We scattered them (all over the region) in isolated bands. There are indeed lessons in this for all who are patient and thankful. [19]

And so it was that Iblis [1439] had used them to prove (the truth of) his notion (that he could corrupt humankind), and they followed him, save for a fragment who believed (in Allah). [20] He had no (real) power over them. (He was only able to corrupt them) because We (had given him permission to try and deceive humanity if he could), in order that We could test (the sincerity) of the one who believes in the next life (and separate) him from the one who doubts in it. Your Lord is a guardian over all things. [21]

Tell Them about the Hour

Say (to them), *"Call upon whatever (false gods) that you like instead of Allah, for they haven't even an atom's weight of power in the heavens or on the earth, nor do they own any part of them, nor has He any supporters among them."* [22]

No intercession will do anyone any good in His sight (on the Day of Judgment), save for (the intercession) of those who've been granted His permission.

(On that day, even those who are given permission to intercede will be in utter shock,) to the point that only when they're released from their own fear (of Allah's absolute presence) will they exclaim, *"What did your Lord say?"*

Then they'll answer (their own question, saying), *"He said the truth, and He's the Highest and the Greatest."* [1440] [23]

So ask them, *"Who gives you your resources (for life) from the heavens and the earth?"* (Answer for them by) saying, *"Allah! And*

---

disruption in food production - caused a large part of the population to flee in all directions, and the local economy never recovered. (*Ibn Kathir*) Though attempts were made to repair the damage, that part of Yemen never regained its wealth and prominence on the peninsula. The effects of that disaster were felt all throughout Arabia.

[1439] This is Satan's personal name.

[1440] The Prophet said, "When Allah decides a matter in heaven, the angels beat their wings in submission to His words, making a sound like a chain striking a smooth stone. When the fear leaves their hearts, they say, 'What is it that your Lord said?' Then they say the truth and that He is the highest and the greatest. Then the listener hears it, and the listeners are standing ranged atop each other. After the listening (angel) hears it, he passes it on to (the angel below him, and so on until (because of a jinn) it reaches the ears of a soothsayer or fortuneteller. Perhaps a shooting star will strike (the jinn) down (who is bringing the news to the fortunetellers) before he can pass it along further, or maybe he will pass it before he is hit. (The fortuneteller) will tell a hundred lies along with it, but people will say, 'Didn't he tell us that on a specific day a specific thing will happen?' So, they'll believe in him because of the one thing that was heard in heaven." (*Bukhari*)

one of us is being guided, while the other is clearly wrong." [24]

Then tell them, "*You won't be asked about our sins, and we won't be asked about what you've done.*" [25]

Then say, "*Our Lord will gather all of us together. Then He's going (to decide this issue) openly between us in all fairness, for He's the Opener (to the truth) and the Knowing.*" [26]

Ask them, "*Show me the (gods) that you've made into His partners. Not so! No way! He's (the only) Allah, the Powerful and the Wise!*" [27]

(Muhammad,) We sent you to be no less than (a prophet) to all of humanity, in order to give them the good news (of salvation) and also to warn them (of the prospect of damnation), but most people don't understand this. [28]

If they ask, "*So when will this promise (come to pass), if you're really being so honest?*" [29] Tell them, "*A day has already been fixed for you, and you can't hold it back for even an hour, nor can you bring it closer.*" [30]

Arrogance and Ignorance Blame Each Other

The faithless boast, "*We're never going to believe in this Qur'an nor in any other (scriptures) that came before it.*" If you could only see it - when the wrongdoers will be made to stand before their Lord. *They'll be blaming each other back and forth!*

The lowly (masses will be yelling) at their arrogant (leaders), saying, "*If it weren't for you, then we would've been believers!*" [31]

Those arrogant (leaders) will answer the lowly (masses), saying, "*Were we the ones who held you back from (Allah's) guidance after it*

came to you? No way! You were (perfectly willing) to be wicked yourselves!*" [32]

The lowly (masses) will reply, "*Not so! It was your (plan all along when you told us every) day and night to reject Allah and to make others equal with Him!*" [1441]

When they see the punishment (that awaits them), they're going to be speechless in their remorse. Then We'll drape (iron) collars around the necks of those who suppressed (their faith), for they deserve no less for their deeds. [33]

What of Wealth?

We never sent a warner to any settlement without the influential people among them saying, "*We don't believe in that with which you've been sent.*" [34] They would go on saying, "*We have more wealth and sons (than you), and we'll never be punished.*" [35]

(Their warners used to answer them), saying, "*My Lord is the One Who increases the resources of whomever He wants, or He restricts them,*" but most people don't understand. [36]

It's neither your money nor your sons that will bring you closer to Us in Our sight.

Rather, it's those who believe and do what's morally right who will have their reward doubled on account of their deeds, (and who will live within) secure mansions (in Paradise). [37] Those who try to thwart (the progress) of Our revealed messages will be brought back for punishment. [38]

Say to them, "*My Lord is the One Who increases the resources of whomever of His servants that He wants, or He restricts them (as He wants).* [1442] *There's no (amount of money) that you spend*

[1441] The Prophet said, "A person who acts as (a mischievous) go-between and tries to get two people to fight over something will not enter Paradise." (*Bukhari*)

[1442] The Prophet said, "The successful person is the one who becomes a Muslim and is given just enough resources upon which to survive, so that Allah can make him content with what He's given to him." (*Muslim*)

in His cause without Him replacing it, for He's the best of all providers." [1443] [39]

Foolish Denials

$\mathcal{O}$ne day, We're going to gather them all together and ask the angels, *"Are you the ones these men used to worship?"* [40]

"Glory be to You!" they'll cry. *"You're our protector, not them! No way! They were just worshipping jinns, and most of them believed in them."* [1444] [41]

So on that day (the faithless) will have no control over each other for good or ill. We're going to tell the wrongdoers, *"Suffer the punishment of the Fire, the very thing you used to call a lie!"* [42]

When Our clear verses are read out to them, they say, *"This is just a man who wants to steer you away from the traditions of your ancestors."*

Then they say, *"This is all just an invented pack of lies."* The faithless describe the truth when it comes to them, saying, *"This is nothing more than obvious magic!"* [43]

However, We neither sent them any books to study nor any messengers to warn them before you, (Muhammad), [44] and their predecessors (in the region) denied (their prophets, as well). (Your people) haven't even been given ten percent of what they had. When they denied My

messengers, oh, how terrible was My revulsion (against them)! [45]

Muhammad is the Sincere Messenger of Allah

$\mathcal{S}$ay (to them), *"I'm only asking for you to do one thing, that you stand up before Allah, whether in groups or alone, and think deeply - (ask yourself) if your companion might not be possessed by a jinn. (Consider the possibility) that he just might be a (true) warner sent to you in the face of an extreme punishment."* [46]

Say to them, *"I'm not asking you for any rewards; everything that I'm doing is for your own welfare. My reward is due from no one besides Allah, and He's a witness to all things."* [1445] [47]

Then tell them, *"Truly, my Lord spreads the truth, and He knows what's beyond perception."* [48]

Tell them, *"The truth has arrived, and falsehood neither creates anything new, nor does it reestablish anything."* [49]

Finally, say to them, *"If I'm wrong, then my mistake is nobody's loss but my own. If I'm guided, it's because of my Lord's inspiration given to me, for He indeed listens closely."* [50]

If you could just see it – the time when they'll be shaking in terror, but by then there'll be no escape, for they'll be seized from a very near place. [51]

[1443] The Prophet said, "Charity extinguishes bad deeds as water extinguishes fire." (*Ibn Kathir*)

[1444] *Jinns* are usually thought of as the hidden beings that inhabit the realm of unseen energy. The word can also apply to unknown foreigners or strangers. (The Arabic term *jinn* literally means 'hidden or obscure ones.') As for the race of energy beings known as *jinn*, they often pose as supernatural spirits or contact fortune-tellers and shamans to convince them to abandon reason and believe in mystical forces instead of a single, all-powerful God. The idol-worshippers of Arabia venerated many such false ideas. They anthropomorphized the forces of nature and their mini-gods while also elevating the angels to be Allah's daughters. As is typical for a sound court of law, Allah will cross examine the objects of worship and establish that such objects or beings, in this case the angels, are innocent of making people worship them.

[1445] This is a point with which it has been difficult for critics of Islam to deal with. Muhammad neither accumulated wealth nor worldly possessions. Whatever he had, he always quickly gave away to the benefit of others, especially the poor and needy. Even the one-fifth of all war booty that was assigned to the Prophet was always given away to help in good causes. If Muhammad were merely a charlatan, then wouldn't he have lived like a king? Even his wives lived in a constant state of poverty! (See 33:29, also see 8:41.)

"*Now we believe in it!*" they'll cry out (in panic); yet, how could they demonstrate (genuine faith then), when they'll be so far removed from the place (in which their faith could have been proven sincere)? [52]

They had already rejected it before and ridiculed what was beyond their perception, even though (the reality of the next life) was still far away from them. [1446] [53] And so a wall will be erected between them and that for which they'll so desperately wish, even as the same thing will be done to those factions who went before them, for in the end they were (all) lost in suspicious misgivings. [54]

[1446] They will beg to have their faith in Allah accepted, even though they're far away from the world in which they had a chance to believe. This is juxtaposed with the fact that while they were in the world, they rejected forcefully the truth of Allah, even though Judgment Day and the afterlife were still far away from them. They're doubly in loss, for they want to accept something that they should've done in another place, and they rejected something far from them when they should've accepted it.

The Initiator

35 Al Fatir
Early to Middle Meccan Period

The exact place of this chapter in the Meccan period is not entirely certain, but it seems to suggest a transition for the Prophet into a more desperate circumstance, given that Meccan opposition to his message of monotheism was growing steadily. The tone of the chapters that were revealed after this also seem to present a more impassioned plea for common sense on the part of the pagans. The frequent call to observe Allah's signs that this and other chapters promote is one of the primary ways in which the Qur'an tried to get across to the pagans that an idol made with their own hands was no creator of anything. Rather, the unseen Allah, Whose creative will could be detected within the natural environment and within their own hearts, was the only Allah to Whom submission is worthy.

In the Name of Allah,
the Compassionate, the Merciful

*P*raise be to Allah Who initiated the (creation of) the heavens and the earth, and Who made messengers out of the angels with two, three or four (pairs) of wings. [1447] He adds to creation whatever He wills, for Allah has power over all things. [1]

Whatever (good fortune) that Allah opens up for people out of His mercy, no one can hold back. Whatever He holds back, no one can give after (He's withheld it). [1448] He's the Powerful and the Wise. [2]

O people! Remember the favors of Allah that have come down upon you. Is there any other creator besides Allah who can give you resources from the sky and the earth? There is no other god than He, so why are you so deceived? [3]

If they reject you, (Muhammad,) then know that other messengers were rejected before you. Yet, all issues will return (to Allah) for a resolution. [4]

An Appeal to Humanity

O people! Allah's promise is true. Don't let the life of this world fool you, nor let the Great Deceiver [1449] fool you about Allah. [5] Satan is truly your enemy, so treat him as an enemy! He only invites his

---

[1447] The Old Testament describes angels with four wings in Ezekiel 1:5, 9:3 and 10:3.

[1448] The Prophet said, "There are four areas (of essential practice). If you succeed in adopting them, then you will no longer care about anything you happen to miss out on in this world: keeping your trusts, speaking the truth, having good manners, and learning to eat moderately." (*Ahmad*) On this topic, a companion named 'Amir ibn 'Abd-Qays said, "Once I recite the following four verses of the Qur'an in the morning, I no longer worry about what happens from morning to evening. These are verses: (35:2, 6:17, 65:7, and 11:6)." (*Ma'ariful Qur'an*)

[1449] This would be Satan, who seeks to corrupt people into worshipping idols instead of Allah. This is his desire, so that he can 'prove' to Allah that his kind, the jinns, are superior to humans. See 7:14-17 for example.

followers to become companions of the raging blaze. [6]

Those who reject Allah will find an awful punishment awaiting them, but those who believe and do what's morally right will have forgiveness and a huge reward. [7]

Is the one who thinks his bad behavior is proper, so much so that he sees it as good, (equal to the one who is righteous)? [1450] Allah lets whomever He wants go astray, and He guides whomever He wants (to the truth). So don't be distressed over (their callous attitude towards your message, Muhammad,) for Allah knows what they're up to. [8]

Allah is the One Who sends the winds that whip up the clouds. Then We push them to a barren land and revive the earth with (the rain that falls), even though it was dead before. [1451] *That's how the regeneration (of the dead) will be!* [9]

Whoever wants power (and glory for himself should know that) all power (and glory) belongs to Allah! All the choicest words (of praise) rise up to Him, and He elevates (the status of) moral deeds. [1452] Those who plan to do wrong will suffer a terrible punishment, and their planning will go nowhere. [10]

The Many Signs of Allah

Allah created you from dust and then from a drop of fluid. Then He made you into pairs. [1453] No female conceives or gives birth without Him knowing about it, nor is an elderly man given a longer life or a shortened one, without its being recorded in a decree – and that's easy for Allah. [1454] [11]

The two types of flowing water are also not alike. One of them is fresh and good to drink, while the other is salty and bitter. Yet, (even though the two types of water

---

[1450] In the early hard years in Mecca, the Prophet had made a prayer to Allah asking for his persecuted movement to be strengthened by either the conversion of 'Umar ibn al-Khattab or Abu Jahl. This verse was revealed in response. (*Ma'ariful Qur'an*) It was 'Umar who would convert in answer to this prayer.

[1451] A man named Abu Razeen asked the Prophet, "Messenger of Allah, how is Allah going to bring the dead back to life? Where is an example of that in His creation?" The Prophet answered, "Abu Razeen, don't you ever pass through your people's valley and find it arid and dry; then later you pass through it, and it's filled with green growth?" The man said, "Yes." Thereupon the Prophet said, "That's how Allah will bring the dead back to life." (*Ahmad*) The Prophet said on another occasion, "Every part of the son of Adam will rot away except for the tailbone, from which he was created and from it he will be made afresh." (*Muslim*) The tailbone, or coccyx, is a vestigial part of our bodies. In other words, it serves no real function in our bodies now, but it did serve a purpose in an earlier form of our species (if you accept that human beings might have gone through different forms over the eons). It is a hardened, dense bone that is sometimes one of the bones that archeologists find when they uncover ancient skeletons (usually along with the skull, some parts of the spine, a rib or two, and the pelvic bone). It is interesting that this *hadith* says we were created (or grew) from this, for the developing fetus in its earliest stages looks like it has a tail for some time.

[1452] The *choicest words* are things such as supplications, chanting of Allah's names, reading the Qur'an aloud, saying the testimony of faith, etc. The Prophet said, "Those who remember Allah and glorify Him by saying, 'Glory be to Allah, Allah is the Greatest, all praise be to Allah and there is no god other than Allah' - these words go around the throne like buzzing bees, mentioning those who said them. Wouldn't you all like to have something (there) with Allah that's making mention of him (to Allah)?" (*Ahmad*)

[1453] This can mean that He made humans into males or females, or, since it is chronologically after insemination and before the birthing mentioned in the next sentence, it can possibly be a reference to the even dividing of the cells as the egg grows: one becomes two, two becomes four and so on in the development of the fetus.

[1454] The Prophet said, "Whoever would like to have sufficient resources and a long life, then let him keep solid relationships with his relatives." (*Nisa'i*) Modern research into life spans has proven that this is, indeed, a true proposition.

are so different,) you're still able to get fresh meat from both, as well as ornaments with which to wear (as decorations).

You watch the ships that sail through the waves. You use them to go in search of His bounty, and thus you (should learn to) be thankful. [12]

He merges the night into day and merges the day into night. He's subjected the sun and the moon (to His command) - each one follows its computed orbit. That's your Lord Allah. All dominion belongs to Him. The (false gods) that you call upon besides Him haven't even a sliver of a date seed's (worth of power). [13]

When you call upon them, they don't hear your cry, and even if they did hear you, they wouldn't be able answer you.

On the Day of Assembly, they're going to decline your (assertion - that they were somehow) 'partners' (with Allah). No one can tell you (the truth) like (Allah can, because He's) the Well-informed. [14]

Humanity Must Realize Its True Situation

O people! You're the ones in need of Allah, while Allah Doesn't Need Anything and (is already being) Praised. [15] If it were ever His desire, He could erase you and bring some new kind of creation, [16] and that's not hard for Allah (to do). [17]

The one who has to bear his own load (of deeds) cannot be made to bear the load of another. If someone is already carrying his load, and then he asks someone else to take some of his load for him, none of it can be transferred, even though (the other person) might be a close relative.

You can only warn those who fear their Lord, even though they don't see (Him) yet, and who establish (the regular practice of) prayer. Whoever cleanses his own soul does it for his own good, for (all beings) will (eventually) go back to Allah (for judgment). [18]

The blind and the seeing are not the same, [19] nor are the darkness and the light, [20] nor are the shade and the burning sunlight, [21] nor are the living and the dead.

Allah can make anyone He wants hear (the message), but you can't force them to listen – *they're the ones who might as well be in their graves already*, [1455] [22] for you're no more than a warner. [23]

We've sent you with the truth (so you can) give good news (to people of Allah's forgiveness), and also (so that you can) warn (them of Allah's punishment). No community has ever existed without having a warner who lived in their midst. [24]

If they reject you, (Muhammad,) so did their predecessors who had messengers come to them with clear evidence, holy writings and the illuminated Book (of Allah). [25] I seized all those who rejected (faith) – *and oh, how great was My condemnation (upon them)!* [26]

Accepting the Existence of Signs Leads to Knowledge

Don't you see how Allah sends down water from the sky? We use it to produce the many colored plants (you cultivate).

(Don't you see) how in the mountains there are separate and distinct bands of color in the rock layers, some white or red, others tinted or jet-black? [27]

[1455] The interpreters say this is a metaphor for living people who are as good as dead when it comes to their ability to understand the truth of Allah's message.

The same holds true for people, animals and livestock – they all come in many different colors! [1456]

Those who are well-informed among His servants are the ones who fear Allah, for Allah is powerful and forgiving. [28] Those who recite the Book of Allah, who establish prayer and who spend (in charity) out of what We've given them, whether in secret or in public, can hope for a transaction that will never run out. [29]

He will indeed pay them what they're owed – and even more besides out of His bounty, for He's forgiving and appreciative. [30]

Whatever We've revealed to you of the Book, (Muhammad), is the truth, and it confirms (the truth of the scriptures) that came before it. Allah is well-informed and watches over His servants. [1457] [31] And that's (the way it is). We've given the Book

---

[1456] A light-skinned man went to the Prophet and complained strongly that his wife bore him a dark-complexioned child, insinuating she must have been unfaithful. The Prophet asked the man if he owned any commonly colored camels. The man said that he did. Then the Prophet asked, "Is there a spotted one among them?" When the man affirmed that there was, the Prophet asked, "So how was it born to reddish colored parents?" The man said, "It could have been a trait from earlier generations." The Prophet then said, "This could be the cause of your son's dark complexion." (*Bukhari, Muslim*) Through his deductive reasoning, the Prophet brought out of the man the understanding of recessive genes. Using this prophetic pronouncement and Qur'anic verse, early Muslims understood that all humans were genetically diverse even as they were all equally human. The famous early essayist al-Jahiz (d. 869) even noted that it was the environment that altered skin color and caused superficial differences among humans and that such racial and ethnic variations were not the blessing or curse of Allah. (From his book written about 830 C.E. entitled *The Essays*.) See 16:13 and footnote for a discussion on the meaning of evolution in Islamic terms.

[1457] Oftentimes, non-Muslim critics raise an objection to Islam, saying that the Qur'an mentions things that previously appeared in the Bible, such as the stories of prophets and some moral teachings, but the Qur'an says that this is precisely the point! The same God that revealed the Torah and Gospel is revealing His message yet again! If it were completely different in subject matter, then how could it be called a message from the same God? The Gospel contains elements of the Torah, which came before it, and the Qur'an contains elements of both of its predecessors, with some new material, as well. With that said, it must also be pointed out that the Qur'an, in style, has no similarity with the Torah or Gospel, neither of which were written completely in a poetic, Socratic style. In this regard, the Qur'an is closer to the style of the Psalms of David, another revelation of Allah. Yet, the Psalms are more passionate and ecstatic, while the Qur'an combines many different styles and themes within its pages, rather than being random poems of praise. So the Qur'an is from the same God that gave the previous revelations, but its style and format is fresh, compelling and new. Those who assume that Muhammad wrote the Qur'an himself are not thinking realistically, for anyone who has ever opened a Qur'an and flipped through its pages can see that it would be challenging, to say the least, to believe it could ever be the product of an ordinary, uneducated man living in a desert oasis in the seventh century. It's just too big and too expansive. Its message is too poignant, and its ultimate success as a religious scripture is too spectacular. All from the hand of a middle-aged man in the Arabian desert? From a man who never went to school or read a book in his life? From a man who lived in a society of uncivilized idolaters? From an orphan who was barely lucky enough to survive into adulthood? A message so compelling it caused the overthrow of the mighty Roman and Persian Empires in a very short time? A way of life so satisfying that its teachings continue to attract multitudes of converts all over the world at a record pace every year? All from the hand of a man like this - a man whose entire life was an open book to his enemies, and whose dramatic story is preserved for us to this day? I think not. Critics seek to 'understand' what 'influences' worked on Muhammad, but they rarely even dare to 'understand' what 'influences' worked on Moses (since, by their standards he would have had to 'make up' the Torah) or what 'influences' worked on Jesus or David. These are the same types of critics who regularly dispute that William Shakespeare wrote all the works attributed to his name, simply because they cannot find any plausible way (based upon his time, environment and humble birth) for him to have been so well-grounded in history and literature. It is not always the case that a man or woman must be tied to their times or governed by surrounding 'influences,' and it is not always the case that such 'influences' even matter.

as an inheritance to whichever of Our servants that We chose. [1458]

There are some (people) who have done wrong against their own souls, while others have followed a middle path, and there are yet others, by Allah's leave, who race ahead to do the best – and that's the greatest foundation (for amassing spiritual) bounty. [1459] [32]

(As a reward), they'll enter gardens of eternity! Inside they'll be adorned with bracelets of gold and pearls, and their clothes will be made of silk. [33]

They'll say, "*Praise be to Allah, Who made all heartache depart from us, for our Lord is truly forgiving and appreciative* [34] – *the One Who, out of His bounty, settled us in a realm that will last forever. Never shall we have to struggle or feel exhausted within.*" [35]

Those who reject (Allah) will have the fires of Hell (as a reward). They won't be given any release date from their sentence, nor will they ever die, for its punishment will never be alleviated. That's how we pay back every thankless (wretch)! [36]

They'll scream inside (for help, saying), "*Our Lord! Get us out of here! We'll be good! (We won't do) what we used to do!*"

(Then they'll be told), "*Didn't We give you enough of a lifespan (there on earth) already, so that whoever would (have had enough common sense to) accept a reminder could have been reminded?* [1460] *The warner already came to you, as well, so now you will suffer (the punishment)!*"

The wrongdoers will have no one to help them! [37]

Allah's Warning is Clear

*A*llah knows what's hidden in the heavens and the earth, even as He knows precisely what's in the hearts (of all His creatures). [38]

He's the One Who made you inheritors in the earth, so if anyone rejects (Allah), then they're really rejecting themselves.

Their rejection adds nothing more for them in their Lord's sight except greater revulsion (of them by Him). Their rejection adds nothing more for them except (endless) failure. [39]

Ask them, "*Have you ever even seen these 'partners' of yours upon whom you call in place of Allah? Show me what they've created in the world - or do they own a share of the heavens?*"

Have We ever given (the idol-worshippers) a scripture from which they can offer evidence?

No way! The wrongdoers promise each other nothing more than delusions. [40] Allah - (*and not your idols*) - maintains the heavens and the earth so they won't fail.

If they did fail, there would be no one who could maintain them after that. Indeed, Allah is forbearing and forgiving. [41]

[1458] The divine scripture was given to previous prophets such as Abraham, Moses, David and Jesus. When their followers lost or distorted those messages, Allah bestowed His message yet again as an 'inheritance' upon some other community. Thus, the Prophet received the Qur'an, and his companions carried it forward to the world successfully.

[1459] The Prophet's widow A'ishah was asked about the three types of people mentioned in this verse. She explained that all of them will go to Paradise with varying degrees of review on Judgment Day, but due to her modesty, she said she considered herself to be part of the category that did wrong to their own souls. (*Ma'ariful Qur'an*)

[1460] The Prophet said, "Allah has left no excuse for the person who lives to be sixty or seventy years old. Allah has left no excuse for him! Allah has left no excuse for him!" (*Ahmad*) In other words, if you've lived that long, you have no excuse for denying Allah. Surely in that time you've thought about Allah at least a few times, heard messages about Allah or had the chance to consider how you feel about life and its meaning.

People will be Held to Account

The (idol-worshippers) swore their most sacred oaths that if a warner ever came to them, they would follow his guidance even better than any other nation, but when a warner did come to them, it only made them run away that much faster! [42] They were arrogant in the earth and plotted evil, *but evil plots only trap those who weave them!*

Are they waiting for the fate that ancient (civilizations) suffered? You'll never find any change in Allah's methods, nor will you ever find any other way except Allah's way. [43]

Haven't they ever traveled through the earth and noticed how those who came before them were punished, even though those (earlier civilizations) were stronger than they could ever be? Allah is never thwarted (in His actions) in the heavens or on the earth, for He's full of knowledge and is able to determine events. [44]

If Allah were to punish people according to what they deserved, then He wouldn't leave one single thing alive on the surface of (the earth)! [1461]

However, He gives (people) time for a set duration. When that time limit expires, then (you're going to see) how much Allah was watching (what) His servants (were doing)! [45]

[1461] People are capable of utter evil and depravity. The injustice we inflict upon each other and upon all the wildlife that lives around us is unimaginable in scale. Imam Abu Hanifa (d. 765) once said, "Who are we to wish for Paradise? It will be enough if Allah spares us from His wrath." Yet, even still, Allah gives us time to repent. The Prophet said, "If the believer knew the extent of Allah's punishment, no one would ever have any hopes of entering Paradise. If the rejecter knew of the extent of Allah's mercy, no one would ever feel hopeless of gaining Paradise. Allah created a hundred degrees of mercy. He sent down just one of them to His creation, and (all creatures are capable of being) merciful to each other from that alone. With Allah, the other ninety-nine (degrees) of mercy remain." (*Ahmad*)

514

Ya Seen

36 Ya Seen
Middle Meccan Period

This very poetic and rhythmic chapter is one of the more famous ones in this part of the Qur'an. It is often displayed on posters or other artwork, as well. The Prophet once described it as the heart of the Qur'an. In another tradition, he said, "Recite the chapter of *Ya Seen* to the dying ones among you," because it so beautifully sums up the different features of the trials that people face in both this life and the next. (*Ahmad*) In another narration, the Prophet said that Allah wrote chapters 20 (Ta Ha) and 36 (Ya Seen) a thousand years before He created the universe. When the angels heard the lines being uttered, they said, "Blessed be the community to which it will be sent down, blessed are the minds that will bear it, and blessed are the tongues that will recite it." (*Tabari*)

In the Name of Allah,
the Compassionate, the Merciful

Yā. Seen. [1]

By the Qur'an filled with wisdom, [1462] [2] you're indeed one of the messengers, [3] (guided) on a straight path. [4] It's a (revelation) sent down by the Powerful and the Merciful, [5] so you can warn a nation whose ancestors never received any warning before, leaving them heedless (of Allah's truth). [6]

And so it has come to pass that the truth of (Allah's) pronouncement has now been proven true against most of them, for they don't believe. [1463] [7] We've encircled their necks with collars up to their chins, so they must straighten their heads (under the weight of their sins). [8]

We've put a wall (of uncertainty) in front of them and behind them and covered them (in the darkness of ignorance), so they can't see a thing. [1464] [9]

[1462] In the formal (not chronological) arrangement of the Qur'an, this is one of the first instances of a type of 'oath' that was common among mystic fortune tellers of the desert, who were called *kahin*. Many early Meccan chapters make use of this device, which essentially uses an oath to impress upon the listener the importance or truthfulness of a subject. This would have been an oral technique that the more superstitious Meccans were attuned to, and thus its usage in that period was relevant in the Prophet's ministry. In the Medinan period such usages are generally not found in the revelations and are, in fact, unnecessary given the more cosmopolitan and sophisticated nature of that new city where logic was often all that was needed to prove a point - not a call to some natural or esoteric phenomenon. The Qur'an was an evolutionary book in that regard, as it spoke to its changing audience in terms to which each successive group could relate.

[1463] Allah has promised that those who do not listen to the truth when it comes to them bring ruin upon themselves in both this world and the next. This saying of His has been 'proven true' time and time again. See 38:84-85 for the actual pronouncement and also 32:13.

[1464] By rejecting faith in Allah, the heedless bring upon themselves an inability to be open-minded about the truths of Allah all around them. The description used here to express what their state is like

515

It's all the same whether you warn them or don't warn them, for they won't believe. [10]

You can only warn those who will obey the message and who fear (to displease) the Compassionate, (even though He's) beyond their perception. Give good news to them of forgiveness and a generous reward. [11]

Indeed, We're going to give life to the dead, and We're recording whatever (deeds) they've sent ahead, as well as what they've left behind, [1465] for We've recorded everything in a clear ledger. [1466] [12]

The Example of the City Dwellers

*P*resent to them the example of the city dwellers who had messengers sent to them. [1467] [13] We dispatched two messengers (to their city), but the (people within) rejected them, so We reinforced (the two messengers) with a third one. They told (their people), "*We've truly been sent to give you (a message).*" [14]

The (people) answered, "*You're only mortal men like us, and the Compassionate never sends anything down. You're no more than liars!*" [15] (The messengers) replied, "*Our Lord knows that we've been sent to give you (a message).*

[16] *Our only duty is to convey the message clearly.*" [17]

"*We see a bad omen in you,*" the people said, "*so if you don't stop what you're doing, we'll stone you (to death) and punish you terribly!*" [18]

(The messengers) answered, "*Your 'bad omens' are really within your own selves. (Do you think it's a bad thing) that you're being reminded? Certainly not! It's just that you're a people who are out of control!*" [19]

The Unknown Martyr

*T*hen a man came running from a far corner of the city. [1468] He told (the gathered crowds):

"*My people! Obey the messengers.* [20] *Obey those who ask you for no reward and who themselves have been guided.* [21] *It would make no sense to me if I didn't serve the One Who created me and to Whom you will all return.* [22] *Should I take other gods in place of Him?*

"*If the Compassionate wanted to bring some harm down upon me, (those gods) wouldn't be able to intercede for me at all, nor could they save me.* [23] *If I (worshipped idols), then I'd be clearly wrong.* [24] *So as for me, I believe in your Lord, so listen to me!*" [25]

(Then the mob killed him in their fury, but because of his great faith) he'll be told,

---

is that of a haughty person who doesn't even know all the hidden fetters there are upon his understanding and intellect.

[1465] 'Left behind' refers to deeds left unfinished or unfulfilled.

[1466] The children of a man named Salamah went to the Prophet one day, complaining that they lived too far from the mosque in Medina. They wanted to know if they could move closer. The Prophet told them, "Children of Salamah, stay where you are, for your footsteps will be recorded. Stay where you are, for your footsteps will be recorded." (*Muslim, Ahmad*). In other words, living closer or farther from the mosque doesn't make one a better or worse Muslim.

[1467] At-Tabari, quoting reports contained in Ibn Is-haq, explains that two messengers of Allah, who were named (or nicknamed) Sadiq and Saduq, began preaching in their hometown, but when they were ignored and ridiculed, Allah sent a third messenger named Shalum (or Sham'un) to back them up. Some early scholars suggested that the city was Antioch, in Syria, but many classical scholars such as Ibn Kathir have disproved this view. Thus, the city's identity remains a mystery. (*Ma'ariful Qur'an*)

[1468] The unknown man introduced in this passage has been traditionally named *Habib,* or Beloved, and it is thought he was a carpenter. Other commentators suggest he was a leper who prayed to idols for decades to be cured, but by chance he heard the preaching of the three prophets and was cured. Thus, he approached the crowd, pleading with them and was thus killed. He was able to enter Paradise straightaway for martyrs are given that blessing (though for Judgment Day they come for a brief appearance as a formality). (*Ibn Kathir*)

"*Enter the Garden.*" Then he'll (look around and exclaim in wonderment and surprise), "*Oh my! If only my people knew (about all of this),* [26] *that my Lord has forgiven me and set me up among the honored.*" [27]

After he (was unjustly killed,) We sent no armies from the sky down upon his people, for We didn't need to do that. [28] It was no more than a tremendous boom, and then there they were – *eradicated!* [29]

How unfortunate for (My) servants! No messenger ever comes to them without them mocking him! [30] Don't they see how many generations before them We destroyed? None of them will ever return. [1469] [31] Yet, every single one of them will be brought back before Us (for Judgment)! [32]

Signs for Them to Ponder

$\mathcal{A}$ sign (to prove) to them that (this message is true) can be found within the lifeless earth. We bring life to it and cause grain to grow for you to eat. [33]

We placed within it orchards of date palms and grape vines, and We cause bubbling springs to flow [34] for (people), so they can enjoy the fruits (that grow from Our bounty). It wasn't their hands that did all of this, so won't they be thankful? [35]

Glory be to Allah, Who created all things that the earth produces in pairs, even their own (human species, as well), along with other things they know nothing about. [36]

(Another) sign for them is the night that falls when We withdraw the day, leaving them in utter darkness. [37]

The sun has its own set course to follow, as well, and that's the measured power of the Powerful and the Knowing (Allah). [38]

We've determined the moon's course through its phases until it returns looking like a curved date stalk. [39] The sun isn't allowed to get ahead of the moon, nor can the night get ahead of the day. Each of (those heavenly bodies) swims along in its own rounded orbit. [40]

(Another) sign for them is that We carried their ancestors on a loaded boat [1470] [41] and that We also created for (humanity, in general), similar (modes of transportation) upon which they ride. [42]

If We ever wanted, We could (overwhelm all their ships) and drown them (when they set sail).

Then there would be no one they could call to (for help), nor could they ever be saved, [43] apart from an act of Our mercy, allowing them to enjoy (life) for a little while longer. [44]

They Scoff at the Concept of Judgment

$\mathcal{W}$hen they're told, "*Be mindful of what's coming up and what's left behind, so you can receive mercy,*" (they ignore you). [45]

[1469] Some commentators say this verse means that the lineage of those wrongdoers was destroyed. Other commentators take it more generically to say that those civilizations will never rise to prominence again.

[1470] Most translators render this verse to mean that Allah carried our *seed* or *race* on Noah's loaded boat. The term *dhuriya* means one's ancestors, offspring or descendants. Some translators have stretched the meaning of *dhuriya* to assume this passage is talking about modern ships and the descendants of Noah being carried on them. The entire context of verses 33-42 is somewhat generic and non-specific. Thus, ships used for trade are mentioned in a general sense, and the next verse, which references generic land transportation, seems to support their view. Translators such as Muhammad Asad follow this more expansive conclusion and render it accordingly.

Indeed, no proof from their Lord's signs ever reaches them without them turning away from it. [46]

When they're told, *"Spend (in charity) from (the wealth) that Allah has provided for you,"* the faithless say to the believers, *"Should we feed the people that Allah could've fed Himself, if only He had wanted to? You're clearly mistaken!"* [47]

Then they add, *"When will this promise (of judgment come to pass), if you're really so honest?"* [48]

They won't have to wait for more than a single boom, and it will overtake them, even as they're still arguing with each other. [49]

They'll have no more (time) to decide (for themselves), nor will they be able to return to their families again. [50]

The trumpet will sound, and suddenly they'll be rushing out of their graves straight back to their Lord! [51]

They'll cry out (in amazement), *"We're doomed! Who raised us up from our resting places?"*

(Then a voice will say,) *"This is what the Compassionate promised, and the messengers spoke the honest truth!"* [52]

It'll be no more than a single blast, and then they'll all come out together before Us! [53]

No soul will be wronged in the least on that day, for you won't be rewarded except by what you did (in the world). [54]

The Two Possibilities on Judgment Day

*O*n that day, the companions of the Garden will be occupied with pleasure! [55]

They and their spouses will relax upon couches nestled in shady nooks. [56]

There will be fruits for them, and whatever else they ask for will be theirs. [57]

"Peace," (is the) saying (that they'll hear) from a merciful Lord! [58]

(On the other hand, the sinners will be told:)

"Get back this day, all you wicked ones! [59] *Didn't I make an agreement with you, all you children of Adam, that you were not to serve Satan, for he was your obvious enemy?* [1471] [60]

"(Didn't I order you) to serve Me, for that was a straight path? [61] *However, he led a huge number of you astray. Was there something (in what I said) that you didn't understand?* [62] *So this is the Hellfire about which you were warned!* [63] *Embrace it today because you rejected (the truth)!"* [64]

On that day, We're going to seal their mouths shut, but their hands will speak to Us, and their feet will testify to what they earned. [1472] [65]

If We had wanted, We could've blinded their eyes, and then they would've been left (hopelessly) stumbling along the

---

[1471] See 2:37-39.

[1472] The Prophet was sitting with his companions one day when he suddenly began to smile broadly. He asked those with him if they knew what made him smile. When they answered in the negative, he said, "Because of the way a servant will argue with his Lord on the Day of Judgment. He's going to say, 'Lord! Are you going to protect me from suffering injustice?' (Allah) will answer, 'Of course.' Then (the servant) will say, 'I'm not going to accept the testimony of any witnesses against me other than myself.' (Allah) will say, 'This day you'll be enough of a witness against yourself, and the noble writers (angels who watch you and record your deeds) will serve as witnesses against you.' Then his mouth will be sealed up, his body parts will be commanded to speak, and they'll talk about what he did. Then, when the (servant) is allowed to talk again, he'll say to his own body, 'You're doomed! It was for your sake that I was contending!'" (*Muslim, Nisa'i*)

path (of life), for how could they have seen clearly then? [1473] [66]

And if We had wanted, We could've transformed them on the spot into motionless (statues), so they would've been unable to move forward or return back. [1474] [67]

The Nature of Disbelief

If We give long life to someone, We reverse (the nature) of (his) creation (by means of senility, as if he were a helpless infant again), so won't they understand? [68]

We aren't teaching (the Prophet) mere poetry, [1475] nor does it suit him. [1476] This is no less than a reminder and a clear reading [69] to warn the living and also to show that the truth of the sentence will be

---

[1473] The point is that they didn't use their insight to guide them in life, even though Allah gave people the power to see the truth, so it would have been all the same if Allah had blinded them. But even though their hearts were dead, they could still see the signs of Allah's handiwork all around them. For all they were worth, though, they might just have well been statues, as the next verse suggests.

[1474] In other words, if Allah wasn't going to test us and let us choose right from wrong, He would have created us with no ability to discern right from wrong or good from evil. Likewise, if He wasn't going to let us choose to do good or evil, then He might just as well have made us into statues who can't ever do wrong. Thus, we would never be able to return to goodness or seek the pardon of Allah.

[1475] A pagan named 'Uqbah ibn Abi Mu'ayt accused the Prophet one day of being a mere poet. This passage was revealed in response. (*Zamakhshari*)

[1476] Although the Prophet loved to hear good poetry, he was not a poet himself, and his widow A'ishah reported that the Prophet never recited original poetry but on a couple of occasions. There are only a few examples of poetry that are attributed to the Prophet, and they are not imaginative or particularly clever. Here is one of those pieces: "I am the Prophet; that's no lie. I am the son of 'Abdel Muttalib." (*Zamakhshari*) As for quoting other people, once the Prophet recited a couplet composed by the poet Ibn Tarfah, but he was off on the rhyme scheme. Abu Bakr (diplomatically) said to him, "Messenger of Allah, that line is not like that." The Prophet replied, "I'm not a poet, nor does poetry suit me." (*Ma'ariful Qur'an*) Interestingly enough, the Qur'an is not like the poetry typical of its time, and this is another proof against those foolish people who think the Prophet 'made it all up.' He was an Arab, who grew up in west-central Arabia, and he could neither read nor write nor had any reputation as a literary or poetic composer. How could he have invented a new form of literature all of a sudden in the year 610? In fact, many studies have proven that the Qur'an has no relationship to the poetry that existed around him. One study points out: "Thomas Bauer (2010) argues that Qur'anic diction deliberately avoids any semblance with the form, style or content of the poetry of its time. As a result of this 'negative intertextuality', a text came into being which 'is, in many ways, the complete antithesis of contemporary poetry' (2010: 705-6). Bauer points out, however, that there are instances where the Qur'an, in a tone of disparagement, appears to evoke phrases found in pre-Islamic verse." (*The Qur'an and Arabic Poetry*. Sperle, 2017) In other words, sometime the Qur'an mocks Arabic poetry and its lowly emphasis on tribal loyalty, bravado in war and the romance of lost causes. "Bauer's findings corroborate the work of earlier scholars, notably Toshihiko Izitsu (1959), who have argued that the Qur'anic message was intended to overcome the tribalist ethos of pre-Islamic Arabia... Having established poetry as the repository of the ethos to which the Qur'an is opposed, Neuwirth repeatedly highlights how standard poetic themes are countered and implicitly nullified by passages in the Qur'an. Thus the transitory bliss of lost love conjured up by the *nasīb*, the erotic prelude of the *qasīda*, is inverted by the 'counter-image of everlasting bliss' and amorous delight granted to the souls in Paradise (2014:79). Similarly, the *atlāl*, the ruins of the abandoned campsite bemoaned by the pre-Islamic poet, have a superior Qur'anic counterpart in the *umam khāliya*, the communities destroyed by divine retribution (2014,26). These and numerous other examples in Neuwirth's work go to show that in the Qur'an a pessimistic, anthropocentric world-view internalized by the tribal ethos of *muruwwa* and voiced through the medium of poetry, is effectively and deliberately countered by a theocentric vision in which the individual is answerable only to God and faced with the prospect of eternal punishment or reward." (Sperl, 2017) Now we can better understand the challenge made to the Arabs to make a surah or verse like the Qur'an: it was an art form completely new to them so they couldn't do it!

proven against those who suppress (their faith). [1477] [70]

Don't they see that We created for them - out of all the things Our hands have made - the livestock that are under their control [71] and that We made (those animals) docile for them?

They use (some animals) for riding and others for eating. [72] They have other benefits, as well, in addition to providing (milk) to drink. So won't you be thankful? [73]

Instead, they set up other gods in place of Allah, thinking they might help them. [74] (Those false gods) have no power to help them, even if they raised a whole army (to help). [75]

Ignore the Taunts of the Foolish

Don't let what they're saying bother you, for We know exactly what they're keeping in secret and what they're (saying) openly. [1478] [76]

Doesn't the human being see that We created him from a drop? Yet, he's clearly defiant. [77]

He sets up depictions of Us, all the while forgetting his own creation. He asks, *"Who can bring old rotted bones back to life?"* [78]

Say to him, *"The One Who gave them life the first time will give them life again, for He knows about every type of creation. [79] He's the One who can produce a fire from green trees when you kindle it.* [1479] [80] *Doesn't the One Who created the heavens and the earth have the power to create something like (a human being again)? Definitely! He's the Creator and the Knowing!"* [81]

Whenever He commands something to come into existence, all He says is, *"Be,"* and it is! [1480] [82] So all glory be to the One in Whose hands is all dominion, and you're going to go back to Him. [83]

[1477] See 38:84-85 and 32:13 for the 'sentence' or proclamation of Allah.

[1478] An idolater named Ubayy ibn Khalaf approached the Prophet one day while holding a dry bone in his hand. (Some reports say it was 'As ibn Wa'il.) He broke the bone and pulverized some of it in his hand. Then he asked the Prophet, "Do you think Allah can raise to life something like this after it's all smashed to bits?" The Prophet said, "Yes. He can raise that up, and He can raise you to life again and send you to Hellfire." Then this passage was revealed in response. (*Ibn Kathir*)

[1479] There were two different types of trees that were commonly used for making fires by the Arabs. They were called the *markh* and *afar* trees. Even though both trees might be green, when twigs from each were rubbed together it would create enough heat to cause a fire. This is what this verse is alluding to. (*Qurtubi*)

[1480] The Prophet said, "Allah, the Exalted, once said, 'My servants, you're all sinners, except for those whom I protect from sin. Seek My forgiveness, and I will forgive you. All of you are in need, except for those whom I make independent. I am the Generous and the Majestic, and I do whatever I want. My giving is a word, and My punishment is a word. When I want something to happen, I merely say, 'Be,' and it is." (*Ahmad*)

The Rows

37 As-Saffat
Middle Meccan Period

The main theme of this chapter is constant throughout its various sub-arguments, namely that Allah reaches out to humanity in many ways, despite humanity's insistence on turning its face from Allah. From dabbling in astrology and fortune-telling to making up invented theological doctrines, humanity rarely opens their collective eyes to the One Who created them and will judge them. The call for people to listen to the words and deeds of the ancient prophets, in order to reaffirm in their hearts the truth of Allah's last prophet Muhammad, is accompanied by a note of hope for the faithful believers who stand up unflinchingly for Allah.

In the Name of Allah,
the Compassionate, the Merciful

By those who align themselves in rows [1481] [1]
and drive away the driven (foe), [1482] [2]
reciting the reminder [3]
that your God is One alone! [4]

(He's) the Lord of the heavens and the earth and all in between, and the Lord of the two Easts! [1483] [5]

We adorned the lowest sky with the glittering streaks (of falling) meteorites, [1484] [6] as a guard against

---

[1481] The Prophet said, "We've been favored over the rest of humanity in three ways: our rows have been made like the rows of the angels, the entire earth has been made a place of prostration for us, and its soil has been made a means to achieve ritual purity for us if we can't find any water for ablution." (*Muslim*) The rows of the angels means the way we line up for group prayers in lines and rows. The entire earth as a place of bowing means that a Muslim is not restricted to praying in a temple, tabernacle or other dedicated building, and the earth's soil can be used to purify ourselves symbolically (*tayamum*) if we can't find water to clean up.

[1482] Some commentators hold that the imagery in the first four verses of this chapter is of a line of powerful horsemen who never waver under an enemy assault. They push ahead and never crumble in their resolve to press their cause, which is rooted in their religious beliefs. (That is an example of how a believer is supposed to be in his commitment to his religion.) Other commentators are of the opinion that this dramatic opening refers to the angels and that it is a message to the Meccans that just as the angels will not waver, so too will Islam succeed. In my humble view, it is more likely that the imagery of charging horsemen is more plausible, as the average Meccan would not have cared about forceful allusions to unseen angels, but they would have understood the thrill of a bold charge by dedicated warriors, albeit ones chanting religious slogans as they rode.

[1483] This refers to the two extreme points north and south from which the sun will rise throughout the year. This is called the solar equinox.

[1484] The Arabic word used here is Kaukab, which is usually reserved for celestial bodies other than stars, such as planets, meteors, and planetoids. (Najm is the word normally used for light-producing stars.) Falling stars, planets and their movements, and other celestial bodies form the basis of astrology, which evil jinn and people use to predict the future, based on knowledge from Heaven. Verse eight mentions being pelted. Some commentators hold that chunks of rock in space (falling meteorites) are driving the jinns away. Others assume it is the falseness of astrology that is chasing them away and thwarting them.

every relentless devil, [1485] [7]
to prevent them from eavesdropping
on the higher assembly (of angels). [1486]

They're pelted from every side [8]
and thrown back (in a rush)!

And what's more,
they'll have
an endless torment
to suffer besides! [9]

Though some may
manage to snatch away
(some of the secrets
of the angels) by stealth,
they're pursued by
flaming fireballs. [1487] [10]

Questions for the Skeptics

So ask them their opinion. Are they harder to create or the (other) things that We created? In fact, We made their (ultimate ancestor) from sticky clay! [11]

But no! You're amazed (at Allah's creative power), while they just ridicule (it). [12] When they're reminded, they don't accept the reminder, [13] and when they see a miracle, they belittle it. [14]

Then they say, *"This is clearly no more than wizardry.* [15] *Huh? When we die and become dust and bones, are we really going to be raised up (to life) again* [16] *- and our ancestors, too?"* [17]

Tell (them), *"Yes, and then you'll be in disgrace!"* [18] It'll take just a single cry, and then they'll be staring (in disbelief). [19]

"We're doomed!" they'll cry out. *"This is the Day of Judgment!"* [20]

"This is the Day of Sorting," (they'll hear a voice say), *"the day that you said was a lie."* [21]

(Then the angels will be told), *"Bring them, all the tyrants, and their counterparts, and all the things they used to worship* [22] *besides Allah. Direct them to the path that leads to the flame* [23] *- but stop them first, for they must be asked,* [24] *'What's wrong with you? Why aren't you helping each other now?'"* [1488] [25]

By no means! (They won't be able to help each other at all), for on that day they'll have to submit (to their punishment). [26]

[1485] Satan has an army of other jinns who believe in him and assist him in his mission to corrupt as many humans as possible. The existence of jinns has spawned an entire body of lore and legend in the Muslim world that is equivalent to the Western preoccupation with ghosts. Despite the fervent nature of the countless "jinn stories" prevalent in the Muslim world, Islamically speaking, it is all but impossible for any human being to see a jinn, save for a prophet. The famous Muslim legal jurist, Imam ash-Shafi'i (d. 820), commented on this when he said, "Whoever is of sound character and claims to have seen the jinn, his testimony is no longer valid, because Allah says: '*Truly, he (Satan) and his minions see you from where you cannot see them*'" (Qur'an 7:27)

[1486] When angels receive divine decrees from Allah, they sometimes discuss the affairs of those on earth. The jinns try to eavesdrop on the angels by ascending towards the higher heavens. They want to know what Allah has planned for people, in order to use that knowledge for mischief. Fiery meteorites repel most of them, but occasionally some jinns sneak a tidbit of information. They go back to the earth's surface and pour that information into the ears of fortune-tellers who then make predictions that 'come true.' This causes people to believe in them, and they follow the fortune-teller's advice in other areas of which they have no knowledge. The Prophet was once asked about the fact that fortune-tellers were sometimes right, and he said, "A jinn snatches that true word and pours it into the ear of his friend (the fortune-teller) as one puts something into a bottle. The fortune-teller then mixes with that word one hundred lies." (*Bukhari*)

[1487] This is commonly understood to be shooting stars or meteors that burn up in earth's atmosphere. (*Shihabun thaqibun* literally means 'shooting chunks that are lit up,' i.e., flaming fireballs.)

[1488] On earth, allies in sin offer to back each other up if they ever get caught, but just as there is no honor among thieves, on the Day of Judgment, wicked wrongdoers will be powerless to aid each other, even if they wanted to.

They'll turn on each other and start making accusations, [27] saying, *"It was you! You were the ones who used your influence (to goad us into disbelief and sin)."* [28]

(The accused) will answer, *"Not a chance! You, yourselves, had no faith! [29] We had no authority over you (to make you do what you weren't willing to do already). No way! You were a stubborn group of people. [30] So now the sentence of our Lord has been proven true against us. We're going to suffer (the terrible result of our sin all together). [31] We led you astray, yes, but only because we, ourselves, were astray."* [1489] [32]

On that day they'll indeed share in the punishment all together, [33] for that's how We deal with the wicked. [34]

They became arrogant whenever they were told that there's no god but the (One True) God, [1490] [35] and they said, *"What! Should we give up all our gods for the sake of a crazy poet?"* [36]

Not so! He's coming with the truth (of Allah), and he's confirming the (validity of) the messengers (that came before him). [37]

(Each of) you will certainly experience the awful punishment, [38] but it's no less than a payback for (the sins) you committed. [39]

The Possible Results of Judgment Day

The sincere servants of Allah, however, (are exempted from the punishment). [40] They're going to have well-measured supplies [41] of fruit, and they'll be held in honor [42] among gardens of delight. [1491] [43]

They'll be facing each other on couches, [44] passing around a cup filled from a crystal-clear fountain [45] - a drink of such sparkling clarity - *a delight to the drinker!* [46] No hangover will it cause, nor will it intoxicate them. [1492] [47]

(Distinctive-mates) with coy glances and expressive eyes will linger in their presence, [48] as if they were eggs nestled in safety. [49] They'll turn to each other and ask each other questions. [1493] [50]

One of the speakers will say, *"I had a close (friend in the world) [51] who used to say, 'What! Are you one of the people who assert that this (message) is true? [52] So when we die and become dust and bones, are we really going to be judged?'"* [53]

[1489] See 38:84-85 for the proverbial 'sentence' or verdict of Allah.

[1490] Prophet Jesus also taught the same message of monotheism or *tawheed* in Arabic (lit. oneness). See Mark 12:29.

[1491] The Prophet said, "On the Day of Judgment, a person who was devoted to the Qur'an will be told, 'Begin reciting the Qur'an and start to ascend upwards through the levels of Paradise. Recite it in a slow, measured way as you did in your worldly life. Your final resting place will be where you reach the last verse of your recitation.'" (*Tirmidhi*)

[1492] The pure wine of Paradise will be purified of all negative side-effects. It will give all the pleasure of earthly wine – and then some – but it won't cause any headaches, vomiting, urine or hangovers. It will be crystal clear, not dark red or purple, as are the wines of earth. (*Ibn Kathir*)

[1493] There is an obscure reference to an account that some Muslims in the second generation of Islam used to circulate that is purported to reveal the identity of the two men mentioned in this passage. Apparently, there were two businessmen in the Meccan period, with one being a convert to Islam, while the other was a pagan. They split their profits evenly, and while the pagan used his money to buy land and build a house, the convert was busy giving his money in charitable causes. Eventually, the convert fell on hard times, and he went to his old partner for help. The pagan inquired as to how his old friend could have lost so much money, and when the Muslim explained that he had given it away for the sake of Allah, the pagan said to him, "Do you really believe that it's true that when we die and become dust and bones, that we're really going to be brought to life again and be paid back for what we did here on earth? Get out of here! I'm not going to give you anything!" Then both men later died, and the dialogue contained in verses 51-61 will take place after Judgment Day. (From *As-Suyuti* as mentioned in *Ma'ariful Qur'an*)

"Would you care to look down?" (a hidden voice) will ask, [54] and when he does look down, he'll (be surprised) to see (his old friend) in the middle of the burning flame! [55]

He'll say, *"By Allah! You almost ruined me!* [56] *If it wasn't for the grace of my Lord, I would surely have been one of those put in there!"* [57]

(Then he'll look to his companions around him and say), *"Isn't it true that we won't ever die again,* [58] *save for our first death, and that we'll never be punished? [59] This is the greatest success of all!"* [60]

And so for (a reward) like this, let those who would make an effort give it their best effort! [61]

Is that a better welcome or the tree of *Zaqqum?* [1494] [62] We made its (mention) to be a trial for the wrongdoers, (who would likely reject the notion that such a thing existed). [1495] [63]

It's a tree whose roots grow out of the very pit of the flame, [64] the fruits of which are like the heads of devils. [65]

They'll most assuredly be made to eat from it, and what's more, they'll fill their stomachs with it! [66] Then after all that, they'll (drink) a mixture made of filthy muck (to help it all go down). [67] Then

(after they've finished their meal), they'll be forced back into the flames! [1496] [68]

They certainly found their forefathers on the wrong path, [69] so they hurried onward in their footsteps! [70]

Before them, many ancient (civilizations) went astray, [71] even though We sent them (messengers) to warn them, as well. [72]

Then see what ultimately happened to those who were warned, [73] (a fate that befell them all), save for the sincere servants of Allah. [74]

Recognizing Noah

*A*nd so it was that Noah called out to Us, and We're the best to respond. [75] We saved him and his family from the great tragedy [76] and caused his descendants to endure (in the world). [77]

We left (his story) among the generations that followed after him. [78] *So peace be upon Noah throughout all the worlds!* [79]

That's how We reward the good, [80] for he was one of Our faithful servants. [81] All the rest (of his people) were drowned (in the Flood). [82]

[1494] What is the tree of *Zaqqum?* The Arabic term from which the name is derived is *zaqama.* It literally means to swallow, gobble or be forced to do those things; thus, the tree of Zaqqum would be the tree of *forced feeding.* Given that the taste is reputed to be the most horrible thing imaginable, it would not be a pleasant meal. The Prophet said, "If a single drop from the tree of *Zaqqum* were to fall on a house in this world, it would spoil all the food on the planet, so what will it be like for the one who has to eat it as his meal?" (*Tirmidhi*) Also see 17:60 and footnote.

[1495] After the tree of *Zaqqum* was mentioned in 44:43-46, Abu Jahl had publicly taunted the idea of a tree in Hellfire, saying, "Your friend (Muhammad) is saying that there is a tree in the fire, even though fire consumes trees. We know for sure that *zaqqum* is nothing more than dates and butter! So come and eat these dates and butter!" This passage was revealed in response. (*Ibn Kathir*)

[1496] The Prophet said, "There will be some for whom the fire will reach their ankles (only); others will have it come to the knees, others to the waist, and some will have the fire come up to their neck." (*Muslim*) Ibn Kathir records that one companion of the Prophet, Sa'id ibn Jubayr, described a typical day in Hell, saying, "When the people of Hellfire get hungry, they'll ask for food from the tree of Zaqqum. They'll eat from it, and the skin will fall off their faces…they'll ask for a drink (when they're thirsty), and they'll be given water like boiling oil that's been superheated. When it comes near their mouths, the remaining flesh on their faces will be baked by its heat, and whatever was in their stomachs will melt. They'll walk with their guts falling out and with their skin dragging, and then they'll be beaten with hooked iron rods, causing every part of their bodies to burst in loud lamentations."

Abraham Adopts Noah's Ways

$\mathcal{A}$braham [1497] was among those factions that stood for (Noah's) [1498] ideals, [83] for he approached his Lord with a submissive heart. [1499] [84] He had said to his father and to his people, *"What are you worshiping? [85] Is it all a fraud? Do you really want gods other than the (One True) God? [86] So what do you think of the Lord of All the Worlds?"* [87]

(When his people called to him to join them in their annual ritual outside the city,) he raised his glance towards the stars above [88] and said, *"I feel ill."* [89] So his people turned away from him and left. [90]

Then he made his way (into the main temple to confront) their gods, and he said to them, *"Why won't you eat (the food that's been offered before you)? [91] What's wrong with you that you don't speak?"* [92]

Then he took a swing at them with his right hand (and kept at it until he destroyed them all - save for the biggest one). [93] (The temple priests) came rushing back and (soon they found him and) confronted him. [94] (Abraham heard their accusations and responded, saying), *"Are you worshipping things that you carved yourselves? [95] Allah created you and your crafts."* [96]

"Build a bonfire!" they cried. *"Throw him in the burning flames!"* [97] (When he escaped unharmed from it), they made a plan to do away with him, but We (foiled their plan) and made them (look foolish and) humiliated. [1500] [98]

(Abraham) said, *"I will go to my Lord (and leave this wicked land)! He will surely guide me (on my way).* [99]

Abraham Benefits from His Faith

$\mathcal{I}$n later years, Abraham prayed,) *"My Lord! Grant me a righteous son!"* [100] Then We gave him the good news of a resolute boy. [101] At length, when (the

---

[1497] Abraham was an adherent of the way of Noah, namely uncompromising monotheism and social justice. Abraham was also born into the same land as Noah and would have heard the tales of the great flood and how Noah escaped harm due to help from heaven. By Abraham's time, the flood story was well-known and written in many versions – some more monotheistic than others.

[1498] Abraham lived many centuries after the flood of Noah. How could he know what Noah's ideals were? Remember that Noah was a messenger of Allah who received revelations from Him, and also recall that he lived and preached for many centuries in ancient Mesopotamia. Noah, as we explained before, was most probably Ziasudra, a king of the city of Shuruppak, which was obliterated in a dramatic flood on account of the wickedness of the people, as ancient texts assert. Miraculously, the teachings of Ziasudra's *father* Currupag (or Ubara-tutu) were collected and written down in a text known as *the Instructions of Shuruppak*. This is the oldest written book in the world and dates to the time of the flood. (In fact, in ancient Sumerian records, Currupag was the last king to rule before the flood.) In this book, Currupag gives good advice to his son Ziasudra, much like Luqman did for his son. This work became a popular text and was circulated in many cities. It contains over two hundred lines of moral precepts that are remarkably similar to the exhortations of all three of the 'Abrahamic' faiths: *do not steal; do not curse; to have authority, to have possessions and to be steadfast are princely divine powers. You should submit to the respected; you should be humble before the powerful. My son, you will then survive against the wicked,* etc. Thus, we can read the kinds of teachings with which Noah was instructed as a young man, and furthermore we can know what kinds of practical teachings Noah was probably circulating among the people – teachings with which a young Abraham would have come into contact in the scribe schools of ancient Mesopotamia.

[1499] Muhammad ibn Sirin (d. 728), an early scholar most famous for compiling a dictionary of dream interpretation, was once asked what type of a heart it was that Abraham had, as mentioned in this verse. He answered, "(A submissive heart) is one that knows that Allah is real, that the Hour (of Judgment) will surely come to pass and that Allah will resurrect those who are in their graves." (As quoted by *al-Qurtubi* in his commentary.)

[1500] This is a reference to events mentioned in 2:258.

boy) was old enough to work alongside of him, (Abraham said), "*My son! I saw in a dream that I offered you as a sacrifice.* [1501] *What do you see in that?*" [1502]

(The boy) answered, "*My father! Do what you've been ordered to do. You'll find that, by Allah's will, I'll be patient.*" [102]

When they both resolved to submit (to the ritual, Abraham) laid his (son bound) and prostrate on his forehead. [103] (However, just as he was about to sacrifice him), We called out to him, saying, "*Abraham!* [104] *You've already fulfilled the dream!*"

That's how We reward the good, [105] and this was clearly a difficult trial. [106] Then We substituted in his (son's) place the substantial sacrifice (of a ram). [1503] [107]

We left his (story) among the generations that followed after him, [108] so, "*Peace be upon Abraham!*" [109] That's how We reward the good, [110] for he was one of our faithful servants. [111]

We also gave him the good news about Isaac, that he would (one day) become a righteous prophet. [112] We blessed both him and Isaac, and while some of their descendants (remained on the right path and were) good, (others, however), were unjust to the detriment of their own souls. [113]

Moses and Aaron were of the Righteous

And so it was that We also granted Our favor upon Moses and Aaron. [114] We saved them and their people from the great tragedy (of bondage in Egypt). [115]

[1501] By Abraham seeing this vision in a dream, Allah is saved from being accused of verbally ordering a man to sacrifice his son. Thus, when Abraham is stopped at the last moment from doing the deed, it was rightly said that he had already mimicked his dream far enough and that the dream is where the deed was conceived.

[1502] Which son of Abraham was about to be sacrificed, Ishmael or Isaac? The Qur'an does not say, and this issue was the subject of much debate among classical scholars. One opinion, noted by at-Tabari and others, was that it was Isaac, while the majority of scholars, such as Ibn Kathir, preferred Ishmael. (The commentator al-Qurtubi (d. 1273) lists a whole range of arguments for both sides in his voluminous work of *tafseer*.) Of course, the exact identification has no bearing on Islamic theology, and the scholars of yore have admitted as such. Be that as it may, the most favored position today is that it was Ishmael. Although the Hebrew Old Testament in Genesis 22:2 and 22:16 asserts that it was Isaac who was to be sacrificed, the very text itself is contradictory, as Isaac is called Abraham's *only* son, while that is not a true statement, for Ishmael was already a teenager by that time. Some scholars have postulated that somewhere in the deep recesses of time someone might have switched the name from Ishmael to Isaac in the Bible. The Biblical text reads, "And He said, take now thy son, thine only son, Isaac, whom thou lovest...and offer him there for a burnt offering..." As was mentioned before, Isaac was not his only son, for Ishmael was born before him, and Hebrew law makes no distinction about the status of the birth mother, whether she was a free woman, a second wife or a slave, when assigning who has the first-born status and all the rights and privileges thereunto. (See Deuteronomy 21:15-17.)

[1503] There is a ritual performed during the Islamic Pilgrimage in Mecca called Stoning the Devil, and its roots go back to an action of Abraham. It is said that when Abraham was commanded to sacrifice his son, he headed for the appointed place just outside of the small encampment his wife and son had made in the Valley of Becca (Mecca), but Satan raced him to the place of sacrifice. Abraham arrived first, and Satan kept assailing Abraham's mind with doubts, so Abraham threw seven stones at him several times to drive him off. Then Abraham laid his son down prostrate. The boy was wearing a white shirt, and he said, "Father, I don't have any cloth for you to wrap me in other than this, so take it off of me so you can shroud me with it (for burial)." It was when Abraham began to remove his son's shirt that the angel came and told him to stop the proceedings. Then they found the ram and sacrificed it, instead. The horns of that ram remained in Mecca as it slowly grew into a trading town over the centuries. After the Conquest of Mecca, the Prophet left the horns where they were hanging in the Ka'bah. He merely ordered them to be covered up with a sheet, so there would be no distraction inside the House of Allah. The horns were destroyed in later years during a fire that struck the Ka'bah. (*Ahmad*)

We helped them so they could triumph, [116] gave them the Book to clarify (their affairs) [117] and guided them to the straight path. [118]

We left their (story) among the generations that followed after them, [119] so, *"Peace be upon Moses and Aaron!"* [120]

That's how We reward the good, [121] for they both were Our faithful servants. [122]

The Struggle of Elijah

$\mathcal{E}$lijah [1504] was also one of those who were sent. [1505] [123] He announced to his people, *"Won't you be mindful (of your duty to Allah)?* [124] *Will you call upon Ba-al-im* [1506] *and forsake the best of all creators?* [125] *(Will you forsake) Allah, your Lord and the Lord of your ancient ancestors?"* [126]

However, they denied him, and thus they'll be brought back (for punishment), [127] all except for the sincere servants of Allah (among them). [128]

And We left his (story) among the generations that followed after him, [129] so, *"Peace be upon (all who are like) Elijah!"* [1507] [130]

That's how We reward the good, [131] and he was one of Our faithful servants. [132]

The Lesson of Prophet Lot

$\mathcal{L}$ot was also one of those who were sent. [133] We saved him and his entire family, [134] all except for an old woman who remained behind. [135] Then We destroyed the rest (of his people). [136]

You (Meccans) still pass by the (ruins of their domain on your caravan journeys) by day [137] and by night. [1508] So won't you think deeply on it? [138]

Jonah Fulfilled His Mission

$\mathcal{J}$onah was one of those sent, as well. [139] He fled (from his mission) and embarked on a crowded ship. [140] (After a storm at sea threatened to sink the ship), he (agreed) to the luck of the draw (to see which man would be thrown overboard to calm the angry sea), and he was condemned (to drown). [141] Then a huge fish swallowed him whole, for he was still to be blamed (for disobeying Allah). [142]

[1504] Elijah (Ilyas in Arabic) lived in the ninth century BCE during the reign of the Jewish kings Ahab and Ahaziah. Elijah opposed both kings (who had adopted idolatry) and who had promoted it among the Israelites. When Elijah first appeared in Israel, he convinced many of the people to believe in his message, including King Ahab. Yet, within a short time, Elijah was forced into hiding as the leaders of his people vowed to kill him (see I Kings 19:1-3). He wound up hiding in a cave, fearing for his life. See I Kings 19:10 where Elijah cries out to Allah that he is the last prophet of Allah left in the land.

[1505] The Old Testament mentions Elijah in I Kings 17-19 and II Kings 1-2. He was succeeded, according to II Kings 2:1-15, by Elisha (Al Yas'a in Arabic).

[1506] Elijah warned the people of Israel not to maintain their worship of the Babylonian god, Ba-al-im. See I Kings 18:18. The term used here, *ba'lan*, was also understood by early Muslims to mean an owner, head controller, husband, or any false god or idol, not necessarily one specific idol. Ibn 'Abbas (d. 687) held that idols in general is the proper understanding of this term (*Lisan al Arab* 13.62).

[1507] In the Arabic text, Elijah's name is mentioned here in the plural, so it would read, "Peace be upon (all) the Elijahs," which could be a poetic way of saying peace be upon all *who are like* Elijah. Other commentators explain that making the name Elijah plural is merely a linguistic technique of showing magnified status and that it still refers to the original Elijah. (*Ma'ariful Qur'an*)

[1508] There was an ancient trade route, still used by Muhammad's time, that passed along the southeastern side of the Dead Sea and steadily rose upwards. This is the area where it is commonly assumed the destroyed cities of Sodom and Gomorrah lay.

If it wasn't for his glorification of Allah, [1509] [143] then he would've surely remained inside that fish until the Day of Resurrection. [144] However, We threw him out on a deserted beach, sick and weary, [145] and We made a gourd vine grow over him (for shade.) [1510] [146]

Then We sent him (on his mission to preach) to a hundred thousand or more. [1511] [147] They believed (in what he had to say), so we allowed them to enjoy a little more time (in this world). [148]

Allah has No Children

So now ask them what they think about this. Does your Lord have only daughters, while they get to have (their coveted) sons? [149] Did they witness Us making the angels as females? [150] Aren't they making up the claim that, [151] *"Allah has given birth to children."* They're really just liars! [152]

Would He have chosen daughters rather than sons, (especially since you think sons are better)? [1512] [153] What's the matter with you? How do you figure? [154]

Won't you take a hint, [155] or do you have some clear authority (for your false ideas)? [156] So then bring your scripture if you're so honest! [157]

(Worse still), they've invented blood-ties between Him and the jinns, though the jinns themselves have already accepted (the fact) that they'll be brought back (to Him for judgment). [158] Glory be to Allah! (He's high above) what they're making Him out to be. [159]

The sincere servants of Allah, however, don't (ascribe such foolishness to Him). [160] Neither you (idol-worshippers) nor what you worship [161] can lure anyone into temptation (against Allah), [162] except for those (who let themselves fall into error) and will thus be made to enter the flames (of Hell). [163]

(The firm believers stand united together and say), *"We all have our assigned place, [164] and we're lined up, (ready for service). [165] We declare the glory (of Allah)!"* [166]

(The sinners, though), will say, [167] *"If only we would've had a message in front of our eyes like one of those from ancient (times), [168] then we*

[1509] While in the belly of the great fish (possible a large sturgeon, sea dog or sperm whale), Jonah cried out, "There is no god but You! All Glory belongs to You! I was truly wrong!" (Also see 21:87 where the possibility of being swallowed by a fish is discussed.)

[1510] The gourd vine provided squash for Jonah to eat, and its broad leaves sheltered him from the hot sun while he recuperated from his ordeal. Squash was one of Prophet Muhammad's favorite foods.

[1511] The city of Nineveh was, according to Biblical accounts, inhabited by about 120,000 persons. (See the book of Jonah in the Old Testament: 4:11) It was an early capital of the Assyrian Empire located on the eastern bank of the Tigris river in what is today called northern Iraq. Historical records from the Babylonian Empire reveal that something of the story of Jonah was remembered long after his time. The name of the Assyrian fish-god was Oannes, according to the Babylonian writer Berosus, who wrote his historical accounts in the fourth century BCE, long after the Assyrians had been vanquished. This fish-god, whom the Assyrians also knew as Dagon, is depicted as a fish with the head of a man coming out of its mouth and arms and legs coming out of the body of the fish. Obviously, the ancients over many centuries transformed a human who was swallowed by a fish into a composite of a fish-man, and this is indicative of the habit of humanity – to mythologize and warp true stories into fantastic legends. The connection is clear, however, for the Arabic name of Jonah is Yunus, an obvious relation to the Assyrian name Oannes (and the Greek New Testament uses the name Joannes for Jonah, and scholars such as Dr. Herman V. Hilprecht have made the connection between the two names). The name *Yunas* also appears in inscriptions in the ruins of old Nineveh, which were discovered under an old mound the locals had nicknamed *Nabi Yunus*, or 'the prophet Jonah.' Such was the impact of Jonah upon the imagination of Nineveh that later generations turned his story into that of a man-fish-god!

[1512] The pagans said that the angels were the daughters of Allah and that female jinns were the mothers of the angels; thus, they were Allah's concubines! This passage was revealed to address this position. (*At-Tabari*)

would surely have become sincere servants of Allah, as well." [169]

However, they're rejecting this (very Qur'an that has since come to them)! Soon they'll know (their folly)! [170] And so it was that long ago Our word was passed along to Our messenger servants [171] that they would certainly be helped [172] and that Our forces will triumph in the end. [173]

So turn away from them for a little while, [174] but watch them, for they'll soon see (who was right). [175] Do they really want to hurry on Our punishment? [176] Oh, but when it does descend before them in their own front yard - *how terrible will that morning be for the forewarned (and heedless)!* [177]

So turn away from them for a while; [178] watch them, for soon they'll see (just who was right). [1513] [179] Let your Lord be glorified, for (He's) the Lord of all majesty. (He is far above) what they're making Him out to be. [180] So, peace be upon the messengers, [181] and praise be to Allah, the Lord of All the Worlds! [1514] [182]

[1513] 'Abdul Qadir al-Jilani (d. 1166) once wrote, "If someone devotes himself completely to Allah, then He provides him with everything he needs. If a person devotes himself entirely to this world, Allah leaves him in the middle of it."

[1514] 'Ali ibn Abi Talib said, "Whoever wants to have a greater amount of reward on the Day of Judgment, let him say (the following verses) at the end of any gathering." Then he recited verses 37:180-182. (*Ibn Kathir*) These verses are often used by preachers and speakers at the end of their speeches.

Sawd

38 Sawd
Late Meccan Period

The Prophet's uncle, Abu Talib, had fallen ill and was unlikely to recover. The leaders of the Quraysh, believing that he might yet still exert some influence upon his nephew Muhammad before he passed away, approached him and asked him to intercede on their behalf. Accordingly, Abu Talib sent for Muhammad, and he arrived a short time later.

He wanted to take a seat close to his uncle's bed, but Abu Jahl prevented him. "My nephew," Abu Talib began in a raspy voice, "these people have just one request of you, so don't ignore them."

Muhammad looked at the pagan leaders in the room around him and said, "What is it?" One of the pagans said, "To let us have our gods, and we'll leave you alone with your God."

Then Abu Talib asked Muhammad, "What do you want of your people?" The Prophet said, "Just to say one statement by which all the Arabs would become obedient to them, and all the foreigners would pay tribute to them.

"Just one *statement!?*" Abu Jahl interrupted hastily, "We'll give you your one statement - and ten more like it!" Then Muhammad said, "Say that there's no god other than the One God."

The pagan became angry and shouted, "Do you deny all of our gods and say there's only one? How can one God create all these people?"

This chapter was then revealed to the Prophet, and as he recited the verses aloud, the pagans began to leave the meeting in disgust. Thus, this chapter presents us with a message of patient perseverance in the face of unreasonable and relentless opposition. The Meccan pagans took every opportunity to taunt and ridicule the Prophet and his small band of followers.

Yet, in the examples of Allah's prophets of old, who suffered tests, trials and hardships of their own, Muhammad and his followers learned that struggle and hardship were inevitable, but manageable, if they truly placed their hope in Allah's ultimate plan of victory.

In the Name of Allah,
the Compassionate, the Merciful

Sawd.

By (this) Qur'an, filled with reminders [1] - *but oh, the faithless (persist in boosting their) reputations and fomenting division!* 1515 [2] How many generations did We destroy before

---

1515 The quotes mentioned in this passage are what the leaders of the Quraysh said when they disparaged the Prophet and walked away from him in contempt. This passage was revealed in response. (*Asbab ul-Nuzul*)

them who cried out (for deliverance) when there was no longer time to be saved? [3]

So are they surprised that a warner should come to them from their own people? Yet, the faithless only say, "*Just a lying wizard!* [4] *Has he lumped all the gods together into just one God? That's a strange thing, indeed!*" [5]

Their leaders turn and leave (impatiently, saying), "*Let's get out of here. Stay true to your gods. This is what you have to do.* [6] *We've never heard anything like this from the other (religious) sect of late,* 1516 *so this is no more than an invented (religion)!* [7] *Has (Allah's) message been sent to him, out of all of us?*"

But no! They're in a quandary about My message. No way! They haven't even begun to feel My punishment! [8]

Do they control the treasures of your Lord's mercy, the Powerful and the Giving? [9] Do they have control over the heavens and the earth and everything in between? If they do, then let them climb up to (the sky) with ropes (and prove it), [10] but their hordes will be routed no matter how many allies (they bring)! [11]

Before these (Meccans here with you), there were many (other nations) who rejected their messengers: the people of Noah, of 'Ad and of Pharaoh, lord of (an army of) staked (tents), [12] and also the Thamud, the people of Lot, and the Companions of the Thicket. 1517 They were all allies (in sin). [13] There wasn't a single one of them that didn't deny the messengers, so My fitting outcome (came swiftly down upon them)! [14]

Now these (Meccans here with you now) are just waiting for that single, loud boom (signaling the Last Day)! Then there will be no further delays. [15] "*Our Lord!*" (they mockingly sneer). "*Come on and hurry up our verdict (so we can be punished even) before the Day of Account!*" [16]

The Patience of David

*H*ave patience with what they're saying. Remember (the example of) Our servant David, the sturdy one, for he always turned (to Allah). [17] We tamed the hills and made them declare Our glory along with him throughout the evening and at the rising of the day. [18]

The gathered birds turned along with him (to praise Allah), as well. 1518 [19] We strengthened his rule and granted him wisdom and common sense in his speeches. [20]

Have you ever heard the story of the arguers? They climbed over the wall of his private chamber [21] and entered into his presence.

He was startled, but they said, "*Don't be afraid!* We *have a dispute (for you to solve) involving one doing wrong against the other. Judge*

1516 Some commentators believe this verse was revealed about Abu Talib, when the other Meccan leaders advised him not to abandon the idols. (Ibn Hisham) They were already used to fighting threats to their beliefs. Indeed, a generation before Muhammad's time, the Meccans had already squashed the introduction of Christianity into Mecca for much the same reasons that they were opposing Islam now. The idol-worshippers of Mecca pointed out that such a strict monotheism, as promoted by the Qur'an, was not even taught by Christianity, the latest religion with which they had come into contact. Indeed, Christianity held that Allah was divided into three persons, each with his own name, powers, image and function, and one of whom was born as a baby and raised in a house on earth. If the well-organized religion of Christianity can have room for many gods, (after a fashion,) then how, the idol-worshippers were asking, could Islam, which just came on the scene, insist that Allah is completely without peer, partner or rival?

1517 The Companions of the Thicket were the ancient Midianites who worshipped a knotted tangle of trees.

1518 David was known for his poetic expressions of faith. The Psalms (*Zabur*) is considered a masterwork of religious and spiritual expression. Even the birds, we are told, sang the praises of Allah when he did. See Psalm 148:1-14.

between us truthfully, and don't treat us unfairly. Guide us to an even path." [22]

"This man," (the claimant continued), "is my brother. He has ninety-nine sheep, while I have only one. Yet, then he said to me, 'Hand it over to me!' and he was overbearing in his speech." [23]

(David, without even hearing the other man's side of the story, abruptly made his judgment,) saying, "He's done you wrong by demanding that your sheep be added to his flock. There are certainly many (business) partners who wrong each other, except for those who believe (in Allah) and do what's morally right, but there aren't many like that!"

Then David realized that We were testing him, and he asked forgiveness from his Lord (for rendering his verdict without hearing the other man's defense). He bowed and repented in earnest. [1519] [24] Then We forgave him for that (hastiness), and (soon) he'll have close access to Us in a wonderful place of welcome. [25]

David! We made you a caretaker on the earth, so judge between people in truth. Don't follow (your own) whims, for they'll mislead you from the path of Allah. Those who stray from the path of Allah will find a sorrowful punishment because they forgot about the Day of Account. [26]

Differing Results are Logical

*W*e didn't create the sky and the earth and everything in between them without purpose; yet, those who suppress (their faith in Allah's signs) think otherwise.

Those who reject (their awareness of Allah's truth), however, will be doomed on account of the Fire! [27]

Should We treat the believers, who do what's morally right, in the same way as those who cause chaos throughout the earth? Should We treat those who make a conscious effort (to avoid doing wrong) the same way as deviants (who do evil at every turn)? [28] This is a blessed Book that We've sent down to you, so they can ponder over its verses and so that intelligent people can be reminded. [29]

Solomon was of the Righteous

*W*e granted (a son) to David (named) Solomon, and he was an excellent servant (to his Lord) who always turned (towards Us). [30] One late afternoon a troop of fine horses was presented before him. [31] He (inspected them proudly until the sun) was veiled in darkness, (but then he realized, after a while, that he had missed his prayers). "I fell in love with the love of finery, instead of remembering my Lord!" he exclaimed. [32]

(After he performed his prayers, he returned to the courtyard and said), "Bring those (horses) back to me." Then he began to run his hands over their necks and legs (until he had admired them all). [33]

We tested Solomon when We placed a lifeless body on his throne, but then he turned (to Us in repentance), [34] saying, "My Lord! Forgive me (for being an absent-minded ruler)! [1520] Grant me a kingdom (so

---

[1519] When the Prophet recited this verse in a gathering, he prostrated, and the people in the audience did so, likewise. On another occasion he recited it, and the people stood up to prostrate, but he said, "This is the repentance of a prophet, but I see you're preparing to prostrate." Then he came down from his pulpit and prostrated. (*Abu Dawud*) All schools of thought are in agreement that when anyone reads this verse [38:24] that he or she should prostrate and praise Allah, also.

[1520] There is no definitive explanation for the meaning of this verse. However, there are several conjectures among the commentators, some of them drawn from Jewish fables. The most seemingly plausible among them is as follows. For a time Solomon ruled, but without imagination or a proactive policy. Therefore, idolatry, imported from surrounding nations, crept into Israel. In this way, he was as a "lifeless" body, until he repented to Allah and became an effective and assertive ruler again. The commentator, ar-Razi (d. 1209), explained it to mean that Solomon was so weak that he became like a

powerful) that no one after me will have one like it, for You're the One Who Grants (all things)." [35]

Then We tamed the wind for him so he could command it to flow in whatever direction he willed. [36] (We also gave him control) over demons, (including) every type of builder and (underwater) diver, [37] and even others bound in binding shackles. [38]

"This is Our gift to you, (Solomon), so whether you use it or withhold it, you won't be asked about how you used it." [39]

He will have very near access to Us in a wonderful place of welcome. [40]

The Patience of Job and Others

$\mathcal{R}$emember Our servant Job when he cried out to his Lord, *"Satan has afflicted me with anguish and suffering!"* [1521] [41]

"Stomp (the ground) with your foot," (the order came). *"There's a spring (below you) to wash yourself and to drink."* [42] Then We restored to him his family and doubled their number as a mercy from Us, and that's something thoughtful people should remember. [43]

"(Job), take a bunch (of grass) [1522] in your hand, and hit (your wife) with that, (instead of your hand), so you won't have to break (the foolish oath you made in anger during your days of hardship)." [1523] We found him to be truly patient and persevering, and He was an excellent servant, for he always turned (to Us). [44]

Remember Our servants, Abraham, Isaac, and Jacob who possessed ability and clear vision. [1524] [45] We chose them specifically to remind (their people) of (their ultimate) home (in the next life). [46]

They were each in Our sight and were among the chosen and exceptional. [47] Also remember Ishmael, [1525] Elisha and

---

skeleton and took no interest in his affairs. The Old Testament (I Kings 11:1-6) records that in his old age, Solomon became overly infatuated with his alleged 700 wives and 300 concubines and thus let idolatry creep into the land, even into his own practice. This would explain the "lifeless body" reference. However, Muslim theologians would disagree that Solomon would have been so corrupted by such things as idols, preferring rather to assert that he had become distracted with this worldly life (as in the horses incident in verses 38:31-33) and ineffectual in his rule before repenting to Allah of those lapses.

[1521] The Hebrew Bible records that the Devil made a challenge with Allah that he could corrupt Job, Allah's most ardent servant. Therefore, Allah allowed him to do his worst to Job. (See Job 1:7-12.) The Prophet explained that Job suffered for eighteen long years before finally proving his faith was complete. He lost his children and fortune during that time and was afflicted with sickness. When Allah removed his trial, he showered Job with good fortune, new children and good health.

[1522] The Arabic word used here to describe the size of the grass bundle that he was to take is *dighthan*, which means a bunch or a bouquet. Thus, it was a flimsy amount of grass that could be held by a lightly closed hand.

[1523] In the Hebrew Bible we learn that Job was patient when afflicted with suffering but that his wife was bitter and even taunted him. (See Job 2:9-10). Islam has a different take on her behavior, finding her more noble than that. Commentators of this verse, using traditions of the Prophet to guide them, have understood that during the darkest hour of his affliction, Job, in his frustration with his wife (when she was apparently tricked by Satan into saying something spiteful to him), swore that he would hit her 100 times with a stick if he ever recovered from the loss of his children, health and fortune. (*Ahmad*) During his many years of suffering, however, his wife remained by his side and cared for him, so how could he keep such a foolish oath? When Allah blessed him with more than he had before (as a reward for his patience,) Job felt remorseful for his hasty promise. Allah gave Job a way to fulfill his oath without actually physically hurting his wife, as no prophet of Allah would ever hurt a woman so. Thus, he would hit her with "a few harmless blades of grass." (*Ibn Kathir*)

[1524] The addendum to Jacob here, mentioning that he possessed ability and clear vision, is a reference to verses 12:67-68 and 12:96.

[1525] In addition to being a prophet, Ishmael had another talent, as well. Once when the Prophet was passing by some people of Medina practicing archery, he said to them, "Shoot, you sons of Ishmael,

Ezekiel; each one of them was exceptional, as well. [48]

The Reward and Punishment of Our Choices

*T*his is a reminder, and those who were mindful (of Allah) will certainly find themselves in a beautiful place of welcome [49] - in everlasting gardens whose doors will be open for them. [50] They'll relax within and call for loads of fruits and drinks. [51]

In their presence, they'll have bashful (attendants) of equal age. [52] This is the promise that's been made to you for the Day of Account. [53] This is what We'll provide to you, and it's (a reward that will) never run out. [54]

That's it! However, the disobedient will find themselves in a terrible place of welcome [55] - Hellfire! They'll burn in it, and what an evil bed (upon which to rest)! [56] That's it! They'll feel it, the scalding water and icy dark muck [57] and other tortures, as well! [58]

"Here's another group rushing head first along with you! There's no greeting here for them! They're certainly going to burn in the Fire!" [59]

(Those who were misled will cry out to those who mislead them), *"No way! There's no greeting here for you either! You brought this down upon us! What a vile place in which to stay!"* [60]

Then they'll say, *"Our Lord! Whoever brought this upon us, double their punishment in the Fire!"* [61]

They'll also say, *"What's the matter with us? Why don't we see here the people we used to think of as bad? [62] Didn't we laugh at them? Is it that our eyes just don't see them?"* [63]

Isn't that the truth! The people of the Fire pointing fingers at each other! [64]

Muhammad is no More than a Warner

*S*ay (to them), *"Truly, I am a warner, and there is no god except Allah, the One and Irresistible, [65] Lord of the heavens and the earth and all in between, the Powerful and Forgiving."* [1526] [66]

Then tell (them), *"This is a serious prophetic message, [67] and yet you're just turning away from it! [68] I don't know what the (angels) up above are saying when they talk amongst themselves (about the fate of human beings). [69] All that I've been inspired to do is to warn (everyone) as clearly as possible."* [70]

Iblis Makes a Challenge

*Y*our Lord said to the angels, *"I'm going to create mortal humans from clay. [71] After I've formed him completely and then breathed into him of My spirit, you must all fall down prostrate before him."* [72]

So all the angels fell down together in prostration, [73] but (a jinn named) Iblis did not (join in), for he became proud and lost his faith. [74]

(Allah) asked him, *"Iblis! Why haven't you prostrated yourself to a being that I've created with My Own hands? Are you too proud, or are you so high and mighty?"* [75]

"I'm better than him," (Iblis) answered, *"You made me from fire, while You made him from clay."* [76]

---

for your father was an archer." (*Bukhari*) Also see Genesis 21:20, which also mentions Ishmael's skill with a bow.

[1526] The Meccan chiefs used to taunt the Prophet, asking him all kinds of questions about people's secrets, their futures and other such things. This passage tells the Prophet to inform them clearly that Allah is not giving him those kinds of secrets. Rather, Allah sent him to warn people and reform their conduct and belief.

"Get out of here," (Allah) commanded, *"for you shall be an outcast!* [77] *My curse will mark you until the Day of Judgment!"* [78]

"My Lord!" (Iblis) cried. *"Give me time until the day You resurrect (them)."* [79]

"You shall have your time," (Allah) replied, [80] *"until the day the scheduled event comes to pass."* [81]

"Then," Iblis said, *"by the token of Your Own Power, know that I'm going to seduce them all,* [82] *except for Your sincere servants, of course."* [83]

"Then that's the truth of it, and what I say is true," (Allah) declared. [84] *"I will fill Hellfire with you and all who follow you, all together."* [85]

Say (to them), *"I'm not asking you for any reward for this (preaching), nor am I some kind of pretender.* [86] *This is no less than a reminder to all the worlds,* [87] *and you're going to know the truth of it, after some time has passed."* [88]

The Crowds

39 Az-Zumar
Middle Meccan Period

This majority of the verses in this chapter were revealed before the immigration to Abyssinia (in the year 615) of a large company of Muslim refugees fleeing persecution in Mecca. The clue is in verse ten where the believers are told that "Allah's earth is wide." Verses 52-54, however, were revealed in the early Medinan period. The main subject matter revolves around issues of the next life and how Allah will classify and sort people according to their faith and deeds. A'ishah reported that the Prophet would recite this chapter (along with chapter 17) every night. (*Ahmad, Nisa'i*)

In the Name of Allah,
the Compassionate, the Merciful

The revelation of this Book is from Allah, the Powerful and the Wise. [1] We've revealed this Book to you in all truth, so serve Allah sincerely, for He owns all religion. [2]   To whom is sincere devotion due, if not to Allah?

Those who take protectors other than Allah (say), "*We're only serving (the idols) so they can bring us closer to Allah.*"

Allah will certainly judge between them in their disagreements, and Allah doesn't guide any who lie or reject (the truth). [3]

If Allah had wanted to take a son for Himself, He could've chosen anyone out of all the beings He created. Let Him be glorified!   He is Allah, the One, the Irresistible! [4] He created the heavens and the earth for a truthful purpose.

He coils the night upon the day and coils the day upon the night. He tamed the sun and the moon, and each one follows a specific orbit. Isn't He the Powerful and Forgiving One? [5]

Who Needs Whom?

He created all of you from a single soul, and from it He created its mate. [1527] He sent down for you the eight types of livestock (animals) in pairs (of male and female). [1528]

He creates you in your mothers' wombs in stages that follow in sequence, (protected) under three veils of darkness.

[1527] Adam was the first human being, and his spouse was Eve, or *Hawwa*. Men and women share many similarities, both biological and physical, though they are not exactly alike. Prophet Muhammad once remarked, "Women are the twin-halves of men." (*Abu Dawood*)

[1528] The eight types are bovines (cows or oxen), sheep, goats and camels, a male and female of each. Thus, there are eight types of herd animals or "cattle" from which humanity derives benefit (even to this day). A distinction is made between male and female herd animals because each has its own special qualities: a female cow gives milk, while a male cow (bull or ox) is used to plow, etc...

[1529] That's (the work of) Allah, your Lord. All dominion belongs to Him, and there is no god besides Him, so why do you turn away? [6]

If you reject (Him, then know that) Allah doesn't need you at all. [1530] However, He's not pleased that His servants should be so thankless. Thus, if you're grateful (for all that He's done for your benefit), then He'll be pleased with you.

No soul can bear the burdens of another, and in the end you're going to go back to your Lord. Then He's going to tell you the meaning of everything you did, *and He knows the innermost secrets of the heart.* [7]

When a human being feels the effects of some misfortune (upon his life), he cries to his Lord in earnest.

Yet, when He directs some favor of His Own towards him, (the person) forgets all about what he cried for (the day) before!

Then he sets up rivals with Allah in order to mislead others away from His path.

Say (to such a person), *"Enjoy your rejection (of the truth) for a while, but in the end you'll be among the companions of the Fire!"* [8]

Serving Allah without Hesitation

The one who is devoted to Allah, who prostrates and stands (in devotion) throughout the night, who is cognizant of the (seriousness) of the next life and who desires the mercy of his Lord, (is that kind of noble person equal to someone who does the opposite)?

Ask them, *"Are they equal, the ones who know and the ones who don't know?"* Only the thoughtful are influenced by reminders. [9]

(Muhammad), tell them (that I have said), *"My believing servants! Be mindful of your Lord! Good is for those who do good in this world.* [1531] *Allah's earth is wide (so you always have somewhere to go to escape evil)! Those who patiently persevere will certainly be given a reward without limit!"* [10]

Say (to them), *"I am indeed commanded to serve Allah sincerely, for He owns all religion.* [11] *I'm commanded to be the first among those who surrender to Allah."* [12]

Then say, *"If I ever disobeyed my Lord, then I would be terrified of the punishment on a momentous day."* [13]

Then tell (them), *"I serve Allah sincerely, for He owns my religion.* [14] *So go ahead and worship whatever else you want to besides Him."*

Then say, *"The real losers are those who will lose their own souls and the souls of their families on the Day of Assembly! Oh, how clearly a loss that will be!"* [15]

There will be layers of fire above them and layers (of fire) below them. This is (the imagery) that Allah uses to scare His servants (into taking His warning seriously). *"My servants! Be mindful of Me!"* [16]

The Righteous shall Prevail

Those who shunt falsehood aside, and thus avoid becoming its servants, and who turn themselves towards Allah - *good*

[1529] There are, in fact, three protective layers shielding the developing child in the darkened, yet vibrantly alive, womb: (a) the anterior abdominal wall, (b) the uterine wall, and (c) the amniochorionic membrane.

[1530] The Prophet said that Allah, Himself, said, "My servants, if the first and the last of you, from both humans and jinns, all acted as evil as the most evil one among you, it wouldn't take away anything at all from My absolute dominion." (*Muslim*)

[1531] This line is echoed in verse 2:201, and it is put in the form of a supplication there.

news for them! [1532] So give the good news to those who would serve (Allah). [17]

They're the ones who listen to this speech and follow the best of it. They're the ones who've been guided by Allah, and they're the thoughtful ones. [18]

(Consider this question): is the one who had the verdict of punishment legitimately leveled against him (equal to the one who will be saved)? Can you rescue someone like that from the Fire? [19]

However, lofty mansions with rivers flowing throughout have been built exclusively for those who were mindful of their Lord. (This is what) Allah has promised, and Allah never breaks a promise! [20]

Don't you see that Allah sends down water from the sky and leads it through sources in the ground; then He uses (such groundwater) to produce the multi-colored plants?

Then it all withers; then you see it turning pale yellow, and then ultimately He dries it all into crumbled dust. There is definitely a reminder in this for the thoughtful (to reflect upon). [21]

This Message is Serious

*I*s the one who's had his understanding so broadened [1533] by Allah that he surrendered (his will to Him), and who's been enlightened by His Lord, (equal to someone whose mind is closed to it)? Ruin to those whose hearts have been hardened against the remembrance of Allah! They're clearly in the wrong. [22]

The Qur'an is the Best Reminder

*A*llah has revealed the best narration in the form of a book that retains harmony with itself, even as it repeats (its teachings in many different ways). [1534] Those who fear their Lord tremble in their skins, from (understanding its true significance).

Then their skins and their hearts soften towards the remembrance of Allah. This is Allah's guidance, and He guides whomever He wants with it. For those whom Allah leaves to stray, there can be no one to guide such a one! [23]

Is the one who must be wary of the worst penalty on the Day of Assembly, being made to lie down on his face, (equal to someone who will be safe that day)? The oppressors will be told, "*Suffer for what you've earned!*" [24]

Those who came before them also denied (Allah's truth), and so the punishment came upon them from where they least expected it. [25]

Allah gave them a taste of humiliation in the life of this world, but far greater is the punishment of the next life, if they only knew! [26]

And so We've laid out for people in this Qur'an every kind of example, so they can get the message. [27] This is a Qur'an (expressed) in the best form of the Arabic

---

[1532] It is thought that this passage was revealed concerning the righteousness of three especially noble companions: Abu Dharr al-Ghifari, Salman al-Farsi and Zayd ibn 'Amr ibn Nufayl - the last of whom was known for his piety even before the coming of Islam. (*Ma'ariful Qur'an*)

[1533] This passage is a reference to the Prophet's teenage cousin, 'Ali ibn Abi Talib, and his uncle Hamza, who both accepted Islam. On the flip side, his other uncle, Abu Lahab, and Abu Lahab's son rejected it. (*Ibn Kathir*)

[1534] A man went to the Prophet and asked him to recite something of the Qur'an for him. This verse was revealed in response. (*Asbab ul-Nuzul*) Asma', the daughter of Abu Bakr, once quoted this verse and explained that this was the constant state of the companions, for whenever they heard the words of the Qur'an being recited, they softened their hearts, began to weep, and felt their hair standing on end. (*Qurtubi*)

language, so they can be cognizant (of its truth.) [28]

Now Allah lays out the example of a man who belongs to many partners, all with conflicting agendas, as opposed to a man who belongs entirely to one master.

Are both examples equally similar? All praise be to Allah! But no! Most (people) don't know (the difference). [29]

It's a fact that you will die and also a fact that they will die. [30] Then all of you will settle your disputes on the Day of Assembly in the presence of your Lord. [31]

So who's doing more wrong than the one who says a lie against Allah and who denies the honest (truth) when it's presented to him? Isn't Hellfire the residence of those who rejected (the truth)? [32]

The one who brings the honest (truth) and the one who affirms it are the ones who are mindful (of their duty to Allah). [33]

They're going to have everything they ever wanted in the presence of their Lord, for that's the reward of the good [34] – (and they're rewarded) so that Allah can erase from (their record) the worst of what they ever did and reward them according to the best of what they ever did. [35]

Fear no Idols of Wood or Stone

$\mathcal{I}$sn't Allah enough for His servants? Yet, (the idol-worshippers) try to scare you with others besides Him! [1535]

For those whom Allah leaves astray, there can be no one to guide such a one, [36] and whomever Allah guides, there can be no one to lead such a one astray. Isn't Allah powerful enough to be a master at retribution? [37]

Allah is Your Only Rightful Lord

$\mathcal{I}$f you asked them: "*Who created the heavens and the earth?*" they would (be quick) to say, "*Allah.*" So tell them, "*Now look here - all those (goddesses) that you call upon besides Allah - if Allah wanted to penalize me in some way, could they avert His punishment? If He wanted to grant me some kind of mercy, could they hold His mercy back?*" Then say to them, "*Allah is quite enough for me, and those who would trust (in something) should trust in Him.*" [38]

Tell them, "*My people! Do whatever you can (to hinder me), and I will likewise act (in my capacity), but soon you're going to know* [39] *who will get a disgraceful punishment – and upon whom an enduring punishment will descend.*" [40]

We've revealed this Book to you in all truth (as a guide) for people. The one who accepts this guidance does so for the good of his own soul, while the one who veers away (from it) only harms his own soul. You're not responsible for (which path) they (choose). [41]

Allah is the One Who collects (all) souls at the time of death, and (He collects) the souls of those who are asleep, even though they're not dead. [1536] Then He holds back the souls of those whom He

---

[1535] The idolaters of Mecca used to threaten the Prophet, saying that the idols would cause him harm if he continued to speak against them. This passage was revealed in response. (*Ma'ariful Qur'an*)

[1536] In Islamic parlance, sleep is considered something of a preview of death. When you sleep, you are present but not present. When the Prophet was asked if the people in Paradise ever sleep, he replied: "No, for sleep is the brother of death." (Reported in *Al Kashf* of *ath-Thalabi*) The Prophet said on another occasion, "When any of you goes to bed, let him brush down the bed with his garment, for he doesn't know what's come on his bed since he left it. Then let him say, 'In Your Name, Lord, I lay down on my side, and in Your Name, I will rise back up. If You take my soul, have mercy on it. If you send it back, protect it with what You use to protect Your righteous servants." (*Bukhari, Muslim*)

decreed must die, but the rest He returns (to their slumbering bodies) for a fixed time limit. There are signs in this for people who think. [42]

Are they taking (demigods and saints) for intercessors besides Allah? Ask them, *"(Are you doing that) even though they have no power or understanding?"* [43] Then say to them, *"It's Allah's exclusive (right to choose someone to be) an intercessor, for the control of the heavens and the earth belongs to Him, and then you're all going to go back to Him."* [44]

When the One God is mentioned, the hearts of the faithless, who suppress (their belief in the existence) of the next life, become filled with revulsion, but when other (names) are mentioned besides His - *oh, how overjoyed they get!* [45]

Pray then, *"O Allah! Originator of the heavens and the earth! Knower of the unseen and the clear! You're the One Who will judge between Your servants in that which they differ."* [1537] [46]

If the wrongdoers had everything on earth - *and even more besides* - they would try to offer it as a bribe (to escape) the worst punishment on the Day of Assembly. However, what they didn't expect from Allah will confront them (face to face)! [47]

The terrible nature of what they've earned will confront them, and they'll be completely surrounded by what they used to ridicule! [48]

Weak Human Nature

*W*henever some setback afflicts a human being, he cries out to Us (for help), but when We grant him one of Our favors, he says, *"This (success) has been given to me from my own knowledge (and skill)."* Not so! It's all just a test, but most of them don't understand. [49] This is (how the nations) who came before them boasted, but nothing they did (on their own) ever brought them any benefit. [50]

On the contrary, the bad consequences of what they earned overtook them, even as they're going to overtake the wrongdoers here (before you now) because of what they've earned. They'll never be able to thwart Us! [51] Don't they know that Allah increases or restricts the resources of anyone He wants? There are certainly signs in this for people who believe. [52]

Don't Despair of Allah's Mercy even upon Sinners

O Prophet!) [1538] Tell (people that I, Myself, have said), *"All My servants who have acted excessively against their own souls! Don't lose hope of Allah's mercy, for Allah can forgive all sins. He truly is the Forgiving and the Merciful!* [1539] [53] *Turn towards your Lord, and surrender to*

A shorter bedtime supplication, which also comes from the Prophet, is to say, "O Allah, in Your Name I die, and I live." (*Bukhari*)

[1537] One famous early Muslim by the name of Ibn Jubayr, who was a student of the surviving companions in later days, was of the opinion that a prayer to Allah coupled with the recitation of this verse would be sure to be answered. (*Ma'ariful Qur'an*)

[1538] There were some Meccans who wanted to accept Islam, but they had indulged in very wicked behavior in their lives before, having murdered people, committed adultery, theft and other crimes. They felt that their sins were too enormous for Allah to forgive merely by their accepting Islam. "How can we become Muslims when we did all that?" one of them even asked. Just after the Muslims migrated to Medina, the concerns of such sympathetic but despairing Meccans were discussed by many. These verses were revealed, and 'Umar ibn al Khattab, who knew how to write, wrote them on a paper and sent it secretly back to Mecca. The first person who read it was a man named Hisham who said in later days, "I took it and went to (a place named) Thitawa, and I asked Allah to make me understand it. When I realized it was for us, I returned to where my mount was tethered and resolved to follow the Prophet." Many others also joined Islam and made their way to Medina.

[1539] Ibn 'Abbas (d. 687) said that this verse also applies to Jews and Christians, the first of which called themselves as Allah's only beloved people and the second of which worshipped a man as god.

Him before the punishment overwhelms you, for then you'll have no one to help you." [54]

"Follow the best of what's being revealed to you from your Lord before the punishment overwhelms you all of a sudden without your even realizing what's happening, [55] *for then your soul will cry out, 'I'm doomed! I neglected my duty to Allah, and I scoffed!'* [56]

"Or it might cry out, 'If only Allah had guided me, I would surely have been one of the mindful.' [57] *Or it might cry out, the moment it sees the punishment approaching, 'If only I had a second chance, I would surely be with those who are good.'"* [58]

"But no! My signs came to you, and you denied them! You were arrogant, and you tried to cover (the truth that was all around you)." [59]

On the Day of Assembly, you're going to see those who told lies against Allah with darkened faces. Isn't Hellfire the residence of the arrogant? [60]

Allah will deliver those who were mindful (of Him) to their ultimate achievement. Nothing bad will touch them, nor will they have any cause for sorrow. [61]

Allah is the Creator of all things, and He manages all affairs. [62]

The keys of the heavens and the earth belong to Him. Whoever rejects the signs of Allah, they'll be the ones who lose. [63]

Don't Add Partners with Allah

$\mathcal{A}$sk them, *"Are you foolish people ordering me to serve someone other than (the One True) God?* [64] *You've already been given the revelation - the same (revelation) that (nations) before you got, namely that if you join (false gods with the One True God), your life's work will be a waste, and you'll be placed with the losers.* [65] *By no means! Serve Allah, and be among the thankful."* [66]

Don't Underestimate Allah

$\mathcal{T}$hey haven't estimated (the power of) Allah (to the extent) that (His power) should be considered. [1540] On the Day of Assembly, the entire earth will be but a handful to Him, and the heavens will be rolled up in His right hand (like a scroll). All glory is His! He's high above the 'partners' they assign to Him! [67]

The Arrival of Judgment Day

$\mathcal{T}$he trumpet will be blown, and then every creature in the heavens and on the earth will faint, save for any whom Allah will (exempt). [1541]

Then a second note will sound, and all of a sudden, they'll be standing right there all together, staring (in disbelief)! [68]

The earth will shine with the light of its Lord, and the Record will be set at the

---

[1540] A rabbi came to visit the Prophet and told him, "Did you know, O father of Qasim, that Allah holds all creatures on one finger, the earth and sky on another finger, the trees on another finger, and the soil on another finger? Then He says, 'I am the King.'" Then the Prophet smiled wide. This verse was then revealed in response making the case that Allah is even more exalted than that. (*Asbab ul-Nuzul*)
[1541] An angel named Israfil will blow the proverbial "trumpet" signaling the end of time and the beginning of Judgment Day. This "blast" will echo through the world with such force that all living things in the sky and on the earth will faint and die, even the angels will swoon and die. Israfil will be exempted, as he has to blow the trumpet once more, after which all living beings with a soul and a responsibility to Allah will be standing in arranged rows, waiting for their turn to receive their verdict from Allah. The angels will revive, as well.

ready. Prophets and witnesses will be brought forward (to give their testimony), and decisions will be made in all truth between them (and their people). No one will be wronged even in the slightest, [69] and every soul will be paid back for its deeds. He knows best what they did. [70]

A Tale of Two Crowds

*T*hose who suppressed (their faith in Allah) will be led towards Hellfire in crowds, (and they'll march along) until they arrive at its gates, which will be opened. Its guards will ask, *"Didn't any messengers ever come to you from among you, who spoke of the signs of your Lord, and warned you of the meeting of this day of yours?"*

(The guardians of Hellfire will then answer their own question), saying, *"Definitely (they did)! The order of punishment has been proven true against the faithless."* [71]

Then (the sinners) will be told, *"Enter the gates of Hell, and stay there. Oh, how terrible is the home of the arrogant!"* [72]

Meanwhile, those who were mindful of their Lord will be escorted towards the Garden in crowds, (and they'll stroll along) until they arrive at its gates, which will be opened. Its guards will announce, *"Peace be upon you! You've done well, so enter here and remain."* [1542] [73]

(As they go in, the righteous) will say, *"Praise be to Allah, the One Who fulfilled His promise to us, and Who gave us this land as our inheritance. We can now settle in the Garden as we wish. Oh, how excellent a reward for those who worked (hard)!"* [1543] [74]

You're also going to see the angels surrounding the throne on all sides, glorifying and praising their Lord. (On Judgment Day all) shall receive an honest verdict, and (those who will enter Paradise will lift up their voices) and cry, *"Praise be to Allah, the Lord of All the Worlds!"* [75]

[1542] The Prophet said, "I will come to the gate of Paradise on the Day of Judgment and will ask for it to be opened. The gatekeeper will ask, 'Who are you?' I will answer, 'Muhammad.' He will say, 'I was told about you and that I wasn't to open the gate for anyone before you.'" (*Ahmad*) The Prophet also said that Paradise has eight gates and that each gate is named for a particular virtue or good deed, such as *struggling in Allah's cause, charity, prayer* or *fasting* (this last gate is called the Gate of *Rayan*). Abu Bakr asked the Prophet if there would be any people who could enter through any gate they chose, and the Prophet replied in the affirmative and said he hoped that he (Abu Bakr) would be one of them. (*Ahmad*) The Prophet also mentioned that the distance between each of the gates of Paradise was the distance of a forty-year journey. (*Muslim*)

[1543] The Prophet once told a gathering, "A group from my community numbering seventy thousand will enter Paradise with their faces shining like the moon on a night when it's full." A man named 'Ukaashah ibn Mihsan stood up and said, "Messenger of Allah, pray to Allah to make me one of them." The Prophet said, "O Allah, make him one of them." Then a man from the Helpers stood up and said, "Messenger of Allah, pray to Allah to make me one of them, too." The Prophet answered, "'Ukaashah has beaten you to it." (*Bukhari, Muslim*)

The Forgiver

40 Al Ghafir
(aka Al Mu'min)
Late Meccan Period

This chapter begins a series of seven chapters that all start with the abbreviated letters, *Ha Meem*. The early Muslims considered these seven chapters to be a very special portion of the Qur'an. Ibn 'Abbas (d. 687) said the *Ha Meems* were the essence of the Qur'an. 'Abdullah ibn Mas'ud (d. 653) said, "When I reach the family of *Ha Meem*, it's like reaching a beautiful garden, so I take my time." Some people used to call these chapters "the brides," and more than one early scholar likened them to a family or a refreshing destination. The recurring theme in this series is the importance of faith and how it can overcome disbelief. Accordingly, there is a generous mix of examples from previous peoples, as well as vivid arguments to convince the listener that the next life is a concrete reality. These seven chapters present something of an extended argument for non-believers to consider – almost in a way that gives them an opportunity to look at the issues from a variety of perspectives.

In the Name of Allah,
the Compassionate, the Merciful

Ḥā. Meem. [1]

The revelation of this Book is from Allah, the Powerful and the Knowing. [2]

(He) erases sins, accepts repentance, punishes sternly and towers over (all others). There is no god but He, and to Him is the ultimate conclusion. [3]

Arguments can Lead to Disbelief

*N*o one argues about the signs of Allah, except for those who cover (their capacity to believe in Him). [1544] So don't let their seeming ability to do whatever they want in the land fool you! [4] Before them, other people denied (the truth), like the people of Noah and all the allies of evil who followed after them.

Every community plotted against their prophet in an effort to take hold of him [1545]

[1544] One day the Prophet found two companions arguing over the meaning of a Qur'anic verse in an overly aggressive way. He became angry and told them that nations before their time were ruined because of that kind of quarrelling. The first part of this verse was revealed to comment upon that. The second sentence of this verse refers to the pagans of Mecca who were still able to make their lucrative caravan journeys despite the rising power of Islam. (*Ma'ariful Qur'an*)

[1545] The Prophet was praying near the Ka'bah, and a pagan man named 'Uqbah ibn Abi Muaty happened along and found him there. He became so angry at seeing the Prophet deep in prayer that he took a cloth he was carrying, wrapped it around Muhammad's neck from behind and proceeded to

or engaged him in endless argument using fallacious logic in their quest to refute the truth. However, it was I Who took hold of them, *and, oh, how (severe) was My retribution!* [5] Thus, the sentence of your Lord was carried out against the faithless that they'll be companions of the Fire! [6]

The (angels), who uphold the throne (of Allah), and those who encircle about it glorify the praises of their Lord. They believe in Him and ask forgiveness for those who believe (on earth).

"Our Lord," (they pray), *"You encompass everything with mercy and knowledge, so forgive those who repent and those who follow Your path. Save them from the punishment of the raging blaze!"* [7]

"Our Lord, let them enter the eternal Garden that You've promised to them, along with the righteous among their parents, spouses and descendants! [1546] *Truly, You are the Powerful and the Wise,* [8] *so protect them from hardship! Anyone whom You protect from hardship on the Day (of Judgment) will have indeed received mercy from You, and that's the greatest success!"* [9]

Hellfire is Earned

The faithless (residing in Hellfire) will be told, *"Allah is more disgusted with you than you're disgusted with yourselves, given that you had been called to faith and you refused it."* [10]

"Our Lord," they'll reply. *"You made us exist twice without life and twice with life! Now that we know we did wrong, is there any way out of here?"* [11]

"This is what you get," (they'll be told), *"because when the call was (made to believe) in the* One God, you rejected it, but when 'partners' were added to Him, you believed, even though it's Allah's exclusive right (to be believed in, for He's) the Most High and Most Great." [12]

He's the One Who shows you His signs and sends down resources for you from the sky, but the only ones who reflect upon this are those who incline (towards their Lord). [13]

Call upon Allah sincerely, for He owns all religion, no matter how much the faithless may hate it. [14] Higher in status than all others, (Allah is) the Lord of the throne. He sends the Spirit (i.e., Angel Gabriel) by His command to any of His servants that He wills, so (the chosen messenger) can warn people about the Day of the Encounter. [15]

(That's) the day when they'll emerge (from their graves). There won't be anything at all about them that will be hidden from Allah. So who's going to be in charge that day? It will be Allah's (day alone), the One, the Irresistible! [16]

That day every soul will be paid back for what it earned, and there won't be any unfairness on that day, for Allah is quick to settle accounts. [17] So warn them of the day that's fast approaching, (the day) when (people's) hearts will leap up to their throats and gag them. The wrongdoers will have no sympathizers nor intercessors who will be heard. [18]

He knows every trick of the eye and every secret hidden in the mind. [19] Allah (won't be fooled by such antics), but will rather judge truthfully. Those whom (people) called upon besides Him won't be able to judge at all! Truly, Allah is the Hearing and the Watchful. [20]

---

strangle him. Abu Bakr was passing by, and he stopped in horror when he saw what was happening. He rushed at 'Uqbah and wrestled with him, saying, "Will you kill a man just because he says, 'Allah is my Lord!'" Then 'Uqbah scampered away. (*Bukhari*)

[1546] Sa'id ibn Jubayr explained this verse by saying that when a believer enters into Paradise, he will ask about his parents, children and siblings, wanting to know where they are. He will be told, "They didn't reach the same level of good deeds that you did." Then the believer will say, "But I did all of them for my sake and for theirs." Then they will all be brought to join him in that higher level of Paradise. (*Ibn Kathir*)

The Lesson of the Pharaoh's Arrogance

$\mathcal{H}$aven't they traveled all over the world and seen how (the civilizations) that came before them were ended? (Those past nations) were stronger than they in might, and yet in the ruins they left behind throughout the world, (you can see) how Allah seized them for their sins, *and they had no defense against Allah.* [21]

That (fate was bound to befall them) because messengers were sent to them, bringing clear evidence (of the truth); yet, they rejected them. Thus, Allah took hold of them, and He is indeed mighty and stern in bringing about final conclusions. [22]

And so it was that We sent Moses with Our signs and a clear mandate [23] to Pharaoh, Haman and Korah, but they said, "*A lying wizard.*" [24] When he went to them in all truth, (the Pharaoh and his men) said, "*Kill the sons of those who believe with him, but keep their females alive,*" but the plans of the faithless always go awry. [25]

Pharaoh then said (to his court attendants), "*Leave me to kill Moses. Just let him try and call upon his Lord (for help)! I'm only afraid that he might convert you away from your religion or that he might cause dissension in the land.*" [26]

"*I've called upon my Lord,*" Moses answered him, "*(to protect me) from every arrogant (tyrant) who disbelieves in the Day of Account.*" [27]

A believing man from among Pharaoh's family, who had been hiding his faith, came forward and asked, "*Are you going to kill a man simply because he says, 'My Lord is Allah' - especially since he's come to you with clear evidence from your Lord? If he's lying, then his lie will be on him, but if he's telling the truth, then some of the (consequences) that he's promised you will befall you. Allah gives no guidance to outrageous liars. [28] My people! You have control (over a kingdom) today and are*

ascendant in the earth, but who will help us against the penalty of Allah if it ever came upon us?*"

"*I see nothing but that which I see,*" Pharaoh answered. "*I'm doing nothing more than guiding you correctly.*" [29]

Then the one who believed said, "*My people! I fear that a similar fate might befall you like the day that befell the allies (of sin), [30] something like (what befell) the peoples of Noah or 'Ad or Thamud and all those who came after them, though Allah never wills injustice to His servants.*" [31]

"*My people! I fear for you the Day of Summoning [32] - a day when you'll turn and run (for your lives). You'll have no defense against Allah, and whomever Allah leaves astray, there is no one who can guide him. [33] And so it was that long before, Joseph had come to you with clear evidence, but you never stopped doubting (the reason) why he had come. When he passed away, you said, 'Allah won't raise up any more messengers after him.' This is how Allah let's outrageous doubters go astray.*" [34]

Those who quibble over the signs of Allah without being given any authority (to debate them) - oh, how greatly hated is that in Allah's sight - even as the faithful (hate it, as well). This is how Allah seals up the hearts of every arrogant oppressor! [35]

"*Haman!*" Pharaoh commanded, "*Build for me a tall tower so I can find a way [36] - a way to reach up and enter into the heavens, so I'll be able to rise up to the God of Moses. As for me, I think he's a liar.*"

Thus, Pharaoh's awful deeds seemed justified in his eyes. He was blocked from the path (of Allah), and whatever Pharaoh planned brought him nothing but ruin. [37]

The one who believed declared, "*My people! Follow me, and I'll lead you to the right way. [38] My people! The life of this world is nothing more than a passing convenience, while the next life is the realm of permanence. [39] Whoever works for evil will be paid back with nothing but the same. Whoever behaves in a moral fashion, whether a man or a woman, and then has faith, they're the ones who will enter the Garden and have resources without end.*" [40]

"My people," (he continued), *"Why am I calling you to salvation, while you're calling me to the Fire?* [41] *You're calling for me to reject Allah and to make partners with Him - adopting things that I know nothing about — even as I'm calling you (to believe) in the Powerful and the Forgiving One!"* [42]

"You're blatantly calling me to (pray to) something that has no legitimacy for receiving supplication, neither in this life nor in the next. Our only (legitimate) appeal is to Allah, and those who are outrageous (in their claims) will be companions of the Fire! [43] *Soon you'll remember what I'm saying to you now. I'm placing my affair with Allah, for indeed Allah watches over His servants."* [44]

Then Allah saved him from whatever harm they planned against him, and the reality of the (ultimate) punishment will soon surround the people of Pharaoh. [45] They'll be brought in front of the Fire from morning to evening on the day when the Hour (of Judgment) will be established. *"Admit the people of Pharaoh into the worst torment!"* [46]

Then they're going to argue with each other (as they're being marched into) the Fire. The weak-minded followers will say to their arrogant (leaders), *"But we followed you (willingly)! Can't you take some of our burden of fire from us?"* [47]

"We're all in this together," the arrogant (leaders) will reply, *"and Allah has indeed made judgments among (His) servants."* [48] Then those who are (plunged) into the Fire will plead with the wardens of Hell, *"Call upon your Lord to ease the punishment for us - (at least) for a day!"* [49]

"Didn't any messengers ever come to you with clear evidence?" (the wardens) will ask. *"Absolutely,"* (the damned) will reply. *"Then call out as much as you like,"* (the wardens) will say, *"for what is the call of the faithless except mistaken (hopes)!"* [50]

We're going to aid Our messengers and the believers in this worldly life, as well as on the day when the witnesses will stand (forth to testify). [1547] [51] (That) day the wrongdoers will gain nothing from their excuses and will instead be left with a curse and a terrible home. [52]

Accountability is the Only Constant

And so it was that We gave guidance to Moses, and We let the Children of Israel inherit (it as a) Scripture, [53] to be a source of guidance and a remembrance for (people) who use their intellect. [54]

So patiently persevere, for Allah's promise is true. Ask forgiveness for your shortcomings, and glorify the praises of your Lord at night and in the morning. [55]

Those who argue about the signs of Allah without being given any authority have nothing in their hearts save an inflated view of their own importance, (and that's a status) they'll never be able to achieve. So seek the protection of Allah (from ever falling victim to false pride), for He's the Hearing and the Watchful. [56]

Without a doubt, the creation of the heavens and the earth is a more impressive accomplishment than the creation of people. Yet, most people don't understand (that truth). [57] The blind and the seeing are not the same, nor are those who believe and do what's morally right (the same as) the depraved. How little you learn when you're reminded! [58]

The Hour (of Judgment) will definitely arrive, and there's no doubting it. Yet, even still most people don't believe (in it), [59] even though your Lord says, *"Call upon Me! I will answer you! Those who are too proud*

[1547] While many prophets and messengers achieved a great measure of success, others had difficult times, and some were even killed. In that case, Allah's aid will consist of getting justice for them through others on earth or recompensing them in full for their suffering on the Day of Judgment. (Ma'ariful Qur'an)

to serve Me will find themselves in humiliating Hellfire!" 1548 [60]

This is What Allah Did for You

Allah is the One Who made the night for you so you can rest, and (He made the) day for you to see clearly. Allah is the source of every favor for people; yet, most people are thankless. [61]

That's Allah for you, your Lord, the Creator of everything. There is no other god than He, so why are you so deceived? [62] So that's how they're deceived, those who are determined to work against the signs of Allah! [63]

Allah is the One Who made the earth to be your resting place and the sky to be your canopy. He's given you your shapes, and He's made your shapes well. Then He provided for all your needs with wholesome resources.

That's Allah for you - your Lord - so glory be to Allah, the Lord of All the Worlds! [64] He's the Living; there is no god but He. So call upon Him sincerely, for He owns all religion. Praise be to Allah, the Lord of All the Worlds! [65]

Say to them, *"I've been forbidden to call upon those whom you call upon besides Allah. Clear evidence has come to me from my Lord. I've been commanded to surrender myself to the Lord of All the Worlds."* [66]

He's the One Who created you from dust, then from a drop of fluid and then from a clinging thing. Then he brings you out (of the womb) as a child. Then He lets you mature until you become strong. Then He lets you descend into old age, though some of you will die earlier, (and this process continues) until (each of) you arrives at your (own individual) deadline.

(This cycle continues onward throughout human society) so you can learn to use your reason. [67] He's the One Who gives life and death, and when He decides to do something, all He has to do is say, *'Be,'* and it is. [68]

Sinners will Learn the Truth

Don't you see how much those who argue about the signs of Allah are turned away? [69] They're the ones who deny the Book and whatever else We've sent down to Our messengers.

Soon they'll know (their folly), [70] when the shackles will be draped around their necks and the chains will be dragging along behind them, (as they march along) [71] through the scalding muck - only to be burnt up in the Fire! [72]

They'll be asked, *"Where are the ones that you made partners [73] in place of Allah?"* They'll answer, saying, *"They've left us to languish. Oh no! Whatever we called upon before wasn't even real!"* That's how Allah leaves the faithless to stray. [74]

(They'll be told), *"This (is your fate) because in the world you looked approvingly upon everything else (but the truth), and you were brazen (in your arrogance)! [75] So enter the gates of*

1548 A group of people went to a scholar named Ibrahim ibn Adham (d. 777). One of them quoted this verse [40:60] to him and said, "We pray to Allah, but why are we not answered?" The scholar said to them, "You know about Allah; yet, you don't obey Him. You read the Qur'an; yet, you don't act according to it. You know how bad Satan is; yet, you have joined with him. You say that you love the Messenger of Allah; yet, you abandon his example. You declare that you love Paradise; yet, you don't do anything to obtain it. You declare that you're afraid of the Fire; yet, you don't keep yourselves from committing sins. You agree that we will all die; yet, you're not prepared for it. You're busy finding faults with others; yet, you don't look at your own faults. You eat the food Allah provided for you; yet, you don't thank Him. You bury your dead; yet, you take no lesson from it."

Hellfire, and stay inside. Oh, how terrible is the home of the arrogant!" [1549] [76]

Then patiently persevere, (Muhammad,) for Allah's promise is true. Whether We show you now some (of the punishment) that We've promised them or We take your soul instead, (all of you) will come back to Us. [77]

And so it was that We sent messengers before you. We've told you some of their stories, but the stories of others We have not. It wasn't the place of any messenger to bring a (revealed) verse without Allah's permission. When the command of Allah was given, the matter was decided fairly, and those who clung to falsehood were destroyed. [78]

When Belief is too Late

$\mathcal{A}$llah is the One who made domesticated herd animals for you, so you can ride some and eat others, [79] along with the many other benefits they offer besides. You can use them to gain whatever your hearts desire. You're carried on them, just as you're carried on ships (at sea). [80] He's (always) presenting His evidence to you, so which of the signs of Allah are you going to deny? [81]

Don't they ever travel over the earth and see how (all the civilizations that went) before them came to an end? They were more numerous than these (people in Mecca) and more powerful, (as evidenced) by all the ruins they left behind in the earth. Clearly, whatever (marvels of engineering) they accomplished brought them nothing. [82]

When their messengers came to them with clear evidence, (the people) relied on whatever knowledge they already had, and the (punishment that they laughed off) came upon them from all sides. [83] When they saw Our punishment, they cried out, *"Now we believe in the One God! We reject whatever partners we made with Him!"* [84]

However, their (clamoring) affirmations of faith, in the face of the coming punishment, were worth nothing for them. This has been Allah's pattern in dealing with His servants, and so those who rejected Allah were completely lost! [85]

[1549] A companion of the Prophet named Abu Hurairah reported the following: "While we were in the company of Allah's Messenger, we heard a terrible sound. Thereupon, Allah's Messenger asked, 'Do you know what that sound was?' We answered, 'Allah and His Messenger know best.' Then he said, "That's a stone that was thrown into Hell seventy years ago and that's been constantly falling until now when it finally reached the bottom.'" (*Muslim*)

Clear Explanation

41 Fussilat
(aka *Ha Meem as-Sajdah*)
Late Meccan Period

The leaders of Mecca were sitting in the courtyard of the Ka'bah on their pavilion, as was their custom, when their discussions turned to the matter of Muhammad and what to do about him. They noticed that he was also in the courtyard, sitting alone. 'Utbah ibn Rabi'ah, who was Abu Sufyan's father-in-law, suggested that he would go and speak with Muhammad and try to convince him to change his course of action. (The Prophet's uncle Hamza had recently embraced Islam, and due to his vaunted reputation the Muslims were enjoying a temporary boost in status for their fledgling movement.)

The pagan leaders agreed with 'Utbah's suggestion, and he accordingly approached Muhammad and said, "Nephew, you know the high status that you enjoy in the community on account of your ancestry and family relations, but you've put your people in a bad situation. You've created divisions among them, and you even consider them to be fools! You talk badly about their religion and gods and say things as though all our forefathers were mere superstitious followers. Now listen to me, for I'm going to make some suggestions. Consider them well, for maybe you could accept one of them."

The Prophet said, "Abu Walid, say what you want to say, and I'll listen to you." So 'Utbah said, "Nephew, if by what you are doing you want money, we'll give you enough of it so that you'll be the richest man among us. If you want to become an important man, we'll make you our chief and will never decide a matter without you. If you want to be a king, we'll accept you as our king. If you're being visited by a jinn whom you can't get rid of by your own power, we'll arrange the best shamans and have you treated at our own expense."

'Utbah went on speaking in this fashion while the Prophet continued to listen quietly. Then he said, "Abu Walid, have you said everything that you had to say?" He replied that he had.

Then the Prophet said, "So now listen to me." Then after saying, "In the Name of Allah, the Compassionate, the Merciful," he began to recite this chapter. 'Utbah kept on listening to it, putting his hands behind his back and leaning on them as he listened. When he came to verse 38, the Prophet prostrated himself, then raised his head and said, "This is my answer, Abu Walid; now you may do as you please."

'Utbah then arose and walked back towards the gathered Meccan chiefs. As he approached them, they saw him from afar and said, "By Allah! 'Utbah's face has changed. He doesn't look the same as he was when he left from here." When he came back and sat down, the people asked, "What have you heard?"

He replied, "By Allah! I've heard something the like of which I've never heard before. By Allah, it's neither poetry nor sorcery nor magic. Chiefs of the Quraysh, listen to what I say and leave this man to himself. I think what he recites is going to have its effect. If the other Arabs overcome him, you'll be saved from raising your hand against your brother, and the others will deal with him. If he overcomes Arabia, his rule would be your rule and his honor your honor." Hearing this the chiefs spoke out, saying, "You, too, Abu Walid, have been bewitched by his tongue." 'Utbah replied, "I've given you my opinion. Now you may do as you please." (*Ibn Is-haq*)

In the Name of Allah,
the Compassionate, the Merciful

Ḥā. Meem. [1]

(This is) a revelation from the Compassionate and Merciful [2] - a book with clearly explained verses and a recitation in Arabic for people who understand. [3]

It gives good news and warnings. Yet, most (people) turn away and fail to listen. [4]

They say, *"Our hearts are immune to what you're inviting us, and our ears are deaf (to what you say). There's a veil between us and you, so do (whatever you like), and we'll do whatever we like, as well!"* [5]

Say to them, *"I'm just a mortal man like you. Revelation has come to me that (compels me to say that) your god is only One God, so stand firmly for Him, and ask for His forgiveness! Ruin to those who make partners (with Allah)* [6] *- those who make no effort to cleanse themselves through charity and who reject (the concept of) an afterlife!* [7] *However, those who believe and do what's morally right will receive a reward that will never end."* [8]

The Creation of Earth

Say (to them), *"Are you rejecting the One Who created the earth in two stages? Are you making others equals with Him? That's the Lord of All the Worlds!"* [9]

He placed well-rooted highlands upon (the earth) and (put many) blessings within them. Then He measured out every (physical and ecological system), so there would be sufficient resources (for all things, a process that was accomplished) in four stages. (This is an answer) for all those who ask (about this matter). [10]

And He also applied His design upon the sky, which was (filled with a kind of) smoke. He said to it and the earth, *"You will come together willingly or unwillingly."*

They responded, *"We come willingly."* [11] And so, He completed (crafting) them as seven (layers of) atmosphere in two stages, and He assigned to each (layer) its function. We adorned the lowest level of the sky with radiant (lights) and made it secure. [1550] This is the command of the Powerful and the Knowing. [12]

[1550] Early commentators, reflecting an Aristotelian view, have usually understood the unnamed 'lights' or 'lamps' to be starlight or stars, which can be seen from the earth's surface. The term used here, which is derived from the root word *sahaha*, doesn't actually mean starlight, however, but rather terms akin to radiance, morning light or to light something up as with the glow of a lamp. So this verse is not saying that God literally placed "stars" right next to the earth in a dome like the ancient Greeks supposed (and many early Muslims accepted as accurate), but rather that the sky has the *capacity* to reflect radiance from many external or general sources. The northern lights, or Aurora Borealis, is an example, as is the tendency of the earth's atmosphere to reflect a constant, soft pale light above the horizon, even in the darkest night. What does it mean that the sky was made *secure*? (The word *hafeez* is used here, which is also used for a memorizer or *guardian* of the Qur'an.) Scientifically, the sky above the earth is "secure" or guarded in that gravity holds it in place against the vacuum of space. Early commentators, not knowing these things, assumed that 'the sky being made secure' refers to the fact that jinns are repelled from spying on the angels who move around the sky on their errands.

The Disaster of the 'Ad and Thamud

*I*f they turn away, then say to them, *"I'm warning you of a disaster, like the disaster that befell the people of 'Ad and Thamud."* [13]

Messengers came (and warned them) from their fronts and from their backs, saying, *"Don't serve anyone except Allah!"* The (people scoffed) and said, *"If our Lord (really) wanted to (warn us), He would've sent angels (instead of you mortal men). So we reject your message completely."* [14]

As for the (people of) 'Ad, they acted arrogantly throughout the land against all right. They boasted, *"Who is stronger in power than we are?"* Didn't they see that Allah, the One Who created them, was infinitely mightier than they (could ever be)?

They worked against Our signs with determination, [15] so We sent a terrible sandstorm against them, causing many days of disaster, in order to give them a taste of the most degrading punishment this life can offer. The punishment of the next life will be even more degrading still, *and they'll have no one to help them.* [16]

As for the (people of) Thamud, We offered them guidance, but they preferred blindness over guidance, so a sudden humiliating disaster overtook them as a consequence of what they earned. [17] However, We saved those who believed and who were mindful (of Allah among both nations). [18]

The Body Betrays its Owner

*O*n the day when Allah's enemies will be gathered together (to be sent) to the Fire, they'll be (forced to) march in tight formations [1551] [19] until they reach it. Their hearing, their sight and *even their own skins* will testify against them about their deeds. [20]

They'll say to their skins, *"Why are you testifying against us?"*

Their (skins) will reply, *"Allah, the One Who can make anything speak, has given us the power to speak. He created you the first time, and back to Him you had to return. [21] You never tried to hide your (sins from us, never realizing) that your hearing, sight and skins would testify against you, and you didn't think that Allah knew about all the things you used to do! [22] This (neglect) in your thinking about your Lord has now brought you to ruin, and now you're among those who have lost completely!"* [23]

If they would just be patient, the Fire will be their home soon enough! If they beg to be allowed to make amends (for their sinful lives), they won't be indulged. [1552] [24]

On the contrary, We've assigned for them (diabolical) associates who make them feel satisfied with what's coming up ahead of them and with what they've left behind.

And in this way the verdict (that was leveled against) them will be proven true, even as it was (proved true) against all the preceding generations of jinns and humans, for they were thoroughly lost. [25]

[1551] A man named 'Abdullah reports that he was hiding under the large curtain that was always draped over the Ka'bah when three pagan men came along. He overheard part of their conversation, and one of the men asked his fellow, "Do you think Allah can hear what we're saying right now?" The other man answered, "If we talk loudly, then He will hear us, but if we don't talk loudly, He won't hear us." The third man said, "If He can hear one thing from us, then He can hear everything." After the men left, 'Abdullah snuck away and reported what he overheard to the Prophet. Then this passage was revealed in comment. (*Ahmad*)

[1552] The Prophet said that every new day that arrives comes with the following implicit message: "I am a new day, and I will be a witness to whatever you do this day. Therefore, you must do some kind of good deed before I come to an end, so that I can give evidence. Once I'm gone, you'll never find me again." Then the Prophet explained that each new day comes with the same announcement. (*Qurtubi*)

The Taunts of the Faithless

*T*he faithless say, *"Don't listen to this Qur'an! Talk nonsense over it when it's being recited, so that you can come out on top!"* [1553] [26]

We're going to give the faithless a taste of harsh punishment, and We're going to pay them back for the worst of their deeds! [27]

This is the payback that Allah's enemies will get - *the Fire!* That'll be their permanent home, and that's a payback (they deserve), for they campaigned against Our signs with utter determination. [28] The faithless will cry out, *"Our Lord! Show us those jinns and people who misled us! We'll crush them underfoot so they'll be less than nothing!"* [29]

On the contrary, those who said, *"Our Lord is Allah,"* and then stood firmly, will have angels descending upon them, (strengthening their hearts, inspiring them with messages such as), *"Have no fear! Have no sorrow! Accept the good news of the Garden that you've been promised!* [1554] [30] *We're your protectors in this life, as well as in the next life, within which you'll receive everything your souls ever desired and everything you ever asked for!"* [31]

That's a welcome gift from the (One Who) forgives and shows mercy! [1555] [32]

Which is more Equal?

*W*hose word is better than the one who calls (people) to Allah, does what's morally right and then says, *"I'm with those who surrender (to Allah)"?* [1556] [33] Good and evil are not equal, so ward off (evil) by doing good. That's how you can turn your enemy into your close supporter and ally. [34]

However, no one will achieve (the results of this principle) unless they're patient, and no one will achieve it unless they're granted the utmost good fortune. [35] If Satan ever tries to involve you in dissension, ask for Allah's protection, for He's the Hearing and the Knowing. [36]

The Truth of Allah's Signs

*A*mong His signs are the night and the day and the sun and the moon. Don't bow down to the sun or the moon, but bow down to Allah Who created them, if you really aim to serve Him. [37]

If they're too arrogant (to bow before Allah, it doesn't matter), because in your Lord's presence (are many who already) glorify Him throughout the night and the day, and they never get worn out (from doing it). [1557] [38]

Among His signs is the way in which you see the lifeless earth revive itself after

---

[1553] Abu Jahl is the one who said the statement quoted in verse 26, and he tried to get people to make noise and commotion whenever the Prophet was reciting Qur'anic verses in public, in order to drown out his preaching. (*Ma'ariful Qur'an*)

[1554] A man named Sufyan ibn 'Abdullah ath-Thaqafi once asked the Prophet to tell him something so comprehensive about Islam that he would never need to ask anyone else for advice on how to follow Islam again. The Prophet replied, "Say, 'I believe in Allah,' and then stand firm on that." (*Ma'ariful Qur'an*)

[1555] The Prophet said, "The angels will say to the soul of a believer (when they take it), 'Come out, you good soul from the good body you used to live in. Come out to rest, to provision and to a Lord Who is not angry.'" (*Ahmad*)

[1556] Apparently, someone had questioned the integrity of Abu Bakr, and instead of insulting the man back, Abu Bakr prayed for Allah to forgive him from whatever shortcomings the man's tirade must have implied. This passage was revealed in comment on this. (*Ma'ariful Qur'an*)

[1557] After reading this verse it is customary for the one who has faith in Allah to prostrate himself on the floor and praise Allah.

the rain showers that We send down upon it. It stirs to life, and (plants) grow (profusely over its surface). Surely, the One Who gives life to the dead earth can give life once again to the dead, for He has power over all things. [39]

Those who pervert the meaning of Our (revealed) verses are not hidden from Us. Therefore, is the one who is thrown in the Fire better than the one who skirts it safely on the Day of Assembly? Do whatever you like, for He's watching everything you do. [40]

Those who reject the message when it comes to them (are going to lose), for truly (this is) a powerful Book. [41]

Falsehood cannot enter it, neither from the front nor the back, for it's being sent down by a wise and praiseworthy (Lord). [42]

Nothing is being said to you that's any different from what was said to the messengers who came before you, namely that your Lord is a master of forgiveness and a master of dire results. [43]

Why was the Qur'an Revealed in Arabic?

$\mathcal{I}$f We would've sent this Qur'an in any other (language) besides Arabic, then (the Arabs, who received it first), would've said, *"Why aren't its verses clearly explained? Huh? Not in Arabic, and (the man bringing it to us) is an Arab?"* [1558]

Say (to them), *"It's a guidebook and a source of healing for the faithful. However, for those who reject (it), it's a source of deafness in their ears and blindness (in their eyes) - as if they were being called from a place far off in the distance!"* [44]

Fickle Faith

$\mathcal{A}$nd so it was that We gave the Book to Moses, but arguments sprang up concerning it. If it wasn't for a sentence (of principle) that had already been issued from your Lord, then there would've been a settlement among them, but there remained suspicions and doubts among them concerning (their scripture). [45] Whoever does what's morally right does so for the good of his own soul. Whoever does what's evil works against (his own soul), and Allah is never unfair to His servants. [46]

The knowledge of the Hour (of Judgment) is directly (with) Him. No date-fruit comes out of its sheath or female becomes pregnant or delivers (her offspring) without Him knowing about it.

On the day when Allah directs (the question) to them, *"Where are My 'partners' (that you made equal) with Me?"*

They'll answer, *"We have no one here to testify to that!"* [47] The (false idols) that they used to call upon before will leave them to languish, and they'll finally realize that they have no way of escape. [48]

Human beings never tire of asking for good, but if hardship comes upon one of them, he gives up all hope and is lost in despair. [49]

Then, when We give him a taste of mercy after some hardship that has come upon him, he says, *"This (turn of fortune) is of my own doing. I don't think the (final) Hour will ever come, and even if I'm ever brought back to my Lord, I'm sure I'll have many good (rewards) waiting there for me in His presence."*

On the contrary, We'll show the faithless the real meaning of everything they did, and We'll give them a taste of

---

[1558] Some pagans in Mecca suggested to Muhammad that if a portion of the Qur'an were revealed in a foreign language that he did not know, this would indeed truly be a miracle. This verse was revealed in answer, pointing out that it would have been a useless exercise, for the Arabs would have then complained that the Qur'an was unintelligible. (*Asbab ul-Nuzul*)

brutal punishment! [50] Whenever We grant good fortune to a human being, he (takes it and) turns away (from Us), moving far off to the side. But when misfortune comes upon him, (he rushes back to us) filled with intense supplication. [51]

Honest Faith is Not a Mistake

Say (to them), *"Don't you see that this is from Allah, and then you just reject it? Who's making the bigger mistake than the one who breaks away in opposition (to Allah)?"* [1559] [52]

We're going to show them Our signs soon enough in locations far away on the horizon [1560] and also within their own souls, until it becomes clear to them that this is the truth.

Isn't it enough (for them) that (Allah) witnesses everything? [53] *Oh, how much they doubt meeting their Lord! Oh, how much He surrounds everything!* [54]

[1559] The Meccan idol-worshippers used to accuse Muhammad of being mistaken in his beliefs. Thus, the retort is given that the mistakes are all theirs. (*Ibn Kathir*)

[1560] Even though this chapter was revealed in the Meccan period, it foreshadows future events in faraway places and tells the pagans to watch and see what will happen. As it turned out, when the Muslims moved to the far city of Yathrib (Medina), quite a few important events took place there that shook Mecca to its core, even as they strengthened the hearts of the believers.

Consultation

42 Ash-Shura
Late Meccan Period

This chapter was revealed immediately after the previous one, though verses 23-24 and 27 were revealed in Medina. Given the chronological order of this series of seven Ha Meem chapters, it is apparent that this chapter is something of a continuation of the arguments of the past, with a special emphasis on exposing the recalcitrance of the chiefs of the Quraysh. This would have had propaganda value in the countryside, where the position of Islam was already hotly debated.

In the Name of Allah,
the Compassionate, the Merciful

Ḥā. Meem. [1] *'Ayn. Seen. Qāf.* [2]

And so He's inspiring you, (Muhammad,) just as (He inspired) the (ancient prophets) who went before you, and Allah is Powerful and Wise. [3]

Whatever is in the heavens and whatever is on the earth belongs to Him, for He's the Exalted and the Great. [4] The heavens above them are nearly ripped to shreds (by His presence), and the angels magnify the praise of their Lord and pray for the forgiveness of whomever is on the earth.

Without a doubt He's truly the Forgiving and the Merciful. [5] Those who take protectors other than Him - *Allah is the guardian of even them* - and you're not responsible for them at all. [6]

And so We've inspired you with a Qur'an in Arabic, so you can warn the mother of all settlements (Mecca) [1561] and all of the other places around it about the Day of Gathering, (which will arrive) without a doubt. Some of them will be in the Garden, and some of them will be in the burning flames. [7]

If Allah had wanted, He could've made all (the people of the earth) into a single community, but He (allows them to differ and divide in order to test them) and also so that He can admit to His mercy whomever He wants. The wrongdoers won't find anyone to protect them or help them. [8]

What? Are they taking protectors other than Him? Allah is the (only One Who can) protect! He's the One Who gives life to the dead, for He has power over all things. [9]

[1561] The term used here, *mother of all settlements*, is a reference to Mecca. The Prophet had not left the city yet, but the Meccan persecution was reaching an unbearable level for the small Muslim community. In Arabic idiom, the addition of the phrase, "The Mother of" means the most important of that category. Sometime after the Muslims had peacefully taken over Mecca, the Prophet walked through its main bazaar and said aloud, "By Allah, you're the best of Allah's lands, the most beloved land of Allah. If it wasn't for the fact that I was driven out from you, I would have never left you." (*Ahmad, Tirmidhi, Nisa'i*)

All True Religion Came from Allah

*M*uhammad, say to them), *"Whatever you're all arguing about, Allah will be the One to solve it. That's my Lord, Allah. I trust Him, and I turn myself towards Him (for guidance).* [10] *(He's) the originator of the heavens and the earth, and He made you all into pairs (of male and female) among your own kind, even as He made herd animals in pairs."*

"That's how He made it possible for you to multiply. There's really nothing like Him at all, for He's the Hearing and the Watchful. [11] *The keys of the heavens and the earth belong to Him. He increases or restricts the resources of whomever He wants, for He knows about all things."* [12]

He has established the same way of life for you that He ordained for Noah. It's the same one that We're inspiring you with, (Muhammad,) and the same one that We ordained for Abraham, Moses and Jesus, namely to institute the (moral) way of life and not to make any divisions in it. 1562

The idol-worshippers find that what you're asking of them is hard, though Allah draws to Himself whomever He wants, and He guides to Himself (all) who turn (their hopes towards Him). [13]

(The people of the past) didn't divide up (into many competing sects) until *after* knowledge came to them, (and this division was solely) out of selfish envy among themselves. If it wasn't for an order that your Lord had already decreed that gave (humanity) a fixed time limit, then the issue would've been resolved among them. (Later generations) who had inherited the scripture are filled with uncertainty about its (meaning). [14]

So for that (confusion on their part), do call them (to believe in the Qur'an), and remain committed (to the cause) as you've been commanded.

Don't follow their whims, but rather say to them, *"I believe in the Book that Allah has sent down. I'm commanded to judge fairly between you. Allah is our Lord and your Lord. To us our deeds, and to you your deeds. There's no disagreement between us and you. Allah will bring us all together, and the final destination is back with Him."* [15]

Those who argue about Allah after His (existence) has already been accepted (by all parties concerned) are arguing pointlessly in their Lord's sight. His wrath is drawn over them, and they'll receive a strong punishment besides. [16]

Allah is the One Who sent down the Book in all truth, as well as the balance (of justice). 1563 Then how can you be made to understand that the Hour (of Judgment) might be close? [17]

The only ones who want it to come sooner are those who don't believe in it, but the faithful are in awe of it and know that it will be a reality. Isn't it (true) that those who are disregarding the Hour are grossly mistaken? [18]

Allah is Fair to His Servants

*A*llah is subtly (gracious) to His servants, and He gives resources to whomever He wants. He is the Capable and the Powerful. [19] Whoever desires the harvest of the next life, We add to his

---

1562 Muhammad never claimed that he was starting a new religion. In this regard, his example is the same as that of Jesus, who likewise never claimed to be founding a new religion. Both men called people to remember the pure faith and teachings of the godly men of the past. Muhammad called upon the Arabs to remember Ishmael and by extension Abraham and his pure religion. Jesus called on the Jews to remember Moses and by extension Abraham, as well. (See 2:127-129.) Interestingly enough, Muhammad called upon both the Jews and Christians to return to the Original Religion of Abraham, the religion that was being renewed by Allah through the Qur'anic revelation. (See 2:135-136.)

1563 The balance is thought to be the Prophet's example, sayings, interpretations and rulings.

harvest. [1564] Whoever desires the harvest of this world, We'll give him some of it, but he'll have no share of the next life. [1565] [20]

What! Do they have partners (as powerful as Allah) who can establish a religion for them without Allah's permission? If it wasn't for the order of sorting (right from wrong), then the issue would've been decided between them. Truly, the corrupt will have a painful punishment. [21]

You're going to see the wrongdoers trembling in fear for (all the sins) they've earned, and that's something they'll have to bear. Those who believed, however, and did what was morally right, will rest in the pleasures of the Garden.

In their Lord's presence, they'll have everything they ever wanted, *and that's the greatest bounty!* [22] That's the same one about which Allah is giving good news to His servants – to those who believe and do what's morally right.

The Prophet Seeks No Personal Wealth or Gain

$\mathcal{S}$ay (to them), *"I'm not asking you for any reward for this, but at least extend to me the love that is due to a member of your own family!"* [1566]

Whoever accumulates good (deeds), then We'll multiply the goodness within them, for Allah is forgiving and appreciative. [23]

What! Are they saying, *"He's making up lies about Allah"*? If Allah had wanted, He could've sealed up your heart, as well. Allah blots out falsehood and proves by His Own words that the truth is true, for He knows the secrets (that lurk within all people's) hearts. [24]

He's the One Who accepts repentance from His servants, and He also forgives sins. He knows what you're doing. [25] He listens to those who believe and who do what's morally right, and He increases (their fortune) from His largess, but for those who suppressed (their awareness of the truth), there will be a strong punishment. [26]

Never Discount Your Own Responsibility

$\mathcal{I}$f Allah ever increased the resources of His servants (to the maximum limit), they would surely go out of control in the world. [1567] However, He sends (resources)

[1564] A man once went to the Prophet, while he was leading people on a journey, and said loudly, "Hey, Muhammad!" The Prophet answered back, "Here I am!" Then the man asked, "When will the Hour come?" The Prophet replied, "Woe to you! It will certainly come to pass. What have you done to prepare for it?" The man answered, "I love Allah and His Messenger." The Prophet then said, "You will be with those whom you love." (*Bukhari, Muslim*)

[1565] The Prophet said, "Wealth consists of a variety of treasures, and those treasures have keys. Blessed be he whom Allah has made a key for good and a lock for evil, but woe to the one whom Allah has made a key for evil and a lock for good." (*Ibn Majah*)

[1566] Some of the pagans charged that Muhammad was doing what he was doing as some sort of scheme to get rich. It was a preposterous charge, of course, for Muhammad lived in self-imposed poverty throughout his entire ministry. Muhammad was bringing to the people of Mecca a new religion to replace idolatry and ignorant superstition; he never asked for any wages. Here in this verse, he is instructed to tell them that he's not asking them for their money, only for their faith and open hearts. Some of Muhammad's bitterest and most violent foes were his own relatives: uncles, aunts, cousins, etc. This verse, which was revealed to address this situation, suggests that it is shameful for his relatives to persecute him so blatantly while he was still a member of their own extended family. That is a serious indictment of the Meccans, who always asserted that 'blood is thicker than water' and that they would aid any relative no matter who he might have wronged or how.

[1567] When the Meccan refugees were settled in Medina, they were generally stricken with poverty, having lost everything they owned in Mecca. (Some were even forced to sleep in the mosque at night for they had no homes.) According to a companion named Khabab ibn al-'Aratt, when the refugees

down in measured increments as He wills, for He is well-informed and watchful over His servants. [27]

He's the One Who sends down rain even after (people) have given up all hope for it. He scatters His mercy (in every direction), for He is the Protector and the Praiseworthy. [28] Among His signs is the creation of the heavens and the earth and all the living creatures that He spread throughout them. He has the ability to collect them all together again when He wills. [29]

Whatever misfortune that befalls you is the result of what your own hands have earned, but for many (of your mishaps) there is forgiveness from (Allah). [1568] [30]

You can't frustrate (suffering from the results of your bad decisions) by running all over the world, for there is no one who can protect you or help you besides Allah. [31]

Among His signs are the ships that sail smoothly through the oceans like mountain peaks. [32] If it were ever His desire, He could stop the wind (that propels them), and they would be rendered immobile on the (ocean's) surface. Truly, there are signs in this (example) for every patient and thankful person. [33]

(If it were ever His desire), He could (sink those ships) as a (punishment) for (the sins) that (the people on board) have earned, though He forgives many things. [34] Inform those who argue about Our signs that they'll have no escape (from Allah's judgment!) [35]

Whatever you're given in this world is only a trifle to use in this life, but whatever is with Allah is better and more lasting for those who believe and who trust in their Lord. [1569] [36]

They're the ones who avoid the most serious sins and shameful acts, and they forgive others, even when they're angry. [37] They're the ones who respond to their Lord and establish prayer.

They decide their communal affairs by consulting each other, and they spend (in Allah's cause) out of that which We've supplied to them. [38] They're the ones who help themselves when they're wronged. [39]

The payback for an injury is to get back an equal amount of compensation from the (guilty party), unless (the injured party) forgives (the one who wronged him) and reconciles (with him). His compensation will then be with Allah, and He has no love for wrongdoers. [1570] [40]

Whoever helps himself after he's been wronged, such (people) won't be blamed for it. [41] Blame will only be directed against those who oppress people and defy all norms of justice in the earth against all right. [1571] A painful punishment awaits them! [42] Whoever is patient and forgives (the wrongs that were done against him) is

---

saw the wealth and opulence of the three Jewish tribes of Medina, they longed for such wealth and spoke about their desire publicly. Soon, this passage was revealed to tell the believers that Allah is in control and that there are dangers and temptations in too much wealth. (*Ma'ariful Qur'an*)

[1568] After this verse was revealed, the Prophet commented on its meaning, saying, "By the One Who holds my soul in His hand, no believer is stricken with fatigue, exhaustion, worry or grief, but Allah will forgive him for some of his sins on account of it, even if a thorn pricks him." (*Ahmad*)

[1569] The Prophet said, "It is a part of the excellence of a person's practice of self-surrender (Islam) that he discards what is of no use to him either in this world or in the next." (*Tirmidhi*)

[1570] The Prophet said, "When two people start to abuse each other, the one who started the misbehavior is to blame, unless the one who is being wronged oversteps the bounds of proper retaliation." (*Muslim*)

[1571] This is another one of those passages that takes the arguments of religious extremists and shows them as hollow, for in seeking redress for an injustice done to a person, the wronged party is not allowed to go overboard, and is further counseled to consider forgiveness and reconciliation, if at all possible.

truly courageous in resolving the matter. [1572] [43]

Let them Decide for Themselves

Whomever Allah leaves astray, he will have no protector after that. You're going to see the wrongdoers saying, just as they see the punishment (ahead of them), *"Isn't there any road back?"* [44]

You're going to see them brought to the front with eyes darting about in utter humility at their shame. Those who believe (in Allah) will exclaim, *"Truly, the losers are the ones who lost themselves and their families on this Day of Assembly."*

The punishment that the wrongdoers must endure will be firmly set. [45] They'll have no supporter to help them in the sight of Allah, and anyone whom Allah leaves astray will have no way (to escape). [46]

Respond to your Lord before the day comes that cannot be delayed, (for it will come) by Allah's will. What safe place will you have that day? What further defense can you offer? [47] If they turn away, then (it's not your fault), for We haven't appointed you to be their guardian. Your only duty is to convey (the message).

Truly, when We give a human being a taste of Our mercy, he celebrates in it, but when some miscalculation of his backfires against him as a result of his own handiwork, he's truly thankless! [48]

The control of the heavens and the earth belongs to Allah. He creates whatever He wants. He bestows female children upon whomever He wants and male children upon whomever He wants, [49] or He bestows both males and females, while leaving barren whomever He wants, for He is full of knowledge and measured ways. [1573] [50]

How does Allah Reveal His Messages?

It's not for a mortal that Allah should speak to him directly, [1574] unless it's through inspired revelation, (inspiration)

[1572] This passage [42:40-43] has been misused by extremists in the modern era to justify their attacks on the civilians of their enemies. Incredibly, they assume that since the military of their enemies harms Muslim civilians, they have the right, according to this principle of equal retaliation, to do the same with the innocents of their enemies. Traditional Muslim scholarship has never advanced such an illogical and mean-spirited view. This verse, in the main, is referring to injuries done on the personal level. If someone damages your car, you get the value of that damage from a judge's verdict. If someone hits you, you can fight back – though forgiveness is better. Once a companion of the Prophet named Abu Dharr al-Ghiffari got angry at Bilal and called him the son of a black woman. (He meant it in an insulting way.) Bilal went to the Prophet complaining, and after the Prophet scolded Abu Dharr, he (Abu Dharr) ran back to Bilal, put his face on the ground and asked Bilal to put his foot on it. Bilal forgave the man, instead. (*Bukhari*) This passage above has never been used by Muslim governments of antiquity as a matter of state policy against enemy nations or populations. For issues of getting justice for the unjust killing of one's own civilians in war, only the ones actually guilty of the crime, such as the soldiers who did it or the leaders who actually ordered attacks upon civilians can be held responsible (see 2:178-179). The Prophet, himself, had many instances when enemies attacked and harmed innocent Muslims, and he never demanded an equal number of innocents from the other side to be killed.

[1573] Some women bear children of one sex only, while others have both male and female offspring, while yet others can bear no children at all. Allah knows and plans according to His just will. The point of this verse is that we must accept graciously any children that are born to us, regardless of gender, and that those who are barren should bear their condition with patience, for Allah rewards patience in suffering.

[1574] A Jewish man went to the Prophet and said, "If you're a prophet, then you have to see and speak to Allah directly like Moses did. Until you do that, we will never believe in you." The Prophet replied, "But Moses didn't see Allah, either." Then this verse was revealed. (*Asbab ul-Nuzul, Ma'ariful Qur'an*)

from behind a veil, [1575] or through the agency of a message-bearer (like an angel), who will reveal, by Allah's permission, whatever Allah wills him (to reveal), for He is highly exalted and wise. [51]

And so it is that We're inspiring you, (Muhammad,) through (the agency of a) spirit (under) Our command. You didn't know what revelation and faith were (before being made a prophet). We've sent down to you a light, which you can use to guide whomever of Our servants that We will.

You're imparting guidance (to them) that will lead (them) towards a straight path, [52] - (*towards*) *the path of Allah* - the One to Whom belongs all that is within the heavens and all that is upon the earth, and all affairs will eventually go back to Allah (for their resolution). [53]

The Ornaments

43 Az-Zukhruf
Late Meccan Period

This is the fourth chapter in the *Ha Meem* series. It was revealed at a time when the Meccans were laying various plans to assassinate the Prophet, as evidenced by verses 79-80. Even though a dire situation was rapidly developing, the final arguments against idolatry were still coming in rapid succession and from so many different angles that the pagans were literally being wonder-struck by the challenges and could no longer simply rebut them. This is why the violence began to reach a fever pitch. For those whose intellectual arguments are laid to waste, there are only two choices: accept the message, or lash out. The Meccan leadership chose the latter.

*In the Name of Allah,
the Compassionate, the Merciful*

Ḥā. Meem. [1]

By the Book that makes things clear [2] – We've made it an Arabic Qur'an so you could understand it. [3] It (originated) in the Mother of the Book, which is kept in Our presence, transcendent and full of wisdom. [4]

Should we take Our message away from you (Arabs) simply because you're a nation that's out of control? [5] Yet, how many prophets did we send in ancient times? [6]

No prophet ever came to them except that they ridiculed him. [7] Therefore, We destroyed (those nations), which were even mightier than this (one of yours). Thus, the example of the ancients passes on. [8]

Recognizing His Favors

If you asked them, *"Who created the heavens and the earth?"* they would (swiftly) reply, *"They were created by the Powerful and the Knowledgeable One."* [9]

(They would be right, of course), for He's the One Who spread the earth out wide for you and made many pathways within it so you could find the right direction. [10]

(He's) the One Who sends down sufficient rain from the sky, and We revive the dead land with it, *and that's also how you'll be brought (up at the resurrection)*. [11]

(He's) the One Who created all living things in pairs.

He sent down (the knowledge of) shipbuilding, and He gave you livestock (animals), as well, so you can ride upon them, [12] sitting securely on their flat backs.

Whenever you're seated upon (some mode of travel), you can remember the favors of your Lord, saying *"Glory be to the One Who subjected this to our (use), for we never could've mastered this by ourselves, [13] and we're certainly going to return to our Lord."* [14]

They Claim Ignorance

*Y*et, they give a share of (divine power) to some of His servants! [1576] Truly, humanity is obviously thankless! [15] Has He taken daughters out of everything He created and then given you the choice to have sons? [16]

When one of (those pagans) is told the good news of (the birth of a daughter) - *the same (gender) that he so readily adds to the likeness of the Compassionate*, his face becomes downcast, and he's filled with terrible disappointment. [1577] [17]

(Is it right that you would ascribe the qualities of a female), whom (you consider) to be raised merely among ornaments (and baubles) and (whom you consider) to be incapable of speaking with directness, (with the qualities of Allah)? [18]

And so they turn the angels into females, (even though the angels were made) only to serve Allah. Were they there to witness when they were created? (If they were), then their evidence will be noted, and they could be questioned about it. [19]

Then (the idol-worshippers) say, "*Oh, if it had only been the Compassionate's will, then we would've never worshipped (any idols).*" They don't know what (they're saying), and they do nothing more than speculate. [20] Did We give them some scripture in the past to which they're committed? [21]

Not so! (Their only excuse is to) say, "*This is the cultural tradition that we found our ancestors following, so we're following in their tracks.*" [22]

This is how it's always been: whenever We sent a warner before you to any nation, the well-to-do among them said, "*This is the cultural tradition that we found our ancestors following, so we're following in their footsteps.*" [23]

(And their warner would always) say, "*What! Even though I'm bringing you better guidance than what you inherited from your ancestors?*"

(To which the people would always) reply, "*As far as we're concerned, we don't accept that you've been sent (on any mission at all).*" [24]

Thus, We took payback from them – *and, oh, how (stunning) was the end of those who denied (the truth)!* [25]

How to Make a Clean Break from Idolatry

*A*braham said to his father and his people, "*I'm free of what you're worshipping!* [26] *(I'll serve) no one besides the One Who made me, for He's going to guide me.*" [27] (Abraham) left this doctrine to posterity, so that (those who came after his time) could turn back (to Allah). [28]

Allah Chooses Whomever He Wants

*B*ut no! [1578] I've given (the luxuries of this world) to these (ungrateful people),

---

[1576] The Arab idol-worshippers claimed Allah had daughters. The Arabs then worshipped these daughters as mini-gods. Here the Qur'an is pointing out that the Arabs valued sons higher than daughters, so it was blatant hypocrisy to ascribe to Allah what they themselves didn't want. (*Asbab ul-Nuzul*)

[1577] The Prophet said, "If a man has a daughter born to him, and he does not bury her alive, as the pagans did, and he's never treated her with contempt or preferred his son over her, he will be granted entry into Paradise by Allah." (*Abu Dawud*)

[1578] Mecca and the nearby town of Ta'if were the two most important cities in the immediate region. The idol-worshippers couldn't believe that Allah would choose someone like Muhammad, who wasn't wealthy or particularly important, to be a message-bearer. Better someone wealthy or politically connected, they charged, and then they suggested that Allah would do better if he chose 'Utbah ibn

as well as to their ancestors, until now when an obvious messenger (comes to them), bringing them the truth. [29] So now that the truth has come to them, they (deny it), saying, *"It's just some kind of magic, and we reject it."* [30]

Then they say, *"Why isn't this Qur'an being sent down to a more important man (than him) from either of the two (largest) cities (around here)?"* [1579] [31]

Are they the ones who parcel out your Lord's mercy? In fact, We're the One who parcels out among them their livelihood in the life of this world. We only promote some (people) above the rest in status, so they can coerce labor from them, but the mercy of your Lord is far better than what they accumulate. [32]

If it wasn't for the fact that all (people) would (merge together) into one community (of greedy misers), We would've given everyone who rejects the Compassionate silver roofs for their houses, (ornate) stairs upon which to climb, [33] (massive) doors on their houses, couches upon which to rest [34] and golden ornaments, as well! However, all those things are nothing more than objects for use in the life of this world. The next life, in Allah's view, is for those who were aware (of the difference). [35]

Separation from Allah

𝒲hoever blinds himself to the remembrance of the Compassionate (One) will have a devil assigned to him by Us to be his intimate confidant. [36] They'll steer them away from the path, even as they think they're being rightly guided. [37]

(This goes on) until he comes back to Us and then says (to his devil), *"If only we were as far apart as the east and then another east!"* [1580] What a horrible confidant (he had)! [38] (All the) wrong you did together won't help you at all on that day, for both of you will be partners in the punishment! [39]

Can you make the deaf hear or show the way to the blind or to someone who is clearly wrong? [40] Even if We took you away (from them, as they wish to get rid of you), We would still get our due out of them, [41] or We just might show you (the retribution) that We've promised them, for indeed We have complete power over them. [42] So hold tight to the inspiration that's coming down to you, for you're on a straight path. [43]

The Example of Moses

𝒯his (Qur'an) is indeed the (noble) message (intended) for you and your people, and soon you'll be questioned (about how well you followed it). [44] You should ask Our messengers whom We sent before your time if We ever set up any gods for worship other than the Compassionate. [1581] [45]

And so it was that We sent Moses with Our signs to Pharaoh and his nobles, and he said to them, *"I'm a messenger from the Lord of All the Worlds."* [46] However, even though He went to them with Our signs, they ridiculed them. [47]

Rab'iah of Mecca or some other leading man from the nearby city of Ta'if. This passage was revealed in response. (*Ma'ariful Qur'an*)

[1579] It is assumed that the Quraysh were referring to a man like al-Walid ibn al-Mughirah. (*Ibn Hisham*)

[1580] In other words, if a person travels due east as far as he can, this person will cry to be removed from the terror of Judgment Day by a distance equal to that. Most commentators say this verse means as far apart as one could possibly be.

[1581] How can previous messengers be 'asked?' By reading the stories of their lives from previous holy books. That's why, after making this statement, the chapter then proceeds into one of those previous messenger's stories. See Deuteronomy 4:35, 6:4, Isaiah 45:5-6, Mark 12:29 or Matthew 22:36. All these verses from the Bible give the testimony of previous prophets that Allah is only one without any partners.

We showed them miracle after miracle, with each one being more impressive than the last, until We finally seized them with punishing (plagues), so they could (at least have a chance) to return (to Allah). [48]

(In their fear), they cried out, *"You wizard! Call upon your Lord for us by His covenant with you (and remove this plague from us), then we'll accept (your) guidance."* [49] However, (every time) We relieved them of the punishment, they went back on their word. [50]

Pharaoh declared to his people, *"My people! Doesn't the kingdom of Egypt belong to me? Look at these streams flowing below my (realm). Don't you see them?* [51] *Aren't I better than this (Moses), that vagabond who can't even speak properly?*[1582] [52] *Why aren't gold bracelets being laid upon him, and why isn't he flanked by angels?"* [53]

This is how he persuaded his people, and they obeyed him. They were truly a rebellious nation. [54] When they provoked Us, We took Our due from them and drowned all (their army). [55] We caused them to recede (into history) and made them an example for those (civilizations that would arise) later. [56]

The Example of Jesus

When the son of Mary is held up as an example, your people complain loudly,

[57] saying, *"Are our gods better, (or this Jesus, whom the Christians worship)?"*

They're offering this (objection) against you for no other reason than (they like) to argue, for they're a very argumentative people. [1583] [58]

(Jesus) was no more than a servant to whom We granted Our favor. We made him an example for the Children of Israel. [59] If We had wanted, We could've sent angels to live among you on the earth, and they would've (eventually) replaced you. [1584] [60]

(Jesus) is a portent of the Hour, so have no doubt about (its arrival). Rather, you should follow Me, for that is a straight path. [61] *Don't let Satan get in your way, for he's your obvious enemy.* [62]

Jesus came with clear evidence (of the truth). He said (to his people), *"I've come to you with wisdom, so I can resolve those issues that cause you to differ. Therefore, be mindful of Allah and obey me.* [63] *Truly, Allah is my Lord and your Lord, so serve Him alone, for that's a straight path."* [64]

(However, after Jesus was gone from the world), sects arose over differences among them. So ruin upon those who do wrong, (for they're going to suffer) from the punishment of a dreadful day. [65]

[1582] Moses sometimes stuttered.

[1583] The idol-worshippers of Mecca often objected strongly whenever the Qur'anic revelations made references to Jesus, charging that Christianity was a foreign religion and thus not an equal comparison with their own beliefs. Once the Prophet told the Meccans that there is no goodness in anyone unless he serves Allah. Then the Meccans asked, "Do you think Jesus was a servant? How could he have been such a good servant while he's held by them to be their god?" (*Qurtubi*) A man named 'Abdullah ibn Az-Zab'ari then tried to corner the Prophet into saying that Jesus would be in Hell because he was worshipped as were the idols of Mecca, which were also promised Hellfire. (See 21:98-103 and notes.) After the Prophet won that portion of the debate, Az-Zab'ari accused Muhammad of wanting to be worshipped as a part of Allah, like the Christians called Jesus a part of Allah. Thereafter, to the amazement of the pagans who had accompanied az-Zab'ari to watch, the Prophet recited these new verses [57-62], which laid out a clear doctrine of separation between Allah and any mortal man.

[1584] To the Meccans, who said that the angels were Allah's children, the argument is made that a human is sent as a messenger to other humans. If Allah would have wanted to send angels as proof of His power, then He might just as well have created angels to live on the earth.

Paradise Described

*A*re they waiting for the Hour (of Judgment) to come upon them all of a sudden, without their even realizing it? [66] Friends will become enemies on that day, except for those who were mindful (of Allah). [67]

"My servants! You shall have nothing to fear on that day, nor will you feel any sadness, [68] *(for you were) the ones who believed in Our signs and surrendered (to Us).* [69] *So now enter the Garden, you and your spouses together, in celebration."* [70]

Dishes (of food) and golden cups will be passed around among them! Everything that a soul could want will be there - *everything in which eyes could take pleasure* - and there you shall remain! [71] This is the Garden that you'll inherit (as a reward) for what you used to do (in the world), [72] and in it you'll have an endless supply of fruits from which to eat. [73]

Hellfire Described

*T*he wicked will remain in the punishment of Hellfire. [74] Its (torments) won't be lightened for them, even as they're engulfed by sadness and despair. [75] It's not that We were unfair to them; rather, they're the ones who were unfair to themselves. [76]

"O Master!" they'll cry out (to the chief warden of Hell), *"If only your Lord would put an end to us!"*

(Then the warden will) reply, *"(No), you must linger on."* [77]

And so We've brought the truth to all of you; yet, most of you have an aversion to the truth. [78] Have they made some kind of plan (to thwart Us), when We're the One Who decides matters? [79] Do they think that We don't hear their secrets and private consultations? No way! Our (angelic) messengers are very close to them, recording (what they say against Allah). [80]

Say to them, *"If the Compassionate ever had a son, then I would be the first to worship him."* [81] Glory to the Lord of the heavens and the earth! The Lord of the throne is (far removed) from what they're making Him out to be. [82] So leave them to speculate and play until they come upon that day of theirs that they've been promised. [83]

He's the One Who is God in the heavens and God on the earth. He's the Wise and the Knowing. [84] Blessed be the One Who controls the heavens and the earth and everything in between! He has knowledge of the Hour, and you're going to go back to Him. [85]

Those whom they call upon besides Allah have no power to intercede, save for any who testify to the truth, and they know (that Allah is their Lord). [86] If you were to ask (the pagans) who it was that created them, they would be sure to say, *"Allah did."* So how can they be so far off the mark (in their veneration of idols)? [87]

(Allah knows what His Prophet) said (of them when he cried out), *"My Lord! This is a nation that truly won't believe!"* [88] So turn away from them, (Muhammad,) and say, *"Peace,"* for soon they'll know (the truth). [1585] [89]

[1585] Even after many years of preaching and teaching patiently and gently, Muhammad felt exasperated that the bulk of his people were not listening to him. This passage acknowledges that Allah had heard his concern, and it also gives him the command to leave them be if they won't listen. In effect, saying, "Peace," to the ignorant in this instance is like saying, "I'm done with you," in English.

The Smoky Haze

44 Ad-Dukhan
Late Meccan Period

According to 'Abdullah ibn Mas'ud (d. 653), during the early days of the Prophet's ministry, the Quraysh used to ask him many irrelevant questions, such as when it would rain, what would happen with market prices in the future and so on. When the persecution began, the Prophet asked Allah to inflict the Quraysh with seven years of famine, as He had done in the time of Prophet Joseph to the Egyptians. (Apparently, verses 1-11 were then revealed.) A famine then did, in fact, befall the region, and the Meccans were reduced to eating whatever hardscrabble food they could come by, even animal bones. The heat and hunger were so great that many Meccans complained of seeing a hazy smoke in the air (which was probably a result of their weakened state). Abu Sufyan was driven by desperation to plead with Muhammad to ask Allah to intercede and remove the punishment. If the famine lifted, he explained, then the Meccans would believe in him. Verses 12-42 were then revealed, which mention the punishment that Muhammad had invoked against them. These verses also predicted, however, that the Meccans would continue to reject faith, and that is exactly what they did.

This episode then leads into a discussion of how other peoples of the past, most notably the pharaoh of Egypt, failed to pay heed to the warnings of Allah. Thus, they, too, suffered a heavy price. Finally, the chapter closes with a description of the ultimate penalty that unmindful people will have to face, namely the trials of Hellfire. Thus, the central message is that people have time while they are alive to see the signs and take the warnings. Better to listen while there is a chance to enter into Allah's fellowship, rather than be filled with regret when it is impossible to make amends. The Prophet said of this chapter, "Whoever recites (this chapter) on a Friday, whether by day or night, then Allah will build an abode for him or her in Paradise." (*Qurtubi*)

In the Name of Allah,
the Compassionate, the Merciful

Ḥā. Meem. [1]

By the Book that makes things clear, [2] We sent it down on a blessed night, [1586] and We're (constantly giving you) warning. [3]

On that (night), every wise command was made apparent [4] by a command from Our presence, for We're indeed sending (revelation) [5] as a mercy from your Lord.

[1586] This is a reference to the Night of Power mentioned in chapter 97. According to the majority of commentators, Allah commissions His prophets in the month of Ramadan and has always followed that pattern. (*Ma'ariful Qur'an*) The Prophet said that Allah forgives all Muslims their sins on this night with the exception of fortune-tellers (*kahin*), sorcerers, people prone to argumentation, those who imbibe intoxicants, those who disobey their parents and those who are unchaste. (*Zamakhshari*)

He's the Hearing and the Knowing [6] - the Lord of the heavens and the earth and everything in between!

(So, accept this revelation if) you're certain of your convictions. [7] There's no other god than He; He gives life and death – (He's) your Lord and the Lord of your earliest ancestors! [8]

The Meccans Receive a Warning

*B*ut no! They still dabble in uncertainty. [1587] [9] Then watch for the day when a smoky haze will be clearly evident in the sky, [10] enveloping people's (senses with heat, stale air and hunger); that will be an awful punishment. [11]

(Now that it's come upon them, they've come to you and cried), *"Our Lord! Take this punishment away from us, and then we'll believe!"* [12]

Yet, how could this reminder really convince them, given that a clear messenger had already come to them? [13] They just turned away from him and said, *"He's being taught by someone, or he's just crazy!"* [14]

We'll relieve them of the punishment for a while, (but just see how fast) you'll revert (to your old ways)! [15] One day We're going to take hold of you (Meccans) in a great onslaught, and then We'll get Our due from you. [1588] [16]

The Pharaoh did not Heed the Warning

*A*nd so it was that before them we tested the people of Pharaoh.

An honorable messenger [1589] came to them, [17] saying, *"Release to me the servants of Allah, for I'm a trustworthy messenger (that's been sent) to you. [18] Don't be arrogant against Allah, for I stand before you with the clear power (to command)."* [19]

"As for me, I've sought the protection of my Lord and your Lord against your ability to do me harm. [20] If you don't believe (what I'm telling you), then at least don't interfere (with my mission)." [21]

(The Egyptians worked against him, however), so he called out to his Lord, *"They're a wicked people!"* [22]

"Set out with My servants by night," (came the command,) *"for you'll certainly be pursued. [23] Leave the (parted) sea (that you'll have to cross through) alone, for (the Egyptian) forces that will (pursue you through it will) be drowned (when it collapses in on them)."* [24]

How many gardens and bubbling springs did they leave behind, [25] and fields of grain, fine buildings [26] and richness in which they delighted? [27]

That's (how it ended), and We let other peoples inherit (those things). [28] Neither heaven above nor the earth shed a

---

[1587] 'Abdullah ibn Mas'ud (d. 653), one of the Prophet's most prominent companions, said of the famine that came, "(The people of western Arabia) became so exhausted and hungry that they ate bones and dead carcasses. A man would look at the sky and would see nothing between him and the sky except a smoky haze on account of his exhaustion." (*Ibn Kathir*) Sometime after the drought began, many desperate people began beseeching the Prophet for relief. One man approached the Prophet and begged him to pray for rain for the people of his district. The Prophet then prayed for rain, and soon thereafter the rain came, and the drought was broken.

[1588] 'Abdullah ibn Mas'ud (d. 653) once mentioned five predictions or miracles mentioned in the Qur'an that came true. He said, "Five things have come to pass: the smoky haze [44:10-11], the (victory) of the Romans [30:1-6], the (splitting of the) moon [54:1-2], the great *seizure* (the death of the Qurayshi leadership at the Battle of Badr, see 32:28-30 and 76:23-24), and the great tie-down (at Badr, when the Meccan defeat tied shame and torment to their hearts and minds, see 25:77)." (*Bukhari, Muslim, Ibn Kathir*)

[1589] The honorable messenger was Moses.

tear for them, nor were they given any chance to recover. [29]

And so it was that We delivered the Children of Israel from the pain and humiliation [30] caused by Pharaoh, for He was more outrageous than other tyrants. [31]

Moreover, We deliberately chose (the Children of Israel) over all the other people of the world, [32] and We gave them some signs that were an obvious challenge. [33]

Arrogance is No Substitute for Faith

*N*ow as for these (Meccans), they say, [34] *"There's nothing more to come after we die the first time, and we're certainly never going to be raised to life again!* [35] *If you're so honest, then bring our ancestors back (from the dead)!"* [36]

Are they better than the people of Tuba and all those (ancient ones) who came before them? [1590] We destroyed them all because of their wickedness! [37] We didn't create the heavens and the earth and all in between them merely for fun. [38] We didn't create them except for a truthful purpose, but most of them don't know that. [39]

The Day of Sorting is a time that's reserved for all of them. [40] (It's) a day when no defender can aid his client in the least and when no help will come to them, [41] save for the one who receives Allah's mercy, for truly He's the Powerful, the Merciful. [42]

The Trials and Delights of the Afterlife

*T*he tree of *Zaqqum* [1591] [43] will be the food of the sinful. [1592] [44] Like molten brass it will curdle in their guts, [45] rippling like scalding water. [46] *"Seize him!"* (a voice will command). *"Drag him in the middle of the raging blaze!* [47] *Punish him with scalding water poured over his head.* [48] *Suffer it now! Oh, you were so strong and respectable!* [49] *Now this (punishment you're receiving) is what you used to doubt (before)!"* [50]

Those who were mindful (of Allah), however, will be in a safe position [51] among gardens and fountains, [52] dressed in silk and rich brocade. They'll gaze upon each other (in satisfaction). [53]

That's (how it will be)! We're going to join them (with attendants), who will have intense, expressive eyes. [54] They can call for every type of fruit to be brought to them in a secure environment. [55]

[1590] There are two possible groups to whom this verse could refer. Some classical Islamic scholars have suggested that this refers to an ancient people from the land of Yemen who had many successive dynasties several centuries before the time of the Prophet. One of these dynasties was headed by a family that used the term *Tuba* as their word for a ruler. It is even suggested that the specific evil king was a man named As'ad Abu Kurayb ibn Madikarab Yamani, who ruled in the first century B.C.E. Supposedly, this king attempted to attack the city of Yathrib (later Medina), but local Jewish rabbis warned him that this city would one day host a prophet, so King As'ad decided to convert to Judaism and believe in One God. After he died, his people reverted to idolatry, and their country later fell into ruin. (*Ibn Kathir*) The Prophet reportedly stated that no one should revile (the king of) Tuba, for he had become a believer in God. (*Ahmad, Tabarani*) Another possible connection has recently been uncovered by archeologists working in northern Syria since the 1990s. An ancient city known as Tuba existed in that area, as attested to by ancient records from the city of Ebla that date as far back as 2400 B.C.E. At a site known as Tell Umm el-Marra, archeologists have uncovered the remains of tombs, city walls and artifacts that have led them to believe that this, in fact, may be the site of the ancient city spoken of in the old clay tablets. That area, near the Euphrates River and in the midst of the Jabbul Plain, is known as the original cradle of civilization. Perhaps legends of that ancient city still survived in the lore of the region.

[1591] See 37:62-68 for information about the tree of *Zaqqum*.

[1592] This passage was revealed after the Prophet's foe, Abu Jahl, told him, "I'm the strongest man around here and the most respectable." (*Asbab ul-Nuzul*)

They'll never again (feel the sensation) of death, other than for the first time they died, and He'll protect them from the punishment of the raging blaze. [56] *That's a generous gift from your Lord, and that's the ultimate success!* [57]

Truly, We've made this (Qur'an) easy on your tongue [1593] so they could be reminded, [58] so keep watch, for they'll be keeping watch, also. [59]

[1593] In Arabic, the Qur'an has many qualities that are akin to music, poetry, rhyme and dramatic prose. It would be an easy message to get across to its first listeners. Even for those who do not understand Arabic, the tones, rhymes and obvious charm of the melody are evident.

Kneeling

45 Al Jathīyah
Late Meccan Period

This chapter was most likely revealed after the preceding one, as it seems like a continuation of the themes raised there. Its main message revolves around answering any lingering doubts about the Qur'an's conception of Allah, as well as making it clear that wicked behavior will not be rewarded in either this life or in the next.

In the Name of Allah,
the Compassionate, the Merciful

Hā. Meem. [1]

The revelation of this Book is from Allah, the Powerful and the Wise. [2] Signs (of His power) exist all throughout the heavens and the earth for the believers (to see), [3] even as they exist in the creation of your own selves and in the wide dispersal of living creatures (all around the world). There are indeed signs in all of these things for those who are certain of their convictions. [4]

The alternation of night and day, the pouring down from the sky of life-giving rain with which the dead earth is revived, and the changing wind patterns – all of these are signs for those who reflect. [5]

These are the signs of Allah that We're enumerating for you in all truth. So then in what kind of presentation will they believe after rejecting Allah and His signs? [6]

Ruin to every sinful charlatan! [7] He hears the signs of Allah enumerated for him; yet, he becomes stubborn and arrogant, acting as if he never heard them! Tell him about a painful punishment! [8]

For sure, whenever he learns about some of Our (revealed) verses, he takes them as a joke! Well, a humiliating punishment will be waiting for him! [1594] [9]

Hellfire will be standing right in front of (those fakers)! Nothing they earned will do them any good, and no close allies they arranged, besides Allah, will be there to help, for a terrible punishment will be waiting for them. [10]

(Therefore you should know that) this (Book) is a source of guidance. Whoever rejects the (revealed) verses of their Lord will suffer the punishment of complete annihilation. [11]

We are only Responsible for Ourselves

Allah is the One Who tamed the ocean for you, so that ships could sail throughout it by His permission, thus

---

[1594] Abu Jahl, Abu Lahab, an-Nadr ibn al-Harith and others are representative of the kinds of enemies of the Prophet that are referenced here. Abu Jahl was the most sarcastic of all the Prophet's foes, so it is possible he is the main focus of this passage.

allowing you to seek His bounty and express your gratitude. [12] He has tamed for you, from His Own Self, whatever is in the heavens and on the earth. Truly, the signs are there for those who think. [1595] [13]

We are All Judged for Our Faith and Our Actions

*T*ell the believers to forgive those who don't look forward to the days of Allah. [1596] He's the One Who rewards every community according to what they've earned. [14]

Whoever does what's morally right does so for the benefit of his own soul. Whoever does evil is in reality working against (his own future welfare). Soon enough you all will be brought back to your Lord. [15]

Stand Firmly despite the Ignorant

*A*nd so it was that We granted the Children of Israel the Book (of scripture), the power to act, and the gift of prophethood. We also provided them with wholesome (food) and favored them above all others in the universe. [16]

We also gave them clear directions in all their affairs, but it was only after they received such knowledge that they fell into competing groups, due to arrogant jealousy among themselves.

Their Lord will judge between them concerning these points of difference on the Day of Judgment. [17]

Then we put you, (Muhammad,) on the path of authority. So follow it, and don't follow the whims of the ignorant. [18] They won't be of any use to you in the sight of Allah.

Wrongdoers protect no one but themselves, while Allah protects those who are mindful (of Him). [19] These (verses) are plain truths for people and a source of guidance and mercy to those who are confident in their convictions. [20]

Supreme Justice

*D*o people who are wicked think that We're going to measure them by the same standard as believers who practice morality and goodness? Do they think that they're going to be treated the same way both here and after their deaths? *If so, then they're making the worst kind of assumption!* [21]

Allah created the heavens and the earth for a clear purpose, so that every soul may find its just reward for what it's earned, and no one will be treated unfairly. [22]

Have you seen the kind of person who takes his own whims as his god? Allah has left that one astray - sealing his hearing, veiling his heart and covering his sight. So who can now guide him after Allah (has withdrawn His support)? Won't you take a reminder? [23]

The (faithless) say, "*What else is there but this life here and now? We're all going to die. So we just live for now, and nothing but time can destroy us.*" [1597] However, they have no

---

[1595] The Prophet said, "One learned person is harder on Satan than a thousand (simple) worshippers." (*Nisa'i, Tirmidhi*)

[1596] There are two complimentary stories connected to this verse. In the late Meccan period, a pagan insulted 'Umar ibn al-Khattab, and the latter wanted to get back at the pagan, but this verse was revealed counseling self-control and patience with those who deal in insults; thus, 'Umar relented. (*Asbab ul-Nuzul*)

[1597] In Pre-Islamic times, when some hardship would come upon people, they would say, "Curses to the passage of time!" (*Ibn Kathir*) The Prophet said not to curse time, for Allah is the embodiment of time. He also said that Allah, Himself, said, "The son of Adam annoys Me when he curses Time, even

solid information (about this) and thus do no more than speculate. [24]

When Our clear verses are presented to them, their only defense is to say, "*So bring our ancestors back to life if what you're saying is true.*" [25]

Say (to them), "*Allah is the One Who gives you life, and then He gives you death. He's going to collect you all back together on the Day of Judgment, a day of which there is no doubt. Yet, most people don't understand.*" [26]

The Regret of the Foretold Day

𝒯he control of the heavens and the earth belongs to Allah, as well as the day upon which the Hour (of Judgment) will be established.

On that day, the deceitful will surely perish. [27] You will see every community kneeling, and every community will be called to make an account of its record. "*This day you're being paid back for all that you did. [28] Our record here faithfully describes all of your (actions), for We've kept track of everything you've ever done!*" [29]

Those who believed and did what was morally right will be admitted into their Lord's mercy, *and that will be a success for all to see!* [30]

The faithless, however, (will be told), "*Weren't Our signs ever presented to you? Oh, but you were arrogant and inclined towards evil. [31] When you were told that Allah's promise was true and that there was no mistaking the reality of the Hour, you said, 'We don't know anything about this 'Hour.' It's nothing but a fancy notion, and we have no confidence in its (reality).'*" [32]

Then they're going to see the (amount of) wickedness that they've amassed, and they'll be surrounded by what they used to ridicule! [1598] [33]

They'll be told, "*Today We're going to forget you, just like you forgot the appointment on this day of yours! Your home is in the Fire, and no one will ever help you. [34] You used to take the (revealed) verses of Allah as a joke, and the physical life of the world deceived you.*"

From that day onward, they'll never be released from it, nor will they ever have their repentance accepted. [1599] [35]

So all praise be to Allah, the Lord of the Heavens, the Lord of the Earth and the Lord of All the Worlds! [36] To Him belongs all greatness throughout the heavens and the earth, and He's the Powerful and the Wise. [37]

---

though I am Time. In My hands are all things, and it is I who alternates the day and the night." (*Bukhari*)

[1598] On the Day of Resurrection, Allah will ask some of His servants, "Didn't I give you a spouse, honor you and put horses and camels under your control? Didn't I let you become a leader and a master?" The servant will say, "Yes, Lord." Then Allah will say, "Didn't you think you would ever meet Me?" The servant will say, "No." Then Allah will say, "Then I will forget you today, even as you forgot Me." (*Muslim*)

[1599] The Prophet said, "When a deceased person is carried to his grave, he is followed by three, two of which return, leaving only one to remain with him. His relatives, his property and his deeds follow him. His relatives and property will leave him, while his deeds are all that remain with him." (*Bukhari*)

The Sand Dunes

46 Al Ahqaf
Late Meccan Period

This chapter, which internal evidence dates to about the year 620, is the last in the seven part *Ha Meem* series. During this time the Meccans had agreed to boycott the Prophet's clan and one other, from whom most of the converts came, and they forced the two groups to flee into a barren valley. They were only allowed to emerge to buy food during sacred months. At any other time, if any of the boycotted members were seen in the markets, Abu Jahl and others would shout to the merchants not to sell them anything.

After the Meccans were shamed into lifting the boycott by visiting bedouin chiefs, the Prophet suffered the loss of both his beloved wife Khadijah and his uncle and protector, Abu Talib. When Meccan persecution became unbearable, the Prophet traveled to the nearby city of Ta'if in the year 619 to seek asylum. However, he was cruelly ejected from that city, which had an equally strong tradition of idolatry as that of Mecca. On his return journey to Mecca, he stopped and made camp one night. There he recited some new verses of the Qur'an. A company of jinn heard what he was saying, and they converted. (See verses 46:29-32 and also introduction to chapter 72.)

In the Name of Allah, the Compassionate, the Merciful

Ḥā. Meem. [1]

This revelation is from Allah, the Powerful and the Wise. [2] We didn't create the heavens and the earth and everything else in between them save for a truthful purpose, and even then only for a fixed time limit. Still the faithless turn away from what they've been forewarned about. [3]

So ask (them), *"Don't you see (with your own eyes the foolishness of what) you're calling on besides Allah? Show me something – anything - that (your idols) created on this earth, or do (your false gods) own a part of the heavens, instead? Bring me some (kind of proof) from a book that came (to you) before this (Qur'an), or (show me)* some scrap of (ancient) knowledge (to confirm your claims), if you're really so honest!" [1600] [4]

Who can be more mistaken than the one who calls upon something other than Allah - something that won't even answer him on the Day of Assembly and that is oblivious to his cries? [5]

On the contrary, when all people are gathered together, those (false gods) will be hostile to them, and they're going to reject all acts of worship (offered to them). [6]

Answering those who Doubt

*W*hen Our clearly evident verses are read out to them, the faithless say of

---

[1600] The pagans would criticize Muhammad (p) for his views; yet they could not produce any authority for their beliefs and practices other than to say, "These are the customs of our ancestors."

this truth that has reached them, *"It's obviously magic,"* [7] or they claim, *"He made it all up!"*

Say (to them), *"If I had invented (this Qur'an on my own), then you wouldn't be able to get one good thing for me from Allah.* [1601] *He knows better what you're talking about, and He's quite enough of a witness between you and me. He's the Forgiving and Merciful."* [8]

Then tell (them), *"I'm not (some peddler) of new doctrines that are out of sync with the rest of the messengers (of Allah), nor do I know what will happen to you or to me.* [1602] *I'm only following what's been revealed to me. I'm no less than a clear warner."* [9]

Thereafter ask (them), *"Look here. If (what I'm bringing to you) is, in fact, from Allah, and you reject it, even though a witness from the Children of Israel has confirmed that (this message) is similar (to what the prophets of old brought) and has believed in it, are you still too*

proud (to accept it)? [1603] *Truly, Allah doesn't guide people who are corrupt."* [10]

Social Class is no Barrier to Equality before Allah

The faithless have this to say about the believers: *"If this (message) were a good thing, then (lower class people) would not have accepted it first before us!"* [1604]

Since they won't let themselves be guided by it, they add, *"These (teachings) are an old fraud!"* [11] Long before this (Qur'an) came, the Book of Moses (was revealed) as a source of direction and mercy. This Book (that you have now) reaffirms its (truths), though in the Arabic language. It's a warning to those who do wrong and good news for the good. [12]

Those who say, *"Our Lord is Allah,"* and then stand resolved (in their declaration) will have nothing to fear or regret. [13]

[1601] The argument is made that if Muhammad merely invented a new religion, then Allah would not put any blessings in it, nor would He bring success to it. This was something of a bold assertion given that at the time of this chapter's revelation, the Prophet and his followers were suffering under the constant bullying and persecution of the Meccans. Amazingly enough, within a few short years Islam triumphed and paganism failed. So which way of life seemed to have Allah's support?

[1602] When the Muslim refugees from Mecca fled to Medina in the year 622, they were impoverished. The Prophet asked the Medinan converts to parcel out the refugees and take them in and shelter them. One women named Umm al-'Ala had this story to tell about it: "When the Helpers drew lots to see which Immigrants would live with them, our lot was to have Uthman ibn Maz'un. Later he fell sick in our house, so we took care of him until he died. Then we wrapped him up in his burial shroud. The Messenger of Allah came in (for the funeral), and then I said (of the deceased man), 'Father of Sa'ib, may Allah have mercy on you. I testify that Allah has truly honored you.' The Messenger of Allah asked, 'How do you know that Allah has honored him?' I said, 'I don't know, may my parents be ransomed for you!' Then the Messenger of Allah said, 'As for him, what is certain has reached him from his Lord, and I wish him well. But by Allah, even though I am Allah's Messenger, I don't know what will happen to me (after death).' Then I said, 'I will never claim to be a pious person again after hearing this.' I was distressed over this incident, and when I went to sleep I saw in a dream that same man, Uthman, and he owned a running spring. I went to the Messenger of Allah and told him about it, and he said, 'That was his good deeds.'" *(Bukhari, Ahmad)*

[1603] The identity of the Jewish visitor to Mecca who vouched for the teachings of Muhammad is unknown, though the Meccans obviously knew of him for the Qur'an to point him out so prominently to them. In those days, Jewish travelers were as common as any others passing through Mecca.

[1604] The bulk of the Prophet's converts were drawn from what were considered to be the middle and lower rungs of society, including freed slaves, women, poor people, foreigners and people with lesser social influence. It is thought that this verse references one female convert in particular, a slave girl named Zunayrah, who was owned by 'Umar ibn al-Khattab in the days while he was still a pagan. When he found out she had converted to Islam, 'Umar used to beat her until his arm got tired. The pagans commented on her suffering, saying, "If accepting Islam were such a good thing, then this worthless woman Zunayrah would not have accepted it before us." This verse was revealed to answer this charge. (Imagine the shock of the pagans later on when 'Umar finally did convert – and repented of all the evil he had done before!) *(Ma'ariful Qur'an)*

They're the companions of the Garden, and there they shall remain as a reward for their (good) deeds. [14]

Respecting Our Parents for their Sacrifices

$\mathcal{W}$e've made it an obligation upon every human being to show kindness to his parents. [1605] His mother carried him painfully and gave birth to him in pain. It took thirty months (for his mother) to carry him and finally wean him.

Then, when he reaches the age of his full strength at forty years, he says, *"O My Lord! Let me show my thanks to You for the favor You've given to me and to my parents, so that I can do the right thing as You would have me do. Be good to me in (the raising of) my own descendants. I have indeed turned myself to You, and I am among those who submit (to You)."* [1606] [15]

These are the ones from whom We will accept the best of their deeds and also overlook their faults. [1607] (They'll) be among the companions of the Garden - *an honest promise that was made to them (while they were still in the world).* [16]

(There is another type of person) who says to his parents, *"To heck with you! Are you trying to convince me that I'll be resurrected, even though generations before me have passed away (and disappeared)?"* (His parents) will ask for Allah's relief (as they tell him,) *"You're doomed! (For Allah's sake) believe! The promise*

of Allah is real." However, (their child) only says, *"What is all of this but ancient fables?"* [17]

It's these who've had the truth of the sentence proven against them. (It's a sentence) that was levied against the many previous generations of jinns and humans that have passed away – *(the promise) that they'll all be utterly lost.* [1608] [18] Everyone is assigned a different rank based upon the deeds (they did in life), so that (Allah) can repay them for their deeds (fairly), and no injustice will be done to anyone. [19]

On the day when the faithless will be placed by the Fire, (they're going to be told), *"You had your good things in the life of the world, and you had a good time with them, but today you're going to be paid back (for your failures) with a humiliating punishment, for you were arrogant in the world - for no good reason - and you behaved poorly."* [20]

The Story of Prophet Hūd

$\mathcal{R}$emember (the story of the people of) 'Ad when a brother of theirs [1609] warned his people about their (dependence on the irrigation channels that snaked through) the winding tracts of sand. There were warners who came before him, and there would be some after him, (who said), *"Don't serve anything other than Allah. I fear for you the penalty of a momentous day."* [21]

They said, *"Did you come here in order to make us turn away from our gods? Then bring*

[1605] A man once asked the Prophet, "Messenger of Allah, is there any kindness left that I can do for my parents after their death?" He replied, "Yes, you can invoke blessings upon them, implore forgiveness for them, carry out their final instructions after their death, honor ties of relationship that were dependent on them, and honor their friends." (*Abu Dawud*)

[1606] A man went to the Prophet and asked him for permission to join a military expedition. The Prophet asked him if he had a mother still living. When he replied that he had, he said, "Stay with her, for Paradise is at her feet." (*Ahmad*)

[1607] The Prophet said, "A believer will approach his Lord on the Day of Judgment and will be covered with His mercy. He will ask him about his sins saying, 'Do you remember such and such a sin?' He will answer, 'O Lord, I do remember.' Then Allah will say, 'I kept it secret for you in the world, and I pardon you today.' Then the record of his good deeds will be given him." (*Bukhari, Muslim*) 'Ali ibn Abi Talib, in later years, once told some people who were criticizing Uthman ibn Affan that 'Uthman was one of those about whom this verse mentioned. (*Ibn Kathir*)

[1608] The 'sentence' or verdict of which this verse speaks can be found in 38:84-85 and 32:13.

[1609] This is a reference to prophet Hud, who was raised up among them.

down upon us this (disaster) with which you've been threatening us, that is if you're really so honest!" [22]

"The knowledge of (when it will come) is with Allah alone," he replied. *"I'm only conveying to you what's been sent down to me, but now I finally see that you're an ignorant people."* [23]

Then when they saw the great cloud moving in the sky, coming nearer to their valleys, they said, *"Oh, that's just an advancing rain cloud!"*

"Not so!" (their prophet cried). *"It's the very thing that you dared to come sooner - a terrible, destructive sandstorm* [24] *that will destroy everything in its path by its Lord's command!"*

In the morning, there was nothing left to see, save for (the wreckage) of their homes. That's how We repay wicked nations. [1610] [25]

And so We had established (their powerful civilization) in a way that We haven't done for you (people of Mecca). We blessed them with (the same) ability to hear, see and understand (with which We've blessed you), but their hearing, seeing and understanding did them no good, for they kept on rejecting the signs of Allah. Thus, they were completely engulfed by what they used to ridicule. [26]

And so it was that We destroyed (many) towns that existed in your very region. [1611] We've shown the signs in so many ways, so you might (be influenced) to return (to Us). [27]

Why didn't the gods they worshipped in place of Allah help them or make an opening for them (to gain Allah's favor)? No way! They left them to languish, but that was their charade and that was their invention. [28]

Some Jinns Accepted the Message

𝓘t came to pass [1612] that We turned a company of *hidden ones* towards you, [1613] (Muhammad), and they listened to the recitation of this Qur'an as they stood by.

(After hearing it), they exclaimed (to each other), *"Listen quietly!"*

[1610] The ruins of their city are located at a site in present-day Oman.
[1611] The ruined cities of the Thamud and some others in Yemen were known to the Arabs.
[1612] Background on verses 29-32: Many scholars believe that the following narrative refers to the same incident mentioned in Surah Al-Jinn, when the Prophet was reciting Surah Ar-Rahman in the valley of Nakhlah after being chased out of Ta'if. The jinn overheard his recitation and immediately embraced his message. In another narration, it is said that the Prophet had traveled with some companions to attend a trade fair at a place named Ukaz. (This was the site of a battle that he had witnessed as a ten-year-old boy during the Fijar War between the Quraysh and the Hawazin.) It was his intention to preach to the throngs who would gather there for business and diversion. While the Prophet was leading his men in prayer in their camp, a group of 'hidden ones' (jinns) happened by and heard the recitation of the Qur'an. They converted to Islam and went to their own people to try and convert them. The Prophet was not immediately aware of this until chapter 72 was revealed. Then he understood that the hidden ones (jinns) could also hear him and convert. This passage was then revealed, informing the Prophet that this phenomenon happened once before, even before chapter 72 and its events were mentioned. (Ma'ariful Qur'an) Some scholars have postulated that the hidden ones in question might have been desert nomads, as unknown people can be given this designation in Arab parlance.
[1613] The term for 'Hidden Ones' is *jinn* in Arabic. It can refer to hidden spiritual beings, or even unknown human strangers. Some modern scholars have postulated that the 'Hidden Ones' mentioned here were human travelers who heard the Prophet preaching somewhere and, without introducing themselves to the Prophet, returned home and brought the message of monotheism to their people. The majority opinion however is that this refers to the classic fiery energy beings (*jinns*) that populate another spectrum.

When the recitation was finished, they returned to their own kind to warn them. [1614] [29]

They said, *"Our people! We've just heard a book, one revealed after Moses, that confirms what came before it. It guides towards the truth and to a straight path. [30] Our people! Respond to the one who invites you to Allah, and believe him. (Allah) will forgive you your faults and save you from a terrible punishment.* [31]

"If any of you don't respond to the one who's inviting (us) to Allah, (then he should know that) he can't frustrate (Allah's plan) on earth, nor will He find any protectors besides Allah. They're clearly mistaken (if they think they can thwart Him)." [32]

The Signs of Truth will Strengthen You

*D*on't they see that Allah, the One Who created the heavens and the earth and Who never tired from doing that work, is able to give life to the dead? Yes, indeed! He has power over all things! [33]

On the day when the faithless will be placed near the Fire, (they'll be asked), *"Isn't this all true?"* *"Absolutely,"* they'll cry, *"by our Lord it is!"*

(Then they'll be told,) *"So now suffer the punishment for all your suppression (of the truth that you did)."* [34]

Persevere in patience, as did (all the) resolute messengers (of the past). [1615] Don't be impatient over them, (waiting for the faithless to be punished).

When the day comes and they see what they were promised, it'll seem as if they lingered (in the world) no more than an hour on a single day. So convey (the message). Is anyone ever destroyed except for rebellious nations? [35]

[1614] The Prophet had traveled with some companions to attend a trade fair at a place named Ukaz. (This was the site of a battle that he had witnessed as a ten year old boy during the Fijar War between the Quraysh and the Hawazin.) It was his intention to preach to the throngs who would gather there for business and diversion. While the Prophet was leading his men in prayer in their camp, a group of 'hidden ones' (*jinns*) happened by and heard the recitation of the Qur'an. They converted to Islam and went to their own people to try and convert them. The Prophet was not immediately aware of this until chapter 72 was revealed. Then he understood that the hidden ones (*jinns*) could also hear him and convert. This passage was then revealed, informing the Prophet that this phenomenon happened once before, even before chapter 72 and its events were mentioned. (*Ma'ariful Qur'an*) Some scholars have postulated that the hidden ones in question might have been desert nomads, as unknown people can be given this designation in Arab parlance.

[1615] The resolute messengers were Noah, Abraham, Moses and Jesus. (See 33:7 and 42:13.) The Prophet needed such counsel as it looked as if he had no options for his weak following in the face of relentless Meccan persecution. Indeed, the Muslims in Mecca were enduring very harsh conditions at the hands of the idolaters. One night, however, the Prophet had a dream in which he saw a land full of palm trees situated in between two rocky lava fields. (*Bukhari*) When he told his followers, they immediately felt that it was a sign from Allah that they were to move somewhere to escape the predations of their pagan neighbors. (Far away Yathrib, or *Medina,* as it would later be called, was not even thought of as an option for refuge.) Some months passed, and the Prophet gave no order about migrating anywhere. His followers began to ask him about it. "When should we leave our homes?" they would inquire. He explained that he was waiting for a more definitive order from Allah. Later, when the Yathrib option opened up, the meaning of his dream became clear to all, for Yathrib was a fertile oasis town surrounded by many orchards of palms in all directions – situated between two large lava fields.

The Praised One

47 Muhammad
aka Al-Qital
Early Medinan Period

This chapter is the first of three Medinan chapters that deal with issues the fledgling community had to face. This first one promotes the idea that self-defense is sometimes necessary in the face of a relentless oppressor. Indeed, even though previous verses of the Qur'an mentioned to the believers that they might have to fight back against their persecutors, by this time no such action had taken place (see 2:190 for example). Even though the Muslims had abandoned Mecca, the pagans were not in any mood to live and let live. They began to initiate raids on the outskirts of Medina and also upon tribes that had allied with the Prophet. This was normal Arabian custom, to raid one's enemies, but the Muslim community, which stood for civilization and order, could not tolerate such banditry and murder. This chapter, then, was meant to rally the believers, even though the number of their able-bodied fighting men was measured only in hundreds, not thousands like the pagans had.

In the Name of Allah,
the Compassionate, the Merciful

Those who reject Allah and hinder (others) from (joining) the path of Allah will find that Allah will nullify the value of their deeds. [1]

Those who believe, who do what's morally right and who believe in what was sent down to Muhammad, *for it's the truth from their Lord*, will find that (Allah) will erase their faults and improve their overall condition. [2]

This (difference in treatment) is because the faithless follow foolishness, while the believers follow the truth from their Lord. This is the manner in which Allah compares the different conditions among people. [3]

Don't Hesitate Against an Enemy

Whenever you meet the faithless (in battle), aim for the lethal blow, (fighting aggressively and without hesitation). [1616]

[1616] The Prophet said, "There will always be a group from my community who will be victorious in the promotion of truth, until the last of them fight the Anti-Christ." (*Abu Dawud*) In another similar report, the Prophet added that Syria is the center of the domain of belief. (*Ahmad*) Also see 9:14-15. Tyranny and injustice always require sacrifice to confront. That is the way of the world. In 2:251 we read: "Truly, if Allah didn't enable one nation to deter another, then the world would indeed be filled with chaos, but Allah is unfailingly bountiful to all the worlds." Of course, the victorious group in question, that fights against injustice and promotes truth, must adhere to the Prophet's injunctions concerning just warfare. Among these is that non-combatants are not to be harmed, and neither trees nor buildings

Then, after you've thoroughly subdued them, tie them up with firm restraints.

Afterwards, (you can either) choose to be magnanimous (by freeing your prisoners outright), or (you can seek) release payments (by bargaining them back to their own side). [1617]

(This is the proper procedure to follow in your campaigns) until hostilities are over, and thus (you've been commanded.)

If Allah had wanted, He could've taken His retribution from them, (Himself), but (He lets you struggle in His cause) so that He can test some of you by way of others.

Allah will never let those who are killed (struggling) in His way lose any value in their deeds. [4] Soon He'll guide them, enhance their status [5] and then enter them into the Garden that He's already made known to them. [6]

Lessons about True Success

O you who believe! If you help in (the cause of) Allah, then He'll help you and plant your feet firmly. [7] However, those who reject (Allah) will be destroyed, and the value of their deeds will be nullified. [1618] [8]

That's because they hate what Allah has revealed. Therefore, He's going to render their deeds worthless. [9]

Don't they ever travel through the world and consider how (the wicked nations that came) before them were ended? Allah brought disaster down upon them, and a similar (fate awaits these Meccans who are trying to) suppress (the faith of Allah)! [10]

That's because Allah is the Protector of those who believe, while those who suppress (their awareness of) Allah have no protector at all. [1619] [11]

---

are allowed to be damaged if it can be helped at all. (Compare this with biblical injunctions on warfare such as in I Samuel 15:3 or Deuteronomy 20:16, where even the infants of one's enemies are to be executed, supposedly on Allah's orders!) Warfare for a just cause, according to Islamic principles, is between fighting units, not civilians, and chivalry (a Muslim-originated concept, by the way,) is the order of the day.

[1617] Islam forbids the unnecessary killing of captives taken in war. Freeing them, which was the Prophet's preferred custom, often had the effect of making people take a second look at Islamic principles and would oftentimes result in further conversions. Releasing prisoners upon the payment of a fine from their own people was a way to lift the fortunes of the poor among the community, who would be allowed to make individual bargains for their share of the captives. (It seems, however, that during the Battle of Badr, some of the Muslim fighters were a little *too* eager to gain captives, as 8:67-68 suggests, and this may have actually emboldened the enemy the next year at Uhud.) In either case, there is no concept in Islam of a lengthy confinement or imprisonment for prisoners of war; either free them outright for goodwill, exchange them for Muslim POWs, release them upon payment, execute proven war criminals or enter the prisoners into bonded servitude – a condition from which they may earn their way out later on (see 24:33). (*Ma'ariful Qur'an*)

[1618] The Prophet said, "Misery awaits the servant of the dollar (*dinar*); misery awaits the servant of the coin (*dirham*); misery awaits the servant of velvet. Misery awaits him and decline, and if he's stabbed by a thorn, may he not find anyone to pull it out for him." (*Ibn Majah*)

[1619] When the pagans of Mecca stood upon the field of battle at Uhud in the year 625, they were cheering and claiming victory, as they saw the Muslims fleeing up the side of Mount Uhud to seek safety. Dozens of Muslims lay dead, and the failure of some of Muhammad's men to obey orders and hold their positions enabled the crushing counterattack of Meccan cavalry that effectively forced them from the battlefield under fire. Abu Sufyan, the chief of Mecca (after nearly all other Meccan leaders had perished after the Battle of Badr in 624), called up the slopes, asking about the fate of the Prophet, Abu Bakr and 'Umar. When there was no response, he shouted that he thought all three were dead. 'Umar called back loudly, "You're a liar, you enemy of Allah! Allah saved those whom you don't like, for they're all alive!" Then Abu Sufyan shouted back, saying, "Today makes up for the day of Badr, and war always has ups and downs. Mutilation (of your dead) is what you will find, though I didn't encourage or restrain (my men from it)." Then he turned to his own men and began chanting, "Glory

Allah will admit those who believe and do what's morally right into gardens beneath which rivers flow, while those who reject (Allah) will enjoy (this shallow life), grazing (on its bounty) like cattle, (until) the Fire becomes their final home. [12]

Standing for Truth Involves Hardships

$\mathcal{H}$ow many cities have We destroyed (for their sins) that had more power than your city (of Mecca), (whose people) drove you out? [1620] Those (previous civilizations) had no one to help them (against Us). [13]

Is the one who (follows) clear evidence from his Lord no better than the one who thinks his bad conduct is fabulous? (Such people) only follow their own whims. [14]

Here is the likeness of the Garden that's been promised to those who were mindful (of Allah). Within it are sparkling rivers that never get stale, rivers of milk that never lose their flavor, rivers of wine that are pure bliss to drinkers, and rivers of sweet golden honey. [1621]

They'll also have every kind of fruit, as well as forgiveness from their Lord. (How can this be compared to the condition of) the one who must live in the Fire forever, and who'll be given a drink so scalding hot that it will tear his organs to shreds? [15]

The Doubters and the Faithful

$\mathcal{A}$mong (the faithless) are some who listen to you, but then leave your presence to ask those who received (religious) knowledge (from Allah) before, "*What did he just say?*" [1622] This is how those who've had their hearts sealed up by Allah behave, for they only follow their own whims. [16]

In contrast, those who (open their hearts) to guidance have their understanding (of the truth) heightened by Him, and He gives them a sense of mindfulness (about their duty to Him). [17]

Are they holding out for the Hour (of Judgment) to just spring upon them? They've already been given some portents of its coming, so when it's actually upon them, what use will all their reminders be? [1623] [18]

---

to Hubal!" (A prominent Meccan idol.) The Prophet asked his followers, "Well, aren't you going to answer them?" "What should we say," they asked. "Say, 'Allah is Most High and Exalted!'" Then Abu Sufyan said, "We have the goddess of honor (al-'Uzza), and you have no honor at all." The Prophet again asked his followers to respond. When they asked what they should say, he said, "Tell them, 'Allah is our Protector, and you have no protector at all!'" (*Ibn Kathir*)

[1620] Ibn 'Abbas (d. 687) said that this verse was revealed in Mecca just as the Prophet was leaving the city on his clandestine migration. The Prophet had paused under the cover of darkness, looked back upon Mecca as he was about to leave it for good, and then said, "You're the most beloved to Allah among all of Allah's settlements, and you're the most beloved to me among all of Allah's settlements. If it wasn't for the idolaters driving me away from you, I would never have left you." This verse was revealed in response to give the Prophet hope. (*Ibn Kathir, Ma'ariful Qur'an*)

[1621] The Prophet said, "In Paradise there is a lake of milk, a lake of water, a lake of honey and a lake of wine. Rivers flow forth from them." (*Ahmad*) He also insisted that honey had good healthful benefits for us. He said, "Make use of the two remedies: honey and the Qur'an." (*Tirmidhi, Ibn Majah, Bayhaqi*)

[1622] Some low class people would listen to the Prophet's teachings, then go to more experienced men who had already heard some of the stories of the Jews and Christians, and try to curry favor with them by mocking what they heard. This verse was revealed in response. (*Ibn Kathir*)

[1623] The Prophet spoke of many signs that would signal the coming of the Last Day. Among some of the more well-known portents culled from Bukhari and Muslim are these: women will outnumber men by fifty-to-one, it will be hard to tell men and women apart because they will dress so similarly, poor nations will waste their resources building tall buildings they can ill-afford, children will no longer respect their parents, knowledge will decrease, alcohol consumption will be widespread, tyrants will

Know then, (O Prophet), that there is no other god than Allah. Ask forgiveness for your faults and for the men and women who believe. Allah knows how you move around (in daily life) and how you dwell (in your homes). [1624] [19]

The Condition of Hypocrisy Described

(Some of) the believers say, "*If only a chapter (of the Qur'an) were sent down (to give us permission to fight back against our enemies)!*" Yet, when a decisive chapter is revealed, one that talks about fighting, suddenly you'll see the faint of heart looking at you like they were on the verge of death!

It would've been more appropriate [20] for them to obey and say the right thing, and when an issue has been decided upon, it would've been best for them if they would've been sincere to Allah. [21]

Then what would happen if you (hypocrites) were put in charge? Would you cause disorder in the land and betray your family ties? [22] These are (the kinds of people) whom Allah has cursed. He's deafened them and blinded them (from ever understanding anything). [23]

Are they even making an effort to understand the Qur'an, or are there padlocks on their hearts? [24] Those who turn their backs and renounce their faith, even after guidance was made self-evident to them, have been stirred up by Satan, who's filled them with false hopes. [25] This is (their condition) because they told those who hate what Allah has revealed, "*We'll obey you sometimes, too.*" Allah knows their deepest secrets. [26]

Then how will it be when the angels take (their souls at death) and raise (their hands to strike) towards their faces and their backs (to punish them)? [27]

This (fate awaits them) because they went along with what makes Allah angry. They hated to please Allah, so that's why He's going to render their deeds worthless. [28]

Do the (hypocrites, who are) weak at heart think that Allah will never expose their bitterness? [29] If We had wanted, We could've pointed all of them out to you, and you would've known them by their traits. Oh, but you will know them *by their tone of voice at least!* Allah knows whatever you're doing. [30]

Expect to be Tested

We're going to test you until We distinguish who strives the most and who's the most persevering. [1625] We're going to test your reputations, as well. [31]

Those who reject (Allah), who obstruct others from adopting the path of Allah and who resist His Messenger, even after guidance has clearly been shown to them - well, they do no harm to Allah, but He (can do harm to them) by rendering all their deeds worthless. [32]

O you who believe! [1626] Obey Allah and obey the Messenger, and don't let

---

be common, leaders will be devoid of intelligence, and war and conflict will increase causing great chaos.

[1624] Sufyan ibn 'Uyaynah was once asked about the importance of knowledge, and he replied, "Haven't you read verse 19 of chapter Muhammad?" After he quoted the verse, Ibn 'Uyaynah explained that knowledge must come before action. (*Ma'ariful Qur'an*)

[1625] This passage, according to Ibn 'Abbas (d. 687), refers to the hypocrites of Medina and some men of the two Jewish tribes of Banu Nadir and Banu Qurayzah who secretly sent food deliveries to the Meccans before the Battle of Badr. (*Ma'ariful Qur'an*)

[1626] Some of the Prophet's companions used to think that no sins would be recorded for someone who becomes a Muslim. This verse was revealed to tell them that even a Muslim can have bad deeds added

your deeds be made worthless. [33] Those who reject (Allah), who obstruct others from adopting the path of Allah and who die while still rejecting (faith) won't be forgiven by Allah. [1627] [34]

Don't lose heart and cry out for peace when you're the ones who should be on top. Allah is with you, and He'll never let you be cheated out of your deeds. [35]

The life of this world is no more than frolicking and entertainment. If you believe and are mindful (of your duty to Allah), then He'll grant you your due reward, and He won't ask you to give up (all) your (worldly) wealth, either. [36]

If He *were* to ask you for all of it and insisted upon it, *then, oh, how you would greedily cling to it!* That's how He could expose all of your lowly tendencies, (if He ever wanted to do that). [37]

You're the ones who are being invited to spend in the cause of Allah. Yet, there are some very stingy (people) among you.

Whoever is stingy does so to the loss of his own soul. Allah (is the One Who) Needs Nothing; rather, you are the ones who are in need.

If you turn back (from faith), then He'll just replace you with another group of people who won't be (as unreliable) as you! [1628] [38]

---

to his record. After this, the people who had thought this way became much more careful in their deeds. (*Asbab ul-Nuzul*)

[1627] Verse 4:48 was revealed later on after this verse to let the believers know that Allah will forgive all sins, save for making partners with Him, for those who truly repent. (*Ibn Kathir*)

[1628] When the Prophet recited this last line, one of his companions, the Persian convert, Salman al-Farsi, asked him, "Who are those people who will replace us if we, Allah forbid, turn away from Allah's commands, and who will not be (as unreliable) as we?" The Prophet slapped Salman's thigh (in a friendly way) and said, "If faith were to fly away to the stars, then a man from Persia will get it down from there and act upon it." (*Ma'ariful Qur'an*)

Victory

48 Al Fet-h
Middle Medinan Period

The Muslims who had fled from Meccan oppression in the year 622 and found refuge in Medina suffered three major assaults by the Meccan pagans: the Battle of Badr [624]; the debacle at Uhud [625]; and an attack and siege on Medina, itself [627]. In the year 628, in response to a prophetic dream he had, the Prophet announced that he would be leading a sacred pilgrimage to visit the Ka'bah in Mecca. Some thought that this bold course of action, walking into the stronghold of the enemy virtually unarmed, would be suicide, but, nevertheless, over 1,400 followers, both male and female, accompanied the Prophet on his journey towards Mecca.

Arab custom had always held that certain months were to be sacred truce months when all fighting and wars among the tribes had to be suspended. The Meccans were thus alarmed when they heard that the Muslims were using this custom as cover for such a bold visit. They sent their cavalry out to turn the Muslims back, but the Prophet led his followers, with the help of a scout, through trackless valleys and confounded the Meccan force sent to seek them out. When the Prophet and his followers arrived at a field above the hills of Mecca named Hudaybiyyah, the Prophet's camel suddenly stopped. Everyone thought the animal was being stubborn or at least tired, but Muhammad said, "No, the camel isn't tired. It has stopped by the order of Allah. By the One Who created me, I will accept any offers the Meccans make for peace." When the Meccan cavalry finally realized they had lost their prey, they returned home and stood down. When the location of the Muslims was finally found out, a message was sent to them, ordering them not to enter the city.

One of Muhammad's trusted companions, Uthman ibn Affan (d. 656), entered the city to talk to some of the Meccans about letting his people in for a pilgrimage, but then he was delayed for a while. Many Muslims thought he had been killed, and they were angry and wanted to fight. The Prophet swore that if they killed Uthman, he would invade the city. He moved under a tall acacia tree and took a pledge from all the Muslims there that they would fight to the last man if the Meccans had killed Uthman and violated the holy months of pilgrimage. This is called the Pledge of Ridwan.

A short time later, Uthman returned from his discussions, and a Meccan representative named Sahal soon arrived to begin the negotiations. After heated discussions, the two sides hammered out a ten-year truce. When the Prophet's secretary drew up the treaty, Sahal objected to Muhammad being referred to as a "Messenger of Allah" in the treaty, and he refused to sign it. (He also disliked the name of Allah being used in the preamble.) The Prophet said, "By Allah, I am His Messenger, even if your people don't believe it." Then he asked his secretary, 'Ali ibn Abi Talib, to blot out the words "Messenger of Allah" on the document, but when he hesitated, the Prophet took the quill in his own hand and asked where the words were located. When it was pointed out to him, he crossed them out with his own hand, all in the interests of getting some peace dividends for his beleaguered community.

Afterwards, many Muslims thought the Treaty of Hudaybiyyah, as it was called, was too favorable to the Meccans. What was worse, it stipulated that the Muslim pilgrims would not even be allowed to enter Mecca *until the following year*. In addition, a troubling clause made it incumbent upon the Muslims to return to Mecca any Meccan man who thereafter converted to Islam and fled to Medina. (They would most likely face torture and even death.) The prominent companions were quite alarmed by this and other provisions that seemed like a capitulation, but a Qur'anic revelation announced that the treaty was a great victory.

'Umar ibn al-Khattab is reported to have said incredulously, "*This* is a victory?" Yet it was, as later events would bear out. For his part, Muhammad ordered the pilgrims to sacrifice their animals and complete their pilgrimage rites there at Hudaybiyyah, but the people hesitated. Muhammad went into his tent despondently, and his wife, Umm Salamah, comforted him and told him to set the example for the others by completing the pilgrimage rites himself. He went out and did so, and the rest followed suit.

'Umar ibn al-Khattab and a number of other companions were still upset, and 'Umar went to ask the Prophet about the treaty while the pilgrims were completing their long journey back to Medina. He didn't get any reply from the Prophet, so he thought he might have been too forward and impolite. He quickly rode ahead of the column, fearing that a Qur'anic revelation might be sent down scolding him. The next day a rider rushed to him as they neared their city and called him to return to the Prophet. 'Umar rode back to the Prophet apprehensively, but the Prophet said, "Last night a chapter was revealed to me that's dearer to me than this life and all it contains." Then the Prophet began reciting this chapter to him. (*Bukhari, Nisa'i, Tirmidhi*)

The next year [629], as promised, the Meccans allowed the Prophet to lead a pilgrimage to the Ka'bah. The Meccan leadership departed from the city because they didn't want to see the Muslims involved in their devotions, but the commoners of the city remained and watched the Muslims perform their rites from their rooftops. One man from the Helpers led the Prophet's camel by the bridle and recited a poem loudly that included the line, "In the Name of the One for Whom Muhammad is His Messenger…"

One year later [630], when the Prophet led a column of ten thousand followers to force the peaceful surrender of Mecca (after the Meccans had broken the truce), he recited this very same chapter of Victory once again as he rode into the city triumphantly. One pagan witness said that the Prophet recited this chapter so beautifully and so loudly to the gathered throngs that day that people were thronging around him mesmerized. (*Bukhari, Muslim*)

In the Name of Allah,
the Compassionate, the Merciful

(Muhammad,) We've truly granted you a clear victory (through the signing of a truce with the Meccans)! [1] Allah will forgive you your past shortcomings and any that may follow. [1629]

He'll also fulfill His favor towards you and guide you on a straight path. [2]

Furthermore, Allah will help you with potent assistance. [3]

He's the One Who sent down tranquility into the hearts of the believers, so they could add even more faith to their

---

[1629] The Prophet used to offer prayers throughout the night, standing so long that his feet often became swollen. Somebody said to him, "But Allah has already forgiven you your past and future sins." On that, he replied, "Then shouldn't I be a thankful servant?" (*Bukhari, Muslim*)

faith. [1630] The forces of the heavens and the earth belong to Allah, and Allah is full of knowledge and wisdom. [4]

Believers will be Rewarded for their Efforts

$\mathcal{H}$e's going to admit the believers, both male and female, into gardens beneath which rivers flow, *and there they shall remain!* [1631] (He'll) also erase from them their shortcomings, and that's the ultimate success in Allah's sight! [5]

He's also going to punish the hypocrites, both male and female, and the idol-worshippers, both male and female, who have a perverted understanding of Allah. Evil surrounds them - *even the very wrath of Allah, Himself, is upon them*!

He's cursed them and prepared Hellfire for them, *and it's the worst destination!* [6] To Allah belongs the forces of the heavens and the earth, and Allah is powerful and wise. [7]

We sent you, (Muhammad,) to be a witness, a bringer of good news and also a warner, [8] so that (all of) you can believe in Allah and His Messenger, and so you can revere and honor Him and glorify Him morning and night. [9]

Indeed, those who pledge their allegiance to you, (Muhammad,) do no less than pledge their allegiance to Allah. [1632] The hand of Allah is over their hands!

Thereafter, the one who violates his pledge does so to the harm of his own soul, while the one who fulfills what he's promised to Allah, then Allah will soon give him a valuable reward. [10]

Excuses for Weakness

$\mathcal{T}$he (bedouin) Arabs who lagged behind, (avoiding the dangerous journey towards Mecca,) will tell you, "*We were busy with our property and our families – so just ask for our forgiveness.*" They're saying with their tongues what's not in their hearts. [1633]

So tell (them), "*Who has any power (to come to) your side against Allah if He wanted to give you some loss or give you some gain? No way! Allah is well-informed of everything you do.* [11] *No way! You thought that the Messenger and the faithful would never (survive the trip) and that they would never come back to their families. Your hearts were delighted with that prospect, and you harbored such ill-thoughts because you're a worthless group of people.*" [12]

Whoever has no faith in Allah and His Messenger (should know that) We've

---

[1630] The interpreters say that the Muslim pilgrims became resolved and full of spirit during their enterprise, when it is quite possible that they could have become fearful, since they were virtually unarmed in the countryside and at the mercy of the Meccans. The commentators say that this verse is proof that a believer can go through ups and downs in their level of faith. This is confirmed by a popular saying of the Prophet in which he said that hearts can get rusty just like metal. When people asked him how it could be prevented, he said by engaging in the habit of remembering Allah repeatedly (*dhikr*) and remembering death.

[1631] Despite the symbolic and practical value of winning a truce with the powerful Meccans, many of the companions were quite upset that they wouldn't be allowed to enter Mecca that year. They pointed out that the opening verses were good news for the Prophet. When they asked what good news was for them, the Prophet recited this new verse. (*Ibn Kathir*)

[1632] This refers to the Pledge at 'Aqabah.

[1633] The Prophet had asked that all of his able-bodied followers should accompany him on an unprecedented pilgrimage toward Mecca. However, because Mecca was still under enemy control, many of the weak in faith, especially from the bedouins, avoided taking part in the journey for fear of getting hurt. After the Prophet and the men and women who followed him returned unscathed to Medina, along with a new truce deal in hand, the bedouins began offering their excuses for not joining before. Among these were that they were too busy to participate. This passage was revealed in response. (*Ibn Hisham*)

prepared a raging blaze for all those who reject (Allah)! [13]

The control of the heavens and the earth belongs to Allah.

He forgives whomever He wants, and He punishes whomever He wants, though Allah is forgiving and merciful. [14]

No Reward for those who are Slow to do Their Duty

*A*h, but when it's time for you to march out and collect some gains, those who lagged behind will say, "*Let us go along with you, too.*" [1634] They want to change the very decree of Allah!

Tell them, "*You can't follow us just like that. Allah has already imposed (this prohibition) before.*"

Then they'll say, "*Oh! Well, you're just jealous of us.*"

Not so! They just don't understand very much. [15]

Tell the (bedouin) Arabs who lagged behind, "*You're (soon) going to be called (to fight) against a people who are fierce in warfare.* [1635] *Then you'll (really have) a fight (on your hands, unless they happen to) surrender first. If you're obedient (at that time), then Allah will give you an excellent reward. However, if you turn back like you did before, then He'll punish you with a painful punishment.*" [16]

There's no blame, however, on the blind, the handicapped or on a sick person (if he doesn't serve in the militia).

Whoever obeys Allah and His Messenger will be admitted into gardens beneath which rivers flow, while whoever turns back will be punished with a painful punishment. [17]

The Pledge of Ridwan

*A*llah's good pleasure was upon the believers when they pledged their allegiance to you [1636] under the tree (at

---

[1634] Prior to the Battle of Badr, some hypocrites and shifty bedouins used to pretend they were part of the Muslim effort. However, when any fighting would actually occur, such as during small patrols to intercept Meccan raiders, these people would melt away, offering excuses. Then when it would be time to distribute captured goods, they would come forward for their 'share.' Later on, when the Prophet subdued Khaybar, a den of intrigue from which the Siege of Medina was hatched, he forbade such bedouins from accompanying him or sharing in the spoils, based on this verse. (*Ibn Kathir*)

[1635] Some commentators hold that the '*people who are fierce in warfare*' were various peoples ranging from the Thaqif and Hawazin tribes (later encountered at the Battle of Hunayn in 630) or even the Persians, whom the Muslims fought later on after the Prophet passed away. Given the context, however, it's possible to suggest accurately to whom this prediction refers, especially given that the two Arab tribes mentioned were not so fierce as to warrant special mention. It seems that both the Byzantines and the Persians were being referenced, for by this time the Prophet had begun giving veiled hints that one day the Muslims would face those foes and beat them both, (much to the astonishment of some companions), and this has been the view of many commentators. (*Ma'ariful Qur'an*)

[1636] Uthman ibn Affan (d. 656) had entered the city of Mecca to deliver the Prophet's message that he just wanted to lead his followers in pilgrimage rites and meant no harm. The pagan chiefs, who all respected Uthman, offered to let him perform the pilgrimage rite of walking around the Ka'bah right there, but Uthman insisted he would never engage in any pilgrimage rite before the Prophet could do so. The Meccans then delayed him with their words, so he didn't return to the Muslim camp when he was supposed to. When the Muslims thought that Uthman might have been murdered by the Meccans, the Prophet stood under a tree as the throngs lined up and came to him, one at a time, and pledged to fight to the death if the treachery were true. The Prophet said, "No one who gave his pledge under the tree will enter Hellfire." (*Ahmad*) He also called those 1400 followers of his that day, "The best people on the face of the earth." (*Ma'ariful Qur'an*) Also see 9:111.

Hudaybiyyah, while the fate of your emissary was still in question). [1637]

He knew what was in their hearts, and He sent tranquility down upon them and rewarded them with a quick victory (through the signing of the truce deal). [18] There will be many more benefits they will take from it, (as well,) and Allah is powerful and wise. [19]

Allah promises you that you will take many benefits from (this treaty), and He's already given you some of them with regards to how He's restrained the hands (of the Meccans) from (attacking) you (while you were virtually defenseless), so that it could be a sign for the faithful, and also so He could guide you to a straight path. [20] There are other benefits (from this treaty) that are not within your power to achieve. Yet, Allah has accomplished them, and Allah has power over all things. [21]

If the faithless should fight you now, they would certainly turn their backs (and run away), and then they would surely have no supporters nor defenders (to protect them from Allah). [22] (This is) the method that was (approved) by Allah in the past, and you won't find any change in the methodology of Allah. [23]

Allah Protected the Believers

*H*e's the One Who restrained their hands from you and your hands from them - *right in the midst (of their own territory) of Mecca.* [1638] Then, afterwards, He gave you victory over them (through the truce), and Allah is watching whatever you do. [24]

The (Meccan idol-worshippers) are the ones who've rejected (Allah), held you back from the Sacred Mosque, and kept the sacrificial animals delayed from reaching their place of sacrifice.

If it wasn't for the fact that there were believing men and believing women (living clandestinely among the Meccans), about whom you knew nothing, and whom you might have rampaged through unknowingly and had embarrassing blunders recorded against you, (then Allah would have allowed you to force your way into Mecca, but He restrained you) so He could admit into His mercy whomever He willed.

If the (secret believers in Mecca) were separated (and in safety), then We would've certainly penalized the faithless among (the Meccans) with a painful punishment! [25]

While the faithless had hearts filled with rage - *the rage of ignorance* - Allah was sending His tranquility down upon His Messenger and also upon the believers, helping them to obey the order to restrain themselves. They were true to it and were more entitled to it, and Allah has knowledge of all things. [26]

Good Strategy Sometimes Requires Compromise

*A*nd so Allah fulfilled the vision of His Messenger (when he had seen himself in a dream leading the believers on a pilgrimage to hostile Mecca).

Now you can enter the Sacred Mosque, (next year) as Allah wills, with peace of mind, with your heads shaved or

---

[1637] The exact tree under which the pledge was taken was soon forgotten in the heady years of action that followed these events; however, a few of the companions in their senior years spoke wistfully of a desire to see it again. They were unable to identify the tree despite numerous visits. (*Ibn Kathir*)

[1638] While they were making camp on the plain of Hudaybiyyah, the Muslims captured a raiding party of some eighty Meccans who were aiming to ambush the Prophet in his camp. The Prophet forgave them and let them go without ransom so as not to provoke further needless hostility from the Meccans. That is what this next verse is referencing. (*Muslim, Abu Dawud, Tirmidhi, Ahmad*)

hair cut short and without fear, (on account of the truce deal).

He knew what *you* didn't know, and He granted you an early victory besides this, as well. [27] He's the One Who sent His Messenger with guidance and the true way of life, to proclaim it over all other ways of life, and Allah is enough as a witness. [28]

Muhammad is the Messenger of Allah. [1639] Those who are with him are hard on the faithless but compassionate among each other. [1640] You'll see them bowing and prostrating themselves (in prayer),

seeking the grace of Allah and (His) pleasure. On their faces are the marks of their prostrations, and this is their example in the Torah. [1641]

Their example in the Gospel is like a seed that sends out its blade and then makes itself strong. It then thickens and stands on its own stem, [1642] filling the farmers with satisfaction.

However, (such firm belief) fills the faithless with rage against (the believers). Allah has promised those among them who believe and do what's morally right forgiveness and a great reward. [1643] [29]

[1639] This is perhaps the first chronological use of the term "Messenger of Allah" as an attachment to the Prophet's name. The timing is probably due to the fact that before this chapter was revealed, the Meccan negotiators at Hudaybiyyah insisted that this phrase be stricken from the treaty of peace (under threat that they wouldn't sign it otherwise.) Imam ash-Shafi'i (d. 820), who loved the Prophet very deeply, was influenced by this verse. He never liked people to refer to Muhammad by his first name alone or as merely "the Messenger." Whenever he heard this, he would ask those people to refer to the Prophet as "The Messenger of Allah."

[1640] The Prophet said, "The example of the believers in their kindness and mercy for each other is like that of a body. When one of its parts becomes ill, the rest of the body responds with fever and sleeplessness." (*Muslim*) The Prophet also said, "One believer to another is like a house whose different parts reinforce each other." Then he interlaced his fingers together to show people what he meant. (*Bukhari*)

[1641] The book of Numbers in verse 16:22 records how Moses and Aaron prostrated on their faces to God. In fact, there are many such verses in the Bible that show this to be the most humble way to pray to God. Those who are given to frequent prayer actually begin to get small calluses or bruises on their foreheads from their constant prostrations. This spiritually-induced blemish is considered an honorable mark in much of the Muslim world.

[1642] See Mark 4:26-33, where Jesus is quoted as comparing faith to a seed that sprouts and multiplies. Also see Matthew 13:31-32 for a similar report.

[1643] The commentators have generally held that this (and other similar verses) make it a sin to ever curse or belittle the companions of the Prophet. (*Ma'ariful Qur'an*) The Prophet said of his companions: "(Remember) Allah. (Remember) Allah with regards to my companions. Don't make them the object of your criticism after I'm gone. He who loves them does so for love of me. He who hates them, hates them because they hate me. Whoever insults them, insults me, and whoever insults me, insults Allah. Whoever desires to insult Allah will be punished by Him." (*Tirmidhi*)

The Inner Rooms

49 Al Hujurat
Late Medinan Period

This chapter, which was revealed either late in the year 630 or early in the year 631, takes its name from the apartments of the Prophet's wives. These apartments were attached to the mosque in Medina. The main incident in question concerns a group of visitors from the tribe of Banu Tameem, who arrived in Medina and were shouting for the Prophet to come out of one of the apartments to meet them. Thus, this series of verses lays out basic rules of conduct in both official and personal capacities.

In the Name of Allah,
the Compassionate, the Merciful

O you who believe! [1644] Don't put yourselves ahead of Allah and His Messenger. Rather, be mindful of Allah, for Allah hears and knows (all things). [1]

O you who believe! Don't raise your voices above the voice of the Prophet, or speak loudly to him in the same way that you would speak loudly to each other. Otherwise, your (good) deeds might become worthless without your even realizing it. [2]

Those who lower their voices in the presence of Allah's Messenger have had their hearts examined by Allah, and (He affirms that) they're aware (of their duty to Him). They're going to receive forgiveness and a great reward. [3]

There is No Need to be Rude

*M*ost of those who shout out to you from outside (your) inner rooms have no sense. [1645] [4] If only they would be

---

[1644] Abu Bakr and 'Umar ibn al-Khattab got into a heated argument over a petty matter involving either the identification of an incoming caravan, the choosing of a greeter to go out and meet it, or the selection of a leader for the newly converted tribe of Tameem. (The reports differ, or they could all be correct and reflect a chain of small disagreements that led to the eventual quarrel.) The Prophet tried to calm them down, but they both kept shouting at one another. After they finally cooled down, this passage was revealed. Abu Bakr, ever afterwards, only spoke softly when he was talking with the Prophet, and Umar resolved never to speak to the Prophet unless he was spoken to first. (*Bukhari, Bayhaqi, Ma'ariful Qur'an*)

[1645] There are slightly differing reports as to the exact background for this verse. The basic idea in most of them is that a prominent man named Al-'Aqra Al-Tameemi arrived in Medina, along with his many sons. After they had all entered the mosque, Al-'Aqra began calling for Muhammad to come out of his inner chambers to meet him and hear about his reputation. (Muhammad's home was attached to the mosque.) He came out rather annoyed, and the men of the Tameemi family convinced him to listen to one of their poets who praised them and their noble qualities, victories and abundant resources. The Prophet then called for one of his own more eloquent companions, Hassan ibn Thabit, and he asked him to compose poetry in answer. (*Ibn Kathir*) Ibn Thabit spoke of Allah's favor and the renown of the Muslims, and he did so well that Al-'Aqra and his sons accepted Islam. This is the same Al-

patient until you could come out (to see) them, it would be so much better for them, though Allah is forgiving and merciful. [5]

Don't Rush to Judgment

O you who believe! [1646] If a deceitful person comes to you with some news, verify the truth of it (before you act upon it), so that you don't hurt people unknowingly and become remorseful the next morning for what you've done. [6]

Know that Allah's Messenger is in your midst. If he followed (your opinions) in most situations, you would certainly fall into dissension.

Even still, Allah has endeared the faith to you and has made it attractive in your hearts.

He's made disbelief, disobedience and rebellion something that you hate, and these are the kinds (of people) who are rightly guided. [7]

(This is) a grace and a favor from Allah, and Allah is full of knowledge and wisdom. [8]

Learn to Respect Each Other

If two factions among the faithful get into a disagreement, then you must make peace between them.

If one of them goes beyond (what's fair) against the other (group), then you must fight against the one that's going out of bounds until they comply with the command of Allah. If they do comply, then make peace between them with justice, and be sure to be evenhanded, for Allah loves those who are evenhanded. [9]

Make Peace Among the Community

Truly, all believers are a single brotherhood, [1647] so patch things up between your brothers, and be mindful of Allah so you can receive mercy. [1648] [10]

'Aqra who once saw the Prophet kiss his grandson Hassan. At that, Al-'Aqra commented, "I have ten children, and I've never kissed any of them." The Prophet looked at him and said, "The one who doesn't show mercy will not be shown mercy."

[1646] The Prophet sent a man named Walid ibn 'Uqbah to the tribe of Banu Mustaliq to collect alms. (Some reports say he was sent to teach them more about Islam.) Walid had been an enemy to them before the days of Islam. As such, he let suspicion get the better of him, and he fancied that the tribe was planning to kill him. Therefore, he cut short his visit and promptly returned to Medina. He also told the Prophet that he feared for his life from them. The Prophet dispatched Khalid ibn Walid and a few men to investigate this claim. Khalid's men observed the tribe from hidden places and returned to Medina to report that they saw the tribe behaving as faithful Muslims and observing their regular prayers. A few days later, representatives of the tribe came to Medina and explained that Walid had left them so abruptly that they felt that the Prophet must have been angry at them. They knew nothing of a plot to kill Walid. Thus, it was only Walid's irrational fear that led him to make a false charge. This verse was revealed in response. (*Asbab ul-Nuzul, Ma'ariful Qur'an*)

[1647] Anas asked the Prophet to pay a visit to 'Abdullah ibn Ubayy, who had sore feelings at the Prophet's arrival, for it deflected his own plans to be crowned king of the city. Muhammad mounted a donkey and trailed by a number of followers set out over the fields until he approached Ibn Ubayy's home. When Ibn Ubayy saw him, he said, "Get away from me, for your stinky donkey is hurting (my nose)." One of the Helpers, as Muhammad's Medinan followers were known, shouted back that the Prophet's donkey smelled better than he. One of Ibn Ubayy's men became enraged, and then men from both sides charged at each other and began hitting each other with palm fronds and shoes. Muhammad calmed them down, and this verse was revealed. (*Bukhari, Muslim*)

[1648] The Prophet said, "A Muslim is a brother to another Muslim; he does not oppress him nor forsake him." (*Bukhari*) He also said, "A believer is the mirror of his brother. A believer is the brother of another believer. He protects him against loss and defends him behind his back." (Abu *Dawoud*)

Men Should not Mock each Other

 $\mathcal{O}$ you who believe! [1649] Don't let some men among you make fun of other men, for it may be that the (ones who are being made fun of) are better than the (ones making fun of them). [1650]

Women Should not Mock each Other

 $\mathcal{A}$ nd don't let some women (make fun of) other women, either, for it may be that the (ones being made fun of) are better than the (ones who are making fun of them). [1651]

Don't Use Nicknames that Belittle

 $\mathcal{D}$ on't damage each other's reputations nor be sarcastic [1652] with each other, and don't call each other by (cruel) nicknames. It's terrible to use an insulting nickname for someone after he's become a believer. Whoever doesn't stop this practice is doing wrong. [11]

O you who believe! Avoid being overly suspicious (of your fellow believers), for suspicion in some cases is a sin. [1653]

[1649] A partially deaf man named Thabit ibn Kais made it his habit to sit near the Prophet when he spoke, so Thabit could hear him better. One day he walked into a gathering in which the Prophet was lecturing, and he asked people to move out of his way so he could sit close to the Prophet. One man said, "Just sit where you are." Thabit got angry, and while winking at someone else he asked the man who told him to sit down in the back what his name was. The man said his name, and then Thabit said, "You're the son of so-and-so, who is the son of so-and-so." (The names were of mocked men from pre-Islamic times, so Thabit was insulting him.) The man lowered his head in embarrassment, and the first part of this verse was revealed, telling the believers not to mock each other. (*Asbab ul-Nuzul*)

[1650] 'Abdullah bin Mas'ud was not a large or muscled man. He was very slight of stature and a bit on the short side. One day a strong gust of wind came and made him fall, exposing his legs from under his robe. When some of the Companions saw this, they laughed. The Messenger of Allah said, "What are you laughing at?" They responded, "O Prophet of Allah, look at his tiny shins." The Prophet said, "By the one in whose hand is my soul, they will both be heavier on the Scale (of measuring deeds) than the mountain of Uhud." (*Ahmad*)

[1651] An addendum asking women not to mock each other was soon added to this verse after it became known that some of the Prophet's wives were teasing others among them. A'ishah and Hafsah had teased Umm Salamah about her drab choice of clothes, and A'ishah, in particular, had taken to insulting Muhammad's Jewish wife Safiyah, making fun of her short stature and ethnicity. Hafsah also once angrily called Safiyah a 'Jew's daughter,' and this made Safiyah weep. This news displeased the Prophet greatly, and he comforted Safiyah, saying, "You are the daughter of a prophet, your paternal uncle was a prophet, and you're married to a prophet, so what has she got to brag about over you?" (The Prophet was referencing Safiyah's ancestors Moses and Aaron in the first part of his saying.) The Prophet then told Hafsah, in particular, "Be mindful of Allah, O Hafsah." (*Tirmidhi, Nisa'i*)

[1652] A companion named Abu Jabirah explained that the last part of this verse was revealed for the following reason. After the Prophet and his Meccan followers had migrated to Medina, they found that many people in the city had two or even three nicknames or *kunyahs*. (Some were affectionate in nature, and others were public names meant to belittle the person in question.) The Prophet innocently would sometimes call people by these nicknames, not knowing that some of the names were hurtful to the people who were being called upon. Someone informed the Prophet that the nicknames among the people of Medina were not all mutually benign. Sometime later, this verse was revealed banning all hurtful nicknames. The Prophet thereafter only used nicknames for people of which they expressly approved. (*Ma'ariful Qur'an*)

[1653] The Prophet said, "Beware of suspicion, for suspicion is the worst of false tales. Don't look for faults in each other, and don't spy on each other. Don't raise the price on an object for sale merely to create interest in it. Don't be jealous of one another. Don't hate each other, and don't have bad blood with each other, causing you to stop talking to one another. O servants of Allah, be brothers." (*Bukhari*)

Don't spy on each other, nor speak badly about each other behind their backs.

Would any of you like to eat the flesh of his dead brother? In fact, you would detest it! Be mindful of Allah, for Allah accepts repentance and is merciful. [12]

made you into different races and tribes so you can come to know one another.

The noblest among you in the sight of Allah is the one who is the most mindful (of his duty to Him). Truly, Allah knows and is aware. [1655] [13]

There is no Preference by Race or Ethnic Group

O people! [1654] We created you from a single (pair of) a male and a female and

Joining Islam is not Doing Allah a Favor

The (bedouin) Arabs (are quick) to say, "*We believe!*" [1656]

[1654] On the day when the Muslims marched victoriously into Mecca, (after the Meccans had agreed to surrender control of their city peacefully,) Muhammad sent Bilal, one of his African companions, to the roof of the Ka'bah to announce the call to prayer. Three of the Meccans, including Harith ibn Hisham and Abu Sufyan, commented on this out of their disdain that a black man (and a former slave) should be given the honor to climb atop the Ka'bah. The Prophet heard about their remarks and called the men to a meeting to explain to him why they made their racist comments. They admitted to making disparaging remarks, and then this verse was revealed, abolishing judging people by race, class or any other yardstick besides personal piety and righteousness. (*Ibn Kathir*)

[1655] During the Prophet's last pilgrimage to Mecca, near the end of his life, he gave a major address in which he said: "All you people, indeed your Lord is One and your ancestor is one. All of you belong to the line of Adam, and Adam was created from dust. An Arab is not better than a non-Arab, nor is a white better than a black, nor a black better than a white except in consciousness (of Allah). The best among you is the one who is the most conscious of Allah." This pronouncement of the Prophet and this particular verse are both an unequivocal declaration of the universal equality of all humanity. Razi said that this verse declares "the equality of human dignity." Zamakhshari said of this verse that we "all belong to one human family, without any inherent superiority of one over another." In our own times, critics of Islam often assert that Islam needs to undergo some form of 'reformation' or 'enlightenment' to make it more compatible with the modern world; yet, Islam asserted the idea of religious freedom a thousand years before the Protestant Reformation (see 2:256), and it proclaimed universal human equality (49:13) twelve centuries before the European Enlightenment. During the Protestant Reformation, when the northern half of Europe broke away from the Catholic Church to form its own brand of Christianity, European writers such as Micheal Servetus (d. 1553) were praising Islam for its logic and remarkable religious tolerance. During the Enlightenment Period (1740-1789), when secular-humanists tried to vanquish completely the power of the medieval-minded church in Europe, the advanced ideas of Islamic philosophers such as Averroes (d. 1198) and Avicenna (d. 1037) were well-known through longstanding translations. Translations of the Qur'an, though highly inaccurate, as well as other documents were also widely available to the educated classes. Voltaire, although having written a play that made fun of Muhammad, nevertheless praised Islamic egalitarian ideals in his book *Essai sur les Moeurs* (1756). Edward Gibbon, the great English historian, also wrote positively about Islam's emphasis on human equality and the lack of a priestly class. It is ironic, however, that Europeans, after extolling the basic rights of all people, were filled with a spirit of triumphalism when their secular governments invaded, conquered and subjugated the rest of the world in the age of Imperialism, and they used doctrines of racial superiority to do it! ! To be fair, other civilizations have behaved similarly and conquered those of other races and cultures in the name of divine or cultural right, such as the Incan Empire, the ancient Chinese Dynasties, and the Romans.

[1656] During a year of famine, members of the bedouin tribe of Banu Asad arrived in Medina and professed to be Muslims in order to receive donations to help their tribe. They said they had never fought the Muslims and that they had always donated to the Muslims and helped them in the past, which was only partially true. Their behavior in the city was culturally reprehensible, and they also conducted themselves in obvious ignorance of Islamic manners and values. Finally, they made it seem as if they were doing the Muslims a favor by joining them. While their profession of faith may or may not have been real, they had not let the full effect of faith seep into their hearts in a genuine fashion. This passage was revealed in response. (*Asbab ul-Nuzul*)

Yet, say to them, *"You have no faith, for you're only saying, 'We're surrendered to Allah,' but (sincere) faith hasn't yet entered your hearts. If you obey Allah and His Messenger, He won't decrease (the value) of any of your (good) deeds, for Allah is forgiving and merciful."* [14]

The only people who are (true) believers are those who've placed their full faith in Allah and His Messenger, and who have since never doubted. They've struggled with their wealth and their own selves in the cause of Allah, and that makes them the trustworthy ones. [15]

Ask them, *"Are you really going to lecture Allah about (the sincerity of) your religion?"*

Allah already knows about all things within the heavens and on the earth, for Allah knows all about everything. [16] They make it seem as if they're doing you a favor by accepting Islam. [1657]

Tell them, *"Don't think that your (joining) Islam is a favor to me. No way! It's Allah Who has done a favor to you by guiding you to the faith – that is, if you're really honest."* [17]

Without a doubt, Allah knows what's beyond perception within the heavens and the earth, and Allah is watching everything you do. [18]

[1657] A group of the Prophet's companions approached him one day and started praising the religious devotion of a man they knew. They said of him, "We've never seen someone like him. While we travel, he recites the Qur'an at all times, and whenever we camp somewhere, we always find him engaged in prayer." The Prophet asked them, "Who took care of his baggage and fed his camel and flocks while he was at prayer?" The people replied that it was they who did these things for him. Thereupon the Prophet said, "Then you are all better than he." (*Ibn Qutaybah*)

Qawf

50 Qawf
Early Meccan Period

This chapter, which was revealed in approximately 615, covers a wide variety of themes related to the theology of Islam. In later years, the Prophet often read this chapter (along with chapter 54) in the 'Eid holiday prayers. In fact, he so often recited this chapter in prayers, especially the pre-dawn one, that one woman named Umm Hisham bint al-Harith reported that this was the reason why she memorized it so easily. As it encompasses so many important themes, it is easy to see why the Prophet favored it so much.

In the Name of Allah,
the Compassionate, the Merciful

 Qâwf.

By the glorious Qur'an [1] – but no! they're still amazed that a warner has come to them from their own people.

The faithless cry out, "*This is really something astounding!* [2] *What? After we're dead and crumbled to dust, (are we really to be raised to life again?) That's a distant return.*" [3]

We already know how much of their (bodies) the earth will consume, for We've recorded it all in a secure record. [4] But no! They deny the truth when it comes to them, and thus they remain confused. [5] Don't they ponder over the sky above them and how We built it and adorned it? There are no flaws in it at all! [6]

(Don't they see) the earth and how We spread it out wide and set firm mountains within it, or how We produced in (the land) all kinds of pleasing pairs? [1658] [7] For every seeking servant, (these signs) are noticed and remembered! [8]

We send blessed water down from the sky and use it to produce gardens and grains for harvest [9] and tall palm trees with shoots of stalks, piled high on top of each other, [10] all as resources for (Our) servants. (That's how) We give life to the earth that was once dead, and that's how the emergence (from the grave) will be! [11]

Many were those Who were Brought Low

*B*efore (these faithless Meccans), there were others who denied (exclusive allegiance to the One God) like the people of Noah, the Companions of the Shallow Pool [1659] and (the peoples) of Thamud [12]

[1658] This refers to the plants, animals, etc. that have paired qualities either through gender or similar counterparts.

[1659] The Companions of the Shallow Pool are not exactly identified. There are divergent views as to which people they reference, though most classical commentators consider them to be a tribe in Yemen that had control over some productive wells in an area known as Hadramawt. This tribe is thought to be a remnant of the previously destroyed Thamud tribe that moved from northern Arabia to Yemen.

and 'Ad [1660] and of Pharaoh, along with the brothers of Lot, [13] the Companions of the Thicket and the People of Tuba.

Each one of them denied their messengers, so My promise (of destruction) was carried out against (them). [14]

How Close is Allah?

*W*ere We so worn out from the initial creation (of the universe that We could never do it again)? No way! They're baffled by (the thought of) a new creation! [15] We created (every) human being, and We know what (kind of lowly) suggestions his soul makes to him, for We're closer to him than his own jugular vein. [16]

There are two (angels) assigned to learn (and record his actions) - one perched on his right (side) and one on his left. [17] He doesn't say a word without a watcher being there, ready to jot it down. [18] The haze of death will bring the reality (to his eyes): *"This is what you were trying to avoid."* [19]

Then the trumpet will be blown – that will be a day whose arrival has long been foretold. [20] Every soul will then (be made to) come forward (on the Day of Judgment), accompanied (by an angel) to drive (him) ahead and (an angel) to testify. [21]

(They will be told,) *"(O human being!) You didn't think about this at all. Now We've removed your blinders, and your sight is crystal-clear today!"* [22]

(Then the angel holding his record) will say, *"This (person's record) needs to be examined!"* [23]

(Then the command will come), *"Throw every arrogant one who suppressed (their faith in Allah) into Hellfire, [24] all those who prevented good and acted aggressively, who instilled doubt [25] and made others equal with Allah. Throw him into the most severe punishment (imaginable)!"* [26]

Then his (jinn) companion will cry out, *"Our Lord! I didn't make him rebel (against you)! He was already clearly in the wrong (well enough by himself)!"* [27]

(Allah) will reply, *"Don't argue with each other in My presence. I already sent you (both) enough warning in advance. [28] My decree doesn't change with Me, and I'm never unjust to My servants."* [29]

The Final Payback

*O*ne day We're going to ask Hellfire, *"Are you full yet?"* to which it will reply, *"Are there any more (to come)?"* [1661] [30]

The name of their area, Hadramawt, which means, "Death Came," is reflective of what befell their ancestors. (*Ma'ariful Qur'an*)

[1660] The more prominent tribes of 'Ad and the original Thamud are mentioned several times in various places in the Qur'an. The 'Ad were a powerful people who dominated trade routes in southeastern Arabia from 2800 BCE to 300 CE. Their capital was a city named Iram, or Ubar as the Greeks called it. The Thamud were a tribal group that existed in an area known as Al-Hijr, today located in southern Jordan and northern Arabia. The Companions of the Thicket were the people of Prophet Shu'ayb of Madyan, so named because they worshipped a knotted thicket of trees as their goddess. The people of Tuba were either a group who lived in present-day Yemen some centuries before the coming of Islam and who called their kings by the honorific title *Tuba*, or they are the people of the Bronze Age city of Tuba, which has possibly been discovered in northern Syria at a site known as Tell Umm el-Marra. The latter city suffered severe devastation from foreign invasion in the 14th century B.C.E. and was inexplicably and abruptly abandoned by its people by about 1200 B.C.E. Also see 44:37 and footnote.

[1661] The Prophet said, "The inmates (of Hell) will be thrown into the fire (continuously), and (the Pit of Hell) will keep on saying, 'Are there any more to come?' This will go on until the Lord of All the Worlds puts His foot over it, causing its sides to contract. It will say, 'Enough! Enough! By Your power and Your generosity!' Paradise, on the other hand, will have more than enough room to accommodate everyone who enters until the time comes when Allah creates more people to inhabit the empty tracts within Paradise." (*Bukhari*)

The Garden will be brought near to those (who were) mindful (of Allah); it won't be so distant any more. [31]

"This is what you were promised (as a reward for) all who repented and guarded (their morality), [32] *who feared the Compassionate, even though they couldn't see (Him), and who approached (Him with) a devoted heart.* [33] *Enter (Paradise) in peace and safety, for this is the day of eternal life!"* [34]

They'll have everything they ever wished for - *and more besides* - all within Our presence. [35]

How many generations did We wipe out before them (on account of their sins, nations) who were stronger in power than they? Only (a few) survivors were left to wander through the land. Was there any refuge for them? [36]

There is a reminder in this for anyone who has a heart that understands, ears that hear and who can witness (to the fate of past civilizations). [37]

We created the heavens and the earth and everything in between them in six stages, and We never felt any fatigue. [1662] [38]

So be patient with all the (discouraging things) they say, and glorify the praises of your Lord before the rising of the sun, before its setting [1663] [39] and during a part of the night. [1664] Glorify Him whenever you finish (your prostrations). [40]

Listen for the day when the announcer will cry out from a very near place. [41] (That will be) the day when they'll hear the blast of reality. *That (cry will signal) the Day of Emergence (from the grave)!* [42]

Truly, We give life and death, and back to Us is the ultimate end. [43] The day when the world will be split open (from the dead) rushing out (of their graves) in a frenzy, that will be a time of gathering, and it's easy for Us to do. [44]

We know better what they're saying (about you). You have never tried to be a tyrant with them, so instead remind them with this Qur'an all those who will fear My warning (of what is to come). [1665] [45]

[1662] Some Jews who were visiting Mecca went to Muhammad and asked him what Allah did on the seventh day of creation. The Hebrew Bible states that God rested on the seventh day, after six days of creating the universe. The Qur'an does not accept the personification of Allah into something like a human being who labors and then rests. In fact, the Qur'an doesn't even mention anything about a seventh 'day,' other than to say that Allah 'took control' after He created everything in six "days" or stages. This verse was revealed in response to those who asked about it. (*Asbab ul-Nuzul*)

[1663] A man named Jarir said, "We were with the Prophet, and he was looking at the full moon. He turned to us and said, 'You will certainly see your Lord as you see this moon, and you won't have any difficulty in seeing Him. Therefore, if you can avoid missing a prayer before sunrise and sunset, you must do so.' Then he recited the verse [50:39] from Allah that said, 'Glorify the praises of your Lord before the rising of the sun and before its setting.'" (*Bukhari*)

[1664] The Prophet said, "Allah, the Most High descends every night to the lowest heaven when the last third of the night remains, and He says, 'Is there anyone repenting so I can accept his repentance? Is there anyone seeking forgiveness so I can forgive him? Is there anyone asking of Me so I can grant him his request?' This goes on until the start of the predawn prayer." (*Bukhari, Muslim*)

[1665] A man named Jarir ibn Abdullah gave an account of something he witnessed, saying: "On the day when the Muslims entered Mecca victoriously after the Quraysh surrendered without a fight, a Meccan man was brought to the Prophet trembling and in fear. The Prophet saw how he was terrified of retribution for what he may have done in the past to the Muslims. The Prophet said to him kindly, 'Listen. Be at ease. I'm not a king. I'm the son of a woman of Quraysh who used to eat dried meat strips in this very valley.' Then Jarir recited this verse (50:45). (*Sahih Hadith*) This verse is another of the many proofs that Islam is not to be imposed by force on others, nor are Muslims to be tyrants when their enemies fall into their hands. Too many extremists have hearts filled with hate and they become unjust oppressors themselves. The Prophet's noble example is of a leader who took decisive action when a crisis or enemy threatened the community, but when the opportunity for mercy and tolerance presented itself, he embraced it.

The Dispersal

51 Adh-Dharīyat
Early Meccan Period

This chapter was revealed in the same basic time period as the previous one, a time before the full force of Meccan persecution came to bear. As such, the arguments are more philosophically inclined and make the basic call to those who don't believe to consider their world and the One Who created it.

In the Name of Allah,
the Compassionate, the Merciful

By (the winds) that scatter everywhere [1] and those that push the heavy (clouds) [2] and those that flow with gentle ease [3] and those that allocate by need [4] - indeed, what you've been told is true [5] that judgment will surely come (to you). [6]

So by (the vastness) of the sky and its (countless) streaking paths, [1666] [7] truly, your conclusions are ever lost in argument. [8] Whoever falls away by them will surely fall away, [9] so doomed are those who speculate [10] and those whose (thoughts) are dazed. [11]

The Faithless are Unconcerned

They (mockingly) ask, *"When will this Day of Judgment come to pass?"* [12] (When it does come upon them), it will be a day in which they'll be tested over the Fire! [13]

"Suffer your trial! This is what you dared to come sooner!" [14]

Truly, those who were mindful (of Allah) will be among gardens and springs, [15] partaking in what their Lord has given them, for they lived an exemplary life before. [16] They used to sleep only a little at night, [17] and in the early hours of dawn they were (praying for) forgiveness. [18]

In their wealth, (they remembered) the right of the (poor) who asked and also that of those who were prevented (from asking). [1667] [19]

All throughout the world are signs for those who are confident (in their faith), [20] even as the (proofs of Allah's handiwork) are also within yourselves, so won't you notice them? [21]

The source of your (ultimate) survival is in the sky, even as (the Last Day) that you were promised (will become plainly visible there). [22]

[1666] This refers to all the many objects one can see in the night sky, such as the constellations and the moon that each follow a different trajectory.

[1667] Beyond merely giving in charity to those who ask, the Qur'an asks us to actually seek out the poor to help them, for there are many needy people who are too shy or who have too much self-respect to ask when they are in need. The Prophet said, "The poor person is not the one who goes around people begging for a mouthful or a date fruit or two. Rather, a poor person is one who doesn't have enough to satisfy his needs, and others don't know about his situation, which would make them give him something in charity." (*Bukhari, Muslim*) Also see 2:273.

And so, by the Lord of the heavens and the earth, this is the very truth, even as you're able to communicate with each other through (intelligent) speech. [23]

The Guests of Abraham

*H*ave you ever heard about the story of Abraham's honored guests? [1668] [24] They came before him and said, *"Peace be to you,"* and *"Peace be to you too, strangers,"* he answered back. [25]

Then he rushed to his family, and soon he came out with (a platter of) roasted meat. [26] He placed it in front of them and said, *"Why don't you eat?"* [27]

(When they didn't take anything,) he became afraid of them. [1669] They said, *"Have no fear,"* and then they gave him the good news that he would have a son filled with knowledge. [28]

Then his wife came forward and made a loud scene; then she slapped her forehead and exclaimed, *"From a barren old woman like me!"* [29]

They replied, *"So it shall be, for your Lord has decreed it, and He's full of wisdom and knowledge."* [30] (Then Abraham asked), *"Now messengers, what's your next task?"* [31]

"We're being sent to a wicked people" they answered, [32] *"to bring a shower of splintered rock down upon them,* [33] *(which is) intended from your Lord upon those who do an outlandish crime."* [34]

Then We set about to evacuate all those who had faith, [35] though We found no one surrendered (to Allah in that city,) save for in one house. [36]

We left a portent in (that city's destruction) for all those who would fear the painful punishment (of Allah). [37]

(Here's an example) with Moses. We sent him to Pharaoh with clear authority, [38] but (Pharaoh) turned back with his nobles and said (of Moses), *"A wizard or a crazy man!"* [39] Then We took him and his legions and threw them in the open sea, *and all the blame was on him.* [40]

In the (people) of 'Ad (is another example). We sent against them a devastating sandstorm. [41] It left nothing standing in its path and reduced everything to ruin. [42]

In the (people) of Thamud (is a further sign). They were told, *"Enjoy yourselves for a little while!"* [43]

Then they boldly disobeyed the order of their Lord. So the great rumbling blast (of an earthquake) seized them even as they were looking on. [44] They couldn't even stand up, let alone help themselves. [45] The people of Noah who came before them were just as bad. [46]

Allah must be Our Final Goal

*W*e built the sky above with Our (special) ability, and We're expanding it. [47] We laid out the earth, and how excellently We spread it! [48] We created every (living) thing in pairs so you could take a reminder. [49]

"So rush to (be safe with) Allah. I'm a clear warner from Him to you. [50] *Don't set up any other gods with Allah.* [1670] *(Again), I'm a clear warner from Him to you."* [51]

[1668] The 'guests' were three angels who took on the form of perfect young men.
[1669] Hospitality is the universal language, so when these strange guests refused all offers of food, Abraham became apprehensive about their identity and intentions.
[1670] Ibn 'Abbas (d. 687) said that this verse means: "Rush away from your sins, and take shelter with Allah through repentance to Him." (*Ma'ariful Qur'an*)

In the same way, no messenger came to any previous (nation) without them saying of him, "*A wizard or a crazy man!*" [52]

Is this the tradition they've handed down to each other? No way! They're a people who are out of control! [53] So turn away from them, for there's no blame on you. [54] However, keep reminding, for reminders benefit the believers. [55]

I didn't create jinns and human beings for any other purpose than to serve Me. [56] I don't need any resources from them, nor do I want them to feed Me. [57] Allah is the Giver of Resources, *the master of everlasting might!* [58]

Those who do wrong will get a similar share of what their fellow (wrongdoing predecessors) got, so they shouldn't ask Me to bring it on sooner! [59]

Those who suppress (their awareness of the truth) are truly doomed because of that day of theirs that they've been promised. [60]

The (Mountain of) Tur

52 At-Tur
Early Meccan Period

This chapter, which was revealed in the same general time period as the last chapter, continues the themes raised concerning the reality of the next life and our accountability in this life. So powerful is the message of this chapter that a man named Jubayr ibn Mu'tim converted to Islam merely upon hearing it being recited. It happened shortly after the Battle of Badr when he went to Medina to pay a ransom to free one of his relatives who had been captured by the Muslims. As he was standing outside the mosque at nightfall, waiting to speak to the Prophet, he heard him reciting this chapter in the congregational prayer. When the Prophet reached verse 37, Jubayr said of it, "I felt my heart was about fly away." A short time after he returned to Mecca, he declared his conversion to Islam and quickly rejoined the Muslims in Medina. (*Bukhari*)

In the Name of Allah,
the Compassionate, the Merciful

*B*y the (mountain of) Tūr, [1] by the written order [2] on an open sheet, [3] by the frequently visited House, [1671] [4] by the canopy (of the sky) so high [5] and by the constant swelling of the sea [6] – (by these tokens know that) the punishment of your Lord will surely come to pass. [7]

No one can avoid it [8] on the day when the sky will swirl apart [9] and the mountains will move all around. [10]

Ruin that day to those who denied [11] and who played their shallow games. [1672] [12] On that day, they'll be forcefully thrown into the fires of Hell. [13]

"This is the Fire - the one you used to deny! [14] Is this an illusion, or do you still not see it? [15] Then burn in it. It doesn't matter if you can take it or not, for you're only getting your due payback for what you did." [16]

What is Heaven Like?

*A*s for those who were mindful (of their duty to Allah), they'll reside within gardens and delight, [17] enjoying what their Lord gave them.

Indeed, their Lord protected them from the punishment of the raging blaze! [18]

[1671] The 'frequently visited House' is a place in Paradise called the *Bayt ul-Mamur*, which is like a parallel Ka'bah, or house of worship, akin to the one on Earth. 70,0000 angels a day visit it and encircle it in an act of worship to Allah. (*Bukhari*) When he was taken to see Paradise on his ascension, the Prophet said that he was able to see this 'House' with his own eyes. Some commentators hold that this verse is referring to the Ka'bah on earth, though Allah knows best. (*Ibn Kathir*)

[1672] A young man once stood up and asked the Prophet, "Who is the most diligent among the believers?" The Prophet replied, "The one who remembers death the most and is best prepared for it. Such are the most diligent ones." (*Hilyat ul-Awliya wa Tabaqat al-Asfiya*)

"Eat and drink with ease on account of your (good) deeds." [19]

They'll relax on couches lined up in ranks, and We'll pair them with (mates) who will have intense, expressive eyes. [20]

Those who believe and whose relatives follow them in belief will be reunited (in Paradise) with their relatives.

We won't deprive them of (the value) of their (good) deeds, although everyone is responsible only for his own actions. [1673] [21]

We'll give them fruit and meat and anything else they desire. [22]

They'll pass around a cup (of wine whose pleasurable after-effects) carry with it neither the prospect of talking nonsense nor of being belligerent. [23]

All around them youths will go about (serving them), and their (appearance will) remind them of expensive pearls. [24]

They'll approach each other and ask about (new) things. [25]

They'll say, *"We used to worry about our families before,* [26] *though Allah was good to us and protected all of us from the punishment of the searing heat.* [27] *We used to call upon Him before*

(in our lives on earth), and He certainly is Benevolent and Merciful." [28]

Why won't they Use Their Sense?

$\mathcal{K}$eep reminding (people about Allah), for by your Lord's grace, you're not a fortune-teller, nor are you crazy. [29] Are they saying, *"(He's just) a poet. Let's just wait for some misfortune to take care of him"*? [30] Say to them, *"Keep waiting, for I, too, will wait along with you."* [31]

Is it their own whims that prompt them to make these (accusations), or are they really just a people who are out of control? [32] Are they saying, *"He's making it all up"*?

Certainly not! They just have no faith! [33] *Then let them compose a chapter like this, if they're really being so honest!* [1674] [34]

Were they created from nothing, or did they make themselves? [35] Did they create the heavens and the earth?

Not so! They just have no conviction. [36] Are the treasures of your Lord with them, or are they somehow in charge? [37] Do they have a ladder they can use to

---

[1673] The Prophet said that in Heaven an announcer will say, "For you there is everlasting health, and you will never be sick. For you there is everlasting life, and you will never die. For you is eternal youth, and you will never grow old. For you is everlasting happiness, and you will never go without ever again." (*Muslim*)

[1674] The poets of the Quraysh were unable to craft verses like the Qur'an, for they were skilled only in satire, family odes and epic poems. Later, a false prophet arose in central Arabia named Musaylima. He made his initial claims some years after the Muslim migration from Mecca to Medina, and he claimed equal status with Muhammad. He once sent a letter to the Prophet in Medina, offering to divide Arabia between them. The Prophet sent a note back that said the entire earth belongs to Allah, and He gives it to whom He wills. The Prophet then dubbed Musaylima "the Liar." In order to increase his stature among his followers, Musaylima used to ask about what Muhammad was saying and doing, in order to emulate it as best he could. One day Musaylima met a visitor from Mecca named 'Amr ibn al-'As, who had not yet embraced Islam, and he asked him about any new chapters of the Qur'an that had been revealed to Muhammad. 'Amr recited chapter 103, and Musaylima, after thinking for some time, said, "A similar chapter was revealed to me!" Then he began reciting: "O Wabr O Wabr (i.e., a type of wild cat), you are only two ears and a chest, and the rest of you is unworthy and thin." 'Amr listened politely and said, "By Allah! I know now that you're a liar!" (*Ibn Kathir*) For a time, Musaylima was married to a woman named Sajjah, who also claimed to be a prophetess, and the two plotted to attack the Muslims. She left him after becoming disenchanted with him. She later became an observant Muslim and lived to an old age in Iraq. Musaylima's forces were defeated at the Battle of Yamamah in the year 633 during the rule of Abu Bakr.

(climb up to the sky) and listen? If so, then let the listener produce his evident authority! [38]

Does (Allah) have daughters while you (idol-worshippers) claim sons? [39] Are you asking them for some kind of payment so they'll be burdened down with a load of debt? [40]

Is the unseen (realm) there before them, so they can somehow write about it? [41] Do they want to make a plan against you? - but those who reject (Allah) are themselves (trapped) in a plan! [42] Do they have a god other than Allah? Allah is far above what they associate with Him! [43]

If they saw a piece of the sky falling down upon them, they would merely say, *"Oh, it's just a pile of clouds."* 1675 [44]

So leave them alone until they come to that day of theirs in which they'll faint [45] - *the day when their scheming won't help them and no help will be given them.* [46] Indeed, for those who do wrong there's yet another punishment besides this, but most of them don't understand. [47]

So wait patiently upon the command of your Lord, for you're present under Our watchful eye. 1676 Glorify the praises of your Lord whenever you stand up (for prayer), [48] and glorify Him for part of the night, as well, and also after the stars have set. [49]

1675 The pagans had asked for the sky to be brought down upon them as proof of Muhammad's prophethood, but this verse is pointing out that they were so lacking in sense and humility that they would find some sort of rational explanation for such a sign as that, as well. (*Ma'ariful Qur'an*)

1676 The use of the word "eye" to refer to God is understood to mean a variety of things such as His knowledge, His support, under His protection, the angels watching over us, etc. (*Tafseer al Jalalayn*) The Prophet said, "When Allah, the Exalted, intends to do something, He makes all worldly causes act accordingly." (*Ma'ariful Qur'an*)

The Star

53 An-Najm
Early Meccan Period

Meccan persecution had become more serious by the year 615, forcing some of the weaker Muslims to emigrate to Abyssinia for safety. Up to this point, the Prophet had never recited a full or lengthy chapter of the Qur'an in a large public gathering. One day he stood in front of the Ka'bah and recited this chapter to the gathered throngs. When he came to the last verse, he prostrated. Then the people who had listened prostrated, as well, both believers and a few pagans. Although the pagans were not affirming the truth of the message, they were so mesmerized by its eloquence that when the Muslims mingled among them bowed, many of them also did so automatically, though one pagan merely rubbed some dust on his forehead, saying, "This is enough." *(Ibn Kathir)*

Some of their fellow pagans teased their compatriots, saying that they opposed Muhammad but then bowed when he recited the Qur'an. Then the embarrassed pagans, who had bowed unthinkingly, invented a story to cover their lapse in judgment. They let it be known that they thought Muhammad was *praising* their main goddesses, Al-Lat, Manat and Al-'Uzza, and that this was why they prostrated. This is the basis of the famous 'Satanic Verses' incident, for which modern critics of Islam take so much unearned delight.

Such critics accept this version of events without further investigation in their efforts to disparage the Prophet, by making it seem as if he wavered in his commitment to monotheism and was willing to 'compromise.' However, the idea that 'Satan' injected some words in the Prophet's recitation or that the Prophet was willing to compromise with the pagans is easily dismissible as the fabrication of the Meccans that it is. Verses 21-22 would be out of synch with the rest of the rhyme scheme in the chapter if their proposed verses were 'accidentally' substituted for what was actually there, and there was no letup in Meccan persecution after the day the Prophet recited this chapter. In addition, if the Prophet could have been persuaded to compromise with the pagans, one would wonder for what reason it would be. They had already offered him wealth, women and even kingship of the city before, and he refused.

If it were to save himself from danger or persecution, he would come to endure a lot worse in the coming years, and he never wavered then, either. Thus, the fabrication invented by the pagans, that the Prophet somehow was willing to compromise with them on an ordinary day without any back up story as to what incentive they possibly could have offered him, is most probably a sham or at the very least an incomplete tale. The spontaneous prostration of some of the pagans that day did have an effect, however. When word of this public incident reached the Muslim refugees in Abyssinia, they took the seeming pagan acquiescence as a sign that the Meccans would be more tolerant of Islam. Thus, they returned home within weeks, but if anything, the persecution grew more heated after that.

One man who had witnessed that day, and who didn't bow along with his pagan fellows (another proof that the Meccan leadership was merely acting on its own, for if the Prophet had really recited verses tolerant of idolatry, then all would have bowed) said in later years, "When the Prophet recited the chapter of the Star and performed a prostration and the whole assembly fell down in prostration along with him, I didn't prostrate. Now to compensate for the same, whenever I recite this chapter I make sure never to abandon its performance." (*Nisa'i, Ahmad*)

In the Name of Allah,
the Compassionate, the Merciful

*B*y the star when it declines, [1] your companion is not mistaken, nor is he being misled, [2] and he says nothing on his own. [3] It's no less than revelation revealed! [4]

An irresistible and compelling (angel) teaches him [5] – a master of wisdom. He stood forth (clearly) [6] while on the highest part of the horizon. [1677] [7] Then he came down and approached [8] and was only two bow-draws distant - *or even lower!* [9]

So, (Allah) revealed whatever revelation to His servant (that He willed). [10] His heart didn't fool him about what he saw, [11] so are you going to argue with him about what he saw? [12]

As it happened, he saw (the angel) yet again during a second descent [13] near the lote tree, (in a place) beyond which none may pass. [14] Close by is the Garden of Sanctuary. [1678] [15] The lote tree was shrouded (in a shimmering light), [16] but his sight never swerved, nor did it fail, [17] for he really saw the greatest sign of his Lord! [18]

Idols and Angels as Demigods

*H*ave you seen (the idols named) Al-Lat and Al-'Uzza, [19] and the third one named Manat? [1679] [20]

[1677] A'ishah was sitting with the Prophet, and she asked him about this passage, saying, "Did you see your Lord (Allah)?" The Prophet replied, saying that he only saw Gabriel and that the angel was so huge that he covered the entire horizon between the sky and the earth. (*Ibn Kathir*) According to 'Abdullah ibn Mas'ud (d. 653), the Prophet said that when he first saw Gabriel, he was a being of pure light with 600 wings. The Prophet fainted on that night in the year 610 when he was first contacted by this representative from the supernatural realm, and then Gabriel approached him and revived him. (*At-Tabari, Bukhari, Ahmad*)

[1678] This is a reference to the Prophet's journey into Paradise to see the realms of the other world. See chapter 17.

[1679] The Arabs believed that Allah had daughters. They worshipped these deities as intercessors with Allah for good luck, protection, and good fortune. Al-Lat (lit. *the one to bend towards* or *rotate around*) was the patron goddess of the city of Ta'if. (She was also worshipped as far north as Syria.) The idol was represented as a white stone with mysterious writing on it, and it was kept in a small structure with curtains around it next to the workplace of a Jewish barley grinder. The early commentators say that Al-Lat originally was the name of a man from ancient pagan days who was similarly a grain grinder, and whose legend of generosity transformed him over time into a patron goddess for traveling pilgrims. When he/she died, the people erected a large square tombstone and began to pray at the site of his/her grave. (This same kind of process is how most ancient deities were invented!) Some pagans held that Al-Lat was the wife of Allah, but even though the names seem like dual complements, the term for *Allah* is derived from *al-elah*, which means *to be possessed of God*. After Muhammad sent some Companions to destroy the stone, one of them named Shadid warned the people of Ta'if thusly: "Come not to Al-lat, for Allah has doomed her to destruction. How can you stand by one which does not triumph? Verily that which, when set on fire, resisted not the flames, nor saved her stones, is shameful and worthless. Hence when the Prophet in your place shall arrive and then leave, not one of her followers shall be left." (*al-Kalbi* d. 819) Al-Uzza (lit. *the great one*) was a sacred group of three palm trees with a monument set upon a dias shrouded in curtains. It was located in a valley named Hurad in the district of Nakhlah, which lay at a point between Mecca and Ta'if. The Quraysh were her principal worshippers. They supported an oracle who lived there in a hut, dispensing fortunes. Manat (lit. *the one for whom blood is spilled*, or

604

What! For you, (you prefer) males (as sons), but then you assign to (Allah) females (for children)! [21]

That's hardly a fair deal! [22] In fact, they're nothing more than names you've made up - *you and your ancestors.*

Allah sent down no permission for (you to do) that. They're only following their own opinions and what they themselves (foolishly) desire.

And so it is that guidance has now come to them from their Lord, (so see if they will obey Allah now, as they always claimed they would)! [23]

Are human beings going to have whatever they want? [24]

The end and the beginning of everything belongs to Allah. [25]

No matter how many angels there are in the heavens, their intercession won't matter at all unless Allah gives His permission to whomever He wants - and then only if he's acceptable (to Him). [26]

Those who don't believe in the next life give feminine names to the angels, [27] but they have no certain knowledge in this.

They're only following their own whims, and whims don't stand a chance against the truth. [28] So avoid those who turn away from Our message and who only desire the life of this world. [29]

That's as far as knowledge will ever reach them. Truly, your Lord knows best who is straying from His path, and He knows best who is guided. [30]

To Allah belongs whatever is in the heavens and on the earth.

He repays those who do wrong according to (the severity of) their deeds, and He rewards those who do good with the very best. [31]

Those who avoid the major sins and shameful deeds, only (straying into) minor sins, 1680 (should remember) that your Lord is surrounded with forgiveness.

He knows you well when He brings you out of the earth and when you're hidden in your mother's wombs. Therefore, don't try to justify yourselves (by your deeds), for He knows who is mindful (of their duty to Him). [32]

---

alternatively, *the storm-bringer*) was an idol in the shape of a large stone that was located closer to the sea in between Mecca and Yathrib, and the tribes of Hudhayl, Aws, Khajraj and Khuza'a used to venerate it. When they went to Mecca for pilgrimage in pre-Islamic days, they would not shave their hair in Mecca, but only on the return journey while visiting Manat. She controlled fate and death in their lore. Eight years after the Prophet had fled to Medina, and while he was leading his followers back to Mecca seeking final victory, he dispatched 'Ali ibn Abi Talib to destroy the idol. 'Ali did so and returned with the treasures of the shrine, which included two fancy swords. The Prophet gave one of them, which had two prongs, to him, and so 'Ali earned the nickname of the holder of the "Double Sword, or *Dhul Fiqar.* (Some sources say the sword was obtained when 'Ali destroyed a different idol named al-Fals in the same general area.) These aforementioned deities were three of the most prominent idols of the Arabs, though there were dozens of other idols in the diverse Arab pantheon. Hubal, the god of fertility, spring, and agriculture, was also important in Mecca, as was al-Zuhara, the goddess of love, often associated with al-'Uzza. (*Zamakhshari*)

1680 The companions and commentators who discussed the meaning of what the minor sins (mentioned in this verse) are have said they pertain to flirting, longing stares, kissing and embracing someone of the opposite sex when it is unlawful for them to do so, given that they are not married to each other. If they go beyond this to actual intimacy, then it rises to the more serious level of a "shameful deed." (*Ibn Kathir*) It must be remembered that even the minor sins must be avoided, for they lead to more serious sins. This verse is just pointing out that Allah will forgive the truly repentant, and it counsels people to be mindful of anything that leads to more serious sins down the line. Verse 3:135 also gives hope that major sins can be forgiven to the truly penitent.

What the Past Can Teach

ℋave you seen the one who turns back, [33] gives a little, then hardens (his heart against faith)? [1681] [34]

What! Does he know what's beyond perception so he can see it? [35] Doesn't he know what's been prophesized in the scrolls of Moses [36] and of Abraham, the one who fulfilled his agreements? [37]

All True Religion Teaches the Same Truth

(Those previous revelations clearly taught that) no bearer of burdens can bear the burden of another, [38] And that human beings shall have nothing more than what they strive for, [39] and that the results of (each person's) efforts will soon be seen [40] - and then (each of them) will be paid back in full - [41]

And that the final destination is back to your Lord, [42] for He's the One Who grants laughter and tears [43] and both death and life. [44]

(Allah is the One Who) created pairs of males and females [45] out of an ejected drop (of fluid), [46] and He will orchestrate a second creation. [47] He's the One Who gives wealth and prosperity. [48] He's the Lord of (the great star) Sirius. [49] He's the One Who destroyed the ancient (peoples of) 'Ad [50] and Thamud, leaving nothing untouched. [51]

The people of Noah had lived even before them, and most of them were corrupt and stubborn. [52] He also obliterated the overthrown towns (of Sodom and Gomorrah), [53] so much so that even (their ruins) are covered up. [54]

So now which of the favors of your Lord will you bicker about? [55] This (man Muhammad) is a warner just like the warners of old. [56] (The Day of Judgment) is getting closer and closer, [57] and no one can move it forward save Allah. [58]

So are you amazed at this narrative? [59] Will you laugh and not cry, [60] wasting all your time in useless distractions? [61] Then (know that you should) bow down prostrate before Allah and serve Him. [62]

[1681] This passage was revealed regarding al-Waleed ibn al-Mughirah, who had accepted Islam, but who then reverted to idolatry after his pagan friends convinced him to rejoin his original religion. At first, they tried to entice him with offers of increasing his wealth. When Waleed said he was afraid that Allah would punish him for the many sins he had done in the past, one of his friends asked for some money in exchange for taking some of Waleed's expected punishment upon his own self. After Waleed paid him, his friend demanded more money. The two men got into a scuffle, and then Walid agreed to pay the extra amount. A contract was recorded, witnesses signed it, and thus Waleed remained a pagan. (*Asbab ul-Nuzul*)

The Moon

54 Al Qamar
Early Meccan Period

In approximately the year 614, the Prophet was addressing a gathering of pagans and Muslims during the evening at a field called Mina just outside of Mecca. The pagans had been fiercely disputing with the Prophet for some days, demanding a miracle to prove his prophethood, and this meeting was heated, as well. Suddenly, the Prophet raised his hand and pointed his finger to the moon. To the amazement of all, the moon appeared to separate into two halves, and then just as quickly, the Prophet declared, "Be witnesses!" Then the line of separation disappeared.

The Quraysh were left speechless, but within a few days they discounted the miracle and called it some kind of an illusion. One source quotes a pagan man as saying, "Muhammad has merely bewitched us, but he can't bewitch the entire world. Let's wait for people to come from faraway places and hear what reports they bring." (*Bayhaqi, Abu Dawud*) Some travelers who arrived in Mecca a few days later did report to the Quraysh that they saw an unusual occurrence with the moon. (*Ibn Kathir*)

There are two proofs to support that something unusual did take place. The first is that it was witnessed by the enemies of the Prophet, and they dismissed it as an illusion of some type. (The Qur'an quotes what they said, and the Qur'an has been proven to be the best record of the give-and-take between Muhammad and his critics.) In addition, the scholars of *hadith* have found this report to be so numerous, traceable to so many companions, that it clearly could not be false. Secondly, in the same year, a king in Malabar, India, named Cheruman Perumel (aka Chakrawati Farmas or Rama Kulasekhara) saw the moon seem to split in half for a moment. In amazement, he asked his religious scholars what it meant. They said it was a portent signaling the rise of a prophet in Arabia.

Given that there had been Sanskrit predictions of such a prophet, the king named his son as regent, and then he set out for Arabia in the company of Arab traders who were journeying home on the monsoon winds. (His report and travels are documented from old manuscripts such as the cyclical *Tarikh-e-Fareshtah* and others that still exist in India and England. See document labeled Arabic, 2807, 152-173 in the India Office Library in London.) After a long journey, he met with the Prophet and embraced Islam. He even brought the Prophet a gift of jarred pickles with ginger, and, according to Abu Sa'eed al-Khudri, the Prophet shared it among his companions. (*Hakim*)

The king died on the return journey while having a stopover in Zafar, Yemen; there he was buried. His retainers returned to Malabar, and the people of that island were the first Indians to embrace Islam.

The Hour (of Judgment) is near, and the moon has split in half. [1682] [1] However, if they see a miracle, they turn away and say, *"Just some kind of fading magic."* [1683] [2] They deny (such miracles) and follow their own vain desires, but all affairs have a resolution. [3]

And so it is that enough (stories of the past) have already come to them for them to consider [4] - (stories and reports) filled with wisdom; yet, warnings do them no good. [1684] [5]

So turn away from them. On the day when the Announcer will call (them) to something awful, [6] they'll come out of their graves with their eyes downcast, looking like scattered locusts in a frenzy. [7]

They'll hurry forward with their sight locked upon the Announcer! *"This will be a hard day!"* the faithless will cry. [8]

The Lesson of Noah

Before them the people of Noah denied (the truth). They denied Our servant and said, *"He's crazy!"* Then he was ostracized. [9] (Noah had to) call upon his Lord, saying, *"I'm overwhelmed! Help!"* [10]

So We opened the doors of the sky and let the water rain down in torrents. [11] Then We caused the earth to overflow with springs so the waters would meet at the determined level. [1685] [12]

We carried (Noah and his followers) on a (ship) made of boards bound with fiber cords. [13] It floated under Our watchful eye, and that was the reward for (a man) who had been rejected! [14] We left this (story) as a sign (for future generations), so will anyone be reminded? [15]

Oh, how (terrible) was My punishment and My warning! [16]

And so, We've made this Qur'an easy to remember, so will anyone be reminded? [17]

The Nations of 'Ad and Thamud

The (people of) 'Ad denied (the warning). *Oh, how (terrible) was My punishment and My warning!* [18]

[1682] The moon is seen at night only because it reflects the light of the Sun. The moon may have appeared to have been split or divided in half due to a shadow caused by an event associated with the Sun such as a solar flare, the crossing of an errant comet across the space between the Sun and the moon, perhaps a meteorite or even a shadow caused by some object passing between the earth and moon. Given that the event happened over a thousand years ago, there is little chance of identifying a possible cause for this event.

[1683] Some Meccans met with the Prophet one evening in a field named Mina, and they asked him to perform a physical miracle to prove his claims. He directed their attention to the moon, which quickly took on the appearance of having some type of crack or thin shadow over its middle, dividing it in half. Given the fact that this chapter was soon recited to the Meccans some days later and that none of them disputed the reference to the moon being split, (rather they attributed it to magic), it can be assumed either that some type of rare and possibly natural phenomena did occur to make the moon's appearance seem unusual or that a genuine supernatural occurrence took place to show the Quraysh a mighty sign!

[1684] The Meccans should have already heard enough scattered tales of the past and perhaps some of the stories of the Jews and Christians to know that idolatry was false and that human actions, both good and evil, really do mean something to Allah.

[1685] So a deluge of rain came to the region that caused the sources of the Tigris and Euphrates rivers to overflow, which in turn caused the rivers to overflow their banks (see 11:40). This is the mechanism of the great flood, and it is a scientifically plausible explanation.

We sent a sandstorm against them on a disastrous day, [19] snatching people up like they were palm trees, ripped from their roots. [20] *Oh, how (terrible) was My punishment and My warning!* [21]

And so, We've made this Qur'an easy to remember, so will anyone be reminded? [22]

The (people of) Thamud denied the warning. [23] They scoffed, saying, *"What! A mortal like us! A single (man) from our own! Should we follow someone like him? We would truly be mistaken and out of our minds! [24] Why should he get the message over any of the rest of us? No way! He's just a reckless liar!"* [25]

Oh, how they'll know the very next day just who the reckless liar was! [26] We will send a female camel, as a test for them. So watch them, (Salih,) and have patience! [1686] [27]

Tell them that the well-water is to be divided among them and that all will have the right to come forward to water (their flocks by turns). [1687] [28]

But the (arrogant chiefs) called upon (one of) their (worst) fellows (to take action), and he took a blade and cut (the legs of the camel). [29]

Oh! How (terrible) was My punishment and My warning! [30]

We sent against them a single blast, (and when the dust cleared) they looked like dry matchsticks. [31] We made this Qur'an easy to remember, so will anyone be reminded? [32]

Prophet Lot and His Mission

The people of Lot denied the warning. [33] Thus, We sent against them a violent sandstorm carrying showers of stones, (which destroyed them) all, except for Lot's own family, for We had rescued them at daybreak, [34] by Our grace, for that's how We reward the thankful. [35]

(Lot) had already warned (his people) about Our coming attack, but they argued (with him) about the warning. [36] They wanted to accost his guests (the disguised angels,) but We blinded their eyes. *"Now taste (the results of) My punishment and My warning."* [37]

Then early the next morning a lasting punishment overcame them. [38] *"Taste (the results of) My punishment and My warning."* [39]

We made this Qur'an easy to understand and remember, so will anyone be reminded? [40]

Moses and Aaron and Their Mission

And so it was that warners came to the people of Pharaoh, [41] but the (Egyptians) denied all of Our signs, so We seized them with the kind of seizure (that comes) from a powerful being Who can do whatever He wants. [42]

[1686] This is a good example (in translation) of the absolute charm of the Qur'an when it's recited orally. Verses 54:23-25 start off in a straightforward informational style, but by verse 26 we are suddenly thrust in the middle of an ongoing story – right in the middle of the action, as if it were unfolding before us in the hands of an expert storyteller. You can almost taste how it draws the listener in. This is a wonderful way of weaving together different literary techniques to keep the listener's attention. In the hands of a very skilled reciter, the Arabic text can make native listeners literally drop everything to hear more, in the same way that the troubadours of Europe used to enthrall audiences with their tales and speeches, or like modern docudramas that weave together story lines, human interest material, and informational segments into one seamless production.

[1687] The chiefs of the tribe had a monopoly on the water supply and used it to enrich themselves at the expense of the poor. The test of the camel was that they had to let an animal drink when it was thirsty, not when its owner could afford to pay. Would they obey Allah's command?

The Arrogance of Faithlessness

*A*re you faithless (people of Mecca) better than those (peoples of the past)? [1688] Do you have a special exemption (from punishment) in some holy scripture somewhere? [43]

Are they saying, "*If we act together, we can help ourselves*"? [44] Soon their mobs will be forced to turn their backs and flee. [45]

But no! The (final) Hour is a time that they've been promised, and that Hour will be full of sorrow and terrible bitterness. [46] Truly, it's the wicked who are mistaken and out of their minds. [47]

On the day when they'll be dragged through the Fire flat on their faces, (they'll be told), "*Now taste the burning flames!*" [48]

The Power of Allah is without Limits

*T*ruly, We've created everything in a predetermined manner. [1689] [49] Our command is (carried out) in a single (moment) - *like the twinkling of an eye.* [50]

And so it was that We destroyed partisans (of disbelief) just like you (idol-worshippers of Mecca). So now will anyone accept the reminder? [1690] [51]

Everything they do is noted in (their) record (of deeds). [52] All things small and great are recorded. [1691] [53] As for the righteous, they'll be among gardens and rivers [54] in a truthful meeting place in the presence of a sovereign and capable (Lord). [55]

[1688] On the night before the Battle of Badr commenced, the Prophet called out to Abu Bakr after a long night of prayer and said, "Abu Bakr! There's good news for you! Gabriel is standing by that cliff and saying [the words of this passage]." (*Ibn Kathir*)

[1689] The Arabic word *qadar* means primarily to measure the outcome of things. In a religious sense, (according to the Prophet's sayings,) it means that Allah has predetermined certain things such as the length of our lives, the lands in which we will die, the amount of wealth we will gain, and other such broad factors. It isn't exactly the same thing as fatalistic destiny, though, for we're still responsible for our individual actions, intentions and measure of faith. (Modern geneticists have discovered that we are literally born with predispositions in our genes that affect us our entire lives.) Does Islam teach fatalism or a lazy reliance on what Allah planned for us? No, it does not (although some rustic Muslim cultures assume that it does). Islam merely gives an explanation for many of the broad trends that we will all experience in life. When the Prophet saw a camel wandering in the streets of Medina, the owner told him he didn't tie it because he was trusting in Allah to look after it. The Prophet then famously said, "Tie your camel, and then rely upon Allah." Indeed, the Prophet once described it as a wrong notion to say that we should just rely on fate and abandon our actions. The Prophet also said, "Seek Allah's help, and don't succumb to weakness. When an affliction strikes you, you should say, 'Allah has planned this, and He does what He wills.' Don't say, 'If I would have done this or that, then this or that would've happened,' because saying, 'if' opens the door wide open for Satan." (*Muslim*) Compare the Islamic teaching on Allah's power over earthly affairs with the following Biblical quote: "I well know, O Jehovah, that to earthling man his way does not belong. It does not belong to a man who is walking *even to direct his step.*" (Jeremiah 10:23) In Islam, Allah knows the outcome, but we decide how we *feel* about it and interpret our actions and reactions.

[1690] Some pagans had been arguing with the Prophet about the meaning of Allah's ability to determine the future. This passage was revealed in response. (*Muslim, Tirmidhi*) Believing in this concept, which is known as *taqdir*, is a requirement of faith, according to several prophetic traditions.

[1691] The Prophet once said to A'ishah, "A'ishah, beware of small sins, for there is someone assigned by Allah who records them." (*Ahmad*)

The Compassionate

55 Ar-Rahman
Early to Middle Meccan Period

This chapter is one of the more famous ones due to its very beautiful rhythm and rhyme scheme, which under the command of a skilled Arabic reciter comes as close to audible art as one can get. When this chapter was revealed to the Prophet, he had not yet gone public with the message of Islam, and he had busied himself with inviting friends, relatives and close associates to the new faith.

The total number of Muslims by this time might have numbered less than fifty persons, and the opposition of the Quraysh was mostly from their leadership and from individual families who might have opposed their members joining what they considered to be a new cult. Indeed, it was mostly the young who were responding to Muhammad's call, and he had quite a few young men and women in his following.

One day in a secret meeting, several of Muhammad's followers began to point out that the general public had never heard anyone recite the Qur'an in the public square before, and they wondered aloud who among them should be the first to do it. A young man named 'Abdullah ibn Mas'ud (d. 653) volunteered, but many in the meeting were scared for his safety and suggested that someone who was stronger or who had better family connections should do it, as he might be attacked by the pagans.

'Abdullah merely said, "Leave me alone, for Allah is my protector." The next morning, he entered into the courtyard of the Ka'bah where the various tribal elders were holding their counsels, and he began to recite this very chapter, raising his voice as he went along. At first the Quraysh didn't know what he was saying, but soon they realized that he was reciting some of the Qur'an that Muhammad was preaching in private to people all over the city.

They arose and set upon him with their palms and their fists, but 'Abdullah, staggering under their blows, kept on reciting. When he could bear it no more, he returned to the companions of the Prophet, and they said they expected what occurred to befall him.

'Abdullah said, "Allah's enemies were never so light for me as they were today. If you give the word, then I'll recite the Qur'an to them again tomorrow." They all said, "No, you've done enough; you've made them listen to what they didn't want to hear." (*Ibn Hisham*)

In the Name of Allah,
the Compassionate, the Merciful

The Compassionate [1] taught the Qur'an. [2]

He created (every woman and) man. [3]

He taught (them) communication. [4]
The sun and moon follow a fixed rotation. [5]

Even the stars [1692] and trees bow down in adoration! [1693] [6]

He raised the cosmos on high and set up the balance (of justice) [7]
so that you wouldn't go out of balance (in your own behavior). [8]

So calculate weights and measures honestly,
and don't fall short on the scale. [9]

He's the One Who spread the earth out
wide for (grazing) animals, [1694] [10]
and there are fruits (to be had) and date palms piled high, [11]
and grains with stalks and leaves (for animal feed)
and fragrant flowers indeed! [12]

So which of the favors
of your Lord will you deny? [1695] [13]

What are His Favors upon You?

*H*e created human beings from molded clay, [14]

and He created jinns from smokeless fire. [15]

So which of the favors
of your Lord will you deny? [16]

(He's) the Lord of the two Easts
and Lord of the two Wests. [1696] [17]

So which of the favors
of your Lord will you deny? [18]

[1692] The Arabic word *najm* usually means stars, but it can also mean plants with no trunks, such as grass and shrubbery. Some commentators favor the former meaning, some the latter. (*Ma'ariful Qur'an*)

[1693] The Prophet had recited this chapter at night in his makeshift camp after his abortive mission to the nearby city of Ta'if, and it was overheard by some jinns who converted. See introduction to chapter 72.

[1694] The Arabic word used here that is often translated generically as 'creatures' is actually *an'am*, which denotes domesticated herd animals that people depend upon, such as cattle, sheep, horses, camels, oxen and the like. So this verse is making a veiled reference to the wide pasture lands that people use to feed their flocks and herds. Also see Genesis 1:26, 29-30 for comparison.

[1695] The Prophet once heard a person reciting this chapter in company. Whenever the reciter came to a line like this one (verse 13), he noticed that no one was responding, so he said to the gathering, "How is it that I'm not hearing from you the kind of good answer that the jinn had given to their Lord?" When the companions asked what the reply they gave was, he replied, "As I recited the divine words, '...so which of the favors of your Lord will you deny?', the jinn would respond by saying, '*La bi shai'in min ni'mati Rabbina nukadhdhib*' (We do not deny any of our Lord's blessings.)" (*At-Tabari, Daraqutni*)

[1696] In other words, since the earth rotates on its axis and orbits around the sun, there are two extreme points at which the sun will rise from the east and two more extreme points into which it will set to the west during the course of the year, so there are 'two Easts' and 'two Wests.' These are called equinoxes.

He caused the two seas to flow,
(one being salty and the other fresh,)
and when they meet together, [19] behold –
there's a barrier between them they don't traverse. [1697] [20]

So which of the favors
of your Lord will you deny? [21]

From them pearls and corals are produced. [22]

So which of the favors
of your Lord will you deny? [23]

The ships that sail smoothly through the sea, (whose sails)
tower as high as mountains - they all belong to Him! [24]

So which of the favors
of your Lord will you deny? [25]

What does the Lord Provide?

*A*ll who are on (the earth) shall pass away, [1698] [26]

but the face of your Lord will last (forever) -
full of Majesty and Honor! [27]

So which of the favors
of your Lord will you deny? [28]

Every creature in the heavens and the earth
gets what it needs from Him,
and He's active every day. [29]

So which of the favors
of your Lord will you deny? [30]

Soon We're going to settle the important
affairs of both (your worlds)! [31]

So which of the favors
of your Lord will you deny? [32]

Reach Him if You Think You Can!

*Y*ou gathered assembly
of jinns and human beings!

[1697] See 25:53.
[1698] The term used here for 'pass away' or *fana*, is the term adopted by Sufis for losing one's self through contemplation in the vastness of Allah's majesty.

If you can pass beyond
the heavens and the earth (into space),
then pass through them!

Yet, you'll never be able to pass beyond them
until you (invent the right type) of power. [1699] [33]

So which of the favors
of your Lord will you deny? [34]

A flaming heat will
meet (the wicked amongst)
you (on Judgment Day),
and a (choking) smoke, against which
you'll have no defense. [35]

So which of the favors
of your Lord will you deny? [36]

When the sky is torn apart
and resembles smeared rose petals... [37]

So which of the favors
of your Lord will you deny? [38]

On that day no human or jinn
will be asked any more about his guilt. [1700] [39]

So which of the favors
of your Lord will you deny? [40]

The wicked will be known
by their marks (of shame);
they'll be seized
by their forelocks and their feet. [41]

So which of the favors
of your Lord will you deny? [42]

This is Hellfire, (the fate) the wicked denied! [43]
They'll wander around in the midst of it
- smothered in burning (flames)! [44]

So which of the favors
of your Lord will you deny? [45]

[1699] This is a challenge for people to venture beyond the zone of earth into the heavens, though the caveat is given that we must first develop the proper type of power (*sultan*). It is interesting that the Qur'an envisioned rocket fuel and space exploration at a time (the seventh century) when it was never even imagined by any society.

[1700] In other words, their guilt will be evident and recognizable by their faces, as verse 41 states.

Rewards for the Righteous

𝒯or those who feared the time
when they would stand before their Lord,
there will be two gardens. [46]

So which of the favors
of your Lord will you deny? [47]

They will hold many (wonderful) things. [1701] [48]

So which of the favors
of your Lord will you deny? [49]

Each of them will have two free-flowing springs. [50]

So which of the favors
of your Lord will you deny? [51]

There will be fruits of every kind in doubled pairs. [52]

So which of the favors
of your Lord will you deny? [53]

They'll relax within on carpets lined with rich brocade,
and the fruit of the gardens will hang within easy reach. [54]

So which of the favors
of your Lord will you deny? [55]

Chaste (attendants) [1702] will wait there - bashful,
whom no human or jinn has ever touched. [56]

So which of the favors
of your Lord will you deny? [57]

(They're stunning and dazzling to behold)
like rubies or coral! [58]

[1701] The Prophet said, "In Paradise there is a pavilion made of a single hollow pearl sixty miles wide, in each corner of which are people who will not see those in the other corners. The faithful will go around and visit them. There are two gardens, the utensils and contents of which are made of silver; and two other gardens, the utensils and contents of which are made of gold. Nothing will prevent the people who are in this Garden of Eden from seeing their Lord except the curtain of majesty over His face." (*Bukhari*)

[1702] These mates will be of human form, the most beautiful of women or handsome of men, but they will lack a soul and are created only to please us. There is no question in heaven of fidelity to one's earthly spouse, as the mates are not equal to full human beings, and both males and females get such mates. The idea is that all of the carnal delights that are forbidden or restricted on earth are allowed in heaven. (Verse 60 explains why succinctly and elegantly.) The emphasis on bashfulness is to put forward the concept that they will be dedicated solely to the individual to whom they are assigned.

So which of the favors
of your Lord will you deny? [59]

How Can you Deny?

Can there be any other reward
for goodness except good? [60]

So which of the favors
of your Lord will you deny? [61]

And besides these there will
be even two more gardens. [1703] [62]

So which of the favors
of your Lord will you deny? [63]

They'll have deep green leaves. [64]

So which of the favors
of your Lord will you deny? [65]

And there will be two springs within, as well,
from which cool water will gush forth. [66]

So which of the favors
of your Lord will you deny? [67]

Fruits, dates and pomegranates
will be there in them both! [68]

So which of the favors
of your Lord will you deny? [69]

There will be (mates) there,
noble and fine. [70]

So which of the favors
of your Lord will you deny? [71]

They're bashful companions,
waiting in raised pavilions. [72]

So which of the favors
of your Lord will you deny? [73]

No human or jinn has
ever touched them. [74]

[1703] The Prophet gave the interpretation of the two verses in this chapter (verses 46 and 62) that mention two gardens each as follows: "There are two gardens made of gold for believers who will be granted special nearness to Allah, and there are two gardens made of silver for the People of the Right (the regular righteous believers)." (*Ma'ariful Qur'an*)

So which of the favors
of your Lord will you deny? [75]

They're reclining on green cushions
and richly patterned carpets. [76]

So which of the favors
of your Lord will you deny? [77]

Blessed be the Name of your Lord,
full of majesty and honor. [78]

The Inevitable

56 Al Waqi'ah
Early Meccan Period

This chapter, which has a sense of urgency to it when one hears it recited in Arabic, even if one doesn't understand the language, explains more fully the Qur'anic concept of 'sorting' on Judgment Day. In other words, based upon what people do in this life, they will be among one of three categories: the ultra-righteous, the good, or the wicked. The latter two being personified with the idea of being on either the right or left side of a gathering. The fate of each is also mentioned in a concise yet compelling way. 'Abdullah ibn Mas'ud (d. 653) reports that the Prophet said of this chapter, "Whoever recites the chapter named the Inevitable every night will never suffer from poverty." (*Ibn Kathir*)

In the Name of Allah,
the Compassionate, the Merciful

*W*hen the shattering

(Moment of Judgment)
comes crashing down [1]
- *and there will be no denying it,* [2]
(many are those) who will be brought low,
and (many are those) who will be raised. [3]

The earth will be shaken to its very core; [4]
the mountains will be ground to dust [5]
and then be swept away! [6]

Then you're going to be sorted into three groups. 1704 [7]

(Some will be called) the *Companions of the Right,*
and who are the Companions of the Right? [8]

(Some will be called) the *Companions of the Left,*
and who are the Companions of the Left? [9]

While the foremost (in doing righteous deeds)
will be called the *Outstanding Ones.* [10]

The (Outstanding Ones)
will be nearest (to Allah) [11]
in gardens of delight. [12]

1704 'Umar ibn al-Khattab said that the meaning of this passage is that people will be grouped together based on the similarity of their deeds. (*Ma'ariful Qur'an*)

A large number (of them will be)
from the early (generations of believers), [13]
and a few will come from later times. [14]

(They'll rest) upon decorated couches, [15]
watching each other as they recline; [16]
ageless youths will scurry in their midst [17]
with glasses, pitchers and cups filled from pure fountains [18]
that will cause them neither hangover nor drunkenness. [19]

They'll choose from every variety of fruit [20]
and the meat of any type of fowl, as they will, [21]
and (they'll be joined by special mates) who will have intense,
expressive eyes [22] that resemble treasured pearls. [23]

All this is a reward for their deeds (in their former lives). [24]

Neither sinful talk nor criticism will be heard, [25]
only the saying of, "*Peace. Peace.*" [26]

Now the Companions of the Right
– and just who are the Companions of the Right? [27]

(They'll be) among lote trees where
there's neither thorn nor bramble, [28]
amidst wildly flowering acacia trees [29]
that provide cool, expansive shade, [1705] [30]
near flowing brooks [31] and abundant fruits [32]
that never go out of season or diminish. [33]

(They'll recline) on raised couches, [34]
with specially produced (mates) [35]
who are made virgin pure, [36]
playfully affectionate and of a similar age. [37]

(All this) is for the Companions of the Right, [38]
a large number from the early (generations of believers), [39]
and a large number from later times.   [40]

The Unfortunate Ones

𝒩ow as for the Companions of the Left
– and just who are the Companions of the Left? [41]

(They'll reside among) scorching blasts and scalding muck, [42]
under the shade of choking, black smoke. [43]

(They'll find) neither refreshment nor enjoyment, [44]
even as they were indulgent and living

[1705] The Prophet said, "In Paradise there is a tree under whose shade a rider can travel for a hundred years, and he still won't be able to come out of it. Recite if you will, '*that provide cool, expansive shade…*'" (*Bukhari*)

comfortably in their former (lives) [45]
- all the while they were extremely depraved! [46]

They're the ones who used to scoff:
"What? After we've died and crumbled to bones and dust,
are we really going to be resurrected, [47] *and our ancestors, too? Ha!"* [48]

Say (to them), *"Yes, indeed, both the ancient ones and all who came after!* [49]
All of you will be gathered together to stand on a well-known day! [50]
Then all of you mistaken deniers [51] *will eat from the (cursed) tree of Zaqqum.* [52]
You'll be stuffed with it, [53] *and then you'll wash it down*
with scalding muck, [54] *drinking like thirsty camels!"* [55]

This will be their welcome on the Day of Judgment. [56]

Consider the Signs of Allah

$\mathcal{W}$e created (all of) you,

so why won't you accept the truth? [57]

Have you ever thought about
(the seminal fluid) that you throw out? [58]

Did you create it, or did We? [59]
We've ordained for all of you to die (one day),
and We won't be held back [60] from transforming
you from one form into another,
the likes of which you can't even comprehend. [61]

You've already witnessed
(the complexity) of your first creation,
so why won't you accept this reminder? [62]

Have you ever seen the seed
that you plant in the ground? [63]
Do you make it sprout, or do We? [64]
If We wanted, We could make it crumble to dust.
Then you would be left speechless, [65] saying,
"We've gone into debt (for the sake of our farms). [66]
Oh no! We've been thwarted!" [67]

Have you ever thought about the water that you drink? [68]
Do you bring it down from the clouds, or do We? [69]
If We wanted, We could make it salty.
So why aren't you thankful? [70]

Have you looked at the fire that you kindle? [71]
Do you grow the trees that feed (its flames), or do We? [72]
We bestowed (the knowledge of how to control fire with you)
as a reminder (of Our power) and also as a source of
comfort for travelers in the wilderness. [73]
So now glorify the name
of your Lord, the Almighty! [74]

This is a Message to be Taken Seriously

*A*nd so I swear by the setting of the stars [75]

- and that's a mighty oath if you only knew [76]
- that this Qur'an is an honorable one. [77]

It's (preserved) in a protected Book [78]
that no one can touch save the pure. [79]
(It's no less) than revelation from the Lord of All the Worlds! [80]

Are you taking its narratives lightly? [81]
Have you made denying it your career? [82]
(But if you're so strong), then why are you helpless
when a person chokes (up his soul at death), [83]
while all you can do is stand around and watch? [84]

We're even closer to him than you are,
though you don't see it! [85]

And why, if you're so safe from (any future) review, [86]
is it impossible for you to bring him back to life,
if you're really so sure? [87]

And so, for whoever is among those nearest (to Allah), [88]
there will be rest and satisfaction within gardens of delight. [89]

Whoever is among the Companions of the Right, [90]
"Peace be upon you," from the companions of the right! [91]

While whoever denied (the truth) in error, [92]
his welcome will be scalding muck [93] and roasting flames. [94]

This is the certain truth, [95]
so glorify the name of your Lord, the Almighty! [96]

Iron

57 Al Hadeed
Late Medinan Period

This chapter was revealed sometime after the Battle of Uhud (in 625), but before the Treaty of Hudaybiyyah (in 628). During this time the Muslim community in Medina was trying to establish itself on a solid footing, both socially and politically, as well as financially. Thus, we see in this chapter various exhortations to the believers to take a more active role in shaping the affairs of their fledgling civilization. It is reported that the Prophet said that there is a verse in this chapter that is better than a thousand other verses, and most scholars are of the opinion that it is verse number three.

In the Name of Allah,
the Compassionate, the Merciful

All things within the heavens and the earth reflect the glory of Allah, and He's the Powerful and the Wise. [1]

To Him belongs the control of the heavens and the earth. He alone grants life, and He alone takes it, for He has power over all things. [2]

He's the First and the Last, the Evident and the Hidden, and He knows about all things. [1706] [3]

He's the One Who created the heavens and the earth in six stages, and He's entrenched upon the seat (of power).

He knows everything that goes into the earth and everything that leaves it,

And (He knows) everything that descends from the sky and everything that goes back into it.

He's with you wherever you are, and Allah is watching everything you do. [4]

The control of the heavens and the earth belongs to Him, and all issues go back to Allah (for resolution). [5]

He merges the night into day and the day into night, and He knows the innermost secrets of the heart. [6]

[1706] The Prophet taught people to say special supplications before falling asleep. One of them is as follows: "O Allah, Lord of the seven heavens and Lord of the Glorious Throne! Our Lord and the Lord of everything, revealer of the Torah, the Gospel and the Standard, the splitter of grain seeds and date stones! I seek Your protection from the evil of everything whose forehead you control. O Allah, You are the First, and there is nothing before You, the Last, for there is nothing after You, the Evident, for nothing is above You, and the Hidden, for nothing is below You. Remove the burden of debt from us, and free us from poverty." (*Muslim*) Among the shortest bedtime supplications is, "*Bismika Allahumma amutu wa ahya,*" or "In Your Name, O Allah, we die and we live." Supplications to Allah may be made in any language, as per the unanimous agreement of the scholars, both modern and classical.

Supporting the Faith Financially

*B*elieve in Allah and His Messenger, and spend (in charity) from the inheritance that He's placed with you. For those who believe among you and who spend (their money in Allah's cause), there is a vast reward. [7]

So what's keeping you from believing in Allah, seeing that the Messenger is calling you to believe in your Lord, and has taken your oath? Are you (really) believers? [8]

He's the One Who sends His self-evident verses to His servant so He can bring you out of darkness and into light, for Allah is kind and merciful to you. [9]

So now what's keeping you from spending in the path of Allah, (knowing that) the (final) inheritance of the heavens and the earth belongs to Allah?

Those who spent and fought before the victory (over the Meccans are more than) equal (with those who came later). 1707

They're truly higher in status than those who spent and fought afterwards, though Allah has promised a fine reward to both. Allah is well-informed of everything you do. [10]

Who will lend to Allah a beautiful loan for which He will multiply its value many times and reward him generously? [11] One day you're going to see the believers, both men and women, preceded by their light shining before them and by their right hand, (being told), *"There's good news for you today: gardens beneath which rivers flow in which to stay! That's the ultimate success!"* [12]

One day, the hypocrites, both men and women, (will be calling desperately to the believers), saying, *"Wait for us! Lend us some of your light!"* But they'll be told, *"Turn back around, and find your own light."*

Then a wall will be laid between them having but a (single) gate. Inside it mercy abounds; outside it punishment is all around. [13]

The (hypocrites on the other side) will cry out, *"But weren't we with you (before on earth)?"*

To which (the believers) will answer, *"Of course, but you led yourselves into temptation, and you were hesitant and doubtful, so your false hopes deluded you until the command of Allah arrived. The Deceiver tricked you (into rejecting) Allah!"* 1708 [14]

"So no bribe will be accepted from you today nor from those who openly rejected (faith). Your home is in the Fire, and it's your only home now, and, oh, how dreadful a place to stay!" [15]

The Nature of the Physical World

*I*sn't it time for the hearts of the believers to humble themselves to the remembrance of Allah?

(Shouldn't they now recognize) the truth bestowed upon them, so they won't become like those who received revelation in the past, but whose hearts have hardened with time, so much so that many of them are now hopelessly rebellious? [16]

Know that Allah brings life to the earth after it was dead. We've made Our proofs clear to you so you can understand. [17]

Indeed, those men and women who give in charity and who have lent to Allah a beautiful loan, will be amply repaid with a generous reward. [18]

1707 This refers to the surrender of Mecca to the Muslims in the year 630. Allah accounts the deeds of those who struggled for Islam when it was hardest to do so on a higher scale than those who became Muslim later when it was easier to do so, though both will have an ample reward.
1708 This would be Satan. See 4:118-121 for an explanation of his plan to deceive as much of humanity as he can.

Those who believe in Allah and in His messengers are the truthful and the witnesses in the presence of their Lord. For them is their reward and their light, but those who reject (the truth) and deny Our signs, they're going to be companions of Hellfire. [19]

Know that the life of this world is nothing more than distraction and games; an alluring show of boasting and accumulating wealth and children. Its example is like plentiful vegetation (growing) after a constant rain - *a delight to the gardener!*

However, it soon withers, and you see it turning yellow; then it crumbles into dust. In the next life, there's either stern punishment or forgiveness from Allah and His good pleasure. Now what is the life of this world but the illusion of material goods? [20]

So race ahead towards the forgiveness of your Lord and to a garden as vast as the heavens and the earth that's been prepared for those who believe in Allah and His messengers.

This is the bounty of Allah, and He grants it to whomever He wants, *and Allah is the master of incredible bounty!* [21]

No misfortune can come upon the earth nor upon yourselves that isn't already recorded by Us in a ledger before We even let it happen, and that's easy for Allah. [22]

(Remember this) so you don't despair over what you've lost or brag about what you've gained, for Allah has no love for

conceited show offs. [23] They're miserly and urge others to be miserly, also. Whoever turns away (from faith should know) that Allah is Self-sufficient and is (already being) Praised. [24]

The Chain of Prophethood

*A*nd so it was that We sent Our messengers with clear evidence. We revealed along with them the Book and the balance (of right and wrong) so that people could stand up for justice.

We've also sent iron down (to earth) as both a source of grim strength and (economic) benefit for people. (This material was given to you) so that Allah could (use it) to distinguish who would help Him and His messengers, even though they don't perceive (the unseen world, yet). Allah is strong and powerful. [1709] [25]

We sent Noah and Abraham and instituted prophethood among their descendants, granting them scriptures, as well. Although some of them were guided (in the succeeding generations), most of the rest were disobedient. [26]

After them, We sent more of Our messengers in succession and (followed them up) with Jesus, the son of Mary, giving to him the Gospel. We also placed compassion and mercy into the hearts of his followers.

However, some of them began to practice monasticism on their own, even though We never prescribed it for them. [1710]

[1709] Iron is a strong metal that can be put to grim uses, such as in making war materials. It can also be used for peaceful purposes, such as in manufacturing and construction. Our test is in how we use it, for good or evil.

[1710] Throughout history, many pious men and women have sought to come closer to Allah through asceticism, or giving up the pleasures of the world for a life of poverty and prayer. Christians and Buddhists, in particular, have taken this one step further by establishing centers called monasteries where such people can gather. The monks (and nuns) are forbidden to marry (a Catholic practice enforced since the Second Lateran Council of 1139). They wear coarse clothes and generally withdraw from the world to meditate, pray and lead a simple life. While it may seem like a peaceful path, Islam discourages this as an unnatural lifestyle for a creature of the earth. Instead, Islam asks its followers to be engaged in the world, but to do so with the understanding that their lives are short. Thus, life

Rather, (We only asked them) to seek the good pleasure of Allah, but they didn't practice it as it should have been practiced! Although We rewarded those among them who believed, still most of them were rebellious. [27]

All you (Jews and Christians) who have faith! Be mindful (of Allah) and believe in His Messenger, for He will grant you a double portion of His mercy and will send down upon you a light wherein you can walk. [1711] He will forgive you (your sins), for Allah is forgiving and merciful. [28]

(This call) is made to the Followers of Earlier Revelation so they can know that they have no power at all over the bounty of Allah, [1712] for it's in His hand to give to whomever He wills, *and Allah is the master of incredible bounty!* [29]

must be lived simply, honestly and without pretension. The Prophet said, "Giving up the world does not mean making lawful things unlawful or wasting possessions. Rather, giving up the world means that you do not put more reliance on what is in your hand than what is in the hand of Allah and that when you are stricken with adversity, you actually want it to continue for the sake of the rewards that grow on account of it." *(Ibn Majah, Tirmidhi)* On another occasion, when the Prophet had heard that some of his followers wanted to become more pious by giving up meat, marriage and the comfort of a bed upon which to lie, the Prophet forbade them, saying he engaged in all those things. He added that whoever is not content with following his example is not of him. *(Bukhari)*

[1711] Jesus is quoted as saying that a new prophet after his time can be known to be authentic or not by the fruits that he bears. If the prophet in question is good, then his teachings will be good, but if he is evil, then his teachings will bring out the worst in people. Muhammad was a moral and thoughtful man who spent his time in worship of Allah, struggling against superstition and in reforming an ignorant and backward people. He stopped infanticide and alcohol consumption and gave women rights they never had before. He taught people to reject idols, to give in charity and to let go of materialistic desires, along with many, many other noble things. Just look at this statement of the Prophet: "If you can guarantee me six things on your part, I shall guarantee you Paradise: speak the truth when you talk, keep a promise when you make it, when you are trusted with something fulfill your trust, avoid sexual immorality, lower your gaze (so as not to stare lustfully), and restrain your hands from injustice." *(Tirmidhi)* Is this not the proof of Jesus' test? (See Matthew 7:15-20) So what tremendous benefit will a Jew or Christian receive for accepting Muhammad as Allah's last prophet? The Prophet said, "Any person who is from the Followers of Earlier Revelation (the Jews and Christians), who believes in his own prophet (Moses or Jesus) and then believes in me (Muhammad), as well, will get a double reward. Any servant who fulfils his duty to his master and also to his Lord will get a double reward, as well." *(Bukhari)*

[1712] There are three implications here. The first is that even if Jews and Christians object to Muhammad's prophethood on the grounds that he is an Arab, they have no control over whom Allah appoints as a prophet. Secondly, if they object, saying that Allah only favors Jews or Christians, again, it's in Allah's hand to give to whom He pleases. Lastly, if they claim that only Jesus can forgive, it's not in their power to make it so, just because they wish it. Only Allah can forgive, and only Allah can reward – not a supposed son (or wife) of His.

The Petitioner

58 Al Mujadilah
Middle Medinan Period

A woman named Khuwaylah bint Thalabah went to the Prophet and complained that her husband (and cousin), Auws ibn as-Samit, had divorced her using an old Arab custom in which the man swore that he had the same kind of feelings towards his wife that he had towards his mother. In other words, he wouldn't sleep with his own mother, so he rejected ever cohabitating with his wife on the same grounds. In her own words she said, "By Allah, that Allah sent down the beginning of (chapter 58) with regard to me and Auws ibn as-Samit. He was my husband and had grown old and difficult. One day he came to me, and I argued with him about something.

He said, 'You are like my mother's back to me.' (Which was a pre-Islamic practice known as *zihar*.) Then he went out and sat with some people. Then he came back in and wanted to sleep with me, and I said, 'No, by the One Who holds my soul! You won't have your way with me after you said what you said to me until after Allah and His Messenger make a judgment in our case.' He wanted to have his way with me anyway, but I pushed him away for he was a weak old man. Then I went to my neighbor, borrowed a cloak from her and then went to the Messenger of Allah and kept complaining to him of the ill treatment I received from Auws." (*Ahmad, Abu Dawud*)

A'ishah, who was in another room, overheard Khuwaylah and reports that she said to the Prophet, "Messenger of Allah! He spent my wealth and exhausted my youth. My womb produced abundantly for him. When I became old and unable to bear any more children, he pronounced Zihar on me! O Allah! I make my complaint to You." (*Bukhari*) The Prophet said to her, "Khuwaylah! Your cousin is an old man, so have mindfulness of Allah about him." As Khuwaylah continues the story, she said, "By Allah, before I left parts of the Qur'an were revealed about me.

The Messenger of Allah felt the tension of receiving revelation, as he usually did, and then he relaxed and said to me, 'Khuwaylah! Allah has revealed something about you and your husband.' Then he recited to me (verses 1-4). Then the Prophet said to me, 'Order him to free a slave.' I replied, 'Messenger of Allah, he doesn't have any to free.' Then the Prophet told me, 'Let him fast for two months.' I said, 'By Allah, he's an old man and is unable to fast.' Then the Prophet told me, 'Let him feed sixty poor people a camel-load of dates.' I said, 'By Allah, he doesn't have any of that.' Then the Prophet said, 'We will help him with a basket of dates.' I said, 'Messenger of Allah, I will help him with another.' The Prophet then said, 'You have done a noble thing. Now go and give away the dates on his behalf and take care of your cousin.'" (*Ahmad, Abu Dawud*)

Thus, Khuwaylah's husband was taken to task and shamed for what he did. Yet, the situation turned around with everyone trying to help him to atone for his sin. A woman's complaint was addressed to her satisfaction, and she received the credit of a great reward on her record of deeds. In later years, during the rule of 'Umar ibn al-Khattab, Khuwaylah saw 'Umar walking in the streets of Medina followed by an attendant.

She approached him and boldly said, "When you were young, we used to call you 'Umayr. Then when you became older we called you 'Umar. Now we call you Commander of the Faithful!" With that she left. The attendant was amazed at her boldness and asked 'Umar how he could keep silent and listen to her speak to him like that. 'Umar replied, "If she spoke to me for the whole day, I would listen to her. Do you know who she was? Allah revealed a chapter about her, and if Allah can listen to her from the heavens, then who am I not to listen to her!"

In the Name of Allah,
the Compassionate, the Merciful

Allah has heard the appeal of (the woman) who brought her petition to you about her husband. Thus, she's bringing her case to Allah (for a resolution). Allah has heard what both sides have said, for Allah listens and observes. [1]

(So from now on), those (men) who distance themselves from their wives (by saying, *"You're no more my wife than my own mother,"* must realize that their wives) can never be equated with their mothers, for no one can be called their mothers except those who gave birth to them. [1713]

When they say such things, they're speaking absurdly and falsely, though Allah erases sins and forgives (those who repent). [1714] [2]

Those (men) who try to divorce their wives in this way, but who later want to take back what they pronounced, must free a bonded-servant before they can go back to each other again. [1715] You're required to do this, and Allah is well-informed of everything you do. [1716] [3]

Whoever can't afford to do this must fast for two months in a row before (the couple) can touch each other again. (If even this task is too much of a hardship to be fulfilled), then he should feed sixty poor people.

That's how you can demonstrate your faith in Allah and His Messenger. These are the rules set by Allah, and the faithless (who disregard these rules) will have a painful punishment. [4]

Those who oppose Allah and His Messenger will be brought low just like all

---

[1713] This pre-Islamic custom outlined here was truly degrading and hurtful to women. A man could tell his wife he's not attracted to her any more than he is to his own mother, but then he would not divorce her, thus keeping her in social and marital limbo. She wasn't even free to marry another, as women in pre-Islamic times had next to no divorce rights. Thus, it was a great injustice. This Qur'anic revelation abolished this practice.

[1714] A married couple approached the Prophet one day and explained that they often quarreled and were close to divorcing. They asked the Prophet for advice on how they could stop their cycle of fighting, for the husband was quick to anger and often became abusive, while the wife had a sharp tongue and said hurtful things that provoked him. The Prophet told the man that whenever his wife started saying things that made him upset, he should take a drink of water, but not swallow it, until his wife had calmed down. The couple practiced this technique, and the husband visited the Prophet a few months later to report that the method had worked, and he no longer became so easily angered and enjoyed harmony in his home.

[1715] i.e., before they can be intimate or affectionate with each other again.

[1716] A man went to the Prophet and said, "Messenger of Allah! I said *zihar* to my wife, but then I slept with her before I paid the penalty." The Prophet asked, "May Allah be merciful to you. What made you do that?" The man said, "I saw the nice clothes and bangles she was wearing by the light of the moon." The Prophet said, "Then don't touch her again until you do what Allah, the Exalted and Honored, has ordered you to do." (*Tirmidhi, Abu Dawud, Nisa'i*)

those (sinners) who were brought low before them. As it is, We've sent clear verses (that already demonstrate this truth).

Those who covered over (their awareness of the truth) will have a humiliating punishment [5] on the day when Allah will resurrect them all and make them realize the meaning of what they did. (Even though they may have forgotten their deeds,) Allah has kept track of their accounts, and Allah is a witness over all things. [6]

On Secret Meetings

$\mathcal{D}$on't you see that Allah knows everything in the heavens and on the earth? 1717 There is no secret gathering of three without Him being the fourth or between five except that He's the sixth, and whether they be fewer or greater, He's in their midst wherever they may be. 1718

On the Day of Assembly, He's going to inform them about what they did. Indeed, Allah has knowledge of all things. [7]

Haven't you noticed those who were forbidden to engage in secret talk? 1719 Yet, they continue to do what they've been told not to do! They secretly make plans to indulge in sin and to be hostile and disobedient to the Messenger.

Don't Speak in Secret or Convey False Meanings

$\mathcal{W}$hen they come to you, (Muhammad,) they address you (in a kind of haughty manner) that even Allah doesn't use. 1720 Then they think to themselves, *"So why isn't Allah punishing us for what we said?"*

Hellfire is enough to take care of them. They're going to burn in it – and, oh, how horrible a destination! [8]

O you who believe! When you hold secret meetings, don't discuss sin, hostility or disobedience to the Messenger.

Rather, talk about virtue and mindfulness (of Allah). Be mindful then (of Allah), to Whom you will be brought back. [9]

1717 Some of the hypocrites used to take secret counsels together in order to find ways to harass and annoy the Muslims. When a sincere believer would pass by them, they would wink at each other and make up stories that the relatives of that believer, who might have been out on patrol or traveling, had died. This vexed the Muslims greatly, and they complained to the Prophet about that. This verse was revealed to comfort them. (*Asbab ul-Nuzul*)

1718 The Prophet said, "If you were three (in a gathering), then two of you shouldn't hold secret counsel in the presence of the third person without his permission, because that would cause him to be distressed." (*Muslim*) Many modern scholars say that this tradition of the Prophet applies when two people speak in a language that a third person in their midst doesn't understand, for the exclusionary effect remains the same.

1719 This verse refers to the habit of the Jews of Medina who used to whisper and look menacingly upon any Muslim who passed by them. Many Muslims complained about this habit, for the way they were being looked at and whispered about made them feel that the Jews might attack them. The Prophet repeatedly asked the Jews to stop doing it, but they ignored his requests. (*Asbab ul-Nuzul*)

1720 A group of Jews approached the Prophet one day while he was sitting with his wife A'ishah and some other people. They greeted him by saying in a quick voice, "As-sa'mu 'alayka," which means, "Death be upon you." The customary Muslim greeting was, "As-salamu 'alaykum," so the Jews were trying to insult him. A'ishah got angry, and she spoke out before the Prophet could, saying, "And upon you and may Allah do it!" The Prophet looked at her and said, "Be quiet, A'ishah, for Allah doesn't like the shameful and excessiveness in that." A'ishah protested, "But don't you know what they said to you?" The Prophet answered, "But don't you know I replied to them for what they said?" A'ishah was about to argue further, but then this verse was revealed. Ever afterward, by the Prophet's orders, the Muslim reply to a non-Muslim's greeting has been merely to say, "And the same be to you," or "wa 'alayk." (*Asbab ul-Nuzul*)

(All other kinds of) secret meetings are inspired by Satan so he can create disharmony among the believers, though he can do them no harm at all except as Allah allows. The believers should trust in Allah! [10]

Make Room for Others

O you who believe! [1721] When you're asked to make room in your gatherings (for others), then make room, for then Allah will make room for you. [1722] When you're asked to rise up (to leave or to make more space), then arise, for Allah will raise by degrees those who believe among you and those who achieve deep insight. Allah is well-informed of all that you do. [11]

Give in Charity before Seeking Advice

O you who believe! [1723] Before going to ask the Messenger privately for advice,

give something in charity before your consultation.

That's best for you and closer to purity. If you don't have the means (to give, then know) that Allah is forgiving and merciful. [12]

Are you afraid that you won't be able to give in charity before meeting privately with the Messenger? At the least, if you have to skip the charity, and Allah has forgiven you, then at least remain diligent in your prayers, [1724] practice regular charity and obey Allah and His Messenger, for Allah is well-informed of all that you do. [13]

On Choosing Friends Who Actively Oppose Allah

*H*aven't you noticed those people who turn (in friendship) to those at whom

---

[1721] The Prophet said, "None of you should make someone move from their spot and sit in it. Rather, spread out and make room." (*Ahmad*)

[1722] Sometime after the conquest of Mecca, the Prophet was giving a Friday congregational sermon by the side of Safa Hill. It was a narrow place that had very little room to accommodate a large crowd. Many of the people who had fought in the Battle of Badr were sitting near to him, and this pleased him greatly. A large group of others, both from among the Helpers of Medina and the Immigrants from Mecca, arrived late, and they stood near the side, waiting for people to make room for them. No one in the crowd moved or shifted at all, and the Prophet was upset by this. He wound up asking those nearest to him to move off to the side, so the latecomers could join the congregation. As it happened, many of the Badr veterans happened to be the ones who were asked to move from their places. Many of them were annoyed at having been moved farther back away from their beloved leader, and the Prophet noticed the grimaces on many of their faces. After the service was concluded, some of the Meccans who had not yet converted and were still idol-worshippers said to the Muslims, "Do you think your Prophet is fair? Has he just sent away the people who want to sit near to him in favor of those who arrived late?" This verse was revealed to make it easier for the believers to accommodate each other in crowded places with no ill feelings. (*Asbab ul-Nuzul*)

[1723] Some of the more influential and wealthy Muslims began to monopolize the Prophet's time, and this left the poor with less access to him. This situation bothered Muhammad greatly, in addition to the fact that so many people came to him with questions that he had scarcely a moment to himself. This verse was revealed, asking the wealthy to donate to charity before seeking a private audience with the Prophet, in order to purify their intentions and also to discourage the miserly from trying to tie up his schedule for their own vainglory. Thus, only those who sincerely wanted to grow in piety would come to see him. The poor, of course, were exempted from this rule, unless they could afford it. (*Asbab ul-Nuzul*)

[1724] The Prophet said that Allah, Himself, said, "I accept the prayers of the person who performs (their prayers) in a state of humility, recognizing My greatness, and who fulfills their obligations to My creatures, is not persistent in sinning against Me, spends his day remembering Me, and is kind to the poor, travelers, the weak and those who are suffering." (*Hadith Qudsi*)

Allah is angry? [1725] They're neither fully with you nor with them, and they knowingly swear to lies. [14]

Allah has prepared a terrible punishment for them because what they're doing is evil. [15] They use their promises as a screen (to hide their deceit), and thus they turn others away from the path of Allah. Humiliating punishment awaits them! [16] Neither (the extent) of their fortune nor (the size) of their families will help them in the least against Allah.

They're going to be companions of the Fire, *and that's where they're going to stay!* [17] On the day when Allah resurrects them, they'll swear to Him (as to their innocence), even as they're swearing before you now, thinking they're fully justified.

But no! They're truly liars! [18] Satan has won them over and made them forget the remembrance of Allah, [1726] so they're on Satan's team, and Satan's team will surely lose! [19]

Without a doubt, those who oppose Allah and His Messenger will be humiliated in shame, [20] for Allah has decreed, *"My messengers and I shall prevail."* Without a doubt, Allah is strong and powerful. [21]

You won't find any people who believe in Allah and the Last Day loving those who oppose Allah and His Messenger, even if they're from among their own parents, children, siblings or other relatives. They've had faith written upon their hearts, and they've been strengthened with a spirit from His Own Self.

He's going to admit them into gardens beneath which rivers flow, and there they shall remain! Allah will be pleased with them, and they with Him. They're on Allah's side, and Allah's side will achieve success! [22]

[1725] A hypocrite named 'Abdullah ibn Nabtal had been sitting in a gathering listening to the Prophet giving a speech. Then he left, went straight to some Jewish friends of his and began telling them everything the Prophet had said (in a disrespectful and mocking manner). Then he went to return to the mosque to get more information. Meanwhile, the Prophet was sitting inside with some companions, and he told them, "A man is about to enter with an arrogant heart and eyes that have the look of Satan." Ibn Nabtal entered, and the Prophet said to him, "Why are you insulting me?" Ibn Nabtal swore repeatedly that he had not. He called for some of his friends to be brought in to swear also that he had not, and they all backed each other's stories. Ibn Nabtal left, and then this passage was revealed. (*Hakim*)

[1726] The hypocrites would only pray when they were in public. Otherwise, they disregarded prayer along with most other Islamic injunctions.

The Gathering
59 Al Hashr
Early Medinan Period

In the year 624, an outnumbered force of Muslims defeated a Meccan army at the Wells of Badr. This elevated the status of the Muslims in the eyes of the Arabs and caused a great amount of embarrassment for the Meccans. In Medina, it also gave pause for the three Jewish tribes to reconsider Muhammad's rising power. Even though each had signed a city charter with him guaranteeing the mutual safety of all, none of them had considered Muhammad or his religion to be a permanent fixture in Arabia.

The tribe of Banu Qaynuqa decided to scrap the treaty first, and they challenged the Muslims to a fight, but they were defeated and banished from the city. Meanwhile, among the Banu Nadir there were those who were impressed with the Muslim victory at Badr. A few even took it as a sign that Muhammad might just be a true prophet, and a few of those even converted to Islam, given that he apparently had the favor of Allah. However, the majority of the tribe were content to remain quietly opposed in their attitude.

The embittered Meccans soon began to send messages to the Banu Nadir, one of which said, "You're the people who have fortresses and military might. You had better fight the Prophet, otherwise we'll attack (him and then you), and nothing will prevent us from seizing your women." This only added to the internal debate among the Banu Nadir about what to do about Islam.

After the Muslims were defeated by the Meccans the following year at the Battle of Uhud (in the year 625), the leaders among the Banu Nadir felt that this showed that Muhammad did not have the favor of Allah after all. Thus, they increased in their quiet resistance to Islam. A delegation of forty men led by a chief of the Banu Nadir, Ka'b ibn Ashraf, traveled to Mecca and pledged support to the pagans in their fight against Islam.

When they returned to Medina, they began to make secret pledges of support with some factions of hypocrites within the city, even extracting a promise from 'Abdullah ibn Ubayy that if they fought the Muslims, then Ibn Ubayy's men would back them up - and even share their fate if their side lost. (The Meccans had also written a similar threatening letter to Ibn Ubayy to force his support.)

Eventually, the Banu Nadir faction resolved to assassinate the Prophet. They asked the Prophet to come with thirty followers - and they would join him with thirty followers of their own - to hold a summit meeting. When the meeting was underway, some of the rabbis, realizing that Muhammad's followers were fervent enough to fight to the death, reconsidered attacking him there. Thus, one of them told Muhammad, "How can we come to an agreement when we're a mass of sixty men? Come and visit us with three of your men, and we'll bring three of our good people. If any of them believe in you, at least one of us will have believed in you."

When the time for the next meeting was at hand, three Jewish men with swords awaited to ambush the Prophet. A Jewish woman of the Banu Nadir, whose own son had converted to Islam, warned her son of the plot to kill the Prophet, and he went to the Prophet right away with the news. The Prophet refrained from attending that meeting and took to avoiding the neighborhood of the Banu Nadir. It is reported that the Prophet publicly called to be 'relieved' of Ka'b ibn Ashraf and his plotting and propagandizing, and he was killed in a clandestine ambush by one of the companions a short time later.

Eventually, the Prophet would have to pay a visit to the Banu Nadir's district, and here is the background for that story. A man named 'Amr ibn Umayyah Damuri had survived a massacre in which almost seventy of the Prophet's missionaries had been ambushed and killed, despite promises of safe passage from an ostensibly sincere tribe that was secretly allied to the Meccans. On his way back to Medina with the grim news, 'Amr, who was the sole survivor, encountered two pagans and attacked them, thinking they had been involved in the massacre.

When he finally returned to the city, he found out that the two men were not a part of the ambush and that their tribe was allied to both the Muslims and the Banu Nadir. The Prophet then ordered blood-money to be collected to compensate the victims' families for the unintended loss of their two men, and he also went to pay a visit to the district of the Banu Nadir to collect money from them for the same purpose, as they were contractually obligated to pay.

Apparently, the men who received the Prophet and his companions asked him to sit in the shade of a wall and wait for them to meet with him. A young Jewish man named 'Umar ibn Jahash was tapped by the Jewish elders to drop a heavy stone from the roof in an attempt to kill the Prophet, but the Prophet noticed the activity from above and quickly retreated with his followers back into the Muslim district of the city. Thereupon, the Prophet called for his followers to arm themselves, and they went to the fortress complex of the Banu Nadir and besieged it.

The Prophet ordered them to leave Medina within ten days, or he would attack. The Banu Nadir sent a desperate message to 'Abdullah ibn Ubayy to reinforce them, but he remained in his own neighborhood and forsook them. (Not even their Jewish cousins, the Banu Qurayzah, came to their aid, preferring to sign a renewed mutual security agreement with Muhammad.)

The resourceful men of the Banu Nadir held out for about fifteen days by raining arrows down upon the Muslims to keep them at bay. Finally, after a spirited defense of their position, they saw the Muslims uprooting some of their precious orchards, and they quickly lost the will to fight. Eventually the pressure of the siege forced the Banu Nadir to sue for peace. Trusting in Muhammad's lenient reputation, they surrendered some days later, and he gave them quite generous terms, considering what they tried to do to him.

The tribe was ordered to leave Medina because of their betrayal of the treaty. Yet, they would have the originally ordered ten days to pack, and they could take whatever they could load onto their camels. Before they left, the Banu Nadir practically demolished their homes to keep the Muslims from enjoying them.

Most of the tribe then moved to Syria, though a remnant went to a Jewish settlement named Khaybar far to the north. (From there they would later seek revenge by cobbling a coalition of pagans together to besiege the city of Medina!)

*A*ll things within the heavens and on the earth glorify Allah. He's the Powerful and the Wise. [1]

He's the One Who drove the faithless from among the Followers of Earlier Revelation away from their homes - even at the first gathering (for battle)!

You never thought (the Banu Nadir) would leave, even as they thought their fortresses could stand against Allah.

Then Allah came upon them from every direction and from where they least expected!

He cast fear into their hearts, causing them to destroy their homes with their own hands – (even helping) the believers' efforts in the process! [1727]

You who have eyes
to see, take heed! [2]

If Allah had not already decreed their exile, He would've certainly imposed upon them far greater punishment in this world, though the punishment of the Fire awaits them in the next life. [3]

That's because they opposed Allah and His Messenger, and anyone who opposes Allah (should know) that Allah is severe in retribution. [1728] [4]

Whether you had cut the palm trees or let them stand firmly, it was all by the will of Allah, (though He commanded them to be cut) so that the rebels could be disgraced. [1729] [5]

(The property) that Allah (removed from their control) and transferred to His Messenger required no expedition of cavalry or camelry on your part, for Allah grants His messengers power over whomever He wants, for Allah has power over all things. [6]

[1727] During the fighting, as the Muslim forces slowly advanced on Jewish held buildings, the Jews would set fire to the buildings before retreating in an effort to stall the Muslims. Though it was a sound military tactic, the end result was that the Jews were destroying their own homes and thus diminishing their own holdings, regardless of the result of their battle.

[1728] The Jews of the Banu Nadir had decided to kill the Prophet after mistakenly assigning the meaning of some verses from their Torah against him. Those verses command that Jews must kill any prophet who comes to them with suggestions to worship any other God than the God who delivered them from Egypt. (See Deuteronomy 13:1-5) The problem with assigning that sentence against Muhammad is the same with their ancestors assigning it against Jesus. Neither of those men were telling the Jews to abandon God or worship idols. Both of them were teaching greater dedication to God and using appeals to ancient scripture to back up their claims. (See Matthew 21:42 where Jesus is using Torah quotations to advance his message, and see Qur'an 2:40-41 where Allah is making the case that Muhammad's message is from the same source as the Torah.)

[1729] The Prophet quickly realized that the Banu Nadir were fighting so resolutely on account of their extensive land holdings and orchards, which they wanted to protect. He ordered his men to begin uprooting the date palms within sight of the fortress, in order to demoralize its defenders. One of the men of the Banu Nadir called down from his position, "Are you pretending to ask people to practice goodness? Is it goodness to cut fruit trees and palm trees? Do you think you have the right to corrupt the earth, according to what's been revealed to you?" (The Jews were perhaps unaware that their own scripture allowed for the cutting of trees in a long siege if needed for military reasons, though only of non fruit-bearing trees. See Deuteronomy 20:19-20) The Prophet and the Muslims were troubled by the accusations made against them, and many took to asking each other if it were right to cut down such useful trees. Finally, the Prophet announced that Allah, Himself, willed it, as a way to defeat the enemy. After this event was over, the Prophet forbade future Muslim armies from cutting trees during wartime unless absolutely necessary. The allowance to cut some of the trees in this instance was a dispensation to aid Allah's Prophet. Not all of the trees were destroyed, only enough to make the Banu Nadir realize there was no hope of their holding on to them any further.

Whatever (property) Allah transferred to His Messenger from the people of the (Banu Nadir and their) settlement belongs to Allah and His Messenger and to relatives, to orphans, to the needy and to travelers, so that the money doesn't remain circulating among the wealthy alone. [1730]

So take what the Messenger apportions for you, and refrain from what he withholds from you. Be mindful of Allah, for Allah is severe in retribution. [7]

(Also distribute something) to the poor refugees (from Mecca) who were driven from their homes and deprived of their properties in their pursuit of the grace and pleasure of Allah, and also because they were helping Allah and His Messenger. They were sincere (in their intentions). [8]

Don't be Jealous of the Fortunes of Others

*T*hose who already had homes here (in Medina) and who believed (in Islam), extended their heartfelt hospitality to those (Meccan refugees) who came to them seeking a safe haven. They're not inwardly jealous of the portions (that the refugees) are receiving. [1731]

And even though they might be needy themselves, they give preference to others first. [1732] Whoever is saved from the greed of his own soul will be successful. [1733] [9]

Those (believers) who came after them said, "*Our Lord, forgive us and our brothers (in faith) who came before us. Don't let any malice against other believers take root within our hearts,*

[1730] Whether wealth comes into the community through default (when an enemy abandons an area) or through war (when an enemy is vanquished on the battlefield), it is not meant to enrich those who are in charge. There are five groups who can benefit especially, as noted here, from the Prophet (to fund his communally-based activities) to orphans and so on. (This is a delineation known as the *khums*, of one-fifth distribution. Also see 8:41 for an identical distribution for booty.) This speaks to a wider principle in Islamic economic theory: wealth should not remain concentrated in the hands of the rich at the expense of the rest of society. At the same time, Islam is not unjust and does not forbid people from amassing profits gained from their own honest efforts. Islam is not against capitalism in its most basic form, nor is it communistic in nature. Islam is somewhere in between. Beyond the principles of this verse, which lay down rules for distributing unexpected windfalls, the institution of *zakah*, or mandatory charity based on annual savings, ensures that those who have more in normal life must share something with the needier portions of society. (*Ma'ariful Qur'an*)

[1731] After the Banu Nadir left Medina and headed northwards, the Prophet gave a speech about the distribution of the lands they left behind to the gathered throngs of jubilant (and expectant) believers. He told the crowd, which was made up mostly of Helpers (natives of Medina who took in the Meccan refugees), "Allah has granted you the wealth of the Banu Nadir. If you like, I will divide the wealth among the Immigrants and Helpers equally, and the Immigrants will continue to dwell in the homes of the Helpers, or if you like, the wealth can be distributed among the homeless Immigrants, and they can thus move out of your homes and into their own new ones." The Helpers generously deferred all the wealth to the Immigrants, who were thus able to establish themselves in the city in their own dwellings. (*Ma'ariful Qur'an*)

[1732] The Prophet sent a hungry Immigrant to a Helper's house for a meal. (The Prophet had first asked his own wives if they had any food for the man, and they had nothing in their apartments except water!) The Helper who volunteered to feed the Immigrant went inside his home and asked his wife if there was any food in the house. She answered that there was only enough for the children. So he asked her to blow out the lamp in their room and put the children to bed. Then he invited the Immigrant in and fed the food to his visitor. When the Prophet heard about this, he told the Helper that the (angels) in the sky were astonished at what he had done, and then the second half of this verse along with verse ten was revealed for him. (*Bukhari, Muslim*)

[1733] The Prophet said, "The best charity is that given when one is in need himself and struggling (to make ends meet)." (*Abu Dawud*)

for You are, Our Lord, kind and merciful." [1734]
[10]

An Unholy Alliance

$\mathcal{H}$aven't you noticed how the hypocrites behave towards their 'brothers' among the Followers of Earlier Revelation?

(They conspired with them), saying, *"If you're banished (for breaking your treaty with the Muslims), then we'll all go into exile together. We'll never listen to anyone else ever. If war is waged against you, then we'll come to your aid."*

Allah is a witness that they're all liars, [11] for if the (Banu Nadir) are banished, (the hypocrites) would never follow them, and if war is made, (the hypocrites) would never help them.

If a (few of them) did, then they would turn back (in cowardice) and find no one to help them themselves! [12]

Truly, you're stronger than they are, for their minds are afflicted with dread from Allah!

That's because they're a people who lack understanding. [1735] [13]

They'll never fight you in united front, except from behind fortified areas or mighty ramparts, and even though their bravado might make it seem as if they're strong and united, in reality their hearts are divided, for they're a people devoid of sense. [14]

They're like those nearby (Jews of the Banu Qaynuqa) who felt the results of their affair.

They're going to have a painful punishment (in the afterlife), as well. [1736] [15]

Their (friends fooled them) just like Satan does when he entices human beings, saying, *"Hide (the truth)!"*

However, as soon as someone suppresses (his natural belief in Allah and suffers His wrath,) Satan shouts, *"I'm not responsible for you. I fear Allah, the Lord of All the Worlds!"* [16]

In the end, they'll both be in the Fire, and they're going to remain within, for that's the reward of the wrongdoers. [17]

Mind Your Real Investment Returns

$\mathcal{O}$ you who believe!

Be mindful (of Allah), and let every soul consider what it has invested for the future. [1737]

[1734] It is thought that the last sentence of this verse references future Muslims who will come to Medina and who might not be recipients of the kind of bonanza that the Immigrants got when the Banu Nadir tribe was defeated. Instead of looking on what they gained with jealousy or envy, they are instead asked to pray for their forgiveness.

[1735] As it turned out, despite these promises that the hypocrites made to the Jews, when war did come, the hypocrites didn't come to their aid and rather sat and watched. Didn't the Jews realize that a group who pretended to be Muslim, but who secretly worked against that in which they professed to believe, would likewise make the worst kind of ally?

[1736] The Jewish tribe of Banu Qaynuqa challenged the Muslims after they had returned from the Battle of Badr. The Muslim forces then besieged their neighborhood causing them to surrender. The tribe packed up its possessions and resettled themselves in Syria.

[1737] Some impoverished bedouins from the tribe of Mudar came into Medina in the early morning, dressed in rags and looking pitiful. The Prophet became distressed upon seeing them and asked Bilal to announce the call to prayer, so the faithful would come for their pre-dawn prayer. Afterwards the Prophet addressed the people by first reciting verse 4:1, and then he recited this passage. The people saw the poor bedouins and got the point. They immediately began a collection pile in front of the Prophet and started putting in coins, dates, articles of clothing and such. As the hour progressed, more

Be mindful (of Allah), for Allah is well-informed of all that you do. [18]

Don't be like those who forgot about Allah, for Allah then allowed them to forget (what was best) for their own souls.

They're truly the disobedient ones. [19]

The companions of the Fire can never be (thought of as) equal to the companions of the Garden, for only the companions of the Garden will achieve complete bliss. [20]

If We had sent this Qur'an down upon a mountain, you would've seen it humble itself and break apart for fear of Allah. [1738]

These are the kinds of examples We lay out for people, so they can use their reason. [21]

A Song of Praise

He is Allah, before
Whom there are no others.

*He knows what's beyond perception
and also what's plainly seen.*

He's the Compassionate, the Merciful. [22]

He is Allah, before Whom there are no others:

*the Master, the Holy, the Source of Peace,
the Guardian of Faith,
the Protector, the Powerful,
the Compeller,* [1739] *the Majestic.*

Glory be to Allah!

*He's far above what
they attribute to Him.* [23]

*He is Allah, the Creator,
the Evolver, the Fashioner.
The most beautiful names* [1740] *are His.*

*All things within the heavens
and the earth declare His praise,
for He is the Powerful, and the Wise.* [24]

and more people came and donated – one man brought two big money bags all by himself! The Prophet then began to look pleased. As he handed over the donations to the poor bedouins, he addressed the crowd, saying, "Whoever sets a good example in Islam, there is a reward for him and a reward for those who act after that by its example, without any deduction from the rewards of the (person who initiated the good act). Whoever sets an evil example, there is upon him the burden of that evil and the burden of the one who also acted upon his example, without the latter having anything deducted from their own burden." (*Ahmad*)

[1738] In other places the Qur'an is described as a "weighty message." (See 73:5) If a mountain were the intended recipient of the full responsibility and honor of bearing the Qur'an, the implication is that the mountain, which is an inanimate object following nature's laws (and thus a 'Muslim') would recognize the seriousness and humble itself by shattering into pieces.

[1739] This attribute of Allah, *al-Jabbar*, which I have translated as the *Compeller*, is derived from the root *jabara*, from which various meanings are extracted. These range from *one who forces an action, a setter of broken bones*, and even *the mixing of numbers*, an art that we call today the science of Algebra (*al-jibr*), a branch of mathematics greatly advanced by Muslims in the Middle Ages!

[1740] The famed Ninety-Nine Names (or Qualities) of Allah', or *al-Asma' al-Husna*, is a collection of ninety-nine separate adjectives describing Allah and His attributes. The Prophet said, "Allah has ninety-nine names (or qualities) – one hundred less one. Whoever preserves them (in his memory) will go to Paradise." (*Bukhari*) These famed Ninety-Nine Names are often displayed on posters and in artwork in homes, mosques and schools all over the Muslim world.

She Who is Interviewed
60 Al Mumtahinah
Middle to Late Medinan Period

This chapter was revealed just after the Meccans had broken the terms of the Treaty of Hudaybiyyah, and just before the Prophet led an army to Mecca to force its capitulation. It reiterates the need for group solidarity and warns them of the cruelty they would suffer if the pagans ever had power to inflict it upon them. It also offers the caveat that enemies may one day be friends, so believers must not go to extremes in their zealousness against their opponents.

In the Name of Allah,
the Compassionate, the Merciful

O you who believe! [1741] Don't take our mutual enemies for close allies!

You're friendly towards them, even though they're denying the truth that's come to you. They expelled you and the Messenger (from Mecca) only because you believed in your Lord Allah.

If you've really committed yourselves to struggle in My cause and to seek My pleasure, then don't secretly build bonds of friendship with them, for I know what you conceal and what you reveal. Whoever

---

[1741] Sometime after the Battle of Badr but before the Conquest of Mecca, a pagan woman from Mecca named Sarah, who had been a singer and entertainer, entered Medina and pleaded poverty, calling upon the Prophet to show her mercy due to her being a member of his tribe. The Prophet asked her if she had converted to Islam, and she replied in the negative. He asked her why she didn't continue her singing profession in Mecca, and she complained that business was down and she had no more invitations to sing. The Prophet let her stay in Medina, even though she admitted she was a non-Muslim, and he asked some of the Immigrants to give her food and clothes. Later on, after the Meccans violated the terms of the treaty of Hudaybiyyah, and while the Prophet was making preparations to march on the city, a concerned Immigrant Muslim named Hatib ibn Abi Balta'a was afraid for his relatives in Mecca, for they were not members of the tribe of Quraysh but were from another smaller tribe. He thought that he should warn them because the bulk of the other Immigrants were from the Quraysh tribe and could protect their own relatives in the event of an assault on the city, even though their own Meccan relatives were pagans. So Hatib approached Sarah and hired her to carry a secret letter to Mecca, warning the Quraysh of Muhammad's impending arrival, in the hopes of getting them to look after his non-Qurayshi relatives. The Prophet learned of this scheme (reportedly from Gabriel) and sent some of his followers to find the woman, who was passing through a meadow on her way back to Mecca. She was intercepted before she got far, and the letter was confiscated. (At first she hid it in her braided hair and denied having it. Then she gave it up and was allowed to go free.) Hatib explained to the Prophet why he wrote the letter, reiterating profusely that he wasn't a traitor. The Prophet excused him, but this verse warned the believers to be wary of taking in a refugee in the future without first ascertaining their intentions and religious loyalty. 'Umar asked permission to cut off Hatib's head, because his traitorous action would have cost many lives, but the Prophet forbade him, saying, "He was at Badr, and perhaps Allah saw the people at Badr and said, 'Do whatever you want after this, for I will forgive you.'" This verse was revealed in response to this incident. (*Asbab ul-Nuzul*)

among you disobeys Me, then he has strayed far from the way. [1]

Why Support Those Who Would Ruin You?

*O*f they were ever to gain an advantage over you, they would treat you like enemies - harming you with their hands and tongues in their relentless efforts to destroy your faith. [1742] [2]

(And if you were then to reject your faith), neither your relatives nor your children would be of any use to you on the Day of Assembly when He will judge between you, and Allah is watching everything you do. [3]

Be Firm and be Open at the Same Time

*T*here's an excellent example for you that can be found in (the life of) Abraham and his (followers) when he declared to his people, *"We're not going to have anything more to do with you or the idols you*

worship in place of Allah. We reject your (traditions)! Never again shall there be any friendship or family ties between us and you until you believe in the One God."

However, (it wasn't an appropriate act) when Abraham said to his father, *"I'm going to ask forgiveness for you, but it's not in my power to obtain anything from Allah on your behalf."* [1743]

(Abraham later realized his error and prayed), *"Our Lord, we place our trust in You, and we repent to You, for our final end is with You. [4] Our Lord, don't make us a test for the faithless; rather, forgive us (our shortcomings), for You are the Powerful and the Wise."* [1744] [5]

And so in their example there is a fine pattern for you to emulate – for anyone who hopes in Allah and the Last Day. However, if anyone turns away, (know that) Allah is the Self-sufficient and is Worthy of All Praise. [6]

(One day) Allah will create a warm bond between you and your opponents, [1745] for Allah is capable enough (to bring that about), and Allah is forgiving and merciful. [1746] [7]

[1742] This passage is a rebuke to Hatib, who thought he might tell Allah on Judgment Day that he did what he did for the sake of his relatives and children. He didn't realize that the Meccans were not honorable and that if they felt they could get away with it or get some gain from it, they would kill his relatives, as well. (*Asbab ul-Nuzul*)

[1743] When verses 4-6 were revealed, the Prophet told the believers that they had to take Abraham as an example, for he severed relations with his idolatrous relatives. Thus, the Muslims, both Immigrant and Helper, resolved to cut off relations with their non-Muslim relatives. When Asma', the daughter of Abu Bakr, received an unexpected visitor in the person of her pagan mother, she refused to see her or accept her gifts. (Abu Bakr had divorced Asma's mother long before Islam arose in Mecca.) Asma' said of this incident: "My mother, who was an idol-worshipper at the time, came to visit me (in Medina) after the peace treaty (of Hudaybiyyah) that the Prophet concluded with the Quraysh had gone into effect. I went to the Prophet and said, 'Messenger of Allah, my mother has come to visit me, seeking something from me, so should I keep good relations with her?' The Prophet said, 'Yes, keep good relations with your mother.'" (*Ahmad, Bukhari, Muslim*)

[1744] Some Muslims began to ask forgiveness for their dead ancestors who had been pagans, based on verses 60:4-5, but then verses 9:113-114 were later revealed, banning that practice. A man went to the Prophet and asked him about the fate of his dead father, who had been an idol-worshipper. The Prophet said that he was in the Fire. The man began to walk away, and then the Prophet called him back and told him, "My father and your father are both in the Fire." (*Muslim, Abu Dawud*) Thus, there are no special favors for anyone's parents with Allah, even if the person was a prophet.

[1745] The Prophet said, "Be mild in your love for others, for the one you love too much now, may one day be your mortal enemy, and be mild in your hate, for the one you hate too much now, may one day be your beloved." (*Tirmidhi, Tuhfat al-Ahwadhi*)

[1746] Many of the Prophet's followers were sad that their relatives and friends of old were now unbelievers and hated them. In addition, A'ishah had asked the Prophet about the lawfulness of

Allah doesn't forbid you from being kind and fair to those who don't fight you because of your beliefs or drive you from your homes, for Allah loves the tolerant. [8]

Allah only forbids you from having relationships with those who fought you for your faith and drove you from your homes or aided in your exile. Whoever befriends one of these, then they're wrongdoers. [9]

On Women who Join or Leave the Community

O you who believe! [1747] When believing women come to you as refugees (from enemy territory), interview them to establish the validity of their convictions, although Allah knows best their true level of faith. [1748]

If you determine that they're sincere believers, then don't send them back to the faithless.

(Believing women) are no longer legitimate for them (as wives,) even as (idol-worshippers) are no longer legitimate (as husbands for women of faith). Reimburse (the idol-worshippers) for what they spent (on their marriage gifts to the women who have now deserted them).

Then there will be no blame if you (believing men seek to) marry (such women) after offering them a marriage gift.

There is no Valid Marriage with a Pagan

As for any women (who are idol-worshippers), they're no longer your responsibility), so don't play host to them. Ask for the dowry you gave to them from (the idol-worshippers), even as they may seek what they spent (on the women joining you).

This is the law of Allah and His judgment between you. Allah is full of knowledge and wisdom. [1749] [10]

---

keeping good relations with non-Muslim relatives. Verses 7-9 were revealed allowing believers to have good relations with their non-Muslim family members, just as long as those relatives were not enemies of Islam. It also comforted the sorrow of the others who were told that good relations would be restored one day. (*Ibn Kathir*)

[1747] The Treaty of Hudaybiyyah stipulated (rather unfairly) that the Muslims had to return back to Mecca any Meccan man who joined Islam afterwards, (if the Meccans demanded his return). This was a sore trial for the Muslims, and even at the very moment of signing the treaty, Muhammad was forced to surrender a Meccan convert named Abu Jundal, who had escaped his tormentors and beseeched the Prophet's protection, seeking to join the Muslims in Medina. Abu Jundal was taken into custody by the Meccans, but he escaped again and this time fled to the hills. In time, he came to lead a growing band of other Meccan converts, living as brigands, attacking Meccan caravans of their own accord, while not going to Medina or swearing an oath of allegiance to the Prophet. Eventually, the Meccans dropped their insistence on the return of their own family members, and these 'warriors of the hills' were allowed to enter Medina. Women who wanted to convert, however, left straight for the sanctuary of Medina. One such woman named Umm Kulthum bint 'Uqbah fled to join the Muslims (along with her two brothers). When her pagan relatives came after her and demanded the Prophet return all three of them, the Prophet pointed out that the treaty said, "...any Meccan *man*..." Then this passage was revealed, and the Prophet said that no woman who wanted to join the Muslims would be returned, though he returned the two brothers regretfully. (*Asbab ul-Nuzul, Ma'ariful Qur'an*)

[1748] The women would be asked why they immigrated to insure they weren't coming just because they were angry with their husbands in Mecca or for any other reason than sincere belief. (*Ibn Kathir*) They would also have to swear the oath contained in verse 12.

[1749] Many of the Immigrant Muslims to Medina had left behind pagan wives or husbands when they fled. The question arose as to what ties were to remain after the separation. In addition, many women in Mecca were converting to Islam and fleeing from their pagan husbands to Medina. Did their pagan husbands still have rights on them? This verse, which was revealed just after the Treaty of Hudaybiyyah, declared that marriage between a monotheist and an idolater was invalid. To be fair,

Compensating the Enemy for Women who Join You

$\mathcal{I}$f any of your wives abandon you to be among the faithless, and (one of their women chooses to be among you) in exchange, (even though this absolves both communities of reimbursement), still compensate (the deserted husband) with the value of his (marriage gift) that he had spent.

Be mindful of Allah, the One in Whom you've believed. [1750] [11]

Prophet, when believing women come to you and swear this oath of loyalty:

- That they won't serve anything other than Allah,
- That they won't steal,
- That they won't commit adultery,
- That they won't kill their (newborn) children,
- That they won't produce any lie (of false paternity) that they've concocted between their hands or feet, [1751]
- Or disobey you in any good act…

Then accept their allegiance and pray to Allah for their forgiveness, for Allah is forgiving and merciful. [12]

Don't Betray Your Own Cause

$\mathcal{O}$ you who believe! [1752] Don't take (for friends) people upon whom is the wrath of Allah.

They've already lost all hope of the next life, even as the faithless have lost all hope of ever seeing their buried (ancestors) again. [13]

---

affected husbands had to be compensated, even pagan ones. Then the Muslim men and women were free to seek each other in marriage, as all previous ties with idol-worshippers were severed.

[1750] The Meccans did not believe in the Qur'an, and so when a woman left her Muslim husband in Medina and migrated to Mecca, the Meccans would not send compensation for any dowry to the deserted husband. This verse was revealed to reiterate to the Muslim side that, in any case, they themselves must still do what's right. In practice, though, only six women (five pagan women and a convert named Umm al-Hakim bint Abi Sufyan) left their Muslim husbands to join the Meccan side, whereas women were deserting their pagan husbands in Mecca repeatedly and migrating to Medina, where their status and rights were rising to a level previously unheard of in Arabia. (Umm al-Hakim later reconverted to Islam.) (*Ma'ariful Qur'an*)

[1751] This literally means that if they had a child out of wedlock or through adultery that they wouldn't ascribe it falsely to the wrong man or to their lawful husband if the child wasn't really his.

[1752] Some very poor Muslims were selling information on events within the Muslim community to some local Jews who paid them for the intelligence-gathering. This verse was revealed, forbidding contact with those Jews who were encouraging this trade. (*Asbab ul-Nuzul*)

The Formations

61 As-Saff
Early Medinan Period

~~~~~~

This chapter opens with a reference to the failure of some of Muhammad's followers to obey orders during the Battle of Uhud. Of fifty archers he had placed on a hill to guard his rear position, nearly all of them abandoned their posts to collect the goods the pagans of Mecca dropped when they were fleeing the battlefield in confusion. (The few who had remained at their post were overwhelmed by the advancing Meccan cavalry.) This breach of orders allowed the Meccan cavalry to counterattack and turn the tide against the Muslims, who were nearly crushed in defeat. Only a spirited defense saved the Muslims from being annihilated in the fearsome melee that followed.

In the Name of Allah,
the Compassionate, the Merciful

All things within the heavens and the earth reflect the glory of Allah, for He is the Powerful and the Wise. [1]

All you who (claim) to believe! Why do you say what you don't do? [1753] [2] It's repulsive in Allah's sight to say what you don't do. [3]

Allah loves those who fight in His cause in tight formations, as if they were a brick wall, (rather than those who disobey orders). [4]

Remember when Moses said to his people, "*My people! Why are you causing me so much grief when you know that I'm the Messenger of Allah sent to you?*"

When they wavered (from their duty), Allah allowed their hearts to waver even further, for Allah doesn't guide rebellious people. [5]

Remember that Jesus, the son of Mary, (also faced a similar challenge) when he announced, "*Children of Israel! I'm the Messenger of Allah sent to you. I confirm the truth of the Torah that came before me, and I bring you the good news of a messenger who will come after me, whose name will mean 'praise'.*"

However, when (the foretold prophet) came to them with clear evidence (of the truth), they scoffed, "*This (message he brings) is obviously some kind of magic!*" [1754] [6]

[1753] The Prophet went to pay a social visit on one of his companions named Amr. Then Amr's son 'Abdullah went out to play. Sometime later, his mother began calling for him to come back in the house, and she promised she would give him something if he came in. Afterwards the Prophet asked her what she gave him, and she replied that she gave him some dates. The Prophet, knowing that sometimes parents falsely promise their children rewards for doing something, said, "If you wouldn't have given the dates to him, it would have been recorded as a lie on your record." (*Ahmad*)

[1754] The Jews of Medina were open to considering that Muhammad might be their foretold prophet; yet, after a time the majority of the Jews rejected him. A small segment did accept him and converted to Islam.

Who's more corrupt than the one who invents such lies against Allah, especially when he's only being called to surrender his will (to Allah)? Allah doesn't guide corrupt people. [7]

They want to dim the light of Allah with their mouths (by attacking His revelations), though Allah will spread His light fully, no matter how much the faithless may hate it. [8]

He's the One Who sent His Messenger with guidance and the way of truth, so that he could proclaim it over all (other) ways of life, no matter how much the idol-worshippers may hate it. [9]

The Cause of Allah

O you who believe!

Shall I lead you to a bargain that will save you from a painful punishment? [10] Believe in Allah and His Messenger; then struggle in the cause of Allah with your wealth and your lives.

That's the best (deal) for you if you only knew! [11]

He'll forgive you your sins and admit you to gardens beneath which rivers flow and to stunning mansions in idyllic gardens of eternity. That's the greatest success! [12]

He'll also grant you something else you ardently desire: help from Allah and a swift victory. So then announce the good news to all who believe! [13]

O you who believe! Be disciples in the cause of Allah, even as Jesus, the son of Mary, called for disciples, saying, "*Who will help me (to call the people to) Allah?*"

Then the disciples (joined him and) declared, "*We shall help you (call the people to) Allah.*"

It just so happened that some of the Children of Israel believed, while others rejected, but We reinforced the believers against their enemies, and they ultimately prevailed. [14]

The Congregation
62 Al Jumu'ah
Mixed Medinan Period

The first eight verses of this chapter were sent down in approximately the year 628 after the Muslims forced the capitulation of the northern Jewish settlement of Khaybar. A remnant of the exiled Banu Nadir, who had settled there among their cousins, were responsible for assembling the Grand Alliance of Jews, Meccans and Bedouin pagans that had threatened the very existence of the Muslim community during the Great Siege of Medina the prior year. (The Jews of Khaybar were allowed to remain in their settlement, but they had to pay an annual tribute.) The remaining verses were revealed earlier, perhaps in the first year or two after the migration, and cover a real incident that tested the faithfulness of the believers.

Salman al-Farsi, a Persian convert to Islam, was sitting with the Prophet in a gathering when the first eight verses of this chapter were revealed. When the Prophet reached verse three, Salman asked excitedly, "Messenger of Allah! Who are the (people of the other nations who will accept Islam)?" The Prophet remained silent, and Salman asked the same question again. Then the Prophet placed his hand on Salman's shoulder and told the people, "Even if faith were as far away as the highest stars in the sky, still some of these (Persians) would have accepted it." (*Bukhari*)

In the Name of Allah,
the Compassionate, the Merciful

*A*ll things within the heavens and on the earth reflect the glory of Allah.

He's the King, the Holy, the Powerful and the Wise. [1]

He's the One Who raised a messenger from an unschooled nation [1755] - a messenger from among their own kind to recite revealed verses from Him, to reform them, to teach them the scripture and to give them wisdom, for they lived in obvious error before. [2]

(He wants them to spread this message) from themselves to others among them who haven't joined them yet, for He is Powerful and Wise. [1756] [3]

[1755] Literally, this designation of *unschooled* means a nation that wasn't literate or possessing a scripture. The overwhelming majority of Arabs could neither read nor write, and the only people who ever learned those skills were a handful of urban dwellers. (A rudimentary Arabic script was only introduced to Mecca and the surrounding region in the generation just before Muhammad's birth.) There were no schools or centers of learning in the Arabian Peninsula, nor were there books or libraries. It was, by and large, an oral society.

[1756] Islam is a religion for all humanity, all races, cultures and creeds. The Prophet stressed this in many sayings; the Qur'an affirmed it in numerous verses, and the multiracial and multicultural nature of the companions confirmed this view in the minds of the first generations of Muslims. This verse is one of the motivating factors for the Prophet to send letters of invitation to the rulers of both the Byzantine and Persian Empires, along with other communities near and far. Islam was for all of

That's the favor of Allah that He gives to whomever He wills, and Allah is a master at bestowing great favor. [4]

The example of those who were given the Torah before, but who then failed in their duty, is like that of a donkey that carries a load of books, (oblivious to the value of what it bears).

What a disgraceful metaphor for a nation that denied the signs of Allah! Allah doesn't guide corrupted nations. [5]

Tell (them):

"All you who follow (the religion of) Judaism! If you claim to be the chosen allies of Allah to the exclusion of all other people, then wish for death (so you can go to Heaven straight away), that is if you're speaking the truth!" [6]

However, they would never wish for death on account of what their hands have sent ahead of them (for Judgment Day), and Allah knows who the wrongdoers are. [7]

So say (to them):

"The death you so ardently avoid will surely overtake you! Then you'll go back to the One Who knows everything that's beyond perception, as well as everything that's in plain sight. Then He'll show you (the real meaning) of everything you did." [8]

The Importance of Friday Prayer

O you who believe! [1757]

When the call for Friday prayer is proclaimed, [1758] move along without delay to the remembrance of Allah, and leave off your business. [1759]

That's the best thing for you if you only knew. [1760] [9] When the prayer is completed, you may again disperse throughout the land and seek the bounty of Allah. [1761]

---

humanity. Many commentators believe that this verse also contains a nod towards the Prophet's Persian companion, Salman al-Farsi, for when the companions asked the Prophet about this verse, he put his hand on the shoulder of this foreign convert and said, "If faith were high up in the Pleiades (a group of stars), even then some men of these people (the Persians) would attain to it." (*Ma'ariful Qur'an*).

[1757] The Prophet heard a rushing sound behind him while he was leading the congregation in prayer during one Friday service. After the prayer had ended, he asked about it and was told that some people had rushed in to catch the prayer. The Prophet asked them, "What's the matter with you?" because the rushing of those people disturbed everyone. The people who came late replied, "We were moving along without delay to prayer," citing this verse. The Prophet said, "Don't do it like that. When you come for prayer, you should be calm and peaceful. Pray whatever remains of the prayer, and complete what you missed." (*Muslim*) He also said, "When you come to attend the prayer, don't come in a rush, but rather come to it while walking at ease and gracefully." (*Muslim*)

[1758] The Prophet said, "The best day on which the sun rises is Friday, for on it, Adam was created. On it, he was admitted to the Garden (of Eden), and on it he was expelled from it. The Hour (of the Last Day) will not come to pass except on this day." (*Muslim*)

[1759] The Prophet made it obligatory for everyone over the age of puberty to take a bath on Fridays before the congregational prayer. (*Bukhari, Muslim*) The Prophet used to bathe every day, himself, and wear scented oils when he went out.

[1760] In the centuries before Islam, the Arabs used to call Friday as the Day of the Arabs. During the time of the prominent Qurayshi chieftain (and ancestor of Muhammad), K'ab ibn Lu'ayy, the name was changed to the Day of Gathering, which is *Yawm ul-Jumu'ah,* a name that endured. Ibn Lu'ayy was a monotheist, or *hanif,* and he predicted that one day Allah would raise a prophet among the Arabs. This prophecy was fulfilled centuries later with the advent of Muhammad. (*Ma'ariful Qur'an*)

[1761] The Prophet said, "Whoever takes a bath on Friday, then leaves early (for the mosque), walking and not riding, and sits close to the Imam and listens without talking will earn the reward of fasting and performing prayer for an entire year for every step he takes." (*Ahmad*) He also advised worshippers to come in clean clothes that are specifically reserved for such special occasions. (*Ahmad, Ibn Majah*) He also said, "It's the duty of people who are destined for Paradise to sweep the mosque, keep it tidy, throw the trash outside, and burn incense within it, especially on Fridays." (*Ibn Majah*)

Remember Allah often so that you may be successful. [10]

Yet, even still when they see a chance to make a deal or have some fun, they run straight towards it, leaving you standing there (alone in the mosque)! [1762]

Tell (them), *"What you can get from Allah is far better than any entertainment or bargain, for Allah is the best provider of all."* [1763] [11]

Ibn Kathir reports that some companions claimed that business deals performed after Friday services are given a seventy-fold increase in blessings.

[1762] The Prophet was giving a Friday congregational sermon when the sound of drums beating in the street was suddenly heard. (This was how new caravan arrivals were announced in Medina.) Then someone said that a new caravan from Syria, loaded full of foodstuffs for sale, had arrived in town. There had been a food shortage in the city for a while, so everyone in the congregation (except for twelve men) got up and left the mosque, leaving the stunned Prophet in the middle of his sermon. This verse was revealed to chasten those who forgot their duty to Allah and left a solemn service only for the sake of shopping, which they could have done afterwards. (*Bukhari, Muslim*)

[1763] The Prophet said, "The promised day is the Day of Resurrection. The witnessed day is the Day of Arafat, and the witness is Friday. The sun has neither risen nor set on a day better than it. There is a time (on Friday) in which a faithful servant who is praying to Allah for good will find Allah responding to him. If he seeks to be protected from something, Allah will keep him safe from it." (*Ahmad, Tirmidhi*)

The Hypocrites
63 Al Munafiqun
Early Medinan Period

This chapter was revealed in the year 626 and references events that occurred just after the Prophet's preemptive strike against the bedouin tribe of Banu Mustaliq, specifically the antics of the hypocrite, 'Abdullah ibn Ubayy, and his followers. Ibn Ubayy had already begun plotting in earnest against the Prophet from his earliest arrival in Medina, and he looked for every opportunity to sabotage Islam wherever he could find it.

On the journey back from that expedition, while the Muslim force was encamped, an altercation broke out between an Immigrant named Jahjah and a Medinan convert named Sinan ibn Wabrah al-Juhani over whose camel could drink from a well first. The Immigrant wound up fracturing the Medinan man's jaw.

Some nearby men then began to square off with each other based on their affiliations, and it was only the well-timed intervention of the Prophet that prevented a melee. He even told the men that their calls to tribal solidarity were disgusting and that they should give up tribal affinity as the basis of their allegiance. The original two combatants were also reconciled, though 'Abdullah Ibn Ubayy got angry about the whole affair and looked for an opportunity to raise sedition and dissension.

The next day, while the men were again making camp for the night, Ibn Ubayy approached a gathering of Medinan Muslims and said, "What have you done to yourselves? You let them settle in your land and shared your resources with them. By Allah, if you abandon them, then they'll have to leave and settle in another land." He even suggested that through this tactic they might be able "to throw the beggars," i.e., the Muslims from Mecca, out of their city. He also insulted the Prophet and called him low-class.

One of the Prophet's faithful young companions, Zayd ibn Arqam, heard what Ibn Ubayy said and went to the Prophet to tell him what the hypocrite was saying. 'Umar ibn al-Khattab was upset at the news and asked the Prophet for permission to kill Ibn Ubayy for slander and inciting sedition. However, the Prophet said, "'Umar, what if people started saying that Muhammad kills his companions? No. Just order the people to start the journey (back to Medina)."

When Ibn Ubayy found out that the Prophet knew about what he had said, Ibn Ubayy went to him and denied it, claiming that the informant, who was merely a teenager, must have misheard what he said. The Prophet seemed to be convinced by Ibn Ubayy's denial, and this crushed Zayd's spirit, though he held his tongue.

The next day the Prophet ordered the expedition to move again, but at an odd hour, and a man went to the Prophet to ask him about it. The Prophet explained that Ibn Ubayy wanted to raise his hand against him. The man, a native of Medina, beseeched the Prophet to be understanding with Ibn Ubayy, because the people of his city were about to crown him king before the arrival of the Muslims, and he was sore about it.

Before the expedition reentered Medina, however, Ibn Ubayy's own son, a man also named 'Abdullah, held up his father's camel of his own volition and refused to let it move until his father apologized for insulting the Prophet. Ibn Ubayy finally relented, and the

Prophet asked 'Abdullah to let his father enter the city. (*Ma'ariful Qur'an*) Shortly after the Prophet and his men returned to Medina, this chapter began to be revealed. The Prophet soon sent for Zayd and told him that Allah confirmed that what Zayd had said was true. (*Ibn Hisham, Bukhari*)

In the Name of Allah,
the Compassionate, the Merciful

*W*hen the hypocrites come to you, (Muhammad,) they clamor, *"We declare that you are truly the Messenger of Allah,"* but Allah already knows that you're His Messenger, even as He affirms that the hypocrites are a bunch of liars. [1764] [1]

They use their public affirmations to disguise (their evil intentions), and that's how they obstruct others from the path of Allah. How evil are their actions! [2]

That's because even though they once had faith, they later renounced it, and thus a seal was placed upon their hearts, so that they understand nothing. [3]

When you look at them, their appearance impresses you, and when they speak, their influence inclines you to listen.

Yet, even though they (seem confident), they're as weak as propped up sticks – *and they're constantly paranoid of being accused*!

They're the (real) enemies (of faith), so watch out for them.

Allah's curse be upon them for their careless attitude (towards the truth)! [4]

The Audacity of the Arrogant

*W*hen they're told, *"Come, let the Messenger of Allah pray for your forgiveness,"* you see them turning their heads aside and slipping away arrogantly. [1765] [5]

It's all the same whether you pray for their forgiveness or not; Allah won't forgive them, for Allah doesn't guide the rebellious. [6]

Withholding Support for Allah's Cause

*T*hey're the ones who say to each other, *"Don't spend your money on any (of the followers) of the Messenger of Allah, for perhaps (one day) they'll leave (him)."* [1766]

[1764] Before every Friday sermon, the known hypocrite, 'Abdullah ibn Ubayy, always stood up to speak. No one opposed him because he was a chief. He would praise the Prophet profusely and exhort everyone to follow him, even though behind the scenes he would work against the Muslims. Even the day after the Battle of Uhud, when he took three hundred of his followers back home, abandoning the outnumbered Muslims on the eve of battle, he tried to do the same thing, but the people near him took hold of his robe and tried to make him sit down, saying he wasn't worthy to stand after he did what he did. Ibn Ubayy stormed angrily out of the mosque, and some of the Helpers met him by the gate. Ibn Ubayy said, "I just stood up to support him, and some men, his companions, jumped at me, pulled me back and admonished me, as if I had said something so terrible. I just wanted to support him." The people near him said, "You're doomed! Go back so that the Messenger of Allah will ask Allah to forgive you." Ibn Ubayy said, "By Allah, I don't want him to ask Allah to forgive me." This passage was revealed shortly thereafter. (*Ibn Hisham*)

[1765] After 'Abdullah ibn Ubayy refused to go back to the Prophet and repent, despite the insistent urging of so many of his fellows, this passage was revealed. (*Asbab ul-Nuzul*)

[1766] 'Abdullah ibn Ubayy counseled anyone who would listen to him not to give financial support to Muhammad or to any Muslim, under the hope that economic pressure would force the destitute

To Allah belongs the treasures of the heavens and the earth, even though the hypocrites don't realize it. [7]

(Now during the return journey from the campaign against the Banu Mustaliq), they're saying (to each other):

"When we get back to the city, the affluent will throw those beggars out!"

(Well, they should know that) affluence belongs only to Allah, His Messenger and the faithful, though the hypocrites don't know it. [8]

Don't Let Worldly Concerns Overtake You

O you who believe! Don't let your money or your children distract you from remembering Allah, for anyone who allows that to happen will be losers (in the end). [1767] [9] Spend something (in charity) out of what We've supplied to you before death should come upon one of you, and he cries out:

"My Lord! Why didn't you give me a little more time? I would've given (much more) in charity, and I would've been with the righteous!" [10]

However, no soul will receive from Allah any more time when its deadline has come, and Allah is well-informed of what you're doing. [11]

Muslims to either abandon Muhammad or leave the city. His quotes are in these verses. (*Asbab ul-Nuzul*)

[1767] The Muslims were urged not to cavort too closely with the hypocrites, and 'Abdullah ibn Ubayy's own son, who was a staunch believer, prevented his father from drawing water from a well. Ibn Ubayy went to the Prophet and complained about the way his son had treated him, and the Prophet ordered the son to allow his father to get what he needed. The son sighed and said, "If this is the command of the Prophet, then I'll do it." (*Asbab ul-Nuzul*)

Varied Fortune

64 Al Taghabun
Early Medinan Period

This is something of a transitional chapter that was revealed just after the migration to Medina in the year 622. For this reason, it resembles a Meccan chapter in its subject matter, though its addressing of hardships in verses 11-18 shows that its ultimate purpose was to provide the desperate Muslim refugees with some words of advice on how to view their plight and also on how to rise above it. It cannot be overappreciated how difficult it is for people to leave their homes and cities under a barrage of persecution, and it was extremely arduous and stressful upon the Muslim faithful.

In the Name of Allah,
the Compassionate, the Merciful

Whatever is within the heavens and on earth reflects the glory of Allah. All dominion and praise belong to Him, and He has power over all things. [1]

He's the One Who created you, and among you are some who reject (Allah) and some who believe. Allah is watching whatever you do. [2]

He created the heavens and the earth for a true purpose. He crafted you, and you've been crafted well, and to Him is the journey's end. [3]

He knows what's in the heavens and on the earth, and He knows what you hide and what you show, for Allah knows the secrets of the heart. [4]

Haven't you encountered the tales of all the faithless (nations) who came before you?

They suffered the consequences of their actions, and they're going to have a painful punishment. [5]

That's because whenever messengers went to them with clear evidence (of the truth, they scoffed at it), saying, *"How can a mere mortal show us the way?"*

So they rejected (the message) and turned away. Allah had no need of them, for Allah is self-sufficient and is already being praised. [6]

Those who suppress (their awareness of Allah) assume that they're never going to be resurrected.

Say (to them):

"Absolutely! By my Lord, you're going to be resurrected, and then you'll be made to understand (the meaning of) all that you did. That's easy for Allah to do." [7]

So believe in Allah and His Messenger and in the light that We've sent down, for Allah is well-informed of everything you do. [8]

The day when He gathers you all together for the Day of Gathering - that will be a day of varied fortune. [1768]

Whoever believed in Allah and did what was morally right will have their faults erased by Him.

He'll admit them into gardens beneath which rivers flow, and there they'll remain forever. That's the greatest success! [9]

But those who rejected (the truth) and denied Our signs will be companions of the Fire, and that's where they're going to stay, and that's the worst of all destinations! [10]

How Should We Consider Life's Challenges?

*N*o catastrophe can ever happen except with Allah's permission. Whoever believes in Allah, He will then guide his heart, for Allah knows about everything. [1769] [11]

So obey Allah and obey His Messenger, [1770] though if anyone turns aside, Our Messenger's only duty is to convey (the message) clearly. [12]

*A*llah: there is no god but He, and the faithful should trust in Allah! [13]

Remain True to the Way

O you who believe! [1771]

[1768] Ibn 'Abbas (d. 687) said, "This is one of the names of the Day of Judgment, and that's because the people of Paradise will have an advantage over the people of the Fire." (*At-Tabari*) The Prophet said, "Whoever owes somebody something should pay it or ask the one to whom he owes to forgive his debt here in this world. He won't have any assets or coins in the next life to pay for his liabilities. Those who are owed will be credited with good deeds from the debtor in lieu of their unfulfilled rights. When the debtor's good deeds are exhausted, then the sins of the oppressed will be added to the account of the oppressor." (*Bukhari*)

[1769] The Prophet said, "How excellent is a believer's situation! Unlike all others, there is good in everything he does. If he is prosperous, he thanks Allah, which is good. If misfortune befalls him, he endures it with perseverance, and that is also good for him." (*Bukhari, Muslim*)

[1770] Obeying Allah means to follow the dictates of the Qur'an. Obeying the Messenger means to follow the Prophet's personal instructions as contained in his narrations, or *hadiths*. In the early days of Islam, the Prophet used to forbid people from writing down his sayings for fear that they would get mixed up with Qur'anic verses, which were frequently written down and circulated among the community for learning and study. He had said, "Do not write (whatever oral teaching that you hear directly) from me, and whoever has written something (of my *hadiths*) should erase it. Narrate to others (what you hear) from me. Whoever deliberately attributes a false saying to me should prepare for his seat in the Fire." (*Muslim*) Such was the Prophet's forethought that he only allowed Qur'anic verses to be written, rather than his personal sayings. Later on, when the community in Medina was well-versed in the Qur'an, and when there was no longer any danger of his sayings being mixed up with Qur'anic verses, he lifted the prohibition against writing *hadiths*. One of the Muslims of Medina complained to the Prophet that he sometimes forgot *hadiths* that he heard, and the Prophet said to him, "Seek the help of your right hand," and then the Prophet moved his hand in the air to indicate writing. (*Tirmidhi*)

[1771] This passage was revealed to address the situation of people who converted to Islam in Mecca and who wanted to migrate to Medina, but their unconverted spouses and children refused to let them leave. Later on, when they finally did migrate with their families, they found that those who had preceded them had gained much more knowledge of the religion. Such people then spent much more of their time in the mosque or doing charity or other good deeds. Their families would then berate them, complain and make them feel guilty for going out and learning, preaching, teaching, etc. (*Asbab ul-Nuzul*) Some commentators say this verse is specifically about the case of a companion named 'Auf ibn Malik Ashja'i, who always volunteered whenever there was a call to arms. His wife and children would complain to him, saying, "And in whose care are you going to leave us?" (*Ma'ariful Qur'an*) The Muslims are advised to be patient and to forgive their families, however, for perhaps their fears are legitimate. In a wider sense, this is general advice to be patient with one's family when they seem to be less than supportive. It may be just a test for us to see if we are truly patient and wise.

There are potential adversaries for you among your spouses and children, so watch out! [1772]

However, if you overlook (their faults), gloss over (their shortcomings) and forgive them, (know that) Allah is forgiving and merciful. [14]

Your wealth and your children may be a test for you, but the greatest reward is in Allah's presence! [15]

Be mindful (of your duty) to Allah to the best of your ability, [1773] listen and obey, and spend (in charity) for your own good. Whoever saves himself from the greed of his own soul will be victorious. [16]

If you lend a beautiful loan to Allah, He will double it (to your benefit) and forgive you (your sins), for Allah is appreciative and forbearing. [17]

He knows what's beyond perception, as well as what's plainly visible, (for He is) the Powerful and Wise. [18]

[1772] The Prophet was giving a speech one day when suddenly his two very young grandchildren, Hassan and Husayn, came stumbling and tripping into the gathering wearing red shirts. The Prophet left the pulpit and scooped them both up in his arms. Then he quoted this verse and said, "I saw these two boys walking and tripping and could barely wait until I stopped my speech and picked them up." (*Ahmad, Tirmidhi*)

[1773] The Prophet said, "Whenever I order you to do something, do as much of it as you can, and whatever I forbid you from, then avoid it." (*Bukhari, Muslim*)

Divorce

65 At-Talaq
Middle Medinan Period

This chapter was revealed sometime after the regulations concerning divorce were announced in chapter two. Marriage and divorce are facts of life. It happened that some divorces occurred in the community, most notably that of 'Abdullah, the son of 'Umar ibn al-Khattab, who divorced his wife while she was menstruating. (It is forbidden to divorce women while they are in that state.) The Prophet ordered him to take her back and start the divorce process over again. In addition, some people were misunderstanding the divorce regulations mentioned in chapter two, specifically in verses 228-234. This current chapter was sent as something of an addendum to further clarify and explain the rules governing marriage and divorce.

In the Name of Allah,
the Compassionate, the Merciful

O Prophet! When (any of you men) intend to divorce women, (you must) divorce them after their waiting periods [1774] (are complete) – and count them accurately.

Be mindful of Allah, your Lord! (During the waiting period, men) must not drive (their wives) from their homes or (make them feel) they must leave, except in cases involving clear indecency. [1775]

[1774] The *'iddah*, or waiting period before a divorce is finalized, is a pause for three months to let the estranged couple decide if they might want to reconcile (see 2:238). No intimate relations are allowed during this time, even though the husband and wife must still maintain the household together, though living in separate rooms. (If intimate relations do occur, it nullifies the man's divorce pronouncement, unless he had said it three times.) The cooling off period also serves the practical function of letting both parties know if the woman is pregnant. If she is, it might be further reason for the couple to reconcile. Also, because of the mandatory waiting period, if the woman wants to marry someone else after the divorce is finalized, any issues of legitimate paternity are already cleared up. (By the way, during the waiting period, the man must fully support the living expenses of his estranged wife.)

[1775] What is the *clear indecency* that would be the only grounds for a woman to be sent out of the home during the waiting period before a divorce is finalized? There are three interpretations, and they are as follows. 1) If a wife betrayed her husband sexually with another man before the divorce pronouncement or during the waiting period, and there is no doubt about the facts, then the husband seeking a divorce has the right to ask his wife to leave his house while the waiting period passes. 2) If the woman moves out of the home on her own before the waiting period is over, then she is doing something scandalous, given that the divorce is not yet finalized, and thus the man is absolved of the responsibility to maintain her living expenses. 3) The last interpretation, favored by Ibn 'Abbas, is that the clear indecency refers to abusive behavior on the part of the wife (from hurtful language and name-calling to excessive quarreling). Otherwise, no man is allowed to pressure his wife to leave the home during the waiting period (if he owns it). What of the living arrangements of the divorced wife after the divorce is finalized? There is no principle in Islamic law that stipulates that the husband automatically gets the house in a divorce. If the woman has sole legal ownership of the property, then, according to Islamic law, the man will have to leave upon the completion of the divorce. If the house

These are the rules set by Allah. Anyone who disregards the rules set by Allah brings harm only upon himself.

You don't know if Allah might change your situation (for the better). [1776] [1]

Then, when they've fulfilled their appointed time, either retain (your spouses) in fairness, or let them go in fairness.

Choose two people among you who are known for their evenhandedness as witnesses, and present the case (to them, knowing that you are also) before Allah. [1777]

This is how those who believe in Allah and the Last Day are instructed.

Whoever is mindful of Allah will be shown a way out (of distress), [2] and He'll provide for him from where he least expects it.

Whoever relies upon Allah (should know that) Allah is enough for him. Allah achieves His objective, and Allah has determined the course of all things. [3]

An Exemption on Clothing Restrictions for Elderly Women

$\mathcal{N}$ow as for those women who are too old to menstruate or who don't have it for other reasons, their waiting period, to dispel any doubts, is three months.

Any woman who is pregnant will wait for the birth (of her child, and then her waiting period will end). [1778] Whoever is mindful of Allah (should know that) He will make his affair an easy one. [4]

This is the command of Allah that He's sending down to you. Whoever is mindful of Allah will have his shortcomings erased and his reward increased. [5]

Support (women in their waiting period) in your same standard of living, according to your means, and don't harass them in the hopes of making their situation worse.

If they're pregnant, then pay all their expenses until they give birth. Then afterwards, if they wean (the infant) by themselves, then compensate them, and consult with each other fairly (on issues related to the child). [1779]

---

was held jointly, then a division of assets must occur, with each party getting their lawful share of the property. If the husband is abusive, then he can be ordered from the home by a court judge. There is a lively and dynamic record of Muslim family law that bears testimony to the wide range of latitude given to individual judges to rule on behalf of the legitimate rights of both men and women.

[1776] Fatimah bint Qays, one of the Prophet's companions, said of this verse that it means the husband may regret his divorce pronouncement, feel remorse, and may then desire to take her back. If she's living in the same house, it would be easy for him to rethink his decision. (*At-Tabari*)

[1777] Witnesses must be able to testify to the final decision of the couple regarding either reconciliation or divorce.

[1778] Ubayy ibn K'ab said to the Prophet, "After the verses in the Chapter of the Cow concerning the waiting period were revealed, some people in Medina said that there were still some women whose waiting periods were not mentioned, specifically the old, the young and the pregnant (who might be left widows before their baby is born)." This passage was revealed in response. (*Asbab ul-Nuzul*)

[1779] A man who divorces his pregnant wife must pay child and spousal support to her before and after the child is born, though the father has a right to be consulted on issues regarding his children. Spousal support ends if the woman marries another or when the child is weaned, though the father must still remain liable for at least some of the expenses directly related to his child when they're below the age of puberty. (*Ibn Kathir*) The mother automatically gets custody of any children below the age of eight. Afterwards, the children must be consulted about with whom they want to live. (See 2:233 and footnotes and also *Ma'ariful Qur'an*.)

If (nursing the baby) is a hardship for (any of) you (women), [1780] then (the ex-husband must pay for) the child to be weaned by a wet-nurse. [6]

Let the wealthy spend according to his means, and let those of more modest means do likewise.

Allah doesn't burden any soul beyond what He's given it (to work with), and Allah will soon make things easier. [7]

Take the Lesson While You Can

*H*ow many settlements rebelled against the command of their Lord and His messengers, (despite the fact) that We called them on it and thereafter punished them with unprecedented retribution? [8]

They felt the dire consequences of their conduct, and the final result of their efforts brought about their own downfall. [9]

Allah has prepared a stern punishment for them, so be mindful of Allah, all you reasonable people who believe, for Allah has sent a reminder down to you: [10] a messenger who recites the clearly evident verses of Allah, so he can lead the believers who do what's morally right from darkness into light.

Whoever believes in Allah and does what's morally right will be admitted by Him into gardens beneath which rivers flow to live within forever, and Allah will give them an excellent share! [11]

Allah is the One Who created the seven-layered skies and the similarly ordered (terrain of the) earth. Through them flows His command, so you can know that Allah has power over all things and that Allah has inclusive knowledge of everything. [12]

[1780] If a woman cannot nurse her own child for health or medically related reasons, or if the parents cannot agree on what is best for the child, then the ex-husband must pay the expenses of a wet-nurse that the mother arranges. For custody issues also see footnote to 2:233.

Prohibition

66 At-Tahreem
Middle Medinan Period

There are two incidents that happened in Muhammad's personal life that demonstrated his lively and sometimes challenging marital relations with his wives (and their competing interests and jealousies). At least one of these incidents is the reason for the revelation of this chapter, and the scholars are divided as to which is the primary one. The first report, then, is of a time when Hafsah found the Prophet visiting with Maria in her (Hafsah's) own apartment, even though it was A'ishah's turn to see him.

Hafsah told the Prophet that she was going to tell on him to A'ishah (whom the Prophet never wanted to be upset with him). The Prophet asked her not to tell, and he even promised not to see Maria (his Greek-Egyptian wife, a former slave whom he freed and married), again. Such was his genuine love for A'ishah. (His other wives were not as dear to his heart, for they were generally married for reasons ranging from cementing tribal alliances to supporting widows.) Hafsah agreed to keep silent but later wound up telling A'ishah anyway, and she was upset at the news. The Prophet was informed sometime later by an angel of what had transpired.

He was so bothered by this unnecessary drama and also by some other antics in which his wives were engaging to make his life full of annoyances that he boycotted seeing any of his wives for a month. (This was an application of the principle of *daraba* or separation as explained in 4:34.) After some weeks had passed like this, 'Umar suspected that the Prophet might have already divorced his wives. He approached the Prophet, who was staying in a second floor apartment owned by one of his close companions, and asked him if he had, in fact, divorced all his wives. The Prophet replied that he had not, and 'Umar was relieved, as his own daughter Hafsah was married to the Prophet.

In the second (less likely) incident, the Prophet used to visit with his wives in turn following the afternoon prayer. One day he spent more time than usual in Zaynab bint Jahsh's apartment because of the fact that she had offered him a jar of honey to eat from – honey being one of his favorite foods. His other wives, A'ishah and Hafsah (and possibly Saudah), became jealous and hatched a petty plot to make him stop eating honey by suggesting that it made his breath smell bad. The Prophet was quite sensitive about his personal hygiene, so after they each told him the lie, he swore he would never eat honey again. In addition, so that Zaynab's feelings wouldn't be hurt, the Prophet asked no one to mention to her that her honey might have been spoiled. One of the wives involved in the plot mentioned it to others, anyway.

Whichever incident is the primary cause of this revelation, this chapter makes the case that it is wrong to forbid lawful things for oneself. It also shows that even though Muhammad was a prophet, he was still not immune from the human foibles and drama in his family life with which the rest of us must contend. (Verses 11-12 are a veiled exhortation to the Prophet's wives to improve their conduct, as they're wives of a prophet of Allah.) There are, in fact, several incidents mentioned in the Qur'an that tell him, and by extension all of the rest of us, how to handle such situations and how to avoid them in the future.

In the Name of Allah,
the Compassionate, the Merciful

O Prophet! Why would you forbid yourself from something that Allah has allowed for you? Are you thinking that this is what you have to do to please your spouses?

Allah is forgiving and merciful! [1] Allah has already given you a required method to cancel your (hasty) promises. 1781

Allah is the protector of you all, and He is the Knowing and the Wise. [2]

When the Prophet told something in confidence to one wife, she told it to another, and Allah made this known to him.

Then he had (to tell others about the matter), while leaving some of its (details) vague.

When he confronted her (about her having told the secret), she exclaimed, "*Who told you that (I told someone else)?*" 1782

"*I was informed*," he said, "*by the Knowing and the Well-Informed.*" [3]

Both of you, (the wife who told the secret and the one to whom she told it), should turn to Allah in repentance, if your hearts lead you to do it.

If you try to defend each other against (the Prophet, know that) his protector is Allah, even as is Gabriel, every righteous believer and the very angels themselves, who will all defend him. 1783 [4]

(Wives of the Prophet), if he were to divorce you all, Allah would provide him with wives who are much better than you, who are surrendered (to Allah), who believe, who are devout, penitent, dedicated to (Allah's) service and who are

---

1781 This is a reference to a previously revealed verse in which foolish oaths were given a method of release. When the truth of the matter mentioned in verse 3 was made known to the Prophet, he broke the oath he had made to abstain from what he had sworn to abstain from, and he made up for it as per the directions contained in verse 5:89.

1782 As the introduction notes, the woman being referenced here is most likely Hafsah.

1783 Islam gave women many new dimensions in their personal freedom. 'Umar ibn al-Khattab once explained to Ibn 'Abbas (d. 687) that in Mecca men had absolute authority over women, but in Medina he noticed that women had the better of men and that the Muslim women who immigrated from Mecca started to pick up their habits and joust more frequently with their husbands over their concerns and rights. 'Umar then explained that he once got angry with his wife, and she talked back to him, which was a first for him. When he tried to scold her, she said, "Why don't you like me talking back to you? By Allah, the Prophet's wives talk back to him, and some of them even refuse to talk to him for the whole day." Although this quality is not conducive to marital harmony if it is over-applied, the fact remains that the Prophet did not forbid women from speaking their mind, and this had the effect of a liberation for them. It's no wonder that the Prophet was so supported by women and the young in his mission. As many writers have pointed out, Islam was, in the main, a youth movement for social change. In later years, when 'Umar was the caliph, a man approached his house to complain of his argumentative wife. When he came near the door, he heard 'Umar's wife shouting at him. He turned to leave when 'Umar noticed him out the window and called for him to wait. When 'Umar came and asked him what he wanted, the man said, "I came to complain to you about my wife arguing with me and shouting at me, but now I see you have the same problem as I." When the man asked 'Umar how he could allow it, 'Umar said, "Isn't it true that she cooks for me, washes my clothes and suckles my children? By this she saves me from having to hire a cook, a launderer and a wet-nurse, and she isn't legally obligated to do any of those things (she does for me). Besides, I enjoy peace of mind because of her, and I stay away from immoral acts because of her. Therefore, I tolerate all her excesses on account of these benefits." Then he told the man, "It would be most appropriate for you to adopt this attitude, as well." (Quoted in *The Role of Muslim Women* by Afzalur Rahman.)

outgoing (in spreading the faith), [1784] whether previously married or not. [5]

Save Your Family

O you who believe!

Save yourselves and your families from a fire whose fuel is men and the stone (of idols), over which are appointed stern and severe angels who don't hesitate from thoroughly carrying out the commands they receive from Allah, and they do whatever they're commanded. [1785] [6]

(The angels will scold the inmates of Hell, saying,) *"All you who suppressed (your awareness of the truth)! Make no more excuses today! You're not being punished as much as you're being repaid for what you did!"* [7]

Be True to the Cause

O you who believe! Turn to Allah in repentance with sincere remorse. Your Lord will erase some of your sins and admit you into gardens beneath which rivers flow.

On that day, Allah will shield the Prophet and the believers (who followed) him from any humiliation. The light (of their purity) will shine before them and from their right hands, and they will say:

"Our Lord, perfect our light and forgive us, for You have power over all things." [8]

O Prophet! Strive hard against the faithless and the hypocrites; be firm against them, for their final home is in Hellfire, the worst destination! [9]

For the faithless, Allah points out the example of the wife of Noah and the wife of Lot. They were under (the care) of two of our righteous servants; yet, each betrayed (her husband). [1786]

Their (association with their husbands) did them no good against Allah, for they're going to be told:

"Enter the Fire along with all those who have to enter!" [10]

For the believers, Allah points out the example of Pharaoh's wife who had prayed, *"My Lord, prepare for me a house in the Garden near to You. Save me from the (evil) deeds*

[1784] The word *sa'ihat*, which means *outgoing* or *wandering about*, is believed by some commentators to imply fasting when women are concerned, though linguistically there is no relationship to the Arabic word for fasting (*saimiun*). Thus, we see an example of extreme social conservatism being justified by falsely interpreting a Qur'anic verse. (See 9:112 where the word is also used to mean wandering about or going abroad, and commentators apply the true meaning there, perhaps because men are assumed to be the subject!) So what does it mean for women to wander or *go abroad* in Allah's cause? Some have suggested it means that women should migrate from their homeland if they're being oppressed in their religion. Others imply that it means women should be active in promoting Islam in their society. For conservatives who prefer to believe that this word wandering really implies *fasting*, (as they are distressed by the thought of women engaged actively in society), they offer the proposal that when a woman fasts, she is engaging in an *otherworldly* experience and is thus *wandering* out of her normal life's parameters. Strangely enough, they do not apply this interpretation to men.

[1785] When this verse was revealed, some companions asked the Prophet, "We understand how to save ourselves from Hellfire, by guarding against sins and obeying divine commands, but how do we save our families from Hellfire?" The Prophet replied, "Teach them to avoid doing deeds that Allah has forbidden, and encourage them to do those things that Allah has enjoined. This will save them from Hellfire." (*Ma'ariful Qur'an*) In another narration, the Prophet said, "Allah have mercy upon the person who says, 'O my spouse and children! Mind your prayers, your fasting, your charity, your poor (relatives), your orphans, your neighbors!' Hopefully Allah will gather all of them together in Paradise." (*Ma'ariful Qur'an*)

[1786] Ibn 'Abbas (d. 687) said that the betrayal was in not following the religion of their husbands who were made Allah's prophets. Prophet Noah's wife used to tell her people whenever a new convert joined her husband's religion, so they could beat him, and Prophet Lot's wife used to tell her friends in Sodom whenever her husband had guests, so they could molest or bother them. (*At-Tabari*)

of (my husband), the pharaoh, and save me from the wrongdoers." [1787] [11]

(Yet another example) is that of Mary, daughter of (the house of) Amrām, [1788] who guarded her chastity.

We breathed Our spirit into her (womb), and she accepted the truth of her Lord's words and scriptures, for she was among the compliant. [1789] [12]

[1787] The pharaoh who ruled at the time of Moses' childhood was Khenephres (aka Sobekhotep IV). The pharaoh at the time when Moses returned to Egypt has been identified as the first pharaoh's son, Dudimose. In 28:9 we read that the wife of *that* Pharaoh convinced her husband not to kill the baby that her servants had fished out of the river in a basket. (The wife of Khenephres was named Merris.) The wife of the *new* pharaoh, traditionally named 'Asiyah, *betrayed* her husband by believing in the teachings of Moses when he returned and started preaching. In retaliation, this second pharaoh had her tortured to death. It is said that the angels used to shield her body with their wings to dampen the pain she was feeling at the hands of Pharaoh's torturers and that they showed her a vision of her house in Paradise before she died. (*Ibn Kathir*)

[1788] Mary was a member of the house of Amram ('*Imran* in Arabic). Some people unfamiliar with the poetic usage of Semitic languages with regards to familial relationships have suggested that the Qur'an inaccurately names Mary's father as Amram (the father of Prophets Moses and Aaron) by saying, "...Mary, daughter of Amram..." In Arabic (and Hebrew) a woman who is descended from a distant, famous ancestor can metaphorically be called a 'daughter' or 'sister' of such a person. (Conversely, it works for males, as well.) The Prophet stated this phenomenon in his own words when one of his companions returned from the Christian territory of Najran and reported that the Christians objected to the Qur'an calling Mary the sister of Aaron. The Prophet said, "The (people in ancient days) used to give nicknames (to their people) after the names of prophets and pious persons who had gone before them." (*Muslim*)

[1789] The Prophet was sitting with some people, and he drew four lines on the ground with a stick. "Do you know what these lines mean?" he asked. The people replied, "Allah and His Messenger know best." The Prophet then said, "The best among the women of Paradise are Khadijah bint Khuwaylid, Fatimah bint Muhammad, Maryam bint Amram, and 'Asiyah bint Muzahim, the wife of Pharaoh." (*Ahmad*)

The Dominion

67 Al Mulk
Middle Meccan Period

This chapter was revealed concerning the pagans who continually harassed the Prophet and jeered him when he attempted to preach in the public square of Mecca. Indeed, the common theme of most mid-length Meccan chapters is to provide the Prophet and his followers with a combination of succinct essays to defend themselves from the pagans, as well as to reaffirm the core beliefs of the religion. The Prophet once said of this particular chapter: "There is a chapter in the Qur'an that contains thirty verses that will intercede on behalf of its reciter until he is forgiven: *'Blessed is the One in Whose hands is all dominion...'*" (*Ahmad, Tirmidhi*) He also said of this chapter, "It is my deepest wish that the chapter called *the Dominion* be in every believer's heart." (*ath-Tha'labi*) Finally, it is reported that the Prophet used to recite this chapter before going to sleep, and he said of it that "It rescues people from the punishment of the grave." (*Ma'ariful Qur'an*)

In the Name of Allah,
the Compassionate, the Merciful

Blessed is the One in Whose hand is all dominion. [1790]
He has power over all things. [1]

He's the One Who created death and life
so He could test who among you is the best in their conduct,
and He's the Powerful and Forgiving. [1791] [2]

He created seven skies, one above the other.

You won't see any flaws in the creation of the Compassionate!

So look around again – do you see any flaws? [3]
Look again a second time!

[1790] The "hand' of Allah is considered by all scholars to be allegorical, as Allah has no form we can understand. (See Qur'an 42:11)

[1791] The Prophet once remarked, "Death is enough of a preacher, and certainty (of your ultimate fate) is enough (of a reason) to be free of wants." (*Tabarani*) In my humble opinion, this one saying of the Prophet should be sufficient to guide people in their life choices in all things and in all situations. People who truly reflect on these words must realize that greed should melt away from their hearts and that the inevitable end of their lives should temper their anger and rather make them want to love all living things with every fleeting last moment they have left. Build what you like, go where you want, enjoy your family and accomplishments, but let your heart remain free of the sins of greed and meanness. Love others because love is all that matters to Allah. It is the sign of a purified heart, and no one can truly love their Lord until they have learned to make love a way of life.

(No matter how many times you probe),
your eyesight will return to you worn out and defeated! [4]

And so it was that We've decorated the lowest layer of the sky with streaks of light, [1792]
using them as ammunition to repel devils, [1793]
and We've prepared for them a fiery punishment. [5]

Those who reject their Lord will receive
the punishment of Hell, and that's the worst destination. [6]

As they're being thrown into it, they're going to hear
its overwhelming heave and sigh as it blazes fiercely. [7]

It'll burst forth with the utmost fury!

Every time a crowd is flung inside of it,
its keepers will ask them, *"Didn't any warner ever come to you?"* [8]

To which they'll answer (in despair):
*"Yes, a warner did come to us, but we rejected him and said,
'Allah never revealed anything (to you); you're just greatly mistaken!'"* [9]

Then they'll lament:
*"If only we would've listened or used our reason,
then we wouldn't now be companions of the raging blaze."* [10]

They'll confess their own sins,
but the companions of the raging blaze
will be far (from ever being forgiven). [1794] [11]

[1792] Depending on the context, when the Qur'an uses the plural term *samawat* it is either referring to space beyond the exosphere where the stars and planets reside, or it can refer to the various atmospheric zones above the earth's surface that we think of as *our* sky. Verse 3 seems to be leaning more towards a reference to both the earth's atmosphere and space. We can determine this from the *context*, because when the singular *sama'* is used the Qur'an wants to refer the reader to atmosphere we experience just above us. In those instances, such as here in verse 5, we can translate it as the lower sky. It is not the zone of the planets or the stars, but a part of the earth's atmosphere. Meteors burn up in the mesosphere which is just about at the highest point that humans can see such local things happening. With regards to the number seven, in traditional Arabic parlance, seven is one of those numbers that can mean the same as many, not necessarily an exact quantity. As an aside, the reference to streaks of light can be to the movement of planets, causing astrologers, and their jinn partners, to be misled.

[1793] This verse is most often interpreted in two ways: some say it refers to shooting stars (meteorites) that are said to repel devils from prying into the secrets of the heavens. (Most classical commentators have offered this interpretation). Other more modern commentators such as Muhammad Asad suggest that it refers to the constellations in the night sky, which are used by astrologers to make predictions with the aid of evil jinns who whisper a mixture of truth and lies in their minds. No Muslim has ever believed that the stars, themselves, are what streak across the sky, for as Ibn Kathir states, "The stars are not thrown; rather, the meteorites under them." Thus, the lowest sky is full of meteorites that streak across it like missiles and thus thwart the activities of those who engage in the occult.

[1794] The Prophet said, "The people (destined for Hell) will not be destroyed until they confess their own guilt." (*Ahmad*)

As for those who feared their Lord,
even though He was beyond their perception,
there is forgiveness and a great reward. [1795] [12]

Whether you speak secretly or in public,
(it matters little to Allah), for He knows the secrets of the heart. [13]

Wouldn't the One Who created you know?
He's the Subtle and the Well-informed. [14]

Allah's Power is Absolute

He's the One Who made the earth manageable for you (to live on),

so travel over its broad shoulders [1796] and eat from what He's provided, [1797]
(but remember) that you're going to be brought back to Him. [15]

Do you feel so safe (in your life) from the One Who is (above you)
in the heavens that (you don't think) He would ever make
the earth swallow you up when it quakes? [16]

Do you feel so safe (in your life) that (you don't think) the One Who is (above you)
in the heavens would ever bring down upon you a deadly tornado,
so that you might finally realize (the seriousness) of My warning? [1798] [17]

And so it was that those who lived before (you) also denied (My warning)
- oh, how terrible was My rejection (of them!) [18]

Haven't they seen the birds flying high above them,
how they spread and fold their wings in flight?
No one holds them in place except the Compassionate. [1799]
Without a doubt, He watches over all things. [19]

So whose army can help you better than the Compassionate can?

[1795] The Prophet said, "Love and remember Allah in good times, and He will remember you in difficult times." (*Tirmidhi*)

[1796] The earth's broad *shoulders* are its mountains, according to the commentators. Thus, this is a poetic metaphor evoking the essential way the earth supports us. A follower of the companions named Bashir ibn Ka'b had a maidservant, and he said to her, "If you can tell me what is meant by '*the shoulders of the earth*' you are free." She replied, "Its shoulders are its mountains," and so he set her free.

[1797] The Prophet said, "If you would put your faith completely in Allah, He would provide for your needs in the same way He provides for the birds. They go out in the morning with their stomachs empty and return in the evening with their stomachs full." (*Tirmidhi*)

[1798] The Prophet said, "Whoever folds all of his concerns into just one concern alone, namely the next life, then Allah will satisfy his demands and concerns in this life. Whoever devotes his concerns only to worldly things, then Allah won't care in which valley he dies." (*Ibn Majah*)

[1799] Some critics of Islam have looked at this beautifully poetic verse and concluded that the Qur'an is somehow against the concept of aerodynamics and self-powered flight. They misinterpret this verse to mean that Allah is somehow literally holding the birds with His hands or some other such nonsense. This verse is merely and innocently remarking that it is from Allah's power that birds can fly. In other words, Allah gave them that ability and no one else. No reputable Muslim scholar has ever assumed that this verse is saying that Allah has the birds held by some sort of invisible strings!

Truly, the faithless are deluded! [20]

Who can provide resources for you
if He were to withhold His resources from you?

Oh, but no!

The stubborn persist in their audacity and contempt! [21]

Human Beings are not Thankful

Can the one who looks at only what's right in front of him

be better guided than the one who walks
with his head held high on a straight path? [1800] [22]

Say (to them), *"He's the One Who willed you (to exist),*
and He gave you the abilities of hearing, sight, feeling and understanding
- but you're hardly ever grateful." [23]

Then say, *"He's the One Who populated the earth with your kind,*
but (one day) He's going to gather you all back together." [24]

Yet, still they ask, *"When will this promise come to pass,*
if you're really telling the truth?" [25]

Tell (them), *"That knowledge is with Allah.*
I was sent only as a clear warner." [26]

When they finally see the fulfillment (of that prophecy),
the faces of the faithless will be filled with tremendous grief.
They'll be told, *"This is only what you used to dare to come!"* [27]

Say (to them), *"Look you! If Allah were to obliterate me and those who are with me*
or if He were to shower His mercy down upon us, (in either case, we look to Allah as our savior;)
yet, who will save the faithless, (who put no hope in Allah,) from an awful punishment?" [1801] [28]

Then tell them, *"He's the Compassionate. We believe in Him,*
and we trust Him. Soon you'll know who was so obviously wrong." [29]

Then add, *"Look you! If one morning all your flowing water were (to sink in the earth)*
and be lost, who (besides Allah) could supply you with flowing water again?" [1802] [30]

[1800] This verse is a reference to Abu Jahl, who was known for walking with his head down, looking at the ground in a groveling fashion. The Prophet, by contrast, used to walk with head upright and looked ahead of him. (*Ibn Kathir*)

[1801] The idea here is that whatever happens to believers, good or bad, they place their ultimate hope in Allah and have been promised Paradise as a reward for their faith, hardships, suffering and striving, while those who believe in nothing outside of their own finite selves have no comfort in anything. If bad times befall them, they have no hope other than trusting in blind luck, while if they revel in good times, they fear the death that will take them away from all their good fortune forever. Unbeknownst to them, that is when their real misfortune will start – and there will be no one to save them!

[1802] While still a teenager, Ibn 'Abbas (d. 687) was sitting with the Prophet when the Prophet turned to him and said, "Young man, I'm going to teach you something. Be loyal to Allah, and remember Him

The Pen

68 Al Qalam aka Nun
Early Meccan Period

This very early chapter (second in the order of revelation) addresses the attempts of the pagans of Mecca (especially Abu Jahl) either to bribe, buy off or silence the Prophet through familial pressures. The Muslims were not yet facing the worst of the persecution, so the tone of this chapter is decidedly defiant. In contrast, chapters from the late Meccan period, which were revealed when the Prophet and his followers were being assaulted in the streets, generally attempt to strengthen the Prophet's resolve and steady him psychologically in the face of relentless public scorn and ridicule. This chapter counsels the Prophet to stay the course in the verbal jousting that characterized this phase of his ministry.

In the Name of Allah,
the Compassionate, the Merciful

Nun.

By the pen and what (scribes) record, [1803] [1] by the grace of your Lord, you're not crazy. [1804] [2] On the contrary, you're

---

at all times. Obey His orders, and He will save you from every evil and take care of you in every aspect of your life. Be loyal to Allah, and you will find that He is near. If you ask for something, ask of Allah. If you seek help, seek it from Allah. Know that if all the people in the world got together to help you with something, they won't be able to help you at all, except as much as Allah has allowed for you. If they all got together to bring harm to you, they would not be able to harm you beyond what Allah has allowed for you. The Pens (of Destiny) have stopped writing, and the ink on the pages (of the Book of Orders) has dried." (*Ahmad, Tirmidhi*)

[1803] Usually, this verse is interpreted to mean that the angelic scribes write down the destinies of all things as directed by Allah. A man named Walid ibn 'Ubadah reported that his father called him to his death bed and told him, "I heard the Messenger of Allah say, 'The first thing that Allah created was the pen, and He said to it, 'Write.' The pen asked, 'My Lord, what should I write?' He said, 'Write the outcome of everything that will happen throughout eternity.'" (*Ahmad, Tirmidhi*) In another narration, the Prophet stated that Allah recorded the destinies of all creatures 50,000 years before He created the universe. (*Muslim*) It doesn't mean He is making us do anything, but that He commanded the universe to exist and operate (*qada*), and ultimately, He knows the outcome (*qadr*). Allah knows all outcomes or fates because He is not bound by time. He is outside it, so He sees all time periods at once. It's a hard concept to grasp, but then again, He is Allah, and we are only human.

[1804] The Meccans had taken to taunting Muhammad, accusing him of being *majnun*, i.e., possessed or crazy. This verse seeks to reassure him that not only was he *not* crazy or possessed by a demon, but that he was a nobly disposed person of high character. This is borne out by the numerous reports from his contemporaries illustrating how kind, well-mannered and sensitive he was. He was never cruel, barbaric or crass, nor did he ever do anything but campaign against ignorance and superstition. Once A'ishah was asked about the Prophet's character, and she replied, "Haven't you read the Qur'an? The character of Allah's Messenger was the Qur'an." (*Muslim*)

going to have an unfailing reward, [3] for you have a most excellent character. 1805 [4]

Soon you and your critics will see [5] who it was that was really being challenged the most. [6]

Don't Compromise with Falsehood

*T*ruly, your Lord knows best who forsakes His way, and He knows best who accepts guidance. 1806 [7]

So don't follow (the suggestions) of those who deny (Allah). [8] They only want to make you compromise (in your beliefs), so they could compromise in return. [9]

Don't follow (the suggestions) of a contemptuous scoundrel who is eager to make promises [10] - all the while slandering and disrespecting, [11] obstructing good, sinning brazenly [12] and abusing others when he's already so despised as illegitimate himself [13] - (all because he thinks) he's rich and has so many sons (to back him up)! 1807 [14]

When Our revelations are read to him, he scoffs, *"Tales from long ago!"* [15] Soon We'll brand him (like a beast) on the nose! [16]

The Lesson of the Gardeners

*W*e're only testing them like We tested the gardeners who vowed to harvest their fruits in the morning [17] without making any allowance (for the will of Allah). 1808 [18] And so, while they slept, a catastrophe from your Lord overwhelmed (the garden), [19] and by morning it was left bare. [20]

When they arose early the next day, they called to one another, [21] *"Come on, let's harvest our produce while it's still early!"* [22]

Then as they set out, they whispered in hushed tones, [23] *"Let's not allow any poor beggars into (our garden) today."* [24]

Then they hurried off early, firm in their intent. [25] (However, when they came upon their plot) and saw its

---

1805 The Prophet was so gentle mannered in his personal life that one of his attendants, a companion man named Anas bin Malik, said in later years, "I served the Messenger of Allah for ten years, and he never once said a word of displeasure to me, nor did he ever look at something I did and ask me why I did it or notice something I forgot to do and ask me why I didn't do it." (*Muslim, Tirmidhi*) He also said, "The Prophet was so gentle in his demeanor that any maidservant in Medina could have taken hold of his hand and taken him wherever she liked." (*Ma'ariful Qur'an*) A'ishah, on another occasion, described the Prophet thusly: "The Prophet never abused or spoke ill of anybody. He forgave faults and refrained from retaliation. He never thought of taking personal revenge. He forgave non-believers promptly upon their conversion to Islam, never fought on personal grounds, took an interest in his household affairs, condemned vendettas and blood-feuds, and never beat anyone – not even a servant." (*Tabaqat of Ibn Sa'd*)

1806 This passage is thought to be referring to Abu Jahl, one of the Prophet's bitterest and most uncouth critics from the start. Other scholars believe it refers to Walid ibn al-Mughirah, another bitter foe. In heated discussions, some of the idol-worshippers counseled Muhammad to be tolerant of their religion and idols, and they would be tolerant of his monotheistic beliefs.

1807 The Prophet said, "This world is the believer's prison and the unbeliever's paradise. (*Muslim*)

1808 Most commentators hold that this passage was revealed in Medina and that the 'them' in the first sentence is referring to the Meccans who were suffering from a famine that the Meccans blamed on Muhammad. (See chapter 44 introduction.) Thus, the Meccans were being 'tested like' the owners of the garden. Who were those owners? Ibn 'Abbas (d. 687) and others asserted that the garden in question was located in Yemen, was owned by either Jews or Christians, and that its events took place sometime after the era of Jesus. According to the generally accepted story, a righteous man used to own an abundant plot of land. After harvesting, he used to leave some produce behind intentionally for the poor to pick through. When he died, his three sons inherited the land and felt that it would no longer be prudent to leave any food unharvested, due to the demands of their large families. Therefore, the rest of the story is about the lesson they learned on account of their stinginess. (*Ma'ariful Qur'an*)

condition, they said (in confusion), "*We must have taken a wrong turn somewhere!*" [26]

(Then when they realized the truth), they cried, "*This can't be! We've been thwarted!*" [27]

Thereafter, the nobler (man) among them said, "*Didn't I tell you to glorify (Allah)?*" [28] (So in repentance) they cried, "*Glory to our Lord! We were truly at fault.*" [29]

Then they fell to blaming each other, [30] though at last they said, "*We're ruined, for we went beyond (what was fair).* [31] *Our Lord will provide us with a better garden than this, for now we're turning towards our Lord in repentance.*" [32]

That's the kind of punishment (to be had in this life), but far greater is the punishment of the next, if they only knew. [33]

For those who were mindful (of their duty to Allah), there will be delightful gardens in the presence of their Lord. [34]

Good and Evil are Not Equal

Do you expect Us to treat those who surrendered their wills to Us in the same way We treat the wicked? 1809 [35] What's wrong with you that you would assume that? [36]

Do you have some scripture to study from [37] that tells you what you want (to hear)? [38] Have you taken agreements from Us, binding until the Day of Assembly, which let you decide as you please? [39]

Ask which of them will vouch for this! [40] Do they have some partners (who will support them)? Then let them produce their 'partners' if they're really so honest! [41]

On the day when the shin will be exposed, 1810 prostration will be commanded, and some (people) will be unable to comply. [42]

Their eyes will lower in shame, knowing that when they were (safe and) secure (in the world), they refused to comply) when they were called to bow down. 1811 [43]

So leave them to Me – and whoever denies this narrative, We're slowly going to lead them to their ruin without their even knowing it. [44] Although I might give them time for a while, My plan is unyielding. [45]

Are you asking them for some kind of payment or to burden them under a load of debt? [46] Do they have insight into the unseen so they can write (about the mysteries of the supernatural)? [47]

1809 The Prophet said, "Should I tell you about the people of Paradise? They're every weak and oppressed person who fulfills his promises when he swears in Allah's name. Should I tell you about the people of Hellfire? They're every cruel, rude and arrogant person." (*Ahmad*)

1810 The Prophet said, "Our Lord will uncover His shin (to signal all must bow), and every believing male and female will prostrate to Him. The only ones who will remain standing are those who prostrated in the worldly life only to be seen and heard. They'll try to prostrate themselves at that time, but their backs will be transformed into one stiff plate." (*Bukhari, Muslim*) So this is a poetic way of saying that when all must bow without question, some will be surprised to find that just as they disobeyed Allah before, on this day they can't comply, even though they desperately will want to. The commentators explain that the 'shin being exposed' is an old idiom that refers to all secrets being revealed, even though they were kept under wraps in the life of the world. Some ancient monarchs would take their seat on their throne and open the front of their robe exposing their shin to demand people to bow.

1811 The Prophet once posed this question to a group of people, "Can anyone walk in water without getting his feet wet?" They answered in the negative. Then he said, "So, too, this is the condition of the worldly oriented person; he cannot avoid making mistakes." (*Bayhaqi*)

So wait patiently upon the judgment of your Lord, and don't be like (Jonah) of the fish, who cried out in distress. [1812] [48]

If the grace of His Lord hadn't reached him, then he would've been deposited on the empty beach while still in disgrace. [49] However, your Lord chose him and placed him among the ranks of the righteous. [1813] [50]

For sure, the faithless try to put you off balance with their venomous stares [1814] when they hear this reminder, and they shout, *"He's crazy!"* [51] However, this (message) is no less than a reminder to all the worlds. [52]

[1812] Verse 21:87 contains the words of his plea. Also see 37:139-148 for his summarized story.

[1813] Due to all he suffered and his redemption, the Prophet once said, "It's not right for any of you to say that he's better than Jonah, the son of Matta (*Heb.* Ammitai)." (*Bukhari, Ahmad*)

[1814] As part of their superstitions, the pagan Arabs believed in the practice of giving the "evil eye" to someone. The Quraysh asked some people who said they could do that to do it to the Prophet. They tried their techniques of staring menacingly and chanted their spells with fearsome looks on their faces, but it never worked. The Prophet advised that if someone feels they've been afflicted with a venomous stare from someone, or 'evil eye,' that they should pray to Allah for relief from it (a practice called *ruqyah*). In addition, reciting chapters 113 and 114 are also recommended in this regard. (*Muslim, Ibn Majah*)

The Reality

69 Al Haqqah
Middle Meccan Period

'Umar ibn al-Khattab was a prominent idolater. When opposition to Islam grew, he also reflected on how to put a stop to the Prophet's teachings. As it happened, he was given several opportunities to hear the Qur'an being recited, and after each one he slowly became more inclined towards the message, though he tried hard to suppress it. In later years he told of one of these incidents, and it just so happens that it involved this chapter.

'Umar said, "Before embracing Islam I came out of my house one day with the intention of causing trouble for the Prophet, but he had entered the sacred courtyard before I got there. When I arrived, I found that he was reciting chapter 69 aloud as he stood praying. I stood behind him and listened. As he recited the Qur'an, I wondered at its literary charm and beauty. Then suddenly an idea came to my mind that he must be a poet, as the Quraysh alleged. Just at that moment he recited the words: 'this is truly the word of an honored messenger. These aren't the words of a mere poet,' and I thought to myself: 'Then, he must be a fortune-teller, if not a poet.' Thereupon he recited the words: '...neither are these the words of a fortune-teller – oh, how few reminders you take! This is being sent down (to you) from the Lord of All the Worlds!' On hearing this, (an interest in) Islam entered deep into my heart." 'Umar still did not convert, however, until sometime later in a famous incident involving his sister, who had converted first. (Read the story of his conversion in the appendices under the section entitled *Biographical Sketches of Muhammad's Major Companions*.)

In the Name of Allah,
the Compassionate, the Merciful

The Reality! [1]

And just what *is* the Reality, [2]
and how can you understand
what the Reality is? [3]

The Thamud and the 'Ad (said)
the coming disaster was a lie, [4]
but the Thamud were destroyed
by a stunning (blast), [5]
while the 'Ad were destroyed
by a violent sandstorm. [6]

He made it rage against them
seven nights and eight days in a row.

In the end, you could've seen the (whole) population
lying flat in its (path) like uprooted palm trees all strewn about! [7]

Could you have even seen any survivors? [8]

Then came Pharaoh and those before him,
and the depraved overthrown (towns of Sodom and Gomorrah). [9]

They disobeyed the messenger of their Lord,
so He seized them with utter destruction. [10]

When the waters overflowed (the land) beyond their limits,
We carried (some of your ancestors) in a floating boat [11]
so We could make it a reminder for you now,
as well as (an enduring example),
so that ears (could hear the story)
and preserve its (lessons for posterity). 1815 [12]

When the Final Days Come

*W*hen the trumpet sounds a single blast [13]

and the earth is moved and its mountains
are crushed to powder in an instant [14]
– on that day, the Inevitable Event will come to pass! [15]

The very sky itself will be torn apart,
for it will be flimsy on that day. [16]

The angels will be perched on its edges,
and eight of them will be carrying the throne
of your Lord above them that day. 1816 [17]

That will be the day when you're
going to be presented (before Him).

None of what you did and then hid
will remain secret any longer. 1817 [18]

1815 The flood of Noah occurred in ancient Mesopotamia. Versions of this tale exist in cuneiform
tablets that are almost five thousand years old!

1816 The Prophet was brought to heaven during his night journey and ascension in order for Allah to
show him the wonders of the afterlife. (See chapter 17:1) When he returned, he was able to tell people
much of what he saw. One of the reports he gave was about the eight angels that will bear Allah's
throne on the Last Day. He said, "I was allowed to speak to one of the angels among those angels who
carry the throne of Allah. Between his ear and his shoulder is the distance of seven hundred years of
traveling." (*Abu Dawud*)

1817 The Prophet said, "People will have three appearances (before Allah) on the Day of Judgment. The
first two appearances will be for them to argue and offer excuses. During the final presentation, the
pages (of their record) will fly into their hands. Some will receive their records in their right hands,
and some will receive their records in their left hands." (*Ibn Majah, Tirmidhi*) If we combine this
hadith with the description contained in 50:21-23, then we see a more complete picture that shows
people being brought forward from the crowds for their first appearance, with the angels escorting the
person forward and holding his records at the ready. When the person's third appearance before the
throne comes, then the angel gives his record to him.

Then the one who will receive his record
in his right hand will say:

"Here it is! Go ahead and read my record! [19]
I realized that (one day) I would have to give an account!" [20]

Then he'll enter into a life of pleasure [21]
within a high garden [22]
where the fruits will hang
within easy reach. [23]

(A Voice will say):

"Eat and drink with full satisfaction
because of the (good) that you sent ahead of you
in the days that have passed away!" [24]

However, the one who will receive his record
in his left hand will cry out: [1818]

"Oh no! If only my record hadn't come back (to haunt) me! [25]
I never knew my account (stood so poorly)! [26]
Oh, if only (death) would've been the end of me! [27]
My money has done no good for me! [28]
All my power has left me!" [29]

(Then a voice will say):

"Take him! Tie him at the neck! [30]
Burn him in the raging blaze! [31]
Tie him to a chain seventy links long!" [32]

This was someone who wouldn't believe
in Allah, the Almighty, [33]
and who never encouraged
the feeding of the poor! [34]

He has no friends here today, [35]
nor will he have any food
save for slimy muck, [36]
which no one eats but the depraved." [37]

[1818] The idea of a "left" and "right" hand signifying two definite destinies is an old idea in human history. In ancient Hindu, Buddhist, Sikh, and Jain beliefs, there are left handed (*vamacara*) and right handed paths (*daksinacara*). The left is associated with alcohol, lack of control and living a carnal lifestyle, while the right is geared towards meditation, morality and spirituality. In 1875 a philosophical sect was created in Europe by Madame Blavatsky with similar connotations. Islam does not make any value judgment on a person being left-handed or right-handed.

Don't be Too Proud to Take a Warning

So now I call to witness what you can see [38]

and also what you can't see, [39]
(to demonstrate) that this is truly the word
of an honored messenger. [40]

These aren't the words of a mere poet
- oh, how little you believe! [41]

Neither are these the words of a fortune-teller
- oh, how few reminders you take! [42]

This is being sent down (to you)
from the Lord of All the Worlds! [43]

If this messenger, (Muhammad),
were ever to invent any teachings
(on his own and then pass them off) in Our name, [44]
We would take him by his right hand [45]
and cut off the artery (of his heart). [46]

None of you could save him (from Our vengeance)! [47]

This (Qur'an) is no less than a reminder
for all who are mindful (of their duty to Allah)! [48]
We already know that some of you deny it. [49]

(Without doubt, Divine revelation) is always
a source of distress for the faithless, [50]
but this is the absolute truth... [51]

So now glorify the Name
of your Lord, the Almighty. [52]

The Ascent

70 Al Ma'arij
Early Meccan Period

This chapter, which continues the themes raised in the previous one, boldly takes on the satirizing that the Prophet suffered at the hands of the chiefs and the poets of Mecca. The Arabs used poetry as both entertainment and propaganda, and the city of Mecca was the scene of a yearly contest for all the aspiring poets of the land. All throughout the year, people would also engage in mini-poetry contests in various towns and villages.

Some of these men who made their livelihood from poetry began to poke fun at the Prophet, and in time they took to outright slander and venomous hostility, much to the delight of their pagan sponsors. This chapter addresses one incident where the leaders and poets of the Quraysh cajoled the crowds into mocking the Prophet by literally running to the right and left, pretending they were entering into Paradise.

In the Name of Allah,
the Compassionate, the Merciful

A questioner asked about the Moment (when punishment) will befall [1819] [1] the faithless – (a punishment) that cannot be turned aside [2] (and that will come directly) from Allah, the master of the ascent. [1820] [3]

The angels and the Spirit [1821] will ascend up to Him (on the) Day (of

---

[1819] An-Nadr ibn al-Harith was a famed poet of the Quraysh. In the early days of Islam, the leaders of the Quraysh tribe asked him to ridicule Muhammad whenever he was preaching in the public square. When the Prophet began to speak of Allah and His ancient prophets, an-Nadr would follow him and speak about the heroes and kings of Persia, saying, "By Allah, Muhammad can't tell a better story than I, and his talk is only of old fables that he's copied, as have I." An-Nadr's harassment became so intense that the Prophet engaged some of his followers to recite poetry back at him. An-Nadr was unfazed and continued to ridicule the Prophet, even to the point of inciting people to do him and his followers physical harm. Many Muslims were tortured, and a few were killed partly due to an-Nadr's prodding. He is the one mentioned here in this passage, having asked for the punishment of Allah in a mocking way. (*Asbab ul-Nuzul*) His actual statement is recorded in verse 8:32. When the pagans and Muslims fought at Badr in the year 624, two years after this revelation, an-Nadr was among those captured from the Meccans. Although the Muslims eventually freed their Meccan prisoners on payment of ransom or by letting literate pagans earn their way free by teaching people to read, an-Nadr was one of two men executed for their cruel incitement of the Meccans to harm the believers who were living among them. (Some reports say he was killed in the battle itself.) (*Ibn Abi Hatim*)

[1820] This means Allah is above all things, and if any beings wish to ascend to His presence, they must go through many levels of elevation in the spiritual realm to get to Him.

[1821] There are two possible interpretations of what the 'spirit' mentioned here refers to. The majority of commentators believe it is a reference to Angel Gabriel, who is referred to as the Holy Spirit in other places in the Qur'an. A few obscure commentators have suggested it can mean the collective spirit of all humanity together, which emanated originally from Allah, which will return back to Him for Judgment Day. (See 15:29).

Judgment), and its duration will be fifty thousand (of your) years. [1822] [4]

So be patient, for patience is a beautiful thing. [5]

They see the Day (of Judgment) as a far off prospect, [6] but We see it quite near. [7] That day the sky will be like molten brass, [8] and the mountains will be (tossed about) like tufts of wool. [9] No close ally will ask about another close ally, [10] even if they saw each other clearly.

Every sinner's wish will be to save himself from the punishment of that day, even if he had to (sacrifice) his own children, [11] spouse, brother [12] or nurturing relatives. [13] *(He'd even sacrifice) everything on earth if it could save him!* [14]

Certainly not! It will be the scorching flame (for him) [15] - plucking out (his flesh) right down to the skull! [16] It beckons all who turned their backs and their faces (from the truth) [17] and who greedily gathered (wealth) and stowed it away! [18]

Truly, human beings are insatiable from the moment they're created, [19] for they're worried when misfortune comes, [20] yet greedy when times are good. [21]

However, it's not the same with those who are inclined to prayer, [22] who are diligent in their devotions [23] and who know that there's a claim on their wealth [24] from (the poor) who ask and from the (poor) who are held back (from asking). [25]

They accept the reality of the Day of Judgment, [26] and they're afraid of the punishment of their Lord, [27] (knowing that) their Lord's punishment is the opposite of contentment. [28]

(They're the ones) who guard their chastity, [29] except with their spouses and those (servants) who are under their authority (and whom they've married), [1823] for (with lawful mates) they're not to be blamed. [30]

Whoever goes beyond (these allowances) is a rule-breaker. [31] (Furthermore, the righteous) are those who respect their trusts and agreements, [32] who stand firm (in the truth) whenever they testify [33] and who guard their prayers strictly. [1824] [34] Those who (embody all of these qualities) will be among the honored ones in the Garden. [35]

The Mocking of the Faithless

*W*hat's the matter [1825] with those who suppress (their inner awareness of Allah), that they rush around in front of you [36] to the right and to the left in crowds, (mocking the idea that the believers will be directed into Paradise)? [37]

[1822] The Prophet said, "There won't be any owner of treasure who failed to pay his due charity tax without having his treasure transformed into heated metal plates that will brand him in the fires of Hell on his forehead, sides and back. This will continue until Allah judges between His servants on a Day whose measure is fifty thousand years of what you count. Then he will see his path either to Paradise or (back) into the Fire." (*Ahmad*)

[1823] Opinion is divided as to whether this refers to a *concubine* or to a maidservant who has been taken in marriage.

[1824] The Prophet once saw a man praying. He wasn't praying carefully and failed to complete his bowing and his prostrations. The Prophet remarked of him, "If he were to die in that state, then he would have died (following a religion) other than the religion of Muhammad. The example of the one who prays and does not complete his bowing and prostrations properly is that of a starving person who eats nothing but one or two dates – it doesn't stop his hunger at all." (*Abu Ya'la, Ibn Khuzaymah*)

[1825] While the Prophet was giving a public speech one day in the center of Mecca, a crowd of idol-worshippers, after hearing what kind of people will enter Paradise, insulted the Prophet and ran back and forth in a wild rush, acting as if they were entering Paradise. The poets laughed and had a good time of it, as well! However, as Allah points out, they didn't really want to enter Paradise. They were making fun of it! Some of them even boasted that if there was a Paradise, they would enter it first because they were better than the Muslims. This passage was revealed in response. (*Asbab ul-Nuzul*)

Doesn't each of those men want to enter the garden of delight? [38]

But no! We created them from lowly (compounds), and they know it. [39]

Now I swear by the Lord of all points in the East and the West that We surely can [40] substitute in their place better (people) than them, and We won't be frustrated. [41]

So leave them to fall into more vain talk and useless play until they come upon their day, which they've been promised [42] - the day when they'll come out of their graves all of a sudden, as if they were rushing towards some kind of finish line! [43]

Their eyes will be lowered in dejection, and humiliation will overshadow them! That's (what will happen) on the day they've been promised! [44]

Noah

71 Nuh
Early Meccan Period

This chapter is entirely concerned with a summary of the mission of Prophet Noah. Given that it was sent down in the early Meccan period, it was probably meant as a lesson for the Quraysh. It also served as a boost for the Prophet's self-esteem and an assurance that Allah would help him achieve victory in the end. In later years, the Prophet explained how idolatry began among Noah's people by narrating that there were five famous people in their past named: *Wadd, Suwa, Yaghuth, Ya'uq* and *Nasr.* They each lived at different times and were known for different qualities. After they passed away, legends and stories grew up around them, and they were passed on by village storytellers from generation to generation. Some people eventually erected statues in their honor to remember them and to inspire them. (*The Book of Idols,* al-Kalbi d. 819)

A generation passed, and Satan introduced the idea to them that their forefathers actually worshipped these images. Then people began to believe that these idols were real gods and that they made the rain fall on the crops and brought other benefits, as well. In time, rituals and prayers were introduced, and people virtually forgot about the Supreme God. It was in this circumstance that Allah chose Noah to reform his people. A simple villager in our remote past was given the duty to proclaim Allah's message to a network of farming villages steeped in ignorance.

In the Name of Allah,
the Compassionate, the Merciful

$\mathcal{W}$e sent Noah to his people (with this instruction), [1826] *"Warn your people before a painful punishment overtakes them."* [1827] [1]

"My People!" (Noah) said to them. *"I'm a clear warner (who's been sent to tell you)* [2] *that you should serve Allah! So be mindful of Him and obey me.* [3] *He'll forgive you your sins and give your (civilization) an extra amount of time, but when the time limit given by Allah is reached, it can't be extended any further, if you only knew!"* [4]

(He was ignored, however, and in his despair he cried out to Allah), saying, *"My Lord! I've called to my people through the night and through the day,* [5] *but my invitation only (seems to) make them drift further away."* [6]

"Every time I've called to them so You could forgive them, they've stuck their fingers in their ears

---

[1826] Noah lived in ancient Mesopotamia, in an age when civilization was still a novel concept. His tale was told orally in the generations that came after his time, and it was eventually set down in writing in the cuneiform system of script. Although the story has undergone many changes over successive Mesopotamian cultures, the basic outline of the story has remained the same.

[1827] Ibn 'Abbas (d. 687) said that Noah was commissioned as a prophet at the age of 40. (*Ma'ariful Qur'an*)

674

and wrapped themselves up in their cloaks, growing more stubborn and arrogant!" [1828] [7]

"Then I called them in public, [8] spoke to them at large and also privately in secret, [9] saying, 'Ask forgiveness from your Lord, for He is certainly forgiving. [10] He'll send water down upon you from the sky, [11] increase your wealth and children and grant you gardens and rivers. [12] So what's the matter with you that you don't stand in awe of Allah's majesty?'" [13]

'He created you (in the womb) in diverse stages! [14] Don't you see how Allah created the seven skies, one above the other, [15] and how He made the moon a light in their midst and the sun like a shining lamp? [16]

'Allah grew you from the earth slowly, [17] and in the end He's going to send you back into it and then raise you up (again on the Day of Resurrection). [18] Allah spread the earth out wide for you, [19] so you can move through its roads (and mountain) passes.'" [20]

Noah's Desperation

(After his people firmly rejected him,) Noah cried out, "My Lord! They've disobeyed me! They're following those whose wealth and children do them no good and lead them into loss. [21] They've devised an elaborate plan (to oppose my mission)." [1829] [22]

"They say (to each other), 'Don't abandon your gods! Don't abandon the god of Adoration or the goddess of Beauty or the Bull god, the Stallion god or the Eagle god.' [1830] [23] They've already misled so many, so don't let the wrongdoers have anything more besides greater mistakes." [24]

On account of their sins, they were drowned (in the flood) and entered into a fire. [1831] They found no one to help them besides Allah. [25]

"My Lord!" Noah had prayed. "Don't leave any realm for the faithless on the earth, [26] for if You did, then they would mislead Your servants again and give birth to nothing more than thankless hedonists." [27]

"My Lord, forgive me and my parents, and anyone who enters my house in faith, and (forgive) all believing men and believing women. Grant nothing more to the wrongdoers - unless it's more destruction!" [28]

[1828] The pagans among the Quraysh also treated Prophet Muhammad in a similar fashion, and chapters like this were meant as a source of solace for him to let him know he was not the first to be ignored by his people.

[1829] Ibn 'Abbas (d. 687) reports that Noah's people used to beat him up until he passed out whenever he preached to them. Then they would wrap him in a blanket and put him in his house, leaving him for dead. When Noah revived and recovered, he would preach to them again. Ibn Is-haq includes a similar report in his *tafseer*, with the addition that when Noah woke up, he would pray for his people, saying, "O Allah, forgive them, for they don't know what they're doing." (*Ma'ariful Qur'an*)

[1830] These gods mentioned here were originally heroes from ancient times who lived long before Noah's generation was born. They had many followers who obeyed their commandments. After each of those men died, their followers first made pictures of them and later erected statues (to help them to remember their example and teachings), but later generations took these statues as gods. (*Bukhari, Ibn Kathir*) These names, which were passed along to the Arabs after Noah's people were destroyed, were represented by the following shapes: *Wadd*, a man; *Suwa*, a beautiful woman; *Yaghuth*, a bull and sometimes a lion; *Ya'uq*, a horse; and *Nasr*, an eagle and sometimes another such bird of prey like a vulture. (*Zamakhshari*) Each of these five idols was worshipped in various places in the Arabian Peninsula.

[1831] Many commentators understand the term "a fire" mentioned here not to refer to Hellfire, which will come after the Day of Judgment, but to the punishment of the grave. (*Ma'ariful Qur'an*)

The Jinn

72 Al Jinn
Late Meccan Period

This chapter was revealed about two years before the Prophet immigrated to Medina. Muhammad had paid a visit to the nearby city of Ta'if in the year 619, seeking permission from its elders to allow him to preach in their city. The daily persecution he and his followers suffered in Mecca compelled the Prophet to seek out a place of refuge for his movement, especially since his protective uncle, Abu Talib, and supportive wife Khadijah had both recently passed away, leaving him vulnerable. (He went there either alone or in the company of his adopted son Zayd - the reports differ).

Situated in fertile and well-watered country, the wealthy city of Ta'if was a center of idolatry, even as Mecca was, though not as prominent. Thus, the masters of the city, including one of Muhammad's distant relatives, 'Abdiyah Layl, not only refused to accept Muhammad's message, despite many days of talks, but they forbade their people from listening to him. When Muhammad realized he was getting nowhere, before leaving, he asked the leaders not to tell the Meccans they had rejected him. In spite, they ordered their servants and the rabble of the streets to chase him away under a barrage of thrown stones. The mobs then forcibly expelled Muhammad, while pelting him mercilessly, forcing him to flee for his life.

By the time he escaped, he was cut, bloodied and bruised. Then Muhammad, along with his adopted son, Zayd ibn Harith, began the long journey back to Mecca. After some miles, he sought refuge in a walled orchard not far from Mecca, and remained hiding there for some time. While he was resting and nursing his bruised body, a woman happened by, and the Prophet complained to her of how his people treated him.

The pair of brothers who owned the orchard, his enemies 'Utbah and Shaybah, who saw him near their orchard, had thought at first to drive him out, as well, but they felt some sympathy for him. They sent a Christian slave of theirs to offer him grapes, and the slave was mightily impressed to hear Muhammad say grace before eating.

The Prophet then traveled a little north of Mecca, worried about how he would re-enter the city safely. In desperation the Prophet then called out to Allah, saying, "O Allah, to You I complain of my weakness, my poverty and lowliness before men. O Merciful One, You're the Lord of the weak, and You're my Lord. To whom will You give me, to one far away who will misuse me or to an enemy to whom You've given power over me? If You're not angry with me, I don't care to whom You give me. Your favor is expansive enough for me. I take refuge in the light of Your glance by which the darkness is illuminated and the things of this world and the next are rightly ordered, lest Your anger descend upon me or Your wrath light upon me. It is for You to be satisfied until You're pleased as much as You should be. There is no power and no might save in You." (As quoted in Qadi Panipati's book entitled *Tafsir al-Mazhari*.)

It is said that angel Jibra'il appeared and offered to send an angel to destroy the idolaters, but the Prophet refused, exclaiming that in the future their descendants would be believers. Muhammad remained camped out in the desert, while Zayd continued to look for new hideouts for him. The Prophet was afraid terribly that the Meccans might try to kill him if he were caught out in the open. To occupy his mind in the darkness of each night, the Prophet would recite the Qur'an. One night he was reciting chapter 55 from the Qur'an in his prayers.

As this chapter here tells it, a company of wandering jinns, or hidden beings, happened along and stopped in wonder to listen. (Verses 46:29-32 mention this incident, as well) The jinns repented of their evil and became believers. Muhammad spent some weeks out in the desert and approached a total of sixteen tribal leaders, asking for protection before one of them (the sheikh of the Nawfal branch of the Quraysh tribe) agreed to sponsor him under his protection. Thus, Muhammad was able to return safely to Mecca.

In the Name of Allah,
the Compassionate, the Merciful

(*M*uhammad,) say (to them), *"It's been revealed to me that a group of hidden ones heard (this Qur'an being recited."* [1832] They (listened to it and) said:

"We've just heard an amazing speech! [1] *It guided (us) towards the right direction, so now we believe in it. We'll never hold anyone else the equal of our Lord ever again.* [2] *Exalted is the majesty of our Lord! He hasn't taken any female consort nor any son!"* [3]

"Fools among us used to say outrageous things against Allah. [4] *However, now we feel that no human or jinn should ever say anything that's untrue about Allah.* [5] *Even though some individual humans have sought the protection of some individual jinns, (calling to them for supernatural aid), their vanity was only magnified.* [1833] [6] *Then they begin to think like you (jinns in*

this gathering used to) think, namely that Allah wouldn't raise anyone (to life again)." [7]

"We used to peer into the secrets of the sky, but we found it filled with unyielding obstacles and streaks of fire. [8] *We used to wait in (hidden) places to eavesdrop on news (of the future), but anyone who listens now will get a flaming fireball waiting to ambush him!* [9] *Even still, we never knew if misfortune was intended for those on earth or if their Lord wanted to direct them to the right."* [10]

"Among us are some who are morally inclined, while others of us are not, for we all follow different paths. [11] *Now we know that we can't frustrate Allah in the earth, nor can we frustrate Him by running away.* [12] *As for us, since we've now heard the guidance, we believe in it, and whoever believes in his Lord should not fear having a deficient (record) nor suffering any unfair (verdict)."* [13]

[1832] Ibn 'Abbas (d. 687) said, "When they heard the Prophet reciting the Qur'an, (the jinns) almost mounted on top of the Prophet due to their excitement. They drew very near to him, and he was unaware of their presence until the messenger (Angel Gabriel) came to him and made him recite the opening verses of this chapter." (*Ahmad*) They were also amazed at the way the Prophet prayed. Later, when they saw how his companions followed him obediently in prayer, the jinns were again impressed. (*Ibn Kathir*)

[1833] Before the coming of Islam, the Arabs were so fearful of *jinns*, both the human and incorporeal kind, that before they would enter any valley on their travels, it was customary to say the following invocation: "I seek protection with the leader of this valley from the foolish troublemakers of his people." (*Ibn Kathir*) One Companion of the Prophet named Rafi' ibn 'Umayr reports that before he was a Muslim he was on a journey through the desert. As he approached a valley at night, he uttered the customary invocation of refuge and then made camp. In his dream he saw a vision in which an old man said to him, "You fool, when you seek safety in a valley, or you're afraid of jinns, say this invocation, instead, 'I seek the protection of Allah, the Lord of Muhammad, from the tribulations of this valley.' Don't seek the protection of jinns any longer, for the time is over when humans must seek safety with jinns." The voice in his dream then told him that he was Muhammad and also told him where he could find him. When he awoke, Rafi' rode straightaway to Medina where he met the Prophet and told him about his dream. The Prophet invited him to Islam, and he accepted. This verse [72:6] references the pre-Islamic custom of jinn invocation. (*Ma'ariful Qur'an*)

677

"Among us are some who surrender themselves (to Allah) and some who avoid (accepting Him). Whoever surrenders himself (to Allah) has moved towards (the path) of right guidance, [14] *but those who avoid (accepting faith) will be mere fuel for Hellfire."* [15]

Final Words to the Obstinate

$\mathcal{I}$f (only the faithless) had committed themselves to the path (of goodness), We would've granted them abundant rain (for their dry land), [16] so We could've tested them (with their good fortune). If anyone turns away from remembering his Lord, then He'll bring upon him a devastating punishment! [17]

Places of worship (like Mecca) belong to Allah, so don't call upon anything at all besides Allah. [18] Yet, when (Muhammad) the servant of Allah stands up to call upon Him, (you idol-worshippers) just crowd around him (to taunt him). [19]

Say (to them), *"I'm not doing anything more than calling on my Lord, and I don't make anything else His equal."* [20] Then say, *"It's not in my power to cause you any harm nor to direct you."* [21]

Say (to them), *"No one can save me from Allah (if I disobeyed Him), nor could I ever find any shelter save with Him.* [22] *If I don't deliver the message that I've received from Allah, then Hellfire is reserved for the one who disobeys Allah and His Messenger, and he'll remain in it forever."* [23]

When they finally see what they were promised, then they'll know who really had the weakest support and the smallest number. [24] So now say to them, *"I don't know whether the (punishment) you've been promised is close at hand or whether my Lord will set it far off in the future."* [25]

"He knows what's beyond perception, and He doesn't share His hidden (knowledge) with anyone, [26] *except for a messenger that He chooses. Even then, He appoints sentinels* [1834] *who tread in front of them and behind them,* [27] *so (the messengers) can be sure that they're carrying and delivering the messages of their Lord. (Allah) surrounds (everything) that's with them, and He calculates all things."* [28]

[1834] These are angels.

Enfolded

73 Al Muzzammil
Early Meccan Period

This chapter is the third installment of revelation the Prophet received after a smattering of verses from chapters 96, 74 and 68. As to the opening lines of this chapter, Muhammad had been accused by his pagan neighbors of being a magician who was trying to make divisions among friends. He felt despondent and then wrapped himself in his cloak, hoping for more revelation to guide him and tell him what he should do next. Thus, he is addressed appropriately and told to be patient and to get himself ready for a weighty body of teachings to come.

Verse number 2 asked him to begin nightly devotions, and his slow but growing body of followers began joining him. It was a trial, of course, to stay up most of the night in prayer, but it prepared the foundation of spirituality that Muhammad needed to sustain him for the struggle that was ahead of him. After a year, verse 20 was revealed that relaxed the duty of nightly prayer and made it optional.

In the Name of Allah,
the Compassionate, the Merciful

*Y*ou there! The one covered up (in a cloak)! [1] Stand up (in prayer) at night, but not all night [2] - half of it or a little less [3] or more. [1835] Recite the Qur'an in slow, measured tones, [1836] [4] for soon We're going to send you momentous teachings. [1837] [5]

[1835] It is considered praiseworthy for people to rise from their sleep in the middle of the night to pray, read the Qur'an and meditate on life. In the earliest days of his mission, the Prophet was very eager to please Allah, to the point of exhausting himself. The world at night is a different place from the day, and thoughts and feelings flow more easily for the one devoted to Allah. The Muslim poet, Jalaluddin Rumi (d. 1273), once wrote, "Listen, stand up and pray at night, because you're a candle, and at night a candle stands and burns." (*Mathnawi*)

[1836] A'ishah was once asked about the way in which the Prophet recited the Qur'an, and she said, "He used to recite each chapter slowly, so much so that it would seem longer than chapters that were actually longer than it." (*Muslim*) Umm Salamah said, "He used to pause in between verses." (*Ahmad*) This verse is generally taken as the advice that the Qur'an should be recited beautifully and with feeling. (*Ma'ariful Qur'an*)

[1837] Zayd ibn Thabit once told of a time when the Prophet was sitting with him, dictating some verses while leaning on (Zayd's) thigh, when suddenly the Prophet seemed to increase in weight and made Zayd feel as if he would crush his leg. The Prophet then became lighter, and he had received a new revelation. Thus, the force of revelation was weighty upon the Prophet physically. (*Bukhari*) 'Abdullah ibn 'Amr once asked the Prophet if he ever felt anything when revelation came to him. The Prophet replied, "I hear a ringing, and then I remain quiet when I hear it. There hasn't been a single time that I've received revelation except that I thought my soul was about to be taken." (*Ahmad*) Another man asked the Prophet the same question, and he said, "Sometimes it comes to me like the ringing of a bell, and that's the hardest on me. Then this state passes away from me when I grasp what's being inspired. Sometimes the angel comes to me in the form of a man and talks to me, and I

Rising at night is truly a powerful (way) for taming (the soul), and it's the best (time) for composing words (of praise). [6] You're far too busy in the day with ordinary duties (to be able to concentrate). [7]

Remember the name of your Lord, and devote yourself completely to Him. [1838] [8] (He's the) Lord of the East and the West; there is no god but He! So look upon Him as the One Who can take care of (your) affairs. [9]

Have patience with what the (Meccans) are saying, and distance yourself from them in an amiable way. [10]

Let Me (deal with) those deniers who have the finest things in life. [1839] Bear with them – for just a little while longer. [11]

We have chains (ready to bind them), a fire (to burn them), [12] food that will choke (them) and even more terrible punishments besides! [13]

(Know that) a day will come when the earth and the mountains will shake so violently that the mountains will turn to shifting sand. [14]

We've sent you (people) a messenger to be a witness over you, even as We sent a messenger to Pharaoh (of Egypt). [15] Pharaoh disobeyed the messenger, so We took hold of him harshly. [16]

Now if you reject (the truth of Allah), how are you going to protect yourselves against a day (so terrifying that it) will cause children to sprout gray hair [17] - (a day when) the sky will literally be torn apart? (Without a doubt,) His promise will be fulfilled! [18]

Truly, this is no less than a reminder (for all people to consider), so whoever wants to (listen to it) should take a path that leads towards his Lord! [19]

Regulating One's Extra Prayers

Your Lord knows that you've been standing (for prayer) almost two-thirds of the night, or half the night, or a third of the night, and that a group of your followers have been joining you. [1840]

---

grasp what he says." A'ishah once remarked that if the Prophet ever received revelation while he was riding on a camel, the camel would suddenly drop its neck (under the increased weight). (*Bukhari*)

[1838] Long after the Prophet had passed away, two men went to ask A'ishah about the Prophet's practice of night prayer. She explained that when this verse was revealed the Prophet would pray for a large part of the night and that his followers, as they converted, would also join him praying so long that their feet would swell up. Twelve months later, verse 20 was revealed, making the night prayer voluntary rather than obligatory. (*Muslim, Ahmad*) There is no value in Islam to abandoning the world and performing unending religious rituals such as monks do. Our bodies, families and community also have rights upon us. (See 57:27)

[1839] At this stage of his mission, the Prophet had not yet gone public with his teachings, and the Qur'an at this time consisted of only a smattering of small chapters and miscellaneous verses. However, a few dozen people that the Prophet did approach in private scoffed at him. Little did he realize how much hardship and persecution he would soon face! For the Prophet, the advice in this verse is to be nobler than his critics and not to demean himself by arguing with them on their level. Rather, he is asked to be kind and courteous with his critics, even as he ignores their taunting and ridicule. The Prophet once told a companion named 'Ubadah ibn as-Samit, "Should I tell you about the thing that Allah will use to honor your household?" When 'Ubadah expressed his eagerness to know, the Prophet said, "Be patient towards the one who treats you ignorantly; forgive the one who oppresses you; give to the one who deprives you, and build ties with those who sever them with you." (*At-Tabari*)

[1840] This prayer in the middle of the night became known as *tahajjud* prayer. It is an extra prayer one can perform out of piety. It is not obligatory. The Prophet made it his habit to do this prayer in the dead of night in the mosque after the Muslims migrated to Medina. Soon, as the word spread, more and more followers began to join him at night. One night he didn't go into the mosque to perform that prayer. The next morning his followers were confused, and they asked him why he missed it. He replied that he didn't want Allah to make it an obligatory prayer, so he was showing his followers it

Allah measures the night and the day for a set length of time, and He knows that you, yourself, haven't been able to keep track of (the time that you've spent in prayer). Therefore, He's turning towards you (in mercy. So now you can) read from the Qur'an only as much as is easy for you.

He knows there may be some among you who will be sick, while others will be on the road, traveling in search of Allah's bounty, while others will be fighting in the cause of Allah. [1841] So read as much of the Qur'an as is easy (for you).

Establish the prayer, give in charity and loan to Allah a beautiful loan. Whatever good you send ahead for your souls, you will find it in Allah's presence, and it will be an even better and greater reward, besides! Seek Allah's forgiveness, for Allah is forgiving and merciful. [1842] [20]

---

was optional, even as praying late at night was optional when he was living in Mecca. The Prophet once said of it either to do it regularly or leave it off. In other words, don't do it occasionally and haphazardly.

[1841] The night has always been a time of prayer and deep meditation reserved for the most pious people in all religions and in all places. Prophet Muhammad took advantage of the night, as well, and spent nearly every night of his ministry in prayer. In the early days he sometimes passed most of the night in this way, and this prevented him from getting proper rest. Some of his more ardent followers used to join him and also suffered from the same effect. The Qur'an is, in effect, telling the Prophet that he need only do as much prayer and meditation at night as he is able. Then this is further explained by making reference to the future, where it is pointed out that lengthy night prayers would be overly burdensome on people who might be doing all sorts of things with their lives. Therefore, night prayer is not required of Muslims, and those who wish to engage in it are encouraged not to overdo it beyond their capacity.

[1842] The Prophet said that Allah, Himself, said, "I am as My servant thinks I am, and I am with him when he remembers Me. If he remembers Me to himself, then I remember him to Myself. If he remembers Me in a group, then I remember him in a better group than that. If he comes a foot closer to me, I come a yard closer to him. If he comes a yard closer to me, I come two arm length's closer to him. If he comes to me walking, I go to him in a rush." (*Bukhari*)

Enwrapped

74 Al Muddathir
Early Meccan Period

This was the fourth chapter to be revealed to the Prophet. It came in the first year of his prophethood at a time when he was still uncertain about what had happened to him. By this time, he accepted that supernatural contact had been made to him, but he was still unused to the coming of revelation and especially to the sight of angels, blazing in their glory.

Then a period of about six months came in which he received no further communications from Allah, and the Prophet began to feel increasingly despondent. He sometimes climbed up into the craggy hills outside the city and in despair thought to throw himself off a cliff. Every time that thought would occur, he would hear Angel Gabriel telling him to stop and that he really was Allah's chosen prophet.

Muhammad soon made it his habit to return to Mount Hira, where he had received his first communication from Allah, feeling that it was an appropriate place to be. On one outing, he wound up camping at the foot of the mountain for about a month. One night, while he was walking alone, he heard someone call his name in a loud voice. He looked all around the perimeter and saw no one. Agitated, he stood up to investigate. He happened to glance up at the sky and was astounded to see the image of Angel Gabriel, shining brightly and sitting on a throne, and this image filled the entire night sky.

Muhammad was startled and shook in fear. He turned, ran back to his home and burst in the door, crying, "Cover me in a sheet! Cover me in a sheet!" His wife wrapped his shivering body in a cloak-like blanket (called a *dithar*), and then she brought water for him. He was sweating hard in concentration. Suddenly, verses 1-5 were revealed to him, and he recited them to her. *(Bukhari, Muslim, Ahmad)* Verses 11-25 were revealed later on with regards to a wealthy Meccan noble named Walid ibn Mughirah, when he called to his fellows to denounce Muhammad loudly in an upcoming trade fair. He was a man who boasted of his wealth and lineage to such an extent that he used to call himself '*the One and Only, son of the One and Only.*' *(Qurtubi)*

In the Name of Allah,
the Compassionate, the Merciful

*Y*ou there! The one wrapped up (in a blanket)! [1]

Arise and warn! [2] Magnify your Lord! [3] Keep your clothes clean, [4] and shun the idols. [5] Don't give (in charity) with the expectation of receiving anything back. [6] For your Lord's sake, be patient. [7]

(On the day) when the trumpet is sounded, [1843] [8] that day will be a day of

---

[1843] The Prophet said, "How can I be relaxed when the one with the trumpet has placed it in his mouth, leaned his forehead forward and is waiting to be commanded so that he can blow?" Some of his

anguish, [9] *and it won't be easy for those who suppressed (their natural inclination to believe in Allah).* [1844] [10]

Allah will Confront the Schemers

*L*et Me deal with that (creature) whom I created, (who will then be) all alone himself! [1845] [11] I granted him ample wealth, [12] sons (to stand) by him, [13] and I made his (path in life) smooth! [14] Yet, he was greedy for more and more! [15]

By no means! He's been stubborn against Our signs! [16] Soon I'll bring waves of disaster down upon him! [17]

He pondered, and he schemed (against Me), [18] so now he's doomed! *Oh, how he schemed!* [19] Once again, he's doomed! *Oh, how he schemed!* [20]

Then he looked around (and saw the truth of Allah's signs), [21] but then he frowned and scowled, [22] turning arrogantly away, [23] saying, *"This (Qur'an) is no more than some remnant of the magic of ancient days.* [24] *This is no more than the speech of a mortal man!"* [25]

Soon will I roast him in a burning blaze [26] - *and how can you understand what that burning blaze is?* [27]

It leaves nothing unscathed nor leaves anything alone! [28] (It reduces) mortal men (to a lifeless, blank) slate, [29] *and there are nineteen (guardian angels watching) over (Hellfire).* [30]

A Riddle for the Willfully Blind

*W*e've not appointed anyone besides angels to be the guardians of the Fire, and We didn't fix their exact number

---

followers asked what they should do, and the Prophet replied, "Say, 'Allah is enough for us. He is the Best One in Whom to trust, and we put our trust in Allah.'" (*Ahmad*)

[1844] This is chronologically the first use of the term *kafir* in the Qur'an. It means to hide, withhold, conceal or thanklessly suppress something.

[1845] Muhammad was reciting the few passages of the Qur'an that he had received, and he began calling people to believe in him as a prophet of the One True God. The Meccans didn't know what to do with him afterwards. One Meccan notable, Walid ibn Mughirah, accepted an invitation to have dinner with Muhammad and Abu Bakr. The Prophet recited verses 40:1-3 to him, and Walid came away stunned and praised the verses, saying, "By Allah, I've heard a recital from him that's not from any mortal or jinn! It has sweetness and elegance; its height is juicy, and its descent is as well. It's more beautiful than any other recital, and it can't be outdone. It's not the speech of any human being." Abu Jahl found out about what he said and went to Walid the next day, saying, "Your family wants to give you some money so you can forget about what Muhammad said, because you (only praised his words because you) need to collect food from him and the son of Abu Quhafah (Abu Bakr)." Walid was affronted and answered that he was already the richest man in the city. Then he swore by some idols that he needed no handouts of food from Muhammad. (This was how Abu Jahl riled Walid up.) So Abu Jahl pressed him, saying, "So say something that shows you deny him and hate him." Walid answered, "What can I say? None of you are as skilled at poetry, and you think Muhammad is a madman. What Muhammad is saying is not the same as poetry. It's finer and more graceful, light at the top and deep at the bottom, better than any other verse and nothing can outdo it. Do you see him predicting anything?" Abu Jahl said, "No." Walid then asked, "Do you think he's a poet? Have you ever seen him reciting poetry before?" Abu Jahl again answered, "No." Walid next asked, "Do you think he's a liar? Have you ever caught him in a lie?" Abu Jahl replied a third time in the negative. Then Abu Jahl warned Walid that his clan was murmuring behind his back, and he asked him one last time, "What do you think it is? Say something against it." So Walid pondered about his position and what he should do. Then he abruptly said, "I think it's witchcraft, and the words are nothing but magic." Then he counseled his friends that they should be unified in denouncing Muhammad at the upcoming trade fair. Later on, either he or Abu Jahl publicly declared the words contained in verses 24-25. This passage was revealed in response to their conversation and public declaration. (*Asbab ul-Nuzul*)

except as a test for those who suppress (their ability to understand the truth). [1846]

(We gave this exact number also) so that those who received earlier revelation can know for sure, and further so that the believers can increase in their faith, and even further so that no doubts can remain among those who received earlier revelation and among the believers. [1847]

The (weaker believers, who are) infirm at heart, [1848] and the faithless, however, will (hear this figure and just complain), saying *What does Allah mean by giving us this (exact number)?* That's how Allah leaves to stray whom He wants and guides whom He wants.

No one can know the forces of the Lord except He, and this (message) is no less than a reminder to all mortals (everywhere). [31]

Personal Responsibility and its Consequences

*B*ut no!

By the moon [32] and by the night as it recedes [33] and by the dawn as it shines ever brighter [34] - *and this is just one of the greater (signs)* [35] - (know that this) is a warning to all mortals, [36] for anyone who chooses to move forward (in Allah's cause) or to fall behind. [37]

Every soul will be (held) as collateral for what it earned, [38] all except for the companions of the right. [39] (They're going to rest) in gardens, asking each other [40] about the wicked ones (below them in Hell, saying), [41] *"What landed you in such an inferno?"* [42]

The (inmates of Hell) will answer, *"We were not among those who prayed,* [43] *and we didn't feed the poor.* [44] *Instead, we used to talk uselessly with useless people,* [45] *and we denied the Day of Judgment* [46] *even until its certainty came upon us."* [47]

(On that day), no one's intercession will do them any good. [48] So what's the matter with them that they're turning away from the reminders [49] - *as if they were scared donkeys* [50] *running from a lion!* [51]

Not so!

Every one of them wants to have unrolled scrolls (of revelation tailored just for him)! [52]

Absolutely not! No way!

They're not (even the slightest bit) afraid of (what awaits them) in the next life! [53] There's no question but that this is a grave reminder all the same! [54]

Whoever wants to be reminded by it will be reminded, [55] but no one will be reminded by it except as Allah wills, for He's the essence of mindfulness and the essence of forgiveness. [1849] [56]

[1846] When the Meccans heard verse 30, Abu Jahl addressed the young men of the Quraysh tribe, telling them that since Muhammad only has nineteen followers (the angels mentioned in verse 30), they have nothing to worry about. (*Ma'ariful Qur'an*) When he came to know that there were nineteen guardian angels as the wardens of Hellfire, one powerful warrior among the Quraysh named Kaladah ibn Usayd boasted that he could take on seventeen of the angels himself and that the other two could be beaten by the rest of the tribe. (*Ibn Kathir*) Another Meccan warrior by the name of Abu al-Asalayn boasted that he could vanquish ten of the nineteen angels with his right arm, and the rest with his left arm. Verse 31 was revealed in response to these taunts of the Quraysh. (*Ma'ariful Qur'an*)

[1847] Much has been made of this enigmatic figure of nineteen in modern days. Some modern researchers have used mathematical models, based on the number nineteen, to show the numerical wonders of the Qur'an. A modern scholar named Abu Ameenah Bilal Phillips has shown much of this research to be fanciful.

[1848] This refers to the Muslims in Mecca during the days of persecution. They were not hypocrites, but their faith was constantly challenged, and some were weak.

[1849] The Prophet said, "Whoever spends the night safely in his abode of rest, is healthy and has enough resources for his day, it's as if he has achieved the whole world and everything in it." (*Tirmidhi*)

The (Day of) Standing

75 Al Qiyamah
Early Meccan Period

This is one of the earliest revealed chapters, and the internal evidence contained in verses 16-19 is clearly in favor of this view. When the Prophet first began receiving his revelations, he tried to speak quickly when the angel said them to him, in an attempt to memorize the words as fast he could. Here he is instructed to slow down and let Allah fix it in his memory. The stark subject matter in the preceding and following verses, covering themes of death and resurrection, are also indicative of the themes of the earliest chapters.

As for the way the chapter begins, a man named 'Adi ibn Rabi'ah went to the Prophet and said, "Tell me about the resurrection. When will it be, and what will occur on it?" The Prophet told him about it, but 'Adi merely said, "I'll never believe you, for how can Allah reassemble these bones?" and he held up his fingertips. The chapter starts with the word 'no' as a negation of the claim of the man that people won't be resurrected, and then in the second verse the 'no' is negating the wider pagan objection to moral responsibility. That is the unspoken implication that starts the chapter off like it was in the middle of an argument.

In the Name of Allah,
the Compassionate, the Merciful

*A*h, no!

But I swear by the Day of Standing, [1850] [1]
and again no! I swear by the accusing voice of the soul! [1851] [2]
Does the human assume that We're unable
to gather his bones back together? [3]
No way! We can reconfigure him down to his very fingertips! [4]

But, oh, the human being wants to go on violating (Allah's laws endlessly), [5]
and he (dismissively) asks, "*Where is this 'Day of Assembly?'*" [6]

[1850] The Arabic word *qiyamah* is often translated as resurrection, although it actually means to stand up. Once a man went to the Prophet and asked what the word *qiyamah* meant and why the Day of Judgment is also called the Day of *Qiyamah*. The Prophet replied, "Because on that day living things will stand up and give an account (of their deeds)." (*Tafseer Noor ath-Thaqalayn*). Thus, in this translation wherever the word *qiyamah* appears, I have translated it as the assembly, because that's the time when all will be made to stand up (for judgment), i.e., all will be standing at attention as if in an assembly.
[1851] Hasan al-Basri explained that this verse implies that Allah is praising those people who listen to their inner conscience and avoid bad deeds. (*Ma'ariful Qur'an*)

When sight is clouded (by fear) [7] and the moon is darkened [8]
and the sun and moon are merged together, [1852] [9]
that day the human being will cry,
"Where can I find safety?" [10]

But no!

There'll be no safe place, [11]
for that day all will be set before their Lord. [12]
Then that day (every) human being will be shown
what he sent ahead and left behind. [1853] [13]

But no!

The human being will be
an eye-witness against his own self, [14]
though he may try to offer excuses. [1854] [15]

How to Learn the Qur'anic Recitation

*D*on't move your tongue too fast, [1855]

(Muhammad, trying to memorize
the verses) in a rush. [1856] [16]
It's Our duty to assemble (the Qur'an)
and also (to teach its proper) recitation. [17]

So as We recite it,
follow along with the recital. [18]
Moreover, it's Our duty to explain it. [19]

When Realization is too Late

*B*ut no!

Without a doubt, (you human beings)
love this temporal life, [20]
and you give no thought to the next life. [21]

[1852] Possibly this means an eclipse.

[1853] Sent ahead refers to deeds that will be examined on Judgment Day, and left behind refers to lost opportunities, regrets and missed chances to do good. (*Qatadah*)

[1854] The Prophet said, "Get a hold of five things before five things happen: your youth before old age, your health before sickness, your riches before poverty, your leisure before business and your life before your death." (*Al-Hakim*)

[1855] When the Prophet was receiving these earliest revelations, he used to try to memorize them quickly by repeating the verses as fast as he could. Here he is being told to take his time, for Allah will enable him to remember them. After this passage was revealed, the Prophet used to recite new verses more slowly. (*Bukhari*)

[1856] A'ishah narrates that the Prophet said, "A person who recites the Qur'an and masters it by heart will be with the honorable and obedient scribes (in Paradise). A person who has to work very hard in learning the Qur'an by heart and recites it with great difficulty will have a double reward." (*Bukhari*)

Some faces will be beaming that day, [22]
as they gaze (expectantly) upon their Lord, [23]
and some faces will be gloomy that day, [24]
thinking that some terrible blow will soon befall them. [25]

Truly, when (a dying soul) reaches the collarbone at last, [26]
and when, *"Can any miracle worker save him?"* (is asked), [27]
then (in the pangs of death) he'll know his time to leave is due. [28]

Then his legs will be pushed together (as death approaches). [1857] [29]
That's the day (when all) will be driven back to your Lord. [30]

(It'll be too late for repentance then),
for he never donated, nor did he pray. [31]
Rather, he denied and turned away [32]
and then strutted arrogantly back to his family. [33]

You're ruined – *ruined!* [34]

Once more, you're ruined – *ruined!* [1858] [35]

Does the human being still think he'll just be left alone? [36]
Wasn't he a mere spewed drop of sperm, [37]
then a clinging thing, then formed in correct proportion, [38]
and set as one of two genders, male or female? [39]

(If this is how Allah made you the first time),
then isn't it possible for Him to bring
the dead to life (once again)? [1859] [40]

[1857] When a person is about to die on his deathbed, the normal custom is for his legs to be pushed together and his arms to be either folded on his chest or left at his sides.

[1858] Jalaluddin Rumi once wrote of this verse in these words: "For years Death has been beating the drum; only when time is running out do you listen? In his anguish, the careless person will cry out from deep within, saying, 'Oh my! I'm dying!' Has Death only made you aware of that now? Death's throat is hoarse from all the shouting; his drum is cracked from the severe blows he's laid upon it. But you've wrapped yourself up in trivial things. Only now will you realize the mystery of dying." (*Mathnawi* VI, 774-776)

[1859] Whenever the Prophet finished reciting this verse, he would say, "All glory is Yours, and Most definitely (you can do it)!" (*Abu Dawud*) In another narration, he advised people to respond to verse 40 after they've recited it by saying, "Most definitely! I testify that He has the power to do that!" (*Ma'ariful Qur'an*)

Passing Time

76 Ad-Dahr aka *Al Insan* or *Al Abrar*
Early to Middle Meccan Period

This chapter, which the Prophet used to recite often in Friday morning prayers, takes its title from the Arabic word for endless time. The Arabs had a notion that time was everlasting and that it was the only constant in the universe. In 45:24 the Meccans are even quoted as saying, "Nothing but time can destroy us." It was a contradictory belief for the simple fact that these same people then took to worshipping idols to get luck in their everyday affairs, while at the same time affirming that there was, somewhere out there, a Supreme God Who made the universe. Time had to be under the command of that Supreme God, and the pagans who made their own idols with their own hands were calling to them for aid, when only the Creator could accurately be said to hear. So time is not the overarching power in the universe, and one day even time will end when Allah decrees.

The actual occasion for revelation for the opening verse of this chapter revolves around an old black African man who approached the Prophet in a gathering one day and said, "Messenger of Allah, may the blessings (of Allah) be upon you, for not only are you handsome in body and skin tone, but you are also a prophet and messenger of Allah. Now if I were to believe in what you believe, and were I to do what you do, can I (as a black man) have the honor of being with you in Paradise?"

The reason why the man asked the question in this way was a reflection of the society in which he lived and suffered through for so long. The pre-Islamic Arabs generally felt superior to Africans, and from time immemorial Africans were seen as inferior.

Of course, the Prophet had been teaching the equality of all races; yet, in the early Meccan Period, the prevailing ideas of the day were still the major influence in Meccan society. By this time, the number of converts to Islam was still small, and Muhammad's willingness to embrace people of all colors and classes was a sticking point the Meccan chiefs had often used against him in the court of public opinion.

Turning to the man, the Prophet replied, "Absolutely! I swear by the One Who holds my life in His hands that all members of the black race will be bright and beautiful, so much so that their radiance will shine over a distance that will take a thousand years to travel. Allah will take it upon Himself to ensure the success of (every) person who says, 'There is no god other than Allah,' and moreover, the one who says, 'Glory be to Him and all praise is His,' will have 124,000 good deeds written in his record of deeds."

One of the men in the gathering was astonished, and he exclaimed, "Messenger of Allah! When Allah is so generous in rewarding people for even such small things as that, how could we ever be in danger of being destroyed or punished?"

The Prophet replied, "The fact is that some people will come on the Day of Judgment with so many good deeds that, if they were all placed on a mountain, even the mountain would strain under their weight. However, when all those (good deeds) will be compared to all the blessings of Allah (that were bestowed on that person in the world,) the person's deeds and good acts will not measure up at all (as enough to get him into Paradise), unless

Allah, the Almighty, decides to be generous and merciful to him." At that moment, the first verse of this chapter was revealed, and the African man asked excitedly, "Messenger of Allah, will my eyes see the same blessings that your holy eyes will see?" To which the Prophet replied, "Absolutely!"

The African declared his conversion and wept tears of joy for some time. Given his age and weakened condition, he soon passed away, while still weeping in gratitude to Allah. The Prophet performed his last rites, bathing and shrouding his body with his own hands, and then he led the small community of believers in the funeral oration. (*Tabarani*)

In the Name of Allah,
the Compassionate, the Merciful

$\mathcal{D}$idn't many ages pass before human beings were even something mentioned? 1860 [1]

We created (every) human being from mingled fluids so We could test him (in life), and thus We've endowed him with the faculties of hearing and sight. [2]

Then We lead him towards the path (of this world's life), so he can (choose by his own actions) whether to be effortlessly thankful or full of spite. 1861 [3]

For those who suppressed (their awareness of the truth), We've prepared chains, shackles and a scorching flame. [4]

However, the righteous will drink from a cup sweetened with camphor, 1862 [5] drawn from an ever-flowing spring from which the servants of Allah drink. [6]

They were the ones who fulfilled their oaths 1863 and feared an awful day whose ill-effects would be widely felt. [7]

Selfless Faith for the Sake of Allah

$\mathcal{T}$hey fed the needy, the orphans and the captives for love of (Allah) alone, 1864 [8] saying, "*We're feeding you only for Allah's face (to see), and we expect nothing in*

1860 The earth is thought to be four and a half billion years old. Human beings, at least of our current form, have only been around for less than the last two hundred thousand years or even less. Therefore, many ages have indeed passed in earth's history before our kind was even 'something mentioned.' Some scholars believe the "many ages" mentioned here should be understood to be the time before a person was conceived in his or her mother's womb, when they were indeed nothing *even mentioned*. (*Ma'ariful Qur'an*)

1861 The words used here that are usually translated as grateful and ungrateful imply more than just being thankful or thankless, but to be easily and effortlessly grateful for Allah's blessings, or to be actively spiteful against them. Also see 34:13.

1862 *Kaafur*, which is basically an early form of henna, was a valuable commodity in the Prophet's time. He recommended people use it when giving their last respects to someone who just passed away. It can also be used as a flavoring.

1863 Many commentators are quick to point out that the oaths in question must be good promises for legitimate purposes and not oaths to do evil. (*Ma'ariful Qur'an*)

1864 Some commentators feel that this passage was revealed in Medina regarding 'Ali ibn Abi Talib, and they cite the following story. 'Ali once labored hard all day watering some palm trees in exchange for a bag of barley grain. In the morning he was paid, so he went home to prepare a meal of three barley cakes out of it. When he finished preparing the first one, a poor man approached him, asking for something to eat. 'Ali gave it to him. After he left, he started cooking again with some more of the grain. When that cake was ready, an orphaned child came and asked for food. 'Ali gave it to him. After he left, he cooked the last of the grain and was about to eat the cake when a man who had been kidnapped and held for ransom by the Quraysh happened along and complained of hunger. 'Ali gave him the last of his cakes and spent the rest of the day hungry. (*Asbab ul-Nuzul*)

return from you, neither compensation nor thanks. [9] *We fear a day from our Lord that will be gloomy and distressing."* [1865] [10]

Allah will protect them from the malevolence of that day, and He'll bathe them in (the light of) brilliance and joy. [11]

Then He'll reward them with the Garden and silk robes for their perseverance. [12]

They'll relax upon raised thrones in a temperate climate where they'll neither bake under a hot sun nor suffer from a cold chill. [13]

Shade will cascade over them, and abundant (fruit) will hang within easy reach. [14] Silver flasks will be passed around, and crystal glasses, [15] shining like silver, will be filled according (to their desire). [16]

Even further, they'll be served with a cup (of wine) flavored with ginger, [17] (drawn from a unique) spring called *Seek the Way.* [1866] [18]

Ageless young servants will tend to them, and if you saw them they would seem (to scurry about) like scattered pearls. [19]

Everywhere you look, delight and magnificence will be what you see in every place! [20]

They'll be draped in lush green silk and rich brocade, adorned with silver bracelets, and their Lord will offer them the purest beverages, [21] (saying), *"This is your reward, for (Allah) appreciates your efforts!"* [22]

Be Patient, O Prophet

We're the One sending this Qur'an to you in installments, [23] so wait patiently upon the command of your Lord. [1867]

Don't (be seduced into) following the sinful and the faithless among (your opponents). [1868] [24]

Remember the name of your Lord morning and evening. [1869] [25] Prostrate yourself to Him during part of the night, and glorify Him all night long. [26]

[1865] It is often said that this passage is a reference to 'Ali ibn Abi Talib giving away a day's wages to help the needy. The poet, Hakim Sanai (d. 1150), wrote of this incident and passage in these words: "Whatever you have, give it up for the sake of Allah, for charity is even more marvelous when it comes from beggars. Bestow your life and soul, for the work of the poor is the best gift of mortal clay. The prince and chief of the Family of the Cloak was honored by the verse, *'Hasn't there come…'* He became so valuable in Allah's sight merely for the sake of three barley cakes." (The 'prince' is an allusion to 'Ali, and the 'Family of the Cloak' is the Prophet's family. See 33:33 and footnote.) Other commentators suggest that these verses were really revealed in Mecca long before this incident and that people later on applied them to 'Ali's act of generosity.

[1866] *Salsabil,* which literally means to go towards the way or path, is a unique fountain in Paradise.

[1867] The expected command of Allah was understood to be the definitive moment when Allah would make it clear to the Prophet's enemies that Allah's word would triumph over idolatry. Thus, even though the Meccans became harsh and oppressive, the Muslims were told frequently in Qur'anic revelations to wait and see, for Allah would make the final move. The Muslim victory over the Meccans at the Battle of Badr in the year 624 is considered to be the fulfillment of this awaited sign.

[1868] The allure of our physical desires is strong, and Satan uses this weakness of ours to cause our downfall. Other people who don't understand the predicament that they've stumbled into try to drag down all those around them who are noble and good so they, themselves, can validate for themselves the rightness of their sinfulness. At such times when our faith and resolve are sorely tested, we can call upon Allah for inner strength. A woman named Asma' bint Umays said of such times, "The Messenger of Allah said to me, 'Should I teach you a phrase that you can say when you're in distress? It is: Allah! Allah! My Lord. I don't make any partners alongside of Him.'"

[1869] The ninth-century poet, Ibn 'Abdus-Samad, wrote: "Love deafens me to every voice but His. Was love ever so strange as this? Love blinds me, and on Him alone I gaze. Love blinds me, and from a hidden place it overwhelms me completely."

Human Beings cannot Outrun the Reach of Allah

*A*s for these (people), they love the temporal (life), putting off a hard day that will surely come. [1870] [27]

We created them and gave them boundless energy, but whenever We wish, We can exchange (those people) for others like them. [28]

This is a warning, so anyone who so chooses can follow a path (that leads) to his Lord. [29]

Not as you will, however, but as Allah wills, for He is full of knowledge and wisdom. [30]

He enters into His mercy whomever He wants, but for the wrongdoers He's prepared a painful punishment. [31]

[1870] This passage is referring to the Meccans. They thought they were so powerful, strong and virile, and they often bullied the Muslims, who were forbidden to fight back, even if some of them had wanted to. The Qur'anic response is basically saying that they may have strong and burly men; yet, Allah can bring about their end and bring a new group of people in their place.

The Sent Ones
77 Al Mursalat
Early Meccan Period

This early Meccan chapter is one of a series that consists of chapters 75-79. The themes are all interrelated and seek to impress upon the Meccans the concepts of an afterlife and personal accountability. One of the more dramatic features of this chapter, which is a tightly woven poem in its original Arabic, is the frequent repetition of the refrain, *"So ruin that day to those who denied!"* which occurs after nearly every five verses.

As to the moment of revelation, a man named 'Abdullah ibn Mas'ud (d. 653) reported that he and some others were sitting and chatting with the Prophet in a small cave in a place known as Mina, when this chapter was revealed to the Prophet, and he began reciting it. 'Abdullah said that he himself repeated the words as they were coming from the Prophet's mouth. Suddenly a snake leapt out of a crevice, and the Prophet said, "Kill it!" The snake got away, however, and the Prophet said, "It was saved from being harmed by you, just as you were saved from being harmed by it." (*Bukhari*)

Umm Fadl, the mother of 'Abdullah ibn 'Abbas (d. 687), once heard her son reciting this chapter, and she said, "My son, you reminded me of something by your recitation of this chapter. It's the last thing I heard from the Messenger of Allah. He recited it in the sunset prayer (before he passed away)." (*Bukhari*)

In the Name of Allah,
the Compassionate, the Merciful

*B*y the (winds) sent with a purpose, [1]
reaching the speed of a tempest, [2]
scattering (clouds) far and wide, [3]
separating and dividing, [4]
offering reminders [5] of validation and warning [1871] [6]
– indeed, what you've been promised will surely come to pass. [7]

When the stars are put out, [8]
when the sky is ripped to shreds, [9]
when the mountains dissolve to dust, [10]
and when the messengers are given their tasks [11]

[1871] Opinion is divided as to what verses 1-6 refer. The four main interpretations are: 1) angels, 2) winds, 3) charging horsemen, and 4) the growth of revelation through the interlinked missions of successive prophets. Given that the verses in question do not seem to describe angelic activities, and given that the concept of evolving revelation wasn't really stressed or conceptualized definitively at the time when this chapter was revealed, I am of the opinion that it is most probably a reference to either cavalry charges or the forces of nature around the audience. I chose the latter, though the former could work as well.

\- for what day are all these (events) waiting? [12]
For the Day of Sorting, [13]
and how can you understand
what the Day of Sorting is? [14]

Ruin that day to those who denied! [15]

Didn't We destroy ancient (civilizations that denied Us)? [16]
And so, shall We follow them with later (generations), as well. [17]
That's how We deal with the wicked! [18]

So ruin that day to those who denied! [19]

Didn't We create you from a lowly fluid [20]
and lodge you safely in a nestled place [21]
for a measured term? [22]

We measure (the time you spend in the womb),
and how excellently We measure! [23]

So ruin that day to those who denied! [24]

Didn't We make the earth as a gathering place [25]
for both the living and the dead, [26]
setting within it soaring highlands
and offering you fresh water? [27]

So ruin that day to those who denied! [28]

"Now go towards what you used to deny! [29]
Go to the three tiers of darkness, [30]
under which there is neither cooling shade
nor protection from the flames!" [31]

The (fires of Hell) will throw out
streaking sparks as big as logs, [32]
(streaking outward) like fiery yellow ropes! [33]

So ruin that day to those who denied! [34]

And on that day they'll get no chance
to speak (in their defense), [35]
nor will they be able to justify (their actions). [36]

So ruin that day to all those who denied! [37]
And that's (how it will be on) the Day of Sorting!

We're going to gather you all together,
along with the ancient (peoples of the past), [38]
so if you want to make a plan against Me,
then go ahead and make your plans! [39]

So ruin that day to those who denied! [40]

Now as for those who were mindful (of their Lord),
they'll live within cooling shade
and bubbling springs [41]
with every kind of fruit they desire. [42]

"(All you who believed!):
Eat and drink joyfully
in return for your deeds before!" [43]

That's how We reward the good. [1872] [44]
Oh, but ruin that day to those who denied! [45]

(All you sinners!):

"Eat and enjoy yourselves for a little while now,
but without a doubt you're the wicked ones." [46]

So ruin that day to those who denied! [47]

When they're asked to bow (down to Allah),
they don't bow (to Him)! [48]

So ruin that day to those who denied! [49]

Now in what message
will they believe, after this? [1873] [50]

[1872] Abu Ayyoub al Ansari reports that someone went to the Messenger of Allah and asked him for some brief advice. He replied, "When you stand up for prayer, pray as if it were your last. Don't say anything for which you'll have to make an excuse tomorrow, and resolve to give up all hopes of what people possess." (*Ahmad, Bayhaqi*)

[1873] The Prophet said that after reciting this last line, a person should respond to the question posed by saying, "I believe in Allah." (*Ma'ariful Qur'an*)

The Prophecy
78 An-Naba'
Middle Meccan Period

Most early to middle Meccan chapters focus upon three main themes: monotheism, the prophethood of Muhammad and the coming doomsday and resurrection. This chapter makes a reference to the fact that the general public in Mecca was discomfited with these ideas and would often argue about them, both with the Prophet and among themselves. Some were accepting the message, while others were rejecting it outright. It even divided families. Thus, the people were arguing about it, but they would learn soon whether or not Islam was a divine way of life by its ultimate success or failure.

In the Name of Allah,
the Compassionate, the Merciful

What are they arguing about? [1874] [1]

It's about the great prophecy (of resurrection), [2]
and it makes them disagree. [3]

Oh no, but they'll soon know, [4]
and then, oh no, they'll soon know! [5]

Didn't We spread the earth out wide [6]
and stake it down with strong mountains? [7]

(Didn't We) create you in pairs [8]
and give you sleep as your way to rejuvenate? [9]

(Didn't We) make the night for covering up [10]
and the day for earning a living? [11]

(Didn't We) build high above you the seven skies [12]
and place a blazing lamp within, [1875] [13]
and (don't We) cause the heavy rains to fall from the clouds [14]
to produce grains, vegetables [15] and verdant gardens? [16]

[1874] According to Ibn 'Abbas, in the early days of revelation, the Meccans would form discussion circles to debate the merit and meaning of Muhammad's revelations. Sometimes they would get into heated arguments, especially with those who were inclined to believe in Muhammad's message. At other times, certain pagans would feign interest in Muhammad's message just to cause an argument with him. These incidents are what the opening passage here is referencing. (*Ma'ariful Qur'an*)
[1875] The sun.

Truly, the Day of Sorting
(good from evil) is a confirmed date. [17]

That day the trumpet will sound,
and you'll come forward in huge crowds. [18]

The sky will open wide like it was full of doors, [19]
and the mountains will shift and vanish like a mirage. [20]

Hellfire will be ready to ambush (the sinners), [21]
for it's the final destination of the rebellious. [1876] [22]

They're going to stay in there for ages, [1877] [23]
having neither (pleasant) coolness
nor anything to quench their thirst [24]
- save for boiling muck and numbing cold! [25]

That's the payback they deserve, [26]
for they never expected to be called
to answer (for what they did), [27]
and they denied Our (revealed) verses as false. [28]

Oh, but We recorded everything in a ledger! [29]

"Suffer (the results of your actions!)
Nothing more will you get besides added punishment!" [30]

Those who were mindful (of their duty to Allah)
will have their greatest wish: [31]
reserved gardens and vineyards, [32]
splendid companions of equal age, [33]
every cup *filled* to overflowing, [34]
and no more useless talk or lies to be heard. [1878] [35]

(All this) will be a reward from your Lord.
That's an excellent compensation [36]
from the Lord of the heavens,
the earth and everything in between
- the Compassionate!

[1876] Hasan al-Basri said that there will be guardian angels waiting on the bridge that runs over the chasm of Hellfire. They will push anyone off the bridge who is not allowed to approach heaven on the other side. (*Qurtubi*)

[1877] The term *ahqab*, or ages, is thought by some commentators (as mentioned by Ibn Kathir) to equal anywhere from forty to eighty years in Arabic parlance. The Prophet said, "Those who will be put in Hellfire to be punished for their sins will not be able to come out until they've passed a few ages there. One age is a little over eighty years, and each year has three hundred and sixty days according to your estimation." (*Ma'ariful Qur'an*) Generally, those who had at least a small amount of faith will be released from Hell and entered in Heaven after they've paid the penalty for their sins. Some inmates, however, will never get out, and the Qur'an used other terminology to describe their stay and its permanence. See 4:169.

[1878] This life is filled with people who lie to us and who assault our ears with useless talk. Thus, one of the benefits of heaven is that we will no longer have to hear such painful discourse ever again! The Prophet said, "Whoever believes in Allah and the Last Day, if he has nothing good to say, he should keep quiet." (*Bukhari, Muslim*)

No one will dare argue with Him [37]
on the day when the Spirit [1879]
and the (other) angels assemble in ranks,
and no one will speak save for
those whom the Compassionate allows,
and even then, only the truth will be spoken. [1880] [38]

That will be the day of ultimate truth!
So whoever chooses, let them take the path
that leads directly back to their Lord. [1881] [39]

For sure, We've warned you of a penalty near,
the day when each person will be the witness over
everything their hands have sent ahead of them.

Then the one who denied (the truth) will cry,
"I'm doomed! If only I were dust!" [1882] [40]

[1879] The majority of commentators, such as Ibn 'Abbas (d. 687), usually state that the Spirit, or *ruh*, mentioned here refers to Angel Gabriel. Others like Ibn Kathir have speculated that it refers to the collective spirit of all of humanity.

[1880] People will try to lie and will offer excuses for their behavior. (See 6:23) When this happens, Allah will seal their mouths up tight, and then their limbs will testify to the truth. (See 36:65) Thus, the truth will take precedence, as this verse attests, over any lies. (*Ma'ariful Qur'an*)

[1881] Uthman ibn Affan, the third caliph of Islam (d. 656), reports that once while he was standing by a grave and crying so much that his beard was wet, someone asked him, "You don't cry over discussions of Paradise and Hell, but you are crying over a grave?" He replied that the Messenger of Allah said, "Truly, the grave is the first step in the journey towards the next life. If one finds salvation (at this stage), then the succeeding ones become easy for him. If one doesn't find salvation there, what follows becomes very difficult."

[1882] When the Day of Judgment begins, all the animals will also appear, and any animal that was wronged by another will be able to take its revenge. They will also be allowed to take revenge on people who mistreated them, as proven by several sayings of the Prophet. Then when all that is finished, the animals will be reduced to dust, and sinful people, seeing that animals will not suffer any punishment in Hell for their earthly misdeeds, will cry out that they wish they would become dust, too. (*Ma'ariful Qur'an*)

Those Who Pull Roughly

79 An-Nazi'at
Early Meccan Period

This chapter was revealed immediately after the previous one and continues to expound upon the importance of personal conduct and its relationship to our fate on Judgment Day. The story of Pharaoh and his rejection of Moses plays a central role. Egyptian ruins and the mummified remains of their rulers are indeed powerful relics for future civilizations to ponder. The opening verses of this chapter reference either riders on horses pulling reins, or angels and how they take the souls of people at death.

In the Name of Allah,
the Compassionate, the Merciful

By those who pull roughly [1]
and those who gently slide through. [1883] [2]

By those who glide serenely, [3]
then race (each other) at stride, [4]
bringing on the final score! [5]

(By these tokens consider)
the day when violent convulsions [6]
will repeatedly engulf (the earth). [7]

That day hearts will be racing, [8]
and eyes will be downcast. [9]

Yet, (some people) ask,
"Huh? Are we really going to be
brought back as good as new? [10]

Huh? Even after our bones have rotted away? [11]
Such a return would be a total waste!" [12]

Oh, but when a single cry goes forth, [13]
they'll suddenly (find themselves)
awake (on a vast empty plain)! [14]

[1883] There are two interpretations of this opening passage. The first is that it refers to angels taking the souls of the doomed (roughly) and the blessed (gently). The other is that it evokes a calvary charge with all the nuanced excitement of a full on blitz having some riders pulling the reins harshly, and others in a more subtle way.

An Example of a Tyrant

$\mathcal{H}$ave you ever heard the story of Moses? [15]

His Lord called out to him in the double-blessed vale, [1884]
saying, [16] "Go to Pharaoh for he's out of control." [17]

"Say to him,
'Would you like to cleanse yourself (from sin)? [18]
I will guide you to your Lord so you can revere Him.'" [19]

(Then Moses went to Pharaoh)
and showed him the great sign (of Allah's power), [1885] [20]
but he denied it and disobeyed [21]
and harshly turned his back away. [22]

Then he assembled (his court)
and made an announcement (to all his people). [23]

He said, "It is I who am your supreme lord!" [24]

Then Allah took hold of him
and made an example of him
in the next life, as well as in the first. [25]

There's an important lesson in this
for those who fear (displeasing their Lord). [1886] [26]

Are you harder to create than the sky He built? [27]

He raised its expansive height in proportion
and balanced it in precision. [28]
He made its night obscure and its day revealing. [29]

He shaped the earth as an egg [1887]
after that [30] and brought out its waters and plains. [31]
He also steadied it with firm mountains, [32]
all as a convenience for you and your livestock. [33]

[1884] This is the small covered vale on the mountain where Moses communed with Allah for forty days and nights. Tuwa means doubly-blessed.

[1885] Moses was granted a number of miracles that he could use to convince Pharaoh that he was speaking the truth. 17:101 mentions nine signs in total. Which one was the great sign? Some commentators are of the opinion that it was the glowing white hand mentioned in 20:22-23. Others offer the rod that changed into a snake, as described in 20:17-21.

[1886] The Prophet said, "Whoever avoids doubtful things (that are actions whose legality is uncertain) protects his honor and his way of life. Whoever indulges in doubtful things will eventually indulge in forbidden things." (*Ma'ariful Qur'an*)

[1887] Though most translators render the Arabic term *dahaha* as to expand or spread out (with regards to the earth,) the ancient usage of the word is a reference to an egg or an egg-like shape, and this word is still used to this day to refer to eggs in some parts of Arabic-speaking North Africa. Early Muslim commentators, who might have assumed that the earth was flat, glossed over the meaning of this word and interpreted it to mean that the earth was unrolled or at best *spread out*. What is the significance of this? It could mean that the Qur'an was correctly deducing the shape of the earth (which is not a perfect sphere) long before the truth of it was discovered by modern science.

Therefore, when the colossal event comes to pass, [34]
that day the human being will recall clearly what he labored for. [35]

Then the raging blaze will be presented for all to see. [36]
Whoever went beyond the bounds
(of what was moral and right), [37]
and who preferred the life of this world, [38]
then he'll make his home in the raging blaze. [39]

In contrast to this, whoever feared standing
in the presence of his Lord,
and who controlled his passions, [40]
he'll make his home in Paradise. [1888] [41]

(And now, Muhammad,)
they're asking you about the Hour:
"When will it come to pass?" [42]

Why would you (need to) remind us about it? [43]
Your Lord has fixed the deadline. [44]

Your duty is only to warn those who fear (its coming). [45]
When they see that the day is finally upon them,
(it will seem) as if they lived but a single night
and at most until the dawn! [46]

[1888] The Prophet said, "None of you is (truly) a believer until even his (fleshly) desires also conform to my teachings." He also said, "Whenever I feel my heart disturbed (by bad thoughts or inclinations), I say, 'Allah forgive me,' a hundred times a day." (*Ma'ariful Qur'an*)

He Frowned

80 'Abasa
Early Meccan Period

The Prophet was engaged in a serious discussion with some of the Meccan leaders, most notably Al-Walid ibn al-Mughirah, Abu Jahl, 'Utbah ibn Rabi'ah and the Prophet's uncle 'Abbas, who was not yet a Muslim, concerning what he was teaching and why. The Prophet earnestly hoped that if he could just convince them of the logic of Islam that their conversion would go a long way towards bringing the rest of the Meccans around to his position. As it happened, an old blind convert named 'Abdullah ibn Shurayh, who was commonly known by the name of his grandmother, Ibn Umm Maktoum, heard the Prophet's voice, and he ambled over to the sound, asking to have some Qur'anic verses explained for him. (He didn't know the Prophet was busy).

The Prophet became annoyed at the interruption, feeling it might make the pagans lose interest in the discussion, given that the pagans considered the Prophet's companions as nothing more than disabled people, low class denizens and slaves, so Muhammad *"frowned and turned away."* This chapter was immediately revealed to him, and he recited it aloud to the astonishment of those watching. The Meccans left in disgust, for they despised the weak and disabled. The Prophet, duly chastened, immediately attended to Ibn Umm Maktoum's question. Ever afterward, the Prophet treated him with the utmost respect and kindness, often saying to him, "Welcome to the one on whose behalf my Lord rebuked me."

In the Name of Allah,
the Compassionate, the Merciful

(Muhammad) frowned and turned away [1]
when the blind man came (and interrupted his preaching), [2]
but for all you knew he could've grown in purity [3]
or received a useful reminder. [4]

The one who thought he needed nothing [5]
was the one to whom you gave your full attention, [6]
though he wasn't your responsibility. [7]

So the one who came to you eagerly (in search of knowledge), [8]
and who feared (Allah), [9] you neglected. [10]

Let it not be!

This (revelation) is a reminder [11]
for anyone who desires to remember (the truth). [12]
(It's) written on honored pages, [13] exalted and holy, [14]

701

by the hands of scribes, [15] both noble and fair. [1889] [16]

Doomed to destruction is the human being! How thankless is he! [17]
From what did (Allah) create him? [18] - from a mere drop!

He proportioned (his unique nature), [19]
and then eased his path (into the world at birth). [20]

Then He makes him die (one day), and then he's buried [21]
- only to be raised up again when (Allah) wills! [22]

But no!

How often does he fail to achieve
the standards He set for him! [1890] [23]

So let humanity observe the
(complexity) of their food (chain). [24]
We cause abundant rain to fall [25]
and (cause plants) to crack the earth (as they grow). [26]

And so, We produce the grains, [27] grapes, herbs, [28] olives and dates. [29]
(We also) bring forth orchards, [30] fruits and grasslands, [31]
both for you and the livestock you raise. [32]

*W*hen there comes the piercing cry [1891] [33]

(signaling the Last) Day, everyone
will run from their own sibling, [34]
mother, father, [35] spouse and children, [36]
for each one will have concern enough
for themselves that day. [37]

Some faces will be bright on that day, [38] laughing
and joyous (for the glad tidings they received), [39]
while other faces will be dusty that day, [40] overcast (in shame). [41]
They're the ones who rejected (faith) and who were insolent. [42]

[1889] The Prophet had a number of literate companions who acted as his secretaries, at one time calling upon the services of dozens of men. Whenever he would receive a new revelation, he would call to one of them and dictate as they wrote the verses down. Sometimes these revelations were copied and distributed.

[1890] The Prophet said, "The children of Adam have a right to only these: a dwelling in which to live, clothes to hide their nakedness, and some bread and water." (*Tirmidhi*)

[1891] This passage was revealed in Medina in response to a question from A'ishah. She asked the Prophet, "Are we all going to be judged while we're *naked*?" The Prophet replied, "Yes." A'ishah became alarmed and said, "But that will be so embarrassing." Then this passage was revealed explaining that no one will have any mind to notice anything except their own troubles. (*Asbab ul-Nuzul*)

The Enveloping
81 At Takwīr
Early Meccan Period

This chapter contains one of the more vivid descriptions of the Last Day. It's designed to counter the charge of the Meccans that Muhammad must have been possessed by a devil or lost in derangement to become so eloquent so quickly. Clearly a man under the thrall of a devil wouldn't call people to remember Allah, (even as Jesus rebutted such a charge saying 'a house divided against itself cannot stand'), nor would a madman promote a code of self-control and morality. Thus, this chapter leaves us with the question: *"So which way will you go?"*

In the Name of Allah,
the Compassionate, the Merciful

*W*hen the sun
is wrapped in darkness, [1]

When the stars
are cast down, [1892] [2]

When the mountains
pass away, [3]

When the livestock
heavy with young
are abandoned, [4]

When the wild beasts
are herded together, [5]

When the seas rise, [6]
When the souls are sorted, [7]

When the baby girl buried alive is asked [8]
for what crime she was killed, [1893] [9]

[1892] There are many sayings traced to the Prophet that describe what will happen to the celestial bodies in the End Times, and they range from things such as they will be thrown in the sea to they will be immersed and lost in Hellfire. The scholars have explained that on the Last Day, when Hellfire bursts forth in the physical universe, it will swallow up the oceans, the earth and all celestial bodies. (*Ma'ariful Qur'an*)

[1893] This is a reference to the pagan custom of murdering unwanted baby girls by burying them alive in the sand. Muhammad detested this cruel practice and opposed the pagans most strongly about it.

When the scrolls are opened, [1894] [10]
when the sky is laid bare, [11]

And when Hell is set ablaze [12]
and Paradise is brought near, [13]

Then every soul will know
what it has prepared. [1895] [14]

And so, by the (heavenly bodies) that withdraw, [15]
move on directly or pass out of sight. [1896] [16]

And by the night as it draws slowly in and out, [1897] [17]
and the dawn as it slowly lets out its breath... [1898] [18]

He taught that both girls and boys were equal as children and should be beloved equally by the parents. He once said, "Whoever becomes the father of a girl, he should neither hurt her nor treat her with contempt nor show preference over her to his sons in kindness and affection. God will grant him Paradise in return for his kind treatment of his daughter." (*Ibn Abbas*) Prophet Muhammad advocated strongly that parents should value and treat their daughters well, saying, "Treat your daughters well, for I am also the father of daughters." On another occasion, he said that whoever has three daughters, cares for them, educates them and teaches them well, then they will enter Paradise. A man asked him about having only two daughters and the Prophet replied the same. (*Bukhari*) At another time, a woman approached the Prophet and asked him who was guaranteed to enter Paradise, and he said, "The Prophets, the martyrs, children and baby girls (who had been murdered by their pagan fathers by) burying them alive in the sand." (*Ibn Abi Hatim*) In addition, Islamic theology teaches that all children above the age of four months in the womb until before the age of puberty will go to Paradise, (if they happen to pass away), regardless of whether or not their parents were Muslims.

[1894] The *scrolls* are the records of deeds for each person. The Prophet even once said, "Do not think that any good deed is too small (to be important,) even if it is just greeting your brother with a smile."

[1895] The Prophet is reported to have said that on the Day of Judgment, all the stars and objects of veneration that people worshipped will be thrown into Hell, except for Jesus and Mary, and they would have been thrown into it themselves if they had *accepted* and *enjoyed* the veneration people had offered them. (*Ibn Abi Hatim*) In other words, no true servant of God is responsible if other people start to worship them or overpraise them. In turn this is a warning to secular and religious leaders in all times. When people start to venerate a beloved leader, it can veer off into hero worship. If the person starts to get a 'big head' and see themselves a special and powerful, they 'set themselves up as lords besides god.' No one, not a celebrity, a king, a president, a religious leader, a businessperson or an entertainer should allow themselves to get a big ego because of the praise of others. This is difficult to fight against, because the Shaytan will whisper in the minds of such people (Qur'an 7:16-17), like he did in the ears of the first couple, that they are better than others. (Qur'an 7:20-22) In reality, we are all the same under our clothes and piles of money, and we all must grow old and whither away, provided fate doesn't take us young first!

[1896] The scholars differ as to what is being referenced here with the Arabic word *khunnas* or withdrawers, with some saying it means stars and others asserting it means planets, especially since the verse continues with these unnamed bodies ultimately hiding or going out of sight. (I have chosen a compromise rendering.) The planets and stars in the night sky have a variety of observable motions based upon the time of year, the position of the earth, the speed of the individual planet or star relative to the earth's orbital speed around the sun, etc. Sometimes they seem to follow an east to west motion across the sky; other times they decline in their orbit, and still other times they are hidden behind the path of other objects. These erratic-seeming motions are explained in the scientific principle known as Kepler's Second Law of Planetary Motion.

[1897] The Arabic word used here denotes both coming and going, as well as sneaking in and stealth. (Ibn Faris)

[1898] Like a soft breath, the dawn is ushered in and gently dispels the darkness of night.

(By these tokens know that) this
is the speech of an honored messenger. [1899] [19]

He has authority and status
before the Lord of the throne; [20]
he is to be obeyed and trusted.   [21]

Your companion is not delirious, [1900]
nor is he deceived, [22]
for he certainly saw the (angel of revelation)
on a clear horizon. [1901] [23]

He doesn't hesitate in disclosing
knowledge of the unseen, [24]
nor are these the words
of an accursed devil. [25]

So which way will you go? [26]
This is no less than a reminder
to all the worlds, [27]

For anyone who seeks
to walk the straight path [28]
– but not as you will, as Allah wills,
the Lord of All the Worlds. [29]

[1899] The honored messenger is usually construed to mean the angel Gabriel from whom the Prophet
was getting Allah's messages.
[1900] *Majnoon*: delirious, crazy, possessed by a jinn.
[1901] Also see 53:5-18.

The Dividing

82 Al Infitar
Early Meccan Period

This chapter succinctly asks people in general to confront their own faith, or lack of it, and to understand that Allah is not unmindful of what they do. This was an important point to make to the pagans of Mecca, who believed that Allah was remote and uncaring and that their idols were more immediate and real. The vivid opening lines describing the Last Day were commented upon especially by the Prophet when he said, "Whoever wants to experience Resurrection Day like one who will really be seeing it with his own eyes should read chapters (and then he said the names of chapters 81, 82 and 84)." (*Ahmad, Tirmidhi*)

In the Name of Allah,
the Compassionate, the Merciful

When the skies are divided [1]

and the stars are dispersed, [2]

When the oceans overflow [3]
and the graves are overturned... [4]

Then every soul will know
what it has sent ahead
and left behind. [1902] [5]

O human!
What has lured you away
from your Generous Lord [6]
- the One Who created you (in the womb),
balanced you (in proportion),
infused within you with a sense of justice [7]
and structured you in whatever form He wished? [8]

Oh, but no! Not so!

Even still you deny the judgment! [1903] [9]
(Know then) that guardians
(are appointed to watch) over you. [10]

[1902] This is a Qur'anic euphemism that refers to the deeds one has accumulated in this life and sent ahead for Judgment Day, and what was left behind or undone. In other words, the deeds that one has earned for himself and the deeds or responsibilities he has missed.

[1903] Hasan al-Basri aptly put it this way: "How many people are there whose shortcomings are concealed (by Allah); yet, they're so thankless!"

(They're) the noble recorders [11]
who know everything you do. [1904] [12]

The righteous will be in ecstasy, [13]
even as the insolent will roast in the flames. [14]
They're going to enter it on the Day of Judgment, [15]
and they won't be able to avoid it. [16]

So how can you appreciate
(the magnitude) of the Day of Judgment, [17]
and how can you understand
what the Day of Judgment will mean? [18]

That day,
no soul will be able
to help another at all.

(On that day),
all power to command
will belong to Allah alone. [1905] [19]

[1904] The Prophet said that the angels only look away when a person is using the bathroom, is engaged in intimate relations or is naked. As such, he asked Muslims to take their showers in private behind a curtain out of respect for them. *(Ibn Abi Hatim)*

[1905] The classical writer, Abu al-Atahiyah (d. 828), once wrote a poem addressed to the Abbasid Caliph Harun ar-Rashid of Baghdad (d. 809), "Live securely as you wish; the palace heights are safe enough. With pleasures flooding day and night, the smooth proves sweeter than the rough. But when your breath begins to clog in sharp contractions in your lungs, then know for certain, my dear sire, that your life was as pointless as an idle tongue."

The Shortchanger

83 At-Tatfeef aka Al Mutaffifīn
Late Meccan Period

This chapter was revealed in the late Meccan period, though verses 1-4 were revealed just after the Prophet arrived in Medina and found many merchants in the marketplace boldly cheating their customers by weighing wrongly and measuring short when they packed up people's orders of grain and other things, while being strict in getting their own full account at the time of payment. (*Nisa'i*) Muhammad was always particular about honest business practices. To drive the point home - that cheating and fraud are heinous sins - the remainder of this chapter proceeds to paint a vivid picture of the ultimate triumph of the faithful believers who are honest.

In the Name of Allah,
the Compassionate, the Merciful

And now a warning to people who shortchange, [1906] [1]

who want every last item from people when they're owed, [2]
but who shortchange when they have to pay. [3]

Don't they realize they're going to be resurrected [4]
on a momentous day [5] - the day when all people must stand
before the Lord of All the Worlds? [1907] [6]

But no!

The account of the decadent
is preserved in the Crevice. [1908] [7]

And how can you understand
what the Crevice is? [8]
It's a written record. [9]

[1906] Although the opening of this chapter is primarily about money and goods used in trade, 'Umar ibn al-Khattab once used the term shortchange with regards to a person cheating Allah out of His due. In the mosque, 'Umar saw a man rushing through his prayers and not completing his bowing and prostration. He told the man afterwards, "You're shortchanging the rights of Allah." (*Muwatta*)

[1907] The Prophet said, "On the day when all humanity must stand before the Lord of All the Worlds, some of them will be covered in their sweat (from nervousness) up to their ears." (*Bukhari*)

[1908] The term *sijjin*, or crevice, means a very narrow, confined and dark place. It is also used in some *hadith* reports to describe the deep crevices in Hellfire that the wicked souls will be put into to suffer. (*Ibn Kathir*) The Prophet is reported to have said that the narrow crevices of Hell are located under the seventh layer of the earth. (*Ma'ariful Qur'an*)

Then ruin that day to those who denied [10]
and (ruin) to those who called
the Day of Judgment a lie, [11]
for only the rebellious
and sinful deny (the truth). [12]

Those Who Deny

𝓦hen Our (revealed) verses
are read to one of them, he says,
"Tales from long ago!" [1909] [13]

Not so! No way!

Their hearts are rusted
by the burden (of the sins)
they've earned. [1910] [14]

Not so!

They're going to be veiled from
the (grace) of their Lord that day. [15]

And then they'll be forced
to enter the raging blaze. [16]

Then they'll be told,
"This is what you were so quick to deny!" [17]

The Account of the Righteous

𝒪n the contrary, the account of the righteous
is preserved in the Summit. [18]

And how can you understand what the Summit is? [1911] [19]

It's (also) a written record, [20]
witnessed over by those nearest (to Allah). [21]

[1909] This passage references what the vile enemy of the Prophet, an-Nadr ibn al-Harith, used to tell his fellow Meccans whenever he saw Muhammad preaching. An-Nadr also used to incite the Meccans to attack the Muslims in their midst and do harm to them. This hateful propaganda resulted in many Muslims suffering persecution and even death. (*Asbab ul-Nuzul*)

[1910] The Prophet said, "When a servant (of Allah) commits a sin, a stain appears on his heart. Then if that person repents, then his heart is cleansed of it. If he repeats the sin once more, then the size of the stain is increased until his heart is completely covered with it. That is the covering that Allah mentions in the Qur'an: 'But no! Their hearts are rusted by the burden (of the sins) they've earned.'" (*Ahmad, Tirmidhi*) Hasan al-Basri (d. 737) said, "Repeated sinning makes the heart go blind until it ultimately dies."

[1911] The *Summit* is thought to be a place in the seventh heaven, beneath the throne of Allah, where the records of the righteous are kept. (*Ma'ariful Qur'an*)

The righteous will be in ecstasy; [22]
gathered upon thrones, they'll be looking around. [23]

You'll recognize the glow of delight
upon their faces. [24]

They'll be served the finest wine sealed [25]
– sealed with musk. [1912]

The ambitious should take note (of this delight)
and exert themselves (to achieve it), [26]
for (it's a drink) mixed with pure bliss, [27]
drawn from a fountain from which
those nearest (to Allah) may drink. [28]

The wicked used to laugh at those who believed. [29]

They winked at each other whenever they passed by, [30]
then hurried back to their associates to laugh and joke, [31]
and whenever they saw them they would say,
"Truly, these are the ones who got it all wrong!" [1913] [32]

However, they weren't sent to look after them! [33]

Yet, on this day, it will be the believers
who will scoff at the faithless [34] from high thrones. [35]

Won't the faithless then be fully repaid
for (the evil) they did? [36]

[1912] This special drink is so pleasurable that it, in itself, is considered one of Paradise's more special rewards. The Prophet once said, "Whoever gives a thirsty Muslim a drink, Allah will give him the sealed nectar to drink. Whoever feeds a hungry Muslim, Allah will feed him from the fruits of Paradise. Whoever clothes a needy Muslim, Allah will clothe him with the green silk of Paradise." (*Ahmad*)

[1913] The Prophet said, "There are five sins, for which there are five punishments. The one who breaks his word, Allah will allow his enemy to gain control over him. The community that abandons the prohibitions of Allah and chooses instead to follow their own ways, then poverty will afflict them in general. The community among which promiscuity and unlawful sex becomes common, Allah will afflict them with epidemics and diseases. Those who shortchange in measurements and weights, Allah will afflict them with deprivation and famine. Those who refrain from paying their required charity (*zakah*), then Allah will withhold rain from them." (*Bazzar, Qurtubi*. A similar report is from *Tabarani*, which adds that wide-spread mortality will be common in a community that deals in interest money.)

The Tearing

84 Al Inshiqaq
Early Meccan Period

This very early chapter was revealed after Islam's main teachings had been made public, but before the period of persecution by the Meccans began. Its message is simple and direct and is one of those chapters whose main purpose was to introduce to the pagans of the city the concept of accountability for one's faith in Allah (or lack thereof) and one's life's work, whether dedicated to good or evil. The concluding question as to why people are not accepting the Qur'an when its author is Allah, Himself, is evidence that at this stage in Muhammad's ministry he faced mere verbal rejection and ridicule from his peers.

In the Name of Allah,
the Compassionate, the Merciful

When the sky is torn away [1]
by the will of its Lord, which it must obey, [2]

When the earth is leveled [1914] [3]
and casts out all it contains [4]
by the will of its Lord, which it must obey... [5]

Then, all you humans, who've been struggling
on the journey back towards your Lord,
will finally meet Him! [1915] [6]

Then, the one who receives his record in his right hand [7]
will soon have an easy review. [1916] [8]

He'll return to his people celebrating... [9]

But the one who receives his record
from behind his back [10]
will soon wish for oblivion [11]

[1914] *Lit.* the earth will be stretched until it becomes a smooth level plain with no mountains or valleys.
[1915] Angel Gabriel went to the Prophet one day and said, "O Muhammad, live as long as you want, but one day you will meet your death. Love whomever you want, but one day you will have to leave them. Do whatever you want, but one day you will have to answer for it. Remember that the honor of a believer is prayer at night, and his source of pride is in not being dependent on others." (*Hakim*)
[1916] One day A'ishah heard the Prophet supplicating, "O Allah, give me an easy assessment." She asked, "What is an easy assessment?" The Prophet explained, "It means that Allah will merely glance over the record of deeds and forgive the sins within, but, A'ishah, whoever is going to have to answer for their record is ruined!" (*Ahmad*)

as he's driven into the raging blaze. [12] [12]

Truly, he spent his life
celebrating with his people, [13]
never thinking he'd be (brought
before his Creator) in the end. [14]

But no!

His Lord was always watching him. [15]

And so by the fleeting afterglow of sunset, [16]
by the night and what it conceals [17]
and by the moon as it grows full... [18]

(Know by these same tokens)
that you're certainly progressing in stages. [19]

So what's the matter with them that they don't believe, [20]
and why won't they bow themselves in wonder
upon hearing the Qur'an read to them? [1918] [21]

But no!

The faithless just deny it outright! [1919] [22]

Allah knows their innermost thoughts, [23]
so give them the 'good news' of a painful doom! [1920] [24]

However, for those who believe and do what's morally right,
there's a reward that will never fail. [25]

[1917] Whenever A'ishah, the Prophet's wife, heard something she didn't understand, she used to ask about it until it was made clear to her. A'ishah reports that once the Prophet said, "Whoever will be interrogated (on Judgment Day concerning his record) will surely be punished." A'ishah said, "Doesn't Allah say, '(he) *will soon have an easy assessment?*'" [84:8] The Prophet replied, "This refers only to the presentation of the record, but whoever will be *interrogated* about his record will be ruined." (*Bukhari*)
[1918] After reading this verse it is customary for the one who has faith in Allah to prostrate himself on the floor and praise Allah. (*Ma'ariful Qur'an*)
[1919] Muhammad al Ghazali (d. 1111) once wrote, "A worldly-oriented person is like an ant crawling on paper. He sees the black lettering and thinks it was made by a pen and nothing more." (*The Alchemy of Happiness*)
[1920] This is a wordplay against those who deny the message. Their 'good' news is actually what they deny!

The Constellations

85 Al Buruj
Early Meccan Period

There is a lengthy story told by the Prophet, as recorded in the *hadith* collections of *Muslim* and *Ahmad*, that fills in the details about which this chapter makes only passing mention. We can summarize the tale as follows: an old wizard, who worked for Yusuf As'ar Yath'ar, the Jewish king of Yemen (d. 525), also known by his honorific title of *Dhu Nuwas*, wanted an apprentice on whom to pass his dark arts.

A certain young man named 'Abdullah ibn Tamir was chosen, but this young man soon fell under the influence of a Christian monk named Faymun who lived on the road between his village and the wizard's workshop. Every day the youth wound up spending time with both men, and he soon fell in love with the monk's teachings about the One God and pure morality.

Later, after he killed a lion with a stone, ostensibly by invoking the name of the monk's god, the young man once and for all renounced sorcery and became something of an evangelist. He began faith-healing people, and his fame grew throughout the land. News of the young man got back to the palace, and he was finally summoned before the king who disliked his beliefs and conspired to kill him.

After many foiled attempts with execution by bow and arrow, the king was finally able to execute the young man, but not before being tricked into saying (in front of a crowd) that the young man's god was in control of our destiny, as shown by the last arrow finally hitting him fatally. Based upon his popularity, the masses took the deceased young man as a saint and began adopting Christianity. The enraged king ordered the new Christians, especially in Najran, to the north of Yemen proper, to be killed if they did not recant their faith. In one episode, his soldiers dug fire pits and began tossing people in them alive. (According to the Prophet, a young boy comforted his mother as they were both thrown in together.)

One man escaped this carnage and fled to Syria where he informed the Byzantine authorities of what was happening. The Byzantine emperor, in turn, wrote to Ella Asbeha, the King of Abyssinia, to do something. Thus, it was this persecution of the Christians that prompted the Christian Abyssinians to invade and depose the Jewish dynasty. This invasion under a general named Azyat, happened sometime between the years 524 and 525 CE and brought down the rule of Dhu Nuwas, leaving a line of Christian, Ethiopian-controlled puppet governors in his place who began to persecute Jews and pagans. (In 575, at the behest of Jewish entreaties, the Persians invaded Yemen and put their own client ruler (Abraha) in place, and chapter 105 of the Qur'an later comes into play about him!) It is said that Dhu Nuwas fled the Ethiopians by sea but drowned when his ship capsized.

In the Name of Allah,
the Compassionate, the Merciful

*B*y the sky filled with constellations, [1921] [1]

by the Promised Day [2]
and by the witness and all that it witnesses… [1922] [3]

(By these same tokens know that)
the pit-diggers will be ruined, [4]
(for they tried to destroy the faithful)
with a well-fed fire. [5]

They gathered around it [6] and witnessed
what they were doing to the faithful. [7]

They persecuted them for no other reason
than that they had faith in Allah,
the Exalted and Praiseworthy, [8]
the One Whose dominion extends
over the heavens and the earth,
and Allah is a witness to everything. [9]

Without a doubt, those who persecute
the believing men and the believing women like that,
and who don't repent (of their evil),
will be punished with the fires of Hell,
and in that manner they'll be punished
with (an even greater) blaze! [10]

While those who believe and do what's morally right,
(they) will have gardens beneath which rivers flow
 – *and that's the greatest success of all!* [1923]   [11]

For sure your Lord has a firm grip. [12]
He starts (every form of creation)
and restores (life to the dead). [13]

He's the Forgiving and the Loving - [14]
the Lord of the throne of glory [15]
and Doer of all He intends! [16]

[1921] The term used here for constellations, *buruj*, also means gleaming castles, and thus the constellations are romantically called gleaming castles in the sky. Some minor exegetes in the early medieval period thought this verse should be interpreted to mean that there were castles in the sky in which angels lived, but no major commentator ever accepted this view. (*Ma'ariful Qur'an*)

[1922] According to a *hadith* found both in Ibn Abi Hatim and Tirmidhi, the 'Promised Day' is the Day of Resurrection; the witness is Friday, and the thing it witnesses is the Day of 'Arafah, which takes place during the pilgrimage.

[1923] The Prophet said, "Allah, the Exalted, has declared, 'Child of Adam! Verily, I shall continue to pardon you as long as you call upon Me and hope for My forgiveness. Whatever your sins may be, I care not. Child of Adam, even if your sins should pile up as high as the sky and you asked for My forgiveness, I would forgive you. Child of Adam, if you came to Me with an earth full of sins but met Me not holding anything as My equal, I would come to you with an earth full of forgiveness.'" (*Tirmidhi*)

Have you ever heard of the stories of the hordes [17]
of Pharaoh and of the (people of) Thamud? [18]

But no!

The faithless still persist in their denial. [19]
Yet, Allah is right behind them! [20]

Regardless (of their rejection of it),
this is a Noble Qur'an [21]
(that's forever preserved)
on a protected tablet. [1924] [22]

[1924] Most commentators hold that this "protected tablet" is the original source book of all of Allah's revelations. In other words, it is Allah's Own Book of Decrees and law. Also see 13:39 where this overarching book is referred to as "the Mother of the Book."

The Night Star

86 At-Tariq
Early Meccan Period

This is an extremely early revelation, as evidenced by its basic theme of introducing the concept of accountability for one's actions. It is said that it was revealed while the Prophet was having a dinner provided by his uncle, Abu Talib. A shooting star streaked down across the sky, and Abu Talib was frightened. "What does it mean?" he asked in fear. Being a pagan, he naturally thought that such phenomena brought with it bad omens. The Prophet merely answered that it was a proof of Allah's existence. Abu Talib became intrigued, and this chapter was then revealed, which the Prophet recited. It is interesting how the various early Meccan chapters begin with a call to nature and then change their focus to moral issues. This was an important technique to reach a people who were already filled with the wonders of nature all around them.

In the Name of Allah,
the Compassionate, the Merciful

*B*y the sky and the visitor by night, [1]

and how can you understand
what the visitor by night is? [2]

It's the bright star (that pierces
through the midnight sky). [1925] [3]

(By this same token, know that) there is no soul
without a guardian set over it. [1926] [4]

Now let (every) human being consider from what he was created, [5]
for he was created from a squirted drop of fluid [6]
emanating from between the spine and the rib cage. [1927] [7]

Truly, (the One Who created people in this way once before)
can surely bring them back again [8]

[1925] This star of piercing brightness is alternatively understood to be either a generic reference to starlight or a reference to a specific star such as Sirius, which would have seemed to be brighter than many of the more distant stars in that quadrant of space. The idea, of course, is that in the same way we see the stars each night above us, so, too, are the angels watching us.

[1926] There is a tradition traced to the Prophet in which he stated that there are 360 angels that watch over us each day and that they steer dangers away from us that we were not decreed to experience. (*Ma'ariful Qur'an*) Also see 13:11.

[1927] The complete system of seminal fluid emission involves many conjoined processes in the lower abdomen, such as the prostate gland, glands attached to the urinary tract, and also other glandular systems whose roots are in the area described here in this verse.

on the day when all secrets will be exposed, [9]
when they'll have no power or anyone to help them. [10]

And so, by the sky as it springs back, [1928] [11]

and by the splitting of the earth (under pressure), [1929] [12]
truly, this speech sorts (the truth from falsehood), [13]
and it's not some kind of game. [14]

(Though the faithless) continue
to weave their schemes, [15]
I'm making a plan, as well. [16]

So give the faithless some time,
and leave them alone (for a while). [17]

[1928] This could refer to the elastic nature of space, or to the annual rotation of all the constellations throughout the course of the year. Some commentators have proposed the idea that this can alternatively refer to the returning seasonal rains. (*Ma'ariful Qur'an*)

[1929] Different meanings can be assumed for the "splitting" of the earth. It can mean the opening of the soil by growing plants, or it can be understood to be the opening made in the earth by springs, or pressure from earthquakes and the like. The classical commentators have offered different interpretations.

The Most High

87 Al A'la
Early Meccan Period

This is one of the earliest chapters of the Qur'an to be revealed. Verses 6-7 even make mention of the fact that Muhammad was unused to getting these supernatural messages. Thus, he was afraid he would forget them or mix them up. He is reassured here and in two other chapters of the Qur'an [20:114, 75:16-19] that he need not worry about it, for Allah will attune his mind and cause him to remember. Then Muhammad is comforted and told he will gain peace of mind eventually, a sure sign that Muhammad was under stress from the vindictive persecution of his people. The truth of his message is given continuity with previous prophets in the mention of Moses and Abraham.

In the Name of Allah,
the Compassionate, the Merciful

Glorify the name [1930] of your Lord, the Most High, [1931] [1]

the One Who creates and completes (all things), [2]
determines (their length) and directs (them to their end). [3]

He's the One Who brings out the lush (green) pastures, [4]
(and He's the One Who) reduces them to scrub. [5]

We'll teach you to recite (this message),
so you won't forget anything, [6] except as Allah wills,
for He knows what's out in the open as well as what's hidden away. [7]

We'll soon make your path (towards peace of mind) an easy one. [8]
So remind (people), for it may be to their benefit. [1932] [9]

Whoever fears (displeasing his Lord) will take the reminder, [10]
while the miserable wretch will avoid it. [11]

[1930] The classical commentator, al-Qurtubi, was of the opinion that the use of the term *ism* (name) here is actually a euphemism for Allah's very being and existence. In that case, we would understand the verse to mean, 'Glorify the very *existence* of your Lord...' (*Ma'ariful Qur'an*)

[1931] After this verse was revealed to him, the Prophet ordered his followers to begin saying a variation of it in their prayers whenever they bowed prostrate on the ground (in a position called *sujud*). In Arabic it is said as, '*Subhana rabbi ul-a'la.*' It means, 'Glory to my Lord, the Most High.' (*Ahmad*) When this verse is heard outside of prayer, it is commendable to say the above phrase, as well. (*Ma'ariful Qur'an*)

[1932] Abu Bakr once said, "There are people who forgot that their lifetime would come to an end. They kept procrastinating about doing good deeds until death came to them. Beware of being like them. Strive hard and hasten towards safety, for a serious matter is coming to you, and your lifespan will quickly pass. Be aware of death and learn lessons from what happened to your fathers, sons and brothers (who have passed away)."

He is the one who will enter the blazing fire, [12]
wherein there is neither living nor dying. [13]

And so it is that the one who tries
to improve himself shall prosper. [1933] [14]
He remembers the name of his Lord and prays. [15]

But no!

It seems that (most of) you
still prefer the life of this world, [16]
even though the next life
is better and more lasting. [17]

Yet, (these truths were revealed) in ancient scrolls before [18]
- in the scrolls of Abraham and of Moses. [1934] [19]

[1933] Jalaluddin Rumi (d. 1273) once wrote, "Yesterday I was clever, so I wanted to change the world. Today I am wide, so I am changing myself."

[1934] A companion named Abu Dharr once asked the Prophet, "Messenger of Allah, has anything from the scrolls of Abraham or Moses been sent down to you?" He replied, "(Yes,) Abu Dharr, such and such verses were revealed." Then he began to read this passage. (*Taysir al-'usul ila Jami` al-'usul*) In a related account, the Prophet actually gave several examples of some of the lines contained in those previous revelations, one of which is, "I'm amazed that there are people who know they're going to die; yet, they live without a care." (*Ma'ariful Qur'an*)

The Overwhelming

88 Al Ghashīyah
Early Meccan Period

This chapter opens with a statement of shock value: something is going to happen that will overwhelm all it touches. Then the verses proceed to describe the state of people in both Hellfire and Heaven. The implication is that there are only two possible fates after Judgment Day. Allah's signs are then offered as proof for this concept. The chapter closes with the instruction to Muhammad that while he must preach, he needn't worry if people listen or not. That is for Allah to handle.

In the Name of Allah,
the Compassionate, the Merciful

*H*ave you heard about

the overwhelming (event)? [1]

It's the day when some
faces will be downcast, [2]
looking worn and haggard [1935] [3]
as they're herded into a raging fire. [4]

They'll quench their thirst from a boiling spring, [5]
having no other food than bitter thorn, [6]
which neither nourishes nor satisfies. [1936] [7]

(Other) faces that day will be overjoyed [8]
and pleased with their result. [9]

(They'll reside) within high gardens, [10]
hearing no foolish talk. [11]

[1935] According to Hasan al-Basri, when 'Umar ibn al-Khattab toured Syria (as part of his duties as caliph,) he met an old Christian monk who lived in abject poverty. He had a wasted and withered body on account of his fasting and constant prayer. At his sight, 'Umar began to weep, and he said, "I feel sorry for this old man's condition. This poor man has worked so hard and kept himself in constant readiness to die for his goal (of seeking Allah's pleasure). In the end, he couldn't accomplish it." Then he recited these verses [88:2-3]. (*Ma'ariful Qur'an*)

[1936] When some of the pagans of Mecca heard verse six, they laughed and boasted that their camels eat bitter thorn (a kind of desert scrub plant) and that they're healthy and fat. Verse seven was revealed in response to make the point that the bitter thorn of Hellfire is not like that on earth. (*Ma'ariful Qur'an*)

A bubbling spring will flow within, [1937] [12]
and high thrones of honor will be there, too, [13]
with cups placed [14] and cushions arranged [15]
on rich carpets spread out. [16]

Don't (the skeptics) ever gaze
at the moisture-laden clouds [1938]
and ponder over their formation [17]
or at the sky and how
it's been raised up so high [18]
or at the mountains and how
they've been firmly set [19]
or at the earth and how
it's been laid out? [20]

So remind them,
for you're truly one to remind, [21]
even though you're not in charge (of their hearts). [22]

If anyone rejects (the truth) and turns away, [23]
Allah will punish him with a punishment most severe. [24]

Truly, they'll come back to Us, [25]
and then We're going to review (all the records). [26]

[1937] The Prophet once described Paradise by saying, "The rivers of Paradise will flow from hills of musk. Paradise will have lofty thrones with *houries* (mates) sitting on them. When the people of Paradise want to sit on the thrones, they will come down from them. They will also enjoy delightful drinks from cups placed in an orderly fashion."

[1938] The Arabic term *ibil* can mean either puffy rain clouds or camels, depending on the context (*Lisan al-'Arab*, etc.) I have chosen to render it as clouds given the context of the items that follow (such as the sky and the mountains). Either choice is correct, though some translators prefer the use of the word 'camel.'

The Dawn

89 Al Fajr
Early Meccan Period

This is one of the earliest chapters of the Qur'an that the Prophet received. The evidence for this is the mention of the 'Ad and Thamud nations and what became of them as a result of their disobeying Allah. The veiled message to the Meccan pagans, who had recently begun persecuting the first Muslims, was that they, too, are not beyond Allah's power to punish. The reader is then asked to consider the wonders of Allah's creation as concrete proof of Allah's existence. An indictment of the fickle and thankless nature of people then follows with a comparison of what will happen ultimately to the wicked and the righteous. It must be remembered that this concept of an *afterlife*, and even further of reward and punishment for one's record of deeds, was entirely new to the Meccans who believed quite sincerely that there was nothing beyond death for anyone.

In the Name of Allah,
the Compassionate, the Merciful

By the dawn, [1] by the ten (sacred) nights, [1939] [2]

by the even and the odd, [3]
and by the cycle of night and its passing, [4]
for those who have sense is there any evidence
more convincing than this? [5]

Don't you see how your Lord dealt
with the people of 'Ad [6]
from (the city of) Iram,
of the tall towers [7] –
(a city) unlike any other built in the land? [8]

And with the (people of) Thamud,
(who lived in cities) made of cut rock? [9]

And what of Pharaoh, master of legions? [10]
All of them acted like tyrants in the land [11]
and caused so much chaos and disorder. [12]

And so then your Lord (brought them down)
with crippling disasters, [13] for your Lord is always watchful. [14]

[1939] The ten sacred nights are the first ten days of the month of *Hajj*. The Prophet said, "No worship is better than the worship done in the first ten days of the month of *Hajj*." One of the companions asked, "Not even *jihad* in the way of Allah?" The Prophet then answered, "No, not even that, except for the one who goes out struggling with his life and wealth, and who returns with neither of them." (*Bukhari*)

Now as for (the average) person,
whenever his Lord generously tests him through honor and prosperity,
he boasts, *"Even My Lord is good to me!"* [15]

Yet, whenever he's tested by having his resources restricted,
he laments, *"Even My Lord is against me!"* [16]

Not so!

There's no way (you can blame Allah for your troubles,)
when you're not even generous with orphans, [17]
nor do you urge each other to feed the poor. [18]

You waste your inheritance eagerly, [19]
and on top of that you crave
wealth more than anything else! [20]

But no!

When the earth is ground to powder [21]
and your Lord comes with hosts of angels in ranks, [22]
and when Hellfire will be brought very close on that day,
then on that very day, (every) human being will realize
(what he's done), but how will it help him then? [23]

(In shame) he will cry,
*"Oh, the misfortune! If only I would've sent something
ahead (to prepare) for this (new) life!"* [24]

On that day, no one will punish like Allah will punish, [25]
and no one will bind like He will bind. [26]

"O soul at rest," (the righteous will be told), [27]
*"return to your Lord completely satisfied,
(even as He is) completely satisfied with you. [28]
So enter now, and be among My servants. [29]
Enter now, (and come) into My Paradise."* [1940] [30]

[1940] When Abu Bakr heard these last two lines he said, "What an excellent address that is." Then the Prophet remarked, "It will be said to you, too." (*Ma'ariful Qur'an*) Some scholars believe that these will be the words that the angels tell a believing soul when they take him or her at the time of death. This view is supported by a *hadith* report that mentions the same. (*Ma'ariful Qur'an*)

The Land

90 Al Balad
Early Meccan Period

The pagans of Mecca, after having been introduced to Islam by Muhammad, resolved to oppose his message by any means necessary. They began with simple verbal abuse and slander and then graduated to assaulting him and his fledgling followers physically. This chapter makes an appeal to the Meccans, in the name of the city of Mecca, Muhammad's hometown. How can they treat a native son so poorly, especially when his call is to goodness? The immorality of greed and cruelty is then compared with the path of spiritual peace- the very path towards which the Prophet was calling his detractors.

In the Name of Allah,
the Compassionate, the Merciful

I swear by this land, [1]

and you belong to this land, [1941] [2]
and I swear by the bond
between a parent and a child... [3]

And so it was that We created human beings
to labor on in toil and hardship. [1942] [4]

Does he think there's no power over him, [5]
and while he may boast, "I have wealth to waste!" [1943] [6]
does he think no one's watching him? [7]

Haven't We given him a pair of eyes, [8]
a tongue and a pair of lips [1944] [9]

[1941] The 'land' in question is considered to be Mecca and its surrounding countryside. The idea is that Muhammad had the right to preach in that ostensibly open city, even though the Meccans tried to silence him, for he was a free citizen (*hillun*) in a free land bound by no unfairly imposed restrictions. The next verse, which alludes to the bond of parents and their children, seems to suggest that bringing Allah's truth to Mecca is a natural thing given that the Ka'bah, a shrine dedicated to Him, is located there.

[1942] This refers to the nature of life in this precarious world. We must work every day for our daily resources and labor on in weary toil. Those who make no effort to secure their daily needs will perish. The Prophet once remarked that if a person has his health, some food to eat and some clothes to wear, then it's like he has all the riches in the world.

[1943] The Prophet said, "True wealth is not having an abundance of possessions. True wealth is a contented heart." (*Bukhari, Muslim*)

[1944] The Prophet said that Allah, Himself, said, "O Son of Adam, I have given you so many advantages that you cannot even count them all, nor are you able to thank Me enough for them. I gave you two

and then shown him
the two roads (of good and evil)? [10]

Yet, he makes no effort
to travel the Steep Road, [11]
and how can you understand
what the Steep Road is? [12]

It's the freeing of a slave [13]
or the feeding on a hungry day [14]
of orphaned relatives [1945] [15]
or of the poor person lying in the dust. [16]

Then he'll be with the believers
who teach each other perseverance and compassion. [17]
Those are the Companions of the Right. [1946] [18]

Those who reject Our signs
are the Companions of the Left. [1947] [19]
They'll have fire engulfing them completely. [1948] [20]

---

eyes and eyelids, so look at what you're allowed to see, and if you come across forbidden things, then close them. I gave you a tongue and a mouth to cover it, so say what you're allowed to say and hold your tongue from speaking about forbidden things." (*Hadith Qudsi*)

[1945] The Prophet said, "The hand that gives is better than the hand that receives, and begin (your charitable giving) with your dependents." (*Tabarani*) The famed medieval poet, Abu A'la of Ma'arri (d. 1057), once wrote, "You strut in piety the while you take that pilgrimage to Mecca. Now beware, for starving relatives befoul the air, and curse, O fool, the threshold you forsake." (*Diwan of Abu A'la*)

[1946] There is no discrimination in Islam against people who are right or left handed. The figurative language used follows common Arabic idiom, which favored the right side as the side of enlightenment and virtue. For a further description of the Companions of the Right see 56:27-40.

[1947] For a further description of the Companions of the Left, see 56:41-56.

[1948] 'Abdullah ibn Mas'ud (d. 653), as quoted in *Ibn Kathir*, *al-Qurtubi* and *at-Tabari*, explained what he thought the meaning of this verse was. He said, "When the companions of Hellfire are thrown into it, each of them will be put in a separate box of fire, so that he won't see anyone else being punished in Hellfire save for himself." Then he recited the following verse: "For them will be nothing more in there than weeping and crushing silence." [21:100]

The Sun

91 Ash-Shamms
Early Meccan Period

Opposition to Islam had been growing among the pagans in the early years of Muhammad's ministry in Mecca. This chapter brought to the Meccans' attention a previous civilization, that of the Thamud, who also rejected their prophet and suffered for it. The implication to the Meccans must have been that if they didn't listen to *this* prophet, then the fate of the ancient Thamud would be their own.

In the Name of Allah,
the Compassionate, the Merciful

*B*y the sun and its radiance, [1]

by the moon as it trails along, [1949] [2]
by the day as it brightens, [3]
by the night as it covers up, [4]
by the sky and what built it, [5]

By the earth and its wide expanse, [6]
and by the soul and its balanced (nature) [7]
and its innate awareness (of right and wrong)... [1950] [8]

(By the same token, know that) the one
who purifies his soul shall prosper, [1951] [9]
while he who corrupts it shall fail. [1952] [10]

The (people of) Thamud
rejected (this truth) in their audacity. [11]

[1949] Alternatively, the moon reflects the sun's light. This is how many early scholars such as ar-Razi (d. 1209) and the *hadith* specialist Muhammad al-Farra' Baghawi (d. 1122) understood this verse and its relationship to the sun mentioned in verse 91:1.

[1950] Whenever the Prophet was reciting verses 7-8 of this chapter (outside of the ritual prayer), he would stop and supplicate, saying, "O Allah! Grant awareness to my soul! You are the guardian and master over it and the best One to make it pure." (*Ma'ariful Qur'an*)

[1951] The Prophet said, "A person is born already inclined to his true nature (as a believer in God), then his parents make him a Jew or a Christian or a Muslim. It's the same way with animals. Each of their offspring is perfect, and you won't see any of them with slit-eared branding marks." (*Bukhari, Muslim*)

[1952] Hasan al Basri once wrote: "The heart becomes corrupt in six ways: (1) by committing sins with the assumption that you will just repent later, (2) seeking knowledge and not applying it, (3) practicing (your religion) without sincerity, (4) eating the sustenance of Allah without appreciating Him, (5) not being pleased with the share Allah has given you, and (6) burying the dead without learning from them." – (Recorded by *Jam'i*)

The worst man among them
rose up (to do an evil deed). [1953] [12]

Their messenger of Allah had told them,
"This camel belongs to Allah,
so let her drink (at the wells)." [13]

Then they called him an impostor,
and (the wicked man) cruelly maimed her.

So their Lord annihilated
all of them equally for their crime, [14]

And He's not afraid
of the consequences
(of His actions). [15]

[1953] 'Abdullah ibn Zam'a narrates that he was listening to a Friday sermon being delivered by the Prophet, and he mentioned in his speech the she-camel and the man who killed it. The Prophet recited verse twelve and then said, "He was a tough man, unusually strong, and he had the protection of his people - a man like Zam'a's father – he went forward (and killed it)." (*Bukhari*)

The Night

92 Al-Layl
Early Meccan Period

This is one of earliest chapters of the Qur'an to be revealed. It is something of a mirror image of the preceding chapter and reiterates every person's responsibility to choose the moral course of his life. A unique concept is introduced with regards to charity: it should be given without any thought to being repaid. The practice in virtually all human societies is to use charity as a way to increase influence and to ensure future favors. This chapter suggests that Allah's knowledge of what you did is sufficient, and that makes your charity completely altruistic in every sense of the word.

In the Name of Allah,
the Compassionate, the Merciful

By the cover of night, [1]

by the day as it shines bright, [2]
and by the creation of male and female, [3]
truly, varied are the goals (which you seek). [4]

And so for the one who gives (in charity),
guards himself (against evil), [5]
and who promotes goodness, [6]
We'll smooth (his path) to an easy end. [1954] [7]

For the greedy miser,
who thinks he's in need of nothing [8]
and who disregards goodness, [9]
We'll smooth (his path) to a miserable end. [1955] [10]

[1954] The Prophet once said, "There are none among you who don't have their place in Hell or in Paradise already reserved." Someone asked, "Messenger of Allah, should we then count on what has already been decided for us and abandon all our actions?" He replied, "Continue to act, because things come easy for those (whose nature is) made for them; good actions come easy for (one who naturally) does good, and evil actions come easy for (one who is) unfortunate." He then recited verses 5-11 of this chapter. (*Bukhari, Muslim*) In other words, Allah knows our future, but we do not. Therefore, we must live our lives and strive as we can. The Prophet did report that Allah can change our slated future if we supplicate to Him frequently, and He knows if He will change our course of action. Thus, our faith, sincerity and actions definitely do count for us.

[1955] The Prophet said, "Allah has forbidden you from the following things: to disobey your mother, to bury your baby daughters alive, to be unmindful of what you owe to others (in charity) and to beg from other people. Allah hates it if you do these things: engage in useless talk like backbiting, or that you talk too much about others, ask too many questions (when there is no use for them), and waste money." (*Bukhari*)

What will all his money do for him then,
as he tumbles headlong (into the pit of Hell)? [1956] [11]

Indeed, We've taken it upon Ourselves to provide guidance, [12]
for the end and the beginning belong to Us. [13]

So now, I *am* warning you of a burning fire [1957] [14]
that no one will enter but the most wretched (of all people), [15]
who deny (the truth) and turn away. [16]

The one who was mindful (of his duty to Allah),

however, will be far away from it. [1958] [17]

Such a one purified his wealth (through charity) [18]
and gave no thought to being repaid with favors. [19]

His only concern was seeking
the approving gaze of his Lord, Most High. [20]
Soon, he will have the greatest satisfaction! [21]

[1956] Layla Akhyaliyya (d. 704) wrote, "If a person has not lived shamefully, then there is no shame in dying. No person, however safe in life, escapes the tomb. Only time is immortal. No life is favored with immortality here, nor are any dead bodies brought back to life. Every period of youth passes through destruction on its way back to Allah. All my dear friends, though eager to live long, depart in disorder, while spheres (of activity) spin all around them and pass them by."

[1957] Nu'man ibn Bashir reported that he heard the Prophet giving a sermon in the mosque, during the course of which he said, "People! I've warned you against Hellfire! People! I'm warning you against Hellfire!" His voice rose when he said it so that it could be heard outside the walls of the mosque in the marketplace. He repeated it so many times his shawl fell off his shoulders. (*Ahmad*)

[1958] It is said that this passage was revealed with regards to Abu Bakr, who bought the freedom of seven convert slaves from the pagans, including one man named Bilal ibn Rabah. The idol-worshippers began saying that Abu Bakr did it only as a favor for Bilal, who suffered great torture at the hands of his master, and this verse makes the point that Abu Bakr did what he did only for Allah's sake. (*al-Itqān*) Abu Bakr often bought the freedom of slaves who had become Muslims, though mostly he worked to free the weaker ones. His father, who was not yet a Muslim, noticed this and asked him of his peculiar habit of preferring to emancipate women and old slaves in preference to strong young slaves who could be an asset for the Muslims in times of distress. Abu Bakr said, "Father, I'm not freeing them for worldly advantage, but only to win Allah's favor." (*At-Tabari*)

Daybreak

93 Ad-Duha
Early Meccan Period

After the initial few revelations, a pause of several months followed in which Muhammad received no more communications from Allah. He therefore began to feel depressed, thinking that he had done something to anger Allah, an explanation that his wife Khadijah discounted. His fellow Meccans, who were also initially skeptical of his claims, even began to ridicule him, saying, "Your God has forgotten about you." One pagan woman, Umm Jamil, even taunted him during this time, saying, "Has your devil left you alone?" When the revelations began to flow again, these words were designed to assure Muhammad that he had, in fact, not done anything wrong to cause the interruption in revelation.

In the Name of Allah,
the Compassionate, the Merciful

*B*y the brilliance of daybreak [1959] [1]

and by the still of the night, [2]
your Lord hasn't forsaken you,
nor is He displeased. [3]

Your future is brighter than your present, [1960] [4]
for your Lord will soon
grant you (what you truly seek),
and you will be well-pleased. [1961] [5]

[1959] Jalaluddin Rumi (d. 1273) used the opening line of this chapter to weave together a summary of our mission in life. He wrote: "Every moment the voice of Love is calling to us from both left and right. We're destined for Heaven; who will see what's up ahead? We were once in Heaven; we've been the friends of angels. Master, let us return there for it's our homeland. We're even greater than Heaven and higher than the angels! Why aren't we surpassing them both? Our goal is the highest glory of all. Oh, how different are the sources of the material and ethereal worlds! Even though we've come down from there, let's hurry back – what kind of place is this world to stay? The fortune of our youth is our friend; giving up the soul is our business. The leader of our caravan is the chosen one, (Muhammad) – the glory of the world! The sweet scent of this wind is from the curls of his hair. Radiant thoughts of (his compassion) are from a cheek as bright as, 'By the brilliance of daybreak.'" (*Divan*)

[1960] 'Abdullah ibn Mas'ud (d. 653) walked into the Prophet's house while the Prophet happened to be sleeping. As usual, the Prophet was lying on a rough reed mat on the floor. When he woke up and sat up, Ibn Mas'ud noticed the marks from the mat all over his back. He touched one of the marks and said in sorrow, "Messenger of Allah! Why don't you let us spread something soft for you?" The Prophet replied, "What have I to do with this world? I'm like a traveler who rests in the shade of a tree for a while, then gets up and moves on." (*Tirmidhi*)

[1961] The Prophet wanted to be vindicated in the eyes of his fellows – a natural human desire - and to be respected by them. Thus, his ardent wish was for acceptance and success. When verse 5 of this chapter

Didn't He find you an orphan
and shelter you? [1962] [6]

Didn't He find you lost
and show you the way? [1963] [7]

Didn't He find you in need
and make you independent? [1964] [8]

Therefore, don't be harsh with an orphan [9]
nor scoff at the requests (of the poor), [1965] [10]
and continue to declare (the mercy)
and blessings of your Lord. [1966] [11]

was revealed to him, the Prophet is reported to have said, "In that case, I won't be pleased as long as one member of my community remains in the Fire." (*Ma'ariful Qur'an*)

[1962] Muhammad's father died before he was born. His mother passed away when he was about six years old. He then came under the care of his grandfather, but he, too, passed away when the boy was only about eight years old. Then the young Muhammad went to live in his uncle's crowded house. This made Muhammad sensitive to the travails of orphans. He once said that the best house is one in which an orphan is treated with kindness and love, and the worst house is one in which an orphan is being mistreated. (*Bukhari*)

[1963] The Prophet said, "I asked Allah about something that I wished I had never asked about. I said to him, 'There were prophets before me, and You placed the wind under the command of some of them. Some raised the dead to life, like Jesus, the son of Mary...' and on I went. So He revealed to me, 'Didn't I find you an orphan and care for you?' I said, 'Yes.' 'Didn't I find you lost and guide you?' Again I said, 'Yes.' 'Didn't I provide for you?' I replied 'Yes,' yet again. Then He said, 'Didn't We broaden your understanding and free you of the burden...' I said, 'Yes.'" (*Ma'ariful Qur'an*)

[1964] When he married the wealthy widow Khadijah, Muhammad was elevated out of economic uncertainty.

[1965] The Prophet said, "The one who looks after a widow or a poor person is like a struggler who fights for Allah's cause or like a person who prays all night and fasts all day." (*Bukhari*)

[1966] The Prophet said, "Whoever is given a great bounty (from Allah) should mention it, for whoever conceals it is thankless." (*Ahmad*)

The Broadening

94 Ash-Sharh aka Al Inshirah
Early Meccan Period

This chapter was revealed almost immediately after chapter 93 and is considered something of a continuation of the general message to Muhammad in the earliest days of his ministry. It instructs him that he should be brave and look to Allah for strength and inner peace in the face of the difficult task of preaching in a hostile environment.

In the Name of Allah,
the Compassionate, the Merciful

(Muhammad,) didn't We
broaden your understanding [1]
and free you of the burden [2]
that weighed heavily on your back? [1967] [3]
(Didn't We) raise your reputation, as well? [4]

And so it is that every hardship has its relief. [5]
(In spite of everything), hardship always has its relief. [1968] [6]

Therefore, even when you're free (from all your other duties),
remain resolute, [7] and turn attentively towards your Lord. [1969] [8]

[1967] The Prophet once told his followers of a time when he was eleven years old and was out in the hills tending his uncle's sheep. He heard a strange voice from above saying, "Is he the one?" Then he saw two people appear before him with faces so bright and clothes so fine that they looked unworldly. They took hold of his arms and laid him on the ground gently. Then they opened his chest, though the boy felt no pain, nor was there any blood. Then one of them said, "Remove all envy, anger and hatred from it." The other took something that looked like a clot from his heart and threw it away. Then the first one said, "Fill it with love, mercy and affection." Then a shiny silvery thing was put in his chest. Then his chest was sealed back up, and one of the beings yanked his toe and said, "Go and live in peace." The Prophet then told his audience, "After that, I always had a heart filled with mercy towards children and affection towards the elderly." (*Ahmad*)

[1968] A famous Muslim writer once counseled those who feel like hope is gone to consider the following advice: "Do not lose hope in adversity and complain that God singled you out for punishment, letting others off who are guilty of worse sins. Your present state could very well be His intent to elevate your spiritual station; or He could just be testing your faith. Every day that you persevere, you grow closer to perfection. Thus your present despair may be beginning of an infinite blessing." - Shaykh Abdul Qadir Jilani (d. 1166)

[1969] One day the angel Jibra'il (Gabriel) went to the Prophet and said, "Muhammad, live as you wish, for one day you will die. Work as you wish, for you will be repaid accordingly. Love whomever you wish, for you will be separated. Remember that the nobility of the believer is in prayer at night, and his honor is in his independence from people." (*al-Muj'am al-Aswat*)

The Fig

95 At-Teen
Early Meccan Period

This is another short chapter that introduces the concept that every person has a basic responsibility to reform his conduct. The four symbols mentioned in the beginning of this passage (olive, fig, Mount Tur and Mecca) can be interpreted in any number of ways, but the general thread among them is that of integrated destinies and cultural continuity. It is thought that the olive represents Christianity through Jesus, Mount Tur represents Moses, and the secure city (Mecca) represents Muhammad. The designation of the fig is uncertain, and many suggestions have been offered, from Buddha to other lesser known religious figures, though there is no definitive consensus. Other commentators suggest that the fig and the olive are a generic reference to Palestine and Syria – the lands of the ancient prophets.

In the Name of Allah,
the Compassionate, the Merciful

By the fig and the olive, [1]

by the Mountain of Tur, [1970] [2]
and by this city secure... [3]
(By these tokens know that)
We've created the human being
in the best form. [4]

Then We bring him down
to the lowest of the low [5]
- all except for those who believe
and do what's morally right.

For them is a reward that won't expire. [6]

So how can (the coming) judgment be denied? [7]
Isn't Allah the most fit to decide? [1971] [8]

[1970] This would be the mountain, known in Arabic as Mount Tur, to which Prophet Moses brought the Israelites after leading them out of Egypt. See 2:47-49 and 4:153-162 for incidents that occurred there.
[1971] The Prophet asked people to say the following phrase after reading this last verse: "Most definitely! I testify that He has the power to do that!" (*Ma'ariful Qur'an*)

The Clinging Thing
96 Al 'Alaq aka Iqra'
Early Meccan Period

This chapter contains the first five revealed verses, which Muhammad received while on retreat in a mountain cave just outside of the city of Mecca in the year 610 CE. The remainder of the chapter (verses 6-19) was revealed sometime later after Muhammad began to pray publicly near the Ka'bah. (Verses from chapters 73 and 74 were revealed in the intervening period.) His foe, Abu Jahl, tried to interfere with Muhammad's worship on more than one occasion and is referenced here, as well. The theme of this chapter argues that since human life depends upon Allah, it is foolish for humanity to try and ignore Allah and His moral principles for life. Even more foolish is to try and discourage others out of spite from serving Allah.

In the Name of Allah,
the Compassionate, the Merciful

$\mathcal{R}$ecite in the name of

your Lord Who created [1972] [1]
- created human beings from
a clinging (leech-like) thing. [1973] [2]

Recite, for your Lord is Most Generous. [3]
He taught by the pen; [1974] [4]

[1972] Before Islam, it was the poet who was the voice of authority in the Arabian Peninsula. Poets were the mouthpieces of their tribes, and when they spoke, their words were considered to be deeply important. In this first verse of the Qur'an ever revealed, we see that Allah is setting His revelation apart. This was not the speech of a mere poet, but of the Lord of the Universe. In this way, the Qur'an set itself up against the system of poetry and tribalism that existed. This text and its message would be on a different level altogether. Verses 26:224-226 even address the subordinate nature of poets in comparison to the Words of Allah.

[1973] In previous generations, before the advent of modern science, translators often used the term 'blood-clot' to translate the enigmatic Arabic term, '*alaq*, which literally means *something that clings* or *hangs* (like a leech). Science has revealed that after fertilization, the egg in the womb does in fact adhere itself to the uterine wall and literally *clings* or *hangs* from it, extracting its nutrients from the blood of the mother. Thus, we can now understand more accurately the meaning of the term used here.

[1974] Classical scholars such as al-Qurtubi have interpreted this verse to mean that human beings were created with the biological disposition to employ language and communicate through complex symbols. Writing was the next, logical step. (*Ma'ariful Qur'an*) How ironic then that Allah should raise a prophet and advocate of the written word who was himself illiterate and dwelling within a harsh, dry land practically devoid of books, paper or ink.

He taught human beings
what they didn't know before. [1975] [5]

Yet, the human being is still so utterly rebellious, [6]
even considering himself to be independent! [7]
Yet, back to your Lord is the return. [8]

Sincerity Requires Effort

*H*ave you ever seen the
one who discourages [1976] [9]
a servant (of Allah) from praying? [10]
Do you think he's being guided [11]
or even concerned (about Allah), [12]
or does he deny (the truth) and turn aside? [13]
Doesn't he know that Allah is watching him? [14]

Let him be warned then, [1977]
that unless he changes his ways,

[1975] In other words, the invention of writing six thousand years ago enabled human civilization to progress to never before imagined heights. Written records would enable one generation, by Allah's will, to pass on its knowledge to succeeding generations, and this includes religious teachings. It's no wonder that Islam places great emphasis on literacy. The Prophet once remarked, "A person reading is handsome in Allah's sight." Classical Islamic civilization took this maxim to heart and kept the torch of learning alive while Europe was sunk in its dark ages. The ninth-century poet, 'Ali ibn al-Jahm, sums up the attitude that a believer should have towards books in the following words. "If I find a book to be agreeable and enjoyable, and if I deem it to be beneficial, you will see me hour after hour checking how many pages are left, from fear of being close to the end. If it has many volumes with a great number of pages, my life is complete and my happiness total." The early Umayyad general, Yazid al-Muhallab (d. 720), once told his son, "Don't linger in the marketplace unless it be in the shops of armor makers or book makers." In modern times, the fictional author George R. R. Martin included this quote from a character in one of his novels: "A reader lives a thousand lives before he dies...The man who never reads lives only one." (*A Dance with Dragons*) It is no coincidence that at the height of Islamic civilization, public libraries were a common fixture of life in all cities, large and small. Compare past times with the modern world where bookstores are closing and libraries are forgotten. A nation is only as strong as the amount of knowledge kept in the minds of its people. *Iqra!*

[1976] When Muhammad first began praying near the Ka'bah, his fellow Meccans did not know exactly what he was doing. His foe, Abu Jahl, came to suspect that he had adopted a new religion and tried to drive him away from the Ka'bah precinct. He is reported to have asked a gathered crowd, "Is Muhammad setting his face on the ground in front of you?" When they replied in the affirmative, he said, "By the gods *al-Lat* and *al-'Uzza*, if I ever catch him in that act of worship, I will set my foot on his neck and rub his face in the dust." Abu Jahl wanted to make good on his threat. When he saw the opportunity, he gingerly stepped forward and motioned to put his foot on the Prophet's neck, but suddenly he became frightened and left. When asked about it later, he said that he had seen a vision of a ditch filled with fire and a ghoul with fiery wings. When Muhammad heard about what Abu Jahl said, he remarked, "If he would have come near me, the angels would have struck him down and torn him to pieces." This passage was thus revealed about Abu Jahl (and others like him) who forbid people from making devotions to Allah. (*Ahmad, Tirmidhi, Nisa'i*)

[1977] When Abu Jahl later saw Muhammad praying once again near the Ka'bah, he angrily accosted him and said, "Didn't I tell you not to do this!" The Prophet scolded him and said he had the right to pray there, and then Abu Jahl said, "You dare to scold me! By Allah, with one call I can fill this valley with supporters!" Then this passage was revealed. The commentator, Ibn 'Abbas (d. 687), said, "If (Abu Jahl) would have called his men, the angel of punishment would have seized him." (*Asbab ul-Nuzul*)

We'll drag him down
by the hair of his forehead [15]
- his lying, sinful forehead! [16]

Then let him call upon
his supporters for help, [17]
for We, too, will call –
upon the forces of torment! [18]

Absolutely not!
Don't let yourself get sidetracked
by someone like that.
Rather, bow (in adoration),
and draw closer (to Allah). [1978] [19]

[1978] After reading this verse it is customary for the one who has faith in Allah to prostrate himself on the floor and praise Allah.

Determination

97 Al Qadr
Early Meccan Period

The very first night that a Qur'anic revelation came to the Prophet is called the Night of *Qadr*, which is loosely translated as power, destiny, determination or measurement. (It is so named because that is a night when Allah's will for the denizens of earth comes down in full force, especially with world changing events such as the appointment of a prophet, etc.) Muslims, who observe the annual fast of *Ramadan*, look forward in anticipation to praying and meditating throughout the very same night that coincides with the first revelation. (The first five verses of chapter 96 were the initial verses that Muhammad received.)

In the Name of Allah,
the Compassionate, the Merciful

Truly, We (began) revealing (this revelation)
on the Night of Determination. [1979] [1]
And how can you understand
what the Night of Determination is? [2]

The Night of Determination
is better than a thousand months, [1980] [3]
for in it the angels and the Spirit [1981] descend,

[1979] The exact 'Night of Determination' or 'Power,' (*qadr*), is unknown. According to 'Ubada bin As-Samit, the Prophet went out to tell people on which night it was, but there happened to be a quarrel between two men that distracted him. The Prophet said, "I came out to tell you about the night of *Qadr*, but because those people were arguing, its knowledge was taken away from me. Maybe it's better for you. Now look for it either on the 5th, 7th or 9th night (in the last ten days of the month of *Ramadan*)." (*Bukhari*) Ibn 'Abbas was of the opinion that the special night fell on the 27th of *Ramadan*, and Allah knows best.

[1980] A story circulated in Mecca about an ancient Israelite who worshipped Allah at night and fought in His cause all day for a thousand consecutive months. On hearing this, the Prophet's companions were amazed. This verse references that story and makes the claim that the first night of Allah's revelation of the Qur'an is even better than that. (*Ibn Abi Hatim, At-Tabari*)

[1981] The spirit is commonly held to refer to Angel Gabriel, who is called the Holy Spirit elsewhere in the Qur'an. The Prophet said that on the Night of Power, a huge throng of angels, led by Gabriel, descends upon the earth, praying for the forgiveness of every male and female servant of Allah who is engaged in prayer or remembrance of Allah. (*Mazhari*)

by their Lord's command, [1982] to finish every task. [1983] [4]

Peace prevails until the break of dawn! [1984] [5]

[1982] According to Muslim belief, Allah has a special tablet that is the source for all wisdom and revelation. It is from this tablet that all previous revelations, such as the Torah, the Psalms and the Gospel, originated. When Allah decides to send a new revelation from it to the world, He brings that tablet near to the earth and orders the angel Gabriel to take His words from it. The inspirational words from this tablet, also known as the *Umm ul-Kitab* or *Mother of the Book*, are then revealed to the particular prophet who is to receive them. (Thus, a night of determination!) .

[1983] This is interpreted to mean that the angels bring the divine decrees for all creatures for the coming year. (*Ma'ariful Qur'an*)

[1984] The Prophet said, "Whoever spends the night in prayer on the Night of Determination, as a sign of his faith and seeking the reward of Allah, his previous sins will be forgiven." (*Bukhari*) A'ishah reports that it was the Prophet's habit to pray nearly the entire night in the last ten days of *Ramadan*, and he used to keep his family awake, likewise, for that purpose. (*Bukhari*) When she asked him what words of repentance she should say, the Prophet told her to say, "O Allah! Indeed you are the One Who forgives; You love to forgive, so forgive me." (*Ma'ariful Qur'an, Tirmidhi*)

The Clear Evidence

98 Al Bayyinah
Period Uncertain

When the Prophet recited this chapter to one of his companions named Ubayy ibn Ka'b, he told Ubayy that Gabriel ordered him to recite it to him especially. Ubayy asked excitedly, "Messenger of Allah, was I mentioned by name?" When the Prophet said, "Yes," Ubayy began to weep for joy. Then the Prophet said to him that Allah, Himself, said, "If the son of Adam asked for a valley full of gold, and I gave it to him, then he would ask for a second. If he asked for a second one, and I gave it to him, then he would ask for a third. Nothing can fill his belly except dust. Allah accepts the repentance of one who turns to Him in repentance. The only way of life Allah accepts is the steady and true religion, not idolatry, not Judaism or Christianity, though whoever does good, it shall not be in vain." (*Ahmad*)

In the Name of Allah,
the Compassionate, the Merciful

Those who covered over (the truth)
from among the Followers of Earlier Revelation
and the idol-worshippers couldn't abandon (their mistaken ways)
until clear evidence (of Islam's validity) was presented to them [1]
- a messenger from Allah who could recite (undeniable proof to them)
from sanctified pages [2] that offer straightforward teachings. [3]

However, the Followers of Earlier Revelation didn't break up
into (competing) sects until after (this kind of guidance)
had already reached them before, [1985] [4]
even though they weren't taught anything
more than to serve Allah,
to be sincere to the religion that He owns,
and to establish regular prayer
and to give in charity.
That's the straightest way of life! [1986] [5]

[1985] The Prophet said, "The Jews divided up into 71 sects, the Christians into 72, and my people will divide up into 73 sects. All of them will be in the Fire except one." When he was asked which sect would be spared, he said, "The one that adheres to my way (*sunnah*) and the way of my companions." Thus, the majority Sunni sect of Islam took the name of *Ahl al Sunnah wal Jami'ah*, or the People of the Way and the Main Group. The second largest sect of Islam, the Shi'a, take their name from the term *Shi'at 'Ali*, or the Supporters of 'Ali ibn Abi Talib, who struggled to remain the caliph in the face of armed rebellion some thirty years after the Prophet passed away. Muslims, like Christians, have since divided into even more sects, though the Sunni sect is nearly 85% of all Muslims.

[1986] Many visiting Jews and Christians to whom Muhammad would preach would insist that, although they believed he could be the foretold one in their scriptures, still they would not convert to Islam until they received such crystal clear proofs as to be wholly indisputable. However, as this verse points out,

Truly, those who suppress (the truth,
now that it's come to them once more),
whether they're Followers of Earlier Revelation or idol-worshippers,
have earned for themselves the fire of Hell,
and there they shall remain.

They're the worst of all creatures! [6]

However, those who believe
and do what's morally right
are the best of creatures. [1987] [7]

Their reward lies with their Lord:
everlasting gardens beneath which rivers flow –
and there they get to stay (forever) –
Allah well pleased with them and they with Him.

This is what's in store for the one who adored their Lord. [8]

---

their ancestors had such clear teachings, but then they broke up into competing sects. Thus, by this standard, it is unreasonable for anyone to ask for further proof after initial acceptance, especially if they cannot appreciate or adhere faithfully to what they were already given.

[1987] The Prophet once asked some of his companions, "Should I tell you about the best of people?" They all said, "Yes, Messenger of Allah." So he said, "The best person is the one who is always holding the reins of his horse, waiting to be called to struggle (in Allah's cause), and it is someone who is in the midst of tending his sheep (or business) and who neither misses his prayers nor fails to give the required charity due on it." Then he asked if he should tell them about the worst of all people, and they also asked for his answer. Thereupon the Prophet said, "The one who is asked for something in Allah's name, and he doesn't give it." (*Ahmad*)

The Quaking
99 Al Zilzal aka Al Zalzalah
Period Uncertain

The concept that no good or evil deed is hidden from Allah was very new to the Arabs of seventh-century Arabia. In their traditional religion, there was no concept of Allah (or any supernatural being) as a record keeper. The many demigods they worshipped were bringers of luck and good fortune. The only place where a Supreme God fit in was as a general overlord, who, nevertheless, viewed creation with only passing interest. That the One, Supreme God should destroy the earth to gather its people for a detailed judgment was a weighty concept to ponder. The Prophet considered the message of this chapter to be so weighty that he said, "Whoever recites this chapter earns the reward of reading half of the Qur'an." (*Tirmidhi*)

In the Name of Allah,
the Compassionate, the Merciful

When the earth is shaken to its very core [1988] [1]

and the earth casts out all that it contains. [1989] [2]

And when people cry in bewilderment,
"What's happening to her?" [3]

On that day the earth will reveal many things [4]
by the inspiration of her Lord. [1990] [5]

[1988] Sa'id ibn Jubayr reports that when verses 76:8-10 were revealed, the early Muslims were of the opinion that Allah wouldn't count small amounts of charity, so they began to deny beggars when they had only a date or a small piece of bread to give. They believed that only a large amount of charity would count. Similarly, some of them thought small misdeeds wouldn't be counted. (Chapter 76 was revealed in Mecca when there were only around forty converts or so.) Hellfire, it was thought, was only for major sins. To correct these false impressions, this chapter was revealed. (*Asbab ul-Nuzul*)

[1989] The Prophet said, "The earth will throw out its insides, and gold and silver will streak out like columns. A murderer will say in regret, 'I'm ruined! I murdered on it for that (wealth), and now its lying there, and nobody cares.' A person who cut off contact with his relatives will say, 'For the love of this I behaved poorly with my relatives.' A thief will say, 'For the love of this I lost my hand.' The wealth of the earth will lay there unclaimed." (*Muslim*) In another tradition the Prophet said, "Beware of the earth! It's your mother. Any good or evil act done on its surface will be testified to by it." (*Tabarani*)

[1990] Abu Bakr was sitting with the Prophet when this chapter was revealed. He began to weep when he heard it, and the Prophet asked him why he was filled with sorrow. Abu Bakr replied that the weightiness of the message saddened him, and he was afraid of being punished for every small thing. The Prophet then said, "If no one ever sinned or made mistakes, then Allah would create a people after you who would make mistakes and commit sins so He could forgive them." Then the Prophet explained that all the hardships and troubles we face in this world are payback for our small sins but that our good deeds will be stored for our accounting on Judgment Day. (*At-Tabari*)

On that day, people will come forward in sorted groups
to be shown the full account of their deeds. [1991] [6]

Whoever did a speck of good will see it, [7]
and whoever did a speck of evil will see it. [1992] [8]

[1991] When Abu Sa'id al-Khudri heard the verses of this chapter, he asked the Prophet, "Do I have to watch all my deeds?" The Prophet said, "Yes." Then Abu Sa'id asked, "All the major deeds?" The Prophet said, "Yes." "And all the little deeds?" Abu Sa'id asked. Then the Prophet answered, "Yes," again. "Then I'm doomed!" Abu Sa'id cried out. "Be of good cheer, Abu Sa'id," the Prophet said, "for good deeds will be rewarded from ten to seven hundred times each, or even more if Allah wills, while sinful deeds are counted as only one, or Allah just might forgive them altogether. Listen, no one will be saved on account of his deeds alone." "Not even the Messenger of Allah?" Abu Sa'id asked. "No, not even I," the Prophet replied, "unless Allah showers me with His mercy and favor." (*Bukhari, Muslim*)

[1992] A'ishah once said to the Prophet, "I know the hardest verse in the Qur'an." The Prophet asked, "Which one is it, A'ishah?" Then she recited this verse [99:8]. The Prophet exclaimed, "That's what happens to a believing servant, even the problems that bother him." (*Abu Dawud*) In other words, when a believer makes a mistake or does a sin, it may come back to haunt him or her in this life by causing him or her some hardship.

The Running Stallions

100 Al 'Adiyat
Early Meccan Period

Arabian society was rooted in both trade and tribal warfare. From time immemorial, the clash of mounted horsemen in the desert was the stuff of legend and lore, and many a man held as his dream the chance to raid and war against his neighbors to gain wealth and renown. The literary device this chapter employs to get the listener's attention is a direct evocation of just such an exhilarating scene. However, the charging horses are transformed in the second half of the chapter into a representation of materialistic people, miserably and pathetically clawing their way towards the false dream of wealth and worldly success. The concluding question leaves the reader with a choice: either continue on as a mindless pleasure seeker, or consider one's ultimate fate and see the world for what it really is.

In the Name of Allah,
the Compassionate, the Merciful

By charging (horses), breathless, panting, [1]

striking sparks [2] - assault by dawn, [3]
raising dust, pacing forward, [4]
in the center, storming on! [5]

Thankless man is of his Lord, [6]
and, oh, how well he shows it! [7]
His lust for worldly wealth is real,
and, oh, how fierce and fervent! [1993] [8]

Knows he not when graves lie empty - [9]
when secrets are all shown - [10]
that his Lord about him
on that day will long have known? [1994] [11]

[1993] The Prophet said, "Whoever focuses only upon the world (and its wealth), then Allah will scatter his affairs, and his poverty will be ever present before his eyes. He won't get from the world any more than what's been allotted for him. Whoever focuses his intentions upon the next life, then his affairs will be brought in order for him, and his true wealth will be placed in his heart. The (wealth) of the world will then come to him anyway, (even though he doesn't strive after it)." (*Ibn Majah*)

[1994] Umm Darda reports that she asked her husband, Abu Darda, what was wrong with him because he didn't ask for money and power like some others did. He answered that he had heard the Prophet say, "Before you is a difficult ascent (up to Paradise), over which the heavily-laden cannot climb." So, he explained, he wanted to be light for that climb. (*Bayhaqi*)

The Sudden Disaster

101 Al Qari'ah
Early Meccan Period

To the people of Mecca, surrounded as they were by impermeable deserts, ancient mountains and an equally ancient lifestyle, the notion that it could all pass away in the future was never even entertained. This chapter begins by making a bold statement with just such a concept and then follows with a call to personal responsibility for one's deeds. One can imagine a Meccan idolater hearing this being recited and dismissing it out of hand. In the end, it was Muhammad's message that survived, and not Arab idolatry.

In the Name of Allah,
the Compassionate, the Merciful

The Sudden Disaster! [1]

And just what *is* the Sudden Disaster? [2]
So how can you understand
what the Sudden Disaster will be? [3]

It's the day when people will seem
like moths fluttering about, [4]
when the mountains will be like
tangled tufts of wool. [5]

Then, whoever's scale is heavy (with good), [6]
they will have satisfaction, [1995] [7]
while the one whose scale is scarce (of good) [8]
Their mother will be the Abyss! [9]

And how can you understand
what the Abyss is? [10]
It's a fiercely burning blaze. [11]

[1995] The Prophet said, "The most enviable of my friends in my opinion is the believer with few possessions who finds his pleasure in prayer, who performs well in the service of his Lord and obeys Him in secret, who is anonymous among people and is not pointed out among others and whose supply is just enough, which contents him." He then snapped his fingers and said, "His death will come quickly; few women will mourn him, and he will leave only a little." (*Ahmad, Tirmidhi, Ibn Majah*)

The Race (for Wealth)

102 At-Takathur
Early Meccan Period

This very early chapter introduced, in a definitive way, the concept of punishment in the afterlife. This penalty would be a direct consequence of greed and thoughtless living, centered upon mere materialistic goals. When Allah, morality and our duty to our fellow creatures are forgotten, all that is left is the selfish pursuit of ever greater resources, which results in waste, oppression and injustice. The Prophet declared that the message of this chapter was so weighty that reciting its eight verses is like reciting a thousand other verses. (*Hakim, Bayhaqi*) The immediate cause for its revelation was a boasting match between members of the two rival clans, the Banu Sahm and the Banu 'Abd Manaf, in which each side gloated over its wealth and power in ever greater rivalry.

In the Name of Allah,
the Compassionate, the Merciful

The endless race for (wealth)
distracts you [1] – *even unto the grave.* [1996] [2]

Oh, but you'll soon know
(the foolishness of your goals!) [3]

And then again, oh yes, in time,
you'll soon know! [1997] [4]

If you knew for sure (what lies ahead), [5]
you'd see Hellfire all around you, [6]

Even as you'll no doubt see it clearly [7]
on a day when you'll be questioned
about your (handling of life's) opportunities. [8]

[1996] The Prophet once said, "If the son of Adam has a valley full of gold, he would desire to have two such valleys, for nothing but the dirt of his grave will ever make his mouth full. Allah accepts the repentance of those who turn to Him in repentance." (*Bukhari*)

[1997] A man named 'Abdullah ibn Shikhir visited the Prophet one day, and he found him reciting this chapter. After he finished reciting it, the Prophet turned and said, "The son of Adam says, 'My wealth, my wealth,' but you gain nothing from your wealth save for what you ate and finished, the clothes you wore and then wore out, and the money you gave away in charity and thus secured (as an investment in the next life). Everything else besides these will pass away, and other people will inherit it." (*Muslim*)

The (Passage of) Time
103 Al 'Asr
Early Meccan Period

This is one of the shortest, yet most compelling, chapters of the Qur'an. The passage of human history is filled with war, betrayal, suffering and sorrow brought about from such human failings as greed, anger, depravity and arrogance. Every nation and individual will experience loss at some point or another, and every achievement will pass away to dust.

However, if a person has faith in something greater than himself and weathers the trials, *knowing that no test is endless or without purpose*, then he can transcend both earthly triumph and failure and gain a deep-seated tranquility that can help him detach his mind from the immediacy of the physical world. He can achieve the kind of inner strength and peace that come from wrestling with one's own mortality and realizing that we matter only to Allah.

The classical jurist, Imam Shafi'i, once remarked that if people spent their time pondering over the lessons of this chapter that it would be enough for them to achieve deep understanding. The companions of the Prophet thought so highly of this chapter that it is said that when they would meet each other, they would not part until someone recited this chapter. (*Tabarani*)

In the Name of Allah,
the Compassionate, the Merciful

The passage of time is a witness... [1]

Human beings are in a constant
state of failure; [1998] [2]

All except those who believe
and do what's morally right,

And who teach each other
to be truthful and persevering. [1999] [3]

[1998] Ibn Taymiyyah once enumerated the reasons that hold people back from believing in Allah. These are being assailed by doubts that gnaw at the mind and heart, and then giving in to selfish desires that corrupt the mind and warp the heart. (*Ma'ariful Qur'an*)

[1999] The Prophet said, "You must be truthful, for truthfulness leads to righteousness, and righteousness leads to Paradise. Beware of lying, for lying leads to immorality, and immorality leads to Hellfire. A person will keep on telling the truth and striving to do so until Allah will record him as truthful. Another person will keep telling lies and persist in doing so until Allah records him as a liar." (*Muslim*)

The Slanderer
104 Al Humazah
Early Meccan Period

This is one of several chapters that challenged the Meccans to rethink the significance of certain practices that were taken for granted as a part of everyday life. Although slander and gossip were looked down upon, as they are in every society, for the first time the notion is introduced that such behavior is immoral and ultimately sinful. It is said that this chapter was revealed about a Meccan pagan (either Umayyah ibn Khalf, al-Walid ibn al-Mughirah or Akhnas ibn Shariq ath-Thaqafi), who slandered the Prophet publicly.

In the Name of Allah,
the Compassionate, the Merciful

A warning to every slanderer [2000] and backbiter [2001] [1]

who hoards his money in preparation... [2]
Is he hoping to buy immortality? [3]

No way!
He'll be thrown into the Crusher, [4]
and just how can the Crusher be described? [5]

It's the very wrath of Allah,
kindled (in a blaze), [6]
penetrating to the very core [7]
- overwhelming them [8]
in *endless* columns. [9]

[2000] A man once asked the Prophet to define backbiting for him. The Prophet replied, "It's mentioning your brother in a way that he doesn't like." The man then asked, "What if what I said about my brother was true?" The Prophet answered, "If what you said about him was true, then you still would have engaged in backbiting, and if what you said about him was false, then you would have slandered him." (*Abu Dawud, Tirmidhi*)

[2001] The Prophet said, "Slander is worse than adultery." He was then asked how that can be worse than adultery, to which he replied, "If a person commits adultery, he can be forgiven by Allah if he repents. However, a slanderer will not be forgiven until he is forgiven by the person about whom he was talking (badly)." (*Bayhaqi*) He also said, "The worst of Allah's servants are those who speak ill of another in order to cause hatred between friends, and also those who constantly find faults with other people." (*Ma'ariful Qur'an*) The classical commentator Qatadah described the first verse of this chapter as being about those who torture others with their tongue and eyes (with cruel stares). The Prophet also said, "The worst of Allah's servants are those who speak ill of another in order to cause hatred between friends and also those who constantly find faults with other people." (*Ma'ariful Qur'an*)

The Elephant
105 Al Feel
Early Meccan Period

Somewhere around the year 569 CE, the Abyssinian governor of Yemen, Abrahah al-Ashram, marched an army northwards to Mecca in an effort to occupy the city and demolish the Ka'bah. He had previously opened a huge Christian cathedral in Yemen, constructed of red, white and black marble with jewels set into the walls, hoping to draw the Arabs to his territory for pilgrimage (and also to steer some of Mecca's trade to his own coffers.) However, the Arabs were reluctant to abandon their traditional site of devotion and economic activity. One visitor from a tribe south of Mecca named Nufayl even desecrated Abrahah's cathedral in contempt by urinating in it, provoking Abrahah's wrath even further. While his exact troop strength (a purported mix of 60,000 Yemenis and southern Arab tribesmen) is unknown, Abrahah did bring with him a dozen or so imported African war elephants sent by the Negus of Abyssinia - *no doubt to shock and awe the Meccans* - and also to use their strength to tear down the Ka'bah. A few Arab tribes along the way tried to thwart this invasion, but they were defeated and could not stop the invading army.

When Abrahah's army was on the outskirts of Mecca they captured 200 camels that belonged to 'Abdel-Muttalib. The Meccan leadership, realizing the hopelessness of their situation, sent 'Abdel-Muttalib, their leading man, to open negotiations. The first thing he asked the king was for his camels back! Abrahah expressed surprise that this was the first thing that the Meccan asked for, and 'Abdel-Muttalib replied that the Ka'bah has its own Guardian. Abrahah then explained to 'Abdel-Muttalib (who would later be Muhammad's grandfather) that he didn't want to fight the Quraysh, but only wanted to demolish the Ka'bah.

'Abdel-Muttalib replied that the Ka'bah had its Protector (Allah) and that the Quraysh were not going to fight his army. Abrahah then boasted that no one could protect the Ka'bah from *him*. Before departing, 'Abdel-Muttalib said, "That's between you and *Him*." 'Abdel-Muttalib then returned to Mecca and told his people to hide in the hills, for Abrahah was coming. The Meccans then invoked Allah to protect the Ka'bah and then left. Some citizens remained behind, including 'Abdel-Muttalib's widowed daughter-in-law Aminah, who was pregnant with the unborn child she would later name Muhammad.

The next day, the army's progress was stalled when the elephants refused to enter the outskirts of the city. The gnawing effects of a latent plague also began to spread rapidly throughout Abrahah's army, as this was a constant danger in those days. Abrahah's troops began to weaken and fall ill by the hour. People who were alive at that time say it was a flock of birds that darkened the sky and dropped stones on the men, killing them with bloody wounds. In later times, some Qur'anic commentators have suggested that it was a contagion, borne by fleas, that did the deed. If it was the plague, it may have been small pox or bubonic plague, for it would have left huge welts and open sores on the men's bodies that resembled the wound that a thrown stone would make. In any case, Abrahah was forced to withdraw back to his capital of Sana, thwarted in his goal. He died shortly after his return home, though some say he died in the field. The rejoicing Meccans returned to their city and ever afterwards referred to that year as the *Year of the Elephant*.

In the Name of Allah,
the Compassionate, the Merciful

Haven't you seen how your Lord

dealt with the army of the elephant? [1]
Didn't He foil their evil plans? 2002 [2]

He let loose upon them a horde of fliers, 2003 [3]
which struck them down with stone-smacked (wounds), [4]
leaving their ranks like barren fields - harvested and razed. [5]

2002 Even though the events mentioned in this chapter occurred before the Prophet was born, it speaks in the immediate sense, asking people to notice what Allah did to that invading army. This is because there were still many people alive who witnessed those events, including nearly the entire leadership of Mecca. According to both A'ishah bint Abi Bakr and her sister Asma', there were also two blind beggars still living in Mecca, who were originally among the elephant drivers of Abrahah's army. (*Ibn Is-haq*) The unspoken implication for the Meccans was that this act of power by Allah was a sign for them of the coming of more *signs*. i.e. a dispensation from on High. (*Ibn Kathir*)

2003 Was it birds dropping stones or a plague that destroyed Abrahah's army? The Arabic word used here can mean a bird or anything that flies. This is a debate that is open for discussion until this day, though most traditionally-minded commentators subscribe to the former view. What must be remembered is that the Qur'an did not invent the idea of birds attacking the army. This interpretation of events was already established in the local lore of pagan Mecca even from Muhammad's birth, as evidenced by the matter-of-fact tone in this chapter. It is assumed in the text that the listeners already know of this event and what happened. The chapter is merely asking the listeners to consider Allah's power and thus give up worshipping things besides Him.

The Quraysh
106 Quraysh
Early Meccan Period

The elite members of the Quraysh tribe, who were the rulers of Mecca in the seventh century, began to oppose the ministry of Prophet Muhammad almost immediately. They felt that their longstanding traditions and culture were sacred, and they did not want to anger their idols by rejecting them, nor did they want to alienate the bedouins who housed their own idols in the Ka'bah, (and thus risk their financial livelihood in the process). They also felt that they did not need a new religion, for they assumed they already had every benefit they needed, both materially and spiritually.

Although their ancestors were once poor, the Prophet's great-grandfather Hashim had advised the Meccans to take up the alternating trading seasons as a way of life, and they did so to great economic success. Over the years, the Meccans made alliances and treaties throughout the region, ensuring that their trade caravans to Syria and Yemen in alternate seasons, the source of their wealth, would be safe. They earnestly believed that their capricious gods had to be venerated to ensure their continued success. As this chapter points out, it doesn't matter if they made treaties for safe passage because in the end the One True God is in control, and it is He Who ultimately allows them to prosper.

In the Name of Allah,
the Compassionate, the Merciful

About the treaties of the Quraysh, [2004] [1]

those treaties that protect them [2005]
on their journeys through winter and summer... [2]

They should serve the Lord of this House, [2006] [3]
for He's the One Who provides them
with their rations against hunger
and their security against fear. [4]

[2004] The Quraysh tribe is named after a nickname of Fihr, a celebrated ancestor of theirs who is credited with organizing and gathering together the dispersed clans of his people several generations before Muhammad's birth. Some sources say it was also the nickname of Al-Harith, another forbear.

[2005] The Prophet said, "Allah has given seven advantages to the Quraysh that He didn't give to anyone else (among the Arabs): I am from them, prophethood was instituted among them (over all other Arab tribes), they're the custodians of the Ka'bah, they offer the water of Zamzam, Allah helped them to overcome the Army of the Elephant, they alone had people worshipping Allah for ten years before anyone else (had accepted Islam), and Allah revealed this chapter about them." Then the Prophet recited this chapter. (*Bayhaqi*)

[2006] Being in charge of the holy Ka'bah in Mecca gave the Quraysh tribe certain advantages in making safe-conduct deals with tribes in Arabia and beyond. This chapter is reminding them that they should not forget that it is the presence of Allah's sacred shrine that has given them this perk.

Small Favors

107 Al Ma'un
Early Meccan Period

One day Abu Sufyan, the nominal head of the Quraysh tribe, was slaughtering two lambs. An orphan came and asked him for some food, and Abu Sufyan became angry and hit him with a stick. This chapter was revealed to answer the attitude of such people who feel they don't have any obligation to help their fellows in need.

It equates being selfish and uncaring with denying that people will be held accountable in the next life. After all, if people believe this life is all there is, then they could very easily develop a calloused mind and feel nothing if people weaker than they are needy or are in crisis.

A small side argument is introduced about hypocrisy. Even if a person seems to be praying and doing "religious" rituals, if he or she still doesn't care enough to help others, then they may be praying to make other people think they are "religious" and for no other reason. Such a person denies his obligation to Allah, as well.

In the Name of Allah,
the Compassionate, the Merciful

*H*ave you ever seen someone
who denies the (moral) way of life? [1]

Well, he's the one who pushes orphans aside [2]
and doesn't encourage the feeding of the poor. [3]

So a warning to those who pray [4]
- to those who are careless in their devotions, [2007] [5]
whose prayers are only for show, [6]
and yet who refuse to share even the smallest of favors. [2008] [7]

[2007] The Prophet was asked the meaning of this verse, and he said it was about those who perform their prayers past their due times. (*Ibn Kathir*)

[2008] The term *ma'un* means any small favor or kind gesture. A'ishah once asked the Prophet about this, saying, "Messenger of Allah, what is it unlawful to refuse?" He replied, "Water, fire and salt." Then she asked, "Messenger of Allah, I understand water, but what about fire and salt?" He said, "O rosy-cheeked one, if someone gives fire, it's as if he were giving in charity all that is cooked with that fire. If someone gives salt, it's as if he is giving in charity all that is made tasty by that salt. If he gives a drink of water where there is no water, it's as if he gave life to a soul." (*Kashf al-Asrar*)

Abundance

108 Al Kawthar
Early Meccan Period

Most scholars are of the opinion that this chapter was revealed sometime after Muhammad's infant son 'Abdullah passed away. One of Muhammad's enemies, an ardent idolater named Al 'As ibn Wa'il taunted him cruelly after the tragedy, claiming that because he had no surviving male heirs, his future roots in society were 'cut off' or ended. Ibn Wa'il often said of Muhammad, "Leave him; he has no sons, and no one will remember his name after he dies." Abu Lahab (see chapter 111) also used to taunt the Prophet in this way.

This chapter gives Muhammad a reminder that no matter how poor his material or social situation might have been in Mecca, the guidance and heartfelt contentment of Allah are a greater gift than all of the comforts of this world. Though the faithless may appear to live in luxury and have power in the world, they will have no hope in the *afterlife,* where their power will be meaningless.

As for the exact moment of revelation, the Prophet was sitting with some of his companions, and he appeared to be drowsy. After a while he raised his head, smiled and said, "A chapter has been revealed to me." Then after reciting it, he asked, "Do you know what abundance (*kawthar*) is?"

"Allah and His Messenger know best," they replied. Then the Prophet said, "It is a stream in Paradise, filled with blessings. It has been given to me by Allah. On the Day of Judgment, my people will gather around it, and it will fill as many cups as there are stars in the sky. Some people will be pushed away from it, however, and I'm going to ask, 'But my Lord! They are also my followers!' A voice will say, 'You don't know what happened after you.'" (*Ahmad*)

It is said that when Abu Jahl first heard these few small verses, he exclaimed, "Allah be glorified! How wonderfully each word rhymes with the other!" He then wrote them down on a sheet of leather and took the verses to a poet he knew who read them and said, "Allah be glorified, these are not a man's words."

Then the poet took the sheet and went into the Ka'bah where he removed his own poetry that was hanging there and substituted the new paper in its place. It is said he added the line, "These are not the words of a human being," at the bottom. How ironic that Abu Jahl would grow to be one of the Prophet's worst enemies!

In the Name of Allah,
the Compassionate, the Merciful

Indeed, We've granted you abundance, [2009] [1]

so now turn to your Lord in prayer and sacrifice. [2010] [2]
Truly, it will be your critics whose (future) will be cut off. [3]

[2009] When Muhammad returned from his ascension to Heaven, he told his companions, "I came upon a river there, the banks of which were made of tents of hollowed pearl. I asked Gabriel, 'What is this (river)?' He replied, 'This is (the river of) abundance (*kawthar*).'" (*Bukhari*)

[2010] The sacrifice of animals in Islam is a way to gain piety by providing food for the poor and needy to whom the meat is distributed. (See 22:36) The ritual of sacrifice has many rules to ensure that no cruelty to the animal is done. Animals are to be slaughtered with a quick cut to the neck with a sharpened knife, so the animal dies instantly and painlessly. Animals are not allowed to be slaughtered in front of other animals, as well, so as not to frighten them beforehand. The slaughtered animals are not burnt on an alter, as in ancient Judaism, nor are there any invocations other than calling on Allah's name beforehand. To those who oppose this type of humane slaughter and the benefit it brings to the poor, the Islamic practice is far superior to what befalls the billions of luckless animals that are butchered cruelly in modern slaughterhouses each year and from which society gets most of its meat.

The Faithless
109 Al Kafirun
Early Meccan Period

In the early days of his ministry, the pagans of Mecca tried to convince Muhammad to dilute his teachings or, at the very least, to make an accommodation with them to live and let live, so to speak, by co-opting his beliefs into the religious fabric of the wider community. Some leaders of the Quraysh, namely Al-Walid ibn al-Mughirah, Al-'As ibn Wa'il, Aswad ibn 'Abdul-Muttalib and Umayyah ibn Khalaf, actually made the proposal that if Muhammad were to worship their gods for a year, then they would worship his One God for a year. (*Qurtubi*) Their exact offer was in these words: "Muhammad, we will worship what you worship and you will worship what we worship. If what you worship is better than what we worship, then we will take part in it, and if what we worship is better than what you worship, you can take part in that." (*Ibn Hisham*)

Muhammad declined their offer. When they said, "At least touch some of our gods (in reverence,) and we'll believe in you," this short and concise chapter was revealed in response and laid out the distinct incompatibility of mixing Islam and idolatry.

In the Name of Allah,
the Compassionate, the Merciful

Say (to them):

"O you who suppress (your awareness of the truth)! [1]
I don't serve what you serve, [2]
and you don't serve what I serve. [3]

"And I won't serve what you serve, [4]
nor will you serve what I serve. [5]
To you, your way of life, and to me, mine." [2011] [6]

[2011] Nawfal ibn Mu'awiya said that the Prophet asked him to lodge his (the Prophet's) cousin, Zaynab bint Jahsh, (who was married to his adopted son Zayd) in his home (as the Meccans were beginning to harass members of his household.) Later, Nawfal returned to the Prophet and asked to be given something he could recite before going to sleep. The Prophet taught him the verses of this chapter because they rejected idolatry. (*Ahmad ibn Hanbal*)

The Help (of Allah)

110 An-Nasr aka At-Tawdi'
Late Medinan Period

While some authorities believe that this chapter was revealed after the settlement of Khaybar was captured (and before Mecca was taken), most scholars are of the opinion that this chapter, which is the last complete chapter to have been revealed *as a complete chapter*, was revealed during the Prophet's Farewell Pilgrimage, just two months before his passing. The statement that this religion was now complete, which is contained in verse 5:3 was revealed during the same pilgrimage just a day earlier. After this chapter was revealed, the Prophet said, "The people (of the world) are on one side, and I and my companions are on the other side. There is no more migration after the conquest (of Mecca). All that remains is *jihad* (dedicated devotion to advancing Allah's cause) and good intentions." (*Tabarani*)

In the Name of Allah,
the Compassionate, the Merciful

*W*hen Allah's help arrives

and victory (is achieved), [1]
and when you see people coming
into Allah's way of life in crowds, [2012] [2]

Glorify your Lord and seek His forgiveness,
for He is indeed the acceptor of repentance. [2013] [3]

[2012] According to the Prophet's wife, Umm Salamah, after the conquest of Mecca in the year 630, the Prophet said that Allah ordered him to say the following words in thanks as he observed people accepting Islam in crowds: "All Glory be to Allah, and Praise is His, and we repent to Him." (*Ahmad*) In addition, the Prophet also offered four prayers of two units each as a thanksgiving prayer. The commentators hold that this shows it to be the duty of any Muslim commander to do the same upon the conquest of any city (i.e., to make the same supplication and then pray in thanks as noted). Many years later, during the rule of the caliphs, a man returned to Medina from the north and reported to his friend Jabir that differences were arising among the Muslims there. Jabir burst into tears and said, "I heard the Prophet saying that people would enter into Islam in crowds but would soon leave it in crowds." (*Ahmad*)

[2013] During the rule of the second caliph, 'Umar ibn al-Khattab, he used to invite the young man, 'Abdullah ibn Abbas (d. 687), to sit in on his meetings with the older surviving companions who were veterans of the Battle of Badr. Some of them didn't like to have such a younger man sitting with them on the grounds that he was young and thus, they felt, more inexperienced in matters of statecraft and religion. (Ibn Abbas was only a teenager when the Prophet was living in Medina.) One of the older men even objected to his presence, saying, "He shouldn't join us; we have children who are his age." 'Umar responded, "But you all know him well." One day he called a meeting and asked those older companions, "What do you know about the chapter *'When Allah's help arrives...'*" The men gave answers to the effect that it taught Muslims to be thankful and to praise Allah and seek His forgiveness when any victory is achieved. 'Umar then turned to Ibn 'Abbas and asked him if he held the same opinion. Ibn 'Abbas said, "No." Then 'Umar asked him to give his understanding of it, and Ibn 'Abbas said, "It contains a message about the departure of the Prophet. It informs him that his life is coming

Flame

111 Lahab aka Masad
Early Meccan Period

After the verse was revealed commanding him to go public with his message (Qur'an 26:214), Muhammad climbed up on a small hill called Safa inside the city's limits and started calling his fellow Meccans to come to him urgently. A few moments later a small crowd gathered, with his foul-tempered uncle, Abu Lahab, present as well.

Muhammad announced, "Sons of 'Abdel-Muttalib! Sons of Fihr! If I were to tell you that cavalrymen were approaching on the other side of this hill, would you believe me?" Someone responded, saying, "Yes, for we've never heard you telling a lie." Then Muhammad announced, "So now I'm warning you plainly of a terrible punishment!"

Abu Lahab became furious and denounced him, "You gathered us here just *for this*? May you be cut off!" Then Abu Lahab threw a rock at him. (*Bukhari*) This chapter came in response and made the prediction that it would be *Abu Lahab's* fame and fortune that would be cut down, along with all his power and influence.

The reference to his *lady*, or wife, is connected to her campaign against the Prophet. She would slander Muhammad and incite others to ridicule him; hence *feeding the flame*. She boasted that she would sell her gold necklaces and use the money to fund the persecution of the Prophet. She also used to bring thorny bundles and throw them in front of the Prophet's door at night. Asma', the daughter of Abu Bakr, said that after this chapter of the Qur'an was revealed, Abu Lahab's wife, Urwa bint Harb (aka Umm Jamil), came out looking for Muhammad, holding a sharp edged stone to throw at him. She was shouting, "We reject the blameworthy one! We shun his religion and disobey whatever he commands!"

At the time, Muhammad was sitting with Abu Bakr, who saw her coming, and he said to the Prophet, "I wish you would go and hide, for she's coming to us, and she might hurt you." The Prophet said, "There will be a screen set between you and me and her." Then the Prophet recited verse 17:45 of the Qur'an: "When you recite the Qur'an, We put between you and those who don't believe in the afterlife an invisible screen."

Urwa then approached Abu Bakr, and she didn't notice the Prophet. She asked Abu Bakr, "Abu Bakr! Is your friend saying poetry against me?" Abu Bakr replied, "By Allah, he doesn't say mere poetry." She answered, "Do you really believe that? All the Quraysh know that I'm the daughter of their chief!" Then she left. Abu Bakr turned towards the Prophet and said, "Messenger of Allah, she really didn't see you!" The Prophet replied, "An angel was screening me from her." (*Compiled from Musnad Abu Ya'la, Abi Hatim, Tafseer al-Qurtubi, Ibn Kathir*)

---

to an end and instructs him to get busy in praising Allah and seeking His forgiveness." 'Umar looked at the gathered older gentlemen and said, "I don't know any other interpretation than this." (*Bukhari*)

In the Name of Allah,
the Compassionate, the Merciful

Cut off are (the works)

of Abu Lahab's hands - cut off! [2014] [1]

Neither his money nor his accomplishments
will save him, [2]for in a raging blaze
he shall soon be. [3]

And his woman,
who must feed the flame, [4]
will have 'round her neck
a twisted fiber chain. [2015] [5]

[2014] Abu Lahab, whose real name was Abdul-'Uzza, or slave of the goddess 'Uzza, was an early enemy of the Prophet. A man named Rabi'a ibn 'Abbad Dayli told of what he witnessed in Mecca before he became a Muslim. "I saw the Prophet addressing the people in the bazaar of Dhilmajaz, saying, 'People! Say there is no god but Allah, and you will be saved.' Then I saw behind him a light-skinned man with squinty eyes and parted hair yelling, 'People! He is against our way of life! He's a liar!' Whenever the Prophet called people to believe in one God, that man would follow him, saying what he was saying. I asked who that man was and was told that he was an uncle of the Prophet." (*Ahmad*) The phrase "cut down are his hands," is an idiom meaning his life's work is wasted.

[2015] This is an obvious play on the gold necklace Urwa intended to sell to fund the persecution of the Prophet.

Pure Faith

112 Al Ikhlas
Early Meccan Period

A group of visiting Jews asked Muhammad to describe what his conception of Allah was like, for they wanted to compare his description of Allah with what their own scripture said. They asked him if his God was male or female, made of gold, copper or silver, whether He eats and drinks, how He came to be in control of the earth, and who will control it after Him. The Prophet waited patiently for a few days for a revelation from Allah. Then the Prophet sent word to his followers to assemble in front of his house and then he would recite one-third of the Qur'an for them. (Remember that in the early Meccan period the Qur'an was much smaller.) They gathered at the appropriate time, and after the Prophet recited this chapter to them, he went back in his house.

The people were confused for they thought they were going to hear one-third of the Qur'an, and some thought that the Prophet was inside and was receiving additional revelations. The Prophet came out of his door again and said, "Listen, this chapter is equal to one-third of the Qur'an." (*Tirmidhi*) This chapter was then conveyed to the Jews in answer to their questions. On a later occasion, the Prophet said, "Whoever recites this chapter ten times, Allah will build for him a palace in Paradise." 'Umar said, "In that case, we may have many palaces." The Prophet replied, "Allah may give you even more than that." (*Ahmad*)

In the Name of Allah,
the Compassionate, the Merciful

Say (to them): "He is only one God. [2016] [1]

Allah the Eternal Absolute. [2]

He neither begets nor was He begotten, [2017] [3]
and there is nothing equal to Him." [4]

[2016] Other Qur'anic passages explain the nature of Allah in great detail, but this passage packs a tremendous amount of theology in a very small space. Compare it with lengthier descriptions such as those found in 2:255, 59:22-24 and 62:1. The Prophet advised people to recite chapters 112-114 before going to sleep. He also said that there were no better chapters to say for someone who is seeking Allah's safety. (*Nisa'i*)

[2017] The Prophet said that Allah, Himself, has said, "The son of Adam tells a lie against Me, though he has no right to do so, and he abuses Me, though he has no right to do so. As for his lying against Me, it's because he claims that I cannot recreate him as I created him before. As for his abusing Me, it's because he says that I have a son. Absolutely not! Glory belongs to Me! I am far above taking a wife or a son." (*Bukhari*) The Prophet also said, "No one can surpass Allah in showing patience upon being slighted. He hears people saying He has a son; yet, He still bestows upon them good health and resources." (*Bukhari*) Also see 6:101 and 19:88-95.

Daybreak

113 Al Falaq
Period Uncertain

Chapters 113 and 114 of the Qur'an are known as the *Two Protections*, and they are designed to calm people's fears of the supernatural and the unknown. They were revealed after the Prophet began to suspect that he had become the victim of a hex cast upon him. (He began having daydreams in which he thought he already did things that he hadn't done yet.) Shamanism, witchcraft and hexes were part of Arabian culture in those days, (which is a practice that persists to this day in many parts of the world,) and it is not unreasonable that the Prophet should have looked for an explanation there for the cause of his unusual sensations.

Then one night, he saw two men in a dream discussing the cause of his fear. When he awoke, he followed what he saw in his dream to a tree. Under a rock in a nearby dry well was an old comb that had a single hair of his own wound up on it. He also found a knotted rope. Apparently, a man named Labid ibn A'sam had obtained the Prophet's comb some days earlier, desiring to make incantations before burying it and the strand of hair tangled in it. The Prophet untied the eleven or twelve knots, destroyed these objects and soon thereafter regained his sense of inner balance. His wife A'ishah asked him, "Won't you tell everyone about this?" He replied, "Allah has cured me, and I hate to spread talk of evil occurrences to other people." (*Bukhari*)

In the Name of Allah,
the Compassionate, the Merciful

Say (to them):

"I seek safety with the Lord of the Dawn [1]
from the evil (of the unknown) in creation, [2]
from the evil of approaching darkness, [2018] [3]
from the evil of spell-casters [4]
and from the evil of the envious
whenever they resent." [2019] [5

[2018] One night the Prophet held A'ishah's hand, pointed to the moon and said, "Take refuge from the approaching darkness." (*Ahmad*) Although modern studies on human behavior have sometimes suggested that people become more prone to risk taking at night, the greatest dangers come from more mundane sources, such as nightmares, getting lost, surprise attacks by enemies and theft.

[2019] The Prophet once said to a man named 'Uqbah ibn 'Amir, "Do you know that two chapters have been revealed to me, the likes of which have never been revealed before?" Then he recited chapters 113 and 114. (*Nisa'i, Ahmad ibn Hanbal*)

People
114 An-Nas
Period Uncertain

This chapter is the second in the pair known as the *Two Protections*. Its main theme is to reassure people that Allah is in charge and that only by surrendering our weak wills to His will can we ever hope to keep ourselves out of all the temptations that surround us in this uncertain and decadent world.

In the Name of Allah,
the Compassionate, the Merciful

Say (to them):

"I seek the safety of
the Lord of people, [2020] [1]
the Ruler of people, [2]
the God of people… [3]

From the subtle temptations of evil, [2021] [4]
whispered into the hearts of people [5]
by jinns [2022] and other people." [6]

[2020] The Prophet was riding with a friend on a mule when the mule suddenly stumbled. The man said, "Curse you, Satan!" The Prophet then said, "Don't say that, for it only encourages him, and he says, 'I unhinged him with my strength.'" Then the Prophet said, "Rather, you should say, 'In the Name of Allah,' for it towers over him, and he becomes as small as a fly." (*Ahmad*)

[2021] The Prophet said, "Satan is perched upon the heart of the son of Adam. When he becomes absentminded and heedless, he whispers (for him to do evil). Then, when (the person) remembers Allah, he withdraws." (*At-Tabari*) The Prophet also said, "Allah has accepted my plea to forgive the whispers in the hearts of my followers, unless they put them into action or talk about them." (*Bukhari*)

[2022] The Prophet said, "There is not a single one of you except that he has a companion (jinn) who has been assigned to him (to tempt him)." Those around him said, "What about you, Messenger of Allah?" He replied, "Yes. However, Allah has helped me against him, and he has accepted Islam. Thus, he only commands me to do good." (*Muslim*) On another occasion the Prophet said, "Satan puts his hand on a person's heart. If he finds it filled with the praise of Allah, he removes his hand. If he finds it forgetful of Allah, he overcomes his heart fully, and this is the whispering of the jinns." (*Musnad Abu Ya'la*)

Upon completion of the reading of the Qur'an,
it is customary to say:

And indeed, Allah, the Exalted,
has spoken the truth...

(Sadaq Allahul owzeem)

Then the reader should return to the beginning of the book
and read the first chapter along with a few verses of chapter two.

This signifies that the cycle of searching for Allah's guidance
never ends but begins anew until the day we return to meet our Lord.

Selected Index

Azar, 6:74

B

Babylon, 2:102
Backbiting (see Slander)
Badr (Battle of)
    lesson of, 3:13; 8:5-19, 42-48
    the second Badr, 3:172
Baptism, 2:138
Barrier (Barzakh), 23:100; 15:53; 55:20
Becca, 3:96
Beasts (see Animals)
Bees, 16:68-69
Beliefs (see Doctrines)
Believers
    in general, 3:102; 5:8; 10:62, 4:92-93,
    4:94; 7:45; 8:63; 9:20-21, 33:69-71;
    44:12; 85:6-11
    blessed with a messenger, 3:164
    will gain heaven, 4:175
    hold together, 3:103
    promote goodness, 3:104, 110; 61:14
    true in word, 61:2-3, 9:119
    Will be forgiven, 29:7; 47:2
    must fulfill their obligations, 5:1
    Allah protects them from their enemies,
    3:111; 5:11, 105
    Angels watch over, 41:30-31
    if you're not sincere then Allah will
replace you, 5:54
    don't associate with those who mock
your religion, 4:140; 5:57; 6:68
    don't overindulge in lawful things, 5:87-
88
    cling to faith for Allah's protection, 5:105
    can have beautiful things in this life, 7:32
Bigotry
    avoid people who insult the Qur'an,
6:68-69
Biology, 16:66; 22:5; 23:13-14; 24:45; 32:9; 53:45-46;
    96:1-2
Birds, 2:260; 3:49; 5:10; 6:38; 12:36, 41; 16:79; 21:79;
    22:31; 24:41; 27:16-17; 34:10; 38:19;
        67:19
Boat (of Noah), 7:64; 10:73; 11:37-38; 26:119; 29:15
Boat (of Khidr), 18:71, 79
Boat (of Jonah), 37:139-140
Boats, 2:164; 10:22; 14:32; 16:14; 17:66; 22:65;
    23:22; 29:65; 30:46; 31:31; 35:12; 36:41;
    40:80; 43:12; 45:12
Book, 2:2, 87; 2:121; 3:7; 5:15-16; 6:114; 13:38; 44:3-
    4; 46:2
Booty, 8:1, 41; 48:15; 59:7-8
Borrowing, 4:58
Bribery, 2:188
Brotherhood, 21:92
Business (see Trade)
Burden (see Adversity)
Byzantines (see Romans)

C

Cain, 5:27-32
Calf (the golden), 2:51-52, 4:153
Call to Prayer (Adhan), 62:9
Cattle, (see Animals)
Cave, (Companions of), 18:9-22, 25-26
Charity
    general, 2:179, 195, 219, 254, 261-274;
    3:134; 30:39; 57:18; 63:10; 64:16-17

    the command to give, 2:43, 83, 110, 177,
    277; 9:103-104; 19:31, 55; 21:73; 22:41,
    78; 24:56; 33:33; 58:13; 73:20; 98:5
    quality of a believer, 4:162; 5:55; 8:18;
    9:71; 24:37; 27:3; 31:4
    the reward of doing, 5:12; 7:156; 9:11,
    103; 23:1-4; 30:39
    on those who don't give, 41:6-7
    who to give to, 2:215; 9:60
    give for your own good, 2:254
    multiplies its blessings, 2:261
    don't humiliate the poor, 2:262-264
    should be from love of Allah, 2:265
    don't give poor quality goods, 2:267,
    3:92
    secret or public charity are both good,
    2:270-271
    can be given to unbelievers without
restriction, 2:272
    give to support missionaries, 2:273
    don't be tightfisted, 4:37
    for show, 4:38
    who receives it, 9:60
Children, 2:233; 42:49-50
Childcare, 2:233
Children of Israel (see Jews)
Christ (see Jesus)
Christians
    general, 2:138-140; 5:14
    claim exclusive truth, 2:111-113; 5:18
    deny Judaism, 2:113
    assign a son to Allah, 2:116; 9:30
    seek to convert you, 2:120
    lost most of their revelation, 5:14
    divided up into competing sects, 5:14
    obey priests over Allah, 9:31
    should judge by the Gospel, 5:46-47
    don't take for protectors or close allies,
    5:51-53
    some are sincere, 5:66
    most likely to love Muslims, 5:82-86
Class Conflict
    don't discriminate against the common
people, 6:52-53
    status is merely a test, 6:165
    don't covet what the rich have, 4:32
Cleanliness, 4:42; 5:6; 74:4
Clothing, 7:26, 31-32; 24:31, 60
Contract Law, 2:282-283
Corruption, 5:100
Courteous manners, 4:86
Creation, 8:5; 7:54; 10:4; 14:48; 15:85; 16:3; 17:49,
    98; 21:16-17, 104; 27:64;
    29:19-20; 32:4; 35:16; 39:5; 44:39;
    45:22; 46:3; 51:56-58; 57:4
Creatures (see Animals)
Creature (Sign of the Last Day), 27:82
Cyrus (see Master of the Two Horns)

D

Danger
    believers should not go singly into
dangerous places, 4:71
    brings out hypocrisy, 4:72-73
David, 2:251, 5:78; 6:84; 21:78-80; 34:10-11;
    38:17-26
Da'wah (see Missionaries)
Death
    every soul will experience, 3:185; 4:78;
    21:35; 29:57

sinful souls will regret at, 4:97; 8:50-54;
16:28-29; 56:83-87

by Allah's command, 3:145; 16:70

not the end, 14:24-26

process described, 56:83-87; 75:26-29

experience of the righteous, 16:30-32

wicked will be confused, 6:93-94

Debt, 2:280

Deeds, 6:132, 160, 164

Dietary Guidelines (see Food)

Disciples (of Jesus), 3:52-54; 5:112-115

Disputes

refer them to the Qur'an and the
teachings of the Prophet, 4:59

Diversity, 30:22

Divorce, 2:226-232, 236-237, 241; 4:35; 65:1-7

Doctrines (of Islam)

the main beliefs listed in detail, 2:285

what we must accept, 4:136

Domestic Disharmony

Islam limits domestic violence, 4:34

husband's options, 4:34

wife's options, 4:128

counseling of sympathetic parties, 4:35

Donkey, 2:259

Dowry, 2:229, 236-237; 4:4, 19-21, 24-25

Drugs (see Intoxicants)

E

Earth, 14:48; 15:19-20; 26:7; 29:56; 67:15; 77:25-28;
99:1-6

Ecumenism, 2:62

Elephant, (army of), 105:1-5

Elijah, 6:85; 37:123-132

Elisha, 6:86; 38:48

Equality

both males and females equal before
Allah in reward, 4:124

Eve (see Adam)

Ezekiel, 21:85; 38:48

Ezra, 9:31

F

Faith, 2:28, 177

Faithless, the

described 2:6-7

want believers to fail, 2:105

will be defeated, 3:10-12; 6:6

ask for miracles, 6:8-9

despair when their fellows die, 3:156

only seem to be dominant, 3:178

seem to do as they please, 3:197

would reject miracles anyway, 6:7-10

will have no chance to evade punishment
on Judgment Day, 6:22-24

pretend to listen to the Qur'an, 6:25-26

will be sorry one day, 6:27-32

they cause stress to the Prophet, 6:33

Allah seizes them in punishment, 6:44-45

persist in denial even though friends call
them to faith, 6:71-72

avoid those who take religion as a joke,
6:70

can the spiritually dead be equal to the
aware, 6:122

corrupt leaders in every town, 6:123-124

call to tradition to defend their idolatry,
5:104; 6:148-150, 7:28

Muslims do not worship what others do,

109:1-6

ransom not accepted, 5:36-37

Fair Dealing, 5:8

Family, 2:83; 4:7-9; 8:41; 16:90; 17:26; 24:22; 42:23

Fasting, 2:183-184

Fear (of Allah), 2:2; 3:102; 4:131; 47:17; 67:12; 98:8

Fortune (Fate), 17:13

Fighting (see War)

Fire (Also see Hellfire)

the fire of Hell, 2:24

gift from Allah, 56:72-73

Followers of Earlier Revelation

want to destroy your faith, 2:109

divided themselves and made sects,
3:105

would be better with strong faith, 3:110

overshadowed with shame, 3:111-112

some are sincere and righteous, 3:113-
115, 199; 5:66

their religions required them to preach
openly, 3:187

they bargain with mistakes, 4:45

they should believe in Allah before it's
too late, 4:47-48

Allah taught them to fear Him, 4:131

place too much emphasis on miracles,
4:153

don't create outlandish theology, 4:171

renounce the trinity, 4:171; 5:17

Muslim men can marry a woman of, 5:5

a call from Allah, 5:15-16, 19

they mock the Islamic call to prayer,
5:58-60

they agree with you for deceptive
reasons, 5:61-63

should have sincere faith and follow their
religions properly, 5:65-68

can see the wisdom of the Qur'an, 6:20

Food

restricted foods for believers, 2:168, 172-
173; 5:1, 3-5; 6:118-119, 121,
145-146; 16:114-118

allowed to eat after pronouncing Allah's
name, 6:119

general restrictions, 6:145

what was forbidden to Jews to eat, 6:146

Forgiveness, 2:109; 4:48, 110, 116; 7:199; 39:53; 42:5,
37, 40; 39:53; 40:14; 45:14; 53:32; 57:21

Fornication, 24:2-3

Fortune-telling, 2:102

Fraud, 83:1-6

Friday Prayers, 62:9-11

G

Gabriel, 2:97-98; 26:193; 66:4; 81:19-21

Gambling, 2:219, 5:90-91

Garden (of Eden), 2:35-36; 7:19-25

Garden, the (see Paradise)

God (Allah)

introduced 1:1

only One Who can save, 2:107

is near and everywhere, 2:115, 186;
11:61; 35:40; 50:16; 56:85

has no partners, 6:163; 17:111; 18:26;
25:2

is near the believers, 2:186

created nature, 25:61-62

can create things with a word, 2:117;
3:47; 6:73; 19:35; 36:82; 40:68

is higher than people can conceptualize,

Pilgrimage, 2:196-203; 3:96-97; 5:2; 22:26-33

Plants
    Allah causes them to sprout, 6:95
    Allah sends rain for them, 6:99
Poets, 26:224-227; 36:69; 69:41
Polytheism (Shirk), 2:254-258; 6:125-137; 7:189-206;
    11:96-109; 16:17-34; 25:41-57
Prayer
    general, 2:238-239; 3:8; 4:43; 5:6;
    11:114; 17:78-81; 23:118; 50:39-40;
        52:48-49; 73:1-8
    characteristic of the believers, 2:3
    for the determined, 2:45,
    gives courage, 2:153
    don't neglect, 2:210, 238
    while traveling or in danger, 4:101-104
    for Allah, 13:14-15
    the five, 11:144; 17:78-79; 20:130; 30:17-
    18
    while feeling in danger, 2:239; 4:101-103
    don't pray while inebriated, 4:43
    don't pray while ritually impure, 4:43
    how to perform ablution without water,
    4:43
Prayer Direction, 2:142-150
Promises, 2:224-227; 5:1, 92; 16:94; 24:22; 66:2;
    68:10
    foolish promises, 2:224-225
    how to compensate for breaking a foolish
promise, 5:89
Prophet's household, 33:28-34, 50-62
Prophets
    general, 2:253; 3:33-34, 81; 4:163-165;
    5:19; 6:84-90; 23:23-50; 57:26-27
    believers believe in them all, 2:285;
    4:150-152
    would never claim divinity, 3:79-80
    Allah established a covenant with, 3:82
    fought alongside the faithful, 3:146
    must never be false to their mission,
    3:161
    were sent all over the world, 6:42-44
    always have enemies, 6:112-113; 25:31
    had families, 13:38
    persecuted, 14:13
    only some are named in the Qur'an,
    40:78
Prophethood, 3:144-148; 4:170-175; 6:12-20, 47-55,
    56-82, 130-137, 151-154; 8:20-28
Protectors, (also Close Allies, Close Comrades)
    never prefer a faithless one, 3:28
    don't take them as, 3:118-120
Psalms, 4:163
Publicity, 4:148-149
Punishment
    for waging war on Allah and His
Messenger, 5:33-34
    for theft, 5:38-39
    every community in Hell wants to give it
to others, 7:38-39
Purity of demeanor, 18:81; 19:13
Purpose of life, 2:21,148; 3:14-17, 133; 5:35

Q

Qiblah (see Prayer Direction)
Qarun (see Korah)
Questioning, 5:101-102
Qur'an
    general, 2:23; 4:82; 6:19; 7:204-206;

10:38; 11:13; 17:89; 45:2; 80:11-12
    has both plain and allegorical verses, 3:7
    is flawless, 4:82
    confirms previous revelations, 6:92
    is a revelation like the Torah, 6:155-157
    gives warnings and good news, 7:2
    in Arabic, 12:2; 13:37; 41:44; 42:7; 43:30
    a mercy, 17:82
    follow it, 6:155
    only Allah could construct it, 2:23;
    10:38; 11:13; 17:89
    revealed in stages, 17:106; 25:32; 76:23;
    87:6-7
    instructs people, 39:41; 80:11-12
Quraysh, 106:1-4

R

Rabbis, 5:44
Race
    Allah made all the races, 30:22
    all races are meant to live in harmony,
    49:13
Racism
    Iblis was the first, 7:12
Ramadan, 2:185, 187
Raven, 5:31
Record (of Deeds), 50:4; 69:19; 83:7-9, 18-21; 84:7-15
Religion
    no forcing anyone into Islam, 2:256
    perfected by Allah, 5:3
    Islam described, 3:19-20, 83-84
    not for amusement, 6:70
    not difficult, 22:78
    the correct way, 45:18
    all prophets taught the same, 42:13-15
    do not make divisions, 6:159; 30:32
    no extremism, 4:171; 5:77-81
Religious Sects, 6:159; 23:53-54; 30:32
Remembrance of Allah (in general), 2:152, 198, 200,
203, 231, 239; 3:41; 4:103; 5:7, 11, 20;
    7:69, 74, 205; 13:28; 18:24, 28, 101;
20:14, 42, 124; 23:110; 25:18; 33:35, 41;
    35:3; 43:13; 62:10; 63:9; 73:8; 76:8
Remembrance, (the lack thereof), 25:29; 26:5, 32;
    39:2243:36; 53:29; 58:19; 72:17
Remembrance of Allah (dhikr, zikr), 3:135, 191;
    24:37; 26:227; 29:45; 33:21; 39:23;
        57:16; 87:15
Reminder (from Allah), 3:58; 6:90; 7:2; 11:120;
    12:104; 15:6, 9; 16:44; 20:99; 21:24, 48,
    50; 29:51; 37:3; 38:1, 8, 49, 87; 41:41;
    43:44; 54:25; 68:51-52; 74:31; 77:5;
    81:27
Repentance
    Adam's words of, 2:37-39
    a comprehensive prayer of, 2:286
    after small sins, 3:135
    Allah accepts it, 4:17; 6:54; 42:25
    habitual wrongdoers will not have their
    repentance accepted, 4:18
    of total rejecters not accepted, 4:168-169
Retaliation, 2:178-179; 5:45
Revelation
    Qur'an is in the same vein as others,
    4:163
    solves doubts, 2:23
    is guidance, 3:73
    purpose of, 7:2, 203
    in stages, 16:101
    nature of, 41:2-4, 6-8; 69:50-51; 81:15-

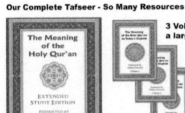

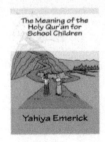

Printed in Great Britain
by Amazon

41631191R00442